THE DYNAMICS OF WORLD POWER

The United Nations

—

Subsaharan Africa

THE DYNAMICS OF WORLD POWER

A DOCUMENTARY HISTORY OF UNITED STATES FOREIGN POLICY 1945–1973

General Editor
ARTHUR M. SCHLESINGER, JR.
Albert Schweitzer Professor
in the Humanities
City University of New York

Volume V

The United Nations

Editor
RICHARD C. HOTTELET
News Correspondent, Columbia
Broadcasting System

Subsaharan Africa

Editor
JEAN HERSKOVITS
Professor of History
State University of New York
at Purchase

New York

CHELSEA HOUSE PUBLISHERS
IN ASSOCIATION WITH
McGRAW-HILL BOOK COMPANY

New York   Toronto   London   Sydney

1973

Managing Editor: *KARYN GULLEN BROWNE*

Consulting Editor: *LEON FRIEDMAN*
Editorial Staff: *BETSY NICOLAUS, ALICE SHERMAN, GRACE CORSO, ELLEN TABAK, IRVING RUDERMAN*

Library of Congress Cataloging in Publication Data
Schlesinger, Arthur Meier, 1917-   comp.
The dynamics of world power.
CONTENTS: v. 1. Western Europe, edited by R. Dallek.
— v. 2. Eastern Europe and the Soviet Union, edited
by W. LaFeber. — v. 3. Latin America, edited by
R. Burr. — v. 4. The Far East, edited by R. Buhite.
— v. 5. The United Nations, edited by R. C. Hottelet.
Subsaharan Africa, edited by J. Herskovits.
1. United States—Foreign relations—1945—
— Sources. I. Dallek, Robert. II. LaFeber, Walter.
III. Burr, Robert N. IV. Title.
E744.S395   327.73   78-150208
ISBN 0-07-079729-3
234567890 HDBP 7654

CONTENTS

Volume V
The United Nations

*The General Introduction to this Series
by Professor Arthur M. Schlesinger, jr. appears
in Volume I.*

THE UNITED STATES JOINS
THE UNITED NATIONS

THE YALTA CONFERENCE

THE SAN FRANCISCO CONFERENCE

BASIC U.N. DOCUMENTS

UNITED STATES ADHERENCE TO THE U.N.

DISARMAMENT AND OUTER SPACE

PROBLEMS OF OUTER SPACE AND THE END OF NUCLEAR TESTING

NON-PROLIFERATION TREATY

PROHIBITION OF NUCLEAR WEAPONS
IN THE OCEANS AND IN OUTER SPACE

TREATY OF TLATELOLCO

PEACEKEEPING

FIRST EFFORTS AT PEACEKEEPING

KOREA

GENERAL ASSEMBLY'S PEACEKEEPING ACTIONS

HUNGARY

GENERAL ASSEMBLY RESOLUTIONS ON HUNGARY

GENERAL ASSEMBLY RESOLUTIONS ON SENDING U.N. OBSERVERS TO HUNGARY

THE CONGO

THE UNITED NATIONS AND THE MIDDLE EAST

WHITE HOUSE STATEMENTS CONCERNING AGGRESSION IN THE MIDDLE EAST ISSUED BY JAMES C. HAGERTY, PRESS SECRETARY TO THE PRESIDENT

*   *   *

THE EISENHOWER DOCTRINE

THE SIX DAY WAR AND ITS AFTERMATH

THE HUMAN DIMENSION

BANNING SPAIN FROM THE U.N.

THE PROBLEM OF SOUTH AFRICA

SANCTIONS AGAINST SOUTHERN RHODESIA

SOUTH WEST AFRICA

PROTECTING HUMAN RIGHTS

ASSISTING FORMER COLONIAL COUNTRIES

SOUTHERN RHODESIA

THE CONSTITUTIONAL STRUGGLE

CONTENTS

Volume V
Subsaharan Africa

*The General Introduction to this Series
by Professor Arthur M. Schlesinger, jr. appears
in Volume I.*

Preface . . . . . Jean Herskovits

SUBSAHARAN AFRICA:
THE LOWEST PRIORITY

UNITED STATES ECONOMIC POLICY
TOWARD SUBSAHARAN AFRICA

BLACK AFRICA:
FROM THE SAHARA TO THE ZAMBEZI

WEST AFRICA

TOGO: FROM TRUSTEESHIP TO INDEPENDENCE

EAST AFRICA

SUDAN

ETHIOPIA AND THE SOMALI REPUBLIC

KENYA, TANZANIA, UGANDA

CENTRAL AFRICA

ZAIRE (THE CONGO-KINSHASA)

SOUTHERN AFRICA: THE WHITE REDOUBT

STATEMENTS OF GENERAL POLICY TOWARD AFRICA SOUTH OF THE ZAMBEZI

SOUTH AFRICA

THE UNITED STATES BAN ON
SALE OF ARMS TO SOUTH AFRICA

*   *   *

The United Nations Condemns Unilateral Declaration of Independence by Southern Rhodesia and Calls for Economic Sanctions

The United States Supports Sanctions Against Southern Rhodesia

*   *   *

Executive Orders Relating to Trade and Other Transactions Involving Southern Rhodesia

PORTUGUESE AFRICA

INDEX

Volume I
Western Europe

Volume II
Eastern Europe and the
Soviet Union

Volume III
Latin America

Volume IV
The Far East

THE UNITED STATES AND
THE UNITED NATIONS

Editor
RICHARD C. HOTTELET
Columbia Broadcasting System

THE UNITED STATES JOINS THE UNITED NATIONS

THE UNITED STATES JOINS THE
UNITED NATIONS

Commentary

The forceful logic of events brought the United States into the enterprise in world order to be called the United Nations—the logic of experience, embracing the consequences which flowed from the moral and political disintegration of the League of Nations and the logic of necessity, which dictated unity to win the Second World War.

One might have imagined the same compelling combination at the end of the First World War. The American approach was the same—the slightly sanctimonious combination of high moral purpose and geographical detachment. But the issue then was not so clearly drawn. The rising power of the New World had still to contend with the old habits of European giants who could not recognize, let alone accept, the beginning of a new era. Lofty principles were there rooted in the age-old dream of just and lasting peace. And as the carnage of the first mechanized war grew more appalling and less decisive, thoughtful leaders everywhere cast about for an alternative.

On January 8, 1918, President Woodrow Wilson, looking ahead to Imperial Germany's last convulsive effort (and to its failure) presented his Fourteen Points. Setting down principles for the peace settlement and the organization of the postwar world, they culminated in the final thesis: "A general association of nations must be formed under specific covenants for the purpose of affording mutual guarantees of political independence and territorial integrity to great and small states alike."

This precept was elaborated at the Versailles Peace Conference as the Covenant of the League of Nations, forming the first 26 articles of the Treaty of Versailles. Combining in one document the two main works of Versailles, ending the war and shaping the peace, the precept was meant to underscore the continuity of the effort and, perhaps, to ennoble the former with the idealism of the latter. It had the opposite effect. The outline of the New World Order was linked with such provisions as Germany's obligation "to hand over to His Britannic Majesty's Government the skull of the Sultan Mkwawa which was removed from the Protectorate of German East Africa and taken to Germany." More important, the Covenant of the League was made part of what many saw as a nineteenth century peace whose fear ridden, vengeful and greedy terms not only registered the absence of a unified ethical or political concept for the reconstruction of Europe but, in fact, helped to make it impossible.

The haggling and bickering of the Peace Conference and the terms of the Treaty adversely affected public opinion in the United States. They also stimulated endemic isolationist sentiment. Despite Woodrow Wilson's utmost effort in a campaign which

3

cost him his health and his Presidency, the Senate refused to ratify the Treaty of Versailles and the American electorate upheld its judgment in the election of 1920. The United States turned its back on the League of Nations.

It is idle to speculate what the League might have become with United States membership. Without it, the organization moved down the scale from grand experiment through nervous frustration to melancholy farce. In the preamble to the League Covenant, the High Contracting Parties explained their adherence: "in order to promote international cooperation and to achieve international peace and security." But the initial exclusion of Germany and the Soviet Union complemented the absence of the United States and turmoil in the Middle East and the League's inability to cope with the problem of armaments (among other things) reflected disagreement on basic terms. Open defiance of the Covenant in Japan's seizure of Manchuria, Mussolini's invasion of Ethiopia, multilateral intervention in the Spanish Civil War, Hitler's march of conquest, the Nazi-Soviet alliance, the partition of Poland and the Soviet invasion of Finland, progressively and utterly destroyed the League. The great economic crisis which raged unchecked around the globe in the early 1930's furthermore underscored the inadequacy of an international organization which had almost completely ignored the economic and social dimensions of life.

In the years between the two World Wars, the United States joined the International Labor Organization, an agency associated with the League. It took part in several futile international conferences on arms limitations and otherwise engaged in the normal traffic of bilateral diplomacy. In the Western Hemisphere, Washington sought to adapt its abiding interest in the Monroe Doctrine to a time in which the role of the Good Neighbor had become more appropriate than gunboat diplomacy and banana republic conspiracy. As for the rest of the world, the Neutrality Acts of 1935, 1936 and 1937 very accurately expressed the national will. Even President Franklin D. Roosevelt, who saw the danger of war so soon and so clearly, had to confine himself to sounding an alarm which his countrymen largely ignored and admonishing Adolf Hitler to adhere to standards of peace and humanity, which the Fuehrer openly ridiculed. On September 5, 1939, under the legislation enacted by Congress, President Roosevelt proclaimed the United States neutrality and applied an arms embargo to all belligerents.

The outbreak of war, early Nazi successes, and growing apprehension in the United States led President Roosevelt to concentrate on ways to meet the emergency. He established the United States as the "Arsenal of Democracy" and devised Lend-Lease to provide military equipment to Britain within the somewhat stretched framework of the neutrality laws. Nevertheless, he also looked ahead to the postwar world, setting up study groups and articulating basic aims, like the Four Freedoms, in his State of the Union speech on January 6, 1941.

Hitler's invasion of the Soviet Union on June 21, 1941 appeared to aggravate the danger of the West. President Roosevelt met Prime Minister Winston Churchill of Great Britain to discuss the accelerated supply of arms and equipment but also to formulate the body of principle in which this prodigious effort was to be made. Meeting at sea off Argentia, Newfoundland, the two men drafted the Atlantic Charter, setting down eight points which concluded in the desire for disarmament and creation of a permanent security system.

Nineteen forty-one was a dark year for the arms of the coalition against the Axis, so much so that Japan seized what looked like the most auspicious moment to clear the way for the conquest of Southeast Asia. On December 7, 1941 Japanese forces attacked Pearl Harbor, destroying the concept of American isolationist neutrality as well as much of the U.S. Pacific Fleet. A new chapter began for American foreign policy in which the pragmatic, informal arrangements of the first two years came to be codified in terms of alliance for war and peace.

Little time was lost in gathering representatives of twenty-six nations together in Washington where on January 1 and 2, 1942 they signed a Joint Declaration of United Nations. The occasion was noteworthy on at least three counts—it established the capital of the United States as the focal point of the war effort; while concentrating on winning the war, it made the Atlantic Charter the common denominator of peace; and it introduced the concept of "United Nations."

At that time, the name "United Nations" was not really stated as a proper noun. No discussion had been held, let alone agreement reached to create a world organization under that title. United Nations—without the article—was conceived as a coalition to prosecute the war: "the sheriff's posse" as President Roosevelt described it in a speech at Ottawa. But a year and a half later, the allied invasion of North Africa and the conquest of Sicily had set the stage for the invasion of Italy. In the Pacific, the tide had turned and Japan was being pushed back. It was a time to look ahead, anticipating doubts and working to preclude a repetition of Woodrow Wilson's defeat. A Joint Resolution of Congress, introduced by Congressman J. William Fulbright of Arkansas, quickly put the Legislature on record together with the Executive Branch as favoring creation of appropriate peace machinery.

Shaping that machinery and making it run required full United States participation, but also—and indispensably—the cooperation of the Soviet Union, which would emerge from the war as the second superpower. Broad guidelines were laid out at meetings in Moscow and Teheran. Explanatory statements issued from Washington. One might have noticed even then certain differences in tone—the U.S. Senate and the President speaking of an "international authority" and an "international force" while the Moscow Delcaration, which the Soviets helped to draft, contented itself with the more static prospect of an "international organization." There was nothing accidental in this variance. It was to affect and, at times, to dominate the work of the United Nations in its first twenty-five years. But, for the moment, United Nations meant only the wartime coalition and there was no quarrel with the way President Roosevelt summed up "the one supreme objective: security."

It was universally taken for granted that the new world organization must include the United States. The steps which were taken to involve this country—holding the preparatory discussions at Dumbarton Oaks, Washington D.C., and the United Nations Conference at San Francisco—reflected this conclusion more than it did the fact that the United States, geographically removed from the fighting, had the facilities to accommodate them.

The Yalta Conference, in February 1945, brought agreement that the Soviet Union should have three seats in the Assembly of the new organization and that the five permanent members of the projected Security Council should have the veto in matters of substance but not of procedure. But as the War moved toward its victorious end and the time for the San Francisco conference approached, the harmony and close cooperation which had, in general, marked relations between the wartime allies (primarily the United States and the Soviet Union) turned into tension and mistrust.

Openly violating its promise at Yalta to permit formation of democratic governments in Eastern Europe through free elections, the Soviet Union imposed communist regimes on Bulgaria, Rumania, Hungary and Poland. In Poland, the tug of war between Soviet intrusion and national opposition, watched with rising dismay by the Western world, delayed the progress so that no Polish delegation, led by Andrei Gromyko, precipitated a crisis. Secretary of State Edward R. Stettinius, Chairman of the U.S. delegation later reported that, toward the end of May, with a new President in the White House and the War ended in Europe, "on instruction from [Foreign Minister Vyacheslav] Molotov, Gromyko insisted at San Francisco that a dispute could not even be discussed by the Security Council without the unanimous vote of the five permanent members unless the situation was one that could be settled by peaceful means. On June 2, I announced at a meeting of Great Britain, the Soviet Union, the United States and China that it would be utterly impossible for the United States to join a world organization that provided for veto power against the introduction of measures purely for discussion. I advised Gromyko that if the Soviet Union insisted on this view, the United States would not join the world organization." Faced with this prospect, the Soviet Union dropped its demand and the U.N. Charter was completed.

President Harry S. Truman flew to San Francisco to attend the ceremony at which the Charter was signed. He spoke with transparent eager hope and determination of a Charter, like the U.S. Constitution: imperfect at birth but capable of improvement and expansion, and upon which could be built "a bigger, a better, a more perfect union."

In 1945, unlike 1919, there was not the slightest doubt that the United States would join the world organization. It was a different world, and the U.N. Charter was deliberately drafted to make up the shortcomings of the League Covenant. The major powers were members. The Charter was not linked in any way to terms of peace liquidating the Second World War. The veto was prudently limited to the five permanent members of the Security Council to be cast, realistically, in matters of substance which affected their vital interests. Without the veto to protect this interest against some contrary majority, there was no question that the United States (like the Soviet Union) would never have joined.

The U.N. was no more designed to be a world government than was the League, and the sovereign rights of its member states were explicitly noted. But the Charter opened with the words "We the Peoples" and extended the organization's activities—albeit without enforceable authority—into many fields of human life. An elaborate system of autonomous specialized agencies, working under the aegis of a new Economic and Social Council, was added to the existing International Telecommunication Union, the Universal Postal Union and the International Labor Organization. Even before the Charter, the U.N. Relief and Rehabilitation Administration was established by a conference in Atlantic City (1943), and the Food and Agriculture Organization at Hot Springs. The International Bank for Reconstruction and Development and the International Monetary Fund, with a new monetary system to replace the chaos of the 1920's and 1930's, were created at Bretton Woods, New Hampshire; the International Civil Aviation Organization at Chicago. Other agencies were formed in such areas as health, education and atomic energy. The U.N. itself embarked ever more actively upon economic development and the protection of human rights, in keeping with Franklin D. Roosevelt's conviction that peace must be based on moral order.

The primary purpose of the United Nations was set down as maintaining international peace and security, which the League had striven more modestly to achieve. The Charter was to make the new instrument more effective than the old, even where it adopted the League's institutions. In Article 25, the members of the U.N. agreed to accept and implement Security Council decisions. In Article 99, the Charter expanded the international civil service character of the Secretariat by giving the Secretary General the highly political power to bring to the Security Council any matter which he thought might threaten international peace and security.

New ground was broken as, for instance, in the Charter's Chapter XI on the treatment of non-selfgoverning territories, preparing the way for the massive and largely peaceful process of decolonization which marked the U.N.'s second decade. Old rules were reinforced to make the Charter more effective than the Covenant. The United States joined in eagerly, with the feeling that it could not tolerate another effort to restore the colonial status quo ante and with the conviction that peace could best be preserved by perpetuating the Grand Alliance which had won the war. But in the latter case, the United States and other like-minded members reasoned on the basis of a faulty premise. In speaking, in the Charter's Preamble, of the "scourge of war, which twice in our lifetime has brought untold sorrow to mankind . . ." and of maintaining "international peace and security" they anticipated a new order based on cooperation; they also assumed that the next threat to peace would resemble the previous one (and the one before that, in 1914). Working only months before the onset of the nuclear age, they could not be expected to anticipate the self-stabilizing forces and the new variations of danger which would characterize an altogether different world. The United States, with its long experience of an elastic Constitution, counted upon being able to deal with the unpredictable as it arose by reinterpreting principles and improvising means to keep and make peace. It did not reckon with the strong disinclination of some members to embark on case-by-case development of the Charter, as in Anglo-Saxon jurisprudence—especially when it ran against their interests and their conception of what the United Nations should be.

No serious opposition met the Charter when President Harry S. Truman sent it to the Senate for approval. After six days, on July 28, 1945, the Senate voted its endorsement, 89 to 2, having overcome certain fears that Article 43 would supersede the "warmaking" power of Congress. The Charter entered into force on October 24 upon ratification by a majority of the signatory states including the big five powers. Congress took somewhat longer to draft the U.N. Participation Act, which defined the legal relationship of the United States with the United Nations: the perquisities and authority of U.S. representatives to its organs, the power of the President to order compliance with Security Council decisions under Article 41 and to engage men and resources in support of peacekeeping operations as well as the U.S. contribution to the U.N. budget. Another important step followed: the decision to accept the jurisdiction of the International Court of Justice. Neither the United States nor the Soviet Union, having ensured its power of veto in the Security Council, felt inclined to submit its sovereign rights to interpretation by an international tribunal, although it was strongly argued that the American commitment to a system of world order would otherwise be incomplete and unconvincing. The Senate's acceptance of the Court's authority was limited to exclude disputes "essentially within the domestic jurisdiction of the United States as determined by the United States"—the so-called Connally Amendment, named after the Chairman of the Foreign Relations Committee. The Soviet Union did not accept the Court's jurisdiction in any form.

With the legal framework of the new U.N. organization completed, a permanent site had to be found. The Court remained at The Hague, where its predecessor had functioned under the League. And there were some who urged that the U.N.'s Secretariat move into the League's old building in Geneva. This suggestion was opposed by China and the Soviet Union as well as by others who wanted a fresh beginning. Most members wanted to link the United States physically with the United Nations, and their suggestion that the headquarters be established in the new world drew a unanimous congressional invitation to come. A number of American states, cities, and communities extended their hospitality. One delegation came to offer the Black Hills of South Dakota. All were refused as being too remote or in other ways inconvenient. But, when the U.N. itself focused on wealthy suburbs east and north of New York City, the residents indignantly rebuffed what they felt was an intrusion on their privacy. The United Nations made do with temporary quarters at Lake Success until John D. Rockefeller, Jr. donated the money to buy land in midtown Manhattan on the East River. A loan, without interest, of $65 million from the United States financed the construction of permanent buildings. A Headquarters Agreement, concluded the next year, laid down the terms on which the United Nations could be located in the United States, as part of a great metropolitan community, and yet retain full freedom to function without hindrance or pressure from the powerful host. With this, the constitutional and physical preliminaries were complete.

WARTIME ORIGINS

*Address by President Franklin D. Roosevelt to the Congress on the Four Freedoms**

January 6, 1941

               *   *   *

In the future days, which we seek to make secure, we look forward to a world founded upon four essential human freedoms.

The first is freedom of speech and expression—everywhere in the world.

The second is freedom of every person to worship God in his own way—everywhere in the world.

The third is freedom from want—which, translated into world terms, means economic understandings which will secure to every nation a healthy peacetime life for its inhabitants—everywhere in the world.

The fourth is freedom from fear—which, translated into world terms, means a world-wide reduction of armaments to such a point and in such a thorough fashion that no nation will be in a position to commit an act of physical aggression against any neighbor—anywhere in the world.

That is no vision of a distant millenium. It is a definite basis for a kind of world attainable in our own time and generation. That kind of world is the very antithesis of the so-called new order of tyranny which the dictators seek to create with the crash of a bomb.

To that new order we oppose the greater conception—the moral order. A good society is able to face schemes of world domination and foreign revolutions alike without fear.

Since the beginning of our American history, we have been engaged in change—in a perpetual peaceful revolution—a revolution which goes on steadily, quietly adjusting itself to changing conditions—without the concentration camp or the quick-lime in the ditch. The world order which we seek is the cooperation of free countries, working together in a friendly, civilized society.

This nation has placed its destiny in the hands and heads and hearts of its millions of free men and women; and its faith in freedom under the guidance of God. Freedom means the supremacy of human rights everywhere. Our support goes to those who struggle to gain those rights or keep them. Our strength is our unity of purpose.

To that high concept there can be no end save victory.

*The Atlantic Charter***

August 14, 1941

The following statement signed by the President of the United States and the Prime Minister of Great Britain is released for the information of the Press:

*S. I. Roseman, *The Public Papers and Address of F.D.R.,* Vol. IX, (New York, 1941), p. 672.
***Foreign Relations of the United States, Diplomatic Papers,* Vol. I, (Washington, 1958), pp. 367-68.

The President of the United States and the Prime Minister, Mr. Churchill, representing His Majesty's Government in the United Kingdom, have met at sea.

* * *

The President and the Prime Minister have had several conferences. They have considered the dangers to world civilization arising from the policies of military domination by conquest upon which the Hitlerite government of Germany and other governments associated therewith have embarked, and have made clear the stress which their countries are respectively taking for their safety in the face of these dangers.

They have agreed upon the following joint declaration:

Joint declaration of the President of the United States of America and the Prime Minister, Mr. Churchill, representing His Majesty's Government in the United Kingdom, being met together, deem it right to make known certain common principles in the national policies of their respective countries on which they base their hopes for a better future for the world.

First, their countries seek no aggrandizement, territorial or other;

Second, they desire to see no territorial changes that do not accord with the freely expressed wishes of the peoples concerned;

Third, they respect the right of all peoples to choose the form of government under which they will live; and they wish to see sovereign rights and self government restored to those who have been forcibly deprived of them;

Fourth, they will endeavor, with due respect for their existing obligations, to further the enjoyment by all States, great or small, victor or vanquished, of access, on equal terms, to the trade and to the raw materials of the world which are needed for their economic prosperity;

Fifth, they desire to bring about the fullest collaboration between all nations in the economic field with the object of securing, for all, improved labor standards, economic advancement and social security;

Sixth, after the final destruction of the Nazi tyranny, they hope to see established a peace which will afford to all nations the means of dwelling in safety within their own boundaries, and which will afford assurance that all the men in all the lands may live out their lives in freedom from fear and want;

Seventh, such a peace should enable all men to traverse the high seas and oceans without hindrance;

Eighth, they believe that all of the nations of the world, for realistic as well as spiritual reasons must come to the abandonment of the use of force. Since no future peace can be maintained if land, sea or air armaments continue to be employed by nations which threaten, or may threaten, aggression outside of their frontiers, they believe, pending the establishment of a wider and permanent system of general security, that the disarmament of such nations is essential. They will likewise aid and encourage all other practicable measures which will lighten for peace-loving peoples the crushing burden of armaments.

Franklin D. Roosevelt
Winston S. Churchill

Declaration by United Nations*

January 1, 1942

A JOINT DECLARATION BY THE UNITED STATES OF AMERICA, THE UNITED KINGDOM OF GREAT BRITAIN AND NORTHERN IRELAND, THE UNION OF SOVIET SOCIALIST REPUBLICS, CHINA, AUSTRALIA, BELGIUM, CANADA, COSTA RICA, CUBA, CZECHOSLO-VAKIA, DOMINICAN REPUBLIC, EL SALVADOR, GREECE, GUATEMALA, HAITI, HONDURAS, INDIA, LUXEMBOURG, NETHERLANDS, NEW ZEALAND, NICARAGUA, NORWAY, PANAMA, POLAND, SOUTH AFRICA, YUGOSLAVIA

The Governments signatory hereto,

Having subscribed to a common program of purposes and principles embodied in the Joint Declaration of the President of the United States of America and the Prime Minister of the United Kingdom of Great Britain and Northern Ireland dated August 14, 1941, known as the Atlantic Charter.

Being convinced that complete victory over their enemies is essential to defend life, liberty, independence and religious freedom, and to preserve human rights and justice in their own lands as well as in other lands, and that they are now engaged in a common struggle against savage and brutal forces seeking to subjugate the world, declare:

(1) Each Government pledges itself to employ its full resources, military or economic, against those members of the Tripartite Pact and its adherents with which such government is at war.

(2) Each Government pledges itself to cooperate with the Governments signatory hereto and not to make a separate armistice or peace with the enemies.

The foregoing declaration may be adhered to by other nations which are, or which may be, rendering material assistance and contributions in the struggle for victory over Hitlerism.

Address by President Roosevelt on "Gangsterism" in the Community of Nations**

Ottawa, August 25, 1943

*   *   *

We have been forced to call out what we in the United States would call the sheriff's posse to break up the gang in order that gangsterism may be eliminated in the community of Nations.

We are making sure—absolutely, irrevocably sure—that this time the lesson is driven home to them once and for all. Yes, we are going to be rid of outlaws this time.

Every one of the United Nations believes that only a real and lasting peace can justify the sacrifices we are making, and our unanimity gives us confidence in seeking that goal.

It is no secret that at Quebec there was much talk of the postwar world. That

*Department of State, *Cooperative War Effort*, Executive Agreement Series 236, Publication 1732, p. 1.
***The Public Papers and Addresses of F.D.R.*, Vol. XII, p. 368.

discussion was doubtless duplicated simultaneously in dozens of Nations and hundreds of cities and among millions of people.

There is a longing in the air. It is not a longing to go back to what they call "the good old days." I have distinct reservations as to how good "the good old days" were. I would rather believe that we can achieve new and better days.

Absolute victory in this war will give greater opportunities to the world, because the winning of the war in itself is certainly proving to all of us up here that concerted action can accomplish things. Surely we can make strides toward a greater freedom from want than the world has yet enjoyed. Surely by unanimous action in driving out the outlaws and keeping them under heel forever, we can attain a freedom from fear of violence.

I am everlastingly angry only at those who assert vociferously that the four freedoms and the Atlantic Charter are nonsense because they are unattainable. If those people had lived a century and a half ago they would have sneered and said that the Declaration of Independence was utter piffle. If they had lived nearly a thousand years ago they would have laughed uproariously at the ideals of Magna Charta. And if they had lived several thousand years ago they would have derided Moses when he came from the Mountain with the Ten Commandments.

*   *   *

House Concurrent Resolution 25 on Aggression and the Maintenance of Peace *

June 15-16, 1943

IN THE SENATE OF THE UNITED STATES
SEPTEMBER 24 (LEGISLATIVE DAY, SEPTEMBER 15), 1943
REFERRED TO THE COMMITTEE ON FOREIGN RELATIONS

Concurrent Resolution

Resolved by the House of Representatives (the Senate concurring), That the Congress hereby expresses itself as favoring the creation of appropriate international machinery with power adequate to establish and to maintain a just and lasting peace, among the nations of the world, and as favoring participation by the United States therein through its constitutional processes.

Passed the House of Representatives September 21, 1943.

Attest:

South Trimble,
Clerk

---

*House Calendar No. 104, H. Con. Res. 25 (Report No. 553), 78th Cong., 1st sess.

Declaration of Four Nations on General Security *

November 1, 1943

The Governments of the United States of America, the United Kingdom, the Soviet Union and China;

united in their determination, in accordance with the Declaration by the United Nations of January 1, 1942, and subsequent declarations, to continue hostilities against those Axis powers with which they respectively are at war until such powers have laid down their arms on the basis of unconditional surrender;

conscious of their responsibility to secure the liberation of themselves and the peoples allied with them from the menace of aggression;

recognizing the necessity of ensuring a rapid and orderly transition from war to peace and of establishing and maintaining international peace and security with the least diversion of the world's human and economic resources for armaments;

jointly declare:

1. That their united action, pledged for the prosecution of the war against their respective enemies, will be continued for the organization and maintenance of peace and security.

2. That those of them at war with a common enemy will act together in all matters relating to the surrender and disarmament of that enemy.

3. That they will take all measures deemed by them to be necessary to provide against any violation of the terms imposed upon the enemy.

4. That they recognize the necessity of establishing at the earliest practicable date a general international organization, based on the principle of the sovereign equality of all peace-loving states, and open to membership by all such states, large and small, for the maintenance of international peace and security.

5. That for the purposes of maintaining international peace and security pending the reestablishment of law and order and the inauguration of a system of general security, they will consult with one another and as occasion requires with other members of the United Nations with a view to joint action on behalf of the community of nations.

6. That after the termination of hostilities they will not employ their military forces within the territories of other states except for the purposes envisaged in this declaration and after joint consultation.

7. That they will confer and cooperate with one another and with other members of the United Nations to bring about a practicable general agreement with respect to the regulation of armaments in the post-war period.

Senate Resolution 192 on Peace and an International Authority to Preserve Peace **

October, 1943

IN THE SENATE OF THE UNITED STATES
OCTOBER 14 (LEGISLATIVE DAY, OCTOBER 12), 1943

Foreign Relations of the United States, Diplomatic Papers, 1943, Vol. 1, (Washington, 1963), pp. 755-56.
**S. Res. 192*, 78th Cong., 1st sess.

MR. CONNALLY SUBMITTED THE FOLLOWING RESOLUTION; WHICH WAS REFERRED
TO THE COMMITTEE ON FOREIGN RELATIONS

OCTOBER 21, 1943

REPORTED BY MR. CONNALLY, WITHOUT AMENDMENT

NOVEMBER 3 (LEGISLATIVE DAY, OCTOBER 25), 1943

MODIFIED AND ORDERED TO BE REPRINTED

NOVEMBER 5 (LEGISLATIVE DAY, OCTOBER 25), 1943

CONSIDERED AND AGREED TO AS MODIFIED

Resolution

Resolved, That the war against all our enemies be waged until complete victory is achieved.

That the United States cooperate with its comrades-in-arms in securing a just and honorable peace.

That the United States, acting through its constitutional processes, join with free and sovereign nations in the establishment and maintenance of international authority with power to prevent aggression and to preserve the peace of the world.

That the Senate recognizes the necessity of there being established at the earliest practicable date a general international organization, based on the principle of the sovereign equality of all peace-loving states, and open to membership by all such states, large and small, for the maintenance of international peace and security.

That, pursuant to the Constitution of the United States, any treaty made to effect the purposes of this resolution, on behalf of the Government of the United States with any other nation or any association of nations, shall be made only by and with the advice and consent of the Senate of the United States, provided two-thirds of the Senators present concur.

Declaration of the Three Powers *

December 1, 1943

We—The President of the United States, the Prime Minister of Great Britain, and the Premier of the Soviet Union, have met these four days past, in this, the Capital of our Ally, Iran, and have shaped and confirmed our common policy.

We express our determination that our nations shall work together in war and in the peace that will follow.

As to war—our military staffs have joined in our round table discussions, and we have concerted our plans for the destruction of the German forces. We have reached complete agreement as to the scope and timing of the operations to be undertaken from the east, west and south.

The common understanding which we have here reached guarantees that victory will be ours.

And as to peace—we are sure that our concord will win an enduring Peace. We recognize fully the supreme responsibility resting upon us and all the United Nations

*Department of State Bulletin, Vol. IX, p. 409.

to make a peace which will command the goodwill of the overwhelming mass of the peoples of the world and banish the scourge and terror of war for many generations.

With our diplomatic advisors we have surveyed the problems of the future. We shall seek the cooperation and active participation of all nations, large and small, whose peoples in heart and mind are dedicated, as are our own peoples, to the elimination of tyranny and slavery, oppression and intolerance. We will welcome them, as they may choose to come, into a world family of Democratic Nations.

No power on earth can prevent our destroying the German armies by land, their U-Boats by sea, and their war plants from the air.

Our attack will be relentless and increasing.

Emerging from these cordial conferences we look with confidence to the day when all peoples of the world may live free lives, untouched by tyranny, and according to their varying desires and their own consciences.

We came here with hope and determination. We leave here, friends in fact, in spirit and in purpose.

Roosevelt, Churchill, and Stalin

*Christmas Eve Fireside Chat by President Roosevelt on Teheran and Cairo Conferences**

December 24, 1943

      *   *   *

Britain, Russia, China, and the United States and their allies represent more than three-quarters of the total population of the earth. As long as these four Nations with great military power stick together in determination to keep the peace there will be no possibility of an aggressor Nation arising to start another world war.

But those four powers must be united with and cooperate with all the freedom-loving peoples of Europe, and Asia, and Africa, and the Americas. The rights of every Nation, large or small, must be respected and guarded as jealously as are the rights of every individual within our own Republic.

The doctrine that the strong shall dominate the weak is the doctrine of our enemies—and we reject it.

But, at the same time, we are agreed that if force is necessary to keep international peace, international force will be applied—for as long as it may be necessary.

      *   *   *

Message to the Congress by President Roosevelt on Security at Home†

January 11, 1944

This Nation in the past two years has become an active partner in the world's greatest war against human slavery.

*The Public Papers and Addresses of F.D.R., Vol. XII, 1943, p. 558.
†Ibid., Vol. XIII, 1944-45, pp. 32-34.

We have joined with like-minded people in order to defend ourselves in a world that has been gravely threatened with gangster rule.

But I do not think that any of us Americans can be content with mere survival. Sacrifices that we and our allies are making impose upon us all a sacred obligation to see to it that out of this war we and our children will gain something better than mere survival.

We are united in determination that this war shall not be followed by another interim which leads to new disaster—that we shall not repeat the tragic errors of ostrich isolationism—that we shall not repeat the excesses of the wild twenties when this Nation went for a joy ride on a roller coaster which ended in a tragic crash.

When Mr. Hull went to Moscow in October, and when I went to Cairo and Teheran in November, we knew that we were in agreement with our allies in our common determination to fight and win this war. But there were many vital questions concerning the future peace, and they were discussed in an atmosphere of complete candor and harmony.

In the last war such discussions, such meetings, did not even begin until the shooting had stopped and the delegates began to assemble at the peace table. There had been no previous opportunities for man-to-man discussions which lead to meetings of minds. The result was a peace which was not a peace.

That was a mistake which we are not repeating in this war.

And right here I want to address a word or two to some suspicious souls who are fearful that Mr. Hull or I have made "commitments" for the future which might pledge this Nation to secret treaties, or to enacting the role of Santa Claus.

To such suspicious souls—using a polite terminology—I wish to say that Mr. Churchill, and Marshal Stalin, and Generalissimo Chiang Kai-shek are all thoroughly conversant with the provisions of our Constitution. And so is Mr. Hull. And so am I.

Of course we made some commitments. We most certainly committed ourselves to very large and very specific military plans which require the use of all Allied forces to bring about the defeat of our enemies at the earliest possible time.

But there were no secret treaties or political or financial commitments.

The one supreme objective for the future, which we discussed for each Nation individually, and for all the United Nations, can be summed up in one word: Security.

And that means not only physical security which provides safety from attacks by aggressors. It means also economic security, social security, moral security—in a family of Nations.

In the plain down-to-earth talks that I had with the Generalissimo and Marshal Stalin and Prime Minister Churchill, it was abundantly clear that they are all most deeply interested in the resumption of peaceful progress by their own peoples—progress toward a better life. All our allies want freedom to develop their lands and resources, to build up industry, to increase education and individual opportunity, and to raise standards of living.

All our allies have learned by bitter experience that real development will not be possible if they are to be diverted from their purpose by repeated wars—or even threats of war.

China and Russia are truly united with Britain and America in recognition of this essential fact:

The best interests of each Nation, large and small, demand that all freedom-loving

Nations shall join together in a just and durable system of peace. In the present world situation, evidenced by the actions of Germany, Italy, and Japan, unquestioned military control over disturbers of the peace is as necessary among Nations as it is among citizens in a community. And an equally basic essential to peace is a decent standard of living for all individual men and women and children in all Nations. Freedom from fear is eternally linked with freedom from want.

There are people who burrow through our Nation like unseeing moles, and attempt to spread the suspicion that if other Nations are encouraged to raise their standards of living, our own American standard of living must of necessity be depressed.

The fact is the very contrary. It has been shown time and again that if the standard of living of any country goes up, so does its purchasing power—and that such a rise encourages a better standard of living in neighboring countries with whom it trades. That is just plain common sense—and it is the kind of plain common sense that provided the basis for our discussions at Moscow, Cairo, and Teheran.

*   *   *

*Secretary of State Edward Stettinius on "Roosevelt and the Russians"**

1949

*   *   *

President Roosevelt sent me to Great Britain on a special mission in April 1944. In the group that accompanied me was Dr. Bowman, who was my adviser on a number of matters including those pertaining to international organization. I reached an agreement with Anthony Eden that the two countries should participate in conversations that summer in the United States on the world security organization. I advised Russian Ambassador Gusev of this agreement before I left London. On my return to Washington, Mr. Hull asked me to take charge of the preparations for the coming Conference.

It was apparent from my conversations in London that the United States would have to assume the initiative on the question of a world organization. I am convinced that if the United States had not continually pushed the plans there would have been no United Nations by the end of the war.

As the result of our initiative we held exploratory talks on world organization at Dumbarton Oaks with the British and the Russians from August 21 to September 28, 1944, and with the British and the Chinese from September 29 to October 7. (The Russians would not sit with the Chinese because of possible complications which might develop with the Japanese.)

The American proposals on world organization were accepted by the other powers as the basic documents of the conversations. At this conference the representatives of the major powers drafted the document that was to be the basis of discussion at San Francisco the following spring. We agreed on a statement of principles and purposes, a General Assembly, a Security Council, a Secretariat, an International Court of Justice, and an Economic and Social Council. It was only the insistence of the United States that secured a provision for an Economic and Social Council. The Soviet Union, and to

*Edward Stettinius, *Roosevelt and the Russians*, (New York, 1949), pp. 16-19.

a lesser extent Churchill, did not seem to understand the American concern for an organization that was broader than just a security organization.

Although we had agreed at Dumbarton Oaks that Great Britain, the Soviet Union, China, the United States, and even finally France should be permanent members of the Security Council, we had come to no agreement as to the voting procedure. There was also complete disagreement with the Russians over their proposal that all sixteen Soviet Republics be admitted as members of the world organization. When I told Mr. Hull of the impossible request which the Soviet Union had placed before the conference, he remarked, "Are these Russians going to break up our hope of a world organization?"

The crucial voting problem at Dumbarton Oaks and after concerned the voting procedure in the Security Council that should be adopted for making the necessary decisions in maintaining peace and security. There was no disagreement at Dumbarton Oaks regarding the desirability of having the Security Council function on the basis of a qualified majority vote, or of the necessity of having all *procedural* questions decided by a majority vote with no distinction made between the permanent and non-permanent members of the Security Council.

On procedural questions the British favored a two-thirds majority vote while the Russians preferred a simple majority. We originally favored a simple majority but were willing to accept the British proposal provided the Russians agreed. There was, however, no agreement on this question. The President told Gromyko at a meeting in the White House on September 8, 1944, that we would accept a simple majority of the eleven members of the Security Council on decisions of procedure. At Dumbarton Oaks we suggested that the number be seven, and this was included in a cable from the President to Stalin on December 5 and later adopted at Yalta.

The sharpest disagreement on voting in the Security Council related to the vote to decide substantive questions. Great Britain, the Soviet Union, China, and the United States had to decide whether or not they would accept as binding all the decisions made by a majority of the Council. A straight majority vote on substantive as well as on procedural matters would mean that the armed forces of any major nation could be used without its consent, quite likely as the result of a vote cast largely by nations which had few armed forces to contribute.

At Dumbarton Oaks none of the four major powers was willing to accept this situation. They all agreed that the only way each of them could be safeguarded was by adding the requirement that any majority of the Security Council had to include the concurring votes of the permanent members— or, in other words, the right of each major power to veto decisions.

The military and naval staffs working with the State Department—including Admirals Russell Willson, Harold Train, and Arthur Hepburn and Generals Stanley D. Embick, George V. Strong, and Muir Fairchild—had insisted on the right of the United States to veto decisions involving the use of American military forces. The armed forces would not recommend to the Senate a world organization that permitted American forces to be used without the express permission of the United States.

*   *   *

THE YALTA CONFERENCE*

Article IX of the Yalta Conference Agreement on "Unity for Peace as for War"

February 11, 1945

*   *   *

Our meeting here in the Crimea has reaffirmed our common determination to maintain and strengthen in the peace to come that unity of purpose and of action which has made victory possible and certain for the United Nations in this war. We believe that this is a sacred obligation which our Governments owe to our peoples and to all the peoples of the world.

Only with continuing and growing co-operation and understanding among our three countries and among all the peace-loving nations can the highest aspiration of humanity be realized—a secure and lasting peace which will, in the words of the Atlantic Charter, "afford assurance that all the men in all the lands may live out their lives in freedom from fear and want."

Victory in this war and establishment of the proposed international organization will provide the greatest opportunity in all history to create in the years to come the essential conditions of such a peace.

Winston S. Churchill
Franklin D. Roosevelt
I. Stalin

Protocol of the Proceedings of the Crimea Conference

March 24, 1947

The Crimea Conference of the Heads of the Governments of the United States of America, the United Kingdom, and the Union of Soviet Socialist Republics which took place from February 4th to 11th came to the following conclusions.

I. World Organisation

It was decided:

(1) that a United Nations Conference on the proposed world organisation should be summoned for Wednesday, 25th April, 1945, and should be held in the United States of America.

(2) the Nations to be invited to this Conference should be:

(*a*) the United Nations as they existed on the 8th February, 1945 and

(*b*) such of the Associated Nations as have declared war on the common enemy by 1st March, 1945. (For this purpose by the term "Associated Nation" was meant the

*Foreign Relations of the U.S., the Conferences at Malta and Yalta, 1945, (Washington, 1955), pp. 975-77.

eight Associated Nations and Turkey). When the Conference on World Organisation is held, the delegates of the United Kingdom and United States of America will support a proposal to admit to original membership two Soviet Socialist Republics, i.e. the Ukraine and White Russia.

(3) that the United States Government on behalf of the Three Powers should consult the Government of China and the French Provisional Government in regard to the decisions taken at the present Conference concerning the proposed World Organisation.

(4) that the text of the invitation to be issued to all the nations which would take part in the United Nations Conference should be as follows:

Invitation

"The Government of the United States of America, on behalf of itself and of the Governments of the United Kingdom, the Union of Soviet Socialist Republics, and the Republic of China and of the Provisional Government of the French Republic, invite the Government of   to send representatives to a Conference of the United Nations to be held on 25th April, 1945, or soon thereafter, at San Francisco in the United States of America to prepare a Charter for a General International Organisation for the maintenance of international peace and security.

"The above named governments suggest that the Conference consider as affording a basis for such a Charter the Proposals for the Establishment of a General International Organisation, which were made public last October as a result of the Dumbarton Oaks Conference, and which have now been supplemented by the following provisions for Section C of Chapter VI:

" 'C. *Voting*
'1. Each member of the Security Council should have one vote.
'2. Decisions of the Security Council on procedural matters should be made by an affirmative vote of seven members.
'3. Decisions of the Security Council on all other matters should be made by an affirmative vote of seven members including the concurring votes of the permanent members; provided that, in decisions under Chapter VIII, Section A and under the second sentence of paragraph 1 of Chapter VIII, Section C, a party to dispute should abstain from voting'.

"Further information as to arrangements will be transmitted subsequently.

"In the event that the Government of   desires in advance of the Conference to present views or comments concerning the proposals, the Government of the United States of America will be pleased to transmit such views and comments to the other participating Governments."

Territorial Trusteeship

It was agreed that the five Nations which will have permanent seats on the Security Council should consult each other prior to the United Nations Conference on the question of territorial trusteeship.

The acceptance of this recommendation is subject to its being made clear that territorial trusteeship will only apply to (a) existing mandates of the League of Nations; (b) territories detached from the enemy as a result of the present war; (c) any other territory which might voluntarily be placed under trusteeship; and (d) no discussion of actual territories is contemplated at the forthcoming United Nations Conference or in the preliminary consultations, and it will be a matter for subsequent agreement which territories within the above categories will be placed under trusteeship.

*   *   *

Address to the Congress by President Roosevelt on the Yalta Conference*

March 1, 1945

*   *   *

Responsibility for political conditions thousands of miles away can no longer be avoided by this great Nation. Certainly, I do not want to live to see another war. As I have said, the world is smaller—smaller every year. The United States now exerts a tremendous influence in the cause of peace throughout all the world. What we people over here are thinking and talking about is in the interest of peace, because it is known all over the world. The slightest remark in either House of the Congress is known all over the world the following day. We will continue to exert that influence, only if we are willing to continue to share in the responsibility for keeping the peace. It will be our own tragic loss, I think, if we were to shirk that responsibility.

The final decisions in these areas are going to be made jointly; and therefore they will often be a result of give-and-take compromise. The United States will not always have its way a hundred percent—nor will Russia nor Great Britain. We shall not always have ideal answers—solutions to complicated international problems, even though we are determined continuously to strive toward that ideal. But I am sure that under the agreements reached at Yalta, there will be a more stable political Europe than ever before.

Of course, once there has been a free expression of the people's will in any country, our immediate responsibility ends—with the exception only of such action as may be agreed on in the International Security Organization that we hope to set up.

The United Nations must also soon begin to help these liberated areas adequately to reconstruct their economy so that they are ready to resume their places in the world. The Nazi war machine has stripped them of raw materials and machine tools and trucks and locomotives. They have left the industry of these places stagnant and much of the agricultural areas are unproductive. The Nazis have left a ruin in their wake.

To start the wheels running again is not a mere matter of relief. It is to the national interest that all of us see to it that these liberated areas are again made self-supporting

**Public Papers and Addresses of F.D.R.*, Vol. XIII, 1944-45, p. 580-81; 585-86.

and productive so that they do not need continuous relief from us. I should say that was an argument based on plain common sense.

*　　　　　　　　　*　　　　　　　　　*

The Conference in the Crimea was a turning point—I hope in our history and therefore in the history of the world. There will soon be presented to the Senate of the United States and to the American people a great decision that will determine the fate of the United States—and of the world—for generations to come.

There can be no middle ground here. We shall have to take the responsibility for world collaboration, or we shall have to bear the responsibility for another world conflict.

I know that the word "planning" is not looked upon with favor in some circles. In domestic affairs, tragic mistakes have been made by reason of lack of planning; and, on the other hand, many great improvements in living, and many benefits to the human race, have been accomplished as a result of adequate, intelligent planning—reclamation of desert areas, developments of whole river valleys, and provision for adequate housing.

The same will be true in relations between Nations. For the second time in the lives of most of us this generation is face to face with the objective of preventing wars. To meet that objective, the Nations of the world will either have a plan or they will not. The groundwork of a plan has now been furnished, and has been submitted to humanity for discussion and decision.

No plan is perfect. Whatever is adopted at San Francisco will doubtless have to be amended time and again over the years, just as our own Constitution has been.

No one can say exactly how long any plan will last. Peace can endure only so long as humanity really insists upon it, and is willing to work for it—and sacrifice for it.

Twenty-five years ago, American fighting men looked to the statesmen of the world to finish the work of peace for which they fought and suffered. We failed them then. We cannot fail them again, and expect the world again to survive.

The Crimea Conference was a successful effort by the three leading Nations to find a common ground for peace. It ought to spell the end of the system of unilateral action, the exclusive alliances, the spheres of influence, the balances of power, and all the other expedients that have been tried for centuries—and have always failed.

We propose to substitute for all these, a universal organization in which all peace-loving Nations will finally have a chance to join.

I am confident that the Congress and the American people will accept the results of this Conference as the beginnings of a permanent structure of peace upon which we can begin to build, under God, that better world in which our children and grandchildren—yours and mine, the children and grandchildren of the whole world—must live, and can live.

And that, my friends, is the principal message I can give you. But I feel it very deeply, as I know that all of you are feeling it today, and are going to feel it in the future.

Undelivered Address by President Roosevelt on "Let Us Move Forward with Strong and Active Faith"*

April 13, 1945

Americans are gathered together this evening in communities all over the country to pay tribute to the living memory of Thomas Jefferson—one of the greatest of all democrats; and I want to make it clear that I am spelling that word "democrats" with a small *d*.

I wish I had the power, just for this evening, to be present at all of these gatherings.

In this historic year, more than ever before, we do well to consider the character of Thomas Jefferson as an American citizen.

As Minister to France, then as our first Secretary of State and as our third President, Jefferson was instrumental in the establishment of the United States as a vital factor in international affairs.

It was he who first sent our Navy into far-distant waters to defend our rights. And the promulgation of the Monroe Doctrine was the logical development of Jefferson's far-seeing foreign policy.

Today this Nation which Jefferson helped so greatly to build is playing a tremendous part in the battle for the rights of man all over the world.

Today we are part of the vast Allied force—a force composed of flesh and blood and steel and spirit—which is today destroying the makers of war, the breeders of hatred, in Europe and in Asia.

In Jefferson's time our Navy consisted of only a handful of frigates headed by the gallant U.S.S. *Constitution—Old Ironsides*—but that tiny Navy taught Nations across the Atlantic that piracy in the Mediterranean—acts of aggression against peaceful commerce and the enslavement of their crews—was one of those things which, among neighbors, simply was not done.

Today we have learned in the agony of war that great power involves great responsibility. Today we can no more escape the consequences of German and Japanese aggression than could we avoid the consequences of attacks by the Barbary Corsairs a century and a half before.

We, as Americans, do not choose to deny our responsibility.

Nor do we intend to abandon our determination that, within the lives of our children and our children's children, there will not be a third world war.

We seek peace—enduring peace. More than an end to war, we want an end to the beginnings of all wars—yes, an end to this brutal, inhuman, and thoroughly impractical method of settling the differences between governments.

The once powerful, malignant Nazi state is crumbling. The Japanese war lords are receiving, in their own homeland, the retribution for which they asked when they attacked Pearl Harbor.

But the mere conquest of our enemies is not enough.

We must go on to do all in our power to conquer the doubts and the fears, the ignorance and the greed, which made this horror possible.

Thomas Jefferson, himself a distinguished scientist, once spoke of "the brotherly

**Public Papers and Addresses of F.D.R.*, Vol. XIII, 1944-45, pp. 613-16.

spirit of Science, which unites into one family all its votaries of whatever grade, and however widely dispersed throughout the different quarters of the globe."

Today, science has brought all the different quarters of the globe so close together that it is impossible to isolate them one from another.

Today we are faced with the preeminent fact that, if civilization is to survive, we must cultivate the science of human relationships—the ability of all peoples, of all kinds, to live together and work together, in the same world, at peace.

Let me assure you that my hand is the steadier for the work that is to be done, that I move more firmly into the task, knowing that you—millions and millions of you—are joined with me in the resolve to make this work endure.

The work, my friends, is peace. More than an end of this war—an end to the beginnings of all wars. Yes, an end, forever, to this impractical, unrealistic settlement of the differences between governments by the mass killing of peoples.

Today, as we move against the terrible scourge of war—as we go forward toward the geatest contribution that any generation of human beings can make in this world—the contribution of lasting peace, I ask you to keep up your faith. I measure the sound, solid achievement that can be made at this time by the straight edge of your own confidence and your resolve. And to you, and to all Americans who dedicate themselves with us to the making of an abiding peace, I say:

The only limit to our realization of tomorrow will be our doubts of today. Let us move forward with strong and active faith.

THE SAN FRANCISCO CONFERENCE

Secretary Stettinius on "Roosevelt and the Russians" (Planning World Security Conference)*

1949

*   *   *

Molotov asked if it would not facilitate the admission of the Ukrainian and the Byelorussian (White Russian) republics as members of the Assembly if they signed the United Nations Declaration before the first of March. Churchill observed that it did not seem quite right to him to allow small countries, which had done so little, to attend the conference by the expedient of their declaring war, and to exclude the two Soviet Republics.

Marshal Stalin agreed that it was illogical, and questioned whether, although the three powers had agreed to recommend the Ukraine and White Russia as members of the Assembly, the fact that they had not signed the United Nations Declaration by March 1 might not furnish an excuse for excluding them from the conference. Both the President and the Prime Minister again assured Stalin that they would support the request of the Soviet delegation at the conference.

The Prime Minister again emphasized that he had preferred confining the conference to the present United Nations but, if others were to be added, he thought the two Soviet Republics also should be added. Stalin declared that he did not want to embarrass the President on this point. If the President would explain his difficulties, the Marshal added, he would see what could be done.

The President replied that it was a technical question but an important one. Up to that moment they had been discussing invitations to separate countries, but now it was not a question of a country but of granting one of the Great Powers three votes instead of one in the Assembly. This was a matter, he said, which should be put before the conference. "We have already agreed," he added, "to support this request at the conference." There had been no briefing of the President by the State Department on this particular question. Throughout this give-and-take, his mind functioned with clarity and conciseness, furnishing excellent proof that he was alert and in full command of his faculties.

Stalin then inquired again whether Ukrainian and Byelorussian signatures to the United Nations Declaration would not be advisable. The President replied that it would not be advisable and the Marshal withdrew his suggestion.

After this discussion the question of the world security organization and the approaching conference required very little of the time of the Crimean Conference. It is, however, of interest to describe how San Francisco was selected at Yalta as the location of the conference.

For months the State Department had surveyed possible locations and had discussed the advantages and disadvantages of many cities. The requirement was a city that could accommodate four to five thousand delegates, advisers, secretariat, and correspondents, with ample auditoriums and conference rooms, and with radio, cable,

*Roosevelt and the Russians, pp. 202-05.

rail, and airfield facilities. We discussed the possibility of Atlantic City, New York, Philadelphia, Chicago, Cincinnati, Miami, French Lick, Hot Springs (Virginia), Pinehurst, and other centers.

For various reasons, either because of the time of year or the lack of hotel facilities and auditoriums, or war congestion, or for questions of security, none of these places quite satisfied Roosevelt. In a final conversation that I had with him on the subject that day, as he lay in bed at the Livadia Palace, he said, "Go back to work, Ed, and come up with a better suggestion, as we haven't hit it yet." I went to bed that night perplexed.

I suddenly wakened at about three o'clock in the morning with a clear picture in my mind of San Francisco playing host to the United Nations. My mind raced with enthusiasm and freshness. I saw Nob Hill, the Opera House, the Veterans Building, the Pacific Union Club, the Mark Hopkins, the Fairmont and the St. Francis Hotel, each filling its purpose. I saw the golden sunshine, and as I lay there on the shores of the Black Sea in the Crimea, I could almost feel the fresh and invigorating air from the Pacific.

I went back to sleep and arose in the morning feeling that a solution to a great dilemma had been found. My mind was clear that the Pacific coast of the United States was the place to convene this historic conference and that San Francisco was the city; that it was directly accessible by air and water to the Latin-American countries and to the Philippines, China, New Zealand, Australia, and other countries across the Pacific; that the Nazis were soon to fall and it would be a striking reminder to the world that Japan was still to be conquered; that emphasis would be placed on the fact that aggression had been only half stamped out by the crushing of Nazi Germany.

I also thought it would be helpful from the standpoint of the whole concept of the United Nations to have the representatives of various countries of the world travel through the United States and see for themselves its magnificence, greatness, and power. I recall now, for instance, Molotov's remark after he had been across San Francisco Bay to visit shipyards that he was at last beginning to understand the greatness of America.

I knew, as I thought of the wisdom of holding the conference in California, that Roosevelt always believed that the Assembly should meet in a different country from time to time so that during the course of fifteen years, for instance, all the delegates would have seen most of the world.

Early that morning I went to see General Marshall to tell him that I would like to propose San Francisco as the site of the meeting. Before doing so I wished to obtain his reaction because of the importance of Army and Navy operations in the San Francisco area at that particular time. Marshall discussed the matter and said he felt that, while San Francisco was terribly congested, there was no place in the United States that was not, and that from the standpoint of facilities this would be a splendid choice. I had a similar conversation with Admiral King, who pledged full co-operation on the part of the Navy.

I tried to find in my mind the reason why San Francisco had come to me so clearly in the middle of the night. I thought back to one of the meetings that Molotov, Eden, and I had had a day or so before when various locations were being discussed and of my analysis of the various sections of the United States where we could hold the meeting. Eden had privately whispered to me that he had never seen California, and my mind had been thus directed toward the West Coast.

*   *   *

Address by President Harry S. Truman to the United Nations Conference*

April 25, 1945

The world has experienced a revival of an old faith in the everlasting moral force of justice. At no time in history has there been a more important Conference, or a more necessary meeting, than this one in San Francisco, which you are opening today.

On behalf of the American people, I extend to you a most hearty welcome.

President Roosevelt appointed an able delegation to represent the United States. I have complete confidence in its Chairman, Secretary of State Stettinius, and in his distinguished colleagues, former Secretary Cordell Hull, Senator Connally, Senator Vandenberg, Representative Bloom and Representative Eaton, Governor Stassen and Dean Gildersleeve.

They have my confidence. They have my support.

In the name of a great humanitarian—one who surely is with us today in spirit—I earnestly appeal to each and every one of you to rise above personal interests, and adhere to those lofty principles, which benefit all mankind.

Franklin D. Roosevelt gave his life while trying to perpetuate these high ideals. This Conference owes its existence, in a large part, to the vision, foresight, and determination of Franklin Roosevelt.

Each of you can remember other courageous champions, who also made the supreme sacrifice, serving under your flag. They gave their lives, so that others might live in security. They died to insure justice. We must work and live to guarantee justice—for all.

You members of this Conference are to be the architects of the better world. In your hands rests our future. By your labors at this Conference, we shall know if suffering humanity is to achieve a just and lasting peace.

Let us labor to achieve a peace which is really worthy of their great sacrifice. We must make certain, by your work here, that another war will be impossible.

We, who have lived through the torture and the tragedy of two world conflicts, must realize the magnitude of the problem before us. We do not need far-sighted vision to understand the trend in recent history. Its significance is all too clear.

With ever-increasing brutality and destruction, modern warfare, if unchecked, would ultimately crush all civilization. We still have a choice between the alternatives: the continuation of international chaos—or the establishment of a world organization for the enforcement of peace.

It is not the purpose of this Conference to draft a treaty of peace in the old sense of that term. It is not our assignment to settle specific questions of territories, boundaries, citizenship and reparations.

The Public Papers of the Presidents of the United States, Harry S. Truman, 1945, April 12-December 31, 1945, (Washington, 1961), pp. 20-23.

This Conference will devote its energies and its labors exclusively to the single problem of setting up the essential organization to keep the peace. You are to write the fundamental charter.

Our sole objective, at this decisive gathering, is to create the structure. We must provide the machinery, which will make future peace, not only possible, but certain.

The construction of this delicate machine is far more complicated than drawing boundary lines on a map, or estimating fair reparations, or placing reasonable limits upon armaments. Your task must be completed first.

We represent the overwhelming majority of all mankind. We speak for people, who have endured the most savage and devastating war ever inflicted upon innocent men, women and children.

We hold a powerful mandate from our people. They believe we will fulfill this obligation. We must prevent, if human mind, heart and hope can prevent it, the repetition of the disaster from which the entire world will suffer for years to come.

If we should pay merely lip service to inspiring ideals, and later do violence to simple justice, we would draw down upon us the bitter wrath of generations yet unborn.

We must not continue to sacrifice the flower of our youth merely to check madmen, those who in every age plan world domination. The sacrifices of our youth today must lead, through your efforts, to the building for tomorrow of a mighty combination of nations founded upon justice—on peace.

Justice remains the greatest power on earth.

To that tremendous power alone will we submit.

Nine days ago, I told the Congress of the United States, and I now repeat it to you:

"Nothing is more essential to the future peace of the world, than continued cooperation of the nations, which had to muster the force necessary to defeat the conspiracy of the axis powers to dominate the world.

"While these great states have a special responsibility to enforce the peace, their responsibility is based upon the obligations resting upon all states, large and small, not to use force in international relations, except in the defense of law. The responsibility of the great states is to serve, and not dominate the peoples of the world."

None of us doubt that with Divine guidance, friendly cooperation, and hard work, we shall find an adequate answer to the problem history has put before us.

Realizing the scope of our task and the imperative need for success, we proceed with humility and determination.

By harmonious cooperation, the United Nations repelled the onslaught of the greatest aggregation of military force that was ever assembled in the long history of aggression. Every nation now fighting for freedom is giving according to its ability and opportunity.

We fully realize today that victory in war requires a mighty united effort. Certainly, victory in peace calls for, and must receive, an equal effort.

Man has learned long ago, that it is impossible to live unto himself. This same basic principle applies today to nations. We were not isolated during the war. We dare not now become isolated in peace.

All will concede that in order to have good neighbors, we must also be good neighbors. That applies in every field of human endeavor.

For lasting security, men of good-will must unite and organize. Moreover, if our friendly policies should ever be considered by belligerent leaders as merely evidence of weakness, the organization we establish must be adequately prepared to meet any challenge.

Differences between men, and between nations, will always remain. In fact, if held within reasonable limits, such disagreements are actually wholesome. All progress begins with differences of opinion and moves onward as the differences are adjusted through reason and mutual understanding.

In recent years, our enemies have clearly demonstrated the disaster which follows when freedom of thought is no longer tolerated. Honest minds cannot long be regimented without protest.

The essence of our problem here is to provide sensible machinery for the settlement of disputes among nations. Without this, peace cannot exist. We can no longer permit any nation, or group of nations, to attempt to settle their arguments with bombs and bayonets.

If we continue to abide by such decisions, we will be forced to accept the fundamental concept of our enemies, namely, that "Might makes right." To deny this premise, and we most certainly do deny it, we are obliged to provide the necessary means to refute it. Words are not enough.

We must, once and for all, reverse the order, and prove by our acts conclusively, that Right Has Might.

If we do not want to die together in war, we must learn to live together in peace.

With firm faith in our hearts, to sustain us along the hard road to victory, we will find our way to a secure peace, for the ultimate benefit of all humanity.

We must build a new world—a far better world—one in which the eternal dignity of man is respected.

As we are about to undertake our heavy duties, we beseech our Almighty God to guide us in the building of a permanent monument to those who gave their lives that this moment might come.

May He lead our steps in His own righteous path of peace.

Secretary Stettinius on "Roosevelt and the Russians" (The Breakdown After Yalta)*

1949

        *   *   *

While Hopkins was in Moscow trying to straighten out the Polish question and a number of other issues, the San Francisco Conference reached an impasse that threatened failure in our attempt to build a world organization. On instruction from Molotov, Gromyko insisted at San Francisco that a dispute could not even be discussed by the Security Council without the unanimous vote of the five permanent members unless the situation was one that could be settled by peaceful means. On June 2, I announced at a meeting of Great Britain, the Soviet Union, the United States, France, and China that it would be utterly impossible for the United States to join a world organization that provided for veto power against the introduction of

---

**Roosevelt and the Russians*, pp. 319-21.

measures purely for discussion. I advised Gromyko that if the Soviet Union insisted on this view the United States would not join the world organization.

I telephoned President Truman that day and explained that the Soviet Union was insisting that one of the five permanent powers in the Security Council could veto the discussion of a situation, in which that Great Power was not involved, when the discussion was merely for the purpose of enabling the Security Council to explore what action, if any, it should take or recommend.

The President wholeheartedly supported me in my stand against the Russian position and approved my proposal to send a cable to Ambassador Harriman instructing him immediately to discuss the question with Marshal Stalin, accompanied by Hopkins if possible. I sent the message to Harriman that afternoon. I put a key sentence in the cable, saying I was aware that Marshal Stalin, in the past, did not know of "some of the decisions" which had been made and "communicated" to us. I instructed Harriman to describe the gravity of the situation to Stalin, saying that the conference would have to be adjourned unless the Russians withdrew their request.

Hopkins had been in Moscow over a week and had had already a number of conferences with Stalin when my message reached Moscow. He and Harriman, at Hopkins' last meeting with Stalin on June 6, raised the issue in my message with Stalin. It was pointed out to Stalin that the United States believed that the Yalta agreement safeguarded freedom of discussion and the right of any member to bring before the Security Council for discussion any situation affecting the peace and security of the world. When Molotov attempted to defend the instructions he had sent to Gromyko, I was told that the Marshal told him not to be ridiculous and that the Soviet Union should accept the American position.

On June 6, while I was presiding at a meeting of the conference in San Francisco, I received a message from Grew that Stalin had accepted the United States position regarding the voting procedure in the Security Council. I immediately talked to Gromyko and advised him of the word we had received from Moscow. His own instructions came in later, and we then proceeded with the final drafting of the Charter.

The entire incident reveals that Stalin could reach a quick decision, even though it meant publicly repudiating the position of his Foreign Minister. If Stalin had adamantly supported Molotov there would have been no United Nations formed at San Francisco. Furthermore, if we had not seized that moment to form the United Nations we would never have succeeded in the trying months that followed the end of the war.

*   *   *

Address by President Truman at the Closing Session of the
United Nations Conference *

San Francisco, June 26, 1945

I deeply regret that the press of circumstances when this Conference opened made it impossible for me to be here to greet you in person. I have asked for the privilege of coming today to express on behalf of the people of the United States our thanks for what you have done here, and to wish you Godspeed on your journeys home.

Public Papers of the Presidents, Harry S. Truman, pp. 138-44.

Somewhere in this broad country, every one of you can find some of our citizens who are sons and daughters, or descendants in some degree, of your own native land. All our people are glad and proud that this historic meeting and its accomplishments have taken place in our country. And that includes the millions of loyal and patriotic Americans who stem from the countries not represented at this Conference.

We are grateful to you for coming. We hope you have enjoyed your stay, and that you will come again.

You assembled in San Francisco nine weeks ago with the high hope and confidence of peace-loving people the world over.

Their confidence in you has been justified.

Their hope for your success has been fulfilled.

The Charter of the United Nations which you have just signed is a solid structure upon which we can build a better world. History will honor you for it. Between the victory in Europe and the final victory in Japan, in this most destructive of all wars, you have won a victory against war itself.

It was the hope of such a Charter that helped sustain the courage of stricken peoples through the darkest days of the war. For it is a declaration of great faith by the nations of the earth—faith that war is not inevitable, faith that peace can be maintained.

If we had had this Charter a few years ago—and above all, the will to use it—millions now dead would be alive. If we should falter in the future in our will to use it, millions now living will surely die.

It has already been said by many that this is only a first step to a lasting peace. That is true. The important thing is that all our thinking and all our actions be based on the realization that it is in fact only a first step. Let us all have it firmly in mind that we start today from a good beginning and, with our eye always on the final objective, let us march forward.

The Constitution of my own country came from a Convention which—like this one—was made up of delegates with many different views. Like this Charter, our Constitution came from a free and sometimes bitter exchange of conflicting opinions. When it was adopted, no one regarded it as a perfect document. But it grew and developed and expanded. And upon it there was built a bigger, a better, a more perfect union.

This Charter, like our own Constitution, will be expanded and improved as time goes on. No one claims that it is now a final or a perfect instrument. It has not been poured into any fixed mold. Changing world conditions will require readjustments—but they will be the readjustments of peace and not of war.

That we now have this Charter at all is a great wonder. It is also a cause for profound thanksgiving to Almighty God, who has brought us so far in our search for peace through world organization.

There were many who doubted that agreement could ever be reached by these fifty countries differing so much in race and religion, in language and culture. But these differences were all forgotten in one unshakable unity of determination—to find a way to end wars.

Out of all the arguments and disputes, and different points of view, a way was found to agree. Here in the spotlight of full publicity, in the tradition of liberty-loving people, opinions were expressed openly and freely. The faith and the hope of fifty peaceful nations were laid before this world forum. Differences were overcome. This

Charter was not the work of any single nation or group of nations, large or small. It was the result of a spirit of give-and-take, of tolerance for the views and interests of others.

It was proof that nations, like men, can state their differences, can face them, and then can find common ground on which to stand. That is the essence of democracy; that is the essence of keeping the peace in the future. By your agreement, the way was shown toward future agreement in the years to come.

This Conference owes its success largely to the fact that you have kept your minds firmly on the main objective. You had the single job of writing a constitution—a charter for peace. And you stayed on that job.

In spite of the many distractions which came to you in the form of daily problems and disputes about such matters as new boundaries, control of Germany, peace settlements, reparations, war criminals, the form of government of some of the European countries—in spite of all these, you continued in the task of framing this document.

Those problems and scores of others, which will arise, are all difficult. They are complicated. They are controversial and dangerous.

But with united spirit we met and solved even more difficult problems during the war. And with the same spirit, if we keep to our principles and never forsake our objectives, the problems we now face and those to come will also be solved.

We have tested the principle of cooperation in this war and have found that it works. Through the pooling of resources, through joint and combined military command, through constant staff meetings, we have shown what united strength can do in war. That united strength forced Germany to surrender. United strength will force Japan to surrender.

The United Nations have also had experience, even while the fighting was still going on, in reaching economic agreements for times of peace. What was done on the subject of relief at Atlantic City, food at Hot Springs, finance at Bretton Woods, aviation at Chicago, was a fair test of what can be done by nations determined to live cooperatively in a world where they cannot live peacefully any other way.

What you have accomplished in San Francisco shows how well these lessons of military and economic cooperation have been learned. You have created a great instrument for peace and security and human progress in the world.

The world must now use it!

If we fail to use it, we shall betray all those who have died in order that we might meet here in freedom and safety to create it.

If we seek to use it selfishly—for the advantage of any one nation or any small group of nations—we shall be equally guilty of that betrayal.

The successful use of this instrument will require the united will and firm determination of the free peoples who have created it. The job will tax the moral strength and fibre of us all.

We all have to recognize—no matter how great our strength—that we must deny ourselves the license to do always as we please. No one nation, no regional group, can or should expect, any special privilege which harms any other nation. If any nation would keep security for itself, it must be ready and willing to share security with all. That is the price which each nation will have to pay for world peace. Unless we are all willing to pay that price, no organization for world peace can accomplish its purpose.

And what a reasonable price that is!

Out of this conflict have come powerful military nations, now fully trained and equipped for war. But they have no right to dominate the world. It is rather the duty of these powerful nations to assume the responsibility for leadership toward a world of peace. That is why we have here resolved that power and strength shall be used not to wage war, but to keep the world at peace, and free from the fear of war.

By their own example the strong nations of the world should lead the way to international justice. That principle of justice is the foundation stone of this Charter. That principle is the guiding spirit by which it must be carried out—not by words alone but by continued concrete acts of good will.

There is a time for making plans—and there is a time for action. The time for action is now! Let us, therefore, each in his own nation and according to its own way, seek immediate approval of this Charter—and make it a living thing.

I shall send this Charter to the United States Senate at once. I am sure that the overwhelming sentiment of the people of my country and of their representatives in the Senate is in favor of immediate ratification.

A just and lasting peace cannot be attained by diplomatic agreement alone, or by military cooperation alone. Experience has shown how deeply the seeds of war are planted by economic rivalry and by social injustice. The Charter recognizes this fact for it has provided for economic and social cooperation as well. It has provided for this cooperation as part of the very heart of the entire compact.

It has set up machinery of international cooperation which men and nations of good will can use to help correct economic and social causes for conflict.

Artificial and uneconomic trade barriers should be removed—to the end that the standard of living of as many people as possible throughout the world may be raised. For Freedom from Want is one of the basic Four Freedoms toward which we all strive. The large and powerful nations of the world must assume leadership in this economic field as in all others.

Under this document we have good reason to expect the framing of an international bill of rights, acceptable to all the nations involved. That bill of rights will be as much a part of international life as our own Bill of Rights is a part of our Constitution. The Charter is dedicated to the achievement and observance of human rights and fundamental freedoms. Unless we can attain those objectives for all men and women everywhere—without regard to race, language or religion—we cannot have permanent peace and security.

With this Charter the world can begin to look forward to the time when all worthy human beings may be permitted to live decently as free people.

The world has learned again that nations, like individuals, must know the truth if they would be free—must read and hear the truth, learn and teach the truth.

We must set up an effective agency for constant and thorough interchange of thought and ideas. For there lies the road to a better and more tolerant understanding among nations and among peoples.

All Fascism did not die with Mussolini. Hitler is finished—but the seeds spread by his disordered mind have firm root in too many fanatical brains. It is easier to remove tyrants and destroy concentration camps than it is to kill the ideas which gave them birth and strength. Victory on the battlefield was essential, but it was not enough. For a good peace, a lasting peace, the decent peoples of the earth must remain determined to strike down the evil spirit which has hung over the world for the last decade.

The forces of reaction and tyranny all over the world will try to keep the United

Nations from remaining united. Even while the military machine of the Axis was being destroyed in Europe—even down to its very end—they still tried to divide us.

They failed. But they will try again.

They are trying even now. To divide and conquer was—and still is—their plan. They still try to make one Ally suspect the other, hate the other, desert the other.

But I know I speak for every one of you when I say that the United Nations will remain united. They will not be divided by propaganda either before the Japanese surrender—or after.

This occasion shows again the continuity of history.

By this Charter, you have given reality to the ideal of that great statesman of a generation ago—Woodrow Wilson.

By this Charter, you have moved toward the goal for which that gallant leader in this second world struggle worked and fought and gave his life—Franklin D. Roosevelt.

By this Charter, you have realized the objectives of many men of vision in your own countries who have devoted their lives to the cause of world organization for peace.

Upon all of us, in all our countries, is now laid the duty of transforming into action these words which you have written. Upon our decisive action rests the hope of those who have fallen, those now living, those yet unborn—the hope for a world of free countries—with decent standards of living—which will work and cooperate in a friendly civilized community of nations.

This new structure of peace is rising upon strong foundations.

Let us not fail to grasp this supreme chance to establish a world-wide rule of reason—to create an enduring peace under the guidance of God.

The Charter of the United Nations*

June 26, 1945

We the peoples of the United Nations determined to save succeeding generations from the scourge of war, which twice in our lifetime has brought untold sorrow to mankind, and

To reaffirm faith in fundamental human rights, in the dignity and worth of the human person, in the equal rights of men and women and of nations large and small, and

To establish conditions under which justice and respect for the obligations arising from treaties and other sources of international law can be maintained, and

To promote social progress and better standards of life in larger freedom,

and for these ends to practice tolerance and live together in peace with one another as good neighbors, and

To unite our strength to maintain international peace and security, and

To ensure, by the acceptance of principles and the institution of methods, that armed force shall not be used, save in the common interest, and

To employ international machinery for the promotion of the economic and social advancement of all peoples,

have resolved to combine our efforts to accomplish these aims; accordingly, our respective Governments, through representatives assembled in the city of San Francisco, who have exhibited their full powers found to be in good and due form, have agreed to the present Charter of the United Nations and do hereby establish an international organization to be known as the United Nations.

CHAPTER I
PURPOSES AND PRINCIPLES

Article 1

The Purposes of the United Nations are:

1. To maintain international peace and security, and to that end: to take effective collective measures for the prevention and removal of threats to the peace, and for the suppression of acts of aggression or other breaches of the peace, and to bring about by peaceful means, and in conformity with the principles of justice and international law, adjustment or settlement of international disputes or situations which might lead to a breach of the peace;

2. To develop friendly relations among nations based on respect for the principle of equal rights and self-determination of peoples, and to take other appropriate measures to strengthen universal peace;

3. To achieve international cooperation in solving international problems of an economic, social, cultural, or humanitarian character, and in promoting and encourag-

*U.S. Participation in the U.N. Report by the President to the Congress for the Year 1946, pp. 195-221.

ing respect for human rights and for fundamental freedoms for all without distinction as to race, sex, language, or religion; and

4. To be a center for harmonizing the actions of nations in the attainment of these common ends.

Article 2

The Organization and its Members, in pursuit of the Purposes stated in Article 1, shall act in accordance with the following Principles.

1. The Organization is based on the principle of the sovereign equality of all its Members.

2. All Members, in order to ensure to all of them the rights and benefits resulting from membership, shall fulfill in good faith the obligations assumed by them in accordance with the present Charter.

3. All Members shall settle their international disputes by peaceful means in such a manner that international peace and security, and justice, are not endangered.

4. All Members shall refrain in their international relations from the threat or use of force against the territorial integrity or political independence of any state, or in any other manner, inconsistent with the Purposes of the United Nations.

5. All Members shall give the United Nations every assistance in any action it takes in accordance with the present Charter, and shall refrain from giving assistance to any state against which the United Nations is taking preventive or enforcement action.

6. The Organization shall ensure that states which are not Members of the United Nations act in accordance with these Principles so far as may be necessary for the maintenance of international peace and security.

7. Nothing contained in the present Charter shall authorize the United Nations to intervene in matters which are essentially within the domestic jurisdiction of any state or shall require the Members to submit such matters to settlement under the present Charter; but this principle shall not prejudice the application of enforcement measures under Chapter VII.

CHAPTER II
MEMBERSHIP

Article 3

The original Members of the United Nations shall be the states which, having participated in the United Nations Conference on International Organization at San Francisco, or having previously signed the Declaration by United Nations of January 1, 1942, sign the present Charter and ratify it in accordance with Article 110.

Article 4

1. Membership in the United Nations is open to all other peace-loving states which accept the obligations contained in the present Charter and, in the judgment of the Organization, are able and willing to carry out these obligations.

2. The admission of any such state to membership in the United Nations will be effected by a decision of the General Assembly upon the recommendation of the Security Council.

Article 5

A Member of the United Nations against which preventive or enforcement action has been taken by the Security Council may be suspended from the exercise of the rights and privileges of membership by the General Assembly upon the recommendation of the Security Council. The exercise of these rights and privileges may be restored by the Security Council.

Article 6

A Member of the United Nations which has persistently violated the Principles contained in the present Charter may be expelled from the Organization by the General Assembly upon the recommendation of the Security Council.

CHAPTER III
ORGANS

Article 7

1. There are established as the principal organs of the United Nations: a General Assembly, a Security Council, an Economic and Social Council, a Trusteeship Council, an International Court of Justice, and a Secretariat.

2. Such subsidiary organs as may be found necessary may be established in accordance with the present Charter.

Article 8

The United Nations shall place no restrictions on the eligibility of men and women to participate in any capacity and under conditions of equality in its principal and subsidiary organs.

CHAPTER IV
THE GENERAL ASSEMBLY

Composition

Article 9

1. The General Assembly shall consist of all the Members of the United Nations.

2. Each Member shall have not more than five representatives in the General Assembly.

Functions and Powers

Article 10

The General Assembly may discuss any questions or any matters within the scope of the present Charter or relating to the powers and functions of any organs provided for in the present Charter, and, except as provided in Article 12, may make recommendations to the Members of the United Nations or to the Security Council or to both on any such questions or matters.

Article 11

1. The General Assembly may consider the general principles of cooperation in the maintenance of international peace and security, including the principles governing disarmament and the regulation of armaments, and may make recommendations with regard to such principles to the Members or to the Security Council or to both.

2. The General Assembly may discuss any questions relating to the maintenance of international peace and security brought before it by any Member of the United Nations, or by the Security Council, or by a state which is not a Member of the United Nations in accordance with Article 35, paragraph 2, and, except as provided in Article 12, may make recommendations with regard to any such question to the state or states concerned or to the Security Council or to both. Any such question on which action is necessary shall be referred to the Security Council by the General Assembly either before or after discussion.

3. The General Assembly may call the attention of the Security Council to situations which are likely to endanger international peace and security.

4. The powers of the General Assembly set forth in this Article shall not limit the general scope of Article 10.

Article 12

1. While the Security Council is exercising in respect of any dispute or situation the functions assigned to it in the present Charter, the General Assembly shall not make any recommendations with regard to that dispute or situation unless the Security Council so requests.

2. The Secretary-General, with the consent of the Security Council, shall notify the General Assembly at each session of any matters relative to the maintenance of international peace and security which are being dealt with by the Security Council and shall similarly notify the General Assembly, or the Members of the United Nations if the General Assembly is not in session, immediately the Security Council ceases to deal with such matters.

Article 13

1. The General Assembly shall initiate studies and make recommendations for the purpose of:

    a. promoting international cooperation in the political field and encouraging the progressive development of international law and its codification;

b. promoting international cooperation in the economic, social, cultural, educational, and health fields, and assisting in the realization of human rights and fundamental freedoms for all without distinction as to race, sex, language, or religion.

2. The further responsibilities, functions, and powers of the General Assembly with respect to matters mentioned in paragraph 1(b) above are set forth in Chapters IX and X.

Article 14

Subject to the provisions of Article 12, the General Assembly may recommend measures for the peaceful adjustment of any situation, regardless of origin, which it deems likely to impair the general welfare or friendly relations among nations, including situations resulting from a violation of the provisions of the present Charter setting forth the Purposes and Principles of the United Nations.

Article 15

1. The General Assembly shall receive and consider annual and special reports from the Security Council; these reports shall include an account of the measures that the Security Council has decided upon or taken to maintain international peace and security.

2. The General Assembly shall receive and consider reports from the other organs of the United Nations.

Article 16

The General Assembly shall perform such functions with respect to the international trusteeship system as are assigned to it under Chapters XII and XIII, including the approval of the trusteeship agreements for areas not designated as strategic.

Article 17

1. The General Assembly shall consider and approve the budget of the Organization.

2. The expenses of the Organization shall be borne by the Members as apportioned by the General Assembly.

3. The General Assembly shall consider and approve any financial and budgetary arrangements with specialized agencies referred to in Article 57 and shall examine the administrative budgets of such specialized agencies with a view to making recommendations to the agencies concerned.

Voting

Article 18

1. Each member of the General Assembly shall have one vote.

2. Decisions of the General Assembly on important questions shall be made by a two-thirds majority of the members present and voting. These questions shall include: recommendations with respect to the maintenance of international peace and security, the election of the non-permanent members of the Security Council, the election of the members of the Economic and Social Council, the election of members of the Trusteeship Council in accordance with paragraph 1(c) of Article 86, the admission of new Members to the United Nations, the suspension of the rights and privileges of membership, the expulsion of Members, questions relating to the operation of the trusteeship system, and budgetary questions.

3. Decisions on other questions, including the determination of additional categories of questions to be decided by a two-thirds majority, shall be made by a majority of the members present and voting.

Article 19

A Member of the United Nations which is in arrears in the payment of its financial contributions to the Organization shall have no vote in the General Assembly if the amount of its arrears equals or exceeds the amount of the contributions due from it for the preceding two full years. The General Assembly may, nevertheless, permit such a Member to vote if it is satisfied that the failure to pay is due to conditions beyond the control of the Member.

Procedure

Article 20

The General Assembly shall meet in regular annual sessions and in such special sessions as occasion may require. Special sessions shall be convoked by the Secretary-General at the request of the Security Council or of a majority of the Members of the United Nations.

Article 21

The General Assembly shall adopt its own rules of procedure. It shall elect the President for each session.

Article 22

The General Assembly may establish such subsidiary organs as it deems necessary for the performance of its functions.

CHAPTER V
THE SECURITY COUNCIL

Article 23

1. The Security Council shall consist of fifteen Members of the United Nations.

The Republic of China, France, the Union of Soviet Socialist Republics, the United Kingdom of Great Britain and Northern Ireland, and the United States of America shall be permanent members of the Security Council. The General Assembly shall elect ten other Members of the United Nations to be non-permanent members of the Security Council, due regard being specially paid, in the first instance to the contribution of Members of the United Nations to the maintenance of international peace and security and to the other purposes of the Organization, and also to equitable geographical distribution.

2. The non-permanent members of the Security Council shall be elected for a term of two years. In the first election of the non-permanent members after the increase of the membership of the Security Council from eleven to fifteen, two of the four additional members shall be chosen for a term of one year. A retiring member shall not be eligible for immediate re-election.

3. Each member of the Security Council shall have one representative.

Functions and Powers

Article 24

1. In order to ensure prompt and effective action by the United Nations, its Members confer on the Security Council primary responsibility for the maintenance of international peace and security, and agree that in carrying out its duties under this responsibility the Security Council acts on their behalf.

2. In discharging these duties the Security Council shall act in accordance with the Purposes and Principles of the United Nations. The specific powers granted to the Security Council for the discharge of these duties are laid down in Chapters VI, VII, VIII, and XII.

3. The Security Council shall submit annual and, when necessary, special reports to the General Assembly for its consideration.

Article 25

The Members of the United Nations agree to accept and carry out the decisions of the Security Council in accordance with the present Charter.

Article 26

In order to promote the establishment and maintenance of international peace and security with the least diversion for armaments of the world's human and economic resources, the Security Council shall be responsible for formulating, with the assistance of the Military Staff Committee referred to in Article 47, plans to be submitted to the Members of the United Nations for the establishment of a system for the regulation of armaments.

Article 27

1. Each member of the Security Council shall have one vote.

2. Decisions of the Security Council on procedural matters shall be made by an affirmative vote of nine members.

3. Decisions of the Security Council on all other matters shall be made by an affirmative vote of nine members including the concurring votes of the permanent members; provided that, in decisions under Chapter VI, and under paragraph 3 of Article 52, a party to a dispute shall abstain from voting.

Procedure

Article 28

1. The Security Council shall be so organized as to be able to function continuously. Each member of the Security Council shall for this purpose be represented at all times at the seat of the Organization.

2. The Security Council shall hold periodic meetings at which each of its members may, if it so desires, be represented by a member of the government or by some other specially designated representative.

3. The Security Council may hold meetings at such places other than the seat of the Organization as in its judgment will best facilitate its work.

Article 29

The Security Council may establish such subsidiary organs as it deems necessary for the performance of its functions.

Article 30

The Security Council shall adopt its own rules of procedure, including the method of selecting its President.

Article 31

Any member of the United Nations which is not a member of the Security Council may participate, without vote, in the discussion of any question brought before the Security Council whenever the latter considers that the interests of that Member are specially affected.

Article 32

Any Member of the United Nations which is not a member of the Security Council or any state which is not a Member of the United Nations, if it is a party to a dispute under consideration by the Security Council, shall be invited to participate, without vote, in the discussion relating to the dispute. The Security Council shall lay down such conditions as it deems just for the participation of a state which is not a Member of the United Nations.

CHAPTER VI
PACIFIC SETTLEMENT OF DISPUTES

Article 33

1. The parties to any dispute, the continuance of which is likely to endanger the maintenance of international peace and security, shall, first of all, seek a solution by negotiation, enquiry, mediation, conciliation, arbitration, judicial settlement, resort to regional agencies or arrangements, or other peaceful means of their own choice.

2. The Security Council shall, when it deems necessary, call upon the parties to settle their dispute by such means.

Article 34

The Security Council may investigate any dispute, or any situation which might lead to international friction or give rise to a dispute, in order to determine whether the continuance of the dispute or situation is likely to endanger the maintenance of international peace and security.

Article 35

1. Any Member of the United Nations may bring any dispute, or any situation of the nature referred to in Article 34, to the attention of the Security Council or of the General Assembly.

2. A state which is not a Member of the United Nations may bring to the attention of the Security Council or of the General Assembly any dispute to which it is a party if it accepts in advance, for the purposes of the dispute, the obligations of pacific settlement provided in the present Charter.

3. The proceedings of the General Assembly in respect of matters brought to its attention under this Article will be subject to the provisions of Articles 11 and 12.

Article 36

1. The Security Council may, at any stage of a dispute of the nature referred to in Article 33 or of a situation of like nature, recommend appropriate procedures or methods of adjustment.

2. The Security Council should take into consideration any procedures for the settlement of the dispute which have already been adopted by the parties.

3. In making recommendations under this Article the Security Council should also take into consideration that legal disputes should as a general rule be referred by the parties to the International Court of Justice in accordance with the provisions of the Statute of the Court.

Article 37

1. Should the parties to a dispute of the nature referred to in Article 33 fail to

settle it by the means indicated in that Article, they shall refer it to the Security Council.

2. If the Security Council deems that the continuance of the dispute is in fact likely to endanger the maintenance of international peace and security, it shall decide whether to take action under Article 36 or to recommend such terms of settlement as it may consider appropriate.

Article 38

Without prejudice to the provisions of Articles 33 to 37, the Security Council may, if all the parties to any dispute so request, make recommendations to the parties with a view to a pacific settlement of the dispute.

CHAPTER VII
ACTION WITH RESPECT TO THREATS TO THE PEACE, BREACHES OF THE PEACE, AND ACTS OF AGGRESSION

Article 39

The Security Council shall determine the existence of any threat to the peace, breach of the peace, or act of aggression and shall make recommendations, or decide what measures shall be taken in accordance with Articles 41 and 42, to maintain or restore international peace and security.

Article 40

In order to prevent an aggravation of the situation, the Security Council may, before making the recommendations or deciding upon the measures provided for in Article 39, call upon the parties concerned to comply with such provisional measures as it deems necessary or desirable. Such provisional measures shall be without prejudice to the rights, claims, or position of the parties concerned. The Security Council shall duly take account of failure to comply with such provisional measures.

Article 41

The Security Council may decide what measures not involving the use of armed force are to be employed to give effect to its decisions, and it may call upon the Members of the United Nations to apply such measures. These may include complete or partial interruption of economic relations and of rail, sea, air, postal, telegraphic, radio, and other means of communication, and the severance of diplomatic relations.

Article 42

Should the Security Council consider that measures provided for in Article 41 would be inadequate or have proved to be inadequate it may take such action by air, sea, or land forces as may be necessary to maintain or restore international peace and security. Such action may include demonstrations, blockade, and other operations by air, sea, or land forces of Members of the United Nations.

Article 43

1. All Members of the United Nations, in order to contribute to the maintenance of international peace and security, undertake to make available to the Security Council, on its call and in accordance with a special agreement or agreements, armed forces, assistance, and facilities, including rights of passage, necessary for the purpose of maintaining international peace and security.

2. Such agreement or agreements shall govern the numbers and types of forces, their degree of readiness and general location, and the nature of the facilities and assistance to be provided.

3. The agreement or agreements shall be negotiated as soon as possible on the initiative of the Security Council. They shall be concluded between the Security Council and Members or between the Security Council and groups of Members and shall be subject to ratification by the signatory states in accordance with their respective constitutional processes.

Article 44

When the Security Council has decided to use force it shall, before calling upon a Member not represented on it to provide armed forces in fulfillment of the obligations assumed under Article 43, invite that Member, if the Member so desires, to participate in the decisions of the Security Council concerning the employment of contingents of that Member's armed forces.

Article 45

In order to enable the United Nations to take urgent military measures, Members shall hold immediately available national air-force contingents for combined international enforcement action. The strength and degree of readiness of these contingents and plans for their combined action shall be determined, within the limits laid down in the special agreement or agreements referred to in Article 43, by the Security Council with the assistance of the Military Staff Committee.

Article 46

Plans for the application of armed force shall be made by the Security Council with the assistance of the Military Staff Committee.

Article 47

1. There shall be established a Military Staff Committee to advise and assist the

Security Council on all questions relating to the Security Council's military requirements for the maintenance of international peace and security, the employment and
command of forces placed at its disposal, the regulation of armaments, and possible
disarmament.

2. The Military Staff Committee shall consist of the Chiefs of Staff of the
permanent members of the Security Council or their representatives. Any Member of
the United Nations not permanently represented on the Committee shall be invited by
the Committee to be associated with it when the efficient discharge of the Committee's responsibilities requires the participation of the Member in its work.

3. The Military Staff Committee shall be responsible under the Security Council
for the strategic direction of any armed forces placed at the disposal of the Security
Council. Questions relating to the command of such forces shall be worked out
subsequently.

4. The Military Staff Committee, with the authorization of the Security Council
and after consultation with appropriate regional agencies, may establish regional
subcommittees.

Article 48

1. The action required to carry out the decisions of the Security Council for the
maintenance of international peace and security shall be taken by all the Members of
the United Nations or by some of them, as the Security Council may determine.

2. Such decisions shall be carried out by the Members of the United Nations
directly and through their action in the appropriate international agencies of which
they are members.

Article 49

The Members of the United Nations shall join in affording mutual assistance in
carrying out the measures decided upon by the Security Council.

Article 50

If preventive or enforcement measures against any state are taken by the Security
Council, any other state, whether a Member of the United Nations or not, which finds
itself confronted with special economic problems arising from the carrying out of
those measures shall have the right to consult the Security Council with regard to a
solution of those problems.

Article 51

Nothing in the present Charter shall impair the inherent right of individual or
collective self-defense if an armed attack occurs against a Member of the United
Nations, until the Security Council has taken measures necessary to maintain interna-

tional peace and security. Measures taken by Members in the exercise of this right of self-defense shall be immediately reported to the Security Council and shall not in any way affect the authority and responsibility of the Security Council under the present Charter to take at any time such action as it deems necessary in order to maintain or restore international peace and security.

CHAPTER VIII
REGIONAL ARRANGEMENTS

Article 52

1. Nothing in the present Charter precludes the existence of regional arrangements or agencies for dealing with such matters relating to the maintenance of international peace and security as are appropriate for regional action, provided that such arrangements or agencies and their activities are consistent with the Purposes and Principles of the United Nations.

2. The Members of the United Nations entering into such arrangements or constituting such agencies shall make every effort to achieve pacific settlement of local disputes through such regional agencies before referring them to the Security Council.

3. The Security Council shall encourage the development of pacific settlement of local disputes through such regional arrangements or by such regional agencies either on the initiative of the states concerned or by reference from the Security Council.

4. This Article in no way impairs the application of Articles 34 and 35.

Article 53

1. The Security Council shall, where appropriate, utilize such regional arrangements or agencies for enforcement action under its authority. But no enforcement action shall be taken under regional arrangements or by regional agencies without the authorization of the Security Council, with the exception of measures against any enemy state, as defined in paragraph 2 of this Article, provided for pursuant to Article 107 or in regional arrangements directed against renewal of aggressive policy on the part of any such state, until such time as the Organization may, on request of the Governments concerned, be charged with the responsibility for preventing further aggression by such a state.

2. The term enemy state as used in paragraph 1 of this Article applies to any state which during the Second World War has been an enemy of any signatory of the present Charter.

Article 54

The Security Council shall at all times be kept fully informed of activities undertaken or in contemplation under regional arrangements or by regional agencies for the maintenance of international peace and security.

CHAPTER IX
INTERNATIONAL ECONOMIC AND SOCIAL COOPERATION

Article 55

With a view to the creation of conditions of stability and well-being which are necessary for peaceful and friendly relations among nations based on respect for the principle of equal rights and self-determination of peoples, the United Nations shall promote:

a. higher standards of living, full employment, and conditions of economic and social progress and development;

b. solutions of international eonomic, social, health, and related problems; and international cultural and educational cooperation; and

c. universal respect for, and observance of, human rights and fundamental freedoms for all without distinction as to race, sex, language, or religion.

Article 56

All Members pledge themselves to take joint and separate action in cooperation with the Organization for the achievement of the purposes set forth in Article 55.

Article 57

1. The various specialized agencies, established by intergovernmental agreement and having wide international responsibilities, as defined in their basic instruments, in economic, social, cultural, educational, health, and related fields, shall be brought into relationship with the United Nations in accordance with the provisions of Article 63.

2. Such agencies thus brought into relationship with the United Nations are hereinafter referred to as specialized agencies.

Article 58

The Organization shall make recommendations for the coordination of the policies and activities of the specialized agencies.

Article 59

The Organization shall, where appropriate, initiate negotiations among the states concerned for the accomplishment of the purposes set forth in Article 55.

Article 60

Responsibility for the discharge of the functions of the Organization set forth in this Chapter shall be vested in the General Assembly and, under the authority of the

General Assembly, in the Economic and Social Council, which shall have for this purpose the powers set forth in Chapter X.

CHAPTER X
THE ECONOMIC AND SOCIAL COUNCIL

Article 61

1. The Economic and Social Council shall consist of twenty-seven Members of the United Nations elected by the General Assembly.

2. Subject to the provisions of paragraph 3, nine members of the Economic and Social Council shall be elected each year for a term of three years. A retiring member shall be eligible for immediate re-election.

3. At the first election after the increase in the membership of the Economic and Social Council from eighteen to twenty-seven members, in addition to the members elected in place of the six members whose term of office expires at the end of that year, nine additional members shall be elected. Of these nine additional members, the term of office of three members so elected shall expire at the end of one year, and of three other members at the end of two years, in accordance with arrangements made by the General Assembly.

4. Each member of the Economic and Social Council shall have one representative.

Functions and Powers

Article 62

1. The Economic and Social Council may make or initiate studies and reports with respect to international economic, social, cultural, educational, health, and related matters and may make recommendations with respect to any such matters to the General Assembly, to the Members of the United Nations, and to the specialized agencies concerned.

2. It may make recommendations for the purpose of promoting respect for, and observance of, human rights and fundamental freedoms for all.

3. It may prepare draft conventions for submission to the General Assembly, with respect to matters falling within its competence.

4. It may call, in accordance with the rules prescribed by the United Nations, international conferences on matters falling within its competence.

Article 63

1. The Economic and Social Council may enter into agreements with any of the agencies referred to in Article 57, defining the terms on which the agency concerned shall be brought into relationship with the United Nations. Such agreements shall be subject to approval by the General Assembly.

2. It may coordinate the activities of the specialized agencies through consultation with and recommendations to such agencies and through recommendations to the General Assembly and to the Members of the United Nations.

Article 64

1. The Economic and Social Council may take appropriate steps to obtain regular reports from the specialized agencies. It may make arrangements with the Members of the United Nations and with the specialized agencies to obtain reports on the steps taken to give effect to its own recommendations and to recommendations on matters falling within its competence made by the General Assembly.

2. It may communicate its observations on these reports to the General Assembly.

Article 65

The Economic and Social Council may furnish information to the Security Council and shall assist the Security Council upon its request.

Article 66

1. The Economic and Social Council shall perform such functions as fall within its competence in connection with the carrying out of the recommendations of the General Assembly.

2. It may, with the approval of the General Assembly, perform services at the request of Members of the United Nations and at the request of specialized agencies.

3. It shall perform such other functions as are specified elsewhere in the present Charter or as may be assigned to it by the General Assembly.

Voting

Article 67

1. Each member of the Economic and Social Council shall have one vote.

2. Decisions of the Economic and Social Council shall be made by a majority of the members present and voting.

Procedure

Article 68

The Economic and Social Council shall set up commissions in economic and social fields and for the promotion of human rights, and such other commissions as may be required for the performance of its functions.

Article 69

The Economic and Social Council shall invite any Member of the United Nations to participate, without vote, in its deliberations on any matter of particular concern to that Member.

Article 70

The Economic and Social Council may make arrangements for representatives of the specialized agencies to participate, without vote, in its deliberations and in those of the commissions established by it, and for its representatives to participate in the deliberations of the specialized agencies.

Article 71

The Economic and Social Council may make suitable arrangements for consultation with non-governmental organizations which are concerned with matters within its competence. Such arrangements may be made with international organizations and, where appropriate, with national organizations after consultation with the Member of the United Nations concerned.

Article 72

1. The Economic and Social Council shall adopt its own rules of procedure, including the method of selecting its President.

2. The Economic and Social Council shall meet as required in accordance with its rules, which shall include provision for the convening of meetings on the request of a majority of its members.

CHAPTER XI
DECLARATION REGARDING NON-SELF-GOVERNING
TERRITORIES

Article 73

Members of the United Nations which have or assume responsibilities for the administration of territories whose peoples have not yet attained a full measure of self-government recognize the principle that the interests of the inhabitants of these territories are paramount, and accept as a sacred trust the obligation to promote to the utmost, within the system of international peace and security established by the present Charter, the well-being of the inhabitants of these territories, and, to this end:

a. to ensure, with due respect for the culture of the peoples concerned, their political, economic, social, and educational advancement, their just treatment, and their protection against abuses;

b. to develop self-government, to take due account of the political aspirations of the peoples, and to assist them in the progressive development of their free political institutions, according to the particular circumstances of each territory and its peoples and their varying stages of advancement.

c. to further international peace and security.

d. to promote constructive measures of development, to encourage research, and to cooperate with one another and, when and where appropriate, with specialized international bodies with a view to the practical achievement of the social, economic, and scientific purposes set forth in this Article; and

e. to transmit regularly to the Secretary-General for information purposes, subject to such limitations as security and constitutional considerations may require, statistical and other information of a technical nature relating to economic, social, and educational conditions in the territories for which they are respectively responsible other than those territories to which Chapters XII and XII apply.

Article 74

Members of the United Nations also agree that their policy in respect of the territories to which this Chapter applies, no less than in respect of their metropolitan areas, must be based on the general principle of good-neighborliness, due account being taken of the interests and well-being of the rest of the world, in social, economic, and commercial matters.

CHAPTER XII
INTERNATIONAL TRUSTEESHIP SYSTEM

Article 75

The United Nations shall establish under its authority an international trusteeship system for the administration and supervision of such territories as may be placed thereunder by subsequent individual agreements. These territories are hereinafter referred to as trust territories.

Article 76

The basic objectives of the trusteeship system, in accordance with the Purposes of the United Nations laid down in Article 1 of the present Charter, shall be:

a. to further international peace and security;

b. to promote the political, economic, social, and educational advancement of the inhabitants of the trust territories, and their progressive development towards self-government or independence as may be appropriate to the particular circumstances of each territory and its peoples and the freely expressed wishes of the peoples concerned, and as may be provided by the terms of each trusteeship agreement;

c. to encourage respect for human rights and for fundamental freedoms for all without distinction as to race, sex, language, or religion, and to encourage recognition of the interdependence of the peoples of the world; and

d. to ensure equal treatment in social, economic, and commercial matters for all Members of the United Nations and their nationals, and also equal treatment for the latter in the administration of justice, without prejudice to the attainment of the foregoing objectives and subject to the provisions of Article 80.

Article 77

1. The trusteeship system shall apply to such territories in the following categories as may be placed thereunder by means of trusteeship agreements:

a. territories now held under mandate.

b. territories which may be detached from enemy states as a result of the Second World War; and

c. territories voluntarily placed under the system by states responsible for their administration.

2. It will be matter for subsequent agreement as to which territories in the foregoing categories will be brought under the trusteeship system and upon what terms.

Article 78

The trusteeship system shall not apply to territories which have become Members of the United Nations, relationship among which shall be based on respect for the principle of sovereign equality.

Article 79

The terms of trusteeship for each territory to be placed under the trusteeship system, including any alteration or amendment, shall be agreed upon by the states directly concerned, including the mandatory power in the case of territories held under mandate by a Member of the United Nations, and shall be approved as provided for in Articles 83 and 85.

Article 80

1. Except as may be agreed upon in individual trusteeship agreements, made under Articles 77, 79, and 81, placing each territory under the trusteeship system, and until such agreements have been concluded, nothing in this Chapter shall be construed in or of itself to alter in any manner the rights whatsoever of any states or any peoples or the terms of existing international instruments to which Members of the United Nations may respectively be parties.

2. Paragraph 1 of this Article shall not be interpreted as giving grounds for delay or postponement of the negotiation and conclusion of agreements for placing mandated and other territories under the trusteeship system as provided for in Article 77.

Article 81

The trusteeship agreement shall in each case include the terms under which the trust territory will be administered and designate the authority which will exercise the administration of the trust territory. Such authority, hereinafter called the administering authority, may be one or more states or the Organization itself.

Article 82

There may be designated, in any trusteeship agreement, a strategic area or areas which may include part or all of the trust territory to which the agreement applies, without prejudice to any special agreement or agreements made under Article 43.

Article 83

1. All functions of the United Nations relating to strategic areas, including the approval of the terms of the trusteeship agreements and of their alteration or amendment, shall be exercised by the Security Council.

2. The basic objectives set forth in Article 76 shall be applicable to the people of each strategic area.

3. The Security Council shall, subject to the provisions of the trusteeship agreements and without prejudice to security considerations, avail itself of the assistance of the Trusteeship Council to perform those functions of the United Nations under the trusteeship system relating to political, economic, social, and educational matters in the strategic areas.

Article 84

It shall be the duty of the administering authority to ensure that the trust territory shall play its part in the maintenance of international peace and security. To this end the administering authority may make use of volunteer forces, facilities, and assistance from the trust territory in carrying out the obligations towards the Security Council undertaken in this regard by the administering authority, as well as for local defense and the maintenance of law and order within the trust territory.

Article 85

1. The functions of the United Nations with regard to trusteeship agreements for all areas not designated as strategic, including the approval of the terms of the trusteeship agreements and of their alteration or amendment, shall be exercised by the General Assembly.

2. The Trusteeship Council, operating under the authority of the General Assembly, shall assist the General Assembly in carrying out these functions.

CHAPTER XIII
THE TRUSTEESHIP COUNCIL

Composition

Article 86

1. The Trusteeship Council shall consist of the following Members of the United Nations.

   a. those Members administering trust territories;
   b. such of those Members mentioned by name in Article 23 as are not administering trust territories; and
   c. as many other Members elected for three-year terms by the General Assembly as may be necessary to ensure that the total number of members of the Trusteeship Council is equally divided between those Members of the United Nations which administer trust territories and those which do not.

2. Each member of the Trusteeship Council shall designate one specially qualified person to represent it therein.

Functions and Powers

Article 87

The General Assembly and, under its authority, the Trusteeship Council, in carrying out their functions, may:

    a. consider reports submitted by the administering authority;

    b. accept petitions and examine them in consultation with the administering authority;

    c. provide for periodic visits to the respective trust territories at times agreed upon with the administering authority; and

    d. take these and other actions in conformity with the terms of the trusteeship agreements.

Article 88

The Trusteeship Council shall formulate a questionnaire on the political, economic, social, and educational advancement of the inhabitants of each trust territory, and the administering authority for each trust territory within the competence of the General Assembly shall make an annual report to the General Assembly upon the basis of such questionnaire.

Voting

Article 89

1. Each member of the Trusteeship Council shall have one vote.

2. Decisions of the Trusteeship Council shall be made by a majority of the members present and voting.

Procedure

Article 90

1. The Trusteeship Council shall adopt its own rules of procedure, including the method of selecting its President.

2. The Trusteeship Council shall meet as required in accordance with its rules, which shall include provision for the convening of meetings on the request of a majority of its members.

Article 91

The Trusteeship Council shall, when appropriate, avail itself of the assistance of the Economic and Social Council and of the specialized agencies in regard to matters with which they are respectively concerned.

CHAPTER XIV
THE INTERNATIONAL COURT OF JUSTICE

Article 92

The International Court of Justice shall be the principal judicial organ of the United Nations. It shall function in accordance with the annexed Statute, which is based upon the Statute of the Permanent Court of International Justice and forms an integral part of the present Charter.

Article 93

1. All Members of the United Nations are *ipso facto* parties to the Statute of the International Court of Justice.

2. A state which is not a Member of the United Nations may become a party to the Statute of the International Court of Justice on conditions to be determined in each case by the General Assembly upon the recommendation of the Security Council.

Article 94

1. Each Member of the United Nations undertakes to comply with the decision of the International Court of Justice in any case to which it is a party.

2. If any party to a case fails to perform the obligations incumbent upon it under a judgment rendered by the Court, the other party may have recourse to the Security Council, which may, if it deems necessary, make recommendations or decide upon measures to be taken to give effect to the judgment.

Article 95

Nothing in the present Charter shall prevent Members of the United Nations from entrusting the solution of their differences to other tribunals by virtue of agreements already in existence or which may be concluded in the future.

Article 96

1. The General Assembly or the Security Council may request the International Court of Justice to give an advisory opinion on any legal question.

2. Other organs of the United Nations and specialized agencies, which may at any time be so authorized by the General Assembly, may also request advisory opinions of the Court on legal questions arising within the scope of their activities.

CHAPTER XV
THE SECRETARIAT

Article 97

The Secretariat shall comprise a Secretary-General and such staff as the Organization may require. The Secretary-General shall be appointed by the General Assembly upon the recommendation of the Security Council. He shall be the chief administrative officer of the Organization.

Article 98

The Secretary-General shall act in that capacity in all meetings of the General Assembly, of the Security Council, of the Economic and Social Council, and of the Trusteeship Council, and shall perform such other functions as are entrusted to him by these organs. The Secretary-General shall make an annual report to the General Assembly on the work of the Organization.

Article 99

The Secretary-General may bring to the attention of the Security Council any matter which in his opinion may threaten the maintenance of international peace and security.

Article 100

1. In the performance of their duties the Secretary-General and the staff shall not seek or receive instructions from any government or from any other authority external to the Organization. They shall refrain from any action which might reflect on their position as international officials responsible only to the Organization.

2. Each Member of the United Nations undertakes to respect the exclusively international character of the responsibilities of the Secretary-General and the staff and not to seek to influence them in the discharge of their responsibilities.

Article 101

1. The staff shall be appointed by the Secretary-General under regulations established by the General Assembly.

2. Appropriate staffs shall be permanently assigned to the Economic and Social Council, the Trusteeship Council, and, as required, to other organs of the United Nations. These staffs shall form a part of the Secretariat.

3. The paramount consideration in the employment of the staff and in the determination of the conditions of service shall be the necessity of securing the highest standards of efficiency, competence, and integrity. Due regard shall be paid to the importance of recruiting the staff on as wide a geographical basis as possible.

CHAPTER XVI
MISCELLANEOUS PROVISIONS

Article 102

1. Every treaty and every international agreement entered into by any Member of the United Nations after the present Charter comes into force shall as soon as possible be registered with the Secretariat and published by it.

2. No party to any such treaty or international agreement which has not been registered in accordance with the provisions of paragraph 1 of this Article may invoke that treaty or agreement before any organ of the United Nations.

Article 103

In the event of a conflict between the obligations of the Members of the United Nations under the present Charter and their obligations under any other international agreement, their obligations under the present Charter shall prevail.

Article 104

The Organization shall enjoy in the territory of each of its Members such legal capacity as may be necessary for the exercise of its functions and the fulfillment of its purposes.

Article 105

1. The Organization shall enjoy in the territory of each of its Members such privileges and immunities as are necessary for the fulfillment of its purposes.

2. Representatives of the Members of the United Nations and officials of the Organization shall similarly enjoy such privileges and immunities as are necessary for the independent exercise of their functions in connection with the Organization.

3. The General Assembly may make recommendations with a view to determining the details of the application of paragraphs 1 and 2 of this Article or may propose conventions of the Members of the United Nations for this purpose.

CHAPTER XVII
TRANSITIONAL SECURITY ARRANGEMENTS

Article 106

Pending the coming into force of such special agreements referred to in Article 43 as in the opinion of the Security Council enable it to begin the exercise of its responsibilities under Article 42, the parties to the Four-Nation Declaration, signed at Moscow, October 30, 1943, and France, shall, in accordance with the provisions of paragraph 5 of that Declaration, consult with one another and as occasion requires with other Members of the United Nations with a view to such joint action on behalf of the Organization as may be necessary for the purpose of maintaining international peace and security.

Article 107

Nothing in the present Charter shall invalidate or preclude action in relation to any state which during the Second World War has been an enemy of any signatory to the present Charter, taken or authorized as a result of that war by the Governments having responsibility for such action.

CHAPTER XVIII
AMENDMENTS

Article 108

Amendments to the present Charter shall come into force for all Members of the United Nations when they have been adopted by a vote of two thirds of the members of the General Assembly and ratified in accordance with their respective constitutional processes by two thirds of the Members of the United Nations, including all the permanent members of the Security Council.

Article 109

1. A General Conference of the Members of the United Nations for the purpose of reviewing the present Charter may be held at a date and place to be fixed by a two-thirds vote of the members of the General Assembly and by a vote of any seven members of the Security Council. Each Member of the United Nations shall have one vote in the conference.

2. Any alteration of the present Charter recommended by a two-thirds vote of the conference shall take effect when ratified in accordance with their respective constitutional processes by two thirds of the Members of the United Nations including all the permanent members of the Security Council.

3. If such a conference has not been held before the tenth annual session of the General Assembly following the coming into force of the present Charter, the proposal to call such a conference shall be placed on the agenda of that session of the General Assembly, and the conference shall be held if so decided by a majority vote of the members of the General Assembly and by a vote of any seven members of the Security Council.

CHAPTER XIX
RATIFICATION AND SIGNATURE

Article 110

1. The present Charter shall be ratified by the signatory states in accordance with their respective constitutional processes.

2. The ratifications shall be deposited with the Government of the United States of America, which shall notify all the signatory states of each deposit as well as the Secretary-General of the Organization when he has been appointed.

3. The present Charter shall come into force upon the deposit of ratifications by the Republic of China, France, the Union of Soviet Socialist Republics, the United Kingdom of Great Britain and Northern Ireland, and the United States of America,

and by a majority of the other signatory states. A protocol of the ratifications deposited shall thereupon be drawn up by the Government of the United States of America which shall communicate copies thereof to all the signatory states.

4. The states signatory to the present Charter which ratify it after it has come into force will become original Members of the United Nations on the date of the deposit of their respective ratifications.

Article 111

The present Charter, of which the Chinese, French, Russian, English, and Spanish texts are equally authentic shall remain deposited in the archives of the Government of the United States of America. Duly certified copies thereof shall be transmitted by that Government to the Governments of the other signatory states.

In faith whereof the representatives of the Governments of the United Nations have signed the present Charter.

Amendments to the Charter of the United Nations and Message from President Lyndon B. Johnson*

April 6, 1965

I request the advice and consent of the Senate to ratification of two amendments to the Charter of the United Nations which are transmitted herewith along with a report to me from the Secretary of State. They are the first amendments adopted by the General Assembly since the founding of the United Nations.

These amendments will strengthen the ability of the United Nations to act as a force for peace and the progress of mankind.

They enlarge the membership of both the Security Council and the Economic and Social Council to bring those bodies into balance with the enlarged membership of the United Nations itself.

History of the Amendments

Amendments to the Charter of the United Nations must first be adopted by a two-thirds vote of the General Assembly, and then ratified by two-thirds of the member states, including all the permanent members, according to their constitutional procedure.

In late 1963, the General Assembly considered resolutions proposing the two amendments in question. These resolutions focused on three points:

First. That the text of the United Nations Charter be changed to increase the size of the Security Council from 11 to 15, to increase the voting majority of the Security

*Congressional Record, Apr. 6, 1965, pp. 7051-52.

Council from 7 to 9, and to increase the size of the Economic and Social Council from 13 to 27. In the Security Council, neither the seats nor the right of veto of the permanent members would be affected.

Second. The resolutions provided that members of the two Councils be elected on the basis of geographic distribution.

In the Security Council, the 10 nonpermanent members would include 5 from Africa and Asia, 1 from Eastern Europe, 2 from Latin America, and 2 from Western Europe and other areas; the 5 permanent members would remain the same. The present nonpermanent membership of the Security Council includes two members from Africa and Asia, two from Latin America, one from Western Europe, and one seat split between Asia and Eastern Europe.

In the Economic and Social Council, there would be the United States, 12 African and Asian States, 5 Latin American States, 3 Eastern European states—including the Soviet Union—and 6 states from Western Europe and other areas. The present composition of the Economic and Social Council, in addition to the United States, is five African and Asian States, four Latin American States, three Eastern European states—including the Soviet Union—and five states from Western Europe and other areas.

Third. The resolutions proposed that member states ratify the amendments by September 1, 1965.

On December 17, 1963, the resolutions were adopted by the General Assembly. On the enlargement of the Security Council, the vote was 97 to 11, with 4 abstentions; on the enlargement of the Economic and Social Council, it was 96 to 11, with 5 abstentions.

In those votes, the United States abstained, not because it doubted the principle of enlargement, but to maintain complete freedom of action while giving deliberate study to the effects of the specific proposals. The Soviet Union and France voted negatively. China voted for enlargement of the Security Council but abstained on enlargement of the Economic and Social Council. The United Kingdom abstained on both resolutions.

Since that time, 63 nations out of the required 76 have ratified the amendments. Other governments are now considering them. Of the permanent members of the Security Council, the Soviet Union has been the first to approve the amendments.

The United States should now move to ratify the charter amendments to enlarge the Security Council and the Economic and Social Council.

First. The amendments are realistic.

The membership of the United Nations has grown from 51 in 1945 to 114 in 1965. Almost all of the newer members are nations which have gained their independence from the peaceful dismantling of empires—a process which brought nationhood to one-third of all the peoples of the world and which is here to stay.

We welcome this growth.

The peoples of the world are more directly represented in the General Assembly of the United Nations today than they were 20 years ago.

We want to work together and cooperate with these new countries, within the United Nations.

If there are differences among us, we want them to be aired and examined within the United Nations.

This is the way to a peaceful and cooperative world.

But just as we welcome the growth of the United Nations, we must also recognize that the present Security Council and the present Economic and Social Council do not now realistically reflect it.

An increase in the representation on both Councils is now clearly necessary to restore the balance which existed between the Council and the General Assembly when the charter came into force. An expansion of 50 percent in the case of the Economic and Social Council and less in the Security Council is a reasonable way to adjust to a membership which has more than doubled. At the same time, the expansion is not such as to make the Councils unwieldy.

Second. The amendments are equitable.   .

When the charter was signed in 1945, the member states from Africa and Asia numbered 13 out of a total of 51—less than a third. Today, the member states from these great continents number 61 out of a total of 114—more than a half. The General Assembly resolutions, necessarily and rightly, take this new arithmetic into account.

Moreover, the explicit allocation of the new seats to geographic areas, as provided by Assembly resolution, is wise. It is designed to eliminate the contentious problem of sharing an inadequate number of seats—which has led to pressures against existing seats, to disputes over the definition of geographic areas, and to split terms in the Security Council to meet competing claims for representation.

Third. The amendments fully protect the basic interests of the permanent members. While we have seen that the work of the Security Council can be hampered seriously by the abuse of the veto provision, it nevertheless remains a wise and realistic feature of the United Nations Charter. The veto provision is maintained.

Fourth. Because the amendments are at once realistic and equitable, they will strengthen the United Nations.

They will increase the vitality of these Councils and of the United Nations itself by permitting more of the newer members to take part in the consideration of major world problems.

The amendments which will insure that the councils represent the whole organization they are intended to serve, will thereby also insure that the councils continue to earn the confidence and support of the membership at large. Without this confidence and support, the councils cannot be fully effective.

The organization as a whole will benefit from fuller participation in the work of the councils by the new members who have much to contribute—as they will benefit from the exercise of shared responsibility.

Fifth and finally, the amendments are a reflection and a demonstration of both the stability and the adaptability of the United Nations Charter.

We Americans have always had a healthy respect for the stability of our institutions and a wariness of change for the sake of change. Our American Constitution, which has been amended only 14 times since the Bill of Rights of 1791, has clearly met the test of stability. The fact that the United Nations Charter has remained as it was written 20 years ago is ample evidence of its stability.

At the same time, we Americans have always recognized the forces of change, and have always known instinctively that the ability of an institution to adapt to changed conditions is a reliable measure of its capacity for survival and growth. Our American Constitution, as evidenced by its amendments, has clearly met this test of adaptability.

Now, with its 20th birthday approaching, the United Nations is seeking the first two amendments to its basic charter. And this is welcome evidence of the inherent flexibility of another great institution.

The State of the United Nations

As we consider these first amendments to the United Nations Charter, it is fitting to review briefly the state of the United Nations itself.

The limitations of the United Nations are apparent. It has not been able to prevent aggression in southeast Asia; it has not been able to rid the world of poverty.

Nor has the United Nations been able to solve all of its internal problems. At the present time a serious financial problem threatens the capacity of the General Assembly to perform its share of peacekeeping.

And if the limitations are clear, the basic reason is plain. The United Nations is not a world government; it is an organization of governments participating by consent. It can move only in the direction and at the pace that its members want it to move.

And yet the United Nations has served well the cause of world peace and progress— and, therefore, the national interest and the personal interest of every American.

Keeping the Peace

Through the United Nations, the members have acted to avert wars on at least a dozen occasions—local wars which could have spread.

In Kashmir, the United Nations obtained and still polices a cease-fire line running through a bitterly contested area.

In Suez, the United Nations deployed an emergency force which enabled the respective national military forces to withdraw.

In the Congo, the United Nations provided 20,000 troops, assisted a new nation to survive its birth, and forestalled an East-West confrontation in the heart of Africa.

In Cyprus, the United Nations has stationed a force of 6,000 to strengthen that nation's security.

The office of the Secretary General has evolved into a sensitive listening post—an ever-ready channel of communication—a potential conciliation service open at all times to the international community of states.

Economic Development

At the same time, the day-to-day work of the United Nations is directed over-whelmingly toward building conditions which make the peace worth keeping.

United Nations experts are now at work in 130 countries or territories—bringing modern knowledge and technology to bear on the universal struggle to liberate man from the slavery of poverty.

The United Nations is in partnership with 89 nations and territories in cooperative pre-investment projects—surveying resources or training men and women in modern skills.

The development lending institutions affiliated with the United Nations have been investing some $1 billion annually in world development.

All in all, the level of development assistance flowing through the United Nations system of agencies now has reached some $1.3 billion a year.

Technological Cooperation

Meanwhile, United Nations agencies are performing the vital task of establishing cooperative ground rules which are required in the age of rapid international transport and instant international communication.

Agencies affiliated with the United Nations have developed standards for international air traffic—and for the safety of life at sea.

They have arranged for orderly use of the airways by allocating available radio frequencies among nations and users.

They have promoted international weather forecasting and are pioneering in the development of a world weather watch of incalculable benefit to peoples of all nations.

They have developed and maintained uniform international quarantine regulations against the spread of communicable diseases—and liberated 800 million people from the threat of the greatest killer of all time: malaria.

In these and other ways—through peacekeeping, through nation building, and through international technical services—the United Nations serves its members. In doing so, the Organization serves the national interest of the United States. It helps us do things we could not do so well alone and encourages other nations to share the burdens.

Conclusion

In one sense, the smallest members are in greatest need of the United Nations.

In another sense, the United Nations is of greatest service to the largest nations—for without the United Nations, the nations with the greatest resources would have to shoulder most of these tasks alone.

And in a combined sense, the United Nations serves simultaneously the large and the small, the rich and the poor—for the peace of one area is but part of world peace, and the prosperity of one country is but an element of the world's well-being.

This is why consistent and effective support for the United Nations has been near the heart of the U.S. foreign policy for two decades.

This is why the Congress and the public, regardless of politics or party, have been ready to stick with the United Nations through thick and thin.

The Organization has reached a point where the Security Council and the Economic and Social Council need to be enlarged to take account of the great growth of the Organization in recent years.

The proposed amendments offer responsible and equitable plans for meeting this problem.

Because the United Nations will continue to be deeply needed by nations which seek peace—by all nations which seek to raise the levels of human welfare—by all nations which seek to cooperate in putting the achievements of modern technology to work for all mankind—it is in the national interest of the United States to ratify these steps toward making more effective the principal councils of the Organization.

I therefore request the consent of the Senate to ratification by the United States of these amendments to the Charter of the United Nations.

Statute of the International Court of Justice*

June 25, 1945

Article 1

The International Court of Justice established by the Charter of the United Nations as the principal judicial organ of the United Nations shall be constituted and shall function in accordance with the provisions of the present Statute.

CHAPTER I: ORGANIZATION OF THE COURT

Article 2

The Court shall be composed of a body of independent judges, elected regardless of their nationality from among persons of high moral character, who possess the qualifications required in their respective countries for appointment to the highest judicial offices, or are jurisconsults of recognized competence in international law.

Article 3

1. The Court shall consist of fifteen members, no two of whom may be nationals of the same state.

2. A person who for the purposes of membership in the Court could be regarded as a national of more than one state shall be deemed to be a national of the one in which he ordinarily exercises civil and political rights.

Article 4

1. The members of the Court shall be elected by the General Assembly and by the Security Council from a list of persons nominated by the national groups in the Permanent Court of Arbitration, in accordance with the following provisions.

2. In the case of Members of the United Nations not represented in the Permanent Court of Arbitration, candidates shall be nominated by national groups appointed for this purpose by their governments under the same conditions as those prescribed for members of the Permanent Court of Arbitration by Article 44 of the Convention of The Hague of 1907 for the pacific settlement of international disputes.

*Department of State Bulletin, June 24, 1945, pp. 1134-42.

3. The conditions under which a state which is the party to the present Statute but is not a Member of the United Nations may participate in electing the members of the Court shall, in the absence of a special agreement, be laid down by the General Assembly upon recommendation of the Security Council.

Article 5

1. At least three months before the date of the action, the Secretary-General of the United Nations shall address a written request to the members of the Permanent Court of Arbitration belonging to the states which are parties to the present statute, and to the members of the national groups appointed under Article 4, paragraph 2, inviting them to undertake, within a given time, by national groups, the nomination of persons in a position to accept the duties of a member of the Court.

2. No group may nominate more than four persons, not more than two of whom shall be of their own nationality. In no case may the number of candidates nominated by a group be more than double the number of seats to be filled.

Article 6

Before making these nominations, each national group is recommended to consult its highest court of justice, its legal faculties and schools of law, and its national academies and national sections of international academies devoted to the study of law.

Article 7

1. The Secretary-General shall prepare a list in alphabetical order of all the persons thus nominated. Save as provided in Article 12, paragraph 2, these shall be the only persons eligible.

2. The Secretary-General shall submit this list to the General Assembly and to the Security Council.

Article 8

The General Assembly and the Security Council shall proceed independently of one another to elect the members of the Court.

Article 9

At every election, the electors shall bear in mind not only that the persons to be elected should individually possess the qualifications required, but also that in the body as a whole the representation of the main forms of civilization and of the principal legal systems of the world should be assured.

Article 10

1. Those candidates who obtain an absolute majority of votes in the General Assembly and in the Security Council shall be considered as elected.

2. Any vote of the Security Council, whether for the election of judges or for the appointment of members of the conference envisaged in Article 12, shall be taken without any distinction between permanent and non-permanent members of the Security Council.

3. In the event of more than one national of the same state obtaining an absolute majority of the votes both of the General Assembly and of the Security Council, the eldest of these only shall be considered as elected.

Article 11

If, after the first meeting held for the purpose of the election, one or more seats remain to be filled, a second and, if necessary, a third meeting shall take place.

Article 12

1. If, after the third meeting, one or more seats still remain unfilled, a joint conference consisting of six members, three appointed by the General Assembly and three by the Security Council, may be formed at any time at the request of either the General Assembly or the Security Council, for the purpose of choosing by the vote of an absolute majority one name for each seat still vacant, to submit to the General Assembly and the Security Council for their respective acceptance.

2. If the joint conference is unanimously agreed upon any person who fulfills the required conditions, he may be included in its list, even though he was not included in the list of nominations referred to in Article 7.

3. If the joint conference is satisfied that it will not be successful in procuring an election, those members of the Court who have already been elected shall, within a period to be fixed by the Security Council, proceed to fill the vacant seats by selection from among those candidates who have obtained votes either in the General Assembly or in the Security Council.

4. In the event of an equality of votes among the judges, the eldest judge shall have a casting vote.

Article 13

1. The members of the Court shall be elected for nine years and may be re-elected; provided, however, that of the judges elected at the first election, the terms of five judges shall expire at the end of three years and the terms of five more judges shall expire at the end of six years.

2. The judges whose terms are to expire at the end of the above-mentioned initial periods of three and six years shall be chosen by lot to be drawn by the Secretary-General immediately after the first election has been completed.

3. The members of the Court shall continue to discharge their duties until their places have been filled. Though replaced, they shall finish any cases which they may have begun.

4. In the case of the resignation of a member of the Court, the resignation shall be addressed to the President of the Court for transmission to the Secretary-General. This last notification makes the place vacant.

Article 14

Vacancies shall be filled by the same method as that laid down for the first election, subject to the following provision: the Secretary-General shall, within one month of the occurrence of the vacancy, proceed to issue the invitations provided for in Article 5, and the date of the election shall be fixed by the Security Council.

Article 15

A member of the Court elected to replace a member whose term of office has not expired shall hold office for the remainder of his predecessor's term.

Article 16

1. No member of the Court may exercise any political or administrative function, or engage in any other occupation of a professional nature.

2. Any doubt on this point shall be settled by the decision of the Court.

Article 17

1. No member of the Court may act as agent, counsel, or advocate in any case.

2. No member may participate in the decision of any case in which he has previously taken part as agent, counsel, or advocate for one of the parties, or as a member of a national or international court, or of a commission of enquiry, or in any other capacity.

3. Any doubt on this point shall be settled by the decision of the Court.

Article 18

1. No member of the Court can be dismissed unless, in the unanimous opinion of the other members, he has ceased to fulfil the required conditions.

2. Formal notification thereof shall be made to the Secretary-General by the Registrar.

3. This notification makes the place vacant.

Article 19

The members of the Court, when engaged in the business of the Court, shall enjoy diplomatic privileges and immunities.

Article 20

Every member of the Court shall, before taking up his duties, make a solemn declaration in open court that he will exercise his powers impartially and conscientiously.

Article 21

1. The Court shall elect its President and Vice President for three years; they may be re-elected.

2. The Court shall appoint its Registrar and may provide for the appointment of such other officers as may be necessary.

Article 22

1. The seat of the Court shall be established at The Hague. This, however, shall not prevent the Court from sitting and exercising its functions elsewhere whenever the Court considers it desirable.

2. The President and the Registrar shall reside at the seat of the Court.

Article 23

1. The Court shall remain permanently in session, except during the judicial vacations, the dates and duration of which shall be fixed by the Court.

2. Members of the Court are entitled to periodic leave, the dates and duration of which shall be fixed by the Court, having in mind the distance between The Hague and the home of each judge.

3. Members of the Court shall be bound, unless they are on leave or prevented from attending by illness or other serious reasons duly explained to the President, to hold themselves permanently at the disposal of the Court.

Article 24

1. If, for some special reason, a member of the Court considers that he should not take part in the decision of a particular case, he shall so inform the President.

2. If the President considers that for some special reason one of the members of the Court should not sit in a particular case, he shall give him notice accordingly.

3. If in any such case the member of the Court and the President disagree, the matter shall be settled by the decision of the Court.

Article 25

1. The full Court shall sit except when it is expressly provided otherwise in the present Statute.

2. Subject to the condition that the number of judges available to constitute the

Court is not thereby reduced below eleven, the Rules of the Court may provide for allowing one or more judges, according to circumstances and in rotation, to be dispensed from sitting.

3. A quorum of nine judges shall suffice to constitute the Court.

Article 26

1. The Court may from time to time form one or more chambers, composed of three or more judges as the Court may determine, for dealing with particular categories of cases; for example, labor cases and cases relating to transit and communications.

2. The Court may at any time form a chamber for dealing with a particular case. The number of judges to constitute such a chamber shall be determined by the Court with the approval of the parties.

3. Cases shall be heard and determined by the chambers provided for in this Article if the parties so request.

Article 27

A judgment given by any of the chambers provided for in Articles 26 and 29 shall be considered as rendered by the Court.

Article 28

The chambers provided for in Articles 26 and 29 may, with the consent of the parties, sit and exercise their functions elsewhere than at The Hague.

Article 29

With a view to the speedy dispatch of business, the Court shall form annually a chamber composed of five judges which, at the request of the parties, may hear and determine cases by summary procedure. In addition, two judges shall be selected for the purpose of replacing judges who find it impossible to sit.

Article 30

1. The Court shall frame rules for carrying out its functions. In particular, it shall lay down rules of procedure.

2. The Rules of the Court may provide for assessors to sit with the Court or with any of its chambers, without the right to vote.

Article 31

1. Judges of the nationality of each of the parties shall retain their right to sit in the case before the Court.

2. If the Court includes upon the Bench a judge of the nationality of one of the parties, any other party may choose a person to sit as judge. Such person shall be chosen preferably from among those persons who have been nominated as candidates as provided in Articles 4 and 5.

3. If the Court includes upon the Bench no judge of the nationality of the parties, each of these parties may proceed to choose a judge as provided in paragraph 2 of this Article.

4. The provisions of this Article shall apply to the case of Articles 26 and 29. In such cases, the President shall request one or, if necessary, two of the members of the Court forming the chamber to give place to the members of the Court of the nationality of the parties concerned, and, failing such, or if they are unable to be present, to the judges specially chosen by the parties.

5. Should there be several parties in the same interest, they shall, for the purpose of the preceding provisions, be reckoned as one party only. Any doubt upon this point shall be settled by the decision of the Court.

6. Judges chosen as laid down in paragraphs 2, 3, and 4 of this Article shall fulfil the conditions required by Articles 2, 17 (paragraph 2), 20, and 24 of the present Statute. They shall take part in the decision on terms of complete equality with their colleagues.

Article 32

1. Each member of the Court shall receive an annual salary.

2. The President shall receive a special annual allowance.

3. The Vice-President shall receive a special allowance for every day on which he acts as President.

4. The judges chosen under Article 31, other than members of the Court, shall receive compensation for each day on which they exercise their functions.

5. These salaries, allowances, and compensation shall be fixed by the General Assembly. They may not be decreased during the term of office.

6. The salary of the Registrar shall be fixed by the General Assembly on the proposal of the Court.

7. Regulations made by the General Assembly shall fix the conditions under which retirement pensions may be given to members of the Court and to the Registrar, and the conditions under which members of the Court and the Registrar shall have their traveling expenses refunded.

8. The above salaries, allowances, and compensation shall be free of all taxation.

Article 33

The expenses of the Court shall be borne by the United Nations in such a manner as shall be decided by the General Assembly.

CHAPTER II: COMPETENCE OF THE COURT

Article 34

1. Only states may be parties in cases before the Court.

2. The Court, subject to and in conformity with its Rules, may request of public international organizations information relevant to cases before it, and shall receive such information presented by such organizations on their own initiative.

3. Whenever the construction of the constituent instrument of a public international organization or of an international convention adopted thereunder is in question in a case before the Court, the Registrar shall so notify the public international organization concerned and shall communicate to it copies of all the written proceedings.

Article 35

1. The Court shall be open to the states parties to the present Statute.

2. The conditions under which the Court shall be open to other states shall, subject to the special provisions contained in treaties in force, be laid down by the Security Council, but in no case shall such conditions place the parties in a position of inequality before the Court.

3. When a state which is not a Member of the United Nations is a party to a case, the Court shall fix the amount which that party is to contribute towards the expenses of the Court. This provision shall not apply if such state is bearing a share of the expenses of the Court.

Article 36

1. The jurisdiction of the Court comprises all cases which the parties refer to it and all matters specially provided for in the Charter of the United Nations or in treaties and conventions in force.

2. The states parties to the present Statute may at any time declare that they recognize as compulsory *ipso facto* and without special agreement, in relation to any other state accepting the same obligation, the jurisdiction of the Court in all legal disputes concerning:

   a. the interpretation of a treaty;
   b. any question of international law;
   c. the existence of any fact which, if established, would constitute a breach of an international obligation;
   d. the nature or extent of the reparation to be made for the breach of an international obligation.

3. The declarations referred to above may be made unconditionally or on condition of reciprocity on the part of several or certain states, or for a certain time.

4. Such declarations shall be deposited with the Secretary-General of the United Nations, who shall transmit copies thereof to the parties to the Statute and to the Registrar of the Court.

5. Declarations made under Article 36 of the Statute of the Permanent Court of International Justice and which are still in force shall be deemed as between the parties to the present Statute, to be acceptances of the compulsory jurisdiction of the International Court of Justice for the period which they still have to run and in accordance with their terms.

6. In the event of a dispute as to whether the Court has jurisdiction, the matter shall be settled by the decision of the Court.

Article 37

Whenever a treaty or convention in force provides for reference of a matter to a tribunal to have been instituted by the League of Nations, or to the Permanent Court of International Justice, the matter shall, as between the parties to the present Statute, be referred to the International Court of Justice.

Article 38

1. The Court, whose function is to decide in accordance with international law such disputes as are submitted to it, shall apply:

    a. international conventions, whether general or particular, establishing rules expressly recognized by the contesting states;

    b. international custom, as evidence of a general practice accepted as law;

    c. the general principles of law recognized by civilized nations;

    d. subject to the provisions of Article 59, judicial decisions and the teachings of the most highly qualified publicists of the various nations, as subsidiary means for the determination of rules of law.

2. This provision shall not prejudice the power of the Court to decide a case *ex aequo et bono*, if the parties agree thereto.

CHAPTER III: PROCEDURE

Article 39

1. The official languages of the Court shall be French and English. If the parties agree that the case shall be conducted in French, the judgment shall be delivered in French. If the parties agree that the case shall be conducted in English, the judgment shall be delivered in English.

2. In the absence of an agreement as to which language shall be employed, each party may, in the pleadings, use the language which it prefers; the decision of the Court shall be given in French and English. In this case the Court shall at the same time determine which of the two texts shall be considered as authoritative.

3. The Court shall, at the request of any party, authorize a language other than French or English to be used by that party.

Article 40

1. Cases are brought before the Court, as the case may be, either by the notification of the special agreement or by a written application addressed to the Registrar. In either case the subject of the dispute and the parties shall be indicated.

2. The Registrar shall forthwith communicate the application to all concerned.

3. He shall also notify the Members of the United Nations through the Secretary-General, and also any other states entitled to appear before the Court.

Article 41

1. The Court shall have the power to indicate, if it considers that circumstances so require, any provisional measures which ought to be taken to preserve the respective rights of either party.

2. Pending the final decision, notice of the measures suggested shall forthwith be given to the parties and to the Security Council.

Article 42

1. The parties shall be represented by agents.

2. They may have the assistance of counsel or advocates before the Court.

3. The agents, counsel, and advocates of parties before the Court shall enjoy the privileges and immunities necessary to the independent exercise of their duties.

Article 43

1. The procedure shall consist of two parts: written and oral.

2. The written proceedings shall consist of the communication to the Court and to the parties of memorials, counter-memorials and, if necessary, replies; also all papers and documents in support.

3. These communications shall be made through the Registrar, in the order and within the time fixed by the Court.

4. A certified copy of every document produced by one party shall be communicated to the other party.

5. The oral proceedings shall consist of the hearing by the Court of witnesses, experts, agents, counsel, and advocates.

Article 44

1. For the service of all notices upon persons other than the agents, counsel, and advocates, the Court shall apply direct to the government of the state upon whose territory the notice has to be served.

2. The same provision shall apply whenever steps are to be taken to procure evidence on the spot.

Article 45

The hearing shall be under the control of the President or, if he is unable to preside, of the Vice-President; if neither is able to preside, the senior judge present shall preside.

Article 46

The hearing in Court shall be public, unless the Court shall decide otherwise, or unless the parties demand that the public be not admitted.

Article 47

1. Minutes shall be made at each hearing and signed by the Registrar and the President.

2. These minutes alone shall be authentic.

Article 48

The Court shall make orders for the conduct of the case, shall decide the form and time in which each party must conclude its arguments, and make all arrangements connected with the taking of evidence.

Article 49

The Court may, even before the hearing begins, call upon the agents to produce any document or to supply any explanations. Formal note shall be taken of any refusal.

Article 50

The Court may, at any time, entrust any individual, body, bureau, commission, or other organization that it may select, with the task of carrying out an enquiry or giving an expert opinion.

Article 51

During the hearing any relevant questions are to be put to the witnesses and experts under the conditions laid down by the Court in the rules of procedure referred to in Article 30.

Article 52

After the Court has received the proofs and evidence within the time specified for the purpose, it may refuse to accept any further oral or written evidence that one party may desire to present unless the other side consents.

Article 53

1. Whenever one of the parties does not appear before the Court, or fails to defend its case, the other party may call upon the Court to decide in favor of its claim.

2. The Court must, before doing so, satisfy itself, not only that it has jurisdiction in accordance with Articles 36 and 37, but also that the claim is well founded in fact and law.

Article 54

1. When, subject to the control of the Court, the agents, counsel, and advocates have completed their presentation of the case, the President shall declare the hearing closed.

2. The Court shall withdraw to consider the judgment.

3. The deliberations of the Court shall take place in private and remain secret.

Article 55

1. All questions shall be decided by a majority of the judges present.

2. In the event of an equality of votes, the President or the judge who acts in his place shall have a casting vote.

Article 56

1. The judgment shall state the reasons on which it is based.

2. It shall contain the names of the judges who have taken part in the decision.

Article 57

If the judgment does not represent in whole or in part the unanimous opinion of the judges, any judge shall be entitled to deliver a separate opinion.

Article 58

The judgment shall be signed by the President and by the Registrar. It shall be read in open court, due notice having been given to the agents.

Article 59

The decision of the Court has no binding force except between the parties and in respect of that particular case.

Article 60

The judgment is final and without appeal. In the event of dispute as to the meaning or scope of the judgment, the Court shall construe it upon the request of any party.

Article 61

1. An application for revision of a judgment may be made only when it is based

upon the discovery of some fact of such a nature as to be a decisive factor, which fact was, when the judgment was given, unknown to the Court and also to the party claiming revision, always provided that such ignorance was not due to negligence.

2. The proceedings for revision shall be opened by a judgment of the Court expressly recording the existence of the new fact, recognizing that it has such a character as to lay the case open to revision, and declaring the application admissible on this ground.

3. The Court may require previous compliance with the terms of the judgment before it admits proceedings in revision.

4. The application for revision must be made at latest within six months of the discovery of the new fact.

5. No application for revision may be made after the lapse of ten years from the date of the judgment.

Article 62

1. Should a state consider that it has an interest of a legal nature which may be affected by the decision in the case, it may submit a request to the Court to be permitted to intervene.

2. It shall be for the Court to decide upon this request.

Article 63

1. Whenever the construction of a convention to which states other than those concerned in the case are parties is in question, the Registrar shall notify all such states forthwith.

2. Every state so notified has the right to intervene in the proceedings; but if it uses this right, the construction given by the judgment will be equally binding upon it.

Article 64

Unless otherwise decided by the Court, each party shall bear its own costs.

CHAPTER IV: ADVISORY OPINIONS

Article 65

1. The Court may give an advisory opinion on any legal question at the request of whatever body may be authorized by or in accordance with the Charter of the United Nations to make such a request.

2. Questions upon which the advisory opinion of the Court is asked shall be laid before the Court by means of a written request containing an exact statement of the question upon which an opinion is required, and accompanied by all documents likely to throw light upon the question.

Article 66

1. The Registrar shall forthwith give notice of the request for an advisory opinion to all states entitled to appear before the Court.

2. The Registrar shall also, by means of a special and direct communication, notify any state entitled to appear before the Court or international organization considered by the Court, or, should it not be sitting, by the President, as likely to be able to furnish information on the question, that the Court will be prepared to receive, within a time limit to be fixed by the President, written statements, or to hear, at a public sitting to be held for the purpose, oral statements relating to the question.

3. Should any such state entitled to appear before the Court have failed to receive the special communication referred to in paragraph 2 of this Article, such state may express a desire to submit a written statement or to be heard; and the Court will decide.

4. States and organizations having presented written or oral statements or both shall be permitted to comment on the statements made by other states or organizations in the form, to the extent, and within the time limits which the Court, or, should it not be sitting, the President, shall decide in each particular case. Accordingly, the Registrar shall in due time communicate any such written statements to states and organizations having submitted similar statements.

Article 67

The Court shall deliver its advisory opinions in open Court, notice having been given to the Secretary-General and to the representatives of Members of the United Nations, of other states and of international organizations immediately concerned.

Article 68

In the exercise of its advisory functions the Court shall further be guided by the provisions of the present Statute which apply in contentious cases to the extent to which it recognizes them to be applicable.

CHAPTER V: AMENDMENT

Article 69

Amendments to the present Statute shall be effected by the same procedure as is provided by the Charter of the United Nations for amendments to that Charter, subject however to any provisions which the General Assembly upon recommendation of the Security Council may adopt concerning the participation of states which are parties to the Statute but are not Members of the United Nations.

Article 70

The Court shall have power to propose such amendments to the present Statute as it may deem necessary, through written communications to the Secretary-General, for consideration in conformity with the provisions of Article 69.

Proclamation by President Truman on the Charter of the United Nations *

October 31, 1945

Charter of the United Nations and Statute of the International Court of Justice. Signed at San Francisco June 26, 1945; ratification advised by the Senate of the United States of America July 28, 1945; ratified by the President of the United States of America August 8, 1945; ratification deposited August 8, 1945; proclaimed by the President of the United States of America October 31, 1945; effective October 24, 1945.

BY THE PRESIDENT OF THE UNITED STATES OF AMERICA
A PROCLAMATION

Whereas the Charter of the United Nations, with the Statute of the International Court of Justice annexed thereto, was formulated at the United Nations Conference on International Organization and was signed in San Francisco on June 26, 1945 by the Plenipotentiaries of the United States of America and the respective Plenipotentiaries of forty-nine other Governments, and was signed in Washington on October 15, 1945 by the Plenipotentiary of one other Government, the original of which Charter, with annexed Statute, in the Chinese, French, Russian, English, and Spanish languages, as certified by the Department of State of the United States of America, is word for word as follows:

*　　　　　　　　*　　　　　　　　*

And whereas the Senate of the United States of America by their Resolution of July 28 (legislative day of July 9), 1945, two-thirds of the Senators present concurring therein, did advise and consent to the ratification of the said Charter, with annexed Statute;

And whereas the said Charter, with annexed Statute, was duly ratified by the President of the United States of America on August 8, 1945, in pursuance of the aforesaid advice and consent of the Senate;

And whereas it is provided by paragraph 3 of Article 110 of the said Charter that the Charter shall come into force upon the deposit of ratifications by the Republic of China, France, the Union of Soviet Socialist Republics, the United Kingdom of Great Britain and Northern Ireland, and the United States of America, and by a majority of the other signatory states, and that a protocol of the ratifications deposited shall thereupon be drawn up by the Government of the United States of America;

And whereas the Secretary of State of the United States of America signed on October 24, 1945 a protocol of deposit of ratifications of the Charter of the United Nations stating that the requirements of the said paragraph 3 of Article 110 with respect to the coming into force of the said Charter have been fulfilled by the deposit of instruments of ratification of the said Charter by the following states:

**United States Statutes at Large*, 79th Cong., 1st sess., 1945, Vol. 59, Pt. 2, pp. 1031; 1213-14.

the Republic of China on September 28, 1945,
France on August 31, 1945,
the Union of Soviet Socialist Republics on October 24, 1945,
the United Kingdom of Great Britain and Northern Ireland on October 20, 1945, and
the United States of America on August 8, 1945;
and by
Argentina on September 24, 1945,
Brazil on September 21, 1945,
the Byelorussian Soviet Socialist Republic on October 24, 1945,
Chile on October 11, 1945,
Cuba on October 15, 1945,
Czechoslovakia on October 19, 1945,
Denmark on October 9, 1945,
the Dominican Republic on September 4, 1945,
Egypt on October 22, 1945,
El Salvador on September 26, 1945,
Haiti on September 27, 1945,
Iran on October 16, 1945,
Lebanon on October 15, 1945,
Luxembourg on October 17, 1945,
New Zealand on September 19, 1945,
Nicaragua on September 6, 1945,
Paraguay on October 12, 1945,
the Philippine Commonwealth on October 11, 1945,
Poland on October 24, 1945,
Saudi Arabia on October 18, 1945,
Syria on October 19, 1945,
Turkey on September 28, 1945,
the Ukrainian Soviet Socialist Republic on October 24, 1945, and
Yugoslavia on October 19, 1945;

Now, therefore, be it known that I, Harry S. Truman, President of the United States of America, do hereby proclaim and make public the said Charter of the United Nations, with the Statute of the International Court of Justice annexed thereto, to the end that the same and every article and clause thereof may be observed and fulfilled with good faith, on and from the twenty-fourth day of October, one thousand nine hundred forty-five, by the United States of America and by the citizens of the United States of America and all other persons subject to the jurisdiction thereof.

In testimony whereof, I have hereunto set my hand and caused the Seal of the United States of America to be affixed.

The Amended United Nations Participation Act*

1945

Text of Public Law 264, 79th Congress [S. 1580], 59 Stat. 619, approved December 20, 1945, as amended by Public Law 341, 81st Congress [H.R. 4708], 63 Stat. 734, approved October 10, 1949, and by Public Law 89-206 [S. 1903], 79 Stat. 841, approved September 28, 1965.

Ibid., 89th Cong., 1st sess., Vol. 79, pp. 841-2.

AN ACT To provide for the appointment of representatives of the United States in the organs and agencies of the United Nations, and to make other provision with respect to the participation of the United States in such organization.

Be it enacted by the Senate and House of Representatives of the United States of America in Congress assembled, That this Act may be cited as the "United Nations Participation Act of 1945."

Sec. 2

(a) The President, by and with the advice and consent of the Senate, shall appoint a representative of the United States to the United Nations who shall have the rank and status of Ambassador Extraordinary and Plenipotentiary and shall hold office at the pleasure of the President. Such representative shall represent the United States in the Security Council of the United Nations and may serve ex officio as representative of the United States in any organ, commission, or other body of the United Nations other than specialized agencies of the United Nations, and shall perform such other functions in connection with the participation of the United States in the United Nations as the President may, from time to time, direct.

(b) The President, by and with the advice and consent of the Senate, shall appoint additional persons with appropriate titles, rank, and status to represent the United States in the principal organs of the United Nations and in such organs, commissions, or other bodies as may be created by the United Nations with respect to nuclear energy or disarmament (control and limitation of armament). Such persons shall serve at the pleasure of the President and subject to the direction of the Representative of the United States to the United Nations. They shall at the direction of the Representative of the United States to the United Nations, represent the United States in any organ, commission, or other body of the United Nations, including the Security Council, the Economic and Social Council, and the Trusteeship Council, and perform such other functions as the Representative of the United States is authorized to perform in connection with the participation of the United States in the United Nations. Any Deputy Representative or any other officer holding office at the time the provisions of this Act, as amended, become effective shall not be required to be reappointed by reason of the enactment of this Act, as amended.

(c) The President, by and with the advice and consent of the Senate, shall designate from time to time to attend a specified session or specified sessions of the General Assembly of the United Nations not to exceed five representatives of the United States and such number of alternates as he may determine consistent with the rules of procedure of the General Assembly. One of the representatives shall be designated as the senior representative.

(d) The President may also appoint from time to time such other persons as he may deem necessary to represent the United States in organs and agencies of the United Nations. The President may, without the advice and consent of the Senate, designate any officer of the United States to act without additional compensation as the representative of the United States in either the Economic and Social Council or the Trusteeship Council (1) at any specified session thereof where the position is vacant or in the absence or disability of the regular representative or (2) in connection with a specified subject matter at any specified session of either such Council in lieu of the regular representative. The President may designate any officer of the Department of State, whose appointment is subject to confirmation by the Senate, to act, without additional compensation, for temporary periods as the representative of the United States in the Security Council of the United Nations in the absence or disability of the representatives provided for under section 2 (a) and (b) or in lieu of such representatives in connection with a specified subject matter.

(e) The President, by and with the advice and consent of the Senate, shall appoint a representative of the United States to the European office of the United Nations with appropriate rank and status who shall serve at the pleasure of the President and subject to the direction of the Secretary of State. Such person shall, at the direction of the Secretary of State, represent the United States at the European office of the United Nations, and perform such other functions there in connection with the participation of the United States in international organizations as the Secretary of State may, from time to time, direct.

(f) Nothing contained in this section shall preclude the President or the Secretary of State, at the direction of the President, from representing the United States at any meeting or session of any organ or agency of the United Nations.

(g) All persons appointed in pursuance of authority contained in this section shall receive compensation at rates determined by the President upon the basis of duties to be performed but not in excess of rates authorized by sections 411 and 412 of the Foreign Service Act of 1946 (Public Law 724, Seventy-ninth Congress) for chiefs of mission and Foreign Service officers occupying positions of equivalent importance, except that no Member of the Senate or House of Representatives or officer of the United States who is designated under subsections (c) and (d) of this section as a representative of the United States or as an alternate to attend any specified session or specified sessions of the General Assembly shall be entitled to receive such compensation.

Sec. 3

The representatives provided for in section 2 hereof, when representing the United States in the respective organs and agencies of the United Nations, shall, at all times, act in accordance with the instructions of the President transmitted by the Secretary of State unless other means of transmission is directed by the President, and such representatives shall, in accordance with such instructions, cast any and all votes under the Charter of the United Nations.

Sec. 4

The President shall, from time to time as occasion may require, but not less than once each year, make reports to the Congress of the activities of the United Nations and of the participation of the United States therein. He shall make special current reports on decisions of the Security Council to take enforcement measures under the provisions of the Charter of the United Nations, and on the participation therein, under his instructions, of the representative of the United States.

Sec. 5

(a) Notwithstanding the provisions of any other law, whenever the United States is called upon by the Security Council to apply measures which said Council has decided, pursuant to article 41 of said Chapter, are to be employed to give effect to its decisions under said Charter, the President may, to the extent necessary to apply such measures, through any agency which he may designate, and under such orders, rules and regulations as may be prescribed by him, investigate, regulate, or prohibit, in whole or in part, economic relations or rail, sea, air, postal, telegraphic, radio, and other means of communication between any foreign country or any national thereof or any person therein and the United States or any person subject to the jurisdiction thereof, or involving any property subject to the jurisdiction of the United States.

(b) Any person who willfully violates or evades or attempts to violate or evade any order, rule, or regulation issued by the President pursuant to paragraph (a) of this section shall, upon conviction, be fined not more than $10,000 or, if a natural person, be imprisoned for not more than ten years, or both: and the officer, director, or agent of any corporation who knowingly participates in such violation or evasion shall be punished by a like fine, imprisonment, or both, and any property, funds, securities, papers, or other articles or documents, or any vessel, together with her tackle, apparel, furniture, and equipment, or vehicle, or aircraft, concerned in such violation shall be forfeited to the United States.

Sec. 6

The President is authorized to negotiate a special agreement or agreements with the Security Council which shall be subject to the approval of the Congress by appropriate Act or joint resolution, providing for the numbers and types of armed forces, their degree of readiness and general locations, and the nature of facilities and assistance, including rights of passage, to be made available to the Security Council on its call for the purpose of maintaining international peace and security in accordance with article 43 of said Charter. The President shall not be deemed to require the authorization of the Congress to make available to the Security Council on its call in order to take action under article 42 of said Charter and pursuant to such special agreement or agreements the armed forces, facilities, or assistance provided for therein: Provided, That, except as authorized in section 7 of this Act, nothing herein contained shall be construed as an authorization to the President by the Congress to make available to the Security Council for such purpose armed forces, facilities, or assistance in addition to the forces, facilities, and assistance provided for in such special agreement or agreements.

Sec. 7

(a) Notwithstanding the provisions of any other law, the President, upon the request by the United Nations for cooperative action, and to the extent that he finds that it is consistent with the national interest to comply with such request, may authorize, in support of such activities of the United Nations as are specifically directed to the peaceful settlement of disputes and not involving the employment of armed forces contemplated by chapter VII of the United Nations Charter—

(1) the detail to the United Nations, under such terms and conditions as the President shall determine, of personnel of the armed forces of the United States to serve as observers, guards, or in any noncombatant capacity, but in no event shall more than a total of one thousand of such personnel be so detailed at any one time: Provided, That while so detailed, such personnel shall be considered for all purposes as acting in the line of duty, including the receipt of pay and allowances as personnel of the armed forces of the United States, credit for longevity and retirement, and all other perquisites appertaining to such duty:

Provided further, That upon authorization or approval by the President, such personnel may accept directly from the United Nations (a) any or all of the allowances or perquisites to which they are entitled under the first proviso hereof, and (b) extraordinary expenses and perquisites incident to such detail;

(2) the furnishing of facilities, services, or other assistance and the loan of the agreed fair share of the United States of any supplies and equipment to the United Nations by the National Military Establishment, under such terms and conditions as the President shall determine;

(3) the obligation, insofar as necessary to carry out the purposes of clauses (1) and (2) of this subsection, of any funds appropriated to the National Military Establishment or any department therein, the procurement of such personnel, supplies, equipment, facilities, services, or other assistance as may be made available in accordance with the request of the United Nations, and the replacement of such items, when necessary, where they are furnished from stocks.

(b) Whenever personnel or assistance is made available pursuant to the authority contained in subsection (a) (1) and (2) of this section, the President shall require reimbursement from the United Nations for the expense thereby incurred by the United States: Provided, That in exceptional circumstances, or when the President finds it to be in the national interest, he may waive, in whole or in part, the requirement of such reimbursement: Provided further, That when any such reimbursement is made, it shall be credited, at the option of the appropriate department of the National Military Establishment, either to the appropriation, fund, or account utilized in incurring the obligation, or to an appropriate appropriation, fund, or account currently available for the purposes for which expenditures were made.

(c) In addition to the authorization of appropriations to the Department of State contained in section 8 of this Act, there is hereby authorized to be appropriated to the National Military Establishment, or any department therein, such sums as may be necessary to reimburse such Establishment or department in the event that reimbursement from the United Nations is waived in whole or in part pursuant to authority contained in subsection (b) of this section.

(d) Nothing in this Act shall authorize the disclosure of any information or knowledge in any case in which such disclosure is prohibited by any other law of the United States.

Sec. 8

There is hereby authorized to be appropriate annually to the Department of State, out of any money in the Treasury not otherwise appropriated, such sums as may be necessary for the payment by the United States of its share of the expenses of the United Nations as apportioned by the General Assembly in accordance with article 17 of the Charter, and for all necessary salaries and expenses of the representatives provided for in section 2 hereof, and of their appropriate staffs, including personal services in the District of Columbia and elsewhere, without regard to the civil-service laws and the Classification Act of 1923, as amended; travel expenses without regard to the Standardized Government Travel Regulations, as amended, the Travel Expense Act of 1949, and section 10 of the Act of March 3, 1933, as amended, and, under such rules and regulations as the Secretary of State may prescribe, travel expenses of families and transportation of effects of United States representatives and other personnel in going to and returning from their post of duty; allowances for living quarters, including heat, fuel, and light, as authorized by the Act approved June 26,

1930 (5 U.S.C. 118a); cost-of-living allowances for personnel stationed abroad under such rules and regulations as the Secretary of State may prescribe; communications services; stenographic reporting, translating, and other services, by contract; hire of passenger motor vehicles and other local transportation; rent of offices; printing and binding without regard to section 11 of the Act of March 4, 1949 (44 U.S.C. 111); allowances and expenses as provided in section 6 of the Act of July 30, 1916 (Public Law 565, Seventy-ninth Congress), and allowances and expenses equivalent to those provided in section 901(3) of the Foreign Service Act of 1946 (Public Law 724, Seventy-ninth Congress); the lease or rental (for periods not exceeding ten years) of living quarters for the use of the representative of the United States to the United Nations referred to in paragraph (a) of section 2 hereof, the cost of installation and use of telephones in the same manner as telephone service is provided for use of the Foreign Service pursuant to the Act of August 23, 1912, as amended (31 U.S.C. 679), and the allotment of funds, similar to the allotment authorized by section 902 of the Foreign Service Act of 1946, for unusual expenses incident to the operation and maintenance of such living quarters, to be accounted for in accordance with section 903 of said Act; and such other expenses as may be authorized by the Secretary of State; all without regard to section 3709 of the Revised Statutes, as amended (41 U.S.C. 5).

Senate Resolution 196 on the Jurisdiction of the International Court of Justice*

November 28, 1945

Mr. Morse (for himself, Mr. Taft, Mr. Green, Mr. Fulbright, Mr. Smith, Mr. Ferguson, Mr. Aiken, Mr. Ball, Mr. Cordon, Mr. Wiley, Mr. Torey, Mr. Magnuson, Mr. Johnston of South Carolina, Mr. Myers, and Mr. McMahon) submitted the following resolution; which was referred to the Committee on Foreign Relations.

Resolved (two-thirds of the Senators present concurring therein), That the Senate advise and consent to the deposit by the President of the United States with the Secretary General of the United Nations, whenever that official shall have been installed in office, of a declaration under paragraph 2 of article 36 of the Statute of the International Court of Justice recognizing as compulsory ipso facto and without special agreement, in relation to any other state accepting the same obligation, the jurisdiction of the International Court of Justice in all legal disputes hereafter arising concerning—

    a. the interpretation of a treaty;
    b. any question of international law;
    c. the existence of any fact which, if established, would constitute a breach of an international obligation;
    d. the nature or extent of the reparation to be made for the breach of an international obligation.

Provided, That such declaration should not apply to—

    a. disputes the solution of which the parties shall entrust to other tribunals by virtue of agreements already in existence or which may be concluded in the future; or

*S. Res. 196, 79th Cong., 1st sess.

    b. disputes with regard to matters which are essentially within the domestic jurisdiction of the United States.

Provided further, That such declaration should remain in force for a period of five years and thereafter until the expiration of six months after notice may be given to terminate the declaration.

Joint Resolution on the Permanent Headquarters of the United Nations *

August 4, 1947

Whereas the Charter of the United Nations was signed on behalf of the United States on June 26, 1945, and was ratified on August 8, 1945, by the President of the United States, by and with the advice and consent of the Senate, and the instrument of ratification of the said Charter was deposited on August 8, 1945; and

Whereas the said Charter of the United Nations came into force with respect to the United States on October 24, 1945; and

Whereas article 104 of the Charter provides that "The Organization shall enjoy in the territory of each of its Members such legal capacity as may be necessary for the exercise of its functions and the fulfillment of its purposes"; and

Whereas article 105 of the Charter provides that:

"1. The Organization shall enjoy in the territory of each of its Members such privileges and immunities as are necessary for the fulfillment of its purposes.

"2. Representatives of the Members of the United Nations and officials of the Organization shall similarly enjoy such privileges and immunities as are necessary for the independent exercise of their functions in connection with the Organization.

"3. The General Assembly may make recommendations with a view to determining the details of the application of paragraphs 1 and 2 of this article or may propose conventions to the Members of the United Nations for this purpose."; and

Whereas article 28 and other articles of the Charter of the United Nations contemplate the establishment of a seat for the permanent headquarters of the Organization; and

Whereas the interim arrangements concluded on June 26, 1945, by the governments represented at the United Nations Conference on International Organization instructed the Preparatory Commission established in pursuance of the arrangements to "make studies and prepare recommendations concerning the location of the permanent headquarters of the Organization"; and

Whereas during the labors of the said Preparatory Commission, the Congress of the United States in H. Con. Res. 75, passed unanimously by the House of Representatives December 10, 1945, and agreed to unanimously by the Senate December 11, 1945, invited the United Nations "to locate the seat of the United Nations Organization within the United States"; and

Whereas the General Assembly on December 14, 1946, resolved "that the permanent headquarters of the United Nations shall be established in New York City in the area bounded by First Avenue, East Forty-eighth Street, the East River, and East Forty-second Street"; and

*Public Laws, Aug. 4, 1947, 80th Cong., 1st sess., pp. 756-68.

Whereas the General Assembly resolved on December 14, 1946, "That the Secretary-General be authorized to negotiate and conclude with the appropriate authorities of the United States of America an agreement concerning the arrangements required as a result of the establishment of the permanent headquarters of the United Nations in the city of New York" and to be guided in these negotiations by the provisions of a preliminary draft agreement which had been negotiated by the Secretary-General and the Secretary of State of the United States; and

Whereas the General Assembly resolved on December 14, 1946, that pending the coming into force of the agreement referred to above "the Secretary-General be authorized to negotiate and conclude arrangements with the appropriate authorities of the United States of America to determine on a provisional basis the privileges, immunities, and facilities needed in connection with the temporary headquarters of the United Nations."; and

Whereas the Secretary of State of the United States, after consultation with the appropriate authorities of the State and City of New York, signed at Lake Success, New York, on June 26, 1947, on behalf of the United States an agreement with the United Nations regarding the headquarters of the United Nations, which agreement is incorporated herein; and

Whereas the aforesaid agreement provides that it shall be brought into effect by an exchange of notes between the United States and the Secretary-General of the United Nations: Therefore be it

Resolved by the Senate and House of Representatives of the United States of America in Congress assembled, That the President is hereby authorized to bring into effect on the part of the United States the agreement between the United States of America and the United Nations regarding the headquarters of the United Nations, signed at Lake Success, New York, on June 26, 1947 (hereinafter referred to as the "agreement"), with such changes therein not contrary to the general tenor thereof and not imposing any additional obligations on the United States as the President may deem necessary and appropriate, and at his discretion, after consultation with the appropriate State and local authorities, to enter into such supplemental agreements with the United Nations as may be necessary to fulfill the purposes of the said agreement: Provided, That any supplemental agreement entered into pursuant to section 5 of the agreement incorporated herein shall be submitted to the Congress for approval. The agreement follows:

AGREEMENT BETWEEN THE UNITED NATIONS AND
THE UNITED STATES OF AMERICA REGARDING THE
HEADQUARTERS OF THE UNITED NATIONS

The United Nations and the United States of America:

Desiring to conclude an agreement for the purpose of carrying out the Resolution adopted by the General Assembly on 14 December 1946 to establish the seat of the United Nations in The City of New York and to regulate questions arising as a result thereof;

Have appointed as their representatives for this purpose:

The United Nations:
Trygve Lie,
Secretary-General,
and
The United States of America:
George C. Marshall,
Secretary of State,

Who have agreed as follows:

Article I—Definitions

Section 1

In this agreement:

(a) The expression "headquarters district" means (1) the area defined as such in Annex 1, (2) any other lands or buildings which from time to time may be included therein by supplemental agreement with the appropriate American authorities;

(b) the expression "appropriate American authorities" means such federal, state, or local authorities in the United States as may be appropriate in the context and in accordance with the laws and customs of the United States, including the laws and customs of the state and local government involved;

(c) the expression "General Convention" means the Convention on the Privileges and Immunities of the United Nations approved by the General Assembly of the United Nations 13 February 1946, as acceded to by the United States;

(d) the expression "United Nations" means the international organization established by the Charter of the United Nations, hereinafter referred to as the "Charter";

(e) the expression "Secretary-General" means the Secretary-General of the United Nations.

Article II—The Headquarters District

Section 2

The seat of the United Nations shall be the headquarters district.

Section 3

The appropriate American authorities shall take whatever action may be necessary to assure that the United Nations shall not be dispossessed of its property in the headquarters district, except as provided in Section 22 in the event that the United Nations ceases to use the same; provided that the United Nations shall reimburse the appropriate American authorities for any costs incurred, after consultation with the United Nations, in liquidating by eminent domain proceedings or otherwise any adverse claims.

Section 4

(a) The United Nations may establish and operate in the headquarters district:

(1) its own short-wave sending and receiving radio broadcasting facilities (including

emergency link equipment) which may be used on the same frequencies (within the tolerances prescribed for the broadcasting service by applicable United States regulations) for radiotelegraph, radioteletype, radiotelephone, radiotelephoto, and similar services;

(2) one point-to-point circuit between the headquarters district and the office of the United Nations in Geneva (using single sideband equipment) to be used exclusively for the exchange of broadcasting programs and interoffice communcations;

(3) low power micro-wave, low or medium frequency facilities for communication within headquarters buildings only, or such other buildings as may temporarily be used by the United Nations;

(4) facilities for point-to-point communication to the same extent and subject to the same conditions as permitted under applicable rules and regulations for amateur operation in the United States, except that such rules and regulations shall not be applied in a manner inconsistent with the inviolability of the headquarters district provided by Section 9 (a);

(5) such other radio facilities as may be specified by supplemental agreement between the United Nations and the appropriate American authorities.

(b) The United Nations shall make arrangements for the operation of the services referred to in this section with the International Telecommunication Union, the appropriate agencies of the Government of the United States and the appropriate agencies of the Government of the United States and the appropriate agencies of other affected governments with regard to all frequencies and similar matters.

(c) The facilities provided for in this section may, to the extent necessary for efficient operation, be established and operated outside the headquarters district. The appropriate American authorities will, on request of the United Nations, make arrangements, on such terms and in such manner as may be agreed upon by supplemental agreement, for the acquisition or use by the United Nations of appropriate premises for such purposes and the inclusion of such premises in the headquarters district.

Section 5

In the event that the United Nations should find it necessary and desirable to establish and operate an aerodrome, the conditions for the location, use and operation of such an aerodrome and the conditions under which there shall be entry into and exit therefrom shall be the subject of a supplemental agreement.

Section 6

In the event that the United Nations should propose to organize its own postal service, the conditions under which such service shall be set up shall be the subject of a supplemental agreement.

Article III—Law and Authority in the Headquarters District

Section 7

(a) The headquarters district shall be under the control and authority of the United Nations as provided in this agreement.

(b) Except as otherwise provided in this agreement or in the General Convention, the federal, state and local law of the United States shall apply within the headquarters district.

(c) Except as otherwise provided in this agreement or in the General Convention, the federal, state and local courts of the United States shall have jurisdiction over acts done and transactions taking place in the headquarters district as provided in applicable federal, state and local laws.

(d) The federal, state and local courts of the United States, when dealing with cases arising out of or relating to acts done or transactions taking place in the headquarters district, shall take into account the regulations enacted by the United Nations under Section 8.

Section 8

The United Nations shall have the power to make regulations, operative within the headquarters district, for the purpose of establishing therein conditions in all respects necessary for the full execution of its functions. No federal, state or local law or regulation of the United States which is inconsistent with a regulation of the United Nations authorized by this section shall, to the extent of such inconsistency, be applicable within the headquarters district. Any dispute, between the United Nations and the United States, as to whether a regulation of the United Nations is authorized by this section or as to whether a federal, state or local law or regulation is inconsistent with any regulation of the United Nations authorized by this section, shall be promptly settled as provided in Section 21. Pending such settlement, the regulation of the United Nations shall apply, and the federal, state or local law or regulation shall be inapplicable in the headquarters district to the extent that the United Nations claims it to be inconsistent with the regulation of the United Nations. This section shall not prevent the reasonable application of fire protection regulations of the appropriate American authorities.

Section 9

(a) The headquarters district shall be inviolable. Federal, state or local officers or officials of the United States, whether administrative, judicial, military or police, shall not enter the headquarters district to perform any official duties therein except with the consent of and under conditions agreed to by the Secretary-General. The service of legal process, including the seizure of private property, may take place within the headquarters district only with the consent of and under conditions approved by the Secretary-General.

(b) Without prejudice to the provisions of the General Convention or Article IV of this agreement, the United Nations shall prevent the headquarters district from becoming a refuge either for persons who are avoiding arrest under the federal, state, or local law of the United States or are required by the Government of the United States for extradition to another country, or for persons who are endeavoring to avoid service of legal process.

Section 10

The United Nations may expel or exclude persons from the headquarters district for violation of its regulations adopted under Section 8 or for other cause. Persons who violate such regulations shall be subject to other penalties or to detention under arrest only in accordance with the provisions of such laws or regulations as may be adopted by the appropriate American authorities.

Article IV—Communications and Transit

Section 11

The federal, state or local authorities of the United States shall not impose any impediments to transit to or from the headquarters district of (1) representatives of Members or officials of the United Nations, or of specialized agencies as defined in Article 57, paragraph 2, of the Charter, or the families of such representatives or officials, (2) experts performing missions for the United Nations or for such specialized agencies, (3) representatives of the press, or of radio, film or other information agencies, who have been accredited by the United Nations (or by such a specialized agency) in its discretion after consultation with the United States, (4) representatives of nongovernmental organizations recognized by the United Nations for the purpose of consultation under Article 71 of the Charter, or (5) other persons invited to the headquarters district by the United Nations or by such specialized agency on official business. The appropriate American authorities shall afford any necessary protection to such persons while in transit to or from the headquarters district. This section does not apply to general interruptions of transportation which are to be dealt with as provided in Section 17, and does not impair the effectiveness of generally applicable laws and regulations as to the operation of means of transportation.

Section 12

The provisions of Section 11 shall be applicable irrespective of the relations existing between the Governments of the persons referred to in that section and the Government of the United States.

Section 13

(a) Laws and regulations in force in the United States regarding the entry of aliens shall not be applied in such manner as to interfere with the privileges referred to in Section 11. When visas are required for persons referred to in that Section, they shall be granted without charge and as promptly as possible.

(b) Laws and regulations in force in the United States regarding the residence of aliens shall not be applied in such manner as to interfere with the privileges referred to in Section 11 and, specifically, shall not be applied in such manner as to require any such person to leave the United States on account of any activities performed by him in his official capacity. In case of abuse of such privileges of residence by any such person in activities in the United States outside his official capacity, it is understood that the privileges referred to in Section 11 shall not be construed to grant him exemption from the laws and regulations of the United States regarding the continued residence of aliens, provided that:

(1) No proceedings shall be instituted under such laws or regulations to require any such person to leave the United States except with the prior approval of the Secretary of State of the United States. Such approval shall be given only after consultation with the appropriate Member in the case of a representative of a Member (or a member of his family) or with the Secretary-General or the principal executive officer of the appropriate specialized agency in the case of any other person referred to in Section 11;

(2) A representative of the Member concerned, the Secretary-General, or the principal executive officer of the appropriate specialized agency, as the case may be, shall have the right to appear in any such proceedings on behalf of the person against whom they are instituted;

(3) Persons who are entitled to diplomatic privileges and immunities under Section 15 or under the General Convention shall not be required to leave the United States otherwise than in accordance with the customary procedure applicable to diplomatic envoys accredited to the United States.

(c) This section does not prevent the requirement of reasonable evidence to establish that persons claiming the rights granted by Section 11 come within the classes described in that section, or the reasonable application of quarantine and health regulations.

(d) Except as provided above in this section and in the General Convention, the United States retains full control and authority over the entry of persons or property into the territory of the United States and the conditions under which persons may remain or reside there.

(e) The Secretary-General shall, at the request of the appropriate American authorities, enter into discussions with such authorities, with a view to making arrangements for registering the arrival and departure of persons who have been granted visas valid only for transit to and from the headquarters district and sojourn therein and in its immediate vicinity.

(f) The United Nations shall, subject to the foregoing provisions of this section, have the exclusive right to authorize or prohibit entry of persons and property into the headquarters district and to prescribe the conditions under which persons may remain or reside there.

Section 14

The Secretary-General and the appropriate American authorities shall, at the request of either of them, consult as to methods of facilitating entrance into the United States, and the use of available means of transportation, by persons coming from abroad who wish to visit the headquarters district and do not enjoy the rights referred to in this Article.

Article V—Resident Representatives to the United Nations

Section 15

(1) Every person designated by a Member as the principal resident representative to the United Nations of such Member or as a resident representative with the rank of ambassador or minister plenipotentiary,

(2) such resident members of their staffs as may be agreed upon between the Secretary-General, the Government of the United States and the Government of the Member concerned,

(3) every person designated by a Member of a specialized agency, as defined in Article 57, paragraph 2, of the Charter, as its principal resident representative, with the rank of ambassador or minister plenipotentiary, at the headquarters of such agency in the United States, and

(4) such other principal resident representatives of members to a specialized agency and such resident members of the staffs of representatives to a specialized agency as may be agreed upon between the principal executive officer of the specialized agency, the Government of the United States and the Government of the Member concerned, shall, whether residing inside or outside the headquarters district, be entitled in the territory of the United States to the same privileges and immunities, subject to corresponding conditions and obligations, as it accords to diplomatic envoys accredited to it. In the case of Members whose governments are not recognized by the United

States, such privileges and immunities need be extended to such representatives, or persons on the staffs of such representatives, only within the headquarters district, at their residences and offices outside the district, in transit between the district and such residences and offices, and in transit on official business to or from foreign countries.

Article VI—Police Protection of the Headquarters District

Section 16

(a) The appropriate American authorities shall exercise due diligence to ensure that the tranquility of the headquarters district is not disturbed by the unauthorized entry of groups of persons from outside or by disturbances in its immediate vicinity and shall cause to be provided on the boundaries of the headquarters district such police protection as is required for these purposes.

(b) If so requested by the Secretary-General, the appropriate American authorities shall provide a sufficient number of police for the preservation of law and order in the headquarters district, and for the removal therefrom of persons as requested under the authority of the United Nations. The United Nations shall, if requested, enter into arrangements with the appropriate American authorities to reimburse them for the reasonable cost of such services.

Article VII—Public Services and Protection of the Headquarters District

Section 17

(a) The appropriate American authorities will exercise to the extent requested by the Secretary-General the powers which they possess with respect to the supplying of public services to ensure that the headquarters district shall be supplied on equitable terms with the necessary public services, including electricity, water, gas, post, telephone, telegraph, transportation, drainage, collection of refuse, fire protection, snow removal, et cetera. In case of any interruption or threatened interruption of any such services, the appropriate American authorities will consider the needs of the United Nations as being of equal importance with the similar needs of essential agencies of the Government of the United States, and will take steps accordingly, to ensure that the work of the United Nations is not prejudiced.

(b) Special provisions with reference to maintenance of utilities and underground construction are contained in Annex 2.

Section 18

The appropriate American authorities shall take all reasonable steps to ensure that the amenities of the headquarters district are not prejudiced and the purposes for which the disrict is required are not obstructed by any use made of the land in the vicinity of the district. The United Nations shall on its part take all reasonable steps to ensure that the amenities of the land in the vicinity of the headquarters district are not prejudiced by any use made of the land in the headquarters district by the United Nations.

Section 19

It is agreed that no form of racial or religious discrimination shall be permitted within the headquarters district.

Article VIII—Matters Relating to the Operation of This Agreement

Section 20

The Secretary-General and the appropriate American authorities shall settle by agreement the channels through which they will communicate regarding the application of the provisions of this agreement and other questions affecting the headquarters district, and may enter into such supplemental agreements as may be necessary to fulfill the purposes of this agreement. In making supplemental agreements with the Secretary-General, the United States shall consult with the appropriate state and local authorities. If the Secretary-General so requests, the Secretary of State of the United States shall appoint a special representative for the purpose of liaison with the Secretary-General.

Section 21

(a) Any dispute between the United Nations and the United States concerning the interpretation or application of this agreement or of any supplemental agreement, which is not settled by negotiation or other agreed mode of settlement, shall be referred for final decision to a tribunal of three arbitrators, one to be named by the Secretary-General, one to be named by the Secretary of State of the United States, and the third to be chosen by the two, or, if they should fail to agree upon a third, then by the President of the International Court of Justice.

(b) The Secretary-General or the United States may ask the General Assembly to request of the International Court of Justice an advisory opinion on any legal question arising in the course of such proceedings. Pending the receipt of the opinion of the Court, an interim decision of the arbitral tribunal shall be observed on both parties. Thereafter, the arbitral tribunal shall render a final decision, having regard to the opinion of the Court.

Article IX—Miscellaneous Provisions

Section 22

(a) The United Nations shall not dispose of all or any part of the land owned by it in the headquarters district without the consent of the United States. If the United States is unwilling to consent to a disposition which the United Nations wishes to make of all or any part of such land, the United States shall buy the same from the United Nations at a price to be determined as provided in paragraph (d) of this section.

(b) If the seat of the United Nations is removed from the headquarters district, all right, title and interest of the United Nations in and to real property in the headquarters district or any part of it shall, on request of either the United Nations or the United States, be assigned and conveyed to the United States. In the absence of such request, the same shall be assigned and conveyed to the subdivision of a state in which it is located or, if such subdivision shall not desire it, then to the state in which it is located. If none of the foregoing desires the same, it may be disposed of as provided in paragraph (a) of this section.

(c) If the United Nations disposes of all or any part of the headquarters district, the provisions of other sections of this agreement which apply to the headquarters district shall immediately cease to apply to the land and buildings so disposed of.

(d) The price to be paid for any conveyance under this section shall, in default of agreement, be the then fair value of the land, buildings and installations, to be determined under the procedure provided in Section 21.

Section 23

The seat of the United Nations shall not be removed from the headquarters district unless the United Nations should so decide.

Section 24

This agreement shall cease to be in force if the seat of the United Nations is removed from the territory of the United States, except for such provisions as may be applicable in connection with the orderly termination of the operations of the United Nations at its seat in the United States and the disposition of its property therein.

Section 25

Wherever this agreement imposes obligations on the appropriate American authorities, the Government of the United States shall have the ultimate responsibility for the fulfillment of such obligations by the appropriate American authorities.

Section 26

The provisions of this agreement shall be complementary to the provisions of the General Convention. In so far as any provision of this agreement and any provisions of the General Convention relate to the same subject matter, the two provisions shall, wherever possible, be treated as complementary, so that both provisions shall be applicable and neither shall narrow the effect of the other; but in any case of absolute conflict, the provisions of this agreement shall prevail.

Section 27

This agreement shall be construed in the light of its primary purpose to enable the United Nations at its headquarters in the United States, fully and efficiently to discharge its responsibilities and fulfill its purposes.

Section 28

This agreement shall be brought into effect by an exchange of notes between the Secretary-General, duly authorized pursuant to a resolution of the General Assembly of the United Nations, and the appropriate executive officer of the United States, duly authorized pursuant to appropriate action of the Congress.

In witness whereof the respective representatives have signed this Agreement and have affixed their seals hereto.

Done in duplicate, in the English and French languages, both authentic, at Lake Success the twenty-sixth day of June 1947.

For the Government of the United States of America:

G. C. Marshall
Secretary of State
For the United Nations:
Trygve Lie
Secretary-General

ANNEX 1

The area referred to in Section 1 (a) (1) consists of (a) the premises bounded on the East by the westerly side of Franklin D. Roosevelt Drive, on the West by the easterly side of First Avenue, on the North by the southerly side of East Forty-eighth Street, and on the South by the northerly side of East Forty-second Street, all as proposed to be widened, in the Borough of Manhattan, City and State of New York, and (b) an easement over Franklin D. Roosevelt Drive, above a lower limiting plane to be fixed for the construction and maintenance of an esplanade, together with the structures thereon and foundations and columns to support the same in locations below such limiting plane, the entire area to be more definitely defined by supplemental agreement between the United Nations and the United States of America.

ANNEX 2—MAINTENANCE OF UTILITIES AND UNDERGROUND CONSTRUCTION

Section 1
The Secretary-General agrees to provide passes to duly authorized employees of The City of New York, the State of New York, or any of their agencies or subdivisions, for the purpose of enabling them to inspect, repair, maintain, reconstruct and relocate utilities, conduits, mains and sewers within the headquarters district.

Section 2
Underground constructions may be undertaken by The City of New York, or the State of New York, or any of their agencies or subdivisions, within the headquarters district only after consultation with the Secretary-General, and under conditions which shall not disturb the carrying out of the functions of the United Nations.

Sec. 2
For the purpose of carrying out the obligations of the United States under said agreement and supplemental agreements with respect to United States assurance that the United Nations shall not be dispossessed of its property in the headquarters district, and with respect to the establishment of radio facilities and the possible establishment of an airport:

(a) The President of the United States, or any official or governmental agency authorized by the President, may acquire in the name of the United States any property or interest therein by purchase, donation, or other means of transfer, or may cause proceedings to be instituted for the acquisition of the same by condemnation.

(b) Upon the request of the President, or such officer as the President may designate, the Attorney General of the United States shall cause such condemnation or other proceedings to be instituted in the name of the United States in the district court of the United States for the district in which the property is situated and such court shall have full jurisdiction of such proceedings, and any condemnation proceedings shall be conducted in accordance with the Act of August 1, 1888 (25 Stat. 357), as amended, and the Act of February 26, 1931 (46 Stat. 1421), as amended.

(c) After the institution of any such condemnation proceedings, possession of the property may be taken at any time the President, or such officer as he may designate, determines is necessary, and the court shall enter such orders as may be necessary to effect entry and occupancy of the property.

(d) The President of the United States, or any officer of governmental agency duly authorized by the President, may, in the name of the United States, transfer or convey possession of and title to any interest in any property acquired or held by the United States, pursuant to paragraph (a) above, to the United Nations on the terms provided in the agreement or in any supplemental agreement, and shall execute and deliver such conveyances and other instruments and perform such other acts in connection therewith as may be necessary to carry out the provisions of the agreement.

(e) There are authorized to be appropriated, out of any money in the Treasury not otherwise appropriated, such sums as may be required to enable the United States to carry out the undertakings hereby authorized: Provided, That any money appropriated under this authorization shall be spent only on a basis of reimbursement by the United Nations in accordance with section 3 of the agreement, and that the money thus reimbursed shall be deposited and covered into the Treasury of the United States as miscellaneous receipts.

Sec. 3

The President, or the Secretary of State under his direction, is authorized to enter into agreements with the State of New York or any other State of the United States and to the extent not inconsistent with State law, with any one or more of the political subdivisions thereof in aid of effectuating the provisions of the agreement.

Sec. 4

Any States, or, to the extent not inconsistent with State law any political subdivisions thereof, affected by the establishment of the headquarters of the United Nations in the United States are authorized to enter into agreements with the United Nations or with each other consistent with the agreement and for the purpose of facilitating compliance with the same: Provided, That, except in cases of emergency and agreements of a routine contractual character, a representative of the United States, to be appointed by the Secretary of State, may, at the discretion of the Secretary of State, participate in the negotiations, and that any such agreement entered into by such State or States or political subdivisions thereof shall be subject to approval by the Secretary of State.

Sec. 5

The President is authorized to make effective with respect to the temporary headquarters of the United Nations in the State of New York, on a provisional basis, such of the provisions of the agreement as he may deem appropriate, having due regard for the needs of the United Nations at its temporary headquarters.

Sec. 6

Nothing in the agreement shall be construed as in any way diminishing, abridging, or weakening the right of the United States to safeguard its own security and completely to control the entrance of aliens into any territory of the United States other than the headquarters district and its immediate vicinity, as to be defined and fixed in a supplementary agreement between the Government of the United States and the United Nations in pursuance of section 13 (3) (e) of the agreement, and such areas as it is reasonably necessary to traverse in transit between the same and foreign countries. Moreover, nothing in section 14 of the agreement with respect to facilitating entrance into the United States by persons who wish to visit the headquarters district and do not enjoy the right of entry provided in section 11 of the agreement shall be construed to amend or suspend in any way the immigration laws of the United States or to commit the United States in any way to effect any amendment or suspension of such laws.

DISARMAMENT AND
OUTER SPACE

DISARMAMENT AND OUTER SPACE

Commentary

The urge to disarm or, at least, to put the process of armament under international control, did not begin with the birth of the nuclear age. Good intentions had ebbed and swelled between the two World Wars. Conferences were held. The Kellogg-Briand Pact of 1928 enjoined its adherents to renounce war. However, such efforts proved futile when the new totalitarians and the old imperialists chose to rearm behind the cloak of disarmament talk. The United States, seeking to turn its back on "power politics" was content to take naval parity formulas at face value and let its military power decline. Only the clear and massive emergency of the Second World War turned this country into the "arsenal of democracy;" but, when the War was over, revulsion against the means of victory more than matched the original effort.

All this, and the drafting of the U.N. Charter, preceded the first atomic explosion at Alamogordo, N.M. on July 16, 1945. The lesson of that climactic occurrence was spelled out in the first use of a nuclear weapon against Hiroshima on August 6th and Nagasaki on August 9th. The resulting horror left no doubt in most minds that the world could not afford a third great conflict. Renewed determination to assist peace by beating swords into plowshares was expressed most urgently by the new U.N. organization.

Approaching the problem with full realism, the three nations—the United States, Britain and Canada—which had combined their talents to build the first atomic bomb, proposed placing its incredible potential under international control. This conclusion was, without delay, submitted to the Soviet Union for its concurrence. The three nations visualized a U.N. Commission to prepare and submit recommendations. The Moscow Declaration of December, 1945 adopted their language and began the process of fulfillment.

The very first resolution of the First General Assembly in London, in a session primarily concerned with organization, did, nevertheless, unanimously establish the Atomic Energy Commission and—in the spirit of the times—instructed it to make specific proposals.

Bernard M. Baruch was appointed U.S. Representative to the Commission and proposed at its first meeting, on June 14, 1946, the creation of an International Atomic Development Authority. Such a body, with unlimited perogatives of licensing, inspection, and control, was to take over the United States nuclear monopoly. The Soviet Union rejected the plan, calling instead for an international convention "prohibiting the production and employment of weapons based on the use of atomic energy." Existing stocks of atomic weapons were to be destroyed within three months, but no provision was made for international control or enforcement. Soviet Foreign Minister

Andrei Gromyko explained shortly afterward that the international control envisaged in the Baruch Plan was not compatible with national sovereignty. The Soviet Union demanded, furthermore, that any control function be subject to the veto in the Security Council. These conditions, manifestly elaborating Soviet strategic doctrine, remained at the core of Moscow's disarmament diplomacy, although the General Assembly in effect approved the essentials of the Baruch Plan.

Nineteen forty-six was not a tranquil year, or one whose varied action lent support to the central premise of the United Nations—the translation of the great powers' wartime partnership into the political terms of the postwar world. The Soviet Union, probing along its periphery in Iran, Turkey, Greece, and Germany, met the unqualified resistance of an increasingly disillusioned United States. When President Harry S. Truman addressed the opening meeting of the resumed First General Assembly on the eve of the U.N.'s first anniversary, his tone was almost grim. The Assembly subsequently adopted a resolution setting forth the "Principles Governing the General Regulation and Reduction of Armaments," the first of many in this and other fields which demonstrated that agreement was more easily achieved in principle than in practice.

Under the U.N. Charter, the General Assembly is authorized to discuss the general principles of disarmament and to make recommendations on the subject. The Security Council, which is charged with "primary responsibility for the maintenance of international peace and security" was also made responsible in Article 26, for formulating plans for the regulation of armaments.

The Military Staff Committee, which was to assist the Security Council in drafting these plans, was a dead letter from the start. The Security Council remained the focal point of all postwar disarmament efforts during the U.N.'s first thirteen years. The U.N. Atomic Energy Commission, which tried to deal with nuclear weapons, and the U.N. Commission for Conventional Armaments each comprised the eleven members of the Security Council (plus Canada in the atomic field). The two bodies were merged, after achieving slight success individually, in a 12-nation U.N. Disarmament Commission. Enlarged in 1958 to include the full membership of the U.N., the new body was no more productive than its predecessors. Nor was the resort, from time to time, to private talks or smaller subcommittees successful. Varying the object of the U.N.'s labors made no difference either. For the first ten years, comprehensive measures were sought on the assumption that a world not armed to the teeth would be more relaxed in coping with its political problems. Then attention turned to specific partial steps, which were seen as ways of building confidence for an assault on the larger question. Such agreements as were concluded in the U.N.'s first quarter century fell in this category and dealt with nuclear testing, the spread of nuclear weapons and outer space. They were only indirectly related to disarmament. If they built any confidence, it remained invisible. Efforts, renewed from time to time, to find a direct approach to general and complete disarmament continued fruitless.

In 1959, the active pursuit of disarmament and arms control formulas was removed from the U.N. and assigned, by the agreement of the United States, the United Kingdom, the Soviet Union and France, to a Disarmament Committee. This group met in Geneva, but reported to the General Assembly. The Assembly took note of its voluminous reports and urged it on to greater effort. But the member nations, moving in these years from one crisis to another, chose to seek security in their own strength and in alliances. After the adoption of the first peacetime draft law, the Senate passed another of those resolutions in which it periodically expressed more good will than understanding of the U.N.'s real limitations. President Truman, addressing the General Assembly on the U.N.'s Fifth Anniversary, stressed the hard reality in a context of hope.

In 1953, President Dwight D. Eisenhower, starting his first term, called for renewed negotiations toward arms reduction, with the money thus saved to be applied to a "total war . . . upon the brute forces of poverty and need" in the world. He called for the limitation of armed forces by absolute numbers or ratios, adequate safeguards, and international control of the atom. Later that year, before the Assembly, he elaborated on the last point in a speech which was given the title "Atoms for Peace."

In 1956, the United States joined with other members of the U.N. and the specialized agencies (a formula which excluded such non-members as Communist China and such unrecognized entities as East Germany) to form the International Atomic Energy Agency. It was designed to serve as a world pool of nuclear fuels like U-235 and plutonium for such peaceful uses as research and atomic power. The fuels were to be given to the Agency by the atomically advanced countries and to be made available by it to others under safety standards and safeguards to ensure against diversion for military use. Inspection was completely voluntary—accepted by the signatories for projects involving the Agency's help or, in the case of the atomic powers, for installations they opened to examination. This first, partial machinery of control was later written into a treaty barring the dissemination of nuclear weapons.

Another proposal that would lead to arms control was advanced by President Eisenhower on July 21, 1955 at a meeting in Geneva with the heads of government of Britain, France and the Soviet Union. Labelled the "Open Skies" proposal, it called for an exchange of blueprints of military establishments and reciprocal aerial reconnaissance to banish the fear of surprise attack. A week later, the Senate urged the President to ask the United Nations to study limitations on military spending in order to improve the world's standard of living. In September, Secretary of State John Foster Dulles touched on both these ideas in an address to the General Assembly. The Soviet Union had already objected to the "Open Skies" plan because it did not include overseas bases and did not refer to the reduction of armaments and the prohibition of nuclear weapons. Moscow asserted that security could be gained against surprise attack by installing observers at certain harbors, airports, railroad stations and road junctions.

This and other familiar elements of the disarmament complex were still under review two years later, but the increasing effort devoted to beginning space exploration was appropriately reflected in the discussion. Man's first earth satellite, the Soviet Sputnik launched on October 4, 1957, added a new dimension to the problem of security and arms control.

Those who hoped for a new stimulus to agreement may have been disappointed. Not for the reason that there was no agreement. In 1959, the United States and the Soviet Union joined ten other states in a treaty reserving Antarctica for peaceful purposes. This was followed, over the next nine years by conventions on the peaceful use of outer space, a partial nuclear test ban and a treaty against the spread of nuclear weapons. Interesting though they were, they were peripheral to disarmament. In fact, the frailty of any agreement which was not foolproof, self-enforcing and of mutual benefit, was demonstrated in September, 1961 when the Soviet Union resumed nuclear testing in the atmosphere despite a tacitly agreed moratorium which the United States had been observing for three years. A special plea from the General Assembly could not dissuade the Soviet government from carrying its test series to a climax with an explosion of nearly sixty megatons.

Outer space, whose drama compelled worldwide attention, was dealt with quickly and effectively. The subject was new, above all, capturing the imagination and stirring emotion on its own dramatic merits uncompromised by historic claims or vested interests. All contestants were starting from scratch and the two superpowers, the United States and the Soviet Union, were provided with a special common purpose. They alone had the technology to explore and to utilize outer space under military as well as scientific auspices. Each, therefore, was interested in establishing a code of conduct which would keep the other from preempting rights or territory. The other nations, seeing little or no chance of competing, wanted a framework of law to preserve their security and their own opportunity in the future.

The United Nations first considered the question of outer space in 1958. Three years later, an Assembly resolution set down the principle that international law, including the U.N. Charter, applied to outer space and the celestial bodies; and that both were free for exploration and use by all states and not subject to national appropriation. It also provided for systematic international cooperation, with the U.N. as a focal point.

High tension over Berlin in 1961 and the Cuban missile crisis of 1962 did not exactly stimulate cooperation. Nevertheless, consultations continued quietly. In the Fall, 1961, the United States and the Soviet Union submitted to the XVI General Assembly a Joint Statement of Agreed Principles for Disarmament Negotiations, based on an American draft. Unanimously adopted in that session, it provided the foundation for the work of a new Disarmament Commission in Geneva composed at first of eighteen nations but later expanded by agreement of the Soviet and American co-chairmen. In 1961, the Kennedy administration created an Arms Control and Disarmament Agency to lend purpose as well as coherence to its efforts. In September 1963, President John F. Kennedy was able to renew the call with fresh hope, suggesting new steps toward arms control and a joint Soviet-American expedition to the moon. The Assembly moved quickly to formulate the principles that should govern activities in space, including the prohibition of weapons of mass destruction being stationed in space or on celestial bodies. (Stationed was the operative word, since it did not cover intercontinental ballistic missiles, whose high trajectory only traversed space; or the lower-slung fractional orbital missile which did not remain in space long enough to be "stationed.") The principles were then written into a historic space treaty, which came into force on October 10, 1967.

A year after endorsing this treaty, the Assembly was able to vote its approval of an international agreement on the rescue and return of astronauts in distress and the return of space objects. A parallel agreement, on liability for damage in space accidents, proved more difficult to conclude, taking another three years. The former seemed to hold more urgency and greater mutual advantage to the two operating space powers. As for the latter, of the thousands of objects, including boosters and instrument packages, which had gone into earth orbit since the birth of the space age, only a few had not been totally consumed, according to plan, in their fiery reentry into the atmosphere.

Disarmament talks continued all the while in Geneva and in bilateral contacts between the United States and the Soviet Union. While no agreement could be reached on reducing the level of armament, or even freezing it, both countries regarded with anxiety the likelihood that other nations would develop nuclear weapons. As far back as 1958, China had announced its operation of an atomic reactor and a cyclotron. France had declared it would not be bound by a test ban agreement among the United States, the United Kingdom and the Soviet Union. Peking took the same position.

There were those who saw in Moscow's expression of anxiety about the spread of nuclear weapons a political broadside aimed particularly at West Germany, which had remained a special target of Soviet propaganda. Seen in that light, it was a device to split the western alliance. Whatever the doubts on that score, they were more than overcome by Washington's own desire to put the cork in the nuclear bottle. Mutuality of interest led to the conclusion by the United States and the Soviet Union of a Treaty on the Non-Proliferation of Nuclear Weapons. They explicitly opened it to all states to permit Peking to join. And they cooperated closely in securing the endorsement of the General Assembly against the strong reluctance of members like India, Japan and Brazil—not to mention other nuclear-threshold countries like West Germany and Switzerland. These raised three main objections. For one, in not imposing any brake on the nuclear development of the "have" nations, the treaty promised only to widen the armaments gap between them and the "have-nots." Secondly, the nations which renounced their own nuclear capability were afraid of thereby relegating themselves to perpetual and increasing scientific and technical inferiority. Lastly, the non-nuclear countries feared that they would be exposed to blackmail by nonsignatories who developed weapons.

The United States, Britain and the Soviet Union answered the first of these objections with assurances written into the treaty. The third was met by a formal identical statement of the three governments in the Security Council and by the passage of a resolution intended to convey a psychological guarantee against nuclear pressure or attack. Some members, pointing out that such security was inherent in the Charter, remained unimpressed. But President Lyndon Johnson flew to New York on the day the General Assembly voted its endorsement, by a somewhat hesitant 95 to 4 with 21 abstentions, to hail its importance on its merits and as a prelude to the limitation of strategic arms. Unhappily, two months later, on August 21, 1968, the day the President intended to announce the start of substantive talks with the Soviet Union on this subject, troops of the Warsaw Pact nations invaded Czechoslovakia. The spirit of confidence which such talks required was blighted. It was not until the following year that the administration of President Richard M. Nixon joined the Soviets alternately at Helsinki and Vienna in formal Strategic Arms Limitation Talks.

Work continued in the United Nations system also on other aspects of arms control. Agreement was reached on a treaty doing for the vast expanse of the sea bed what had earlier been done for Antarctica as well as for Outer Space and celestial bodies, viz. proscribing the emplacement of nuclear and other weapons of mass destruction.

A convention on liability for damage done in space accidents—a contingency brought close to home by the impacting of unconsumed satellite and rocket booster fragments at several points in the United States—was approved by the General Assembly. Like so many consensus documents, worthy as it was, it gained the indispensable endorsement of the Soviet Union only because it had no teeth.

The one true disarmament measure in decades, drafted in Geneva and commended by the General Assembly, was the treaty outlawing biological weapons. The United States had already unilaterally renounced their use.

The Assembly also noted with satisfaction Washington's ratification of Protocol II of the Treaty of Tlatelolco (Mexico) which was designed to make Latin America a prohibited zone for nuclear weapons.

AMERICAN MONOPOLY ON ATOMIC WEAPONS

Declaration by the United States, the United Kingdom and Canada on Atomic Energy *

November 18, 1945

The President of the United States, the Prime Miniser of the United Kingdom, and the Prime Minister of Canada have issued the following statement.

1. We recognize that the application of recent scientific discoveries to the methods and practice of war has placed at the disposal of mankind means of destruction hitherto unknown, against which there can be no adequate military defence, and in the employment of which no single nation can in fact have a monopoly.

2. We desire to emphasize that the responsibility for devising means to ensure that the new discoveries shall be used for the benefit of mankind, instead of as a means of destruction, rests not on our nations alone, but upon the whole civilized world. Nevertheless, the progress that we have made in the development and use of atomic energy demands that we take an initiative in the matter, and we have accordingly met together to consider the possibility of international action:

(a) To prevent the use of atomic energy for destructive purposes

(b) To promote the use of recent and future advances in scientific knowledge, particularly in the utilization of atomic energy, for peaceful and humanitarian ends.

3. We are aware that the only complete protection for the civilized world from the destructive use of scientific knowledge lies in the prevention of war. No system of safeguards that can be devised will of itself provide an effective guarantee against production of atomic weapons by a nation bent on aggression. Nor can we ignore the possibility of the development of other weapons, or of new methods of warfare, which may constitute as great a threat to civilization as the military use of atomic energy.

4. Representing as we do, the three countries which possess the knowledge essential to the use of atomic energy, we declare at the outset our willingness, as a first contribution, to proceed with the exchange of fundamental scientific information and the interchange of scientists and scientific literature for peaceful ends with any nation that will fully reciprocate.

5. We believe that the fruits of scientific research should be made available to all nations, and that freedom of investigation and free interchange of ideas are essential to the progress of knowledge. In pursuance of this policy, the basic scientific information essential to the development of atomic energy for peaceful purposes has already been made available to the world. It is our intention that all further information of this character that may become available from time to time shall be similarly treated. We trust that other nations will adopt the same policy, thereby creating an atmosphere of reciprocal confidence in which political agreement and cooperation will flourish.

6. We have considered the question of the disclosure of detailed information concerning the practical industrial application of atomic energy. The military exploita-

Department of State Bulletin, Nov. 18, 1945, pp. 781-82.

tion of atomic energy depends, in large part, upon the same methods and processes as would be required for industrial uses.

We are not convinced that the spreading of the specialized information regarding the practical application of atomic energy, before it is possible to devise effective, reciprocal, and enforceable safeguards acceptable to all nations, would contribute to a constructive solution of the problem of the atomic bomb. On the contrary we think it might have the opposite effect. We are, however, prepared to share, on a reciprocal basis with others of the United Nations, detailed information concerning the practical industrial application of atomic energy just as soon as effective enforceable safeguards against its use for destructive purposes can be devised.

7. In order to attain the most effective means of entirely eliminating the use of atomic energy for destructive purposes and promoting its widest use for industrial and humanitarian purposes, we are of the opinion that at the earliest practicable date a Commission should be set up under the United Nations Organization to prepare recommendations for submission to the Organization.

The Commission should be instructed to proceed with the utmost dispatch and should be authorized to submit recommendations from time to time dealing with separate phases of its work.

In particular the Commission should make specific proposals:

(a) For extending between all nations the exchange of basic scientific information for peaceful ends,

(b) For control of atomic energy to the extent necessary to ensure its use only for peaceful purposes,

(c) For the elimination from national armaments of atomic weapons and of all other major weapons adaptable to mass destruction,

(d) For effective safeguards by way of inspection and other means to protect complying states against the hazards of violations and evasions.

8. The work of the Commission should proceed by separate stages, the successful completion of each one of which will develop the necessary confidence of the world before the next stage is undertaken. Specifically it is considered that the Commission might well devote its attention first to the wide exchange of scientists and scientific information, and as a second stage to the development of full knowledge concerning natural resources of raw materials.

9. Faced with the terrible realities of the application of science to destruction, every nation will realize more urgently than before the overwhelming need to maintain the rule of law among nations and to banish the scourge of war from the earth. This can only be brought about by giving wholehearted support to the United Nations Organization, and by consolidating and extending its authority, thus creating conditions of mutual trust in which all peoples will be free to devote themselves to the arts of peace. It is our firm resolve to work without reservation to achieve these ends.

Harry S. Truman
President of the United States
C. R. Attlee
Prime Minister of the United Kingdom
W. L. Mackenzie King
Prime Minister of Canada

*Report by President Truman to Congress on the Establishment
of the Atomic Energy Commission**

1947

When the United Nations met at San Francisco to draw up the Charter of the United Nations, atomic energy as a deadly weapon was as yet unknown to the world. After the surrender of Japan, this Government moved to establish machinery, both domestic and international, for control of the new and devastating weapon, and to insure that atomic energy would be used only for peaceful and productive purposes. In the President's message to the Congress on October 3, 1945, domestic legislation was recommended, which has already come into being, and the need was stressed for international arrangements looking to the renunciation of the use of the atomic bomb and the encouragement of the use of atomic energy for peaceful and humanitarian ends.

With these purposes in mind the President met with the Prime Ministers of the United Kingdom and Canada during the following month. The result of these conversations by the Governments which had collaborated in the wartime development of the atomic bomb was an Agreed Declaration citing the urgent need for international action under the auspices of the United Nations to control atomic energy to the extent necessary to insure its use only for peaceful purposes, to outlaw atomic weapons and other major weapons adaptable to mass destruction, and to provide for effective safeguards by way of inspection and other means to protect complying states against the hazards of violations and evasions.

The signatories of the Agreed Declaration, recognizing the magnitude of the task outlined and the need for having the other states which share under the Charter the primary responsibility for maintaining international peace and security join in the undertaking, took steps to accomplish this end.

As a result of a conference among the Secretary of State of the United States and the Foreign Ministers of the United Kingdom and the Soviet Union at Moscow in December 1945, the Soviet Union concurred in the principles outlined in the Agreed Declaration and became a co-sponsor of the Resolution which was introduced into the General Assembly at its First Session in London in January 1946. France and China also readily joined in introducing the resolution which called for the establishment of a United Nations Atomic Energy Commission. The General Assembly, taking note of the urgency and importance of the objectives of the proposed commission, approved the Resolution on January 24, 1946 without a dissenting vote. The objectives are stated in the terms of reference of the Commission which require it to make specific proposals:

"(a) for extending between all nations the exchange of basic scientific information for peaceful ends;

"(b) for control of atomic energy to the extent necessary to ensure its use only for peaceful purposes;

"(c) for the elimination from national armaments of atomic weapons and of all other major weapons adaptable to mass destruction;

"(d) for effective safeguards by way of inspection and other means to protect complying States against the hazards of violations and evasions."

*Department of State, *The United States and the United Nations Report Series* No. 7, (Washington, 1947), pp. 44-45.

The resolution specifies that the work of the Commission should proceed by separate stages, the successful completion of each of which will develop the necessary confidence of the world before the next stage is undertaken. The Commission was duly constituted, consisting of the representatives of the members of the Security Council and Canada. It began its meetings in New York on June 14, 1946.

By the terms of reference of the General Assembly resolution, the Commission shall submit its reports and recommendations to the Security Council, and such reports and recommendations shall be made public unless the Security Council, in the interest of peace and security, otherwise directs. In the appropriate cases the Security Council shall transmit these reports to the General Assembly and the Members of the United Nations, as well as to the Economic and Social Council and other organizations within the framework of the United Nations.

Speech by Bernard M. Baruch to the United Nations Atomic Energy Commission on Control of Atomic Energy*

June 14, 1946

We are here to make a choice between the quick and the dead.

That is our business.

Behind the black portent of the new atomic age lies a hope which, seized upon with faith, can work our salvation. If we fail, then we have damned every man to be the slave of Fear. Let us not deceive ourselves: We must elect World Peace or World Destruction.

Science has torn from nature a secret so vast in its potentialities that our minds cower from the terror it creates. Yet terror is not enough to inhibit the use of the atomic bomb. The terror created by weapons has never stopped man from employing them. For each new weapon a defense has been produced, in time. But now we face a condition in which adequate defense does not exist.

Science, which gave us this dread power, shows that it can be made a giant help to humanity, but science does not show us how to prevent its baleful use. So we have been appointed to obviate that peril by finding a meeting of the minds and the hearts of our people. Only in the will of mankind lies the answer.

It is to express this will and make it effective that we have been assembled. We must provide the mechanism to assure that atomic energy is used for peaceful purposes and preclude its use in war. To that end, we must provide immediate, swift, and sure punishment of those who violate the agreements that are reached by the nations. Penalization is essential if peace is to be more than a feverish interlude between wars. And, too, the United Nations can prescribe individual responsibility and punishment on the principles applied at Nürnberg by the Union of Soviet Socialist Republics, the United Kingdom, France, and the United States—a formula certain to benefit the world's future.

In this crisis, we represent not only our governments but, in a larger way, we represent the peoples of the world. We must remember that the peoples do not belong to the governments but that the governments belong to the peoples. We must answer their demands; we must answer the world's longing for peace and security.

*The United States and the United Nations Report Series, 7, Supplement, pp. 169-78.

In that desire the United States shares ardently and hopefully. The search of science for the absolute weapon has reached fruition in this country. But she stands ready to proscribe and destroy this instrument—to lift its use from death to life—if the world will join in a pact to that end.

In our success lies the promise of a new life, freed from the heart-stopping fears that now beset the world. The beginning of victory for the great ideals for which millions have bled and died lies in building a workable plan. Now we approach fulfillment of the aspirations of mankind. At the end of the road lies the fairer, better, surer life we crave and mean to have.

Only by a lasting peace are liberties and democracies strengthened and deepened. War is their enemy. And it will not do to believe that any of us can escape war's devastation. Victor, vanquished, and neutrals alike are affected physically, economically, and morally.

Against the degradation of war we can erect a safeguard. That is the guerdon for which we reach. Within the scope of the formula we outline here there will be found, to those who seek it, the essential elements of our purpose. Others will see only emptiness. Each of us carries his own mirror in which is reflected hope—or determined desperation—courage or cowardice.

There is a famine throughout the world today. It starves men's bodies. But there is a greater famine—the hunger of men's spirit. That starvation can be cured by the conquest of fear, and the substitution of hope, from which springs faith—faith in each other, faith that we want to work together toward salvation, and determination that those who threaten the peace and safety shall be punished.

The peoples of these democracies gathered here have a particular concern with our answer, for their peoples hate war. They will have a heavy exaction to make of those who fail to provide an escape. They are not afraid of an internationalism that protects; they are unwilling to be fobbed off by mouthings about narrow sovereignty, which is today's phrase for yesterday's isolation.

The basis of a sound foreign policy, in this new age, for all the nations here gathered, is that anything that happens, no matter where or how, which menaces the peace of the world, or the economic stability, concerns each and all of us.

That, roughly, may be said to be the central theme of the United Nations. It is with that thought we begin consideration of the most important subject that can engage mankind—life itself.

Let there be no quibbling about the duty and the responsibility of this group and of the governments we represent. I was moved, in the afternoon of my life, to add my effort to gain the world's quest, by the broad mandate under which we were created. The resolution of the General Assembly, passed January 24, 1946 in London, reads:

"Section V. Terms of Reference of the Commission

"The Commission shall proceed with the utmost despatch and enquire into all phases of the problems, and make such recommendations from time to time with respect to them as it finds possible. In particular the Commission shall make specific proposals:

"(a) For extending between all nations the exchange of basic scientific information for peaceful ends;

"(b) For control of atomic energy to the extent necessary to ensure its use only for peaceful purposes;

"(c) For the elimination from national armaments of atomic weapons and of all other major weapons adaptable to mass destruction;

"(d) For effective safeguards by way of inspection and other means to protect complying States against the hazards of violations and evasions.

"The work of the Commission should proceed by separate stages, the successful completion of each of which will develop the necessary confidence of the world before the next stage is undertaken. . . ."

Our mandate rests, in text and in spirit, upon the outcome of the Conference in Moscow of Messrs. Molotov of the Union of Soviet Socialist Republics, Bevin of the United Kingdom, and Byrnes of the United States of America. The three Foreign Ministers on December 27, 1945 proposed the establishment of this body.

Their action was animated by a preceding conference in Washington on November 15, 1945, when the President of the United States, associated with Mr. Attlee, Prime Minister of the United Kingdom, and Mr. Mackenzie King, Prime Minister of Canada, stated that international control of the whole field of atomic energy was immediately essential. They proposed the formation of this body. In examining that source, the Agreed Declaration, it will be found that the fathers of the concept recognized the final means of world salvation—the abolition of war. Solemnly they wrote:

"We are aware that the only complete protection for the civilized world from the destructive use of scientific knowledge lies in the prevention of war. No system of safeguards that can be devised will of itself provide an effective guarantee against production of atomic weapons by a nation bent on aggression. Nor can we ignore the possibility of the development of other weapons, or of new methods of warfare, which may constitute as great a threat to civilization as the military use of atomic energy."

Through the historical approach I have outlined, we find ourselves here to test if man can produce, through his will and faith, the miracle of peace, just as he has, through science and skill, the miracle of the atom.

The United States proposes the creation of an International Atomic Development Authority, to which should be entrusted all phases of the development and use of atomic energy, starting with the raw material and including—

1. Managerial control or ownership of all atomic-energy activities potentially dangerous to world security.

2. Power to control, inspect, and license all other atomic activities.

3. The duty of fostering the beneficial uses of atomic energy.

4. Research and development responsibilities of an affirmative character intended to put the Authority in the forefront of atomic knowledge and thus to enable it to comprehend, and therefor to detect, misuse of atomic energy. To be effective, the Authority must itself be the world's leader in the field of atomic knowledge and development and thus supplement its legal authority with the great power inherent in possession of leadership in knowledge.

I offer this as a basis for beginning our discussion.

But I think the peoples we serve would not believe—and without faith nothing counts—that a treaty, merely outlawing possession or use of the atomic bomb, constitutes effective fulfillment of the instructions to this Commission. Previous failures have been recorded in trying the method of simple renunciation, unsupported by effective guaranties of security and armament limitation. No one would have faith in that approach alone.

Now, if ever, is the time to act for the common good. Public opinion supports a world movement towward security. If I read the signs aright, the peoples want a program not composed merely of pious thoughts but of enforceable sanctions—an international law with teeth in it.

We of this nation, desirous of helping to bring peace to the world and realizing the heavy obligations upon us arising from our possession of the means of producing the bomb and from the fact that it is part of our armament, are prepared to make our full contribution toward effective control of atomic energy.

When an adequate system for control of atomic energy, including the renunciation of the bomb as a weapon, has been agreed upon and put into effective operation and condign punishments set up for violations of the rules of control which are to be stigmatized as international crimes, we propose that—

1. Manufacture of atomic bombs shall stop;

2. Existing bombs shall be disposed of pursuant to the terms of the treaty; and

3. The Authority shall be in possession of full information as to the know-how for the production of atomic energy.

Let me repeat, so as to avoid misunderstanding: My country is ready to make its full contribution toward the end we seek, subject of course to our constitutional processes and to an adequate system of control becoming fully effective, as we finally work it out.

Now as to violations: In the agreement, penalties of as serious a nature as the nations may wish and as immediate and certain in their execution as possible should be fixed for—

1. Illegal possession or use of an atomic bomb;

2. Illegal possession, or separation, of atomic material suitable for use in an atomic bomb;

3. Seizure of any plant or other property belonging to or licensed by the Authority;

4. Wilful interference with the activities of the Authority;

5. Creation or operation of dangerous projects in a manner contrary to, or in the absence of, a license granted by the international control body.

It would be a deception, to which I am unwilling to lend myself, were I not to say to you and to our peoples that the matter of punishment lies at the very heart of our present security system. It might as well be admitted, here and now, that the subject goes straight to the veto power contained in the Charter of the United Nations so far as it relates to the field of atomic energy. The Charter permits penalization only by concurrence of each of the five great powers—the Union of Soviet Socialist Republics, the United Kingdom, China, France, and the United States.

I want to make very plain that I am concerned here with the veto power only as it affects this particular problem. There must be no veto to protect those who violate their solemn agreements not to develop or use atomic energy for destructive purposes.

The bomb does not wait upon debate. To delay may be to die. The time between a violation and preventive action or punishment would be all too short for extended discussion as to the course to be followed.

As matters now stand several years may be necesssary for another country to produce a bomb, *de novo*. However, once the basic information is generally known, and the Authority has established producing plants for peaceful purposes in the several countries, an illegal seizure of such a plant might permit a malevolent nation to produce a bomb in 12 months, and if preceded by secret preparation and necessary facilities perhaps even in a much shorter time. The time required—the advance warning given of the possible use of a bomb—can only be generally estimated but obviously will depend upon many factors, including the success with which the Authority has been able to introduce elements of safety in the design of its plants and the degree to which illegal and secret preparation for the military use of atomic energy will have been eliminated. Presumably no nation would think of starting a war with only one bomb.

This shows how imperative speed is in detecting and penalizing violations.

The process of prevention and penalization—a problem of profound statecraft—is, as I read it, implicit in the Moscow statement, signed by the Union of Soviet Socialist Republics, the United States, and the United Kingdom a few months ago.

But before a country is ready to relinquish any winning weapons it must have more than words to reassure it. It must have a guarantee of safety, not only against the offenders in the atomic area but against the illegal users of other weapons—bacteriological, biological, gas—perhaps—why not?—against war itself.

In the elimination of war lies our solution, for only then will nations cease to compete with one another in the production and use of dread "secret" weapons which are evaluated solely by their capacity to kill. This devilish program takes us back not merely to the Dark Ages but from cosmos to chaos. If we succeeed in finding a suitable way to control atomic weapons, it is reasonable to hope that we may also preclude the use of other weapons adaptable to mass destruction. When a man learns to say "A" he can, if he chooses, learn the rest of the alphabet too.

Let this be anchored in our minds:

Peace is never long preserved by weight of metal or by an armament race. Peace can be made tranquil and secure only by understanding and agreement fortified by sanctions. We must embrace international cooperation or international disintegration.

Science has taught us how to put the atom to work. But to make it work for good instead of for evil lies in the domain dealing with the principles of human duty. We are now facing a problem more of ethics than of physics.

The solution will require apparent sacrifice in pride and in position, but better pain as the price of peace than death as the price of war.

I now submit the following measures as representing the fundamental features of a plan which would give effect to certain of the conclusions which I have epitomized.

1. *General.* The Authority should set up a thorough plan for control of the field of atomic energy, through various forms of ownership, dominion, licenses, operation, inspection, research, and management by competent personnel. After this is provided for, there should be as little interference as may be with the economic plans and the present private, corporate, and state relationships in the several countries involved.

2. *Raw Materials.* The Authority should have as one of its earliest purposes to obtain and maintain complete and accurate information on world supplies of uranium and thorium and to bring them under its dominion. The precise pattern of control for various types of deposits of such materials will have to depend upon the geological, mining, refining, and economic facts involved in different situations.

The Authority should conduct continuous surveys so that it will have the most complete knowledge of the world geology of uranium and thorium. Only after all current information on world sources of uranium and thorium is known to us all can equitable plans be made for their production, refining, and distribution.

3. *Primary Production Plants.* The Authority should exercise complete managerial control of the production of fissionable materials. This means that it should control and operate all plants producing fissionable materials in dangerous quantities and must own and control the product of these plants.

4. *Atomic Explosives.* The Authority should be given sole and exclusive right to conduct research in the field of atomic explosives. Research activities in the field of atomic explosives are essential in order that the Authority may keep in the forefront of knowledge in the field of atomic energy and fulfil the objective of preventing illicit manufacture of bombs. Only by maintaining its position as the best-informed agency will the Authority be able to determine the line between intrinsically dangerous and non-dangerous activities.

5. *Strategic Distribution of Activities and Materials.* The activities entrusted exclusively to the Authority because they are intrinsically dangerous to security should be distributed throughout the world. Similarly, stockpiles of raw materials and fissionable materials should not be centralized.

6. *Non-Dangerous Activities.* A function of the Authority should be promotion of the peacetime benefits of atomic energy.

Atomic research (except in explosives), the use of research reactors, the production of radioactive tracers by means of non-dangerous reactors, the use of such tracers, and to some extent the production of power should be open to nations and their citizens under reasonable licensing arrangements from the Authority. Denatured materials, whose use we know also requires suitable safeguards, should be furnished for such purposes by the Authority under lease or other arrangement. Denaturing seems to have been overestimated by the public as a safety measure.

7. *Definition of Dangerous and Non-Dangerous Activities.* Although a reasonable dividing line can be drawn between dangerous and non-dangerous activities, it is not hard and fast. Provision should, therefore, be made to assure constant reexamination of the questions and to permit revision of the dividing line as changing conditions and new discoveries may require.

8. *Operations of Dangerous Activities.* Any plant dealing with uranium or thorium after it once reaches the potential of dangerous use must be not only subject to the most rigorous and competent inspection by the Authority, but its actual operation shall be under the management, supervision, and control of the Authority.

9. *Inspection.* By assigning intrinsically dangerous activities exclusively to the Authority, the difficulties of inspection are reduced. If the Authority is the only agency which may lawfully conduct dangerous activities, then visible operation by others than the Authority will constitute an unambiguous danger signal. Inspection will also occur in connection with the licensing functions of the Authority.

10. *Freedom of Access.* Adequate ingress and egress for all qualified representatives of the Authority must be assured. Many of the inspection activities of the Authority should grow out of, and be incidental to, its other functions. Important measures of inspection will be associated with the tight control of raw materials, for this is a keystone of the plan. The continuing activities of prospecting, survey, and research in relation to raw materials will be designed not only to serve the affirmative development functions of the Authority but also to assure that no surreptitious operations are conducted in the raw-materials field by nations or their citizens.

11. *Personnel.* The personnel of the Authority should be recruited on a basis of proven competence but also so far as possible on an international basis.

12. *Progress by Stages.* A primary step in the creation of the system of control is the setting forth, in comprehensive terms, of the functions, responsibilities, powers, and limitations of the Authority. Once a charter for the Authority has been adopted, the Authority and the system of control for which it will be responsible will require time to become fully organized and effective. The plan of control will, therefore, have to come into effect in successive stages. These should be specifically fixed in the charter or means should be otherwise set forth in the charter for transitions from one stage to another, as contemplated in the resolution of the United Nations Assembly which created this Commission.

18. *Disclosures.* In the deliberations of the United Nations Commission on Atomic Energy, the United States is prepared to make available the information essential to a reasonable understanding of the proposals which it advocates. Further disclosure must be dependent, in the interests of all, upon the effective ratification of the treaty. When the Authority is actually created, the United States will join the other nations in making available the further information essential to that organization for the performance of its functions. As the successive stages of international control are reached, the United States will be prepared to yield, to the extent required by each stage, national control of activities in this field to the Authority.

14. *International Control.* There will be questions about the extent of control to be allowed to national bodies, when the Authority is established. Purely national authorities for control and development of atomic energy should to the extent necessary for the effective operation of the Authority be subordinate to it. This is neither an endorsement nor a disapproval of the creation of national authorities. The Commission should evolve a clear demarcation of the scope of duties and responsibilities of such national authorities.

And now I end. I have submitted an outline for present discussion. Our consideration will be broadened by the criticism of the United States proposals and by the plans of the other nations, which, it is to be hoped, will be submitted at their early convenience. I and my associates of the United States Delegation will make available to each member of this body books and pamphlets, including the Acheson-Lilienthal report, recently made by the United States Department of State, and the McMahon Committee Monograph No. 1 entitled "Essential Information on Atomic Energy" relating to the McMahon bill recently passed by the United States Senate, which may prove of value in assessing the situation.

All of us are consecrated to making an end of gloom and hopelessness. It will not be an easy job. The way is long and thorny, but supremely worth traveling. All of us want to stand erect, with our faces to the sun, instead of being forced to burrow into the earth, like rats.

The pattern of salvation must be worked out by all for all.

The light at the end of the tunnel is dim, but our path seems to grow brighter as we actually begin our journey. We cannot yet light the way to the end. However, we hope the suggestions of my Government will be illuminating.

Let us keep in mind the exhortation of Abraham Lincoln, whose words, uttered at a moment of shattering national peril, form a complete text for our deliberation. I quote, paraphrasing slightly:

"We cannot escape history. We of this meeting will be remembered in spite of ourselves. No personal significance or insignificance can spare one or another of us.

The fiery trial through which we are passing will light us down in honor or dishonor to the latest generation.

"We say we are for Peace. The world will not forget that we say this. We know how to save Peace. The world knows that we do. We, even we here, hold the power and have the responsibility.

"We shall nobly save, or meanly lose, the last, best hope of earth. The way is plain, peaceful, generous, just—a way which, if followed, the world will forever applaud."

FIRST DISARMAMENT EFFORTS

Address by President Truman at Opening Session of United Nations
General Assembly *

New York, October 23, 1946

On behalf of the Government and the people of the United States I extend a warm and hearty welcome to the delegates who have come here from all parts of the world to represent their countries at this meeting of the General Assembly of the United Nations.

I recall with great pleasure the last occasion on which I met and spoke with the representatives of the United Nations. Many of you who are here today were present then. It was the final day of the Conference at San Francisco, when the United Nations Charter was signed. On that day the constitutional foundation of the United Nations was laid.

For the people of my country this meeting today has a special historic significance. After the first world war the United States refused to join the League of Nations and our seat was empty at the first meeting of the League Assembly. This time the United States is not only a member; it is the host to the United Nations.

I can assure you that the Government and the people of the United States are deeply proud and grateful that the United Nations has chosen our country for its headquarters. We will extend the fullest measure of cooperation in making a home for the United Nations in this country. The American people welcome the delegates and the Secretariat of the United Nations as good neighbors and warm friends.

This meeting of the Assembly symbolizes the abandonment by the United States of a policy of isolation.

The overwhelming majority of the American people, regardless of party, support the United Nations.

They are resolved that the United States, to the full limit of its strength, shall contribute to the establishment and maintenance of a just and lasting peace among the nations of the world.

However, I must tell you that the American people are troubled by the failure of the Allied nations to make more progress in their common search for a lasting peace.

It is important to remember the intended place of the United Nations in moving toward this goal. The United Nations—as an organization—was not intended to settle the problems arising immediately out of the war. The United Nations was intended to provide the means for maintaining international peace in the future after just settlements have been made.

The settlement of these problems was deliberately consigned to negotiations among the Allies as distinguished from the United Nations. This was done in order to give the United Nations a better opportunity and a freer hand to carry out its long-range task of providing peaceful means for the adjustment of future differences, some of which might arise out of the settlements made as a result of this war.

The United Nations cannot, however, fulfill adequately its own responsibilities until

The Public Papers of the Presidents, Harry S. Truman, pp. 457-63.

the peace settlements have been made and unless these settlements form a solid foundation upon which to build a permanent peace.

I submit that these settlements, and our search for everlasting peace, rest upon the four essential freedoms.

These are freedom of speech, freedom of religion, freedom from want, and freedom from fear. These are fundamental freedoms to which all the United Nations are pledged under the Charter.

To the attainment of these freedoms—everywhere in the world—through the friendly cooperation of all nations, the Government and people of the United States are dedicated.

The fourth freedom—freedom from fear—means, above all else, freedom from fear of war.

This freedom is attainable now.

Lately we have all heard talk about the possibility of another world war. Fears have been aroused all over the world.

These fears are unwarranted and unjustified.

However, rumors of war still find willing listeners in certain places. If these rumors are not checked they are sure to impede world recovery.

I have been reading reports from many parts of the world. These reports all agree on one major point—the people of every nation are sick of war. They know its agony and its futility. No responsible government can ignore this universal feeling.

The United States of America has no wish to make war, now or in the future, upon any people anywhere in the world. The heart of our foreign policy is a sincere desire for peace. This nation will work patiently for peace by every means consistent with self-respect and security. Another world war would shatter the hopes of mankind and completely destroy civilization as we know it.

I am sure that every delegate in this hall will join me in rejecting talk of war. No nation wants war. Every nation wants peace.

To avoid war and rumors and danger of war the peoples of all countries must not only cherish peace as an ideal but they must develop means of settling conflicts between nations in accordance with the principles of law and justice.

The difficulty is that it is easier to get people to agree upon peace as an ideal than to agree upon principles of law and justice or to agree to subject their own acts to the collective judgment of mankind.

But difficult as the task may be, the path along which agreement may be sought is clearly defined. We expect to follow that path with success.

In the first place, every member of the United Nations is legally and morally bound by the Charter to keep the peace. More specifically, every member is bound to refrain in its international relations from the threat, or use, of force against the territorial integrity of political independence of any state.

In the second place, I remind you that 23 members of the United Nations have bound themselves by the Charter of the Nuremberg Tribunal to the principle that planning, initiating or waging a war of aggression is a crime against humanity for which individuals as well as states shall be tried before the bar of international justice.

The basic principles upon which we are agreed go far, but not far enough, in removing the fear of war from the world. There must be agreement upon a positive, constructive course of action as well.

The peoples of the world know that there can be no real peace unless it is peace with justice for all—justice for small nations and for large nations and justice for individuals without distinction as to race, creed or color—a peace that will advance, not retard, the attainment of the four freedoms.

We shall attain freedom from fear when every act of every nation, in its dealings with every other nation, brings closer to realization the other freedoms—freedom of speech, freedom of religion, and freedom from want. Along this path we can find justice for all, without distinction between the strong and the weak among nations, and without discrimination among individuals.

After the peace has been made, I am convinced that the United Nations can and will prevent war between nations and remove the fear of war that distracts the peoples of the world and interferes with their progress toward a better life.

The war has left many parts of the world in turmoil. Differences have arisen among the Allies. It will not help us to pretend that this is not the case. But it is not necessary to exaggerate these differences.

For my part, I believe there is no difference of interest that need stand in the way of settling these problems and settling them in accordance with the principles of the United Nations Charter. Above all, we must not permit differences in economic and social systems to stand in the way of peace, either now or in the future. To permit the United Nations to be broken into irreconcilable parts by different political philosophies would bring disaster to the world.

So far as Germany and Japan are concerned, the United States is resolved that neither shall again become a cause for war. We shall continue to seek agreement upon peace terms which ensure that both Germany and Japan remain disarmed, that Nazi influence in Germany be destroyed and that the power of the war lords in Japan be eliminated forever.

The United States will continue to seek settlements arising from the war that are just to all states, large and small, that uphold the human rights and fundamental freedoms to which the Charter pledges all its members, and that do not contain the seeds of new conflicts.

A peace between the nations based upon justice will make possible an early improvement in living conditions throughout the world and a quick recovery from the ravages of war. The world is crying for a just and durable peace with an intensity that must force its attainment at the earliest possible date.

If the members of the United Nations are to act together to remove the fear of war, the first requirement is for the Allied Nations to reach agreement on the peace settlements.

Propaganda that promotes distrust and misunderstanding among the Allies will not help us. Agreements designed to remove the fear of war can be reached only by the cooperation of nations to respect the legitimate interests of all states and act as good neighbors toward each other.

And lasting agreements between allies cannot be imposed by one nation nor can they be reached at the expense of the security, independence or integrity of any nation. There must be accommodation by all the Allied Nations in which mutual adjustments of lesser national interests are made in order to serve the greater interest of all in peace, security and justice.

This Assembly can do much toward recreating the spirit of friendly cooperation and toward reaffirming these principles of the United Nations which must be applied to the peace settlements. It must also prepare and strengthen the United Nations for the tasks that lie ahead after the settlements have been made.

All member nations, large and small, are represented here as equals. Wisdom is not the monopoly of strength or size. Small nations can contribute equally with the large nations toward bringing constructive thought and wise judgment to bear upon the formation of collective policy.

This Assembly is the world's supreme deliberative body.

The highest obligation of this Assembly is to speak for all mankind in such a way as to promote the unity of all members in behalf of a peace that will be lasting because it is founded upon justice.

In seeking unity we should not be concerned about expressing differences freely. The United States believes that this Assembly should demonstrate the importance of freedom of speech to the cause of peace. I do not share the view of those who are fearful of the effects of free and frank discussions in the United Nations.

The United States attaches great importance to the principle of free discussion in this Assembly and in this Security Council. Free and direct exchange of arguments and information promotes understanding and therefore contributes in the long run to the removal of the fear of war and some of the causes of war.

The United States believes that the rule of unanimous accord among the five permanent members of the Security Council imposes upon these members a special obligation. This obligation is to seek and reach agreements that will enable them and the Security Council to fulfill their responsibilities under the Charter toward their fellow members of the United Nations and toward the maintenance of peace.

It is essential to the future of the United Nations that the members should use the Council as a means of promoting settlement of disputes as well as for airing them. The exercise of neither veto rights nor majority rights can make peace secure. There is no substitute for agreements that are universally acceptable because they are just to all concerned. The Security Council is intended to promote that kind of agreement and it is fully qualified for that purpose.

Because it is able to function continuously, the Security Council represents a most significant development in international relations—the continued application of the public and peaceful methods of a council chamber to the settlement of disputes between nations.

Two of the greatest obligations undertaken by the United Nations toward the removal of the fear of war remain to be fulfilled.

First, we must reach an agreement establishing international controls of atomic energy that will ensure its use for peaceful purposes only, in accordance with the Assembly's unanimous resolution last winter.

Second, we must reach agreements that will remove the deadly fear of other weapons of mass destruction, in accordance with that same resolution.

Each of these obligations is going to be difficult to fulfill. Their fulfillment will require the utmost in perseverance and good faith, and we cannot succeed without setting fundamental precedents in the law of nations. Each will be worth everything in perseverance and good faith that we can give to it. The future safety of the United Nations, and of every member nation, depends upon the outcome.

On behalf of the United States I can say we are not discouraged. We shall continue to seek agreement by every possible means.

At the same time we shall also press for preparation of agreements in order that the

Security Council may have at its disposal peace forces adequate to prevent acts of aggression.

The United Nations will not be able to remove the fear of war from the world unless substantial progress can be made in the next few years toward the realization of another of the four freedoms—freedom from want.

The Charter pledges the members of the United Nations to work together toward this end. The structure of the United Nations in this field is now nearing completion, with the Economic and Social Council, its commissions and related specialized agencies. It provides more complete and effective institutions through which to work than the world has ever had before.

A great opportunity lies before us.

In these constructive tasks which concern directly the lives and welfare of human beings throughout the world, humanity and self-interest alike demand of all of us the fullest cooperation.

The United States has already demonstrated in many ways its grave concern about economic reconstruction that will repair the damage done by war.

We have participated actively in every measure taken by the United Nations toward this end. The structure of the United Nations in this field is now nearing completion, with the Economic and Social Council, its commissions and related specialized agencies. It provides more complete and effective institutions through which to work than the world has ever had before.

A great opportunity lies before us.

In these constructive tasks which concern directly the lives and welfare of human beings throughout the world, humanity and self-interest alike demand of all of us the fullest cooperation.

The United States has already demonstrated in many ways its grave concern about economic reconstruction that will repair the damage done by war.

We have participated actively in every measure taken by the United Nations toward this end. We have in addition taken such separate national action as the granting of large loans and credits and renewal of our reciprocal trade-agreements program.

Through the establishment of the Food and Agriculture Organization, the International Bank for Reconstruction and Development and the International Monetary Fund, members of the United Nations have proved their capacity for constructive cooperation toward common economic objectives. In addition, the International Labor Organization is being brought into relationship with the United Nations.

Now we must complete that structure. The United States attaches the highest importance to the creation of the International Trade Organization now being discussed in London by a Preparatory Committee.

This country wants to see not only the rapid restoration of devastated areas but the industrial and agricultural progress of the less well-developed areas of the world.

We believe that all nations should be able to develop a healthy economic life of their own. We believe that all peoples should be able to reap the benefits of their own labor and of their own natural resources.

There are immense possibilities in many parts of the world for industrial development and agricultural modernization.

These possibilities can be realized only by the cooperation of members of the United Nations, helping each other on a basis of equal rights.

In the field of social reconstruction and advancement the completion of the Charter for a World Health Organization is an important step forward.

The Assembly now has before it for adoption the constitution of another specialized agency in this field—the International Refugee Organization. It is essential that this Organization be created in time to take over from UNRRA as early as possible in the new year the tasks of caring for and repatriating or resettling the refugees and displaced persons of Europe. There will be similar tasks, of great magnitude, in the Far East.

The United States considers this a matter of great urgency in the cause of restoring peace and in the cause of humanity itself.

I intend to urge the Congress of the United States to authorize this country to do its full part, both in financial support of the International Refugee Organization and in joining with other nations to receive those refugees who do not wish to return to their former homes for reasons of political or religious belief.

The United States believes a concerted effort must be made to break down the barriers to a free flow of information among the nations of the world.

We regard freedom of expression and freedom to receive information—the right of the people to know—as among the most important of those human rights and fundamental freedoms to which we are pledged under the United Nations Charter.

The United Nations Educational, Scientific and Cultural Organization, which is meeting in November, is a recognition of this fact. That Organization is built upon the premise that since wars begin in the minds of men, the defense of peace must be constructed in the minds of men, and that a free exchange of ideas and knowledge among peoples is necessary to this task. The United States therefore attaches great importance to all activities designed to break down barriers to mutual understanding and to wider tolerance.

The United States will support the United Nations with all the resources that we possess.

The use of force or the threat of force anywhere in the world to break the peace is of direct concern to the American people.

The course of history has made us one of the stronger nations of the world. It has therefore placed upon us special responsibilities to conserve our strength and to use it rightly in a world so interdependent as our world today.

The American people recognize these special responsibilities. We shall do our best to meet them, both in the making of the peace settlements and in the fulfillment of the long-range tasks of the United Nations.

The American people look upon the United Nations not as a temporary expedient but as a permanent partnership—a partnership among the peoples of the world for their common peace and common well-being.

It must be the determined purpose of all of us to see that the United Nations lives and grows in the minds and the hearts of all people.

May Almighty God, in His infinite wisdom and mercy, guide and sustain us as we seek to bring peace everlasting to the world.

With His help we shall succeed.

Resolutions Adopted by the General Assembly on Principles
Governing the General Regulation and Reduction of Armaments*

December 14, 1946

1. In pursuance of Article 11 of the Charter and with a view to strenghtening international peace and security in conformity with the Purposes and Principles of the United Nations,

The General Assembly recognizes the necessity of an early general regulation and reduction of armaments and armed forces.

2. Accordingly, the General Assembly recommends that the Security Council give prompt consideration to formulating the practical measures, according to their priority, which are essential to provide for the general regulation and reduction of armaments and armed forces and to assure that such regulation and reduction of armaments and armed forces will be generally observed by all participants and not unilaterally by only some of the participants. The plans formulated by the Security Council shall be submitted by the Secretary-General to the Members of the United Nations for consideration at a special session of the General Assembly. The treaties or conventions approved by the General Assembly shall be submitted to the signatory States for ratification in accordance with Article 26 of the Charter.

3. As an essential step towards the urgent objective of prohibiting and eliminating from national armaments atomic and all other majors weapons adaptable now and in the future to mass destruction, and the early establishment of international control of atomic energy and other modern scientific discoveries and technical developments to ensure their use only for peaceful purposes,

The General Assembly urges the expeditious fulfilment by the Atomic Energy Commission of its terms of reference as set forth in section 5 of the General Assembly resolution of 24 January 1946.

4. In order to ensure that the general prohibition, regulation and reduction of armaments are directed towards the major weapons of modern warfare and not merely towards the minor weapons,

The General Assembly recommends that the Security Council expedite consideration of the reports which the Atomic Energy Commission will make to the Security Council and that it facilitate the work of that Commission, and also that the Security Council expedite consideration of a draft convention or conventions for the creation of an international system of control and inspection, these conventions to include the prohibition of atomic and all other major weapons adaptable now and in the future to mass destruction and the control of atomic energy to the extent necessary to ensure its use only for peaceful purposes.

5. The General Assembly, further recognizes that essential to the general regulation and reduction of armaments and armed forces, is the provision of practical and effective safeguards by way of inspection and other means to protect complying States against the hazards of violations and evasions.

Accordingly, the General Assembly, recommends to the Security Council that it give prompt consideration to the working out of proposals to provide such practical and effective safeguards in connexion with the control of atomic energy and the general regulation and reduction of armaments.

*U.N. General Assembly, *Official Records*, 1947.

6. To ensure the adoption of measures for the early general regulation and reduction of armaments and armed forces, for the prohibition of the use of atomic energy for military purposes and the elimination from national armaments of atomic and all other major weapons adaptable now or in the future to mass destruction, and for the control of atomic energy to the extent necessary to ensure its use only for peaceful purposes,

There shall be established, within the framework of the Security Council, which bears the primary responsibility for the maintenance of international peace and security, an international system, as mentioned in paragraph 4, operating through special organs, which organs shall derive their powers and status from the convention or conventions under which they are established.

7. The General Assembly, regarding the problem of security as closely connected with that of disarmament,

Recommends the Security Council to accelerate as much as possible the placing at its disposal of the armed forces mentioned in Article 43 of the Charter;

Recommends the Members to undertake the progressive and balanced withdrawal, taking into account the needs of occupation, of their armed forces stationed in ex-enemy territories, and the withdrawal without delay of their armed forces stationed in the territories of Members without their consent freely and publicly expressed in treaties or agreements consistent with the Charter and not contradicting international agreements;

Further recommends a corresponding reduction of national armed forces, and a general progressive and balanced reduction of national armed forces.

8. Nothing herein contained shall alter or limit the resolution of the General Assembly passed on 24 January 1946, creating the Atomic Energy Commission.

9. The General Assembly, calls upon all Members of the United Nations to render every possible assistance to the Security Council and the Atomic Energy Commission in order to promote the establishment and maintenance of international peace and collective security with the least diversion for armaments of the world's human and economic resources.

Senate Resolution 239 on Armed Force and Removal of Veto Power on Questions Involving Pacific Settlements of International Disputes*

June 11, 1948

Whereas peace with justice and the defense of human rights and fundamental freedoms require international cooperation through more effective use of the United Nations: Therefore be it

Resolved, That the Senate reaffirm the policy of the United States to achieve international peace and security through the United Nations so that armed force shall not be used except in the common interest, and that the President be advised of the sense of the Senate that this Government, by constitutional process, should particularly pursue the following objectives within the United Nations Charter:

(1) Voluntary agreement to remove the veto from all questions involving pacific

*S. Res. 239, 80th Cong., 2d sess.

settlements of international disputes and situations, and from the admission of new members.

(2) Progressive development of regional and other collective arrangements for individual and collective self-defense in accordance with the purposes, principles, and provisions of the Charter.

(3) Association of the United States, by constitutional process, with such regional and other collective arrangements as are based on continuous and effective self-help and mutual aid, and as affect its national security.

(4) Contributing to the maintenance of peace by making clear its determination to exercise the right of individual or collective self-defense under article 51 should any armed attack occur affecting its national security.

(5) Maximum efforts to obtain agreements to provide the United Nations with armed forces as provided by the Charter, and to obtain agreement among member nations upon universal regulation and reduction of armaments under adequate and dependable quaranty against violation.

(6) If necessary, after adequate effort toward strengthening the United Nations, review of the Charter at an appropriate time by a General Conference called under article 109 or by the General Assembly.

INTERNATIONAL CONTROL OF ATOMIC POWER

Statement Issued by Representatives of Canada, China, France, the United Kingdom and the United States on International Control of Atomic Energy [*]

October 25, 1949

On 24 October 1949, the representatives of Canada, China, France, the Union of Soviet Socialist Republics, the United Kingdom and the United States of America agreed to send to the Secretary-General of the United Nations, for transmission to the General Assembly, the following interim report on the consultations of the six permanent members of the Atomic Energy Commission:

"In paragraph 3 of General Assembly resolution 191 (III) of 4 November 1948, the representatives of the Sponsoring Powers, who are the Permanent Members of the Atomic Energy Commission, namely, Canada, China, France, the Union of Soviet Socialist Republics, the United Kingdom of Great Britain and Northern Ireland and the United States of America, were requested to hold consultations "in order to determine if there exist a basis for agreement on the international control of atomic energy to ensure its use only for peaceful purposes, and for the elimination from national armaments of atomic weapons'.

"The first meeting took place on 9 August 1949. The consultations have not yet been concluded and are continuing but, in order to inform the General Assembly of the position which has so far been reached, the six Sponsoring Powers have decided to transmit to it the summary records of the first ten meetings."

It was agreed by the group that any of the representatives of the Governments taking part in these consultations retained the right to submit to the Assembly their observations on the course of the consultations so far. The representatives of Canada, China, France, the United Kingdom and the United States accordingly submit to the General Assembly this statement, which represents their joint views, in the hope that it may ask the Assembly in its consideration of this problem.

Basis of Discussion

It was found desirable to approach these consultations from the viewpoint of general principle rather than specific proposals which had been the basis of most of the discussion in the United Nations Atomic Energy Commission. To this end, the representative of the United Kingdom offered a list of topics as a basis for discussion. Included in this paper was a Statement of Principles relating to each topic (Annex I). It was pointed out that the United Kingdom Statement of Principle was based on the plan approved by the General Assembly, but at the same time covered the essential topics with which any plan for the prohibition of atomic weapons and the control of atomic energy would have to deal. The list of topics was thus adopted as the basis for discussion. The representatives of Canada, China, France, the United Kingdom and the United States made it clear that their Governments accepted the Statement and Principles set forth in this paper and considered them essential to any plan of effective prohibiting of atomic weapons and effective control of atomic energy for peaceful

[*]*Department of State Bulletin*, Nov. 7, 1949, pp. 686-89.

purposes. They expressed the readiness of their Governments to consider the alternative proposals which might be put forward but emphasized that they would continue to suggest the plan approved by the General Assembly and until proposals were made which would provide equally or more effective and workable means of control and prohibition.

Prohibition of Atomic Weapons

At the request of the Soviet representative, the question of the prohibition of atomic weapons was taken up first. The texts which served as a basis for the discussion were point four of the Statement of Principles, and a Soviet amendment submitted to replace that text (Annex II). In the course of the discussion, the Soviet representative declared that the representatives of all six Sponsoring Powers were in agreement in recognizing that atomic weapons should be prohibited, and he therefore drew the conclusion that his amendment should be accepted. The other representatives pointed out that it had always been agreed that the production, possession or use of atomic weapons by all nations must be prohibited. But it was also agreed that prohibition could only be enforced by means of an effective system of control. This was recognized even in the Soviet amendment, but the remainder of the amendment contained a repetition of the earlier Soviet proposals for control which were deemed inadequate.

The Soviet representative insisted that two separate conventions, one on prohibition and the other on control, should be put into effect simultaneously. The other representatives maintained that the important point to be resolved was what constitutes effective control, and that this control had to embrace all uses of atomic materials in dangerous quantities. In their view the Soviet proposals would not only fail to provide the security required but they would be so inadequate as to be dangerous. They would delude the peoples of the world into thinking that atomic energy was being controlled when in fact it was not. On the other hand, under the approved plan, the prohibition of the use of atomic weapons would rest not only on the pledge of each nation, but no nation would be permitted to possess the materials with which weapons could be made. Furthermore, the Soviet Government took an impracticable stand as regards the question of timing or stages by which prohibition and control would be brought into effect.

Stages for Putting Into Effect
Prohibition and Control

On this topic, the Soviet representative maintained that the entire system of prohibition and control must be put into effect simultaneously over the entire nuclear industry.

The representatives of the other Powers pointed out that this would be physically impossible. The development of atomic energy is the world's newest industry, and already is one of the most complicated. It would not be reasonable to assume that any effective system of control could be introduced and enforced overnight. Control and prohibition must, therefore, go into effect over a period of time and by a series of stages.

The plan approved by the General Assembly on 4 November 1948 does not attempt to define what the stages should be, the order in which they should be put into effect, or the time which the whole process of transition would take. The reason for this is that no detailed provisions on stages could be drawn up until agreement is reached on what the control system should be, and the provisions would also depend on the state of development of atomic energy in the various countries at the time agreement is reached. Until then, detailed study of the question of stages would be unrealistic.

Meanwhile, the approved plan covers the question of stages in so far as it can usefully be carried at present. The plan provides that the schedule of stages of application of control and prohibition over all the many phases of the entire nuclear industry is to be written into the treaty, with the United Nations Atomic Energy Commission as the body to supervise their orderly implementation. No other commitment or position on this question is contained in the approved plan.

Control

(a) Means of Control

The Soviet representative insisted, as in the past, that any plan of control, to be acceptable to the Soviet Union, must be based on the Soviet proposals for control, originally put forward in June 1947 (Document AEC/24, 11 June 1947), which provide for periodic inspection of nationally owned plants producing or using atomic materials, when declared to an international control organ by the Governments concerned.

The representatives of Canada, China, France, the United Kingdom and the United States recalled that the nuclear fuels produced or used in such plants are the very nuclear explosives used in the manufacture of weapons. A new situation therefore was created in the field of armaments where the conversion of a peaceful industry into a war industry could take place rapidly and without warning.

In dealing with such materials a system of control depending merely on inspection would be ineffective. For ordinary chemical or mineral substances and their processing inspection might provide adequate guarantees, but atomic development presented special problems which could not be solved in this way. Materials used in the development of atomic energy were highly radioactive and could not, therefore, be handled except by remote control. The process of measuring atomic fuels was extremely intricate and, at the present stage of our knowledge, subject to appreciable error. It would be impracticable to rely on the inspection of plants and impossible to check the actual amounts of atomic materials inside piles or reactors against the amounts shown in the records.

A system of inspection alone would not prevent the clandestine diversion of atomic materials to war purposes from plants designed for peaceful use and would provide no guarantee that, in spite of any treaty, a nation which was determined to continue the secret manufacture of atomic weapons would be prevented from doing so. A plan based on periodic inspection, on which the Soviet Union insists, would be even less adequate than one based on continuous inspection.

The Soviet representative dismissed these arguments as exaggerated or non-existent.

Since there was evidence that an atomic explosion had been produced in the Soviet Union, the Soviet representative was asked whether he had any new evidence derived from Soviet experience to support his contention that periodic inspection would be sufficient to assure control. No answer has yet been received to this question.

The five Powers remain convinced that any system of inspection alone would be inadequate and that in order to provide security the International Control Agency must itself operate and manage dangerous facilities and must hold dangerous atomic materials and facilities for making or using dangerous quantities of such materials in trust for Member States.

(b) Ownership

During the consultations, the question of ownership, which has often been represented as the real obstacle to agreement on control, was the subject of an extended exchange of views.

The Soviet representative argued that international management and operation were equivalent to international ownership; and that neither international ownership nor international management and operation was essential to control. He stated that his Government would not accept either.

The representatives of the other Sponsoring Powers refuted the interpretation put by the Soviet representative on ownership, management and operation. For the reasons given they believed that the management and operation of dangerous facilities must be entrusted to the International Agency. Management and operation were clearly among the more important rights conferred by ownership. Since effective control would be impossible unless these rights were exercised by the Agency, the nations on whose territories such facilitires were situated would have to renounce important rights normally conferred by ownership. This did not necessarily mean the complete devolution of the rights of ownership to the Agency; for example, the Agency would not have the right arbitrarily to close atomic power plants it would have to conform to national legislation as regards public health and working conditions it could not construct plants at will but only agreement with the nation concerned. Moreover, the Agency would not be free to determine the production policy for nuclear fuel since they would follow provision to be laid down in advance in the treaty. The treaty would also determine the quotas for production and consumption of atomic fuel. Finally, the Agency would leave materials and facilities in trust and would therefore be able to manage or dispose of them arbitrarily or for its own profit but only for the benefit of Member States.

There might well be other rights which would normally be conferred by ownership and which were not specifically mentioned in the approved plan. Their disposition would follow a simple principle. If there were rights, the exercise of which could impair the effectiveness of control individual nations would be required to renounce them. Otherwise they might retain them.

If individual nations agreed to renounce national ownership of dangerous atomic material and the right of managing and operating planes making or using them, in favor of an International Agency acting for the international community, such agreement would be on the basic principles and there would be no need to quarrel over terminology.

(c) Sovereignty

A further argument put forward by the Soviet representative was that to confer on any international agency the powers suggested in the Statement of Principles would constitute a gross infringement of national sovereignty and would permit the International Agency to interfere in the internal economy of individual nations.

In answer to this argument it was pointed out that any plan for international prohibition and control must involve some surrender of sovereignty. The representatives of the other Powers argued that it was indefensible to reject a plan for the international control of atomic energy on the purely negative ground that it would infringe national sovereignty. The ideal of international co-operation and, indeed, the whole concept on which the United Nations was based would be meaningless if States insisted on the rigid maintenance of all their sovereign rights. The question was not one of encroachment on sovereignty, but of assuring the security of the world, which could only be attained by the voluntary association of nations in the exercise of certain rights of sovereignty in an open and co-operating world community.

The Soviet representative remarked that, while some representatives had stated that their Governments were prepared to waive sovereignty provided that the majority plan was accepted, the government of the USSR would not agree to do so.

Obstacles in the Way of Agreement

It appears from these consultations that, as in the pact, the Soviet Union will not negotiate except on the basis of the principles set forth in the proposals of June 1947.

The essential points in the Soviet control provide and the reasons for their rejection by the other five Powers, as brought out in the consultations, are as follows:

The Soviet Union proposes that nations should name to own explosive atomic materials.

The other five Powers feel that under such conditions there would be no effective protection against the sudden use of these materials as atomic weapons.

The Soviet Union proposes that nations continue, as at present, to own, operate and manage facilities making or using dangerous quantities of atomic materials.

The other Five powers believe that, under such conditions, it would be impossible to detect or prevent the diversion of such materials for use in atomic weapons.

The Soviet Union proposes a system of control depending on periodic inspection of facilities the existence of which the national Government concerned reports to the international agency, supplemented by special investigations on suspicion of treaty violations.

The other five Powers believe that periodic inspection would not prevent the diversion of dangerous materials and that the special investigations envisaged would be wholly insufficient to prevent clandestine activities.

Other points of difference, including Soviet insistence on the right to veto the recommendation of the International Control Agency, have not yet been discussed in the consultations.

Conclusions

These consultations have not yet succeeded in bringing about agreement between the U.S.S.R. and the other five Powers, but they have served to clarify some of the points on which there is no agreement.

It is apparent that there is a fundamental difference not only on methods but also on aims. All the Sponsoring Powers other than the U.S.S.R. want world security first and are prepared to accept reservations in traditional concepts of international co-operation, national sovereignty and economic organization where these are necessary for security. The Government of the U.S.S.R. put its sovereignty first and is unwilling to accept measures which may impinge upon or interfere with its rigid exercise of unimpeded state sovereignty.

If this fundamental difference could be overcome, other differences which have hitherto appeared insurmountable could be seen in true perspective, and reasonable ground might be found for their adjustment.

Address by President Truman to the United Nations on Disarmament *

October 24, 1950

* * *

Five years ago, after the bloodshed and destruction of World War II, many of us hoped that all nations would work together to make sure that war could never happen again. We hoped that international cooperation, supported by the strength and moral authority of the United Nations, would be sufficient to prevent aggression.

But this was not to be the case, I am sorry to say.

Although many countries promptly disbanded their wartime armies, other countries continued to maintain forces so large that they posed a constant threat of aggression. And this year, the invasion of Korea has shown that there are some who will resort to outright war, contrary to the principles of the charter, if it suits their ends.

In these circumstances, the United Nations, if it is to be an effective instrument for keeping the peace, has no choice except to use the collective strength of its members to curb aggression.

To do so, the United Nations must be prepared to use force. The United Nations did use force to curb aggression in Korea, and by so doing has greatly strengthened the cause of peace. I am glad that additional steps are being taken at this session to prepare for quick and effective action in any future case of aggression.

The Resolution on the United Action for Peace which is now being considered by the General Assembly recognizes three important principles:

To maintain the peace, the United Nations must be able to learn the facts about any threat of aggression.

Next, it must be able to call quickly upon the member nations to act if the threat becomes serious.

Above all, the peace-loving nations must have the military strength available, when called upon, to act decisively to put down aggression.

The peace-loving nations are building that strength.

However much they may regret the necessity, they will continue to build up their

Public Papers of the Presidents, Harry S. Truman, 1950, pp. 685-87.

strength until they have created forces strong enough to preserve the peace under the United Nations. They will do all that is required to provide a defense against aggression. They will do that because, under the conditions which now exist in the world, it is the only way to maintain peace.

We intend to build up strength for peace as long as it is necessary. But at the same time, we must continue to strive, through the United Nations, to achieve international control of atomic energy and the reduction of armaments and armed forces. Cooperative and effective disarmament would make the danger of war remote. It would be a way of achieving the high purposes of the United Nations without the tremendous expenditures for armaments which conditions in the world today make imperative.

Disarmament is the course which the United States would prefer to take. It is the course which most nations would like to adopt. It is the course which the United Nations from its earliest beginnings has been seeking to follow.

For nearly 5 years, two commissions of the United Nations have been working on the problem of disarmament. One commission has been concerned with the elimination of atomic weapons and the other with the reduction of other types of armaments and of armed forces. Thus far, these commissions have not been successful in obtaining agreement among all the major powers. Nevertheless, these years of effort have served to bring to the attention of all nations the three basic principles upon which any successful plan of disarmament must rest.

First, the plan must include all kinds of weapons. Outlawing any particular kind of weapon is not enough. The conflict in Korea bears tragic witness to the fact that aggression, whatever the weapons used, brings frightful destruction.

Second, the plan must be based on unanimous agreement. A majority of nations is not enough. No plan of disarmament can work unless it includes every nation having substantial armed forces. One-sided disarmament is a sure invitation to aggression.

Third, the plan must be foolproof. Paper promises are not enough. Disarmament must be based on safeguards which will insure the compliance of all nations. The safeguards must be adequate to give immediate warning of any threatened violation. Disarmament must be policed continuously and thoroughly. It must be founded upon free and open interchange of information across national borders.

These are simple, practical principles. If they were accepted and carried out, genuine disarmament would be possible.

It is true that, even if initial agreement were reached, tremendous difficulties would remain. The task of working out the successive steps would still be a complex one and would take a long time and much effort. But the fact that this process is so complex and so difficult is no reason for us to give up hope of ultimate success.

The will of the world for peace is too strong to allow us to give up in this effort. We cannot permit the history of our times to record that we failed by default.

We must explore every avenue which offers any chance of bringing success to the activities of the United Nations in this vital area.

Much valuable work has already been done by the two disarmament commissions on the different technical problems confronting them. I believe it would be useful to explore ways in which the work of these commissions could now be more closely brought together. One possibility to be considered is whether their work might be revitalized if carried forward in the future through a new and consolidated disarmament commission.

But until an effective system of disarmament is established, let us be clear about the task ahead. The only course the peace-loving nations can take in the present situation is to create the armaments needed to make the world secure against aggression.

That is the course to which the United States is now firmly committed. That is the course we will continue to follow as long as it is necessary.

The United States has embarked upon the course of increasing its armed strength only for the purpose of helping to keep the peace. We pledge that strength to uphold the principles of the Charter of the United Nations. We believe that the peace-loving members of the United Nations join us in that pledge.

I believe that the United Nations, strengthened by these pledges, will bring us nearer to the peace we seek.

We know that the difficulties ahead are great. We have learned from hard experience that there is no easy road to peace.

We have a solemn obligation to the peoples we represent to continue our combined efforts to achieve the strength that will prevent aggression.

At the same time, we have an equally solemn obligation to continue our efforts to find solutions to the major problems and issues that divide the nations. The settlement of these differences would make possible a truly dependable and effective system for the reduction and control of armaments.

Although the possibility of attaining that goal appears distant today, we must never stop trying. For its attainment would release immense resources for the good of all mankind. It would free the nations to devote more of their energies to wiping out poverty, hunger, and injustice.

If real disarmament were achieved, the nations of the world, acting through the United Nations, could join in a greatly enlarged program of mutual aid. As the cost of maintaining armaments decreased, every nation could greatly increase its contributions to advancing human welfare. All of us could then pool even greater resources to support the United Nations in its war against want.

In this way, our armaments would be transformed into foods, medicine, tools for use in underdeveloped areas, and into other aids for human advancement. The latest discoveries of science could be made available to men all over the globe. Thus, we could give real meaning to the old promise that swords shall be beaten into plowshares, and that nations shall not learn war any more.

Then, man can turn his great inventiveness, his tremendous energies, and the resources with which he has been blessed, to creative efforts. Then we shall be able to realize the kind of world which has been the vision of man for centuries.

This is the goal which we must keep before us—and the vision in which we must never lose faith. This will be our inspiration, and, with God's help, we shall attain our goal.

Statement by Ambassador Benjamin V. Cohen in Subcommittee I of the Disarmament Commission*

April 4, 1952

In dealing with this item—regulation of armed forces and armaments—we come to what we all agree is the heart of the disarmament problem.

*United States Mission to the United Nations, Press Release 1455.

It seems to me that at the very outset, we must distinguish between the goal we wish to reach and the practical ways and means of reaching the goal.

We would propose that we should at the outset define our goal so that we may have some principles and standards by which to judge the specific proposals which may be submitted to us. If we define our goal first, we should be able to avoid many of the difficulties involved in the debates in the General Assembly. As we review those debates, we find that agreement or partial agreement on our objectives was obscured by differences regarding the ways and means of achieving them.

Let me cite a few examples. The Soviet representatives have argued that the United States was opposed to any general reduction in armed forces and armaments because the United States was unwilling to accept the Soviet proposals that a decision should be taken to reduce by one-third the armed strength of the great powers and to prohibit the use of atomic weapons and other weapons capable of mass destruction. Now it is true that the United States opposed the specific Soviet proposals. But it does not follow from this that the United States is opposed to a general and drastic reduction in the armed forces and armaments of all powers. On the contrary, the United States favors the elimination of all mass armed forces. Nor is it true that the United States is opposed to the prohibition of all instruments capable of mass destruction. The United States favor the prohibition not only of mass armies but of atomic and bacteriological weapons. The United States, however, believes that such prohibitions can be effective only when they are accompanied by safeguards—international controls—which will ensure their observance.

The objective of the United States is, in fact, much more far reaching than that of the Soviet Union. The United States is not interested in merely taking a decision at a meeting declaring that these things are unlawful. The United States desires to find ways and means of devising safeguards which will ensure that the obligations undertaken will be kept. The United States objects to the Soviet proposals because their objectives are too limited and arbitrary, and because the ways and means of reaching them appear to us to be wholly inadequate and unreliable in practice.

If we want to make progress now or in the future, we must not be content to declare that we want peace and an end of the armaments race. We must be honest and courageous enough to inform ourselves and our peoples what it is necessary that we all must do to secure peace and to end the armaments race. There has been no aggressor in history who would not accept peace on his own terms and at his own price. And we all know that Hitler and his minions financed and supported pacifist movements for all peoples other than those members of their chosen race of supermen.

In my opening statement in the Disarmament Commission, I tried to outline some of the objectives and principles which we all must accept if we wish to do something about, and not merely talk about, disarmament.

I shall try briefly to restate some of these objectives and principles which I think ought to be agreed upon at the outset if we are to make progress in this difficult field.

1. We should agree that the goal of disarmament is not to regulate but to prevent war, by making war inherently and constitutionally impossible as a means of adjusting disputes between nations.

Disarmament discussions should not degenerate into horse-trades in which the participants try to improve their relative armed strength.

2. We must accept the fourth of the Four Freedoms—freedom from fear—as embracing, in the words used by President Roosevelt, "a worldwide reduction of

armaments to such a point and in such a thorough fashion that no nation will be in a position to commit an act of aggression against any neighbor anywhere in the world."

That means that we must eliminate mass armies and all instruments of mass destruction. That means that no nation should be in such a state of armed prepared-ness as to be able to undertake a major war. We believe that armed forces and armaments should be reduced by international agreement to these levels:

(a) Necessary for the maintenance of internal order.

(b) Necessary for the maintenance of peace through the United Nations collective security system.

3. We all must agree and accept such foolproof safeguards so that we can all feel safe and sure that no nation is in a position to wage a successful war.

That means an open world with no secret armies, no secret weapons and no secret war plans. No nation must have any reason to suspect or fear that any other nation is covertly making preparations to fight a war. No new aggressor should be in a position to flout the laws of a disarmed world without all other nations having fair warning long before the aggressor could put himself in a position to fight a major war.

It may be difficult for nations accustomed to living in the dark to trust themselves in the light, but that is what we all must learn to do if we want to rid ourselves of the burden of armaments.

The objectives and principles which I have outlined are not far different from the objectives and principles that Maxim Litvinov pleaded for before the last war. They are the objectives and principles which we all must accept if we wish to achieve peace through disarmament.

Speech by President Dwight D. Eisenhower Before the General Assembly on Peaceful Uses of Atomic Energy*

New York, December 8, 1953

*   *   *

I feel impelled to speak today in a language that in a sense is new—one which I, who have spent so much of my life in the military profession, would have preferred never to use.

That new language is the language of atomic warfare.

The atomic age has moved forward at such a pace that every citizen of the world should have some comprehension, at least in comparative terms, of the extent of this development of the utmost significance to every one of us. Clearly, if the peoples of the world are to conduct an intelligent search for peace, they must be armed with the significant facts of today's existence.

My recital of atomic danger and power is necessarily stated in United States terms, for these are the only incontrovertible facts that I know. I need hardly point out to this Assembly, however, that this subject is global, not merely national in character.

On July 16, 1945, the United States set off the world's first atomic explosion. Since that date in 1945, the United States of America has conducted 42 test explosions.

The Public Papers of the Presidents of the United States, Dwight D. Eisenhower, Jan 20 1953-Dec. 3, 1953, (Washington, 1960), pp. 815-22.

Atomic bombs today are more than 25 times as powerful as the weapons with which the atomic age dawned, while hydrogen weapons are in the ranges of millions of tons of TNT equivalent.

Today, the United States' stockpile of atomic weapons, which, of course, increases daily, exceeds by many times the explosive equivalent of the total of all bombs and all shells that came from every plane and every gun in every theatre of war in all of the years of World War II.

A single air group, whether afloat or land-based, can now deliver to any reachable target a destructive cargo exceeding in power all the bombs that fell on Britain in all of World War II.

In size and variety, the development of atomic weapons has been no less remarkable. The development has been such that atomic weapons have virtually achieved conventional status within our armed services. In the United States, the Army, the Navy, the Air Force, and the Marine Corps are all capable of putting this weapon to military use.

But the dread secret, and the fearful engines of atomic might, are not ours alone.

In the first place, the secret is possessed by our friends and allies, Great Britain and Canada, whose scientific genius made a tremendous contribution to our original discoveries, and the designs of atomic bombs.

The secret is also known by the Soviet Union.

The Soviet Union has informed us that, over recent years, it has devoted extensive resources to atomic weapons. During this period, the Soviet Union has exploded a series of atomic devices, including at least one involving thermo-nuclear reactions.

If at one time the United States possessed what might have been called a monopoly of atomic power, that monopoly ceased to exist several years ago. Therefore, although our earlier start has permitted us to accumulate what is today a great quantitative advantage, the atomic realities of today comprehend two facts of even greater significance.

First, the knowledge now possessed by several nations will eventually be shared by others—possibly all others.

Second, even a vast superiority in numbers of weapons, and a consequent capability of devastating retaliation, is no preventive, of itself, against the fearful material damage and toll of human lives that would be inflicted by surprise aggression.

The free world, at least dimly aware of these facts, has naturally embarked on a large program of warning and defense systems. That program will be accelerated and expanded.

But let no one think that the expenditure of vast sums for weapons and systems of defense can guarantee absolute safety for the cities and citizens of any nation. The awful arithmetic of the atomic bomb does not permit of any such easy solution. Even against the most powerful defense, an aggressor in possession of the effective minimum number of atomic bombs for a surprise attack could probably place a sufficient number of his bombs on the chosen targets to cause hideous damage.

Should such an atomic attack be launched against the United States, our reactions would be swift and resolute. But for me to say that the defense capabilities of the United States are such that they could inflict terrible losses upon an aggressor—for me to say that the retaliation capabilities of the United States are so great that such an aggressor's land would be laid waste—all this, while fact, is not the true expression of the purpose and hope of the United States.

To pause there would be to confirm the hopeless finality of a belief that two atomic colossi are doomed malevolently to eye each other indefinitely across a trembling world. To stop there would be to accept helplessly the probability of civilization destroyed—the annihilation of the irreplaceable heritage of mankind handed down to us generation from generation—and the condemnation of mankind to begin all over again the age-old struggle upward from savagery toward decency, and right, and justice.

Surely no sane member of the human race could discover victory in such desolation. Could anyone wish his name to be coupled by history with such human degradation and destruction.

Occasional pages of history do record the faces of the "Great Destroyers" but the whole book of history reveals mankind's never-ending quest for peace, and mankind's God-given capacity to build.

It is with the book of history, and not with isolated pages, that the United States will ever wish to be identified. My country wants to be constructive, not destructive. It wants agreements, not wars, among nations. It wants itself to live in freedom, and in the confidence that the people of every other nation enjoy equally the right of choosing their own way of life.

So my country's purpose is to help us move out of the dark chamber of horrors into the light, to find a way by which the minds of men, the hopes of men, the souls of men everywhere, can move forward toward peace and happiness and well being.

In this quest, I know that we must not lack patience.

I know that in a world divided, such as ours today, salvation cannot be attained by one dramatic act.

I know that many steps will have to be taken over many months before the world can look at itself one day and truly realize that a new climate of mutually peaceful confidence is abroad in the world.

But I know, above all else, that we must start to take these steps—now.

*   *   *

There is at least one new avenue of peace which has not yet been well explored—an avenue now laid out by the General Assembly of the United Nations.

In its resolution of November 18th, 1953, this General Assembly suggested—and I quote—"that the Disarmament Commission study the desirability of establishing a sub-committee consisting of representatives of the Powers principally involved, which should seek in private an acceptable solution . . . and report on such a solution to the General Assembly and to the Security Council not later than 1 September 1954."

The United States, heeding the suggestion of the General Assembly of the United Nations, is instantly prepared to meet privately with such other countries as may be "principally involved," to seek "an acceptable solution" to the atomic armaments race which overshadows not only the peace, but the very life, of the world.

We shall carry into these private or diplomatic talks a new conception.

The United States would seek more than the mere reduction or elimination of atomic materials for military purposes.

It is not enough to take this weapon out of the hands of the soldiers. It must be put into the hands of those who will know how to strip its military casing and adapt it to the arts of peace.

The United States knows that if the fearful trend of atomic military buildup can be reversed, this greatest of destructive forces can be developed into a great boon, for the benefit of all mankind.

The United States knows that peaceful power from atomic energy is no dream of the future. That capability, already proved, is here—now—today. Who can doubt, if the entire body of the world's scientists and engineers had adequate amounts of fissionable material with which to test and develop their ideas, that this capability would rapidly be transformed into universal, efficient, and economic usage.

To hasten the day when fear of the atom will begin to disappear from the minds of people, and the governments of the East and West, there are certain steps that can be taken now.

I therefore make the following proposals:

The Governments principally involved, to the extent permitted by elementary prudence, to begin now and continue to make joint contributions from their stockpiles of normal uranium and fissionable materials to an International Atomic Energy Agency. We would expect that such an agency would be set up under the aegis of the United Nations.

The ratios of contributions, the procedures and other details would properly be within the scope of the "private conversations" I have referred to earlier.

The United States is prepared to undertake these explorations in good faith. Any partner of the United States acting in the same good faith will find the United States a not unreasonable or ungenerous associate.

Undoubtedly initial and early contributions to this plan would be small in quantity. However, the proposal has the great virtue that it can be undertaken without the irritations and mutual suspicions incident to any attempt to set up a completely acceptable system of world-wide inspection and control.

The Atomic Energy Agency could be made responsible for the impounding, storage, and protection of the contributed fissionable and other materials. The ingenuity of our scientists will provide special safe conditions under which such a bank of fissionable material can be made essentially immune to surprise seizure.

The more important responsibility of this Atomic Energy Agency would be to devise methods whereby this fissionable material would be allocated to serve the peaceful pursuits of mankind. Experts would be mobilized to apply atomic energy to the needs of agriculture, medicine, and other peaceful activities. A special purpose would be to provide abundant electrical energy in the power-starved areas of the world. Thus the contributing powers would be dedicating some of their strength to serve the needs rather than the fears of mankind.

The United States would be more than willing—it would be proud to take up with others "principally involved" the development of plans whereby such peaceful use of atomic energy would be expedited.

Of those "principally involved" the Soviet Union must, of course, be one.

I would be prepared to submit to the Congress of the United States, and with every expectation of approval, any such plan that would:

First—encourage world-wide investigation into the most effective peacetime uses of fissionable material, and with the certainty that they had all the material needed for the conduct of all experiments that were appropriate;

Second—begin to diminish the potential destructive power of the world's atomic stockpiles;

Third—allow all peoples of all nations to see that, in this enlightened age, the great powers of the earth, both of the East and of the West, are interested in human aspirations first, rather than in building up the armaments of war;

Fourth—open up a new channel for peaceful discussion, and initiate at least a new approach to the many difficult problems that must be solved in both private and public conversations, if the world is to shake off the inertia imposed by fear, and is to make positive progress toward peace.

Against the dark background of the atomic bomb, the United States does not wish merely to present strength, but also the desire and the hope for peace.

The coming months will be fraught with fateful decisions. In this Assembly; in the capitals and military headquarters of the world; in the hearts of men everywhere, be they governors or governed, may they be the decisions which will lead this world out of fear and into peace.

To the making of these fateful decisions, the United States pledges before you—and therefore before the world—its determination to help solve the fearful atomic dilemma—to devote its entire heart and mind to find the way by which the miraculous inventiveness of man shall not be dedicated to his death, but consecrated to his life.

I again thank the delegates for the great honor they have done me, in inviting me to appear before them, and in listening to me so courteously. Thank you.

*Address by Secretary of State John Foster Dulles Before the General Assembly on Peaceful Uses of Atomic Energy**

September 22, 1955

*   *   *

Last September I mentioned four activities which we promised to commence immediately. Since that time, we have made good progress in each of these fields.

The negotiations for establishment of an International Atomic Energy Agency have led to the preparation of a draft statute establishing such an agency.

An International Conference on the Peaceful Uses of Atomic Energy was held with outstanding success last month at Geneva. This conference was so successful that the United States will again propose a similar conference to be held in 3 years or earlier if the increasing development of the peaceful uses of atomic energy will so warrant.

The first reactor training course at our Argonne National laboratory is nearing completion, and an enlarged course is about to begin.

Distinguished doctors and surgeons from other countries are visiting our hospitals and research establishments where atomic energy is used for the cure of cancer and other diseases.

The Soviet Union is now taking a more cooperative attitude, and we gladly note the recent offer of Premier Bulganin to set aside fissionable material for the work of the proposed International Agency when it comes into existence.

Much has happened, we see, to give reality to the vista of hope which President Eisenhower portrayed when he spoke to our Eighth Session.

Department of State Bulletin, Oct. 3, 1955, pp. 527-29.

The United States also plans at this session to propose the establishment of an international technical body on the effects of atomic radiation upon human health. It would be composed of qualified scientists who would collate and give wide distribution to radiological information furnished by states members of the United Nations, or specialized agencies.

The United States is itself giving much study to this matter. We believe that properly safeguarded nuclear testing and the development of peaceful uses of atomic energy do not threaten human health or life. But this is a subject of such transcendent concern that we believe that all available data should be sought out and pooled under United Nations auspices.

On July 21st of this year, at Geneva, the President of the United States took still another major initiative. Dealing with disarmament, and addressing himself for the moment principally to the delegates from the Soviet Union, he proposed that, as a beginning, each of our two nations should provide the other with information as to its military establishments and with facilities for unrestricted aerial reconnaissance of the other.

The logic of this proposal is simple and clear. Major aggression is unlikely unless the aggressor can have the advantage of surprise and can hope to strike a blow which will be devastating because unexpected. But the preparation of an attack of such magnitude could hardly be concealed from aerial inspection. Aerial inspection would not, of course, detect everything. We do not think of it as itself a final comprehensive system of inspection. But aerial inspection would detect enough to exclude the greatest risk. Because it would do that, it would open the way to further steps toward inspection and disarmament which we all, and I emphatically include the United States, want to see taken.

Long experience makes it apparent that, when there is a sense of insecurity, when there is an ominous unknown, then arms seem needed and limitation of armament becomes virtually unattainable. Reductions of armament occur when fear is dissipated, when knowledge replaces exaggerated speculation, and when in consequence arms seem less needed.

It was, I believe, immediately sensed by all that, if the United States were to permit Soviet overflights of its territory and if the Soviet Union were to permit the United States overflights of its territory, that would go far to show that neither had aggressive intentions against the other. Then, as President Eisenhower pointed out in his plea at Geneva, it would be easier to move on to a comprehensive, scientific system of inspection and disarmament. The essence of the President's proposal was that it would, as a beginning, do what is required of a beginning; namely, make it more possible to take subsequent steps.

I hope that the sentiment of this General Assembly will make clear that this beginning should be made as simply as may be and as quickly as may be. From such a beginning can come, and I believe will come, solid advance toward our charter goal of reducing the "diversion for armaments of the world's human and economic resources." Then we can realistically look forward to fulfilling the desire close to the hearts of all our people—a desire voiced by President Eisenhower at our recent meeting in San Francisco—that more of this earth's resources should be used for truly constructive purposes, which would particularly benefit the underdeveloped areas of the world.

It was 10 years ago last month that the fighting stopped in World War II. We have lived through the subsequent decade without another world war. That is something for which to be profoundly thankful. But true peace has not been enjoyed. There have been limited wars; free nations have been subverted and taken over; there has been the piling up of armament, and the rigidities of position which are imposed upon those who regard each other as potential fighting enemies.

That phase may now be ending. I believe that all four of the Heads of Government, who were at Geneva, wanted that result and that each contributed to it. In consequence, a new spirit does indeed prevail, with greater flexibility and less brittleness in international relations.

Some find it interesting to speculate as to which nations gained and which lost from this development. I would say that if the "spirit of Geneva" is to be permanent, then all the world must be the gainer. The "summit" meeting, if it is to be historic rather than episodic, must usher in an era of peaceful change.

It will not be an era of placidity and stagnancy, in the sense that the *status quo*, with its manifold injustices, is accepted as permanent. It will be an era of change, and it will have its strains and its stresses. But peoples and governments will renounce the use of war and of subversion to achieve their goals. They will accept orderly evolution toward the realization of legitimate national aspirations. They will develop wider economic intercourse among themselves. They will increasingly respect human rights and fundamental freedoms. And human effort will be dedicated to what is creative and benign.

The United Nations, too, will change. Given good will and mutual confidence, many provisions of the charter will gain new meaning and new vitality.

Let us together strive that the next decade shall be known as the healing decade of true peace.

General Assembly Resolution 914 (X) on Regulation of Armed Forces and an International Treaty on Reduction of Armaments*

December 16, 1955

The General Assembly,

Recalling its resolution 808(IX) of 4 November 1954, which established the conclusion that a further effort should be made to reach agreement on comprehensive and co-ordinated proposals to be embodied in a draft international disarmament convention providing for:

(a) The regulation, limitation and major reduction of all armed forces and all conventional armaments,

(b) The total prohibition of the use and manufacture of nuclear weapons and weapons of mass destruction of every type, together with the conversion of existing stocks of nuclear weapons for peaceful purposes,

(c) The establishment of effective international control, through a control organ with rights, powers and functions adequate to guarantee the effective observance of the agreed reductions of all armaments and armed forces and the prohibition of nuclear and other weapons of mass destruction, and to ensure the use of atomic energy for peaceful purposes only,

the whole programme to be such that no State would have cause to fear that its security was endangered,

*U.N. General Assembly, *Official Records*, 10th sess., 1965, Supplement 19, pp. 5-6.

Expressing the hope that efforts to relax international tensions, to promote mutual confidence and to develop co-operation among States, such as the Geneva Conference of the Heads of Government of the four Powers, the Banding Conference of African and Asian countries and the United Nations tenth anniversary commemorative meeting at San Francisco, will provide effective in promoting world peace,

Desirous of contributing to the lowering of international tensions, the strengthening of confidence between States, the removal of the threat of war and the reduction of the burden of armaments,

Convinced therefore of the need to continue to seek agreement on a comprehensive programme for disarmament which will promote international peace and security with thy least diversion for armaments of the world's human and economic resources,

Welcoming the progress which has been made towards agreement on objectives during the meetings in 1955 of the Sub-Committee of the Disarmament Commission,

Noting that agreement has not yet been reached on the rights, powers, and functions of a control system, which is the keystone of any disarmament agreement, nor on other essential matters set out in General Assembly resolution 808 (IX),

Noting also that special technical difficulties have arisen in regard to the detection and control of nuclear weapons material,

Recognizing further that inspection and control of disarmament can best be achieved in an atmosphere which is free of fear and suspicion,

1. Urges that the States concerned and particularly those on the Sub-Committee of the Disarmament Commission:

(a) Should continue their endeavours to reach agreement on a comprehensive disarmament plan in accordance with the goals set out in General Assembly resolution 808 (IX);

(b) Should, as initial steps, give priority to early agreement on and implementation of:

(i) Such confidence-building measures as the plan of Mr. Eisenhower, President of the United States of America, for exchanging military blueprints and mutual aerial inspection, and the plan of Mr. Bulganin, Prime Minister of the Union of Soviet Socialist Republics, for establishing control posts at strategic centres,

(ii) All such measures of adequately safeguarded disarmament as are now feasible;

2. Suggests that account should also be taken of the proposals of the Prime Minister of France for exchanging and publishing information regarding military expenditures and budgets, of the Prime Minister of the United Kingdom of Great Britain and Northern Ireland for seeking practical experience in the problems of inspection and control, and of the Government of India regarding the suspension of experimental explosions of nuclear weapons and an "armaments truce";

3. Calls upon the States concerned, and especially those on the Sub-Committee of the Disarmament Commission, to study the proposal of the Prime Minister of France for the allocation of funds resulting from disarmament for improving the standards of living throughout the world and, in particular, in the less-developed countries;

4. Recommends further that scientific search should be continued by each State, with appropriate consultation between Governments, for methods that would make possible thoroughly effective inspection and control of nuclear weapons material, having as its aim to facilitate the solution of the problem of comprehensive disarmament;

5. Suggests that the Disarmament Commission reconvene its Sub-Committee and that both pursue their efforts to attain the above objectives;

6. Decides to transmit to the Disarmament Commission, for its information, the records of the meetings of the First Committee at which the disarmament problem was discussed during the tenth session of the General Assembly, and requests the Disarmament Commission and the Sub-Committee to give careful and early consideration to the views expressed in those documents.

*Statute of the International Atomic Energy Agency**

September 20–October 26, 1956

Article XII

Agency Safeguards

A. With respect to any Agency project, or other arrangement where the Agency is requested by the parties concerned to apply safeguards, the Agency shall have the following rights and responsibilities to the extent relevant to the project or arrangement:

1. To examine the design of specialized equipment and facilities, including nuclear reactors, and to approve it only from the viewpoint of assuring that it will not further any military purpose, that it complies with applicable health and safety standards, and that it will permit effective application of the safeguards provided for in this article;

2. To require the observance of any health and safety measures prescribed by the Agency;

3. To require the maintenance and production of operating records to assist in ensuring accountability for source and special fissionable materials used or produced in the project or arrangement;

4. To call for and receive progress reports;

5. To approve the means to be used for the chemical processing of irradiated materials solely to ensure that this chemical processing will not lend itself to diversion of materials for military purposes and will comply with applicable health and safety standards; to require that special fissionable materials recovered or produced as a by-product be used for peaceful purposes under continuing Agency safeguards for research or in reactors, existing or under construction, specified by the member or members concerned; and to require deposit with the Agency of any excess of any special fissionable materials recovered or produced as a by-product over what is needed for the above-stated uses in order to prevent stockpiling of these materials, provided that thereafter at the request of the member or members concerned special fissionable materials so deposited with the Agency shall be returned promptly to the member or members concerned for use under the same provisions as stated above;

6. To send into the territory of the recipient State or States inspectors, designated by the Agency after consultation with the State or States concerned, who shall have access at all times to all places and data and to any person who by reason of his occupation deals with materials, equipment, or facilities which are required by this Statute to be safeguarded, as necessary to account for source and special fissionable materials supplied and fissionable products and to determine whether there is compli-

Statute of the International Atomic Energy Agency, Conference on the Statute Held at Headquarters of the United Nations, September 20 to October 26, 1956, TAEA/13, Nov. 1, 1956.

ance with the undertaking against use in furtherance of any military purpose referred to in sub-paragraph F-4 of article XI, with the health and safety measures referred to in sub-paragraph A-2 of this article, and with any other conditions prescribed in the agreement between the Agency and the State or States concerned. Inspectors designated by the Agency shall be accompanied by representatives of the authorities of the State concerned, if that State so requests, provided that the inspectors shall not thereby be delayed or otherwise impeded in the exercise of their functions;

7. In the event of non-compliance and failure by the recipient State to take requested corrective steps within a reasonable time, to suspend or terminate assistance and withdraw any materials and equipment made available by the Agency or a member in furtherance of the project.

B. The Agency shall, as necessary, establish a staff of inspectors. The staff of inspectors shall have the responsibility of examining all operations conducted by the Agency itself to determine whether the Agency is complying with the health and safety measures prescribed by it for application to projects subject to its approval, supervision or control, and whether the Agency is taking adequate measures to prevent the source and special fissionable materials in its custody or used or produced in its own operations from being used in furtherance of any military purpose. The Agency shall take remedial action forthwith to correct any non-compliance or failure to take adequate measures.

C. The staff of inspectors shall also have the responsibility of obtaining and verifying the accounting referred to in sub-paragraph A-6 of this article and of determining whether there is compliance with the undertaking referred to in sub-paragraph F-4 of article XI, with the measures referred to in sub-paragraph A-2 of this article, and with all other conditions of the project prescribed in the agreement between the Agency and the State or States concerned. The inspectors shall report any non-compliance to the Director General who shall thereupon transmit the report to the Board of Governors. The Board shall call upon the recipient State or States to remedy forthwith any non-compliance which it finds to have occurred. The Board shall report the non-compliance to all members and to the Security Council and General Assembly of the United Nations. In the event of failure of the recipient State or States to take fully corrective action within a reasonable time, the Board may take one or both of the following measures: direct curtailment or suspension of assistance being provided by the Agency or by a member, and call for the return of materials and equipment made available to the recipient member or group of members. The Agency may also, in accordance with article XIX, suspend any non-complying member from the exercise of the privileges and rights of membership.

*Statement by Henry Cabot Lodge, U.S. Representative in
Committee I, on Disarmament**

October 10, 1957

All of us here present today must feel the urgent need for progress in solving a problem as vital to world peace as is the disarmament problem.

No country feels that need more urgently than the United States, which must bear

*United States Delegation to the General Assembly, Press Release 2763.

a heavy load of military preparedness. We have long and earnestly sought a way to be rid of that costly burden.

But we seek more than that, Mr. Chairman. Through a safe disarmament program we seek to build a world in which all nations, large and small, will be free from the danger of war and surprise attack, and can devote themselves confidently to the arts of peace.

Every nation, Mr. Chairman, understands how vitally important that is in this dangerous time.

We have had that goal in mind in all our work on disarmament, including the sessions of the Disarmament Subcommittee in London this year. The five and a half months of the Subcommittee's work, although it recessed in disappointment, produced something of value. During its 71 meetings progress was made in narrowing disagreements, and new proposals of the greatest importance were presented to the world. Both the Foreign Secretary of the United Kingdom and the United States Secretary of State took part directly, and the Foreign Minister of France went to London for consultations in connection with the negotiations. This was without precedent in the Subcommittee's history.

We have noted with interest the proposal of the Belgian representative for action to inform and enlighten the peoples of the world of the dangers which may confront us all if a solution to the problem of disarmament is not found. It is well that all peoples should know the terrible facts of modern warfare. These facts have been brought forcefully, through every medium of information, to the people of my country. We hope that this may be the case with all the other countries represented here. Perhaps in this way the collective conscience of the United Nations will have its effect on the progress of the disarmament negotiations.

Disarmament discussions are so difficult that we run the risk of giving way to despair. Fortunately there is no need for us now to entertain such fears.

We were disappointed, of course—indeed, some people were shocked—when the Soviet representative said "No" to the new four-power proposals of August 29 without even studying them. But that fact, whatever else it may suggest, is surely no cause for despair. Indeed the fact that there has not yet been a thoroughly considered analytical response from the Soviet Union to these proposals as a whole leaves room for further progress during this session of the General Assembly.

I. The London Meetings

Since we hear doubts expressed now and then on the value of the Subcommittee's work, the United States feels it important that the Assembly should have a clear appreciation of what was done at London. The full record is available. Let me indicate some of the important points where the Subcommittee succeeded in narrowing the differences which we faced last year in the General Assembly.

Here are some forward steps which the Soviet representative took during the Subcommittee meetings.

1. He reaffirmed acceptance of the idea of a limited "first-stage" agreement on various aspects of the disarmament problem, instead of insisting that there must be agreement immediately on a complete disarmament program before any steps are taken.

2. He seemed to see the value of the "Open Skies" air and ground inspection plan

as a safeguard against surprise attack. And he accepted the idea of beginning with agreed zones of inspection—even though these zones remain to be defined.

3. He seemed willing to have a "first-stage" agreement without the Soviet demand for so-called "elimination" of nuclear weapons, which he agrees would be impossible to verify.

4. He agreed that if nuclear testing were suspended there should be a monitoring system with inspection posts inside our countries in order to check on compliance.

5. He indicated that the Soviet Union would accept the ideas of international disarmament depots for the storage of arms.

Those, Mr. Chairman, are five concrete points on which the Soviet Union made advances from its earlier stand. It is entitled to credit for having shown this spirit of accommodation, at least in the earlier stages of the talks. We trust that the Soviet delegate's more negative position at the end does not imply that his government has changed its policy regarding these earlier advances.

The other four members of the Subcommittee showed an equal or even greater spirit of accommodation. We made a number of changes in our position to meet Soviet objections. All these are reflected in the four-power working paper of August 29. Here are the chief new points in our proposals:

1. We agreed to move beyond discussion of a purely "first-stage" agreement, and proposed specific target levels for a further reduction in the size of armed forces in the second and third stages of a disarmament program.

2. As an alternative to complete initial inspection, we suggested limited inspection zones as a beginning for the proposed "open sky" inspection plan thus making it easier for the Soviet Union to agree.

3. To meet the concern expressed over existing stocks of nuclear weapons, we made more specific our proposal not merely to stop adding to these stocks of weapons, but to begin at once to reduce them by transferring successive amounts of fissionable material from military stockpile to peaceful uses, under international supervision.

4. We agreed to transfer large amounts of such material to peaceful uses than the Soviet Union was willing to do. We agreed to negotiate the quantities on a basis that is fair and equitable. That, Mr. Chairman, is a proposal of great significance.

5. We agreed that immediately upon the ratification of the first-stage disarmament program nuclear tests could be suspended for an initial period without waiting until the other portions of the program were actually in operation. Moreover, when the Soviet Union objected that the initial Western proposal for a test suspension of 10 months was not long enough, we agreed to accept the period of 24 months put forward by the Soviet Union.

I think that is a most important point, Mr. Chairman, and will come back to it later on.

These forward steps are substantial, and prove the value of the Subcommittee. It is a body in which serious negotiations can take place and have taken place. It is, of course, not complete proof against temptations to score propaganda points, but then no body is proof against that. We frankly admit that we were startled and surprised, as was most of the world at the abrupt change in the Soviet attitude toward the end of the meetings, and the biggest jolt of all was Mr. Zorin's abrupt rejection of our very serious joint proposals before he or his government had even studied them. But that action, strange as it was, by no means discredits the Subcommittee. The Soviet Representative himself, in a more reasonable frame of mind, has proved it a practical body for real negotiation. All that is needed is the spirit of reasonableness.

The United States does not agree that the prospects for progress in disarmament can be improved, as some say, if only the present bodies dealing with the question can be expanded. Proposals to this end have been made at this and the last Assembly.

We believe that the Assembly decided wisely when, in 1953, it suggested establishment of a Subcommittee of the powers "principally involved." This principle is as valid today as it was then. A disarmament agreement can be hammered out only through negotiations among the parties who, in the first instance, have to submit to inspection and control and who, in the first instance, have to accept reductions and limitations. This is an indispensable first requirement. Basic issues of national security are involved. Accommodation must be achieved by and among these powers to begin with.

This, of course, is not to say that disarmament is the exclusive preserve of the "Big Powers." It is not. While the nations possessing armaments are, to use the language of the 1953 resolution, "principally involved," the whole world, in the larger sense, is vitally involved. It is of deep and legitimate interest to every state represented in this room. All will be affected, and many will have in some way to participate.

We think that the way disarmament is handled in the United Nations fully reflects this widening circle of interest.

In addition to the Subcommittee, there is the Assembly in which all members are heard and have ample opportunity to express their views.

The Assembly itself established the Disarmament Commission of smaller membership that can go more deeply into the issues and which can follow the negotiations closely. Furthermore, there has always been an opportunity for any member which desires it to appear before the Disarmament Commission for a hearing—a right which was exercised during the last year.

II. The Question of Nuclear Tests

The United States believes that a solution to this problem can be found.

Our tests are carried on for defensive purposes. We would not conduct them if we were not deeply convinced that under present circumstances they were necessary for the security of the free world and of our own country. The danger of war will only increase if offensive capabilities are allowed further to outstrip defensive capabilities.

Without moving into a discussion of political issues, it seems fair to say that the United States Government is looked to not alone by the American people, but by the peoples of many other free countries as well, as a safeguard of their security against possible military attack. We cannot carry out the responsibility which has fallen upon us if we are less strong than the potential attacker. What is the basic reason for all of our military defense activity—all of it, Mr. Chairman, including that involving the tests of nuclear weapons.

Now, although we share the concern of other countries about nuclear weapons testing, we believe that this subject must be seen in its context, including the military and technical dangers that confront us. In this connection a few observations about nuclear weapons tests may be in order.

1. Because of our concern over the radiation effects of nuclear tests, however slight they might be, and also because of the importance of understanding atomic radiation

as atomic energy is increasingly developed for peaceful purposes, the United States proposed two years ago in the General Assembly that a United Nations Committee on Radiation be established to report to the world on the whole question. This committee's report is due next year. From what is already known and published, we expect that the Committee's full report will answer many of the fears now being expressed about radiation from nuclear testing.

No environmental hazard nor substance to which human beings are exposed is receiving such thorough investigation as radiation and radioactive materials. While some leading medical and genetic authorities differ on the effects of radioactive fallout at low levels, all agree that the effects are small compared to the effects of radiation from other sources.

The present levels of radiation exposure from weapons testing fallout are extremely low. They are but a fraction of the natural radiation to which man has always been exposed. They are far lower than the levels we customarily receive voluntarily from other man-made sources such as medical and dental X-rays, and even the luminescent dials of our wrist watches. The danger to the world lies in the possible use of the nuclear weapons, and not in some small addition to natural radiation because of testings. We think that is a fundamental point—the possible use of weapons. That is the real danger.

2. What is seldom realized is that the tests themselves are enabling us to develop weapons with reduced fallout so that radiation hazards in the event of hostilities may be restricted to military targets. Thus if our testing program should continue at the present rate the radiation it puts into the world's atmosphere would be less in future years. Indeed, as Secretary Dulles pointed out on September 19, in the General Assembly, since a percentage of radioactivity dies away each year we have reason to hope that in the future any needed testing can be done without materially raising the levels of radioactivity in the world. A practical demonstration of this achievement should result from our plan to invite United Nations observers to witness a nuclear test explosion.

Mr. Chairman, the United States has given a great deal of serious thought to this subject. We do not treat our responsibility lightly in this matter of nuclear tests. Indeed, we have shown what I think lawyers call "an abundance of caution" on this subject.

But we go further than that, Mr. Chairman. We know how anxious people have become about this unfamiliar force. The quickest and most obvious way to allay that anxiety would be to suspend nuclear tests on a sound basis. In fact, in conjunction with our British, French, and Canadian colleagues in the Subcommittee we have proposed that it be done through an immediate suspension taking effect upon there being in existence a treaty for initial measures of disarmament.

III. How to Suspend Nuclear Tests

Since there is agreement on all sides that nuclear tests could be suspended, the question is—how can we do it? There are two approaches to this problem. One is to concentrate on this point alone and attempt to by-pass other questions in the armaments field, hoping that by this one step international confidence would be so strengthened that other steps would follow. Whoever considers this line of approach will have also to consider the following points.

1. Even if the agreement were obeyed by all concerned, and all test explosions

stopped, the efforts to pile up more and more atomic and hydrogen bombs would go right on. That is something to think about.

2. Moreover, under such conditions the efforts to reduce the radioactive fallout in such weapons would also be suspended—you would cut that whole work down—and consequently the weapons added to the stockpiles would contain a larger amount of radioactive fallout than they would otherwise. We ought to consider that.

3. Finally, additional nations could and probably would, without the aid of nuclear tests, nevertheless manufacture and acquire their own nuclear weapons, using techniques which are now known.

These points alone, Mr. Chairman, are enough to dramatize the fact that, a separate approach to the nuclear testing problem does not go to the heart of the matter. The heart of the matter, in this world filled with conflict and mistrust, is the danger of war and the use of weapons of any kind on a mass scale. To deal effectively with this danger, a bolder and a more comprehensive approach is imperative.

It is tragically true that the danger of war imposes on the defender the same iron military necessities as it does upon a would-be aggressor.

Like the aggressor, the defender must have weapons.

Like the aggressor, the defender must draft able young men into the military service.

Like the aggressor, the defender must take away from his civilian economy large amounts of valuable raw materials, iron, steel, aluminum, rubber, and textiles, manufacturing plants, scientific research facilities, and great tracts of useful land.

We in the United States know all these facts very well because we have experienced them in defense against aggression.

Believe me, Mr. Chairman, if it were not for the danger of a great war, the American people would never consent to the continuation of this huge burden on our national life. They and their freely-elected representatives in Congress unceasingly plead for us to find some way by which the burden can safely be laid down. In the meantime they recognize the need to bear it, as do other free peoples, because they know it is the price of liberty.

Consequently, we would not conduct nuclear tests if we did not have to. Let us remove the necessity for nuclear tests and suspend the tests at the same time. That means making at least a beginning on removing the danger of an all-out nuclear war. And that, Mr. Chairman, is the heart and the soul of the proposals which the United States joined in submitting to the Soviet Union in London on August 29. It is just as simple as that.

IV. The London Proposals

Let me review very briefly what the London proposals consist of, as we renew our offer to the Soviet Union. These proposals are not so complicated as they are sometimes made to seem. I shall try to sum them up, in ordinary language, under five headings.

1. Atoms for Peace, Not War. We want to put an end to production of fissionable materials for war purposes. We propose that no country shall make any more fissionable material for weapons, and that all new production of fissionable material should be devoted to peaceful purposes. This program would begin as soon as an inspection system is in existence to see it carried out. We then propose that a start be

made on transferring fissionable materials from weapons stockpiles to peaceful uses, again under international supervision. Mr. Chairman, that is the vision which President Eisenhower presented right here in this building when he urged "that the miraculous inventiveness of man . . . not be dedicated to his death but consecrated to his life." We could not take a greater step for peace than this. This is the practical and only realistic way of first stopping and then reversing the trend towards ever increasing stockpiles of nuclear weapons. Unless we get this problem under control soon, it may become entirely unmanageable as more and more countries begin the production of nuclear weapons.

2. Suspend Nuclear Tests. This would be done immediately upon there being a treaty in existence, and would be followed by the prompt installation of an agreed monitoring system with inspection posts within our respective countries.

3. Reduce Armed Forces and Armaments. On this essential part of the disarmament problem we have made definite proposals, not only for the first stage of a disarmament program, but also for second and third stages as well. The troop limit which we suggest for the Soviet Union and the United States in the first stage is 2.5 million men; in the second stage, assuming satisfactory fulfillment of the first step and progress toward settlement of the problems that cause world tension, we would reduce to 2.1 million, and in the third stage to 1.7 million. As to armaments, we propose a practical method of reduction—setting up storage depots in which specified and agreed modern armaments of land, sea, and air would be deposited under international supervision. This plan would reduce the requirements of inspection to a minimum. We are prepared to negotiate at any time on the types and quantities of arms to be deposited in these depots.

4. Prevent Surprise Attack. We continue to urge adoption of an "Open Sky" ground and air inspection system to make a massive surprise attack impossible. Under such a system the fear of war would decrease and further reductions in armaments would be encouraged. That is what we are striving for. We are willing to begin inspection on a progressive basis beginning in areas where safeguarding against surprise attack is of the greatest importance. In addition, we have reaffirmed the proposal originally made by President Eisenhower at Geneva in 1955. This proposal would embrace the entire territory of the United States and the entire territory of the Soviet Union. With the consent of the countries concerned, we have also agreed to include territory of Canada and important areas in Europe. We are ready also to include areas in the free world where military bases are located provided the countries concerned also agree. Thus we have given the Soviet Union a considerable range of choice on how to begin this vital process of inspection against surprise attack. We are ready to begin modestly and expand later.

5. Control Outer Space Weapons. Finally, Mr. Chairman, we seek agreement on ways to control the newest creation of science—the outer space missile. Like atomic energy, this device can serve the purposes of peace or it can be used to blow us to bits. We have only begun to learn about its possibilities, but we already know that the prospect of outer space missiles armed with nuclear warheads is too dangerous to ignore.

Mr. Chairman, in 1946 when the United States alone had nuclear weapons, it proposed to the United Nations—and there are men in this room who remember this—a plan to ensure the peaceful use of the new and tremendous force of atomic energy by putting it under international control. We made that proposal. The world knows now that a decade of anxiety and trouble could have been avoided if that plan had been accepted. We now have a similar opportunity to harness for peace man's new pioneering efforts in outer space. We must not miss *this* chance. We have therefore proposed that a technical committee be set up to work out an inspection system which will assure the use of outer space for exclusively peaceful and scientific purposes. If there is general agreement to proceed with this study on a multilateral basis, the United States is prepared to join in this initiative without awaiting the conclusion of negotiations on the other substantive proposals.

These, Mr. Chairman, are the highlights of the London proposals.

Before leaving this subject of the London proposals, let me make clear that we are ready to begin the entire first-phase disarmament program without any political conditions whatsoever—without demanding that a single political issue be met. That includes all of the five headings which I just finished summarizing. We are dealing here with a disarmament program on which the United States and its three co-sponsors are ready to embark without delay.

Also, we intend that the very first part of this program to go into effect would be the suspending of nuclear tests. The necessary inspection system for the test ban should be in operation before the end of the first year of suspension.

V. Conclusion

No part of the agreement which we have in mind could be other than welcome to any country which truly works for peace. I have outlined its main parts—nuclear production for peace, not war; prompt suspension of nuclear bomb tests; reduction of troops levels and armaments; a start on inspection to prevent surprise attack, and a start on control of outer space missiles. Mr. Chairman, who can object to any of these points?

The question of prompt suspension of nuclear testing lies today in the hands of the Soviet Union. It can bring the tests to a halt if it wants to. It can do more than that. It can relieve the world's anxiety about the inexpressibly greater perils of surprise attack and nuclear war involving the most dread devices that the genius of science has provided.

The United States has always devoutly wished, and wishes today, for a world in which all nations, including very definitely the Soviet Union, may feel secure from any external danger. We would be defeating our own purpose if we made a proposal designed to impair the security of the Soviet Union, since our aim is the very opposite of that. We trust that the Soviet Union will believe that. Surely, it is to the interest of the Soviet Union to remove distrust of its motives. Indeed, not to do so would leave a world such as that described by President Eisenhower here at the United Nations in 1953, when he spoke of "two atomic colossi eyeing each other malevolently across a trembling world." If that trembling world were to erupt in war, the bombs that fell would be no respectors of persons, nor of ideologies either.

It is not the American people alone, Mr. Chairman, but the peoples of the whole world who request today that the Soviet Union consider the alternatives facing all of us. Especially this request comes from the small nations of the world, whose prospects for a peaceful life lie, not in their own armed might, but in their hope for an ordered world—a world of openness and a world of confidence, free from the fear of sudden and overwhelming attack.

There is no reason for us to despair of a change of mind by the Soviet Union. To their credit let it be said that we have seen them change their minds before. They changed their minds about "atoms for peace." They changed their minds about considering the "Open Sky" plan. Surely they can change their minds again when their security and self-interest as well as ours so clearly demand it.

In essence, we, that is to say Canada, France, the United Kingdom, and the United States, have made, and do make, this offer to the Soviet Union:

We will suspend nuclear tests for an initial period expected to be two years but also subject to further extension, provided you, the Soviet Union, agree on establishing an effective inspection system, air and ground; on stopping production of fissionable material for weapons purposes and reducing present stocks; on starting outer-space missile control; and not reducing armed forces.

Now we do not insist, Mr. Chairman, that all these things be done at once. An agreement that they should be done in acceptable stages is enough to get this program under way and suspension of testing would be the first thing to happen.

So, Mr. Chairman, I conclude by simply saying this:

We think sincerely that our position is fair and far-sighted and that, if endorsed by this Assembly, it will help to move the world forward to a broad plateau of peace.

PROBLEMS OF OUTER SPACE
AND THE END OF NUCLEAR TESTING

*Address by President Eisenhower Before the 15th General Assembly
on Outer Space**

September 22, 1960

*   *   *

Another problem confronting us involves outer space.

The emergence of this new world poses a vital issue: will outer space be preserved for peaceful use and developed for the benefit of all mankind? Or will it become another focus for the arms race—and thus an area of dangerous and sterile competition?

The choice is urgent. And it is ours to make.

The nations of the world have recently united in declaring the continent of Antarctica "off limits" to military preparations. We could extend this principle to an even more important sphere. National vested interests have not yet been developed in space or in celestial bodies. Barriers to agreement are now lower than they will ever be again.

The opportunity may be fleeting. Before many years have passed, the point of no return may have passed.

Let us remind ourselves that we had a chance in 1946 to ensure that atomic energy be devoted exclusively to peaceful purposes. That chance was missed when the Soviet Union turned down the comprehensive plan submitted by the United States for placing atomic energy under international control.

We must not lose the chance we still have to control the future of outer space.

I propose that:

1. We agree that celestial bodies are not subject to national appropriation by any claims of sovereignty.

2. We agree that the nations of the world shall not engage in warlike activities on these bodies.

3. We agree, subject to appropriate verification, that no nation will put into orbit or station in outer space weapons of mass destruction. All launchings of space craft should be verified in advance by the United Nations.

4. We press forward with a program of international cooperation for constructive peaceful uses of outer space under the United Nations. Better weather forecasting, improved world-wide communications, and more effective exploration not only of outer space but of our own earth—these are but a few of the benefits of such cooperation.

Agreement on these proposals would enable future generations to find peaceful and scientific progress, not another fearful dimension to the arms race, as they explore the universe.

*Public Papers of the Presidents, Dwight D. Eisenhower, 1960-61, pp. 714-18.

VI

But armaments must also be controlled here on earth, if civilization is to be assured of survival. These efforts must extend both to conventional and non-conventional armaments.

My country has made specific proposals to this end during the past year. New United States proposals were put forward on June 27, with the hope that they could serve as the basis for negotiations to achieve general disarmament. The United States still supports these proposals.

The communist nations' walk-out at Geneva, when they learned that we were about to submit these proposals, brought negotiations to an abrupt halt. Their unexplained action does not, however, reduce the urgent need for arms control.

My country believes that negotiations can—and should—soon be resumed.

Our aim is to reach agreement on all the various measures that will bring general and complete disarmament. Any honest appraisal, however, must recognize that this is an immense task. It will take time.

We should not have to wait until we have agreed on all the detailed measures to reach this goal before we begin to move toward disarmament. Specific and promising steps to this end were suggested in our June 27 proposals.

If negotiations can be resumed, it may be possible to deal particularly with two pressing dangers—that of war by miscalculation and that of mounting nuclear weapons stockpiles.

The advent of missiles, with ever shorter reaction times, makes measures to curtail the danger of war by miscalculation increasingly necessary. States must be able quickly to assure each other that they are not preparing aggressive moves—particularly in international crises, when each side takes steps to improve its own defenses, which actions might be misinterpreted by the other. Such misinterpretation in the absence of machinery to verify that neither was preparing to attack the other, could lead to a war which no one had intended or wanted.

Today the danger of war by miscalculation could be reduced, in times of crisis, by the intervention, when requested by any nation seeking to prove its own peaceful intention, of an appropriate United Nations surveillance body. The question of methods can be left to the experts.

Thus the vital issue is not a matter of technical feasibility but the political willingness of individual countries to submit to inspection. The United States has taken the lead in this field.

Today, I solemnly declare, on behalf of the United States, that we are prepared to submit to any international inspection, provided only that it is effective and truly reciprocal. This step we will take willingly as an earnest of our determination to uphold the preamble of the United Nations Charter which says its purpose is "to save succeeding generations from the scourge of war, which twice in our lifetime has brought untold sorrow to mankind . . ."

The United States wants the Soviet Union and all the nations of the world to know enough about United States defense preparations to be assured that United States forces exist only for deterrence and defense—not for surprise attack. I hope the Soviet Union will similarly wish to assure the United States and other nations of the nonaggressive character of its security preparations.

There is a more basic point: in an age of rapidly developing technology, secrecy is not only an anachronism—it is downright dangerous. To seek to maintain a society in which a military move can be taken in complete secrecy, while professing a desire to reduce the risk of war through arms control, is a contradiction.

A second danger which ought to be dealt with in early negotiations is posed by the growth and prospective spread of nuclear weapons stockpiles.

To reverse this trend, I propose that the nations producing nuclear weapons immediately convene experts to design a system for terminating, under verification procedures, all production of fissionable materials for weapons purposes.

That termination would take effect as soon as the agreed inspection system has been installed and is operating effectively, while progress in other disarmament fields is also being sought.

The United States is prepared, in the event of a termination of production, to join the USSR in transferring substantial quantities of fissionable materials to international stockpiles. The United Nations Disarmament Commission has already heard the proposal of Ambassador Lodge, to set aside not pounds, as was proposed by the United States in 1954, but tons of fissionable materials for peaceful purposes. Additional transfers would be made as progress in other aspects of disarmament is accomplished.

If the USSR will agree to a cessation of production of fissionable materials for weapons purposes, some production facilities could be closed without delay. The United States would be willing to match the USSR in shutting down major plants producing fissionable materials, one by one, under international inspection and verification.

The proposed working group of experts could also consider how to verify the complete elimination of nuclear weapons, which is part of the third stage of our proposed disarmament program of June 27. There is as yet no known means of demonstrably accomplishing this; we would hope that the experts could develop such a system.

United States officials are willing to meet immediately with representatives of other countries for a preliminary exchange of views on these proposals.

Some who have followed closely the many fruitless disarmament talks since the war tend to become cynical—to assume that the task is hopeless. This is not the position of the United States.

Men everywhere want to disarm. They want their wealth and labor to be spent not for war, but for food, for clothing, for shelter, for medicines, for schools.

Time and again, the American people have voiced this yearning—to join with men of good will everywhere in building a better world. We always stand ready to consider any feasible proposal to this end. And as I have said so many times, the United States is always ready to negotiate with any country which in integrity and sincerity shows itself ready to talk about any of these problems. We ask only this—that such a program not give military advantage to any nation and that it permit men to inspect the disarmament of other nations.

A disarmament program which was not inspected and guaranteed would increase, not reduce, the risk of war.

The international control of atomic energy and general and complete disarmament can no more be accomplished by rhetoric than can the economic development of newly independent countries. Both of these immense tasks facing mankind call for serious, painstaking, costly, laborious and non-propaganda approaches.

*   *   *

*Address by President John F. Kennedy Before the General Assembly on Nuclear Weapons**

September 25, 1961

Today, every inhabitant of this planet must contemplate the day when this planet may no longer be habitable. Every man, woman and child lives under a nuclear sword of Damocles, hanging by the slenderest of threads, capable of being cut at any moment by accident or miscalculation or by madness. The weapons of war must be abolished before they abolish us.

Men no longer debate whether armaments are a symptom or a cause of tension. The mere existence of modern weapons—ten million times more powerful than any that the world has ever seen, and only minutes away from any target on earth—is a source of horror, and discord and distrust. Men no longer maintain that disarmament must await the settlement of all disputes—for disarmament must be a part of any permanent settlement. And men may no longer pretend that the quest for disarmament is a sign of weakness—for in a spiraling arms race, a nation's security may well be shrinking even as its arms increase.

For 15 years this organization has sought the reduction and destruction of arms. Now that goal is no longer a dream—it is a practical matter of life or death. The risks inherent in disarmament pale in comparison to the risks inherent in an unlimited arms race.

It is in this spirit that the recent Belgrade Conference—recognizing that this is no longer a Soviet problem or an American problem, but a human problem—endorsed a program of "general, complete and strictly an internationally controlled disarmament." It is in this same spirit that we in the United States have labored this year, with a new urgency, and with a new, now statutory agency fully endorsed by the Congress, to find an approach to disarmament which would be so far-reaching yet realistic, so mutually balanced and beneficial, that it could be accepted by every nation. And it is in this spirit that we have presented with the agreement of the Soviet Union—under the label both nations now accept of "general and complete disarmament"—a new statement of newly-agreed principles for negotiation.

But we are well aware that all issues of principle are not settled, and that principles alone are not enough. It is therefore our intention to challenge the Soviet Union, not to an arms race, but to a peace race—to advance together step by step, stage by stage, until general and complete disarmament has been achieved. We invite them now to go beyond agreement in principle to reach agreement on actual plans.

The program to be presented to this assembly—for general and complete disarmament under effective international control—moves to bridge the gap between those who insist on a gradual approach and those who talk only of the final and total

*Public Papers of the Presidents of the United States, John F. Kennedy, Jan. 20, 1961-Dec. 31, 1961, pp. 620-22.

achievement. It would create machinery to keep the peace as it destroys the machinery of war. It would proceed through balanced and safeguarded stages designed to give no state a military advantage over another. It would place the final responsibility for verification and control where it belongs, not with the big powers alone, not with one's adversary or one's self, but in an international organization within the framework of the United Nations. It would assure that indispensable condition of disarmament—true inspection—and apply it in stages proportionate to the stage of disarmament. It would cover delivery systems as well as weapons. It would ultimately halt their production as well as their testing, their transfer as well as their possession. It would achieve, under the eyes of an international disarmament organization, a steady reduction in force, both nuclear and conventional, until it has abolished all armies and all weapons except those needed for internal order and a new United Nations Peace Force. And it starts that process now, today, even as the talks begin.

In short, general and complete disarmament must no longer be a slogan, used to resist the first steps. It is no longer to be a goal without means of achieving it, without means of verifying its progress, without means of keeping the peace. It is now a realistic plan, and a test—a test of those only willing to talk and a test of those willing to act.

Such a plan would not bring a world free from conflict and greed—but it would bring a world free from the terrors of mass destruction. It would not usher in the era of the super state—but it would usher in an era in which no state could annihilate or be annihilated by another.

In 1945, this Nation proposed the Baruch Plan to internationalize the atom before other nations even possessed the bomb or demilitarized their troops. We proposed with our allies the Disarmament Plan of 1951 while still at war in Korea. And we make our proposals today, while building up our defenses over Berlin, not because we are inconsistent or insincere or intimidated, but because we know the rights of free men will prevail—because while we are compelled against our will to rearm, we look confidently beyond Berlin to the kind of disarmed world we all prefer.

I therefore propose, on the basis of this Plan, that disarmament negotiations resume promptly, and continue without interruption until an entire program for general and complete disarmament has not only been agreed but has been actually achieved.

The logical place to begin is a treaty assuring the end of nuclear tests of all kinds, in every environment, under workable controls. The United States and the United Kingdom have proposed such a treaty that is both reasonable, effective and ready for signature. We are still prepared to sign that treaty today.

We also proposed a mutual ban on atmospheric testing, without inspection or controls, in order to save the human race from the poison of radioactive fallout. We regret that that offer has not been accepted.

For 15 years we have sought to make the atom an instrument of peaceful growth rather than of war. But for 15 years our concessions have been matched by obstruction, our patience by intransigence. And the pleas of mankind for peace have met with disregard.

Finally, as the explosions of others beclouded the skies, my country was left with no alternative but to act in the interests of its own and the free world's security. We cannot endanger that security by refraining from testing while others improve their arsenals. Nor can we endanger it by another long, uninspected ban on testing. For three years we accepted those risks in our open society while seeking agreement on inspection. But this year, while we were negotiating in good faith in Geneva, others were secretly preparing new experiments in destruction.

Our tests are not polluting the atmosphere. Our deterrent weapons are guarded against accidental explosion or use. Our doctors and scientists stand ready to help any nation measure and meet the hazards to health which inevitably result from the tests in the atmosphere.

But to halt the spread of these terrible weapons, to halt the contamination of the air, to halt the spiralling nuclear arms race, we remain ready to seek new avenues of agreement, our new Disarmament Program thus includes the following proposals:

—First, signing the test-ban treaty by all nations. This can be done now. Test ban negotiations need not and should not await general disarmament.

—Second, stopping the production of fissionable materials for use in weapons, and preventing their transfer to any nation now lacking in nuclear weapons.

—Third, prohibiting the transfer of control over nuclear weapons to states that do not own them.

—Fourth, keeping nuclear weapons from seeding new battlegrounds in outer space.

—Fifth, gradually destroying existing nuclear weapons and converting their materials to peaceful uses; and

—Finally, halting the unlimited testing and production of strategic nuclear delivery vehicles, and gradually destroying them as well.

To destroy arms, however, is not enough. We must create even as we destroy—creating worldwide law and law enforcement as we outlaw worldwide war and weapons. In the world we seek, the United Nations Emergency Forces which have been hastily assembled, uncertainly supplied, and inadequately financed, will never be enough.

Therefore, the United States recommends that all member nations earmark special peace-keeping units in their armed forces—to be on call of the United Nations, to be specially trained and quickly available, and with advance provision for financial and logistic support.

In addition, the American delegation will suggest a series of steps to improve the United Nations' machinery for the peaceful settlement of disputes—for on-the-spot fact-finding, mediation and adjudication—for extending the rule of international law. For peace is not solely a matter of military or technical problems—it is primarily a problem of politics and people. And unless man can match his strides in weaponry and technology with equal strides in social and political development, our great strength, like that of the dinosaur, will become incapable of proper control—and like the dinosaur vanish from the earth.

As we extend the rule of law on earth, so must we also extend it to man's new domain—outer space.

All of us salute the brave cosmonauts of the Soviet Union. The new horizons of outer space must not be driven by the old bitter concepts of imperialism and sovereign claims. The cold reaches of the universe must not become the new arena of an even colder war.

To this end, we shall urge proposals extending the United Nations Charter to the limits of man's exploration in the universe, reserving outer space for peaceful use, prohibiting weapons of mass destruction in space or on celestial bodies, and opening

the mysteries and benefits of space to every nation. We shall propose further cooperative efforts between all nations in weather prediction and eventually in weather
control. We shall propose, finally, a global system of communications satellites linking
the whole world in telegraph and telephone and radio and television. The day need not
be far away when such a system will televise the proceedings of this body to every
corner of the world for the benefit of peace.

*   *   *

*Report by President Kennedy to the Congress on Disarmament
and the Soviet Union**

1961

*   *   *

The Soviet Union initially took the position that there could be no negotiations
until the United States and the Soviet Union had reached a basic understanding on a
disarmament program. During June and July the Soviet Representative submitted
several papers which described the Soviet position in considerable detail. None of them
differed significantly from the proposal for general and complete disarmament submitted by the Soviet Union to the General Assembly on September 23, 1960. The
Soviet Representative was unwilling at first to discuss the composition of the negotiating forum until the United States and the Soviet Union agreed on a disarmament plan.
The United States pointed out that specific plans should not be discussed in the
absence of other states whose interests were affected.

Just before the conclusion of the Moscow phase of the talks, the Soviet Representative commented briefly on the question of the forum. He then proposed the addition
of five neutral states to the Ten Nation Committee. This proposal, which the Soviet
Union had originally made at the 15th General Assembly, was unacceptable to the
United States because it incorporated the "troika" principle of dividing the world into
three blocs. The question of the composition of the forum thus remained unsettled
until December 1961, when the Soviet Union finally agreed to the establishment of an
18 Nation Committee embodying geographic representation essentially on the basis
advocated by the U.S. Representative during the talks.

The outcome of the bilateral talks was the following Joint Statement of Agreed
Principles for Disarmament Negotiations based on an American draft. The joint
statement was submitted by the United States and the Soviet Union to the 16th
General Assembly on September 20, 1961:

The United States and the USSR have agreed to recommend the following principles as the basis for future multilateral negotiations on disarmament and to call upon
other States to co-operate in reaching early agreement on general and complete
disarmament in a peaceful world in accordance with these principles.

*   *   *

1. The goal of negotiations is to achieve agreement on a programme which will
ensure that (a) disarmament is general and complete and war is no longer an instru-

*U.S. Participation in the U.N., Report by the President to the Congress for the Year 1961,
(Washington, 1962) pp. 21-23.

ment for settling international problems, and (b) such disarmament is accompanied by the establishment of reliable procedures for the peaceful settlement of disputes and effective arrangements for the maintenance of peace in accordance with the principles of the United Nations Charter.

2. The programme for general and complete disarmament shall ensure that States will have at their disposal only those non-nuclear armaments, forces, facilities, and establishments as are agreed to be necessary to maintain internal order and protect the personal security of citizens; and that States shall support and provide agreed manpower for a United Nations peace force.

3. To this end, the programme for general and complete disarmament shall contain the necessary provisions, with respect to the military establishment of every nation, for:

(a) Disbanding of armed forces, dismantling of military establishments, including bases, cessation of the production of armaments as well as their liquidation or conversion to peaceful uses;

(b) Elimination of all stockpiles of nuclear, chemical, bacteriological, and other weapons of mass destruction and cessation of the production of such weapons;

(c) Elimination of all means of delivery of weapons of mass destruction;

(d) Abolishment of the organization and institutions designed to organize the military effort of States, cessation of military training, and closing of all military training institutions;

(e) Discontinuance of military expenditures.

4. The disarmament programme should be implemented in an agreed sequence, by stages until it is completed, with each measure and stage carried out within specified time limits. Transition to a subsequent stage in the process of disarmament should take place upon a review of the implementation of measures included in the preceding stage and upon a decision that all such measures have been implemented and verified and that any additional verification arrangements required for measures in the next stage are, when appropriate, ready to operate.

5. All measures of general and complete disarmament should be balanced so that at no stage of the implementation of the treaty could any State or group of States gain military advantage and that security is ensured equally for all.

6. All disarmament measures should be implemented from beginning to end under such strict and effective international control as would provide firm assurance that all parties are honouring their obligations. During and after the implementation of general and complete disarmament, the most thorough control should be exercised, the nature and extent of such control depending on the requirements for verification of the disarmament measures being carried out in each stage. To implement control over and inspection of disarmament, an International Disarmament Organization including all parties to the agreement should be created within the framework of the United Nations. This International Disarmament Organization and its inspectors should be assured unrestricted access without veto to all places as necessary for the purpose of effective verification.

7. Progress in disarmament should be accompanied by measures to strengthen institutions for maintaining peace and the settlement of international disputes by peaceful means. During and after the implementation of the programme of general and complete disarmament, there should be taken, in accordance with the principles of the United Nations Charter, the necessary measures to maintain international peace and

security, including the obligation of States to place at the disposal of the United Nations agreed manpower necessary for an international peace force to be equipped with agreed types of armaments. Arrangements for the use of this force should ensure that the United Nations can effectively deter or suppress any threat or use of arms in violation of the purposes and principles of the United Nations.

8. States participating in the negotiations should seek to achieve and implement the widest possible agreement at the earliest possible date. Efforts should continue without interruption until agreement upon the total programme has been achieved, and efforts to ensure early agreement on and implementation of measures of disarmament should be undertaken without prejudicing progress on agreement on the total programme and in such a way that these measures would facilitate and form part of that programme.

The joint statement included several principles which the United States had strongly advocated during the bilateral talks: the development of international peacekeeping machinery, an adequate control system, and possible implementation of initial measures before final agreement on a complete program. The Soviet Union, however, insisted on deleting one clause which the United States considered vital. This was the verification of retained forces and armaments at each stage.

In a letter of September 20 to Ambassador Zorin, Ambassador McCloy declared:

> This ... expresses a key element in the United States position which we believe is implicit in the entire joint statement of agreed principles that whenever an agreement stipulates that at a certain point certain levels of forces and armament may be retained, the verification machinery must have all the rights and powers necessary to ensure that those levels are not exceeded.

Ambassador McCloy made it clear that the omission of this provision from the joint statement in no way prejudiced the position of the United States. Ambassador Zorin, following the same line that he had taken in the Ten Nation Committee during the 1960 negotiations, told Ambassador McCloy in a letter of the same date that control of retained forces and arms amounted to "legalized espionage, which of course, cannot be accepted. . . ."

General Assembly Resolutions 1721 (XVI) on Peaceful Uses of Outer Space *

December 20, 1961

A

The General Assembly,

Recognizing the common interest of mankind in furthering the peaceful uses of outer space and the urgent need to strengthen international co-operation in this important field,

Believing that the exploration and use of outer space should be only for the betterment of mankind and to the benefit of States irrespective of the stage of their economic or scientific development,

*U.N. General Assembly, *Official Records*, 16th sess., 1961-62, Supplement 17, p. 6.

1. Commends to States for their guidance in the exploration and use of outer space the following principles:

(a) International law, including the Charter of the United Nations, applies to outer space and celestial bodies;

(b) Outer space and celestial bodies are free for exploration and use by all States in conformity with international law and are not subject to national appropriation;

2. Invites the Committee on the Peaceful Uses of Outer Space to study and report on the legal problems which may arise from the exploration and use of outer space.

B

The General Assembly,

Believing that the United Nations should provide a focal point for international co-operation in the peaceful exploration and use of outer space,

1. Calls upon States launching objects into orbit or beyond to furnish information promptly to the Committee on the Peaceful Uses of Outer Space, through the Secretary-General, for the registration of launchings;

2. Requests the Secretary-General to maintain a public registry of the information furnished in accordance with paragraph 1 above;

3. Requests the Committee on the Peaceful Uses of Outer Space, in co-operation with the Secretary-General and making full use of the functions and resources of the Secretariat:

(a) To maintain close contact with governmental and non-governmental organizations concerned with outer space matters;

(b) To provide for the exchange of such information relating to outer space activities as Governments may supply on a voluntary basis, supplementing but not duplicating existing technical and scientific exchanges;

(c) To assist in the study of measures for the promotion of international co-operation in outer space activities;

4. Further requests the Committee on the Peaceful Uses of Outer Space to report to the General Assembly on the arrangements undertaken for the performance of those functions and on such developments relating to the peaceful uses of outer space as it considers significant.

C

The General Assembly,

Noting with gratification the marked progress for meteorological science and technology opened up by the advances in outer space,

Convinced of the world-wide benefits to be derived from international co-operation in weather research and analysis,

1. Recommends to all Member States and to the World Meteorological Organization and other appropriate specialized agencies the early and comprehensive study, in the light of developments in outer space, of measures:

(a) To advance the state of atmospheric science and technology so as to provide greater knowledge of basic physical forces affecting climate and the possibility of large-scale weather modification;

(b) To develop existing weather forecasting capabilities and to help Member States make effective use of such capabilities through regional meteorological centres;

2. Requests the World Meteorological Organization, consulting as appropriate with the United Nations Educational, Scientific and Cultural Organization and other specialized agencies and governmental and non-governmental organizations, such as the International Council of Scientific Unions, to submit a report to the Governments of its Member States and to the Economic and Social Council at its thirty-fourth session regarding appropriate organizational and financial arrangements to achieve those ends, with a view to their further consideration by the General Assembly at its seventeenth session;

3. Requests the Committee on the Peaceful uses of Outer Space, as it deems appropriate, to review that report and submit its comments and recommendations to the Economic and Social Council and to the General Assembly.

D

The General Assembly,

Believing that communication by means of satellites should be available to the nations of the world as soon as practicable on a global and non-discriminatory basis,

Convinced of the need to prepare the way for the establishment of effective operational satellite communication,

1. Notes with satisfaction that the International Telecommunication Union plans to call a special conference in 1963 to make allocations of radio frequency bands for outer space activities;

2. Recommends that the International Telecommunication Union consider at that conference those aspects of space communication in which international co-operation will be required;

3. Notes the potential importance of communication satellites for use by the United Nations and its principal organs and specialized agencies for both operational and informational requirements;

4. Invites the Special Fund and the Expanded Programme of Technical Assistance, in consultation with the International Telecommunication Union, to give sympathetic consideration to requests from Member States for technical and other assistance for the survey of their communication needs and for the development of their domestic communication facilities, so that they may make effective use of space communication;

5. Requests the International Telecommunication Union, consulting as appropriate with Member States, the United Nations Educational, Scientific and Cultural Organization and other specialized agencies and governmental and non-governmental organizations, such as the Committee on Space Research of the International Council of Scientific Unions, to submit a report on the implementation of these proposals to the Economic and Social Council at its thirty-fourth session and to the General Assembly at its seventeenth session;

6. Requests the Committee on the Peaceful Uses of Outer Space, as it deems appropriate, to review that report and submit its comments and recommendations to the Economic and Social Council and to the General Assembly.

E

The General Assembly,

Recalling its resolution 1472 (XIV) of 12 December 1959,

Noting that the terms of office of the members of the Committee on the Peaceful Uses of Outer Space expire at the end of 1961,

Noting the report of the Committee on the Peaceful Uses of Outer Space,

1. Decides to continue the membership of the Committee on the Peaceful Uses of Outer Space as set forth in General Assembly resolution 1472 (XIV) and to add Chad, Mongolia, Morocco and Sierra Leone to its membership in recognition of the increased membership of the United Nations since the Committee was established;

2. Requests the Committee on the Peaceful Uses of Outer Space to meet not later than 31 March 1962 to carry out its mandate as contained in General Assembly resolution 1472 (XIV), to review the activities provided for in resolutions A, B, C and D above and to make such reports as it may consider appropriate.

Address by President Kennedy Before the 18th General Assembly on Outer Space*

September 20, 1963

We meet again in the quest for peace.

Twenty-four months ago, when I last had the honor of addressing this body, the shadow of fear lay darkly across the world. The freedom of West Berlin was in immediate peril. Agreement on a neutral Laos seemed remote. The mandate of the United Nations in the Congo was under fire. The financial outlook for this organization was in doubt. Dag Hammarskjold was dead. The doctrine of troika was being pressed in his place, and atmospheric nuclear tests had been resumed by the Soviet Union.

Those were anxious days for mankind—and some men wondered aloud whether this organization could survive. But the 16th and 17th General Assemblies achieved not only survival but progress. Rising to its responsibility, the United Nations helped reduce the tensions and helped to hold back the darkness.

Today the clouds have lifted a little so that new rays of hope can break through. The pressures on West Berlin appear to be temporarily eased. Political unity in the Congo has been largely restored. A neutral coalition in Laos, while still in difficulty, is at least in being. The integrity of the United Nations Secretariat has been reaffirmed. A United Nations Decade of Development is under way. And, for the first time in 17 years of effort, a specific step has been taken to limit the nuclear arms race.

I refer, of course, to the treaty to ban nuclear tests in the atmosphere, outer space, and under water—concluded by the Soviet Union, the United Kingdom, and the United States—and already signed by nearly 100 countries. It has been hailed by people the world over who are thankful to be free from the fears of nuclear fallout, and I am confident that on next Tuesday at 10:30 o'clock in the morning it will receive the overwhelming endorsement of the Senate of the United States.

*Public Papers of the Presidents, John F. Kennedy, pp. 693-96.

The world has not escaped from the darkness. The long shadows of conflict and crisis envelop us still. But we meet today in an atmosphere of rising hope, and at a moment of comparative calm. My presence here today is not a sign of crisis, but of confidence. I am not here to report on a new threat to the peace or new signs of war. I have come to salute the United Nations and to show the support of the American people for your daily deliberations.

For the value of this body's work is not dependent on the existence of emergencies —nor can the winning of peace consist only of dramatic victories. Peace is a daily, a weekly, a monthly process, gradually changing opinions, slowly eroding old barriers, quietly building new structures. And however undramatic the pursuit of peace, that pursuit must go on.

Today we may have reached a pause in the cold war—but that is not a lasting peace. A test ban treaty is a milestone—but it is not the millennium. We have not been released from our obligations—we have been given an opportunity. And if we fail to make the most of this moment and this momentum—if we convert our new-found hopes and understandings into new walls and weapons of hostility—if this pause in the cold war merely leads to its renewal and not to its end—then the indictment of posterity will rightly point its finger at us all. But if we can stretch this pause into a period of cooperation—if both sides can now gain new confidence and experience in concrete collaborations for peace—if we can now be as bold and farsighted in the control of deadly weapons as we have been in their creation—then surely this first small step can be the start of a long and fruitful journey.

The task of building the peace lies with the leaders of every nation, large and small. For the great powers have no monopoly on conflict or ambition. The cold war is not the only expression of tension in this world—and the nuclear race is not the only arms race. Even little wars are dangerous in a nuclear world. The long labor of peace is an undertaking for every nation—and in this effort none of us can remain unaligned. To this goal none can be uncommitted.

The reduction of global tension must not be an excuse for the narrow pursuit of self-interest. If the Soviet Union and the United States, with all of their global interests and clashing commitments of ideology, and with nuclear weapons still aimed at each other today, can find areas of common interest and agreement, then surely other nations can do the same—nations caught in regional conflicts, in racial issues, or in the death throes of old colonialism. Chronic disputes which divert precious resources from the needs of the people or drain the energies of both sides serve the interests of no one—and the badge of responsibility in the modern world is a willingness to seek peaceful solutions.

It is never too early to try; and it's never too late to talk; and it's high time that many disputes on the agenda of this Assembly were taken off the debating schedule and placed on the negotiating table.

The fact remains that the United States, as a major nuclear power, does have a special responsibility in the world. It is, in fact, a threefold responsibility—a responsibility to our own citizens; a responsibility to the people of the whole world who are affected by our decisions; and to the next generation of humanity. We believe the Soviet Union also has these special responsibilities—and that those responsibilities require our two nations to concentrate less on our differences and more on the means of resolving them peacefully. For too long both of us have increased our military budgets, our nuclear stockpiles, and our capacity to destroy all life on this hemisphere —human, animal, vegetable—without any corresponding increase in our security.

Our conflicts, to be sure, are real. Our concepts of the world are different. No service is performed by failing to make clear our disagreements. A central difference is the belief of the American people in self-determination for all people.

We believe that the people of Germany and Berlin must be free to reunite their capital and their country.

We believe that the people of Cuba must be free to secure the fruits of the revolution that have been betrayed from within and exploited from without.

In short, we believe that all the world—in Eastern Europe as well as Western, in Southern Africa as well as Northern, in old nations as well as new—that people must be free to choose their own future, without discrimination or dictation, without coercion or subversion.

These are the basic differences between the Soviet Union and the United States, and they cannot be concealed. So long as they exist, they set limits to agreement, and they forbid the relaxation of our vigilance. Our defense around the world will be maintained for the protection of freedom—and our determination to safeguard that freedom will measure up to any threat or challenge.

But I would say to the leaders of the Soviet Union, and to their people, that if either of our countries is to be fully secure, we need a much better weapon than the H-bomb—a weapon better than ballistic missiles or nuclear submarines—and that better weapon is peaceful cooperation.

We have, in recent years, agreed on a limited test ban treaty, on an emergency communications link between our capitals, on a statement of principles for disarmament, on an increase in cultural exchange, on cooperation in outer space, on the peaceful exploration of the Antarctic, and on tempering last year's crisis over Cuba.

I believe, therefore, that the Soviet Union and the United States, together with their allies, can achieve further agreements—agreements which spring from our mutual interest in avoiding mutual destruction.

There can be no doubt about the agenda of further steps. We must continue to seek agreements on measures which prevent war by accident or miscalculation. We must continue to seek agreement on safeguards against surprise attack, including observation posts at key points. We must continue to seek agreement on further measures to curb the nuclear arms race, by controlling the transfer of nuclear weapons, converting fissionable materials to peaceful purposes, and banning underground testing, with adequate inspection and enforcement. We must continue to seek agreement on a freer flow of information and people from East to West and West to East.

We must continue to seek agreement, encouraged by yesterday's affirmative response to this proposal by the Soviet Foreign Minister, on an arrangement to keep weapons of mass destruction out of outer space. Let us get our negotiators back to the negotiating table to work out a practicable arrangement to this end.

In these and other ways, let us move up the steep and difficult path toward comprehensive disarmament, securing mutual confidence through mutual verification, and building the institutions of peace as we dismantle the engines of war. We must not let failure to agree on all points delay agreements where agreement is possible. And we must not put forward proposals for propaganda purposes.

Finally, in a field where the United States and the Soviet Union have a special capacity—in the field of space—there is room for new cooperation, for further joint efforts in the regulation and exploration of space. I include among these possibilities a joint expedition to the moon. Space offers no problems of sovereignty; by resolution of this Assembly, the members of the United Nations have foresworn any claim to territorial rights in outer space or on celestial bodies, and declared that international law and the United Nations Charter will apply. Why, therefore, should man's first flight to the moon be a matter of national competition? Why should the United States and the Soviet Union, in preparing for such expeditions, become involved in immense duplications of research, construction, and expenditure? Surely we should explore whether the scientists and astronauts of our two countries—indeed of all the world— cannot work together in the conquest of space, sending some day in this decade to the moon not the representatives of a single nation, but the representatives of all of our countries.

All these and other new steps toward peaceful cooperation may be possible. Most of them will require on our part full consultation with our allies—for their interests are as much involved as our own, and we will not make an agreement at their expense. Most of them will require long and careful negotiation. And most of them will require a new approach to the cold war—a desire not to "bury" one's adversary, but to compete in a host of peaceful arenas, in ideas, in production, and ultimately in service to all mankind.

The contest will continue—the contest between those who see a monolithic world and those who believe in diversity—but it should be a contest in leadership and responsibility instead of destruction, a contest in achievement instead of intimidation. Speaking for the United States of America, I welcome such a contest. For we believe that truth is stronger than error—and that freedom is more enduring than coercion. And in the contest for a better life, all the world can be a winner.

*   *   *

Statement by President Johnson Announcing Agreement on a Space Treaty *

December 8, 1966

I am glad to confirm on the basis of Ambassador Goldberg's report to me this morning that agreement has been reached at the United Nations among members of the Outer Space Committee, including the United States, on a draft text of a treaty governing the exploration of outer space, including the moon and other celestial bodies.

In accordance with U.N. procedures, it is expected that a resolution endorsing the treaty will be submitted formally early next week with broad co-sponsorship along with the agreed text of the Outer Space Treaty.

We look forward to early action by the Assembly on this matter.

Progress toward such a treaty commenced on May 7 of this year when I requested Ambassador Goldberg to initiate consultation for a treaty in the appropriate U.N. body.

Weekly Compilation of Presidential Documents, Dec. 12, 1966, pp. 1781-82.

After business-like negotiations within the U.N. Outer Space Committee in Geneva and at the U.N. in New York, this important step toward peace has been achieved.

It is the most important arms control development since the Limited Test Ban Treaty of 1963. It puts in treaty form the "no bombs in orbit" resolution of the U.N.

It guarantees access to all areas and installations of celestial bodies.

This openness taken with other provisions of the treaty should prevent war-like preparations on the moon and other celestial bodies.

This treaty has historical significance for the new age of space exploration.

I salute and commend all members of the U.N. who contributed to this significant agreement.

In the expectation that formal U.N. action will have been completed at an early date, I plan to present the treaty to the Senate for advice and consent at the next session of Congress and I hope that the United States will be one of the first countries to ratify it.

Treaty on Principles Governing the Activities of States in the Exploration and Use of Outer Space*

December 8, 1966

The States Parties to this Treaty,

Inspired by the great prospects opening up before mankind as a result of man's entry into outer space,

Recognizing the common interest of all mankind in the progress of the exploration and use of outer space for peaceful purposes,

Believing that the exploration and use of outer space should be carried on for the benefit of all peoples irrespective of the degree of their economic or scientific development,

Desiring to contribute to broad international co-operation in the scientific as well as the legal aspects of the exploration and use of outer space for peaceful purposes,

Believing that such co-operation will contribute to the development of mutual understanding and to the strengthening of friendly relations between States and peoples,

Recalling resolution 1962 (XVIII), entitled "Declaration of Legal Principles Governing the Activities of States in the Exploration and Use of Outer Space," which was adopted unanimously by the United Nations General Assembly on 13 December 1963,

Recalling resolution 1884 (XVIII), calling upon States to refrain from placing in orbit around the earth any objects carrying nuclear weapons or any other kinds of weapons of mass destruction or from installing such weapons on celestial bodies, which was adopted unanimously by the United Nations General Assembly on 17 October 1963,

Taking account of United Nations General Assembly resolution 110 (II) of 3 November 1947, which condemned propaganda designed or likely to provoke or encourage any threat to the peace, breach of the peace or act of aggression, and considering that the aforementioned resolution is applicable to outer space,

Department of State Bulletin, Dec. 26, 1966. pp. 953-55.

Convinced that a Treaty on Principles Governing the Activities of States in the Exploration and Use of Outer Space, including the Moon and Other Celestial Bodies, will further the Purposes and Principles of the Charter of the United Nations,

Have agreed on the following:

Article I

The exploration and use of outer space, including the moon and other celestial bodies, shall be carried out for the benefit and in the interests of all countries, irrespective of their degree of economic or scientific development, and shall be the province of all mankind.

Outer space, including the moon and other celestial bodies, shall be free for exploration and use by all States without discrimination of any kind, on a basis of equality and in accordance with international law, and there shall be free access to all areas of celestial bodies.

There shall be freedom of scientific investigation in outer space, including the moon and other celestial bodies, and States shall facilitate and encourage international co-operation in such investigation.

Article II

Outer space, including the moon and other celestial bodies, is not subject to national appropriation by claim of sovereignty, by means of use or occupation, or by any other means.

Article III

States Parties to the Treaty shall carry on activities in the exploration and use of outer space, including the moon and other celestial bodies, in accordance with international law, including the Charter of the United Nations, in the interest of maintaining international peace and security and promoting international co-operation and understanding.

Article IV

States Parties to the Treaty undertake not to place in orbit around the earth any objects carrying nuclear weapons or any other kinds of weapons of mass destruction, install such weapons on celestial bodies, or station such weapons in outer space in any other manner.

The moon and other celestial bodies shall be used by all States Parties to the Treaty exclusively for peaceful purposes. The establishment of military bases, installations and fortifications, the testing of any type of weapons and the conduct of military manoeuvres on celestial bodies shall be forbidden. The use of military personnel for scientific research or for any other peaceful purposes shall not be prohibited. The use of any equipment or facility necessary for peaceful exploration of the moon and other celestial bodies shall also not be prohibited.

Article V

States Parties to the Treaty shall regard astronauts as envoys of mankind in outer space and shall render to them all possible assistance in the event of accident, distress, or emergency landing on the territory of another State Party or on the high seas. When astronauts make such a landing, they shall be safely and promptly returned to the State of registry of their space vehicle.

In carrying on activities in outer space and on celestial bodies, the astronauts of one State Party shall render all possible assistance to the astronauts of other States Parties.

States Parties to the Treaty shall immediately inform the other States Parties to the treaty or the Secretary-General of the United Nations of any phenomena they discover in outer space, including the moon and other celestial bodies, which could constitute a danger to the life or health of astronauts.

Article VI

States Parties to the Treaty shall bear international responsibility for national activities in outer space, including the moon and other celestial bodies, whether such activities are carried on by governmental agencies or by non-governmental entities and for assuring that national activities are carried out in conformity with the provisions set forth in the present Treaty. The activities of non-governmental entities in outer space, including the moon and other celestial bodies, shall require authorization and continuing supervision by the State concerned. When activities are carried on in outer space, including the moon and other celestial bodies, by an international organization, responsibility for compliance with this Treaty shall be borne both by the international organization and by the States Parties to the Treaty participating in such organizations.

Article VII

Each State Party to the Treaty that launches or procures the launching of an object into outer space, including the moon and other celestial bodies, and each State Party from whose territory or facility an object is launched, is internationally liable for damage to another State Party to the Treaty or to its natural or juridical persons by such object or its component parts on the Earth, in air space or in outer space, including the moon and other celestial bodies.

Article VIII

A State Party to the Treaty on whose registry an object launched into outer space is carried shall retain jurisdiction and control over such object, and over any personnel thereof, while in outer space or on a celestial body. Ownership of objects launched into outer space, including objects landed or constructed on a celestial body, and of their component parts, is not affected by their presence in outer space or on a celestial body or by their return to the Earth. Such objects or component parts found beyond the limits of the State Party to the Treaty on whose registry they are carried shall be returned to that State, which shall, upon request, furnish identifying data prior to their return.

Article IX

In the exploration and use of outer space, including the moon and other celestial bodies, States Parties to the Treaty shall be guided by the principle of co-operation and mutual assistance and shall conduct all their activities in outer space, including the moon and other celestial bodies, with due regard to the corresponding interests of all other States Parties to the Treaty. States Parties to the Treaty shall pursue studies of outer space, including the moon and other celestial bodies, and conduct exploration of them so as to avoid their harmful contamination and also adverse changes in the environment of the Earth resulting from the introduction of extraterrestrial matter and, where necessary, shall adopt appropriate measures for this purpose. If a State Party to the Treaty has reason to believe that an activity or experiment planned by it or its nationals in outer space, including the moon and other celestial bodies, would cause potentially harmful interference with activities of other States Parties in the peaceful exploration and use of outer space, including the moon and other celestial bodies, it shall undertake appropriate international consultations before proceeding with any such activity or experiment. A State Party to the Treaty which has reason to believe that an activity or experiment planned by another State Party in outer space, including the moon and other celestial bodies, would cause potentially harmful interference with activities in the peaceful exploration and use of outer space, including the moon and other celestial bodies, may request consultation concerning the activity or experiment.

Article X

In order to promote international co-operation in the exploration and use of outer space, including the moon and other celestial bodies, in conformity with the purposes of this Treaty, the States Parties to the Treaty shall consider on a basis of equality any requests by other States Parties to the Treaty to be afforded an opportunity to observe the flight of space objects launched by those States.

The nature of such an opportunity for observation and the conditions under which it could be afforded shall be determined by agreement between the States concerned.

Article XI

In order to promote international co-operation in the peaceful exploration and use of outer space, States Parties to the Treaty conducting activities in outer space, including the moon and other celestial bodies, agree to inform the Secretary-General of the United Nations as well as the public and the international scientific community, to the greatest extent feasible and practicable, of the nature, conduct, locations and results of such activities. On receiving the said information, the Secretary-General of the United Nations should be prepared to disseminate it immediately and effectively.

Article XII

All stations, installations, equipment and space vehicles on the moon and other celestial bodies shall be open to representatives of other States Parties to the Treaty on a basis of reciprocity. Such representatives shall give reasonable advance notice of a projected visit, in order that appropriate consultations may be held and that maximum precautions may be taken to assure safety and to avoid interference with normal operations in the facility to be visited.

Article XIII

The provisions of this Treaty shall apply to the activities of States Parties to the Treaty in the exploration and use of outer space, including the moon and other celestial bodies, whether such activities are carried on by a single State Party to the Treaty or jointly with other States, including cases where they are carried on within the framework of international inter-governmental organizations.

Any practical questions arising in connexion with activities carried on by international inter-governmental organizations in the exploration and use of outer space, including the moon and other celestial bodies, shall be resolved by the States Parties to the Treaty either with the appropriate international organization or with one or more States members of that international organization, which are Parties to this Treaty.

Article XIV

1. This Treaty shall be open to all States for signature. Any State which does not sign this Treaty before its entry into force in accordance with paragraph 3 of this article may accede to it at any time.

2. This Treaty shall be subject to ratification by signatory States. Instruments of ratification and instruments of accession shall be deposited with the Governments of the Union of Soviet Socialist Republics, the United Kingdom of Great Britain and Northern Ireland and the United States of America, which are hereby designated the Depositary Governments.

3. This Treaty shall enter into force upon the deposit of instruments of ratification by five Governments including the Governments designated as Depositary Governments under this Treaty.

4. For States whose instruments of ratification or accession are deposited subsequently to the entry into force of this Treaty, it shall enter into force on the date of deposit of their instruments of ratification or accession.

5. The Depositary Governments shall promptly inform all signatory and acceding

States of the date of each signature, the date of deposit of each instrument of ratification of and accession to this Treaty, the date of its entry into force and other notices.

6. This Treaty shall be registered by the Depositary Governments pursuant to Article 102 of the Charter of the United Nations.

Article XV

Any State Party to the Treaty may propose amendments to this Treaty. Amendments shall enter into force for each State Party to the Treaty accepting the amendments upon their acceptance by a majority of the States Parties to the Treaty and thereafter for each remaining State Party to the Treaty on the date of acceptance by it.

Article XVI

Any State Party to the Treaty may give notice of its withdrawal from the Treaty one year after its entry into force by written notification to the Depositary Governments. Such withdrawal shall take effect one year from the date of receipt of this notification.

Article XVII

This Treaty, of which the Chinese, English, French, Russian and Spanish texts are equally authentic, shall be deposited in the archives of the Depositary Governments. Duly certified copies of this Treaty shall be transmitted by the Depositary Governments to the Governments of the signatory and acceding States.

In witness whereof the undersigned, duly authorized, have signed this Treaty.

Done in   at the cities of London, Moscow and Washington, the   day of   one thousand nine hundred and

*General Assembly Resolution 2345 (XXII), on the Rescue
of Astronauts and Return of Objects Launched into Outer Space**

December 19, 1967

The General Assembly,

Bearing in mind its resolution 2260 (XXII) of 3 November 1967, which calls upon the Committee on the Peaceful Uses of Outer Space to continue with a sense of urgency its work on the elaboration of an agreement on liability for damage caused by the launching of objects into outer space and an agreement on assistance to and return of astronauts and space vehicles,

Referring to the addendum to the report of the Committee on the Peaceful Uses of Outer Space,

Desiring to give further concrete expression to the rights and obligations contained

*U.N. General Assembly, Official Records, 22d sess., 1967, Supplement 16, pp. 5-7.

in the Treaty of Principles Governing the Activities of States in the Exploration and Use of Outer Space, including the Moon and Other Celestial Bodies,

1. Commends the Agreement on the Rescue of Astronauts, the Return of Astronauts and the Return of Objects Launched into Outer Space, the text of which is annexed to the present resolution;

2. Requests the Depositary Governments to open the Agreement for signature and ratification at the earliest possible date;

3. Expresses its hope for the widest possible adherence to this Agreement;

4. Calls upon the Committee on the Peaceful Uses of Outer Space to complete urgently the preparation of the draft agreement on liability for damage caused by the launching of objects into outer space and, in any event, not later than the beginning of the twenty-third session of the General Assembly, and to submit it to the Assembly at that session.

ANNEX

Agreement on the Rescue of Astronauts, the Return of Astronauts and the Return of Objects Launched into Outer Space

The Contracting Parties,

Noting the great importance of the Treaty on Principles Governing the Activities of States in the Exploration and Use of Outer Space, including the Moon and Other Celestial Bodies, which calls for the rendering of all possible assistance to astronauts in the event of accident, distress or emergency landing, the prompt and safe return of astronauts, and the return of objects launched into outer space,

Desiring to develop and give further concrete expression to these duties,

Wishing to promote international co-operation in the peaceful exploration and use of outer space,

Prompted by sentiments of humanity,

Have agreed on the following:

Article 1

Each Contracting Party which receives information or discovers that the personnel of a spacecraft have suffered accident or are experiencing conditions of distress or have made an emergency or unintended landing in territory under its jurisdiction or on the high seas or in any other place not under the jurisdiction of any State shall immediately:

(a) Notify the launching authority or, if it cannot identify and immediately communicate with the launching authority, immediately make a public announcement by all appropriate means of communication at its disposal;

(b) Notify the Secretary-General of the United Nations, who should disseminate the information without delay by all appropriate means of communication at his disposal.

Article 2

If, owing to accident, distress, emergency or unintended landing, the personnel of a spacecraft land in territory under the jurisdiction of a Contracting Party, it shall immediately take all possible steps to rescue them and render them all necessary assistance. It shall inform the launching authority and also the Secretary-General of the United Nations of the steps it is taking and of their progress. If assistance by the launching authority would help to effect a prompt rescue or would contribute substantially to the effectiveness of search and rescue operations, the launching authority shall co-operate with the Contracting Party with a view to the effective conduct of search and rescue operations. Such operations shall be subject to the direction and control of the Contracting Party, which shall act in close and continuing consultation with the launching authority.

Article 3

If information is received or it is discovered that the personnel of a spacecraft have alighted on the high seas or in any other place not under the jurisdiction of any State, those Contracting Parties which are in a position to do so shall, if necessary, extend assistance in search and rescue operations for such personnel to assure their speedy rescue. They shall inform the launching authority and the Secretary-General of the United Nations of the steps they are taking and of their progress.

Article 4

If, owing to accident, distress, emergency or unintended landing, the personnel of a spacecraft land in territory under the jurisdiction of a Contracting Party or have been found on the high seas or in any other place not under the jurisdiction of any State, they shall be safely and promptly returned to representatives of the launching authority.

Article 5

1. Each Contracting Party which receives information or discovers that a space object or its component parts has returned to Earth in territory under its jurisdiction or on the high seas or in any other place not under the jurisdiction of any State, shall notify the launching authority and the Secretary-General of the United Nations.

2. Each Contracting Party having jurisdiction over the territory on which a space object or its component parts has been discovered shall, upon the request of the launching authority and with assistance from that authority if requested, take such steps as it finds practicable to recover the object or component parts.

3. Upon request of the launching authority, objects launched into outer space or their component parts found beyond the territorial limits of the launching authority shall be returned to or held at the disposal of representatives of the launching authority, which shall, upon request, furnish identifying data prior to their return.

4. Notwithstanding paragraphs 2 and 3 of this article, a Contracting Party which has reason to believe that a space object or its component parts discovered in territory under its jurisdiction, or recovered by it elsewhere, is of a hazardous or deleterious

nature may so notify the launching authority, which shall immediately take effective steps, under the direction and control of the said Contracting Party, to eliminate possible danger of harm.

5. Expenses incurred in fulfilling obligations to recover and return a space object or its component parts under paragraphs 2 and 3 of this article shall be borne by the launching authority.

Article 6

For the purposes of this Agreement, the term "launching authority" shall refer to the State responsible for launching, or, where an international intergovernmental organization is responsible for launching, that organization, provided that that organization declares its acceptance of the rights and obligations provided for in this Agreement and a majority of the States members of that organization are Contracting Parties to this Agreement and to the Treaty on Principles Governing the Activities of States in the Exploration and Use of Outer Space, including the Moon and other Celestial Bodies.

Article 7

1. This Agreement shall be open to all States for signature. Any State which does not sign this Agreement before its entry into force in accordance with paragraph 3 of this article may accede to it at any time.

2. This Agreement shall be subject to ratification by signatory States. Instruments of ratification and instruments of accession shall be deposited with the Governments of the Union of Soviet Socialist Republics, the United Kingdom of Great Britain and Northern Ireland, and the United States of America, which are hereby designated the Depositary Governments.

3. This Agreement shall enter into force upon the deposit of instruments of ratification by five Governments including the Governments designated as Depositary Governments under this Agreement.

4. For States whose instruments of ratification or accession are deposited subsequently to the entry into force of this Agreement, it shall enter into force on the date of the deposit of their instruments of ratification or accession.

5. The Depositary Governments shall promptly inform all signatory and acceding States of the date of each signature, the date of deposit of each instrument of ratification of and accession to this Agreement, the date of its entry into force and other notices.

6. This Agreement shall be registered by the Depositary Governments pursuant to Article 102 of the Charter of the United Nations.

Article 8

Any State Party to the Agreement may propose amendments to this Agreement. Amendments shall enter into force for each State Party to the Agreement accepting the amendments upon their acceptance by a majority of the States Parties to the Agreement and thereafter for each remaining State Party to the Agreement on the date of acceptance by it.

Article 9

Any State Party to the Agreement may give notice of its withdrawal from the Agreement one year after its entry into force by written notification to the Depositary Governments. Such withdrawal shall take effect one year from the date of receipt of this notification.

Article 10

This Agreement, of which the Chinese, English, French, Russian and Spanish texts are equally authentic, shall be deposited in the archives of the Depositary Governments. Duly certified copies of this Agreement shall be transmitted by the Depositary Governments to the Governments of the signatory and acceding States.

In witness whereof the undersigned, duly authorized, have signed this Agreement.

NON-PROLIFERATION TREATY

Treaty on the Non-Proliferation of Nuclear Weapons*

June 12, 1968

The General Assembly,

Recalling its resolutions 2346 A (XXII) of 19 December 1967, 2153 A (XXI) of 17 November 1966, 2149 (XXI) of 4 November 1966, 2028 (XX) of 19 November 1965 and 1665 (XVI) of 4 December 1961,

Convinced of the urgency and great importance of preventing the spread of nuclear weapons and of intensifying international co-operation in the development of peaceful applications of atomic energy,

Having considered the report of the Conference of the Eighteen-Nation Committee on Disarmament, dated 14 March 1968, and appreciative of the work of the Committee on the elaboration of the draft non-proliferation treaty, which is attached to that report,

Convinced that, pursuant to the provisions of the treaty, all signatories have the right to engage in research, production and use of nuclear energy for peaceful purposes and will be able to acquire source and special fissionable materials, as well as equipment for the processing, use and production of nuclear material for peaceful purposes,

Convinced further that an agreement to prevent the further proliferation of nuclear weapons must be followed as soon as possible by effective measures on the cessation of the nuclear arms race and on nuclear disarmament, and that the non-proliferation treaty will contribute to this aim,

Affirming that in the interest of international peace and security both nuclear-weapon and non-nuclear-weapon States carry the responsibility of acting in accordance with the principles of the Charter of the United Nations that the sovereign equality of all States shall be respected, that the threat or use of force in international relations shall be refrained from and that international disputes shall be settled by peaceful means,

1. Commends the Treaty on the Non-Proliferation of Nuclear Weapons, the text of which is annexed to the present resolution;

2. Requests the Depositary Governments to open the Treaty for signature and ratification at the earliest possible date,

3. Expresses the hope for the widest possible adherence to the Treaty by both nuclear-weapon and non-nuclear-weapon States;

4. Requests the Conference of the Eighteen-Nation Committee on Disarmament and the nuclear-weapon States urgently to pursue negotiations on effective measures relating to the cessation of the nuclear arms race at an early date and to nuclear disarmament, and on a treaty on general and complete disarmament under strict and effective international control;

5. Requests the Conference of the Eighteen-Nation Committee on Disarmament to report on the progress of its work to the General Assembly at its twenty-third session.

*U.N. General Assembly, *Official Records*, 22d sess., 1967, Supplement 16A, pp. 5-7.

ANNEX

Treaty on the Non-Proliferation of Nuclear Weapons

The States concluding this Treaty, hereinafter referred to as the "Parties to the Treaty,"

Considering the devastation that would be visited upon all mankind by a nuclear war and the consequent need to make every effort to avert the danger of such a war and to take measures to safeguard the security of peoples,

Believing that the proliferation of nuclear weapons would seriously enhance the danger of nuclear war,

In conformity with resolutions of the United Nations General Assembly calling for the conclusion of an agreement on the prevention of wider dissemination of nuclear weapons,

Undertaking to co-operate in facilitating the application of International Atomic Energy Agency safeguards on peaceful nuclear activities,

Expressing their support for research, development and other efforts to further the application, within the framework of the International Atomic Energy Agency safeguards system, of the principle of safeguarding effectively the flow of source and special fissionable materials by use of instruments and other techniques at certain strategic points,

Affirming the principle that the benefits of peaceful applications of nuclear technology, including any technological by-products which may be derived by nuclear-weapon States from the development of nuclear explosive devices, should be available for peaceful purposes to all Parties to the Treaty, whether nuclear-weapon or non-nuclear-weapon States,

Convinced that, in furtherance of this principle, all Parties to the Treaty are entitled to participate in the fullest possible exchange of scientific information for, and to contribute alone or in co-operation with other States to, the further development of the applications of atomic energy for peaceful purposes,

Declaring their intention to achieve at the earliest possible date the cessation of the nuclear arms race and to undertake effective measures in the direction of nuclear disarmament,

Urging the co-operation of all States in the attainment of this objective,

Recalling the determination expressed by the Parties to the 1963 Treaty banning nuclear weapon tests in the atmosphere, in outer space and under water in its Preamble to seek to achieve the discontinuance of all test explosions of nuclear weapons for all time and to continue negotiations to this end,

Desiring to further the easing of international tension and the strengthening of trust between States in order to facilitate the cessation of the manufacture of nuclear weapons, the liquidation of all their existing stockpiles, and the elimination from national arsenals of nuclear weapons and the means of their delivery pursuant to a treaty on general and complete disarmament under strict and effective international control,

Recalling that, in accordance with the Charter of the United Nations, States must refrain in their international relations from the threat or use of force against the territorial integrity or political independence of any State, or in any other manner inconsistent with the Purposes of the United Nations, and that the establishment and maintenance of international peace and security are to be promoted with the least diversion for armaments of the world's human and economic resources,

Have agreed as follows:

Article I

Each nuclear-weapon State Party to the Treaty undertakes not to transfer to any recipient whatsoever nuclear weapons or other nuclear explosive devices or control over such weapons or explosive devices directly, or indirectly; and not in any way to assist, encourage, or induce any non-nuclear-weapon State to manufacture or otherwise acquire nuclear weapons or other nuclear explosive devices, or control over such weapons or explosive devices.

Article II

Each non-nuclear-weapon State Party to the Treaty undertakes not to receive the transfer from any transferor whatsoever of nuclear weapons or other nuclear explosive devices or of control over such weapons or explosive devices directly, or indirectly; not to manufacture or otherwise acquire nuclear weapons or other nuclear explosive devices; and not to seek or receive any assistance in the manufacture of nuclear weapons or other nuclear explosive devices.

Article III

1. Each non-nuclear-weapon State Party to the Treaty undertakes to accept safeguards, as set forth in an agreement to be negotiated and concluded with the International Atomic Energy Agency in accordance with the Statute of the International Atomic Energy Agency and the Agency's safeguards system, for the exclusive purpose of verification of the fulfilment of its obligations assumed under this Treaty with a view to preventing diversion of nuclear energy from peaceful uses to nuclear weapons or other nuclear explosive devices. Procedures for the safeguards required by this article shall be followed with respect to source or special fissionable material whether it is being produced, processed or used in any principal nuclear facility or is outside any such facility. The safeguards required by this article shall be applied on all source or special fissionable material in all peaceful nuclear activities within the territory of such State, under its jurisdiction, or carried out under its control anywhere.

2. Each State Party to the Treaty undertakes not to provide: (a) source or special fissionable material, or (b) equipment or material especially designed or prepared for the processing, use or production of special fissionable material, to any non-nuclear-weapon State for peaceful purposes, unless the source or special fissionable material shall be subject to the safeguards required by this article.

3. The safeguards required by this article shall be implemented in a manner designed to comply with article IV of this Treaty, and to avoid hampering the

economic or technological development of the Parties or international co-operation in the field of peaceful nuclear activities, including the international exchange of nuclear material and equipment for the processing, use or production of nuclear material for peaceful purposes in accordance with the provisions of this article and the principle of safeguarding set forth in the Preamble of the Treaty.

4. Non-nuclear-weapon States Party to the Treaty shall conclude agreements with the International Atomic Energy Agency to meet the requirements of this article either individually or together with other States in accordance with the Statute of the International Atomic Energy Agency. Negotiation of such agreements shall commence within 180 days from the original entry into force of this Treaty. For States depositing their instruments of ratification or accession after the 180-day period, negotiation of such agreements shall commence not later than the date of such deposit. Such agreements shall enter into force not later than eighteen months after the date of initiation of negotiations.

Article IV

1. Nothing in this Treaty shall be interpreted as affecting the inalienable right of all the Parties to the Treaty to develop research, production and use of nuclear energy for peaceful purposes without discrimination and in conformity with articles I and II of this Treaty.

2. All the Parties to the Treaty undertake to facilitate, and have the right to participate in, the fullest possible exchange of equipment, materials and scientific and technological information for the peaceful uses of nuclear energy. Parties to the Treaty in a position to do so shall also co-operate in contributing alone or together with other States or international organizations to the further development of the applications of nuclear energy for peaceful purposes, especially in the territories of non-nuclear-weapon States Party to the Treaty, with due consideration for the needs of the developing areas of the world.

Article V

Each Party to the Treaty undertakes to take appropriate measure to ensure that, in accordance with this Treaty, under appropriate international observation and through appropriate international procedures, potential benefits from any peaceful applications of nuclear explosions will be made available to non-nuclear-weapon States Party to the Treaty on a non-discriminatory basis and that the charge to such Parties for the explosive devices used will be as low as possible and exclude any charge for research and development. Non-nuclear-weapon States Party to the Treaty shall be able to obtain such benefits, pursuant to a special international agreement or agreements, through an appropriate international body with adequate representation of non-nuclear-weapon States. Negotiations on this subject shall commence as soon as possible after the Treaty enters into force. Non-nuclear-weapon States Party to the Treaty so desiring may also obtain such benefits pursuant to bilateral agreements.

Article VI

Each of the Parties to the Treaty undertakes to pursue negotiations in good faith on effective measures relating to cessation of the nuclear arms race at an early date and to nuclear disarmament, and on a treaty on general and complete disarmament under strict and effective international control.

Article VII

Nothing in this Treaty affects the right of any group of States to conclude regional treaties in order to assure the total absence of nuclear weapons in their respective territories.

Article VIII

1. Any Party to the Treaty may propose amendments to this Treaty. The text of any proposed amendment shall be submitted to the Depositary Governments which shall circulate it to all Parties to the Treaty. Thereupon, if requested to do so by one third or more of the Parties to the Treaty, the Depositary Governments shall convene a conference, to which they shall invite all the Parties to the Treaty, to consider such an amendment.

2. Any amendment to this Treaty must be approved by a majority of the votes of all the Parties to the Treaty, including the votes of all nuclear-weapon States Party to the Treaty and all other Parties which, on the date the amendment is circulated, are members of the Board of Governors of the International Atomic Energy Agency. The amendment shall enter into force for each Party that deposits its instrument of ratification of the amendment upon the deposit of such instruments of ratification by a majority of all the Parties, including the instruments of ratification of all nuclear-weapon States Party to the Treaty and all other Parties which, on the date the amendment is circulated, are members of the Board of Governors of the International Atomic Energy Agency. Thereafter, it shall enter into force for any other Party upon the deposit of its instrument of ratification of the amendment.

3. Five years after the entry into force of this Treaty, a conference of Parties to the Treaty shall be held in Geneva, Switzerland, in order to review the operation of this Treaty with a view to assuring that the purposes of the Preamble and the provisions of the Treaty are being realized. At intervals of five years thereafter, a majority of the Parties to the Treaty may obtain, by submitting a proposal to this effect to the Depositary Governments, the convening of further conferences with the same objective of reviewing the operation of the Treaty.

Article IX

1. This Treaty shall be open to all States for signature. Any State which does not

sign the Treaty before its entry into force in accordance with paragraph 3 of this article may accede to it at any time.

2. This Treaty shall be subject to ratification by signatory States. Instruments of ratification and instruments of accession shall be deposited with the Governments of the Union of Soviet Socialist Republics, the United Kingdom of Great Britain and Northern Ireland and the United States of America, which are hereby designated the Depositary Governments.

3. This Treaty shall enter into force after its ratification by the States, the Governments of which are designated Depositaries of the Treaty, and forty other States signatory to this Treaty and the deposit of their instruments of ratification. For the purposes of this Treaty, a nuclear-weapon State is one which has manufactured and exploded a nuclear weapon or other nuclear explosive device prior to 1 January 1967.

4. For States whose instruments of ratification or accession are deposited subsequent to the entry into force of this Treaty, it shall enter into force on the date of the deposit of their instruments of ratification or accession.

5. The Depositary Governments shall promptly inform all signatory and acceding States of the date of each signature, the date of deposit of each instrument of ratification or of accession, the date of the entry into force of this Treaty, and the date of receipt of any requests for convening a conference or other notices.

6. This Treaty shall be registered by the Depositary Governments pursuant to article 102 of the Charter of the United Nations.

Article X

1. Each Party shall in exercising its national sovereignty have the right to withdraw from the Treaty if it decides that extraordinary events, related to the subject-matter of this Treaty, have jeopardized the supreme interests of its country. It shall give notice of such withdrawal to all other Parties to the Treaty and to the United Nations Security Council three months in advance. Such notice shall include a statement of the extraordinary events it regards as having jeopardized its supreme interests.

2. Twenty-five years after the entry into force of the Treaty, a conference shall be convened to decide whether the Treaty shall continue in force indefinitely, or shall be extended for an additional fixed period or periods. This decision shall be taken by a majority of the Parties to the Treaty.

Article XI

This Treaty, the Chinese, English, French, Russian and Spanish texts of which are equally authentic, shall be deposited in the archives of the Depositary Governments. Duly certified copies of this Treaty shall be transmitted by the Depositary Governments to the Governments of the signatory and acceding States.

In witness whereof the undersigned, duly authorized, have signed this Treaty.

Speech by President Johnson Before the General Assembly Following
Its Endorsement of the Nuclear Non-Proliferation Treaty*

June 12, 1968

I have asked for the privilege of addressing you this afternoon

—to acknowledge this momentous event in the history of nations; and

—to pledge, on behalf of the United States, our determination to make this but a first step toward ending the peril of nuclear war.

Four and a half years ago, shortly after the awesome responsibility of leadership was thrust into my hands, I instructed our negotiators at Geneva to seek a treaty to prevent the spread of nuclear weapons.

I recalled the modest and mutual reductions in arms spending that had been achieved by the United States and the Soviet Union. And I said then, "Let us pray that the tide has turned—that further and far-reaching agreements lie ahead—and that future generations will mark 1964 as the year the world turned for all time away from the horrors of war and constructed new bulwarks for peace."

Four and a half years of patient and painstaking negotiations in Geneva—and of further debate and refinement here in the United Nations—were to follow. Now, at last, the work of many governments has become one instrument of international peace and sanity. The hands of many peoples have written a testament to reason—and to the will of mankind to endure.

The resolution that you have just approved commends to the governments of the world for their speedy ratification the treaty for the nonproliferation of nuclear weapons.

It is the most important international agreement in the field of disarmament since the nuclear age began.

It goes far to prevent the spread of nuclear weapons.

It commits the nuclear powers to redouble their efforts to end the nuclear arms race and to achieve nuclear disarmament.

It will insure the equitable sharing of the peaceful uses of nuclear energy—under effective safeguards—for the benefit of all nations.

On behalf of the Government and the people of the United States, let me congratulate all who have contributed to this historic event.

But we should not linger long in mutual congratulations. The quest—and the need—for disarmament is too urgent for that.

Many further steps are needed if this treaty is to fulfill its great purposes, and if we are to move beyond it toward the ultimate goal that we all seek—peace in the world.

As regards the treaty itself, no time should be lost in bringing it into force. I pledge you this afternoon that we of the United States will move rapidly

—to open the treaty for signature,

—to sign it on behalf of our own Government, and

—to seek its prompt ratification in accordance with our Constitution.

We shall urge other nations to complete their ratification speedily so that the treaty can enter into force at the earliest possible date.

*Public Papers of the Presidents, Lyndon B. Johnson, pp. 712-15.

I have further pledged that, as soon as the treaty has entered into force, we of the United States will carry out our responsibilities under it—in full measure.

First, we shall fully and scrupulously discharge our obligations as a nuclear-weapon party:

—not to transfer nuclear weapons, or control over them, to any recipient whatsoever; and

—not to help any nonnuclear state acquire such weapons.

Second, we shall cooperate fully in bringing the treaty's safeguards into being—safeguards that will prevent the diversion of nuclear energy from peaceful uses to weapons.

Third, we shall, as the treaty requires, facilitate the fullest possible exchange of equipment, materials, scientific and technical information for the peaceful uses of nuclear energy. We shall give particular attention to the needs of the developing nations.

We shall share our technical knowledge and experience in peaceful nuclear research fully, and we shall share it without reservation. This will include very important new developments in electrical power generation, agriculture, medicine, industry, and in the desalting of sea water.

Fourth, we shall continue our research and development into the use of nuclear explosions for peaceful purposes. We shall make available to the nonnuclear treaty partners—without delay, and under the treaty's provisions—the benefits of such explosions.

Finally—in keeping with our obligations under the treaty—we shall, as a major nuclear-weapon power, promptly and vigorously pursue negotiations on effective measures to halt the nuclear arms race and to reduce existing nuclear arsenals.

It is right that we should be so obligated. The nonnuclear states—who undertake with this treaty to forgo nuclear weapons—are entitled to the assurance that powers possessing them, particularly the United States and the Soviet Union, will lose no time in finding the way to scale down the nuclear arms race.

We desire—yes, we urgently desire—to begin early discussions on the limitation of strategic offensive and defensive nuclear weapons systems.

We shall search for an agreement that will not only avoid another costly and futile escalation of the arms race, but will de-escalate it.

I believe that this treaty can lead to further measures that will inhibit the senseless continuation of the arms race. I believe that it can give the world time—very precious time—to protect itself against Armageddon. If my faith is well founded, as I believe that it is, then this treaty will truly deserve to be recorded as the most important step toward peace since the founding of the United Nations.

Further, the nonproliferation treaty will serve not only as a deterrent to the spread of nuclear weapons, but also as a powerful stimulus for the peaceful use of the atom.

When this treaty comes into force, the growing number of nuclear-power reactors around the world—with their inevitable by-product of plutonium—need no longer cause anxiety as potential sources of nuclear weapons material. Under the safeguards of the treaty, those reactors will be pledged and will be guaranteed as peaceful sources of energy—as vital instruments of growth and development.

My fellow citizens of the world, what we have achieved here today few men would have dared to even hope for a decade ago.

Nations that were long beset by differences have—in this great treaty—found common ground in their need to use the incredible force of the atom for peace, and not for war.

From this ground that we have won here together, then let us press forward

—to halt and to reverse the buildup of nuclear arsenals;

—to find new ways to eliminate the threat of conventional conflicts that might grow into nuclear disaster.

In the name of our common humanity, let us insure our survival—so that we may achieve our high destiny on earth. Let us work for the ultimate self-interest of mankind: for that peace in which future generations may build a world without fear, and without want—a world that is fit for the sons of man.

In closing, Mr. President, permit me to pay my cordial respects to you. In your conduct of the affairs of this Assembly, Mr. President, you have won new honors for your country and for yourself.

Mr. Secretary General, we of the United States are very grateful for your contributions to the United Nations and to its universal goals of peace.

To all of the delegates here assembled, to all of you who have labored hard and fruitfully throughout this historic session, we extend our sincere good wishes; and to those who are about to leave our shores, we bid each of you Godspeed and a safe and pleasant journey home.

Thank you.

Security Council Resolution 255 on International Peace and Security *

June 19, 1968

The Security Council,

Noting with appreciation the desire of a large number of States to subscribe to the Treaty on the Non-Proliferation of Nuclear Weapons, and thereby to undertake not to receive the transfer from any transferor whatsoever of nuclear weapons or other nuclear explosive devices or of control over such weapons or explosive devices directly, or indirectly; not to manufacture or otherwise acquire nuclear weapons or other nuclear explosive devices; and not to seek or receive any assistance in the manufacture of nuclear weapons or other nuclear explosive devices,

Taking into consideration the concern of certain of these States that, in conjunction with their adherence to the Treaty on the Non-Proliferation of Nuclear Weapons, appropriate measures be undertaken to safeguard their security,

Bearing in mind that any aggression accompanied by the use of nuclear weapons would endanger the peace and security of all States,

1. Recognizes that aggression with nuclear weapons or the threat of such aggression against a non-nuclear-weapon State would create a situation in which the Security Council, and above all its nuclear-weapon State permanent members, would have to act immediately in accordance with their obligations under the United Nations Charter,

2. Welcomes the intention expressed by certain States that they will provide or support immediate assistance, in accordance with the Charter, to any non-nuclear-

*U.N. Security Council, *Official Records*, 23d yr., p. 13.

weapon State Party to the Treaty on the Non-Proliferation of Nuclear Weapons that is a victim of an act or an object of a threat of aggression in which nuclear weapons are used;

3. Reaffirms in particular the inherent right, recognized under Article 51 of the Charter, of individual and collective self-defence if an armed attack occurs against a Member of the United Nations, until the Security Council has taken measures necessary to maintain international peace and security.

Letter from Representatives of the Soviet Union, The United Kingdom and the United States to the President of the Security Council on the Nuclear Non-Proliferation Treaty *

June 12, 1968

The General Assembly has today adopted resolution 2373 (XXII) by which it commends the Treaty on the Non-Proliferation of Nuclear Weapons. In the Preamble of this Treaty it is recalled that, "in accordance with the Charter of the United Nations, States must refrain in their international relations from the threat or use of force against the territorial integrity or political independence of any State, or in any other manner inconsistent with the Purposes of the United Nations, and that the establishment and maintenance of international peace and security are to be promoted with the least diversion for armaments of the world's human and economic resources."

As was stated during the course of debate during the resumed twenty-second session of the General Assembly, it is our intention to sponsor a resolution in the Security Council responsive to the desire of many members that appropriate measures be taken to safeguard their security in conjunction with their adherence to the Treaty on the Non-Proliferation of Nuclear Weapons.

The delegations of the Union of Soviet Socialist Republics, the United Kingdom of Great Britain and Northern Ireland, and the United States of America accordingly herewith request an early meeting of the Council to consider the attached draft resolution.

We have the honour to request that this letter be circulated as a document of the Security Council.

Yakov Aleksandrovich Malik
Permanent Representative of the
Union of Soviet Socialist Republics
to the United Nations
Lord Caradon
Permanent Representative of the
United Kingdom of Great Britain
and Northern Ireland to the
United Nations
Arthur J. Goldberg
Permanent Representative of the
United States of America
to the United Nations

*U.N. Security Council, S/8601-8707; S/8630.

PROHIBITION OF NUCLEAR WEAPONS IN THE OCEANS AND IN OUTER SPACE

*Treaty on the Prohibition of the Emplacement of Nuclear Weapons and Other Weapons on the Sea Bed and Ocean Floor**

December 7, 1970

The General Assembly,

Recalling its resolution 2602 F (XXIV) of 16 December 1969,

Convinced that the prevention of a nuclear arms race on the sea-bed and the ocean floor serves the interests of maintaining world peace, reducing international tensions and strengthening friendly relations among States,

1. Commends the Treaty on the Prohibition of the Emplacement of Nuclear Weapons and Other Weapons of Mass Destruction on the Sea-Bed and the Ocean Floor and in the Subsoil Thereof, the text of which is annexed to the present resolution;

2. Requests the depositary Governments to open the Treaty for signature and ratification at the earliest possible date;

3. Expresses the hope for the widest possible adherence to the Treaty.

ANNEX

Treaty on the Prohibition of the Emplacement of Nuclear Weapons and Other Weapons of Mass Destruction on the Sea-Bed and the Ocean Floor and in the Subsoil Thereof

The States Parties to this Treaty,

Recognizing the common interest of mankind in the progress of the exploration and use of the sea-bed and the ocean floor for peaceful purposes,

Considering that the prevention of a nuclear arms race on the sea-bed and the ocean floor serves the interests of maintaining world peace, reduces international tensions and strengthens friendly relations among States,

Convinced that this Treaty constitutes a step towards the exclusion of the sea-bed, the ocean floor and the subsoil thereof from the arms race,

Convinced that this Treaty constitutes a step towards a treaty on general and complete disarmament under strict and effective international control, and determined to continue negotiations to this end,

Convinced that this Treaty will further the purposes and principles of the Charter of the United Nations, in a manner consistent with the principles of international law and without infringing the freedoms of the high seas,

Have agreed as follows:

Article I

1. The States Parties to this Treaty undertake not to emplant or emplace on the sea-bed and the ocean floor and in the subsoil thereof beyond the outer limit of a

*U.N. General Assembly, Agenda Item 27, 25th sess., A/RES/2660 (XV).

sea-bed zone, as defined in article II, any nuclear weapons or any other types of weapons of mass destruction as well as structures, launching installations or any other facilities specifically designed for storing, testing or using such weapons.

2. The undertakings of paragraph 1 of this article shall also apply to the sea-bed zone referred to in the same paragraph, except that within such sea-bed zone, they shall not apply either to the coastal State or to the sea-bed beneath its territorial waters.

3. The States Parties to this Treaty undertake not to assist, encourage or induce any State to carry out activities referred to in paragraph 1 of this article and not to participate in any other way in such actions.

Article II

For the purpose of this Treaty, the outer limit of the sea-bed zone referred to in article I shall be coterminous with the twelve-mile outer limit of the zone referred to in part II of the Convention on the Territorial Sea and the Contiguous Zone, signed at Geneva on 29 April 1958, and shall be measured in accordance with the provisions of part I, section II, of that Convention and in accordance with international law.

Article III

1. In order to promote the objectives of and ensure compliance with the provisions of this Treaty, each State Party to the Treaty shall have the right to verify through observation the activities of other States Parties to the Treaty on the sea-bed and the ocean floor and in the subsoil thereof beyond the zone referred to in article I, provided that observation does not interfere with such activities.

2. If after such observation reasonable doubts remain concerning the fulfilment of the obligations assumed under the Treaty, the State Party having such doubts and the State Party that is responsible for the activities giving rise to the doubts shall consult with a view to removing the doubts. If the doubts persist, the State Party having such doubts shall notify the other States Parties, and the Parties concerned shall co-operate on such further procedures for verification as may be agreed, including appropriate inspection of objects, structures, installations or other facilities that reasonably may be expected to be of a kind described in article I. The Parties in the region of the activities, including any coastal State, and any other Party so requesting, shall be entitled to participate in such consultation and co-operation. After completion of the further procedures for verification, an appropriate report shall be circulated to other Parties by the Party that initiated such procedures.

3. If the State responsible for the activities giving rise to the reasonable doubts is not identifiable by observation of the object, structure, installation or other facility, the State Party having such doubts shall notify and make appropriate inquiries of States Parties in the region of the activities and of any other State Party. If it is ascertained through these inquiries that a particular State Party is responsible for the activities, that State Party shall consult and co-operate with other Parties as provided in paragraph 2 of this article. If the identity of the State responsible for the activities cannot be ascertained through these inquiries, then further verification procedures,

including inspection, may be undertaken by the inquiring State Party, which shall invite the participation of the Parties in the region of the activities, including any coastal State, and of any other Party desiring to co-operate.

4. If consultation and co-operation pursuant to paragraphs 2 and 3 of this article have not removed the doubts concerning the activities and there remains a serious question concerning fulfilment of the obligations assumed under this Treaty, a State Party may, in accordance with the provisions of the Charter of the United Nations, refer the matter to the Security Council, which may take action in accordance with the Charter.

5. Verification pursuant to this article may be undertaken by any State Party using its own means, or with the full or partial assistance of any other State Party, or through appropriate international procedures within the framework of the United Nations and in accordance with its Charter.

6. Verification activities pursuant to this Treaty shall not interfere with activities of other States Parties and shall be conducted with due regard for rights recognized under international law, including the freedoms of the high seas and the rights of coastal States with respect to the exploration and exploitation of their continental shelves.

Article IV

Nothing in this Treaty shall be interpreted as supporting or prejudicing the position of any State Party with respect to existing international conventions, including the 1958 Convention on the Territorial Sea and the Contiguous Zone, or with respect to rights or claims which such State Party may assert, or with respect to recognition or non-recognition of rights or claims asserted by any other State, related to waters off its coasts, including, *inter alia*, territorial seas and contiguous zones, or to the sea-bed and the ocean floor, including continental shelves.

Article V

The Parties to this Treaty undertake to continue negotiations in good faith concerning further measures in the field of disarmament for the prevention of an arms race on the sea-bed, the ocean floor and the subsoil thereof.

Article VI

Any State Party may propose amendments to this Treaty. Amendments shall enter into force for each State Party accepting the amendments upon their acceptance by a majority of the States Parties to the Treaty and, thereafter, for each remaining State Party on the date of acceptance by it.

Article VII

Five years after the entry into force of this Treaty, a conference of Parties to the

Treaty shall be held at Geneva, Switzerland, in order to review the operation of this Treaty with a view to assuring that the purposes of the preamble and the provisions of the Treaty are being realized. Such review shall take into account any relevant technological developments. The review conference shall determine, in accordance with the views of a majority of those Parties attending, whether and when an additional review conference shall be convened.

Article VIII

Each State Party to this Treaty shall in exercising its national sovereignty have the right to withdraw from this Treaty if it decides that extraordinary events related to the subject-matter of this Treaty have jeopardized the supreme interests of its country. It shall give notice of such withdrawal to all other States Parties to the Treaty and to the United Nations Security Council three months in advance. Such notice shall include a statement of the extraordinary events it considers to have jeopardized its supreme interests.

Article IX

The provisions of this Treaty shall in no way affect the obligations assumed by States Parties to the Treaty under international instruments establishing zones free from nuclear weapons.

Article X

1. This Treaty shall be open for signature to all States. Any State which does not sign the Treaty before its entry into force in accordance with paragraph 3 of this article may accede to it at any time.

2. This Treaty shall be subject to ratification by signatory States. Instruments of ratification and of accession shall be deposited with the Governments of the Union of Soviet Socialist Republics, the United Kingdom of Great Britain andd Northern Ireland and the United States of America, which are hereby designated the Depositary Governments.

3. This Treaty shall enter into force after the deposit of instruments of ratification by twenty-two Governments, including the Governments designated as Depositary Governments of this Treaty.

4. For States whose instruments of ratification or accession are deposited after the entry into force of this Treaty, it shall enter into force on the date of the deposit of their instruments of ratification or accession.

5. The Depositary Governments shall promptly inform the Governments of all signatory and acceding States of the date of each signature, of the date of deposit of each instrument of ratification or of accession, of the date of the entry into force of this Treaty, and of the receipt of other notices.

6. This Treaty shall be registered by the Depositary Governments pursuant to Article 102 of the Charter of the United Nations.

Article XI

This Treaty, the Chinese, English, French, Russian and Spanish texts of which are equally authentic, shall be deposited in the archives of the Depositary Governments. Duly certified copies of this Treaty shall be transmitted by the Depositary Governments to the Governments of the States signatory and acceding thereto.

In witness whereof the undersigned, being duly authorized thereto, have signed this Treaty.

Done in   , at   , this   day of   ,   .

*General Assembly Resolution 2777 (XXVI) on International Liability for Damage Caused by Space Objects**

November 29, 1971

The General Assembly,

Reaffirming the importance of international co-operation in the field of the exploration and peaceful uses of outer space, including the Moon and other celestial bodies, and of promoting the law in this new field of human endeavour,

Desiring that the rights and obligations pertaining to liability for damage as laid down in the Treaty on Principles Governing the Activities of States in the Exploration and Use of Outer Space, including the Moon and Other Celestial Bodies, should be elaborated in a separate international instrument,

Recalling its resolutions 1963 (XVIII), of 13 December 1963, 2130 (XX) of 21 December 1965, 2222 (XXI) of 19 December 1966, 2345 (XXII) of 19 December 1967, 2453 B (XXIII) of 20 December 1968, 2601 B (XXIV) of 16 December 1969 and 2733 B (XXV) of 16 December 1970 concerning the elaboration of an agreement on the liability for damages caused by the launching of objects into outer space.

Recalling also that in resolution 2733 B (XXV) it urged the Committee on the Peaceful Uses of Outer Space to reach early agreement on a draft convention on liability, to be submitted to the General Assembly at its twenty-sixth session, embodying the principles of a full measure of compensation to victims and effective procedures which would lead to prompt and equitable settlement of claims,

Having considered the report of the Committee on Peaceful Uses of Outer Space,

Taking note with appreciation of the work accomplished by the Committee on the Peaceful Uses of Outer Space, and in particular that of its Legal Sub-Committee,

1. Commends the Convention on International Liability for Damage Caused by Space Objects, the text of which is annexed to the present resolution;

2. Requests the Depositary Governments to open the Convention for signature and ratification at the earliest possible date;

3. Notes that any State may, on becoming a party to the Convention, declare that it will recognize as binding, in relation to any other State accepting the same obligation, the decision of a claims commission concerning any dispute to which it may become a party;

4. Expresses its hope for the widest possible adherence to this Convention.

Ibid., Res. 2777 (XXVI).

ANNEX

Convention on International Liability for Damage Caused by Space Objects

The States Parties to this Convention,

Recognizing the common interest of all mankind in furthering the exploration and use of outer space for peaceful purposes,

Recalling the Treaty on Principles Governing the Activities of States in the Exploration and Use of Outer Space, including the Moon and Other Celestial Bodies,

Taking into consideration that, notwithstanding the precautionary measures to be taken by States and international intergovernmental organizations involved in the launching of space objects, damage may on occasion be caused by such objects,

Recognizing the need to elaborate effective international rules and procedures concerning liability for damage caused by space objects and to ensure, in particular, the prompt payment under the terms of this Convention of a full and equitable measure of compensation to victims of such damage,

Believing that the establishment of such rules and procedures will contribute to the strengthening of international co-operation in the field of the exploration and use of outer space for peaceful purposes,

Have agreed on the following:

Article I

For the purposes of this Convention:

(a) The term "damage" means loss of life, personal injury or other impairment of health; or loss of or damage to property of States or of persons, natural or juridical, or property of international intergovernmental organizations;

(b) The term "launching" includes attempted launching;

(c) The term "launching State" means:

(i) A State which launches or procures the launching of a space object;

(ii) A State from whose territory or facility a space object is launched;

(d) The term "space object" includes component parts of a space object as well as its launch vehicle and parts thereof.

Article II

A launching State shall be absolutely liable to pay compensation for damage caused by its space object on the surface of the earth or to aircraft in flight.

Article III

In the event of damage being caused elsewhere than on the surface of the earth to a space object of one launching State or to persons or property on board such a space object by a space object of another launching State, the latter shall be liable only if the damage is due to its fault or the fault of persons for whom it is responsible.

Article IV

1. In the event of damage being caused elsewhere than on the surface of the earth to a space object of one launching State or to persons or property on board such a space object by a space object of another launching State, and of damage thereby being caused to a third State or to its natural or juridical persons, the first two States shall be jointly and severally liable to the third State, to the extent indicated by the following:

(a) If the damage has been caused to the third State on the surface of the earth or to aircraft in flight, their liability to the third State shall be absolute;

(b) If the damage has been caused to a space object of the third State or to persons or property on board that space object elsewhere than on the surface of the earth, their liability to the third State shall be based on the fault of either of the first two States or on the fault of persons for whom either is responsible.

2. In all cases of joint and several liability referred to in paragraph 1, the burden of compensation for the damage shall be apportioned between the first two States in accordance with the extent to which they were at fault; if the extent of the fault of each of these States cannot be established, the burden of compensation shall be apportioned equally between them. Such apportionment shall be without prejudice to the right of the third State to seek the entire compensation due under this Convention from any or all of the launching States which are jointly and severally liable.

Article V

1. Whenever two or more States jointly launch a space object, they shall be jointly and severally liable for any damage caused.

2. A launching State which has paid compensation for damage shall have the right to present a claim for indemnification to other participants in the joint launching. The participants in a joint launching may conclude agreements regarding the apportioning among themselves of the financial obligation in respect of which they are jointly and severally liable. Such agreements shall be without prejudice to the right of a State sustaining damage to seek the entire compensation due under this Convention from any or all of the launching States which are jointly and severally liable.

3. A State from whose territory or facility a space object is launched shall be regarded as a participant in a joint launching.

Article VI

1. Subject to the provisions of paragraph 2, exoneration from absolute liability shall be granted to the extent that a launching State establishes that the damage has resulted either wholly or partially from gross negligence or from an act or omission done with intent to cause damage on the part of a claimant State or of natural or juridical persons it represents.

2. No exoneration whatever shall be granted in cases where the damage has resulted

from activities conducted by a launching State which are not in conformity with international law including, in particular, the Charter of the United Nations and the Treaty on Principles Governing the Activities of States in the Exploration and Use of Outer Space, including the Moon and Other Celestial Bodies.

Article VII

The provisions of this Convention shall not apply to damage caused by a space object of a launching State to:

(a) Nationals of that launching State;

(b) Foreign nationals during such time as they are participating in the operation of that space object from the time of its launching or at any stage thereafter until its descent, or during such time as they are in the immediate vicinity of a planned launching or recovery area as the result of an invitation by that launching State.

Article VIII

1. A State which suffers damage, or whose natural or juridical persons suffer damage, may present to a launching State a claim for compensation for such damage.

2. If the State of nationality has not presented a claim, another State may, in respect of damage sustained in its territory by any natural or juridical person, present a claim to a launching State.

3. If neither the State of nationality nor the State in whose territory the damage was sustained has presented a claim or notified its intention of presenting a claim, another State may, in respect of damage sustained by its permanent residents, present a claim to a launching State.

Article IX

A claim for compensation for damage shall be presented to a launching State through diplomatic channels. If a State does not maintain diplomatic relations with the launching State concerned, it may request another State to present its claim to that launching State or otherwise represent its interests under this Convention. It may also present its claim through the Secretary-General of the United Nations, provided the claimant State and the launching State are both Members of the United Nations.

Article X

1. A claim for compensation for damage may be presented to a launching State not later than one year following the date of the occurrence of the damage or the identification of the launching State which is liable.

2. If, however, a State does not know of the occurrence of the damage or has not been able to identify the launching State which is liable, it may present a claim within one year following the date on which it learned of the aforementioned facts; however, this period shall in no event exceed one year following the date on which the State

could reasonably be expected to have learned of the facts through the exercise of due diligence.

3. The time-limits specified in paragraphs 1 and 2 shall apply even if the full extent of the damage may not be known. In this event, however, the claimant State shall be entitled to revise the claim and submit additional documentation after the expiration of such time-limits until one year after the full extent of the damage is known.

Article XI

1. Presentation of a claim to a launching State for compensation for damage under this Convention shall not require the prior exhaustion of any local remedies which may be available to a claimant State or to natural or juridical persons it represents.

2. Nothing in this Convention shall prevent a State, or natural or juridical persons it might represent, from pursuing a claim in the courts or administrative tribunals or agencies of a launching State. A State shall not, however, be entitled to present a claim under this Convention in respect of the same damage for which a claim is being pursued in the courts or administrative tribunals or agencies of a launching State or under another international agreement which is binding on the States concerned.

Article XII

The compensation which the launching State shall be liable to pay for damage under this Convention shall be determined in accordance with international law and the principles of justice and equity, in order to provide such reparation in respect of the damage as will restore the person, natural or juridical, State or international organization on whose behalf the claim is presented to the condition which would have existed if the damage had not occurred.

Article XIII

Unless the claimant State and the State from which compensation is due under this Convention agree on another form of compensation, the compensation shall be paid in the currency of the claimant State or, if that State so requests, in the currency of the State from which compensation is due.

Article XIV

If no settlement of a claim is arrived at through diplomatic negotiations as provided for in article IX, within one year from the date on which the claimant State notifies the launching State that it has submitted the documentation of its claim, the parties concerned shall establish a Claims Commission at the request of either party.

Article XV

1. The Claims Commission shall be composed of three members: one appointed by

the claimant State, one appointed by the launching State and the third member, the Chairman, to be chosen by both parties jointly. Each party shall make its appointment within two months of the request for the establishment of the Claims Commission.

2. If no agreement is reached on the choice of the Chairman within four months of the request for the establishment of the Claims Commission, either party may request the Secretary-General of the United Nations to appoint the Chairman within a further period of two months.

Article XVI

1. If one of the parties does not make its appointment within the stipulated period, the Chairman shall, at the request of the other party, constitute a single-member Claims Commission.

2. Any vacancy which may arise in the Claims Commission for whatever reason shall be filled by the same procedure adopted for the original appointment.

3. The Claims Commission shall determine its own procedure.

4. The Claims Commission shall determine the place or places where it shall sit and all other administrative matters.

5. Except in the case of decisions and awards by a single-member Commission, all decisions and awards of the Claims Commission shall be by majority vote.

Article XVII

No increase in the membership of the Claims Commission shall take place by reason of two or more claimant States or launching States being joined in any one proceeding before the Commission. The claimant States so joined shall collectively appoint one member of the Commission in the same manner and subject to the same conditions as would be the case for a single claimant State. When two or more launching States are so joined, they shall collectively appoint one member of the Commission in the same way. If the claimant States or the launching States do not make the appointment within the stipulated period, the Chairman shall constitute a single-member Commission.

Article XVIII

The Claims Commission shall decide the merits of the claim for compensation and determine the amount of compensation payable, if any.

Article XIX

1. The Commission shall act in accordance with the provisions of article XII.

2. The decision of the Commission shall be final and binding if the parties have so agreed; otherwise the Commission shall render a final and recommendatory award, which the parties shall consider in good faith. The Commission shall state the reasons for its decision or award.

3. The Commission shall give its decision or award as promptly as possible and no later than one year from the date of its establishment unless an extension of this period is found necessary by the Commission.

4. The Commission shall make its decision or award public. It shall deliver a certified copy of its decision or award to each of the parties and to the Secretary-General of the United Nations.

Article XX

The expenses in regard to the Claims Commission shall be borne equally by the parties, unless otherwise decided by the Commission.

Article XXI

If the damage caused by a space object presents a large-scale danger to human life or seriously interferes with the living conditions of the population or the functioning of vital centres, the States Parties, and in particular the launching State, shall examine the possibility of rendering appropriate and rapid assistance to the State which has suffered the damage, when it so requests. However, nothing in this article shall affect the rights or obligations of the States Parties under this Convention.

Article XXII

1. In this Convention, with the exception of articles XXIV to XXVII, references to States shall be deemed to apply to any international intergovernmental organization which conducts space activities if the organization declares its acceptance of the rights and obligations provided for in this Convention and if a majority of the States members of the organization are States Parties to this Convention and to the Treaty on Principles Governing the Activities of States in the Exploration and Use of Outer Space, including the Moon and other Celestial Bodies.

2. States members of any such organization which are States Parties to this Convention shall take all appropriate steps to ensure that the organization makes a declaration in accordance with the preceding paragraph.

3. If an international intergovernmental organization is liable for damage by virtue of the provisions of this Convention, that organization and those of its members which are States Parties to this Convention shall be jointly and severally liable; provided, however, that:

   (a) Any claim for compensation in respect of such damage shall be first presented to the organization;
   (b) Only where the organization has not paid, within a period of six months, any sum agreed or determined to be due as compensation for such damage, may the claimant State invoke the liability of the members which are States Parties to this Convention for the payment of that sum.

4. Any claim, pursuant to the provisions of this Charter, for compensation in respect of damage caused to an organization which has made a declaration in accord-

ance with paragraph 1 of this article shall be presented by a State member of the organization which is a State Party to this Convention.

Article XXIII

1. The provisions of this Convention shall not affect other international agreements in force in so far as relations between the States Parties to such agreements are concerned.

2. No provision of this Convention shall prevent States from concluding international agreements reaffirming, supplementing or extending its provisions.

Article XXIV

1. This Convention shall be open to all States for signature. Any State which does not sign this Convention before its entry into force in accordance with paragraph 3 of this article may accede to it at any time.

2. This Convention shall be subject to ratification by signatory States. Instruments of ratification and instruments of accession shall be deposited with the Governments of the Union of Soviet Socialist Republics, the United Kingdom of Great Britain and Northern Ireland and the United States of America, which are hereby designated the Depositary Governments.

3. This Convention shall enter into force on the deposit of the fifth instrument of ratification.

4. For States whose instruments of ratification or accession are deposited subsequent to the entry into force of this Convention, it shall enter into force on the date of the deposit of their instruments of ratification or accession.

5. The Depositary Governments shall promptly inform all signatory and acceding States of the date of each signature, the date of deposit of each instrument of ratification of and accession to this Convention, the date of its entry into force and other notices.

6. This Convention shall be registered by the Depositary Governments pursuant to Article 102 of the Charter of the United Nations.

Article XXV

Any State Party to this Convention may propose amendments to this Convention. Amendments shall enter into force for each State Party to the Convention accepting the amendments upon their acceptance by a majority of the States Parties to the Convention and thereafter for each remaining State Party to the Convention on the date of acceptance by it.

Article XXVI

Ten years after the entry into force of this Convention, the question of the review of this Convention shall be included in the provisional agenda of the United Nations

General Assembly in order to consider, in the light of past application of the Convention, whether it requires revision. However, at any time after the Convention has been in force for five years, and at the request of one-third of the States Parties to the Convention, and with the concurrence of the majority of the States Parties, a conference of the States Parties shall be convened to review this Convention.

Article XXVII

Any State Party to this Convention may give notice of its withdrawal from the Convention one year after its entry into force by written notification to the Depositary Governments. Such withdrawal shall take effect one year from the date of receipt of this notification.

Article XXVIII

This Convention, of which the Chinese, English, French, Russian and Spanish texts are equally authentic, shall be deposited in the archives of the Depositary Governments. Duly certified copies of this Convention shall be transmitted by the Depositary Governments to the Governments of the signatory and acceding States.

In witness whereof the undersigned, duly authorized, have signed this Convention.

Done in   , at the cities of London, Moscow and Washington, the   day of one thousand nine hundred and

General Assembly Resolution 2826 (XXVI) on Prohibition of the Development, Production and Stockpiling of Bacteriological (Biological) and Toxin Weapons and Their Destruction*

December 16, 1971

The General Assembly,

Recalling its resolution 2662 (XXV) of 7 December 1970,

Convinced of the importance and urgency of eliminating from the arsenals of States, through effective measures, such dangerous weapons of mass destruction as those using chemical or bacteriological (biological) agents,

Having considered the report of the Conference of the Committee on Disarmament dated 1 October 1971, and being appreciative of the work of the Conference on the draft Convention on the Prohibition of the Development, Production and Stockpiling of Bacteriological (Biological) and Toxin Weapons and on Their Destruction, annexed to the report,

Recognizing the important significance of the Protocol for the Prohibition of the Use in War of Asphyxiating, Poisonous and other Gases, and of Bacteriological Methods of Warfare, signed at Geneva on 17 June 1925, and conscious also of the contribution which the said Protocol has already made, and continues to make, to mitigating the horrors of war,

*Ibid., Res. 2826 (XXVI).

Noting that the Convention provides for the parties to reaffirm their adherence to the principles and objectives of that Protocol and calls upon all States to comply strictly with them,

Further noting that nothing in the Convention shall be interpreted as in any way limiting or detracting from the obligations assumed by any State under the Geneva Protocol,

Determined, for the sake of all mankind, to exclude completely the possibility of bacteriological (biological) agents and toxins being used as weapons,

Recognizing that an agreement on the prohibition of bacteriological (biological) and toxin weapons represents a first possible step towards the achievement of agreement on effective measures also for the prohibition of the development, production and stockpiling of chemical weapons,

Noting that the Convention contains an affirmation of the recognized objective of effective prohibition of chemical weapons and, to this end, an undertaking to continue negotiations in good faith with a view to reaching early agreement on effective measures for the prohibition of their development, production and stockpiling and for their destruction, and on appropriate measures concerning equipment and means of delivery specifically designed for the production or use of chemical agents for weapons purposes,

Convinced that the implementation of measures in the field of disarmament should release substantial additional resources, which should promote economic and social development, particularly in the developing countries,

Convinced that the Convention will contribute to the realization of the purposes and principles of the Charter of the United Nations,

1. Commends the Convention on the Prohibition of the Development, Production and Stockpiling of Bacteriological (Biological) and Toxin Weapons and on Their Destruction, the text of which is annexed to the present resolution;

2. Requests the depositary Governments to open the Convention for signature and ratification at the earliest possible date;

3. Expresses hope for the widest possible adherence to the Convention.

ANNEX

Convention on the Prohibition of the Development, Production
and Stockpiling of Bacteriological (Biological) and Toxin
Weapons and on Their Destruction

The States Parties to this Convention,

Determined to act with a view to achieving effective progress towards general and complete disarmament, including the prohibition and elimination of all types of weapons of mass destruction, and convinced that the prohibition of the development, production and stockpiling of chemical and bacteriological (biological) weapons and their elimination, through effective measures, will facilitate the achievement of general and complete disarmament under strict and effective international control,

Recognizing the important significance of the Protocol for the Prohibition of the Use in War of Asphyxiating, Poisonous or Other Gases, and of Bacteriological Methods of Warfare, signed at Geneva on 17 June 1925, and conscious also of the contribution which the said Protocol has already made, and continues to make, to mitigating the horrors of war,

Reaffirming their adherence to the principles and objectives of that Protocol and calling upon all States to comply with them,

Recalling that the General Assembly of the United Nations has repeatedly condemned all actions contrary to the principles and objectives of the Geneva Protocol of 17 June 1925,

Desiring to contribute to the strengthening of confidence between peoples and the general improvement of the international atmosphere,

Desiring also to contribute to the realization of the purposes and principles of the Charter of the United Nations,

Convinced of the importance and urgency of eliminating from the arsenals of States, through effective measures, such dangerous weapons of mass destruction as those using chemical or bacteriological (biological) agents,

Recognizing that an agreement on the prohibition of bacteriological (biological) and toxin weapons represents a first possible step towards the achievement of agreement on effective measures also for prohibition of the development, production and stockpiling of chemical weapons, and determined to continue negotiations to that end,

Determined, for the sake of all mankind, to exclude completely the possibility of bacteriological (biological) agents and toxins being used as weapons,

Convinced that such use would be repugnant to the conscience of mankind and that no effort should be spared to minimize this risk,

Have agreed as follows:

Article I

Each State Party to this convention undertakes never in any circumstances to develop, produce, stockpile or otherwise acquire or retain:

(1) Microbial or other biological agents, or toxins whatever their origin or method of production, of types and in quantities that have no justification for prophylactic, protective or other peaceful purposes;

(2) Weapons, equipment or means of delivery designed to use such agents or toxins for hostile purposes or in armed conflict.

Article II

Each State Party to this Convention undertakes to destroy, or to divert to peaceful purposes, as soon as possible but not later than nine months after the entry into force of the Convention all agents, toxins, weapons, equipment and means of delivery specified in Article I of the Convention, which are in its possession or under its jurisdiction or control. In implementing the provisions of this Article all necessary safety precautions shall be observed to protect populations and the environment.

Article III

Each State Party to this Convention undertakes not to transfer to any recipient whatsoever, directly or indirectly, and not in any way to assist, encourage, or induce any State, group of States or international organizations to manufacture or otherwise acquire any of the agents, toxins, weapons, equipment or means of delivery specified in Article I of the Convention.

Article IV

Each State Party to this Convention shall, in accordance with its constitutional processes, take any necessary measures to prohibit and prevent development, production, stockpiling, acquisition or retention of the agents, toxins, weapons, equipment and means of delivery specified in Article I of the Convention, within the territory of such States, under its jurisdiction or under its control anywhere.

Article V

The States Parties to the Convention undertake to consult one another and to co-operate in solving any problems which may arise in relation to the objective of, or in the application of the provisions of, this Convention. Consultation and co-operation pursuant to this Article may also be undertaken through appropriate international procedures within the framework of the United Nations and in accordance with its Charter.

Article VI

(1) Any State Party to the Convention which finds that any other State Party is acting in breach of obligations deriving from the provisions of this Convention may lodge a complaint with the Security Council of the United Nations. Such a complaint should include all possible evidence confirming its validity, as well as a request for its consideration by the Security Council.

(2) Each State Party to the Convention undertakes to co-operate in carrying out any investigation which the Security Council may initiate, in accordance with the provisions of the Charter of the United Nations, on the basis of the complaint received by the Council. The Security Council shall inform the States Parties to the Convention of the results of the investigation.

Article VII

Each State Party to the Convention undertakes to provide or support assistance, in accordance with the United Nations Charter, to any Party to the Convention which so requests, if the Security Council decides that such party has been exposed to danger as a result of violation of this Convention.

Article VIII

Nothing in this Convention shall be interpreted as in any way limiting or detracting from the obligations assumed by any State under the Protocol for the Prohibition of the Use in War of Asphyxiating, Poisonous or Other Gases, and of Bacteriological Methods of Warfare, signed at Geneva on 17 June 1925.

Article IX

Each State Party to this Convention affirms the recognized objective of effective prohibition of chemical weapons and, to this end, undertakes to continue negotiations in good faith with a view to reaching early agreement on effective measures for the prohibition of their development, production and stockpiling and for their destruction, and on appropriate measures concerning equipment and means of delivery specifically designed for the production or use of chemical agents for weapons purposes.

Article X

(1) The States Parties to the Convention undertake to facilitate, and have the right to participate in the fullest possible exchange of equipment, materials and scientific and technological information for the use of bacteriological (biological) agents and toxins for peaceful purposes. Parties to the Convention in a position to do so shall also co-operate in contributing individually or together with other States or international organizations to the further development and application of scientific discoveries in the field of bacteriology (biology) for prevention of disease, or for other peaceful purposes.

(2) This Convention shall be implemented in a manner designed to avoid hampering the economic or technological development of States Parties to the Convention or international co-operation in the field of peaceful bacteriological (biological) activities, including the international exchange of bacteriological (biological) agents and toxins and equipment for the processing, use or production of bacteriological (biological) agents and toxins for peaceful purposes in accordance with the provisions of this Convention.

Article XI

Any State Party may propose amendments to this Convention. Amendments shall enter into force for each State Party accepting the amendments upon their acceptance by a majority of the States Parties to the Convention and thereafter for each remaining State Party on the date of acceptance by it.

Article XII

Five years after the entry into force of this Convention, or earlier if it is requested by a majority of Parties to the Convention by submitting a proposal to this effect to the Depositary Governments, a conference of States Parties to the Convention shall be held at Geneva, Switzerland, to review the operation of this Convention, with a view to assuring that the purposes of the preamble and the provisions of the Convention including the provisions concerning negotiations on chemical weapons, are being realized. Such review shall take into account any new scientific and technological developments relevant to this Convention.

Article XIII

(1) This Convention shall be of unlimited duration.

(2) Each State Party to this Convention shall in exercising its national sovereignty have the right to withdraw from the Convention if it decides that extraordinary events, related to the subject matter of this Convention, have jeopardized the supreme interests of its country. It shall give notice of such withdrawal to all other States Parties to the Convention and to the United Nations Security Council three months in advance. Such notice shall include a statement of the extraordinary events it regards as having jeopardized its supreme interests.

Article XIV

(1) This Convention shall be open to all States for signature. Any State which does not sign the Convention before its entry into force in accordance with paragraph 3 of this Article may accede to it at any time.

(2) This Convention shall be subject to ratification by signatory States. Instruments of ratification and instruments of accession shall be deposited with the Governments of the Union of Soviet Socialist Republics, the United Kingdom of Great Britain and Northern Ireland and the United States of America, which are hereby designated the Depositary Governments.

(3) This Convention shall enter into force after the deposit of the instruments of ratification by twenty-two Governments, including the Governments designated as Depositaries of the Convention.

(4) For States whose instruments of ratification or accession or deposited subsequent to the entry into force of this Convention, it shall enter into force on the date of the deposit of their instruments of ratification or accession.

(5) The Depositary Governments shall promptly inform all signatory and acceding States of the date of each signature, the date of deposit of each instrument of ratification or of accession and the date of the entry into force of this Convention, and of the receipt of other notices.

(6) This Convention shall be registered by the Depositary Governments pursuant to Article 102 of the Charter of the United Nations.

Article XV

This Convention, the Chinese, English, French, Russian and Spanish texts of which are equally authentic, shall be deposited in the archives of the Depositary Governments. Duly certified copies of this Convention shall be transmitted by the Depositary Governments to the Governments of the signatory and acceding States.

In witness whereof the undersigned, duly authorized, have signed this Convention.
Done in   copies at   , this   day of   ,   .

TREATY OF TLATELOLCO

General Assembly Resolution 2830 (XXVI) on Ratification of Additional Protocol II of the Treaty for Prohibition of Nuclear Weapons in Latin America*

December 16, 1971

The General Assembly,

Recalling its resolutions 1911 (XVIII) of 27 November 1963, 2286 (XXII) of 5 December 1967, 2456 B (XXIII) of 20 December 1968 and 2666 (XXV) of 7 December 1970,

Recalling in particular that in its resolution 2286 (XXII) it declared that the Treaty for the Prohibition of Nuclear Weapons in Latin America (Treaty of Tlatelolco) constitutes an event of historic significance in the efforts to prevent the proliferation of nuclear weapons and to promote international peace and security and that in its resolution 2666 (XXV) it repeated the appeals which on two previous occasions it had addressed to the nuclear-weapon States to sign and ratify additional Protocol II of the Treaty as soon as possible and it urged them to avoid further delay in the fulfilment of such appeals,

1. Reaffirms its conviction that, for the maximum effectiveness of any treaty establishing a nuclear-weapon-free zone, the co-operation of the nuclear-weapon States is necessary and that such co-operation should take the form of commitments likewise undertaken in a formal international instrument which is legally binding, such as a treaty, convention or protocol;

2. Notes with satisfaction that the United States of America deposited its instrument of ratification of Additional Protocol II of the Treaty for the Prohibition of Nuclear Weapons in Latin America on 12 May 1971, thus becoming a State Party to the Protocol, as the United Kingdom of Great Britain and Northern Ireland has been since 11 December 1969;

3. Deplores the fact that the other nuclear-weapon States have not yet heeded the urgent appeals which the General Assembly has made in three different resolutions and it urges them once again to sign and ratify without further delay Additional Protocol II of the Treaty for the Prohibition of Nuclear Weapons in Latin America;

4. Decides to include in the provisional agenda of its twenty-seventh session an item entitled "Implementation of resolution 2830 (XXVI) concerning the signature and ratification of Additional Protocol II of the Treaty for the Prohibition of Nuclear Weapons in Latin America (Treaty or Tlatelolco)";

5. Requests the Secretary-General to transmit the present resolution to the nuclear-weapon States and to inform the General Assembly at its twenty-seventh session of any measure adopted by them in order to implement it.

---

*U.N. General Assembly, 26th sess., agenda item 31, A/8582, Dec. 14, 1971. Adopted on Dec. 16, 1971 by vote of 101-0-12.

*Remarks by Vice President Humphrey on Signing of Protocol II
to Treaty of Tlatelolco**

April 1, 1968

On behalf of the Government of the United States, I am honored to sign protocol II to the Treaty for the Prohibition of Nuclear Weapons in Latin America.

It is appropriate that we hold this ceremony here.

No nation has done more than Mexico to convert this hope into reality. And no leader has contributed more to the successful negotiation of this treaty than President Diaz Ordaz.

It is a special privilege for me to sign on behalf of my country.

Over a decade ago, while serving as chairman of the Disarmament Subcommittee of the Foreign Relations Committee of the United States Senate, I proposed that a regional arms agreement should be negotiated by the nations of our hemisphere.

Our support for this regional treaty parallels our support for a worldwide treaty which would halt the dissemination of nuclear weapons.

The protocol which we sign today calls upon the powers possessing nuclear weapons to respect the statute of denuclearization in Latin America, not to contribute to violations of the basic provision of the treaty, and not to use or threaten to use nuclear weapons against the Latin American states parties to the treaty.

Upon ratification of protocol II, the United States is preapred to assume these obligations with respect to those countries in the region which undertake and meet the treaty's requirements.

I wish to emphasize the willingness of the United States to make nuclear-explosion services for peaceful purposes available to Latin American countries under appropriate international arrangements.

This offer will be reinforced under the proposed nonproliferation treaty, under which such countries as the United States will undertake to cooperate in contributing to the development by other states of the many other peaceful applications of nuclear energy.

We hope this treaty will also give new impetus to the efforts of Latin American governments to reach agreement on other limitations on the acquisition of military equipment.

If Latin American nations could agree that there are certain costly and sophisticated non-nuclear weapons they do not need—and will not buy—this alone would be an important contribution to economic and social growth and political harmony.

For so long as such weapons are considered the best guarantee of security in any one nation, the security of all nations has no guarantee. And precious resources are diverted from the works of peace.

My own country is prepared to cooperate with its neighbors in meeting this problem.

With the successful negotiation of this treaty, the inter-American system, the oldest functioning regional system in the world, has once again demonstrated its capacity to advance the peace and security of the peoples of this hemisphere.

Our presence here today affirms our continued support for that cause.

*Department of State Bulletin, Apr. 29, 1968, pp. 554-55. The United States was not a signatory to the treaty, which was signed by 14 Latin American nations at Mexico City on Feb. 14, 1967.

Protocol II*

The undersigned Plenipotentiaries, furnished with full powers by their respective Governments,

Convinced that the Treaty for the Prohibition of Nuclear Weapons in Latin America, negotiated and signed in accordance with the recommendations of the General Assembly of the United Nations in Resolution 1911 (XVIII) of 27 November 1963, represents an important step towards ensuring the non-proliferation of nuclear weapons,

Aware that the non-proliferation of nuclear weapons is not an end in itself but, rather, a means of achieving general and complete disarmament at a later stage, and

Desiring to contribute, so far as lies in their power, towards ending the armaments race, especially in the field of nuclear weapons, and towards promoting and strengthening a world at peace, based on mutual respect and sovereign equality of states,

Have agreed as follows:

Article 1

The statute of denuclearization of Latin America in respect of warlike purposes, as defined, delimited and set forth in the Treaty for the Prohibition of Nuclear Weapons in Latin America of which this instrument is an annex, shall be fully respected by the Parties to this Protocol in all its express aims and provisions.

Article 2

The Governments represented by the undersigned Plenipotentiaries undertake, therefore, not to contribute in any way to the performance of acts involving a violation of the obligations of article 1 of the Treaty in the territories to which the Treaty applies in accordance with article 4 thereof.

Article 3

The Governments represented by the undersigned Plenipotentiaries also undertake not to use or threaten to use nuclear weapons against the Contracting Parties of the Treaty for the Prohibition of Nuclear Weapons in Latin America.

Article 4

The duration of this Protocol shall be the same as that of the Treaty for the Prohibition of Nuclear Weapons in Latin America of which this Protocol is an annex, and the definitions of territory and nuclear weapons set forth in articles 3 and 5 of the Treaty shall be applicable to this Protocol, as well as the provisions regarding ratification, reservations, denunciation, authentic texts and registration contained in articles 26, 27, 30 and 31 of the Treaty.

*Ibid. p. 555.

Article 5

This Protocol shall enter into force, for the States which have ratified it, on the date of the deposit of their respective instruments of ratification.

In witness whereof, the undersigned Plenipotentiaries, having deposited their full powers, found to be in good and due form, hereby sign this Additional Protocol on behalf of their respective Governments.

United States Statement Accompanying Protocol II*

In signing Protocol II of the Treaty of Tlatelolco, the United States Government makes the following statement:

I

The United States understands that the Treaty and its Protocols have no effect upon the international status of territorial claims.

The United States takes note of the Preparatory Commission's interpretation of the Treaty, as set forth in the Final Act, that, governed by the principles and rules of international law, each of the Contracting Parties retains exclusive power and legal competence, unaffected by the terms of the Treaty, to grant or deny non-Contracting Parties transit and transport privileges.

As regards the undertaking in Article 3 of Protocol II not to use or threaten to use nuclear weapons against the Contracting Parties, the United States would have to consider that an armed attack by a Contracting Party, in which it was assisted by a nuclear-weapon State, would be incompatible with the Contracting Party's corresponding obligations under Article 1 of the Treaty.

II

The United States wishes to point out again the fact that the technology of making nuclear explosive devices for peaceful purposes is indistinguishable from the technology of making nuclear weapons and the fact that nuclear weapons and nuclear explosive devices for peaceful purposes are both capable of releasing nuclear energy in an uncontrolled manner and have the common group of characteristics of large amounts of energy generated instantaneously from a compact source. Therefore we understand the definition contained in Article 5 of the Treaty as necessarily encompassing all nuclear explosive devices. It is our understanding that Articles 1 and 5 restrict accordingly the activities of the Contracting Parties under paragraph 1 of Article 18.

The United States further notes that paragraph 4 of Article 18 of the Treaty permits, and that United States adherence to Protocol II will not prevent, collaboration by the United States with Contracting Parties for the purpose of carrying out explosions of nuclear devices for peaceful purposes in a manner consistent with our policy of not contributing to the proliferation of nuclear weapons capabilities. In this

*Ibid., pp. 555-56.

connection, the United States reaffirms its willingness to make available nuclear explosion services for peaceful purposes on a non-discriminatory basis under appropriate international arrangements and to join other nuclear-weapon States in a commitment to do so.

III

The United States also wishes to state that, although not required by Protocol II, it will act with respect to such territories of Protocol I adherents as are within the geographical area defined in paragraph 2 of Article 4 of the Treaty in the same manner as Protocol II requires it to act with respect to the territories of Contracting Parties.

PEACEKEEPING

PEACEKEEPING

Commentary

No aspiration in the U.N. Charter flew higher or fell flatter than that expressed in Article 43 and subsequent articles—to provide the United Nations with the means of enforcing its mandate to preserve international peace. This was a novelty in human experience and a qualitative step forward from the indecisive shuffle of competing sovereignties that had been the League of Nations.

One of the Security Council's first actions on January 25, 1946, was to establish the Military Staff Committee as a form of U.N. general staff. The Committee set to work at once to formulate the terms on which armed forces were to be made available to the organization, but could not agree on certain essentials. The Soviet Union, with weak naval and air forces, insisted that none of the other permanent members provide components stronger than its own in any force to be organized under Article 43. It demanded that forces be garrisoned at home and refused to make any of its own bases available to the U.N. On July 2, 1948 the Committee reported its deadlock to the Council and met regularly thereafter only as a formality.

Although its main instrumentality was never forged, the U.N. asserted its peace-keeping role in other ways. The General Assembly had the right to discuss any issue and to make recommendations. The Security Council also could encourage the pacific settlement of disputes under Chapter VI; but it retained some teeth as well, in Chapter VII, to impose political, economic and even military sanctions on breakers of the peace through the cooperation of the member states. Between the two lay a broad legal no man's land which had to be traversed with improvisations from case to case.

The very first problem brought to the Security Council two days after it was constituted, was Iran's complaint that Soviet troops had not been withdrawn from the northern provinces where they had been stationed to guard the allied wartime supply route to the Soviet Union. Not only had they not been withdrawn in accordance with an agreement that this would be done after the war was over, but Moscow had also installed a regime of its own and had blocked Iranian troops from returning. Iran pressed its case in the face of Soviet objections. The United States urged negotiations upon both parties but insisted that the Council keep the matter under discussion. At one point, when the Council overrode a Soviet motion to adjourn, the Soviet delegate, Andrei Gromyko, rose from his seat and walked out of the chamber. After three meetings, however, he returned and Soviet troops were pulled out of Iran. A Council resolution to this end would certainly have evoked a Soviet veto. The outcome was taken as evidence that mere discussion in the Council had moral force—and as vindication of Washington's insistence at San Francisco that no member be allowed to veto debate.

217

The first use of the veto had, meanwhile, shown this prerogative of the five Permanent Members of the Council to be much broader than had been imagined. At San Francisco, the Big Five met the expressed fears of the smaller members with the assurance that they would use this exclusive power judiciously to guard their vital interests. But then, early in 1946, the Soviet Union vetoed a resolution on the withdrawal of French and British troops from Syria and Lebanon only because the language did not condemn France and Britain strongly enough. Later that spring the Soviet representative cast six vetoes in the same spirit on the issue of whether the Franco regime in Spain endangered international peace.

Another important case which set a far-reaching precedent was Greece. The Soviet Union called the presence of British forces there a threat to peace. Then the Ukraine accused Greece of provoking incidents along the Albanian border. The United States proposal of an investigation commission was vetoed by the Soviet Union but later adopted by the Council. When a majority of the commission reported that Albania, Bulgaria and Yugoslavia were helping the guerrilla side in the Greek civil war, the Soviet Union vetoed further investigation and public censure. Thereupon the United States initiated transfer of the matter to the General Assembly, which had no veto, and the Assembly kept a special committee in Greece as an international eye on intervention from the north and a stabilizing presence until the breach between Belgrade and Moscow ended the problem. However, an effort, initiated by Secretary of State George Marshall to institutionalize expanded jurisdiction for the Assembly through an Interim Committee, nicknamed the Little Assembly, was boycotted from the start by the Soviet Union and came to naught.

Although the U.N. military force envisaged in Article 43 was never established, two armed conflicts which came to the United Nations brought forth a stopgap—the U.N. military observer. In the collision between India and Pakistan over Kashmir and the fighting in Palestine, the U.N.'s first concern was to obtain a cease fire. Truce arrangements needed supervision. Modest numbers of officers and men, recruited from various countries, were assigned this responsibility—in the one instance, under the U.N. Commission for India and Pakistan; in the other, as the U.N. Truce Supervision Organization (UNTSO).

Also in 1949, the Assembly authorized the formation of a 300 man U.N. Field Service to provide logistical services—transport, communications and headquarters security—for U.N. missions. It was a technical service hardly worth mentioning in the context of peacekeeping, except for the objections raised by the Soviet Union in the constitutional crisis of 1964.

Two important conditions were given as the United Nations approached its first great test in Korea. One was the impotence of the Security Council in the face of the Soviet veto. The other was a strong western majority in the General Assembly, a body lacking enforcement power but able to talk and to recommend practically without limit. The two combined to shift action to the Assembly. However, some of the gravest confrontations and open emergencies of the immediate postwar period were removed from U.N. jurisdiction altogether. Moscow's violation of the Yalta and Potsdam agreements came to the Assembly only indirectly and inconclusively. The Berlin Blockade, which the United States called a Soviet threat to peace in the meaning of Chapter VII, and the Communist seizure of power in Czechoslovakia in 1948 were kept out of the Council by the Soviet veto. The Western world sought its security in the North Atlantic Treaty Organization and its economic revival in the Marshall Plan.

The bombshell that burst in Korea when Communist troops marched south across the 38th parallel on June 25, 1950 found the picture in the Security Council newly and drastically changed. The Soviet representative had been boycotting meetings of the Council and all other U.N. organs since the previous January in a vain effort to make them seat the Communist Chinese Peoples' Republic in place of the Nationalist Republic of China. Also, a United Nations body was on the scene in Korea. A U.N. Commission on Korea, established earlier to help in the unification of that country, was able authoritatively to report what had happened. On the basis of this information and at the request of the United States, an urgent meeting of the Security Council was called. In the absence of the Soviet Union it quickly adopted a U.S. draft resolution laying the foundation for the kind of force which the framers of the U.N. Charter—or, most of them—had envisaged. In the circumstances, it used the language of Chapter VII without explicitly invoking it. Calling for a ceasefire and immediate Communist withdrawal, the resolution asked all member states to render every assistance. All told, fifty-two nations responded to the call, with sixteen of them providing armed forces under the U.N. flag. Two subsequent resolutions underscored the voluntary nature of the contribution and the supreme command of the United States, without whose swift response to the first alarm the Council would have had little to do except to deplore the disappearance of the Republic of Korea.

The Soviet Union's return to its Council seat in August blocked further action there on Korea. Later that year, for instance, after Chinese Communist troops in large numbers crossed the Yalu River into Korea, the United States endorsed an invitation to Peking, over Nationalist China's objections, to join in the debate. A Chinese Communist emissary took his place at the Council table. But a six nation draft resolution calling for the withdrawal of Chinese forces from Korea, while reaffirming the inviolability of the Yalu River boundary, was struck down by the Soviet veto.

Supported by a strong desire among member states to preserve some veto-proof peacekeeping capacity, the United States originated the Acheson Plan, the Uniting for Peace resolution. Secretary of State Dean Acheson spelled out its principles to the Fifth General Assembly and it was adopted later in the session. It amended the Assembly's rules of procedure to permit emergency action in the face of a veto; using the Assembly's right under the Charter's Article 11 to make recommendations, a right specifically affirmed by the International Court of Justice in 1962. It tried to fill the vacuum of Article 43 with a scheme whereby member states might in future systematically contribute military contingents to the kind of force so hastily pulled out of the hat for Korea. Finally, the resolution sought to anchor the Assembly's self-assertion in two new bodies: the Peace Observation Commission and the Collective Measures Committee. As things developed, they followed the Interim Committee into oblivion; but the Uniting for Peace emergency procedures were used repeatedly in later years, invoked by Communist as well as by Western nations, even though the Soviet Union bitterly disputed an active peacekeeping role for the General Assembly.

The General Assembly went on to pass two further resolutions which, though advisory, had practical consequences over a long period. It found the Chinese People's Republic to have engaged in aggression in Korea and, for the first time, recommended that all members apply an embargo on the shipment of arms and war materials to the

CPR. However, Mainland China's intervention in Korea had given most of the Asian members serious second thoughts about the U.N.'s involvement. Impressed by the initial Chinese success, they urged negotiation for an armistice, with no reference to the ultimate goal of Korea's reunification. Their action under India's leadership marked the first appearance of what later came to be designated the nonaligned group.

A 1953 armistice was finally concluded in Korea after U.N. successes had redressed the military balance and clear hints by President Dwight Eisenhower that the United States would not simply sit on its (nuclear) weapons superiority in the face of Peking's intransigence.

South Korea was saved, aggression was checked, the U.N. did rise to new heights of authority—but there was no blinking the fact that only the Soviet boycott of the Security Council had made this possible, a contingency not likely to recur. And a major casualty of the episode was Secretary General Trygve Lie. He had expressed himself wholeheartedly with the U.N. effort. When his term expired, the Soviet Union vetoed his reappointment and boycotted him after the Assembly continued him in office. For all the sympathy and support of most of the membership, Soviet ostracism made his position untenable and he resigned on November 10, 1952. The Korean armistice remained just that, a patchwork truce frequently torn.

Dag Hammarskjold of Sweden, who succeeded Lie, sought through quiet efficiency to gain the confidence of all factions and repair the damage done to his office by Soviet pressure and by the ravages of the McCarthy period in the United States. Early in his first term, acting at the request of the General Assembly, he flew to Peking and secured the release of eleven American fliers held prisoner in Communist China.

His prestige was high when the crises over Suez and Hungary gripped the U.N. in 1956. In the case of Suez, which is dealt with elsewhere, the Secretary General made himself the rallying point for the forces of peace and marshalled the U.N. Emergency Force, the organization's first large peacekeeping contingent. In the case of Hungary, where sharply different circumstances prevailed, the U.N. could do nothing but protest.

The essential difference between the two was this: in Hungary, the imperial interests of the Soviet Union dictated intervention at any cost. The west was in utter disarray, and a counterforce which might have checkmated Soviet power did not exist. In Suez, where the imperial interests of France and Britain were engaged, the United States and the Soviet Union joined to provide that counterforce.

The Hungarian uprising was brought to the Security Council on October 27th, two days before Israel's invasion of Egypt, with the United States, Britain and France demanding an urgent meeting. On this issue the three remained united. But the strongest words and deepest indignation, amplified by the tragic appeals of Prime Minister Imre Nagy, could not bend Soviet determination to stamp out heresy by any and every means.

When the Soviet Union vetoed a U.S. draft resolution demanding that it stop interfering in Hungary's affairs and withdraw its troops, the United States invoked the Uniting for Peace procedure to convene the Second Emergency Special General Assembly later that day. In short order, still on November 4, while the final Soviet offensive against the Nagy government was in full swing, the Assembly adopted a ringing resolution calling upon the Soviets to withdraw. When they ignored it, the Assembly renewed its call and passed a third resolution, submitted by the United States, to deal with the refugee problem and other human suffering.

A month later, at the regular Eleventh General Assembly, with still no cooperation forthcoming from the Soviet Union or Hungary, the United States and nineteen other members introduced yet a further resolution—the strongest ever until then against a member state—condemning the Soviet action. It was no more effective.

In all this parliamentary activity, so much of it at the emotional boiling point, no one ever suggested sanctions or armed action against the Soviet Union along the lines of Korea. That theoretical possibility would have split the United Nations. Thirteen or more nonaligned states abstained consistently when the resolutions were voted. The admission of new members and their search for collective identity, marked by the Bandung Conference of 1955, had altered the political composition of the General Assembly. When the smoke and the fury cleared away, all that remained of the western resolve was for the next fifteen years the presence of the Roman Catholic Primate of Hungary, Josef Cardinal Mindszenty, in asylum in the U.S. Legation in Budapest. Also, for seven years, the United States rallied enough votes in successive General Assemblies to block acceptance of the Hungarian delegation's credentials—a gesture all the more platonic for being left to the end of each session. And, thirdly, resolutions on Hungary and reports by the General Assembly's Special Representative on the Hungarian Problem were adopted annually until the 16th Assembly in 1962, with some relief, ended what had become an empty ritual with one last vote.

The haphazard history of U.N. peacekeeping continued in the Middle East, with the classic stopgap of the U.N. Emergency Force after the Suez crisis and the unilateral intervention by United States forces in Lebanon which brushed aside a U.N. observer operation there. In 1960, the problem of the Congo dwarfed everything that had gone before, sending the U.N. off on a zigzag enterprise that was—and shall probably remain—unique.

After twenty-three years as the personal property of King Leopold I of Belgium and fifty-two years as a Belgian colony, the Congo was abruptly given independence on June 30, 1960. Embracing one of the great river basins of the world, with enormous natural wealth in a territory one third the size of the United States, the Congo had a population of 13,500,000 of whom fewer than ten had a college education. Such political system as there was crumbled under the weight of unfamiliar responsibility. The native armed force, called an army, mutinied in wild disorder. Belgium rushed troops back to its former colony to protect its nationals. Katanga province, with its rich copper mines, seceded. President Joseph Kasavubu and Prime Minister Patrice Lumumba looked for help. They turned first to the United States, but President Eisenhower refused their appeal for U.S. troops to help restore order. American assistance, he said, would be given only through the United Nations. On July 12, the Congolese leaders cabled Secretary General Dag Hammarskjold to request protection "against the present external aggression."

Hammarksjold used his power under Article 99 of the Charter to convene the Security Council. With the United States and the Soviet Union voting together, it authorized the Secretary-General to provide military assistance. In less than 48 hours, the first element of a United Nations force which, at its peak, was to number 20,000 men, was on its way. It was called the U.N. Operation in the Congo and referred to by its French acronym, ONUC. This seemed phonetically less objectionable than the English UNOC, which would, as things turned out, not have done the force adequate justice. ONUC's men came mainly from Asian and African members, with important Irish and Swedish contingents added, but its chief logistic support in the four years it remained in the field came from the United States. The U.S. Air Force furnished the biggest continuous airlift in the history of military aviation, pre-Vietnam. The U.S. Treasury contributed $132,298,000 of the total cost of $368,200,000. The U.S. State Department supplied strong diplomatic backing for the Secretary General's mission to mount a neutral peacekeeping force in the face of Soviet efforts to obtain a position of special influence in the Congo. Of all the U.N. members, only the Soviet Union chose to supply aid to Lumumba directly instead of through the U.N.—trucks and planes, with Soviet technicians to operate them and, it was charged, to do other, more political work.

Secretary General Dag Hammarskjold saw this so-called technical assistance as an additional threat to peace and security. His view was shared by President Dwight Eisenhower, who declared that "the United States takes a most serious view of this action by the Soviet Union." It was a crisis of the most bizarre and ominous sort, changing with every shake of the political kaleidoscope and charged with the peculiar drama that attends a confrontation of the superpowers. It was further compounded, even as smaller climacterics were, by all the devices of traditional diplomacy—silent efforts to change votes in the Council or the Assembly; nagging persuasion to withdraw or maintain troops, to prevent or permit planes to land, to grant or to withhold support from one faction or another.

The Soviet Union joined the United States in adopting the first Security Council resolutions authorizing Dag Hammarskjold to create and deploy ONUC. It appeared that Moscow saw the U.N. force as an instrument to expel the Belgians and to preserve the unity of the Congo under the authority of Patrice Lumumba, with whom the Kremlin had established a special relationship. When, instead, ONUC was seen to function as a neutral agency warding off all foreign intervention, the Soviet Union turned against it, hinted at sending "volunteers" to help Lumumba and vetoed the Council's reaffirmation of the Secretary General's mandate.

The United States led the call for an emergency special session of the General Assembly to carry on from there. James J. Wadsworth became U.S. Representative when Henry Cabot Lodge resigned to accept the Republican Party's nomination for Vice President in the 1960 election. The 15th General Assembly, which followed the emergency session, thickened the already glutinous plot.

Seventeen newly independent states joined the United Nations in that Assembly, sixteen from Africa and the island Republic of Cyprus. Their admission raised the membership to ninety-nine and gave what came to be known as the Third World of uncommitted countries numerical predominance as well as great atmospheric influence in the Assembly and subsidiary organs. The occasion attracted heads of government from the four corners of the earth to the Assembly chamber, with Soviet Prime Minister Nikita Khrushchev the most active of all. Where others addressed sober homilies to the new members, Khrushchev made himself the spokesman of "decolonization" and turned his role to specific use. He inveighed against "western imperialism" and denounced both the Secretary General and ONUC as its creatures. His purpose was clearly to destroy the U.N. force in the Congo and, beyond that, to nullify the power of the organization to establish or to sustain any peacekeeping operation in the face of Soviet opposition. His tactics in the Assembly to gain psychological ascendancy included throwing sessions into pandemonium by hammering his desk with his fists and even with his shoe.

Soviet attacks on Dag Hammarskjold recalled the campaign against Trygve Lie. In 1961, Hammarskjold was killed in a plane crash in Northern Rhodesia. His death foreclosed a precise repetition of that contest; but it precipitated a struggle over the office and its powers in the choice of his successor. Three years later, the still broader issue of the peacekeeping authority of the United Nations, brought to a head by his success in the Congo, was fought out in the constitutional crisis of the 19th General Assembly. The Congo operation was, in fact, a success. Over a period of four years, the U.N. kept the country united and in control of its affairs. The new nation experienced further bloodshed and disorder—as did much of the rest of Africa—but the U.N. technical assistance program, the largest in history, helped to set the Congo on the road of development.

While the Congo problem boiled in Africa, the question of Cuba also engaged the United States and the United Nations. Under the regime of Fidel Castro, relations between Cuba and the United States went from bad to worse, with Cuba accusing Washington and the United Nations of "Various plans of aggression and acts of intervention," until the Bay of Pigs operation capped the climax. Adlai Stevenson, the new U.S. representative, floundering in a welter of misinformation, did his eloquent best to stress that U.S. forces were not directly involved and that the United States sympathized with the efforts of Cubans to rid their country of a new dictatorship. Latin American friends helped to shelve the matter, but nothing could conceal the diplomatic fiasco added to the failure of the undertaking itself.

The Cuban problem returned to the United Nations a year and a half later, when the Soviet Union was found to be installing nuclear missiles on the island. Washington's resort to the U.N. as well as to the Organization of American States was not naive. The United States had long since shed its last illusion about Soviet cooperation for peace in the framework of the Charter. Adlai Stevenson had, in Summer, 1962, used the occasion of the 100th Soviet veto—a resolution urging India and Pakistan to negotiate their dispute over Kashmir—to review the Soviet record in the most cutting terms. But the U.N. formed one of the dimensions of modern diplomacy, even the diplomacy of confrontation. Stevenson, addressing the Council in opening the debate on Cuba, used it as a platform to place the emergency in the perspective of a longer and deeper conflict of principle. When the Soviet representative scoffed, Stevenson proclaimed the Council chamber "the courtroom of world opinion." But in this most serious crisis of the post-World War II period, a climax with the overtones of nuclear Armageddon, the U.N.'s utility was indirect. Secretary General U Thant helped to pry the contending giants apart by offering his good offices, and U.N. headquarters served as a convenient, neutral site for negotiations. U Thant did not succeed in persuading Fidel Castro to accept U.N. supervision of the removal of the Soviet rockets. But the danger passed and little more than two months later, on January 7, 1963, the United States and the Soviet Union registered with the U.N. the conclusion of this sinister episode.

In December, 1963, one of those political volcanoes that helped to shape human affairs burst through the paper crust of treaties meant to contain it. Charged with ethnic animosity going back centuries, aflame with communal strife and carrying the implications of war between Greece and Turkey, the Cyprus question came to the U.N. Turkey maintained its treaty rights to intervene in behalf of the Turkish community on Cyprus. Greece openly backed the Greek Cypriot majority. With

Greece and Turkey members of NATO, the Alliance tried to devise some means of making and keeping peace that would avert a fatal breach in its southeastern anchor, while keeping the U.N. at arm's length. The United Kingdom, which, together with Greece and Turkey, had troops stationed on Cyprus, took the lead in setting up a joint force under British command to police a ceasefire and disengage the Greek and Turkish regular force. The three nations concurred in Cyprus' request that the Secretary General send an observer to the island, but they sought no other U.N. action.

The Soviet Union raised hue and cry against the establishment of a western, predominantly NATO, force in the Eastern Mediterranean, calling it "a serious danger to general peace." Archbishop Makarios, the President of Cyprus, fearing above all any further infringement of his sovereignty, opposed it as well. A British and American compromise proposal to place the force "within the framework of the United Nations," as Adlai Stevenson explained it, but still not subordinating it to U.N. authority, was equally controversial. Makarios, with Soviet support, refused to countenance it and, on February 15, after two months of friction in mounting uncertainty, Britain and Cyprus brought the issue to the Security Council.

Many contradictions and much confusion compounded the negotiations. The sovereign state of Cyprus had its sovereignty limited by the treaty which created it; the North Atlantic Treaty Organization saw two of its members at daggers drawn; the Soviet Union, while most reluctant to approve further U.N. peacekeeping operations not subject to its veto, was seeking to gain influence in the region. It could not oppose Makarios, who insisted on precisely this intervention. In the end, the Council adopted a resolution recommending the creation of UNFICYP—the U.N. Force in Cyprus—with the Soviet Union and France abstaining on paragraph four, which put it under the operational control of the Secretary General. Neither the Soviet Union nor France ever made the requested voluntary contributions to pay for UNFICYP, but they never opposed the periodic extension of its mandate.

The erratic course of the Cyprus struggle brought the hostile state twice to the brink of war. While UNFICYP did its best, open conflict was averted in August 1965 probably in the main by President Lyndon Johnson's direct threat to interpose the U.S. Sixth Fleet between Cyprus and a Turkish invasion force. His action was bitterly resented in Ankara and painfully damaged U.S.-Turkish relations. When a new possibility of Turkish invasion became acute in November, 1967, the United States did not repeat its warning, but joined with others in diplomatic effort to gain time for tempers to cool. All the while, it contributed some 40 percent of the cost of UNFICYP, which totalled about $110,000,000 by the end of 1969.

When the U.N. Charter was hammered into its final form in 1945, the countries of the Western Hemisphere placed great emphasis on Article 52, which defined the role of regional organizations within the framework of the United Nations. This article governed the United States approach toward those hemisphere problems which came to the U.N.—and toward none more than the matter of the Dominican Republic. This was, in essence, that the U.N., and especially the Security Council with its Soviet member, had no right to intervene in American affairs unless asked to do so by the Organization of American States or, where U.S. interests were directly involved, by the United States. The Soviet Union and France, for all their strict construction of the U.S.'s peacekeeping mandate, were eager in this case to introduce the Security

Council—and themselves with it—into Western hemisphere concerns. They tried, after the Security Council invited the Secretary General to send a representative to Santo Domingo, to expand that presence into at least an investigating mission. The Soviet Union even proposed that the Security Council constitute itself a visiting mission and meet in Santo Domingo, a proposal similar to one it had first advanced, also unsuccessfully, in the early stages of the Congo crisis. In the end, the situation in the Dominican Republic calmed down and the Council shelved the issue without seriously challenging the competence of the OAS.

When the smoldering animosity between India and Pakistan burst into open conflict in August, 1965, the United States and the Soviet Union found themselves working, if not together, at least for the same objective, a ceasefire and stability on the subcontinent. Some observers were moved, thereupon, to develop a hopefully hypothetical doctrine of "parallelism" as a key to new efficiency of the Security Council. But this episode, like all the other active U.N. peacekeeping efforts, was an improvisation, *sui generis*, not part of any codified procedure or accepted formula nor even a brick in a structure of precedent for the future.

That point was driven home in 1971 when war broke out between India and Pakistan over the secession of East Pakistan as the independent state of Bangladesh. The United States and the Soviet Union found themselves on opposite sides. The Security Council, paralyzed by this clash of interests and, specifically, by the Soviet veto of several ceasefire resolutions, was able in the end to do no more than to register the accomplished fact. Pakistan, although supported diplomatically by the United States and the Peoples' Republic of China was forced to swallow its defeat.

As in the Vietnam issue, perhaps the United Nations' most conspicuous and fateful nonfeasance, and in the Soviet-led 1968 invasion of Czechoslovakia, the Security Council remained impaled on the horns of its great-power dilemma.

FIRST EFFORTS AT PEACEKEEPING

Speech by Secretary of State George C. Marshall Before the General Assembly on a Program for a More Effective United Nations*

September 17, 1947

I have been asked by the President of the United States to extend to you the cordial greetings of the Government and people of the United States, as well as his own warm personal welcome. We are happy to have you with us in this country. We trust that your stay will be productive of the far-reaching results which the peoples of all countries expect from this gathering.

Our point of departure for the deliberations of this Assembly might well be the annual report of the Secretary-General on the work of the Organization. It is a noteworthy document. It records realistically the progress and development of the United Nations, and its failures. It reflects the diligent efforts of the Secretary-General and his staff to expedite the rapidly growing volume of United Nations business.

The situation we face today may be summarized by the statement that more than two years after the end of the war, the fruits of peace and victory are still beyond our grasp. Men look anxiously toward the future, wondering whether a new and more terrible conflict will engulf them. We have not yet succeeded in establishing a basis for peace with Germany and Japan, nor have we restored Austria as an independent state. Reconstruction lags everywhere; the basic requirements of life are scarce; there is desperate need throughout great areas. The complex economic machinery which was thrown out of joint by the war has not yet been put back into running order. In place of peace, liberty, and economic security, we find menace, repression, and dire want.

A supreme effort is required from us all if we are to succeed in breaking through the vicious circles of deepening political and economic crisis. That is why the United States has placed on the agenda of this Assembly the question of threats to the political independence and territorial integrity of Greece.

The history of the Greek case in the United Nations is well known in this Assembly. You are aware that the Security Council last December adopted a resolution establishing an investigating commission to inquire into the situation along the northern frontier of Greece and report the facts to the Security Council. You know that that commission and its subsidiary group, by large majorities, have attributed the disturbances principally to the illegal assistance and support furnished by Yugoslavia, Albania, and Bulgaria to guerrilla forces fighting against the Greek Government. The extent or effectiveness of such assistance to the Greek guerrillas is not the point at issue here.

*   *   *

U.S. Participation in the U.N., Reports 1946-49, Appendix III, Selected Addresses, (Washington, 1948), p. 261.

Letter from Ambassador Warren Austin to Secretary General Trygve Lie on the Berlin Question*

September 29, 1948

I have the honor, on behalf of the Government of the United States of America, in agreement with the Governments of the French Republic and the United Kingdom, to draw your attention to the serious situation which has arisen as the result of the unilateral imposition by the Government of the Union of Soviet Socialist Republics of restrictions on transport and communications between the Western zones of occupation in Germany and Berlin. Quite apart from the fact that it is in conflict with the rights of the Government of the United States of America and the Governments of France and the United Kingdom with regard to the occupation and administration of Berlin, this action by the Soviet Government is contrary to its obligations under Article II of the Charter of the United Nations and creates a threat to the peace within the meaning of Chapter VII of the Charter.

It is clear from the protracted exchange of notes and the conversations which have taken place on the initiative of the three governments between them and the Soviet Government that the three governments, conscious of their obligation under the Charter to settle their disputes by peaceful means, have made every effort to resolve their differences directly with the Soviet Government. Copies of the relevant documents are submitted separately. In particular, attention is drawn to the summary of the situation which is contained in the notes of the United States Government and the Government of France and the United Kingdom, dated September 26-27, 1948, as follows:

> The issue between the Soviet Government and the Western occupying powers is therefore not that of technical difficulties in communications nor that of reaching agreement upon the conditions for the regulation of the currency for Berlin. The issue is that the Soviet Government has clearly shown by its actions that it is attempting by illegal and coercive measures in disregard of its obligations to secure political objectives to which it is not entitled and which it could not achieve by peaceful means. It has resorted to blockade measures; it has threatened the Berlin population with starvation, disease and economic ruin; it has tolerated disorders and attempted to overthrow the duly elected municipal government of Berlin. The attitude and conduct of the Soviet government reveal sharply its purpose to continue its illegal and coercive blockade and its unlawful actions designed to reduce the status of the United States, the United Kingdom and France as occupying powers in Berlin to one of complete subordination to Soviet rule, and thus to obtain absolute authority over the economic, political and social life of the people of Berlin, and to incorporate the city in the Soviet zone.
>
> The Soviet Government has thereby taken upon itself sole responsibility for creating a situation, in which further recourse to the means of settlement prescribed in Article XXXIII of the Charter of the United Nations is not, in existing circumstances, possible, and which constitutes a threat to international peace and security. In order that international peace and security may not be further endangered the Governments of the United States, the United Kingdom and France, therefore, while reserving to themselves full rights to take such measures as may be necessary to maintain in these circumstances their position in Berlin, find themselves obliged to refer the action of the Soviet Government to the Security Council of the United Nations.

Accordingly, the Government of the United States requests that the Security Council consider this question at the earliest opportunity.

**Department of State Bulletin*, Vol., XIX, p. 455.

KOREA

Security Council Resolution S/1501 Concerning the Complaint of Aggression Upon the Republic of Korea*

June 25, 1950

The Security Council

Recalling the finding of the General Assembly in its resolution of 21 October 1949 that the Government of the Republic of Korea is a lawfully established government "having effective control and jurisdiction over that part of Korea where the United Nations Temporary Commission on Korea was able to observe and consult and in which the great majority of the people of Korea reside; and that this Government is based on elections which were a valid expression of the free will of the electorate of that part of Korea and which were observed by the Temporary Commission; and that this is the only such Government in Korea";

Mindful of the concern expressed by the General Assembly in its resolutions of 12 December 1948 and 21 October 1949 of the consequences which might follow unless Member States refrained from acts derogatory to the results sought to be achieved by the United Nations in bringing about the complete independence and unity of Korea; and the concern expressed that the situation described by the United Nations Commission on Korea in its report menaces the safety and well being of the Republic of Korea and of the people of Korea and might lead to open military conflict there;

Noting with grave concern the armed attack upon the Republic of Korea by forces from North Korea,

Determines that this action constitutes a breach of the peace,

I. Calls for the immediate cessation of hostilities; and

Calls upon the authorities of North Korea to withdraw forthwith their armed forces to the thirty-eighth parallel;

II. Requests the United Nations Commission on Korea

(a) To communicate its fully considered recommendations on the situation with the least possible delay;

(b) To observe the withdrawal of the North Korean forces to the thirty-eighth parallel; and

(c) To keep the Security Council informed on the execution of this resolution;

III. Calls upon all Members to render every assistance to the United Nations in the execution of this resolution and to refrain from giving assistance to the North Korean authorities.

Security Council Resolution S/1508 on Aggression Upon Korea*

June 27, 1950

The Security Council,

Having determined that the armed attack upon the Republic of Korea by forces from North Korea constitutes a breach of the peace,

*U.N. Security Council, *Official Records*, 5th Year, Jan.-Aug. 1950, pp. 459-63.

Having called for an immediate cessation of hostilities, and

Having called upon the authorities of North Korea to withdraw forthwith their armed forces to the 38th parallel, and

Having noted from the report of the United Nations Commission for Korea that the authorities in North Korea have neither ceased hostilities nor withdrawn their armed forces to the 38th parallel and that urgent military measures are required to restore international peace and security, and

Having noted the appeal from the Republic of Korea to the United Nations for immediate and effective steps to secure peace and security,

Recommends that the Members of the United Nations furnish such assistance to the Republic of Korea as may be necessary to repel the armed attack and to restore international peace and security in the area.

*Security Council Resolution 84(1950) on Aggression Upon Korea**

July 7, 1950

The Security Council,

Having determined that the armed attack upon the Republic of Korea by forces from North Korea constitutes a breach of the peace,

Having recommended that Members of the United Nations furnish such assistance to the Republic of Korea as may be necessary to repel the armed attack and to restore international peace and security in the area,

1. Welcomes the prompt and vigorous support which governments and peoples of the United Nations have given to its Resolutions of 25 and 27 June 1950 to assist the Republic of Korea in defending itself against armed attack and thus to restore international peace and security in the area;

2. Notes that Members of the United Nations have transmitted to the United Nations offers of assistance for the Republic of Korea;

3. Recommends that all Members providing military forces and other assistance pursuant to the aforesaid Security Council resolutions make such forces and other assistance available to a unified command under the United States;

4. Requests the United States to designate the commander of such forces;

5. Authorizes the unified command at its discretion to use the United Nations flag in the course of operations against North Korean forces concurrently with the flags of the various nations participating;

6. Requests the United States to provide the Security Council with reports as appropriate on the course of action taken under the unified command.

State Department Memorandum on Use of United Nations Forces in Korea†

July 3, 1950

This memorandum is directed to the authority of the President to order the Armed Forces of the United States to repel the aggressive attack on the Republic of Korea.

*U.N. Security Council, *Official Records*, 5th Year, 1965, pp. 5-6.
†*Department of State Bulletin*, July 31, 1950, pp. 173-77.

As explained by Secretary Acheson to the press on June 28, as soon as word of the attack on Korea was received in Washington, it was the view of the President and of all his advisers that the first responsibility of the Government of the United States was to report the attack to the United Nations.

Accordingly, in the middle of the night of Saturday, June 24, 1950, Ambassador Gross, the United States deputy representative at the Security Council of the United Nations, notified Mr. Trygve Lie, the Secretary-General of the United Nations, that armed forces from North Korea had commenced an unprovoked assault against the territory of the Republic of Korea.

*   *   *

The President, as Commander in Chief of the Armed Forces of the United States, has full control over the use thereof. He also has authority to conduct the foreign relations of the United States. Since the beginning of United States history, he has upon numerous occasions, utilized these powers in sending armed forces abroad. The preservation of the United Nations for the maintenance of peace is a cardinal interest of the United States. Both traditional international law and article 39 of the United Nations Charter and the Revolution pursuant thereto authorize the United States to repel the armed aggression against the Republic of Korea.

The President's control over the Armed Forces of the United States is based on article 2, section 2 of the Constitution which provides that he "shall be Commander in Chief of the Army and Navy of the United States."

In *United States v. Sweeny*, the Supreme Court said that the object of this provision was "evidently to vest in the President the supreme command over all the military forces—such supreme and undivided command as would be necessary to the prosecution of a successful war."

That the President's power to send the Armed Forces outside the country is not dependent on Congressional authority has been repeatedly emphasized by numerous writers.

For example, ex-President William Howard Taft wrote:

> The President is made Commander in Chief of the Army and Navy by the Constitution evidently for the purpose of enabling him to defend the country against invasion, to suppress insurrection and to take care that the laws be faithfully executed. If Congress were to attempt to prevent his use of the Army for any of these purposes, the action would be void. . . . Again, in the carrying on of war as Commander in Chief, it is he who is to determine the movements of the Army and of the Navy. Congress could not take away from him that discretion and place it beyond his control in any of his subordinates, nor could they themselves, as the people of Athens attempted to carry on campaigns by votes in the market-place.

Not only is the President Commander in Chief of the Army and Navy, but he is also charged with the duty of conducting the foreign relations of the United States and in this field he "alone has the power to speak or listen as a representative of the Nation."

Obviously, there are situations in which the powers of the President as Commander in Chief and his power to conduct the foreign relations of this country complement each other.

The basic interest of the United States is international peace and security. The United States has, throughout its history, upon orders of the Commander in Chief to the Armed Forces and without congressional authorization, acted to prevent violent and unlawful acts in other states from depriving the United States and its nationals of the benefits of such peace and security. It has taken such action both unilaterally and in concert with others. A tabulation of 85 instances of the use of American Armed Forces without a declaration of war was incorporated in the *Congressional Record* for July 10, 1941.

It is important to analyze the purposes for which the President as Commander in Chief has authorized the despatch of American troops abroad. In many instances, of course, the Armed Forces have been used to protect specific American lives and property. In other cases, however, United States forces have been used in the broad interests of American foreign policy, and their use could be characterized as participation in international police action.

The traditional power of the President to use the Armed Forces of the United States without consulting Congress was referred to in debates in the Senate in 1945. Senator Connally remarked: "The historical instances in which the President has directed armed forces to go to other countries have not been confined to domestic or internal instances at all." Senator Millikin pointed out that "in many cases the President has sent troops into a foreign country to protect our foreign policy ... notably in Central and South America." "That was done," he continued, "in order to keep foreign countries out of there—was not aimed at protecting any particular American citizen. It was aimed at protecting our foreign policy." To his remark that he presumed that by the Charter of the United Nations we had laid down a foreign policy which we could protect, Senator Connally replied that that was "absolutely correct." He added:

> I was trying to indicate that fact by reading the list of instances of intervention on our part in order to keep another government out of territory in this hemisphere. That was a question of carrying out our international policy, and not a question involving the protection of some American citizen or American property at the moment.

During the Boxer Rebellion in China in 1900-1901, the President sent about 5,000 troops to join with British, Russian, German, French, and Japanese troops to relieve the siege of the foreign quarters in Peking and reestablish the treaty status. This was done without express congressional authority. In defining United States policy at the time Secretary of State Hay said:

> ... The purpose of the President is, as it has been heretofore, to act concurrently with the other powers; first, in opening up communication with Peking and rescuing the American officials, missionaries, and other Americans who are in danger; secondly, in affording all possible protection everywhere in China to American life and property; thirdly, in guarding and protecting all legitimate American interests; and fourthly, in aiding to prevent a spread of the disorders to the other provinces of the Empire and a recurrence of such disasters. It is of course, too early to forecast the means of attaining this last result; but the policy of the Government of the United States is to seek a solution which may bring about permanent safety and peace to China, preserve Chinese territorial and administrative entity, protect all rights guaranteed to friendly powers by treaty and international law, and safeguard for the world the principle of equal and impartial trade with all parts of the Chinese Empire.

After the opening up of Japan to foreigners in the 1850's through the conclusion of commercial treaties between Japan and certain Western powers, antiforeign disturbance occurred. In 1863, the American Legation was burned following previous attacks on the British Legation. The commander of the U.S.S. *Wyoming* was instructed to use all necessary force for the safety of the legation or of Americans residing in Japan. Secretary of State Seward said that the prime objects of the United States were:

> First, to deserve and win the confidence of the Japanese Government and people, if possible, with a view to the common interest of all the treaty powers; secondly, to sustain and cooperate with the legations of these powers, in good faith, so as to render their efforts to the same end effective.

In 1864, the Mikado, not recognizing the treaties with the Western powers, closed the straits of Shimonoseki. At the request of the Tycoon's government (opposed to the Mikado), American, British, French, and Netherlands forces, in a joint operation, opened the straits by force. The object of the Western powers was the enforcement of treaty rights, with the approval of the government that granted them.

Again, in 1868, a detachment of Japanese troops assaulted foreign residents in the streets of Hiogo. One of the crew of the *Oneida* was seriously wounded. The safety of the foreign population being threatened, naval forces of the treaty powers made a joint landing and adopted measures to protect the foreign settlement.

Former Assistant Secretary of State James Grafton Rogers has characterized these uses of force as "international police action," saying:

> They amounted to executive use of the Armed Forces to establish our own and the world's scheme of international order. Two American Presidents used men, ships and guns on a large and expensive scale.

In 1888 and 1889, civil war took place in Samoa where the United States, Great Britain, and Germany had certain respective treaty rights for the maintenance of naval depots. German forces were landed, and the German Government invited the United States to join in an effort to restore calm and quiet in the islands in the interest of all the treaty powers. The commander of the United States naval forces in the Pacific was instructed by the Secretary of the Navy that the United States was willing to cooperate in restoring order "on the basis of the full preservation of American treaty rights and Samoan authority, as recognized and agreed to by Germany, Great Britain, and the United States." He was to extend full protection and defense to American citizens and property, to protest the displacement of the native government by Germany as violating the positive agreement and understanding between the treaty powers, but to inform the British and German Governments of his readiness to cooperate in causing all treaty rights to be respected and in restoring peace and order on the basis of the recognition of the Samoan right to independence.

On July 7, 1941, the President sent to the Congress a message announcing that as Commander in Chief he had ordered the Navy to take all necessary steps to insure the safety of communications between Iceland and the United States as well as on the seas between the United States and all other strategic outposts and that American troops had been sent to Iceland in defense of that country. The United States, he said, could not permit "the occupation by Germany of strategic outposts in the Atlantic to be used as air or naval bases for eventual attack against the Western Hemisphere." For the same reason, he said, substantial forces of the United States had been sent to the bases acquired from Great Britain in Trinidad and British Guiana in the South to forestall any pincers movement undertaken by Germany against the Western Hemisphere.

Thus, even before the ratification of the United Nations Charter, the President had used the Armed Forces of the United States without consulting the Congress for the purpose of protecting the foreign policy of the United States. The ratification of the United Nations Charter was, of course, a landmark in the development of American foreign policy. As noted above, Senator Connally and Senator Millikin agreed that the President was entitled to use armed forces in protection of the foreign policy represented by the Charter. This view was also expressed in the Senate debates in connection with the ratification of the Charter. For example, Senator Wiley made the following pertinent statement:

> It is my understanding, according to the testimony given before the Foreign Relations Committee of the Senate, that the terms "agreement or agreements as used in article 43 are synonymous with the word "treaty." On the other hand, I recognize that Congress might well interpret them as agreements brought about by the action of the Executive and ratified by a joint resolution of both Houses. These agreements would provide for a police force and the specific responsibility of each nation. But outside of these agreements, there is the power in our Executive to preserve the peace, to see that the "supreme laws" are faithfully executed. When we become a party to this charter, and define our responsibilities by the agreement or agreements, there can be no question of the power of the Executive to carry out our commitments in relation to international policing. His constitutional power, however, is in no manner impaired.

An even fuller exposition of the point was made by Senator Austin, who stated:

> Mr. President, I am one of those lawyers in the United States who believe that the general powers of the President—not merely the war powers of the President but the general authority of the President—are commensurate with the obligation which is imposed upon him as President, that he take care that the laws are faithfully executed. That means that he shall take all the care that is required to see that the laws are faithfully executed.
>
> Of course, there are other specific references in the Constitution which show that he has authority to employ armed forces when necessary to carry out specific things named in the Constitution; but the great over-all and general authority arise from his obligation that he take care that the laws are faithfully executed. That has been true throughout our history, and the Chief Executive has taken care, and has sent the armed forces of the United States, without any act of Congress preceding their sending, on a great many occasions. I have three different compilations of those occasions. One of them runs as high as 150 times; another of them 72 times, and so forth. It makes a difference whether we consider the maneuvers which were merely shows of force as combined [*comprised?*] in the exercise of this authority—as I do—or whether we limit the count to those cases in which the armed forces have actually entered upon the territory of a peaceful neighbor. But there is no doubt in my mind of his obligation and authority to employ all the force that is necessary to enforce the laws.
>
> It may be asked, How does a threat to international security and peace violate the laws of the United States? Perhaps, Mr. President, it would not have violated the laws of the United States previous to the obligations set forth in this treaty. Perhaps we have never before recognized as being true the fundamental doctrine with which I opened my remarks. But we are doing so now. We recognize that a breach of the peace anywhere on earth which threatens the security and peace of the world is an attack upon us; and after this treaty is accepted by 29 nations that will be the express law of the world. It will be the law of nations, because according to its express terms it will bind those who are nonmembers, as well as members, and it will be the law of the United States, because we shall have adopted it in a treaty. Indeed, it will be above the ordinary statuses of the United States, because it will be on a par with the Constitution which provides that treaties made pursuant thereto shall be the supreme law of the land.
>
> So I have no doubt of the authority of the President in the past, and his authority in the future, to enforce peace. I am bound to say that I feel that the President is the officer under our Constitution in whom there is exclusively vested the responsibility for maintenance of peace.

Action contrary to the Charter of the United Nations is action against the interests of the United States. Preservation of peace under the Charter is a cornerstone of American foreign policy. President Truman said in his inaugural address in 1949:

> In the coming years, our program for peace and freedom will emphasize four major courses of action.
>
> First, we will continue to give unfaltering support to the United Nations and related agencies, and we will continue to search for ways to strengthen their authority and increase their effectiveness.

In the Korean situation, the resolution of the Security Council of June 25 determined, under article 39 of the Charter, that the action of the North Koreans constituted a breach of the peace and called upon "the authorities in North Korea (a) to cease hostilities forthwith; and (b) to withdraw their armed forces to the thirty-eighth parallel." It also called upon "all Members to render every assistance to the United Nations in the execution of this resolution." This is an application of the principles set forth in article 2, paragraph 5 of the Charter, which states: "All Members shall give the United Nations every assistance in any action it takes in accordance with the present Charter . . ." The Security Council resolution of June 27, passed after the North Korean authorities had disregarded the June 25 resolution, recommended "that Members of the United Nations furnish such assistance to the Republic of Korea as may be necessary to repel the armed attack and to restore international peace and security in the area." This recommendation was also made under the authority of article 39 of the Charter.

The President's action seeks to accomplish the objectives of both resolutions.

The continued defiance of the United Nations by the North Korean authorities would have meant that the United Nations would have ceased to exist as a serious instrument for the maintenance of international peace. The continued existence of the United Nations as an effective international organization is a paramount United States interest. The defiance of the United Nations is in clear violation of the Charter of the United Nations and of the resolutions adopted by the Security Council of the United Nations to bring about a settlement of the problem. It is a threat to international peace and security, a threat to the peace and security of the United States and to the security of United States forces in the Pacific.

These interests of the United States are interests which the President as Commander in Chief can protect by the employment of the Armed Forces of the United States without a declaration of war. It was they which the President's order of June 27 did protect. This order was within his authority as Commander in Chief.

Report by President Truman to Congress on Korea and Uniting for Peace*

1950

KOREA

During 1950 the United Nations met the most serious test in its history. This test was open, armed aggression, carefully prepared in advance and directed first against a peaceful state and later on against the collective forces of the United Nations itself.

U.S. Participation in the U.N., Report by the President to Congress for the Year 1950, (Washington, 1951), pp. 3-8.

The test went to the very foundations of the United Nations. Article 1, paragraph 1, of the Charter states the first of the purposes of the United Nations as follows:

> "To maintain international peace and security, and to that end: to take effective collective measures for the prevention and removal of threats to the peace, and for the suppression of acts of aggression or other breaches of the peace, and to bring about by peaceful means, and in conformity with the principles of justice and international law, adjustment or settlement of international disputes or situations which might lead to a breach of the peace."

It seemed likely that a failure to take effective collective measures would greatly increase the danger of future war and weaken—perhaps irreparably—the determination of the free nations of the world to stand together in support of the United Nations.

The United Nations had to meet aggression without the means which had originally been expected to be available. Chapter VII of the Charter envisages that the Security Council, working mainly through its Military Staff Committee, will build up means of effective United Nations action against aggression. Article 43 contemplates the negotiation of an agreement or agreements between the Security Council and members which would fix the contribution which each member would make on the call of the Council. The failure of the Council, during the first 5 years of the United Nations, to make any progress toward building up United Nations means of resistance against aggression has been recounted in previous annual reports. It will suffice here to recall that this failure occurred because agreement could not be reached between the U.S.S.R. on the one hand and the four other permanent members of the Security Council—China, France, the United Kingdom, and the United States—on the other, on even the rudimentary principles of organizing collective action. Accordingly, while during its first 5 years the United Nations accomplished much in the adjustment and settlement of disputes and other special political problems, no United Nations forces existed when on June 25, 1950, the North Korean Communists launched an armed attack upon the Republic f Korea. The United States and many other members carried out their Charter obligations loyally and courageously. However, as will be seen, their entire collective action had to be improvised.

As soon as the United States Government learned of the North Korean attack, it requested an emergency meeting of the Security Council. The Council met within a few hours, on a Sunday afternoon. The representative of the U.S.S.R. was absent: his government had since January boycotted meetings of the Council in an effort to force the other members to agree to replace the representative of the Chinese National Government in the Council with a representative of the Chinese Communists. Unhampered by Soviet obstruction, the Council quickly determined that the attack constituted a breach of the peace. The Council also called for immediate cessation of hostilities and withdrawal of North Korean forces to the 38th parallel and requested all United Nations members to lend every assistance in carrying out the resolution.

Backing up the United Nations action, President Truman on June 27 authorized aid to forces of the Republic of Korea by United States sea and air forces. The Council on the same day recommended to members that they furnish to the Republic of Korea such assistance as was necessary to repel the attack and restore peace and security in the area. President Truman later authorized action by United States ground forces.

Fifty-two other member nations pledged support to this United Nations action. On July 7 the Security Council recommended that offers of aid be made available to a

Unified Command under the United States, requested the United States to designate a commander of the unified forces, and authorized the use of the United Nations flag by the Unified Command. The President appointed Gen. Douglas MacArthur as the commander of the unified forces. In the bitter days of retreat which followed, as well as in the days of success, these forces battled under the flag of the United Nations, which flew side by side with their own nations' flags. It was the first time this flag had flown over an army on an official United Nations mission to restore peace and security.

While the United Nations was stiffening its resistance to the thrusts of the North Koreans and building up its forces, the Russians acknowledged the failure of their boycott of United Nations organs by returning to assume the presidency of the Security Council for the month of August. The Soviet representative, Jacob Malik, then used his position to obstruct Council action for the entire month.

In September after weeks of repeated Communist attacks, the surprise United Nations landings at Inchon on the west coast of the Korean peninsula turned the tide of battle. In a coordinated strategic move, United Nations troops soon broke out from the south-eastern corner of the peninsula. On September 29 the Government of the Republic of Korea returned to its capital, Seoul. As the Korean Communists retreated northward the prospects of completing the United Nations military mission were bright. It seemed that the invasion of the territory of the Republic of Korea had been definitively repelled and that soon international peace and security would be restored in the area. Indeed it appeared that, incidentally to accomplishing its military objective in Korea, the United Nations might be able also to fulfill what had been its political objective for a number of years—unification of Korea.

On October 7 the Assembly adopted a many-sided program providing for the establishment of an independent, democratic, and unified Korea. As its agent in these matters the Assembly set up a new seven-government commission to succeed the former United Nations Commission on Korea.

Thus the Assembly responded to the proposal made by Secretary of State Acheson that Korea should be the first place to demonstrate the creative and productive possibilities at the command of the United Nations.

Member states likewise demonstrated their cooperation by offering generous quantities of food, clothing, and supplies in answer to the Secretary-General's appeal on behalf of the emergency relief program of the Unified Command. On December 1 the General Assembly passed a resolution creating a relief organization—the United Nations Korean Reconstruction Agency—to assume relief and rehabilitation functions from the Unified Command as soon as military conditions would permit.

On November 5 when the success of the United Nations mission seemed assured, the Commander of the Unified Forces reported increased intervention by the Chinese Communists, who were crossing the border from Manchuria and appearing in the North Korean lines. At the request of the United States, the Security Council called a special meeting to consider this threatening development. United Nations forces, it now appeared, could at any moment be faced by a huge new army of Chinese Communists, based in and supplied from adjacent Manchuria. It was immediately realized that the Chinese Communists had dangerously widened the scope of military operations.

The Chinese Communist intervention was "aggression, outright and naked," according to the United States representative in the Security Council who described the problem created thereby as "the gravest one now confronting the world." The Communist delegation, which had been invited to the Council originally on the question of Formosa, did not defend itself against the charge of intervention by the Chinese People's Republic. Instead it parroted the preposterous Soviet charges that the United States was the aggressor in both Korea and China.

Six Council members, including the United States, introduced a resolution calling on all nations to desist from any encouragement to the North Koreans and giving China every assurance that its legitimate interests along and above the Manchurian border would be safeguarded. Although nine members supported the resolution, it was vetoed by the U.S.S.R. on November 30.

Since Soviet opposition had rendered the Security Council unable to take further action, the General Assembly, at the request of the United States, considered the Chinese Communists' intervention in Korea and their attack upon the forces engaged in carrying out United Nations suppression of North Korean aggression. Despite repeated attempts to obtain agreement to a cease-fire the Chinese Communists refused to halt the fighting. At the year's end the fact of Chinese aggression was clear, although views differed among the members of the United Nations concerning what effective measures could be taken to meet it.

Thus the results of the first united action against aggression taken by the United Nations were at the end of 1950 still uncertain. The effort against the North Korean aggression had almost achieved complete success when the new and graver intervention took place. While as between the forces of the United Nations and of the Chinese aggressors military fortunes fluctuated on the winter battlefields of Korea, it was clear that, in any case, a tremendous deterrent to future aggression had been created. No group contemplating aggression could be sure that it would not find itself in a military struggle with combined forces of the United Nations. It could also not be denied that the quick and courageous action of the United States—the only member with substantial military forces available in the area—had furnished an example of great import for the future.

Appreciation of this country's decisive action was eloquently expressed by Sir Carl Berendsen, the representative of New Zealand in the General Assembly:

"The United States has proved to all that care to hear that it is still possible for a great power at once and unerringly to choose the path of honor and the path of right and at once to set its feet upon that path with faith and in the confident knowledge that it will be supported by countless millions who hold the same ideals, the same beliefs. And the immediate response of the United Kingdom—indeed, of so many nations of the free world—has proved that there is indeed hope for mankind and for the eternal principles of right and justice. Our special gratitude—and let us not forget it for one moment—is due to those United States combat troops who, in South Korea, have held the ramparts of civilization against overwhelming odds."

UNITING FOR PEACE

In addition to its collective armed resistance to aggression in Korea, the United Nations in effect made a new start in the effort to create forces and measures for repelling future aggressions. The General Assembly took this major step through its adoption, by an overwhelming majority of votes, of the resolution on Uniting for Peace. The original proposal was placed before the General Assembly by Secretary of State Acheson on behalf of the United States; the draft resolution was submitted by eight members, one of which was the United States. Recognizing expressly primary responsibility of the Security Council for the maintenance of international peace and security, the resolution provides, broadly speaking, for the more effective and consistent exercise of its Charter functions in this field by the General Assembly if failure of the Security Council to exercise its responsibilities makes this necessary. One major section of the resolution declares the intention of the Assembly, if the Security Council is unable to exercise its responsibilities in a case where there appears to be a breach of the peace or act of aggression, to consider the matter immediately with a view to making appropriate recommendations. In the resolution the Assembly amended its rules of procedure to provide that it will meet in emergency special session within 24 hours upon receipt of a request of the Security Council on the vote of any seven members, or by a majority of members of the United Nations. By another major section of the resolution, the Assembly established a Peace Observation Commission which can dispatch observers to watch and report on developments at points of international tension. Finally, the resolution provides for a new program having in view the creation of United Nations forces and the preparation of measures of collective security. To this end, it established the Collective Measures Committee which is to study what measures can be taken to strengthen international peace and security and report to the General Assembly and the Security Council by September 1, 1951. An important provision recommends that members maintain within their armed forces elements which could be made available to the United Nations pursuant to recommendations of the Security Council or the General Assembly.

Although it was the United States which originally proposed measures of this character, the resolution as finally adopted embodies ideas from a number of members and represents the consensus of practically all members of the United Nations except the Soviet bloc. It is a new effort by the whole United Nations to make concrete progress in the long task of establishing an effective system of collective security, the need for which was sharply disclosed during 1950. The effectiveness of the "Uniting for Peace" resolution will depend upon the measures which member states take to carry out a program based on its provisions.

Although the crucial problem of aggression—present and future—dominated the discussion at Lake Success during the second half of the year, the manifold activities of the United Nations, political and nonpolitical, were carried on as before. Some new problems were brought to the United Nations for consideration. Many other problems were continued from previous years. In a number of instances action on behalf of the United Nations was carried forward mainly by special commissions in the field.

GENERAL ASSEMBLY'S PEACEKEEPING ACTIONS

General Assembly Resolution 377 (V) on Uniting for Peace *

November 3, 1950

The General Assembly,

Recognizing that the first two stated Purposes of the United Nations are:

> "To maintain international peace and security. and to that end: to take effective collective measures for the prevention and removal of threats to the peace, and for the suppression of acts of aggression or other breaches of the peace, and to bring about by peaceful means, and in conformity with the principles of justice and international law, adjustment or settlement of international disputes or situations which might lead to a breach of the peace", and
>
> "To develop friendly relations among nations based on respect for the principle of equal rights and self-determination of peoples, and to take other appropriate measures to strengthen universal peace,"

Reaffirming that it remains the primary duty of all Members of the United Nations, when involved in an international dispute, to seek settlement of such a dispute by peaceful means through the procedures laid down in Chapter VI of the Charter, and recalling the successful achievements of the United Nations in this regard on a number of previous occasions,

Finding that international tension exists on a dangerous scale,

Recalling its resolution 290 (IV) entitled "Essentials of peace," which states that disregard of the Principles of the Charter of the United Nations is primarily responsible for the continuance of international tension, and desiring to contribute further to the objectives of that resolution,

Reaffirming the importance of the exercise by the Security Council of its primary responsibility for the maintenance of international peace and security, and the duty of the permanent members to seek unanimity and to exercise restraint in the use of the veto,

Reaffirming that the initiative in negotiating the agreements for armed forces provided for in Article 43 of the Charter belongs to the Security Council, and desiring to ensure that, pending the conclusion of such agreements, the United Nations has at its disposal means for maintaining international peace and security,

Conscious that failure of the Security Council to discharge its responsibilities on behalf of all the Member States, particularly those responsibilities referred to in the two preceding paragraphs, does not relieve Member States of their obligations or the United Nations of its responsibility under the Charter to maintain international peace and security,

Recognizing in particular that such failure does not deprive the General Assembly of its rights or relieve it of its responsibilities under the Charter in regard to the maintenance of international peace and security,

Recognizing that discharge by the General Assembly of its responsibilities in these respects calls for possibilities of observation which would ascertain the facts and expose aggressors; for the existence of armed forces which could be used collectively;

*U.N. General Assembly, *Official Records*, 5th sess., 1950-51, Supplement 20, pp. 10-12.

and for the possibility of timely recommendation by the General Assembly to Members of the United Nations for collective action which, to be effective, should be prompt,

A

1. Resolves that if the Security Council, because of lack of unanimity of the permanent members, fails to exercise its primary responsibility for the maintenance of international peace and security in any case where there appears to be a threat to the peace, breach of the peace, or act of aggression, the General Assembly shall consider the matter immediately with a view to making appropriate recommendations to Members for collective measures, including in the case of a breach of the peace or act of aggression the use of armed force when necessary, to maintain or restore international peace and security. If not in session at the time, the General Assembly may meet in emergency special session within twenty-four hours of the request therefor. Such emergency special session shall be called if requested by the Security Council on the vote of any seven members, or by a majority of the Members of the United Nations;

2. Adopts for this purpose the amendments to its rules of procedure set forth in the annex to the present resolution;

B

3. Establishes a Peace Observation Commission which, for the calendar years 1951 and 1952, shall be composed of fourteen Members, namely: China, Colombia, Czechoslovakia, France, India, Iraq, Israel, New Zealand, Pakistan, Sweden, the Union of Soviet Socialist Republics, the United Kingdom of Great Britain and Northern Ireland, the United States of America and Uruguay, and which could observe and report on the situation in any area where there exists international tension the continuance of which is likely to endanger the maintenance of international peace and security. Upon the invitation or with the consent of the State into whose territory the Commission would go, the General Assembly, or the Interim Committee when the Assembly is not in session, may utilize the Commission if the Security Council is not exercising the functions assigned to it by the Charter with respect to the matter in question. Decisions to utilize the Commission shall be made on the affirmative vote of two-thirds of the members present and voting. The Security Council may also utilize the Commission in accordance with its authority under the Charter;

4. Decides that the Commission shall have authority in its discretion to appoint sub-commissions and to utilize the services of observers to assist it in the performance of its functions;

5. Recommends to all governments and authorities that they co-operate with the Commission and assist it in the performance of its functions;

6. Requests the Secretary-General to provide the necessary staff and facilities, utilizing, where directed by the Commission, the United Nations Panel of Field Observers envisaged in General Assembly resolution 297 B (IV);

C

7. Invites each Member of the United Nations to survey its resources in order to

determine the nature and scope of the assistance it may be in a position to render in support of any recommendations of the Security Council or of the General Assembly for the restoration of international peace and security;

8. Recommends to the States Members of the United Nations that each Member maintain within its national armed forces elements so trained, organized and equipped that they could promptly be made available, in accordance with its constitutional processes, for service as a United Nations unit or units, upon recommendation by the Security Council or the General Asembly, without prejudice to the use of such elements in exercise of the right of individual or collective self-defence recognized in Article 51 of the Charter;

9. Invites the Members of the United Nations to inform the Collective Measures Committee provided for in paragraph 11 as soon as possible of the measures taken in implementation of the preceding paragraph;

10. Requests the Secretary-General to appoint, with the approval of the Committee provided for in paragraph 11, a panel of military experts who could be made available, on request, to Member States wishing to obtain technical advice regarding the organizations, training, and equipment for prompt service as United Nations units of the elements referred to in paragraph 8;

D

11. Establishes a Collective Measures Committee consisting of fourteen Members, namely: Australia, Belgium, Brazil, Burma, Canada, Egypt, France, Mexico, Philippines, Turkey, the United Kingdom of Great Britain and Northern Ireland, the United States of America, Venezuela and Yugoslavia, and directs the Committee, in consultation with the Secretary-General and with such Member States as the Committee finds appropriate, to study and make a report to the Security Council and the General Assembly, not later than 1 September 1951, on methods, including those in section C of the present resolution, which might be used to maintain and strengthen international peace and security in accordance with the Purposes and Principles of the Charter, taking account of collective self-defence and regional arrangements (Articles 51 and 52 of the Charter);

12. Recommends to all Member States that they co-operate with the Committee and assist it in the performance of its functions;

13. Requests the Secretary-General to furnish the staff and facilities necessary for the effective accomplishment of the purposes set forth in sections C and D of the present resolution;

E

14. Is fully conscious that, in adopting the proposals set forth above, enduring peace will not be secured solely by collective security arrangements against breaches of international peace and acts of aggression, but that a genuine and lasting peace depends also upon the observance of all the Principles and Purposes established in the Charter of the United Nations, upon the implementation of the resolutions of the Security Council, the General Assembly and other principal organs of the United Nations intended to achieve the maintenance of international peace and security, and

especially upon respect for and observance of human rights and fundamental freedoms for all and on the establishment and maintenance of conditions of economic and social well-being in all countries; and accordingly

15. *Urges* Member States to respect fully, and to intensify, joint action, in co-operation with the United Nations, to develop and stimulate universal respect for and observance of human rights and fundamental freedoms, and to intensify individual and collective efforts to achieve conditions of economic stability and social progress, particularly through the development of under-developed countries and areas.

ANNEX

The rules of procedure of the General Assembly are amended in the following respects:

1. The present text of rule 8 shall become paragraph (a) of that rule, and a new paragraph (b) shall be added to read as follows:

"Emergency special sessions pursuant to resolution 377 A (V) shall be convened within twenty-four hours of the receipt by the Secretary-General of a request for such a session from the Security Council, on the vote of any seven members thereof, or of a request from a majority of the Members of the United Nations expressed by vote in the Interim Committee or otherwise, or of the concurrence of a majority of Members as provided in rule 9."

2. The present text of rule 9 shall become paragraph (a) of that rule and a new paragraph (b) shall be added to read as follows:

"This rule shall apply also to a request by any Member for an emergency special session pursuant to resolution 377 A (V). In such a case the Secretary-General shall communicate with other Members by the most expeditious means of communication available."

3. Rule 10 is amended by adding at the end thereof the following:

". . . In the case of an emergency special session convened pursuant to rule 8 (b), the Secretary-General shall notify the Members of the United Nations at least twelve hours in advance of the opening of the session."

4. Rule 16 is amended by adding at the end thereof the following:

". . . The provisional agenda of an emergency special session shall be communicated to the Members of the United Nations simultaneously with the communication summoning the session."

5. Rule 19 is amended by adding at the end thereof the following:

". . . During an emergency special session additional items concerning the matters dealt with in resolution 377 A (V) may be added to the agenda by a two-thirds majority of the Members present and voting."

6. There is added a new rule to precede rule 65 to read as follows:

"Notwithstanding the provisions of any other rule and unless the General Assembly decides otherwise, the Assembly, in case of an emergency special session, shall convene in plenary session only and proceed directly to consider the item proposed for consideration in the request for the holding of the session. without previous reference to the General Committee or to any other Committee; the President and Vice-Presidents for such emergency special sessions shall be, respectively, the Chairman of those delegations from which were elected the President and Vice-Presidents of the previous session."

B`

For the purpose of maintaining international peace and security, in accordance with the Charter of the United Nations, and, in particular, with Chapters V, VI and VII of the Charter,

The General Assembly

Recommends to the Security Council:

That it should take the necessary steps to ensure that the action provided for under the Charter is taken with respect to threats to the peace, breaches of the peace or acts of aggression and with respect to the peaceful settlement of disputes or situations likely to endanger the maintenance of international peace and security;

That it should take the necessary steps to ensure that the action provided for under 47 of the Charter of the United Nations regarding the placing of armed forces at the disposal of the Security Council by the States Members of the United Nations and the effective functioning of the Military Staff Committee;

The above dispositions should in no manner prevent the General Assembly from fulfilling its functions under resolution 377 A (V).

C

The General Assembly,

Recognizing that the primary function of the United Nations Organization is to maintain and promote peace, security and justice among all nations,

Recognizing the responsibility of all Member States to promote the cause of international peace in accordance with their obligations as provided in the Charter,

Recognizing that the Charter charges the Security Council with the primary responsibility for maintaining international peace and security,

Reaffirming the importance of unanimity among the permanent members of the Security Council on all problems which are likely to threaten world peace,

Recalling General Assembly resolution 190 (III) entitled "Appeal to the Great Powers to renew their efforts to compose their differences and establish a lasting peace,"

Recommends to the permanent members of the Security Council that:

(a) They meet and discuss, collectively or otherwise, and, if necessary, with other States concerned, all problems which are likely to threaten international peace and hamper the activities of the United Nations, with a view to their resolving fundamental differences and reaching agreement in accordance with the spirit and letter of the Charter;

(b) They advise the General Assembly and, when it is not in session, the Members of the United Nations, as soon as appropriate, of the results of their consultations.

General Assembly Resolution 498 (V) on Intervention of Central People's Government of People's Republic of China in Korea*

February 1, 1951

(Resolution Adopted on the Report of the First Committee)

The General Assembly,

Noting that the Security Council, because of lack of unanimity of the permanent members, has failed to exercise its primary responsibility for the maintenance of international peace and security in regard to Chinese Communist intervention in Korea,

Noting that the Central People's Government of the People's Republic of China has not accepted United Nations proposals to bring about a cessation of hostilities in Korea with a view to peaceful settlement, and that its armed forces continue their invasion of Korea and their large-scale attacks upon United Nations forces there,

1. Finds that the Central People's Government of the People's Republic of China, by giving direct aid and assistance to those who were already committing aggression in Korea and by engaging in hostilities against United Nations forces there, has itself engaged in aggression in Korea;

2. Calls upon the Central People's Government of the People's Republic of China to cause its forces and nationals in Korea to cease hostilities against the United Nations forces and to withdraw from Korea;

3. Affirms the determination of the United Nations to continue its action in Korea to meet the aggression;

4. Calls upon all States and authorities to continue to lend every assistance to the United Nations action in Korea;

5. Calls upon all States and authorities to refrain from giving any assistance to the aggressors in Korea;

6. Requests a Committee composed of the members of the Collective Measures Committee as a matter of urgency to consider additional measures to be employed to meet this aggression and to report thereon to the General Assembly, it being understood that the Committee is authorized to defer its report if the Good Offices Committee referred to in the following paragraph reports satisfactory progress in its efforts;

7. Affirms that it continues to be the policy of the United Nations to bring about a cessation of hostilities in Korea and the achievement of United Nations objectives in Korea by peaceful means, and requests the President of the General Assembly to designate forthwith two persons who would meet with him at any suitable opportunity to use their good offices to this end.

The President of the General Assembly, on 19 February 1951, informed (A/1779) the members of the General Assembly that Dr. Luis Padilla Nervo (Mexico) and Mr. Sven Grafstrom (Sweden) had accepted his invitation to form with him the Good Offices Committee, as provided in the above resolution.

*Ibid., Supplement 20A, p. 1.

General Assembly Resolution 500 (V) on Additional Measures to Meet the Aggression in Korea*

May 18, 1951

(Resolution Adopted on the Report of the First Committee)

The General Assembly,

Noting the report of the Additional Measures Committee dated 14 May 1951,

Recalling its resolution 498 (V) of 1 February 1951,

Noting that:

(a) The Additional Measures Committee established by that resolution has considered additional measures to be employed to meet the aggression in Korea,

(b) The Additional Measures Committee has reported that a number of States have already taken measures designed to deny contributions to the military strength of the forces opposing the United Nations in Korea,

(c) The Additional Measures Committee has also reported that certain economic measures designed further to deny such contributions would support and supplement the military action of the United Nations in Korea and would assist in putting an end to the aggression,

1. Recommends that every State:

(a) Apply an embargo on the shipment to areas under the control of the Central People's Government of the People's Republic of China and of the North Korean authorities of arms, ammunition and implements of war, atomic energy materials, petroleum, transportation materials of strategic value, and items useful in the production of arms, ammunition and implements of war;

(b) Determine which commodities exported from its territory fall within the embargo, and apply controls to give effect to the embargo;

(c) Prevent by all means within its jurisdiction the circumvention of controls on shipments applied by other States pursuant to the present resolution;

(d) Co-operate with other States in carrying out the purposes of this embargo;

(e) Report to the Additional Measures Committee, within thirty days and thereafter at the request of the Committee, on the measures taken in accordance with the present resolution;

2. Requests the Additional Measures Committee:

(a) To report to the General Assembly, with recommendations as appropriate, on the general effectiveness of the embargo and the desirability of continuing, extending or relaxing it;

(b) To continue its consideration of additional measures to be employed to meet the aggression in Korea, and to report thereon further to the General Assembly, it being understood that the Committee is authorized to defer its report if the Good Offices Committee reports satisfactory progress in its efforts;

3. Reaffirms that it continues to be the policy of the United Nations to bring about a cessation of hostilities in Korea, and the achievement of United Nations objectives in Korea by peaceful means, and requests the Good Offices Committee to continue its good offices.

*Ibid., p. 2.

Report by President Eisenhower to Congress on the Resignation of Trygve Lie*

1952

*   *   *

On November 10, 1952, Mr. Lie, in letters to the Presidents of the General Assembly and the Security Council, submitted his resignation as Secretary-General. In a statement to the Assembly Mr. Lie made the following explanation of his decision:

> First of all, I ask you to remember that I wanted to retire in 1950 at the end of my five-year term. I agreed to continue only because the aggression in Korea created circumstances that put me under an obligation to carry on.
>
> Now I feel the situation is somewhat different. The United Nations has thrown back aggression in Korea. There can be an armistice if the Soviet Union, the Chinese People's Republic and the North Koreans are sincere in their wish to end the fighting.
>
> If they are sincere, then a new secretary-general, who is the unanimous choice of the five great Powers, the Security Council and the General Assembly, may be more helpful than I can be. On the other hand, if the world situation should go from bad to worse, at least I would not want the position of secretary-general to hinder in the slightest degree any hope of reaching a new understanding that would prevent world disaster.

The General Assembly on February 1, 1946, accepting the recommendation of the Security Council, had appointed Trygve Lie as the first Secretary-General of the United Nations for a term of 5 years. Since Mr. Lie's term was due to expire in February 1951, the Security Council in October 1950 held a number of private meetings in an effort to make a recommendation on his reappointment or on the appointment of a successor. Because the Soviet Union was determined to oust Mr. Lie and a number of other members, including the United States, refused to agree to this, the Council was unable to make any recommendation. In these circumstances the Assembly, which had fixed Mr. Lie's original term of office, adopted on November 1, 1950, a resolution under which Mr. Lie was continued in office for a further period of 3 years. The United States was one of the 15 cosponsors of this resolution and strongly supported its adoption. As Ambassador Austin pointed out at the time, the Soviet Union, which had vetoed the reappointment of Mr. Lie in the Security Council, had intended to punish him for carrying out faithfully the Security Council decisions to resist aggression in Korea. The issue had thus become focused on principles, and the use of the veto to punish Mr. Lie had made it impossible to consider new nominations on their merits. Adoption of the Assembly's resolution was necessary, the United States representative explained, to maintain the integrity and independence of the office of the Secretary-General. The Soviet-bloc members vigorously opposed Mr. Lie's continuation in office and have not recognized him as the Secretary-General since the expiration of his initial term.

The General Assembly on November 13 decided to include the question of the appointment of the Secretary-General on its agenda. However, this question had not been considered when the session recessed on December 22 and therefore remained for discussion at the resumed seventh session.

*   *   *

*U.S. Participation in the U.N., Report by the President to Congress for the Year 1952, (Washington, 1953), pp. 95-96.

HUNGARY

Report on Hungary *

1956

What began as a peaceful student demonstration in Budapest on October 23, 1956, was to precipitate a series of fateful events culminating in a wholesale uprising of the Hungarian people against their Communist masters, crushed only by massive Soviet armed intervention. From the outset there were demands for withdrawal of Soviet troops from Hungary, free multiparty elections, and a new independent government. Late in the evening of October 23 the first bloodshed occurred, and fighting went on intermittently between the people on the one hand, and units of the AVH (the Hungarian secret police) and the Soviet army on the other. Many Hungarian troops threw their support to the people. Additional Soviet units entered Hungary, and by October 26 fairly heavy fighting was going on in Budapest and throughout Hungary.

Security Council Consideration

It was in these circumstances that the United States, France, and the United Kingdom, on October 27, submitted "The Situation in Hungary" for the agenda of the Security Council and requested an urgent meeting. They explained that this request was based upon the situation "created by the action of foreign military forces in Hungary in violently repressing the rights of the Hungarian people which are secured by the Treaty of Peace to which the Governments of Hungary and the Allied and Associated Powers are parties." A number of other members addressed individual communications to the Security Council President associating themselves with this tripartite initiative.

On October 28 the Security Council inscribed the Hungarian item on its agenda by a vote of 9 to 1 (U.S.S.R.), with 1 abstention (Yugoslavia), despite the contention in a communication circulated to Council members from the Permanent Representative of Hungary that the events there and the measures taken were exclusively within Hungary's domestic jurisdiction. Supporting Council consideration, the U.S. representative, Ambassador Henry Cabot Lodge, pointed out that the Hungarian people were doing no more than to demand the rights and freedoms affirmed in the U.N. Charter and specifically guaranteed by the peace treaty. The Council's anxiety reflected the deep and worldwide concern over the bloodshed in Hungary. The United States, he said, was prepared to join in considering what the Council could do to bring an end to this situation and to establish conditions under which the Hungarian people could enjoy their fundamental human rights.

The next day Israel invaded Egypt's Sinai Peninsula. Its action was followed on October 30 by Anglo-French ultimatums to Egypt and Israel, implemented on October 31 by Anglo-French military action for the declared purpose of separating the combatants and securing freedom of passage through the Suez Canal. These far-reach-

*U.S. Participation in the U.N., 1956 Reports, pp. 82-106.

ing events required urgent United Nations action and tended to draw attention to some extent from the developing crisis in Hungary.

Moreover, at this precise moment it apeared that Soviet units were withdrawing from Hungary. On October 28 a Soviet-Hungarian agreement was announced for the immediate withdrawal of Soviet forces from Budapest. Another apparently encouraging development was the announcement on October 30 by Hungarian Premier Imre Nagy, who had formed a new government on October 27, of the abolition of the one-party system, the reestablishment of the democratic cooperation of the coalition parties as they existed in 1945, and the formation of a new cabinet. Significance was likewise attached to a Soviet policy declaration in Moscow issued on October 30 stating Soviet agreement to the withdrawal of Soviet military units from Budapest and Soviet readiness to start negotiations with the Government of Hungary and with the governments of other states participating in the Warsaw Pact concerning the stationing of Soviet troops in Hungary. By October 31 Soviet units began to pull out of Budapest. Their departure was followed by large popular demonstrations and the destruction of Soviet monuments and Communist insignia throughout the city; many political prisoners, including Cardinal Mindszenty, were released.

By November 1 the outward situation was peaceful. With the Nagy Government in power there appeared to be a basis for a greater expression of national independence. At that moment, however, the Hungarian Government learned of the entry of new Soviet units. Premier Nagy called in the Soviet Ambassador to demand their immediate withdrawal and to inform him that Hungary was giving immediate notice of its withdrawal from the Warsaw Pact and was appealing to the United Nations and the four great powers to guarantee Hungarian neutrality. Late that day the United Nations Secretary-General received a cablegram from Premier Nagy reporting this development and requesting that an item be placed on the agenda of the forthcoming General Assembly entitled "The Question of Hungary's Neutrality and the Defense of this Neutrality by the Four Great Powers."

In these confused circumstances the Security Council met again November 2. No Hungarian representative participated because it was questioned whether the permanent Hungarian delegation in New York still represented Hungary, particularly since it was without instructions or first-hand information on the situation in Hungary.

Ambassador Lodge referred to the emergency General Assembly session convened the previous day to consider the grave crisis in Egypt, a situation requiring continued close attention but which could not, he said, justify the Council's ignoring the equally urgent and dangerous situation developing in Hungary. Praising the "valiant struggle of the Hungarian people ... to assert their right to an independent national existence," he regarded the news of the entry of new Soviet units with foreboding, but he also recalled the significant October 30 Soviet declaration regarding relations of the nations of Eastern Europe and the U.S.S.R. since it emphasized that "the countries of the great commonwealth of Socialist nations can build their relations only on the principle of full equality, respect of territorial integrity, state independence and sovereignty, and noninterference with the domestic affairs of one another." He observed that President Eisenhower on October 31 had emphasized that "if the Soviet Union indeed faithfully acts upon its announced intention, the world will witness the greatest forward stride towards justice, trust, and understanding among nations in our generation." He stressed the need for early arrangements to obtain a clearer picture of events in Hungary and suggested that the Secretary-General might appropriately communicate urgently with Budapest to this end.

Later the same evening a second communication was received from Hungary reporting new large-scale movements of Soviet troops and requesting the Secretary-General "to call upon the great powers to recognize the neutrality of Hungary and ask the Security Council to instruct the Soviet and Hungarian Governments to start the negotiations [for withdrawal of troops] immediately."

The Security Council reconvened on November 3. Ambassador Lodge addressed a series of questions, first to the Hungarian representative (a member of the permanent Hungarian delegation was present) to provide further details on the events reported in the Hungarian communications and, second, to the Soviet representative on whether new Soviet units were entering Hungary or negotiations for Soviet wthdrawal were under way. He submitted a draft resolution calling upon the U.S.S.R. to desist forthwith from any form of intervention in Hungary's internal affairs, and expressing the earnest hope that, under appropriate arrangements with Hungary, it would withdraw all Soviet forces from Hungary without delay. This proposal also affirmed the right of the Hungarian people to a government "responsive to its national aspirations and dedicated to its independence and well-being." Finally, it requested the Secretary-General to explore urgently the need of the Hungarian people for emergency supplies. At the very end of the meeting the Soviet representative, in response to probing questions from other Council members, stated that he could confirm that negotiations were going on in Budapest between Hungarian and Soviet representatives in regard to Soviet troops in Hungary. Consequently, the Council did not then vote on the U.S. proposal.

That same evening the General Assembly was pursuing its consideration of the critical Middle Eastern situation. During the meeting reports of large-scale Soviet military intervention in Hungary came in. Ambassador Lodge, supported by others, immediately requested an emergency Security Council meeting. The Council convened at 3:00 a.m. on Sunday, November 4.

Ambassador Lodge expressed concern at information received from the American Legation in Budapest reporting large-scale fighting and bombing. He reported that the Legation had granted asylum to Cardinal Mindszenty. He urged immediate action on the pending draft resolution, revised by the substitution of a provision calling upon the U.S.S.R. to cease the introduction of additional forces into Hungary and to withdraw all its forces without delay in place of the expression of hope previously included that the U.S.S.R., under appropriate arrangements with the Government of Hungary, would withdraw its forces.

Except for the Yugoslav representative who did not speak and the Soviet representative who contended no Council action was necessary, the other Council members strongly supported the U.S. proposal. It received nine affirmative votes (Australia, Belgium, China, Cuba, France, Iran, Peru, the United Kingdom, the United States) and one negative vote (U.S.S.R.). Yugoslavia did not participate. The Soviet veto blocked adoption.

Ambassador Lodge at once tabled a resolution calling for an emergency special session of the General Assembly under the "Uniting for Peace" procedure "in order to make appropriate recommendations concerning the situation in Hungary." The Soviet representative alone opposed it, arguing again that such Assembly consideration meant interference in Hungary's internal affairs. The resolution was adopted by a vote of 10 to 1 (U.S.S.R.).

General Assembly Action at Special Session

The General Assembly convened in special emergency session again at 4:00 p.m. Sunday, November 4. The Soviet representative immediately opposed inclusion in the agenda and any discussion of the Hungarian item on the ground it would involve intervention in Hungary's domestic affairs contrary to article 2 (7) of the Charter. His position was challenged by the Australian representative who considered that certain provisions of the Hungarian peace treaty gave the situation international character, particularly because through the Warsaw Pact the Soviet Union was seeking to use its troops to circumvent treaty provisions. By a vote of 53 to 1, with 7 abstentions, the item was inscribed.

Ambassador Lodge, speaking early in the debate, drew attention to the appeal of Hungarian Prime Minister Nagy for help from the United Nations. After several days of ominous reports, the United Nations now saw revealed a "sickening picture of duplicity and double dealing" on the part of the U.S.S.R. In this connection he noted statements in the Soviet and Eastern European press on October 28 and 29 welcoming the new liberalized leadership in Hungary that is now denounced as counterrevolutionary. He urged that the Assembly not be deceived by the cynical and wanton Soviet aggression against the Hungarian people and its government or by the creation of a puppet clique to serve the Soviet masters of Hungary.

Ambassador Lodge submitted a draft resolution upon which he sought prompt action. In its preambular paragraphs the resolution recalled those provisions of the peace treaty guaranteeing the enjoyment of human rights and fundamental freedoms and apposite Charter principles, expressed the conviction that recent events in Hungary manifested the desire of the Hungarian people to exercise and enjoy fully these rights, and condemned the use of Soviet military forces to suppress the efforts of the Hungarian people to reassert their rights. It called upon the U.S.S.R. to desist forthwith from all armed attack on the peoples of Hungary and from any form of intervention, particularly armed intervention, in Hungary's internal affairs and to cease introduction of additional armed forces and withdraw its forces without delay from Hungary and affirmed the right of the Hungarian people to a government responsive to its national-aspirations and dedicated to its independence and well-being. The Secretary-General was requested to investigate and to observe the situation directly, through representatives named by him, to report to the Assembly at the earliest moment, and to suggest means to bring an end to the situation in accordance with Charter principles. The resolution also called upon Hungary and the U.S.S.R. to admit observers to Hungary and to permit them to travel freely, and upon all members to cooperate with the Secretary-General and his representatives; it requested the Secretary-General, in consultation with heads of appropriate specialized agencies, to inquire on an urgent basis into the needs of the Hungarian people for food, medicine, and other similar supplies and to report as soon as possible, asking all members to cooperate in making available emergency supplies to the Hungarian people.

The Soviet representative sought to answer the charges of Soviet intervention by alleging that the legitimate and progressive movement of the Hungarian workers was joined by "dark forces of reaction and counterrevolution" attempting to undermine Hungary's popular democracy and to reestablish capitalism. The legitimate Hungarian "people's government" required assistance from the Soviet Union, he contended, to combat these counterrevolutionary forces, aided by imperialist powers. The Soviet representatives argued further that by bringing the Hungarian situation to the United Nations, France, the United Kingdom, and the United States were seeking "to create a smoke screen in order to divert attention from the armed aggression undertaken by the United Kingdom and France against Egypt."

On French initiative the operative paragraph of the U.S. draft resolution was amplified to request the Secretary-General to investigate "the situation caused by foreign intervention in Hungary." Ambassador Lodge immediately accepted this amendment.

The resolution was adopted by a vote of 50 to 8 (Albania, Byelorussia, Bulgaria, Czechoslovakia, Poland, Rumania, Ukraine, U.S.S.R.), with 15 abstentions (Afghanistan, Burma, Ceylon, Egypt, Finland, India, Indonesia, Iraq, Jordan, Libya, Nepal, Saudi Arabia, Syria, Yemen, Yugoslavia). Hungary did not participate, having received no official information or instructions from Budapest.

Later on November 4, however, the Secretary-General received a cable from Budapest declaring tha "the Revolutionary Workers' and Peasants' Government of Hungary" regarded the requests of the Nagy Government for United Nations discussion of the Hungarian question as having "no legal force" and that it objected to U.N. consideration because the question was within Hungary's exclusive jurisdiction.

Meantime, fighting continued in Hungary. Despite large-scale Soviet military activities the Hungarian people resisted heroically. By November 7, however, in the fact of enormous odds and heavy casualties, fighting began to subside. Refugees flooded across Hungary's borders.

During these 3 days the United Nations was occupied exclusively with the equally critical situation in the Middle East: the U.N. Emergency Force was established; on November 6 the British and French announced a cease-fire in Egypt; on November 7 the Assembly called for immediate withdrawal of British, French, and Israeli forces from Egypt; and the Secretary-General began arrangements for putting UNEF into the area.

With one critical phase of the Middle Eastern situation behind it, the General Assembly, on November 8, resumed consideration of the Hungarian situation. At the outset a number of delegates explained their vote on the November 4 resolution. Most of the delegations abstaining based their position on lack of information, obscurity of the actual situation in Hungary, and the desirability of not acting hastily. However, all expressed grave concern over the armed intervention of the Soviet Union.

Following up the November 4 resolution, Italy, Cuba, Ireland, Pakistan, and Peru jointly submitted a resolution whereby, after noting with deep concern the nonimplementation of the November 4 resolution, the Assembly would again call upon the U.S.S.R. to withdraw its forces. It would further consider that free elections should be held in Hungary under U.N. auspices as soon as law and order had been restored and would reaffirm the request to the Secretary-General to continue to investigate the situation through his representatives and to report on compliance in the shortest possible time.

Many delegations also expressed their willingness to contribute to the relief needs of the Hungarian people. These sentiments were given form in a two-part resolution submitted by the United States on November 9 dealing with the needs of the Hungarian people for emergency assistance. The resolution called upon the U.S.S.R. to cease actions against the Hungarian people in violation of accepted standards and principles of international law, justice, and morality. It called upon the Hungarian authorities to facilitate, and the Soviet Union not to interfere with, the distribution of relief supplies and to cooperate fully with the U.N. specialized agencies and other international organizations, such as the International Red Cross. The second part of the resolution requested the Secretary-General to call upon the U.N. High Commissioner for Refugees to consult with other appropriate international agencies and interested governments with a view to making speedy and effective arrangements for emergency assistance to the increasingly large number of refugees seeking asylum in neighboring countries and urging members to make special contributions for this purpose.

In introducing this resolution, Ambassador Lodge called attention to President Eisenhower's announcement the preceding evening that 5,000 refugees would be admitted to the United States. He also announced that the United States would vote for the five-power resolution.

Meantime, Austria introduced another resolution dealing with relief activities. It was drafted to eliminate all references to the cause of the fighting in Hungary, particularly Soviet armed intervention, on the assumption that greater relief assistance might be forthcoming if placed exclusively on humanitarian grounds. This assumption was also reflected in amendments to the two-part U.S. draft resolution proposed by Indonesia, Ceylon, and India which deleted all references to Soviet intervention.

These amendments were strongly opposed by Cuba and the United States. Ambassador Lodge pointed out that his Government possessed first-hand information regarding Soviet interference with the distribution of relief supplies and Soviet actions against Hungarian civilians in violation of accepted international standards. There was no point in saying that certain things were not happening when in fact they were; the United Nations was a moral organization with a moral standard, and morality could not be ignored. The Indian representative rejoined that a remedy to the Hungarian situation could "not be found in throwing political stones at people whom one does not like"; moreover, all delegations did not have access to information confirming Soviet actions in Hungary and the Secretary-General had not yet reported to the Assembly on the situation.

The Assembly voted on the three draft resolutions and amendments on November 9. The five-power resolution was adopted by a vote of 48 to 11 (Albania, Bulgaria, Byelorussia, Czechoslovakia, Hungary, India, Poland, Rumania, Ukraine, U.S.S.R., Yugoslavia), with 16 abstentions (Afghanistan, Austria, Burma, Cambodia, Ceylon, Egypt, Finland, Haiti, Indonesia, Jordan, Lebanon, Libya, Nepal, Saudi Arabia, Syria, Yemen). Next the Assembly rejected the amendments submitted by Ceylon, Indonesia and India to the U.S. resolution by a vote of 45 to 18 (Afghanistan, Austria, Burma, Cambodia, Ceylon, Finland, Hungary, India, Indonesia, Jordan, Lebanon, Libya, Nepal, Poland, Saudi Arabia, Syria, Yemen, Yugoslavia), with 12 abstentions (Albania, Bulgaria, Byelorussia, Czechoslovakia, Egypt, Iran, Iraq, Laos, Rumania, Thailand, Ukraine, U.S.S.R.). The U.S. resolution was then adopted by a vote of 53 to 9

(Albania, Bulgaria, Byelorussia, Czechoslovakia, Hungary, Poland, Rumania, Ukraine, U.S.S.R.), with 13 abstentions (Afghanistan, Burma, Cambodia, Ceylon, Egypt, India, Indonesia, Jordan, Lebanon, Saudi Arabia, Syria, Yemen, Yugoslavia).

Finally the Assembly adopted the Austrian resolution by a vote of 67 to 0, with 8 abstentions (Albania, Bulgaria, Byelorussia, Czechoslovakia, Liberia, Rumania, Ukraine, U.S.S.R.).

Following the vote, Ambassador James J. Wadsworth, referring to both the U.S. and the Austrian resolutions, announced that the U.S. Government was immediately making available $1,000,000 to the Secretary-General for use through appropriate channels for assistance to Hungarian refugees.

On November 10, to enable the imminent 11th regular session of the General Assembly to continue consideration of the Hungarian situation, the United States submitted a proposal to place the situation in Hungary on the agenda of that session. The Hungarian delegation opposed this resolution on the grounds that the subject fell within Hungary's domestic jurisdiction. Supporting this contention, the Soviet representative charged that certain circles in the United States, the United Kingdom, and France were intervening in Hungary's domestic affairs in violation of the Charter and to divert the Assembly's attention from current international questions of "utmost importance." However, the United States proposal received widespread support, with India, among others, noting that the Assembly had requested the Secretary-General to report and clearly was obligated to receive his report. After acceptance of an Italian amendment adding a provision referring to the 11th session the relevant records of the second emergency special session, the resolution was adopted by a vote of 53 to 9, with 8 abstentions.

Secretary-General's Efforts

Acting under the November 4 resolution, the Secretary-General on November 8 addressed an aide memoire to the Hungarian Foreign Minister asking whether Hungary was willing to admit his observers. On November 10 he addressed a second aide memoire to the Hungarian Foreign Minister. Noting that he had received no reply to the question whether Hungary would be willing to permit his observers to enter its territory in pursuance of the Assembly's November 4 resolution, he asked for a reply without further delay. He added that a copy of the aide memoire had also been given to the Soviet representative, with a request for his assistance. If a reply were not forthcoming shortly, the Secretary-General stated he would be obliged to submit the situation to the Assembly. The same day he received a cable from the Deputy Foreign Minister of Hungary acknowledging receipt of the aide memoire and stating that its contents were being studied. On November 11 a second cable from the Hungarian Deputy Foreign Minister stated that the text of the November 4 resolution "for technical reasons" was not yet available. Finally, on November 12 the Acting Minister of Foreign Afairs of Hungary replied in detail but completely negatively. The Hungarian cable alleged that, in the course of mass demonstrations in Hungary, organized Fascist elements and ordinary criminals had taken over the government. To restore law and order and to prevent the danger of fascism, the Revolutionary Workers' and Peasants' Government had been obliged to request the aid of Soviet troops. After restoration of order it would immediately negotiate with the U.S.S.R. for their withdrawal. The settlement of the situation in Hungary lay "exclusively within the internal legal competence of the Hungarian state," and any Assembly resolution was "illegal." Since Soviet troops were present at Hungarian request, the sending of representatives by the Secretary-General was "not warranted." Elections fell entirely within Hungary's competence. The cable went on to state that the Hungarian Government would make it possible for those Hungarians who fled abroad "as a result of the battles" to return freely and without harm. It also expressed Hungary's intention to facilitate the receipt and distribution of food and medicine, its cooperation with the International Red Cross, and its readiness to cooperate fully with U.N. agencies. After final assessment of the damages and the needs to meet them the Hungarian Government would inform the Secretary-General and meanwhile would accept gratefully all food, clothing, and medicine for Hungarian families who faced a difficult winter.

On November 10 the Secretary-General had addressed another aide memoire to the Hungarian Foreign Minister referring exclusively to the provisions of the various resolutions regarding relief assistance and aid to refugees and requesting information concerning needs of the Hungarian people for medical supplies foodstuffs and clothing from abroad. The next day a cablegram was received listing the most urgent needs in foodstuffs and medical supplies. It concluded by stating the readiness of the Hungarian Government "to conduct talks on the best means of providing the assistance required, as well as how the representatives appointed by the Secretary-General might participate in organizing assistance on the spot."

The Secretary-General replied to the Hungarian cable of November 12 on November 13, noting with satisfaction the observations on the resolutions regarding relief activities. With regard to the views expressed on the Assembly's resolution of November 4, he stated that "it would not be to the purpose" for him to enter upon a discussion concerning the Assembly's decision on November 4. The Secretary-General invited Hungary to reconsider its judgment that the sending of representatives appointed by him was not warranted "in the light of the opposite views so widely expressed by member governments in the General Assembly and reflected in the vote and, as a member of the United Nations, to cooperate with the great majority in the clarification of a situation which has given rise to such concern in the General Assembly."

On November 13 the Permanent Soviet Mission, in a note verbale to the Secretary-General replying to the latter's November 10 memorandum, stated that the Soviet position on the November 4 resolution had already been made clear and remained unchanged. As regards the dispatch of observers, the U.S.S.R. considered that this matter lay exclusively within Hungarian jurisdiction.

On November 15 the Hungarian Government again cabled the Secretary-General. Referring to his cable of November 13 and to discussions he had carried on in New York with the Hungarian Foreign Minister, it stated that Hungarian representatives would be glad to meet him in Rome at a convenient time to negotiate on aid and to "exchange views about the position taken by the Hungarian Government regarding the resolutions of the United Nations."

The next day the Secretary-General responded from Cairo to the suggested meeting in Rome. Noting that this represented a counterproposal to his own oral offer in New York to come to Budapest for a discussion of the basis for humanitarian activities by

would not disregard a request for cooperation if it came from virtually all sections of opinion in the General Assembly without any attempt to condemn or to interfere. He the United Nations, he explained that he had made the offer "to discuss in Budapest in

accepted the Belgian changes in the preamble but regarded the request for the Secretary-General to report within 72 hours as impractical, suggesting instead the phrase "without delay," which Belgium accepted. The other Belgian amendments were not acceptable, he said, and, in particular, the phrase "without prejudice to its sovereignty," which was proposed for deletion, was vital to the Indian concept of Hungary's independence and national sovereignty.

In response to inquiries, the Secretary-General stated that Hungary had replied to his communications in such a way as not to exclude the possibility of his discussing both the humanitarian and the broader aspects of the problem.

The Ceylonese representative urged unanimous action on the three-power resolution. If Hungary refused to accept observers, the Assembly would then be obliged to conclude that Hungary had done something that it should not have done. He stressed the necessity for proceeding step by step and argued that it was illogical to call upon Hungary and the Soviet Union to cease deportations since that implied deportations had occurred prior to the establishment of this fact by impartial investigation.

Late in the afternoon of November 21 the Assembly came to the vote. The Hungarian representative stated Hungary would vote against both pending resolutions and specified that Hungary's willingness to hold discussions with the Secretary-General related solely to relief problems.

The Cuban resolution as amended was adopted by a vote of 55 to 10 (Albania, Bulgaria, Byelorussia, Czechoslovakia, Hungary, Poland, Rumania, Ukraine, U.S.S.R., Yugoslavia), with 14 abstentions (Afghanistan, Egypt, Finland, India, Indonesia, Jordan, Lebanon, Libya, Morocco, Saudi Arabia, Sudan, Syria, Tunisia, Yemen).

Next the Indian resolution was put to the vote. At the request of the Philippines, a separate vote was taken on the words "without prejudice to its sovereignty" in the first operative paragraph. India indicated that if this section were deleted, the proposal would be withdrawn. The words, however, were adopted by a vote of 43 to 6, with 30 abstentions. After being voted upon in parts, the Indian resolution was adopted by a vote of 57 to 8 (Albania, Bulgaria, Byelorussia, Czechoslovakia, Hungary, Rumania, Ukraine, U.S.S.R.) with 14 abstentions (Chile, China, Cuba, Dominican Republic, Egypt, Ethiopia, Jordan, Panama, Paraguay, Poland, Saudi Arabia, Syria, Yemen, Yugoslavia).

Assistance to Refugees

The Assembly then turned to the refugee problem on the basis of a joint resolution submitted by Argentina, Belgium, Denmark, and the United States. That resolution, after preambular paragraphs noting the grave situation described in the report of the U.N. High Commissioner for Refugees and recognizing the urgent need of the tens of thousands of refugees for care and resettlement, took note with appreciation of the actions of the Secretary-General and of the Office of the High Commissioner for Refugees to assist the Hungarian refugees and requested the Secretary-General and the High Commissioner to continue their efforts. It also urged governments and non-governmental organizations to make contributions to the Secretary-General and High Commissioner or to other appropriate agencies for the care and resettlement of Hungarian refugees and to coordinate their aid programs in consultation with the High

Commissioner, requested the Secretary-General and the High Commissioner to make an immediate appeal to governments and nongovernmental agencies to meet the minimum present needs, and authorized them to make subsequent appeals on the basis of plans and estimates made by the High Commissioner with the concurrence of his Advisory Committee. Hungary submitted an amendment deleting the preambular paragraphs except for the last provision which would be modified to read "recognizing the urgent need of Hungarian refugees for care" and adding a further operative paragraph which, after taking note of the Hungarian declaration calling upon the refugees to return, would recommend to the governments of the countries concerned "to take urgent measures in order to secure a speedy return to Hungary of Hungarian nationals who as a result of the present situation became refugees."

The Assembly also had before it an interim report submitted by the Secretary-General on the problem of Hungarian refugees, stating that from October 28 to November 18, 34,000 refugees had entered Austria and that, although some of these had now gone to other countries, the flow of refugees from Hungary averaged 2,000 a day. A few other refugees had gone to Yugoslavia, but the problem in that country was by no means as serious as that in Austria. An increased effort was required to provide resources through which emergency assistance could be given to those refugees arriving in Austria. Financial estimates covering all aspects of the situation resulted in an estimated cost for 6 months of $6,530,000.

In introducing the four-power resolution the U.S. representative, Senator William Knowland, explained that the purpose was to provide for coordination and planning of the relief operations in Austria through a single organization, the Office of the High Commissioner for Refugees. He opposed the Hungarian amendments, emphasizing that the free nations of the world would certainly not agree to forced repatriation.

This resolution also was voted on November 21. The Hungarian amendments were decisively rejected. Thereafter, the four-power resolution was adopted by a vote of 69 to 2 (Hungary, Rumania), with 8 abstentions (Albania, Bulgaria, Byelorussia, Czechoslovakia, Poland, Sudan, Ukraine, U.S.S.R.). [See also Part II, p. 189.]

Report of the Secretary-General

On November 30 the Secretary-General submitted a comprehensive report on his activities under the various resolutions on Hungary adopted by the General Assembly. He recalled that the main decisions covered withdrawal of troops from Hungary and related questions, including deportations, investigation of the situation caused by foreign intervention in Hungary, and humanitarian activities, including assistance to refugees. His report of November 19, he noted, had covered the refugee problem.

On the political aspects of the problem, the Secretary-General explained that on November 28 he had transmitted letters to the Hungarian and Soviet delegations, respectively, drawing attention to the several resolutions adopted on November 21 and requesting information on points to be taken into account in an interim report. On November 29 the Soviet delegation had replied, recalling its November 13 communication, and, as regards the November 19 resolution, drawing attention to the Soviet speech of November 19 contending that "allegations of the deportation of Hungarian citizens to the U.S.S.R. are based on slanderous rumors circulated by certain groups for the purpose of misleading public opinion." No reply from Hungary had been received. No information was available concerning steps to establish compliance with Assembly decisions regarding troop withdrawal and related political matters.

The Secretary-General also reviewed his efforts to obtain permission for observers to enter Hungary. He continued to hope for a positive reaction to his offer to go personally to Budapest, which was still under consideration by the Hungarian Government. If he were invited, he would organize his visit to cover not only the humanitarian activities but also the other Assembly resolutions. His contact with the Hungarian Government should also be considered "as based on his position under the Charter, with the wider scope that such a standpoint might give to his approach." He also explained that the group of three individuals engaged in investigation of the situation had been examining material available to the Secretariat, but that the group would be unable to report until it could coordinate its findings with those that might result from the process of direct observations in Hungary. Humanitarian assistance, he reported, was well in hand.

On December 3 the Secretary-General received and circulated a cable from the Acting Hungarian Foreign Minister. It maintained that permission for observers to enter Hungary would violate its sovereignty, contrary to Charter principles. It reiterated Hungary's willingness to instruct its representatives to negotiate with the Secretary-General in Rome or New York and added that it was "ready to welcome" the Secretary-General in Budapest "at a later date as appropriate for both parties."

Further Assembly Consideration

On December 2 a new resolution submitted jointly by Argentina, Australia, Belgium, Cuba, Denmark, El Salvador, Ireland, Italy, the Netherlands, Norway, Pakistan, Sweden, Thailand, and the United States was circulated. Preambular provisions recalled the earlier Assembly resolutions and noted the report of the Secretary-General and also the failure of the Soviet Union to comply with provisions calling upon it to desist from intervention in Hungary's internal affairs, to cease deportations, and to withdraw its armed forces and cease its repression in Hungary. The operative provisions reiterated the call upon the U.S.S.R. and the Hungarian authorities to comply with the Assembly's resolutions and to permit observers to enter Hungarian territory, travel freely therein, and report their findings to the Secretary-General; requested the two governments to communicate to the Secretary-General not later than December 7 their consent to receive U.N. observers; recommended that meantime the Secretary-General arrange for dispatch of his observers to Hungary and other countries as appropriate; and requested all members to cooperate with the Secretary-General's representative for this purpose.

The General Assembly resumed consideration of the situation in Hungary on December 3. The Hungarian representative, while again protesting Assembly consideration, emphasized that Hungary was ready to receive the Secretary-General in Hungary, the date of his visit to be fixed by agreement. He was careful, however, not to make a specific commitment.

In the ensuing discussion a number of delegations took the position that the

General Assembly must continue to do everything within its power to assist the Hungarian people and that it clearly could not defer to the "shameless flouting of its injunctions" and maintain its integrity. Since the Secretary-General still hoped to achieve compliance with the Assembly's earlier resolutions, there was a general consensus that the Assembly should also make one last effort to this end before moving on to more drastic measures. The 14-power resolution met this view by repeating the call on the Hungarian and Soviet authorities but also setting a deadline for compliance after which, in the absence of compliance, the Assembly could consider what additional steps should be taken.

Ambassador Lodge emphasized the need for the Secretary-General to visit Hungary early enough and with sufficient freedom to do some good; an invitation from Hungary for a visit at a distant date would not constitute compliance. The complete contempt of the Soviet Union and of the Hungarian authorities for the provisions of the Charter, as well as their callous disregard for human decency, had been amply demonstrated. No one could argue that the Assembly had acted hastily or failed to give both governments every opportunity to fulfill their Charter obligations. The time had now come, Ambassador Lodge said, "for one final appeal," but the Assembly must also set a deadline for response.

Many other delegations, from all areas, appealed for Hungarian cooperation and for the admission of observers. There was widespread sentiment that Hungary's continued refusal to cooperate with the Secretary-General raised serious questions concerning the true state of affairs there. Serious doubts were also expressed about the representative character of the Kadar regime.

Seeking to answer some of these charges, the Hungarian representative argued at length that the only difficulties Hungary was now experiencing came about as a consequence of Western interference and because Western countries had sent arms to Fascist elements within Hungary. All the United Nations should do, he contended, was "to help the Hungarian people to return to normalcy." He announced that Hungary was ready and willing to cooperate in any international humanitarian mission and to receive the Secretary-General of the United Nations. He had been instructed, he said, to keep in continuous contact with the latter concerning his journey to Hungary, humanitarian relief, relevant information, and other questions. To implement the invitation he was ready at any time convenient to the Secretary-General to meet with him "to discuss the settlement of the date and arrangements for the visit."

The Secretary-General expressed gratification at this clarification and indicated his intention of immediately getting in touch with the Hungarian representative. The situation remained sufficiently unclear, however, that Ambassador Lodge, in pointing out that the Hungarian representative had limited his commitment to discussing the settlement of a date rather than to setting a date, proposed a 1 hour recess during which the Secretary-General and the Hungarian representative could fix a definite date. If within that period no arrangements were completed, he believed that the Assembly should act on the pending resolution. Because of other commitments, however, the President of the Assembly without dissent recessed the Assembly for a period of approximately 4 hours.

When the Assembly reconvened, the Secretary-General reported on his discussion with the Hungarian representative. Since other matters made it impossible for him to be absent from headquarters for another week, he had proposed arriving in Budapest on December 16, remaining there through December 18. Meantime, he planned to send a Secretariat representative to Budapest to make advance arrangements.

The delay involved in these arrangements led a number of delegations to conclude that action on the 14-power resolution was still relevant. Ambassador Lodge, for example, pointed out that the pending proposal did not in any way conflict with the prospective arrangements for the Secretary-General's visit but was complementary. The Indian representative took the opposite position, though he emphasized the moral duty of every member to admit the Secretary-General at any time except on grounds involving his personal safety. Moreover, he objected to provisions of the resolution for sending observers into neighboring countries. He formally moved that the Assembly accepted the statement of the Secretary-General.

The Assembly, however, decided to proceed with the vote on the 14-power resolution. Following a paragraph by paragraph vote, it was adopted by a vote of 54 to 10 (Albania, Bulgaria, Byelorussia, Czechoslovakia, Hungary, Poland, Rumania, Ukraine, U.S.S.R., Yugoslavia), with 14 abstentions (Afghanistan, Burma, Ceylon, Egypt, Finland, India, Indonesia, Jordan, Morocco, Saudi Arabia, Sudan, Syria, Tunisia, Yemen).

The Indian delegate then reminded the President of his pending motion for acceptance of the Secretary-General's statement. Ambassador Lodge expressed his intention of voting affirmatively. Despite some question concerning the propriety of such action since the Assembly as a matter of practice always accepted reports from the Secretary-General without voting upon them, the Indian motion was adopted by a vote of 54 to 9, with 23 abstentions.

Condemnatory Action

On December 12 the Permanent Hungarian Mission, in a note to the Secretary-General, stated that December 16, the date designated by the Secretary-General for a visit to Budapest, was "not appropriate' for Hungary. "On the other hand," the note concluded, Hungary would "at a later date, set forth a proposal through its representative in New York for the purpose of reaching agreement" on the Secretary-General's visit.

In the meantime the Secretary-General had communicated the text of the Assembly's resolution of December 5 not only to the Hungarian and Soviet representatives but also, pursuant to the recommendation that observers should be dispatched to neighboring countries, to the permanent representatives of Austria, Czechoslovakia, Rumania, and Yugoslavia. Except for Austria, the replies were negative.

In these circumstances consultations on further action took place among the cosponsors of the December 5 resolution. On December 9 Argentina, Australia, Belgium, Chile, Denmark, El Salvador, Ireland, Italy, the Netherlands, Norway, Pakistan, Peru, the Philippines, Sweden, Thailand, and the United States tabled a draft resolution. Later Colombia, the Dominican Republic, Spain, and Turkey were added to the cosponsors. As finally revised the resolution recalled the previous Assembly decisions, and reports of the Secretary-General, and noted with grave concern the absence of a reply to the latest appeal for admission of observers. Its operative portions went beyond any action ever taken by the Assembly. First, the Assembly would declare that "by using its armed force against the Hungarian people the Government of the U.S.S.R. is violating the political independence of Hungary"; and would condemn "the violation of the Charter by the Government of the U.S.S.R. in depriving Hungary of its liberty and independence and the Hungarian people of the exercise of their fundamental rights." The resolution went on to reiterate the Assembly's call on the U.S.S.R. to desist from intervention in Hungary's internal affairs and to call upon the U.S.S.R. to make immediate arrangements for withdrawal of its armed forces from Hungary under United Nations observation and to permit reestablishment of Hungary's political independence. Finally, it would request the Secretary-General "to take any initiative that he deems helpful in relation to the Hungarian problem in conformity with the principles of the Charter and the resolutions of the General Assembly."

On December 10 Ceylon, India, and Indonesia submitted a series of amendments to the 20-power proposal primarily designed to remove the sharp condemnation of the Soviet Union. A new preambular paragraph, subsequently accepted by the cosponsors, was proposed that would note "the overwhelming demand of the Hungarian people for the cessation of intervention of foreign armed forces and the withdrawal of foreign troops." The amendments sought to substitute for the first operative paragraph a provision whereby the Assembly would declare "that intervention of Soviet armed forces in Hungary should cease and that arrangements for their withdrawal should be made so that violence and noncooperation will cease and the restoration of peaceful conditions be rendered possible." For the second operative paragraph (condemning the U.S.S.R.), it was proposed that the Assembly simply urge Hungary and the U.S.S.R. "to promote the realization of the above in accordance with the purposes of the Charter and the declared intentions of the two countries." Deletion of the final operative paragraph of the 20-power draft was also proposed, substituting for it provisions declaring that recent events in Hungary "have shown that the use of force and violence cannot bring about or promote a solution of the grave situation in Hungary, but have aggravated it and imposed severe privations and denials of freedom on the Hungarian people"; expressing the conviction that "the interests and freedom of the Hungarian people can only be furthered if there is neither foreign intervention nor the apprehension of external pressure from any quarter"; and requesting the Secretary-General to initiate efforts, both with Hungary and the U.S.S.R. in New York, and to consider without delay the question of visiting Moscow, as well as Budapest, to assist in promoting a speedy solution. These amendments were also embodied in a separate draft resolution.

Austria submitted a resolution according to which the Assembly would authorize the Secretary-General to undertake immediately "to achieve a constructive solution of the Hungarian problem" based on Charter principles, for this purpose to enter into appropriate negotiations with members, and to report to the Assembly on the results of his efforts, if possible before the end of the first part of the 11th session.

As Assembly debate began on December 10, the Cuban representative explained that his delegation had not cosponsored the 20-power resolution because it added nothing to past resolutions and failed to deal with the pressing deportation problem. Moreover, at the least, the resolution should provide for temporary suspension of the Hungarian representatives, if not for their expulsion.

The Indian representative contended that the time had come to use the whole machinery of the United Nations for conciliation. He saw value in reiterating the general principles involved in the Assembly's actions and particularly the widespread sentiment that intervention by force in Hungary's affairs should not be tolerated. However, as regards the 20-power resolution, he made plain that, while in agreement with many parts of it, he could not subscribe either to its phraseology or the implications of certain paragraphs and would consequently abstain unless the "constructive" amendments proposed by Ceylon, India, and Indonesia were adopted. The Indian representative stated that the separate resolution embodying these amendments would not be pressed to a vote if the cosponsors incorporated the amendments in their resolution.

A different approach was urged by the Austrian representative who believed, in line with the Austrian proposal, that the Secretary-General should be authorized to use his ability as a mediator in solving the Hungarian question.

A number of delegations expressed support for all three pending proposals. Only the Soviet bloc continued to oppose any action.

At the morning session on December 11, the Hungarian representative announced that continued discussion of the Hungarian question by the Assembly was "incompatible with Hungary's sovereignty and the national honor of the Hungarian people" and declared that his delegation would not participate in the work of the 11th session "so long as the discussion of the Hungarian question did not proceed in the spirit of the U.N. Charter." He thereupon withdrew from the Assembly, and representatives from Hungary participated in no further meetings of the 11th session on the Hungarian question or any other subject.

On the final day of the discussion Ambassador Lodge made clear that while there was much in the amendments that the United States approved, they tended to give the impression that the Assembly was retreating from principles previously agreed upon. He believed that the time had come not only for reaffirmation of previous decisions but also for a deliberate expression of the Assembly's convictions about the true character of the situation. In particular he strongly opposed the amendment deleting the condemnation of the U.S.S.R.; it was now time for the Assembly to condemn Soviet action in depriving Hungary of its freedom and independence. He also objected to the amendment relating to further initiatives by the Secretary-General, prospectively in Moscow and Budapest, since such authority was inherent in the office of the Secretary-General, and the Assembly had already asked the Secretary-General, in its November 4 resolution, to suggest means to bring an end to the foreign intervention in Hungary. However, there was one basic consideration behind this amendment that the 20 cosponsors had incorporated in the final operative paragraph of their draft, i.e., the request to the Secretary-General to take any initiative that he might deem helpful.

Except for points incorporated by agreement in the 20-power text, the Indian amendments were decisively rejected. The 20-power resolution, after a paragraph-by-paragraph vote on individual provisions, was adopted on December 12 by a vote of 55 to 8 (Albania, Bulgaria, Byelorussia, Czechoslovakia, Poland, Rumania, Ukraine, U.S.S.R.), with 13 abstentions (Afghanistan, Cambodia, Egypt, Finland, India, Indonesia, Jordan, Morocco, Saudi Arabia, Sudan, Syria, Yemen, Yugoslavia).

Following the vote the Indian representative announced that because of the defeat of the three-power amendments, India, Ceylon, and Indonesia would not press their own draft resolution. He contended that, the Assembly having already adopted a contrary resolution, the constructive steps envisaged in the three-power approach were no longer possible.

The Austrian representative had announced previously that he would not seek a vote on his draft if the 20-power proposal were adopted. His reason was the incorporation in the latter of the provision for further initiative by the Secretary-General in the situation.

There were no further developments on the situation in Hungary before the Assembly recessed for Christmas.

Special Committee of Investigation

On January 5, the Secretary-General reported again on his action pursuant to the various Assembly resolutions. He explained that the three individuals appointed by him to investigate the situation in Hungary had reported on December 15 that they had been able to do no more than examine the available and generally known material in New York about the situation in Hungary which had not put them "in a position to add anything significant to what is common knowledge about the situation in Hungary." They also noted that only one country had found it possible to offer facilities for observation. Consequently, the investigators concluded that in the absence of observation in Hungary and cooperation from the governments directly concerned "there would be little purpose" in their attempting "an assessment of the present situation or of recent events." In these circumstances they questioned whether it was not best to suspend the investigation process for the present and to reexamine it later.

The Secretary-General drew special attention to this latter point, emphasizing that there had still been no opportunity for U.N. representatives to make direct observations in Hungary, and the only new and direct source of information might be hearings of Hungarian refugees conducted in neighboring countries. He reported that Austria was prepared to receive observers for this purpose and that the United States and Italy had also offered to cooperate in making refugees available for hearings. While additional points of significance might be established in this way, he pointed out that in order to yield valuable results, such hearings would have to be extensive and organized "in a juridically satisfactory form." Meantime he would continue to try to further the aims of the General Assembly pursuant to its resolution of December 12 but hesitated to initiate further investigatory activities, including hearings for refugees. He specifically raised the question whether the Assembly should not establish a special *ad hoc* committee to assume the activities of the investigators and pursue them under broader terms of reference; such a committee could observe developments on a continuing basis and thereby facilitate further Assembly consideration.

On January 8 a new resolution was submitted, taking account of the Secretary-General's report. As finally revised by its cosponsors (Argentina, Belgium, Canada, Chile, Colombia, Dominican Republic, El Salvador, France, Ireland, Italy, Japan, Liberia, the Netherlands, New Zealand, Norway, Pakistan, Peru, the Philippines, Spain, Sweden, Thailand, Turkey, the United Kingdom, and the United States), the resolution established a special committee composed of representatives of Australia, Ceylon, Denmark, Tunisia, and Uruguay "to investigate, and to establish and maintain direct observation in Hungary and elsewhere, taking testimony, collecting evidence, and receiving information, as appropriate" in order to report to the 11th session of the Assembly and thereafter to prepare additional reports. It further called for Soviet and Hungarian cooperation with the committee; requested all members to assist it in any appropriate way, making available relevant information including testimony and evidence; invited the Secretary-General to render the committee appropriate assistance; called upon all members to give effect to this and previous Assembly resolutions on Hungary; and reaffirmed the request to the Secretary-General to "continue to take any initiative that he deems helpful" in relation to the Hungarian question.

The Assembly took up the draft resolution on January 9. Ambassador Lodge drew attention to the Secretary-General's observations with respect to the problem of observation in Hungary. He emphasized the need for the Assembly to receive "the fullest information regarding the situation created by the attack of the Soviet Union on the Hungarians and on the developments which relate to the recommendations of the General Assembly on this subject." Consequently the United States favored, he said, establishment of a committee of governments to investigate and report on these matters to the present Assembly and thereafter as appropriate. He expressed the belief that adoption of the 24-power resolution would reaffirm the Assembly's objectives and provide it with a means of insuring a flow of information on Hungarian developments.

The overwhelming majority of members supported the draft resolution, and again only the Soviet bloc opposed it, on the grounds of intervention in Hungary's internal affairs.

On January 10 the Assembly adopted the 24-power resolution on a rollcall vote of 59 to 8 (Albania, Bulgaria, Byelorussia, Czechoslovakia, Poland, Rumania, Ukraine, U.S.S.R.), with 10 absentions (Afghanistan, Cuba, Egypt, Finland, India, Jordan, Saudi Arabia, Sudan, Syria, Yugoslavia).

On January 11 a note verbale was circulated by the Secretary-General to all members on behalf of the Hungarian delegation protesting the draft resolution establishing the special committee as violating Hungarian sovereignty.

The special committee established by this resolution held its first meeting in New York January 17, 1957. Alsing Andersen of Denmark was elected chairman and K.C.O. Shann of Australia, rapporteur. The other three representatives were R.S.S. Gunewardene of Ceylon, Mongi Slim of Tunisia, and E. R. Fabregat of Uruguay. On February 20 the special committee submitted an interim report to the General Assembly describing its initial activities. It explained that on January 28 a communication was addressed to all members requesting information relevant to its task. It had also requested governments with diplomatic representatives in Budapest to submit any special information they might have. The committee reported that the Hungarian regime had denied entrance to Hungary to its members. In the meantime the committee had proceeded to hear witnesses from among Hungarian refugees in the United States and proposed to follow up these hearings in Europe. Early in March the committee left for Geneva and planned to visit Vienna, Rome, London, and Paris and to make further efforts to gain admission to Hungary.

Having in mind the prospect of a further report from the special committee, the General Assembly when it recessed on March 8, specifically provided for its reconvening as necessary to consider the situation in Hungary, as well as the situation in the Middle East.

Status of Hungary in the Assembly

The Hungarian delegation never resumed participation in the Assembly after its walkout early in December. When the Assembly's Credentials Committee examined the credentials of all Assembly delegations on February 12, 1957, the U.S. representative, Ambassador James J. Wadsworth, submitted a motion "that the Committee take no decision regarding the credentials submitted on behalf of the representatives of Hungary." He pointed out that the Hungarian credentials had been issued by authorities established through military intervention by a foreign power whose forces remained in Hungary despite requests by the Assembly for their withdrawal. His motion was adopted by a vote of 8 to 1. Plenary action was taken on the Credentials Committee report on February 21, and its decision approved.

Appeal from the Representatives of France, the United Kingdom and the United States to the President of the Security Council on Hungary *

November 4, 1956

The President: In accordance with the decision taken by the Council at its 746th meeting, I invite the representative of Hungary to take a seat at the Council table.

Mr. Szabo, representative of Hungary, took a place at the Council table.

Mr. Lodge (United States of America): If ever there was a time when the action of the United Nations could literally be matter of life and death for a whole nation, this is that time. If ever there was a question which clearly raised a threat to the peace, this is the question. A few minutes ago, we received word of the appeal of the Prime Minister of Hungary for help from the whole world while his capital city is burning. We learned that Budapest, according to its own radio broadcasts, is at this moment surrounded by a thousand Soviet tanks, which are firing phosphorus shells into the city in order to burn it out. Over Radio Budapest, between news bulletins, can be heard the Hungarian national anthem, which ends with the words: "Here is where you live, and here is where you must die."

Here is what *Pravda* is quoted as saying in the typical upside-down talk of Soviet Communism:

"Imre Nagy turned out to be, objectively speaking, an accomplice of the reactionary forces. Imre Nagy cannot and does not want to fight the dark forces of reaction. The task of barring the way to reaction in Hungary has to be carried out without the slightest delay. Such is the course dictated by events. It was Nagy who had requested bringing Russian troops into Budapest, as it was vital for the interests of the Socialist regime. In other words, he admitted that there was a danger from counter-revolutionaries. But in fact he turned out to be an accomplice of the reactionary forces, and this aggravated the situation in Budapest and in the whole country. The Soviet Government, seeing that the presence of Soviet troops in Budapest might lead to further aggravation of the situation, ordered that the troops should leave Budapest. But the further course of events has shown that reactionary forces, taking advantage of the tolerance shown by the Nagy cabinet, let themselves go even more. The blood terror against the working class has reached an unprecedented scale. The Nagy government in

**U.N. General Assembly, *Official Records*, 754th Meeting, pp. 1-3, 12-14.

fact fell apart, making way for anti-people's elements. A state of chaos prevails in Hungary, with economic and cultural life paralysed."

A few hours ago in the Security Council, in this very chamber, the representative of the Soviet Union finally responded to the questioning of his colleagues concerning reported negotiations between the Soviet Union and Hungary for the withdrawal of Soviet forces from Hungary. His answer was:

"I have been asked to comment on the report that negotiations are being conducted between Hungarian and Soviet representatives concerning the Soviet troops in Hungary. I can confirm that such negotiations are going on."

In the light of what we now know is going on at this moment in Hungary, that statement can scarcely be equalled for its total lack of candour and its indifference to human suffering. It should be matched against the fact that it is the Soviets who, all over Asia, have been proclaiming their fealty to the so-called five principles of peaceful coexistence. How far apart can actions and words be?

Shortly after midnight I requested a Sunday meeting of the Security Council to deal with this agony of the Hungarian people. Five minutes later the fact of this request was broadcast by Radio Budapest. That shows how quickly what we say and do here affects the people of Hungary in their struggle.

As I stated in the General Assembly an hour or so ago, we have had word from our Legation in Budapest that large-scale bombing is taking place on Budapest and that the staff has had to take refuge in the cellar of the Legation building.

I have just been handed the following information, which comes from our Legation in Budapest:

"Cardinal Mindszenty and his secretary presented themselves to the offices of the American Legation and have been given refuge at their request."

There is a fact of profound significance.

We can truly say to the Hungarian people, "By your heroic sacrifice you have given the United Nations a brief moment in which to mobilize the conscience of the world on your behalf. We are seizing that moment, and we will not fail you."

I have presented a revised version of our draft resolution on the situation in Hungary, and hope that it will be adopted.

The President: We shall now vote on the United States draft resolution.

A vote was taken by show of hands.

In favour: Australia, Belgium, China, Cuba, France, Iran, Peru, United Kingdom of Great Britain and Northern Ireland, United States of America.

Against: Union of Soviet Socialist Republics.

Present and not voting: Yugoslavia.

The result of the vote was 9 in favour and 1 against.

The draft resolution was not adopted, the negative vote being that of a permanent member of the Council.

Mr. Lodge (United States of America): The Soviet Union has added another veto to the list of more than eighty by which it has thwarted the Security Council as the main organ for the maintenance of international peace and security. Soviet troops and tanks at this moment are annihilating the patriots of Hungary. We cannot afford to temporize over this cynical and brutal breach of the peace.

I therefore make the following motion to call an emergency special session of the General Assembly in accordance with rule 8 (b) of the rules of procedure of the General Assembly:

"The Security Council,

Considering that a grave situation has been created by the use of Soviet military forces to suppress the efforts of the Hungarian people to reassert their rights,

Taking into account that because of the lack of unanimity among its permanent members the Security Council has been unable to exercise its primary responsibility for the maintenance of international peace and security.

Decides to call an emergency special session of the General Assembly, as provided in General Assembly resolution 377A (V) of 3 November 1950, in order to make appropriate recommendations concerning the situation in Hungary."

Mr. Sobolev (Union of Soviet Socialist Republics) (*translated from Russian*): We have already stated that any examination of the "situation in Hungary" in the Security Council is totally unjustified and constitutes an act of intervention in the domestic affairs of Hungary. The same criticism also applies to the proposal to refer the question to the General Assembly. The only purpose of the proposal to refer the situation in Hungary to a special session of the General Assembly can be to exacerbate still further a situation which is already difficult enough. It will not help to restore normal conditions, but is intended to fan still higher the flames of the recent disorders.

There is a further purpose behind the proposal to refer this question to a special session of the General Assembly. The Council is aware that a special session is now examining the question of a cease-fire and of the cessation of the hostilities undertaken against Egypt. The authors of this action, those who are chiefly responsible for the aggression committed against Egypt, are understandably feeling somewhat uncomfortable. They need a smoke-screen, and that is the purpose of the proposed discussion on the situation in Hungary.

It will, I believe, be understood why I shall vote against this proposal.

Mr. Brilej (Yugoslavia): My delegation is going to vote in favour of the proposal to call an emergency special session of the General Assembly. Its vote will not, naturally, imply any judgement on the substance of the question.

The President: We shall now vote on the United States draft resolution.

A vote was taken by show of hands.

In favour: Australia, Belgium, China, Cuba, France, Iran, Peru, United Kingdom of Great Britain and Northern Ireland, United States of America, Yugoslavia.

Against: Union of Soviet Socialist Republics.

The draft resolution was adopted by 10 votes to 1.

GENERAL ASSEMBLY RESOLUTIONS ON HUNGARY*

Resolution 1004 (ES-II)

November 4, 1956

[Document A/RES/393]

The General Assembly,

Considering that the United Nations is based on the principle of the sovereign equality of all its Members,

*U.N. General Assembly, *Official Records*, 2nd Emergency sess., Annex, 1956, pp. 6-7.

Recalling that the enjoyment of human rights and of fundamental freedom in Hungary was specifically guaranteed by the Peace Treaty between Hungary and the Allied and Associated Powers signed at Paris on 10 February 1947 and that the general principle of these rights and this freedom is affirmed for all peoples in the Charter of the United Nations,

Convinced that recent events in Hungary manifest clearly the desire of the Hungarian people to exercise and to enjoy fully their fundamental rights, freedom and independence.

Condemning the use of Soviet military forces to suppress the efforts of the Hungarian people to reassert their rights,

Noting moreover the declaration of 30 October 1956 by the Government of the Union of Soviet Socialist Republics of its avowed policy of non-intervention in the internal affairs of other States,

Noting the communication of 1 November 1956 (A/3251) of the Government of Hungary to the Secretary-General regarding demands made by that Government to the Government of the Union of Soviet Socialist Republics for the instant and immediate withdrawal of Soviet forces,

Noting further the communication of 2 November 1956 (S/3726) from the Government of Hungary to the Secretary-General asking the Security Council to instruct the Government of the Union of Soviet Socialist Republics and the Government of Hungary to start the negotiations immediately on withdrawal of Soviet forces,

Noting that the intervention of Soviet military forces in Hungary has resulted in grave loss of life and widespread bloodshed among the Hungarian people,

Taking note of the radio appeal of Prime Minister Imre Nagy of 4 November 1956,

1. Calls upon the Government of the Union of Soviet Socialist Republics to desist forthwith from all attack on the people of Hungary and from any form of intervention, in particular armed intervention, in the internal affairs of Hungary;

2. Calls upon the Union of Soviet Socialist Republics to cease the introduction of additional armed forces into Hungary and to withdraw all of its forces without delay from Hungarian territory;

3. Affirms the right of the Hungarian people to a government responsive to its national aspirations and dedicated to its independence and well-being;

4. Requests the Secretary-General to investigate the situation caused by foreign intervention in Hungary, to observe the situation directly through representatives named by him, and to report thereon to the General Assembly at the earliest moment, and as soon as possible suggest methods to bring an end to the foreign intervention in Hungary in accordance with the principles of the Charter of the United Nations;

5. Calls upon the Government of Hungary and the Government of the Union of Soviet Socialist Republics to permit observers designated by the Secretary-General to enter the territory of Hungary, to travel freely therein, and to report their findings to the Secretary-General;

6. Calls upon all Members of the United Nations to co-operate with the Secretary-General and his representatives in the execution of his functions;

7. Requests the Secretary-General in consultation with the heads of appropriate specialized agencies to inquire, on an urgent basis, into the needs of the Hungarian people for food, medicine and other similar supplies, and to report to the General Assembly as soon as possible;

8. Reuqests all Members of the United Nations, and invites national and international humanitarian organizations to co-operate in making available such supplies as may be required by the Hungarian people.

Resolution 1005 (ES-II)

November 9, 1956

[Document A/RES/397]

The General Assembly,

Noting with deep concern that the provisions of its resolution 1004 (ES-II) of 4 November 1956 have not yet been carried out and that the violent repression by the Soviet forces of the efforts of the Hungarian people to achieve freedom and independence continues,

Convinced that the recent events in Hungary manifest clearly the desire of the Hungarian people to exercise and to enjoy fully their fundamental rights, freedom and independence,

Considering that foreign intervention in Hungary is an intolerable attempt to deny to the Hungarian people the exercise and the enjoyment of such rights, freedom and independence, and in particular to deny to the Hungarian people the right to a government freely elected and representing their national aspirations,

Considering that the repression undertaken by the Soviet forces in Hungary constitutes a violation of the Charter of the United Nations and of the Peace Treaty between Hungary and the Allied and Associated Powers,

Considering that the immediate withdrawal of the Soviet forces from Hungarian territory is necessary,

1. Calls again upon the Government of the Union of Soviet Socialist Republics to withdraw its forces from Hungary without any further delay;

2. Considers that free elections should be held in Hungary under United Nations auspices, as soon as law and order have been restored, to enable the people of Hungary to determine for themselves the form of government they wish to establish in their country;

3. Reaffirms its request to the Secretary-General to continue to investigate, through representatives named by him, the situation caused by foreign intervention in Hungary and to report at the earliest possible moment to the General Assembly;

4. Requests the Secretary-General to report in the shortest possible time to the General Assembly on compliance herewith.

Resolution 1006 (ES-II)

November 9, 1956

[Document A/RES/398]

The General Assembly,

I

Considering that the military authorities of the Union of Soviet Socialist Republics are interfering with the transportation and distribution of food and medical supplies urgently needed by the civilian population in Hungary,

1. Calls upon the Union of Soviet Socialist Republics to cease immediately actions against the Hungarian population which are in violation of the accepted standards and principles of international law, justice and morality;

2. Calls upon the Hungarian authorities to facilitate, and the Union of Soviet Socialist Republics not to interfere with, the receipt and distribution of food and medical supplies to the Hungarian people and to co-operate fully with the United Nations and its specialized agencies, as well as with other international organizations such as the International Red Cross, to provide humanitarian assistance to the people of Hungary;

3. Urges the Union of Soviet Socialist Republics and the Hungarian authorities to co-operate fully with the Secretary-General and his duly appointed representatives in the carrying out of the tasks referred to above.

II

Considering that, as a result of the harsh and repressive action of the Soviet armed forces, increasingly large numbers of refugees are being obliged to leave Hungary and to seek asylum in neighbouring countries,

1. Requests the Secretary-General to call upon the United Nations High Commissioner for Refugees to consult with other appropriate international agencies and interested Governments with a view to making speedy and effective arrangements for emergency assistance to refugees from Hungary;

2. Urges Member States to make special contributions for this purpose.

Resolution 1007 (ES-II)

November 9, 1956

[Document A/RES/399]

The General Assembly,
Considering the extreme suffering to which the Hungarian people are subjected,
Urgently wishing effectively to eliminate this suffering,

Convinced that humanitarian duties can be fulfilled most effectively through the international co-operation stipulated in Article 1, paragraph 3, of the Charter of the United Nations,

1. Resolves to undertake on a large scale immediate aid for the affected territories by furnishing medical supplies, foodstuffs and clothes;

2. Calls upon all Member States to participate to the greatest extent possible in this relief action;

3. Requests the Secretary-General to undertake immediately the necessary measures;

4. Urgently appeals to all countries concerned to give full assistance to the Secretary-General in the implementation of this task.

GENERAL ASSEMBLY RESOLUTIONS ON SENDING U.N. OBSERVERS TO HUNGARY*

Resolution 1130 (XI)

December 4, 1961

The General Assembly,

Recalling its resolutions 1004 (ES-II) of 4 November 1956, 1005 (ES-II) and 1007 (ES-II) of 9 November 1956, and 1127 (XI) and 1128 (XI) of 21 November 1956 relating to the tragic events in Hungary,

Having received and noted the report of the Secretary-General that United Nations observers have not been permitted to enter Hungary,

Noting with deep concern that the Government of the Union of Soviet Socialist Republics has failed to comply with the provisions of the United Nations resolutions calling upon it to desist from its intervention in the internal affairs of Hungary, to cease its deportations of Hungarian citizens and to return promptly to their homes those it has already deported, to withdraw its armed forces from Hungary and to cease its repression of the Hungarian people,

1. Reiterates its call upon the Government of the Union of Soviet Socialist Republics and the Hungarian authorities to comply with the above resolutions and to permit United Nations observers to enter the territory of Hungary, to travel freely therein and to report their findings to the Secretary-General;

2. Requests the Government of the Union of Soviet Socialist Republics and the Hungarian authorities to communicate to the Secretary-General, not later than 7 December 1956, their consent to receive United Nations observers;

3. Recommends that in the meantime the Secretary-General arrange for the immediate dispatch to Hungary, and other countries as appropriate, of observers named by him pursuant to paragraph 4 of General Assembly resolution 1004 (ES-II) of 4 November 1956;

4. Requests the Governments of all Member States to co-operate with the representatives named by the Secretary-General by extending such assistance and providing such facilities as may be necessary for the effective discharge of their responsibilities.

*U.N. General Assembly, *Official Records*, 11th sess., 1956-57, Supplement 17, pp. 63-65.

Resolution 1132 (XI)

January 10, 1957

The General Assembly,

Recalling its previous resolutions on the Hungarian problem,

Reaffirming the objectives contained therein and the continuing concern of the United Nations in this matter,

Having received the report of the Secretary-General of 5 January 1957,

Desiring to ensure that the General Assembly and all Member States shall be in possession of the fullest and best available information regarding the situation created by the intervention of the Union of Soviet Socialist Republics, through its use of armed force and other means, in the internal affairs of Hungary, as well as regarding developments relating to the recommendations of the General Assembly on this subject,

1. Establishes, for the above-mentioned purposes, a Special Committee, composed of representatives of Australia, Ceylon, Denmark, Tunisia and Uruguay, to investigate and to establish and maintain direct observation in Hungary and elsewhere, taking testimony, collecting evidence and receiving information, as appropriate, in order to report its findings to the General Assembly at its eleventh session, and thereafter from time to time to prepare additional reports for the information of Member States and of the General Assembly if it is in session;

2. Calls upon the Union of Soviet Socialist Republics and Hungary to co-operate in every way with the Committee and, in particular, to permit the Committee and its staff to enter the territory of Hungary and to travel freely therein;

3. Requests all Member States to assist the Committee in any way appropriate in its task, making available to it relevant information, including testimony and evidence, which Members may possess, and assisting it in securing such information;

4. Invites the Secretary-General to render the Committee all appropriate assistance and facilities;

5. Calls upon all Member States promptly to give effect to the present and previous resolutions of the General Assembly on the Hungarian problem;

6. Reaffirms its request that the Secretary-General continue to take any initiative that he deems helpful in relation to the Hungarian problem, in conformity with the principles of the Charter of the United Nations and the resolutions of the General Assembly.

THE CONGO

Security Council Resolutions on the Congo *

July 13, 1960

The Security Council,

Considering the report of the Secretary-General on a request for United Nations action in relation to the Republic of the Congo,

Considering the request for military assistance addressed to the Secretary-General by the President and the Prime Minister of the Republic of the Congo (document S/4382),

1. Calls upon the Government of Belgium to withdraw their troops from the territory of the Republic of the Congo;

2. Decides to authorize the Secretary-General to take the necessary steps, in consultation with the Government of the Republic of the Congo, to provide the Government with such military assistance, as may be necessary, until, through the efforts of the Congolese Government with the technical assistance of the United Nations, the national security forces may be able, in the opinion of the Government, to meet fully their tasks;

3. Requests the Secretary-General to report to the Security Council as appropriate.

July 22, 1960

The Security Council,

Having considered the first report by the Secretary-General on the implementation of Security Council resolution S/4387 of 14 July 1960 (document S/4389),

Appreciating the work of the Secretary-General and the support so readily and so speedily given to him by all Member States invited by him to give assistance,

Noting that as stated by the Secretary-General the arrival of the troops of the United Nations force in Leopoldville has already had a salutary effect,

Recognizing that an urgent need still exists to continue and to increase such efforts,

Considering that the complete restoration of law and order in the Republic of the Congo would effectively contribute to the maintenance of international peace and security,

Recognizing that the Security Council recommended the admission of the Republic of the Congo to membership in the United Nations as a unit,

1. Calls upon the Government of Belgium to implement speedily the Security Council resolution of 14 July 1960, on the withdrawal of their troops and authorizes the Secretary-General to take all necessary action to this effect;

2. Requests all States to refrain from any action which might tend to impede the restoration of law and order and the exercise by the Government of Congo of its authority and also to refrain from any action which might undermine the territorial integrity and the political independence of the Republic of the Congo;

*U.N. Security Council, *Official Records*, 14th and 15th Years, Supplement, 1959-1960, p. 16; pp. 34-35; pp. 91-92.

3. Commends the Secretary-General for the prompt action he has taken to carry out resolution S/4387 of the Security Council and his first report;

4. Invites the specialized agencies of the United Nations to render to the Secretary-General such assistance as he may require;

5. Requests the Secretary-General to report further to the Security Council as appropriate.

August 9, 1960

The Security Council,

Recalling its resolution of 22 July 1960 (S/4405), inter alia, calling upon the Government of Belgium to implement speedily the Security Council resolution of 14 July (S/4387) on the withdrawal of their troops and authorizing the Secretary-General to take all necessary action to this effect,

Having noted the second report by the Secretary-General on the implementation of the aforesaid two resolutions and his statement before the Council,

Having considered the statements made by the representatives of Belgium and the Republic of the Congo to this Council at this meeting,

Noting with satisfaction the progress made by the United Nations in carrying out the Security Council resolutions in respect of the territory of the Republic of the Congo other than the Province of Katanga,

Noting however that the United Nations had been prevented from implementing the aforesaid resolutions in the Province of Katanga although it was ready, and in fact attempted, to do so,

Recognizing that the withdrawal of Belgian troops from the Province of Katanga will be a positive contribution to and essential for the proper implementation of the Security Council resolutions,

1. Confirms the authority given to the Secretary-General by the Security Council resolutions of 14 July and 22 July 1960 and requests him to continue to carry out the responsibility placed on him thereby;

2. Calls upon the Government of Belgium to withdraw immediately its troops from the Province of Katanga under speedy modalities determined by the Secretary-General and to assist in every possible way the implementation of the Council's resolutions;

3. Declares that the entry of the United Nations force into the Province of Katanga is necessary for the full implementation of this resolution;

4. Reaffirms that the United Nations force in the Congo will not be a party to or in any way intervene in or be used to influence the outcome of any internal conflict, constitutional or otherwise;

5. Calls upon all Member States, in accordance with Articles 25 and 49 of the Charter, to accept and carry out the decisions of the Security Council and to afford mutual assistance in carrying out measures decided upon by the Security Council;

6. Requests the Secretary-General to implement this resolution and to report further to the Security Council as appropriate.

Statement by Ambassador Wadsworth to the Fourth Emergency Special Session of the General Assembly on the Congo*

September 17, 1960

Since the night of July 13 the Security Council has dealt with the crisis of the Congo, the breakdown of public order, the outside intervention, and all the urgent and far-reaching consequences of those events. Under the Council's mandate the Secretary-General has assembled in the Congo a United Nations Force of some 18,000 soldiers, deployed in every province of the Congo. Despite enormous difficulties the United Nations Force has made significant progress in restoring public order and security. It has acted with strict impartiality to protect all those, of whatever faction, whose lives were threatened by mob violence. All of these steps have been reported meticulously and faithfully to the Security Council by the Secretary-General.

In addition the Secretary-General has been able to report activities by the United Nations in providing emergency food rations, emergency medical services, administrative support to departments of the Congolese Government, and many other services which have helped to save lives and prevent even more widespread suffering among the people of the Congo.

Never in the history of international organization has such a great operation been mounted so quickly. The selfless dedication of the Secretary-General and his entire staff in carrying on this operation, and the ready response and great self-sacrifice—not to say physical bravery—of the men and women serving the United Nations all the way from Ireland to Ethiopia are all beyond praise. In this "year of Africa" we who have supported the United Nations in this great undertaking believe that the future of freedom in Africa, and even the peace of the world, is to a great extent in the hands of the United Nations and that we could not afford to fail. That knowledge has inspired exertions which can well be described, in many instances, as heroic.

One of the premises on which the Security Council's action was based, and by which the Secretary-General was guided in assembling the United nations Force, was that no permanent member of the Security Council should contribute troops to the force. This, in turn, was based on an even more fundamental premise: that, if the Congo was to have any future at all, it must not become a battleground in a conflict between great powers.

U.S. Faithful to U.N. Principle

The United States has been faithful to that principle. We have sent no troops and no weapons to the Congo. We have sent no personnel or material of any kind except at United Nations request and under United Nations authority. We have made extraordinary efforts to support the United Nations action and have placed at the disposal of the Secretary-General and his staff our transport aircraft and many other services. We have not taken one single step in the Congo independent of the United Nations.

We followed this course not only out of respect for this organization but also because the avoidance of needless conflict between great powers is a matter of the most elementary prudence. And we honestly hoped that all others would do the same.

The United States was by no means alone in expressing this hope and in warning against the danger of great-power conflict in Africa. The record of the Security Council debates is full of statements on this subject. The same point was made very clearly by the recent conference of independent African states in Leopoldville, which warned that the territory of the Republic of the Congo must not become a cold-war arena.

Soviet Defiance of Council's Decisions

If that advice had been heeded by all concerned, the General Assembly would not be in session tonight. But it was not heeded. The Soviet Union, alone among the great powers of the world, chose to defy the Security Council decisions for which it had voted and to strike out on its own path.

In direct violation of the Security Council's proceedings the Soviet Union dispatched to the Congo hundreds of so-called "technicians"—whose character may be judged by the fact that only a few days ago the Congolese authorities ordered these men to leave the Congo. Meanwhile, nearly two dozen Soviet transport aircraft and 100 Soviet trucks appeared in the Congo—not to participate in the United Nations program, not to put themselves under the United Nations authorities there, but to promote strife and bloodshed between Congolese tribes and factions.

All the while the Soviet propaganda machine beamed inflammatory broadcasts to Africa inciting civil strife and slandering the United Nations, its Secretary-General, and his representatives. Soviet propaganda pamphlets bearing the same message were distributed in the Congo itself, with Comrade Khrushchev's picture on the front page.

Consequences of Soviet Action

The United Nations operation in the Congo has so far withstood that assault, but the consequences which flowed from the Soviet action have made it necessary to act without delay if we are to prevent attempts to subvert the Congo and thwart the United Nations. This, and the necessity of providing funds to support the United Nations action in the Congo, was the primary focus of the recent series of Security Council meetings.

The Council, after considering the situation, took up a draft resolution sponsored by Tunisia and Ceylon. It contained several important provisions but none more urgent than that of paragraph 5, which I now quote:

> Reaffirms specifically—
> (a) its request to all States to refrain from any action which might tend to impede the restoration of law and order and the exercise by the Government of the Congo of its authority and also to refrain from any action which might undermine the territorial integrity and the political independence of the Republic of the Congo and decides that no assistance for military purposes be sent to the Congo except as part of the United Nations action.

That draft resolution was vetoed by the Soviet Union, and the purpose of the veto was made clear by Mr. [Valerian] Zorin [Soviet representative] in a statement from which I now quote:

> The representatives of Ceylon and later the representative of Tunisia themselves stated that we—

in this case he meant the Soviet Union—

have no right to deprive the Government of military assistance. They also said that such assistance should, according to our proposal, be provided exclusively through United Nations channels. . . . We feel that it is not at all possible to take such a course.

Thereby the Soviet Union asserted a unilateral right to introduce military personnel and material into the Congo in defiance of the Security Council and in total disregard of the consequences. The issue, Mr. President, was clearly joined.

Actions Needed to Reinforce U.N. Mandate

The General Assembly has now met to clarify and reinforce the mandate of the United Nations.

Let me now summarize briefly what we believe the General Assembly must do if it is to preserve the vital momentum of the United Nations operation and thereby save the Congo from chaos.

First, we believe that the Assembly should uphold the principle that the United Nations in this critical period must be the source of outside assistance to the Republic of the Congo. In this respect we seek to affirm and strengthen the mandate already given to the Secretary-General by the Security Council.

Secondly, we would urge member states to make voluntary financial contributions to a United Nations fund for the Congo to be used under United Nations control. The present disruption of the economic, administrative, and judicial machinery of the Congo makes it imperative to furnish aid as rapidly and as generously as possible. The Republic of the Congo faces a dire threat of imminent bankruptcy. Its economic life has been disrupted and crippled by civil strife. The United Nations must forestall the disaster of hopelessness and hunger which hangs over the Congo. Aid must be forthcoming immediately.

Thirdly, we would place the full weight of the United Nations behind an appeal to all Congolese to avoid further recourse to violence. There have been encouraging signs recently in this respect. But the threat of civil war still hangs over certain areas of the country, and this threat should now be removed.

Fourthly—and this is vital—unilateral actions from whatever source must not be permitted to obstruct the United Nations effort in the Congo. It would be particularly dangerous if any power were again to send personnel or equipment into the Congo which would frustrate the purposes of the United Nations. The alternative to United Nations action to prevent this is unilateral action, with all the grave consequences this would entail.

This is a critical and vital moment for the future of Africa, and perhaps even more for the future of the United Nations. It is not a moment to falter. We must maintain the authority and the momentum of the efforts we have begun. We must insure that the Congo is not made the scene of international conflict as the result of outside interference with the United Nations effort. The issue is clearly drawn, not between great powers that belong to the United Nations but between those who would foment war in the Congo to promote their own ambitions and the community of nations which would seek to place the Congo on the path of true independence and peace. The decision between the two will go far to determine the fate and future of us all.

Mr. President, in this year of destiny for Africa may this Assembly make the right decision.

General Assembly Resolution 1474 (ES-IV) Adopted on the Congo*

September 20, 1960

The General Assembly,

Having considered the situation in the Republic of the Congo,

Taking note of the resolutions of 14 July, 22 July and 9 August 1960 of the Security Council,

Taking into account the unsatisfactory economic and political conditions that continue in the Republic of the Congo,

Considering that, with a view to preserving the unity, territorial integrity and political independence of the Congo, to protecting and advancing the welfare of its people, and to safeguarding international peace, it is essential for the United Nations to continue to assist the Central Government of the Congo,

1. Fully supports the resolutions of 14 and 22 July and 9 August .1960 of the Security Council;

2. Requests the Secretary-General to continue to take vigorous action in accordance with the terms of the aforesaid resolutions and to assist the Central Government of the Congo in the restoration and maintenance of law and order throughout the territory of the Republic of the Congo and to safeguard its unity, territorial integrity and political independence in the intersts of international peace and security;

3. Appeals to all Congolese within the Republic of the Congo to seek a speedy solution by peaceful means of all their internal conflicts for the unity and integrity of the Congo, with the assistance, as appropriate, of Asian and African representatives appointed by the Advisory Committee on the Congo, in consultation with the Secretary-General, for the purpose of conciliation;

4. Appeals to all Member Governments for urgent voluntary contributions to a United Nations Fund for the Congo to be used under United Nations control and in consultation with the Central Government for the purpose of rendering the fullest possible assistance to achieve the objective mentioned in the preamble;

5. Requests:

(a) All States to refrain from any action which might tend to impede the restoration of law and order and the exercise by the Government of the Republic of the Congo of its authority and also to refrain from any action which might undermine the unity, territorial integrity and the political independence of the Republic of the Congo;

(b) All Member States, in accordance with Articles 25 and 49 of the Charter of the United Nations, to accept and carry out the decisions of the Security Council and to afford mutual assistance in carrying out measures decided upon by the Security Council;

6. Without prejudice to the sovereign rights of the Republic of the Congo, calls upon all States to refrain from the direct and indirect provision of arms or other materials of war and military personnel and other assistance for military purposes in the Congo during the temporary period of military assistance through the United Nations, except upon the request of the United Nations through the Secretary-General for carrying out the purposes of this resolution and of the resolutions of 14 and 22 July and 9 August 1960 of the Security Council.

*U.N. General Assembly *Official Records*, 4th Emergency sess., Supplement 1, p. 1.

CUBA

Report by President Kennedy to the Congress on Cuba*

1962

         *   *   *

From the beginning it was clear that in the political and diplomatic realm the implementation of U.S. policy involved two immediate tasks. The first and most proximate task of U.S. diplomacy was to show that the Soviets had in fact used guile and deception to emplace in Cuba offensive nuclear weapons, and that our evidence was conclusive. The second was to halt further shipments and bring about rapidly and effectively the removal of the offensive weapons under U.N. supervision before the quarantine could be lifted. The United States was prepared to negotiate on modalities and to consider various formulas but not to abandon the goals of the removal of the offensive weapons.

From the start, both the OAS and the United Nations were involved. Resources and institutions of this hemisphere were used to underline its solidarity and determination, and to convince the Soviet Union that elimination of the offensive weapons was a purpose to which the hemisphere was solidly committed. From the start, too, it was clear that the United Nations would have a crucial role. It was the forum in which the evidence of Soviet guilt could be most convincingly exposed to a worldwide audience, and where world opinion could be mobilized, and the world verdict pronounced. It was, also, a ready and efficient mechanism for diplomatic communications. The United Nations served as a site where U.S. and Soviet negotiators could easily meet. The Secretary-General himself supplied an important link between the parties particularly during the first days when tension was highest. Thirdly, although Cuba prevented their employment, the United Nations proved itself willing and able to devise acceptable mechanisms for inspection and verification of dismantling and removal of the offensive waapons and for safeguards against their reintroduction. The United Nations was also prepared to carry out the necessary operational responsibilities. Simultaneously with the President's speech, therefore, the United States took diplomatic steps to set in motion the political machinery of the OAS and the United Nations.

         *   *   *

THE CUBAN MISSILE CRISIS

Speech by Ambassador Stevenson Before the Security Council*

October 23, 1962

I have asked for an emergency meeting of the Security Council to bring to your attention a grave threat to the Western Hemisphere and to the peace of the world.

---

*U.S. Participation in the U.N., Report by the President to the Congress for the Year 1962, (Washington, 1963), pp. 103-04.
*Vital Speeches of the Day, Adlai Stevenson, pp. 70-76.

Last night, the President of the United States reported the recent alarming military developments in Cuba. Permit me to remind you of the President's sobering words:

> "Within the past week, unmistakable evidence has established the fact that a series of offensive missile sites is now in preparation on that imprisoned island. The purpose of these bases can be none other than to provide a nuclear strike capability against the Western Hemisphere. Upon receiving the first preliminary hard information of this nature last Tuesday morning at 9 a.m., I directed that our surveillance be stepped up. And having now confirmed and completed our evaluation of the evidence and our decision on a course of action, this Government feels obliged to report this new crisis to you in full detail.
>
> "The characteristics of these new missile sites indicate two distinct types of installations. Several of them include medium range ballistic missiles, capable of carrying a nuclear warhead for a distance of more than 1,000 nautical miles. Each of these missiles, in short, is capable of striking Washington, D.C., the Panama Canal, Cape Canaveral, Mexico City, or any other city in the Southeastern part of the United States, in Central America or in the Caribbean area.
>
> "Additional sites not yet completed appear to be designed for intermediate range ballistic missiles—capable of travelling more than twice as far—and thus capable of striking most of the major cities in the Western Hemisphere, ranging as far north as Hudson's Bay, Canada, and as far south as Lima, Peru. In addition, jet bombers, capable of carrying nuclear weapons, are now being uncrated and assembled in Cuba, while the necessary air bases are being prepared."

In view of this transformation of Cuba into a base for offensive weapons of sudden mass destruction, the President announced the initiation of a strict quarantine on all offensive military weapons under shipment to Cuba. He did so because, in the view of my Government, the recent developments in Cuba—the importation of the Cold War into the heart of the Americas—constitute a threat to the peace of this hemisphere, and, indeed, to the peace of the world.

II

Mr. President, seventeen years ago the representatives of fifty-one nations, gathered in San Francisco to adopt the Charter of the United Nations. These nations stated with clarity and eloquence the high purpose which brought them together.

They announced their common determination "to save succeeding generations from the scourage of war . . . to reaffirm faith in fundamental human rights . . . to establish conditions under which justice and respect for the obligations arising from treaties and other sources of international law can be maintained, and to promote social progress and better standards of life in larger freedom." And in one sentence, Paragraph 4, Article 2, they defined the necessary condition of a community of independent peoples:

> "All members shall refrain in their international relations from the threat or use of force against the territorial integrity or political independence of any state, or in any other manner inconsistent with the Purposes of the United Nations."

In this spirit, these fifty-one nations solemnly resolved to band together in a great cooperative quest for world peace and world progress. The adventure of the United Nations held out to humanity the bright hope of a new world—a world securely founded in international peace, in national independence, in personal freedom, in respect for law, for social justice and betterment, and, in the words of the Charter, for "equal rights and self-determination of peoples."

The vision of San Francisco was the vision of a world community of independent nations, each freely developing according to its own traditions and its own genius, bound together by a common respect for the rights of other nations and by a common loyalty to the larger international order. This vision assumes that this earth is quite large enough to shelter a great variety of economic systems, political creeds, philosophical beliefs and religious convictions. This faith of the Charter is in a pluralistic world, a world of free choice, respecting the infinite diversity of mankind and dedicated to nations living together as good neighbors, in peace.

Like many peoples, we welcomed the world of the Charter, for our society is based on principles of choice and consent.

We believe the principles of an open society in the world order survive and flourish in the competitions of peace. We believe that freedom and diversity are the best climate for human creativity and social progress. We reject all fatalistic philosophies of history and all theories of political and social predestination. We doubt whether any nation has so absolute a grip on absolute truth that it is entitled to impose its idea of what is right on others. And we know that a world community of independent nations accepting a common frame of international order offsets the best safeguard for the safety of our shores and the security of our people. Our commitment to the world of the Charter expresses both our deepest philosophical traditions and the most realistic interpretation of our national interest.

III

Had we any other vision of the world, had we sought the path of empire, our opportunities for self-aggrandizement immediately after the war were almost unparalleled. In 1945, we were incomparably the greatest military power in the world. Our troops and planes were dispersed at strategic points around the globe. We had exclusive possession of the terror and promise of atomic energy. Our economic strength was unmatched. If the American purpose had been world dominion, there could have been no more propitious moment to set out on such a course.

Instead, our commitment, then as now, was to the world of the Charter—the creation of a community of freely cooperating independent states bound together by the United Nations. In the service of this commitment, and without waiting for the peace treaties, we dismantled the mightiest military force we had ever assembled. Armies were disbanded wholesale. Vast supplies of war equipment were liquidated or junked. Within two years after the end of the war, our defense spending had fallen by nearly $70 billion. Our armed forces were slashed from more than 12 million to one and a half million men. We did not retain a single division in a state of combat readiness. We did not have a single military alliance anywhere in the world. History has not seen, I believe, a more complete and comprehensive demonstration of a great nation's hope for peace and amity.

Instead of using our monopoly of atomic energy to extend our national power, we offered in 1946 to transfer the control of atomic energy to the United Nations.

Instead of using our overwhelming economic strength to extend our national power, we contributed more than $2.6 billion to the United Nations Relief and Rehabilitation Administration, much of which went to the relief of suffering in the Communist countries. And after 1948, we contributed many more billions to the economic restoration of Europe—and invited the Communist countries to participate as recipients of our assistance.

Instead of using our substance and strength to extend our national power, we supported the movement for independence which began to sweep through Asia and Africa—the movement which has added 59 new members to the United Nations in the years since 1945. Since the war, we have contributed $97 billion of economic and military assistance to other nations—and, of this sum, $53 billion has gone to the nations of Asia, Africa, and Latin America.

I have often wondered what the world would be like today if the situation at the end of the war had been reversed—if the United States had been ravaged and shattered by war, and if the Soviet Union had emerged intact in exclusive possession of the atomic bomb and overwhelming military and economic might. Would it have followed the same path and devoted itself to realizing the world of the Charter?

IV

To ask this question suggests the central paradox of the United Nations. For among the states which pledged their fidelity to the idea of a pluralistic world in San Francisco were some who had an incompatible vision of the future world order.

Has the Soviet Union ever really joined the United Nations? Or does its philosophy of history and its conception of the future run counter to the pluralistic concept of the Charter?

Against the idea of diversity, Communism asserts the idea of uniformity; against freedom, inevitably; against choice, compulsion; against democracy, dogma; against independence, ideology; against tolerance, conformity. Its faith is that the iron laws of history will require every nation to traverse the same predestined path to the same predestined conclusion. Given this faith in a monolithic world, the very existence of diversity is a threat to the Communist future.

I do not assert that Communism must always remain a messianic faith. Like other fanaticisms of the past, it may in time lose its sense of infallibility and accept the diversity of human destiny. Already in some countries we see Communism subsiding into a local and limited ideology. There are those who have discerned the same evolution in the Soviet Union itself; and we may all earnestly hope that Chairman Khrushchev and his associates will renounce the dream of making the world over in the image of the Soviet Union. It must be the purpose of other nations to do what they can to hasten that day.

But that day has not yet arrived. The conflict between absolutist and pluralistic conceptions of the destiny of mankind remains the basic source of discord within the United Nations. It has given rise to what is known as the Cold War. Were it not for this conflict, this Organization would have made steady progress toward the world of choice and justice envisaged at San Francisco.

But because of the Soviet rejection of an open world, the hope for progress and for peace has been systematically frustrated. And in these halls we spend much of our time and energy either engaged in or avoiding this incessant conflict.

It began even before the nations gathered at San Francisco. As soon as the defeat of the Nazis appeared certain, the Soviet Union began to abandon the policy of war-time cooperation to which it had turned for self-protection. In early 1945, Moscow instructed the communist parties of the West to purge themselves of the sin of cooperation, and to return to their pre-war view that democratic governments were by definition imperialistic and wicked. Within a few weeks after the meeting at Yalta, the Soviet Union took swift action in Rumania and Poland in brutal violation of the Yalta pledges of political freedom.

At the same time, it began a political offensive against the United States, charging that the American government—the government of Franklin Roosevelt—was engaged in secret peace negotiations with Hitler. Roosevelt replied to Stalin that he deeply resented these "vile misrepresentations." At the end of March 1945, Roosevelt cabled Winston Churchill that he was "watching with anxiety and concern the development of the Soviet attitude" and that he was "acutely aware of the dangers inherent in the present course of events, not only for immediate issue but also the San Francisco Conference and future world cooperation."

It is important to recall these facts, because the Soviet Union has tried in the years since to pretend that its policy of aggression was a defensive response to the change of administration in the United Nations, or to Churchill's 1946 speech at Fulton, Missouri, or to some other event after the death of Roosevelt. But the historical record is clear. As soon as the Soviet government saw no further military need for the wartime coalition, it set out on its expansionist adventures.

The ink was hardly dry on the Charter before Moscow began its war against the world of the United Nations. The very first meeting of the Security Council—and I was there—was called to hear a complaint by Iran that Soviet troops had failed to withdraw from the northern part of that country on the date on which they had agreed to leave. Not only had they declined to go; they had installed a puppet regime on Iranian soil and had blocked Iranian troops from entering part of Iran's territory. The Soviet Union, in short, was violating the territorial integrity and denying the political independence of Iran—and doing so by armed force. Eventually the United Nations forced a reluctant agreement from the Soviet Union to live up to its pledge.

This was only the beginning. At the time of the German surrender, the Red Army was in occupation of Rumania, Bulgaria, Hungary, Poland, Eastern Germany and most of Czechoslovakia. And there the Red Army stayed. It stayed in violation of the agreement reached at Yalta by the heads of the allied powers—the agreement which pledged the independence and promised free elections to these nations. By 1948, five nations and half of a sixth, with a combined population of more than 90 million people, had been absorbed into the communist empire. To this day the peoples of Eastern Europe have never been permitted to exercise the Charter rights of self-determination.

Before the suppression of Eastern Europe was complete, the Soviet Union was fomenting guerrilla warfare and sabotaging economic recovery—in Greece and Turkey —assailing neighboring regimes through all the instrumentalities of propaganda and subversion.

Nor were such activities confined to Europe. In Malaya—in the Philippines—in Burma—in Indo-China the communists encouraged and supported guerrilla uprisings against constituted governments.

In one event after another, on one stage after another—the rejection in the United Nations of the American plan for the internationalization of atomic energy, the rejection of the Marshall Plan, the blockade of Berlin and, finally, the invasion of South Korea—the Soviet Union assailed political independence, resisted the world of the Charter and tried to impose its design of a communist future.

Let me recall to this Council, Mr. President, the record with regard to international agreements.

The Soviet government has signed treaties of non-aggression, as it did with the Baltic states and Finland—and then systematically invaded the countries whose integrity it had solemnly promised to respect.

At Yalta and in a succession of peace treaties, it pledged to the liberated countries of Eastern Europe "the right of all peoples to choose the form of government under which they will live—the restoration of sovereign rights and self-government to those peoples who have been forcibly deprived of them"—and then it systematically denied those rights and consolidated that deprivation.

In 1945 it signed a thirty-year pact of mutual assistance and non-aggression with China, pledging that its military aid and economic support would be "given entirely to the National Government as the Central Government of China"—and violated that treaty almost before the Chinese negotiators had left Moscow.

At Potsdam it promised that "all democratic political parties with rights of assembly and of public discussion shall be allowed and encouraged throughout Germany"—and within its own zone promptly repudiated that promise. At Geneva in 1954 it agreed not to introduce arms into Vietnam—and sent guns and ammunition to the Viet Minh.

It denounced nuclear testing—and then violated the moratorium which for three years had spared the world the danger of nuclear tests.

Within this Council, it has thwarted the majority will 100 times by the use of the veto.

The record is clear: treaties, agreements, pledges and the morals of international relations were never an obstacle to the Soviet Union under Stalin. No one has said so more eloquently than Chairman Khrushchev.

VI

With the death of Stalin in 1953, the world had a resurgence of hope. No one can question that Chairman Khrushchev has altered many things in the Soviet Union. He has introduced welcome measures of normalization in many sectors of Soviet life. He has abandoned the classic communist concept of the inevitability of war. He has recognized—intermittently, at least—the appalling danger of nuclear weapons.

But there is one thing he has not altered—and that is the basic drive to abolish the world of the Charter, to destroy the hope of a pluralistic world order. He has not altered the basic drive to fulfill the prophecies of Marx and Lenin and make all the world communist. And he has demonstrated his singleness of purpose in a succession of aggressive acts—the suppression of the East German uprisings in 1953 and the Hungarian Revolution in 1956, in the series of manufactured crises and truculent demands that the Allies get out of West Berlin, in the resumption of nuclear testing, in the explosion—defying a resolution of the General Assembly—of a 50-megaton bomb, in the continued stimulation of guerrilla and subversive warfare all over the globe, in the compulsive intervention in the internal affairs of other nations, whether by diplomatic assault, by economic pressure, by mobs and riots, by propaganda, or by espionage.

The world welcomed the process known as "de-Stalinization" and the movement toward a more normal life within the Soviet Union. But the world has not yet seen compatible changes in Soviet foreign policy.

VII

It is this which has shadowed the world since the end of the second World War—which has dimmed our hopes of peace and progress, which has forced those nations determined to defend their freedom to take measures in their own self-defense. In this effort, the leadership has inevitably fallen in large degree on the United States. I do not believe that every action we have taken in the effort to strengthen the independence of nations has necessarily been correct; we do not subscribe to the thesis of national infallibility for any nation. But we do take great pride in the role we have performed.

Our response to the remorseless Soviet expansionism has taken many forms.

We have sought loyally to support the United Nations, to be faithful to the world of the Charter, and to build an operating system that acts, and does not talk, for peace.

We have never refused to negotiate. We have sat at conference after conference seeking peaceful solutions to menacing conflicts.

We have worked for general and complete disarmament under international supervision. We have tried earnestly and—we won't stop trying—to reach an agreement to end all nuclear testing.

We have declined to be provoked into actions which might lead to war—in face of such challenges as the Berlin blockade, such afronts to humanity as the repression of the Hungarian revolt, such atrocities as the erection of that shameful wall to fence in the East Germans who had fled to the West in such vast multitudes.

We have assisted nations, both allied and unaligned, who have shown a will to maintain their national independence. To shield them and ourselves, we have rebuilt our armed forces—established defensive alliances—and, year after year, reluctantly devoted a large share of our resources to national defense.

Together with our allies, we have installed certain bases overseas as a prudent precaution in response to the clear and persistent Soviet threats. In 1959, 18 months after the boasts of Chairman Khrushchev had called the world's attention to the threat of Soviet long range missiles, the North Atlantic Treaty Organization—without concealment or deceit—as a consequence of agreements freely negotiated and publicly declared, placed intermediate-range ballistic missiles in the NATO area. The warheads of these missiles remain in the custody of the United States, and the decision for their use rests in the hands of the President of the United States of America in association with the governments involved.

VIII

I regret that people here at the United Nations seem to believe that the Cold War is a private struggle between two great super-powers. It isn't a private struggle; it is a world civil war—a contest between the pluralistic world and the monolithic world—a contest between the world of the Charter and the world of Communist conformity. Every nation that is now independent and wants to remain independent is involved, whether they know it or not. Every nation is involved in this grim, costly, distasteful division in the world, no matter how remote and how uninterested.

We all recognized this in 1950, when the Communists decided to test how far they could go by direct military action and unleashed the invasion of South Korea. The response of the United Nations taught them that overt aggression would produce not appeasement, but resistance. This remains the essential lesson. The United Nations stood firm in Korea because we knew the consequences of appeasement.

The policy of appeasement is always intended to strengthen the moderates in the country appeased; but its effect is always to strengthen the extremists. We are prepared to meet and reconcile every legitimate Soviet concern; but we have only contempt for blackmail. We know that every retreat before intimidation strengthens those who say that the threat of force can always achieve Communist objectives—and undermines those in the Soviet Union who are urging caution and restraint, even cooperation.

Reluctantly and repeatedly, we have to face the sad fact that the only way to reinforce those on the other side who are for moderation and peaceful competition is to make it absolutely clear that aggression will be met with resistance, and force with force.

The time has come for this Council to decide whether to make a serious attempt to bring peace to the world—or to let the United Nations stand idly by while the vast plan of piecemeal aggression unfolds, conducted in the hopes that no single issue will seem consequential enough to mobilize the resistance of the free peoples. For my own government, this question is not in doubt. We remain committed to the principles of the United Nations Charter, and we intend to defend them.

IX

We are engaged today in a crucial test of those principles. Nearly four years ago a revolution took place on the island of Cuba. This revolution overthrew a hated dictatorship in the name of democratic freedom and social progress. Dr. Castro made explicit promises to the people of Cuba. He promised them the restoration of the 1940 constitution abandoned by the Batista dictatorship; a "provisional government of entirely civilian character that will return the country to normality and hold general elections within a period of no more than one year"; "truly honest" elections along with "full and untrammeled" freedom of information and political activity.

That is what Dr. Castro offered the people of Cuba. That is what the people of Cuba accepted. Many in my own country and throughout the Americas sympathized with Dr. Castro's stated objectives. The United States Government offered immediate diplomatic recognition and stood ready to provide the revolutionary regime with economic assistance.

But a grim struggle took place within the revolutionary regime, between its democratic and its predominant Communist wings—between those who overthrew Batista to bring freedom to Cuba, and those who overthrew Batista to bring Cuba to

Communism. In a few months the struggle was over. Brave men who had fought with Castro in the Sierra Maestra and who had organized the underground against Batista in the cities were assailed, arrested, and driven from office into prison or exile, all for the single offense of anti-communism, all for the single offense of believing in the principles of the revolution they fought for. By the end of 1959, the Communist Party was the only party in Cuba permitted freedom of political action. By early 1960, the Castro regime was entering into intimate economic and political relations with the Soviet Union.

It is well to remember that all those events took place months before the United States stopped buying Cuban sugar in the summer of 1960—and many more months before exactions upon our Embassy in Havana forced the suspension of diplomatic relations in December 1960.

As the communization of Cuba proceeded, more and more democratic Cubans, men who had fought for freedom in the front ranks, were forced into exile. They were eager to return to their homeland and to save their revolution from betrayal. In the spring of 1961, they tried to liberate their country, under the political leadership of Dr. Castro's first Prime Minister, and of a Revolutionary Council composed without exception of men who had opposed Batista and backed the Revolution. The people and government of the United States sympathized with these men—as throughout our history Americans have always sympathized with those who sought to liberate their native lands from despotism. I have no apologies to make for that sympathy, or for the assistance which these brave Cuban refugees received from our hands. But I would point out, too, that my Government, still forbearing, refrained from direct intervention. It sent no American troops to Cuba.

In the year and a half since, Dr. Castro has continued the communization of his unfortunate country. The 1940 constitution was never restored. Elections were never held and their promise withdrawn—though Dr. Castro's twelve months have stretched to forty-two. The Castro regime fastened on Cuba an iron system of repression. It eradicated human and civil rights. It openly transformed Cuba into a communist satellite and a police state. Whatever benefit this regime might have brought to Cuba has long since been cancelled out by the firing squads, the drumhead executions, the hunger and misery, the suppression of civil and political and cultural freedom.

Yet even these violations of human rights, repellent as they are—even this dictatorship, cruel as it may be—would not, if kept within the confines of one country, constitute a direct threat to the peace and independence of other states. The threat lies in the submission of the Castro regime to the will of an aggressive foreign power. It lies in its readiness to break up the relations of confidence and cooperation among the good neighbors of this hemisphere—at a time when the Alliance for Progress, that vast effort to raise living standards for all peoples of the Americas, has given new vitality and hope to the inter-American system.

Let me make it absolutely clear what the issue of Cuba is. It is not an issue of revolution. This hemisphere has seen many revolutions, including the one which gave my own nation its independence.

It is not an issue of reform. My nation has lived happily with other countries which have had thorough-going and fundamental social transformations like Mexico and Bolivia. The whole point of the Alliance for Progress is to bring about an economic and social revolution in the Americas.

It is not an issue of socialism. As Secretary of State Rusk said at Punta del Este in February: "Our hemisphere has room for a diversity of economic systems."

It is not an issue of dictatorship. The American republics have lived with dictators before. If this were his only fault, they could even live with Dr. Castro.

The foremost objection of the states of the Americas to the Castro regime is not because it is revolutionary, not because it is socialistic, not because it is dictatorial, not even because Dr. Castro perverted a noble revolution in the interests of a squalid totalitarianism. It is because he has aided and abetted an invasion of this hemisphere— and an invasion at just the time when the hemisphere is making a new and unprecedented effort for economic progress and social reform.

The crucial fact is that Cuba has given the Soviet Union a bridgehead and staging area in this hemisphere—that it has invited an extra-continental, anti-democratic and expansionist power into the bosom of the American family—that it has made itself an accomplice in the communist enterprise of world dominion.

There are those who seek to equate the presence of Soviet bases in Cuba with the presence of NATO bases in parts of the world near the Soviet Union.

Let us subject this facile argument to critical consideration.

It is not only that the Soviet action in Cuba has created a new and dangerous situation by sudden and drastic steps which imperil the security of all mankind.

It is necessary further to examine the purposes for which missiles are introduced and bases established.

Missiles which help a country defend its independence—which leave the political institutions of the recipient countries intact—which are not designed to subvert the territorial integrity or political independence of other states—which are installed without concealment or deceit—assistance in this form and with these purposes is consistent with the principles of the United Nations. But missiles which introduce a nuclear threat into an area now free of it—which threaten the security and independence of defenceless neighboring states—which are installed by clandestine means— which result in the most formidable nuclear base in the world outside existing treaty systems—assistance in this form and with these purposes is radically different.

Let me state this point very clearly. The missile sites in NATO countries were established in response to missile sites in the Soviet Union directed at the NATO countries. The NATO states had every right and necessity to respond to the installation of these Soviet missiles by installing missiles of their own. These missiles were designed to deter a process of expansion already in progress. Fortunately, they have helped to do so.

The United States and its Allies established their missile sites after free negotiation, without concealment and without false statements to other governments.

There is, in short, a vast difference between the long-range missile sites established years ago in Europe and the long-range missile sites established by the Soviet Union in Cuba during the last three months.

There is a final significant difference. For one hundred and fifty years the nations of the Americas have painfully labored to construct a hemisphere of independent and cooperating nations—free from foreign threats. An international system far older than this one—the Inter-American system—has been erected on this principle. The principle of the territorial integrity of the Western hemisphere has been woven into the history, the life and the thought of all the people of the Americas. In striking at that principle the Soviet Union is striking at the strongest and most enduring strain in the policy of this hemisphere. It is disrupting the convictions and aspirations of a century and a half. It is intruding on the firm policies of twenty nations. To allow this challenge to go unanswered would be to undermine a basic and historic pillar of the security of this hemisphere.

Twenty years ago the nations of the Americas were understandably disturbed by the threat of Nazism. Just as they would have reacted with vigor had any American republic given itself over to the doctrines and agents of Nazism, so today they look with equal concern on the conquest of Cuba by a foreign power and an alien ideology. They do not intend to applaud and assist while Dr. Castro and his new friends try to halt the march of free and progressive democracy in Latin America.

Yet, despite the ominous movement of affairs in Cuba, the reaction of the hemisphere, and of my own Government continued to be marked by forbearance. Despite Dr. Castro's verbal assaults on other nations in the hemisphere, despite his campaign of subversion against their governments, despite the insurrectionary expeditions launched from Cuba, the nations of the Americas retained their hope that the Cuban Revolution would free itself. But Dr. Castro's persistence in his campaigns against the governments of this hemisphere—his decision to become the junior partner of Moscow—finally destroyed that hope.

If Cuba has withdrawn from the American family of nations, it has been Dr. Castro's own act. If Cuba is today isolated from its brethren of the Americas, it is self-inflicted isolation. If the present Cuban government has turned its back on its own history, tradition, religion and culture, if it has chosen to cast its lot with the Communist empire, it must accept the consequences of its decision. The Hemisphere has no alternative but to accept the tragic choice Dr. Castro has imposed on his people—that is, to accept Cuba's self-exclusion from the Hemisphere.

One after another, the other governments of this hemisphere have withdrawn their diplomatic representatives from Cuba. Today only three still have their ambassadors in Havana. Last February the American states unanimously declared that the Castro regime was incompatible with the principles on which the Organization of American States had been founded and, by a two-thirds vote, excluded that regime from participation in the Inter-American system.

XIII

All this took place before Soviet arms and technicians began to move into Cuba in a massive, continuous stream. But, even then, the governments of the hemisphere were willing to withhold final judgment so long as the Soviet weapons were defensive. And my Government—and the United Nations—were solemnly assured by the representatives of both Soviet Russia and Cuba that the Soviet arms pouring into the island were, in fact, purely defensive weapons.

On September 22, the Soviet Government said in an official statement: "The armaments and military equipment sent to Cuba are designed exclusively for defensive purposes." The Soviet Government added that Soviet rockets were so powerful that "there is no need to search for sites for them beyond the boundaries of the Soviet Union." And last week, on October 18th, Mr. Gromyko, the Soviet Foreign Minister, told the President of the United States at the White House that Soviet assistance to Cuba, "pursued solely the purpose of contributing to the defense capabilities of Cuba," that "training by Soviet specialists of Cuban nationals in handling defensive armaments was by no means offensive," and that "if it were otherwise, the Soviet Government would have never become involved in rendering such assistance." This once peaceable island is being transformed into a formidable missile and strategic air base armed with the deadliest, far-reaching modern nuclear weapons.

The statement issued by the Soviet Government this morning does not deny these facts—which is in refreshing contrast to the categoric assurances on this subject which they had previously given.

However, this same statement repeats the extraordinary claim that Soviet arms in Cuba are of a "defensive character." I should like to know what the Soviets consider "offensive" weapons. In the Soviet lexicon evidently all weapons are purely defensive, even weapons that can strike from 1,000 to 2,000 miles away. Words can be stretched only so far without losing their meaning altogether. But semantic disputes are fruitless, and the fact remains that the Soviet has upset the precarious balance and created a new and dangerous situation in a new area.

This is precisely the sort of action which the Soviet Government is so fond of denouncing as "a policy of positions of strength." Consequently, I invite the attention of the Council to another remark in the Soviet Government's statement of this morning: "Only madmen bank on a policy of positions of strength and believe that this policy will bring any success, will help make it possible to impose their orders on other States."

I need only mention one other curious remark in the Soviet Government's statement of today, and I quote once more: "Who gave the United States the right to assume the role of the master of destinies of other countries and peoples? . . . Cuba belongs to the Cuban peoples and only they can be masters of their destiny." This latter sentence is, of course, a succinct statement of United States policy toward Cuba. It is, however, very far from being Soviet policy toward Cuba.

When the Soviet Union sends thousands of military technicians to its satellite in the Western Hemisphere—when it sends jet bombers capable of delivering nuclear weapons —when it installs in Cuba missiles capable of carrying atomic warheads and of obliterating the Panama Canal, Mexico City and Washington—when it prepares sites for additional missiles with a range of 2,200 miles and a capacity to strike at targets from Peru to Hudson's Bay—when it does these things under the cloak of secrecy and to the accompaniment of premeditated decpetion—when its actions are in flagrant violation of the policies of the Organization of American States and of the Charter of the United Nations—this clearly is a threat to this hemisphere. And when it thus upsets the precarious balance in the world, it is a threat to the whole world.

We now know that the Soviet Union, not content with Dr. Castro's oath of fealty, not content with the destruction of Cuban independence, not content with the extension of Soviet power into the Western Hemisphere, not content with a challenge to the Inter-American system and the United Nations Charter, has decided to transform Cuba into a base for Communist aggression, into a base for putting all of the Americans under the nuclear gun and thereby intensify the Soviet diplomacy of blackmail in every part of the world.

In our passion for peace, we have forborne greatly. But there must be limits to forbearance, if forbearance is not to become the diagram for the destruction of this Organization. Dr. Castro transformed Cuba into a totalitarian dictatorship with impunity—he extinguished the rights of political freedom with impunity—he aligned himself with the Soviet bloc with impunity—he accepted defensive weapons from the Soviet Union with impunity—he welcomed thousands of Communists into Cuba with impunity—but, when, with cold deliberation, he turns his country over to the Soviet Union for a long-range missile launching base, and thus carries the Soviet program for aggression into the heart of the Americas, the day of forbearance is past.

XIV

If the United States and the other nations of the Western Hemisphere should accept this new phase of aggression, we would be delinquent in our obligations to world peace. If the United States and the other nations of the Western Hemisphere should accept this basic disturbance of the world's structure of power, we would invite a new surge of Communist aggression at every point along the frontier which divides the Communist world from the democratic world. If we do not stand firm here, our adversaries may think that we will stand firm nowhere—and we guarantee a heightening of the world civil war to new levels of intensity and danger.

We hope that Chairman Khrushchev has not made a miscalculation, that he has not mistaken forbearance for weakness. We cannot believe that he has deluded himself into supposing that though we have power, we lack nerve; that, though we have weapons, we are without the will to use them.

We still hope, we still pray that the worst may be avoided—that the Soviet leadership will call an end to this ominous adventure. Accordingly, the President has initiated steps to quarantine Cuba against further imports of offensive military equipment. Because the entire inter-American system is challenged, the President last night called for an immediate meeting of the Organ of Consultation of the Organization of the American States, to consider this threat to hemispheric security and to invoke Article 6 and 8 of the Rio Treaty in support of all necessary action. They are meeting now. The results of their deliberations will soon be available to you.

Mr. President, I am submitting today a resolution to the Security Council designed to find a way out of this calamitous situation.

This resolution calls, as an interim measure under Article 40 of the Charter, for the immediate dismantling and withdrawal from Cuba of all missiles and other offensive weapons.

It further authorizes and requests the Acting Secretary General to despatch to Cuba a United Nations observer corps to assure and report on compliance with this resolution.

Upon U.N. certification of compliance, it calls for the termination of the measures of quarantine against military shipments to Cuba.

And, in conclusion, it urgently recommends that the United States of America and the Soviet Union confer promptly on measures to remove the existing threat to the security of the Western Hemisphere and the peace of the world, and to report thereon to the Security Council.

XV

Mr. President, I have just been informed that the Organization of American States this afternoon adopted a resolution by 19 affirmative votes containing the following operative paragraphs:

> "The Council of the Organization of Inter-American States, meeting as the Provisional Organ of Consultation, resolved:
> 1. To call for the immediate dismantling and withdrawal from Cuba of all missiles and other weapons with any offensive capability;
> 2. To recommend that the Member States in accordance with Articles 6 and 8 of the Inter-American Treaty of Reciprocal Assistance take all measures individually and collectively, including the use of armed force, which they may deem necessary, to insure that the government of Cuba cannot continue to receive from the Sino-Soviet power military material and related supplies which may threaten the peace and the security of the continent and to prevent the missiles in Cuba with offensive capability from ever becoming an active threat to the peace and the security of the continent;
> 3. Decides to inform the Security Council of the United Nations of this resolution in accordance with Article 54 of the Charter of the United Nations, and expresses the hope that the Security Council will, in accordance with the resolution introduced by the United States, dispatch United Nations observers to Cuba at the earliest moment."

XVI

Mr. President, the issue which confronts the Security Council today is grave. Since the end of the Second World War, there has been no threat to the vision of peace so profound—no challenge to the world of the Charter so fateful. The hopes of mankind are concentrated in this room. The action we take may determine the future of civilization. I know that this Council will approach the issue with a full sense of our responsibility and a solemn understanding of the import of our deliberations.

There is a road to peace. The beginning of that road is marked out in the resolution I have submitted for your consideration. If we act promptly we will have another chance to take up again the dreadful questions of nuclear arms and military bases and the means and causes of aggression and war—to take them up and do something about them.

This is a solemn and significant day for the life of the United Nations and the hope of world community. Let it be remembered, not as the day when the world came to the edge of nuclear war, but as the day when men resolved to let nothing thereafter stop them in their quest for peace.

*Speech by Acting Secretary General U Thant**

October 24, 1962

Today the United Nations faces a moment of grave responsibility. What is at stake is not just the interests of all member states, but the very fate of mankind. If today the United Nations should prove itself ineffective, it may have proved itself so for all time.

In the circumstances, not only as Acting Secretary General of the United Nations but as a human being, I would be failing in my duty if I did not express my profound

---

Ibid., pp. 76-77.

hope and conviction that moderation, self-restraint and good sense will prevail over all other considerations.

In this situation, where the very existence of mankind is in the balance, I derive some consolation from the fact that there is some common ground in the resolutions introduced in the Council. Irrespective of the fate of those resolutions, that common ground remains. It calls for urgent negotiations between the parties directly involved, though, as I said earlier, the rest of the world is also an interested party.

In this context I cannot help expressing the view that some of the measures proposed or taken, which the Council is called upon to approve, are very unusual, and I might say even extraordinary, except in wartime.

At the request of the permanent representatives of a large number of member governments, who have discussed the matter amongst themselves and with me, I have sent, through the permanent representatives of the two governments, the following identically worded message to the President of the United States of America and the Chairman of the Council of Ministers of the USSR:

"I have been asked by the permanent representatives of a large number of member governments of the United Nations to address an urgent appeal to you in the present critical situation. These representatives feel that in the interest of international peace and security all concerned should refrain from any action which may aggravate the situation and bring with it the risk of war. In their view it is important that time should be given to enable the parties concerned to get together with a view to resolving the present crisis peacefully and normalizing the situation in the Caribbean.

"This involves on the one hand the voluntary suspension of all arms shipments to Cuba, and also the voluntary suspension of the quarantine measures involving the searching of ships bound for Cuba. I believe that such voluntary suspension for a period of two or three weeks will greatly ease the situation and give time to the parties concerned to meet and discuss with a view to finding a peaceful solution of the problem.

"In this context I shall gladly make myself available to all parties for whatever services I may be able to perform. I urgently appeal to Your Excellency to give immediate consideration to this message. I have sent an identical message to the President of the United States of America (Chairman of the Council of Ministers of the USSR)."

I should also like to take this occasion to address an urgent appeal to the President and the Prime Minister of the Revolutionary Government of Cuba. Yesterday Ambassador Garcia—Inchaustegui of Cuba recalled the words of his President, words which were uttered from the rostrum of the General Assembly just over two weeks ago, and I quote:

"Were the United States able to give us proof, by word and deed, that it would not carry out aggression against our country, then, we declare solemnly before you here and now, our weapons would be unnecessary and our army redundant."

Here again I feel that on the basis of discussion, some common ground may be found through which a way may be traced out of the present impasse. I believe it would also contribute greatly to the same end if the construction and development of major military facilities and installations in Cuba could be suspended during the period of negotiations.

Mr. President, I now make a most solemn appeal to the parties concerned to enter into negotiations immediately, even this night, if possible, irrespective of any other procedures which may be available or which could be invoked.

I realize that if my appeal is heeded, the first subject to be discussed will be the modalities, and that all parties concerned will have to agree to comply with those responsibilities which fall on them before any agreement as a whole could become effective. I hope, however, that the need for such discussion will not deter the parties concerned from undertaking these discussions. In my view it would be shortsighted for the parties concerned to seek assurances on the end result before the negotiations have even begun.

I have stated in my message to both the President of the United States of America and the Chairman of the Council of Ministers of the USSR that I shall gladly make myself available to all parties for whatever services I may be able to perform. I repeat that pledge now.

During the 17 years that have passed since the end of World War II, there has never been a more dangerous or closer confrontation of the major powers. At a time when the danger to world peace was less immediate or so it appears by comparison, my distinguished predecessor said:

"The principles of the Charter are, by far, greater than the organization in which they are embodied, and the aims which they are to safeguard are holier than the policies of any single nation or people."

He went on to say: "The discretion and impartiality . . . imposed on the Secretary General by the character of his immediate task may not degenerate into a policy of expedience . . . A Secretary General cannot serve on any other assumption than that—within the necessary limits of human frailty and honest differences of opinion— all member nations honor their pledge to observe all articles of the Charter . . ."

It is after considerable deliberation that I have decided to send the two messages to which I have referred earlier, and likewise I have decided to make this brief intervention tonight before the Security Council including the appeal to the President and Prime Minister of Cuba.

I hope that at this moment, not only in the Council chamber but in the world outside, good sense and understanding will be placed above the anger of the moment or the pride of nations. The path of negotiation and compromise is the only course by which the peace of the world can be secured at this critical moment.

*United Nations Debate by Ambassador Stevenson and Valerian A. Zorin**

October 25, 1962

Mr. Stevenson: Today we must address our attention to the realities of the situation posed by the build-up of nuclear striking power in Cuba. In this connection I want to say at the outset that the course adopted by the Soviet Union yesterday to avoid direct confrontations in the zone of quarantine is welcome to my Government. We welcome also the assurance by Chairman Khrushchev in his letter to Earl Russell that the Soviet Union will take no reckless decisions with regard to this crisis. And we welcome most of all the report that Mr. Khrushchev has agreed to the proposals

Ibid., pp. 77-83.

advanced by the Secretary-General. Perhaps that report will be confirmed here today.

My Government is most anxious to effect a peaceful resolution of this affair. We continue to hope that the Soviet Union will work with us to diminish not only the new danger which has suddenly shadowed the peace but all of the conflicts that divide the world.

I shall not detain the Council with any detailed discussion of the Soviet and the Cuban responses to our complaint. The speeches of the communist representatives were entirely predictable. I shall make brief comment on some points suggested by those speeches and some other points which may have arisen in the minds of Members of the United Nations.

Both Chairman Khrushchev, in his letter to Earl Russell, and Ambassador Zorin, in his remarks to this Council, argued that this threat to the peace had been caused not by the Soviet Union and Cuba but by the United States.

We are here today, and have been this week, for one single reason: because the Soviet Union secretly introduced this menacing offensive military build-up into the island of Cuba while assuring the world that nothing was further from its thoughts.

The argument of the Soviet Union, in essence, is that it was not the Soviet Union which created this threat to peace by secretly installing these weapons in Cuba, but that it was the United States which created this crisis by discovering and reporting these installations. This is the first time, I confess, that I have ever heard it said that the crime is not the burglary but the discovery of the burglary, and that the threat is not the clandestine missiles in Cuba but their discovery and the limited measures taken to quarantine further infection. The peril arises not because the nations of the Western Hemisphere have joined together to take necessary action in their self-defence but because the Soviet Union has extended its nuclear threat into the Western Hemisphere.

I note that there are still some representatives in the Council—very few, I suspect—who say that they do not know whether the Soviet Union has in fact built in Cuba installations capable of firing nuclear missiles over ranges from 1,000 to 2,000 miles. As I say, Chairman Khrushchev did not deny these facts in his letter to Earl Russell, nor did Ambassador Zorin on Tuesday evening, and, if further doubt remains on this score, we shall gladly exhibit photographic evidence to the doubtful.

One other point I should like to make is to invite attention to the casual remark of the Soviet representative claiming that we have thirty-five bases in foreign countries. The fact is that there are missiles comparable to those being placed in Cuba with the forces of only three of our allies. They were established there only by a decision of the Heads of Government meeting in December 1957, which was compelled to authorize such arrangements by virtue of a prior Soviet decision to introduce its own missiles capable of destroying the countries of Western Europe.

In the next place, there are some troublesome questions in the minds of Members that are entitled to serious answers. There are those who say that, conceding the fact that the Soviet Union has installed these offensive missiles in Cuba, conceding the fact that this constitutes a grave threat to the peace of the world, why was it necessary for the nations of the Western Hemisphere to act with such speed? Why could not the quarantine against the shipment of offensive weapons have been delayed until the Security Council and the General Assembly had a full opportunity to consider the situation and make recommendations?

Let me remind the Members that the United States was not looking for some pretext to raise the issue of the transformation of Cuba into a military base. On the contrary, the United States made no objection whatever to the shipment of defensive arms by the Soviet Union to Cuba, even though such shipments offended the traditions of this hemisphere. Even after the first hard intelligence reached Washington concerning the change in the character of Soviet military assistance to Cuba, the President of the United States responded by directing an intensification of surveillance, and only after the facts and the magnitude of the build-up had been established beyond all doubt did we begin to take this limited action of barring only those nuclear weapons, equipment and aircraft.

To understand the reasons for this prompt action, it is necessary to understand the nature and the purposes of this operation. It has been marked, above all, by two characteristics: speed and stealth. As the photographic evidence makes clear, the installation of these missiles, the erection of these missile sites, has taken place with extraordinary speed. One entire complex was put up in twenty-four hours. This speed not only demonstrates the methodical organization and the careful planning involved, but it also demonstrates a premeditated attempt to confront this hemisphere with a *fait accompli*. By quickly completing the whole process of nuclearization of Cuba, the Soviet Union would be in a position to demand that the status quo be maintained and left undisturbed—and, if we were to have delayed our counteraction, the nuclearization of Cuba would have been quickly completed.

This is not a risk which this hemisphere is prepared to take. When we first detected the secret and offensive installations, could we reasonably be expected to have notified the Soviet Union in advance, through the process of calling a meeting of the Security Council, that we had discovered its perfidy, and then to have done nothing but wait while we debated, and then have waited further while the Soviet representative in the Security Council vetoed a resolution, as he has already announced he will do? In different circumstances, we would have done so, but today we are dealing with dread realities and not with wishes.

One of the sites, as I have said, was constructed in twenty-four hours. One of these missiles can be armed with its nuclear warhead in the middle of the night, pointed at New York, and landed above this room five minutes after it was fired. No debate in this room could affect in the slightest the urgency of these terrible facts or the immediacy of the threat to peace.

There was only one way to deal with the emergency and with the immediacy, and that was to act, and to act at once, but with the utmost restraint and consistent with the urgency of the threat to the peace. We came to the Security Council, I would remind you, immediately and concurrently with the Organization of the American States. We did not even wait for the Organization of American States to meet and to act. We came here at the same time.

We immediately put into process the political machinery that we pray will achieve a solution of this grave crisis, and we did not act until the American Republics had acted to make the quarantine effective. We did not shirk our duties to ourselves, to the hemisphere, to the United Nations or to the rest of the world.

We are now in the Security Council on the initiative of the United States, precisely because having taken the hemispheric action which has been taken, we wish the political machinery, the machinery of the United Nations, to take over to reduce these tensions and to interpose itself to eliminate this aggressive threat to peace and to ensure the removal from this hemisphere of offensive nuclear weapons and the corresponding lifting of the quarantine.

There are those who say that the quarantine is an inapproprriate and extreme remedy; that the punishment does not fit the crime. But I would ask those who take this position to put themselves in the position of the Organization of American States and to consider what they would have done in the face of the nuclearization of Cuba. Were we to do nothing until the knife was sharpened? Were we to stand idly by until it was at our throats? What were the alternatives available? On the one hand, the Organization of American States might have sponsored an invasion or destroyed the bases by an air strike, or imposed a total blockade of all imports into Cuba, including medicine and food. On the other hand, the Organization of American States and the United States might have done nothing. Such a course would have confirmed the greatest threat to the peace of the Americas known to history and would have encouraged the Soviet Union in similar adventures in other parts of the world. It would have discredited our will and our determination to live in freedom and to reduce, not increase, the perils of this nuclear age.

The course we have chosen seems to me to be perfectly graduated to meet the character of the threat. To have done less would have been to fail in our obligation to peace.

To those who say that a limited quarantine was too much, in spite of the provocation and the danger, let me tell them a story, attributed, like so many stories of America, to Abraham Lincoln. It is a story about a passerby in my part of the country who was charged by a farmer's ferocious boar. He picked up a pitchfork and met the boar head on and it died. The irate farmer denounced him and asked him why he did not use the blunt end of the pitchfork. The man replied by asking why the boar did not attack me with his blunt end.

Some here have attempted to question the legal basis of the defensive measures taken by the American Republics to protect the Western Hemisphere against Soviet long-range nuclear missiles, and I would gladly expand on our position on this, but in view of the proposal now before us, presented last night by the Acting Secretary-General, perhaps this is a matter for discussion which, in view of its complexity and length, could be more fruitfully delayed to a later time.

Finally, let me say that no twisting of logic, no distortion of words can disguise the plain and obvious and compelling, commonsense conclusion that the installation of nuclear weapons by stealth, the installation of weapons of mass destruction in Cuba poses a dangerous threat to peace, a threat which contravenes paragraph 4 of Article 2 of the Charter, and a threat which the American Republics are entitled to meet, as they have done, by appropriate regional defensive methods.

Nothing has been said here by the representatives of the communist States which alters the basic situation. There is one fundamental question to which I solicit your attention. The question is this: what action served to strengthen the world's hope of peace? Can anyone claim that the introduction of long-range nuclear missiles into Cuba strengthens the peace? Can anyone claim that the speed and the stealth of this operation strengthens the peace? Can anyone suppose that this whole undertaking is anything more than an audacious effort to increase the nuclear striking power of the Soviet Union against the United States and thereby magnify its frequently reiterated threats against Berlin? When we are about to debate how to stop the dissemination of nuclear weapons, does their introduction into a new hemisphere by an outside State advance sanity and peace? Does anyone suppose that if this Soviet adventure went unchecked, the Soviet Union would refrain from similar adventures in other parts of the world?

The one action in the last few days which has strengthened the peace is the determination to stop this further spread of weapons in this hemisphere. In view of the situation that now confronts us, and the proposals made here yesterday by the Acting Secretary-General, I am not going to further extend my remarks this afternoon. I wish only to conclude by reading to the members of the Council the letter from the President of the United States which was delivered to the Acting Secretary-General just a few minutes ago in reply to his appeal of last night. He said to U Thant:

"I deeply appreciate the spirit which prompted your message of yesterday. As we made clear in the Security Council, the existing threat was created by the secret introduction of offensive weapons into Cuba, and the answer lies in the removal of such weapons. In your message and in your statement to the Security Council last night, you have made certain suggestions and have invited preliminary talks to determine whether satisfactory arrangements can be assured. Ambassador Stevenson is ready to discuss promptly these arrangements with you. I can assure you of our desire to reach a satisfactory and a peaceful solution of this matter."

That letter is signed "John F. Kennedy." I have nothing further to say at this time.

Mr. Zorin, The President (interpretation from Russian): Does any other representative wish to speak?

Mr. Garcia-Inchaustegui (Cuba) (interpretation from Spanish): I shall be very brief.

The statement made a few moments ago by the representative of the United States Government constitutes the strongest proof that the grave international crisis provoked by the United States Government in deciding on a unilateral warlike measure against the Revolutionary Government and people of Cuba was based on mere bluff. The representative of the United States presented no valid proof of the affirmation by the President that Cuba constitutes a nuclear threat to the countries of the Western Hemisphere.

The weapons that Cuba possesses are exclusively defensive weapons. They are weapons that we have been forced to acquire because of the aggressive and interventionist policy pursued by the United States Government against Cuba.

This attitude of the United States is another proof of its maneouvres designed to cover up attacks and aggression against our territory, our sovereignty and our independence.

Mr. Zorin, The President (interpretation from Russian): We have listened to the statement by the representative of the United States, Mr. Stevenson. As distinct from the statement which he made at the first meeting of the Council, Mr. Stevenson has not attempted this time to prove the rightness of the position of the United States with regard to the basic motive for having brought up the question of alleged aggressive intentions on the part of Cuba and the Soviet Union. The whole of Mr. Stevenson's speech at today's meeting was obviously defensive in character. He sought to assure the Council that the actions of the United States which have precipitated the serious crisis in the world had in fact some justification. He attempted to prove that the United States could not have acted in any other manner than to declare this self-instituted blockade and to undertake these piratical acts on the high seas, and that the Organization of American States likewise could not have acted in any other manner—the organization which, in this instance, was acting under the pressure of the United States.

The principal motive for the action of the United States, as Mr. Stevenson attempted to prove today, was allegedly the action of the Soviet Union and of Cuba itself through the introduction of nuclear weapons in Cuba, the establishment of offensive military installations on Cuba, and so forth. Mr. Stevenson wished to show that it is universally recognized and axiomatic that in these circumstances the only thing that could have been undertaken was the declaration of a blockade, in violation of the Charter of the United Nations and the universally recognized principles of international law.

The groundlessness of such a position is altogether too clear. The Soviet delegation in its first statement explained in great detail that the point here does not lie in what the United States Press and the President of the United States labelled "the incontrovertible facts of offensive weapons being installed in Cuba," but in the aggressive intentions of the United States with respect to Cuba. That is where the core of the matter lies.

But when the United States attempted to launch these aggressive actions and to put them into effect, they were met with the resistance of world public opinion on the part of the overwhelming majority of the Members of the United Nations, who were deeply concerned by these aggressive actions and who have exerted great pressure upon the United States and all the countries supporting it in order to avert any further dangerous actions by the United States. Following this, Mr. Stevenson was obliged, on the directives of his Government, to change his tone. His statement today—and all those present in the Council today heard this—was quite different from the aggressive speech that he made at the first meeting of the Council on this matter, a speech which found some support only on the part of the direct allies of the United States, which, although they speak a great deal about their own independent policies, are nevertheless obliged to follow the course dictated by Washington. Those representatives of the independent countries that are not associated with any military blocs have openly stated in the Council—and we heard their statements yesterday—that the blockade is an unlawful act, and that it runs counter to the Charter of the United Nations and to the universally recognized principles of international law. The representatives spoke in defence of the right of Cuba to set up its defences in a manner which it considers necessary for itself. They spoke in defence of the right of the Cuban people to independence and of the right of the Cuban State to its independent existence. They openly condemned these aggressive actions of the United States. They were not speaking only on their own behalf. They spoke—as the representative of the United Arab Republic stated—on behalf of more than forty countries of Africa and Asia which are not connected with any military blocs. Their voice forced the United States to reflect and ponder on any further steps that it may take.

In connection with Mr. Stevenson's attempt today to accuse the Soviet Union of being the main cause of these aggressive actions on the part of the United States, I should like to draw the attention of all the members of the Council to the shocking fact of the provocative actions of the United States Government, actions which are completely unjustified. I wish to draw the attention of the Council to the following cirumstance. In the statement of the President of the United States on 22 October 1962, Mr. Kennedy said:

> "Within the past week unmistakable evidence has established the fact that a series of offensive missile sites is now in preparation on that imprisoned island.
> The purpose of these bases can be none other than to provide a nuclear strike capability against the Western Hemisphere."
> Mr. Kennedy went on to say:
> Upon receiving the first preliminary hard information of this nature last Tuesday morning at 9 a.m."–Last Tuesday morning was 16 October–"I directed that our surveillance be stepped up. And having now confirmed and completed our evaluation of the evidence and our decision on a course of action, this Government feels obliged to report this new crisis to you in fullest detail."

Let us establish the first fact. On 16 October the President of the United States had in his hands incontrovertible information. What happened after that? On 18 October the President of the United States was receiving the representative of the Soviet Union, the Minister for Foreign Affairs, Gromyko, two days after he had already in his hands incontrovertible evidence. One may well ask, Why did the President of the United States–in receiving the Minister of another Power which the Government of the United States is now accusing of dispatching offensive arms to Cuba against the United States–not say a word to the Minister for Foreign Affairs of the Soviet Union with respect to these incontrovertible facts? Why? Because no such facts exist. The Government of the United States has no such facts in its hand except the falsified information of the United States Intelligence Agency which are being displayed for review in halls and which are sent to the Press. Falsity is what the United States has in its hands–false evidence.

If there were any incontrovertible facts, the elementary rules of relations between States would have required that the President of the United States–in receiving the Minister for Foreign Affairs of another Power which it is now accusing–present such facts. These are the elementary requirements of normal relations between States in our dangerous times, particularly when the United States considers that it is essential to adopt such extraordinary measures as the declaring of a blockade. On 18 October, the President of the United States said nothing at all to the Minister for Foreign Affairs of the Soviet Union, whereas on 22 October he declared a blockade and also that he would sink Soviet ships. Are these normal relations of one great Power with another–a great Power which is observing the principles of the Charter and the norms of international law? No, this is highway robbery. But one cannot enter into normal relations with such highway robbers.

That is why the more reasonable representatives of the United States Press today are speaking to the effect that this has been a grave error. I should like to refer to an article by Mr. Walter Lippmann, who is wise as a result of considerable experience and is very well informed. Mr. Lippmann wrote today the following:

> "I see the danger of this mistake in the fact that when the President saw Mr. Gromyko on Thursday"–this was on 18 October, precisely–"and had the evidence of the missile build-up in Cuba, he refrained from confronting Mr. Gromyko with this evidence. This was to suspend diplomacy."

Mr. Stevenson, at the session of the General Asesmbly, you said that the United

States is in favour of peaceful, normal and quiet diplomacy, that you are against the cold war, that you are against any actions that might upset the peace and might create tensions. Where is your diplomacy—where is it? Instead of resorting to diplomatic processes at the highest levels—for the President to confront the representative of a country against which it intends to use armed force—instead of confronting that representative with facts which call for examination, instead of that, your President said nothing to Gromyko on this subject. And I can say more: he was assuring that nothing was being contemplated by the United States against Cuba and that the information which the Soviet Government has published is one which he trusts. How is it that you can act in this fashion, that you keep a double accounting system? You say one thing in your official talks, and two days later you declare: "the Soviet Union has deceived us."

No, I beg your pardon, you are the ones who are deceiving your own people and the whole world. In fact, this is precisely what is being written by the United States Press itself. I should like to draw attention to the *New York Herald Tribune* where the following is written:

"Today, on Friday"—on 19 October—the Newspaper writes "as well as the whole of the week-end, the Defense Department had declared that it has no information indicating the presence of any offensive armaments in Cuba."

And yet, the President stated in his speech that he had discovered such rockets at 9 a.m., on Tuesday, 16 October, in other words, six days earlier.

Then, citing a whole series of other official statements, the newspaper posed the question—and I ask this question again here:

"If the lie must be pronounced, then the public has also the right to put the question: when did the lie begin? When did the lie stop?"

This is a legitimate question by the American Press.

I shall not go further on this subject. But from what I have already said, from the facts which are incontrovertible and which cannot be denied by Mr. Stevenson, it will be obvious that the Government of the United States has deliberately intensified the crisis, it has deliberately prepared this provocation and it has tried to cover up this provocation by means of a discussion in the Security Council at a time when there was no foundation for that whatsoever; and now you cannot advance any justification either, apart- from the falsified information supplied by your Intelligence Agency. But you cannot conduct world policies and world politics on such a basis. Such opportunistic steps can lead you to catastrophic consequences for the whole world and the Soviet Government has issued a warning to the United States and to the world on that score.

Mr. Stevenson referred to Mr. Khrushchev's letter to Bertrand Russell. His interpretation of that letter is completely out of keeping with the letter's contents. I should like to read out a portion of the letter so that the Council may see what is the actual position of the Soviet Union.

In the fact of the provocation of the United States, which is threatening the world with thermonuclear war, Mr. Khrushchev declared the following in his letter of 24 October to Bertrand Russell:

"... We shall do everything possible to prevent this catastrophe. But it must be borne in mind that our efforts may prove insufficient. Indeed. our efforts and possibilities are efforts and possibilities of one side. If the United States Government carries out the programme of piratic actions outlined by it, we shall have to resort to means of defence against the aggressor to defend our rights and international rights which are written down in international agreements and expressed in the United Nations Charter. We have no other way out. It is well known that if one tries to appease a robber by giving him at first one's purse, and then one's coat, the robber will not become more merciful, will not stop robbing. On the contrary, he will become increasingly insolent. Therefore, it is necessary to curb the highwayman in order to prevent the law of the jungle from becoming the law governing relations between civilized people and States.

The Soviet Government considers that the Government of the United States of America must display reserve and stay the execution of its piratical threats, which are fraught with most serious consequences.

The question of war and peace is so vital that we consider useful a top-level meeting in order to discuss all the problems which have arisen, to do everything to remove the danger of unleashing a thermonuclear war. As long as rocket nuclear weapons are not put into play, it is still possible to avert war. When aggression will have been unleashed by the Americans, such a meeting will already have become impossible and useless."

That is the position of the Soviet Union on this matter. It has been consistently expressed by the Soviet delegation, from the very outset of the discussion of the question.

In connection, with the initiative of the Acting Secretary-General, U Thant, we have handed over to Mr. Thant an answer which has been sent today by the Chairman of the Council of Ministers of the Union of Soviet Socialist Republics, Mr. N. S. Khrushchev, to the letter to which the Acting Secretary-General referred yesterday. I shall no read out the text of that answer:

"Esteemed U Thant,
I have received your appeal and carefully studied the proposals it contains. I welcome your initiative. I understand your concern about the situation obtaining in the Caribbean, since the Soviet Government also considers this situation as highly dangerous and requiring an immediate intercession by the United Nations.
I wish to inform you that I agree with your proposal, which meets the interests of peace.
Respectfully,
N. Khrushchev

I should like to conclude my statement with that reply from Mr. Khrushchev.

Mr. Stevenson (United States of America): I want to say to you, Mr. Zorin, that I do not have your talent for obfuscation, for distortion, for confusing language and for double-talk—and I must confess to you that I am glad I do not. But, if I understood what you said, you said that my position had changed; that today I was defensive because we do not have the evidence to prove our assertions that your Government had installed long-range missiles in Cuba. Well, let me say something to you, Mr. Ambassador: We do have the evidence. We have it, and it is clear and incontrovertible. And let me say something else: Those weapons must be taken out of Cuba.

Next, let me say to you that, if I understand you, you said—with a trespass on credulity that excels your best—that our position had changed since I spoke here the other day because of the pressures of world opinion and a majority of the United Nations. Well, let me say to you, sir: You are wrong again. We have had no pressure from anyone whatsoever. We came here today to indicate our willingness to discuss U Thant's proposals—and that is the only change that has taken place.

But let me also say to you, sir, that there has been a change. You, the Soviet Union, have sent these weapons to Cuba. You, the Soviet Union, have upset the balance of power in the world. You, the Soviet Union, have created this new danger—not the United States.

You asked, with a fine show of indignation, why the President did not tell Mr. Gromyko last Thursday about our evidence, at the very time that Mr. Gromyko was blandly denying to the President that the USSR was placing such weapons on sites in the New World. Well, I will tell you why: because we were assembling the evidence—and perhaps it would be instructive to the world to see how far a Soviet official would go in perfidy. Perhaps we wanted to know whether this country faced another example of nuclear deceit like the one a year ago, when in stealth the Soviet Union broke the nuclear test moratorium. And, while we are asking questions, let me ask you why your Government, your Foreign Minister, deliberately, cynically deceived us about the nuclear build-up in Cuba.

Finally, Mr. Zorin, I remind you that the other day you did not deny the existence of these weapons. Instead, we heard that they had suddenly become defensive weapons. But today—again, if I heard you correctly—you say that they do not exist, or that we have not proved they exist—and you say this with another fine flood of rhetorical scorn. All right, sir, let me ask you one simple question: Do you, Ambassador Zorin, deny that the USSR has placed and is placing medium and intermediate-range missiles and sites in Cuba? Yes or no? Do not wait for the interpretation. Yes or no?

The President (interpretation from Russian): I am not in an American courtroom, sir, and therefore I do not wish to answer a question that is put to me in the fashion in which a prosecutor puts questions. In due course, sir, you will have your reply.

Mr. Stevenson (United States of America): You are in the courtroom of world opinion right now, and you can answer "Yes" or "No." You have denied that they exist—and I want to know whether I have understood you correctly.

The President (interpretation from Russian): Will you please continue your statement, sir? You will have your answer in due course.

Mr. Stevenson (United States of America): I am prepared to wait for my answer until Hell freezes over, if that is your decision. I am also prepared to present the evidence in this room.

The President (interpretation from Russian): I call on the representative of Chile.

Mr. Schweitzer (Chile) (interpretation from Spanish): I did not expect the incident which has just occurred, Mr. President, but since it has occurred I would prefer to yield the floor to you and to ask for the floor again when you feel it is necessary or after you have been good enough to reply to the question put to you by the United States representative. Therefore, that being the case, I am quite willing to yield the floor to you.

Mr. Stevenson (United States of America): I had not finished my statement. I asked you a question, Mr. President, and I have had no reply to that question. I will now proceed, if I may, to finish my statement.

The President (interpretation from Russian): By all means, you may proceed.

Mr. Stevenson (United States of America): I doubt whether anyone in this room, except possibly the representative of the Soviet Union, has any doubt about the facts, but in view of his statements and the statements of the Soviet Government up until last Thursday, when Mr. Gromyko denied the existence of or any intention of installing such weapons in Cuba, I am going to make a portion of the evidence available right now. If you will indulge me for a moment, we will set up an easal here in the back of the room where I hope it will be visible to everyone.

The first of these exhibits shows an area north of the village of Candelaria, near San Cristóbal in the island of Cuba, southwest of Havana. The map, together with a small photograph shows precisely where the area is in Cuba. The first photograph shows the area in late August 1962. It was then, if you can see from where you are sitting, only a peaceful countryside. The second photograph shows the same area one day last week. A few tents and vehicles had come into the area, new spur roads had appeared, and the main road had been improved.

The third photograph, taken only twenty-four hours later, shows facilities for a medium-range missile battalion installed. There are tents for four or five hundred men. At the end of the new spur road there are seven 1,000-mile missile trailers. There are four launcher-erector mechanisms for placing these trailers in erect firing position. This missile is a mobile weapon which can be moved rapidly from one place to another. It is identical with the 1,000-mile missiles which have been displayed in Moscow parades.

All of this, I remind you, took place in twenty-four hours.

The second exhibit, which you can all examine at your leisure, shows three successive photographic enlargements of another missle base of the same type in the area of San Cristóbal. These enlarged photographs clearly show six of these missiles on trailers and three erectors. That is only one example of the first type of ballistic missile installation in Cuba.

A second type of installation is designed for a missile of intermediate range, a range of about 2,200 miles. Each site of this type has four launching pads. The exhibit on this type of missile shows a launching area being constructed near Guanajay, southwest of the city of Havana. As in the first exhibit, a map and small photograph show this area as it appeared in late August 1962, when no military activities were apparent. A second large photograph shows the same area about six weeks later. Here you will see a very heavy construction effort to push the launching area to rapid completion. The pictures show two large concrete bunkers or control centres in process of construction, one between each pair of launching pads. They show heavy concrete retaining walls being erected to shelter vehicles and equipment from rocket blast-off. They show cable scars leading from the launching pad to the bunkers. They show large, reinforced-concrete buildings under construction. A building with a heavy arch may well be intended as the storage area for the nuclear warheads. The installation is not yet complete and no warheads are yet visible.

The next photograph shows a closer view of the same intermediate-range launching site. Here you can clearly see one of the pairs of large, concrete launching pads with the concrete building from which launching operations for three pads are controlled. Other details are visible, such as fuel-tanks. That is only one example, one illustration of the work going forward in Cuba on intermediate-range missile bases.

Now, in addition to missiles, the Soviet Union is installing other offensive weapons in Cuba. The next photograph is of an airfield at San Julián in western Cuba. On this field you will see twenty-two crates designed to transport the fuselages of Soviet Ilyushin-28 bombers. Four of the aircrraft are uncrated and one is partially assembled. These bombers, sometimes known as Beagles, have an operating radius of about 750 miles and are capable of carrying nuclear weapons. At the same field you can see one of the surface-to-air anti-aircraft guided-missile bases, with six missiles per base, which now ring the entire coastline of Cuba.

Another set of two photographs covers still another area of deployment of medium-range missiles in Cuba. These photographs are on a larger scale than the others and reveal many details of an improved field-type launching site. One photograph provides an over-all view of most of the site. You can see clearly three of the four launching pads. The second photograph displays details of two of these pads. Even an eye untrained in photographic interpretation can clearly see the buildings in which the missiles are checked out and maintained ready to fire. A missile trailer, trucks to move missiles out to the launching pad, erectors to raise the missiles to launching position, tank-trucks to provide fuel, vans from which the missile firing is controlled—in short, all of the requirements to maintain, load and fire these terrible weapons.

These weapons, these launching pads, these planes—of which we have illustrated only a fragment—are part of a much larger weapon complex, of what is called a weapon system. To support this build-up, to operate these advanced weapon systems, the Soviet Union has sent a large number of military personnel to Cuba, a force now amounting to several thousand men.

These photographs, as I say, are available to members for detailed examination in the Trusteeship Council room, following this meeting. There I shall have one of my aides who will gladly explain them to you in such detail as you may require.

I have nothing further to say at this time.

The President (interpretation from Russian): I should like to make a short statement in my capacity as representative of the Soviet Union.

Mr. Stevenson has asked me to answer his question about the sending of nuclear weapons to Cuba and has demonstrated what he called proof which the United States could present as evidence. I shall limit myself to a brief answer. The answer to Mr. Stevenson has already been given by the Government of the Soviet Union, and I shall recall the content of that reply.

The Government of the Soviet Union—this was stated in *Tass* on 11 September and the statement was authorized by the Government—does not need to relocate in any other country, for example in Cuba, its available means to repel aggression or to make a retaliatory blow. Our nuclear means are so powerful in their explosive capability and the Soviet Union has such powerful delivery vehicles for these nuclear weapons that there is no need to seek any further sites for them anywhere outside the borders of the Soviet Union.

This is the answer to the question. We have no need to deploy anywhere, including Cuba, any of our powerful rockets and delivery vehicles. Accordingly, the questions which Mr. Stevenson attempted to put are in fact purely rhetorical.

In addition, Mr. Stevenson himself said that Mr. Gromyko, in his conversations with President Kennedy, denied the presence of such offensive weapons in Cuba. What else would you need, sir? This is my answer to your question.

The second comment that I wish to make deals with the so-called evidence and photographs that have been demonstrated here by Mr. Stevenson. Tactics of that kind, of course, have been utilized previously by Mr. Stevenson, but not very successfully. At the meeting of the First Committee, on 15 April 1961—and this can be verified by the verbatim record—Mr. Stevenson displayed photographs of a Cuban aircraft which allegedly had fired upon Havana, an aircraft which was supposed to have been part of the Cuban Air Force. Mr. Stevenson showed us these photographs and said: these planes have "the markings of the Castro Air Force . . ." I hope that Mr. Stevenson will not deny that this was so.

However, on 1 May, after the failure of the whole enterprise, *The New York Times* wrote as follows:

> "The operation began with an attack upon the Cuban air fields by light bombers of the B-26 tye. In accordance with the best cloak and dagger traditions, in order to ensure the plausibility of the version that the bombings were carried out by pilots who had fled from Castro army, an old Cuban B-26 plane was shot through with a few bullets of 0.3 calibre."

The photograph of this aircraft, which was put together by the United States Intelligence Agency, was presented as evidence to the First Committee to show that allegedly the Cubans themselves and Cuban aircraft were firing upon Havana. This is a fact, and this fact cannot be denied.

What value is there in all your photographs? One who has lied once will not be believed a second time. Accordingly, Mr. Stevenson, we shall not look at your photographs. If you had anything in the way of serious evidence, you should have presented it, as Mr. Lippmann recommended, in accordance with diplomatic practice to the Government which you are accusing. You have not done so. You have utilized the Security Council for a display of your photographs.

I think that this lacks seriousness. And I had a higher opinion of you, personally. Unfortunately, I was in error. I regret this very much.

And the last thing I wish to say, I presume that all this performance, that all this display illustrates but one thing: the wish to detract the Council from the principal issue, namely, the violation by the United States of the universally recognized norms of international law and of the Charter of the United Nations, and from the institution of a blockade in an arbitrary fashion which in fact constitutes an act of war—to detract the Council from this is your principal task. That is why you are displaying all sorts of forged photographs of this kind. I do not wish to enter into a discussion of these photographs and of this evidence because I do not wish to abet your detracting the Council from the important task before it. That, in fact, is my answer to your statements and to your question.

As for the proposal that has been made by the representative of the United Arab Republic, I take it that we would need to have an exchange of opinions on this subject, and after that we shall be able to adopt the decision that might be called for.

If there is no objection, I shall call on the representative of Ghana after the interpretation.

The President (interpretation from Russian): Before calling on the representative of Ghana, I shall call on the United States representative, who has asked to speak and to whom the representative of Ghana has ceded his place.

Mr. Stevenson (United States of America): I shall detain the Council only a moment.

I have not had a direct answer to my question. The representative of the Soviet Union said that the official answer of the Soviet Union was the *Tass* statement that the USSR does not need to locate missiles in Cuba. I agree: the USSR does not need to do that. But the question is not whether the USSR needs missiles in Cuba. The question is: has the USSR missiles in Cuba? And that question remains unanswered. I knew it would remain unanswered.

As to the authenticity of the photographs, about which Mr. Zorin has spoken with such scorn, I wonder if the Soviet Union would ask their Cuban colleagues to permit a United Nations team to go to these sites. If so, Mr. Zorin, I can assure you that we can direct them to the proper places very quickly.

And now I hope that we can get down to business, that we can stop this sparring. We know the facts, Mr. Zorin, and so do you, and we are ready to talk about them. Our job here is not to score debating points: our job, Mr. Zorin, is to save the peace. If you are ready to try, we are.

*Report by President Kennedy to the Congress on Cuba**

1962

*   *   *

The formula for terminating Security Council consideration of the Cuban crisis was finally agreed between the Governments of the United States and the Soviet Union on January 7, 1963. The two Governments agreed to send a joint letter to the Secretary-General which he, in turn, transmitted to the Security Council for the information of its members. The text of the letter read:

> On behalf of the Governments of the United States and the Soviet Union, we desire to express to you our appreciation of your efforts in assisting our Governments to avert the serious threat to the peace which recently arose in the Caribbean area.
>
> While it has not been possible for our Governments to resolve all the problems that have arisen in connection with this affair, they believe that, in view of the degree of understanding reached between them on the settlement of the crisis and the extent of progress in the implementation of this understanding, it is not necessary for this item to occupy further the attention of the Security Council at this time.
>
> The Governments of the United States of America and of the Soviet Union express the hope that the actions taken to avert the threat of war in connection with this crisis will lead toward the adjustment of other differences between them and the general easing of tensions that could cause a further threat of war.

The same day, January 7, 1963, the Cuban Representative addressed a letter to the Secretary-General, which he requested be transmitted to U.N. members, expressing a dissenting view on the conclusion of the affair. Cuba, the letter declared, "does not consider as effective any agreement other than one which would include the consideration of the five points or measures which, as minimum guarantees to peace in the Caribbean, our Prime Minister Fidel Castro stresses in his declaration of 28 October, 1962. . . ."

As the Security Council concluded its consideration of the Cuban item, the situation remained as follows:

1. The Soviet Union had withdrawn its offensive missiles, its bombers, and some of its military personnel. The United States and participating American Republics had lifted the quarantine.

*U.S. Participation in the U.N., Report by the President . . . 1962, pp. 125-27.

2. The Cubans had refused to accept on-site inspection and post-removal verification or to agree on a system of continuing safeguards against reintroduction of offensive weapons under U.N. auspices.

3. In the absence of adequate inspection and safeguards, the United States continued other methods of surveillance of military activities in Cuba in the interests of hemispheric security.

4. The continued presence of Soviet military personnei in Cuba constituted an unacceptable intervention by a foreign military power in the Western Hemisphere. Efforts continued with the U.S.S.R. to obtain their removal.

5. The United States continued to be seriously concerned about Cuban subversive efforts directed against other American Republics.

6. The U.S. position with regard to assurance against invasion remained that stated by the President on November 20 as outlined above.

7. With the conclusion of the New York talks and the joint U.S.-U.S.S.R. letter terminating Security Council consideration of the matter, responsibility for further action remained with the OAS Organ of Consultation in its hemispheric context.

     *   *   *

Security Council Resolution 186 (1964) on Cyprus*

March 4, 1964

The Security Council,

Noting that the present situation with regard to Cyprus is likely to threaten international peace and security and may further deteriorate unless additional measures are promptly taken to maintain peace and to seek out a durable solution.

Considering the positions taken by the parties in relation to the Treaties signed at Nicosia on August 16, 1960,

Having in mind the relevant provisions of the Charter of the United Nations and its Article 2, paragraph 4, which reads: "All Members shall refrain in their international relations from the threat or use of force against the territorial integrity or political independence of any State, or in any other manner inconsistent with the Purposes of the United Nations,"

1. Calls upon all member states, in conformity with their obligations under the Charter of the United Nations, to refrain from any action or threat of action likely to worsen the situation in the sovereign Republic of Cyprus, or to endanger international peace;

2. Asks the Government of Cyprus, which has the responsibility for the maintenance and restoration of law and order, to take all additional measures necessary to stop violence and bloodshed in Cyprus;

3. Calls upon the communities in Cyprus and their leaders to act with the utmost restraint;

4. Recommends the creation, with the consent of the Government of Cyprus, of a United Nations peace-keeping force in Cyprus. The composition and size of the force shall be established by the Secretary-General, in consultation with the Governments of Cyprus, Greece, Turkey and the United Kingdom. The commander of the force shall be appointed by the Secretary-General and report to him. The Secretary-General, who shall keep the governments providing the force fully informed, shall report periodically to the Security Council on its operation;

5. Recommends that the function of the force should be, in the interest of preserving international peace and security, to use its best efforts to prevent a recurrence of fighting and, as necessary, to contribute to the maintenance and restoration of law and order and a return to normal conditions;

6. Recommends that the stationing of the force shall be for a period of three months, all costs pertaining to it being met, in a manner to be agreed upon by them, by the governments providing the contingents and by the Government of Cyprus. The Secretary-General may also accept voluntary contributions for that purpose;

7. Recommends further that the Secretary-General designate, in agreement with the Government of Cyprus and the Governments of Greece, Turkey and the United Kingdom, a mediator, who shall use his best endeavors with the representatives of the communities and also with the aforesaid four Governments, for the purpose of

*U.N. Security Council, *Official Records*, 19th Year, Jan.-June, 1964, Supplement, pp. 102-03.

promoting a peaceful solution and an agreed settlement of the problem confronting Cyprus, in accordance with the Charter of the United Nations, having in mind the well-being of the people of Cyprus as a whole and the preservation of international peace and security. The mediator shall report periodically to the Secretary-General on his efforts;

8. Requests the Secretary-General to provide, from funds of the United Nations, as appropriate, for the remuneration and expenses of the mediator and his staff.

DOMINICAN REPUBLIC

Statement by Ambassador Stevenson Before the Security Council on the Dominican Republic Question*

May 3, 1965

Mr. President, we have heard from the distinguished representative of the Soviet Union about the Congo, about Viet-Nam, about Panama, about Cuba. We have even heard some comments about Alabama and about American business. After the recent experience that we have had in the bodies of the United Nations with Soviet polemics reminiscent of the days of Stalin and Vishinsky, I must say that I am not surprised that the Soviet Union has again used a United Nations body, this time the Security Council, to digress into a whole catalogue of complaints about United States resistance to communist expansion or assistance to those resisting aggression.

I used to marvel at the audacity of the Soviet Union in pointing an accusing finger at others—the Soviet Union which signed a pact with Hitler, which forcibly added 264,000 square miles and over 24 million people to its own territory and population in the aftermath of World War II, which subjugated all of Eastern Europe, crushed the uprisings in East Germany and Hungary, and which has persistently sought to enlarge its domination elsewhere beyond its borders.

When one hears, as we did this morning, the Soviet Union, which has politically enslaved more people than any nation in this century, attack the good faith, the sincerity and honesty of the government of the United Kingdom, which has politically liberated more people than any nation in this century, one gets the measure of the Soviet's cynical disdain for fact or fairness in the pursuit of its goals.

Whenever there are difficulties in the Western Hemisphere in which the United States is in any way involved, we know from experience that the Soviet Union will issue a loud and self-righteous blast accusing the United States of aggression or intervention—or both. Of course, it did not do so when it itself installed long-range nuclear missiles in Cuba. Nor does it hesitate to denounce the United States while itself aiding and abetting the Castro regime to foment the forceful overthrow of established governments throughout the Caribbean area. But whenever any defensive action against subversion or disorder is taken, it is the first to cry "aggression."

Of course, the Soviet Government knows perfectly well that the Western Hemisphere has an active and effective regional organization, the OAS, to which the Republics of the Western Hemisphere are deeply attached, and which they prefer to be the vehicle for resolving the problems of this hemisphere. The Soviet Government also knows that the OAS has for several days been dealing with the situation in the Dominican Republic and has made substantial progress.

But since the Soviet Union cannot use the OAS Council for its customary attacks, it always hastens to bring such matters to the United Nations Security Council, where it can. Most of the members of the United Nations are quite familiar with these tactics and the traditional charges they always involve. You will remember similar charges last year, that the United States was committing aggression against Panama. I believe it is

*United States Mission to the United Nations, Press Release No. 4538, May 3, 1965.

now apparent to all that Panama continues to enjoy its full sovereignty and independence. The same will be true of the Dominican Republic—if the agents of the Cuban
dictator do not succeed in first exploiting and then taking over a democratic revolution as they did in Cuba, and as they have tried and are trying to do in Venezuela and
in other countries of the region. That this is the objective in the Dominican Republic is
apparent from the very eagerness of the Soviet Union and of Cuba to exploit the
present ambiguous situation in the Security Council before the full facts about this
desperate strike for a Communist take-over in the Dominican Republic becomes more
obvious.

I do not propose here to review in great detail the history of the Dominican
Republic over the past five years or to speculate at any length on the origins or the
political motivations of the mixed forces which have led to a state of anarchy in that
unfortunate country. However, I do believe it relevant to our discussions to recall that
the people of the Dominican Republic have suffered from constant turmoil and
political conflict following in the wake of the long tyrannical reign of the former
dictator, Trujillo.

It is also relevant to recall that the final overthrow of that regime was brought
about, in part, by the action of the Organization of American States in adopting
diplomatic sanctions against the Trujillo dictatorship. At that time, and in the period
both preceding and following the election of Juan Bosch as President of the Dominican Republic, the Government of the United States supported every effort of the
Dominican people to establish a representative democracy.

After the last remnants of the Trujillo regime had departed and the Council of State
was established, my Government in conjunction with the OAS, assisted in the preparation of an electoral code, made available information and procedures on the mechanics
of elections and finally, again in conjunction with the OAS, observed the actual
elections, the first free elections held in the Dominican Republic in over 30 years.
Both prior to and following this election my Government has pursued extensive efforts
to build a stable and free society capable of economic, social and political development. Let there be no doubt in anybody's mind of our devotion to the cause of
representative government.

The members of this Council know well the instability which often follows the end
of authoritarian regimes and the difficulties of a people unfamiliar with the practices
of democracy in establishing effective government. The Soviet Union itself has had
some experience with the difficulties of transferring power without public participation and approval.

About a week ago the instability which has plagued the Dominican Republic since
the fall of Trujillo erupted and the officials who had governed there for a year and a
half were violently forced out; rival groups strove to capture power: Fighting broke
out between and among them; and the Dominican Republic was left without effective
government for some days.

As the situation deteriorated, certain of the contending forces indiscriminately
distributed weapons to civilians; armed bands began to roam the streets of Santo
Domingo—looting, burning, and sniping—law and order completely broken down.

The Embassies of Mexico, Guatemala, Peru, Ecuador and the United States were
violated and the Embassy of El Salvador burned.

The great majority of those who joined in this insurgent cause in the Dominican

Republic are not communists. In particular, my Government has never believed that the "P.R.D."—the Dominican Republican Party led by President Bosch—is an extremist party. United States cooperation with President Bosch and his government during his tenure following the ouster by Trujillo speaks for itself.

But while the "P.R.D." planned and during its first hours led the revolutionary movement against the government of Reid Cabral, a small group of well-known communists, consistent with their usual tactics, quickly attempted to seize control of the revolution and of the armed bands in the street.

Quite clearly this group was acting in conformity with directives issued by a communist conference that met in Havana in late 1964 and printed in Pravda last January 18. These called for assistance and continuing campaigns in support of the so-called "freedom fighters" to be organized "on a permanent basis so that this work will not dwindle to sporadic manifestations or disunited statements."

"Active aid" it went on to say, "should be given to those who are subject at present to cruel repressions—for instance, the freedom fighters in Venezuela, Colombia, Guatemala, Honduras, Paraguay and Haiti."

This deliberate effort of Havana and Moscow to promote subversion and overthrow governments in flagrant violation of all norms of international conduct is responsible for much of the unrest in the Caribbean area.

In the face of uncontrollable violence, the government which had replaced the Reid Cabral government also quickly crumbled in a few days. Many of its leaders, and also others from the initial leadership of the revolt against the Reid Cabral government, also sought asylum.

In the absence of any governmental authority Dominican law enforcement and military officials informed our embassy that the situation was completely out of control, that the police and the government could no longer give any guarantee concerning the safety of Americans or of any foreign nationals and that only an immediate landing of American forces could safeguard and protect the lives of thousands of Americans and thousands of other citizens of some thirty other countries.

At that moment, the United States Embassy was under fire; the death toll in the city, according to estimates of the Red Cross, had reached four hundred; hospitals were unable to care for the wounded; medical supplies were running out; the power supply was broken; and a food shortage threatened.

Faced with this emergency, the threat to the lives of its citizens, and a request for assistance from those Dominican authorities still struggling to maintain order, the United States on April 28th dispatched the first of the security forces we have sent to the island. Since their arrival, nearly 3,000 foreign nations from 30 countries have been evacuated without loss, although a number of United States military personnel have been killed and wounded.

We have made a full report to the Organization of American States; we have successfully evacuated some 2,000 Americans and about 1,000 persons of other nationality; we have established the secure zone of refuge called for by the OAS; we have supported the dispatch by the OAS of a committee which is at present in Santo Domingo; we have proposed that other American states make military forces available to assist in carrying out the mission of the committee—and OAS is considering such a resolution today.

To refresh your recollection of last weeks events, let me remind the Council of the sequence.

On Tuesday, April 27th, this situation was considered by the Peace Committee of the OAS. On Wednesday, April 28th, also, the OAS was formally notified by the Ambassador of the Dominican Republic about the situation in this country, and my Government called for an urgent meeting of the Council of the Organization of American States to consider ways to bring an end to the bloodshed by a cease-fire and to restore order so that the people of the Dominican Republic could settle their own political affairs without further recourse to arms.

At the same time my government notified the President of the Security Council of the action it had taken to evacuate its citizens and other foreign nationals and to set in motion the machinery of the Organization of American States.

The Council of the OAS met on Thursday, April 29, and as a first step called for an immediate cease fire on all sides, and addressed an appeal to the Papal Nuncio in Santo Domingo requesting him to use his good offices to help effect a cease fire and a return to peace.

The Council continued in session and in the early hours of April 30, took a second action urgently calling upon all parties to "pursue immediately all possible means by which a cease fire may be established and all hostilities and military operations suspended in order to prevent any further tragic loss of life." This same resolution made "an urgent appeal to the same authorities, political groupings and forces on all sides to permit the immediate establishment of an international neutral zone of refuge encompassing the geographic area of the City of Santo Domingo immediately surrounding the embassies of foreign governments, the inviolability of which will be respected by all opposing forces within which nations of all countries will be given safe haven."

At the same time, on the initiative of the Delegate of Venezuela, an urgent meeting of the Foreign Ministers of the Organization of American States was called for May 1 to consider what further measures should be taken to restore peace to the Dominican Republic.

The Security Council was immediately informed by the OAS of all these actions in accordance with Article 54 of the Charter. In accordance with the OAS Resolution of April 30, U.S. Forces in the Dominican Republic have now established a zone of safety. Three thousand persons, as I have said, have now been evacuated—not only United States citizens, but nations of 30 countries, including 14 countries of this hemisphere. More than five thousand persons, fifteen hundred of whom are American. The others of other foreign nationality, are still awaiting evacuation.

These evacuations continue, and efforts are being made to secure the safety of some 5000 people awaiting evacuation, including more than a thousand American citizens and 500 citizens of other countries who remain in peril throughout the Dominican Republic.

In addition, my government has distributed more than six thousand tons of food and medical supplies, to all elements in Santo Domingo, to relieve the suffering of the population.

The Council of the OAS on the afternoon of April 30, dispatched the Secretary-General of the Organization, Dr. Jose Mora, to the Dominican Republic. He departed on Saturday and is now working with the Papal Nuncio and others to restore order.

On Saturday the OAS again convened as a meeting of consultation of ministers of foregin affairs. This time it despatched a five-member committee composed of Argentina, Brazil, Colombia, Guatemala, and Panama "to go immediately to the city of Santo Domingo, to do everything possible to obtain re-establishment of peace and normal conditions." The committee was directed to give priority to two tasks: In the first place, to offer its good offices "to the Dominican armed groups and political groups and to the diplomatic representatives, for the purpose of obtaining: A cease-fire, the orderly evacuation of the persons who have taken asylum in the embassies and of all foreign citizens who desire to leave the Dominican Republic." Second, "to carry out an investigation of all of the aspects of the situation existing in the Dominican Republic that has led to the convocation of this meeting." This Committee is now actively at work in the Dominican Republic.

Members are no doubt aware that as a result of these repeated appeals a cease-fire was first agreed to—on the initiative of the Papal Nuncio—late in the afternoon of April 30 by the military leaders and by some of the leaders of the opposition forces, and on May 1 also by Colonel Camana. Although the leaders of the opposition forces declare that they no longer control many elements who are still shooting in Santo Domingo, this agreement began to take effect among organized forces Saturday and Sunday, and the situation in the city was much improved by Sunday afternoon.

However, lawlessness and disorder have by no means been eliminated. It has become clear that communist leaders, many trained in Cuba, have taken increasing control of what was initially a democratic movement, just as they once did in Cuba, and many of the original leaders of the rebellion, the followers of President Bosch, have taken refuge in foreign embassies. The American nations will not permit the establishment of another communist government in the Western Hemisphere. This was the unanimous view of all the American nations when in January, 1962, they declared, and I quote, "The principles of Communism are incompatible with the principles of the inter-American system."

This is and this will be the common action and the common purpose of the democratic forces of the hemisphere, as President Johnson has said. For the danger is also a common danger and the principles are common principles. So we have acted to summon the resources of this entire hemisphere to this task.

At the same time, we have increased our own forces in the light of the urgency of the situation.

The OAS Committee now in the Dominican Republic has called for the urgent shipment of more food and medical supplies to be made available to Dr. Mora, Secretary-General of the Organization, and the OAS adopted a resolution to that effect this morning. The United States will respond promptly.

The OAS has before it today a resolution which would "request governments of the American States that are capable of doing so to make available to the OAS contingents of their military, naval or air forces—to assist in carrying out the mission of the committee." The same resolution also would provide for the meeting of consultation "to continue in session in order to—take the necessary steps to facilitate the prompt restoration of constitutional government in the Dominican Republic and the withdrawal of foreign forces."

In this connection, I want to reaffirm the statement made by Ambassador Bunker, representing the United States, in the OAS meeting on Saturday:

"My Government regrets that there was no Inter-American force available to respond to the request of the authorities and the needs of the people of the Dominican Republic, and for the protection of the lives and the safety of other nationals. And my Government would welcome the constitution of such a force, as soon as possible."

Mr. President, the efforts of the OAS to deal with this tragic crisis in the Dominican Republic have been carefully considered, prudent and reasonable. Heroic efforts to end the bloodshed by cease-fire have been made by the Papal Nuncio. The Secretary General of the OAS, Dr. Mora, is on the island contributing his prestige and abilities to this effort. The inter-American Committee is also in Santa Domingo and functioning actively.

The Soviet effort—in the face of these energetic and productive steps—to exploit the anarchy in the Dominican Republic for its own ends is regrettable, if familiar.

But, my delegation welcomes the discussion in the Security Council of the situation in the Dominican Republic. Members of the Council are well aware, however, that Article 33 of our Charter states that efforts should be made to find solutions to disputes "first of all" by peaceful means, including "resort to regional agencies or arrangements."

This, of course, does not derogate from the authority of this Council. It merely prescribes the procedures and priorities envisaged by the authors of the Charters of the United Nations and the OAS for dealing with disputes of a local nature, procedures and priorities that have been followed consistently in analogous situations in the past.

In light of all the action by the OAS, it would be prudent, constructive, and in keeping with the precedents established by this Council to permit the regional organization to continue to deal with this regional problem. The United Nations Charter in Article 52 specifically recognizes the authority of regional organizations in dealing with regional problems. The Council recognizes the desirability of encouraging regional efforts, and I may add, the confidence of this Council in the abilities of regional organizations to deal with their own problems has been justified by the historical record.

In closing, Mr. President, I wish to make two things clear.

First, the United States Government has no intention of seeking to dictate the political future of the Dominican Republic. We believe that the Dominican people under the established principle of self-determination should elect their own government through free elections. It is not our intention to impose a military junta or any other government. Our interest lies in the reestablishment of constitutional government and to that end to assist in maintaining the stability essential to the expression of the free choice of the Dominican people. This intent is in full accord with the basic democratic tenets of the OAS and the inter-American system, the Charter of which calls for the maintenance of systems of political organization "on the basis of the effective exercise of representative democracy."

The United States intends to continue to work with the OAS in assisting the Dominican people to return as soon as possible to constitutional government.

With the good will and sincere support of all parties concerned, we are confident that the Dominican people will ultimately be able to have the democratic and progressive government which they seek. And we feel that the members of this body should encourage such a peaceful and orderly evolution in this small republic which has suffered so long from tyranny and civil strife.

Second, as President Johnson has emphasized, the United States "will never depart from its commitment to the preservation of the right of all of the free people of this hemisphere to choose their own course without falling prey to international conspiracy from any quarter."

"Our goal in the Dominican Republic is the goal which has been expressed again and again in the treaties and agreements which make up the fabric of the inter-American system. It is that the people of that country must be permitted to freely choose the path of political democracy, social justice and economic progress. Neither the United States, nor any nation, can want or permit a return to that brutal and oppressive despotism which earned the condemnation and punishment of this hemipshere and of all civilized humanity. We intend to carry on the struggle against tyranny no matter in what ideology it cloaks itself. This is our mutual responsibility under the agreements we have signed, and the common values which bind us together."

"Third, we believe that change comes, and we're glad that it does, and it should come through peaceful process."

"But revolution in any country is a matter for that country to deal with. It becomes a matter calling for hemispheric action only, repeat only, when the object is the establishment of a communistic dictatorship."

"Let me also make clear that we support no single man or any single group of men in the Dominican Republic. Our goal is a simple one: we are there to save the lives of our citizens and to save the lives of all people."

"Our goal in keeping the principles of the American system is to help prevent another communist state in the hemisphere, and we would like to do this without bloodshed or without large-scale fighting."

"The form and the nature of a free Dominican Government I assure you is solely a matter for the Dominican people, but we do know what kind of government we hope to see in the Dominican Republic. For that is carefully spelled out in the treaties and agreements which make up the fabric of the entire inter-American system.

"It is expressed time and time again in the words of our statesmen and the values and hopes which bind us all together.

"We hope to see a government freely chosen by the will of all the people. We hope to see a government working every hour of every day to feeding the hungry, to educating the ignorant, to healing the sick, a government whose only concern is the progress, the elevation and the welfare of all the people."

*Statement by Ambassador Stevenson in the Security Council in Reply to the Statement of the Soviet Union Representative on the Dominican Republic Question**

May 3, 1965

I do not intend to detain the Council but briefly at this time, but I must preserve the right to speak again at somewhat more length as the discussion proceeds in view of some of the statements that I have heard here this afternoon by the representative of the Soviet Union and of Cuba.

I do want to say, however, that I have been interested by the fact that lately my

Ibid., No. 4538, May 3, 1965.

distinguished colleague, the representative of the Soviet Union, seems to always bring two documents with him. One is his speech and the other is his right of reply—prepared in advance. I wonder if we had not better relabel the right of reply the right to reply by unlimited extension of one's speech!

I should like to inquire: Did I cast any shadows on the gallant struggle of the Soviet armies in the last war? No, not a word. Indeed, my colleague could have found some words of mine to quote, had he wished to do so.

Yet no such diversionary rhetoric can I think change the facts of history, that since the war the world has been afflicted by some aggressive powers and that the United States has not been one of them.

But he has mentioned some moths in the lion skin as examples of United States sins—Viet-Nam, Congo, Korea. I point out to the Council that all were cases of attempts to protect the integrity and the independence of states from outside interference.

I am not surprised, Mr. President, that the representative of the Soviet Union is touchy about some of the record of the past twenty years, including its acquisition of great amounts of territory, its alliance with Nazi Germany, but I am surprised at exactly how touchy he has turned out to be.

The Soviet army, as I have said, did, indeed, fight most gallantly in the second world war, for which we are all profoundly indebted, although I would hardly ascribe the entire credit to the Soviet army, as he seemed to do. We were, indeed, prepared to continue in the post-war world the cooperation with the Soviet Union that had prevailed during the war. The blame for the great gulf which followed that war lies squarely and solely on the policies of the Soviet Union during that time.

I regret that in recent weeks my colleague has revived first in the Committee of 33, then in the Committee on Aggression, and then in the Disarmament Commission, and now in the Security Council, the language and the techniques of the Stalin era. I hope this is only a passing phase and that the frustrations of their troubles with their former ally will not continue to plague us here.

And I will not talk more about the history of the Soviet Union, as he has seen fit to do about the history of my country, because Russia expanded from Duchy of Moscow to the Arctic to Central Asia and all the way to the Pacific. Facts that I think are familiar to all of us hardly need repetition here.

Now if I may turn for only a moment to the extensive remarks of the representative of Cuba. Well, it is not easy. I shall disregard the extreme offensiveness of many of his remarks, such as "pirates in Washington" and "liars in the White House committing criminal acts." If he had spent as much time learning facts as epithets and insults, I think he would have had some trouble getting quite so emotional about the United States imperialist objectives in the Dominican Republic.

History I think will speak on the full significance of the present situation in the Dominican Republic just as it will on the rescue mission in the Congo, and when it has spoken it will be clear that the role of American forces in the Dominican Republic will have been constructive and not destructive of the freedom of the Dominican Republic.

I remind him, too, that it has been necessary, as I have said, for American troops to be sent to several countries since the second world war to Korea, to Lebanon, to the evacuation of foreigners from the Congo and to Viet-Nam. In no case have they derogated from the sovereignty and the independence of the country in which they have been employed. Indeed, one of the main reasons for their dispatch has been to help preserve that independence, whether threatened by direct aggression or by the modern forces of subversion and totalitarian techniques.

He has used so freely some extreme language to express his conclusions about the sins of the United States and our malevolent purposes in the Dominican Republic, but few facts to support him and his conclusions and a good many false statements. Let me assure the representative of Cuba that he is misinformed and that I can categorically deny that the United States has done any bombing in the Dominican Republic, nor have we been fighting against constitutionalists, to use his word. We have been fighting against fighting, trying to stop bloodshed and to restore order. And I can assure him that unless there are nations, to pick up an argument of his, in international organizations that will denounce aggression and will protect against aggression, whether by armies or by acts, there surely will be no free states left. This is the danger in the future, not conquest of anybody by the United States.

We have not invaded the Dominican Republic. We have acted to protect foreigners in a revolution in concert with our fellow representatives in this hemisphere, and to protect the Dominican people from a communist seizure of the country while the Dominicans themselves determine their future.

But his extensive attacks may be germane, in a way, to what is before us. It may be very pertinent to the subject before us for they serve to remind us how easily, how quickly a revolution offered to and accepted by a people in the name of democratic freedom and social progress can be betrayed. It reminds us of the grim struggle which took place within the revolutionary Cuban regime which overthrew Batista, a struggle between those who overthrew Batista to bring freedom to Cuba and those who overthrew Batista to bring freedom to communism. It reminds us of the tragic outcome of that struggle that brave men who had fought for the revolution with Castro were turned on, suddenly assailed, arrested, driven from office into prison or exile all for the singular offense of bringing in the principles of the revolution they had fought for. This stark reminder of a revolution betrayed will remain forever in the minds and hearts of all of the citizens of the Western Hemisphere and it cannot but influence actions which are taken to bring order out of chaos in the Dominican Republic.

I had no thought to refer to the contemptuous epithets that he has used with respect to sister republics of this hemisphere, "lackeys and spittles" and so on, but it was curious that he first quoted with approval what they said when they expressed concern and doubt about our urgent response to the call for help and then denounced them in these repulsive epithets, when they discovered the facts and joined to help stop the bloodshed and to restore order to the Dominican Republic and give the people of that beleaguered land a chance to restore constitutional democracy to their country.

(In a further intervention, Ambassador Stevenson said:)

Mr. President, with some sense of mercy for the members, I reserve the right to speak further in reply to the speeches I have heard this afternoon, although that sense of restraint was not evidently understood by my Soviet colleague. And I regret, I must say, that his concern for the endurance of the Security Council has not changed for the better, like my speech. If I would have thought that truth was revealed in even one or two rights of reply, I should be most happy. The thought that it may take several more is, I must confess, deeply depressing!

Now, let me conclude the afternoon's ceremonies, if that is possible, by reading you one paragraph that I have just received from a news report: "President Johnson said tonight"—if this is of any assurance to the Soviet and Cuban representatives—"that U.S. troops would be withdrawn from the Dominican Republic as soon as the Organization of American States can get a plan into effect to bring peace and stability there."

I have nothing further to say.

GENERAL PROBLEMS OF PEACEKEEPING

Address by President Johnson at the Twentieth Anniversary of the United Nations Charter*

June 25, 1965

On my journey across the continent, I stopped in the state of Missouri, and there I met with the man who made the first such pilgrimage here twenty years ago as the thirty-third President of the United States—Harry S. Truman.

Mr. Truman sent to this Assembly his greetings and good wishes on this anniversary commemoration. He asked that I express to you for him—as for myself and for my countrymen—the faith which we of the United States hold firmly in the United Nations and in the ultimate success of its mission among men.

On this historic and happy occasion we have met to celebrate twenty years of achievement and to look together at the work that we face in future meeings. I come to this anniversary not to speak of futility or failure nor of doubt and despair—I come to raise a voice of confidence in both the future of these United Nations and the fate of the human race.

The movement of history is glacial. On two decades of experience, none can presume to speak with certainty of the direction or the destiny of man's affairs. But this we do know and this we do believe.

Futility and failure are not the truth of this Organization brought into being here twenty years ago.

Where, historically, man has moved fitfully from war toward war, in these last two decades man has moved steadily away from war as either an instrument of national policy or a means of international decision.

Many factors have contributed to this change. But no one single factor has contributed more than the existence and the enterprise of the United Nations itself.

For there can be no doubt that the United Nations has taken root in human need and has established a shape, and a purpose, and a meaning of its own.

By providing a forum for the opinions of the world, the United Nations has given them a force and an influence that they have never had before. By shining the light of inquiry and discussion upon very dark and isolated conflicts, it has pressed the nations of the world to conform their courses to the requirements of the United Nations Charter.

And let all remember—and none forget—that now more than fifty times in these twenty years the United Nations has acted to keep the peace.

By persuading nations to justify their own conduct before all countries, it has helped, at many times and in many places, to soften the harshness of man to his fellow man.

By confronting the rich with the misery of the poor and the privileged with the despair of the oppressed, it has removed the excuse of ignorance—unmasked the evil of indifference, and has placed an insistent, even though still unfulfilled, responsibility upon the more fortunate of the earth.

*White House Press Release, June 25, 1965.

By insisting upon the political dignity of man, it has welcomed 63 nations to take their places alongside the 51 original members—a historical development of dramatic import, achieved mainly through peaceful means.

And by binding countries together in the great declarations of the Charter, it has given those principles a strengthened vocabulary in the conduct of the affairs of man.

Today, then—at this time of anniversary—let us not occupy ourselves with parochial doubts or with passing despair. The United Nations—after twenty years—does not draw its life from the asembly halls or the committee rooms. It lives in the conscience and the reason of mankind.

The most urgent problem we face is the keeping of the peace.

Today, as I speak, clear and present dangers in Southeast Asia cast their shadow across the path of all mankind.

The United Nations must be concerned.

The most elementary principle of the United Nations is that neighbors must not attack their neighbors—and that principle today is under challenge.

The processes of peaceful settlement today are blocked by willful aggressors contemptuous of the opinion and the will of mankind.

Bilateral diplomacy has yielded no result.

The machinery of the Geneva Conference has been paralyzed.

Resort to the Security Council has been rejected.

The efforts of the distinguished Secretary General have been rebuffed.

An appeal for unconditional discussion was met with contempt.

A pause in bombing operations was called an insult.

The concern for peace of the Commonwealth Prime Ministers has received little and very disappointing results.

Therefore, today I put to this World Assembly the facts of aggression, the right of a people to be free from attack, the interest of every member in safety against molestation, the duty of this Organization to reduce the dangers to peace, and the unhesitating readiness of the United States of America to find a peaceful solution.

I now call upon this gathering of the nations of the world to use all their influence, individually and collectively, to bring to the tables those who seem determined to make war. We will support your efforts, as we will support effective action by any agent or agency of these United Nations.

*   *   *

Statement by Ambassador Arthur J. Goldberg on the Question of Peacekeeping*

November 24, 1965

The item before us—the "Comprehensive Review of the Whole Question of Peacekeeping"—is surely one of the key items before this General Assembly.

Peacekeeping is at the heart of this organization's work. For if the United Nations failed to fulfill its responsibilities under the Charter for the maintenance of peace and security, there would be little hope for the other noble aims of the Charter. Prospects

*United States Mission to the United Nations, *Press Release 4719*, Nov. 24, 1965.

for peace in the world and a better life for men everywhere would be immeasurably darkened.

It might be well at this point to define exactly what the term "United Nations Peacekeeping" means.

The Secretary General has provided us with a useful definition. "Peacekeeping forces," he told the Harvard Alumni in 1963, "are of a very different kind and have little in common with the forces foreseen in Chapter VII—but their existence is not in conflict with Chapter VII. They are essentially peace and not fighting forces and they operate only with the consent of the parties directly concerned."

The United Nations has a long history of establishing such peacekeeping forces—in Greece, in 1947; in Kashmir, in 1948; along the borders of Israel, in 1949; in the Gaza Strip, in 1956; in Lebanon, in 1958; in the Congo, in 1960; in West Iran, in 1962; in Yemen, in 1963; in Cyprus, in 1964; and in India and Pakistan in 1965.

The report of the Secretary General and the President of the General Assembly to the Committee of 33, and the discussion in that committee, have helped to define the nature of these peacekeeping operations. Unlike enforcement actions, they are voluntary in two fundamental respects:

> They do not place obligations on member states to contribute personnel, materials, or services.
> They are introduced into the territory of a country only with the consent of that country.

Such operations have taken various forms—observers on a frontier; supervision of a ceasefire line; fact-finding and observation to clarify a factual situation or to investigate charges of interference and infiltration from the outside; and assistance to a country to maintain or restore law and order where requested by that country and in conditions in which international peace and security might otherwise be threatened.

It is remarkable—and heartening to my Government—that UN peacekeeping operations of all these kinds have gone forward even in the face of deep differences over issues of principle. This is a tribute to the diplomatic and executive talents of the Secretary-General and to the generosity and dedication of participating countries. Above all, it is a tribute to the underlying good sense of the overwhelming majority of Member States which have insisted that the UN carry out its responsibilities, though none of us may have been fully satisfied with all the arrangements for initiating, supervising and financing a particular operation.

Mr. Chairman, this success, this partial success, is instructive for our deliberations on the peacekeeping issue. We must avoid the fallacy of assuming that total agreement on all issues of principle is a precondition of cooperating in UN activities. Here, as elsewhere, the pragmatic adaptation of arrangements on a case-by-case basis may offer the best hope of progress.

In any event, we must not allow our search for new and improved ground rules to impair the procedures and arrangements that we already have.

Nor should we permit the considerable progress already made in developing peacekeeping procedures to be frustrated by a small minority. As we said to the Committee of 33 on August 16: "My Government . . . is not prepared to accept a situation in which the capacity of the United Nations to act for peace could be stopped by the negative vote of a single member. Nor should the effectiveness of this Organization be determined by the level of support forthcoming from its least cooperative members."

What are the ground rules for authorizing, supervising and financing peacekeeping operations which have developed in the past—and which can guide us in the future?

From the statements of delegations in this and recent General Assemblies, from the deliberations in the Special Committee on Peacekeeping Operations, from the report jointly submitted to that Committee by the Secretary-General and the President of the 19th General Assembly, and from the comments of governments on that report, there appears to be widespread support for the following major principles:

First, the Security Council has the primary responsibility for initiating and supervising peacekeeping operations—and everything should be done to enable it to exercise that responsibility.

Certainly there is widespread agreement—in which my Government strongly concurs—that the maximum possible use should be made of the Security Council.

Recent experience—in the Congo, in Cyprus, in Kashmir—has demonstrated that the Council *can* meet its responsibilities for dealing with threats to international peace and security. The enlargement of the Council to make it more representative of the membership as a whole should encourage the further strengthening of its peacekeeping work.

The United States continues to favor the suggestion we submitted in September 1964 to the Working Group of 21 that all proposals to initiate peacekeeping operations should be considered first in the Security Council. The Assembly would not authorize or assume control of such operations unless the Council had demonstrated its inability to act.

Second, the General Assembly has authority to initiate and supervise peacekeeping operations where the Security Council is unable to act.

Everyone apparently agrees that the General Assembly can make recommendations to the Security Council with respect to peacekeeping in the event the Council is unable to act. But the real question is whether, in the face of veto by a permanent member, the Assembly can authorize the establishment of such operations.

From the comments made by member states in recent months, it appears that the overwhelming majority of UN members answer this question in the affirmative. Only a small minority of members continue to insist that the negative vote of one permanent member can prevent 116 other members of the organization from initiating voluntary action to protect their common interests in the maintenance of peace.

I will not repeat here all the arguments—fully confirmed by the International Court of Justice—in support of the complementary powers of the Assembly pursuant to various articles of the Charter. I wish only to emphasize, as so many others have already done, that the acceptance of the minority view on this subject would be absurd in theory and intolerable in practice.

All of our countries, in accepting membership in the UN, agreed to refrain from the use of force save in self-defense, in support of UN action and pursuant to Chapter VIII of the Charter. These Charter restraints were undertaken on the assumption that the United Nations could act successfully when peace and security—and hence our common interests—were seriously threatened. It would be unreasonable to expect members to entrust peacekeeping responsibility to a UN which could be rendered impotent by the intransigence of a single member. Such an interpretation would do violence to the

Charter and would disappoint the legitimate hopes in this organization of the peoples of the world.

The United States, though itself a permanent member of the Security Council, has never considered that any one member should have the power unilaterally, and without recourse, to frustrate the initiation of peacekeeping operations not involving enforcement action. Some have argued that, on a narrow calculation of our interests and having regard to the fact that we have but one vote of 117 while paying 32% of the regular budget, we should be disposed to do so.

Nevertheless, we have defended the authority of the Assembly to undertake peacekeeping operations free from veto by ourselves or others because we recognize the long term interest of all mankind in developing this means of containing violence in the nuclear age. We have not considered that our interests require us to have a veto over recommendations to members that they contribute to UN operations taking place on the territory of a state with its consent. We appeal to others to take the same long view of their own interests.

Third, the General Assembly has the exclusive authority under the Charter to apportion the expenses of peacekeeping operations among the members of the United Nations.

This principle, like those I have mentioned earlier, is supported by a large majority of United Nations members. It is fully confirmed by the language of Article 17, by twenty years of practice in the United Nations, and by the Advisory Opinion of the International Court of Justice accepted by the General Assembly. With respect to financing as well as authorization, the powers of the Assembly should be preserved. No member should have the right to veto a financial plan accepted by everyone else.

Fourth, the expenses of UN peacekeeping operations should be, so far as possible, the collective financial responsibility of the entire membership.

This principle, asserted without any qualification in General Assembly Resolution 1874 (S-IV), has been supported by the U.S. and a majority of other members for very practical reasons:

> It offers the best way of sharing the financial burden fairly among the membership.
>
> It recognizes that every member has an interest in the preservation of peace and should therefore pay something—no matter how little—toward its preservation.
>
> It takes account of the fact that member states will be more likely to contribute military contingents for an operation when it has broad political support as reflected in widely shared financial participation.

Many, to be sure, have expressed optimism that voluntary financing of peacekeeping can do the job. The voluntary method of financing certainly offers one possibility to be considered on a case-by-case basis. But experience indicates that it often places unfair burdens on troop-supplying countries and may even fail to produce sufficient funds to assure the continuance of the operation.

At this very moment the Secretary-General is short some $7 million for the United Nations operation in Cyprus. Those who believe voluntary financing is the answer have an obligation to demonstrate that it can work in specific situations. As Ambassador Stevenson once said, it would be irresponsible for the members to sit back while the Secretary-General has to search for funds like a beggar on the street.

Fifth, the cost of peacekeeping operations should be shared fairly among the members in accordance with their capacity to pay and with due regard for the international character of these operations.

General Assembly Resolution 1874 (S-IV) included two propositions on which there is broad support—that economically developed countries are in a position to make relatively larger contributions than countries that are economically less developed and that the special responsibilities of the permanent members of the Security Council should be borne in mind in connection with their contributions to financing. There is widespread support for the concept of a special scale of assessment for peacekeeping operations which could give effect to these propositions.

The United States has already expressed support for a special scale. We reaffirm that support today.

Sixth, General Assembly procedures for authorizing, supervising, and financing peacekeeping operations should provide an appropriate voice for those members which bear the principal responsibility for supporting them.

With this in mind, we included in our submission to the Committee of 21 in September, 1964, a proposal for a Special Finance Committee of the General Assembly. This Committee would include the permanent members of the Security Council and a relatively high percentage of those member states in each geographic area that are large contributors. The General Assembly, in approving financial arrangements for peacekeeping operations, would act only on recommendations from this Committee passed by a two-thirds majority of the Committee's membership.

The United States is not irrevocably wedded to this particular proposal. We note that other proposals addressed to this same problem have been put forward by the delegations of Nigeria and France. Here, as in the case of other principles I have mentioned, we are prepared to consider any reasonable procedure for implementing the overall objective.

Seventh, the Secretary-General is the most appropriate executive agent for managing peacekeeping operations, and should be given every support within the scope of his mandate.

As the chief executive officer of the United Nations, the Secretary-General has the right and the duty to implement the directives of the Security Council, the General Assembly, and other organs. At various times in the past two decades he has carried out this responsibility under broad mandates in United Nations peacekeeping operations in the Middle East, the Congo, Cyprus, and Kashmir. We are of the firm conviction tha he should continue to exercise this responsibility in the best interest of effective United Nations peacekeeping.

These, then, are the general principles which we believe should guide this organization in dealing with the peacekeeping problem. These principles are broadly compatible with the guideline set forth in paragraph 52 of the Report submitted by the Secretary-General and the President of the General Assembly to the Special Committee on Peacekeeping Operations—guidelines which have had the widespread support of the members of the United Nations.

The tide of historical evolution of this organization which is reflected in these principles cannot be reversed by a few recalcitrant members. The peacekeeping work of the United Nations must continue and it will continue.

*   *   *

Statement by Ambassador Goldberg Before the Committee on Foreign Relations on the Responsibility of the U.N. in Vietnam *

November 2, 1967

I appreciate your invitation to appear before this Committee and give testimony on the important subject of the responsibility of the United Nations in the search for peace in Vietnam. This is the gravamen of Senate Concurrent Resolution 44, introduced by Senator Morse, and of Senate Resolution 180, introduced by Senator Mansfield and other Senators.

At the very outset let me say that I agree completely with the concept of the responsibility of the United Nations which underlies both resolutions.

In preparing my testimony I have taken note of Senator Morse's comment in the hearings before this Committee on October 26, referring to the Mansfield resolution: "I think it probably would be the most appropriate type of resolution to send to the President, for, after all, this ought to be a teamwork play."

It is my considered view as the United States Representative to the United Nations that the adoption of Senator Mansfield's resolution at this time will support the efforts I have been making at the United Nations at the direction of the President to enlist the Security Council in the search for peace in Vietnam.

UN Responsibility Under the Charter

Any analysis of the problem of UN involvement in Vietnam must start with the United Nations Charter. Under the Charter, the United Nations and its members have a specific obligation to cooperate in the maintenance of international peace and security. This obligation is clearly set forth in the provisions of the Charter, including specifically the following:

Article 1, paragraph 1, which states the first purpose of the United Nations as:

"To maintain international peace and security, and to that end: to take effective collective measures for the prevention and removal of threats to the peace, and for the suppression of acts of aggression or other breaches of the peace, and to bring about by peaceful means, and in conformity with the principles of justice and international law, adjustment or settlement of international disputes or situations which might lead to a breach of the peace."

Article 2, paragraph 3, which includes among the principles binding upon all members the following:

"All Members shall settle their international disputes by peaceful means in such a manner that international peace and security, and justice, are not endangered."

Article 24, paragraph 1:

"In order to ensure prompt and effective action by the United Nations, its Members confer on the Security Council primary responsibility for the maintenance of international peace and security, and agree that in carrying out its duties under this responsibility the Security Council acts on their behalf.

Ibid., USUN-174, Nov. 2, 1967.

Article 25:

"The Members of the United Nations agree to accept and carry out the decisions of the Security Council in accordance with the present Charter."

And to these provisions should be added all of Chapters VI and VII which confer broad powers on the Security Council for the maintenance of international peace and security.

Moreover, it is obvious that these powers and obligations of the United Nations apply to the situation in Southeast Asia in general and Vietnam in particular.

In saying this I am mindful of the argument that is sometimes made, both in and out of the United Nations, that several of the principal parties—the Democratic Republic of Vietnam, the Republic of Vietnam, and the People's Republic of China—are not in the United Nations and that it is therefore not a suitable place to deal with the Vietnam question. The premise is, of course, a fact, but the conclusion is incorrect. The Charter explicitly provides for the responsibility and participation of non-members; for example:

Article 2, paragraph 6, provides: "The Organization shall ensure that states which are not Members of the United Nations act in accordance with these principles so far as may be necessary for the maintenance of international peace and security."

And Article 32 provides in part that "any state which is not a member of the United Nations, if it is a party to a dispute under consideration by the Security Council, shall be invited to participate, without vote, in the discussion relating to the dispute."

It is clear, therefore, Mr. Chairman, that the United Nations has a duty to act for peace in Vietnam, and that the involvement of non-members is no obstacle to such action. The question therefore arises: Why has such action not taken place?

I believe it would be useful to the Committee if I review briefly the record of our endeavors in the Security Council to obtain such action.

Cambodian Complaint, 1964

In May 1964 Cambodia brought to the Security Council a complaint over incidents on its border with South Vietnam. After extended debate the Council decided by a vote of 9 in favor (Bolivia, Brazil, China, France, Ivory Coast, Morocco, Norway, United Kingdom, United States), none against, and two abstentions (Czechoslovakia and the USSR) to send three of its members as a mission to the scene of the trouble. As the tally shows, the Soviet Union abstained on this step. Its representative contended that the existing machinery set up under the Geneva Agreements was sufficient and a Security Council mission was therefore "not justified."

Nevertheless, the mission was sent. Its recommendations included sending a group of United Nations observers to Cambodia. Both the U.S. and the South Vietnamese Government supported this proposal. But at that point the Cambodian Government termed the proposal "unacceptable to Cambodia" and asked that its complaint "should be placed on file." The matter was thereupon dropped at the request of Cambodia, the original complaintant.

Tonkin Gulf Incident

In August 1964 the United States took the initiative in requesting a Security Council meeting to consider the Tonkin Gulf incident. The Soviet Union proposed that North Vietnam be invited to take part in the discussion. The United States made no objection to such an invitation, but further proposed that South Vietnam also be invited. The President of the Council thereupon consulted with the members and reported to the Council that his consultations had resulted in agreement among the members on the participation of both North and South Vietnam in the proceedings. He made clear that under this agreement the North and South Vietnamese Government would both be welcome to give information to the Council either by taking part in the discussions or in such form as they might prefer. It should be added that the question of participation by Peking was not raised.

In response to this invitation, the Foreign Minister of South Vietnam replied to the Council in a long letter on August 15, giving his Government's side of the dispute and placing the South Vietnamese Permanent Observer to the United Nations at the Council's disposal.

The response from Hanoi was a flat rejection of the competence of the United Nations to deal with the matter at all. I quote from the North Vietnamese telegram to the President of the Security Council, dated August 19, 1964:

> "The consideration of the problem of the acts of war by the United States Government against the Democratic Republic of Vietnam and of the problem of the United States war of aggression in South Vietnam lies within the competence of the 1954 Geneva Conference on Indo-China, and not of the Security Council;
> "Should the Council take an illegal decision on the basis of the United States 'complaint', the Government of the Democratic Republic of Vietnam would regretfully find itself obliged to consider that decision null and void."

In view of this attitude of Hanoi, the members of the Council determined that it would be useless to proceed further.

Efforts in Summer 1965

On June 25, 1965, President Johnson invited members of the United Nations "to use all their influence individually and collectively to bring to the table those who seem determined to make war."

On my appointment as United States Representative in July 1965, in the spirit of this statement by the President and at his direction, I made the Vietnam question my first order of business. On July 30, I sent a letter to the President of the Security Council, summarizing previous United States efforts to open a path to peace in Vietnam and expressing our willingness "to collaborate unconditionally with members of the Security Council in the search for an acceptable formula to restore peace and security to that area of the world." And I added in conclusion: "It is the hope of my Government that the members of the Security Council will somehow find the means to respond effectively to the challenge raised by the present state of affairs in Southeast Asia."

I then initiated an intensive personal canvass of members of the Security Council, with a view to gaining their support for a move by the Council on Vietnam. This canvass disclosed a broad consensus among the members, regardless of their views on the substance of the Vietnam issue, that any effort to have the matter considered in the Council at that time would be unproductive.

Efforts in Connection with the 1965-66 Bombing Pause

In December 1965, as the Committee will recall, the United States suspended the bombing of North Vietnam, and accompanied this step with an intensive diplomatic effort for peace in Vietnam. The bombing pause lasted 37 days, during which, at the direction of the President, I went to Europe to consult with the heads of government of several countries. Upon my return, in January 1966, while the pause was still in effect, I again consulted with members of the Security Council to determine whether action by the Council would, in their view be appropriate and helpful in the cause of peace. My canvass disclosed a general view that a meeting of the Council at that point would jeopardize diplomatic efforts which were then under way.

These diplomatic efforts failed late in January, and the bombing of North Vietnam was resumed. On January 31, I requested a meeting of the Security Council on Vietnam. The Council convened the next day February 1. We laid before it a United States draft resolution, the text of which is as follows:

"The Security Council,

Deeply concerned at the continuation of hostilities in Vietnam,

Mindful of its responsibilities for the maintenance of international peace and security,

Noting that the provisions of the Geneva Accords of 1954 and 1962 have not been implemented,

Desirous of contributing to a peaceful and honorable settlement of the conflict in Vietnam,

Recognizing the right of all peoples, including those in Vietnam, to self-determination,

1. Calls for immediate discussions without preconditions at   on   date, among the appropriate interested governments to arrange a conference looking toward the application of the Geneva Accords of 1954 and 1962 and the establishment of a durable peace in Southeast Asia;

2. Recommends that the first order of business of such a conference be arrangements for a cessation of hostilities under effective supervision;

3. Offers to assist in achieving the purposes of this resolution by all appropriate means, including the provision of arbitrators or mediators;

4. Calls on all concerned to cooperate fully in the implementation of this resolution;

5. Requests the Secretary General to assist as appropriate in the implementation of this resolution."

The Security Council discussed the matter for two days, on February 1 and 2, 1966. The position of the Soviet Union with respect to United Nations competence to deal with the Vietnam conflict was stated by its representative, Ambassador Fedorenko, during the debate in these words:

"The Soviet delegation deems it essential to state that it objects to the convening of the Security Council for the discussion of the question of Vietnam and declares itself to be against the inclusion of the present item in the agenda of the Security Council."

And at a later point in the debate Ambassador Fedorenko went on to say:

"I should like to quote a message stating the position of the National Liberation Front of South Vietnam. This organization today published a statement in reply to the decision of the United States of America to bring the problem of Vietnam to the Security Council. In that statement it is pointed out that the Security Council has no right to take any decisions on questions involving South Vietnam and that all resolutions of the Security Council on the question of Vietnam will be null an void as far as the National Liberation Front is concerned."

It is also pertinent to note the observations of the Representative of France, Ambassador Seydoux, on this question:

"My Government does not believe that the United Nations constitutes the proper framework for achieving a peaceful solution of the Vietnam conflict. . . . A debate before the Security Council might run the risk of resulting ultimately—as has happened in the past—only in a vain confrontation and in demonstrations of purely formal character."

I submit to the Committee the verbatim records of the three Council meetings which took place on those dates.

As the Committee knows, the inscription of an item on the agenda of the Security Council is, under the Council's rules, a procedural question. It is therefore not subject to the veto under Article 27 of the Charter, but can be accomplished by any nine affirmative votes. On the afternoon of February 2 we proceeded to a vote. The result was:

For inscription, 9:   Argentina, China, Japan, Jordan, New Zealand, Netherlands, United Kingdom, United States, Uruguay

Opposed, 2:   Bulgaria, Soviet Union

Abstentions, 4:   France, Mali, Nigeria, Uganda

Let me point out that a number of the favorable votes on inscription were cast on the understanding that the Council would not proceed forthwith to consider the matter substantively, but that instead informal consultations would be held as to the future course of action. Only on this basis was it possible to obtain the necessary nine votes for inscription.

Accordingly, immediately after the vote the President of the Council, Ambassador Matsui of Japan, adjourned the Council with the consent of the members so that the agreed-upon consultations could be held. Intensive consultations were then held by Ambassador Matsui over the three weeks that followed. He summed up the results of these consultations in a letter to the members of the Council dated February 26. He reported that he had found differences of view among the members, principally on "the wisdom of the Council considering the problem of Vietnam at this particular juncture." He added that these differences had "given rise to a general feeling that it would be inopportune for the Council to hold further debate at this time."

Ambassador Matsui's entire letter is pertinent to the Committee's inquiry and I therefore submit it for your records, Mr. Chairman.

It is important to note also that the Soviet Union and Bulgaria refused throughout to join in the consultations which Ambassador Matsui held among the Council members. The Soviet representative, Ambassador Fedorenko, sent a letter to the President of the

Council stating his "strong objections" to the letter of Ambassador Matsui and charging him with "steps which go beyond the limit of his competence and violate the Security Council's rules of procedure and established practice." A similar letter was also sent by the Bulgarian representative.

My own canvass, taken independently of that of Ambassador Matsui, confirmed his assessment that the members of the Council were generally unwilling to proceed with a substantive discussion despite the strong and express preference of the United States that we get on with the debate. Indeed, this unwillingness was found even among those members who had voted affirmatively on inscription in the hope that such a vote might sway the negative attitude of the Soviet Union and France.

Recent Efforts

Since that time, a year and a half ago, my associates and I at the United States Mission have periodically reviewed the possibility of renewed consideration of Vietnam by the Security Council. We made a particular point of this during the Tet bombing pause at the beginning of 1967. This also happened to be the time when several of the non-permanent seats on the Council changed hands, and we engaged in detailed consultations with the members just coming on the Council as well as with those remaining on the Council. But the results of this canvass were no more encouraging than those that had preceded it.

Then, as recently as September of this year, scarcely two months ago, at the request of the President I once again conducted an intensive canvass of the members of the Security Council. In these informal consultations we discussed the possibility of Council action either on the resolution we had offered in January 1966, or on a new formulation. This new draft was as follows:

"The Security Council,

Having considered the problem of Vietnam,

Deeply concerned at the situation in Vietnam and the threat it poses to international peace and security,

Believing in the principle of the inviolability of, and respect for, the sovereignty and territorial integrity of states,

Convinced that a solution to this problem is to be found through political and not military means, and that a peaceful solution should be found through negotiations,

Considering, that the Geneva Agreements of 1954 and 1962 constitute a workable basis for peace in Southeast Asia.

1. Reaffirms, on the basis of the Geneva Agreements, the following principles:

(a) That there should be a complete cease-fire and disengagement by all armed personnel throughout North and South Vietnam at an agreed upon date.

(b) That there should be no military forces or bases maintained or supported in North and South Vietnam other than those under the control of the respective governments, and all other troops and armed personnel should be withdrawn or demobilized, and all other military bases abolished as quickly as possible and in accordance with an agreed time schedule, during which introductions of additional armed personnel should be prohibited.

(c) That the international frontiers of the states bordering on North and South

Vietnam and the demilitarized zone between North and South Vietnam should be fully respected.

(d) That the question of reunification of Vietnam should be settled peacefully by the Vietnamese people in both North and South Vietnam, without any foreign interference.

(e) That there should be international supervision of the foregoing through such machinery as may be agreed upon.

2. Calls for the convening of an international conference for the purpose of establishing a permanent peace in Southeast Asia based upon the principles of the Geneva Agreements."

I regret to report that this recent canvass shows a general unwillingness for the Security Council either to resume its consideration of the agenda item and draft resolution which we proposed in early 1966, or to consider this new draft, or to take any other action on the matter.

Attitudes of Hanoi, NLF and Peking to UN Involvement

It is relevant at this point to note the attitudes of Hanoi and Peking, as well as the National Liberation Front, toward United Nations involvement in the search for peace in Vietnam. All of these have made known their views on the subject many times. I shall cite only a few representative examples.

In late January 1966, the North Vietnamese Foreign Ministry declared:

> "The Government of the Democratic Republic of Vietnam reaffirms once again that on the international plane, the consideration of the United States war acts in Vietnam falls within the competence of the 1954 Geneva conference on Indochina and not the United Nations Security Council. Any resolution by the United Nations Security Council intervening in the Vietnam question will be null and void."

In June 1966 the North Vietnamese Foreign Ministry said:

> "The United Nations has absolutely no competence in the Vietnam problem. The fact that the Saigon puppet administration, at U.S. bidding, proposed that the United Nations send its observers to supervise the election farce in South Vietnam is completely illegal and runs counter to the 1954 Geneva agreements on Vietnam and international law."

Then in September 1966, the Premier of North Vietnam, Pham Van Dong, said in a speech:

> "On the occasion of the current session of the United Nations General Assembly, they are trying again to use the United Nations as an instrument for their aggressive policy in Vietnam. But the United Nations has absolutely no right whatsoever to intervene in the Vietnam issue."

And recently, when I was conducting soundings in late August and early September of this year among members of the Security Council, and this fact became known, Hanoi's major daily, Nhan Dan, which reflects the official view, said:

> "The United States ruling circles are actively trying to get the United Nations to interfere in the Vietnam problem on the occasion of the forthcoming 22nd Session of the United

Nations General Assembly. United States delegate to the United Nations Arthur Goldberg has met a number of representatives of various countries. . . .

The Vietnamese people have many times clearly stated that the United Nations has no right whatsoever to interfere in Vietnam. The Vietnam question can only be settled on the basis of the four-point stand of the DRV Government and the five-point statement of the NFLSV."

The position of the National Liberation Front has been identical with that of Hanoi, as illustrated by the following statement by the central committee of the Front on February 2, 1966:

"The NFLSV is determined to expose before the public the United States imperialists' perfidious plot to hide behind the United Nations flag to accelerate the aggressive war in South Vietnam and the war of destruction against North Vietnam. The NFLSV solemnly declares: the United Nations has no right to make decisions concerning the affairs of the South Vietnamese people."

A similar attitude has been expressed by the Peking Government, as can be seen in the following examples.

In April 1965, the People's Daily in Peking ran an editorial which stated:

"The Vietnam question has nothing to do with the United Nations. The 1954 Geneva agreements were reached outside the United Nations and the latter has no right whatsoever to interfere in the affairs of Vietnam and Indochina. It is the duty of the countries participating in the Geneva conference to safeguard the Geneva agreements and no meddling by the United Nations is called for, nor will it be tolerated. This is the case today as it was in the past, and so will it remain in the future."

Then, on August 7, 1965—just as I was holding my first consultations with members of the Security Council—the People's Daily said in an editorial:

"It is . . . clear to everyone that the United Nations has no right whatever to meddle in the Vietnam question, nor can it solve the issue. The Vietnam question has nothing to do with the United Nations."

We have many other statements from Peking to the same effect, including some of quite recent date.

Conclusion

Mr. Chairman, this is the record of the Administration's efforts to enlist the United Nations, and specifically the Security Council, in the search for peace in Vietnam.

I must confess that the failure of these efforts has been my keenest disappointment and my greatest frustration during my service for our Government at the United Nations. But in spite of these rebuffs, I do not intend, as long as I occupy my present post, to diminish my efforts in this cause.

I repeat my conviction that the Mansfield resolution will support the efforts I am making at the United Nations at the President's direction. The resolution, as I understand it, is intended to express the sense of the Senate and appropriately leaves the timing and circumstances of action in the Security Council for Presidential determination.

For my part, I promise, in keeping with the spirit of that resolution, to persevere with all the resources at my command to the end that the Security Council may carry out its clear responsibilities under the Charter with respect to Vietnam. I shall do so in the conviction that if there is any contribution that diplomacy—in or out of the United Nations—can make to hasten the end of this conflict, none of us can in good conscience spare any effort or any labor to make that contribution—no matter how frustrating past efforts may have been, or how many new beginnings may be required. The admirable courage and perseverance of our men on the battlefield must be fully matched by our perseverance in seeking, through diplomacy, to find the common ground on which a fair and honorable political settlement can be built.

THE UNITED NATIONS
AND THE MIDDLE EAST

THE UNITED NATIONS
AND THE MIDDLE EAST

Commentary

The problem of the Middle East—primarily, the tragic conflict between Jews and Arabs over Palestine—consumed more time and nervous energy than any other in the U.N.'s first 25 years. For all its biblical aspects and antecedents, the Arab-Israeli struggle was relatively new. United States involvement in it was no older than the U.N. But there was nothing shallow about this drama. Its actors, while no strangers to the simple emotions of vanity and ambition, were moved by primordial drives of fear and self-preservation.

Tragedy lay in the fact that, by historical coincidence, two kindred, semitic peoples, strove to recover their identity at the same time, after centuries of dispersal and oppression for the one, and oppression and stagnation for the other. Their striving, acted out in the terms of an age of nationalism, focused on the same small space on the eastern shore of the Mediterranean, for reasons 3,000 years old and beyond the control of their latter-day exponents. This meant that the antagonists sought the satisfaction of noble aims necessarily at each other's expense. Making matters worse, they pursued their goals not according only to their own devices, in the geographical proportions of that small arena, but in the context of a much larger competition among the great powers of the time. Germany, Turkey, Britain, France, the Soviet Union and the United States—pursuing that combination of accident and design, high purpose and low cunning which is called national strategy—intervened, each in its time, as they chose. In doing so, they compounded a dilemma murderous enough without them, amplifying its passions and broadening its scope.

All this, crystallized in an epic record of bungling and malfeasance, came to the United Nations in 1947 when Great Britain decided to divest itself of the responsibility it had assumed so readily less than thirty years before as the League of Nations Palestine Mandate. Britain no longer had either the power or the desire to maintain control of the territory; in addition, a large part of the original reason for holding it, protection of the route to India, had vanished with India's independence.

In 1947, the grand halls of the U.N. were thick with chickens coming home to roost. Britain had solicited Arab and Jewish help in the First World War. It had offered the Arabs independence in most of the Arabian peninsula, implicitly including the region of Palestine, which for 400 years had been a district of the Ottoman Turkish province of Syria. At the same time, in the Balfour Delcaration, it had promised "the establishment in Palestine of a national home for the Jewish people."

Britain obviously hoped to resolve this contradiction in the administration of its mandate. But the Arabs, bitter and resentful, would not cooperate in what they saw as their betrayal. They particularly opposed the arrival of Jewish refugees and settlers, an influx which Nazi persecution in Germany increased sharply. And, with the end of the Second World War, Jewish survivors flooded out of Europe to Palestine, which built up to a condition of intercommunal war.

The United States had, until then, played no national role in the Middle East, although it was an interested spectator. A considerable emotional pull was felt by the American Jewish community as well as, in terms of the Holy Land, by a gentile nation whose founders were deeply rooted in the Old as well as the New Testament, and which saw itself as part of the Judaeo-Christian tradition. In the face of the misery which marked Europe and the uprooted victims of the war in 1945, the diplomatic assurances which President Franklin D. Roosevelt had given King Ibn Saud were not observed by President Harry S. Truman.

On April 2, 1947, against a background of violence and bloodshed in Palestine, Britain asked for a special session of the General Assembly to see how this unhappy responsibility might be taken off its hands. The Assembly established a special committee of inquiry on Palestine, which came to be known as UNSCOP. Its majority report (a minority report proposed an independent federal state of Palestine, with Arab and Jewish components) was adopted by the regular session of the General Assembly on November 29, 1947.

This Plan of Partition with Economic Union envisaged a double entity whose Arab state would cover 4,500 square miles with a population of 804,000 Arabs and 10,000 Jews. The Jewish state would have 5,500 square miles and a population of some 540,000 Jews as well as nearly 400,000 Arabs. The Jewish Agency for Palestine accepted the plan; the Arabs turned it down.

The Palestine Commission, created by the Assembly to carry out the Partition Plan found itself an impotent spectator of open warfare. It appealed for help from the Security Council, only to be checked by the United States representative, who declared, "The Charter of the United Nations does not empower the Security Council to enforce a political settlement whether it is pursuant to a recommendation of the General Assembly or of the Council itself. . . . The Council's action, in other words, is directed to keeping the peace and not to enforcing partition." Others shared this view. That was the end of the Plan, although it remained on paper.

With the situation degenerating in violence and bloodshed, Britain decided to surrender its mandate earlier, on May 15, 1948, and the United States, taking its first major initiative, proposed that the U.N. impose a temporary trusteeship on Palestine in order to forestall chaos. The Arabs favored the idea, which preserved a unitary state. The Jews did not. The Special Assembly called to consider this proposal rejected it.

As the last day of the British mandate approached, Arabs and Jews fought for advantage. Security Council appeals to cease acts of violence addressed directly to them were ignored. The U.S. member of a Truce Commission created by the Council was shot dead by a sniper. On May 14, the last British soldiers left Palestine. The Jews proclaimed the State of Israel. Accepting this at once as irreversible and as a legitimate step toward filling the vacuum, President Truman gave Israel *de facto* recognition. In New York, the Special Assembly ended its session that day with a resolution establishing a U.N. Mediator for Palestine, who was to use his good offices to promote a peaceful settlement—an unenviable post that went to Count Folke Bernadotte, President of the Swedish Red Cross.

The next day, Egypt informed the Security Council that "Egyptian armed forces have started to enter Palestine to establish security and order . . ." Transjordan, Iraq, Syria and Lebanon also sent troops to help the Arabs. The Arab League ordered an economic blockade of Israel, including denial of passage through the Suez Canal, and two years later, through the Gulf of Aqaba. A new ceasefire order had no effect and on May 29 the Council felt compelled to back still another with practical measures and a far-reaching threat. It gave the Mediator a corps of military observers to supervise a truce and warned of action under the Charter's Chapter VII to make it hold. The observers, who later became the U.N. Truce Supervision Organization (UNTSO), reached a strength of seven-hundred and fifty officers and men from France, the United States and Belgium—with the United States lending the Mediator three destroyers as picket vessels off the coast as well as furnishing transport and communications.

The ceasefire lasted only the prescribed four weeks. Then the Arabs renewed the offensive, but found the Israelis better organized and driving a corridor through to Jerusalem. The Security Council, using still more emphatic language, succeeded this time in gaining acceptance of a truce of indefinite duration. It was a truce, however, frequently broken in local clashes and disturbing enough to the efforts of the Mediator to move him to seek and to obtain yet another Security Council resolution. Then he himself added his recommendations to the principles and admonitions which swelled the record of the Middle East problem. Israeli extremists, considering Count Bernadotte pro Arab, assassinated him and an assistant on the day his report was forwarded to the United Nations. His conclusions were endorsed by Secretary of State Dean Acheson.

On October 14, Israeli forces supplied with arms and aircraft by the Soviet bloc, launched a general offensive against Egyptian forces which had occupied the Negev. This was territory, for the most part, allocated to Israel in the Partition Plan; and Israel's claim to it was reaffirmed by President Truman, then at the end of his election campaign. A fourth Council resolution, calling upon all governments (but, in practice affecting only Israel) to return to previously held positions, had no effect. The Israelis had shown their military superiority; the Arabs were exhausted. Acting Mediator Ralph Bunche, who had succeeded Bernadotte, was able to establish provisional truce lines in the Negev and the Council called upon the parties to the conflict to seek agreement forthwith. On December 11, the General Assembly created a Conciliation Commission for Palestine (France, Turkey, United States) to help attain it and formulated certain guidelines to help. Included, in paragraph 11, was a reference to the refugee problem which remained a central point of controversy for decades—the Arabs demanding repatriation, the Israelis resettlement with compensation.

During months of effort, while the ceasefire was broken by major and minor clashes, Ralph Bunche managed to bring Israel and its Arab neighbors—Lebanon, Syria, Jordan and Egypt—together in similar armistice agreements, an accomplishment which won him the Nobel Peace Prize. On May 11, 1949, Israel was admitted to membership in the United Nations.

A real and, as it developed, lasting part of the Palestine tragedy was the flight of Arab civilians from the areas occupied by Israel. Driven by their own fears and by the brutalities of war, they sought refuge in unoccupied territory and in the adjacent Arab states. In November, 1948 the General Assembly established the U.N. Relief for Palestine Refugees to tide 500,000 of them over the period of emergency. A year later it was apparent that, while catastrophe had been averted, the problem could not be liquidated quickly. On December 8, 1949 the General Assembly created the United Nations Relief and Works Agency for Palestine Refugees in the Near East, UNRWA, to follow the recommendations of an Economic Survey Mission that the direct relief program be carried out on a diminishing scale and that the refugees be helped to become self supporting. It was the problem, however, which proved to be self sustaining. The Arab governments were economically unable and politically unwilling to assimilate the refugees. Left in their camps as wards of the U.N. and encouraged to think of going home, they were a strong element of irredentism highly convenient to Arab policy, which asserted that there could be no peace until they returned. Israel declaring that repatriating large numbers of refugees would raise an insuperable security problem, argued that they could not return until there was peace. Israel offered and the Arabs refused peace negotiations. UNRWA was extended until the war of 1967 completely disjointed what had by then become a *status quo*.

UNRWA was, from the beginning, financed by voluntary contributions. By the end of 1968, it had cost $640 million, of which the United States had contributed $425 million—almost 70 percent, not to mention additional millions in emergency and private donations. The Soviet Union, by comparison, made some token gifts in kind, such as tents and blankets, directly to governments but nothing to UNRWA.

For a time it seemed as though there could be a quasi-peaceful consolidation. The three western powers, in a joint declaration, set themselves up as the guardians of peace; and there were discussions between Israel and the Arab States under the auspices of the Conciliation Commission. But the foundation of genuine peace could not be laid. Friction, complaints and skirmishes poisoned the atmosphere; the Arab blockade continued and there was no interest on the Arab side in exploring schemes for regional development—like the Jordan River water project—which might have served as a roundabout, functional road to peace. In this period, too, the policy of the Soviet Union underwent a profound change—from pro-Israeli to pro-Arab.

In September 1951, the Soviet Union joined the other members of the Security Council in calling on Egypt to end restrictions on Israeli shipping through the Suez Canal. But in January, 1954, it cast its veto on the opposite side in a dispute over water between Israel and Syria. And in March it vetoed a resolution urging compliance with the resolution of September, 1951. Whatever motivated the Kremlin—whether it was the distinct anti-semitism of Stalin's last years, the "progressive" turn in the Arab world with the Egyptian revolution of 1952, the increased friction with the west exemplified in NATO and Korea, a projected Middle East Defense Command or entirely different considerations, the Soviet position on Middle East questions was henceforth reversed.

Tension built up in the area, primarily between Israel and Egypt, with Britain and France tending to take Israel's side because of their own difficulties with Egypt over the Suez Canal and Algeria, respectively. Arab commando raids into Israel alternated with strong retaliatory strikes, one of which, against Syria, was condemned by the Security Council. In this crescendo of violence and propaganda, the Soviet bloc commenced large scale arms shipments to Egypt, the United States abruptly cancelled an offer to help finance the Aswan Dam and Gamal Abdel Nasser, who had come to power in Egypt, assumed full control of the Suez Canal. Hectic and elaborate efforts at conciliation failed. On October 29, 1956, Israeli forces moved into the Sinai Peninsula as British and French troops made ready to occupy the Suez Canal zone.

The United States, not consulted by its allies, called an emergency session of the Security Council. It introduced a resolution calling on Israel immediately to withdraw behind the armistice lines and on all members to refrain from the threat or use of force. Britain and France vetoed this and a similar Soviet resolution, whereupon Yugoslavia, with Soviet approval, invoked the Uniting for Peace procedure, which the Communists had so resolutely opposed, to summon the U.N.'s First Emergency Special General Assembly. Secretary of State John Foster Dulles presented the American complaint and introduced a resolution for ceasefire and withdrawal which the Assembly adopted before the night was out. Britain, France and Israel did not comply, but London did say it would welcome a U.N. police force taking over. In the Assembly, Canada started the wheels turning and authorization for what became the United Nations Emergency Force, UNEF, was voted on November 5. The Soviet bloc abstained, but the United States warmly supported it with a vote and then with money, airlift, shipping, transport and supplies.

In this fashion, Secretary General Dag Hammarskjold improvised the first of the great U.N. peacekeeping operations. He set down basic principles: 1) No permanent members of the Security Council and no interested party could contribute troops, and the U.N. command should be responsible to the Secretary General; 2) The U.N. force should not influence the political or military balance in the area; 3) It should use weapons only in self defense; 4) The force could function only with the consent of the countries contributing troops and the countries on whose territory it was stationed; 5) The cost would be outside the regular budget but generally shared.

Israel, in control of the field, wanted no part of the force. Egypt, while eager for help in regaining control of its territory, wanted assurances that the U.N. force would not be imposed on it. The United States, issuing repeated warnings against Soviet threats to send "volunteers" to the Middle East, pressed for quick action to fill the vacuum. Washington used its influence to speed the withdrawal of the occupying troops, taking special pains to overcome Israel's doubts about surrendering positions such as those at Sharm el Sheikh which controlled the entrance to the Gulf of Aqaba. At the same time, the administration, noting the limitations of the U.N. as a "dependable protector of freedom," formulated the Eisenhower Doctrine in the hope of stabilizing the area. So controversial were its thrust and its terms, however, that not a single state in the Middle East except Lebanon and Libya endorsed it—not even Israel.

Arab-Israeli relations lapsed into the fitful, snarling pugnacity that passed for normal between the two sides. But the Arab world, taking stock after eight years of dismal performance, moved to pull itself together. A surge of nationalism focussed on Egypt and Colonel Nasser. Egypt and Syria joined in the United Arab Republic. King Hussein of Jordan became the target of subversion, while the Hashemite Kingdom in Iraq was swept away in a blood bath. On May 22, 1958 Lebanon came to the Security Council to complain of intervention by the UAR in its internal affairs. The Council instructed the Secretary General urgently to send a U.N. Observer Group (UNOGIL) to Lebanon. Fighting continued. The head of the U.N. team, finding no evidence of incursions from Syria, called it civil war. On July 14, the day of the revolution in Iraq, the President of Lebanon requested immediate military help from the United States. The next day, U.S. Marines landed at Beirut. Two days later, two battalions of British paratroopers were flown to Jordan at the government's request. On August 13,

President Eisenhower appeared before the Third Emergency Session of the General Assembly to explain American intervention and to make other proposals for normalization of the region. They fell on deaf ears.

Upheavals in Yemen, Aden, Cyprus, Iraq, Algeria and elsewhere took the spotlight from what the U.N. still called the Palestine Problem. Recurrent border incidents there only occasionally went beyond what had come to be considered routine—as when Israel reacted quickly and sharply to Arab hints at diverting the headwaters of the Jordan. Between 1949 and 1966 more than 100,000 incidents were reported to the Mixed Armistice Commissions. Even so, the scale of violence rose steeply in 1966 and into 1967, to the accompaniment of more threatening political and diplomatic activity.

In Spring, 1967, for reasons which were never made clear, the Soviet Union convinced President Nasser that Israel was mobilizing to attack Syria. A check by UNTSO established that this was not true. Nasser nevertheless felt compelled to mobilize his army and to order the withdrawal of UNEF from the buffer position it had held for ten years between Israel and Egypt on the Sinai Peninsula. On May 22, he declared the Gulf of Aqaba closed to Israeli shipping—as U Thant flew to Cairo to tell him that this was a *casus belli.* President Lyndon Johnson was later to say, "If a single act of folly was more responsible for this explosion than any other, it was the arbitrary and dangerous announced decision that the Straits of Tiran would be closed." On June 5th, Israel's armed force plunged into the Sinai.

The Security Council met on May 24 and again, repeatedly, as the crisis thickened. The United States and the other western members urged support for the Secretary General's efforts to secure a breathing spell in which disaster might be averted. The Soviet Union accused the United States of trying to dramatize the situation. When the war began and the Council convened, the Arab States and the Soviet Union opposed the immediate adoption of a simple ceasefire resolution; but agreed to it the following day when the extent of the Israeli victory became clear. Efforts by the Soviet Union to add to this and later ceasefire resolutions, a condemnation of Israel and a call for withdrawal to the positions of June 4 failed. The United States, having moved Israel to withdraw in 1957 with assurances that later proved empty, now insisted on an unbreakable link between the removal of Israeli forces and the end of Arab belligerency.

The diplomatic struggle over this balance dominated the fruitless Fifth Emergency Special General Assembly in July, 1967 and the work in the Security Council which followed. The Council finally set down a list of ambiguous guidelines for peace and authorized the Secretary General to appoint a representative who would promote agreement between the parties. President Johnson spelled out the United States interpretation of these principles and it appeared, substantially, to be adopted by the administration of President Richard Nixon. Both sought to be evenhanded. In December, 1968, the United States joined in condemning Israel for a retaliatory commando raid on Beirut airport which caused great material damage. And, in July 1969, it supported, for the first time, a resolution censuring Israel for annexing the Arab Old City of Jerusalem. But, throughout this time increasingly serious clashes along the ceasefire lines and sterile diplomacy reflected the inability of the United States and of the United Nations to move the Middle East toward genuine peace.

Ambassador Gunnar Jarring of Sweden, the Secretary General's Special Representative to the Middle East, found himself unable to establish a common denominator on which negotiations could move forward, an agreed basis involving Israel's withdrawal from occupied Arab territory and the Arabs' commitment to a peaceful settlement. As his failure became apparent, the United States explored the theoretical possibility of agreement with the Soviet Union—on the assumption that if these two could find a formula, the parties to the dispute could not ignore it. Britain and France entered these discussions, but they remained fruitless.

It was not until June 19, 1970 that the United States found an effective means to move things forward one step. In a massive effort of diplomacy, Secretary of State William Rogers persuaded Israel, Egypt and Jordan to start discussions under Jarring's auspices. He also secured a ninety day ceasefire on the Suez Canal front to stop a rising spiral of combat and create a favorable climate for these talks. The ceasefire continued through 1971. In its early stages the United States and Israel accused Egypt and the Soviet Union of breaking it by moving anti-aircraft missiles into the ceasefire zone although Egypt's new President, Anwar Sadat, formally terminated it in March. Nevertheless, negotiations did not begin. The United States tried and failed to break the deadlock by bringing Israel and Egypt together in an interim agreement to reopen the Suez Canal. In December, 1971, the General Assembly asked the Secretary General to reactivate the Jarring mission on the basis of a proposal he had made in February—that Israel agree, in principle, to withdraw to the old international border between the Palestine Mandate and Egypt while Egypt commit itself to a peace agreement with Israel.

One new and unpredictable element was added to the diplomatic search for peace when the Peoples' Republic of China took China's seat in the United Nations. Peking did not formally define its position but suggested clearly that it would: 1) not join the Big Four in any negotiation of peace terms; 2) not accept Security Council Resolution 242, with its emphasis on peaceful settlement, as the basis for a solution; 3) strongly support the Palestine guerrilla organizations' insistence on solution only through struggle against "Zionism" and "imperialism."

ATTEMPTS AT NEUTRALITY

*Letter from President Franklin D. Roosevelt to King Ibn Saud of Saudi Arabia on Palestine**

April 5, 1945

I have received the communication which Your Majesty sent me under date of March 10, 1945, in which you refer to the question of Palestine and to the continuing interest of the Arabs in current developments affecting that country.

I am grateful that Your Majesty took this occasion to bring your views on this question to my attention and I have given the most careful attention to the statements which you make in your letter. I am also mindful of the memorable conversation which we had not so long ago and in the course of which I had an opportunity to obtain so vivid an impression of Your Majesty's sentiments on this question.

Your Majesty will recall that on previous occasions I communicated to you the attitude of the American Government toward Palestine and made clear our desire that no decision be taken with respect to the basic situation in that country without full consultation with both Arabs and Jews. Your Majesty will also doubtless recall that during our recent conversation I assured you that I would take no action, in my capacity as Chief of the Executive Branch of this Government, which might prove hostile to the Arab people.

It gives me pleasure to renew to Your Majesty the assurances which you have previously received regarding the attitude of my Government and my own, as Chief Executive, with regard to the question of Palestine and to inform you that the policy of this Government in this respect is unchanged.

I desire also at this time to send you my best wishes for Your Majesty's continued good health and for the welfare of your people.

Report of the Anglo-American Committee of Inquiry on Palestine†

April 20, 1946

PREFACE

We were appointed by the Governments of the United States and of the United Kingdom, as a joint body of American and British membership, with the following Terms of Reference:

1. To examine political, economic and social conditions in Palestine as they bear upon the problem of Jewish immigration and settlement therein and the well-being of the peoples now living therein.

2. To examine the position of the Jews in those countries in Europe where they have been the victims of Nazi and Fascist persecution, and the practical measures taken or contemplated to be taken in those countries to enable them to live free from

*Department of State Bulletin, Oct. 21, 1945, p. 623.
†Ibid., May 12, 1946, pp. 783-87.

discrimination and oppression and to make estimates of those who wish or will be impelled by their conditions to migrate to Palestine or other countries outside Europe.

3. To hear the views of competent witnesses and to consult representative Arabs and Jews on the problems of Palestine as such problems are affected by conditions subject to examination under paragraphs 1 and 2 above and by other relevant facts and circumstances, and to make recommendations to His Majesty's Government and the Government of the United States for *ad interim* handling of these problems as well as for their permanent solution.

4. To make such other recommendations to His Majesty's Government and to the Government of the United States as may be necessary to meet the immediate needs arising from conditions subject to examination under paragraph 2 above, by remedial action in the European countries in question or by the provision of facilities for emigration to and settlement in countries outside Europe.

The Governments urged upon us the need for the utmost expedition in dealing with the subjects committed to us for investigation, and requested to be furnished with our Report within one hundred and twenty days of the inception of our Inquiry.

We assembled in Washington on Friday, 4th January, 1946 and began our public sessions on the following Monday. We sailed from the United States on 18th January and resumed our public sessions in London on 25th January. We left for Europe on 4th and 5th February, and, working in Subcommittees, proceeded to our investigations in Germany, Poland, Czechoslovakia, Austria, Italy and Greece. On 28th February we flew to Cairo and, after sessions there, reached Jerusalem on 6th March. In Palestine, our sessions were interspersed with personal visits to different parts of the country, during which we sought to acquaint ourselves at first hand with its various characteristics and the ways of life of its inhabitants. Subcommittees visited the capitals of Syria, Lebanon, Iraq, Saudi-Arabia and Trans-Jordan to hear the views of the Arab Governments and representatives of bodies concerned with the subjects before us. We left Palestine on 28th March and have concluded our deliberations in Switzerland. The detailed itinerary is shown in Appendix I.

We now submit the following Report.

Chapter I
Recommendations

The European Problem

Recommendation No. 1. We have to report that such information as we received about countries other than Palestine gave no hope of substantial assistance in finding homes for Jews wishing or impelled to leave Europe.

But Palestine alone cannot meet the emigration needs of the Jewish victims of Nazi and Fascist persecution; the whole world shares responsibility for them and indeed for the resettlement of all "displaced persons."

We therefore recommend that our Governments together, and in association with other countries, should endeavor immediately to find new homes for all such "displaced persons," irrespective of creed or nationality, whose ties with their former communities have been irreparably broken.

Though emigration will solve the problems of some victims of persecution, the overwhelming majority, including a considerable number of Jews, will continue to live in Europe. We recommend therefore that our Governments endeavor to secure that immediate effect is given to the provision of the United Nations Charter calling for "universal respect for, and observance of, human rights and fundamental freedoms for all without distinction as to race, sex, language, or religion."

Refugee Immigration Into Palestine

Recommendation No. 2. We recommend (a) that 100,000 certificates be authorized immediately for the admission into Palestine of Jews who have been the victims of Nazi and Fascist persecution; (b) that these certificates be awarded as far as possible in 1946 and that actual immigration be pushed forward as rapidly as conditions will permit.

Principles of Government: no Arab, no Jewish State

Recommendation No. 3. In order to dispose, once and for all, of the exclusive claims of Jews and Arabs to Palestine, we regard it as essential that a clear statement of the following principles should be made:

I. That Jew shall not dominate Arab and Arab shall not dominate Jew in Palestine. II. That Palestine shall be neither a Jewish state nor an Arab state. III. That the form of government ultimately to be established, shall, under international guarantees, fully protect and preserve the interests in the Holy Land of Christendom and of the Moslem and Jewish faiths.

Thus Palestine must ultimately become a state which guards the rights and interests of Moslems, Jews and Christians alike; and accords to the inhabitants, as a whole, the fullest measure of self-government, consistent with the three paramount principles set forth above.

Mandate and United Nations Trusteeship

Recommendation No. 4. We have reached the conclusion that the hostility between Jews and Arabs and, in particular, the determination of each to achieve domination, if necessary by violence, make it almost certain that, now and for some time to come, any attempt to establish either an independent Palestinian state or independent Palestinian states would result in civil strife such as might threaten the peace of the world. We therefore recommend that, until this hostility disappears, the government of Palestine be continued as at present under mandate pending the execution of a trusteeship agreement under the United Nations.

Equality of Standards

Recommendation No. 5. Looking towards a form of ultimate self-government, consistent with the three principles laid down in recommendation No. 3, we recommend that the mandatory or trustee should proclaim the principle that Arab economic, educational and political advancement in Palestine is of equal importance with that of the Jews; and should at once prepare measures designed to bridge the gap which now exists and raise the Arab standard of living to that of the Jews; and so bring the two peoples to a full appreciation of their common interest and common destiny in the land where both belong.

Future Immigration Policy

Recommendation No. 6. We recommend that pending the early reference to the United Nations and the execution of a trusteeship agreement, the mandatory should administer Palestine according to the mandate which declares with regard to immigration that "The administration of Palestine, while ensuring that the rights and position of other sections of the population are not prejudiced, shall facilitate Jewish immigration under suitable conditions."

Land Policy

Recommendation No. 7. (a) We recommend that the land transfers regulations of 1940 be rescinded and replaced by regulations based on a policy of freedom in the sale, lease, or use of land, irrespective of race, community or creed; and providing adequate protection for the interests of small owners and tenant cultivators. (b) We further recommend that steps be taken to render nugatory and to prohibit provisions in conveyances, leases and agreements relating to land which stipulate that only members of one race, community or creed may be employed on or about or in connection therewith. (c) We recommend that the Government should exercise such close supervision over the Holy Places and localities such as the Sea of Galilee and its vicinity as will protect them from desecration and from uses which offend the conscience of religious people; and that such laws as are required for this purpose be enacted forthwith.

Economic Development

Recommendation No. 8. Various plans for large-scale agricultural and industrial development in Palestine have been presented for our consideration; these projects, if successfully carried into effect, could not only greatly enlarge the capacity of the country to support an increasing population, but also raise the living standards of Jew and Arab alike.

We are not in a position to assess the soundness of these specific plans; but we cannot state too strongly that, however technically feasible they may be, they will fail unless there is peace in Palestine. Moreover their full success requires the willing cooperation of adjacent Arab states, since they are not merely Palestinian projects. We recommend therefore that the examination, discussion and execution of these plans be conducted, from the start and throughout, in full consultation and cooperation not only with the Jewish agency but also with the governments of the neighboring Arab states directly affected.

Education

Recommendation No. 9. We recommend that, in the interests of the conciliation of the two peoples and of general improvement of the Arab standard of living, the educational system of both Jews and Arabs be reformed including the introduction of compulsory education within a reasonable time.

The Need for Peace in Palestine

Recommendation No. 10. We recommend that, if this report is adopted, it should be made clear beyond all doubt to both Jews and Arabs that any attempt from either side, by threats of violence, by terrorism, or by the organization or use of illegal armies to prevent its execution, will be resolutely suppressed.

Furthermore, we express the view that the Jewish agency should at once resume active cooperation with the mandatory in the suppression of terrorism and of illegal immigration, and in the maintenance of that law and order throughout Palestine which is essential for the good of all, including the new immigrants.

*   *   *

Statement by President Truman on Immigration into Palestine *

October 4, 1946

I have learned with deep regret that the meetings of the Palestine Conference in London have been adjourned and are not to be resumed until December 16, 1946. In the light of this situation it is appropriate to examine the record of the administration's efforts in this field, efforts which have been supported in and out of Congress by members of both political parties, and to state my views on the situation as it now exists.

It will be recalled that, when Mr. Earl Harrison reported on September 29, 1945, concerning the condition of displaced persons in Europe, I immediately urged that steps be taken to relieve the situation of these persons to the extent at least of admitting 100,000 Jews into Palestine. In response to this suggestion the British Government invited the Government of the United States to cooperate in setting up a joint Anglo-American Committee of Inquiry, an invitation which this Government was happy to accept in the hope that its participation would help to alleviate the situation of the displaced Jews in Europe and would assist in finding a solution for the difficult and complex problem of Palestine itself. The urgency with which this Government regarded the matter is reflected in the fact that a 120-day limit was set for the completion of the Committee's task.

The unanimous report of the Anglo-American Committee of Inquiry was made on April 20, 1946, and I was gratified to note that among the recommendations contained in the Report was an endorsement of my previous suggestion that 100,000 Jews be admitted into Palestine. The administration immediately concerned itself with devising ways and means for transporting the 100,000 and caring for them upon their arrival. With this in mind, experts were sent to London in June 1946 to work out provisionally the actual travel arrangements. The British Government cooperated with this group but made it clear that in its view the Report must be considered as a whole and that the issue of the 100,000 could not be considered separately.

On June 11, I announced the establishment of a Cabinet Committee on Palestine and Related Problems, composed of the Secretaries of State, War, and Treasury, to assist me in considering the recommendations of the Anglo-American Committee of Inquiry. The alternates of this Cabinet Committee, headed by Ambassador Henry F. Grady, departed for London on July 10, 1946, to discuss with British Government representatives how the Report might best be implemented. The alternates submitted on July 24, 1946 a report, commonly referred to as the "Morrison plan," advocating a scheme of provincial autonomy which might lead ultimately to a bi-national state or to partition. However, opposition to this plan developed among members of the major political parties in the United States—both in the Congress and throughout the

*Ibid., Oct. 13, 1946, pp. 669-70.

country. In accordance with the principle which I have consistently tried to follow, of having a maximum degree of unity within the country and between the parties on major elements of American foreign policy, I could not give my support to this plan.

I have, nevertheless, maintained my deep interest in the matter and have repeatedly made known and have urged that steps be taken at the earliest possible moment to admit 100,000 Jewish refugees to Palestine.

In the meantime, this Government was informed of the efforts of the British Government to bring to London representatives of the Arabs and Jews, with a view to finding a solution to this distressing problem. I expressed the hope that as a result of these conversations a fair solution of the Palestine problem could be found. While all the parties invited had not found themselves able to attend, I had hoped that there was still a possibility that representatives of the Jewish Agency might take part. If so, the prospect for an agreed and constructive settlement would have been enhanced.

The British Government presented to the Conference the so-called "Morrison plan" for provincial autonomy and stated that the Conference was open to other proposals. Meanwhile, the Jewish Agency proposed a solution of the Palestine problem by means of the creation of a viable Jewish state in control of its own immigration and economic policies in an adequate area of Palestine instead of in the whole of Palestine. It proposed furthermore the immediate issuance of certificates for 100,000 Jewish immigrants. This proposal received wide-spread attention in the United States, both in the press and in public forums. From the discussion which has ensued it is my belief that a solution along these lines would command the support of public opinion in the United States. I cannot believe that the gap between the proposals which have been put forward is too great to be bridged by men of reason and good-will. To such a solution our Government could give its support.

In the light of the situation which has now developed I wish to state my views as succinctly as possible:

1. In view of the fact that winter will come on before the Conference can be resumed I believe and urge that substantial immigration into Palestine cannot await a solution to the Palestine problem and that it should begin at once. Preparations for this movement have already been made by this Government and it is ready to lend its immediate assistance.

2. I state again, as I have on previous occasions, that the immigration laws of other countries, including the United States, should be liberalized with a view to the admission of displaced persons. I am prepared to make such a recommendation to the Congress and to continue as energetically as possible collaboration with other countries on the whole problem of displaced persons.

3. Furthermore, should a workable solution for Palestine be devised, I would be willing to recommend to the Congress a plan for economic assistance for the development of that country.

In the light of the terrible ordeal which the Jewish people of Europe endured during the recent war and the crisis now existing, I cannot believe that a program of immediate action along the lines suggested above could not be worked out with the cooperation of all people concerned. The administration will continue to do everything it can to this end.

Report by President Truman to Congress on Palestine*

1947

*   *   *

The small country of Palestine, about the size of Vermont, has been a center of international rivalry intermittently since the beginning of human history. It lies near the crossroads of the Old World, where the continents of Europe, Asia, and Africa meet. Its shrines are sacred to Christians, Jews, and Moslems throughout the world; yet its soil has been the battleground of many different nations and empires. Today the Holy Land tests the ability of the world community to make a peaceable disposition of this problem, now marked by strife.

The problem of Palestine in modern times arose after the first World War as a result of the collapse of the Ottoman Empire. Palestine was placed under a League of Nations mandate with the United Kingdom as the mandatory power. On a number of occasions in the 25 years thereafter the United Kingdom attempted, unsuccessfully, to persuade the inhabitants of Palestine to agree upon their future status. More recently, the United Kingdom and the United States tried jointly—through the Anglo-American Committee of Inquiry and the Morrison-Grady conversations in 1946—to find a solution. The conflicting views and desires of the Arabs and Jews made impossible any settlement of this question.

Throughout the period of the mandate, and more recently in debates in the General Assembly during 1947, the Arabs have sought the immediate creation of an independent Palestine. They have insisted that the 1,200,000 Arabs in Palestine, comprising two thirds of the population, have a right, in accordance with the principle of self-determination, to determine the status of that country and to develop an independent state without interference from the outside. The Arabs have also claimed that they acquired special rights in Palestine from certain promises and pledges made during the first World War. They have contended that the League of Nations mandate, providing for the establishment of a Jewish national home in Palestine, was illegal. They have insisted upon curtailment of immigration. They have denied that the United Nations has any right to recommend or impose a solution of the question of the disposition of Palestine which does not recognize what they consider to be the interests of the Arab population in Palestine.

The Jews, on the other hand, have sought unlimited Jewish immigration into Palestine and the establishment of a Jewish state therein. The Jews have based their claims upon their ancient interest in the country, upon their historic quest for a national home, which was recognized by the Balfour declaration, and upon the League mandate. The Jews have maintained that, having devoted their lives and fortunes in the past 30 years to building a community of 600,000 persons in Palestine, they cannot now be deprived of their right to create an independent state. In more recent years they have argued that a Jewish state is needed to assure a refuge for the European victims of Nazi persecution. They have contended that Jewish immigrants alone can develop the country adequately and that these immigrants help, rather than injure, the Arab population.

*U.S. Participation in the United Nations, Report by the President to the Congress, for the Year 1947, (Washington, 1948), pp. 42-44.

For the United States, as for other Members of the United Nations, these rival claims—each based upon historical, political, and legal arguments—have created a dilemma of infinite complexity. Few issues in modern times have taxed statesmanship so heavily; few have offered a greater challenge to an international organization.

* * *

Address by Ambassador Herschel V. Johnson Before the Ad Hoc Committee on the Palestinian Question of the General Assembly on the Future Government of Palestine*

October 11, 1947

The problem of the future government of Palestine confronts the General Assembly of the United Nations with a heavy and complex responsibility. The General Assembly, having assumed responsibility for making recommendations to the United Kingdom on the subject, must do everything within its power to evolve a practical solution consistent with the principles laid down in the United Nations Charter.

The United States Delegation feels that the urgency of the problem is so great that the General Assembly must recommend a solution at this session. The degree of urgency has been brought to our attention by continued violence in Palestine, by the context of the Special Committee's Report, and by the statement of the Delegate from the United Kingdom regarding the recommendations of the Committee and future British responsibilities in Palestine.

During the past weeks this Committee has had the benefit of the views of several members of this Committee, and has heard statements by the Representatives of the Arab Higher Committee and the Jewish Agency for Palestine on behalf of the peoples primarily concerned. The United States Delegation believes that this discussion has been of material assistance and hopes that it will continue on the broadest basis.

It may be recalled that, as a result of the first World War, a large area of the Near East, including Palestine, was liberated and a number of states gained their independence. The United States, having contributed its blood and resources to the winning of that war, felt that it could not divest itself of a certain responsibility for the manner in which the freed territories were disposed of, or for the fate of the peoples liberated at that time. It took the position that these peoples should be prepared for self-government and also that a national home for the Jews should be established in Palestine. The United States Government has subsequently had long and friendly relations with the independent states which were created in the Near East and is happy to note that most of them are Members of the United Nations and have representatives present at this meeting.

It may be recalled, with regard to Palestine, that in 1917 the Government of the United Kingdom, in the statement known as the Balfour Declaration, announced that it viewed with favor the establishment in Palestine of a national home for the Jewish people and that it would use its best endeavors to facilitate the achievement of that object, it being clearly understood that nothing should be done which might prejudice the civil and religious rights of existing non-Jewish communities in Palestine or the rights and political status enjoyed by Jews in any other country. In 1923 the

*Ibid., pp. 291-93.

objectives stated in this declaration were embodied in the League of Nations mandate for Palestine which was entrusted to the Government of the United Kingdom as mandatory. As the United States was not a member of the League of Nations, a convention was concluded between the United States and the United Kingdom in 1924 with regard to American rights in Palestine. The Palestine mandate is embodied in the preamble to this convention. The United States consented to this mandate. Members of this Committee are aware of the situation which subsequently developed in Palestine and of the many efforts which have been made to achieve a settlement. We now have before us a report of the Special Committee of the United Nations with regard to the Palestine question.

The United States Delegation supports the basic principles of the unanimous recommendations and the majority plan which provides for partition and immigration. It is of the opinion, however, that certain amendments and modifications would have to be made in the majority plan in order more accurately to give effect to the principles on which that plan is based. My Delegation believes that certain geographical modifications must be made. For example, Jaffa should be included in the Arab State because it is predominantely an Arab City.

My Delegation suggests that the General Assembly may wish to provide that all the inhabitants of Palestine, regardless of citizenship or place of residence, be guaranteed access to ports and to water and power facilities on a nondiscriminatory basis; that constitutional guaranties, including guaranties regarding equal economic opportunity, be provided for Arabs and Jews alike, and that the powers of the Joint Economic Board be strengthened. Any solution which this Committee recommends should not only be just but also workable and of a nature to command the approval of world opinion.

The United States Delegation desires to make certain observations on the carrying out of such recommendations as the General Assembly may make regarding the future Government of Palestine. The General Assembly did not, by admitting this item to its agenda, undertake to assume responsibility for the administration of Palestine during the process of transition to independence. Responsibility for the Government of Palestine now rests with the mandatory power. The General Assembly, however, would not fully discharge its obligation if it did not take carefully into account the problem of implementation.

Both the majority report and the statement of the United Kingdom Representative in this Committee raise the problem of carrying into effect the recommendations of the General Assembly. We note, for example, that the majority report indicates several points at which the majority thought the United Nations could be of assistance. It was suggested that the General Assembly approved certain steps involved in the transitional period, that the United Nations guarantee certain aspects of the settlement concerning Holy Place and minority rights, that the Economic and Social Council appoint three members of the Joint Economic Board, and that the United Nations accept responsibility as administering authority of the City of Jerusalem under an international trusteeship.

The United States Government is willing to participate in a United Nations program to assist the parties involved in the establishment of a workable political settlement in Palestine. We refer to assistance through the United Nations in meeting economic and financial problems and the problems of internal law and order during the transition period. The latter problem might require the establishment of a special constabulary or police force recruited on a volunteer basis by the United Nations. We do not refer to the possibility of violations by any Member of its obligations to refrain in its international relations from the threat or use of force. We assume that there will be Charter observance.

In the final analysis the problem of making any solution work rests with the people of Palestine. If new political institutions are to endure, they must provide for early assumption by the people themselves of the responsibility for their own domestic order. Acts of violence against constituted authority and against rival elements of the local population have appeared in Palestine over a period of many years and have greatly increased the difficulties of finding a workable solution to this complex problem. Certain elements have resorted to force and terror to obtain their own particular aims. Obviously, this violence must cease if independence is to be more than an empty phrase in the Holy Land.

Mr. Chairman, we must now consider how this Committee is to take the next step in dealing with this question. If the Committee favors the principles of the majority plan, we should establish a subcommittee to work out the details of a program which we could recommend to the General Assembly.

The recommendations reached by the General Assembly will represent the collective opinion of the world. The problem has thus far defied solution because the parties primarily at interest have been unable to reach a basis of agreement. This is a problem in the solution of which world opinion can be most helpful.

THE CREATION OF ISRAEL

*Plan for the Partition of Palestine: General Assembly Resolution 181 (II)**

November 29, 1947

At the 128th plenary meeting of the General Assembly on 29 November 1947, the General Assembly considered the report of the *ad hoc* Committee and adopted the resolution on the future government of Palestine by thirty-three votes in favor, thirteen against, with ten abstentions, as follows:

In favor: Australia, Belgium, Bolivia, Brazil, Byelorussian Soviet Socialist Republic, Canada, Costa Rica, Czechoslovakia, Denmark, Dominican Republic, Ecuador, France, Guatemala, Haiti, Iceland, Liberia, Luxembourg, Netherlands, New Zealand, Nicaragua, Norway, Panama, Paraguay, Peru, Philippines, Poland, Sweden, Ukrainian Soviet Socialist Republic, Union of South Africa, Union of Soviet Socialist Republics, United States of America, Uruguay, Venezuela.

Against: Afghanistan, Cuba, Egypt, Greece, India, Iran, Iraq, Lebanon, Pakistan, Saudi Arabia, Syria, Turkey, Yemen.

Abstained: Argentina, Chile, China, Columbia, El Salvador, Ethiopia; Honduras, Mexico, United Kingdom, Yugoslavia.

At the same meeting the General Assembly elected Bolivia, Czechoslovakia, Denmark, Panama and the Philippines as members of the United Nations Palestine Commission charged with implementing the resolution. It also authorized the Secretary-General to draw from the Working Capital Fund a sum not to exceed $2,000,000 for the purposes set forth in the last paragraph of the resolution on the future government of Palestine.

RESOLUTION ADOPTED ON THE REPORT OF THE AD HOC COMMITTEE ON THE PALESTINIAN QUESTION

A

The General Assembly,

Having met in special session at the request of the mandatory Power to constitute and instruct a special committee to prepare for the consideration of the question of the future government of Palestine at the second regular session;

Having constituted a Special Committee and instructed it to investigate all questions and issues relevant to the problem of Palestine, and to prepare proposals for the solution of the problem, and

Having received and examined the report of the Special Committee (document A/364) including a number of unanimous recommendations and a plan of partition with economic union approved by the majority of the Special Committee,

Considers that the present situation in Palestine is one which is likely to impair the general welfare and friendly relations among nations;

Takes note of the declaration by the mandatory Power that it plans to complete its evacuation of Palestine by 1 August 1948;

*U.N. General Assembly, *Official Records*, 2d sess., Sept.-Nov. 1947, pp. 131-51.

Recommends to the United Kingdom, as the mandatory Power for Palestine, and to all other Members of the United Nations the adoption and implementation, with regard to the future government of Palestine, of the Plan of Partition with Economic Union set out below;

Requests that

(a) The Security Council take the necessary measures as provided for in the plan for its implementation;

(b) The Security Council consider, if circumstances during the transitional period require such consideration, whether the situation in Palestine constitutes a threat to the peace. If it decides that such a threat exists, and in order to maintain international peace and security, the Security Council should supplement the authorization of the General Assembly by taking measures, under Articles 39 and 41 of the Charter, to empower the United Nations Commission, as provided in this resolution, to exercise in Palestine the functions which are assigned to it by this resolution;

(c) The Security Council determine as a threat to the peace, breach of the peace or act of aggression, in accordance with Article 39 of the Charter, any attempt to alter by force the settlement envisaged by this resolution;

(d) The Trusteeship Council be informed of the responsibilities envisaged for it in this plan;

Calls upon the inhabitants of Palestine to take such steps as may be necessary on their part to put this plan into effect;

Appeals to all Governments and all peoples to refrain from taking any action which might hamper or delay the carrying out of these recommendations, and

Authorizes the Secretary-General to reimburse travel and subsistence expenses of the members of the Commission referred to in Part I, Section B, paragraph 1 below, on such basis and in such form as he may determine most appropriate in the circumstances, and to provide the Commission with the necessary staff to assist in carrying out the functions assigned to the Commission by the General Assembly.

B

The General Assembly

Authorizes the Secretary-General to draw from the Working Capital Fund a sum not to exceed $2,000,000 for the purposes set forth in the last paragraph of the resolution on the future government of Palestine.

PLAN OF PARTITION WITH ECONOMIC UNION
PART I

Future Constitution and Government of Palestine

A. *Termination of Mandate Partition and Independence*

1. The Mandate for Palestine shall terminate as soon as possible but in any case not later than 1 August 1948.

2. The armed forces of the mandatory Power shall be progressively withdrawn from Palestine, the withdrawal to be completed as soon as possible but in any case not later than 1 August 1948.

The mandatory Power shall advise the Commission, as far in advance as possible, of its intention to terminate the Mandate and to evacuate each area.

The mandatory Power shall use its best endeavours to ensure that an area situated in the territory of the Jewish State, including a seaport and hinterland adequate to provide facilities for a substantial immigration, shall be evacuated at the earliest possible date and in any event not later than 1 February 1948.

3. Independent Arab and Jewish States and the Special International Regime for the City of Jerusalem, set forth in part III of this plan, shall come into existence in Palestine two months after the evacuation of the armed forces of the mandatory Power has been completed but in any case not later than 1 October 1948. The boundaries of the Arab State, the Jewish State, and the City of Jerusalem shall be as described in parts II and III below.

4. The period between the adoption by the General Assembly of its recommendation on the question of Palestine and the establishment of the independence of the Arab and Jewish States shall be a transitional period.

B. Steps Preparatory to Independence

1. A Commission shall be set up consisting of one representative of each of five Member States. The Members represented on the Commission shall be elected by the General Assembly on as broad a basis, geographically and otherwise, as possible.

2. The administration of Palestine shall, as the mandatory Power withdraws its armed forces, be progressively turned over to the Commission, which shall act in conformity with the recommendations of the General Assembly, under the guidance of the Security Council. The mandatory Power shall to the fullest possible extent co-ordinate its plans for withdrawal with the plans of the Commission to take over and administer areas which have been evacuated.

In the discharge of this administrative responsibility the Commission shall have authority to issue necessary regulations and take other measures as required.

The mandatory Power shall not take any action to prevent, obstruct or delay the implementation by the Commission of the measures recommended by the General Assembly.

3. On its arrival in Palestine the Commission shall proceed to carry out measures for the establishment of the frontiers of the Arab and Jewish States and the City of Jerusalem in accordance with the general lines of the recommendations of the General Assembly on the partition of Palestine. Nevertheless, the boundaries as described in part II of this plan are to be modified in such a way that village areas as a rule will not be divided by state boundaries unless pressing reasons make that necessary.

4. The Commission, after consultation with the democratic parties and other public organizations of the Arab and Jewish States, shall select and establish in each State as rapidly as possible a Provisional Council of Government. The activities of both the Arab and Jewish Provisional Councils of Government shall be carried out under the general direction of the Commission.

If by 1 April 1948 a Provisional Council of Government cannot be selected for either of the States, or, if selected, cannot carry out its functions, the Commission shall communicate that fact to the Security Council for such action with respect to that State as the Security Council may deem proper, and to the Secretary-General for communication to the Members of the United Nations.

5. Subject to the provisions of these recommendations, during the transitional

period the Provisional Councils of Government, acting under the Commission, shall have full authority in the areas under their control, including authority over matters of immigration and land regulation.

6. The Provisional Council of Government of each State, acting under the Commission, shall progressively receive from the Commission full responsibility for the administration of that State in the period between the termination of the Mandate and the establishment of the State's independence.

7. The Commission shall instruct the Provisional Councils of Government of both the Arab and Jewish States, after their formulation, to proceed to the establishment of administrative organs of government, central and local.

8. The Provisional Council of Government of each State shall, within the shortest time possible, recruit an armed militia from the residents of that State, sufficient in number to maintain internal order and to prevent frontier clashes.

This armed militia in each State shall, for operational purposes, be under the command of Jewish or Arab officers resident in that State, but general political and military control, including the choice of the militia's High Command, shall be exercised by the Commission.

9. The Provisional Council of Government of each State shall, not later than two months after the withdrawal of the armed forces of the mandatory Power, hold elections to the Constituent Assembly which shall be conducted on democratic lines.

The election regulations in each State shall be drawn up by the Provisional Council of Government and approved by the Commission. Qualified voters for each State for this election shall be persons over eighteen years of age who are: (a) Palestinian citizens residing in that State and (b) Arabs and Jews residing in the State, although not Palestinian citizens, who, before voting, have signed a notice of intention to become citizens of such State.

Arabs and Jews residing in the City of Jerusalem who have signed a notice of intention to become citizens, the Arabs of the Arab State and the Jews of the Jewish State, shall be entitled to vote in the Arab and Jewish States respectively.

Women may vote and be elected to the Constituent Assemblies.

During the transitional period no Jew shall be permitted to establish residence in the area of the proposed Arab State, and no Arab shall be permitted to establish residence in the area of the proposed Jewish State, except by special leave of the Commission.

10. The Constituent Assembly of each State shall draft a democratic constitution for its State and choose a provisional government to succeed the Provisional Council of Government appointed by the Commission. The constitutions of the States shall embody chapters 1 and 2 of the Declaration provided for in section C below and include *inter alia* provisions for:

(a) Establishing in each State a legislative body elected by universal suffrage and by secret ballot on the basis of proportional representation, and an executive body responsible to the legislature;

(b) Settling all international disputes in which the State may be involved by peaceful means in such a manner that international peace and security, and justice, are not endangered;

(c) Accepting the obligation of the State to refrain in its international relations from the threat or use of force against the territorial integrity or political independence of any State, or in any other manner inconsistent with the purposes of the United Nations;

(d) Guaranteeing to all persons equal and nondiscriminatory rights in civil, political, economic and religious matters and the enjoyment of human rights and fundamental freedoms, including freedom of religion, language, speech and publication, education, assembly and association;

(e) Preserving freedom of transit and visit for all residents and citizens of the other State in Palestine and the City of Jerusalem, subject to considerations of national security, provided that each State shall control residence within its borders.

11. The Commission shall appoint a preparatory economic commission of three members to make whatever arrangements are possible for economic co-operation; with a view to establishing, as soon as practicable, the Economic Union and the Joint Economic Board, as provided in section D below.

12. During the period between the adoption of the recommendations on the question of Palestine by the General Assembly and the termination of the Mandate, the mandatory Power in Palestine shall maintain full responsibility for administration in areas from which it has not withdrawn its armed forces. The Commission shall assist the mandatory Power in the carrying out of these functions. Similarly the mandatory Power shall co-operate with the Commission in the execution of its functions.

13. With a view to ensuring that there shall be continuity in the functioning of administrative services and that, on the withdrawal of the armed forces of the mandatory Power, the whole administration shall be in the charge of the Provisional Councils and the Joint Economic Board, respectively, acting under the Commission, there shall be a progressive transfer, from the mandatory Power of the Commission, of responsibility for all the functions of government, including that of maintaining law and order in the areas from which the forces of the mandatory Power have been withdrawn.

14. The Commission shall be guided in its activities by the recommendations of the General Assembly and by such instructions as the Security Council may consider necessary to issue.

The measures taken by the Commission, within the recommendations of the General Assembly, shall become immediately effective unless the Commission has previously received contrary instructions from the Security Council.

The Commission shall render periodic monthly progress reports, or more frequently if desirable, to the Security Council.

15. The Commission shall make its final report to the next regular session of the General Assembly and to the Security Council simultaneously.

C. Declaration

A declaration shall be made to the United Nations by the provisional government of each proposed State before independence. It shall contain *inter alia* the following clauses:

General provision

The stipulations contained in the declaration are recognized as fundamental laws of the State and no law, regulation or official action shall conflict or interfere with these stipulations, nor shall any law, regulation or official action prevail over them.

CHAPTER 1

Holy Places, Religious Buildings and Sites

1. Existing rights in respect of Holy Places and religious buildings or sites shall not be denied or impaired.

2. In so far as Holy Places are concerned, the liberty of access, visit and transit shall be guaranteed, in conformity with existing rights, to all residents and citizens of the other State and of the City of Jerusalem, as well as to aliens, without distinction as to nationality, subject to requirements of national security, public order and decorum.

Similarly, freedom of worship shall be guaranteed in conformity with existing rights, subject to the maintenance of public order and decorum.

3. Holy Places and religious buildings or sites shall be preserved. No act shall be permitted which may in any way impair their sacred character. If at any time it appears to the Government that any particular Holy Place, religious building or site is in need of urgent repair, the Government may call upon the community or communities concerned to carry out such repair. The Government may carry it out itself at the expense of the community or communities concerned if no action is taken within a reasonable time.

4. No taxation shall be levied in respect of any Holy Place, religious building or site which was exempt from taxation on the date of the creation of the State.

No change in the incidence of such taxation shall be made which would either discriminate between the owners or occupiers of Holy Places, religious buildings or sites, or would place such owners or occupiers in a position less favourable in relation to the general incidence of taxation than existed at the time of the adoption of the Assembly's recommendations.

5. The Governor of the City of Jerusalem shall have the right to determine whether the provisions of the Constitution of the State in relation to Holy Places, religious buildings and sites within the borders or the State and the religious rights appertaining thereto, are being properly applied and respected, and to make decisions on the basis of existing rights in cases of disputes which may arise between the different religious communities or the rites of a religious community with respect to such places, buildings and sites. He shall receive full cooperation and such privileges and immunities as are necessary for the exercise of his functions in the State.

CHAPTER 2

Religious and Minority Rights

1. Freedom of conscience and the free exercise of all forms of worship, subject only to the maintenance of public order and morals, shall be ensured to all.

2. No discrimination of any kind shall be made between the inhabitants on the ground of race, religion, language or sex.

3. All persons within the jurisdiction of the State shall be entitled to equal protection of the laws.

4. The family law and personal status of the various minorities and their religious interests, including endowments, shall be respected.

5. Except as may be required for the maintenance of public order and good government, no measure shall be taken to obstruct or interfere with the enterprise of religious or charitable bodies of all faiths or to discriminate against any representative or member of these bodies on the ground of his religion or nationality.

6. The State shall ensure adequate primary and secondary education for the Arab and Jewish minority, respectively, in its own language and its cultural traditions.

The right of each community to maintain its own schools for the education of its own members in its own language, while conforming to such educational requirements of a general nature as the State may impose, shall not be denied or impaired. Foreign educational establishments shall continue their activity on the basis of their existing rights.

7. No restriction shall be imposed on the free use by any citizen of the State of any language in private intercourse, in commerce, in religion, in the Press or in publications of any kind, or at public meetings.*

8. No expropriation of land owned by an Arab in the Jewish State (by a Jew in the Arab State)† shall be allowed except for public purposes. In all cases of expropriation full compensation as fixed by the Supreme Court shall be paid previous to dispossession.

CHAPTER 3

Citizenship, International Conventions and Financial Obligations

1. *Citizenship.* Palestinian citizens residing in Palestine outside the City of Jerusalem, as well as Arabs and Jews who, not holding Palestinian citizenship, reside in Palestine outside the City of Jerusalem shall, upon the recognition of independence, become citizens of the State in which they are resident and enjoy full civil and political rights. Persons over the age of eighteen years may opt, within one year from the date of recognition of independence of the State in which they reside, for citizenship of the other State, providing that no Arab residing in the area of the proposed Arab State shall have the right to opt for citizenship in the proposed Jewish State and no Jew residing in the proposed Jewish State shall have the right to opt for citizenship in the proposed Arab State. The exercise of this right of option will be taken to include the wives and children under eighteen years of age of persons so opting.

Arabs residing in the area of the proposed Jewish State and Jews residing in the area of the proposed Arab State who have signed a notice of intention to opt for citizenship of the other State shall be eligible to vote in the elections to the Constituent Assembly of that State, but not in the elections to the Constituent Assembly of the State in which they reside.

2. *International conventions.* (a) The State shall be bound by all the international agreements and conventions, both general and special, to which Palestine has become a party. Subject to any right of denunciation provided for therein, such agreements and conventions shall be respected by the State throughout the period for which they were concluded.

(b) Any dispute about the applicability and continued validity of international conventions or treaties signed or adhered to by the mandatory Power on behalf of Palestine shall be referred to the International Court of Justice in accordance with the provisions of the Statute of the Court.

3. *Financial obligations.* (a) The State shall respect and fulfill all financial obliga-

*The following stipulation shall be added to the declaration concerning the Jewish State: "In the Jewish State adequate facilities shall be given to Arabic-speaking citizens for the use of their language, either orally or in writing, in the legislature, before the Courts and in the administration."

†In the declaration concerning the Arab State, the words "by an Arab in the Jewish State" should be replaced by the words "by a Jew in the Arab State."

tions of whatever nature assumed on behalf of Palestine by the mandatory Power during the exercise of the Mandate and recognized by the State. This provision includes the right of public servants to pensions, compensation or gratuities.

(b) These obligations shall be fulfilled through participation in the Joint Economic Board in respect of those obligations applicable to Palestine as a whole, and individually in respect of those applicable to, and fairly apportionable between, the States.

(c) A Court of Claims, affiliated with the Joint Economic Board, and composed of one member appointed by the United Nations, one representative of the United Kingdom and one representative of the State concerned, should be established. Any dispute between the United Kingdom and the State respecting claims not recognized by the latter should be referred to that Court.

(d) Commercial concessions granted in respect of any part of Palestine prior to the adoption of the resolution by the General Assembly shall continue to be valid according to their terms, unless modified by agreement between the concession-holder and the State.

6. In the event of failure of a State to take the necessary action the Board may, by a vote of six members, decide to withhold an appropriate portion of that part of the customs revenue to which the State in question is entitled under the Economic Union. Should the State persist in its failure to cooperate, the Board may decide by a simple majority vote upon such further sanctions, including disposition of funds which it has withheld, as it may deem appropriate.

7. In relation to economic development, the functions of the Board shall be the planning, investigation and encouragement of joint development projects, but it shall not undertake such projects except with the assent of both States and the City of Jerusalem, in the event that Jerusalem is directly involved in the development project.

8. In regard to the joint currency system the currencies circulating in the two States and the City of Jerusalem shall be issued under the authority of the Joint Economic Board, which shall be the sole issuing authority and which shall determine the reserves to be held against such currencies.

9. So far as is consistent with paragraph 2(b) above, each State may operate its own central bank, control its own fiscal and credit policy, its foreign exchange receipts and expenditures, the grant of import licenses, and may conduct international financial operations on its own faith and credit. During the first two years after the termination of the Mandate, the Joint Economic Board shall have the authority to take such measures as may be necessary to ensure that—to the extent that the total foreign exchange revenues of the two States from the export of goods and services permit, and provided that each State takes appropriate measures to conserve its own foreign exchange resources—each State shall have available, in any twelve months' period, foreign exchange sufficient to assure the supply of quantities of imported goods and services for consumption in its territory equivalent to the qualities of such goods and services consumed in that territory in the twelve months' period ending 31 December 1947.

10. All economic authority not specifically vested in the Joint Economic Board is reserved to each State.

11. There shall be a common customs tariff with complete freedom of trade between the States, and between the States and the City of Jerusalem.

12. The tariff schedules shall be drawn up by a Tariff Commission, consisting of

representatives of each of the States in equal numbers, and shall be submitted to the Joint Economic Board for approval by a majority vote. In case of disagreement in the Tariff Commission, the Joint Economic Board shall arbitrate the points of difference. In the event that the Tariff Commission fails to draw up any schedule by a date to be fixed, the Joint Economic Board shall determine the tariff schedule.

13. The following items shall be a first charge on the customs and other common revenue of the Joint Economic Board:

    (a) The expenses of the customs service and of the operation of the joint services;
    (b) The administrative expenses of the Joint Economic Board;
    (c) The financial obligations of the Administration of Palestine consisting of:
        (i) The service of the outstanding public debt;
        (ii) The cost of superannuation benefits, now being paid or falling due in the future, in accordance with the rules and to the extent established by paragraph 3 of chapter 3 above.

14. After these obligations have been met in full, the surplus revenue from the customs and other common services shall be divided in the following manner: not less than 5 per cent and not more than 10 per cent to the City of Jerusalem; the residue shall be allocated to each State by the Joint Economic Board equitably, with the objective of maintaining a sufficient and suitable level of government and social services in each State, except that the share of either State shall not exceed the amount of that State's contribution to the revenues of the Economic Union by more than approximately four million pounds in any year. The amount granted may be adjusted by the Board according to the price level in relation to the prices prevailing at the time of the establishment of the Union. After five years, the principles of the distribution of the joint revenues may be revised by the Joint Economic Board on a basis of equity.

15. All international conventions and treaties affecting customs tariff rates, and those communications services under the jurisdiction of the Joint Economic Board, shall be entered into by both States. In these matters, the two States shall be bound to act in accordance with the majority vote of the Joint Economic Board.

16. The Joint Economic Board shall endeavour to secure for Palestine's exports fair and equal access to world markets.

17. All enterprises operated by the Joint Economic Board shall pay fair wages on a uniform basis.

Freedom of Transit and Visit

18. The undertaking shall contain provisions preserving freedom of transit and visit for all residents or citizens of both States and of the City of Jerusalem, subject to security considerations; provided that each State and the City shall control residence within its borders.

Termination, Modification and Interpretation of the Undertaking

19. The undertaking and any treaty issuing therefrom shall remain in force for a period of ten years. It shall continue in force until notice of termination, to take effect two years thereafter, is given by either of the parties.

20. During the initial ten-year period, the undertaking and any treaty issuing therefrom may not be modified except by consent of both parties and with the approval of the General Assembly.

21. Any dispute relating to the application or the interpretation of the undertaking and any treaty issuing therefrom shall be referred, at the request of either party, to the International Court of Justice, unless the parties agree to another mode of settlement.

E. Assets

1. The movable assets of the Administration of Palestine shall be allocated to the Arab and Jewish States and the City of Jerusalem on an equitable basis. Allocations should be made by the United Nations Commission referred to in section B, paragraph 1, above. Immovable assets shall become the property of the government of the territory in which they are situated.

2. During the period between the appointment of the United Nations Commission and the termination of the Mandate, the mandatory Power shall, except in respect of ordinary operations, consult with the Commission on any measure which it may contemplate involving the liquidation, disposal or encumbering of the assets of the Palestine Government, such as the accumulated treasury surplus, the proceeds of Government bond issues, State lands or any other asset.

F. Admission to Membership in the United Nations

When the independence of either the Arab or the Jewish State as envisaged in this plan has become effective and the declaration and undertaking, as envisaged in this plan, have been signed by either of them, sympathetic consideration should be given to its application for admission to membership in the United Nations in accordance with Article 4 of the Charter of the United Nations.

PART II

Boundaries

A. The Arab State

The area of the Arab State in Western Galilee is bounded on the west by the Mediterranean and on the north by the frontier of the Lebanon from Ras en Naqura to a point north of Saliha. From there the boundary proceeds northwards, leaving the built-up area of Saliha in the Arab State, to join the southernmost point of this village. Thence it follows the western boundary line of the villages of 'Alma, Rihaniya and Teitaba, thence following the northern boundary line of Meirun village to join the Acre-Safad sub-district boundary line. It follows this line to a point west of Es Sammu'i village and joins it again at the northernmost point of Farradiya. Thence it follows the sub-district boundary line to the Acre-Safad main road. From here it follows the western boundary of Kafr I'nan village until it reaches the Tiberia-Acre sub-district boundary line, passing to the west of the junction of the Acre-Safad and Lubiya-Kafr I'nan roads. From the south-west corner of Kafr I'nan village the boundary line follows the western boundary of the Tiberias sub-district to a point close to the boundary line between the villages of Maghar and Eliabun, thence bulging out to the west to include as much of the eastern part of the plain of Battuf as is necessary for the reservoir proposed by the Jewish Agency for the irrigation of lands to the south and east.

The boundary rejoins the Tiberias sub-district boundary at a point on the Nazareth-Tiberias road south-east of the built-up area of Tur'an; thence it runs southwards, at first following the sub-district boundary and then passing between the Kadoorie Agricultural School and Mount Tabor, to a point due south at the base of Mount Tabor. From here it runs due west, parallel to the horizontal grid line 230, to the north-east corner of the village lands of Tel Adashim. It then runs to the north-west corner of these lands, whence it turns south and west so as to include in the Arab State the sources of the Nazareth water supply in Yafa village. On reaching Ginneiger it follows the eastern, northern and western boundaries of the lands of this village to their south-west corner, whence it proceeds in a straight line to a point on the Haifa-Afula railway on the boundary between the villages of Sarid and El Mujeidil. This is the point of intersection.

The south-western boundary of the area of the Arab State in Galilee takes a line from this point, passing northwards along the eastern boundaries of Sarid and Gevat to the north-eastern corner of Nahalal, proceeding thence across the land of Kefar ha Horesh to a central point on the southern boundary of the village of 'Ilut, thence westwards along that village boundary to the eastern boundary of Beit Lahm, thence northwards and north-eastwards along its western boundary to the north-eastern corner of Waldheim and thence north-westwards across the village lands of Shafa'Amr to the south-eastern corner of Ramat Yohanan. From here it runs due north-north-east to a point on the Shafa'Amr-Haifa road, west of its junction with the road to I'Billin. From there it proceeds to the west of the I'Billin-Birwa road. Thence along that boundary to its westernmost point, whence it turns to the north, follows across the village land of Tamra to the north-westernmost corner and along the western boundary of Julis until it reaches the Acre-Safad road. It then runs westwards along the southern side of the Safad-Acre road to the Galilee-Haifa District boundary, from which point it follows that boundary to the sea.

The boundary of the hill country of Samaria and Judea starts on the Jordan River at the Wadi Malih south-east of Beisan and runs due west to meet the Beisan-Jericho road and then follows the western side of that road in a north-westerly direction to the junction of the boundaries of the sub-districts of Beisan, Nablus, and Jenin. From that point it follows the Nablus-Jenin sub-district boundary westwards for a distance of about three kilometres and then turns north-westwards, passing to the east of the built-up areas of the villages of Jalbun and Faqqu'a, to the boundary of the sub-districts of Jenin and Beisan at a point north-east of Nuris. Thence it proceeds first north-westwards to a point due north of the built up area of Zir'in and then westwards to Afula-Jenin railway, thence north-westwards along the district boundary line to the point of intersection on the Hejaz railways. From here the boundary runs south-west-wards, including the built-up area and some of the land of the village of Kh.Lid in the Arab State to cross the Haifa-Jenin road at a point on the district boundary between Haifa and Samaria west of El Mansi. It follows this boundary to the southernmost point of the village of El Buteimat. From here it follows the northern and eastern boundaries of the village of Ar'ara, rejoining the Haifa-Samaria district boundary at Wadi'Ara, and then proceeding south-south-westwards in an approximately straight line joining up with the western boundary of Qaqun to a point east of the railway line on the eastern boundary of Qaqun village. From here it runs along the railway line some distance to the east of it to a point just east of the Tulkarm railway station. Thence the boundary follows a line half-way between the railway and the Tulkarm-

Qalqiliya-Jaljuliya and Ras el Ein road to a point just east of Ras el Ein station, whence it proceeds along the railway some distance to the east of it to the point on the railway line south of the junction of the Haifa-Lydda and Beit Nabala lines, whence it proceeds along the southern border of Lydda airport to its south-west corner, thence in a south-westerly direction to a point just west of the built-up area of Sarafand el'Amar, whence it turns south, passing just to the west of the built-up area of Abu el Fadil to the north-east corner of the lands of Beer Ya'Aqov. (The boundary line should be so demarcated as to allow direct access from the Arab State to the airport.) Thence the boundary line follows the western and southern boundaries of Ramle village, to the north-east corner of Al Na'ana village, thence in a straight line to the southernmost point of El Barriya, along the eastern boundary of that village and the southern boundary of 'Innaba village. Thence it turns north to follow the southern side of the Jaffa-Jerusalem road until El Quabab, whence it follows the road to the boundary of Abu Shusha. It runs along the eastern boundaries of Abu Shusha, Seidun, Hulda to the southernmost point of Hulda, thence westwards in a straight line to the north-eastern corner of Umm Kalkha, thence following the northern boundaries of Umm Kalkha. Qazaza and the northern and western boundaries of Mukhezin to the Gaza District boundary and thence runs across the village lands of El Mismiya. El Kabira, and Yasur to the southern point of intersection, which is midway between the built-up areas of Yasur and Batani Sharqi.

From the southern point of intersection the boundary lines run north-westwards between the villages of Gan Yavne and Barqa to the sea at a point half way between Nabi Yunis and Minat el Qila, and south-eastwards to a point west of Qastina, whence it turns in a south-westerly direction, passing to the east of the built-up areas of Es Sawafir, Esh Sharqiya and Ibdis. From the south-east corner of Ibdis village it runs to a point south-west of the built-up area of Beit 'Affa, crossing the Hebron-El Majdal road just to the west of the built-up area of Iraq Suweidan. Thence it proceeds southwards along the western village boundary of El Faluja to the Beersheba sub-district boundary. It then runs across the tribal lands of 'Arab el Jubarat to a point on the boundary between the sub-districts of Beersheba and Hebron north of Kh. Khuweilifa, whence it proceeds in a south-westerly direction to a point on the Beersheba-Gaza main road two kilometres to the north-west of the town. It then turns south-eastwards to reach Wadi Sab' at a point situated one kilometre to the west of it. From here it turns north-eastwards and proceeds along Wadi Sab' and along the Beersheba-Hebron road for a distance of one kilometre, whence it turns eastwards and runs in a straight line to Kh. Kuseifa to join the Beersheba-Hebron sub-district boundary. It then follows the Beersheba-Hebron boundary eastwards to a point north of Raz Ez Zuweira, only departing from it so as to cut across the base of the indentation between vertical gridlines 150 and 160.

About five kilometres north-east of Ras ez Zuweira it turns north, excluding from the Arab State a strip along the coast of the Dead Sea not more than seven kilometres in depth, as far as Ein Geddi, whence it turns due east to join the Transjordan frontier in the Dead Sea.

The northern boundary of the Arab section of the coastal plain runs from a point between Minat el Qila and Nabi Yunis, passing between the built-up areas of Gan Yavne and Barqa to the point of intersection. From here it turns south-westwards, running across the lands of Batani Sharqi, along the eastern boundary of the lands of Beit Daras and across the lands of Julis, leaving the built-up areas of Batani Sharqi and

Julis to the westwards, as far as the north-west corner of the lands of Beit Tima. Thence it runs east of El Jiya across the village lands of El Barbara along the eastern boundaries of the villages of Beit Jirja, Deir Suneid and Dimra. From the south-east corner of Dimra, the boundary passes across the lands of Beit Hanun, leaving the Jewish lands of Nir-Am to the eastwards. From the south-east corner of Beit Hanun the line runs south-west to a point south of the parallel grid line 100, then turns north-west for two kilometres, turning again in a south-westerly direction and continuing in an almost straight line to the north-west corner of the village lands of Kirbet Ikhza'a. From there it follows the boundary line of this village to its southernmost point. It then runs in a southerly direction along the vertical grid line 90 to its junction with the horizontal grid line 70. It then turns south-eastwards to Kh. el Ruheiba and then proceeds in a southerly direction to a point known as El Baha, beyond which it crosses the Beersheba-El'Auja main road to the west of Kh. el Mushrifa. From there it joins Wadi El Zaiyatin just to the west of El Subeita. From there it turns to the north-east and then to the south-east following this wadi and passes to the east of 'Abda to join Wadi Nafkh. It then bulges to the south-west along Wadi Nafkh, Wadi Ajrim and Wadi Lassan to the point where Wadi Lassan crosses the Egyptian frontier.

The area of the Arab enclave of Jaffa consists of that part of the town-planning area of Jaffa which lies to the west of the Jewish quarters lying south of Tel-Aviv, to the west of the continuation of Herzl street up to its junction with the Jaffa-Jerusalem road, to the south-west of the section of the Jaffa-Jerusalem road lying south-east of that junction, to the west of Miqve Yisrael lands, to the north-west of Holon local council area, to the north of the line linking up the north-west corner of Holon with the north-east corner of Bat Yam local council area and to the north of Bat Yam local council area. The question of Karton quarter will be decided by the Boundary Commission, bearing in mind among other considerations the desirability of including the smallest possible number of its Arab inhabitants and the largest possible number of its Jewish inhabitants in the Jewish State.

B. The Jewish State

The north-eastern sector of the Jewish State (Eastern Galilee) is bounded on the north and west by the Lebanese frontier and on the east by the frontiers of Syria and Transjordan. It includes the whole of the Hula Basin, Lake Tiberias, the whole of the Beisan sub-district, the boundary line being extended to the crest of the Gilboa mountains and the Wadi Malih. From there the Jewish State extends north-west, following the boundary described in respect of the Arab State.

The Jewish section of the coastal plain extends from a point between Minat et Qila and Nabi Yunis in the Gaza sub-district and includes the towns of Haifa and Tel-Aviv, leaving Jaffa as an enclave of the Arab State. The eastern frontier of the Jewish State follows the boundary described in respect of the Arab State.

The Beersheba area comprises the whole of the Beersheba sub-district, including the Negeb and the eastern part of the Gaza sub-district, but excluding the town of Beersheba and those areas described in respect of the Arab State. It includes also a strip of land along the Dead Sea stretching from the Beersheba-Hebron sub-district boundary line to Ein Geddi, as described in respect of the Arab State.

C. The City of Jerusalem

The boundaries of the City of Jerusalem are as defined in the recommendations on the City of Jerusalem. (See Part III, Section B, below.)

PART III

City of Jerusalem

A. Special Regime

The City of Jerusalem shall be established as a *corpus separatum* under a special international regime and shall be administered by the United Nations. The Trusteeship Council shall be designated to discharge the responsibilities of the Administering Authority on behalf of the United Nations.

B. Boundaries of the City

The City of Jerusalem shall include the present municipality of Jerusalem plus the surrounding villages and towns, the most eastern of which shall be Abu Dis; the most southern, Bethlehem; the most western, Ein Karim (including also the built-up area of Motsa); and the most northern Shu'fat, as indicated on the attached sketch-map (annex B).

C. Statute of the City

The Trusteeship Council shall, within five months of the approval of the present plan, elaborate and approve a detailed Statute of the City which shall contain *inter alia* the substance of the following provisions:

1. *Government machinery; special objectives.* The Administering Authority in discharging its administrative obligations shall pursue the following special objectives:

(a) To protect and to preserve the unique spiritual and religious interests located in the city of the three great monotheistic faiths throughout the world, Christian, Jewish and Moslem; to this end to ensure that order and peace, and especially religious peace, reign in Jerusalem;

(b) To foster co-operation among all the inhabitants of the city in their own interests as well as in order to encourage and support the peaceful development of the mutual relations between the two Palestinian peoples, throughout the Holy Land; to promote the security, well-being and any constructive measures of development of the residents, having regard to the special circumstances and customs of the various peoples and communities.

2. *Governor and administrative staff.* A Governor of the City of Jerusalem shall be appointed by the Trusteeship Council and shall be responsible to it. He shall be selected on the basis of special qualifications and without regard to nationality. He shall not, however, be a citizen of either State in Palestine.

The Governor shall represent the United Nations in the City and shall exercise on their behalf all powers of administration, including the conduct of external affairs. He shall be assisted by an administrative staff classed as international officers in the meaning of Article 100 of the Charter and chosen whenever practicable from the residents of the city and of the rest of Palestine on a non-discriminatory basis. A detailed plan for the organization of the administration of the city shall be submitted by the Governor to the Trusteeship Council and duly approved by it.

3. *Local autonomy.* (a) The existing local autonomous units in the territory of the city (villages, townships and municipalities) shall enjoy wide powers of local government and administration.

(b) The Governor shall study and submit for the consideration and decision of the

Trusteeship Council a plan for the establishment of special town units consisting, respectively, of the Jewish and Arab sections of new Jerusalem. The new town units shall continue to form part of the present municipality of Jerusalem.

4. *Security measures.* (a) The City of Jerusalem shall be demilitarized; its neutrality shall be declared and preserved, and no paramilitary formations, exercises or activities shall be permitted within its borders.

(b) Should the administration of the City of Jerusalem be seriously obstructed or prevented by the non-co-operation or interference of one or more sections of the population, the Governor shall have authority to take such measures as may be necessary to restore the effective functioning of the administration.

(c) To assist in the maintenance of internal law and order and especially for the protection of the Holy Places and religious buildings and sites in the city, the Governor shall organize a special police force of adequate strength, the members of which shall be recruited outside of Palestine. The Governor shall be empowered to direct such budgetary provision as may be necessary for the maintenance of this force.

5. *Legislative organization.* A Legislative Council, elected by adult residents of the city irrespective of nationality on the basis of universal and secret suffrage and proportional representation, shall have powers of legislation and taxation. No legislative measures shall, however, conflict or interfere with the provisions which will be set forth in the Statute of the City, nor shall any law, regulation, or official action prevail over them. The Statute shall grant to the Governor a right of vetoing bills inconsistent with the provisions referred to in the preceding sentence. It shall also empower him to promulgate temporary ordinances in case the Council fails to adopt in time a bill deemed essential to the normal functioning of the administration.

6. *Administration of justice.* The Statute shall provide for the establishment of an independent judiciary system, including a court of appeal. All the inhabitants of the City shall be subject to it.

7. *Economic union and economic regime.* The City of Jerusalem shall be included in the Economic Union of Palestine and be bound by all stipulations of the undertaking and of any treaties issued therefrom, as well as by the decisions of the Joint Economic Board. The headquarters of the Economic Board shall be established in the territory of the City.

The Statute shall provide for the regulation of economic matters not falling within the regime of the Economic Union, on the basis of equal treatment and non-discrimination for all Members of the United Nations and their nationals.

8. *Freedom of transit and visit, control of residents.* Subject to considerations of security, and of economic welfare as determined by the Governor under the directions of the Trusteeship Council, freedom of entry into, and residence within, the borders of the City shall be guaranteed for the residents or citizens of the Arab and Jewish States. Immigration into, and residence within, the borders of the city for nationals of other States shall be controlled by the Governor under the directions of the Trusteeship Council.

9. *Relations with the Arab and Jewish States.* Representatives of the Arab and Jewish States shall be accredited to the Governor of the City and charged with the protection of the interests of their States and nationals in connexion with the international administration of the City.

10. *Official language.* Arabic and Hebrew shall be the official languages of the city.

This will not preclude the adoption of one or more additional working languages, as may be required.

11. *Citizenship.* All the residents shall become *ipso facto* citizens of the City of Jerusalem unless they opt for citizenship of the State of which they have been citizens or, if Arabs or Jews, have filed notice of intention to become citizens of the Arab or Jewish State respectively, according to part I, section B, paragraph 9, of this plan.

12. *Freedoms of citizens.* (a) Subject only to the requirements of public order and morals, the inhabitants of the City shall be ensured the enjoyment of human rights and fundamental freedoms, including freedom of conscience, religion and worship, language, education, speech and Press, assembly and association, and petition.

(b) No discrimination of any kind shall be made between the inhabitants on the grounds of race, religion, language or sex.

(c) All persons within the City shall be entitled to equal protection of the laws.

(d) The family law and personal status of the various persons and communities and their religious interests, including endowments shall be respected.

(e) Except as may be required for the maintenance of public order and good government, no measure shall be taken to obstruct or interfere with the enterprise of religious or charitable bodies of all faiths or to discriminate against any representative or member of these bodies on the ground of his religion or nationality.

(f) The City shall ensure adequate primary and secondary education for the Arab and Jewish communities respectively, in their own languages and in accordance with their cultural traditions.

The right of each community to maintain its own schools for the education of its own members in its own language, while conforming to such educational requirements of a general nature as the City may impose, shall not be denied or impaired. Foreign educational establishments shall continue their activity on the basis of their existing rights.

(g) No restriction shall be imposed on the free use by any inhabitant of the City of any language in private intercourse, in commerce, in religion, in the Press or in publications of any kind, or at public meetings.

13. *Holy Places.* (a) Existing rights in respect of Holy Places and religious buildings or sites shall not be denied or impaired.

(b) Free access to the Holy Places and religious buildings or sites and the free exercise of worship shall be secured in conformity with existing rights and subject to the requirements of public order and decorum.

(c) Holy Places and religious buildings or sites shall be preserved. No act shall be permitted which may in any way impair their sacred character. If at any time it appears to the Governor that any particular Holy Place, religious building or site is in need of urgent repair, the Governor may call upon the community or communities concerned to carry out such repair. The Governor may carry it out himself at the expense of the community or communities concerned if no action is taken within a reasonable time.

(d) No taxation shall be levied in respect of any Holy Place, religious building or site which was exempt from taxation on the date of the creation of the City. No change in the incidence of such taxation shall be made which would either discriminate between the owners or occupiers of Holy Places, religious buildings or sites, or would place such owners or occupiers in a position less favourable in relation to the general incidence of taxation than existed at the time of the adoption of the Assembly's recommendations.

14. *Special powers of the Governor in respect of the Holy Places, religious buildings and sites in the City and in any part of Palestine.* (a) The protection of the Holy Places, religious buildings and sites located in the City of Jerusalem shall be a special concern of the Governor.

(b) With relation to such places, buildings and sites in Palestine outside the city, the Governor shall determine, on the ground of powers granted to him by the Constitutions of both States, whether the provisions of the Constitutions of the Arab and Jewish States in Palestine dealing therewith and the religious rights appertaining thereto are being properly applied and respected.

(c) The Governor shall also be empowered to make decisions on the basis of existing rights in cases of disputes which may arise between the different religious communities or the rites of a religious community in respect of the Holy Places, religious buildings and sites in any part of Palestine.

In this task he may be assisted by a consultative council of representatives of different denominations acting in an advisory capacity.

D. *Duration of the Special Regime*

The Statute elaborated by the Trusteeship Council on the aforementioned principles shall come into force not later than 1 October 1948. It shall remain in force in the first instance for a period of ten years, unless the Trusteeship Council finds it necessary to undertake a re-examination of these provisions at an earlier date. After the expiration of this period the whole scheme shall be subject to re-examination by the Trusteeship Council in the light of the experience acquired with its functioning. The residents of the City shall be then free to express by means of a referendum their wishes as to possible modifications of the regime of the City.

PART IV

Capitulations

States whose nationals have in the past enjoyed in Palestine the privileges and immunities of foreigners, including the benefits of consular jurisdiction and protection, as formerly enjoyed by capitulation or usage in the Ottoman Empire, are invited to renounce any right pertaining to them to the re-establishment of such privileges and immunities in the proposed Arab and Jewish States and the City of Jerusalem.

Statement by Ambassador Austin on the United States Position on Palestine*

March 19, 1948

The resolution adopted by the Security Council on 5 March 1948 requested the permanent members of the Security Council "to consult and to inform the Security Council regarding the situation with respect to Palestine . . ."

*Department of State Bulletin, Mar. 28, 1948, pp. 402-08.

The plan proposed by the General Assembly was an integral plan which would not succeed unless each of its parts could be carried out. There seems to be general agreement that the plan cannot now be implemented by peaceful means. From what has been said in the Security Council and in consultations among the several members of the Security Council, it is clear that the Security Council is not prepared to go ahead with efforts to implement this plan in the existing situation. We had a vote on that subject and only five votes could be secured for that purpose.

The Security Council now has before it clear evidence that the Jews and Arabs of Palestine and the mandatory power cannot agree to implement the General Assembly plan of partition through peaceful means. The announced determination of the mandatory power to terminate the mandate on 15 May 1948, if carried out by the United Kingdom, would result, in the light of information now available, in chaos, heavy fighting and much loss of life in Palestine. The United Nations cannot permit such a result. The loss of life in the Holy Land must be brought to an immediate end. The maintenance of international peace is at stake.

The United States fully subscribes to the conclusion reached by the four permanent members that the Security Council should make it clear to the parties and governments concerned that the Security Council is determined not to permit the situation in Palestine to threaten international peace and, further, that the Security Council should take further action by all means available to it to bring about the immediate cessation of violence and the restoration of peace and order in Palestine.

Under the Charter, the Security Council has both an inescapable responsibility and full authority to take the steps necessary to bring about a cease-fire in Palestine and a halt to the incursions being made into that country. The powers of articles 39, 40, 41 and 42 are very great, and the Security Council should not hesitate to use them—all of them—if necessary to bring about peace.

In addition, my Government believes that a temporary trusteeship for Palestine should be established under the Trusteeship Council of the United Nations to maintain the peace and to afford the Jews and Arabs of Palestine, who must live together, further opportunity to reach an agreement regarding the future government of that country. Such a United Nations trusteeship would, of course, be without prejudice to the character of the eventual political settlement, which we hope can be achieved without long delay. In our opinion, the Security Council should recommend the establishment of such a trusteeship to the General Assembly and to the mandatory power. This would require an immediate special session of the General Assembly, which the Security Council might call under the terms of the Charter. Pending the meeting of the special session of the General Assembly, we believe that the Security Council should instruct the Palestine Commission to suspend its efforts to implement the proposed partition plan.

I shall now read three propositions which are being submitted by the United States. I am not making any representation for any other one of the permanent members. The United States propositions are contained in a paper entitled "Additional Conclusions and Recommendations Concerning Palestine," which has been circulated to the members. It reads as follows:

"1. The plan proposed by the General Assembly is an integral plan which cannot succeed unless each of its parts can be carried out. There seems to be general agreement that the plan cannot now be implemented by peaceful means.

"2. We believe that further steps must be taken immediately not only to maintain the peace but also to afford a further opportunity to reach an agreement between the interested parties regarding the future government of Palestine. To this end we believe that a temporary trusteeship for Palestine should be established under the Trusteeship Council of the United Nations. Such a United Nations trusteeship would be without prejudice to the rights, claims or position of the parties concerned or to the character of the eventual political settlement, which we hope can be achieved without long delay. In our opinion, the Security Council should recommend the establishment of such a trusteeship to the General Assembly and to the mandatory power. This would require an immediate special session of the General Assembly, which the Security Council should request the Secretary-General to convoke under article 20 of the Charter.

"3. Pending the meeting of the proposed special session of the General Assembly, we believe that the Security Council should instruct the Palestine Commission to suspend its efforts to implement the proposed partition plan."

Draft resolutions which would give effect to the above suggestions will be circulated shortly for the consideration of the Security Council.

Statement by President Truman on a Temporary United Nations Trusteeship for Palestine*

March 25, 1948

It is vital that the American people have a clear understanding of the position of the United States in the United Nations regarding Palestine.

This country vigorously supported the plan for partition with economic union recommended by the United Nations Special Committee on Palestine and by the General Assembly. We have explored every possibility consistent with the basic principles of the Charter for giving effect to that solution. Unfortunately, it has become clear that the partition plan cannot be carried out at this time by peaceful means. We could not undertake to impose this solution on the people of Palestine by the use of American troops, both on Charter grounds and as a matter of national policy.

The United Kingdom has announced its firm intention to abandon its mandate in Palestine on May 15. Unless emergency action is taken, there will be no public authority in Palestine on that date capable of preserving law and order. Violence and bloodshed will descend upon the Holy Land. Large-scale fighting among the people of that country will be the inevitable result. Such fighting would infect the entire Middle East and could lead to consequences of the gravest sort involving the peace of this Nation and of the world.

These dangers are imminent. Responsible governments in the United Nations cannot face this prospect without acting promptly to prevent it. The United States has proposed to the Security Council a temporary United Nations trusteeship for Palestine to provide a government to keep the peace. Such trusteeship was proposed only after we had exhausted every effort to find a way to carry out partition by peaceful means.

*Ibid., Apr. 4, 1948, p. 451.

Trusteeship is not proposed as a substitute for the partition plan but as an effort to fill the vacuum soon to be created by the termination of the mandate on May 15. The trusteeship does not prejudice the character of the final political settlement. It would establish the conditions of order which are essential to a peaceful solution.

If we are to avert tragedy in Palestine, an immediate truce must be reached between the Arabs and Jews of that country. I am instructing Ambassador Austin to urge upon the Security Council in the strongest terms that representatives of the Arabs and Jews be called at once to the council table to arrange such a truce.

The United States is prepared to lend every appropriate assistance to the United Nations in preventing bloodshed and in reaching a peaceful settlement. If the United Nations agrees to a temporary trusteeship, we must take our share of the necessary responsibility. Our regard for the United Nations, for the peace of the world, and for our own self-interest does not permit us to do less.

With such a truce and such a trusteeship, a peaceful settlement is yet possible; without them, open warfare is just over the horizon. American policy in this emergency period is based squarely upon the recognition of this inescapable fact.

THE FIRST ARAB-ISRAELI WAR

*Security Council Resolution S/801 Calling for a Four Week
Cessation of Armed Force in Palestine**

May 29, 1948

The Security Council,

Desiring to bring about a cessation of hostilities in Palestine without prejudice to the rights, claims and position of either Arabs or Jews,

Calls upon all Governments and authorities concerned to order a cessation of all acts of armed force for a period of four weeks,

Calls upon all Governments and authorities concerned to undertake that they will not introduce fighting personnel into Palestine, Egypt, Iraq, Lebanon, Saudi Arabia, Syria, Transjordan and Yemen during the cease fire and

Calls upon all Governments and authorities concerned, should men of military age be introduced into countries or territories under their control, to undertake not to mobilize or submit them to military training during the cease fire,

Calls upon all Governments and authorities concerned to refrain from importing or exporting war material into or to Palestine, Egypt, Iraq, Lebanon, Saudi Arabia, Syria, Transjordan and Yemen during the cease fire,

Urges all Governments and authorities concerned to take every possible precaution for the protection of the Holy Places and of the City of Jerusalem, including access to all shrines and sanctuaries for the purpose of worship by those who have an established right to visit and worship at them,

Instructs the United Nations Mediator for Palestine in concert with the Truce Commission to supervise the observance of the above provisions, and decides that they shall be provided with a sufficient number of military observers,

Instructs the United Nations Mediator to make contact with all parties as soon as the cease fire is in force with a view to carrying out his functions as determined by the General Assembly,

Calls upon all concerned to give the greatest possible assistance to the United Nations Mediator,

Instructs the United Nations Mediator to make a weekly report to the Security Council during the cease fire,

Invites the States Members of the Arab League and the Jewish and Arab authorities in Palestine to communicate their acceptance of this resolution to the Security Council not later than 6.00 p.m. New York Standard Time on 1 June 1948,

Decides that if the present resolution is rejected by either party or by both, or if, having been accepted, it is subsequently repudiated or violated, the situation in Palestine will be reconsidered with a view to action under Chapter VII of the Charter,

Calls upon all Governments to take all possible steps to assist in the implementation of this resolution.

*U.S. Participation in the U.N., Appendix III, pp. 241-2.

Security Council Resolution Ordering a Ceasefire in Palestine*

July 15, 1948

The Security Council

Taking into consideration that the Provisional Government of Israel has indicated its acceptance in principle of a prolongation of the truce in Palestine: that the States members of the Arab League have rejected successive appeals of the United Nations Mediator, and of the Security Council in its resolution of 7 July 1948, for the prolongation of the truce in Palestine; and that there has consequently developed a renewal of hostilities in Palestine;

Determines that the situation in Palestine constitutes a threat to the peace within the meaning of Article 39 of the Charter;

Orders the Governments and authorities concerned, pursuant to Article 40 of the Charter of the United Nations, to desist from further military action and to this end to issue cease-fire orders to their military and para-military forces, to take effect at a time to be determined by the Mediator, but in any event not later than three days from the date of the adoption of this resolution;

Declares that failure by any of the Governments or authorities concerned to comply with the preceding paragraph of this resolution would demonstrate the existence of a breach of the peace within the meaning of Article 39 of the Charter requiring immediate consideration by the Security Council with a view to such further action under Chapter VII of the Charter as may be decided upon by the Council;

Calls upon all Governments and authorities concerned to continue to co-operate with the Mediator with a view to the maintenance of peace in Palestine in conformity with the resolution adopted by the Security Council in 29 May 1948;

Orders as a matter of special and urgent necessity an immediate and unconditional cease-fire in the City of Jerusalem to take effect 24 hours from the time of the adoption of this resolution, and instructs the Truce Commission to take any necessary steps to make this cease-fire effective;

Instructs the Mediator to continue his efforts to bring about the demilitarization of the City of Jerusalem, without prejudice to the future political status of Jerusalem, and to assure the protection of and access to the Holy Places, religious buildings and sites in Palestine;

Instructs the Mediator to supervise the observance of the truce and to establish procedures for examining alleged breaches of the truce since 11 June 1948, authorizes him to deal with breaches so far as it is within his capacity to do so by appropriate local action, and requests him to keep the Security Council currently informed concerning the operation of the truce and when necessary to take appropriate action;

Decides that, subject to further decision by the Security Council or the General Assembly, the truce shall remain in force, in accordance with the present resolution and with that of 29 May 1948, until a peaceful adjustment of the future situation of Palestine is reached;

Reiterates the appeal to the parties contained in the last paragraph of its resolution of 22 May and urges upon the parties that they continue conversations with the

*Ibid. pp. 241-42.

Mediator in a spirit of conciliation and mutual concession in order that all points under dispute may be settled peacefully;

Requests the Secretary-General to provide the Mediator with the necessary staff and facilities to assist in carrying out the functions assigned to him under the resolution of the General Assembly of 14 May, and under this resolution; and

Requests that the Secretary-General make appropriate arrangements to provide necessary funds to meet the obligations arising from this resolution.

Conclusions from Progress Report of the United Nations Mediator on Palestine*

September 16, 1948

(A) MEDIATION EFFORT

VIII. Conclusions

1. Since I presented my written Suggestions to the Arab and Jewish authorities on 27 June, I have made no formal submission to either party of further suggestions or proposals for a definitive settlement. Since that date, however, I have held many oral discussions in the Arab capitals and Tel Aviv, in the course of which various ideas on settlement have been freely exchanged. As regards my original Suggestions, I hold to the opinion that they offered a general framework within which a reasonable and workable settlement might have been reached, had the two parties concerned been willing to discuss them. They were flatly rejected, however, by both parties. Since they were put forth on the explicit condition that they were purely tentative, were designed primarily to elicit views and countersuggestions from each party, and, in any event, could be implemented only if agreed upon by both parties, I have never since pressed them. With respect to one basic concept in my Suggestions, it has become increasingly clear to me that however desirable a political and economic union might be in Palestine, the time is certainly not now propitious for the effectuation of any such scheme.

2. I do not consider it to be within my province to recommend to the Members of the United Nations a proposed course of action on the Palestine question. That is a responsibility of the Members acting through the appropriate organs. In my role as United Nations Mediator, however, it was inevitable that I should accumulate information and draw conclusions from my experience which might well be of assistance to Members of the United Nations in charting the future course of United Nations action on Palestine. I consider it my duty, therefore, to acquaint the Members of the United Nations, through the medium of this report, with certain of the conclusions on means of peaceful adjustment which have evolved from my frequent consultations with Arab and Jewish authorities over the past three and one-half months and from my personal appraisal of the present Palestinian scene. I do not suggest that these conclusions would provide the basis for a proposal which would readily win the willing approval of both parties. I have not, in the course of my intensive efforts to achieve agreement

---

*Department of State Bulletin, Oct. 3, 1948, pp. 436-40.

between Arabs and Jews, been able to devise any such formula. I am convinced, however, that it is possible at this stage to formulate a proposal which, if firmly approved and strongly backed by the General Assembly, would not be forcibly resisted by either side, confident as I am, of course, that the Security Council stands firm in its resolution of 15 July that military action shall not be employed by either party in the Palestine dispute. It cannot be ignored that the vast difference between now and last November is that a war has been started and stopped and that in the intervening months decisive events have occurred.

Seven Basic Premises

3. The following seven basic premises form the basis for my conclusions:

Return to Peace

(a) Peace must return to Palestine and every feasible measure should be taken to ensure that hostilities will not be resumed and that harmonious relations between Arab and Jew will ultimately be restored.

The Jewish State

(b) A Jewish State called Israel exists in Palestine and there are no sound reasons for assuming that it will not continue to do so.

Boundary Determination

(c) The boundaries of this new State must finally be fixed either by formal agreement between the parties concerned or failing that, by the United Nations.

Continuous Frontiers

(d) Adherence to the principle of geographical homogeneity and integration, which should be the major objective of the boundary arrangements, should apply equally to Arab and Jewish territories, whose frontiers should not therefore, be rigidly controlled by the territorial arrangements envisaged in the resolution of 29 November.

Right of Repatriation

(e) The right of innocent people, uprooted from their homes by the present terror and ravages of war, to return to their homes, should be affirmed and made effective, with assurance of adequate compensation for the property of those who may choose not to return.

Jerusalem

(f) The City of Jerusalem, because of its religious and international significance and the complexity of interest involved, should be accorded special and separate treatment.

International Responsibility

(g) International responsibility should be expressed where desirable and necessary in the form of international guarantees, as a means of allaying existing fears, and particularly with regard to boundaries and human rights.

Specific Conclusions

4. The following conclusions, broadly outlined, would, in my view, considering all the circumstances, provide a reasonable, equitable and workable basis for settlement:

(a) Since the Security Council, under pain of Chapter VII sanctions, has forbidden further employment of military action in Palestine as a means of settling the dispute, hostilities should be pronounced formally ended either by mutual agreement of the parties or, failing that, by the United Nations. The existing indefinite truce should be superseded by a formal peace, or at the minimum, an armistice which would involve either complete withdrawal and demobilization of armed forces or their wide separation by creation of broad demilitarized zones under United Nations supervision.

(b) The frontiers between the Arab and Jewish territories, in the absence of agreement between Arabs and Jews, should be established by the United Nations and delimited by a technical boundaries commission appointed by and responsible to the United Nations, with the following revisions in the boundaries broadly defined in the resolution of the General Assembly of 29 November in order to make them more equitable, workable and consistent with existing realities in Palestine.

  (i) The area known as the Negev, south of a line running from the sea near Majdal east southeast to Faluja (both of which places would be in Arab territory), should be defined as Arab territory;
  (ii) The frontier should run from Faluja north northeast to Ramleh and Lydda (both of which places would be in Arab territory), the frontier at Lydda then following the line established in the General Assembly resolution of 29 November;
  (iii) Galilee should be defined as Jewish territory.

(c) The Disposition of the territory of Palestine not included within the boundaries of the Jewish State should be left to the Governments of the Arab States in full consultation with the Arab inhabitants of Palestine, with the recommendation, however, that in view of the historical connection and common interests of Transjordan and Palestine, there would be compelling reasons for merging the Arab territory of Palestine with the territory of Transjordan, subject to such frontier rectifications regarding other Arab States as may be found practicable and desirable.

(d) The United Nations, by declaration or other appropriate means, should undertake to provide special assurance that the boundaries between the Arab and Jewish territories shall be respected and maintained, subject only to such modifications as may be mutually agreed upon by the parties concerned.

(e) The port of Haifa, including the oil refineries and terminal and without prejudice to their inclusion in the sovereign territory of the Jewish State or the administration of the city of Haifa, should be declared a free port, with assurances of free access for interested Arab countries and an undertaking on their part to place no obstacle in the way of oil deliveries by pipeline to the Haifa refineries, whose distribution would continue on the basis of the historical pattern.

(f) The airport of Lydda should be declared a free airport with assurances of access to it and employment of its facilities for Jerusalem and interested Arab countries.

(g) The City of Jerusalem, which should be understood as covering the area defined in the resolution of the General Assembly of 29 November, should be treated separately and should be placed under effective United Nations control with maximum feasible local autonomy for its Arab and Jewish communities, with full safeguards for the protection of the Holy Places and sites and free access to them, and for religious freedom.

(h) The right of unimpeded access to Jerusalem, by road, rail or air, should be fully respected by all parties.

(i) The right of the Arab refugees to return to their homes in Jewish-controlled territory at the earliest possible date should be affirmed by the United Nations, and their repatriation, resettlement and economic and social rehabilitation, and payment of adequate compensation for the property of those choosing not to return, should be supervised and assisted by the United Nations conciliation commission described in paragraph (k) below.

(j) The political, economic, social and religious rights of all Arabs in the Jewish territory of Palestine and of all Jews in the Arab territory of Palestine should be fully guaranteed and respected by the authorities. The conciliation commission provided for in the following paragraph should supervise the observance of this guarantee. It should also lend its good offices, on the invitation of the parties, to any efforts toward exchanges of populations with a view to eliminating troublesome minority problems, and on the basis of adequate compensation for property owned.

(k) In view of the special nature of the Palestine problem and the dangerous complexities of Arab-Jewish relationships, the United Nations should establish a Palestine conciliation commission. This commission, which should be appointed for a limited period, should be responsible to the United Nations and act under its authority. The commission, assisted by such United Nations personnel as may prove necessary, should undertake

(i) To employ its good offices to make such recommendations to the parties or to the United Nations, and to take such other steps as may be appropriate, with a view to ensuring the continuation of the peaceful adjustment of the situation in Palestine;

(ii) Such measures as it might consider appropriate in fostering the cultivation of friendly relations between Arabs and Jews;

(iii) To supervise the observance of such boundary, road, railroad, free port, free airport, minority rights and other arrangements as may be decided upon by the United Nations;

(iv) To report promptly to the United Nations any development in Palestine likely to alter the arrangements approved by the United Nations in the Palestine settlement or to threaten the peace of the area.

General Assembly Resolution A/807 Creating a Conciliation Commission for Palestine*

December 11, 1948

The General Assembly,

Having considered further the situation in Palestine,

1. Expresses its deep appreciation of the progress achieved through the good offices of the late United Nations Mediator in promoting a peaceful adjustment of the future situation of Palestine, for which cause he sacrificed his life; and

Extends its thanks to the Acting Mediator and his staff for their continued efforts and devotion to duty in Palestine;

*U.S. Participation in the U.N., Report by the President for the Year 1948, pp. 195-98.

2. Establishes a Conciliation Commission consisting of three States Members of the United Nations which shall have the following functions:

(a) To assume, insofar as it considers necessary in existing circumstances, the functions given to the United Nations Mediator on Palestine by the resolution of the General Assembly of 14 May 1948;

(b) To carry out the specific functions and directives given to it by the present resolution and such additional functions and directives as may be given to it by the General Assembly or by the Security Council;

(c) To undertake, upon the request of the Security Council, any of the functions now assigned to the United Nations Mediator on Palestine or to the United Nations Truce Commission by resolutions of the Security Council; upon such request to the Conciliation Commission by the Security Council with respect to all the remaining functions of the United Nations Mediator on Palestine under Security Council resolutions, the office of the Mediator shall be terminated;

3. Decides that a Committee of the Assembly, consisting of China, France, the Union of Soviet Socialist Republics, the United Kingdom and the United States of America, shall present, before the end of the first part of the present session of the General Assembly, for the approval of the Assembly, a proposal concerning the names of the three States which will constitute the Conciliation Commission;

4. Requests the Commission to begin its functions at once, with a view to the establishment of contact between the parties themselves and the Commission at the earliest possible date;

5. Calls upon the Governments and authorities concerned to extend the scope of the negotiations provided for in the Security Council's resolution of 16 November 1948 and to seek agreement by negotiations conducted either with the Conciliation Commission or directly with a view to the final settlement of all questions outstanding between them;

6. Instructs the Conciliation Commission to take steps to assist the Governments and authorities concerned to achieve a final settlement of all questions outstanding between them;

7. Resolves that the Holy Places—including Nazareth—religious building and sites in Palestine should be protected and free access to them assured, in accordance with existing rights and historical practice; that arrangements to this end should be under effective United Nations supervision; that the United Nations Conciliation Commission, in presenting to the fourth regular session of the General Assembly its detailed proposal for a permanent international regime for the territory of Jerusalem, should include recommendations concerning the Holy Places in that territory; that with regard to the Holy Places in the rest of Palestine the Commission should call upon the political authorities of the areas concerned to give appropriate formal guarantees as to the protection of the Holy Places and access to them; and that these undertakings should be presented to the General Assembly for approval;

8. Resolves that, in view of its association with three world religions, the Jerusalem area, including the present municipality of Jerusalem plus the surrounding villages and towns, the most Eastern of which shall be Avu Dis; the most Southern, Bethlehem; the most Western, Ein Karim (including also the built-up area of Motsa); and the most Northern, Shufat, should be accorded special and spearate treatment from the rest of Palestine and should be placed under effective United Nations control;

Requests the Security Council to take further steps to ensure the demilitarization of Jerusalem at the earliest possible date;

Instructs the Conciliation Commission to present to the fourth regular session of the General Assembly detailed proposals for a permanent international regime for the Jerusalem area which will provide for the maximum local autonomy for distinctive groups consistent with the special international status of the Jerusalem area;

The Conciliation Commission is authorized to appoint a United Nations representative who shall co-operate with the local authorities with respect to the interim administration of the Jerusalem area;

9. Resolves that, pending agreement on more detailed arrangements among the Governments and authorities concerned, the freest possible access to Jerusalem by road, rail or air should be accorded to all inhabitants of Palestine;

Instructs the Conciliation Commission to report immediately to the Security Council, for appropriate action by that organ, any attempt by any party to impede such access;

10. Instructs the Conciliation Commission to seek arrangements among the Governments and authorities concerned which will facilitate the economic development of the area, including arrangements for access to ports and airfields and the use of transportation and communication facilities;

11. Resolves that the refugees wishing to return to their homes and live at peace with their neighbours should be permitted to do so at the earliest practicable date, and that compensation should be paid for the property of those choosing not to return and for loss of or damage to property which, under principles of international law or in equity, should be made good by the Governments or authorities responsible;

Instructs the Conciliation Commission to facilitate the repatriation, resettlement and economic and social rehabilitation of the refugees and the payment of compensation, and to maintain close relations with the Director of the United Nations Relief for Palestine Refugees and, through him, with the appropriate organs and agencies of the United Nations;

12. Authorizes the Conciliation Commission to appoint such subsidiary bodies and to employ such technical experts, acting under its authority, as it may find necessary for the effective discharge of its functions and responsibilities under the present resolution;

The Conciliation Commission will have its official headquarters at Jerusalem. The authorities responsible for maintaining order in Jerusalem will be responsible for taking all measures necessary to ensure the security of the Commission. The Secretary-General will provide a limited number of guards for the protection of the staff and premises of the Commission;

13. Instructs the Conciliation Commission to render progress reports periodically to the Secretary-General for transmission to the Security Council and to the Members of the United Nations;

14. Calls upon all Governments and authorities concerned to co-operate with the Conciliation Commission and to take all possible steps to assist in the implementation of the present resolution;

15. Requests the Secretary-General to provide the necessary staff and facilities and to make appropriate arrangements to provide the necessary funds required in carrying out the terms of the present resolution.

Egyptian-Israeli Armistice Agreement*

February 24, 1949

PREAMBLE

The Parties to the present agreement, responding to the Security Council resolution of 16 November 1948 calling upon them, as a further provisional measure under Article 40 of the Charter of the United Nations and in order to facilitate the transition from the present truce to permanent peace in Palestine, to negotiate an Armistice; having decided to enter into negotiations under United Nations Chairmanship concerning the implementation of the Security Council resolutions of 4 and 16 November 1948; and having appointed representatives empowered to negotiate and conclude an Armistice Agreement;

The undersigned representatives, in the full authority entrusted to them by their respective Governments, have agreed upon the following provisions:

Article I

With a view to promoting the return of permanent peace in Palestine and in recognition of the importance in this regard of mutual assurances concerning the future military operations of the Parties, the following principles, which shall be fully observed by both Parties during the Armistice, are hereby affirmed:

1. The injunction of the Security Council against resort to military force in the settlement of the Palestine question shall henceforth be scrupulously respected by both Parties.

2. No aggressive action by the Armed forces—land, sea, or air—of either Party shall be undertaken, planned, or threatened against the people or the armed forces of the other; it being understood that the use of the term "planned" in this context has no bearing on normal staff planning as generally practiced in military organizations.

3. The right of each Party to its security and freedom from fear of attack by the armed forces of the other shall be fully respected.

4. The establishment of an armistice between the armed forces of the two Parties is accepted as an indispensable step toward the liquidation of armed conflict and the restoration of peace in Palestine.

Article II

1. In pursuance of the foregoing principles and of the resolutions of the Security Council of 4 and 16 November 1948, a general armistice between the armed forces of the two Parties—land, sea and air—is hereby established.

2. No element of the land, sea or air military or para-military forces of either Party, including non-regular forces, shall commit any warlike or hostile act against the military or para-military forces of the other Party, or against civilians in territory

*U.N. Documents, S/1264-1299, Security Council, S/1264/corr. 1.

under the control of that Party; or shall advance beyond or pass over for any purpose whatsoever the Armistice Demarcation Line set forth in Article VI of this Agreement except as provided in Article III of this Agreement; and elsewhere shall not violate the international frontier; or enter into or pass through the air space of the other Party or through the waters within three miles of the coastline of the other Party.

Article III

1. In pursuance of the Security Council's resolution of 4 November 1948, and with a view to the implementation of the Security Council's resolution of 16 November 1948, the Egyptian Military Forces in the Al Faluja area shall be withdrawn.

2. This withdrawal shall begin on the day after that which follows the signing of this Agreement, at 0500 hours GMT, and shall be beyond the Egypt-Palestine frontier.

3. The withdrawal shall be under the supervision of the United Nations and in accordance with the Plan of Withdrawal set forth in Annex I to this Agreement.

Article IV

With specific reference to the implementation of the resolutions of the Security Council of 4 and 16 November 1948, the following principles and purposes are affirmed:

1. The principle that no military or political advantage should be gained under the truce ordered by the Security Council is recognized.

2. It is also recognized that the basic purposes and spirit of the Armistice would not be served by the restoration of previously held military positions, changes from those now held other than as specifically provided for in this Agreement, or by the advance of the military forces of either side beyond positions held at the time this Armistice Agreement is signed.

3. It is further recognized that rights, claims or interests of a non-military character in the area of Palestine covered by this Agreement may be asserted by either Party, and that these, by mutual agreement being excluded from the Armistice negotiations, shall be, at the discretion of the Parties, the subject of later settlement. It is emphasized that it is not the purpose of this Agreement to establish, to recognize, to strengthen, or to weaken or nullify, in any way, any territorial, custodial or other rights, claims or interests which may be asserted by either Party in the area of Palestine or any part or locality thereof covered by this Agreement, whether such asserted rights, claims or interests derive from Security Council resolutions, including the resolution of 4 November 1948 and the Memorandum of 13 November 1948 for its implementation, or from any other source. The provisions of this Agreement are dictated exclusively by military considerations and are valid only for the period of the Armistice.

*   *   *

Article XI

No provision of this Agreement shall in any way prejudice the rights, claims and positions of either Party hereto in the ultimate peaceful settlement of the Palestine question.

Article XII

1. The present Agreement is not subject to ratification and shall come into force immediately upon being signed.

2. This Agreement, having been negotiated and concluded in pursuance of the resolution of the Security Council of 16 November 1948 calling for the establishment of an Armistice in order to eliminate the threat to the peace in Palestine and to facilitate the transition from the present truce to permanent peace in Palestine, shall remain in force until a peaceful settlement between the Parties is achieved, except as provided in paragraph 3 of this Article.

3. The Parties to this Agreement may, by mutual consent, revise this Agreement or any of its provisions, or may suspend its application, other than Articles I and II, at any time. In the absence of mutual agreement and after this Agreement has been in effect for one year from the date of its signing, either of the Parties may call upon the Secretary-General of the United Nations to convoke a conference of representatives of the two Parties for the purpose of reviewing, revising or suspending any of the provisions of this Agreement other than Articles I and II. Participation in such conference shall be obligatory upon the Parties.

4. If the conference provided for in paragraph 3 of this Article does not result in an agreed solution of a point in dispute, either Party may bring the matter before the Security Council of the United Nations for the relief sought on the grounds that this Agreement has been concluded in pursuance of Security Council action toward the end of achieving peace in Palestine.

5. This Agreement supersedes the Egyptian-Israeli General Cease-Fire Agreement entered into by the Parties on 24 January 1949.

6. This Agreement is signed in quintuplicate, of which one copy shall be retained by each Party, two copies communicated to the Secretary-General of the United Nations for transmission to the Security Council and to the United Nations Conciliation Commission on Palestine, and one copy to the Acting Mediator on Palestine.

In faith whereof the undersigned representative of the Contracting Parties have signed hereafter, in the presence of the United Nations Acting Mediator on Palestine and the United Nations Chief of Staff of the Truce Supervision Organization.

Done at Rhodes Island of Rhodes, Greece, on the twenty-fourth of February nineteen forty-nine.

For and on behalf of the Government of Egypt
Col. Seif El Dine
Col. El Rahmany
For and on behalf of the Government of Israel

Dr. Walter Eytan
Col. Yigael Yadin
Elias Sasson

Tripartite Declaration Regarding Security in the Middle East*

May 25, 1950

The Governments of the United Kingdom, France, and the United States, having had occasion during the recent Foreign Ministers meeting in London to review certain questions affecting the peace and stability of the Arab states and of Israel, and particularly that of the supply of arms and war material to these states, have resolved to make the following statements:

1. The three Governments recognize that the Arab states and Israel all need to maintain a certain level of armed forces for the purposes of assuring their internal security and their legitimate self-defense and to permit them to play their part in the defense of the area as a whole. All applications for arms or war material for these countries will be considered in the light of these principles. In this connection the three Governments wish to recall and reaffirm the terms of the statements made by their representatives on the Security Council on August 4, 1949, in which they declared their opposition to the development of an arms race between the Arab states and Israel.

2. The three Governments declare that assurances have been received from all the states in question, to which they permit arms to be supplied from their countries, that the purchasing state does not intend to undertake any act of aggression against any other state. Similar assurances will be requested from any other state in the area to which they permit arms to be supplied in the future.

3. The three Governments take this opportunity of declaring their deep interest in and their desire to promote the establishment and maintenance of peace and stability in the area and their unalterable opposition to the use of force or threat of force between any of the states in that area. The three Governments, should they find that any of these states was preparing to violate frontiers or armistice lines, would, consistently with their obligations as members of the United Nations, immediately take action, both within and outside the United Nations, to prevent such violation.

United Nations Resolution on Passage of Israeli Ships Through the Suez Canal†

September 1, 1951

The Security Council

1. Recalling that in its resolution of 11 August 1949, (S/1376) relating to the conclusion of Armistice Agreements between Israel and the neighbouring Arab States it drew attention to the pledges, in these Agreements "against any further acts of hostility between the Parties";

*Department of State Bulletin, June 5, 1950, p. 886.
†United Nations S/2322, Sept. 1, 1951.

2. Recalling further that in its resolution of 17 November 1950 (S/1907) it reminded the States concerned that the Armistice Agreements to which they were parties contemplated "the return of permanent peace in Palestine," and therefore urged them and the other States in the area to take all such steps as would lead to the settlement of the issues between them;

3. Noting the report of the Chief of Staff of the Truce Supervision Organization to the Security Council of 12 June 1951 (S/2194);

4. Further noting that the Chief of Staff of the Truce Supervision Organization recalled the statement of the senior Egyptian delegate in Rhodes on 13 January 1949, to the effect that his delegation was "inspired with every spirit of co-operation, conciliation and a sincere desire to restore peace in Palestine," and that the Egyptian Government has not complied with the earnest plea of the Chief of Staff made to the Egyptian delegate on 12 June 1951, that it desist from the present practice of interfering with the passage through the Suez Canal of goods destined for Israel;

5. Considering that since the Armistice regime, which has been in existence for nearly two and a half years, is of a permanent character, neither party can reasonably assert that it is actively a belligerent or requires to exercise the right of visit, search, and seizure for any legitimate purpose of self-defence;

6. Finds that the maintenance of the practice mentioned in paragraph 4 above is inconsistent with the objectives of a peaceful settlement between the parties and the establishment of a permanent peace in Palestine set forth in the Armistice Agreement;

7. Finds further that such practice is an abuse of the exercise of the right of visit, search and seizure;

8. Further finds that that practice cannot in the prevailing circumstances be justified on the ground that it is necessary for self-defence;

9. And further noting that the restrictions on the passage of goods through the Suez Canal to Israel ports are denying to nations at no time connected with the conflict in Palestine valuable supplies required for their economic reconstruction, and that these restrictions together with sanctions applied by Egypt to certain ships which have visited Israel ports represent unjustified interference with the rights of nations to navigate the seas and to trade freely with one another, including the Arab States and Israel;

10. Calls upon Egypt to terminate the restrictions on the passage of international commercial shipping and goods through the Suez Canal wherever bound and to cease all interference with such shipping beyond that essential to the safety of shipping in the Canal itself and to the observance of international conventions in force.

THE SUEZ CRISIS AND THE 1956 WAR

WHITE HOUSE STATEMENTS CONCERNING AGGRESSION IN THE MIDDLE EAST ISSUED BY JAMES C. HAGERTY, PRESS SECRETARY TO THE PRESIDENT*

Statement of October 29, 1956

At the meeting the President recalled that the United States, under this and prior administrations, has pledged itself to assist the victim of any aggression in the Middle East.

We shall honor our pledge.

The United States is in consultation with the British and French Governments, parties with us to the Tripartite Declaration of 1950, and the United States plans, as contemplated by that declaration, that the situation shall be taken to the United Nations Security Council tomorrow morning.

The question of whether and when the President will call a special session of the Congress will be decided in the light of the unfolding situation.

Statement of October 30, 1956

As soon as the President received his first knowledge, obtained through press reports, of the ultimatum delivered by the French and United Kingdom Governments to Egypt and Israel, planning temporary occupation within 12 hours of the Suez Canal Zone, he sent an urgent personal message to the Prime Minister of Great Britain and the Prime Minister of the Republic of France.

The President expressed his earnest hope that the United Nations Organization would be given full opportunity to settle the items in the controversy by peaceful means instead of by forceful ones.

This Government continues to believe that it is possible by such peaceful means to secure a solution which would restore the armistice conditions between Egypt and Israel, as well as bring about a just settlement of the Suez Canal controversy.

Statement of November 5, 1956

The United States will today propose to the General Assembly of the United Nations two additional resolutions with respect to the critical Middle Eastern situation.

Sixty-three other nations—members of the General Assembly—joined with our country on November 2d in approving the United States resolution urging an immediate cessation of hostilities in Egypt. It is the earnest hope of the United States that all parties to the conflict will be guided by this conclusive evidence of world opinion.

The additional resolutions which will be presented deal with the necessity of

---

*Department of State Bulletin, Nov. 12, 1956, p. 749.

seeking promptly solutions to basic problems which have given rise to the present conflict.

The first resolution will propose a new approach to the settlement of major problems outstanding between the Arab States and Israel with a view to establishing conditions of permanent peace and stability in the area.

The second resolution will deal with means of finding a solution to the Suez Canal controversy. It will seek the earliest possible opening of the canal and the working out of permanent arrangements for the functioning of the canal.

The resolutions will be presented to the General Assembly by Ambassador Henry Cabot Lodge, head of the United States delegation.

*United States Proposal in the Security Council (U.N. doc. S/3710)
on Middle East Aggression**

October 30, 1956

The Security Council,

Noting that the armed forces of Israel have penetrated deeply into Egyptian territory in violation of the armistice agreement between Egypt and Israel;

Expressing its grave concern at this violation of the armistice agreement;

1. Calls upon Israel and Egypt immediately to cease fire;

2. Calls upon Israel immediately to withdraw its armed forces behind the established armistice lines;

3. Calls upon all Members

(a) to refrain from the use of force or threat of force in the area in any manner inconsistent with the Purposes of the United Nations;

(b) to assist the United Nations in ensuring the integrity of the armistice agreements;

(c) to refrain from giving any military, economic or financial assistance to Israel so long as it has not complied with this resolution;

4. Requests the Secretary-General to keep the Security Council informed on compliance with this resolution and to make whatever recommendations he deems appropriate for the maintenance of international peace and security in the area by the implementation of this and prior resolutions.

*Report by President Dwight D. Eisenhower on the Developments
in Eastern Europe and the Middle East†*

October 31, 1956

Tonight I report to you as your President.

We all realize that the full and free debate of a political campaign surrounds us. But

---

*Ibid. The vote on Oct. 30 was 7 to 2 (France, U.K.), with Ausralia and Belgium abstaining. Because of the French and British vetoes, the resolution failed of adoption. France and the United Kingdom also vetoed a Soviet-proposed resolution which contained some of the elements of the U.S. draft. Belgium and the United States abstained on the Soviet proposal.

†*Public Papers of the Presidents of the U.S.*, Dwight D. Eisenhower, Jan. 1-Dec. 31, 1956, pp. 1060-66.

the events and issues I wish to place before you this evening have no connection whatsoever with matters of partisanship. They are concerns of every American his present and his future.

I wish, therefore, to give you a report of essential facts so that you—whether belonging to either one of our two great parties or to neither—May give thoughtful and informed consideration to this swiftly changing world scene.

The changes of which I speak have come in two areas of the world—Eastern Europe and the Mid-East.

I

In Eastern Europe there is the dawning of a new day. It has not been short or easy in coming.

After World War II, the Soviet Union used military force to impose on the nations of Eastern Europe, governments of Soviet choice—servants of Moscow.

It has been consistent United States policy—without regard to political party—to seek to end this situation. We have sought to fulfill the wartime pledge of the United Nations that these countries, over-run by wartime armies, would once again know sovereignty and self-government.

We could not, of course, carry out this policy by resort to force. Such force would have been contrary both to the best interests of the Eastern European peoples and to the abiding principles of the United Nations. But we did help to keep alive the hope of these peoples for freedom.

Beyond this, they needed from us no education in the worth of national independence and personal liberty—for, at the time of the American Revolution, it was many of them who came to our land to aid our cause. Now, recently the pressure of the will of these peoples for national independence has become more and more insistent.

A few days ago, the people of Poland—with their proud and deathless devotion to freedom—moved to secure a peaceful transition to a new government. And this government, it seems, will strive genuinely to serve the Polish people.

And, more recently, all the world has been watching dramatic events in Hungary where this brave people, as so often in the past, have offered their very lives for independence from foreign masters. Today, it appears, a new Hungary is rising from this struggle, a Hungary which we hope from our hearts will know full and free nationhood.

We have rejoiced in all these historic events.

Only yesterday the Soviet Union issued an important statement on its relations with all the countries of Eastern Europe. This statement recognized the need for review of Soviet policies, and the amendment of these policies to meet the demands of the people for greater national independence and personal freedom. The Soviet Union declared its readiness to consider the withdrawal of Soviet "advisers"—who have been, as you know, the effective ruling force in Soviet occupied countries—and also to consider withdrawal of Soviet forces from Poland, Hungary and Rumania.

We cannot yet know if these avowed purposes will be truly carried out.

But two things are clear.

First, the fervor and the sacrifice of the peoples of these countries, in the name of freedom, have themselves brought real promise that the light of liberty soon will shine again in this darkness.

And second, if the Soviet Union indeed faithfully acts upon its announced intention, the world will witness the greatest forward stride toward justice, trust and understanding among nations in our generation.

These are the facts. How has your government responded to them?

The United States has made clear its readiness to assist economically the new and independent governments of these countries. We have already—some days since—been in contact with the new Government of Poland on this matter. We have also publicly declared that we do not demand of these governments their adoption of any particular form of society as a condition upon our economic assistance. Our one concern is that they be free—for their sake, and for freedom's sake.

We have also—with respect to the Soviet Union—sought clearly to remove any false fears that we would look upon new governments in these Eastern European countries as potential military allies. We have no such ulterior purpose. We see these peoples as friends, and we wish simply that they be friends who are free.

II

I now turn to that other part of the world where, at this moment, the situation is somber. It is not a situation that calls for extravagant fear or hysteria. But it invites our most serious concern.

I speak, of course, of the Middle East. This ancient crossroads of the world was, as we all know, an area long subject to colonial rule. This rule ended after World War II, when all countries there won full independence. Out of the Palestinian mandated territory was born the new State of Israel.

These historic changes could not, however, instantly banish animosities born of the ages. Israel and her Arab neighbors soon found themselves at war with one another. And the Arab nations showed continuing anger toward their former colonial rulers, notably France and Great Britain.

The United States—through all the years since the close of World War II—has labored tirelessly to bring peace and stability to this area.

We have considered it a basic matter of United States policy to support the new State of Israel and—at the same time—to strengthen our bonds with Israel and with the Arab countries. But, unfortunately through all these years, passion in the area threatened to prevail over peaceful purposes, and in one form or another, there has been almost continuous fighting.

This situation recently was aggravated by Egyptian policy including rearmament with Communist weapons. We felt this to be a misguided policy on the part of the Government of Egypt. The State of Israel, at the same time, felt increasing anxiety for its safety. And Great Britain and France feared more and more that Egyptian policies threatened their "life line" of the Suez Canal.

These matters came to a crisis on July 26th of this year, when the Egyptian Government seized the Universal Suez Canal Company. For ninety years—ever since the inauguration of the Canal—that Company has operated the Canal, largely under British and French technical supervision.

Now there were some among our allies who urged an immediate reaction to this event by use of force. We insistently urged otherwise, and our wish prevailed—through a long succession of conferences and negotiations for weeks—even months—with participation by the United Nations. And there, in the United Nations, only a short while ago, on the basis of agreed principles, it seemed that an acceptable accord was within our reach.

But the direct relations of Egypt with both Israel and France kept worsening to a point at which first Israel—then France—and Great Britain also—determined that, in their judgment, there could be no protection of their vital interests without resort to force.

Upon this decision, events followed swiftly. On Sunday the Israeli Government ordered total mobilization. On Monday, their armed forces penetrated deeply into Egypt and to the vicinity of the Suez Canal, nearly one hundred miles away. And on Tuesday, the British and French Governments delivered a 12-hour ultimatum to Israel and Egypt—now followed up by armed attack against Egypt.

The United States was not consulted in any way about any phase of these actions. Nor were we informed of them in advance.

As it is the manifest right of any of these nations to take such decisions and actions, it is likewise our right—if our judgment so dictates—to dissent. We believe these actions to have been taken in error. For we do not accept the use of force as a wise or proper instrument for the settlement of international disputes.

To say this—in this particular instance—is in no way to minimize our friendship with these nations—nor our determination to maintain those friendships.

And we are fully aware of the grave anxieties of Israel, of Britain and of France. We know that they have been subjected to grave and repeated provocations.

The present fact, nonetheless, seems clear: the action taken can scarcely be reconciled with the principles and purposes of the United Nations to which we have all subscribed. And, beyond this, we are forced to doubt that resort to force and war will for long serve the permanent interest of the attacking nations.

Now—we must look to the future.

In the circumstances I have described, there will be no United States involvement in these present hostilities. I therefore have no plan to call the Congress in Special Session. Of course, we shall continue to keep in contact with Congressional leaders of both parties.

I assure you, your government will remain alert to every possibility of this situation, and keep in close contact and coordination with the Legislative Branch of this government.

At the same time it is—and it will remain—the dedicated purpose of your government to do all in its power to localize the fighting and to end the conflict.

We took our first measure in this action yesterday. We went to the United Nations with a request that the forces of Israel return to their own land and that hostilities in the area be brought to a close. This proposal was not adopted—because it was vetoed by Great Britain and by France.

The processes of the United Nations, however, are not exhausted. It is our hope and intent that this matter will be brought before the United Nations General Assembly. There—with no veto operating—the opinion of the world can be brought to bear in our quest for a just end to this tormenting problem. In the past the United Nations has proved able to find a way to end bloodshed. We believe it can and that it will do so again.

My fellow citizens, as I review the march of world events in recent years, I am ever more deeply convinced that the processes of the United Nations represent the soundest hope for peace in the world. For this very reason, I believe that the processes of the United Nations need further to be developed and strengthened. I speak particularly of increasing its ability to secure justice under international law.

In all the recent troubles in the Middle East, there have indeed been injustices suffered by all nations involved. But I do not believe that another instrument of injustice—war—is the remedy for these wrongs.

There can be no peace—without law. And there can be no law—if we were to invoke one code of international conduct for those who oppose us—and another for our friends.

The society of nations has been slow in developing means to apply this truth.

But the passionate longing for peace—on the part of all peoples of the earth—compels us to speed our search for new and more effective instruments of justice.

The peace we seek and need means much more than mere absence of war. It means the acceptance of law, and the fostering of justice, in all the world.

To our principles guiding us in this quest we must stand fast. In so doing we can honor the hopes of all men for a world in which peace will truly and justly reign.

I thank you, and goodnight.

Speech by Secretary Dulles at the Special Emergency Session on the Palestine Question *

November 1, 1956

I doubt that any delegate ever spoke from this forum with as heavy a heart as I have brought here tonight. We speak on a matter of vital importance, where the United States finds itself unable to agree with three nations with whom it has ties, deep friendship, admiration and respect, and two of whom constitute our oldest, most trusted and reliable allies.

The fact that we differ with such friends has led us to reconsider and reevaluate our position with the utmost care, and that has been done at the highest levels of our government. Even after that reevaluation, we still find ourselves in disagreement. Because it seems to us that that disagreement involves principles which far transcend the immediate issue, we feel impelled to make our point of view known to you and through you to the world.

This is the first time that this Assembly has met pursuant to the Uniting for Peace resolution which was adopted in 1950. I was a member of the United States Delegation and had the primary responsibility for handling that proposal in Committee and on the floor of this Assembly. It was then during the period of the communist attack upon the Republic of Korea, and at that time surely we little thought that it would be invoked for the first time under the conditions which now prevail.

What are the facts that bring us here?

Vital Speeches of the Day, John Foster Dulles, pp. 75-77.

There is, first of all, the fact that there occurred beginning last Monday a deep penetration of Egypt by Israeli forces. Then, quickly following up upon this action, there came action by France and the United Kingdom in subjecting Egypt first to a 12-hour ultimatum and then to armed attack, which is now going on from the air with the declared purpose of gaining temporary control of the Suez Canal, presumably to make it more secure.

Then there is the third fact that the matter, having been brought to the Security Council, was sought to be dealt with by a resolution which was vetoed by the United Kingdom and by France, which cast the only dissenting votes against the resolution. Thereupon, under the provisions of the Uniting for Peace resolution, the matter came here under a call from the Secretary General, instituted by a vote of seven members of the Security Council, requiring that this Assembly convene in emergency session within 24 hours.

Now, Mr. President and fellow delegates, the United States recognizes full well that the facts which I have referred to are not the only facts in this situation. There is a long and a sad history of irritations and of provocations. There have been armistice violations by Israel and against Israel. There have been violations by Egypt of the Treaty of 1888 governing the Suez Canal, and a disregard by Egypt of the Security Council Resolution of 1951, calling for the passage through that canal by Israeli ships and cargoes. There has been a heavy rearmament of Egypt under somewhat ominous circumstances. There was the abrupt seizure by Egypt of the Universal Suez Canal Company, which largely under British and French auspices had been operating that canal ever since it was opened 90 years ago. There have been repeated expressions of hostility by the Government of Egypt toward other governments with whom it ostensibly had, and should have, friendly relations.

We are not blind, Mr. President, to the fact that what has happened in the last two or three days comes out of a murky background. But we have come to the conclusion that these provocations, serious as they are, cannot justify the resort to armed force which has occurred within the last two and three days, and which is going on tonight.

To be sure, the United Nations perhaps has not done all that it should have done. I have often pointed out, particularly in recent weeks, that our Charter by Article 1, Paragraph 1, calls for the settlement of these matters in accordance with the principles of justice and of international law, and it calls not merely for a peaceful solution, but a just solution. The United Nations may have been somewhat laggard, somewhat impotent in dealing with many injustices which are inherent in this Middle Eastern situation. But I think that we ought, and I hope will, perhaps at the next regular meeting of this General Assembly, give our most earnest thought to the problem of how we can do more to establish and to implement principles of justice and of international law. We have not done all that we should have done in that respect, and on that account a part of the responsibility of present events lies here at our doorstep.

But, Mr. President, if we were to agree that the existence of injustices in the world, which this organization so far has been unable to cure, means that the principle of renunciation of force is no longer respected, and that there still exists the right wherever a nation feels itself subject to injustice to resort to force to try to correct that injustice, then, Mr. President, we would have, I fear, torn this Charter into shreds and the world would again be a world of anarchy. And all the great hopes that are placed in this organization and in our Charter would have vanished and we would be, as we were, when World War II began, with only another tragic failure in place of what we hoped would be—and still can hope will be—a barrier against the recurrence of a world war which, as our Preamble says, has "twice in our lifetime . . . brought untold sorrow to mankind."

Now, Mr. President, this problem of the Suez Canal, which lies at the base perhaps in considerable part of the forcible action now being taken, has been dealt with over the past three months in many ways and on many occasions. I doubt if in all history so sincere, so sustained an effort has been made to find a just and a peaceful solution.

When on July 26 the Universal Suez Canal Company was abruptly seized by the Egyptian Government, all the world felt that a crisis of momentous proportions had been precipitated. Within, I think, three days after that event, the Governments of the United States, the United Kingdom, and France met together in London to see what to do about the situation. Already at that time there were voices raised in favor of an immediate resort to force to attempt to restore the *status quo ante* the Egyptian seizure. But it was the judgment of all three of our governments that the resort to force would be unjustified, certainly under the then conditions, and that first efforts should be made to bring about a peaceful and just solution.

Instead of any resort to force at that critical moment, the three governments agreed to call a conference of the principle users of the Suez Canal—24 nations representing the clearly surviving signatories of the Convention of 1888, eight countries who principally used the Canal and eight countries whose pattern of traffic showed particular dependence upon the Canal. And 22 of those 24 nations met, Egypt declined. Out of the 22, 18 agreed upon what they thought were sound principles for arriving at a peaceful solution which would be just and fair and which would secure for the future the open use of this waterway.

That agreement of the 18 was carried as a proposal to Cairo and presented to President Nasser, who rejected it.

Then the 18 met again in London and again considered a proposal to create an association, a cooperative group of the users.

We felt that that association might be able to work out on a practical provisional basis with the Egyptian canal authorities an acceptable arrangement for assuring the operation on a free and impartial basis of the Canal. Then while that was in process of being organized—the Users Association—the matter was brought to the Security Council of the United Nations by France and the United Kingdom. There six principles were unanimously adopted with the concurrence of Egypt, who participated in the proceedings though not a member of the Council. Those principles were in essence the same principles that had been adopted by the 18 nations at London. There was a second part of the resolution which looked forward to the implementation of these principles. That part failed of adoption, this time by a veto of the Soviet Union.

But despite that fact there occurred under the auspices of the Secretary General, to whom I would like to pay tribute for his great contribution in this matter to a just and peaceful solution, there occurred under his auspices exchanges of views as to how to implement these six principles. I do not think it is an exaggeration to say what I am quite sure he would confirm, that very considerable progress was made. It seemed as though a just and peaceful solution acceptable to all was near at hand, and it was hoped that those negotiations would be continued.

I recall that at the close of our session of the Security Council, I made a statement which was concurred in, or acquiesced in, by all present, stating that the Security Council remains seized of the problem and that it was hoped that the exchanges of views with the Secretary General and the three countries most directly concerned– Egypt, France, and the United Kingdom–that those discussions and exchanges of views would continue.

They did not continue, although I am not aware of any insuperable obstacle to such a continuance. Instead, there developed the events which I have referred to, the invocation of violence, first by Israel and then by France and the United Kingdom, the events which again brought the matter to the Security Council and which, in the face of veto, has brought the matter here to us tonight.

Surely I think we must feel that the peaceful processes which the Charter requests every member to follow had not been exhausted. Even in the case of Israel, which has a legitimate complaint due to the fact that Egypt has never complied with the 1951 resolution of the Security Council recognizing Israel's right to use of the Canal–even there, there was a better prospect because the principles adopted by the Security Council, with the concurrence of Egypt called for the passage of ships and cargoes through the Canal without discrimination, and provided that the Canal could not be used or abused for the national purposes of any nation, including Egypt.

So, Mr. President, and fellow delegates, there seemed to be peaceful processes that were at work and which, as I say, had not yet, it seemed to us at least, run their course. And while, Mr. President, I would be the last to say that there can never be circumstances where resort to force may not be employed–and certainly there can be resort to force for defensive purposes under Article 51–it seems to us that under the circumstances which I described, the resort to force, the violent armed attack by three of our members upon a fourth cannot be treated as other than a grave error, inconsistent with the Principles and Purposes of the Charter, and one which if persisted in would gravely undermine our Charter and undermine this organization.

The question then is: What do we do?

It seems to us imperative that something be done because what has been done in apparent contravention of our Charter has not yet gone so far as irretrievably to damage this organization or to destroy it. Indeed, our Uniting for Peace resolution was designed to meet just such circumstances as have arisen. It is still possible for the united will of this organization to have an impact upon the situation and perhaps to make it apparent to the world, not only for the benefit of ourselves, but of all posterity, that there is here the beginning of a world of order. We do not, any of us, live in societies in which acts of disorder do not occur. But we all of us live in societies where, if those acts occur, something is done by constituted authority to deal with them. At the moment we are the constituted authority. And while we do not have under the Charter the power of action, we do have a power of recommendation, a power which, if it reflects the moral judgment of the world community, of world opinion, will, I think, be influential upon the present situation.

It is animated by such considerations, Mr. President, that the United States has introduced a resolution which I should like to read to you:

"The General Assembly
Noting the disregard on many occasions by parties to the Israel-Arab Armistice Agree-ments of 1948 of the terms of such agreements, and that the armed forces of Israel have penetrated deeply into Egyptian territory in violation of the General Armistice Agreement between Egypt and Israel;

Noting that armed forces of France and the United Kingdom are conducting military operations against Egyptian territory;

Noting that traffic through the Suez Canal is now interrupted to the serious prejudice of many nations;

Expressing its grave concern over these developments:

1. Urges as a matter of priority that all parties now involved in hostilities in the area agree to an immediate cease-fire and as part thereof halt the movement of military forces and arms into the area;

2. Urges the parties to the Armistice Agreements promptly to withdraw all forces behind the Armistice lines, to desist from raids across the Armistice lines into neighboring territory, and to observe scrupulously the provisions of the Armistice Agreements;

3. Recommends that all members refrain from introducing military goods in the area of hostilities and in general refrain from any acts which would delay or prevent the implementation of this resolution;

4. Urges that upon the cease-fire being effective steps be taken to reopen the Suez Canal and restore secure freedom of navigation;

5. Requests the Secretary General to observe and promptly report on the compliance with this resolution, to the Security Council and to the General Assembly, for such further action as they may deem appropriate in accordance with the Charter;

6. Decides to remain in emergency session pending compliance with this resolution."

That, Mr. President, is the proposal of the United States Delegation.

Now, I recognize full well that a recommendation which merely is directed to a cease-fire, to getting back of the armistice lines the foreign land forces in Egypt which so far as we are aware today are only those of Israel, of stopping the attacks by air and not bringing new belligerent forces in the area, and then, as rapidly as possible of the reopening of the Suez Canal—that a resolution which puts primary emphasis upon these things is not an adequate or comprehensive treatment of the situation. All of us, I think, would hope that out of this tragedy there should come something better than merely a restoration of the conditions out of which this tragedy came about. There must be something better than that. Surely, this organization has a duty to strive to bring about that betterment.

If we should do only that we too would be negligent and would have dealt only with one aspect of the problem.

I have said and deeply believe that peace is a coin which has two sides—one of which is the avoidance of the use of force and the other is the creation of conditions of justice—and in the long run you cannot expect one without the other.

I do not by the form of this resolution want to seem in any way to believe that this situation can be adequately taken care of merely by the steps that are in this resolution. There needs to be something better than the uneasy armistices which have existed now for these eight years between Israel and the Arab neighbors; there needs to be a greater sense of confidence and security in the free and equal operation of the Canal than has existed since three months ago when President Nasser seized the Suez Canal Company. These things I regard of the utmost importance.

But, Mr. President and fellow delegates, if we say that it is all right for the fighting to go on until these difficult and complicated matters have been settled, then I fear a situation will have been created such that no settlement will be possible, that the war will have intensified and may have spread, that the world will have been divided by new bitternesses, and that the foundations for peace will have been tragically shattered.

These things that I speak of need to be done. I believe that they are in process of being done because the Security Council is already seized of these matters and has been working upon them in a constructive way. But I think we must put first things first. I believe that the first thing is to stop the fighting as rapidly as possible lest it become a conflagration which would endanger us all—and that is not beyond the realm of possibility.

As President Eisenhower said last night, the important thing is to limit and extinguish the fighting insofar as it is possible and as promptly as possible.

I hope, therefore, Mr. President and fellow delegates, that this point of view reflected in this resolution will prevail.

I fear that if we do not act and act promptly, and if we do not act with sufficient unanimity of opinion so that our recommendations carry a real influence, there is great danger that what is started and what has been called a police action may develop into something which is far more grave. Even if that does not happen, the apparent impotence of this organization to deal with this situation may set a precedent which will lead other nations to attempt to take into their own hands the remedying of what they believe to be their injustices. If that happens, the future is dark indeed.

We thought when we wrote the Charter in San Francisco in 1945 that we had seen perhaps the worst in war, that our task was to prevent a recurrence of what had been, and indeed what then had been was tragic enough. But now we know that what can be will be infinitely more tragic than what we saw in World War II.

I believe that at this critical juncture we owe the highest duty to ourselves, to our peoples, to posterity, to take action which will assure that this fire which has started shall not spread but shall promptly be extinguished. Then we shall turn with renewed vigor to curing the injustices out of which this trouble has arisen.

*General Assembly Resolution 997 (ES-I) on a Ceasefire in Egypt and Withdrawal of Military Forces to the 1949 Armistice lines**

November 2, 1956

The General Assembly,

Noting the disregard on many occasions by parties to the Israel-Arab armistice agreements of 1949 of the terms of such agreements, and that the armed forces of Israel have penetrated deeply into Egyptian territory in violation of the General Armistice Agreement between Egypt and Israel of 24 February 1949,

Noting that armed forces of France and the United Kingdom of Great Britain and Northern Ireland are conducting military operations against Egyptian territory,

Noting that traffic through the Suez Canal is now interrupted to the serious prejudice of many nations,

Expressing its grave concern over these developments,

1. Urges as a matter of priority that all parties now involved in hostilities in the area agree to an immediate cease-fire and, as part thereof, halt the movement of military forces and arms into the area; .

---

*U.N. General Assembly *Official Records, 1st Emergency Special Session, Supplement 1*, p. 2. The resolution, introduced by the United States, was adopted by a vote of 64 to 5 (Australia, France, Israel, New Zealand, and the United Kingdom), with 6 abstentions (Belgium, Canada, Laos, the Netherlands, Portugal, and the Union of South Africa).

2. Urges the parties to the armistice agreements promptly to withdraw all forces behind the armistice lines, to desist from raids across the armistice lines into neighbouring territory, and to observe scrupulously the provisions of the armistice agreements;

3. Recommends that all Member States refrain from introducing military goods in the area of hostilities and in general refrain from any acts which would delay or prevent the implementation of the present resolution;

4. Urges that, upon the cease-fire being effective, steps be taken to reopen the Suez Canal and restore secure freedom of navigation;

5. Requests the Secretary-General to observe and report promptly on the compliance with the present resolution to the Security Council and to the General Assembly, for such further action as they may deem appropriate in accordance with the Charter;

6. Decides to remain in emergency session pending compliance with the present resolution.

General Assembly Resolution 1000 (ES-I) on Creation of a United Nations Emergency Force*

November 5, 1956

The General Assembly,

Having requested the Secretary-General, in its resolution 998 (ES-I) of 4 November 1956, to submit to it a plan for an emergency international United Nations Force, for the purposes stated,

Noting with satisfaction the first report of the Secretary-General on the plan, and having in mind particularly paragraph 4 of that report,

1. Establishes a United Nations Command for an emergency international Force to secure and supervise the cessation of hostilities in accordance with all the terms of General Assembly resolution 997 (ES-I) of 2 November 1956;

2. Appoints, on an emergency basis, the Chief of Staff of the United Nations Truce Supervision Organization, Major-General E. L. M. Burns, as Chief of the Command;

3. Authorizes the Chief of the Command immediately to recruit, from the observer corps of the United Nations Truce Supervision Organization, a limited number of officers who shall be nationals of countries other than those having permanent membership in the Security Council, and further authorizes him, in consultation with the Secretary-General, to undertake the recruitment directly, from various Member States other than the permanent members of the Security Council, of the additional number of officers needed;

4. Invites the Secretary-General to take such administrative measures as may be necessary for the prompt execution of the actions envisaged in the present resolution.

*Ibid., pp. 2-3. This resolution, introduced by Canada, Colombia, and Norway on Nov. 4, 1956, was adopted by a vote of 57 (including the U.S.) to 0, with 19 abstentions (the Soviet bloc, Australia, Egypt, France, Israel, Laos, New Zealand, Portugal, Turkey, the Union of South Africa, and the United Kingdom).

General Assembly Resolution 1125 (XI) on General Armistice
Between Egypt and Israel*

February 2, 1957

The General Assembly,

Having received the report of the Secretary-General of 24 January 1957,

Recognizing that withdrawal by Israel must be followed by action which would assure progress towards the creation of peaceful conditions,

1. Notes with appreciation the Secretary-General's report and the measures therein to be carried out upon Israel's complete withdrawal;

2. Calls upon the Governments of Egypt and Israel scrupulously to observe the provisions of the General Armistice Agreement between Egypt and Israel of 24 February 1949,

3. Considers that, after full withdrawal of Israel from the Sharm el Sheikh and Gaza areas, the scrupulous maintenance of the Armistice Agreement requires the placing of the United Nations Emergency Force on the Egyptian-Israel armistice demarcation line and the implementation of other measures as proposed in the Secretary-General's report, with due regard to the considerations set out therein with a view to assist in achieving situations conducive to the maintenance of peaceful conditions in the area;

4. Requests the Secretary-General, in consultation with the parties concerned to take steps to carry out these measures and to report, as appropriate, to the General Assembly.

Aide Memoire from the United States to Israel on the
Withdrawal of Israeli forces from Egypt†

February 11, 1957

The United Nations Generaly Assembly has sought specifically, vigorously, and almost unanimously, the prompt withdrawal from Egypt of the armed forces of Britain, France and Israel. Britain and France have complied unconditionally. The forces of Israel have been withdrawn to a considerable extent but still hold Egyptian territory at Sharm el Shaikh at the entrance to the Gulf of Aqaba. They also occupy the Gaza Strip which is territory specified by the Armistice arrangements to be occupied by Egypt.

We understand that it is the position of Israel that (1) it will evacuate its military forces from the Gaza Strip provided Israel retains the civil administration and police in some relationship to the United Nations; and (2) it will withdraw from Sharm el Shaikh if continued freedom of passage through the Straits is assured.

With respect to (1) the Gaza Strip—it is the view of the United States that the United Nations General Assembly has no authority to require of either Egypt or Israel a substantial modification of the Armistice Agreement, which, as noted, now gives

*Ibid., 11th sess., 1956-57, Supplement 17, p. 62.
†*Department of State Bulletin*, Mar. 11, 1957, pp. 392-93.

Egypt the right and responsibility of occupation. Accordingly, we believe that Israeli withdrawal from Gaza should be prompt and unconditional, leaving the future of the Gaza Strip to be worked out through the efforts and good offices of the United Nations.

We recognize that the area has been a source of armed infiltration and reprisals back and forth contrary to the Armistice Agreement and is a source of great potential danger because of the presence there of so large a number of Arab refugees—about 200,000. Accordingly, we believe that the United Nations General Assembly and the Secretary General should seek that the United Nations Emergency Force, in the exercise of its mission, move into this area and be on the boundary between Israel and the Gaza Strip.

The United States will use its best efforts to help to assure this result, which we believe is contemplated by the Second Resolution of February 2, 1957.

With respect to (2) the Gulf of Aqaba and access thereto—the United States believes that the Gulf comprehends international waters and that no nation has the right to prevent free and innocent passage in the Gulf and through the Straits giving access thereto. We have in mind not only commercial usage, but the passage of pilgrims on religious missions, which should be fully respected.

The United States recalls that on January 28, 1950, the Egyptian Ministry of Foreign Affairs informed the United States that the Egyptian occupation of the two islands of Tiran and Senafir at the entrance of the Gulf of Aqaba was only to protect the islands themselves against possible damage or violation and that "this occupation being in no way conceived in a spirit of obstructing in any way innocent passage through the stretch of water separating these two islands from the Egyptian coast of Sinai, it follows that this passage, the only practicable one, will remain free as in the past, in conformity with international practice and recognized principles of the law of nations."

In the absence of some overriding decision to the contrary, as by the International Court of Justice, the United States, on behalf of vessels of United States registry, is prepared to exercise the right of free and innocent passage and to join with others to secure general recognition of this right.

It is of course clear that the enjoyment of a right of free and innocent passage by Israel would depend upon its prior withdrawal in accordance with the United Nations Resolutions. The United States has no reason to assume that any littoral state would under these circumstances obstruct the right of free and innocent passage.

The United States believes that the United Nations General Assembly and the Secretary General should, as a precautionary measure, seek that the United Nations Emergency Force move into the Straits area as the Israeli forces are withdrawn. This again we believe to be within the contemplation of the Second Resolution of February 2, 1957.

(3) The United States observes that the recent resolutions of the United Nations General Assembly call not only for the prompt and unconditional withdrawal of Israel behind the Armistice lines but call for other measures.

We believe, however, that the United Nations has properly established an order of events and an order of urgency and that the first requirement is that forces of invasion and occupation should withdraw.

The United States is prepared publicly to declare that it will use its influence, in concert with other United Nations members, to the end that, following Israel's withdrawal, these other measures will be implemented.

We believe that our views and purposes in this respect are shared by many other nations and that a tranquil future for Israel is best assured by reliance upon that fact, rather than by an occupation in defiance of the overwhelming judgment of the world community.

White House Statement on Withdrawal of Israeli Troops within Armistice Lines*

February 17, 1957

The President has authorized the following statement:

The Department of State is today making public a memorandum which the United States gave to the Government of Israel on February 11th. It relates to Israeli withdrawal to within the armistice lines as repeatedly called for by the United Nations. The memorandum outlines the policies which the United States would, thereafter, pursue in relation to the two matters—the Gulf of Aqaba and the Gaza Strip—which so far lead Israel not to withdraw.

Israel would prefer to have the future status of the Gulf of Aqaba and the Gaza Strip definitely settled to its satisfaction prior to its withdrawal, and as a condition thereto. But all members of the United Nations are solemnly bound by the Charter to settle their international disputes by peaceful means and in their international relations to refrain from the threat or use of force against the territorial integrity of any state. These undertakings seem to preclude using the forcible seizure and occupation of other lands as bargaining power in the settlement of international disputes.

The United Kingdom and France, which occupied portions of Egypt at about the time of Israel's attack upon Egypt of last October, withdrew promptly and unconditionally in response to the same United Nations Resolution that called for Israeli withdrawal. They deferred to the overwhelming judgment of the world community that a solution of their difficulties with Egypt should be sought after withdrawal and not be made a condition precedent to withdrawal. The United States believes that Israel should do likewise.

President Eisenhower's letter to Prime Minister Ben-Gurion of Israel of November 8, 1956, urged, as a matter of "highest priority" that "Israeli forces be withdrawn to the General Armistice line." "After which," the President said, "new and energetic steps should be undertaken within the framework of the United Nations to solve the basic problems which have given rise to the present difficulty."

Prime Minister Ben-Gurion in his reply said: "In view of the United Nations Resolution regarding the withdrawal of foreign troops from Egypt and the creation of an international force, we will, upon conclusion of satisfactory arrangements with the United Nations in connection with this international force entering the Suez Canal area, willingly withdraw our forces."

The international force referred to by the Prime Minister has been created and, pursuant to arrangements which the United Nations has deemed satisfactory, has entered into and is now within the Suez Canal area. But while there has been a partial withdrawal of Israeli forces from Egypt, Israel persists in its occupation of Egyptian territory around the entrance of the Gulf of Aqaba and of the Gaza Strip.

The United States is aware of the fact that Israel has legitimate grievances and should, in all fairness, see a prospect of remedying them. The United Nations General Assembly by its second resolution of February 2nd, endorsing the Secretary General's report, gave such a prospect. We believe that that prospect is further assured by the view which the United States has formulated and communicated to Israel in its memorandum of February 11th. There, the United States took note of Israeli views with reference to the Gaza Strip and the Straits of Aqaba and made clear what the United States would do, after Israel's withdrawal, to help solve the problems that preoccupy Israel. Our declaration related to our intentions, both as a Member of the United Nations and as a maritime power having rights of our own.

The United States believes that the action of the United Nations of February 2nd and the statements of various governments, including the United States memorandum of February 11th, provide Israel with the maximum assurance that it can reasonably expect at this juncture, or that can be reconciled with fairness to others.

Accordingly, the United States has renewed its plea to Israel to withdraw in accordance with the repeated demands of the United Nations and to rely upon the resoluteness of all friends of justice to bring about a state of affairs which will conform to the principles of justice and of international law and serve impartially the proper interests of all in the area. This, the United States believes, should provide a greater source of security for Israel than an occupation continued contrary to the overwhelming judgment of the world community.

The United States, for its part, will strive to remain true to, and support, the United Nations in its efforts to sustain the purposes and principles of the Charter as the world's best hope for peace.

THE EISENHOWER DOCTRINE

The Eisenhower Doctrine*

January 5, 1957

First may I express to you my deep appreciation of your courtesy in giving me, at some inconvenience to yourselves, this early opportunity of addressing you on a matter I deem to be of grave importance to our country.

In my forthcoming State of the Union Message, I shall review the international situation generally. There are worldwide hopes which we can reasonably entertain, and there are worldwide responsibilities which we must carry to make certain that freedom—including our own—may be secure.

There is, however, a special situation in the Middle East which I feel I should, even now, lay before you.

Before doing so it is well to remind ourselves that our basic national objective in international affairs remains peace—a world peace based on justice. Such a peace must include all areas, all peoples of the world if it is to be enduring. There is no nation, great or small, with which we would refuse to negotiate, in mutual good faith, with patience and in the determination to secure a better understanding between us. Out of such understandings must, and eventually will, grow confidence and trust, indispensable ingredients to a program of peace and to plans for lifting from us all the burdens of expensive armaments. To promote these objectives, our government works tirelessly, day by day, month by month, year by year. But until a degree of success crowns our efforts that will assure to all nations peaceful existence, we must, in the interests of peace itself, remain vigilant, alert and strong.

I

The Middle East has abruptly reached a new and critical stage in its long and important history. In past decades many of the countries in that area were not fully self-governing. Other nations exercised considerable authority in the area and the security of the region was largely built around their power. But since the First World War there has been a steady evolution toward self-government and independence. This development the United States has welcomed and has encouraged. Our country supports without reservation the full sovereignty and independence of each and every nation of the Middle East.

The evolution to independence has in the main been a peaceful process. But the area has been often troubled. Persistent crosscurrents of distrust and fear with raids back and forth across national boundaries have brought about a high degree of instability in much of the Mid East. Just recently there have been hostilities involving Western European nations that once exercised much influence in the area. Also the relatively large attack by Israel in October has intensified the basic differences between that nation and its Arab neighbors. All this instability has been heightened and, at times, manipulated by International Communism.

*Public Papers of the Presidents, Eisenhower, pp. 6-16.

II

Russia's rulers have long sought to dominate the Middle East. That was true of the Czars and it is true of the Bolsheviks. The reasons are not hard to find. They do not affect Russia's security, for no one plans to use the Middle East as a base for aggression against Russia. Never for a moment has the United States entertained such a thought.

The Soviet Union has nothing whatsoever to fear from the United States in the Middle East, or anywhere else in the world, so long as its rulers do not themselves first resort to aggression.

That statement I make solemnly and emphatically.

Neither does Russia's desire to dominate the Middle East spring from its own economic interest in the area. Russia does not appreciably use or depend upon the Suez Canal. In 1955 Soviet traffic through the Canal represented only about three fouths of 1% of the total. The Soviets have no need for, and could provide no market for, the petroleum resources which constitute the principal natural wealth of the area. Indeed, the Soviet Union is a substantial exporter of petroleum products.

The reason for Russia's interest in the Middle East is solely that of power politics. Considering her announced purpose of Communizing the world, it is easy to understand her hope of dominating the Middle East.

This region has always been the crossroads of the continents of the Eastern Hemisphere. The Suez Canal enables the nations of Asia and Europe to carry on the commerce that is essential if these countries are to maintain well-rounded and prosperous economies. The Middle East provides a gateway between Eurasia and Africa.

It contains about two thirds of the presently known oil deposits of the world and it normally supplies the petroleum needs of many nations of Europe, Asia and Africa. The nations of Europe are peculiarly dependent upon this supply, and this dependency relates to transportation as well as to production! This has been vividly demonstrated since the closing of the Suez Canal and some of the pipelines. Alternate ways of transportation and, indeed, alternate sources of power can, if necessary, be developed. But these cannot be considered as early prospects.

These things stress the immense importance of the Middle East. If the nations of that area should lose their independence, if they were dominated by alien forces hostile to freedom, that would be both a tragedy for the area and for many other free nations whose economic life would be subject to near strangulation. Western Europe would be endangered just as though there had been no Marshall Plan, no North Atlantic Treaty Organization. The free nations of Asia and Africa, too, would be placed in serious jeopardy. And the countries of the Middle East would lose the markets upon which their economies depend. All this would have the most adverse, if not disastrous, effect upon our own Nation's economic life and political prospects.

Then there are other factors which transcend the material. The Middle East is the birthplace of three great religions—Moslem, Christian and Hebrew. Mecca and Jerusalem are more than places on the map. They symbolize religions which teach that the spirit has supremacy over matter and that the individual has a dignity and rights of which no despotic government can rightfully deprive him. It would be intolerable if the holy places of the Middle East should be subjected to rule that glorifies atheistic materialism.

International Communism, of course, seeks to mask its purposes of domination by expressions of good will and by superficially attractive offers of political, economic and military aid. But any free nation, which is the subject of Soviet enticement, ought, in elementary wisdom, to look behind the mask.

Remember Estonia, Latvia and Lithuania! In 1939 the Soviet Union entered into mutual assistance pacts with these then independent countries; and the Soviet Foreign Minister, addressing the Extraordinary Fifth Session of the Supreme Soviet in October 1939, solemnly and publicly declared that "we stand for the scrupulous and punctilious observance of the pacts on the basis of complete reciprocity, and we declare that all the nonsensical talk abou the Sovietization of the Baltic countries is only to the interest of our common enemies and of all anti-Soviet provocateurs." Yet in 1940, Estonia, Latvia and Lithuania were forcibly incorporated into the Soviet Union.

Soviet control of the satellite nations of Eastern Europe has been forcibly maintained in spite of solemn promises of a contrary intent, made during World War II.

Stalin's death brought hope that this pattern would change. And we read the pledge of the Warsaw Treaty of 1955 that the Soviet Union would follow in satellite countries "the principles of mutual respect for their independence and sovereignty and noninterference in domestic affairs." But we have just seen the subjugation of Hungary by naked armed force. In the aftermath of this Hungarian tragedy, world respect for and belief in Soviet promises have sunk to a new low. International Communism needs and seeks a recognizable success.

Thus, we have these simple and indisputable facts:

1. The Middle East, which has always been coveted by Russia, would today be prized more than ever by International Communism.

2. The Soviet rulers continue to show that they do not scruple to use any means to gain their ends.

3. The free nations of the Mid East need, and for the most part want, added strength to assure their continued independence.

III

Our thoughts naturally turn to the United Nations as a protector of small nations. Its charter gives it primary responsibility for the maintenance of international peace and security. Our country has given the United Nations its full support in relation to the hostilities in Hungary and in Egypt. The United Nations was able to bring about a cease-fire and withdrawal of hostile forces from Egypt because it was dealing with governments and peoples who had a decent respect for the opinions of mankind as reflected in the United Nations General Assembly. But in the case of Hungary, the situation was different. The Soviet Union vetoed action by the Security Council to require the withdrawal of Soviet armed forces from Hungary. And it has shown callous indifference to the recommendations, even the censure, of the General Assembly. The United Nations can always be helpful, but it cannot be a wholly dependable protector of freedom when the ambitions of the Soviet Union are involved.

IV

Under all the circumstances I have laid before you, a greater responsibility now devolves upon the United States. We have shown, so that none can doubt, our dedication to the principle that force shall not be used internationally for any aggressive purpose and that the integrity and independence of the nations of the Middle East should be inviolate. Seldom in history has a nation's dedication to principle been tested as severely as ours during recent weeks.

There is general recognition in the Middle East, as elsewhere, that the United States does not seek either political or economic domination over any other people. Our desire is a world environment of freedom, not servitude. On the other hand many, if not all, of the nations of the Middle East are aware of the danger that stems from International Communism and welcome closer cooperation with the United States to realize for themselves the United Nations goals of independence, economic well-being and spiritual growth.

If the Middle East is to continue its geographic role of uniting rather than separating East and West; if its vast economic resources are to serve the well-being of the peoples there, as well as that of others; and if its cultures and religions and their shrines are to be preserved for the uplifting of the spirits of the peoples, then the United States must make more evident its willingness to support the independence of the freedom-loving nations of the area.

V

Under these circumstances I deem it necessary to seek the cooperation of the Congress. Only with that cooperation can we give the reassurance needed to deter aggression, to give courage and confidence to those who are dedicated to freedom and thus prevent a chain of events which would gravely endanger all of the free world.

There have been several Executive declarations made by the United States in relation to the Middle East. There is the Tripartite Declaration of May 25, 1950, followed by the Presidential assurance of October 31, 1950, to the King of Saudi Arabia. There is the Presidential declaration of April 9, 1956, that the United States will within constitutional means oppose any aggression in the area. There is our Declaration of November 29, 1956, that a threat to the territorial integrity or political independence of Iran, Iraq, Pakistan, or Turkey would be viewed by the United States with the utmost gravity.

Nevertheless, weaknesses in the present situation and the increased danger from International Communism, convince me that basic United States policy should now find expression in joint action by the Congress and the Executive. Furthermore, our joint resolve should be so couched as to make it apparent that if need be our words will be backed by action.

VI

It is nothing new for the President and the Congress to join to recognize that the national integrity of other free nations is directly related to our own security.

We have joined to create and support the security system of the United Nations. We have reinforced the collective security system of the United Nations by a series of collective defense arrangements. Today we have security treaties with 42 other nations which recognize that our peace and security are intertwined. We have joined to take decisive action in relation to Greece and Turkey and in relation to Taiwan.

Thus, the United States through the joint action of the President and the Congress, or, in the case of treaties, the Senate, has manifested in many endangered areas its purpose to support free and independent governments—and peace—against external menace, notably the meance of International Communism. Thereby we have helped to maintain peace and security during a period of great danger. It is now essential that the United States should manifest through joint action of the President and the Congress our determination to assist those nations of the Mid East area, which desire that assistance.

The action which I propose would have the following features.

It would, first of all, authorize the United States to cooperate with and assist any nation or group of nations in the general area of the Middle East in the development of economic strength dedicated to the maintenance of national independence.

It would, in the second place, authorize the Executive to undertake in the same region programs of military assistance and cooperation with any nation or group of nations which desires such aid.

It would, in the third place, authorize such assistance and cooperation to include the employment of the armed forces of the United States to secure and protect the territorial integrity and political independence of such nations, requesting such aid, against overt armed aggression from any nation controlled by International Communism.

These measures would have to be consonant with the treaty obligations of the United States, including the Charter of the United Nations and with any action or recommendations of the United Nations. They would also, if armed attack occurs, be subject to the overriding authority of the United Nations Security Council in accordance with the Charter.

The present proposal would, in the fourth place, authorize the President to employ, for economic and defensive military purposes, sums available under the Mutual Security Act of 1954, as amended, without regard to existing limitations.

The legislation now requested should not include the authorization or appropriation of funds because I believe that, under the conditions I suggest, presently appropriated funds will be adequate for the balance of the present fiscal year ending June 30. I shall, however, seek in subsequent legislation the authorization of $200,-000,000 to be available during each of the fiscal years 1958 and 1959 for discretionary use in the area, in addition to the other mutual security programs for the area hereafter provided for by the Congress.

VII

This program will not solve all the problems of the Middle East. Neither does it represent the totality of our policies for the area. There are the problems of Palestine and relations between Israel and the Arab States, and the future of the Arab refugees. There is the problem of the future status of the Suez Canal. These difficulties are aggravated by International Communism, but they would exist quite apart from that threat. It is not the purpose of the legislation I propose to deal directly with these problems. The United Nations is actively concerning itself with all these matters, and we are supporting the United Nations. The United States has made clear, notably by

Secretary Dulles' address of August 26, 1955, that we are willing to do much to assist the United Nations in solving the basic problems of Palestine.

The proposed legislation is primarily designed to deal with the possibility of Communist aggression, direct and indirect. There is imperative need that any lack of power in the area should be made good, not by external or alien force, but by the increased vigor and security of the independent nations of the area.

Experience shows that indirect aggression rarely if ever succeeds where there is reasonable security against direct aggression; where the government disposes of loyal security forces, and where economic conditions are such as not to make Communism seem an attractive alternative. The program I suggest deals with all three aspects of this matter and thus with the problem of indirect aggression.

It is my hope and belief that if our purpose be proclaimed, as proposed by the requested legislation, that very fact will serve to halt any contemplated aggression. We shall have heartened the patriots who are dedicated to the independence of their nations. They will not feel that they stand alone, under the menace of great power. And I should add that patriotism is, throughout this area, a powerful sentiment. It is true that fear sometimes perverts true patriotism into fanaticism and to the acceptance of dangerous enticements from without. But if that fear can be allayed, then the climate will be more favorable to the attainment of worthy national ambitions.

And as I have indicated, it will also be necessary for us to contribute economically to strengthen those countries, or groups of countries, which have governments manifestly dedicated to the preservation of independence and resistance to subversion. Such measures will provide the greatest insurance against Communist inroads. Words alone are not enough.

VIII

Let me refer again to the requested authority to employ the armed forces of the United States to assist to defend the territorial integrity and the political independence of any nation in the area against Communist armed aggression. Such authority would not be exercised except at the desire of the nation attacked. Beyond this it is my profound hope that this authority would never have to be exercised at all.

Nothing is more necessary to assure this than that our policy with respect to the defense of the area be promptly and clearly determined and declared. Thus the United Nations and all friendly governments, and indeed governments which are not friendly, will know where we stand.

If, contrary to my hope and expectation, a situation arose which called for the military application of the policy which I ask the Congress to join me in proclaiming, I would of course maintain hour-by-hour contact with the Congress if it were in session. And if the Congress were not in session, and if the situation had grave implications, I would, of course, at once call the Congress into special session.

In the situation now existing, the greatest risk, as is often the case, is that ambitious despots may miscalculate. If power-hungry Communists should either falsely or correctly estimate that the Middle East is inadequately defended, they might be tempted to use open measures of armed attack. If so, that would start a chain of circumstances which would almost surely involve the United States in military action.

I am convinced that the best insurance against this dangerous contingency is to make clear now our readiness to cooperate fully and freely with our friends in the Middle East in ways consonant with the purposes and principles of the United Nations. I intend promptly to send a special mission to the Middle East to explain the cooperation we are prepared to give.

IX

The policy which I outline involves certain burdens and indeed risks for the United States. Those who covet the area will not like what is proposed. Already, they are grossly distorting our purpose. However, before this Americans have seen our nation's vital interests and human freedom in jeopardy, and their fortitude and resolution have been equal to the crisis, regardless of hostile distortion of our words, motives and actions.

Indeed, the sacrifices of the American people in the cause of freedom have, ever since the close of World War II, been measured in many billions of dollars and in thousands of the precious lives of our youth. These sacrifices, by which great areas of the world have been preserved to freedom, must not be thrown away.

In those momentous periods of the past, the President and the Congress have united, without partisanship, to serve the vital interests of the United States and of the free world.

In those momentous periods of the past, the President and the Congress have united, without partisanship, to serve the vital interests of the United States and of the free world.

The occasion has come for us to manifest again our national unity in support of freedom and to show our deep respect for the rights and independence of every nation—however great, however small. We seek not violence, but peace. To this purpose we must now devote our energies, our determination, ourselves.

The Middle East Resolution (As Amended by the Foreign Assistance Act of 1961, Approved September 4, 1961)*

March 9, 1957

Text of Public Law 85-7 [H.J. Res. 117], 71 Stat. 5, approved March 9, 1957, as amended by the Foreign Assistance Act of 1961, P.L. 87-195 [S. 1983], 75 Stat. 424, approved September 4, 1961

JOINT RESOLUTION

To Promote Peace and Stability in the Middle East

Resolved by the Senate and House of Representatives of the United States of America in Congress assembled, That the President be and hereby is authorized to

*Committees on Foreign Relations and Foreign Affairs, *Legislation on Foreign Relations*, 90th Cong., 1st sess., (Washington, 1967), pp. 600-01.

cooperate with and assist any nation or group of nations in the general area of the Middle East desiring such assistance in the development of economic strength dedicated to the maintenance of national independence.

Sec. 2

The President is authorized to undertake, in the general area of the Middle East, military assistance programs with any nation or group of nations of that area desiring such assistance. Furthermore, the United States regards as vital to the national interest and world peace the preservation of the independence and integrity of the nations of the Middle East. To this end, if the President determines the necessity thereof, the United States is prepared to use armed forces to assist any nation or group of such nations requesting assistance against armed aggression from any country controlled by international communism: Provided, That such employment shall be consonant with the treaty obligations of the United States and with the Constitution of the United States.

Sec. 3

The President is hereby authorized to use during the balance of fiscal year 1957 for economic and military assistance under this joint resolution not to exceed $200,000,-000 from any appropriation now available for carrying out the provisions of the Mutual Security Act of 1954, as amended, in accord with the provisions of such Act: Provided, That, whenever the President determines it to be important to the security of the United States, such use may be under the authority of section 401(a) of the Mutual Security Act of 1954, as amended (except that the provisions of section 105(a) thereof shall not be waived), and without regard to the provisions of section 105 of the Mutual Security Appropriation Act, 1957; Provided further, That obligations incurred in carrying out the purposes of the first sentence of section 2 of this joint resolution shall be paid only out of appropriations for military assistance, and obligations incurred in carrying out the purposes of the first section of this joint resolution shall be paid only out of appropriations other than those for military assistance. This authorization is in addition to other existing authorizations with respect to the use of such appropriations. None of the additional authorizations contained in this section shall be used until fifteen days after the Committee on Foreign Relations of the Senate, the Committee on Foreign Affairs of the House of Representatives, the Committees on Appropriations of the Senate and the House of Representatives and, when military assistance is involved, the Committees on Armed Services of the Senate and the House of Representatives have been furnished a report showing the object of the proposed use, the country for the benefit of which such use is intended, and the particular appropriation or appropriations for carrying out the provisions of the Mutual Security Act of 1954, as amended, from which the funds are proposed to be derived: Provided, That funds available under this section during the balance of fiscal year 1957 shall, in the case of any such report submitted during the last fifteen days of the fiscal year, remain available for use under this section for the purposes stated in such report for a period of twenty days following the date of submission of such report. Nothing contained in this joint resolution shall be construed as itself authorizing the appropriation of additional funds for the purpose of carrying out the provisions of the first section or of the first sentence of section 2 of this joint resolution.

Sec. 4

The President should continue to furnish facilities and military assistance, within the provisions of applicable law and established policies, to the United Nations Emergency Force in the Middle East, with a view to maintaining the truce in that region.

Sec. 5

The President shall whenever appropriate report to the Congress his action hereunder.

Sec. 6

This joint resolution shall expire when the President shall determine that the peace and security of the nations in the general area of the Middle East are reasonably assured by international conditions created by action of the United Nations or otherwise except that it may be terminated earlier by a concurrent resolution of the two Houses of Congress.

Address by President Eisenhower to the Third Special Emergency Session of the General Assembly*

August 13, 1958

It has been almost five years since I had the honor of addressing this Assembly. I then spoke of atomic power and urged that we should find the way by which the miraculous inventiveness of man should not be dedicated to his death but consecrated to his life. Since then great strides have been taken in the use of atomic energy for peaceful purposes. Tragically little has been done to eliminate the use of atomic and nuclear power for weapons purposes.

That is a danger.

That danger in turn gives rise to another danger—the danger that nations under aggressive leadership will seek to exploit man's horror of war by confronting the nations, particularly small nations, with an apparent choice between supine surrender, or war.

This tactic reappeared during the recent Near East crisis.

Some might call it "ballistic blackmail."

In most communities it is illegal to cry "fire" in a crowded assembly. Should it not be considered serious international misconduct to manufacture a general war scare in an effort to achieve local political aims?

Pressures such as these will never be successfully practiced against America, but

*Public Papers of the Presidents, Eisenhower, pp. 606-16.

they do create dangers which could affect each and every one of us. That is why I have asked for the privilege of again addressing you.

The immediate reason is two small countries—Lebanon and Jordan.

The cause is one of universal concern.

The lawful and freely elected Government of Lebanon, feeling itself endangered by civil strife fomented from without, sent the United States a desperate call for instant help. We responded to that call.

On the basis of that response an effort has been made to create a war hysteria. The impression is sought to be created that if small nations are assisted in their desire to survive, that endangers the peace.

This is truly an "upside down" portrayal. If it is made an international crime to help a small nation maintain its independence, then indeed the possibilities of conquest are unlimited. We will have nullified the provision of our Charter which recognizes the inherent right of collective self-defense. We will have let loose forces that could generate great disasters.

The United Nations has, of course, a primary responsibility to maintain not only international peace but also "security." That is an important fact. But we must not evade a second fact, namely, that in the circumstances of the world since 1945, the United Nations has sometimes been blocked in its attempt to fulfill that function.

Respect for the liberty and freedom of all nations has always been a guiding principle of the United States. This respect has been consistently demonstrated by our unswerving adherence to the principles of the Charter, particularly in its opposition to aggression, direct or indirect. Sometimes we have made that demonstration in terms of collective measures called for by the United Nations. Sometimes we have done so pursuant to what the Charter calls "the inherent right of collective self-defense."

I recall the moments of clear danger we have faced since the end of the Second World War—Iran, Greece and Turkey, the Berlin blockade, Korea, the Straits of Taiwan.

A common principle guided the position of the United States on all of these occasions. That principle was that aggression, direct or indirect, must be checked before it gathered sufficient momentum to destroy us all—aggressor and defender alike.

It was this principle that was applied once again when the urgent appeals of the governments of Lebanon and Jordan were answered.

I would be less than candid if I did not tell you that the United States reserves, within the spirit of the Charter, the right to answer the legitimate appeal of any nation, particularly small nations.

I doubt that a single free government in all the world would willingly forego the right to ask for help if its sovereignty were imperiled.

But I must again emphasize that the United States seeks always to keep within the spirit of the Charter.

Thus when President Truman responded in 1947 to the urgent plea of Greece, the United States stipulated that our assistance would be withdrawn whenever the United Nations felt that its action could take the place of ours.

Similarly, when the United States responded to the urgent plea of Lebanon, we went at once to the Security Council and sought United Nations assistance for Lebanon so as to permit the withdrawal of United States forces.

United Nations action would have been taken, the United States forces already withdrawn, had it not been that two resolutions, one proposed by the United States, the other proposed by the Government of Japan, failed to pass because of one negative vote—a veto.

But nothing that I have said is to be construed as indicating that I regard the status quo as sacrosanct. Change is indeed the law of life and progress. But when change reflects the will of the people, then change can and should be brought about in peaceful ways.

In this context the United States respects the right of every Arab nation of the Near East to live in freedom without domination from any source, far or near.

In the same context, we believe that the Charter of the United Nations places on all of us certain solemn obligations. Without respect for each other's sovereignty and the exercise of great care in the means by which new patterns of international life are achieved, the projection of the peaceful vision of the Charter would become a mockery.

II

Let me turn now specifically to the problem of Lebanon.

When the United States military assistance began moving into Lebanon, I reported to the American people that we had immediately reacted to the plea of Lebanon because the situation was such that only prompt action would suffice.

I repeat to you the solemn pledge I then made: our assistance to Lebanon has but one single purpose—that is the purpose of the Charter and of such historic resolutions of the United Nations as the "Essentials for Peace" Resolution of 1949 and the "Peace through Deeds" Resolution of 1950. These denounce, as a form of aggression and as an international crime, the fomenting of civil strife in the interest of a foreign power.

We want to prevent that crime—or at least prevent its having fatal consequences. We have no other purpose whatsoever.

The United States troops will be totally withdrawn whenever this is requested by the duly constituted government of Lebanon or whenever, through action by the United Nations or otherwise, Lebanon is no longer exposed to the original danger.

It is my earnest hope that this Assembly, free of the veto, will consider how it can assure the continued independence and integrity of Lebanon, so that the political destiny of the Lebanese people will continue to lie in their own hands.

The United States Delegation will support measures to this end.

III

Another urgent problem is Jordan.

If we do not act promptly in Jordan a further dangerous crisis may result, for the method of indirect aggression discernible in Jordan may lead to conflicts endangering the peace.

We must recognize that peace in this area is fragile, and we must also recognize that the end of peace in Jordan could have consequences of a far-reaching nature. The

United Nations has a particular responsibility in this matter, since it sponsored the Palestine Armistice Agreements upon which peace in the area rests and since it also sponsors the care of the Palestine refugees.

I hope this Assembly will be able to give expression to the interest of the United Nations in preserving the peace in Jordan.

IV

There is another matter which this Assembly should face in seeking to promote stability in the Near East. That is the question of inflammatory propaganda. The United Nations Assembly has on three occasions—in 1947, 1949 and 1950—passed resolutions designed to stop the projecting of irresponsible broadcasts from one nation into the homes of citizens of other nations, thereby "fomenting civil strife and subverting the will of the people in any State." We all know that these resolutions have recently been violated in many directions in the Near East.

If we, the United States, have been at fault we stand ready to be corrected.

I believe that this Assembly should reaffirm its enunciated policy and should consider means for monitoring the radio broadcasts directed across national frontiers in the troubled Near East area and for examining complaints from these nations which consider their national security jeopardized by external propaganda.

V

The countries of this area should also be freed from armed pressure and infiltration coming across their borders. When such interference threatens they should be able to get from the United Nations prompt and effective action to help safeguard their independence. This requires that adequate machinery be available to make the United Nations presence manifest in the area of trouble.

Therefore I believe this Assembly should take action looking toward the creation of a standby United Nations Peace Force. The need for such a force in being is clearly demonstrated by recent events involving imminent danger to the integrity of two of our members.

I understand that this general subject is to be discussed at the 13th General Assembly and that our distinguished Secretary-General has taken an initiative in this matter. Recent events clearly demonstrate that this is a matter for urgent and positive action.

VI

I have proposed four areas of action for the consideration of the Assembly—in respect to Lebanon, Jordan, subversive propaganda and a Standby United Nations force. These measures, basically, are designed to do one thing: to preserve the right of a nation and its people to determine their own destiny, consistent with the obligation to respect the rights of others.

This clearly applies to the great surge of Arab nationalism.

Let me state the position of my country unmistakably. The peoples of the Arab nations of the Near East clearly possess the right of determining and expressing their own destiny. Other nations should not interfere so long as this expression is found in ways compatible with international peace and security.

However, here as in other areas we have an opportunity to share in a great international task. That is the task of assisting the peoples of that area, under programs which they may desire, to make further progress toward the goals of human welfare they have set. Only on the basis of progressing economies can truly independent governments sustain themselves.

This is a real challenge to the Arab people and to us all.

To help the Arab countries fulfill these aspirations, here is what I propose:

First—that consultations be immediately undertaken by the Secretary-General with the Arab nations of the Near East to ascertain whether an agreement can be reached to establish an Arab development institution on a regional basis.

Second—that these consultations consider the composition and the possible functions of a regional Arab development institution, whose task would be to accelerate progress in such fields as industry, agriculture, water supply, and education.

Third—other nations and private organizations which might be prepared to support this institution should also be consulted at an appropriate time.

Should the Arab States agree on the usefulness of such a soundly organized regional institution, and should they be prepared to support it with their own resources, the United States would also be prepared to support it.

The institution would be set up to provide loans to the Arab States as well as the technical assistance required in the formulation of development projects.

The institution should be governed by the Arab States themselves.

This proposal for a regional Arab development institution can, I believe, be realized on a basis which would attract international capital, both public and private.

I also believe that the best and quickest way to achieve the most desirable result would be for the Secretary-General to make two parallel approaches. First, to consult with the Arab States of the Near East to determine an area of agreement. Then to invite the International Bank for Reconstruction and Development, which has vast experience in this field, to make available its facilities for the planning of the organizational and operating techniques needed to establish the institution on a progressive course.

I hope it is clear that I am not suggesting a position of leadership for my own country in the work of creating such an institution. If this institution is to be a success, the function of leadership must belong to the Arab States themselves.

I would hope that high on the agenda of this institution would be action to meet one of the major challenges of the Near East, the great common shortage—water.

Much scientific and engineering work is already under way in the field of water development. For instance, atomic isotopes now permit us to chart the course of the great underground rivers. And new horizons are opening in the desalting of water. The ancient problem of water is on the threshold of solution. Energy, determination and science will carry it over that threshold.

Another great challenge facing the area is disease.

Already there is substantial effort among the peoples and governments of the Near East to conquer disease and disability. But much more remains to be done.

The United States is prepared to join with other governments and the World Health Organization in an all-out, joint attack on preventable disease in the Near East.

But to see the desert blossom again and preventable disease conquered is only a first step. As I look into the future I see the emergence of modern Arab States that would bring to this century contributions surpassing those we cannot forget from the past. We remember that Western arithmetic and algebra owe much to Arabic mathematicians and that much of the foundations of the world's medical science and astronomy was laid by Arab scholars. Above all, we remember that three of the world's great religions were born in the Near East.

But a true Arab renaissance can only develop in a healthy human setting. Material progress should not be an overriding objective in itself; but it is an important condition for achieving higher human, cultural and spiritual objectives.

But I repeat, if this vision of the modern Arab community is to come to life, the goals must be Arab goals.

VII

With the assistance of the United Nations, the countries of the Near East now have a unique opportunity to advance, in freedom, their security and their political and economic interests. If a plan for peace of the kind I am proposing can be carried forward, in a few short years we may be able to look back on the Lebanon and Jordan crises as the beginning of a great new era of Arab history.

But there is an important consideration which must remain in mind today and in the future.

If there is an end to external interference in the internal affairs of the Arab States of the Near East:—

If an adequate United Nations Peace Force is in existence ready for call by countries fearful for their security:—

If a regional development institution exists and is at work on the basic projects and programs designed to lift the living standards of the area, supported by friendly aid from abroad and governed by the Arab States themselves:

Then with this good prospect, and indeed as a necessary condition for its fulfillment, I hope and believe that the nations of the area, intellectually and emotionally, will no longer feel the need to seek national security through spiralling military buildups which lead not only to economic impotence but to war.

Perhaps the nations involved in the 1948 hostilities may, as a first step, wish to call for a United Nations study of the flow of heavy armaments to those nations. My country would be glad to support the establishment of an appropriate United Nations body to examine this problem. This body would discuss it individually with these countries and see what arms control arrangements could be worked out under which the security of all these nations could be maintained more effectively than under a continued wasteful, dangerous competition in armaments. I recognize that any such arrangements must reflect these countries' own views.

VIII

I have tried to present to you the framework of a plan for peace in the Near East which would provide a setting of political order responsive to the rights of the people in each nation; which would avoid the dangers of a regional arms race; which would permit the peoples of the Near East to devote their energies wholeheartedly to the tasks of development and human progress in the widest sense.

It is important that the six elements of this program be viewed as a whole. They are:

(1) United Nations concern for Lebanon.

(2) United Nations measures to preserve peace in Jordan.

(3) An end to the fomenting from without of civil strife.

(4) A United Nations Peace Force.

(5) A regional economic development plan to assist and accelerate improvement in the living standards of the people in these Arab nations.

(6) Steps to avoid a new arms race spiral in the area.

To have solidity, the different elements of this plan for peace and progress should be considered and acted on together, as integral elements of a single concerted effort.

Therefore, I hope that this Assembly will seek simultaneously to set in motion measures that would create a climate of security in the Near East consonant with the principles of the United Nations Charter, and at the same time create the framework for a common effort to raise the standard of living of the Arab peoples.

*　　　　　　*　　　　　　*

THE SIX DAY WAR AND ITS AFTERMATH

Speech by President Lyndon B. Johnson to the National
Foreign Policy Council for Educators on the Middle East*

June 18, 1967

*   *   *

And now finally, let me turn to the Middle East, and to the tumultuous events of the past months. Those events have proved the wisdom of five great principles of peace in the region.

The first and the greatest principle is that every nation in the area has a fundamental right to live, and to have this right respected by its neighbors.

For the people of the Middle East, the path to hope does not lie in threats to end the life of any nation. Such threats have become a burden to the peace, not only of that region, but a burden to the peace of the entire world.

In the same way, no nation would be true to the United Nations Charter or to its own true interests if it should permit military success to blind it to the fact that its neighbors have interests of their own. Each nation, therefore, must accept the right of others to life.

Second, this last month, I think, shows us another basic requirement for settlement. It is a human requirement; justice for the refugees.

A new conflict has brought new homelessness. The nations of the Middle East must at last address themselves to the plight of those who have been displaced by wars.

In the past, both sides have resisted the best efforts of outside mediators to restore the victims of conflict to their homes or to find them other proper places to live and work. There will be no peace, though, for any party in the Middle East unless this problem is attacked with new energy by all and certainly primarily by those that are immediately concerned.

A third lesson from this last month is that maritime rights must be respected. Our nation has long been committed to free maritime passage through international waterways, and we along with other nations were taking the necessary steps to implement this principle when hostilities exploded. If a single act of folly was more responsible for this explosion than any other, I think it was the arbitrary and the dangerous announced decision that the Straits of Tiran would be closed. The right of innocent maritime passage must be preserved for all nations.

And fourth, this last conflict has demonstrated the danger of the Middle Eastern arms race of the last 12 years. Here the responsibility must rest not only on those in the area, but upon the larger states outside the area. We believe that scarce resources could be used much better for technical and economic development. We have always opposed this arms race, and our own military shipments to the area have consequently been severely limited.

Now the waste and futility of the arms race must be apparent to all the peoples of the world. And now there's another moment of choice. The United States of America,

**Vital Speeches of the Day*, Lyndon B. Johnson, pp. 579-80.

for its part, will use every resource of diplomacy, and every counsel of reason and prudence, to try to find a better course.

As a beginning, I should like to propose that the United Nations immediately call upon all of its members to report all shipments of all military arms into this area and to keep those shipments on file for all the peoples of the world to observe.

Fifth, the crisis underlines the importance of respect for political independence and territorial integrity of all the states of the area. We reaffirmed that principle at the height of this crisis. We reaffirm it again today, on behalf of all.

The principle can be effective in the Middle East only on the basis of peace between the parties. The nations of the region have only fragile and violated truce lines for 20 years. What they now need are recognized boundaries and other arrangements that will give them security against terror and destruction and war. Further, there just must be adequate recognition of the special interest of three great religions in the holy places of Jerusalem.

These five principles are not new, but we do think they're fundamental. Taken together they point the way from uncertain armistice to durable peace. We believe there must be progress toward all of them if there is to be progress toward any.

There are some who have urged as a single simple solution an immediate return to the situation as it was on June the fourth. As our distinguished and able Ambassador, Mr. Arthur Goldberg, has already said, this is not a prescription for peace but for renewed hostilities.

So certainly troops must be withdrawn but there must also be recognized rights of national life, progress in solving the refugee problem, freedom of innocent maritime passage, limitation of the arms race and respect for political independence and territorial integrity.

But who will make this peace where all others have failed for 20 years or more?

Clearly the parties to the conflict must be the parties to the peace. Sooner or later it is they—it is they—who must make a settlement in the area. It is hard to see how it is possible for nations to live together in peace if they cannot learn to reason together.

But we must still ask, who can help them? Some say it should be the United Nations, some call for the use of other parties. We have been first in our support of elective peace-keeping in the United Nations, and we also recognize the great values to come from mediation.

We are ready this morning to see any method tried, and we believe that none should be excluded altogether. Perhaps all of them will be useful and all will be needed.

So, I issue an appeal to all to adopt no rigid view on these matters. I offer assurance to all that this Government of our—the Government of the United States—will do its part for peace in every form, at every level, at every hour.

Yet there is no escape from the fact that the main responsibility for the peace of the region depends upon its own peoples and its own leaders of that region. What will be truly decisive in the Middle East will be what is said and what is done by those who live in the Middle East.

They can seek another arms race if they have not profited from the experience of this one if they want to. But they will seek it at a terrible cost to their own people, and to their very long neglected human needs. They can live on a diet of hate, though only at the cost of hatred in return. Or they can move toward peace with one another.

The world this morning is watching—watching for the peace of the world because that is really what is at stake. It will look for patience and justice. It will look for humility and moral courage. It will look for signs of movement from prejudice and the emotional chaos of conflict to the gradual slow shaping steps that lead to learning to live together and learning to help mold and shape peace in the area and in the world.

The Middle East is rich in history, rich in its people and its resources. It has no need to live in permanent civil war. It has the power to build its own life, as one of the prosperous regions of the world in which we live.

And if the nations of the Middle East will turn toward the works of peace, they can count with confidence upon the friendship and the help of all the people of the United States of America.

In a climate of peace, we here will do our full share to help with a solution for the refugees. We here will do our full share in support of regional cooperation. We here will do our share and do more to see that the peaceful promise of nuclear energy is applied to the critical problems of desalting water and helping to make the deserts bloom.

Our country is committed—and we here reiterate that commitment today—to a peace that is based on five principles:

First, the recognized right of national life.

Second, justice for the refugees.

Third, innocent maritime passage.

Fourth, limits on the wateful and destructive arms race.

And fifth, political independence and territorial integrity for all.

This is a time not for malice, but for magnanimity; not for propaganda, but for patience; not for vituperation, but for vision.

On the basis of peace, we offer our help to the people of the Middle East. That land that's known to every one of us since childhood as the birthplace of great religions and learning can flourish once again in our time. And we here in the United States shall do all in our power to help make it so.

*Security Council Resolution 242 on the Arab-Israeli Crisis**

November 22, 1967

The Security Council,

Expressing its continuing concern with the grave situation in the Middle East,

Emphasizing the inadmissibility of the acquisition of territory by war and the need to work for a just and lasting peace in which every State in the area can live in security,

Emphasizing further that all Member States in their acceptance of the Charter of the United Nations have undertaken a commitment to act in accordance with Article 2 of the Charter,

1. Affirms that the fulfilment of Charter principles requires the establishment of a just and lasting peace in the Middle East which should include the application of both the following principles:

*U.N. Security Council, *Official Records*, 22d Year, 1968, pp. 8-9.

(i) Withdrawal of Israeli armed forces from territories occupied in the recent conflict;

(ii) Termination of all claims or states of belligerency and respect for and acknowledgement of the sovereignty, territorial integrity and political independence of every State in the area and their right to live in peace within secure and recognized boundaries free from threats or acts of force;

2. Affirms further the necessity

(a) For guaranteeing freedom of navigation through international waterways in the area;

(b) For achieving a just settlement of the refugee problem;

(c) For guaranteeing the territorial inviolability and political independence of every State in the area through measures including the establishment of demilitarized zones,

3. Requests the Secretary-General to designate a Special Representative to proceed to the Middle East to establish and maintain contacts with the States concerned in order to promote agreement and assist efforts to achieve a peaceful and accepted settlement in accordance with the provisions and principles in this resolution;

4. Requests the Secretary-General to report to the Security Council on the progress of the efforts of that Special Representative as soon as possible.

Security Council Resolution 262 on the Israeli Attack upon Beirut, Lebanon *

December 31, 1968

The Security Council,

Having considered the agenda contained in document S/Agenda/1462,

Having noted the contents of the letter of the Permanent Representative of Lebanon (S/8945),

Having noted the supplementary information provided by the Chief of Staff of the United Nations Truce Supervision Organization contained in documents S/7930/Add.107 and Add.108,

Having heard the statements of the representative of Lebanon and of the representative of Israel concerning the grave attack committed against the civil International Airport of Beirut,

Observing that the military action by the armed forces of Israel against the civil International Airport of Beirut was premeditated and of a large scale and carefully planned nature,

Gravely concerned about the deteriorating situation resulting from this violation of the Security Council resolutions,

Deeply concerned about the need to assure free uninterrupted international civil air traffic,

1. Condemns Israel for its premeditated military action in violation of its obligations under the Charter and the cease-fire resolutions;

2. Considers that such premeditated acts of violence endanger the maintenance of the peace;

3. Issues a solemn warning to Israel that if such acts were to be repeated, the Council would have to consider further steps to give effect to its decisions;

Ibid., 23d Year, 1970, p. 12.

4. Considers that Lebanon is entitled to appropriate redress for the destruction it has suffered, responsibility for which has been acknowledged by Israel.

Security Council Resolution 267 on the Status of Jerusalem*

July 3, 1969

The Security Council,

Recalling its resolution 252 (1968) of 21 May 1968 and the earlier General Assembly resolutions 2253 (ES-V) and 2254 (ES-V) of 4 and 14 July 1967, respectively, concerning measures and actions by Israel affecting the status of the City of Jerusalem,

Having heard the statements of the parties concerned on the question,

Noting that since the adoption of the above-mentioned resolutions Israel has taken further measures tending to change the status of the City of Jerusalem,

Reaffirming the established principle that acquisition of territory by military conquest is inadmissible;

1. Reaffirms its resolution 252 (1968);

2. Deplores the failure of Israel to show any regard for the resolutions of the General Assembly and the Security Council mentioned above;

3. Censures in the strongest terms all measures taken to change the status of the City of Jerusalem;

4. Confirms that all legislative and administrative measures and actions taken by Israel which purport to alter the status of Jerusalem, including expropriation of land and properties thereon, are invalid and cannot change that status;

5. Urgently calls once more upon Israel to rescind forthwith all measures taken by it which may tend to change the status of the City of Jerusalem, and in future to refrain from all actions likely to have such an effect;

6. Requests Israel to inform the Security Council without any further delay of its intentions with regard to the implementation of the provisions of the present resolution;

7. Determines that, in the event of a negative response or no response from Israel, the Security Council shall reconvene without delay to consider what further action should be taken in this matter;

8. Requests the Secretary-General to report to the Security Council on the implementation of the present resolution.

General Assembly Resolution 2799 (XXVI) on the Middle East Situation†

December 13, 1971

The General Assembly,

Deeply concerned at the continuation of the grave situation prevailing in the Middle East, particularly since the conflict of June 1967, which constitutes a serious threat to international peace and security,

---

*Ibid., 24th Year, 1970, pp. 3-4.

†U.N. General Assembly, 26th sess., agenda item 22, A/Res/2799 (XXVI), Dec. 20, 1971. Adopted by vote of 79-7-36.

Convinced that Security Council resolution 242 (1967) of 22 November 1967 should be implemented immediately in all its parts in order to achieve a just and lasting peace in the Middle East in which every State in the area can live in security,

Determined that the territory of a State shall not be the object of occupation or acquisition by another State resulting from the threat or use of force, which is contrary to the Charter of the United Nations and to the principles enshrined in Security Council resolution 242 (1967) as well as in the Declaration on the Strengthening of International Security adopted by the General Assembly on 16 December 1970,

Expressing its appreciation of the efforts of the Committee of African Heads of State undertaken in pursuance of the resolution adopted on 23 June 1971 by the Assembly of Heads of State and Government of the Organization of African Unity,

Gravely concerned at the continuation of Israel's occupation of the Arab territories since 5 June 1967,

Having considered the item entitled "The situation in the Middle East,"

1. Reaffirms that the acquisition of territories by force is inadmissible and that, consequently, territories thus occupied must be restored;

2. Reaffirms that the establishment of a just and lasting peace in the Middle East should include the application of both the following principles:

(a) Withdrawal of Israeli armed forces from territories occupied in the recent conflict;

(b) Termination of all claims or states of belligerency and respect for and acknowledgement of the sovereignty, territorial integrity and political independence of every State in the area and its right to live in peace within secure and recognized boundaries free from threats or acts of force;

3. Requests the Secretary-General to take the necessary measures to reactivate the mission of the Special Representative of the Secretary-General to the Middle East in order to promote agreement and assist efforts to reach a peace agreement as envisaged in the Special Representative's aide-memoire of 8 February 1971;

4. Expresses its full support for all the efforts of the Special Representative to implement Security Council resolution 242 (1967);

5. Notes with appreciation the positive reply given by Egypt to the Special Representative's initiative for establishing a just and lasting peace in the Middle East;

6. Calls upon Israel to respond favourably to the Special Representative's peace initiative;

7. Further invites the parties to the Middle East conflict to give their full co-operation to the Special Representative in order to work out practical measures for:

(a) Guaranteeing freedom of navigation through international waterways in the area;

(b) Achieving a just settlement of the refugee problem;

(c) Guaranteeing the territorial inviolability and political independence of every State in the area;

8. Requests the Secretary-General to report to the Security Council and to the General Assembly, as appropriate, on the progress made by the Special Representative in the implementation of Security Council resolution 242 (1967) and of the present resolution;

9. Requests the Security Council to consider, if necessary, making arrangements, under the relevant Articles of the Charter of the United Nations, with regard to the implementation of its resolution.

THE HUMAN DIMENSION

THE HUMAN DIMENSION

Commentary

The United States joined enthusiastically and with conviction at San Francisco in giving the United Nations a much greater role in human affairs—as distinct from relations between sovereign states—than had been written into the Covenant of the League of Nations. Five chapters of the Charter were devoted to activities centering on the welfare of human beings.

An Economic and Social Council was established as one of the principal organs of the U.N. and, although given no executive authority, was asked to coordinate the activities in this broad sphere of the U.N.'s family of specialized agencies. It was instructed also to set up commissions in economic and social fields and for the promotion of human rights.

The Charter's preamble had spoken of the determination "to reaffirm faith in fundamental human rights . . ."; and "to promote social progress and better standards of life in larger freedom." But the Charter was essentially the political compact of a primarily political organization; and its Article 55 made quite clear that the founders did not have humanitarianism in mind for its own sake but as a contribution to peace and stability.

The language was loose, the lines of authority were fuzzy in the extreme, but the intent was injected by the Charter into the highly political question of the non-self-governing and trusteeship territories. And, from the start, members applied it in debate and in resolutions also to the foreign and domestic policy of sovereign states—whatever the Charter might say in its famous Article 2(7) about nonintervention in domestic matters. They anticipated the broad interpretation advanced by President John F. Kennedy years later: "And is not peace, in the last analysis, basically a matter of human rights—the right to live out our lives without fear of devastation, the right to breathe air as nature provided it, the right of future generations to a healthy existence?"

One powerful resentment which survived the Second World War in the camp of the victors was Franco Spain's benevolent neutrality toward the Axis. In April, 1946 Communist Poland asserted that the activities of the Franco regime endangered international peace and asked the Security Council to call upon members of the United Nations to sever relations with it. The United States saw no objection and, as the case developed in the First General Assembly, proposed that Franco Spain be excluded from the U.N. family of agencies and their work. It suggested also that the people of Spain be invited to establish their eligibility for membership by getting rid of Generalissimo Franco. The U.S. delegation, however, opposed the use of sanctions against Spain to encourage such action; and the difference between word and deed remained the elastic test of the applicability of Article 2(7). The Assembly's resolution was revoked in 1950 and Spain, under the same regime, later admitted to membership in the United Nations.

Southern Africa, especially the Union (later, Republic) of South Africa, was the main target of those who sought to enlist the moral and material power of the United Nations against violations of the spirit of the Charter provisions on human rights. Its racial policies were criticized at each session of the General Assembly, despite its invocation of Article 2(7). In 1952, the issue of South Africa's apartheid policy of racial segregation came to the Assembly in practical terms, placed on the agenda by members who asserted that it created "a dangerous and explosive situation, which constitutes a threat to international peace and a flagrant violation of the basic principles of human rights and fundamental freedoms which are enshrined in the Charter of the United Nations." The United States sided with the majority in asserting the Assembly's right to discuss the matter; and it endorsed an affirmation of those principles but would not go as far as supporting creation of a commission to look into the international aspects and implications of the racial situation in South Africa.

The United States representative, as President Eisenhower later reported to Congress "emphasized the inherent difficulties of the item. It involved the delicate subject of race relations within a member state, as well as the question of the Assembly's authority to deal with this subject . . ." In subsequent Assemblies, the United States again abstained on resolutions which extended the work of the Commission or called upon South Africa to inform the Secretary General of its response to the Assembly's admonitions to mend its ways. It was not until 1958 that the United States felt able to join the majority in adopting a resolution which reaffirmed human rights in ringing terms but went no farther than expressing regret and concern that South Africa had not yet responded. That was four years after the United States Supreme Court ruled against segregation in American public schools in *Brown vs. Board of Education.*

On March 21, 1960, South African police killed 70 Africans and wounded some 200 in putting down mass demonstrations in Sharpeville and Langa against compulsory passes to control movement. For the first time, the Security Council took up the apartheid question and responded to it with a stern resolution. The next General Assembly considered following through with a call for economic and political sanctions against South Africa but failed to adopt a draft resolution to that effect—in part, at the urging of the United States, which argued that harsh measures would only make South Africa's leaders more intransigent and hurt the people they were meant to help. But in November, 1962, the United States could no longer block the Assembly's recommendation of sanctions, together with its request that the Security Council take appropriate measures.

On August 7, 1963, the Council, with only Britain and France abstaining, recommended an embargo on the shipment of arms and military vehicles to South Africa. Four months later, it reaffirmed that appeal and broadened it to cover "the sale and shipment of equipment and materials for the manufacture and maintenance of arms and ammunition in South Africa." Not having been voted under the Charter's Article VII, the embargo was not mandatory. The United States, having voted for both resolutions, felt itself bound by them and enforced their provisions. When the General Assembly, however, sought to move on to promote mandatory economic sanctions, the United States withheld its support.

The African and Asian countries, helped by the Communist bloc, meanwhile carried their campaign against South Africa into some of the U.N. agencies—voting to exclude it from meetings and to deny its voting rights. Under this pressure, South Africa withdrew from the International Labor Organization, the Food and Agriculture Organization and the Economic Commission for Africa. The same forces then tried to expel South Africa from the U.N. Conference on Trade and Development—an action which the Legal Counsel of the United Nations labelled illegal under the Charter. The United States actively and successfully joined others in preventing it.

In the late 1960's, the specific question of racial discrimination in South Africa was set aside in favor of dramatic action on two closely related problems: Rhodesia and South West Africa.

The issue of Rhodesia came to the Security Council when that British territory, formerly Southern Rhodesia, declared its independence on November 11, 1965 with the manifest intention of preserving the political supremacy of the white five percent of its population. The Council called on all member states not to recognize the new regime, not to provide it with arms and to break off all economic relations. This admonition to voluntary compliance proved ineffectual. Commerce continued to flow and in April, 1966 the Council met again to deal with what appeared to be the imminent arrival in Portuguese Mozambique of tankers with oil destined for Rhodesia. At the request of the United Kingdom, which retained legal responsibility in Rhodesia, the Council for the first time authorized the use of force under Chapter VII of the Charter to intercept vessels carrying oil destined for Rhodesia.

The white regime in Rhodesia was hardly shaken by these voluntary sanctions. African and Asian countries demanded that Britain remove it by force of arms; but the western nations preferred to continue the process of economic pressure. On December 16, 1966, the Council made history, imposing on Rhodesia selective mandatory economic sanctions under Chapter VII, Article 41—the effect of which was to embargo trade in twelve of the territory's principal exports and to restrict important military and industrial imports. By executive order of January 5, 1967 the President of the United States, acting in accordance with the United Nations Participation Act of 1945, applied these measures to U.S. trade and other transactions involving Rhodesia.

However, in 1971, Congress voted to exempt U.S. imports of Rhodesian chrome ore from the Security Council's embargo. The explanation was that other nations had been buying it in defiance of the sanctions while the Soviet Union, the main alternative source, was making a killing by raising the price of the chrome ore it sold to the United States. An unanswered constitutional question was the effect of this action on the U.S. obligation under the U.N. Participation Act to accept and carry out (mandatory) decisions of the Security Council. The question was raised by the General Assembly in a resolution containing an unprecedented reproach of the U.S. Congress.

Earlier, in March, 1970, the Rhodesian issue evoked the first U.S. veto in the Security Council. The United States joined the United Kingdom in killing a proposal that all member states immediately sever not only all diplomatic, economic and other relations with the Salisbury regime but also railway, maritime, air transport, postal, telegraphic and radio communications as well as other means of communication. While the U.S. action was clear reaffirmation that Washington did not want the Security Council to go any further than it had already gone in enforcing a political decision, it was taken primarily for domestic reasons—fulfilling an administration promise to

Congress not to permit the total isolation of some 1,000 American missionaries and their families in Rhodesia.

On May 29, 1968 the Council expanded these mandatory economic sanctions but, when they too had no discernible, immediate effect in the face of obvious noncompliance by some members, it was left with the problem of what else to do.

The question of South West Africa was brought to the U.N. in 1946, when South Africa proposed to annex the former German colony which it had held under a League of Nations mandate. The General Assembly did not agree, proposing instead that the territory be placed under the Trusteeship System. This was not acceptable to South Africa, which remained in full possession; but as its racial policy grew more radical, possession became more controversial. Scores of resolutions by various U.N. bodies had no effect. Then the International Court of Justice sidestepped the issue and the General Assembly, on October 27, 1966, by an overwhelming majority which swept the United States along, declared that South Africa's mandate was terminated and that South West Africa henceforth came "under the direct responsibility of the United Nations."

Confronted by South Africa's flat declaration that it would resist with all the forces at its command attempts from outside to impose what it called a dangerous and unwanted system upon the territory, African and Asian members demanded enforcement action by the Security Council under Chapter VII, if necessary, to effect the immediate transfer of authority from South Africa to the United Nations. The United States, warning against resolutions which went far beyond any expectation of fulfilment, and having no desire whatever to apply Chapter VII in such a case, urged the Assembly to pursue its goal with less melodrama, greater realism and within the framework of the "peaceful means" enjoined upon the membership by the Charter. Righteous anger swamped diplomacy, however, and the United States abstained from the resulting resolution, passed by the Fifth Special General Assembly convened primarily for that purpose, setting up an administrative organ for a territory to which it had no access. In consequence, nothing changed—except that the Assembly gave South West Africa the new name of Namibia. The United States felt able to join in a subsequent Security Council rebuke and admonition to South Africa "because," as the U.S. representative put it, "it wisely does not commit the Council to the narrow path of mandatory sanctions under Chapter VII of the Charter." The Soviet Union, also conspicuously unwilling to set a precedent for drastic action in so peripheral an issue as Namibia, hid behind sharp condemnation of western "neocolonialism." Britain, wearily abstaining, declared, "The road to hopeless frustrations is paved with useless resolutions." Nevertheless, activities continued to press the Security Council for Chapter VII measures.

The discrepancy between the principle and the practice of human rights was with the United Nations, as it had been with mankind, from the beginning. In a sense, the U.N. Charter squared the circle when it placed such great emphasis on the individual's dignity in a body of international law which recognized only states as sovereign members. Yet, the urge they felt, after the Second World War, to pay lip service to the great ideal of the new era helped its champions to codify it in a Universal Declaration of Human Rights. The Declaration was adopted in 1948 without a dissenting voice. The Soviet Union abstained. This document was in no way enforceable and day to day experience suggested that, around the world, it was honored much more in the breach than in the observance. Nevertheless, the standard it set became widely known. Nations which adhered to it found in it a specific guide; those which ignored it, found their departures from the standard somewhat more conspicuous.

After years of negotiation, the General Assembly in 1966 unanimously approved two International Covenants—one on Civil and Political Rights, the other on Economic, Social and Cultural Rights—which were to give the principles of the Declaration the legal force of a formal treaty. The United States also joined in approving an Optional Protocol permitting complaints by individuals or private groups; but it took no further action, just as it had failed to ratify—and, in many cases, even to sign—more than a dozen major conventions in the field of human rights adopted by the various organs of the U.N. family. In fact, in the United Nations' first quarter century, the United States ratified only two modest legal instruments. One was a Supplementary Convention on the Abolition of Slavery, the Slave Trade and Institutions and Practices similar to Slavery applied to the original Slavery Convention of 1926. The other was a Protocol on the Status of Refugees, replacing the 1951 Convention. Of all the members of the United Nations, the United States was one which might have been thought most ready to accede to all parts of the so-called International Bill of Rights, flowing from the Declaration, and to the other conventions outlawing such practices as Genocide, Forced Labor and Racial Discrimination. The U.S. delegation at San Francisco had been most active in writing the Charter so as to give human rights a central place. The United States motivated the Genocide Convention, the first human rights treaty to be adopted by the United Nations, in 1948. Presidents Truman and Kennedy urged ratification of specific conventions, but in vain. Opposition rallied around the legal objection that such treaties infringed the constitutional jurisdiction of federal and state government. The Senate ignored appeals that so restrictive an approach would make it hard for the United States convincingly to advocate the rule of law in international affairs.

One of the most farreaching political accomplishments of the United Nations system was its midwifery to a new generation of nation states. The Charter, imbued with a universal concern for human rights, provided the legal framework within which 700,000,000 people who had been under foreign rule in 1945 achieved independence in an orderly process. If it was not always a peaceful one, that was due to colonial powers—primarily France, but also the Netherlands and Portugal—trying to hold their possessions against the winds of change. However, colonial war and competition between imperialist nations bent on filling a vacuum, which would have been a natural reaction in similar circumstances fifty years earlier, were finished. To be sure, the "war of national liberation" which developed after the Second World War had the same object—although its indirect prosecution and ideological cover enabled its practitioners to justify it as a legitimate instrument of peace and progress.

One of the U.N.'s earliest concerns was to adapt the League of Nations mandates to the new standards in a Trusteeship System which aimed directly toward self-rule and independence. South Africa alone refused to conclude a trusteeship agreement for South West Africa. In the other cases, humanitarian impulses were not unmixed with lesser considerations. The United States, seeking the broadest security base in the Pacific, took over the Japanese mandated islands—the Marianas, Marshalls and Carolinas—under special terms which guaranteed U.S. control, and it simply held Okinawa until the evolution of a new relationship with Japan returned the island to the mother country in 1972. The Soviet Union, seeking a foothold in the Mediterranean, unsuccessfully demanded the administration of Tripolitania, the westernmost part of Libya. Instead, all of Libya was made a ward of the U.N. until it gained independence in 1951.

By 1969 all but two of the original trust territories were independent, the U.S. Trust Territory of the Pacific Islands and Australian New Guinea. All told, fifty-four new states swelled the U.N.'s membership to one-hundred-twenty-six in its first twenty-five years. By 1972 the number stood at 132. Most of them were former colonies, transformed in an impetuous surge of decolonization which was also reflected within the U.N. organization. Efforts on behalf of non-selfgoverning territories over the years reached a climax in 1960 when sixteen nations of Africa, plus Cyprus, were admitted to membership. The remarkable 15th General Assembly was dominated, if not obsessed, by the issue of "colonialism." President Eisenhower appealed at its outset for a programmatic, constructive approach to the problems of the new era. Prime Minister Nikita Khrushchev, who led the Soviet delegation, caught the mood of the Assembly better and took the initiative with a "Declaration on the Granting of Independence to Colonial Countries and Peoples." African and Asian states gave this heading to a sweeping resolution of their own which the Assembly passed unanimously—only nine of the 99 members abstaining. Among these was the United States, which expressed approval of the principle but saw the more radical points as demagoguery or as political shafts aimed squarely at its NATO allies.

The process of decolonization, and the admission of independent states to membership in the U.N., continued unabated. Ten years later, with new members becoming progressively smaller and less viable as sovereign entities, the United States proposed to limit admission and to set up a category of Associate Membership which might share in the work and the accomplishments of the U.N. without the expense and responsibility of full membership. The alternative was further to descend the scale of the remaining ministates to the bitter end of logical absurdity in Pitcairn Island, population ninety-two. While that descent was delayed, if not halted, "colonialism" remained a favorite rhetorical target. It focussed in the main on Southern Africa but was also applied, as "neocolonialism," to any activity which aroused the anger of Communist, "progressive" or other revolutionary forces.

The nation-making activity of the U.N., always dramatic, often spectacular, diverted attention from its sober, plodding, indispensable counterpart, nation-building. As early as 1946, the General Assembly authorized the provision of technical assistance for the economic development of underdeveloped (the adjective later softened to undeveloped) countries. It was a modest step, financed from the regular U.N. budget, and was soon followed by an Expanded Program of Technical Assistance, EPTA, conceived on a somewhat larger scale, with voluntary contributions from the members and enlisting the cooperation of the U.N.'s specialized agencies—FAO, WHO, UNESCO, ITU and the rest.

In October, 1958, the General Assembly enlarged the scope of the U.N.'s development work by creating a Special Fund. In doing so, it spelled out a philosophy of multilateral aid which concentrated on pre-investment studies—in effect, taking inventory of a nation's physical and human resources in order to rationalize its development. Fortunately, the Fund acquired as its director Paul Hoffman, an American executive, who had administered the highly successful Marshall Plan for the economic revival of Europe after World War II. He remained in charge when the EPTA and the Fund were combined to form the U.N. Development Program, UNDP, in 1966.

Multilateral aid, dispensed by the international community with no political or economic strings, grew with the years; as bilateral aid, hemmed in with conditions of various kinds, became less acceptable to giver and receiver alike. In the UNDP's first decade, dating back to the founding of the Special Fund, it committed almost $1,500,000,000, which was matched by slightly more in cash and kind from the countries receiving assistance. The pre-investment projects themselves were calculated to have attracted directly or indirectly, a follow up investment of billions more.

The United States, in this period, contributed some $584,000,000, a good 40 percent of the total. The Soviet Union, by comparison, gave $31,000,000—mostly in unconvertible rubles. Expressed in monetary terms, the United States contribution to the U.N. System—including regular budget, peacekeeping activities, specialized agencies and special programs—from the end of the Second World War through 1968 totalled just under $3,200,000,000 and amounted to 43 percent of the U.N.'s total expenditure.

While the U.N. was created and remained primarily a political organization, four-fifths and more of the funds and the staff of the U.N. family were devoted to economic and social ends. As it entered its second quarter century, with its political scope sharply limited, it appeared to seek fulfilment increasingly in non-political problems of such magnitude as to be tackled only by a world body: environmental pollution, population control and the orderly exploitation and use of the sea bed.

BANNING SPAIN FROM THE U.N.

*General Assembly Resolution 39(1) Recommending that
the Franco Government be Barred from Membership in International Agencies**

December 12, 1946

The peoples of the United Nations, at San Francisco, Potsdam and London condemned the Franco regime in Spain and decided that as long as that regime remains, Spain may not be admitted to the United Nations.

The General Assembly, in its resolution of 9 February 1946, recommended that the Members of the United Nations should act in accordance with the letter and the spirit of the declarations of San Francisco and Potsdam.

The peoples of the United Nations assure the Spanish people of their enduring sympathy and of the cordial welcome awaiting them when circumstances enable them to be admitted to the United Nations.

The General Assembly recalls that in May and June 1946, the Security Council conducted an investigation of the possible further action to be taken by the United Nations. The Sub-Committee of the Security Council charged with the investigation found unanimously:

"(a) In origin, nature, structure and general conduct, the Franco regime is a Fascist regime patterned on, and established largely as a result of aid received from Hitler's Nazi Germany and Mussolini's Fascist Italy.

"(b) During the long struggle of the United Nations against Hitler and Mussolini, Franco, despite continued Allied protests, gave very substantial aid to the enemy Powers. First, for example, from 1941 to 1945, the Blue Infantry Division, the Spanish Legion of Volunteers and the Salvador Air Squadron fought against Soviet Russia on the Eastern front. Second, in the summer of 1940, Spain seized Tangier in breach of international statute, and as a result of Spain maintaining a large army in Spanish Morocco large numbers of Allied troops were immobilized in North Africa.

"(c) Incontrovertible documentary evidence establishes that Franco was a guilty party with Hitler and Mussolini in the conspiracy to wage war against those countries which eventually in the course of the world war became banded together as the United Nations. It was part of the conspiracy that Franco's full belligerency should be postponed until a time to be mutually agreed upon."

The General Assembly,

Convinced that the Franco Fascist Government of Spain, which was imposed by force upon the Spanish people with the aid of the Axis Powers and which gave material assistance to the Axis Powers in the war, does not represent the Spanish people, and by its continued control of Spain is making impossible the participation of the Spanish people with the peoples of the United Nations in international affairs;

*The U.S. and the UN, Report by the President to the Congress for the Year 1946, pp. 98-100.
[In this resolution the General Assembly recommends that the Franco Government be barred from membership in international agencies established by or brought into relationship with the United Nations, and that Members recall their ambassadors and ministers plenipotentiary from Madrid. The United States abstained in the vote on one paragraph in the resolution suggesting that the Security Council consider measures to be taken to remedy the Spanish situation if a democratic Spanish Government is not established within a reasonable time. This paragraph was approved by a vote of 29 to 8, with 11 abstentions. The resolution as a whole was adopted on December 12, 1946, 34 to 6, with 13 abstentions, the United States voting for the resolution.]

Recommends that the Franco Government of Spain be debarred from membership in international agencies established by or brought into relationship with the United Nations, and from participation in conference or other activities which may be arranged by the United Nations or by these agencies, until a new and acceptable government is formed in Spain.

Further desiring to secure the participation of all peace-loving peoples, including the people of Spain, in the community of nations,

Recommends that if, within a reasonable time, there is not established a government which derives its authority from the consent of the governed, committed to respect freedom of speech, religion and assembly and to the prompt holding of an election in which the Spanish people, free from force and intimidation and regardless of party, may express their will, the Security Council consider the adequate measure to be taken in order to remedy the situation;

Recommends that all Members of the United Nations immediately recall from Madrid their ambassadors and ministers plenipotentiary accredited there.

The General Assembly further recommends that the States Members of the Organization report to the Secretary-General and to the next session of the Assembly what action they have taken in accordance with this recommendation.

General Assembly Resolution 386(V) to Debar Spain from Membership in International Agencies*

November 4, 1950

The General Assembly,

Considering that:

The General Assembly, during the second part of its first session in 1946, adopted several recommendations concerning Spain, one of which provided that Spain be debarred from membership in international agencies established by or brought into relationship with the United Nations, and another that Member States withdraw their Ambassadors and Ministers from Madrid,

The establishment of diplomatic relations and the exchange of Ambassadors and Ministers with a Government does not imply any judgment upon the domestic policy of that Government,

The specialized agencies of the United Nations are technical and largely non-political in character and have been established in order to benefit the peoples of all nations, and that, therefore, they should be free to decide for themselves whether the participation of Spain in their activities is desirable in the interest of their work,

Resolves:

1. To revoke the recommendation for the withdrawal of Ambassadors and Ministers from Madrid, contained in General Assembly resolution 39 (I) of 12 December 1946;

2. To revoke the recommendation intended to debar Spain from membership in international agencies established by or brought into relationship with the United Nations, which recommendation is a part of the same resolution adopted by the General Assembly in 1946 concerning relations of Members of the United Nations with Spain.

*U.N. General Assembly, *Official Records*, 5th sess., 1950-51, Supplement 20, pp. 16-17.

THE PROBLEM OF SOUTH AFRICA

General Assembly Resolution 616 (VII) on Policies of Apartheid in Union of South Africa*

December 5, 1952

A

The General Assembly,

Having taken note of the communication dated 12 September 1952, addressed to the Secretary-General of the United Nations by the delegations of Afghanistan, Burma, Egypt, India, Indonesia, Iran, Iraq, Lebanon, Pakistan, the Philippines, Saudi Arabia, Syria and Yemen, regarding the question of race conflict in South Africa resulting from the policies of apartheid of the Government of the Union of South Africa,

Considering that one of the purposes of the United Nations is to achieve international co-operation in promoting and encouraging respect for human rights and fundamental freedoms for all, without distinction as to race, sex, language or religion,

Recalling that the General Assembly declared in its resolution 103 (I) of 19 November 1946 that it is in the higher interests of humanity to put an end to religious and so-called racial persecution, and called upon all governments to conform both to the letter and to the spirit of the Charter and to take the most prompt and energetic steps to that end,

Considering that the General Assembly has held, in its resolutions 395 (V) of 2 December 1950 and 511 (VI) of 12 January 1952, that a policy of "racial segregation" (apartheid) is necessarily based on doctrines of racial discrimination,

1. Establishes a Commission, consisting of three members, to study the racial situation in the Union of South Africa in the light of the Purposes and Principles of the Charter, with due regard to the provision of Article 2, paragraph 7, as well as the provisions of Article 1, paragraphs 2 and 3, Article 13, paragraph 1 b, Article 55 c, and Article 56 of the Charter, and the resolutions of the United Nations on racial persecution and discrimination, and to report its conclusions to the General Assembly at its eighth session;

2. Invites the Government of the Union of South Africa to extend its full co-operation to the Commission;

3. Requests the Secretary-General to provide the Commission with the necessary staff and facilities;

4. Decides to retain the question on the provisional agenda of the eighth session of the General Assembly.

At its 411th meeting on 21 December 1952, the General Assembly decided, on the proposal of the President, that the Commission, established under paragraph 1 of the above resolution, should be composed of the following persons: Mr. Ralph Bunche, Mr. Hernán Santa Cruz and Mr. Jaime Torres Bodet.

B

The General Assembly,

Having taken note of the communication dated 12 September 1952, addressed to

*U.N. General Assembly, *Official Records*, 7th sess., 1952, pp. 2-3.

the Secretary-General of the United Nations by the delegations of Afghanistan, Burma, Egypt, India, Indonesia, Iran, Iraq, Lebanon, Pakistan, the Philippines, Saudi Arabia, Syria and Yemen, regarding the question of race conflict in South Africa resulting from the policies of apartheid of the Government of the Union of South Africa,

Considering that one of the purposes of the United Nations is to achieve international co-operation in promoting and encouraging respect for human rights and fundamental freedoms for all, without distinction as to race, sex, language or religion,

Recalling that the General Assembly declared in its resolution 103 (I) of 19 November 1946 that it is in the higher interests of humanity to put an end to religious and so-called racial persecution, and called upon all governments to conform both to the letter and to the spirit of the Charter and to take the most prompt and energetic steps to that end,

1. Declares that in a multi-racial society harmony and respect for human rights and freedoms and the peaceful development of a unified community are best assured when patterns of legislation and practice are directed towards ensuring equality before the law of all persons regardless of race, creed or colour, and when economic, social, cultural and political participation of all racial groups is on a basis of equality;

2. Affirms that governmental policies of Member States which are not directed towards these goals, but which are designed to perpetuate or increase discrimination, are inconsistent with the pledges of the Members under Article 56 of the Charter;

3. Solemnly calls upon all Member States to bring their policies into conformity with their obligation under the Charter to promote the observance of human rights and fundamental freedoms.

General Assembly Resolution 1248 (XIII) on Apartheid in Union of South Africa *

October 30, 1958

The General Assembly,

Recalling its previous consideration of the question of race conflict in South Africa resulting from the policies of apartheid of the Government of the Union of South Africa,

Recalling in particular paragraph 6 of its resolution 917 (X) of 6 December 1955 calling upon the Government of the Union of South Africa to observe its obligations under the Charter of the United Nations,

1. Declares again that, in a multiracial society, harmony and respect for human rights and freedoms and the peaceful development of a unified community are best assured when patterns of legislation and practice are directed towards ensuring equality before the law of all persons regardless of race, creed or colour, and when the economic, social, cultural and political participation of all racial groups is on a basis of equality;

2. Affirms that governmental policies of Member States which are not directed toward these goals, but which are designed to perpetuate or increase discrimination, are inconsistent with the pledges of the Members under Article 56 of the Charter of the United Nations;

3. Solemnly cals upon all Member States to bring their policies into conformity

*Ibid., 13th sess., 1958, pp. 4-5.

with their obligation under the Charter to promote the observance of human rights and fundamental freedoms;

4. Expresses its regret and concern that the Government of the Union of South Africa has not yet responded to appeals of the General Assembly that it reconsider governmental policies which impair the right of all racial groups to enjoy the same rights and fundamental freedoms.

Security Council Resolution 134 (1960) on Racial Murders in South Africa*

April 1, 1960

The Security Council,

Having considered the complaint of twenty-nine Member States contained in document S/4279 and Add.1 concerning "the situation arising out of the large-scale killings of unarmed and peaceful demonstrators against racial discrimination and segregation in the Union of South Africa,"

Recognizing that such a situation has been brought about by the racial policies of the Government of the Union of South Africa and the continued disregard by that Government of the resolutions of the General Assembly calling upon it to revise its policies and bring them into conformity with its obligations and responsibilities under the Charter of the United Nations,

Taking into account the strong feelings and grave concern aroused among Governments and peoples of the world by the happenings in the Union of South Africa,

1. Recognizes that the situation in the Union of South Africa is one that has led to international friction and if continued might endanger international peace and security;

2. Deplores that the recent disturbances in the Union of South Africa should have led to the loss of life of so many Africans and extends to the families of the victims its deepest sympathies;

3. Deplores the policies and actions of the Government of the Union of South Africa which have given rise to the present situation;

4. Calls upon the Government of the Union of South Africa to initiate measures aimed at bringing about racial harmony based on equality in order to ensure that the present situation does not continue or recur and to abandon its policies of apartheid and racial discrimination;

5. Requests the Secretary-General, in consultation with the Government of the Union of South Africa, to make such arrangements as would adequately help in upholding the purposes and principles of the Charter and to report to the Security Council whenever necessary and appropriate.

General Assembly Resolution 1761 (XVII) on Apartheid in South Africa†

November 6, 1962

The General Assembly,

Recalling its previous resolutions on the question of race conflict in South Africa

*U.N. Security Council, *Official Records,* 15th Year, pp. 1-2.
†U.N. General Assembly, *Official Records,* 17th sess., 1962-63, Supplement 17, pp. 9-10.

resulting from the policies of apartheid of the Government of the Republic of South Africa,

Further recalling its resolutions 44 (1) of 8 December 1946, 395 (V) of 2 December 1950, 615 (VII) of 5 December 1952, 1179 (XII) of 26 November 1957, 1302 (XIII) of 10 December 1958, 1460 (XIV) of 10 December 1959, 1597 (XV) of 13 April 1961 and 1662 (XVI) of 28 November 1961, on the question of the treatment of peoples of Indian and Indo-Pakistan origin,

Noting the reports of the Governments of India and Pakistan on that subject,

Recalling that the Security Council in its resolution of 1 April 1960 recognized that the situation in South Africa was one that had led to international friction and, if continued, might endanger international peace and security,

Recalling further that the Security Council in its aforesaid resolution called upon the Government of South Africa to initiate measures aimed at bringing about racial harmony based on equality in order to ensure that the present situation does not continue or recur and to abandon its policies of apartheid and racial discrimination,

Regretting that the actions of some Member States indirectly provide encouragement to the Government of South Africa to perpetuate its policy of racial segregation, which has been rejected by the majority of that country's population,

1. Deplores the failure of the Government of the Republic of South Africa to comply with the repeated requests and demands of the General Assembly and of the Security Council and its flouting of world public opinion by refusing to abandon its racial policies;

2. Strongly deprecates the continued and total disregard by the Government of South Africa of its obligations under the Charter of the United Nations and, furthermore, its determined aggravation of racial issues by enforcing measures of increasing ruthlessness involving violence and bloodshed;

3. Reaffirms that the continuance of these policies seriously endangers international peace and security;

4. Requests Member States to take the following measures, separately or collectively, in conformity with the Charter, to bring about the abandonment of those policies:

(a) Breaking off diplomatic relations with the Government of the Republic of South Africa or refraining from establishing such relations;

(b) Closing their ports to all vessels flying the South African flag;

(c) Enacting legislation prohibiting their ships from entering South African ports;

(d) Boycotting all South African goods and refraining from exporting goods, including all arms and ammunition, to South Africa;

(e) Refusing landing and passage facilities to all aircraft belonging to the Government and companies registered under the laws of South Africa;

5. Decides to establish a Special Committee consisting of representatives of Member States nominated by the President of the General Assembly with the following terms of reference:

(a) To keep the racial policies of the Government of South Africa under review when the Assembly is not in session;

(b) To report either to the Assembly or to the Security Council or to both as may be appropriate from time to time;

6. Requests all Member States:

(a) To do everything in their power to help the Special Committee to accomplish its task;

(b) To refrain from any act likely to delay or hinder the implementation of the present resolution;

7. Invites Member States to inform the General Assembly at its eighteenth session regarding actions taken, separately or collectively, in dissuading the Government of South Africa from pursuing its policies of apartheid;

8. Requests the Security Council to take appropriate measures, including sanctions, to secure South Africa's compliance with the resolutions of the General Assembly and of the Security Council on this subject and, if necessary, to consider action under Article 6 of the Charter.

Vote: 67 in favor, 16 against and 23 abstentions

In favor: Afghanistan, Albania, Algeria, Bulgaria, Burma, Burundi, Byelorussian SSR, Cambodia, Cameroon, Ceylon, Chad, China, Congo (Brazzaville), Congo (Leopoldville), Cuba, Cyprus, Czechoslovakia, Dahomey, Ethiopia, Federation of Malaya, Ghana, Guinea, Haiti, Hungary, India, Indonesia, Iran, Iraq, Israel, Ivory Coast, Jamaica, Jordan, Laos, Lebanon, Liberia, Libya, Madagascar, Mali, Mauritania, Mexico, Mongolia, Morocco, Nepal, Niger, Nigeria, Pakistan, Philippines, Poland, Romania, Rwanda, Saudi Arabia, Senegal, Sierra Leone, Somalia, Sudan, Syria, Tanganyika, Togo, Trinidad and Tobago, Tunisia, Ukrainian SSR, USSR, United Arab Republic, Upper Volta, Yemen and Yugoslavia.

Against: Australia, Belgium, Canada, France, Greece, Ireland, Japan, Luxembourg, Netherlands, New Zealand, Portugal, South Africa, Spain, Turkey, United Kingdom and United States.

Abstaining: Argentina, Austria, Bolivia, Brazil, Chile, Colombia, Costa Rica, Denmark, Dominican Republic, El Salvador, Finland, Guatemala, Honduras, Iceland, Italy, Nicaragua, Norway, Panama, Peru, Sweden, Thailand, Uruguay and Venezuela.

Security Council Resolution 181 (1963) on Apartheid in South Africa*

August 9, 1963

The Security Council,

Having considered the question of race conflict in South Africa resulting from the policies of apartheid of the Government of the Republic of South Africa, as submitted by the thirty-two African Member States,

Recalling the Security Council resolution of 1 April 1960,

Taking into account that world public opinion has been reflected in General Assembly resolution 1761 (XVII) of 6 November 1962 and particularly in its operative paragraphs 4 and 8,

Noting with appreciation the interim reports adopted on 6 May and 16 July 1963 by the Special Committee on the Policies of Apartheid of the Government of the Republic of South Africa,

Noting with concern the recent arms build-up by the Government of South Africa,

*U.N. Security Council, *Official Records*, 18th Year, 1963, pp. 73-74.

some of which arms are being used in furtherance of that Government's racial policies,

Regretting that some States are indirectly providing encouragement in various ways in the Republic of South Africa to perpetuate, by encouraging apartheid,

Regretting the failure of the Government of South Africa to accept the invitation of the Security Council to delegate a representative to appear before it,

Being convinced that the situation in South Africa is seriously disturbing international peace and security,

1. Strongly deprecates the policies of South Africa in its perpetuation of racial discrimination as being inconsistent with the principles contained in the Charter of the United Nations and contrary to its obligations as a Member State of the United Nations;

2. Calls upon the Government of South Africa to abandon the policies of apartheid and discrimination as called for in the Security Council resolution of 1 April 1960, and to liberate all persons imprisoned, interned or subjected to other restrictions for having opposed the policy of apartheid;

3. Solemnly calls upon all States to cease forthwith the sale and shipment of arms, ammunition of all types and military vehicles to South Africa;

4. Requests the Secretary-General to keep the situation in South Africa under observation and to report to the Security Council by 30 October 1963.

SANCTIONS AGAINST SOUTHERN RHODESIA

Security Council Resolution 221 on Oil Embargo in Southern Rhodesia*

April 9, 1966

The Security Council,

Recalling its resolutions Nos. 216 of 12 November 1965 and 217 of 20 November 1965 and in particular its call to all States to do their utmost to break off economic relations with Southern Rhodesia, including an embargo on oil and petroleum products,

Gravely concerned at reports that substantial supplies of oil may reach Rhodesia as the result of an oil tanker having arrived at Beira and the approach of a further tanker which may lead to the resumption of pumping through the CPMR pipeline with the acquiescence of the Portuguese authorities,

Considering that such supplies will afford great assistance and encouragement to the illegal regime in Southern Rhodesia, thereby enabling it to remain longer in being,

1. Determines that the resulting situation constitutes a threat to the peace;

2. Calls upon the Portuguese Government not to permit oil to be pumped through the pipeline from Beira to Rhodesia;

3. Calls upon the Portuguese Government not to receive at Beira oil destined for Rhodesia;

4. Calls upon all States to ensure the diversion of any of their vessels reasonably believed to be carrying oil destined for Rhodesia which may be en route for Beira;

5. Calls upon the Government of the United Kingdom to prevent by the use of force if necessary the arrival at Beira of vessels reasonably believed to be carrying oil destined for Rhodesia, and empowers the United Kingdom to arrest and detain the tanker known as the Joanna V upon her departure from Beira in the event her oil cargo is discharged there.

Security Council Resolution 232 on Breaking Off Relations with Southern Rhodesia†

December 16, 1966

The Security Council,

Reaffirming its resolutions 216 (1965) of 12 November 1965, 217 (1965) of 20 November 1965 and 221 (1966) of 9 April 1966, and in particular its appeal to all States to do their utmost in order to break off economic relations with Southern Rhodesia,

Deeply concerned that the Council's efforts so far and the measures taken by the administering Power have failed to bring the rebellion in Southern Rhodesia to an end,

Reaffirming that to the extent not superseded in this resolution, the measures

*U.N. Security Council, *Official Records*, 21st Year, 1968, pp. 5-6.
†Ibid., pp. 7-9.

provided for in resolution 217 (1965) of 20 November 1965, as well as those initiated by Member States in implementation of that resolution, shall continue in effect,

Acting in accordance with Articles 39 and 41 of the United Nations Charter,

1. Determines that the present situation in Southern Rhodesia constitutes a threat to international peace and security;

2. Decides that all States Members of the United Nations shall prevent:

(a) the import into their territories of asbestos, iron ore, chrome, pig-iron, sugar, tobacco, copper, meat and meat products and hides, skins and leather originating in Southern Rhodesia and exported therefrom after the date of this resolution;

(b) any activities by their nationals or in their territories which promote or are calculated to promote the export of these commodities from Southern Rhodesia and any dealings by their nationals or in their territories in any of these commodities originating in Southern Rhodesia and exported therefrom after the date of this resolution, including in particular any transfer of funds to Southern Rhodesia for the purposes of such activities or dealings;

(c) shipment in vessels or aircraft of their registration of any of these commodities originating in Southern Rhodesia and exported therefrom after the date of this resolution;

(d) any activities by their nationals or in their territories which promote or are calculated to promote the sale or shipment to Southern Rhodesia of arms, ammunition of all types, military aircraft, military vehicles, and equipment and materials for the manufacture and maintenance of arms and ammunition in Southern Rhodesia;

(e) any activities by their nationals or in their territories which promote or are calculated to promote the supply to Southern Rhodesia of all other aircraft and motor vehicles and of equipment and materials for the manufacture, assembly, or mainte-nance of aircraft and motor vehicles in Southern Rhodesia: the shipment in vessels and aircraft of their registration of any such goods destined for Southern Rhodesia: and any activities by their nationals or in their territories which promote or are calculated to promote the manufacture or assembly of aircraft or motor vehicles in Southern Rhodesia;

(f) participation in their territories or territories under their administration or in land or air transport facilities or by their nationals or vessels of their registration in the supply of oil or oil products to Southern Rhodesia;

notwithstanding any contracts entered into or licenses granted before the date of this resolution;

3. Reminds Member States that the failure or refusal by any of them to implement the present resolution shall constitute a violation of Article 25 of the Charter;

4. Reaffirms the inalienable rights of the people of Southern Rhodesia to freedom and independence in accordance with the Declaration on the Granting of Indepen-dence to Colonial Countries and Peoples contained in General Assembly resolution 1514 (XV); and recognizes the legitimacy of their struggle to secure the enjoyment of their rights as set forth in the Charter of the United Nations;

5. Calls upon all States not to render financial or other economic aid to the illegal racist regime in Southern Rhodesia;

6. Calls upon all States Members of the United Nations to carry out this decision of the Security Council in accordance with Article 25 of the United Nations Charter;

7. Urges, having regard to the principles stated in Article 2 of the United Nations

Charter, States not Members of the United Nations to act in accordance with the provisions of paragraph 2 of the present resolution;

8. Calls upon States Members of the United Nations or of the specialized agencies to report to the Secretary-General the measures each has taken in accordance with the provisions of paragraph 2 of the present resolution;

9. Requests the Secretary-General to report to the Council on the progress of the implementation of the present resolution, the first report to be submitted not later than 1 March 1967;

10. Decides to keep this item on its agenda for further action as appropriate in the light of developments.

Security Council Resolution 253 Sanctioning Southern Rhodesia *

May 29, 1968

The Security Council,

Recalling and reaffirming its resolutions 216 (1965) of 12 November 1965, 217 (1965) of 20 November 1965, 221 (1966) of 9 April 1966, and 232 (1966) of 16 December 1966,

Taking note of resolution 2262 (XXII) adopted by the General Assembly on 3 November 1967,

Noting with great concern that the measures taken so far have failed to bring the rebellion in Southern Rhodesia to an end,

Reaffirming that, to the extent not superseded in this resolution, the measures provided for in resolutions 217 (1965) of 20 November 1965, and 232 (1966) of 16 December 1966, as well as those initiated by Member States in implementation of those resolutions, shall continue in effect,

Gravely concerned that the measures taken by the Security Council have not been complied with by all States and that some States, contrary to resolution 232 (1966) of the Security Council and to their obligations under Article 25 of the Charter, have failed to prevent trade with the illegal regime in Southern Rhodesia,

Condemning the recent inhuman executions carried out by the illegal regime in Southern Rhodesia which have flagrantly affronted the conscience of mankind and have been universally condemned,

Affirming the primary responsibility of the Government of the United Kingdom to enable the people of Southern Rhodesia to achieve self-determination and independence, and in particular their responsibility for dealing with the prevailing situation,

Recognizing the legitimacy of the struggle of the people of Southern Rhodesia to secure the enjoyment of their rights as set forth in the Charter of the United Nations and in conformity with the objectives of General Assembly resolution 1514 (XV),

Reaffirming its determination that the present situation in Southern Rhodesia constitutes a threat to international peace and security,

Acting under Chapter VII of the United Nations Charter,

1. Condemns all measures of political repression, including arrests, detentions, trials and executions which violate fundamental freedoms and rights of the people of

*Ibid., 23rd Year, 1970, pp. 5-7.

Southern Rhodesia, and calls upon the Government of the United Kingdom to take all possible measures to put an end to such actions;

2. Calls upon the United Kingdom as the administering Power in the discharge of its responsibility to take urgently all effective measures to bring to an end the rebellion in Southern Rhodesia, and enable the people to secure the enjoyment of their rights as set forth in the Charter of the United Nations and in conformity with the objectives of General Assembly resolution 1514 (XV);

3. Decides that, in furtherance of the objective of ending the rebellion, all States Members of the United Nations shall prevent:

(a) The import into their territories of all commodites and products originating in Southern Rhodesia and exported therefrom after the date of this resolution (whether or not the commodities or products are for consumption or processing in their territories, whether or not they are imported in bond and whether or not any special legal status with respect to the import of goods is enjoyed by the port or other place where they are imported or stored;

(b) Any activities by their nationals or in their territories which would promote or are calculated to promote the export of any commodities or products from Southern Rhodesia; and any dealings by their nationals or in their territories in any commodities or products originating in Southern Rhodesia and exported therefrom after the date of this resolution, including in particular any transfer of funds to Southern Rhodesia for the purposes of such activities or dealings;

(c) The shipment in vessels or aircraft of their registration or under charter to their nationals, or the carriage (whether or not in bond) by land transport facilities across their territories of any commodities or products originating in Southern Rhodesia and exported therefrom after the date of this resolution;

(d) The sale or supply by their nationals or from their territories of any commodities or products (whether or not originating in their territories, but not including supplies intended strictly for medical purposes, educational equipment and material for use in schools and other educational institutions, publications, news material and, in special humanitarian circumstances, food-stuffs) to any person or body in Southern Rhodesia or to any other person or body for the purposes of any business carried on in or operated from Southern Rhodesia, and any activities by their nationals or in their territories which promote or are calculated to promote such sale or supply;

(e) The shipment in vessels or aircraft of their registration, or under charter to their nationals, or the carriage (whether or not in bond) by land transport facilities across their territories of any such commodities or products which are consigned to any person or body in Southern Rhodesia, or to any other person or body for the purposes of any business carried on in or operated from Southern Rhodesia;

4. Decides that all States Members of the United Nations shall not make available to the illegal regime in Southern Rhodesia or to any commercial, industrial or public utility undertaking, including tourist enterprises, in Southern Rhodesia any funds for investment or any other financial or economic resources and shall prevent their nationals and any persons within their territories from making available to the regime or to any such undertaking any such funds or resources and from remitting any other funds to persons or bodies within Southern Rhodesia except payments exclusively for pensions or for strictly medical, humanitarian or educational purposes or for the provision of news material and in special humanitarian circumstances, food-stuffs;

5. Decides that all States Members of the United Nations shall:

(a) Prevent the entry into their territories, save on exceptional humanitarian grounds, of any person travelling on a Southern Rhodesian passport, regardless of its date of issue, or on a purported passport issued by or on behalf of the illegal regime in Southern Rhodesia; and

(b) Take all possible measures to prevent the entry into their territories of persons whom they have reason to believe to be ordinarily resident in Southern Rhodesia and whom they have reason to believe to have furthered or encouraged, or to be likely to further or encourage, the unlawful actions of the illegal regime in Southern Rhodesia or any activities which are calculated to evade any measure decided upon in this resolution or resolution 232 (1966) of 16 December 1966;

6. Decides that all States Members of the United Nations shall prevent airline companies constituted in their territories and aircraft of their registration or under charter to their nationals from operating to or from Southern Rhodesia and from linking up with any airline company constituted or aircraft registered in Southern Rhodesia;

7. Decides that all States Members of the United Nations shall give effect to the decisions set out in operative paragraphs 3, 4, 5 and 6 of this resolution notwithstanding any contract entered into or license granted before the date of this resolution;

8. Calls upon all States Members of the United Nations or of the specialized agencies to take all possible measures to prevent activities by their nationals and persons in their territories promoting, assisting or encouraging emigration to Southern Rhodesia, with a view to stopping such emigration;

9. Requests all States Members of the United Nations or of the specialized agencies to take all possible further action under Article 41 of the Charter to deal with the situation in Southern Rhodesia, not excluding any of the measures provided in that Article;

10. Emphasizes the need for the withdrawal of all consular and trade representation in Southern Rhodesia, in addition to the provisions of operative paragraph 6 of resolution 217 (1965);

11. Calls upon all States Members of the United Nations to carry out these decisions of the Security Council in accordance with Article 25 of the United Nations Charter and reminds them that failure or refusal by any one of them to do so would constitute a violation of that Article;

12. Deplores the attitude of States that have not complied with their obligations under Article 25 of the Charter, and censures in particular those States which have persisted in trading with the illegal regime in defiance of the resolutions of the Security Council, and which have given active assistance to the regime;

13. Urges all States Members of the United Nations to render moral and material assistance to the people of Southern Rhodesia in their struggle to achieve their freedom and independence;

14. Urges, having regard to the principles stated in Article 2 of the United Nations Charter, States not Members of the United Nations to act in accordance with the provisions of the present resolution;

15. Requests States Members of the United Nations, the United Nations Organization, the specialized agencies, and other international organizations in the United Nations system to extend assistance to Zambia as a matter of priority with a view to helping her solve such special economic problems as she may be confronted with arising from the carrying out of these decisions of the Security Council;

16. Calls upon all States Members of the United Nations, and in particular those with primary responsibility under the Charter for the maintenance of international peace and security, to assist effectively in the implementation of the measures called for by the present resolution;

17. Considers that the United Kingdom as the administering Power should ensure that no settlement is reached without taking into account the views of the people of Southern Rhodesia, and in particular the political parties favouring majority rule, and that it is acceptable to the people of Southern Rhodesia as a whole;

18. Calls upon all States Members of the United Nations or of the specialized agencies to report to the Secretary-General by 1 August 1968 on measures taken to implement the present resolution;

19. Requests the Secretary-General to report to the Security Council on the progress of the implementation of this resolution, the first report to be made not later than 1 September 1968;

20. Decides to establish, in accordance with rule 28 of the provisional rules of procedure of the Security Council, a committee of the Security Council to undertake the following tasks and to report to it with its observations:

(a) To examine such reports on the implementation of the present resolution as are submitted by the Secretary-General;

(b) To seek from any States Members of the United Nations or of the specialized agencies such further information regarding the trade of that State (including information regarding the commodities and products exempted from the prohibition contained in operative paragraph 3 (d) above) or regarding any activities by any nationals of that State or in its territories that may constitute an evasion of the measures decided upon in this resolution as it may consider necessary for the proper discharge of its duty to report to the Security Council;

21. Requests the United Kingdom, as the administering Power, to give maximum assistance to the committee, and to provide the committee with any information which it may receive in order that the measures envisaged in this resolution and resolution 232 (1966) may be rendered fully effective;

22. Calls upon all States Members of the United Nations, or of the specialized agencies, as well as the specialized agencies themselves, to supply such further information as may be sought by the Committee in pursuance of this resolution;

23. Decides to maintain this item on its agenda for further action as appropriate in the light of developments.

Security Council Draft Resolution S/9696 on Burundi, Nepal, Sierra Leone, Syria and Zambia *

March 11, 1970

The Security Council,

Recalling and reaffirming its resolutions 216 (1965) of 12 November 1965, 217 (1965) of 20 November 1965, 221 (1966) of 9 April 1966, 232 (1966) of 16 December 1966 and 253 (1968) of 29 May 1968,

*U.N. Security Council Press Release, S/9696, Mar. 11, 1970.

Reaffirming in particular its resolution 232 (1966), in which it determined that the situation in Southern Rhodesia constitutes a threat to international peace and security,

Deeply concerned that the situation in Southern Rhodesia has deteriorated further as a result of the proclamation of a so-called republic and that the measures so far taken have proved inadequate to resolve the situation in Southern Rhodesia,

Gravely concerned further that the decisions taken by the Security Council have not been fully complied with by all States,

Noting that the Governments of the Republic of South Africa and Portugal, in particular, in contravention of their obligation under Article 25 of the Charter of the United Nations, have not only continued to trade with the illegal racist minority regime of Southern Rhodesia, contrary to the terms of Security Council resolutions 232 (1966) and 253 (1968), but have in fact given active assistance to that regime, enabling it to counter the effects of measures decided upon by the Security Council,

Noting in particular the continued presence of South African forces in the territory of Zimbabwe,

Affirming the primary responsibility of the Government of the United Kingdom to enable the people of Zimbabwe to exercise their right of self-determination and independence,

Reaffirming the inalienable right of the people of Zimbabwe to freedom and independence and the legitimacy of their struggle for the enjoyment of that right,

Acting under Chapter VII of the Charter of the United Nations,

1. Condemns the proclamation of a so-called republic in Zimbabwe by the racist minority regime in Salisbury and declares null and void any form of government which is not based on the principle of majority rule;

2. Decides that all States Members of the United Nations shall refrain from recognizing this illegal regime and urges States not Members of the Organization, having regard to the principles set out in Article 2 of the Charter of the United Nations, to act accordingly;

3. Calls upon all States to take appropriate measures, at the national level, to ensure that any act performed by officials and institutions of the illegal regime in Southern Rhodesia shall not be accorded any recognition, official or otherwise, including judicial notice, by the competent organs of their State;

4. Emphasizes the responsibility of the Government of the United Kingdom, as the administering Power, with regard to the situation prevailing in Southern Rhodesia;

5. Condemns the persistent refusal of the Government of the United Kingdom, as the administering Power, to use force to bring an end to the rebellion in Southern Rhodesia and enable the people of Zimbabwe to exercise their right to self-determination and independence in accordance with General Assembly resolution 1514 (XV);

6. Decides that all States shall immediately sever all diplomatic, consular, economic, military and other relations with the illegal racist minority regime in Southern Rhodesia, including railway, maritime, air transport, postal, telegraphic and wireless communications and other means of communication;

7. Requests the Government of the United Kingdom, as the administering Power, to rescind or withdraw any existing agreements on the basis of which foreign consular, trade and other representations may at present be maintained in or with Southern Rhodesia;

8. Condemns the assistance given by the Governments of Portugal and South

Africa and by other imperialist Powers to the illegal racist minority regime in defiance of resolutions of the Security Council and demands the immediate withdrawal of the troops of the South African aggressors from the territory of Zimbabwe;

9. Decides that Member States and members of the specialized agencies shall apply against the Republic of South Africa and Portugal the measures set out in resolution 253 (1968) and in the present resolution;

10. Calls upon all Member States and members of the specialized agencies to carry out the decisions of the Security Council in accordance with their obligations under the Charter of the United Nations;

11. Calls upon all States Members of the United Nations, and, in particular, those with primary responsibility under the Charter for the maintenance of international peace and security, to assist effectively in the implementation of the measures called for by the present resolution;

12. Urges all States to render moral and material assistance to the national liberation movements of Zimbabwe in order to enable them to regain their freedom and independence;

13. Requests all States to report to the Secretary-General on the measures taken to implement the present resolution;

14. Requests the Secretary-General to report to the Security Council on the progress made in implementing the present resolution.

Security Council Resolution 277 on Illegal Trade with Southern Rhodesia *

March 18, 1970

The Security Council,

Reaffirming its resolutions 216 (1965) of 12 November 1965, 217 (1965) of 20 November 1965, 221 (1966) of 9 April 1966, 232 (1966) of 16 December 1966 and 253 (1968) of 29 May 1968,

Reaffirming that, to the extent not superseded in this resolution, the measures provided for in resolutions 217 (1965) of 20 November 1965, 232 (1966) of 16 December 1966 and 253 (1968) of 29 May 1968, as well as those initiated by Member States in implementation of those resolutions, shall continue in effect,

Taking into account the report of the Committee established in pursuance of Security Council resolution 253 (1968) (S/8954 and S/9252),

Noting with grave concern:

(a) That the measures so far taken have failed to bring the rebellion in Southern Rhodesia to an end,

(b) That some States, contrary to resolutions 232 (1966) and 253 (1968) of the Security Council and to their obligations under Article 25 of the Charter, have failed to prevent trade with the illegal regime of Southern Rhodesia,

(c) That the Governments of the Republic of South Africa and Portugal have continued to give assistance to the illegal regime of Southern Rhodesia, thus diminishing the effects of the measures decided upon by the Security Council,

(d) That the situation in Southern Rhodesia continues to deteriorate as a result of the introduction by the illegal regime of new measures, including the purported

*Ibid. S/RES 277 (1970), Dec. 18, 1970.

assumption of republican status, aimed at repressing the African people in violation of General Assembly resolution 1514 (XV),

Recognizing the legitimacy of the struggle of the people of Southern Rhodesia to secure the enjoyment of their rights as set forth in the Charter of the United Nations and in conformity with the objectives of General Assembly resolution 1514 (XV),

Reaffirming that the present situation in Southern Rhodesia constitutes a threat to international peace and security,

Acting under Chapter VII of the United Nations Charter,

1. Condemns the illegal proclamation of republican status of the Territory by the illegal regime in Southern Rhodesia;

2. Decides that Member States shall refrain from recognizing this illegal regime or from rendering any assistance to it;

3. Calls upon Member States to take appropriate measures, at the national level, to ensure that any act performed by officials and institutions of the illegal regime in Southern Rhodesia shall not be accorded any recognition, official or otherwise, including judicial notice, by the competent organs of their State;

4. Reaffirms the primary responsibility of the Government of the United Kingdom for enabling the people of Zimbabwe to exercise their right to self-determination and independence, in accordance with the Charter of the United Nations and in conformity with General Assembly resolution 1514 (XV), and urges that Government to discharge fully its responsibility;

5. Condemns all measures of political repression, including arrests, detentions, trials and executions, which violate fundamental freedoms and rights of the people of Southern Rhodesia;

6. Condemns the policies of the Governments of South Africa and Portugal, which continue to have political, economic, military and other relations with the illegal regime in Southern Rhodesia in violation of the relevant United Nations resolutions;

7. Demands the immediate withdrawal of South African police and armed personnel from the Territory of Southern Rhodesia;

8. Calls upon Member States to take more stringent measures in order to prevent any circumvention by their nationals, organizations, companies and other institutions of their nationality, of the decisions taken by the Security Council in resolutions 232 (1966) and 253 (1968), all provisions of which shall fully remain in force;

9. Decides, in accordance with Article 41 of the Charter and in furthering the objective of ending the rebellion, that Member States shall:

(a) Immediately sever all diplomatic, consular, trade, military and other relations that they may have with the illegal regime in Southern Rhodesia, and terminate any representation that they may maintain in the Territory;

(b) Immediately interrupt any existing means of transportation to and from Southern Rhodesia;

10. Requests the Government of the United Kingdom as the administering Power, to rescind or withdraw any existing agreements on the basis of which foreign consular, trade and other representation may at present be maintained in or with Southern Rhodesia;

11. Requests Member States to take all possible further action under Article 41 of the Charter to deal with the situation in Southern Rhodesia, not excluding any of the measures provided in that Article;

12. Calls upon Member States to take appropriate action to suspend any member-

ship or associate membership that the illegal regime of Southern Rhodesia has in specialized agencies of the United Nations;

13. Urges Member States of any international or regional organizations to suspend the membership of the illegal regime of Southern Rhodesia from their respective organizations and to refuse any request for membership from that regime;

14. Urges Member States to increase moral and material assistance to the people of Southern Rhodesia in their legitimate struggle to achieve freedom and independence;

15. Requests specialized agencies and other international organizations concerned, in consultation with the Organization of African Unity, to give aid and assistance to refugees from Southern Rhodesia and those who are suffering from oppression by the illegal regime of Southern Rhodesia;

16. Requests Member States, the United Nations, the specialized agencies and other international organizations in the United Nations system to make an urgent effort to increase their assistance to Zambia as a matter of priority with a view to helping her solve such special economic problems as she may be confronted with arising from the carrying out of the decisions of the Security Council in this question;

17. Calls upon Member States, and in particular those with primary responsibility under the Charter for the maintenance of international peace and security, to assist effectively in the implementation of the measures called for by the present resolution;

18. Urges, having regard to the principle stated in Article 2 of the United Nations Charter, States not Members of the United Nations to act in accordance with the provisions of the present resolution;

19. Calls upon Member States to report to the Secretary-General by 1 June 1970 on the measures taken to implement the present resolution;

20. Requests the Secretary-General to report to the Security Council on the progress of the implementation of this resolution, the first report not to be made later than 1 July 1970;

21. Decides that the Committee of the Security Council established by resolution 253 (1968), in accordance with rule 28 of the provisional rules of procedure of the Security Council, shall be entrusted with the responsibility of:

(a) Examining such reports on the implementation of the present resolution as will be submitted by the Secretary-General;

(b) To seek from Member States such further information regarding the effective implementation of the provisions laid down in the present resolution as it may consider necessary for the proper discharge of its duty to report to the Security Council;

(c) To study ways and means by which Member States could carry out more effectively the decisions of the Security Council regarding sanctions against the illegal regime of Southern Rhodesia and to make recommendations to the Security Council;

22. Requests the United Kingdom, as the administering Power, to continue to give maximum assistance to the Committee and to provide the Committee with any information which it may receive in order that the measures envisaged in this resolution as well as resolutions 232 (1966), and 253 (1968) may be rendered fully effective;

23. Calls upon Member States as well as the specialized agencies to supply such information as may be sought by the Committee in pursuance of this resolution;

24. Decides to maintain this item on its agenda for further action as appropriate in the light of developments.

SOUTH WEST AFRICA

*General Assembly Resolution 2445 (XXI) on South West Africa**

October 27, 1966

The General Assembly,

Reaffirming the inalienable right of the people of South West Africa to freedom and independence in accordance with the Charter of the United Nations, General Assembly resolution 1514 (XV) of 14 December 1960[1] and earlier Assembly resolutions concerning the Mandated Territory of South West Africa,

Recalling the advisory opinion of the International Court of Justice of 11 July 1960,[2] accepted by the General Assembly in its resolution 449 A (V) of 13 December 1950, and the advisory opinions of 7 June 1955[3] and 1 June 1956[4] as well as the judgement of 21 December 1962,[5] which have established the fact that South Africa continues to have obligations under the Mandate which was entrusted to it on 17 December 1920 and that the United Nations as the successor to the League of Nations has supervisory powers in respect of South West Africa,

Gravely concerned at the situation in the Mandated Territory, which has seriously deteriorated following the judgement of the International Court of Justice of 18 July 1966,[6]

Having studied the reports of the various committees which had been established to exercise the supervisory functions of the United Nations over the administration of the Mandated Territory of South West Africa,

Convinced that the administration of the Mandated Territory by South Africa has been conducted in a manner contrary to the Mandate, the Charter of the United Nations and the Universal Declaration of Human Rights,[7]

Reaffirming its resolution 2074 (XX) of 17 December 1965, in particular paragraph 4 thereof which condemned the policies of apartheid and racial discrimination practised by the Government of South Africa in South West Africa as constituting a crime against humanity,

Emphasizing that the problem of South West Africa is an issue falling within the terms of General Assembly resolution 15:4 (XV),

Considering that all the efforts of the United Nations to induce the Government of South Africa to fulfil its obligations in respect of the administration of the Mandated

---

*U.N. General Assembly Press Release GA/3313, December 20, 1966, Part I, pp. 4-7; adopted by a roll-call vote of 114-2-3, with the United States voting affirmatively. For the context see *The United States in World Affairs, 1966*, p. 259.
[1] Declaration on the Granting of Independence to Colonial Countries and Peoples; text in *Documents, 1960*, pp. 575-77.
[2] *International Status of South West Africa, Advisory Opinion: I.C.J. Reports 1950*, p. 128.
[3] *South West Africa—Voting Procedure, Advisory Opinion of 7th June, 1955: I.C.J. Reports 1955*, p. 67.
[4] *Admissibility of Hearings of Petitioners by the Committee on South West Africa, Advisory Opinion of June 1st, 1956: I.C.J. Reports 1956*, p. 23.
[5] *South West Africa Cases (Ethiopia v. South Africa; Liberia v. South Africa), Preliminary Objections, Judgment of 21 December 1962: I.C.J. Reports 1962*, p. 319.
[6] *South West Africa, Second Phase, Judgment, I.C.J. Reports 1966*, p. 6.
[7] *Documents, 1948*, pp. 430-35.

Territory and to ensure the well-being and security of the indigenous inhabitants have been of no avail,

Mindful of the obligations of the United Nations towards the people of South West Africa,

Noting with deep concern the explosive situation which exists in the southern region of Africa,

Affirming its right to take appropriate action in the matter, including the right to revert to itself the administration of the Mandated Territory,

1. Reaffirms that the provisions of General Assembly resolution 1514 (XV) are fully applicable to the people of the Mandated Territory of South West Africa and that, therefore, the people of South West Africa have the inalienable right to self-determination, freedom and independence in accordance with the Charter of the United Nations;

2. Reaffirms further that South West Africa is a territory having international status and that it shall maintain this status until it achieves independence;

3. Declares that South Africa has failed to fulfil its obligations in respect of the administration of the Mandated Territory and to ensure the moral and material well-being and security of the indigenous inhabitants of South West Africa, and has, in fact, disavowed the Mandate;

4. Decides that the Mandate conferred upon His Britannic Majesty to be exercised on his behalf by the Government of the Union of South Africa is therefore terminated, that South Africa has no other right to administer the Territory and that henceforth South West Africa comes under the direct responsibility of the United Nations;

5. Resolves that in these circumstances the United Nations must discharge those responsibilities with respect to South West Africa;

6. Establishes an Ad Hoc Committee for South West Africa composed of fourteen Member States to be designated by the President of the General Assembly—to recommend practical means by which South West Africa should be administered, so as to enable the people of the Territory to exercise the right of self-determination and to achieve independence, and to report to the General Assembly at a special session as soon as possible and in any event not later than April 1967;

7. Calls upon the Government of South Africa forthwith to refrain and desist from any action, constitutional, administrative, political or otherwise, which will in any manner whatsoever alter or tend to alter the present international status of South West Africa;

8. Calls the attention of the Security Council to the present resolution;

9. Requests all States to extend their whole-hearted co-operation and to render assistance in the implementation of the present resolution;

10. Requests the Secretary-General to provide all assistance necessary to implement the present resolution and to enable the Ad Hoc Committee for South West Africa to perform its duties.

General Assembly Resolution 2248 (S-V) on a Council for South West Africa*

June 14, 1967

The General Assembly,

Having considered the report of the Ad Hoc Committee for South West Africa,

Reaffirming its resolution 1514 (XV) of 14 December 1960 containing the Declaration on the Granting of Independence to Colonial Countries and Peoples,

Reaffirming its resolution 2145 (XXI) of 27 October 1966, by which it terminated the Mandate conferred upon His Britannic Majesty to be exercised on his behalf by the Government of the Union of South Africa and decided that South Africa had no other right to administer the Territory of South West Africa,

Having assumed direct responsibility for the Territory of South West Africa in accordance with resolution 2145 (XXI),

Recognizing that it has thereupon become incumbent upon the United Nations to give effect to its obligations by taking practical steps to transfer power to the people of South West Africa,

I

Reaffirms the territorial integrity of South West Africa and the inalienable right of its people to freedom and independence, in accordance with the Charter of the United Nations, General Assembly resolution 1514 (XV) and all other resolutions concerning South West Africa;

II

1. Decides to establish a United Nations Council for South West Africa (hereinafter referred to as the Council) comprising eleven Member States to be elected during the present session and to entrust to it the following powers and functions, to be discharged in the Territory:

(a) To administer South West Africa until independence, with the maximum possible participation of the people of the Territory;

(b) To promulgate such laws, decrees and administrative regulations as are necessary for the administration of the Territory until a legislative assembly is established following elections conduted on the basis of universal adult suffrage;

(c) To take as an immediate task all the necessary measures, in consultation with the people of the Territory, for the establishment of a constituent assembly to draw up a constitution on the basis of which elections will be held for the establishment of a legislative assembly and a responsible government;

(d) To take all the necessary measures for the maintenance of law and order in the territory;

(e) To transfer all powers to the people of the Territory upon the declaration of independence;

2. Decides that in the exercise of its powers and in the discharge of its functions the Council shall be responsible to the General Assembly;

3. Decides that the Council shall enturst such executive and administrative tasks as it deems necessary to a United Nations Commissioner for South West Africa (hereinafter referred to as the Commissioner), who shall be appointed during the present session by the General Assembly on the nomination of the Secretary-General;

4. Decides that in the performance of his tasks the Commissioner shall be responsible to the Council;

III

1. Decides that:

(a) The administration of South West Africa under the United Nations shall be financed from the revenues collected in the Territory;

(b) Expenses directly related to the operation of the Council and the Office of the Commissioner—the travel and subsistence expenses of members of the Council, the remuneration of the Commissioner and his staff and the cost of ancillary facilities— shall be met from the regular budget of the United Nations;

2. Requests the specialized agencies and the appropriate organs of the United Nations to render to South West Africa technical and financial assistance through a co-ordinated emergency programme to meet the exigencies of the situation;

IV

1. Decides that the Council shall be based in South West Africa;

2. Requests the Council to enter immediately into contact with the authorities of South Africa in order to lay down procedures, in accordance with General Assembly resolution 2145 (XXI) and the present resolution, for the transfer of the administration of the Territory with the least possible upheaval;

3. Further requests the Council to proceed to South West Africa with a view to:

(a) Taking over the administration of the Territory;

(b) Ensuring the withdrawal of South Africa police and military forces;

(c) Ensuring the withdrawal of South African personnel and their replacement by personnel operating under the authority of the Council;

(d) Ensuring that in the utilization and recruitment of personnel preference be given to the indigenous people;

4. Calls upon the Government of South Africa to comply without delay with the terms of resolution 2145 (XXI) and the present resolution and to facilitate the transfer of the administration of the Territory of South West Africa to the Council;

5. Requests the Security Council to take all appropriate measures to enable the United Nations Council for South West Africa to discharge the functions and responsibilities entrusted to it by the General Assembly;

6. Requests all States to extend their whole-hearted co-operation and to render assistance to the Council in the implementation of its task;

V

Requests the Council to report to the General Assembly at intervals not exceeding three months on its administration of the Territory, and to submit a special report to the Assembly at its twenty-second session concerning the implementation of the present resolution;

VI

Decides that South West Africa shall become independent on a date to be fixed in accordance with the wishes of the people and that the Council shall do all in its power to enable independence to be attained by June 1968.

At its 1524th plenary meeting, on 13 June 1967, the General Assembly, in pursuance of section II, paragraph 1, of the above resolution, elected the members of the United Nations Council for South West Africa.

The Council will be composed of the following Member States: Chile, Colombia, Guyana, India, Indonesia, Nigeria, Pakistan, Turkey, United Arab Republic, Yugoslavia and Zambia.

At the same meeting, in pursuance of section II, paragraph 3, of the above resolution, the General Assembly, on the proposal of the Secretary-General, appointed Mr. Constantin A. Stavropoulos, Legal Counsel of the United Nations, as Acting United Nations Commissioner for South West Africa.

PROTECTING HUMAN RIGHTS

*Address by Mrs. Eleanor Roosevelt, U.S. Representative to
the General Assembly on Human Rights**

December 9, 1948

The long and meticulous study and debate, of which this universal Declaration of Human Rights is the product, means that it reflects the composite views of the many men and governments who have contributed to its formulation. Not every man, nor every government, can have what he wants in a document of this kind. There are, of course, particular provisions in the Declaration with which we are not fully satisfied. I have no doubt that this is true of other delegations. It would still be true if we continued our labours over many years. Taken as a whole, the delegation of the United States believes that this is a good document, even a great document, and we propose to give it our full support.

The position of the United States on the various parts of the Declaration is a matter of record in the Third Committee. I shall not burden the Assembly, and particularly my colleagues of the Third Committee, with a re-statement of that position.

I should like to comment briefly on the amendments proposed by the USSR delegation. The language of these amendments has been dressed up somewhat, but the substance is the same as in the amendments which were offered by the USSR delegation in committee and which were rejected after exhaustive discussion. Substantially the same amendments have been previously considered and rejected in the Human Rights Commission.

We, in the United States, admire those who fight for their convictions. And the USSR delegation has fought for its convictions. But, in the older democracies, we have learned that sometimes we bow to the will of the majority. In doing that, we do not give up our convictions; we continue sometimes to persuade, and, eventually, we may be successful. But we know that we have to work together, and we have to progress, so we believe that, when we have made a good fight and the majority is against us, it is perhaps better tactics to try to co-operate.

I feel bound to say that I think that it is perhaps somewhat of an imposition on this Assembly to have these amendments offered again here, and I am confident that they will be rejected without debate. The first two paragraphs of the amendment to article 3 deal with the question of minorities, which the Third Committee decided required further study and which, in a second resolution, it recommended for reference to the Economic and Social Council and the Human Rights Commission. As set out in the USSR amendment this provision clearly states group and not individual rights.

The USSR amendment to article 20 is obviously a very restrictive statement of the right to freedom of opinion and expression. It sets up standards which would enable any state practically to deny all freedom of opinion and expression without violating the article. It introduces the terms "democratic views," "democratic system," "democratic state" and "fascism," which we know all too well from debates in this Assembly over the past two years on warmongering and related subjects are liable to the most

*U.S. Mission to the United Nations, Press Release, Dec. 9, 1948.

flagrant abuse and diverse interpretations. The statement of the representative of the USSR here tonight is a very good case in point of this.

The USSR amendment to article 22 introduces new elements into the article without improving the Committee's text, and again introduces specific references to discrimination. As was repeatedly pointed out in the Third Committee the question of discrimination is comprehensively covered in article 2 of the declaration so that its restatement elsewhere is completely unnecessary and also has the effect of weakening the comprehensive principle stated in article 2.

The new article proposed by the USSR delegation is but a restatement of state obligation which the USSR delegation attempted to introduce into practically every article in the declaration. It would convert the declaration into a document stating obligations on states, thereby changing completely its character as a statement of principles to serve as a common standard of achievement of the members of the United Nations.

The proposal of the USSR for referring consideration of the declaration to the Fourth Session of the General Assembly requires no comment. An identical text was rejected by the Third Committee by a vote of 6 in favour and 26 against. We are all agreed, I am sure, that the declaration which has been worked on with such great effort and devotion over such a long period of time must be approved by this Assembly at this session. Certain provisions of the declaration are stated in such broad terms as to be acceptable only because of the provisions in article 30 providing for limitation on the exercise of the rights for the purpose of meeting the requirements of morality, public order and the general welfare.

An example of this is the provision that everyone has the right to equal access to the public service in his country. The basic principle of equality and of non-discrimination as to public employment is sound, but it cannot be accepted without limitation. My Government, for example, would consider that this is unquestionably subject to limitation in the interests of public order and the general welfare. It would not consider that the exclusion from public employment of persons holding subversive political beliefs and not loyal to the basic principles and practices of the constitution and laws of the country would in any way infringe upon this right. Likewise my Government has made it clear in the course of the development of the declaration that it does not consider that the economic, social and cultural rights stated in the declaration imply an obligation on governments to assure the enjoyment of these rights by direct governmental action.

This was made quite clear in the Human Rights Commission text of article 23 which served as a so-called umbrella article to the articles on economic and social rights. We consider that the principle has not been affected by the fact that this article no longer contains a reference to the articles which follow it. This in no way affects our whole hearted support for the basic principles of economic, social and cultural rights set forth in these articles.

In giving our approval to the declaration today it is of primary importance that we keep clearly in mind the basic character of the document. It is not a treaty, it is not an international agreement, it is not and does not purport to be a statement of law or of legal obligation. It is a declaration of basic principles of human rights and freedoms to be stamped with the approval of the General Assembly by formal vote of its members, and to serve as a common standard of achievement for all peoples of all nations.

We stand today at the threshold of a great event both in the life of the United Nations and in the life of mankind. This universal declaration of human rights may well become the international Magna Carta of all men everywhere. We hope that its proclamation by the General Assembly will be an event comparable to the proclamation of the declaration of the rights of man by the French people in 1789, the adoption of the Bill of Rights by the people of the United States, and the adoption of comparable declarations at different times in other countries.

At a time when there are so many issues on which we find it difficult to reach a common basis of agreement it is a significant fact that 58 States have found a large measure of agreement in the complex field of human rights. This must be taken as testimony of our common aspiration, as voiced in the Charter of the United Nations, to lift men everywhere to a higher standard of life and to greater enjoyment of freedom. Man's desire for peace lies behind this declaration. The realization that the flagrant violation of human rights by nazi and fascist countries sowed the seeds of the last world war has supplied the impetus for the work which brings us to the moment of achievement here today.

In a recent speech in Canada Gladstone Murray said:

> "The central fact is that man is fundamentally a moral being. That the life we have is imperfect does not matter so long as we are always trying to improve it. We are equal in sharing the moral freedom that distinguishes us as men. Man's status makes each individual an end in himself. No man is by nature simply the servant of the state or of another man. The ideal and fact of freedom itself—not technique—are the true distinguishing marks of our civilization."

This declaration is based upon the spiritual fact that man must have freedom in which to development his full stature and, through common effort, to raise the level of human dignity. We have much to do to achieve fully and to assure the rights set forth in this declaration, but having them put before us with the moral backing of 58 nations will be a great step forward. As we here bring to fruition our labours on this declaration of human rights we must, at the same time, rededicate ourselves to the unfinished task which lies before us. We can now move on with new courage and inspiration to the completion of an international covenant of human rights and to measures for the implementation of human rights.

In conclusion I feel that I cannot do better than to repeat the call to action by Secretary Marshall in his opening statement to this General Assembly:

> "Let this Third Regular Session of the General Assembly approve by an overwhelming majority the Declaration of Human Rights as a standard of conduct for all, and let us, as members of the United Nations conscious of our own shortcomings and imperfections, join our effort in good faith to live up to these high standards."

*Universal Declaration of Human Rights**

December 10, 1948

PREAMBLE

Whereas recognition of the inherent dignity and of the equal and inalienable rights

*U.S. Participation in the U.N., Reports 1946-49, Appendix II, pp. 204-11.

of all members of the human family is the foundation of freedom, justice and peace in the world,

Whereas disregard and contempt for human rights have resulted in barbarous acts which have outraged the conscience of mankind, and the advent of a world in which human beings shall enjoy freedom of speech and belief and freedom from fear and want has been proclaimed as the highest aspiration of the common people,

Whereas it is essential, if man is not to be compelled to have recourse, as a last resort, to rebellion against tyranny and oppression, that human rights should be protected by the rule of law,

Whereas it is essential to promote the development of friendly relations between nations,

Whereas the peoples of the United Nations have in the Charter reaffirmed their faith in fundamental human rights, in the dignity and worth of the human person and in the equal rights of men and women and have determined to promote social progress and better standards of life in larger freedom.

Whereas Member States have pledged themselves to achieve, in co-operation with the United Nations, the promotion of universal respect for and observance of human rights and fundamental freedoms,

Whereas a common understanding of these rights and freedoms is of the greatest importance for the full realization of this pledge,

Now therefore

The General Assembly,

Proclaims this Universal Declaration of Human Rights as a common standard of achievement for all peoples and all nations, to the end that every individual and every organ of society, keeping this Declaration constantly in mind, shall strive by teaching and education to promote respect for these rights and freedoms and by progressive measures, national and international, to secure their universal and effective recognition and observance, both among the peoples of Member States themselves and among the peoples of territories under their jurisdiction.

Article 1

All human beings are born free and equal in dignity and rights. They are endowed with reason and conscience and should act towards one another in a spirit of brotherhood.

Article 2

Everyone is entitled to all the rights and freedoms set forth in this Declaration, without distinction of any kind, such as race, colour, sex, language, religion, political or other opinion, national or social origin, property, birth or other status.

Furthermore, no distinction shall be made on the basis of the political, jurisdictional or international status of the country or territory to which a person belongs, whether it be independent, Trust, Non-Self-Governing or under any other limitation of sovereignty.

Article 3

Everyone has the right to life, liberty and the security of person.

Article 4

No one shall be held in slavery or servitude; slavery and the slave trade shall be prohibited in all their forms.

Article 5

No one shall be subjected to torture or to cruel, inhuman or degrading treatment or punishment.

Article 6

Everyone has the right to recognition everywhere as a person before the law.

Article 7

All are equal before the law and are entitled without any discrimination to equal protection of the law. All are entitled to equal protection against any discrimination in violation of this Declaration and against any incitement to such discrimination.

Article 8

Everyone has the right to an effective remedy by the competent national tribunals for acts violating the fundamental rights granted him by the constitution or by law.

Article 9

No one shall be subjected to arbitrary arrest, detention or exile.

Article 10

Everyone is entitled in full equality to a fair and public hearing by an independent and impartial tribunal, in the determination of his rights and obligations and of any criminal charge against him.

Article 11

1. Everyone charged with a penal offence has the right to be presumed innocent until proved guilty according to law in a public trial at which he has had all the guarantees necessary for his defence.

2. No one shall be held guilty of any penal offence on account of any act or omission which did not constitute a penal offence, under national or international law, at the time when it was committed. Nor shall a heavier penalty be imposed than the one that was applicable at that time the penal offence was committed.

Article 12

No one shall be subjected to arbitrary interference with his privacy, family, home or correspondence, nor to attacks upon his honour and reputation. Everyone has the right to the protection of the law against such interference or attacks.

Article 13

1. Everyone has the right to freedom of movement and residence within the borders of each state.

2. Everyone has the right to leave any country, including his own, and to return to his country.

Article 14

1. Everone has the right to seek and to enjoy in other countries asylum from persecution.

2. This right may not be invoked in the case of prosecutions genuinely arising from non-political crimes or from acts contrary to the purposes and principles of the United Nations.

Article 15

1. Everyone has the right to a nationality.

2. No one shall be arbitrarily deprived of his nationality nor denied the right to change his nationality.

Article 16

1. Men and women of full age, without any limitation due to race, nationality or

religion, have the right to marry and to found a family. They are entitled to equal rights as to marriage, during marriage and at its dissolution.

2. Marriage shall be entered into only with the free and full consent of the intending spouses.

3. The family is the natural and fundamental group unit of society and is entitled to protection by society and the Senate.

Article 17

1. Everyone has the right to own property alone as well as in association with others.

2. No one shall be arbitrarily deprived of his property.

Article 18

Everyone has the right to freedom of thought, conscience and religion; this right includes freedom to change his religion or belief, and freedom, either alone or in community with others and in public or private, to manifest his religion or belief in teaching, practice, worship and observance.

Article 19

Everyone has the right to freedom of opinion and expression; this right includes freedom to hold opinions without interference and to seek, receive and impart information and ideas through any media and regardless of frontiers.

Article 20

1. Everyone has the right to freedom of peaceful assembly and association.
2. No one may be compelled to belong to an association.

Article 21

1. Everyone has the right to take part in the government of his country, directly or through freely chosen representatives.

2. Everyone has the right of equal access to public service in his country.

3. The will of the people shall be the basis of the authority of government; this will shall be expressed in periodic and genuine elections which shall be by universal and equal suffrage and shall be held by secret vote or by equivalent free voting procedures.

Article 22

Everyone, as a member of society, has the right to social security and is entitled to the realization, through national effort and international co-operation and in accordance with the organization and resources of each State, of the economic, social and cultural rights indispensable for his dignity and the free development of his personality.

Article 23

1. Everyone has the right to work, to free choice of employment, to just and favourable conditions of work and to protection against unemployment.

2. Everyone, without any discrimination, has the right to equal pay for equal work.

3. Everyone who works has the right to just and favourable remuneration insuring for himself and his family an existence worthy of human dignity, and supplemented, if necessary, by other means of social protection.

4. Everyone has the right to form and to join trade unions for the protection of his interests.

Article 24

Everyone has the right to rest and leisure, including reasonable limitation of working hours and periodic holidays with pay.

Article 25

1. Everyone has the right to a standard of living adequate for the health and well-being of himself and of his family, including food, clothing, housing and medical care and necessary social services, and the right to security in the event of unemployment, sickness, disability, widowhood, old age or other lack of livelihood in circumstances beyond his control.

2. Motherhood and childhood are entitled to special care and assistance. All children, whether born in or out of wedlock, shall enjoy the same social protection.

Article 26

1. Everyone has the right to education. Education shall be free, at least in the elementary and fundamental stages. Elementary education shall be compulsory. Technical and professional education shall be made generally available and higher education shall be equally accessible to all on the basis of merit.

2. Education shall be directed to the full development of the human personality and to the strengthening of respect for human rights and fundamental freedoms. It shall promote understanding, tolerance and friendship among all nations, racial or religious groups, and shall further the activities of the United Nations for the maintenance of peace.

3. Parents have a prior right to choose the kind of education that shall be given to their children.

Article 27

1. Everyone has the right freely to participate in the cultural life of the community, to enjoy the arts and to share in scientific advancement and its benefits.

2. Everyone has the right to the protection of the moral and material interests resulting from any scientific, literary or artistic production of which he is the author.

Article 28

Everyone is entitled to a social and international order in which the rights and freedoms set forth in this Declaration can be fully realized.

Article 29

1. Everyone has duties to the community in which alone the free and full development of his personality is possible.

2. In the exercise of his rights and freedoms, everyone shall be subject only to such limitations as are determined by law solely for the purpose of securing due recognition and respect for the rights and freedoms of others and of meeting the just requirements of morality, public order and the general welfare in a democratic society.

3. These rights and freedoms may in no case be exercised contrary to the purposes and principles of the United Nations.

Article 30

Nothing in this Declaration may be interpreted as implying for any State, group or person any right to engage in any activity or to perform any act aimed at the destruction of any of the rights and freedoms set forth herein.

II

The General Assembly,

Considering that the right of petition is an essential human right as is recognized in the constitution of a great number of countries,

Having considered the draft article on petitions in document A/C.3/306 and the amendments offered thereto by Cuba and France,

Decides not to take any action on this matter at the present session;

Requests the Economic and Social Council to ask the Commission on Human Rights to give further examination to the problem of petitions when studying the draft Covenant on Human Rights and measures of implementation, in order to enable the General Assembly to consider what further action, if any, should be taken at its next regular session regarding the problem of petitions.

III

The General Assembly,

Considering that the United Nations cannot remain indifferent to the fate of minorities,

Considering that it is difficult to adopt a uniform solution of this complex and delicate question, which has special aspects in each State in which it arises,

Considering the universal character of the Declaration of Human Rights,

Decides not to deal in a specific provision with the question of minorities in the text of this Declaration;

Refers to the Economic and Social Council the texts submitted by the delegations of the Union of Soviet Socialist Republics. Yugoslavia and Denmark on this subject contained in document A/C.3/307/Rev. 2 and requests the Council to ask the Commission on Human Rights and the Sub-Commission on the Prevention of Discrimination and the Protection of Minorities to make a thorough study of the problem of minorities in order that the United Nations may be able to take effective measures for the protection of racial, national, religious or linguistic minorities.

IV

The General Assembly,

Considering that the adoption of the Universal Declaration of Human Rights is an historic act destined to consolidate world peace through the contribution of the United Nations towards the liberation of individuals from the unjustified oppression and constraint to which they are too often subjected,

Considering that the text of the Declaration should be disseminated among all peoples throughout the world;

1. Recommends Governments of Member States to show their adherence to Article 56 of the Charter by using every means within their power solemnly to publicize the text of the Declaration and to cause it to be disseminated, displayed, read and expounded principally in schools and other educational institutions, without distinction based on the political status of countries or territories;

2. Requests the Secretary-General to have this Declaration widely disseminated and, to that end, to publish and distribute texts, not only in the official languages, but also, using every means at his disposal, in all languages possible;

3. Invites the specialized agencies and non-governmental organizations of the world to do their utmost to bring this Declaration to the attention of their members.

V

The General Assembly,

Considering that the plan of work of the Commission on Human Rights provides for an International Bill of Human Rights, to include a Declaration, a Covenant on Human Rights and measures of implementation,

Requests the Economic and Social Council to ask the Commission on Human Rights to continue to give priority in its work to the preparation of a draft Covenant on Human Rights and draft measures implementation.

Address by President Truman at the Cornerstone Laying of the United Nations Building*

October 24, 1949

We have come together today to lay the cornerstone of the permanent headquarters of the United Nations. These are the most important buildings in the world, for they are the center of man's hope for peace and a better life. This is the place where the nations of the world will work together to make that hope a reality.

This occasion is a source of special pride to the people of the United States. We are deeply conscious of the honor of having the permanent headquarters of the United Nations in this country. At the same time, we know how important it is that people of other nations should come to know at first hand the work of this world organization. We consider it appropriate, therefore, that the United Nations should hold meetings from time to time in other countries when that can be done. For the United Nations must draw its inspiration from the people of every land; it must be truly representative of and responsive to the peoples of the world whom it was created to serve.

This ceremony marks a new stage in the growth of the United Nations. It is fitting that it should take place on United Nations Day, the fourth anniversary of the day the charter entered into effect. During the 4 years of its existence, this organization has become a powerful force for promoting peace and friendship among the peoples of the world. The construction of this new headquarters is tangible proof of the steadfast faith of the members in the vitality and strength of the organization, and of our determination that it shall become more and more effective in the years ahead.

The charter embodies the hopes and ideals of men everywhere. Hopes and ideals are not static. They are dynamic, and they give life and vigor to the United Nations. We look forward to a continuing growth and evolution of the organization to meet the changing needs of the world's peoples. We hope that eventually every nation on earth will be a fully qualified and a loyal member of this organization.

We who are close to the United Nations sometimes forget that it is more than the procedures, the councils, and the debates, through which it operates. We tend to overlook the fact that the organization is the living embodiment of the principles of the charter—the renunciation of aggression and the joint determination to build a better life for the whole world.

But if we overlook this fact, we will fail to realize the strength and power of this great organization. We will fail to understand the true nature of this new force that has been created in the affairs of our time.

The United Nations is essentially an expression of the moral nature of man's aspirations. The charter clearly shows our determination that international problems must be settled on a basis acceptable to the conscience of mankind.

Because the United Nations is the dynamic expression of what all the peoples of the

*Public Papers of the Presidents, Harry S. Truman, pp. 526-29.

world desire, because it sets up a standard of right and justice for all nations, it is greater than any of its members. The compact that underlies the United Nations cannot be ignored—and it cannot be infringed or dissolved.

We in the United States, in the course of our own history, have learned what it means to set up an organization to give expression to the common desire for peace and unity. Our Constitution expressed the will of the people that there should be a United States. And through toil and struggle the people made their will prevail.

In the same way, I think, the charter and the organization served by these buildings express the will of the people of the world that there shall be a United Nations.

This does not mean that all the member countries are of one mind on all issues. The controversies which divide us go very deep. We should understand that these buildings are not a monument to the unanimous agreement of nations on all things. But they signify one new and important fact. They signify that the peoples of the world are of one mind in their determination to solve their common problems by working together.

Our success in the United Nations will be measured not only in terms of our ability to meet and master political controversies. We have learned that political controversies grow out of social and economic problems. If the people of the world are to live together in peace, we must work together to establish the conditions that will provide a firm foundation for peace.

For this reason, our success will also be measured by the extent to which the rights of individual human beings are realized. And it will be measured by the extent of our economic and social progress.

These fundamental facts are recognized both in the language of the charter and in the activities in which the United Nations has been engaging during the past 4 years. The charter plainly makes respect for human rights by nations a matter of international concern. The member nations have learned from bitter experience that regard for human rights is indispensable to political, economic, and social progress. They have learned that disregard of human rights is the beginning of tyranny and, too often, the beginning of war.

For these reasons, the United Nations has devoted much of its time to fostering respect for human rights. The General Assembly has adopted the Universal Declaration of Human Rights and the Convention on Genocide. Other important measures in this field are under study.

I am confident that this great work will go steadily forward. The preparation of a Covenant on Human Rights by the Human Rights Commission is a task with which the United States is deeply concerned. We believe strongly that the attainment of basic civil and political rights for men and women everywhere—without regard to race, language, or religion—is essential to the peace we are seeking. We hope that the Covenant on Human Rights will contain effective provisions regarding freedom of information. The minds of men must be free from artificial and arbitrary restraints, in order that they may seek the truth and apply their intelligence to making a better world.

Another field in which the United Nations is undertaking to build the foundations of a peaceful world is that of economic development. Today, at least half of mankind lives in dire poverty. Hundreds of millions of men, women, and children lack adequate food, clothing, and shelter. We cannot achieve permanent peace and prosperity in the world until the standard of living in underdeveloped areas is raised.

It is for this reason that I have urged the launching of a vigorous and concerted effort to apply modern technology and capital investment to improve the lot of these peoples. These areas need a large expansion of investment and trade. In order for this to take place, they also need the application of scientific knowledge and technical skills to their basic problems—producing more food, improving health and sanitation, making use of their natural resources, and educating their people.

To meet these needs, the United Nations and its agencies are preparing a detailed program for technical assistance to underdeveloped areas.

The Economic and Social Council last summer defined the basic principles which should underlie this program. The General Assembly is now completing and perfecting its initial plans. The fact that the Economic Committee of the Assembly voted unanimously for the resolution on technical assistance shows that this is a common cause which commands united support. Although differences may arise over details of the program, I fervently hope that the members of the United Nations will remain unanimous in their determination to raise the standards of living of the less fortunate members of the human family.

The United States intends to play its full part in this great enterprise. We are already carrying on a number of activities in this field. I shall urge the Congress, when it reconvenes in January, to give high priority to proposals which will make possible additional technical assistance and capital investment.

I should like to speak of one other problem which is of major concern to the United Nations. That is the control of atomic energy.

Ever since the first atomic weapon was developed, a major objective of United States policy has been a system of international control of atomic energy that would assure effective prohibition of atomic weapons, and at the same time would promote the peaceful use of atomic energy by all nations.

In November 1945, Prime Minister Attlee of the United Kingdom, Prime Minister Mackenzie King of Canada, and I agreed that the problem of international control of atomic energy should be referred to the United Nations. The establishment of the United Nations Atomic Energy Commission was one of the first acts of the first session of the General Assembly.

That commission worked for 3 years on the problem. It developed a plan of control which reflected valuable contributions by almost every country represented on the commission. This plan of control was overwhelmingly approved by the General Assembly on November 4, 1948.

This is a good plan. It is a plan that can work and, more important, it is a plan that can be effective in accomplishing its purpose. It is the only plan so far developed that would meet the technical requirements of control, and would make prohibition of atomic weapons effective, and at the same time promote the peaceful development of atomic energy on a cooperative basis.

We support this plan and will continue to support it unless or until a better and more effective plan is put forward. To assure that atomic energy will be devoted to man's welfare and not to his destruction is a continuing challenge to all nations and all peoples. The United States is now, and will remain, ready to do its full share in meeting this challenge.

Respect for human rights, promotion of economic development, and a system for control of weapons are requisites to the kind of world we seek. We cannot solve these problems overnight, but we must keep everlastingly working at them in order to reach our goal.

No single nation can always have its own way, for these are human problems, and the solution of human problems is to be found in negotiation and mutual adjustment.

The challenge of the 20th century is the challenge of human relations, and not of impersonal natural forces. The real dangers confronting us today have their origins in outmoded habits of thought, in the inertia of human nature, and in preoccupation with supposed national interests to the detriment of the common good.

As members of the United Nations, we are convinced that patience, the spirit of reasonableness, and hard work will solve the most stubborn political problems. We are convinced that individual rights and social and economic progress can be advanced through international cooperation.

Our faith is in the betterment of human relations. Our vision is of a better world in which men and nations can live together, respecting one another's rights and cooperating in building a better life for all. Our efforts are made in the belief that men and nations can cooperate, and that there are no international problems which men of good will cannot solve or adjust.

Mr. President, Mr. Lie, the laying of this cornerstone is an act of faith—our unshakable faith that the United Nations will succeed in accomplishing the great tasks for which it was created.

But "faith without works is dead." We must make our devotion to the ideals of the charter as strong as the steel in this building. We must pursue the objectives of the charter with resolution as firm as the rock on which this building rests. We must conduct our affairs foursquare with the charter, in terms as true as this cornerstone.

If we do these things, the United Nations will endure and will bring the blessings of peace and well-being to all mankind.

ASSISTING FORMER COLONIAL COUNTRIES

General Assembly Resolution 1514 (XV) on the Granting of
Independence to Colonial Countries and Peoples*

December 14, 1960

The General Assembly,

Mindful of the determination proclaimed by the peoples of the world in the Charter of the United Nations to reaffirm faith in fundamental human rights, in the dignity and worth of the human person, in the equal rights of men and women and of nations large and small and to promote social progress and better standards of life in larger freedom,

Conscious of the need for the creation of conditions of stability and well-being and peaceful and friendly relations based on respect for the principles of equal rights and self-determination of all peoples, and of universal respect for, and observance of, human rights and fundamental freedoms for all without distinction as to race, sex, language or religion,

Recognizing the passionate yearning for freedom in all dependent peoples and the decisive role of such peoples in the attainment of their independence,

Aware of the increasing conflicts resulting from the denial of or impediments in the way of freedom of such peoples, which constitute a serious threat to world peace,

Considering the important role of the United Nations in assisting the movement for independence in Trust and Non-Self-Governing Territories,

Recognizing that the peoples of the world ardently desire the end of colonialism in all its manifestations,

Convinced that the continued existence of colonialism prevents the development of international economic co-operation, impedes the social, cultural and economic development of dependent peoples and militates against the United Nations ideal of universal peace,

Affirming that peoples may, for their own ends, freely dispose of their natural wealth and resources without prejudice to any obligations arising out of international economic co-operation, based upon the principle of mutual benefit, and international law,

Believing that the process of liberation is irresistible and irreversible and that, in order to avoid serious crises, an end must be put to colonialism and all practices of segregation and discrimination associated therewith,

Welcoming the emergence in recent years of a large number of dependent territories into freedom and independence, and recognizing the increasingly powerful trends towards freedom in such territories which have not yet attained independence,

Convinced that all peoples have an inalienable right to complete freedom, the exercise of their sovereignty and the integrity of their national territory,

Solemnly proclaims the necessity of bringing to a speedy and unconditional end colonialism in all its forms and manifestations;

And to this end

Declares that:

*U.N. General Assembly, *Official Records,* 15th sess., Supplement No. 16 (A/4684), pp. 66-67.

1. The subjection of peoples to alien subjugation, domination and exploitation constitutes a denial of fundamental human rights, is contrary to the Charter of the United Nations and is an impediment to the promotion of world peace and co-operation.

2. All peoples have the right to self-determination; by virtue of that right they freely determine their political status and freely pursue their economic, social and cultural development.

3. Inadequacy of political, economic, social or educational preparedness should never serve as a pretext for delaying independence.

4. All armed action or repressive measures of all kinds directed against dependent peoples shall cease in order to enable them to exercise peacefully and freely their right to complete independence, and the integrity of their national territory shall be respected.

5. Immediate steps shall be taken, in Trust and Non-Self-Governing Territories or all other territories which have not yet attained independence, to transfer all powers to the peoples of those territories, without any conditions or reservations, in accordance with their freely expressed will and desire, without any distinction as to race, creed or colour, in order to enable them to enjoy complete indepdnence and freedom.

6. Any attempt aimed at the partial or total disruption of the national unity and the territorial integrity of a country is incompatible with the purposes and principles of the Charter of the United Nations.

7. All States shall observe faithfully and strictly the provisions of the Charter of the United Nations, the Universal Declaration of Human Rights and the present Declaration on the basis of equality, non-interference in the internal affairs of all States, and respect for the sovereign rights of all peoples and their territorial integrity.

General Assembly Resolution 2029 (XX) on Consolidation of the Special Fund and Expanded Program of Technical Assistance *

November 22, 1965

The General Assembly,

Having considered the recommendation of the Economic and Social Council, in its resolution 1020 (XXXVII) of 11 August 1964, to combine the Special Fund and the Expanded Programme of Technical Assistance in a United Nations Development Programme,

Being convinced that such a conslidation would go a long way in streamlining the activities carried on separately and jointly by the Expanded Programme of Technical Assistance and the Special Fund, would simplify organizational arrangements and procedures, would facilitate over-all planning and needed coordination of the several types of technical co-operation programmes carried on within the United Nations system of organizations and would increase their effectiveness,

Recognizing that requests for assistance on the part of the developing countries are steadily increasing in volume and in scope,

Believing that a reorganization is necessary to provide a more solid basis for the

*Ibid., 20th sess., 1964-65, Supplement 14, pp. 20-21.

future growth and evolution of the assistance programmes of the United Nations system of organizations financed from voluntary contributions,

Being convinced that the United Nations assistance programmes are designed to support and supplement the national efforts of developing countries in solving the most important problems of their economic development, including industrial development,

Recalling and reaffirming section III of its resolution 1219 (XII) of 14 December 1957 and part C of its resolution 1240 (XIII) of 14 October 1958 concerning the decision and the conditions under which the General Assembly review the scope and future activities of the Special Fund and take such action as it may deem appropriate,

Reaffirming that the proposed consolidation would be without prejudice consideration of the study which the General Assembly, in its resolution 193 (XVIII) of 11 December 1963, requested the Secretary-General to prepare on the practical steps to transform the Special Fund into a capital development fund such a way as to include both pre-investment and investment activities, and without prejudice to the recommendation of the United Nations Conference on Trade Development on the gradual transformation of the Special Fund, so as to include not only pre-investment but also investment proper, or to the recommendation of the Economic and Social Council and of the General Assembly thereon,

Taking note of the message of the Secretary-General in which he stated, inter alia, that, far from limiting the possibilities of a United Nations capital investment programme, the proposals should enhance those possibilities,

Recognizing that the effective working of a United Nations Development Programme depends upon the full and active participation and the technical contribution of all the organizations concerned,

1. Decides to combine the Expanded Programme of Technical Assistance and the Special Fund in a programme to be known as the United Nations Development Programme, it being understood that the special characteristics and operations of the two programmes, as well as two separate funds, will be maintained and that, as hitherto, contributions may be pledged to the two programmes separately;

2. Reaffirms the principles, procedures and provisions governing the Expanded Programme of Technical Assistance and the Special Fund not inconsistent with the present resolution and declares that they shall continue to apply to relevant activities within the United Nations Development Programme;

3. Urges the Governing Council referred to in paragraph 4 below to consider conditions for an effective implementation of the provisions of section III of General Assembly resolution 1219 (XII) and part C of its resolution 1240 (XIII);

4. Resolves that a single inter-governmental committee of thirty-seven members, to be known as the Governing Council of the United Nations Development Programme, shall be established to perform the functions previously exercised by the Governing Council of the Special Fund and the Technical Assistance Committee, including the consideration and approval of projects and programmes and the allocation of funds; in addition, it shall provide general policy guidance and direction for the United Nations Development Programme as a whole, as well as for the United Nations regular programmes of technical assistance, it shall meet twice a year and shall submit reports and recommendations thereon to the Economic and Social Council for consideration

by the Council at its summer session; decisions of the Governing Council shall be made by a majority of the members present and voting;

5. Requests the Economic and Social Council to elect the members of the Governing Council from among States Members of the United Nations or members of the specialized agencies or of the International Atomic Energy Agency, providing for equitable and balanced representation of the economically more developed countries, on the one hand, having due regard to their contribution to the United Nations Development Programme, and of the developing countries, on the other hand, taking into account the need for suitable regional representation among the latter members and in accordance with the provisions of the annex to the present resolution, the first election to take place at the first meeting of the Economic and Social Council after the adoption of this resolution;

6. Decides to establish, in place of the Technical Assistance Board and the Consultative Board of the Special Fund, an advisory committee, to be known as the Inter-Agency Consultative Board of the United Nations Development Programme, to meet under the chairmanship of the Administrator or Co-Administrator referred to in paragraph 7 below and to include the Secretary-General and the executive heads of the specialized agencies and of the International Atomic Energy Agency or their representatives; the Executive Directors of the United Nations Children's Fund and the World Food Programme should be invited to participate as appropriate; in order that the participating organizations may be provided with the opportunity to take part fully in the process of decision- and policy-making in a consultative capacity, the Inter-Agency Consultative Board shall be consulted on all significant aspects of the United Nations Development Programme and in particular it shall:

(a) Advise the management on the programmes and projects submitted by Governments, through the Resident Representative, prior to their submission to the Governing Council for approval, taking into account the programmes of technical assistance being carried out under the regular programmes of the organization represented on the Consultative Board, with a view to ensuring more effective co-ordination; the views of the Consultative Board, when it so requests, shall be conveyed by the Administrator to the Governing Council, together with any comments he may wish to make, when recommending for approval general policies for the Programme as a whole or for programmes and projects requested by Governments;

(b) Be consulted in the selection of agencies for the execution of specific projects, as appropriate;

(c) Be consulted on the appointment of the Resident Representatives and review annual reports submitted by them;
the Inter-Agency Consultative Board shall meet as often and for such periods as may be necessary for the performance of the foregoing functions;

7. Decides that, as a transitional measure, the present Managing Director of the Special Fund shall become the Administrator of the United Nations Development Programme and the present Executive Chairman of the Technical Assistance Board shall become the Co-Administrator of the Programme, each to serve until 31 December 1966 or, pending a further review of arrangmeents at the management level, until such later date as may be determined by the Secretary-General after consultation with the Governing Council;

8. Decides that the present resolution shall come into effect on 1 January 1966 and that such action as may be required in terms of this resolution shall be taken prior to that date.

ANNEX

1. Nineteen seats on the Governing Council of the United Nations Development Programme shall be filled by developing countries, and seventeen seats by economically more developed countries, subject to the following conditions:

(a) The nineteen seats allocated to developing countries of Africa, Asia, Latin American and to Yugoslavia shall be filled in the following manner: seven seats for African countries, six seats for Asian countries and six seats for Latin American countries, it being understood that agreement has been reached among the developing countries to accommodate Yugoslavia;

(b) Of the seventeen seats allocated to the economically more developed countries, fourteen shall be filled by Western European and other countries and three by Eastern European countries;

(c) Elections to these thirty-six seats shall be for a term of three years provided, however, that of the members elected at the first election the terms of twelve members shall expire at the end of the year and the terms of twelve other members at the end of two years.

2. The thirty-seventh seat shall rotate among the groups of countries mentioned in paragraph 1 above in accordance with the following nine-year cycle:

First and second years: Western European and other countries;

Third, fourth and fifth years: Eastern European countries;

Sixth year: African countries;

Seventh year: Asian countries;

Eighth year: Latin American countries;

Ninth year: Western European and other countries.

3. Retiring members shall be eligible for re-election.

*Memorandum from President Johnson to Heads of Departments and Agencies on U.S. Participation in International Organizations and Programs**

March 15, 1966

I have today sent the attached memorandum directing the Secretary of State to take certain actions which I believe are essential to effective participation by the United States in international organizations.

I expect the heads of all departments and agencies that contribute to the Government's activities in this field to give their full cooperation to the Secretary of State in carrying out my instructions.

This work must receive high priority and the personal attention of the responsible officials in all agencies concerned if this Nation's interest in improving international organizations as instruments for peace and progress is to be fulfilled.

*U.S. Participation in the U.N., Report by the President for the Year 1966, Appendix IV, pp. 67-68.

MEMORANDUM

The Federal budget for 1967 contains this statement:

> we intend to play an increasingly active role in reviewing the program and budgetary proposals of the various international organizations.

The purpose of this memorandum is to set forth what I believe that increasingly active role should be.

No nation has been a greater supporter of the United Nations, its specialized agencies, and other international organizations than the United States. We are today a member of some 65 such agencies.

Our continued strong support is necessary and desirable —

> If the world community is to live in peace;
> If we are to cooperate internationally in extending the benefits of modern agriculture, health, and education to the less fortunate; and
> If international problems in such fields as meteorology, telecommunications, and aviation are to be given the joint attention required for their resolution.

The United States has by far been the largest financial contributor to the international organizations.

> Since 1946, we have provided a total of $3.6 billion in direct contributions.
> Since 1956, our annual contributions have grown from $100 million to an estimated $237 million for the next fiscal year, an overall increase of 137 percent.

Moreover, we can expect the programs and budgets of these international agencies to expand further in future years to meet the growing needs of the world community. The United States shall continue to meet its fair share of the financial requirements of these organizations.

If we are to be a constructive influence in helping to strengthen the international agencies so they can meet essential new needs, we must apply to them the same rigorous standards of program performance and budget review that we do to our own Federal programs. Our purpose in this undertaking must be to see that —

> Future expansion of the activities of the international organizations is governed by the tests of feasibility and reasonableness;
> The programs of the organizations are vigorously scrutinized so that funds are allocated only to high priority projects which we are convinced are in the interests of the international community and of our own country; and
> Each international agency operates with a maximum of effectiveness and economy.

To achieve this purpose, we must —

> Decide what we can best accomplish through multilateral action, as compared to action through our own direct programs;
> Clarify the objectives of our membership in each international agency;
> Organize ourselves for more effective participation in each organization; and
> Insist that the money we spend through international agencies is in our national interest and in the best interest of the world community.

I expect you to continue to direct and coordinate the activities of the U.S. departments and agencies involved in international organization affairs and to instruct our representatives to those organizations. I shall look to you to direct this Government's work in—

Reviewing and establishing our long-term policy objectives in each major international organization;

Analyzing and determining the U.S. position on programs and budgetary needs of each organization on a timely and continuing basis; and

Recommending steps to improve the effectiveness of each organization in contributing to the objectives of the world community and the United States.

Ambassador Goldberg has unique responsibilities in a wide range of matters relating to the United Nations system. I shall continue to rely heavily on his advice and counsel.

The heads of other Federal departments and agencies have significant interest in activities of the various international organizations. I expect them to provide you with expert assistance in their specialized fields. In this work, the close cooperation of all agencies is needed to provide the essential unity of our effort.

I expect the Director of the Bureau of the Budget to work with you and other agency heads to help assure that the positions we take on the budgets of international organizations reflect a searching scrutiny of requirements and priorities for the expenditure of funds.

I am sending copies of this memorandum to all department and agency heads.

SOUTHERN RHODESIA

*General Assembly Resolution 2765 (XXVI) on the Question of Southern Rhodesia**

November 16, 1971

The General Assembly,

Having considered the question of Southern Rhodesia,

Recalling its resolution 1514 (XV) of 14 December 1960, containing the Declaration on the Granting of Independence to Colonial Countries and Peoples, and resolution 2621 (XXV) of 12 October 1970, containing the programme of action for the full implementation of the Declaration,

Recalling also the relevant resolutions of the Security Council, particularly its resolutions 232 (1966) of 16 December 1966, 253 (1968) of 29 May 1968, 277 (1970) of 18 March 1970 and 288 (1970) of 17 November 1970,

Recalling further all previous resolutions concerning the question of Southern Rhodesia adopted by the General Assembly and the Special Committee on the Situation with regard to the Implementation of the Declaration on the Granting of Independence to Colonial Countries and Peoples, and also the consensus adopted by the Special Committee at its 828th meeting, on 6 October 1971,

Expressing its grave concern at the recent decision taken by the Congress of the United States of America which, if confirmed, would permit the importation of chrome into the United States from Southern Rhodesia and thus would constitute a serious violation of the above-mentioned Security Council resolutions imposing sanctions against the illegal régime in Southern Rhodesia,

1. Calls upon the Government of the United States of America to take the necessary measures, in compliance with the relevant provisions of Security Council resolutions 253 (1968), 277 (1970) and 288 (1970), and bearing in mind its obligations under Article 25 of the Charter of the United Nations, to prevent the importation of chrome into the United States from Southern Rhodesia;

2. Requests the Government of the United States to inform the General Assembly at its current session of the action taken or envisaged in the implementation of the present resolution;

3. Requests the President of the General Assembly to draw the attention of the Government of the United States to the urgent need for the implementation of the present resolution;

4. Reminds all Member States of their obligations under the Charter to comply fully with the decisions of the Security Council on mandatory sanctions against the illegal régime in Southern Rhodesia;

5. Decides to keep this and other aspects of the question under continuous review.

*U.N. General Assembly, 26th sess., agenda item 68, A/Res/2765 (XXVI), Nov. 17, 1971.

THE CONSTITUTIONAL STRUGGLE

THE CONSTITUTIONAL STRUGGLE

Commentary

Subtly or bluntly—sometimes dramatically and brutally—the member states of the United Nations worked over the years to adapt the organization to their notion of the needs of the times. Under their prodding and under the pressure of events the U.N. underwent changes in the decades that followed the signing of the Charter.

Performance varied and the U.N. experimented with new organs and functions as its response to emergencies met the circumstances of the moment. Power shifted from the Security Council to the General Assembly to the Secretary General and back to the Council. The enlargement in membership, which created a majority of economically— and often socially and politically—undeveloped states, altered the climate of the organization's work and pushed it in new directions. But structurally the organization hardly changed.

The General Conference of the Members for the purpose of reviewing the Charter, as stipulated in Article 109, was never held. The only charter amendment adopted in the first quarter century enlarged the Security Council from eleven to fifteen and its voting majority from seven to nine, while the Economic and Social Council was increased in size from eighteen to twenty-seven. The process of defining exactly what the organization was and what it was meant to do—a process carried on in the United States through amendments to the Constitution—was pursued politically from day to day and from one crisis to another. The *ad hoc* solutions never became binding precedents because they never answered fundamental questions. Was the United Nations to be more than the sum of its parts, "it" rather than "they"? What kind and how much collective sovereignty was it to exercise? And, in one of the most pressing specific questions, how was it to function—if at all—in the broad gap which the Charter had left between Chapter VI, Pacific Settlement of Disputes, and Chapter VII, Action with Respect to Threats of the Peace, Breaches of the Peace, and Acts of Aggression? This was a legal vacuum left by the drafters of the Charter. The years after World War II filled it with turmoil and often required U.N. intervention to keep the peace. But the U.N.'s peacekeeping ability had always to be improvised. It was never legally defined and remained the object of a constitutional struggle.

The principal organs of the United Nations had barely been formed when the Soviet use of the veto power again roused all the misgivings which smaller countries had expressed at the San Francisco Conference. Then they had been forced to accept the Big Power veto as the price of having a U.N. Now it seemed to threaten the efficacy which made the U.N. worth having. Appeals and a formal Assembly resolution asking the big powers to limit its use had no effect. At a later time, shortly before the U.N.'s seventeenth birthday, on the occasion of the 100th Soviet veto, Adlai Stevenson bitterly summed up the United States view of the damage done.

One immediate consequence of the veto policy was a shift in the center of gravity from the Security Council to the General Assembly. In 1947, Britain took its responsibility for Palestine to the Assembly and in 1950 the Uniting for Peace Resolution made the Assembly the legal alternative when the Council was paralyzed by the veto. The natural vehicle of the common will was always the Secretary General. The Charter's Article 43, tailored to the Council, was a dead letter; while no provision of any kind was made for Assembly action. Inevitably the Secretary General, as the U.N.'s chief executive officer, played a major role.

Trygve Lie, the first to hold that office, was an activist. At the beginning of his term, his interventions in the Iranian case were more acceptable to the Soviet Union than to the United States. But in the Korea crisis it was the other way around, and the Soviet Union set out systematically to destroy him politically. The United States supported the stopgap—an Assembly vote—which continued him in office when the Soviet Union vetoed his renomination in the Security Council. (The U.S., incidentally, threatened on this occasion for the first time—as it did once again 10 years later on a related question—to use its veto against any other candidate.) Trygve Lie resigned his office two years later, demonstrating the impossibility of the Secretary General's position in the teeth of a social and political boycott by one of the big powers.

Control of the Secretariat machinery was another aspect of the struggle—whether defensive or offensive. Polarized, as all big issues became, it might be stated in terms of the Soviet Union trying to prevent the Secretariat from cutting across Soviet interests and the United States trying to prevent the Soviet Union from obtaining an administrative veto through undue influence in the Secretariat. Some friction arose over key posts. The Soviet preference for short term contract personnel on the professional staff made formation of a truly independent international civil service more difficult and contributed to the strain. But one of the most serious attacks on the structure of the Secretariat took place during an inglorious episode in American history: the hysteria stirred up by the frantically anti-Communist Senator Joseph McCarthy.

Secretary General Lie resigned after this onslaught. His successor, Dag Hammarskjold spent quiet years patching things up. He was successful to the point where the slogan was coined, "let Dag do it." Having improvised the U.N. Emergency Force after the Suez crisis of 1956, the Security Council and the General Assembly entrusted him with the conduct of the greatest U.N. peacekeeping operation ever in the Congo. But this achievement, which blocked Soviet ambitions in Africa, exposed him to the same furious reprisal that had brought down Trygve Lie. Soviet Prime Minister Nikita Khrushchev demonstrated at the famous 15th General Assembly that his government would never again permit either the Secretary General or the Assembly to guide, let alone initiate, U.N. peacekeeping operations.

Dag Hammarskjold's death in the plane crash in September, 1961 gave the Soviet Union the opportunity to state its argument in constitutional terms. Playing the role of the champion of the undeveloped new nations which had just come to arithmetical and political prominence in the U.N., the Soviet Union proposed that Hammarskjold's post be filled not by one man, but by three—a Troika, in the Russian expression—representing the West, the East and the nominally nonaligned Third World. The United States, together with others, fought this suggestion tooth and nail. Washington again threatened to use the veto against it. Faced with American determination and with the flagrant absurdity of the Troika proposal, the large majority of the membership supported the nomination of U Thant of Burma. The integrity of his office remained unimpaired, but it was clear to all that the climate in which it functioned had permanently changed. The Security Council, with its principle of Big Five unanimity, and the veto to back it up, again became the center of power.

When Kurt Waldheim of Austria succeeded U Thant on January 1, 1972, he faced the old problem of asserting the collective ethos of the U.N. Charter against the individual interests of the member states. These were expressed in political and financial terms.

One problem both pressing and enormous was the chronic shortage of money resulting from the refusal of the Soviet bloc and France to pay for major U.N. peacekeeping operations. In today's world, the amounts were negligible. The contentious issue was the U.N.'s capacity to act. The events of 1964 and 1965 were loosely called the financial crisis—and, indeed, the U.N. was in serious difficulty. Burdened with enormous outlays for the United Nations Emergency Force in the Middle East and for the U.N. Congo Operation which, for a long period, ran higher than the U.N.'s total budget, the General Assembly resorted to an expedient of U.S. devising. It authorized a United Nations bond issue, which ultimately raised about $170 million dollars, having ascertained from the International Court of Justice that the cost of UNEF and ONUC was an "expense of the organization" which the General Assembly might legally apportion. Even with this massive infusion, of which the United States paid 45 percent, the U.N. remained deeply in the red. To be sure, while the words bankruptcy and insolvency were frequently used, the United Nations was not literally in such danger. No bailiff could evict it. There was no court to freeze its assets for its creditors—who were its own member states. The real nature of the financial crisis was political. It was simply fought out in monetary and legal terms.

The issue came to a head in 1964, when the Soviet Union's refusal to countenance peacekeeping activities of which it disapproved, even to the extent of paying for its share of duly assessed costs, raised the question of applying the Charter's Article 19. The Soviet Union stood firm, withholding its payments not only for UNEF and ONUC but also for UNTSO, the U.N. Commission for the Unification and Rehabilitation of Korea, the U.N. Field Service and the U.N. Cemetery in Korea. The United States insisted on the sanctity of charter obligations. The 19th General Assembly, already delayed with an eye to the U.S. presidential election, was postponed further until December. When it finally convened, it did so only on the understanding that there would be no voting—since the United States would not budge from its view that the Soviet Union had forfeited its right to vote in the General Assembly, while the Soviet Union passed the word around that if it were "illegally" punished by having its vote withdrawn, the United Nations would sign its own death warrant. Since the issue ultimately had to be resolved by an Assembly vote, there was a great deal of lobbying and nose counting.

Many countries of Asia and Africa saw the crisis as lethal pedantry. To them the United Nations was important for three main reasons: it served as a clearing house for a growing volume of economic aid; it provided them, as small or weak members, with a platform of equality in world affairs that would not have existed had there been no U.N.; and it served to focus and to translate into action the one impulse that united them all—their overpowering hatred of "colonialism." They considered the economic imbalance between the industrialized Northern and the undeveloped Southern hemispheres of the earth more important than the protracted conflict between East and

West. They saw no relevance to their own welfare in the Article 19 issue. They could or would not accept the United States argument that the weak benefit most from the preservation of law.

Had the U.S. Mission to the U.N. pressed its point to a showdown vote, it might have won the decisive procedural majority. Whether the Soviet Union would then have carried out its threat to break up the organization is at least doubtful. Even had it lost the vote, the United States would have preserved the principle and drawn the lines with a clarity that so crucial an issue deserved. But the U.S. representatives, uncertain of delegate support, had no stomach for this confrontation. An offer by the Soviet Union to make a voluntary contribution toward relieving the U.N.'s very serious fiscal difficulties was seized upon by many as a face-saving way out of the dilemma. They rebuked the United States for having raised the issue in order, they said, to humiliate its adversary in the Cold War. The United States backed away, taking refuge in "consultations." It lost its point and gained no money. The Soviet Union never made its voluntary contribution. In Summer, 1965 the Article 19 issue was set aside, with the likelihood of arising again. The United Nations continued in a state of genteel poverty.

The Soviet Union, supported by Charles DeGaulle's France, had rammed home its interpretation of the Charter that no nation need pay for a U.N. peacekeeping operation of which it did not approve; or, the converse, that any member desiring such action and obtaining the necessary authorization would have to pay for it. The U.N. Force in Cyprus, UNFICYP, was financed precisely that way.

Left open was the ultimate question of how a peacekeeping enterprise was to be authorized against the wishes of one of the permanent members of the Security Council. The Soviet Union had stated its views on July 10, 1964 in these words, "Under the Charter, the only body authorized to take action in the maintenance or restoration of international peace and security is the Security Council. It is likewise within the purview of the Security Council to adopt decisions in all matters relating to the establishment of United Nations armed forces, the definition of their duties, their composition and strength, the direction of their operations, the structure of their command and the duration of their stay in the area of operation, and also matters of financing. No other United Nations body, including the General Assembly, has the right under the Charter to decide these matters." This meant a monopoly of the Council, with its great power veto, not only in mounting an operation but at every step of its work along the way. The Soviet intention was, clearly, not only to forestall a new Congo or Korea venture but also to stifle it should it, by miscalculation, have come into being, or, having been authorized, become undesirable for any reason. Giving the Security Council operational control was very much in keeping with the Soviet view of the Secretary General as the chief administrative rather than executive officer of the United Nations.

The United States differed fundamentally from this approach, as Ambassador Arthur Goldberg pointed out in some detail in November, 1965. However, the difference remained unsolved.

There was little question, as the U.N. completed a quarter century of existence, that American confidence in its political efficacy and respect for its constitutional probity were severely eroded. More frequently, U.S. representatives felt called upon to bemoan the application of a double standard benefitting the anticolonial activists and the Soviet bloc with which they were frequently aligned. It found expression even in procedure, the neutral connective tissue of any serious working body. But it was especially apparent in political questions.

The disparate performance of the U.N. in Suez and in Hungary in 1956 might have been rationalized in complex terms of law and fact. No such justification was possible in one of the few cases after the Second World War which unequivocally called for collective security against aggression. This was the policy of "confrontation," an open declaration of war by Sukarno's Indonesia against the Republic of Malaysia. A Security Council resolution deploring repeated incidents, specifically an attack by Indonesian paratroopers, and stressing the Charter principles of territorial integrity and peaceful settlement was vetoed by the Soviet Union. When Malaysia was then elected a member of the Security Council, as of January 1, 1965, Indonesia withdrew from the United Nations and joined Communist China in making broad hints at the establishment of a rival "progressive" organization not dominated by "colonialists." When Sukarno was overthrown, later that year, Indonesia quietly made its way back to the U.N.

Another bitter disappointment, and one which came much closer to home, was the United States' failure to enlist the United Nations in ending the Vietnam War. The conflict in Southeast Asia had been brought to the United Nations in one or another aspect several times. Thailand asked for the protection of the U.N. Peace Observation Commission against pressure from the Viet Minh in 1954. That request was vetoed by the Soviet Union. In 1959, Laos asked for U.N. help against North Vietnamese aggression and the Security Council infuriated the Soviet Union by creating a subcommittee through a procedural vote and sending it to investigate. In 1961, in his speech to the General Assembly, President Kennedy called attention to the dangerous condition of the region and especially of Laos. In 1963, the General Assembly dispatched a fact-finding mission to South Vietnam to look into alleged violation of human rights in the government's treatment of the Buddhist community. In 1964, a Security Council Commission of inquiry checked Cambodian complaints of aggression by U.S. and South Vietnamese armed forces. The Tonkin Gulf incident later that year, and its aftermath, brought massive U.S. intervention in Vietnam, and President Lyndon Johnson used a visit to San Francisco on the 20th Anniversary of the United Nations to appeal for the U.N.'s help in moving the conflict to the conference table. Ambassador Arthur Goldberg subsequently tried to set the machinery of the Security Council in motion toward this end; but neither his efforts nor the prodding of the Senate had any effect.

The competition over the nature of the U.N. in its first decades had a strong streak of paradox. One aspect, in which the United States was deeply interested was the seating of Communist China, the Peoples Republic of China. From 1951-1960, the U.S. delegation rallied enough support to keep the item off the Assembly's agenda. When that tactic appeared inadequate, with the influx of Asian and African members which wanted at least to debate it, the United States developed a stand which withstood the pressure of Peking's partisans year after year. To be sure, that pressure lost some of its steam after Communist China's invasion of India in 1962 and the development of the historic rift between Peking and Moscow.

In 1971, tactics of all kinds were submerged by the universal judgment that Peking and not the Nationalist Republic of China on Taiwan truly represented China. By then, the Peoples Republic had emerged from the convulsions of its Cultural Revolution which totally preoccupied it in the middle 1960's. Also, engaged in an ideological and conventional power struggle with the Soviet Union, it may well have decided that isolation made it more vulnerable to Soviet pressure. As the decade ended, Peking moved to normalize its relations with the outside world and found general response.

In the United States, a long process of exploration was suddenly quickened when Peking welcomed an American ping pong team and agreed to a visit by President Nixon. This, however, posed a problem. The administration, which sought better relations with Peking, could no longer oppose its presence in the United Nations. Washington tried to resolve the dilemma by giving Peking China's seat in the Security Council while having both the Peoples Republic of China and the Republic of China present in the General Assembly. To no one's surprise, this inherently contradictory expedient was rejected. Peking refused to accept it and so did the majority of the members—many of which quickly established or re-established diplomatic ties with the Peoples Republic. The General Assembly resolution which seated Peking as China in all the organs of the U.N. simultaneously expelled Taiwan—an act seen as a transfer of credentials and not subject to the veto of the Security Council, as either new membership or formal expulsion of a member would have been.

Paradox was even more clearly apparent in the peacekeeping field. The United States, generally supporting the principle of an active United Nations, quickly answered Lebanon's call for help in 1958 despite the presence of a U.N. observer group there and Dag Hammarskjold's chagrin at unilateral intervention. Washington always preferred to let the Organization of American States deal with emergencies in the Western Hemisphere, but would have welcomed a way to bring the U.N.'s stabilizing influence into Vietnam. And the United States, while working to preserve—or establish—the Assembly's power to recommend peacekeeping operations when the Security Council failed, had its grave doubts that the Afro-Asian majority would always act responsibly. American officials wistfully cited the fact that a two-thirds majority in the General Assembly could represent about ten percent of the world's population, five percent of its gross national product and less than five percent of the U.N. budget.

The Soviet Union, for its part, while opposing Security Council intervention in Southeast Asia urgently demanded it in the Dominican Republic. Its objection to the role played there by the Organization of American States, as a regional organization, did not apply to action by the Arab League against Israel or by the Organization of African Unity against the Portuguese territories and South Africa. Furthermore, although Moscow repudiated the Uniting for Peace formula, it supported the procedure in the Suez crisis and invoked the principle for the Fifth Emergency Special Session on the Middle East in 1967. In diplomacy, as in most other human affairs, much depends on whose ox is gored.

Making due allowance for this, the United States attitude toward the United Nations twenty-five years after the happy signing of the Charter reflected the resentful disappointment which marks the end of a cherished dream. The change in composition, with the consequent shift in values; the failure to act in Vietnam and the traumatic episode of the Article 19 crisis seemed to dissuade Washington from placing much reliance in the U.N. as a political instrument. The United States appeared to acquiesce in the view of the United Nations as little more than a conference forum and diplomatic clearing house for its sovereign members. The U.N.'s inability to act more than peripherally, if at all, in such great emergencies as the Berlin blockade and the Berlin Wall, the Sino-Indian crisis of 1962, the Cuban missile crisis, the Nigerian civil war, the Soviet invasion of Czechoslovakia and the India-Pakistan war of 1971 appeared to be a more reliable index of its practical worth than those instances in which it had managed to help keep the peace. A shift was noted to bilateral diplomacy even in the Middle East, in which the U.N. had been directly and intimately concerned from the beginning.

Skeptics were reminded of an old joke that the world lived in the past, present and future, the United Nations in the subjunctive. But in a world of change, whether the U.N. was settling into a role that had been its real one from the start, or whether it was evolving a new one to fit the times and might still rise to the high expectations which attended its birth, it was still functioning. And even skeptics agreed that if it did not exist it would have to be invented.

THE SECURITY COUNCIL

*Speech by Ambassador Stevenson to the Security Council on the 100th Soviet Veto**

June 22, 1962

[On June 22, 1962, the Soviet Union cast its one hundredth veto in the Security Council. Under the terms of the Charter, a negative vote by any one of the five permanent members—the United States, the U.S.S.R., the United Kingdom, France, the Republic of China—is sufficient to kill a proposal. The issue before the Security Council on this occasion involved the India-Pakistan dispute over Kashmir, and the veto prevented the Security Council from urging the governments of India and Pakistan to enter into negotiations and to refrain from actions or statements that would aggravate the situation. In his statement after the vote, Governor Stevenson gave a history of the veto—never resorted to by the United States—and how the Soviet Union has used it.]

I hope the members of the Security Council will not object and will indulge me while I make a few remarks on this historic day in the Security Council. It is a day that should not pass without notice. A permanent member of the Security Council has just cast its one hundredth veto.

From the beginning of the United Nations, one of its special characteristics has been the voting procedure in the Security Council. We all recall the serious deliberations which took place at San Francisco concerning the nature and the import for the future of the veto right for the permanent members of the Security Council. That right was given to them primarily because it would be their military and economic power which would have to be used to sustain and enforce Security Council decisions directly affecting vital world interests.

Representatives of small and middle-sized states emphasized their anxiety that the veto might be used to paralyze the Security Council. In order to meet such fears, the four sponsoring members of the conference set forth their conception at that time of the unanimity rule, with which the delegation of France also associated itself.

The big powers, including the Soviet Union, specifically stated, "It is not to be assumed ... that the permanent members, any more than the non-permanent members, would use their veto willfully to obstruct the operation of the Council."

That was the way we started, Mr. President, at San Francisco seventeen years ago, this very week, I believe. What has happened since? Before the first year was out the Soviet Union had cast nine vetoes. The Soviet member of the Council has today cast its one hundredth veto. For seventeen years the U.S.S.R. on occasion after occasion has sought to obstruct the operations of the Council, sometimes where Soviet plans and prestige were directly and clearly involved and at other times when the continuation of friction might contribute to Soviet objectives.

The Soviet Union has used the veto lavishly to prevent states from assuming their rightful place in the United Nations. In fact, fifty-one of these vetoes were cast on applications for membership in the United Nations.

Ireland, a member of this Council, was denied membership for nine years. So were Jordan and Portugal. Austria, Finland, and Italy were kept out for eight years. Ceylon was kept out for seven years, Nepal for six years. Mauritania was vetoed in 1960, and Kuwait in 1961. Korea is still not a member.

*U.S. Mission to the United Nations, Press Release 4015, June 22, 1962.

The veto has been used to tie the admission of clearly qualified states for which there was widespread support to the admission of states and regimes about whose qualifications for membership there were grave doubts. This, despite the fact that the tying of the admission of one applicant to that of another has been specifically held by the International Court of Justice to be contrary to the Charter.

The Soviet delegate used the veto thirteen times to assist Soviet bloc activities against the territorial integrity and political independence of other states. When the Soviet subverted Czechoslovakia in 1948, the Soviet delegate vetoed Security Council moves to investigate the case. When Communist-supported guerrillas tried to overturn the independence of Greece in 1946 and 1947, the Soviet again vetoed a Security Council resolution. And when Thailand asked the Security Council to act against attempted infiltration from Indochina in 1954, the Soviet again vetoed.

After realizing its mistake in boycotting the Council during the North Korean aggression against the Republic of Korea in 1950, I remind the members of the Council that the Soviet Union finally returned in August and immediately began to veto Security Council decisions designed to uphold the independence of that country. Fortunately for the Korean people and for this organization, that effort failed because we were able to proceed through the General Assembly.

Similarly, in 1956, the United Nations was forced to move in the General Assembly to condemn Soviet intervention in Hungary after the Soviet Union supported its aggression against the Hungarian people by invocation of the veto.

And, most recently, in 1960, the Soviet Union vetoed a resolution on the Congo sponsored by Ceylon and Tunisia because the resolution was designed in part to resist Soviet efforts to intervene in the Congo despite the fact that the United Nations peace-keeping operation was already in action. Again an emergency session of the General Assembly was required before the United Nations could do what was necessary.

There are still more areas in which the veto has been used to obstruct the operation of the Council. On at least four occasions, with the use of six vetoes, the Soviet Union refused, after using the Security Council to air its charges, to let its own assertions be examined.

I invite your attention to 1950; when the Soviet Union charged the United States Air Force with the bombing of Communist-held areas of China it vetoed a commission of investigation.

In 1952, the Soviet representative climaxed one of the most shameless falsehoods in history—the long crescendo of accusations that the United States and the United Nations troops were employing germ warfare in Korea—by bringing the issue before the Security Council, and then promptly vetoing a proposal for an impartial investigation.

In 1958, when the Soviet Union purpoted to be concerned about United States flights over the Arctic Circle, the United States proposed an Arctic Inspection Zone. That, too, was vetoed. In 1960, when Soviet fighter planes destroyed a United States RB-47 airplane over international waters, the Soviet Union vetoed two separate proposals for investigations, one of them asking only that the International Red Cross be permitted to assist any surviving member of the plane.

In each of these cases the Security Council tried to exercise its proper peacekeeping function through systematic investigations. In each case, after having brought the charge, the Soviets vetoed the attempt at a remedy.

One of the most disturbing facts also revealed in the history of a hundred vetoes is the consistent effort to prevent the Security Council from developing processes of peaceful settlement. Not only do many of the vetoes I have referred to fall into this category, but most of the remaining ones were also cast against efforts to promote peaceful settlements: four times with respect to Spain in 1946; once against a resolution on troop withdrawals from Syria and Lebanon in 1946, not because the resolution was wrong, but because it was not extreme enough; twice in connection with problems arising at the time of Indonesian independence; once against the Security Council recommendations for a solution of the Berlin blockade in 1948; once on Goa; twice to prevent extension of United Nations peace-keeping functions in Lebanon in 1958, and five times since 1960 in the Security Council's consideration of the Congo. The U.S.S.R. also vetoed four resolutions in the field of disarmament.

Distortion of the veto power has been a fact of life in this Council. It is the fact that led to the Uniting for Peace procedure, which added to the United Nations peace-keeping machinery a flexible means whereby members can make sure that the United Nations' primary function of preserving the peace will be carried out.

The veto does exist, within its proper context, as a recognition of political reality, but it is a privilege to be used not abused. And abused it has been, for the Soviet Union has willfully obstructed the operation of this Council over and over. It has violated that part of the Four Power Declaration at San Francisco, in which the powers agreed not to use their veto willfully to obstruct the operation of this Council.

Now, so much for yesterday and for today. What of the future? The Council is a vital and purposeful organ of the United Nations in spite of the veto. It provides vital and purposeful direction and leadership. And in areas of its work where the veto does not apply, we believe the Council might well widen its activities and increasingly provide that direction and that leadership to our affairs.

As for the veto itself, we hope that long before the Soviet Union approaches its two hundredth veto, it will realize that its own interests lie not in national obstruction, but in international cooperation, not in willful vetoes for narrow ends, but in willing assents for the broad and common good for which the United Nations stands.

THE SECRETARIAT

Trygve Lie on Communist Issues in the Secretariat *

1954

*   *   *

Then came the Korean War, which added much new emotional fuel to the fires that had been kindled. A million young Americans were taken from their homes to fight in that war. The casualty lists mounted and mounted to make it the third most costly war in American history, next to the Civil War and the Second World War. Such an experience cuts deep. And Americans rarely thought of the war, in the terms of the United Nations resolutions, as a collective international action to repel armed aggression by "the North Korean authorities" and the "so-called Volunteers from the People's Republic of China." It was, quite simply, a war against Communists. They thought of the enemy, killing and wounding more than 130,000 Americans, as Communist far more than as North Koreans and Chinese. The emotions thus aroused were an irresistible temptation to men who did not hesitate to exploit sorrow, hate, and fear in order to advance themselves; and such as these were in full cry in the summer and fall of 1952 when the United Nations Secretariat became involved in a situation that was beyond the control of reasonable and responsible men.

Before this, I had had a few isolated encounters with "red hunters" in America and "capitalist-hunters" from behind the Iron Curtain. As far back as 1947 a brief flurry stirred by rumors reflecting on the objectivity of some members of the Secretariat I had assigned to the staff of the Balkan Commission, which the Security Council dispatched to Greece to investigate border incidents with Greece's Communist neighbors. No government submitted an official complaint or supporting facts, though the rumors appeared to be promoted by Greek sources which were not disinterested. The climax came with the allegation in the column of a leading American journalist that a Pole on the Commission's staff had been caught trying to steal into the room of the British member of the Commission. I was consequently accused of attempting to undermine President Truman's program of aid to Greece and Turkey, or at least of having "packed" the Commission's staff in the Communists' favor. That the allegation and others that followed were altogether false did not silence my critics. I sent William H. Stoneman to Europe to investigate the work of the staff of the Commission, which was under the direction of a Norwegian, Colonel Roscher Lund. He found that, while some of the staff might have been more tactful toward Greek authorities, the sinister chargers against them were nonsense.

Soon afterward, I was belabored from the other side. Mr. Gromyko came to protest against the White Russians—émigrés and children of émigrés—who were employed in the Secretariat as interpreters, translators, and document officers. He submitted no facts which indicated that these people had done anything amiss, and so I declined to discharge them. The next year, the coup in Czechoslovakia brought a similar experience when Vladimir Houdek, representing the new Communist regime, demanded that

*Trygve Lie, *In the Cause of Peace*, (New York, 1954) pp. 393-402.

I dismiss all Czechs and Slovaks in the Secretariat who were regarded with disfavor in Prague, and handed me a list of names. Responding that this was not his government's affair, I refused to consider such action. He pursued the conversation with a letter, to which I replied in the same vein, and that was the last I heard of that.

In 1948 two junior security officials of the State Department charged in widely publicized testimony before a Senate Judiciary subcommittee that "hundreds" of foreign agents were using United Nations employment or accreditation to the delegations as a cover for subversive activities. Secretary of State Marshall responded that the United States did not have knowledge of a single individual associated with the United Nations who was engaged in activity against American security. A year later, again before a Senate Judiciary subcommittee, an unidentified witness, called "Witness Number 8," alleged that the Secretariat was under Communist domination, and that I myself was a Communist tool—among other things, that Commander Jackson's post had been abolished because he had stood up to my alleged pro-Communist doings. I was in Europe at the time, and Byron Price, as Acting Secretary-General, protested the "unfounded and irresponsible" attacks. But, though the relevant authorities of the United States government publicly affirmed their confidence in me, it is doubtful that the repudiation ever caught up with the charge—as is so frequently the case.

All these were mere skirmishes in comparison to what happened next. A federal grand jury, impaneled to investigate Communist activities in the New York area, turned to the American staff of the United Nations Secretariat. Such a jury is supposed to conduct its inquiries in complete secrecy; but there came a succession of "leaks" to the press, especially to newspapers which had consistently attacked the United Nations, with the general purport that the Secretariat was full of subversives who were endangering American security. Soon statements began to come out of certain Congressional committee offices in Washington that the United Nations harbored "a nest of Communist spies" and an immediate housecleaning was demanded. Meanwhile, hearsay reports reached me that some United States members of the Secretariat were refusing to answer questions before the grand jury about Communist affiliations and possible subversive activities, invoking for that purpose the Fifth Amendment to the United States Constitution, which provides, "nor shall any person . . . be compelled in any criminal case to be a witness against himself."

If the distorted and exaggerated stories from New York and Washington had disturbed me in one direction, the reports of United Nations Fifth Amendment cases disturbed me in another. United Nations immunity extended only to acts of Secretariat members in their official capacity. It did not extend to their outside activities or private lives. I felt strongly that a United Nations official should cooperate fully with investigations conducted by an official agency of his own government, at least in those countries where Western democratic traditions protected him from the exercise of arbitrary power. After becoming Secretary-General I had myself returned to Norway in 1946 to answer fully to exhaustive questioning during a parliamentary inquiry into the conduct of the Norwegian government in London during the war. Furthermore by virtue of the very fact that a United Nations official was an international civil servant, special obligations were imposed upon him to conduct himself vis-á-vis the Member governments at all times in a manner above just reproach. This latter opinion was fully shared by the General Assembly when it adopted Article 1.4 of the Staff Regulations, which read:

> Members of the Secretariat shall conduct themselves at all times in a manner of befitting their status as international civil servants. They shall not engage in any activity that is incompatible with the proper discharge of their duties with the United Nations. They shall avoid any action and in particular any kind of public pronouncement which may adversely reflect on their status. While they are not expected to give up their national sentiments or their political and religious convictions, they shall at all times bear in mind the reserve and tact incumbent upon them by reason of their international status.

I believed that to plead a privilege against self-incrimination, though it was a constitutional right, would be clearly in violation of Article 1.4, except in extraordinary circumstances. This was not the only constitutional right that United Nations officials had to waive in becoming international civil servants. Under the staff rules that implemented the Regulations they could not, for instance, campaign for political office or take public part in partisan political campaigns.

For these reasons I immediately sought official information on the grand-jury proceedings upon which I might base further action. This was denied to me on the ground that grand-jury proceedings were secret, although the vague leaks to favored newspaper and radio columnists continued.

Then, in October, 1952, the Internal Security Subcommittee of the United States Senate Judiciary Committee moved to New York and held a series of public hearings. In these a total of eighteen United Nations staff members pleaded the Fifth Amendment. As I read the transcript of the testimony in each case I was more and more convinced that these staff members had gravely and irresponsibly transgressed the Staff Regulations. Furthermore, I knew that the exercise of the constitutional privilege under American law does not imply any similar constitutional right to continued public employment by the one who exercises it. On the contrary, the practice for federal, state, and municipal employment alike in the United States is the opposite—the invocation of the privilege in such circumstances normally leads to dismissal. The United Nations, of course, was not bound to follow this or any other national legal practice. Its rules cannot incorporate those of any single state. But the precedent strengthened my confiction. Furthermore, the attitude of these witnesses tended under the circumstances to discredit the Secretariat as a whole, to cast suspicion on all the staff—and, still more serious, it imperiled the position of the Organization in the host country. The impression that the Secretariat harbored those subversive of American institutions was heightened by the practice of the Internal Security Subcommittee in generally calling only those staff members to testify in *open* session who earlier had refused in closed session to answer questions about Communist party membership, or who had admitted past membership. Although these witnesses were about one in a hundred of the Americans employed by the United Nations, the impression conveyed to the public was that of a parade of Americans working for the United Nations who were Communists, former Communists, or at least had something to hide.

The public outcry in the United States, whipped up by elements of the press which had never been friendly to the United Nations, grew to appalling proportions, while the morale of the Secretariat slumped badly. Mr. Feller and I had been following developments carefully—with Byron Price, we had carried the main load of the "subversive" issue—and we were seriously alarmed. On the one hand, the sweeping attacks upon the standing and integrity of the Secretariat were vicious and distorted and out of all proportion to the facts. On the other hand, there was no question in my mind that the cases involving the Fifth Amendment ought to go, as a matter of sound policy entirely divorced from the public hue and cry. They had not conducted themselves as international civil servants should. Those holding temporary contracts, I dismissed; but I was not certain that I had the legal right under the Staff Regulations to discharge those with permanent contracts. For the time being, therefore, I put them on compulsory leave. It occurred to Mr. Feller and me that a sound procedure would be to seek the advice of an international commission of eminent jurists as to what further action I could and should take. Discussing this idea with my advisers and the Assistant Secretaries-General and a number of the delegations, I met approval on all sides. The delegations, particularly, supported the proposal, even tough some of them later criticized me for acting on the basis of one of the commission's recommendations. In the meantime I was left virtually alone to deal with the American authorities and American public opinion as best I could. In the autumn of 1952 the other governments had litle disposition for getting involved in the defense of the good name of the Secretariat though in the next spring, after it was all over, certain delegations were not slow to suggest how things might have been done in a different way.

Deciding to appoint a commission was one thing; finding prominent jurists to take on such an assignment was another. It seemed to be necessary to have an American member, with an intimate knowledge of American law; we felt an English jurist would provide both the legal capacity and the detachment desirable; and, for a third, we sought a representative of a small power and a legal system other than the Anglo-Saxon. The Legal Department searched ceaselessly for a panel. Leading jurists of the United States, Great Britain, and Belgium were canvassed or suggested, either directly or through their governments. Men like Judge Learned Hand of the United States, Sir Hartley Shawcross of Great Britain, who had been Attorney General in the Labor Government, and Henri Rolin of Belgium, who was later to criticize the Jurists' Report with great severity, were among those we sought. Many of the most illustrious legal minds of the Western world declined the invitation for one reason or another, or the governments advised against our original proposals. Finally, we constituted a panel of three distinguished lawyers: Sir Edwin Herbert of the United Kingdom, a prominent solicitor; William D. Mitchell, who had been Attorney General of the United States under President Hoover; and Paul Veldekens, professor of civil law at the Catholic University of Louvain. It was part and parcel of the atmoshpere of Greek tragedy that pervaded the whole affair that I was later accused of "packing" the Commission of Jurists, whereas in fact my effort from beginning to end was to obtain for it men especially qualified to pass on the issues.

The Commission came together on November 14.

On the day before, the United Nations—and I personally—suffered an incalculable loss. I was at lunch in the Metropolitan Club as the guest of the Foreign Minister of Brazil, with Secretary of State Acheson, Ambassador Gross, and several other ranking delegates among those present, when an urgent summons came to go to the telephone. The call was from Andrew Cordier, with the news that Abe Feller had died in a jump from the window of his twelfth-floor apartment.

Shock and grief engulfed me. Abe Feller had been nearer to me than anyone else outside the circle of my immediate family. He had been a close adviser for seven years, and hardly a day passed at Headquarters when he did not come to see me—most days he would come several times. Whenever something was up, Abe was there, alert, discreet, full of energy and ideas. I had a deep admiration for his intelligence, and an affection for him which was strengthened by his own loyalty and personal regard.

No doubt Abe Feller was a victim of the witch hunt, of the awful pressure of the hysterical assault upon the United Nations that reactionaries were promoting and using for their own ends. He was a liberal in politics, and a conservative in his lawyerlike respect for due process. He knew that no American in the Secretariat had ever been indicted for espionage or any other subversive activity against his country. Although he felt as strongly as I that the United Nations officials who had pleaded the Fifth Amendment had betrayed their obligations and should be removed, he had a genuine sympathy for the victims of the headline-hunting investigations and resented deeply the "smear" against the whole of the Secretariat which was so assiduously advanced. Day after day, he followed the Senate hearings and saw the tragedy unfold. He saw the hysteria invade high places and sweep his country in violation of fundamental principles of fair play and orderly justice by which he had lived all his life. The strain finally grew too strong, and he broke.

At Abe Feller's funeral I was too much under the sway of emotion to speak; but eleven months later I had the honor of dedicating the Abraham Feller Memorial Room in the United Nations Library to the memory of a great and loyal international servant and a great and loyal American.

On November 29 the Commission of Jurists submitted its opinion. Like many legal interpretations, it was controversial. While disagreeing with it in some respects, I appreciated the devotion, good will, and high intelligence they had shown in carrying out so delicate a task.

The main conclusion of the jurists, which I accepted and upon which I acted, was that refusal by the American staff members on grounds of possible self-incrimination to answer questions about Communist party membership, or any subversive activity, constituted a fundamental breach of Article 1.4 of the Staff Regulations. This confirmed the view I later expressed in my report of January 30, 1953, to the General Assembly on Personnel Policy; "Especially in a time of serious political tension and concern over national security, the United Nations staff member has a positive obligation to refrain from conduct which will draw upon himself grave suspicion of being a danger to the security of a particular State. When he has refused to answer official interrogations relating to crimes involving subversive activities, he has by his own free choice violated that obligation; he has thereby contributed substantially to undermining the confidence which the international official is required to maintain."

The jurists found that I had the power to dismiss the nine staff members with permanent contracts who had used the Fifth Amendment in this manner and recommended that I do so. First, however, I decided to give them a second chance. After announcing to the whole staff my acceptance of the jurists' recommendation I notified the suspended staff members that I should have to dismiss them for a fundamental breach of the obligations laid down in Staff Regulation 1.4 unless, within three days, they informed me that they had notified the appropriate United States authorities of their intention to withdraw the plea of privilege and answer the pertinent questions put to them. This they all refused to do. The refusal created, in my opinion, a clear case for summary dismissal for serious misconduct under Article 10 of the Staff Regulations. I decided, however, to give them the normal indemnities and severance pay to which summary dismissal did not entitle them, in order to help them over the difficult time they faced in finding other employment, after all the publicity.

A few days after the Commission of Jurists had presented its report to me, the federal grand jury in New York, which had been seeking evidence of subversive activity by American members of the Secretariat, came to the end of its term. Had there been meaningful evidence of illegal subversive activity against any member of the Secretariat, it would have returned indictments in accordance with its duty. It did not return even one; but its "presentment" made a blanket and indiscriminate finding of "Guilty," charging that there was "infiltration into the United Nations of an overwhelmingly large group of disloyal United States citizens," and that this situation constituted "a menace" to the United States Government. The presentment not only named no names but gave no figures to support the words "an overwhelmingly large group of disloyal United States citizens." This strange use of the judicial process received wide publicity. My formal request for a copy of the records of the grand jury or, if these could not be supplied, an official statement of the specific evidence on which its conclusions might have been based was denied.

Senator McCarran, chairman of the Internal Security Subcommittee, soon introduced a bill "to prevent citizens of the United States of questionable loyalty to the United States Government from accepting any office or employment in or under the United Nations." It provided that any American citizen taking a position with the United Nations would first have to receive a security clearance from the Attorney General of the United States, and citizens who were already in the employ of the United Nations would have to obtain a similar clearance. "Whoever, being a citizen of the United States . . . shall willfully fail to comply . . . shall be fined not more than $10,000, or imprisoned for not more than five years."

To my dismay the only precedent I could discover for such a law was the edict promulgated by Fascist Italy in 1927 to prevent Italians opposed to Mussolini from being members of the League of Nations Secretariat. It too provided for governmental clearance, though the penalties for violation were less severe than those Senator McCarran found appropriate, being only a fine of not more than 5,000 lire and a prison term of not more than one year.

The executive branch of the United States government now moved rapidly into the breach. President Truman's executive order of January 9, two days after Senator McCarran introduced his bill, prescribed "procedures for making available to the Secretary-General of the United Nations certain information concerning United States citizens employed or being considered for employment on the Secretariat of the United Nations," including a full field investigation by the FBI of American members of, or candidates for, the Secretariat's internationally recruited staff, and a less extensive investigation by the Civil Service Commission of other Americans employed in the locally recruited lower echelons of the Secretariat. If a resultant report contained derogatory information the staff member had the right to hearings before United States loyalty review boards. After the investigations were completed, information "in such detail as security considerations permit" would be transmitted to the Secretary-General for use "in exercising the responsibility with respect to the integrity of the personnel employed by the United Nations imposed upon him by the Charter." The investigations, the hearings, if any, and the findings and evidence transmitted to the Secretary-General, all would be conducted without any publicity whatsoever.

There would be no circus, no hysteria, no blackening of reputations. The United States government, by the terms of the order, did not undertake to instruct the Secretary-General as to whom he should or should not employ, nor to imprison any American citizens he might employ contrary to the Attorney General's judgment. The evidence gathered by United States agencies would be submitted to the Secretary-General, and the Secretary-General would make his own decision.

*   *   *

FINANCIAL PROBLEMS

United States Memorandum on "The United Nations Financial Crisis"*

October 8, 1964

I have the honour to enclose a memorandum by the United States of America, dated 8 October 1964, concerning "The United Nations financial crisis." I would appreciate it if you would arrange to have the memorandum circulated as an official document of the General Assembly.

The memorandum deals with the serious extent of the financial issue facing the Organization, the law on the issue as established by the International Court of Justice and the General Assembly, and the implications which a breach of the Charter on the question would entail.

(Signed) Adlai E. Stevenson
Permanent Representative of the United
States of America to the United Nations

THE UNITED NATIONS FINANCIAL CRISIS
(MEMORANDUM BY THE UNITED STATES OF AMERICA)

A. The Financial Crisis

The United States of America is vitally interested in the survival of the United Nations as an effective institution, and is deeply troubled by the financial crisis facing the Organization.

The crisis is painfully clear. The United Nations has a net deficit of $134 million.

On 30 June 1964 the United Nations had on the books unpaid obligations owed to Governments and other outsiders totalling some $117 million. In addition, it owed to its own Working Capital Fund—which it is supposed to have on hand in order to keep afloat and solvent pending the receipt of assessments—$40 million. Other internal accounts were owed $27 million. Against this total of $183 million of obligations it had $49 million in cash resources, or a net deficit of $134 million.

What does this mean?

It means that the United Nations does not have the money to pay its debts, and that it would be bankrupt today if it were not for the forebearance of the Member Governments to which it owes those debts.

It means that, unless something is done, the United Nations will have to default on its obligations to Member Governments which, in good faith and in reliance on the Organization's promises and good faith, have furnished troops and supplies and services to the United Nations, at its request for the safeguarding of the peace. In so doing, these Governments incurred substantial additior.al and extraordinary expenditures which the United Nations agreed to reimburse—an agreement which the Secretary-General referred to in his statement at the opening session of the Working Group of Twenty-one on 9 September 1964 (A/AC.113/29) as "the commitment which the

**Official Records of the General Assembly*, Nineteenth Session, Annexes, Document A/5739.

Organization has accepted, in its collective capacity, towards those of its Members who have furnished the men and material for its successive peace-keeping operations."

Which are those Governments?

The United Nations owes significant amounts to Argentina, Austria, Brazil, Canada, Denmark, Ethiopia, Ghana, India, Indonesia, Iran, Ireland, Italy, Liberia, Malaysia, Mali, Morocco, Netherlands, Nigeria, Norway, Pakistan, Philippines, Sierra Leone, Sudan, Sweden, Tunisia, United Arab Republic, the United Kingdom of Great Britain and Northern Ireland, Yugoslavia, and the United States of America. It is to be noted that nineteen of these twenty-nine countries are developing countries.

As the Secretary-General said in the Working Group of Twenty-one, these twenty-nine Members "are surely entitled to expect the United Nations to keep with them" (ibid.). For the United Nations to up that faith, it must get the money from its Members, or it has no other practicable source.

These twenty-nine countries will suffer if the United Nations is forced, by the default of the Members which owe it, into defaulting to those which it owes; an entire Organization will suffer if it does not ignore its just obligations and becomes morally bankrupt.

The twenty-nine Members would suffer by a default, but the real sufferer would be the United Nations itself. How could an enfeebled and creditless defaulter maintain peace and security? Indeed, how could any institution that had committed such a breach of faith long to survive as a credit-worthy and effective organization?

As the Secretary-General said in the Working Group of Twenty-one, "failure to take care of the past may not leave us with much of a future" (ibid.).

What has caused this crisis?

The crisis has been thrust upon the United Nations by those Members which have refused to pay the assessments for the Middle East (UNEF) and Congo (ONUC) operations as voted by the General Assembly in accordance with the Charter.

It is worthwhile recalling exactly how those operations were authorized and exactly what they were.

B. The Middle East Operation—UNEF

UNEF grew out of the Suez crisis of 1956. The Security Council found itself unable to act because of vetoes by certain of the permanent members. Yugoslavia then, on 31 October 1956, introduced the following draft resolution:

"The Security Council,

Considering that a grave situation has been created by action undertaken against Egypt,

Taking into account that the lack of unanimity of its permanent members at the 749th and 750th meetings of the Security Council has prevented it from exercising its primary responsibility for the maintenance of international peace and security,

Decides to call an emergency special session of the General Assembly, as provided in General Assembly resolution 377 A (V) of 3 November 1950." [Note: The "Uniting for peace" resolution] "in order to make appropriate recommendations."

The Council adopted the draft resolution by 7 votes to 2, with 2 abstentions and the Soviet Union voted for the resolution (S/3721).

Thus the Soviet Union supported the referral by the Security Council of the crisis to the General Assembly for "appropriate recommendations" under the very "Uniting for peace" resolution which the Soviet Union now tries to discredit.

The "appropriate recommendations" began with resolution 997 (ES-I), adopted by 64 votes to 5, with 6 abstentions (the Soviet Union voting for), calling for an immediate cease-fire, and resolution 998 (ES-I), adopted by 57 votes to none, with 19 abstentions (the Soviet Union abstaining), requesting the Secretary-General to submit a plan for the setting up, with the consent of the nations concerned, of an emergency international United Nations Force to secure and supervise the cessation of hostilities in accordance with all the terms of the aforementioned resolution" –i.e., Assembly resolution 997 (ES-I).

There followed resolution 999 (ES-I), adopted by 59 votes to 5, with 12 abstentions (the Soviet Union voting for), authorizing the Secretary-General to arrange for the implementation of the cease-fire, and resolution 1000 (ES-I), which noted with satisfaction the Secretary-Generals plan for the international force (A/3289), and provided as follows:

"The General Assembly

" . . .

1. Establishes a United Nations Command for an emergency international Force to secure and supervise the cessation of hostilities in accordance with all the terms of General Assembly resolution 997 (ES-I) of 2 November 1956."

The vote on the resolution was 57 to none, with 19 abstentions. There was not a single vote against (the Soviet Union abstained).

Further, the General Assembly, by resolution 1001 (ES-I), which was adopted by 64 votes to none, with 12 abstentions, approved the Secretary-General's second report (A/3302). That report specifically indicated: (a) that UNEF was intended only to secure and supervise the cease-fire and the withdrawal of forces, and not to enforce the withdrawal (b) that it was not an enforcement action, nor was UNEF a force with military objectives, and (c) that no use of force under Chapter VII of the Charter was envisaged. The Soviet Union abstained and did not vote against that resolution either.

Yet now the Soviet Union contends that there was something illegal about an operation (a) which was recommended by the General Assembly pursuant to a referral by the Security Council voted for by the Soviets themselves (b) which involved no enforcement or military action whatsoever but merely the securing and supervising of a previously agreed to cease-fire, (c) which was consented to by the Government concerned, and (d) which was authorized by the Assembly without a negative vote by anyone.

Rejecting the Soviet contentions, the International Court of Justice held (see sect. D.1 below) that UNEF was properly authorized by the Assembly.

C. The Congo Operation—ONUC

The United Nations Operation in the Congo was authorized by the Security Council on 14 July 1960, by resolution S/4387, reading in part as follows:

"The Security Council

" . . .

"2. Decides to authorize the Secretary-General to take the necessary steps, in consultation with the Government of the Republic of the Congo, to provide the

Government with such military assistance as may be necessary until, through the efforts of the Congolese Government with the technical assistance of the United Nations, the national security forces may be able, in the opinion of the Government, to meet fully their tasks."

The Soviet Union voted for the resolution, which clearly gave the Secretary-General discretionary authority, in consultation with the Congolese Government, to determine the make-up of ONUC.

On 18 July 1960, the Secretary-General presented to the Security Council his first report (S/4389) in which he recited the steps taken by him to invite Member States to furnish forces for ONUC.

On 22 July 1960, the Security Council adopted resolution S/4405, reading in part as follows:

"The Security Council,

" . . .

"Appreciating the work of the Secretary-General and the support so readily and so speedily given to him by all Member States invited by him to give assistance,

" . . .

"3. Commends the Secretary-General for the prompt action he has taken to carry out resolution 143 (1960) and for his first report."

The Soviet Union voted for the resolution.

In the face of this record, it is difficult to understand the Soviet Union's present claim—contained in section I of the Soviet memorandum of 11 September 1964 (see A/5729) that it was improper for the Secretary-General to invite States to take part in ONUC—when he did so pursuant to direct Security Council authorization and approval, twice voted for by the Soviet Union itself. There was no "bypassing" of the Security Council (ibid.): on the contrary the Secretary-General did exactly what the Council authorized him to do and commended him for having done!

On 9 August 1960, the Security Council adopted resolution S/4426, confirming the authority given to the Secretary-General by the two prior resolutions and requesting him to continue to carry out his responsibility. The Soviet Union voted for that resolution too.

Furthermore, six months later, the Security Council on 21 February 1961, adopted resolution S/4741 which broadened ONUC's mandate and reaffirmed the three earlier Security Council resolutions and an intervening General Assembly resolution. The Soviet Union abstained.

Finally, the Security Council on 24 November 1961, nine months later, adopted resolution S/5002, which in effect again reauthorized the ONUC operation, recalling the earlier Security Council resolutions (and intervening General Assembly resolutions) and again broadened ONUC's mandate. The Soviet Union voted for the resolution.

Against this record of Security Council authorization and repeated reauthorization, it is difficult to understand how the Soviet Union can now contend that the operation was not legal and was not validly authorized.

As for the Soviet contention that ONUC was not conducted in accordance with the five Security Council resolutions, it is enough to point out that ONUC was reauthorized by the Security Council's resolutions on 21 February and 24 November 1961—six months and fifteen months, respectively, after its inception.

If the Security Council had felt that ONUC was not being properly conducted in accordance with its resolutions it could at any time have changed or given further explicit instructions. No such instructions were ever given or even suggested by the Security Council and the record of Security Council authorization and reauthorization, and reaffirmation, of the ONUC operation, remains unchallenged.

The International Court of Justice accordingly held (see sect. D below) that ONUC was properly authorized.

D. Soviet Legal Arguments

Let us now consider the legal arguments which have been made by the USSR.

It should first be noted that every one of the arguments put forward by the Soviet Union in its memorandum of 11 September, 1964, and elsewhere was made by the Soviet representative in his submission and argument before the International Court of Justice in the summer of 1962, when the Court considered the question of whether the UNEF and ONUC assessments voted by the General Assembly were "expenses of the Organization" within the meaning of Article 17, paragraph 2, of the Charter, and therefore binding obligations of the Members.

Every single one of those arguments was specifically rejected in the Court's advisory opinion of 20 July 1962. That Opinion was accepted on 18 December 1962 by the General Assembly [resolution 1854 (XVII)] by the overwhelming vote of 76 to 17, with 8 abstentions, after the Assembly had decisively defeated an amendment which would merely have taken note of the opinion.

Nevertheless, it may be useful to deal briefly with the Soviet contentions.

1. The Claimed "Exclusive" Peace-keeping Rights of the Security Council

The Soviet position is that the Security Council, and only the Security Council, has any right to take any action whatsoever with respect to the keeping of the peace, and that the General Assembly has no rights whatsoever in that area.

It should first be noted that this argument has nothing to do with ONUC, which was authorized and reauthorized by the Security Council by repeated resolutions, four out of five of which were voted for by the Soviet Union—it abstained on the fifth. Further, it will be remembered that UNEF was recommended by the General Assembly pursuant to the Security Council's referral of the problem to the General Assembly for its recommendations, by a resolution which the Soviet Union voted for [see sect. B above].

In any event, there is no basis for the contention that the Security Council has exclusive rights as to peace-keeping, and the General Assembly none. Article 24 of the Charter gives the Security Council "primary responsibility for the maintenance of international peace and security," primary but not exclusive authority.

The Charter provisions set forth unequivocally the authority of the General Assembly in this regard. Subject only to Article 12, paragraph 1:

Article 10 authorizes the General Assembly to discuss and make recommendations on any questions or matters within the scope of the Charter;

Article 11, paragraph 2, authorizes the General Assembly to discuss and make recommendations with regard to any questions relating to the maintenance of international peace and security (except that any question on which "action" is necessary shall be referred to the Security Council);

Article 14 authorizes the General Assembly to recommend measures for the peaceful adjustment of any situation likely to impair the general welfare or friendly relations among nations, including situations resulting from a violation of the purposes and principles of the United Nations; and

Article 35 provides that any dispute or situation which might lead to international friction or give rise to a dispute may be brought to the attention of the Security Council or of the General Assembly, whose proceedings are to be subject to Articles 11 and 12.

The word "action" in the exception to Article 11, paragraph 2, clearly applies only to coercive or enforcement action, and therefore not to recommendations by the General Assembly. So the International Court of Justice held in its Advisory Opinion of 20 July 1962, saying that:

> "The Court considers that the kind of action referred to in Article 11, paragraph 2, is coercive or enforcement action. This paragraph, which applies not merely to general questions relating to peace and security, but also to specific cases brought before the General Assembly by a State under Article 35, in its first sentence empowers the General Assembly, by means of recommendations to States or to the Security Council or to both, to organize peace-keeping operations at the request or with the consent, of the States concerned. This power of the General Assembly is a special power which in no way derogates from its general powers under Article 10 or Article 14, except as limited by the last sentence of Article 11, paragraph 2. This last sentence says that when 'action' is necessary the General Assembly shall refer the question to the Security Council. The word 'action' must mean such action as is solely within the province of the Security Council. It cannot refer to recommendations which the Security Council might make, as for instance under Article 38, because the General Assembly under Article 11 has a comparable power The action' which is solely within the province of the Security Council is that which is indicated by the title of Chapter VII of the Charter namely 'Action with respect to threats of the peace, breaches of the peace. and acts of agression'. If the word 'action' in Article 11, paragraph 2, were interpreted to mean that the General Assembly could make recommendations only of a general character affecting peace and security in the abstract and not in relation to specific cases. the paragraph would not have provided that the General Assembly may make recommendations on questions brought before it by States or by the Security Council. Accordingly, the last sentence of Article 11, paragraph 2, has no application where the necessary action is not enforcement action."

The Security Council does have the sole authority, under Chapter VII, to make binding decisions, obligatory and compulsory on all Members, for coercive or enforcement action, but that does not mean that the General Assembly cannot make recommendations (as opposed to binding decisions) as to the preservation of the peace.

UNEF, as shown by the Secretary-General's report and on the face of the resolutions which authorized it (see sect. B above), involved no enforcement action, and it was clearly within the recommendatory power of the General Assembly as regards a situation turned over to it by the Security Council by a resolution voted for by the Soviet Union.

ONUC was authorized by the Security Council, and reauthorized by the Security Council, and no valid objection can be raised to that authorization.

Few Members of the United Nations would ever agree that, if the Security Council proves itself unable to act in the face of an international emergency, the General

Assembly can only stand by, motionless and powerless to take any step for the preservation of the peace.

Certainly the record of recent years shows that the General Assembly can take and has taken appropriate measures in the interest of international peace, and that it has done so with the support of the overwhelming majority of the Members, who believe that such measures are fully within the letter and the spirit of the Charter.

2. The Claimed "Exclusive" Rights of the Security Council as to Peace-keeping Expenses

The Soviet Union also contends that the Security Council has sole authority to determine the expenses of a peace-keeping operation, and to assess them on the membership, and that the General Assembly has no such right.

We think it unlikely that many Members would ever agree that the eleven members of the Security Council should be able to assess the other 101 Members without any consent or action on their part—surely taxation without representation.

There is not the slightest justification in the Charter for any such contention. The only reference in the Charter to the Organization's expenses is in Article 17, paragraph 2, which provides that "the expenses of the Organization shall be borne by the Members as apportioned by the General Assembly." The Security Council is never mentioned in the Charter in connexion with any expenses of the United Nations.

3. The Claimed "Non-includability" of Peace-keeping Expenses Under Article 17 of the Charter

Article 17 of the Charter reads in part:

"1. The General Assembly shall consider and approve the budget of the Organization.

"2. The expenses of the Organization shall be borne by the Members as apportioned by the General Assembly."

It is clear that if the expenses of UNEF and ONUC, as apportioned by the General Assembly, are "expenses of the Organization," they are obligatory on the Members and must be paid.

This is precisely the question which was decided in the affirmative by the International Court of Justice in its Advisory Opinion of 20 July 1962, accepted by the General Assembly.

Before the Court the Soviet Union contended, as it does in section II of its memorandum of 11 September 1964, that paragraph 2 of Article 17 refers only to the budgetary expenses of the Organization. The Court points out, in its advisory opinion, that "on its face, the term 'expenses of the Organization' means all the expenses and not just certain types of expenses which might be referred to as 'regular expenses'."

The Soviet memorandum refers, in section II, to a proposal made at San Francisco as to costs of enforcement action. In point of fact, the proposal was made by the Union of South Africa, which suggested an amendment to what is now Article 50 of the Charter.

Article 50 deals with the right of a State (whether a Member of the United Nations or not) to consult the Security Council for a solution of any special economic problems arising from preventive or enforcement measures taken by the Council; the

Article obviously relates to the situation where, for example, a Security Council embargo or boycott against an aggressor has the side effect of seriously harming the economy of an innocent third country.

The amendment submitted by the Union of South Africa was to the effect that a guilty country against which United Nations enforcement action is taken should be required to pay the costs of the enforcement action and to make reparation for losses and damages sustained by the economies of innocent third countries as a result. Countries participating in the enforcement action were to submit their claims for costs and reparation to the Security Council for approval and for action required to ensure recovery. The amendment had nothing whatever to do with the payment of peace-keeping costs incurred by the United Nations itself. Furthermore, the amendment was rejected by Committee III/3 by a vote of 19 to 2. The two votes in favour of the amendment were presumably those of the Union of South Africa, the proposer, and Iran, the seconder, which indicates that both the Soviet Union and the United States voted for rejection.

The full text of the report of Committee III/3 on the matter (partially quoted in section II of the Soviet memorandum) was as follows:

> "Economic Problems of Enforcement Action. In conclusion, having heard various explanations on the subject of mutual assistance, between states in the application of the measures determined by the Security Council and having noted the legitimate concern expressed by South Africa that the expenses of enforcement action carried out against a guilty state should fall upon that state the Committee declared itself satisfied with the provisions of paragraphs 10 and 11." [Note the present Articles 49 and 50 of the Charter which contain no provisions as to the treatment of peace-keeping expenses.]
>
> "A desire moreover was expressed that the Organization should, in the future, seek to promote a system aiming at the fairest possible distribution of expenses incurred as a result of enforcement action."
>
> "Having duly noted the explanations and suggestions given, the Committee unanimously adopted paragraphs 10 and 11 of the Dumbarton Oaks Proposals without change."

The Committee's rejection of the proposal of the Union of South Africa that aggressors pay, and the Committee's omission from Articles 49 and 50 of any reference to expenses, left Article 17 as the only Article in the Charter dealing with expenses. That rejection and omission, and the Committee's emphasis on the fairest possible distribution of enforcement expenses buttress the conclusion that such expenses are to be included in Article 17, paragraph 2, and apportioned by the General Assembly, and are to be borne by the Members.

The Soviet memorandum of 11 September 1964 in section II refers to a statement of Goodrich and Hambro in "Charter of the United Nations. Commentary and Documents" (Boston, 1949), that the expenses referred to in Article 17, paragraph 2, do not include the cost of enforcement action. In point of fact the statement is found in a foot-note, foot-note 90 on page 184. The foot-note refers to Article 49 (which provides that Members are obligated to join in affording mutual assistance in carrying out Chapter VII measures decided upon by the Security Council) and to the discussion of that Article on page 295 of the same book. Both references and the discussion make it clear that the authors have in mind enforcement costs that are to be borne by Members themselves in carrying out measures decided upon by the Security Council under Articles 48 and 49, and not the type of non-enforcement peace-keeping expenses involved in UNEF and ONUC, where, by agreement, primary expenses were to be borne by the States furnishing the forces, but their extra and additional expenses were to be reimbursed by the United Nations.

The Soviet memorandum contends, towards the end of section II, that the fact that the General Assembly set up separate accounts for UNEF and ONUC expenses, apart from the regular budget, and, in certain cases, apportioned and assessed those expenses in a manner different from that used in the case of regular budget expenses, took UNEF and ONUC expenses out of the category of "expenses of the Organization" as found in Article 17, paragraph 2.

The International Court of Justice in its advisory opinion of 20 July 1962 decisively rejected this contention, saying with respect to UNEF expenses, after a full review—pages 172 to 175—of the General Assembly UNEF assessment resolutions from 1956 to date:

> "The Court concludes that, from year to year the expenses of UNEF have been treated by the General Assembly as expenses of the Organization within the meaning of Article 17, paragraph 2, of the Charter."

As to ONUC expenses, the Court said:

> "The conclusion to be drawn from these paragraphs is that the General Assembly has twice decided that even though certain expenses are 'extraordinary' and 'essentially different' from those under the 'regular budget', they are none the less 'expenses of the Organization' to be apportioned in accordance with the power granted to the General Assembly by Article 17, paragraph 2. This conclusion is strengthened by the concluding clause of paragraph 4 of the two resolutions just cited" [note General Assembly resolutions 1619 (XV) and 1732 (XVI)] "which states that the decision therein to use the scale of assessment already adopted for the regular budget is made 'pending the establishment of a different scale of assessment to defray the extraordinary expenses.' The only alternative—and that means the 'different procedure'—contemplated was another scale of assessment and not some method other than assessment. 'Apportionment' and 'assessment' are terms which relate only to the General Assembly's authority under Article 17."

The clear conclusion is that the UNEF and ONUC expenses are "expenses of the Organization" as referred to in Article 17, paragraph 2, and, as duly apportioned by the General Assembly, shall be borne by the Members as obligatory obligations.

4. The Claimed "Non-applicability" of Article 19 of the Charter

The first sentence of Article 19 of the Charter reads as follows:

"A Member of the United Nations which is in arrears in the payment of its financial contributions to the Organization shall have no vote in the General Assembly if the amount of its arrears equals or exceeds the amount of the contributions due from it for the preceding two full years."

The Soviet memorandum of 11 September 1964 states in section III that the arrears to which Article 19 refers are arrears in the payment of expenses under Article 17. This is of course true.

But the memorandum contends that since, according to the Soviet claim, UNEF and ONUC expenses are solely within the competence of the Security Council and are not "expenses of the Organization" under Article 17, they cannot be included in the calculation of arrears under Article 19.

But, as the International Court of Justice has held and as the General Assembly confirmed (see sect. D.3 above), UNEF and ONUC expenses are "expenses of the Organization" under Article 17 and were properly apportioned under that Article by the General Assembly. Therefore they are to be included in any calculation of arrears under Article 19.

The memorandum refers, also in section III, to an amendment to the present Article 19 proposed at the San Francisco Conference by Australia. The amendment in question would have added to Article 19 a provision that a Member shall have no vote if it has not carried out its obligations under what is now Article 43. In other words, for example, if a Member has agreed with the Security Council under Article 43 to furnish certain troops on the Council's call, and later refuses to do so, it should lose its vote. The proposed amendment would thus have added to Article 19, which already provided for loss of vote by a member failing to pay its assessments for United Nations expenses, a provision for loss of vote by a Member failing to comply with its Article 43 obligations. Expenses were not involved in the proposed amendment at all.

In point of fact the proposed amendment was withdrawn by Australia and was never voted on. The proposed amendment and its withdrawal have nothing to do with the fact that Article 19 does deprive a member of its vote for failing to pay its assessments for United Nations expenses, and the fact that those expenses include, as the International Court of Justice has held, the UNEF and ONUC peace-keeping expenses incurred by the United Nations itself and duly assessed on all Members by the General Assembly. Those interested in the proposed amendment will find the accurate story in the documents of the United Nations Conference on International Organization, volume 8, pages 470 (II/1/34) and 476 (II/1/35).

So the conclusion is clear that, in the calculation of arrears under Article 19, UNEF and ONUC assessments are to be included.

E. The Attitude of the United Nations Membership

From the foregoing it is clear that UNEF and ONUC arrears are legal and binding obligations of Members. Furthermore, it is the overwhelming conviction of the United Nations membership that they should be paid, and that all Members have a collective responsibility for the financing of such operations.

General Assembly resolution 1854 (XVII), of 19 December 1962, accepting the International Court of Justice Advisory Opinion that UNEF and ONUC expenses are "expenses of the Organization" within the meaning of Article 17, paragraph 2, has already been cited, together with the vote of 76 to 17, with 8 abstentions in its favour.

By resolution 1874 (S-IV), adopted on 27 June 1963 by 92 votes to 11, with 3 abstentions, the General Assembly affirmed, among other principles, the principle that the financing of peace-keeping operations is the collective responsibility of all States Member of the United Nations.

On 27 June 1963, by 79 votes to 12, with 17 abstentions, the General Assembly adopted resolution 1877 (S-IV), reading in part as follows:

"The General Assembly,

". . .

"Noting with concern the present financial situation of the Organization resulting from the non-payment of a substantial portion of past assessments for the United Nations Emergency Force Special Account and the Ad Hoc Account for the United Nations Operation in the Congo,

"Believing that it is essential that all assessments for these accounts be paid as soon as possible,

"1. Appeals to Member States which continue to be in arrears in respect of their assessed contributions for payment to the United Nations Emergency Force Special Account and the Ad Hoc Account for the United Nations Operation in the Congo to pay their arrears, disregarding other factors, as soon as their respective constitutional and financial arrangements can be processed, and, pending such arrangements, to make an announcement of their intention to do so;

"2. Expresses its conviction that Member States which are in arrears and object on political or juridical grounds to paying their assessments on these accounts nevertheless will, without prejudice to their respective positions, make a special effort towards solving the financial difficulties of the United Nations by making these payments."

Despite the overwhelming support for the legal conclusion of the International Court of Justice that UNEF and ONUC expenses are legally binding obligations, and for the political conclusion that these expenses should be paid, regardless of legal dissent, to keep the Organization solvent, the United Nations is still faced with refusals by certain States to pay their shares of these expenses.

F. Article 19 of the Charter

November 10 is the opening of the General Assembly, and November 10 presents the inevitable and inescapable issue of Article 19 unless requisite payments are made before that opening. Article 19 reads as follows:

"A Member of the United Nations which is in arrears in the payment of its financial contributions to the Organization shall have no vote in the General Assembly if the amount of its arrears equals or exceeds the amount of the contributions due from it for the preceding two full years. The General Assembly may, nevertheless, permit such a Member to vote if it is satisfied that the failure to pay is due to conditions beyond the control of the Member."

The first sentence of Article 19 says in simple and clear terms that a Member subject to its provisions shall have no vote in the General Assembly. It does not say that the General Assembly has any discretion with respect to such a Member; it does not say that the General Assembly shall vote as to whether the delinquent shall have no vote; it simply says that the delinquent shall have no vote. The first sentence of Article 19 in the French text is even more emphatic: it says the delinquent Member cannot vote—"ne peut participer au vote."

The second sentence of Article 19 does provide for a vote; a delinquent Member whose failure to pay is due to conditions beyond its control may be permitted by the General Assembly to vote. But there is no discretion as to a delinquent Member whose failure to pay is not due to conditions beyond its control, no discretion as to a Member which refuses to pay.

The United States hopes that those Members about to be confronted by Article 19 will take the action necessary to avoid the confrontation.

The way to avoid the confrontation is for those subject to the terms of Article 19 to make the necessary payments.

The United States does not seek the confrontation—but if on November 10 the plain and explicit terms of Article 19 do become applicable, there is no alternative to its application.

It is not only that Article 19 means what it says—that the Member shall have no vote—it is that failure to apply the Article would be a violation of the Charter which would have far-reaching consequences.

Failure to apply the Article would break faith with the overwhelming majority of Members who are paying their peace-keeping assessments—often at great sacrifice—as obligations binding under the Charter.

Failure to apply the Article would be a repudiation of the International Court of Justice and of that rule of international law whose continued growth is vital for progress toward peace and disarmament.

Failure to apply the Article would mean the discarding of the only sanction which the United Nations has in support of its capacity to collect what its Members owe it.

Failure to apply the Article would undermine the only mandatory power the General Assembly has—the power under Article 17 to assess the expenses of the Organization on the Members.

Failure to apply the Article would tempt Members to pick and choose, with impunity, from among their obligations to the United Nations, refusing to pay for items they dislike even though those items were authorized by the overwhelming vote of the Members. Indeed, the Soviet Union has already said that it will not pay for certain items in the regular budgets. How could any organization function on such a fiscal quicksand?

Failure to apply the Article to a great Power simply because it is a great Power would undermine the constitutional integrity of the United Nations, and could sharply affect the attitude toward the Organization of those who have always been its strongest supporters.

Failure to apply the Article could seriously jeopardize the support of United Nations operations and programmes, not only for the keeping of the peace but for economic and social development.

The consequences of not applying Article 19 would thus be far worse than any conjectured consequences of applying it.

We believe that it is the desire of most Members of the United Nations that the situation not arise which makes Article 19 applicable, and therefore we believe that it is up to the membership to see to it that the confrontation is avoided through the means available under the Charter for avoiding it—the making of the necessary payments.

G. The Fundamental Issue

The United Nations financial crisis is not an adversary issue between individual Members; it is an issue between those who refuse to pay and the Organization itself, the Organization as a whole. It is an issue which involves the future capacity of the United Nations as an effective institution. If the United Nations cannot collect what is due from its Members, it cannot pay what it owes; if it cannot collect what is due from its Members, it will have no means of effectively carrying on its peace-keeping functions and its economic and social programs will be jeopardized.

The issue is one which vitally affects all Members of the United Nations.

The United Nations is of particular importance to its developing Members. It is not only a free and open forum where all can defend what they think and urge what they want, it is an institution which, in response to the interests of all—both large and small—can act. But it cannot act unless it has the funds to support its acts. And if it cannot get from its Members the funds to support its acts, all would be the losers. So it is to all countries that the United Nations must look for a solution.

It has sometimes been said that somehow the United States should work out with the Soviet Union a compromise on some of the fundamental issues.

Could the United States—or should it—agree that Member States which are not members of the Security Council should have nothing at all to say about peace-keeping, even in cases in which the Security Council cannot act? And nothing to say about peace-keeping expenses or their assessment?

Could the United States—or should it—agree that Article 19, despite its plain terms, should not be applied against a great Power in support of General Assembly assessments, simply because it is a great Power?

The United States does not see how, without violating the Charter, anyone could or should agree to any of these propositions.

H. United States Efforts to Find Solutions

The sincere and earnest desire of the United States to find a way out of the United Nations financial crisis, and to avoid confrontation under Article 19, is evidenced by the repeated attempts it has made to reach common ground.

On 6 March of this year the United States proposed to the Soviet delegation certain ideas as to the initiation, conduct and financing of future peace-keeping operations which it was hoped—without sacrificing the rights of the General Assembly—would emphasize the primary role of the Security Council in peace-keeping and the desirability of according full weight to the views and positions of the permanent members of the Security Council and other major contributors to peace-keeping expenses. The United States hope was that agreement as to future peace-keeping operations would facilitate the solution of the present problem.

However, despite frequent inquiries as to when a reply to the United States suggestions could be expected, four months went by without any answer. Then in early July, the Soviet Union circulated a memorandum, dated 10 July 1964 (S/5811), which merely repeated the familiar Soviet thesis that only the Security Council has any rights under the Charter with respect to peace-keeping operation, and that the General Assembly and the Secretary-General have none. There was no mention of the arrears problem or of any of the ideas the United States had suggested for discussion.

On receipt of that memorandum, and later, the United States delegation again endeavoured to enter into a discussion with the Soviet delegation as to the United States suggestions. Unfortunately the unvarying answer was that the uncompromising Soviet memorandum of 10 July was the only reply to be expected.

This sincere effort to enter into a dialogue with the Soviet delegation was in the hope that adjustments as to the arrangements for the initiation and financing of future peace-keeping operations could make it easier to reach some solution as to the present and the past. Unfortunately, there has been no Soviet willingness to enter into that dialogue.

It is common knowledge that representatives of other Member States also have sought to initiate discussions with the Soviet Union on this subject and also have been met with a reiteration of past Soviet contentions.

None the less, the United States has not given up hope, and it intends to continue its attempts to work out new arrangements in the hope that solutions for the future may make it easier for those in arrears on UNEF and ONUC assessments to clear up in some manner these past arrears. The United States intends to continue its efforts in the Working Group of Twenty-one, now meeting under the chairmanship of Chief Adebo of Nigeria, and the United States hopes that all other members of the Group will join in this attempt.

Accordingly, on 14 September 1964, the United States tabled in the Working Group of Twenty-one, as a basis for discussion, a working paper which sets forth examples of the kinds of new arrangements it has in mind as to peace-keeping operations involving the use of military forces. The following elements were mentioned:

"1. All proposals to initiate such peace-keeping operations would be considered first in the Security Council. The General Assembly would not authorize or assume control of such peace-keeping operations unless the Council had demonstrated that it was unable to take action." [This would be a self-denying ordinance on the part of the General Assembly, emphasizing the primary role of the Security Council.]

"2. The General Assembly would establish a standing special finance committee. The composition of this committee should be similar to that of the present Working Group of Twenty-one . . ." [The committee membership would include the permanent members of the Security Council, who would thus have a position more commensurate with their responsibilities than in the General Assembly.]

"3. In apportioning expenses for such peace-keeping operations, the General Assembly would act only on a recommendation from the committee passed by a two-thirds majority of the committee's membership." [The permanent members of the Security Council would have an influence greater than in the Assembly, but no single Member could frustrate, by a veto, action desired by the overwhelming majority.]

"4. In making recommendations, the committee would rather consider various alternative methods of financing, including direct financing by countries involved in a dispute, voluntary contributions, and assessed contributions. In the event that the Assembly did not accept a particular recommendation, the committee would resume consideration of the matter with a view to recommending an acceptable alternative."

"5. One of the available methods of assessment for peace-keeping operations involving the use of military forces would be a special scale of assessments in which, over a specified amount, States having greater ability to pay would be allocated higher percentages, and States having less ability to pay would be allocated smaller percentages than in the regular scale of assessments." (A/AC.113/30.]

The United States hopes that such ideas may lead to a measure of agreement among Members of the United Nations as to how these operations are to be started and paid for in the future. Arrangements of this kind should go a long way toward giving the Soviet Union and others in a similar position such assurances for the future as should make it easier for them to make their payments relating to the past.

I. What Other States Have Done

It is recognized that the Soviet Union and certain other States in arrears for UNEF and ONUC have strongly-held views against paying these arrears. However, the example of what other States have done when in a similar position indicates that loyalty to the Organization, respect for the International Court of Justice and the rule of law, and consideration for the overwhelming views of Members, should be overriding.

On this point, the following was said by Ambassador Piero Vinci, the Permanent Representative of Italy to the United Nations, in the Working Group of Twenty-one on 23 September 1964:

". . . But we feel that the correct line is the one that the Latin American countries have chosen to follow, although they did not consider the International Court's ruling consistent with the views they had been upholding. The working paper submitted by the delegations of Argentina, Brazil and Mexico and circulated as document A/AC.113/3 reads as follows: '. . . also because they wish to maintain the prestige of the Court, whose objectivity in considering the matters submitted to it is one of the most solid guarantees of the maintenance of international peace and security, the Latin American countries accepted the advisory opinion'. In keeping with this well-inspired and wise policy, the distinguished Representative of Mexico informed us, on Thursday, 17 September, that his Government had decided of its own free will—if I understood correctly—by a sovereign act which does not affect its position of principle, to pay its arrears. We have here an example and an implicit suggestion that, I believe should be carefully weighed and even more usefully followed by whomever might still have reservations on the subject."

In 1954 the United States itself faced a somewhat similar predicament in connexion with an issue on which it had very strong convictions. This was a matter involving awards made by the United Nations Administrative Tribunal to certain former officials of the United Nations Secretariat. The United States and a number of other countries objected strongly on legal grounds to the payment of such awards by the General Assembly. To settle the matter, the General Assembly decided to seek an advisory opinion from the International Court of Justice. The United States vigorously argued its position before the Court. Nevertheless, the Court handed down an advisory opinion contrary to that sought by the United States.

Despite its strongly-held views on the issue, the United States voted with the majority to act in accordance with the opinion of the International Court of Justice. It was not easy for the United States to accept the majority view as to the issue, but it saw no real alternative if the rule of law and the Charter, as interpreted by the Court, were to be maintained.

The case illustrates the fact that all Members, large or small, can be called upon and can be expected to comply with an authoritative legal opinion and the clearly demonstrated will of the General Assembly that they should make payments as to which they may have the strongest legal and political reservations.

In insisting that Member States, including great Powers, follow the examples cited and find some way to make the necessary payments, all must be prepared to be flexible with regard to the modalities of payment. The only vitally essential ingredient in any solution is that the funds be made available to the United Nations. Most Member States are undoubtedly prepared to be flexible in approach to such a solution, are inclined to be considerate in the interests and prestige of States which have thus far found difficulty in payment, and are ready to negotiate on any reasonable basis consistent with the relevant provisions of the United Nations Charter and Financial Regulations.

J. Conclusion

The United Nations is faced with a financial and constitutional crisis which must be solved if the Organization is to continue as an effective instrument. The Charter cannot be ignored. Faith cannot be broken. Commitments must be met. Bills must be paid.

The problem is one which is of crucial importance to all Members, and a solution can be found only if all Members work together in a search for common ground.

The issue is one between (a) the countries that have brought on the crisis by their refusals to pay and (b) the other Members of the Organization. It is now the task of all those other Members to get the help of those who have thus far refused to pay in solving the crisis that faces the entire Organization.

This memorandum has dealt, among other things, with Article 19 and its applicability. The consequences of not applying it, if it becomes applicable, would be to undermine the very integrity and capacity of the United Nations. Let all Members co-operate in finding that common ground which would make possible the receipt by the United Nations of the funds which would make Article 19 inapplicable and which would enable the Organization, thus strengthened, to look forward to continued effective usefulness and man's best hope for a peaceful world.

President Johnson's Report to the Congress on the United Nations *

1965

*   *   *

Since no agreement had been reached on the question either of solvency or of future arrangements by June 15, the Committee adopted an interim report, which defined the limits of the consensus as follows:

> The members of the Special Committee agreed that the United Nations should be strengthened through a co-operative effort and that the General Assembly, when it reconvenes, must conduct its work according to the normal procedure established by its rules of procedure.

The report was adopted unanimously but did not provide any ground for hope that a settlement could be reached either on the terms under which the General Assembly

*U.S. Participation in the U.N., Report by the President to the Congress for the Year 1965, pp. 107-09.

would return to normalcy, or on the terms of a settlement for dealing with the article 19 question. Nor did it offer any hope that oft-promised voluntary contributions to restore the United Nations to solvency would be forthcoming from those who had refused to pay their assessed shares for the UNOC and UNEF accounts.

U.S. Statement of August 16

Informal consultations during the summer were unproductive. The members were clearly unwilling to face another General Assembly session in which the Assembly would be unable to transact business normally and yet the majority of the members were also unwilling to force a showdown on the constitutional issue; rightly or wrongly they feared that application of article 19 to the U.S.S.R. and France might lead to the break-up of the United Nations.

Ambassador Arthur J. Goldberg had been sworn in on July 26 as successor to the late Ambassador Stevenson as U.S. Representative to the United Nations.

On August 16 he told the Committee that "the United States adheres to the position that article 19 is applicable in the present circumstances," but said, "the United States recognizes, as it simply must, that the General Assembly is not prepared to apply article 19 in the present situation and that the consensus of the membership is that the Assembly should proceed normally." Declaring that the United States would "not seek to frustrate that consensus, since it is not in the world interest to have the work of the General Assembly immobilized in these troubled days," he then stated:

> At the same time, we must make it crystal clear that if any member can insist on making an exception to the principle of collective financial responsibility with respect to certain activities of the organization, the United States reserves the same option to make exceptions if, in our view, strong and compelling reasons exist for doing so. There can be no double standard among the members of the organization.

In conclusion he said:

> We look forward nonetheless to the not too distant day when the entire membership will resume its full range of collective responsibility for maintaining world peace. In the meantime, it is all the more important for the membership, though unready to apply article 19, to solve the United Nations financial problems and to continue to support in practice the sound principle of collective financial responsibility, and to adopt practical and equitable means by which those willing to share the responsibility for peace can act in concert to maintain and strengthen the indispensable peacekeeping capacity of the United Nations.

The U.S. statement broke the logjam, and hopefully pointed to the possibility of renewed efforts at the 20th General Assembly to deal with two key problems confronting the United Nations: its need to overcome its financial difficulties; and its need to agree on the rules for future peacekeeping operations, including their financing.

A number of delegations were concerned that the understanding not to press for applying article 19 in the present situation should not create a precedent undermining the validity of article 19. The Canadian Representative on August 20 and the Mexican Representative on August 25 emphasized their understanding that the agreement not to enforce article 19 was applicable only to the Congo and Middle East debts.

However, as the U.S. Representative had noted on August 16, in the U.S. view, in not applying article 19, "no one can or should overlook the fact that the exercise of important prerogatives of the Assembly granted to it under the Charter is being impaired."

Consensus Statement of August 31

At the conclusion of the 18th meeting of the Committee on August 31, Chairman Quaison-Sackey made the following statement:

> In the light of the statements made in the Committee, without prejudice to the positions taken therein and on the basis of paragraph 11 of the Committee's report of 15 June, I take it that the consensus is:
> (a) That the General Assembly will carry on its work normally in accordance with its rules of procedure;
> (b) That the question of the applicability of Article 19 of the Charter will not be raised with regard to the United Nations Emergency Force and the United Nations Operation in the Congo;
> (c) That the financial difficulties of the Organization should be solved through voluntary contributions by Member States, with the highly developed countries making substantial contributions.

The 19th General Assembly reconvened on September 1 for one day and endorsed his consensus statement without objection. The President noted that the work of the Committee remained unfinished, and the General Assembly adopted his suggestion that "the modalities for the continuance of the work should be decided upon at the twentieth session."

The U.S. Representative recalled his statement before the Committee of 33 on August 16 regarding the article 19 issue that the United States had been motivated by the realization that every parliamentary body must somehow resolve the issues before it or cease to have any useful existence. The Assembly had determined to do this, and "it is now our hope and conviction that it will get on with the job of helping to build a world of law and reason and peace."

Appeal for Voluntary Contributions

In a memorandum dated March 31 submitted to the Committee the Secretary-General had estimated that an amount of $108.4 million would be needed to (1) permit the organization to meet in full its current obligations (exclusive of the servicing of the U.N. headquarters loan and the U.N. bond issue for which annual repayments provided in the regular budget); (2) meet additional obligations (other than those relating to the regular budget) that would be incurred at the present time and at such time as the General Assembly may be expected to have decided on assessments in respect of the organization's expenses for the current year; and, (3) restore the Working Capital Fund to the authorized level of $40 million.

*　　　　　*　　　　　*

KOREA

General Assembly Resolution 498 (V) on Hostilities in Korea*

February 1, 1951

The General Assembly,

Noting that the Security Council, because of lack of unanimity of the permanent members, has failed to exercise its primary responsibility for the maintenance of international peace and security in regard to Chinese Communist intervention in Korea,

Noting that the Central People's Government of the People's Republic of China has not accepted United Nations proposals to bring about a cessation of hostilities in Korea with a view to peaceful settlement, and that its armed forces continue their invasion of Korea and their large-scale attacks upon United Nations forces there,

1. Finds that the Central People's Government of the People's Republic of China, by giving direct aid and assistance to those who were already committing aggression in Korea and by engaging in hostilities against United Nations forces there, has itself engaged in aggression in Korea;

2. Calls upon the Central People's Government of the People's Republic of China to cause its forces and nationals in Korea to cease hostilities against the United Nations forces and to withdraw from Korea;

3. Affirms the determination of the United Nations to continue its action in Korea to meet the aggression;

4. Calls upon all States and authorities to refrain from giving any assistance to the aggressors in Korea;

5. Calls upon all States and authorities to refrain from giving any assistance to the aggressors in Korea;

6. Requests a Committee composed of the members of the Collective Measures Committee as a matter of urgency to consider additional measures to be employed to meet this aggression and to report thereon to the General Assembly, it being understood that the Committee is authorized to defer its report if the Good Offices Committee referred to in the following paragraph reports satisfactory progress in its efforts;

7. Affirms that it continues to be the policy of the United Nations to bring about a cessation of hostilities in Korea and the achievement of United Nations objectives in Korea by peaceful means, and requests the President of the General Assembly to designate forthwith two persons who would meet with him at any suitable opportunity to use their good offices to this end.

*U.N. Documents, A/1735-1824, General Assembly A/1771. On February 1 the plenary session of the Assembly adopted the United States resolution by a vote of 44 to 7 (Soviet bloc, India, and Burma) with 9 abstentions (Afghanistan, Egypt, Indonesia, Pakistan, Saudi Arabia, Sweden, Syria, Yemen, and Yugoslavia).

COMMUNIST CHINA

*Report by President Truman to Congress on Chinese Representation
in the United States and Soviet Walkouts**

1950

In October 1949 a Chinese Communist regime was proclaimed in Peiping. Before the end of the year it was recognized by the Soviet group, Burma and India and early in 1950 by Pakistan, the United Kingdom, Norway, Denmark, Israel, Afghanistan, Sweden, the Netherlands, Indonesia, Switzerland, and Yugoslavia. The United States, together with a large majority of the other members of the United Nations, continued to recognize the National Government of China, which had in December 1949 moved to Formosa.

In the Security Council the Soviet Union on January 10, 1950, submitted a draft resolution calling upon the Council not to recognize the credentials of the representative of the Chinese National Government and to exclude him from the Council. On January 13, 1950, a telegram from Chou En-lai, Minister of Foreign Affairs of the Chinese Communist regime, informed the Secretary-General of the United Nations that Chiang Wen-t'ien had been appointed the delegate to the United Nations. On the same day the Council rejected the Soviet resolution by a vote of 3 in favor (U.S.S.R., India, and Yugoslavia), 6 against (China, Cuba, Ecuador, Egypt, France, and the United States), and 2 abstaining (Norway and the United Kingdom). Thereupon the Soviet representative declared that the Soviet Delegation would not participate in the work of the Security Council until the "representative of the Kuomintang group" had been removed from the Council and that the U.S.S.R. would not recognize as legal any decisions of the Security Council adopted with the participation of that representative and would not deem itself bound by such decisions. The Soviet representative then left the meeting.

Our representative stated that it was the United States view that the willfull absence of a permanent member from a meeting of the Security Council in no way diminishes its powers or its authority to act and that the Soviet absence could not be permitted to prevent the Security Council from fulfilling its obligation under the Charter to be organized so as to be able to function continuously.

Thereafter, in the various organs and subsidiary bodies of the United Nations in which they and China participated, members of the Soviet group submitted motions practically identical with that made by the U.S.S.R. in the Security Council. When the motion was rejected, the Soviet member or members in each case walked out after declaring they would refuse to participate so long as a representative of the "Kuomintang clique" remained and declared further that the governments of the Soviet group refused to recognize the validity of any subsequent decisions by the body. By September the Soviet Union or members of its group had walked out of almost 40 organs, subsidiary bodies, or conferences.

The Chinese Communist regime in many of the above instances claimed the right to represent China; in other instances there was only a Soviet motion to exclude the Nationalist representative.

U.S. representatives consistently opposed efforts to unseat the representatives of

*U.S. Participation in the U.N., Report by the President for the Year 1950, pp. 30-33.

the Chinese National Government and seat representatives of the Chinese Communist regime in all U.N. and specialized-agency bodies where the Chinese-representation issue was raised. The views of the United States on the Chinese-representation issue were shared by the large majority of U.N. members. During 1950 the Chinese-representation issue was voted upon over 40 times in 37 U.N. and specialized-agency bodies. In every instance but one, motions to unseat the Chinese National representatives and seat Chinese Communists were rejected. In one minor body, the Executive and Liaison Committee of the Universal Postal Union, a Chinese Communist was seated provisionally for the 1950 session only. (This decision was later reversed, and a U.S. proposal to seat the representative of the Chinese National Government was adopted.)

Notwithstanding the absence of the Soviet bloc during the early part of the year, the Security Council and other bodies conducted their business as usual.

On June 25 and 27 the Security Council took action against a breach of the peace in Korea. Throughout July the Security Council continued to deal with this aggression. Under the monthly rotation plan provided in the rules of procedure of the Security Council, the turn of the representative of the U.S.S.R. to be the president of the Council came during the month of August. At the beginning of the month Mr. Malik, the Soviet representative, took over the functions of this position and resumed his attendance at the meetings of the Security Council.

The Soviet representative continued to claim, however, that the proceedings of the Security Council held in his absence were "illegal."

The question of Chinese representation entered a new phase with the opening of the fifth session of the General Assembly in September. At the first meeting India proposed a resolution to seat the Chinese Communist representatives and to recommend that other United Nations organs do likewise. The Soviet Union submitted two resolutions, one providing for the exclusion of the National Government representatives, the other providing for the seating of the Chinese Communist representatives. A Canadian proposal, with an Australian amendment accepted by Canada, provided for a special committee consisting of seven members, nominated by the president of the General Assembly and confirmed by the General Assembly, to consider the question of Chinese representation and to report, with recommendations, to the Assembly after it had considered a Cuban item on the general question of the recognition of the representation of a member state by the United Nations. Pending an Assembly decision on the report of this special committee, the representatives of the National Government of China should be seated in the Assembly. Secretary of State Acheson urged that the matter be decided as soon as possible and expressed his opposition to the seating of the Chinese Communists. In the voting the Indian resolution was rejected by 33 votes to 16, with 10 abstentions. The paragraph of the Canadian resolution establishing the special committee was adopted by 38 votes to 6, with 11 abstentions. The final paragraph, providing for the seating of the representatives of the National Government, was adopted by 42 votes to 8, with 6 abstentions. The two Soviet proposals were rejected by 38 votes to 10, with 8 abstentions, and 37 votes to 11, with 8 abstentions, respectively.

*   *   *

At the year's end the Soviet Union or members of its group had resumed their participation in the principal organs of the United Nations as well as in a number of subsidiary bodies. In most instances they moved that the Chinese Nationalist representative be excluded and that the Communist representative be seated. When these motions were rejected the Soviet-bloc representatives usually stated that they would consider the vote of the Chinese representative in the body illegal.

                    *   *   *

Report by President Truman to the Congress on Chinese Representation in the U.N. *

                                                                    1951

Throughout 1951 the question of Chinese representation continued to confront the United Nations. As in 1950 the Soviet bloc, with the support of certain other countries which recognized the Chinese Communist regime, submitted proposals in the United Nations and certain specialized agencies calling for the unseating of representatives of the National Government of China and the seating of representatives of the Peiping regime. The United States strongly opposed all these proposals. The large majority of United Nations members continued to recognize the National Government of China and shared the United States view on the Chinese representation issue. In addition, some of the members which recognized the Chinese Communist regime refused to support the Soviet-bloc proposals, believing that the armed intervention of this regime against United Nations forces in Korea made it inappropriate to consider setaing Chinese Communist representatives.

The fifth session of the General Assembly had established a Special Committee to consider the Chinese representation question, but such consideration was not undertaken because of the Korean situation. After rejecting a Polish draft resolution designed to replace the National Government representatives by Communist representatives, the Committee decided on October 16, 1951, to report that under the circumstances it would unable to make any recommendation. When the Assembly President proposed on November 5 that the fifth session of the Assembly merely take note of this report, the Soviet representative countered with a draft resolution to refer consideration of the representation question to the sixth session opening the next day. The Assembly rejected this Soviet draft resolution by 20 votes to 11 with 11 abstentions, and thereupon approved the President's suggestion to take note of the Special Committee's report.

Upon the opening of the sixth session of the Assembly, the Soviet Union again demanded the inclusion of the Chinese representation question on the Assembly's agenda. The General Committee on November 10, 1951, adopted a Thailand resolution recommending that the Assembly reject the Soviet request and postpone consideration, for the duration of the meeting in Paris of the sixth regular session, of any further proposals to exclude representatives of the National Government of China from the Assembly or to seat representatives of the Chinese Communist regime. During the Assembly debate on this recommendation Secretary Acheson expressed strong opposition to the Soviet proposal and said:

*Ibid., 1951, pp. 83-84.

I think that the minds of all of us—or almost all of us, at any rate—revolt at the necessity or the proposal even that we should be called upon to debate and consider here the seating of a regime at the very moment when that regime is engaged in defying to the greatest extent that it possibly can the authority of this General Assembly and of this world organization; at a time when that regime is engaged with its troops in killing the countrymen of at least a score of delegations seated in this hall—those countrymen are defending the cause, the prestige, the honor of the United Nations and the cause of world peace—that we should consider this at a time when this regime is under indictment by this very organization in which it is now proposed to sit—under indictment as a party to aggression in Korea; that we should consider seating this regime at the very time when its international conduct is so low that it would take considerable improvement to raise it to the general level of barbarism.

*   *   *

Speech by Secretary Dulles to the General Assembly on the People's Republic of China*

October 3, 1955

In the China area the situation is somewhat less ominous than it was. We hope that the Chinese People's Republic will respond to the manifest will of the world community that armed force should not be used to achieve national objectives.

The record of this Communist regime has been an evil one. It fought the United Nations in Korea, for which it stands here branded as an aggressor. It took over Tibet by armed force. It became allied with the Communist Viet Minh in their effort to take over Indochina by armed force. Then, following the Indochina armistice, it turned its military attention to the Taiwan (Formosa) area. It intended to take this area by force and began active military assaults on its approaches, which assaults, it claimed, were a first step in its new program of military conquest.

This constituted a major challenge to principles to which the United States is committed by our charter. It was also a direct and special challenge to the United States itself. We have a distinctive relationship to these islands, a relationship which is reinforced by a mutual defense treaty with the Republic of China covering Taiwan and Penghu [the Pescadores].

At this point, on January 24, 1955, President Eisenhower asked the Congress of the United States for authority to use the armed forces of the United States in the defense of Taiwan and Penghu and related areas which the President might judge as appropriate to that defense. After full hearings in the House and the Senate of the United States, the requested authority was granted. In the House the vote was 409 to 3, and in the Senate the vote was 85 to 3. The authority terminates whenever peace and security of the area are reasonably assured by international conditions created by action of the United Nations or otherwise.

I am convinced that this timely warning, given with solid, virtually unanimous, national concurrence, served to prevent what could have been a dangerous miscalculation on the part of the Chinese Communists.

Thereafter the Bandung conference was held. There again the peace-loving nations—many of them members of the United Nations—made clear to the Chinese Communists

*Department of State Bulletin, Oct. 3, 1955, pp. 526-27.

their adherence to our charter principle that states should refrain in their international relations from the threat of force.

From the site of the Bandung conference, Mr. Chou En-lai proposed direct discussions with the United States, a proposal which I promptly indicated was acceptable to the United States so long as we dealt only with matters of concern to the two of us, not involving the rights of third parties. That reservation applies particularly, so far as the United States is concerned, to the Republic of China, to which we are loyal as to a long-time friend and ally.

Shortly thereafter the Chinese Communists released 4 and, later, the other 11 of the United States fliers of the United Nations Command whom it had been holding in violation of the Korean Armistice Agreement. This release had been sought by resolution of this General Assembly adopted last December. The outcome justified the confidence which the United States had placed in the United Nations and our restraint in the use or threat of our own national power.

Some 15 months ago the United States had started talks with the Chinese People's Republic at Geneva with regard to getting our civilians home. As a result of the Bandung statement made by Mr. Chou En-lai and my reply, these talks were resumed last August, to deal first with the topic of freeing civilians for return and then with other practical matters of direct concern to the two of us.

All Chinese in the United States who desire to return to their homeland are free to do so. They have always been free to do so except for a few who were temporarily prevented by restrictions arising out of the Korean war. The Chinese People's Republic has now declared that all Americans on the China mainland have the right to return and will be enabled expeditiously to exercise that right.

For the favorable trend of events to which I refer, thanks are due to many. Our Secretary-General worked assiduously to bring about the release of United States fliers of the United Nations Command. Other governments and individuals were helpful in this and other matters. The will of the world community may have operated to avert another war, the scope of which could not surely be limited.

*　　　　　　*　　　　　　*

Letter from George Bush, U.S. Representative to the U.N. to Secretary General U Thant on Representation of China in the U.N. *

August 17, 1971

I have the honour to request, under rule 14 of the rules of procedure of the General Assembly, the inclusion in the agenda of the twenty-sixth session of an item entitled "The representation of China in the United Nations."

An explanatory memorandum is attached in accordance with rule 20.

EXPLANATORY MEMORANDUM

1. In dealing with the problem of the representation of China, the United Nations should take cognizance of the existence of both the People's Republic of China and

*U.N. General Assembly Press Release, A/8442, Aug. 17, 1971, 26th sess.

the Republic of China and reflect that incontestable reality in the manner by which it makes provision for China's representation. In so doing the United Nations should not be required to take a position on the respective conflicting claims of the People's Republic of China or the Republic of China pending a peaceful resolution of the matter as called for by the Charter.

2. Thus the People's Republic of China should be represented and at the same time provision should be made that the Republic of China is not deprived of its representation. If it is to succeed in its peace-keeping role and in advancing the well-being of mankind, the United Nations should deal with the question of the representation of China in a just and realistic manner.

General Assembly Resolution 2758 (XXVI) on Restoration of the Lawful Rights of the People's Republic of China in the U.N. *

October 25, 1971

The General Assembly,

Recalling the principles of the Charter of the United Nations,

Considering that the restoration of the lawful rights of the People's Republic of China is essential both for the protection of the Charter of the United Nations and for the cause that the United Nations must serve under the Charter,

Recognizing that the representatives of the Government of the People's Republic of China are the only lawful representatives of China to the United Nations and that the People's Republic of China is one of the five permanent members of the Security Council,

Decides to restore all its rights to the People's Republic of China and to recognize the representatives of its Government as the only legitimate representatives of China to the United Nations, and to expel forthwith the representatives of Chiang Kai-shek from the place which they unlawfully occupy at the United Nations and in all the organizations related to it.

General Assembly

Roll Call
Subject of Vote: Motion by the United States for priority in voting on A/L 632 (adopted)
Agenda Item 93
Vote Number 2
Date: Oct. 25

Afghanistan no	Bahrain yes	Brazil yes
Albania no	Barbados yes	Bulgaria no
Algeria no	Belgium yes	Burma no
Argentina yes	Bhutan no	Burundi no
Australia yes	Bolivia yes	Byelorussian SSR no
Austria abstain	Botswana abstain	Cameroon no

*U.N. General Assembly, 26th sess., agenda item 93, A/Res/2758 (XXVI), Oct. 26, 1971.

Canada no
Central African Rep yes
Ceylon no
Chad yes
Chile no
China yes
Colombia yes
Congo (Dem. Rep.) yes
Costa Rica yes
Cuba no
Cyprus abstain
Czechoslovakia no
Dahomey yes
Denmark no
Dominican Republic yes
Ecuador abstain
Egypt no
El Salvador yes
Equatorial Guinea no
Ethiopia no
Fiji yes
Finland no
France no
Gabon yes
Gambia yes
Ghana yes
Greece yes
Guatemala yes
Guinea no
Guyana no
Haiti yes
Honduras yes
Hungary no
Iceland no
India no
Indonesia yes
Iran abstain

Iraq no
Ireland yes
Israel yes
Italy yes
Ivory Coast yes
Jamaica yes
Japan yes
Jordan yes
Kenya abstain
Khmer Republic yes
Kuwait no
Laos abstain
Lebanon yes
Lesotho yes
Liberia yes
Libyan A. R. no
Luxembourg yes
Madagascar yes
Malawi yes
Maldives
Mali no
Malta abstain
Mauritania no
Mauritius yes
Mexico yes
Mongolia no
Morocco yes
Nepal no
Netherlands yes
New Zealand yes
Nicaragua yes
Niger yes
Nigeria no
Norway no
Oman
Pakistan no
Panama yes

Paraguay yes
P.D.R. of Yemen no
People's Rep. of Congo no
Peru no
Philippines yes
Poland no
Portugal yes
Qatar abstain
Romania no
Rwanda yes
Saudi Arabia yes
Senegal abstain
Sierra Leone no
Singapore abstain
Somalia no
South Africa yes
Spain yes
Sudan no
Swaziland yes
Sweden no
Syrian Arab Republic no
Thailand yes
Togo abstain
Trinidad and Tobago abstain
Tunisia yes
Turkey abastain
Uganda no
Ukrainian SSR no
USSR no
United Kingdom no
Un. Rep. of Tanzania no
United States yes
Upper Volta yes
Uruguay yes
Venezuela yes
Yemen no
Yugoslavia no
Zambia no

Yes: 61   Abstain: 15   No: 53

THE UNITED STATES AND SUBSAHARAN AFRICA

Editor
JEAN HERSKOVITS
*State University of New York
at Purchase*

PREFACE

No practicing historian can be sanguine about writing contemporary history from available official documents. In our own day especially, the completion of a study based on such documents raises deeply troubling anxieties. Does unclassified documentary evidence reflect in any fundamental sense the true direction of policy? Still, we must work with what we have, and accessible documents do yield insights: they tell us what issues seemed important enough to pronounce on publicly, and what amount of attention was thought appropriate for each issue. Even the phrasing of official pronouncements often reveals unexpressed judgments. One is left in the end with trying to unravel the actual policies, and why and how they have been made and implemented, all with the knowledge that one day more evidence will become available and yield fuller—or even different—answers.

The student of American relations with Africa since 1945 who examines closely what material now exists cannot fail to reach certain conclusions. One is that Subsaharan Africa was the lowest of the United States' international priorities (though some may make that claim equally for Latin America in the last few years). From government sources, certain other points emerge: for low priorities as well as high, the executive branch made policy virtually unfettered by Congress, the Senate taking no active part in the direction of any African policy; and that in dealing with Africa the executive branch was not significantly affected by public pressures.

There was a period in the early 1960's when circumstances brought Africa briefly to the center of the stage: political events there were dramatic enough to reach the front pages; President Kennedy was genuinely interested in Africa; moreover, black Americans were beginning to take an active interest in African affairs. And the new administration was responsive to a public that included black Americans and took notice of their concerns. After the mid-1960's the situation changed, and American citizens concerned about Africa had little influence on policy making. Only business pressures seemed occasionally to pierce the official unresponsiveness. Military considerations and some economic ones were what seemed to matter, and always in the context of America's global thinking, not thinking about Africa.

Within the executive branch of the government, the Department of State looms highest in importance for Africa, at least in public. That the Department of Defense, the Department of Commerce, and other departments and executive agencies play a role is quite clear, but that role is only sometimes officially and openly accessible. The State Department speeches, delivered by spokesmen for five administrations, show remarkable continuity of ultimate unconcern. Despite some shifts in style, official rhetoric maintains a constancy, not to say identity, that makes it difficult to detect movement in policy. All the Africa bureau's efforts of the early and mid-1960's usually changed only some phrases, but even small changes were victories no less hard won. And the efforts themselves, of course, do not make a public appearance in the documents now available. The point is that because, finally, Africa was seen by most men in government to matter so little, there was very little to say.

The distribution of material within this tiny arena of concern is also revealing. Policy, like publicity, emerges from crisis. The crises are always newsworthy, no matter how ultimately important time may show them to be—no matter whether people thousands of miles away from the events really understand or care about what they mean to those living through them. Often, in America as almost everywhere outside an African country itself, the complexities of its crises have not been understood. But a mountain of paper has gone into them anyway.

Sometimes the views expressed touched the nerves of the problem; often they did not. But once the difficulties were apparently stabilized if not resolved, the interest— and the paper—dwindled to nothing or near it, for example in the 1960's with the Congo, and later, with the Nigerian Civil War. I have chosen documents that show the quality of the arguments on these issues but in no way reflect the quantity of feelings passionately expressed. I have done so because the perspective of even a short time has altered the perceptions of the moment; in the end Americans really didn't care much, and policy didn't really change.

As an historian of Africa, I am deeply in the debt of innumerable Africans for insights I have gained both about their countries and about *their* views of *American* views of their problems. My awareness of how important it was for Americans to know Africans' perceptions of them and their possible and actual roles came during my first prolonged stay in Africa. In 1958 I was Peace Corps age before the Peace Corps' time, doing research for my doctorate in Nigerian history. I lived in Nigeria, and visited Ghana and other countries. It was the beginning of continuous contact for me, in many parts of Africa and outside it, with African complexities and the views of Africans incisively expressed. It was only the first of many times when I had to think and think deeply about relations between Americans and Africans, America and Africa. That I have never ceased to do so is, I hope, reflected in this study.

I have learned no less from many Americans, participants in the making of policy, and observers of it, students of it; many who have tried, usually with but limited success, to influence it. All have been generous with time and insight.

I am particularly indebted to J. Wayne Fredericks, Deputy Assistant Secretary of State for African Affairs from 1961 to 1967, and now head of the Middle East and Africa Program, International Division, the Ford Foundation, who listened to a sometimes perplexed Africanist with the sensibility of a statesman who has deep understanding of the importance to the United States and all Africa of an informed and far-sighted policy.

I am most grateful for the counsel of Graham Hovey of *The New York Times* Editorial Board, a masterful commentator on African events against a long background of experience and insight into American policy on the world scene.

I wish also to acknowledge the suggestions of my fellow Africanist, Peter Schwab of the State University of New York, College at Purchase. The responsibility for the views that emerge from this study is, of course, my own.

Much of the work of compiling hitherto uncollected documents I did in two libraries. At both the staffs were singularly generous with time and assistance. I am especially grateful to Wilfred Danielson of the Government Publications section of the Northwestern University Library, and to Gray Peart of *The New York Times* Editorial Reference Library.

It is impossible to name the many others whose conversations challenged my thinking and encouraged me to clarify and expand my ideas. In addition, at Chelsea House, Karyn Browne and Mundy Dana helped in that most laborious of tasks—compiling an index to the thousands of documents so that those ideas might surface through the mass of official prose.

Jean Herskovits
New York

January, 1972

SUBSAHARAN AFRICA:
THE LOWEST PRIORITY

SUBSAHARAN AFRICA:
THE LOWEST PRIORITY

Commentary

The official language in which the United States government has addressed the problems of Subsaharan Africa consistently stressed ties of history and outlook between America and Africa. Links with Liberia's past always come first, a recital of the American role in Liberia's creation in the 1820's as a place to resettle freed slaves; of laggardly American official recognition in 1862, fifteen years after Liberia declared her nationhood and Britain recognized her; of ties of a less-than-colonial sort through the century that followed and beyond. (The bond of centuries of slave-trading that more crucially linked peoples of West Africa and North America by blood is generally ignored.)

Following upon Liberia comes mention of Ethiopia, with acknowledged centuries of history that have made it special in outsiders' eyes, and American diplomatic relations going back to 1903. Through the 1940's and 1950's, inclusion of the Union of South Africa among fully independent nations—and members of the British Commonwealth—precedes an allusion to the semi-independent status of Southern Rhodesia, internally self-governing since 1923. Until the late 1950's, those four countries were Subsaharan Africa to the Department of State, to other United States government officials, and to most Americans, if they thought about Africa at all.

Even in that rudimentary recognition that Africa existed were strands of what American policy would be, strands of contradiction, of explanation and justification and of rhetoric. The duality that has been seen in American official views towards Africa—that is, between self-interest broadly interpreted (usually in related geopolitical, economic, and military terms), and phrases, rooted deep in at least the mythology of the past, of an idealistic commitment to the dignity of all men, political freedom, self-determination for all peoples—that duality must be taken as constant. Nor is it unusual, for in general no country has totally reconciled ideology with *realpolitik*, and, in particular, the United States had been balancing off the words of the Declaration of Independence and the Constitution against concrete national and often private American interests through the decades.

An observer of the African scene in the 1960's once remarked on the pity that no African state had a manageable constitution—no quotable pronouncements, no ringing phrases to memorize or to inspire national pride and purpose. But, however one may view the impact of these idealistic expressions on Americans, they have, through their impact beyond our shores, pointed up contradictions in our policies, led to urgent demands that we subordinate our special interests to them, and opened the possibility for disillusionment when what is called "reality" gains the upper hand.

The duality between ideology and *realpolitik* has emerged from the earliest decades. Though Africa itself was not the prime consideration in this conflict, it figured prominently in the tension over the slave trade and its abolition, or the one over the slightly less crucial question across the sea, America's abolition of slavery. Through late 1940's, American contacts beyond the minor trade that followed the end of slaving were virtually nil. The contradictions were reflected in the gap between words and inaction, not the harsher, crueler kind between words and opposing action. The neglect of Liberia whether or not benign, was clear; only in the 1920's was that country touched by the American interests, in the form of the Firestone Rubber Company, in full accord with ideas of free enterprise and private initiative so long an adjunct of British and American overseas policy.

Sometimes the idealism, deeply and truly felt, had an impact: the campaign to have the Congo Independent State removed from the brutal and arbitrary personal control of King Leopold II and his agents, to literally force responsibility upon a reluctant Belgian parliament, drew impressive strength from humanitarian Americans and Britons. Most eloquent was Mark Twain's *King Leopold's Soliloquy*, published in Boston in 1905 and in London a year later. In an age where the representative assemblies of the western world began to pay attention to public opinion, at home and abroad, the American reaction added important pressure for the change that came in 1908.

The same period produced an early irony. The first American public outcry for self-determination in Africa was against British imperial rule, in favor of the outnumbered yet hardy, courageous people oppressed by the huge, powerful, economic military European giant. But the underdogs in the Anglo-Boer War of 1900-1902—the outnumbered hardy, courageous people—were the Boers, the non-British Europeans of South Africa. No European or American then thought the fight against imperialism concerned the Africans. If the British and the Boers did not worry about the natives, let alone ask them for their ideas, it is not surprising that the Americans, championing the underdog, rallied psychological support for the Afrikaners rather than the black Africans. No one could then foresee the consequences, among which American sentiment favoring white self-government in Africa in the early 20th century has been the most minute example.

When Woodrow Wilson's Fourteen Points emerged from the events of 1914-1918, the impact on the non-western world was scarcely intended and scarcely noticed. And yet those principles brought forth a Pan-African delegation to the Peace Conference at Versailles, a delegation headed by W.E.B. Du Bois "representing" African interests. They hoped to affect the future of the new League of Nations mandated territories, and to influence Jan C. Smuts, the by-then-world-renowned South African leader, himself an Afrikaner. Neither effort was particularly successful; neither attracted the particular interest of the American delegation. Other matters were for them, then as virtually always, of far greater importance.

In the years that followed, the Italian invasion of Ethiopia and the western response to it showed how little Africa counted. There was the rhetoric inside—and for the United States outside—the League; there was action by default, policy by inaction, a total contradiction to the words (nor was there even, as in Spain, an Abraham Lincoln Brigade). Perhaps that only shows how little Africa, even Ethiopia, meant to outsiders —except, of course, to invaders with special interests.

With the coming of the Second World War, President Roosevelt spoke of the "Four Freedoms" and, with Prime Minister Churchill, issued the Atlantic Charter in 1941. For Roosevelt self-determination and other universal rights recognized in the Charter meant to apply to the western-dominated colonies. But colonial liberation, however it might be stimulated or even hastened as a side effect of the conflict, was never a central issue in the American war effort or the policy or popular feeling behind it.

The American commitment to the new United Nations, a commitment begun during the fighting and vigorously advanced to avoid repeating the fiasco with the League of Nations, forced United States policy makers into a few thoughts about "dependent territories." In the earlier shreds of policy towards Africa, contradictions had been latent. Now, in the new climate of the Cold War the inconsistencies were striking even if the priorities were, if anything, lower relatively then before. There was genuine idealism, a belief that did go beyond mere words that Americans had fought a war in which principle and morality had, perhaps uniquely, weighed as heavily as self-interest and self-defense. The words did not make distinctions among peoples; that had been part of what the struggle was about. And yet, to follow those prescriptions logically, consistently, would be to advocate for those under colonial domination what we advocated for those under other domination. And to do that was not just to oppose past interests of our wartime allies; it was to weaken them in a present in which their importance was immediate. For it was a polarized world, and they were on "our side."

As early as 1942, Cordell Hull, President Roosevelt's equally anti-colonial Secretary of State, had shown the loop-hole that would repeatedly justify American policy through later years:

> We have always believed ... that all peoples, without distinction of race, color, or religion, who are *prepared and willing to accept the responsibilities of liberty*, are entitled to its enjoyment.[1] [italics mine.]

The definitional latitude was, then and thereafter, enormous. And there was also the early enunciation of the use of American *influence* to this end; but no experienced diplomat would suppose that even the "full measure of our influence" was a binding commitment to action.

In this postwar climate Subsaharan Africa could arouse little interest. True, African matters did graduate into a Bureau of Near Eastern, South Asian and African Affairs (except for Egypt, Ethiopia, Liberia and the Union of South Africa, all Africa was previously the responsibility of the Bureau of European Affairs). But there, too, they were the lowest of priorities. The United States continued to view Africa as a concern of the colonizers, and to let what little policy we had flow from Europe. The occasional statements issued in the 1950's openly expressed relief that, with Africa under western colonial control, there was at least one place the United States need not fear a penetrating Communist menace. Not until September, 1958 did the State Department, prodded by Ghana's independence, announce a new Bureau of African Affairs, to be headed by its own Assistant Secretary of State.

Informed European opinion in the early and mid-1950's was complacent about the "evolution" of the African territories (how often one heard, both from officials in the metropoles and administrators on the scene, "oh, yes, there will be independence ... in 25 years," or it might be fifty or a hundred). Few Europeans recognized the force of those coming "winds of change"; how could one expect that less knowledgeable Americans would be aware of it?

The African perspective on those years was quite different. A new leadership, most

[1] Cordell Hull, *Memoirs*, Vol. II (New York, 1948) pp. 1484-85.

active in West Africa, listened to Allied rhetoric during the war years, and they had taken it seriously. Some had fought overseas, had seen Europe beleaguered, had seen Europeans in less elevated positions and activities than they assumed in their colonies. Some had seen black Americans, true, still segregated, still not often in command, but in some situations where they and whites were equal in status and in performance. French Equatorial Africa had been a center for the Free French; for over two years they called Brazzaville the provisional capital of France. Charles de Gaulle had spoken there in 1944, had promised rewards for wartime loyalty. Other Africans had gone overseas for higher education, mostly to Europe, but some, from English-speaking territories, to the United States.

These men came back to their countries with goals of self-determination and independence, and even though these goals were not new (Africans had resisted European domination in myriad ways from its first imposition), they carried with them new ideas about political means. Mass based political parties would force Europe and all "mother countries" to keep their promises.

Where there were no white settlers, the African countries followed rapid and, in most cases, orderly steps to internal autonomy and, soon, full independence. The style varied with the policies and practices of the ruling power, but the colonial nations of Europe—at least England and France—were being squeezed by political and economic pressures at home and in other parts of the globe. These combined with steadily stronger African pressure to break the formal bonds.

The movement to self-determination snow-balled, a metaphor no less accurate for its climatic incongruity. Sometimes events worked in unexpected ways: The independence of the Gold Coast as Ghana in March, 1957 gave the great impetus (the independence of the Sudan two years before had had little impact), a psychological one to Africans generally, but with other effects as well. It forced the United Nations to come to specific terms with the status of African trust territories, for once-German-Togoland had been mandated to England and France, and the administration of the British-ruled part had belonged to the Gold Coast. If it were to be independent, what of British Togoland? And if British Togo were to change in political status, what of the French half, for there was considerable sentiment for joining the two (as did later happen). Similar challenges arose from Nigeria's projected independence, and the questions it raised for the Cameroons.

These events and plans forced actions from the French as well as the U.N. First came legislation splitting the federations of French West and French Equatorial Africa into territories, each for the first time with a form of internal self-government. Then in 1958, Charles de Gaulle, with a vision for Subsaharan French-speaking Africa and acting in the context of Algerian events and domestic French politics, produced the French Community. French-ruled peoples were, by a device later to become familiar, suddenly offered a vote on continuing association with France: a "*oui*," vote, for the Community and increased but not total autonomy; "*non*," for independence now. Only Guinea, under the leadership of Sékou Touré, voted "*non*" (and in mere hours the French left, in a chaotic and ill-tempered exit in which they took even the telephones, pulled out by the wires).

The momentum increased; 1960, to be dubbed "the year of Africa," was less than two years off. During that year a shift in French policy would give independence to Community members; one of Africa's two giants, Nigeria, would be totally self-governing; and, in the pressure-cooker panic caused by world opinion, a paternalistic policy gone awry, and escalating African demands from rural as well as urban areas, Belgium rushed to be rid of formal control of the Congo (whatever the plans for a less formal—shall we say a covert—role, events overtook them).

If the colonial powers of Europe were unprepared for the pace of an Africa pushing to self-determination, how much less ready was the United States. True, the American Vice President attended Ghana's Independence celebrations, but it took a year longer for the State Department to have a separate Bureau of African Affairs, and only in 1959 did the Senate and the House of Representatives create sub-committees dealing with Africa. It is scarcely surprising that Guinea's sudden independence produced neither the immediate recognition nor desperately needed and requested aid that would have enhanced the American position so markedly in Africa. The hesitation and inaction were undoubtedly attributable not only to regard for French sensibilities, but also to the sheer difficulty of finding informed American officials familiar with the situation.

By 1960 at least the informational ingredients for making policy were more readily available. State Department activities had expanded; the Senate Foreign Relations Committee had commissioned a separate study on Africa in its 1959 review of United States policies throughout the world. Academic activity was increasing too; no longer was it so difficult to attract students on one side, and, on the other, foundation support for African research by such students and established scholars. The State Department released younger foreign service officers for academic training in African studies.

In early 1961 came another change: the administration of President John F. Kennedy. Africa, with recently independent countries and wracked by crisis in the Congo, could look to the United States and see a President who had been the first chairman of the Senate Foreign Relations Committee's Sub-Committee on Africa. Moreover, his language was different, and his attitudes seemed new. His first appointment was the Assistant Secretary of State for Africa, and neither of them talked of Africa in Cold War terms (though some Cold War attitudes and their expression still loomed large). He launched the Peace Corps, to meet crying needs for education and technical training—to reach the "Third World" directly, not through European intermediaries.

Though Africa remained a low priority in the global context of American foreign relations, Africans sensed, correctly, a change in attitude. It grew partly from Africa's spotlighted appearance on the world scene—new countries, new voices at the U.N. at a time when that organization focused on an African problem. But it also grew from an American domestic consideration—the role of black Americans. The 1960's saw black Americans as an important voting bloc in the internal political equation for the first time in decades. That the incumbent administration was at least somewhat responsive to their existence and problems, even occasionally to their pressures, coincided with an awakening black American interest in Africa. And that coincidence created conditions in which government officials might begin to consider the problems of Africa. It was a set of circumstances that would change in the later 1960's but for the moment it produced at least a different tone.

When before had an high State Department official on African travels said, "Africa for the Africans," and in a country with a European settler population at that? When, for that matter, had senior State Department officials travelled so much in Africa?

When had a President of the United States, asked about that very statement, retorted, "And who else would Africa be for?" Whatever the later explanations ("all Africans, black and white"), the message to many Africans seemed a new commitment.

In fact there were some possibilities for change. Inside the State Department were new men, some young, some older, but with a different outlook on America's role in the world. From the Deputy Assistant Secretary for Africa, Wayne Fredericks, throughout the ranks of the Africa Bureau were men who knew Africa from study and experience. That they had counterparts in the other State Department bureaus made it easier for them to work to change the perspective on Africa. On the European desk there were now men who questioned a continuing role, direct or indirect, for western colonialism—who had themselves a sense of the importance of dealing with African matters in African terms. This sense had not existed for those who conceived policy in the context of earlier eras, men who would recoil from describing Portuguese or Belgian policy in Africa as "bankrupt," a term that came easily to the others.

The real obstacles to these efforts to bring a new emphasis to African affairs came from two directions. First they ran up against those at the top, whose Cold War thinking and whose general analysis of American security and self-interest did not lend itself to elevating Africa to new importance.

The other set of obstacles are familiar ones in any departmentalized government, for not only might other State Department bureaus have special interests, but so clearly did Commerce, Defense, and Treasury, and even such agencies as NASA and the CAB. Their concerns were far different from the men in the Africa Bureau, and one could not expect to find, and did not, knowledge of and sympathy towards African aims and the American image in Africa that had come to exist in other branches of State.

When retired General Lauris Norstad, president of the Owens-Corning Fiberglass Corporation, said in Johannesburg in 1965, "We have full confidence in South Africa—not only we as individuals but the United States and the American people," his white audience might, had they been looking for them, have glimpsed such conflicting strains in American policy towards South Africa. Norstad might have been thought to reflect a favorable inclination of the Pentagon as well as American business towards the South African regime. But that was the very view the "Afro-philes" in the State Department were fighting to reverse, especially because of the key importance for our African policy of our stance towards Southern Africa. Other policies were important of course: politically, the American position on Africa's determined refusal to become involved in Cold War alignments; economically, the assistance, public and private, in aid, trade, investment, training, that the United States could offer. But for international ramifications in Africa itself, no issue mattered more than the fate of the "White Redoubt," and every African nation believed that America could affect that fate if she wanted.

It was because they understood that fact that the men of the Africa Bureau threw all their efforts into obtaining an American declaration of an arms embargo, voluntarily self-imposed, against South Africa, a measure announced five days before the similar U.N. resolution, passed by the Security Council on August 7, 1963. As one of them put it, "We believed that, whatever else, it would some day be very important for an American President to be able to say flatly that we had not armed *white* South Africa for domination of or war with *black* Africa."

Despite such rare successes, successes as much for achieving action as for the content of that action, Subsaharan African matters did not rise in the hierarchy of importance. The reasons grew from internal African events, but more, from global changes far beyond that continent's control.

In the years after 1964 (by then almost thirty countries had become independent since 1960) many of Africa's new nations underwent internal upheavals through military coups d'etat; African states in the throes of political and economic growth could not avoid domestic dissension and difficulty any more than could the world's other peoples through the centuries. This instability tarnished Africa's glow in the eyes of Americans, who were quick to judge "Progress" (or its absence) in an age of rapid change.

More important, Africa was simply eclipsed. Internationally, American public attention focused ever more intensely on Southeast Asia. Whether passions were directed towards a greater involvement in Vietnam (the "finish-the-job" psychology) or, as they increasingly were, towards a withdrawal from a war seen as the epitome of American meddling and violation of fundamental American beliefs and principles—in both cases, a resolve emerged not to become similarly entangled elsewhere, for any, or almost any, reason. And certainly not in Africa. From one side came arguments that African involvement was in no way in America's national interest; it certainly was not crucial to national security. From the other came abhorrence of further American interference in the internal affairs of others, often phrased as passionate opposition to "further American neo-colonialism." For once self-interest and idealism did not contradict—but they reinforced an even further downgrading of African policy on the official side.

There were other domestic factors too. A growing preoccupation with internal problems had an indirect impact on Africa through the insistence that priorities be reordered with the needs of the poor, the unemployed, the cities, the minorities coming ahead of foreign commitments. But those concerns came amid a decreasing willingness to listen to the very people suffering most from these problems. Black Americans were among those whose political power no longer mattered. Further, preoccupied by their massive problems in the United States itself, black Americans were also less inclined to throw their energies into African matters. And so, during the Johnson and particularly the Nixon administrations, there was no pressure to move to formulate active African policy. (The "Black Caucus" in the House of Representatives became in 1970 a vehicle for possible renewed efforts.)

Those administrations, preoccupied as they were with war in Southeast Asia, scarcely needed to think that Africa was again, or perhaps still, the lowest of priorities. President Johnson's move to send three C-130 transport planes to help General Joseph Mobutu out of Portuguese-provoked Congolese trouble in July, 1967, drew an instant roar of indignation from the press and the United States Congress. The planes quickly returned; outcries came from all political sides.

The civil war in Nigeria, breaking out in Summer, 1967 and lasting until January, 1970, brought private American activities, especially to alleviate the suffering of the war's victims. The American government contributed food and medicine, but under two presidents it firmly refused to actively intervene, not allowing even sales of arms.

The United States military commitment to Ethiopia, begun clandestinely in 1953, and escalating to active involvement during the 1960's, came to light only through hearings in June, 1970 before Senator Symington's Subcommittee on U.S. Security Agreements and Commitments Abroad of the Senate Foreign Relations Committee. Although it was a commitment made for reasons of global communications and possibly of Middle Eastern (rather than African) policy, it still aroused Senatorial ire. Thus far, it is the only such American involvement that has come to light in Subsaharan Africa.

Understandably the greatest concern of the African states is their own economic development. It is no exaggeration to say on that all else depends, directly or indirectly. What African states have wanted and needed most from the United States—and from the industrialized world generally—is economic and technical assistance. The economics of colonial rule had been conducted with an eye to raw materials and their exports and, only very late in the colonial era, to a measure of industrialization and diversification aimed at a small step towards self-sufficiency. The efforts of the colonial powers went into building part of an infra-structure: the stress was on roads and railroads, networks within the colonial boundaries, never across them. Such political planning later created continuing economic complications. Another all-important effort, varying from colony to colony, went into education and technical training. In most cases, however, these innovations were largely financed from colonial funds, that is, from taxes raised within the colonies themselves.

Before the late 1950's the United States gave virtually no official thought to African economic or educational problems. Except for Liberia and Ethiopia—and except for all-important private investments in Liberia and in Southern Africa—these matters were considered the concern of the European metropoles. There was fleeting thought that some Marshall Plan money might find its way into the colonies, and thus was any American obligation discharged.

Framed in the context of reconstructing Europe, America's aid policy was thought to be a continuingly useful tool of foreign policy in the Cold War. Again combining self-interest and idealism, officials proposed such aid for new African states in the still-prevailing Cold War climate of the late 1950's and early 1960's. Even within that framework, however, Africa with possibly the greatest needs was again not a priority.

Figures that include aid to the North Africa countries of Algeria, Morocco, and Tunisia, show United States economic assistance (including AID and its predecessors, Export-Import Bank long-term loans, Food for Freedom, and other economic programs) as climbing from approximately $100 million in 1958 to a peak of just under $380 million in 1962; then came a rapid decline to $329.4 million in 1965, a "recovery" to $384 million in 1966, followed by steady decline. Even that recovery was illusory, for the *percentage* of aid to developing countries allotted to Africa has receded: after rising from 3.4 percent in 1958 to 11.2 percent in 1961, it was back to 7.2 percent by 1968.[2]

But at its height, aid to Africa—all of Africa, excluding only Egypt—was a lower percentage of United States economic assistance than that to any other region, though the per capita figures tell a more generous tale.

Further, since American aid had rebuilt war-torn economies in Europe, United States policy makers thought that those same European countries should be the major donors of aid in Africa: they had specific obligations as colonial, or former colonial,

[2] Africa Briefing—1968. Hearing ... before the Subcommittee on Africa of the Committee on Foreign Affairs, 90th Cong. 2d sess., July 23, 1968, and Waldemar A. Nielsen, *The Great Powers and Africa,* (N.Y., 1969), p. 390.

rulers, and the United States, through her contributions to European recovery, had already given assistance—however indirectly—to the underdeveloped colonies or newly independent nations. Thus Liberia and Ethiopia received special American attention, for the very reason that no European country had commitments to their economic growth.

At times the executive branch of the government tried to increase economic aid in general; sometimes there were special references to Africa. But despite repeated speeches emphasizing the importance and necessity of increasing assistance to African states, ambassadors and AID officials and Assistant Secretaries of State and even Presidents were thwarted by Congressional cuts in meager proposals.

Based on a report by the then Ambassador to Ethiopia, Edward M. Korry, President Johnson advanced four important goals early in 1967: 1) "to encourage greater and more effective cooperation among donor agencies in extending aid to Africa and greater use of multi-national agencies"; 2) "to encourage greater economic cooperation among African recipients on a regional basis . . ."; 3) "to support development in all of independent Africa and on a long-term basis"; and 4) "to improve and gradually increase U.S. aid to Africa." As Waldemar Nielson of the African-American Institute has put it, "The Korry Report and President Johnson proposed; but the Congress disposed." (p. 394)

Once again Africa had fallen victim to internal forces in America, and to the ramifications of world events. Despite the idealistic phrases, foreign aid had been largely a Cold War stratagem. Aid to Africa, even at its peak, had been selective; only a few countries received the benefits, and they were often chosen for reasons tinged with Cold War thinking—the Congo, Ghana, Guinea, even Nigeria, are examples. But now, in the late 1960's, Americans cared less about the Cold War. Nor did they see Africa any longer as a Cold War battleground: African nations had proven the legitimacy of their neutral stand in Great Power rivalry; the paradox, unforeseen, was their inability to use the threat of alignment (to either side, as a lever against the other) to gain Great Power aid. That America had pressing problems demanding the use of her economic resources at home was later compounded by a recession that some called a depression, followed by a world monetary crisis.

The 1971 Congressional revolt against foreign aid would stimulate a broad rethinking of policy. But it would also further cut the miniscule economic assistance the United States offered to African countries, and it would cut it for reasons totally un-African. Broadly, the Senate especially wished to reassert its decisive role in making foreign policy, a role it claimed was usurped by the executive branch. More immediately both Senators and Congressmen objected to continuing foreign aid programs on the existing basis; their reasons ran a pragmatic-to-moral gamut.

Liberals opposed *military* assistance throughout the "Third World"; conservatives opposed continuing support for economic development, support which, as they saw it, brought nothing in return to the United States. In compromise, both kinds of programs would be cut, but economic aid would suffer more than military, with African states the more neglected thereby.

Nor did Africa loom large in the totality of American trade. Complicated by problems of Commonwealth preferences, and the associate status of French-speaking nations within the Common Market, commercial possibilities were hemmed in by the intricacies of world-wide international arrangements. Further, given the development needs of most African countries, their exports of primary produce, always subject to

the vagaries of world commodity prices, was unlikely to bring them favorable trade
balances without successful efforts at stabilization, efforts requiring world-wide cooperation.

As for investment, a subject often emotionally charged, Africa has historically been
of little interest to American investors. Even by the late 1960's less than 5 percent of
all American overseas investment was in the African continent. Though that amount
exceeded $2 billion, it had been placed selectively and largely in extractive industries:
notably oil, in Libya and more recently in Nigeria and off-shore Angola (under
Portuguese rule); and rubber, in Liberia; and copper, in Zambia and the Congo. Some
30 percent of American capital invested in Africa has gone to South Africa, there too,
largely but not exclusively in extractive ventures, such as mining gold, diamonds, and
uranium.

This investment pattern, of continued American business and financial interest in
South Africa, is crucial, for despite the changes both in the United States and Africa,
the issue of white domination south of the Zambezi remains the central political one
of the 1970's.

It is there, in dealing with Southern Rhodesia, with Mocambique and Angola
("Portuguese" Africa), with South Africa and Namibia (South West Africa), that the
United States will be tested by the rest of Africa. It is in that region that the United
States can most easily fall back on the tenacious justifications of policy from earlier
years: the crucial nature of military-global consideration; the remnants of the Cold
War rationale, the support of NATO allies and recognition of their "right" to direct
policy, stability as rationalization for supporting the status quo, especially where
American economic interests are present.

Brief efforts to beat back such reasoning, or at least to swamp it with more
Afro-centered considerations, have already receded. Elsewhere on the continent declining American concern has reinforced the tendency to let the ex-colonial powers do it,
whatever "it" may be at any moment. Such an attitude is hardly astonishing in a
climate in which the President devotes to Africa only five out of some 230 pages of
prescriptions to Congress on "U.S. Foreign Policy for the 1970's: Building for Peace."
(Richard Nixon, February 25, 1971.)

In January, 1971, the United States withdrew, it seemed, in the usual tandem with
Britain, from the U.N. Committee on Colonialism—the conclusion of two years' signs
of pique. Americans explained the action in vague terms, in conjunction with mounting complaints about one-sided actions forced through by Afro-Asian and Soviet
efforts. This step did not increase African confidence that United States policy was
without European bias. Even in the early 1960's American officials had been careful
not to tread on French interests in Africa, though it meant catering to the particular
anti-Americanism that policy produced.

Safeguarding the status quo and American economic interests has led to continuing
token activity in places of such apparently diverse ideologies as Touré's Guinea and
Mobutu's Zaire (Congo-Kinshasa). But to shift policy to unquestioning accommodation south of the Zambezi is to risk placing the United States on the white side of a
conflict which, whether it will end in the holocaust of race war or not, could severely
polarize the world along racial lines.

GENERAL POLICY

Address by George C. McGhee, Assistant Secretary for African Affairs, on United States Interests in Africa*

May, 1950

There is no single answer to the problem of formulating an African policy, as there is no single answer to other major problems which confront us today. What then are our objectives in Africa? How can we reconcile the diverse and conflicting influences which demand consideration? How can we, at the same time, establish a position which represents the best interests of the United States and is consistent with the principles which have traditionally motivated our foreign policy?

*   *   *

Because of the dependent status of most of the African territories, the United States conducts relations with them in large measure through our diplomatic missions in the European capitals. Certain aspects of our relations are also carried on through consular establishments in many of the territories, which function primarily to safeguard American nationals, American commercial interests, and treaty rights in Africa. In the case of Egypt, Liberia, Ethiopia, and the Union of South Africa, we maintain direct relations through our Embassies in those countries and through their representatives in Washington.

*   *   *

Before undertaking to outline the general problems of the area, it would be desirable to place it in the context of the present world situation. In the light of the many critical problems which confront us today and against the background of the great struggle which is being waged between the Communist nations and those of the free world, this area occupies comparatively little space in the American press or in the consciousness of the American people. One reason for this is the fact that it is a region in which we have few direct responsibilities. Other nations, chiefly those with whom we are associated under the North Atlantic Treaty, are directly responsible for solution of the day-to-day problems of Africa. Another reason is the fact that, although tensions are increasing in several parts of Africa, it is not a crisis area. Emergency measures are not required to deal with the problems of the area.

In these troubled times, it is gratifying to be able to single out a region of 10 million square miles in which no significant inroads have been made by communism, and to be able to characterize the area as relatively stable and secure. Yet, if one carefully distinguishes between efforts in behalf of normal political and economic aspirations and agitation inspired by Communist elements, that is basically the case. It is difficult to judge whether the failure of communism to make progress is due to resistance or disinterest on the part of the African peoples, to the results of construc-

**Department of State Bulletin*, June 19, 1950, pp. 999-1000.

tive efforts by the governments concerned or their effective vigilance toward Communist propaganda and agitation, or whether the Cominform has been so occupied elsewhere that it has not yet devoted its maximum efforts to the penetration and subversion of the African continent. But, no matter what the reason, if this is one area in the world, where—in the broadest sense—no major crisis exists, then it is imperative that advantage be taken of the absence of pressure to plan against the time when such pressure may be applied.

Advantage must be taken of this period of grace to further the development within Africa of healthy political, economic, and social institutions, to create an understanding on the part of the Africans of the forces of communism which are disturbing the peace and security of hundreds of millions of peoples elsewhere in the world, and to inspire a determination to resist these forces. Advantage must be taken of the time at our disposal to remedy, through foresighted and constructive action, conditions which could otherwise make the Africans receptive to the baleful attractions of communism and thus nullify the peaceful and progressive advancement of its peoples. And, even though we do not have direct responsibilities in the case of much of Africa, we Americans cannot neglect Africa simply because it is quiescent in the present world crisis. We must play, in cooperation with others, the part which our position in the world demands that we play.

*   *   *

Address by Assistant Secretary McGhee on Africa's Role in the Free World*

June 27, 1951

Africa today remains oriented toward the free world both economically and politically, but we must not make light of the difficulties which face us—the peoples of the free world—if it is to remain so oriented. Communism as such appears to have made no substantial progress in the area, but continuation of this state of affairs cannot be taken for granted. Recent developments have focused attention on Africa's increasingly important role in global affairs. It provides a sizable proportion of the strategic materials now required by the Western powers, including such minerals as copper, chrome, cobalt, manganese, bauxite, asbestos, tin, industrial diamonds, and uranium. It also provides rubber, sisal, hardwoods, hides, fats, and oils.

Since three-fourths of the Continent's inhabitants are under European control, and the sovereign countries of Africa are allied both economically and politically with Europe and the United States, Africa is firmly associated with the free world. The Europeans regard their African territories as essential to their economic well-being, their military security, and their political position in the world community. Since the Second World War, Africa's importance to them has been greatly enhanced.

The Soviet rulers have also become increasingly aware of the importance of Africa to the free world and are accelerating their efforts to weaken European prestige and control with the hope of ultimately including the African territories in the Soviet bloc. In Africa there is fortunately time to apply preventive rather than curative methods

Ibid., July 16, 1951, pp. 97-101.

against communism. But, as Elspeth Huxley recently pointed out: "We run a race with time, on the one hand, our good intentions, our needs, and our resolve to remake and enlighten, and, on the other hand, the natural and gathering impatience of the half-educated, fed on the vapor of our own philosophy—to be done with an alien ruler."

Conditions exist in many parts of Africa which could well play into the hands of Communist agitators—low standards of living, attitudes of white supremacy, and disintegration of tribal authority. In the war of propaganda and diplomacy which the Soviets are waging throughout the world, the central purpose is to destroy the unity of the free world, to pit against each other Americans, Europeans, Asians, and Africans. Soviet propagandists accuse Americans and Europeans of talking of democracy and liberty and yet confining their application to a small minority. The Russians accuse the West of preaching justice and practicing inequality, leaving masses of people in poverty. Russia exploits grievances and poverty, incites resistance to authority, and encourages class and race hatred.

While the Russians have not attempted to establish states in Africa based on Communist ideology, they desire to disrupt the existing governments and create revolutionary conditions which would, if successful, react unfavorably on Europe. Communists in Africa infiltrate wherever possible into labor unions and nationalist movements. They attempt to subvert to Communist ends, movements sincerely designed to improve the position of the African.

In meeting the Soviet threat in Africa, the Department of State attempts to expose Communist lies and to reveal the true nature of "Soviet imperialism."

*   *   *

Exposing the falsities of Soviet propaganda, however, is not sufficient. To provide an answer to Russia's propaganda we must reaffirm our faith in the principles of the free world and its way of life. We must show to the Africans and others that their individual and national aspirations can best be achieved in company with the free world community.

We could do much worse than take the advise of Chief Kidahu of Tanganyika, the first African member of the Executive Council in East Africa who recently suggested: "The prime duty of European, Asian, and African leaders is to find and develop points of agreement." He added significantly: "We Africans will not be misled by extremists if the mass of the people come to feel that the Africans are being given fair representation."

If a true partnership can be worked out between Europeans, Africans, Asians, and Americans—based on mutual self-respect and understanding and the acceptance of mutual responsibilities—non-Africans will be less apt to confuse the African of today with his unprivileged grandfather, and Africans will not confuse the present-day European with his less liberal grandfather. Justified resentment against the practices of nineteenth century colonialism, tainted as it was with human exploitation and racial discrimination, will be replaced by a respect for the constant growth of international accountability for dependent peoples under the aegis of the United Nations.

Africans rightly insist, however, that words must be backed up with deeds. On the whole, the postwar performance of the metropolitan powers shows that steps are being taken in the right direction.

*   *   *

Immediate independence is, however, not the cure for all colonial problems. The United States Government has always maintained that premature independence for primitive, uneducated peoples can do them more harm than good and subject them to an exploitation by indigenous leaders, unrestrained by the civic standards that come with widespread education, that can be just as ruthless as that of aliens. Also, giving full independence to peoples unprepared to meet aggression or subversion can endanger not only the peoples themselves but the security of the free world.

It is, however, the traditional policy of the United States to support orderly movements toward self-government. We have followed with interest, therefore, the efforts of the various European governments over the years to promote the political, economic, social, and educational advancement of the peoples in African territorial and the spread of genuine African nationalism. African nationalism derives in part from the acute nationalism prevalent in other parts of the world and, in part, is a reaction to foreign propaganda against colonialism. It is also derived, however, from an emerging belief that Africans as such must stand together.

Of especial interest have been the recent political developments in British West Africa. January 1, 1951, marked an historic day in the Gold Coast. It may well mark an historic day in Africa. It was on this day that a new constitution became effective in the Gold Coast, establishing popular elections and granting to the African himself broad competence over his own affairs for the first time in African colonial history. This last month I had the privilege of welcoming to Washington on behalf of my government two distinguished visitors from the Gold Coast, Mr. Nkrumah, the Leader of Government Business, and Mr. Botsio, the Minister of Education and Social Welfare, following Mr. Nkrumah's reception of an honorary doctorate at his alma mater, Lincoln University.

I took this occasion to point out to our honored guests that, while the far-reaching developments in British colonial policy had produced misgivings in certain quarters, we ourselves had no such misgivings—that we had observed the efficient manner with which the preliminary stages of this bold experiment had been worked out cooperatively between the British officials and the Africans, and the moderation and sense of responsibility shown by the African leaders since the constitution became operative. I pointed out that we were confident that this significant beginning in African administration would succeed; that it must succeed in order to prove that the African is capable of governing himself. I also cautioned that people were watching with some degree of anxiety, knowing that there are serious obstacles to vercome. Foremost among these will be the difficulty of unifying a diverse people, a people differing in language and customs and in degree of political consciousness and economic development. The boldness of the experiment could only be measured in the light of these difficulties.

Mr. Nkrumah in return spoke feelingly of his awareness of the difficulties and the responsibilities, as well as the opportunities, involved in setting up a new government which he hoped in the not too distant future would attain full dominion status within the British Commonwealth.

Elections will soon take place in Nigeria, and a new government will be elected under the new constitution which will, like the Gold Coast Constitution, represent a significant step in the direction of full self-government. These and other constitutional developments in British Africa offer convincing evidence of a sincerity of purpose in carrying out the long-avowed objectives of British colonial policy of advancing dependent peoples to self-government as rapidly as conditions permit. They represent an incontestable denial of the oft-repeated charges of the Kremlin that the British and other European nations are intent on keeping dependent peoples in permanent subjection. Only by helping responsible African leaders create a state of society which the mass of the people will find infinitely preferable to the alternative offered by the Communists, can the full cooperation of the African be assured to the free world.

Among many of the peoples living in Africa, only slightly touched by modern civilization, the immediate problem is not political status but improvement of health, sanitation, living and working conditions, and education and training in the fundamentals upon which successful participation in government can be achieved.

Within the framework of the United Nations, the various Member nations having overseas territories have assumed specific obligations with respect to the dependent peoples of Africa. They have declared that they "recognize the principle that the interests of the inhabitants of these territories are paramount" and that "they accept as a sacred trust the obligation to promote to the utmost ... the well-being of the inhabitants of these territories." Furthermore, in accepting the doctrine of international accountability they agreed to send regularly to the United Nations information on the economic, social, and educational conditions in their colonies. If one reviews these reports and the huge development and welfare schemes of the various metropolitan powers with territories in Africa, as I am sure you plan to, one cannot help but be impressed with the steps that have been taken since World War II to promote the political, economic, social, and educational advancement of the peoples of their territories.

*   *   *

Through ECA, extensive aid has been provided in the form of both grants and loans, to the African dependencies of France, United Kingdom, Belgium, and, to a smaller extent, Portugal.

Since France has elected to utilize a substantial portion of her regularly allotted ECA program funds for recovery and development purposes in her overseas territories, as well as considerable franc allotments from ECA-generated counterpart funds, Morocco, Algeria, Tunisia, and the large French territories south of the Sahara have been the largest recipients of ECA aid. Altogether, the French have used approximately 285 million dollars in ECA country program funds for territorial imports, and, in addition, about 140 million dollars equivalent in local currency counterpart funds to the overseas territories.

The ECA has also provided considerable aid through grants and loans, to the African Dependent Overseas Territories from a special reserve fund for overseas development. Up to the present time, the ECA aid approved from that source to British, French, and Belgian territories has come to more than 62 million dollars. Assistance from this fund, which has been more and more closely related to critical sectors in the current investment programs for the overseas territories, has been provided in support of a wide range of projects including road developments, developments in river navigation and port facilities, agricultural projects, power installations where these are required in support of expanding production, irrigation schemes, and the like.

Aid provided through ECA has also been made available in the form of technical assistance. Through May 31, 1951, 49 technical-assistance projects in the dependent overseas territories had been approved by ECA at a total cost of about $110,000. The scope of assistance thus provided has been quite wide, including surveys of mineral and other resources, engineering aid in planning transportation routes, and recommendations for birth-control measures. In the handling of these projects, ECA has emphasized continuously the importance of transfer of "know-how" to local technicians in order that the benefits of the assistance provided may be permanent in character.

While ECA has given substantial assistance to the dependent overseas territories in Africa, little or no aid has been extended to the neighboring independent countries. The Point Four agreements which have been signed with Liberia, Libya, Eritrea and Ethiopia will tend to fill this gap.

*   *   *

From the foregoing, it may be seen that there is today a vast ferment of cooperative activity in the development of Africa. It will be effective only if all concerned have an appreciation of certain basic facts. Europeans and Americans having responsibilities in Africa must clearly recognize that there is no short and easy path to economic development which ignores the social complex and the psychological needs of African society. The African peoples must realize that if social and economic evolution is to become integrated effectively into African life, then they themselves must be prepared to assume a large share of the burden and responsibilities which it involves. Both African and non-African must realize that each has a separate but valuable contribution to make in the development of this vast Continent, and that maximum results will be obtained only by combining the African peoples' traditional and intuitive knowledge of their country with the European and American heritage of scientific and industrial advance.

The new era of progress and growing independence which has started in Africa with the help of the free nations of the world stands out in bold contrast to the dark spirit of reactionary colonialism which animates Russian expansionist philosophy. The peoples of Africa must realize that the greatest danger to the full realization of their economic, social, and spiritual development lies in the menace of Communist imperialism, which threatens the security of the entire free world and assures for the Africans as colonial peoples—not self-government but a dark future of political and cultural enslavement.

*Address by Henry A. Byrode, Assistant Secretary for African Affairs
on the World's Colonies and Ex-Colonies.* *

October 31, 1953

When we Americans turn our thoughts to international relations, one problem stands out above all others. Our principal concern is the threat of Soviet aggression, which could culminate in the horrible tragedy of atomic warfare. Americans are therefore sometimes surprised to learn that there are vast areas of the world where the Sovie threat is given secondary emphasis. Throughout parts of Africa, the Near East, South Asia, and the Far East, human interests and emotions are focused primarily on such questions as "imperialism," "colonialism," and "nationalism." In many of these areas, the principal motivating force is the desire of dependent peoples to end foreign domination and achieve political and economic self-determination.

This movement toward self-determination is one of the most powerful forces in 20th-century affairs. When the history of our era is finally written it may prove to have been the most significant of all.

There is a paradox in the fact that the upsurge for national self-determination among the dependent peoples comes at this stage of human history. We know that Western nations, which have long possessed sovereign independence, are coming to recognize that self-sufficiency is a myth. We are moving steadily toward increasing association and interdependence among ourselves. In fact, several of the older nations are now engaged in creating new forms of association in which portions of national sovereignty are voluntarily surrendered.

We must frankly recognize that the hands of the clock of history are set at different hours in different parts of the world. We ourselves believe that peace, prosperity, and human freedom can be assured only within a concert of free peoples which transcends national boundaries. However, we must accept the fact that many of our friends in Asia and Africa tend to view national indepdndence as a magic solution to all their difficulties. The problem is to avoid serious conflict between these viewpoints. We hope that the peoples now seeking self-determination will achieve it and exercise it in such a way as to strengthen rather than weaken the bonds of international cooperation. We hope that they will learn at an early stage of their development what we, of the West, have learned so painfully, tha all mankind is "one continent" and that no nation is sufficient unto itself.

The movement toward self-determination has recently encountered an even more strange and potentially more tragic paradox. At the same time that Western colonialism of the old type is disappearing, a new form of imperialism has begun to extend a clutching hand to every quarter of the globe. I am referring to the new Soviet colonialism. This new colonialism is more subtle and more poisonous than the old, because it often masquerades under the guise of nationalism itself. In the name of independence it persuades people to surrender all hope of independence. In the name of security and economic progress it succeeds in establishing a system of slavery.

Ibid., Nov. 16, 1953, pp. 655-60.

*   *   *

Our basic policy, however, is relatively simple. We believe in eventual self-determination for all peoples, and we believe that evolutionary development to this end should move forward with minimum delay.

Our Government must approach colonial questions in terms of the enlightened self-interest of the United States. We recognize that the disintegration of the old colonialism is inevitable. We believe that much blood and treasure may be saved if the Western World determines firmly to hasten rather than hamper the process of orderly evolution toward self-determination. Moreover we believe that healthy, self-governing societies will prove, in the long run, to be stronger bulwarks in the defense of freedom and the preservation of world peace than weak dependent territories. As Secretary Dulles said last June on returning from his trip to the Near East and Asia, "Without breaking from the framework of Western unity, we can pursue our traditional dedication to political liberty. In reality, the Western powers can gain, rather than lose, from an orderly development of self-government."

We recognize that self-determination will not always be exercised in the form of national independence. Some peoples may choose voluntarily to unite or associate themselves, on a free and equal basis, with the nations which have governed them in the past. The British Commonwealth of Nations and more recently the French Union are outstanding examples of the kind of association which new nations may undertake without impairment of their powers to determine their own destinies. The essence of self-determination is not as much the course of action chosen as the right to choose.

At this point, however, one question inevitably arises. People here and abroad frequently ask "Why evolution? Why not grant all dependent peoples immediate sovereignty? By what right does one nation continue to exercise jurisdiction over a foreign territory?"

This question cannot readily be answered on abstract ethical grounds. No government has God-given right to rule peoples other than its own. The old concept of the "white man's burden" is obsolete and provides no valid justification for colonialism. But if the question defies pure ethics it may nevertheless be answered on practical and human grounds. It is a hard, inescapable fact that premature independence can be dangerous, retrogressive, and destructive.

Unless we are willing to recognize that there is such a thing as premature independence, we can not think intelligently or constructively about the status of dependent peoples. For example, there are areas in which there is no concept of community relationships beyond the family or the tribe. There are regions where human beings are unable to cope with disease, famine, and other forces of nature. Premature independence for these peoples would not serve the interests of the United States nor the interests of the free world as a whole. Least of all would it serve the interests of the dependent peoples themselves.

Let us now consider some of the factors which cause the United States to stress the evolutionary aspects of the movement toward self-determination.

In the first place, we know that the world is shrinking community. No territory can escape from this community and isolate itself from man kind. The withdrawal of foreign influence from a territory not yet capable of independent existence does not mean that the area will simply disappear from the world community. Instead, there will be created a power vacuum, an area of weakness which invites internal disorder and external aggression.

Whenever any people attain nominal sovereignty before they are prepared to exercise it, the net result is weakness. There may be weakness in protecting human rights, weakness in maintaining order, weakness in improving social and economic conditions, weakness in preserving independence itself. In this modern world such weakness is usually dangerous, to the strong as well as the weak.

The United States Government is committed to a policy of promoting strength and well-being in other parts of the world. We should be proud that our national self-interest is in harmony with the desire of other free peoples for strength and progress. We have been generous in helping them achieve these things. Therefore we can be proud of our efforts to prevent the development of the weaknesses which could invite international disaster.

Second, when dependent peoples attain self-determination, we want it to be real, and we want it to endure. If they choose independence, we want them to be able to maintain their independence against the new Soviet imperialism and any other form of tyranny. We do not want the vast labor and pain expended in the struggle for freedom to be wasted by the premature creation of a state which will collapse like a stack of cards at the first hint of difficulty. If, on the other hand, the dependent peoples choose an arrangement other than national independence, such as equal union with their former rulers, this choice should be made freely, without deception or coercion. The peoples making this choice should be prepared to pay their proper role in the new relationship. In other words we want these peoples to have freedom of choice and capacity for self-government similar to that possessed by India, Pakistan, and Ceylon when these nations voluntarily chose association with the British Commonwealth. If a few additional years of evolution can make the difference between a self-determination that endures and a reversion to dependency or chaos, the years will not be wasted.

Third, we know that national independence is by no means a cure-all for the perplexing problems of Asia and Africa. Independence, after all, is but a means to an end. The ultimate objective is the welfare of individual human beings. It is important the the dependent peoples develop governments which can truly represent their interests, protect their liberties, and promote social and economic progress.

These peoples will suffer bitter disappointment if an independent political status offers no hope of solving the age-old problems of poverty, disease, and social discrimination. The peoples of Asia and Africa want more food, better houses, more adequate health facilities, and other concrete human benefits as well as self-government. We want to help them achieve the kind of government which can make these things possible.

Fourth, let us be frank in recognizing our stake in the strength and stability of certain European nations which exercise influence in the dependent areas. These European nations are our allies. They share many common interests with us. They will probably represent, for many years to come, the major source of free-world defensive power outside our own. We cannot blindly disregard their side of the colonial question without injury to our own security. In particular, we cannot ignore the legitimate economic interests which European nations possess in certain dependent territories. Nor can we forget the importance of these interests to the European economy which we have contributed so much to support.

There has been much talk about the "economic exploitation" of dependent peoples. Too little attention has been given to the fact that economic relations between European nations and overseas territories are often beneficial to both parties. Just as Europe needs the raw materials and market opportunities of foreign territories, so do these territories need European manufactured goods, technical skills, and educational facilities. A sudden break in economic relations might seriously injure the European economies upon which our Atlantic defense system depends and at the same time prove equally injurious to the dependent territories themselves. In many instances the sudden withdrawal of European influence would remove one of the major hopes of the dependent peoples for continued economic progress.

Let me make one point very clear. Despite our interest in European economic health, we most certainly do not propose that the rights of dependent peoples should be subordinated to this interest. What we propose is that all parties concerned carefully consider their own interests. This is not a question of preserving Europe's strength at the expense of dependent peoples. It is rather a question of finding ways to increase the strength of both. An evolutionary approach to self-determination can help to preserve legitimate European interests in foreign territories while at the same time giving these territories economic opportunities and benefits which would be lost by a complete severance of relations.

Finally, it is extremely important that the political evolution of the dependent areas follow a course which will permit these peoples to take their place as respected and equal citizens of the free world. Self-determination involves obligations and responsibilities as well as rights and privileges. Statehood in the 20th century is more than a matter of independence. It must include recognition of the obligations of interdependence. It is our earnest hope that the movement toward independence in Asia and Africa will achieve the results expected of it without interfering with a still greater and longer-term trend, the movement toward increasing association and cooperation among all free nations and races.

These considerations should explain the emphasis which we place upon the evolutionary aspect of the movement toward self-determination. At the same time, let me say that it would be contrary to United States interests if these considerations should be used as "excuses" for procrastination or delay. The term "orderly evolution" cannot be translated to mean indefinite prolongation of colonial rule. The continued dependence of people who are ready for self-determination involves dangers to world peace and stability fully as serious as those involved in premature action.

This fact is recognized by almost all nations, including the colonial powers themselves, in the charter of the United Nations. Dependent peoples are no longer exclusively a national problem. Their welfare vitally concerns the peace and welfare of the entire world community. Their right to ultimate self-government is fully acknowledged, and the states which administer the dependent territories have accepted the responsibility of helping to prepare these peoples for the task of self-government.

*　　　　　　　*　　　　　　　*

Let us look at the vast region of the continent of Africa lying south of the Sahara desert. This is a region larger than the United States. Except for the Union of South Africa, Ethiopia, and the Republic of Liberia, it is controlled by colonial powers. Conditions of life in a large part of the region are still primitive, and advancement toward complete self-determination on the part of the local population will require political, economic, social, and cultural development. All these factors are inseparable.

The most populous and varied groupings of central African territories are under the British, who have accelerated their policy of encouraging the devolution of power to the colonial territories. One of their major problems is the fact that many different races, tribes, and religious groups live side by side in the same areas. The British are seeking to remove mistrust and fear between the different groups and to promote a spirit of partnership. They are developing, for example, local parliaments which include representatives of different races. It is also significant that an interracial university is planned for the new federation of the Rhodesias and Nyasaland.

The British approach also takes into account such factors as the wealth of resources in an area, the situation of a territory in relation to its neighbors, and the political maturity of the people and their leaders. I believe this approach is paying dividends. In all British areas there now exists a considerable amount of autonomy at local levels. Nigeria and the Gold Coast, for example, now exercise a large measure of responsible representative government. It is possible to foresee the complete self-government of these two countries within the framework of the Commonwealth.

The French approach in tropical Africa has been increasingly progressive since the end of World War II. The Constitution of the Fourth French Republic confers citizenship on the African inhabitants of French overseas territories in tropical Africa, and these Africans are now brought into political activity at all levels, from the municipal and territorial legislatures to the French Union bodies in Paris. No new measures are effected without consultation with African representatives, although the French High Commissioner still retains ultimate authority to carry out decisions of the French Government. The French have also undertaken important social reforms. One of these is the extension of the social benefits of the French labor code to tropical Africa. It should be noted that measure aimed at the evolutionary development of these territories have been greatly facilitated by the traditional tolerance of the French in matters of race relations.

The policy of the Belgians in the Congo represents still another approach to colonial administration. Primary emphasis is given to economic and social development as a foundation for eventual political evolution. In brief, they believe in building from within by local training and by local institutions. They are seeking to transform the Congo into a great producer of minerals and other natural resources. Meanwhile they are introducing a variety of social measures covering minimum wages, health insurance, etc. They are also instituting a broad system of primary education to be followed by the establishment of higher institutions of learning locally. Much has already been done toward creating an African middle class on a solid economic basis. As this economic base is established, it is anticipated that increasing attention will be given to political development. The best-educated Africans in the Congo are now used in local administration.

Finally, we have the approach taken by the Portuguese in Angola and Mozambique. Portuguese policy has never admitted racial distinctions but does recognize a distinction between the civilized and noncivilized portions of the population. Thus tribal Africans who wish to remain attached to tribal traditions and customs, such as polygamy, are refused political rights characteristic of European institutions. On the other hand, when natives meet the standards of citizenship, they are automatically able to participate in the responsibilities of government.

These are but a few of the methods by which the colonial powers are carrying out their responsibilities in Africa south of the Sahara. It is inevitable that there are differences of opinion on the progress being made. But serious observers of the African scene agree that the European governments are making substantial contributions to the evolution of these peoples.

*   *   *

In closing, I would like to remind you that there is no single problem which we can call a "colonial problem." Instead, there are many different kinds of problems which exist in many different areas. As a great American statesman once said, "General propositions do not decide concrete cases," and this statement certainly has direct application when related to colonialism. Our Government must ever be alert to the necessity of doing those things which the circumstances of time and place demand.

The clock of history cannot be turned back. Alien rule over dependent peoples must be replaced as rapidly as possible by self-determination. Of this there can be no question. At the same time, we know that the clock of history cannot be turned forward by a mere twist of the dial. The evolution of the dependent peoples toward full self-determination requires patience, imagination, and hard work—hard work by the governing powers as well as the governed—accompanied by sympathy and assistance from all nations.

We as Americans are prepared to do what we can as a part of this effort. Our ultimate objective, to use the words of a former American President, is to attain "such a concert of free peoples as will encircle the globe and make the world itself at last free."

Except from Africa in World Politics *by Vernon McKay,*
*Professor of African Studies, The Johns Hopkins University**

1963

*   *   *

The dilemma [of U.S. policy] is clear in the 1950 statement by Assistant Secretary McGhee, but the classic masterpiece of American ambiguity on the colonial question is found in our second major policy declaration made three years later by McGhee's successor, Henry A. Byroade. From a technical point of view the Byroade Address of October 30, 1953, was so skillful a production that it has been commended by persons with diametrically opposing views of colonialism. If we strip away the excess verbiage in which the essence of the statement is obscured, however, we will find the following ten passages remaining, five of which tend to nullify the other five:

1. This movement toward self-determination is one of the most powerful forces in twentieth century affairs.

2. We ourselves believe that peace, prosperity, and human freedom can be assured only within a concert of free peoples. . . .

3. We hope that the peoples now seeking self-determination will achieve it. . . .

*Vernon McKay, Africa in World Politics, (N.Y., 1963), pp. 320-21.

4. We recognize that the disintegration of the old colonialism is inevitable. We believe that much blood and treasure may be saved if the Western world determines firmly to hasten rather than hamper the process of orderly evolution towards self-determination.

5. The clock of history cannot be turned back. Alien rule over dependent peoples must be replaced as rapidly as possible by self-determination. Of this there can be no question.

And now the reverse:

1. It will be one of the great tragedies of our time if the peoples of Asia and Africa, just as they are emerging from generations of dependence, should be deluded by the fatal lure of the new [Soviet] imperialism and return thereby to an age of slavery infinitely more miserable than they have ever known before.

2. It is a hard, inescapable fact that premature independence can be dangerous, retrogressive and destructive.

3. Unless we are willing to recognize that there is such a thing as premature independence, we cannot think intelligently or constructively about the status of dependent peoples.

4. Premature independence for these peoples would not serve the interests of the United States nor the interests of the dependent peoples themselves.

5. ... let us be frank in recognizing our stake in the strength and stability of certain European nations which are our allies. They share many common interests with us. They will probably represent, for many years to come, the major source of the free world defensive power outside our own. We cannot blidnly disregard their side of the colonial question without regard to our own security.

*   *   *

Speech by Representative Adam Clayton Powell (New York) before the House of Representatives on the Asian-African (Bandung) Conference*

March 31, 1955

Mr. Speaker, on April 18, in Bandung, Indonesia, representatives of three-fifths of the world's population will gather together the first world conference of free nations representing the colored peoples of Asia and of Africa. The United States naturally has not been invited. This is an Asian-African Conference. But I believe that someone from the United States should be at that conference, unofficially, of course, but nevertheless as a person of good will. Other nations not invited are sending representatives as observers. The conference is of such earthshaking importance that close to 40 members of the press, radio, and television of the United States are already on their way for a meeting within the next few days. I requested the administration that we send an all-American team as observers, spectators, visitors, ambassadors of good will, whatever you want to call them. The Department of State did not agree with my proposal. While they were not opposed to the conference, yet their attitude was one of benevolent indifference. I want to very frankly say that I do not believe that we or any

*Congressional Record, Mar. 31, 1955.

country is strong enough to be indifferent to a conference representing three-fifths of the earth's population. Therefore, I am going to this conference at my own expense, entirely unofficially. I hope that my presence there as an American and above all as a member of the colored peoples of the United States will be of some value for the peace, understanding, and strengthening of brotherhood of our world.

This conference might well mark the most important event of this century. Even if nothing is accomplished by their coming together for the first time in the history of the world, these people will represent a tremendous event.

$$* \qquad\qquad * \qquad\qquad *$$

We might as well face the truth that we have no foreign policy for Asia and Africa. The only thing we are stumbling around with is the slogan "Let's stop communism." If communism is defeated the West will thrive and go forward. But if communism is defeated what will happen to Asia and Africa? Asia and Africa will still be confronted with its problems of colonialism, illiteracy, hunger, and disease. The main problem in the eyes of the East is not communism but is strictly economic. I do not for one moment advocate that we cast aside our fight against communism. It should be pushed forward relentlessly. But I do say, very emphatically, that fighting communism and fighting communism alone is not going to get us allies and win us friends in Asia and Africa. I gravely doubt whether we can continue much longer as a first-class power without the peoples of those two vast continents on our side.

$$* \qquad\qquad * \qquad\qquad *$$

First, let us consult with the Asian and African nations on every aspect of our Eastern policy. This means a complete revaluation of the importance of the East in world politics. We can hope to achieve the solution of their problems only by establishing a relationship of full equality. Even when we proffer aid we must not seek to dictate, although, naturally, we have the right to withhold aid if certain fundamental terms are unattainable.

Second, recognize that the social and political changes in the East mean more than simply supporting a nation against communism. The nationalist revolution of the East cannot succeed without, at the same time, being an economic revolution.

Third, supply adequate assistance for social change. How stupid it is for us to say that we can afford $100 billion a year for armaments but not a few billion for building independent and stable economies that can withstand the lure of the slogans of communism and the menace of Soviet aggression. Such a program would be compatible with the needs of our American economy. Vast new markets for our products would be opened up in the undeveloped areas of the world. Increasing the productivity of the lands of the lands of the East by grants-in-aid and loans would lay the basis for a permanent independent demand for our own products.

Fourth, we should channel as much of our aid as possible into international organizations. We know the United Nations has a limited role, but we should seek to build its strength through a concrete demonstration of our belief in its principles. The people of the East in turn would know the source of this aid and would appreciate the demonstration of our belief in internationalism without strings.

Fifth, we should stage an all-out offensive through public and private funds against economic exploitation, illiteracy, poverty, social degradation, forced labor, unemployment, lack of labor standards, housing, sanitation, and medical care.

Lastly, we should sell—and I mean sell in the Madison Avenue advertising concept of the word—sell the fact that this is not a white man's country. The United States of America is the only power in Western civilization that has a very large minority of colored people, including our Puerto Ricans, Mexicans, and Negro people. There are 23 million American citizens who are colored, who are a racial link between this country and the people of Asia and Africa. Let the people of Asia and Africa know that we are rapidly eradicating second-class citizenship. Let them know what we have done. Let them know, specifically, what we are going to do and let them know we are going to do it as soon as we can.

*   *   *

Report of the Special Study Mission to Africa by Frances P. Bolton, Subcommittee on the Near East and Africa*

1956

RECOMMENDATIONS
UNITED STATES POLICY TOWARD AFRICA

The United States policy toward Africa is differentiated in degree and direction according to the individual country with which she deals. Our purpose is to maintain friendly relations with the many countries of Africa, to be as helpful to them as possible, and to build understanding of America in a continent only beginning to come into the modern world. Of necessity the application must vary greatly because of the wide differences of government in the many countries involved.

As the governmental entities of Africa are so diverse, I have considered them under the following categories. North Africa is not included as this report deals only with the countries visited by the mission.

Sovereign nations:

Egypt	Morocco
Ethiopia	South Africa
Liberia	Sudan
Libya	Tunisia

Nations anticipating self-government in the near future:

Algeria	Nigeria
Central Federation	Somalia
Gold Coast	Uganda

Nations whose independence is not likely in the foreseeable future:

Angola	Gambia
Belgian Congo	Kenya
British Somaliland	Mozambique

*Committee on Foreign Affairs, *Report of the Special Study Mission to Africa, South and East of the Sahara*, (Washington, 1956) 84th Cong., 2d sess., pp. xiii-xiv; xvi; 12-13.

French Equatorial Africa   Portuguese Guinea
French Somaliland   Rio de Oro or Spanish Sahara
French West Africa   Rio Muni
                 Sierra Leone

United Nations trusteeships:
 The Cameroons   Tanganyika
 Ruanda Urundi   Togolands
 Southwest Africa
  (problematical status)

Countries whose future is in dispute:
 Basutoland   Swaziland
 Bechuanaland

Our policy toward each of these territorial entities should be governed by its current status. Accordingly I would suggest that our foreign policy be adapted to these entities as follows:

1. *Sovereign nations:* Treaties of amity and commerce would be valuable. Wherever possible, offers of assistance could be concluded on a bilateral basis in the fields of—

 (a) Health and medical research.
 (b) Education.
 (c) Agriculture, fisheries, and veterinary sciences.
 (d) Emergency preparedness.
 (e) Economic development and technical training programs.
 (f) Conservation.
 (g) Atoms for peace.

2. *Nations anticipating self-government in the near future:* As they are still under foreign control, we can do no more than assure them that similar services will be available to them if and when they are desired.

3. *Nations whose independence is not likely in the foreseeable future:* We can make it clear that we stand ready to do whatever the metropolitan powers invite us to do, in addition to the developmental programs already initiated in their respective areas.

4. *U.N. trusteeships:* In our policy we must recognize the fact that trusteeship areas differ widely from all other groups and amongst themselves.

 (a) Tanganyika and Ruanda Urundi: They are politically mature, having developed the beginnings of indigenous leadership under U.N. tutelage. The U.N. is also fostering economic programs which will lead to their eventual economic emancipation.
 (b) Togolands and Cameroons: These two trusteeship areas are so fragmented that it is probable that they will never exist as entities, but may be given opportunity by the U.N. to choose to join their current administration's authorities or remain under U.N. guardianship.
 (c) Southwest Africa: The only just method of determination would be a referendum under the aegis of the U.N. as to the wishes of the inhabitants.

5. *Countries whose future is in dispute:* We should assist them to acquire and maintain political independence, while recognizing that their economic future is allied with the Union of South Africa.

It can be readily seen that no one specific policy can be applied to all of the vast continent of Africa. However, the feeling we Americans have for the rights of all men to choose their own government and their way of life makes us extremely sympathetic to the aspirations of people to whom these inalienable rights are somehow denied.

* * *

Intent of Good Will

If we are to play a real part in Africa's rebirth—and if we do not, others will—we should do three things:

1. Make it clear to the metropolitan countries that we have no desire to interfere with their methods of bringing more health and education to their people while at the same time encouraging the utilization of more American personnel in Africa, more economic interchange, and a greater exchange of persons.

2. Make it clear to the African that we know from experience his intense desire for freedom, and sympathize with him. But because we had to win our independence and have since learned many of the difficulties of setting up and maintaining high standards of living and justice for all we should do no more than give them all the help we can without hurrying them into a freedom they would not be able to sustain.

3. Above all else we must prove to all races in Africa that we care deeply for them and their well-being and that that is the mainspring of our desire. That we believe that the exchange of their raw material and our know-how will benefit them at least as much if not more, than it will benefit us.

* * *

The United States and Africa

Our National Interests

The United States has certain general goals in Africa, namely, an interest in the evolution of Africa in a manner not inimical to our democratic type of government; the exclusion of influences unfriendly to our way of life; the hope of having access to the raw materials of that continent, especially to safeguard our minimum strategic needs; to increase our trade with all African countries; and to exercise a moral leadership as befits our honorable traditions.

The United States, in its position of leadership in the free world, cannot sidestep its responsibility in the unfoldment of Africa. We must take a deep interest in the social, economic, and political changes taking place in that great continent since they affect our own national goals. The foundations are being laid today upon which Africa will play a new and larger role in the future of the world. We can no longer permit ourselves either apathy or ignorance in the matter of Africa. Already she is moving into today's world, challenging our ignorance at every point.

The Need for Understanding

As we went from country to country it was brought home to us that the impact of

European culture has brought much good but also some evil to Africa. On every side we saw dramatic evidence that the western philosophy of freedom had given the African an ever-increasing sense that not only must he learn the new ways, but he must preserve the best of his own culture. These two urges have been combined giving him incentives to resist European domination while building his own knowledge, capacity, and strength.

These are but some of the matters about which we here in the United States know all too little—matters that we must not only become aware of but must understand, lest we fail to earn the friendship of the people of this great continent for is it not "the continent God has held in reserve."

As the countries are freed from foreign domination and take full responsibility for themselves we shall no longer have to approach the major part of Africa through the metropole colonial powers, but shall be dealing directly with the native Africans themselves. This fact alone should be cause enough for us to use every means in our power to understand them, to win their confidence, their friendship and their regard. The time for this is not next year, not 5 years from now—the time is now.

Although this mission placed its emphasis upon the many millions of native peoples of this vast continent it at no time lost sight of the fact that some 5 million Europeans call Africa their homeland. In South Africa, in the Central Federation, in Kenya, and others as well as in French and Portuguese areas we made every effort to understand their points of view. Certainly they have done and are doing much to raise the standard of living of all the people, to provide education and to combat disease.

In addition to the Europeans there are some 1 million Asians and related peoples whose problems loom large in several areas. Particularly do they want political equality.

Limited United States Representation

Possibly also the fact that we have so few diplomatic posts in Africa And that even these are drastically hampered by too few funds may be a rather fundamental reason for the difficulty one has in securing such information as for instance, comparisons of health and living standards, of gross national products, per capita incomes, etc.

Raw Materials

Africa is of great importance to the free world, especially perhaps to the United States. Its apparently limitless raw materials, almost all of them important to us, would seem to offer a useful exchange; for Africa is today becoming one of the greatest markets of the world not only for all the thousand and one gadgets we make for the easing of life, but for heavy industry as well. Surely this economic potential is one the United States cannot afford to overlook.

Our Relationships

This mission returned from Africa with the impression that—in a general sense— relations are good between our country and the people on the African Continent.

But it was also apparent that Americans today are not prepared to deal with the newly emergent Africa, nor are Africans able to understand the fundamentals of American interests and philosophies—factors which may become more apparent as Americans and Africans have more direct relationships.

Possibly some of our ignorance of Africa here in the United States is somewhat due to the lack of information available and the fact that much of it is scattered about the country in a few libraries and universities.

*   *   *

*Speech by Senator Mike Mansfield (Montana) before the Senate on a Review of Foreign Policy Toward Africa**

June 7, 1956

*   *   *

In previous statements, I discussed in succession our relations with southeast Asia, North Africa, the Middle East, and, most recently, with Latin America. In all those statements, it was possible to describe a pattern of American policy. It was not always an effective or consistent policy. Nevertheless, there was at least an understandable base to build on—frequently a faltering, uncertain base, but at least a recognizable base.

That is less the case with respect to the area which I propose to consider today. For Africa, and for sub-Sahara Africa in particular, we have barely the beginnings of a policy.

I say that, no so much in criticism, but merely to emphasize a fact that is of great pertinence in our relations with that region. Much of Africa has long been beyond the horizon of our direct interest; and, in consequence, we have given it little direct consideration in our policy For the most part, we have approached that continent through the European nations which exercise sovereignty over a great part of it.

That this is the case is clearly reflected in the organization of the Department of State. The African Division has been tacked on, like an afterthought, to the Bureau of Near Eastern, South Asian, and African Affairs. I may also note that, despite his wide and far-flung travels, the Secretary of State has somehow managed virtually to overlook the second largest continent in the world. On second thought, I believe his plane did set down briefly in Cairo, at one time, on the way to somewhere else, or coming from somewhere else.

What might be termed this official unawareness of Africa is not confined to the executive branch; it is shared by the Congress. Africa has been the subject of almost no discussion in the Senate in the last decade. That is, to say the least, a most unusual phenomenon for this body. As the Members know, our range of interest has otherwise been broad enough to cover in great detail a range of such diverse subjects as daylight saving time in the District of Columbia, the awe-inspiring power of atomic energy, and Presidential critiques of music critics.

Very few Senators in their travels abroad have found occasion to retrace the paths of Stanley and Livingstone through Africa, and I hasten to add that I am as guilty as others of this negligence. It has remained for the inrepid gentlewoman from Ohio [Mrs. Bolton], in the other House, to blaze a congressional trail through the dangerous recesses of that vast continent.

*Congressional Record, June 7, 1956.

In all seriousness, this neglect of Africa seems to me to create a gap both in our understanding of the total international situation and in our foreign policies. In the past, the gap might have had few significant consequences. Today, however, it seems to me that it is one which we can ill afford.

*   *   *

What is certain, however, is that the Africa of tomorrow will be vastly different from the Africa of today, just as Africa today bears little resemblance to the Africa of 50 years ago.

I believe it essential that, now, at the beginnings of policy with Africa, we recognize the origin of the concepts which are stimulating these changes. They are not the product of an unseen or conspiratorial hand. They arise out of the total experience of civilized man. They are the lifeblood of freedom, the same concepts which have underlain the development of America and, in a larger sense, of all western culture. They are the same concepts which time and again all over the world have rallied whole peoples to resist or to overthrow tyrannies.

I stress the universal and especially the western source of these concepts. I do so because I believe we are about to witness the beginning of an attempt to twist and turn the transition of Africa into channels of totalitarianism. Press reports indicate that the Soviet drive into the Middle East is moving beyond that area, deeply into Africa, above and below the Sahara. It is being pursued on cultural, diplomatic, and economic fronts, and, as has happened elsewhere, the concepts of freedom itself have been usurped and are being used by the Communists to spearhead this drive.

The free nations may deplore this development. If we are honest with ourselves, however, we shall acknowledge the fact that it has been the inadequacies of western policies in interpreting our own political, social, and economic ideals in Africa that have afforded, in large part, the opening wedge.

The Soviet drive will not be stopped by a wringing of hands. It will not be stopped by military measures so long as it remains nonmilitary in nature. Least of all will it be stopped by a further retreat from our own finest beliefs. If we and other free nations fail to uphold those beliefs in our relations with Africa, in deed as well as word, then we shall have no one to blame but ourselves if the emergent continent turns not toward the West, but toward totalitarianism, Communist or otherwise.

That is the principal reason why this country must remain alert to the present African transition. Until now, Africa has been largely what might be termed a political neutron, inert and acted upon by others. It is now beginning to move as an independent force in international life. What takes place there in the years immediately ahead will, in effect, determine whether the area of human freedom in the world shall be enlarged or contracted by the addition or subtraction of much, if not all, of that continent.

*   *   *

What matters most, however, is not the past. What matters most is whether the policies of the colonial powers, and the policies of other free nations, including our own, are effectively adjusted now and in the future to the transition which has been set in motion by the awakening of the inhabitants of Africa to the modern world.

We ought not to underestimate the complexity and the magnitude of this task of adjustment, particularly for the European colonial powers. I mentioned earlier that the situation in Africa was somewhat analagous to that in Asia a decade ago. It is, in the sense that nationalism versus colonialism was the decisive issue in many Asian countries at the end of World War II. In a similar fashion, it is or is becoming the decisive issue in many parts of Africa.

In drawing the comparison between Asia and Africa, however, we ought not to overlook the differences in the two situations. European colonialism in Asia was superimposed for the most part on sophisticated civilizations with long histories of cultural development. The ideas and the techniques of the West influenced the existing way of Asian life, but they did not obliterate or suffocate it. In Africa, however, the Europeans opened a continent inhabited largely by peoples, who, like the North American Indians, existed apart from the mainstreams of history.

To cite another significant difference: In Asia, colonialism was not accompanied by massive European settlement. There was never—as there are in South Africa, in Kenya, or in Algeria—anywhere near the same large bodies of settled Europeans. These settlers see their future and their children's future in Africa, not in Europe. Many are uncertain of that future. Their fears not infrequently lead them to resist being cut away from sources of military and political power which lie largely in Europe, or the sharing of any significant political power with the indigenous peoples of the continent.

I am not condoning this fear; I am merely recognizing its existence, for it poses a major problem for the European colonial nations. In a previous statement I dealt at some length with this problem as it confronts France in north Africa. But any responsible European government which attempts to adjust its policies to meet the demands of the African transition, faces tremendous internal political pressures over the same question.

If we contrast the peaceful political progress in the Gold Coast and Nigeria on the one hand with the strife in Kenya and the regression in South Africa, the point should be clear. The contrast, I believe, is due in large measure to the fact that in the Gold Coast and Nigeria, there are few permanent European settlers. In Kenya and in South Africa, however, Europeans and descendants of Europeans are settled in great numbers.

If the European nations face a formidable task in adjusting to the transition, so, too, do the leaders of African nationalism. To them falls much of the responsibility for shaping the changes which are bound to occur in Africa. They, too, face tremendous pressures. In some cases, their responsibility involves literally moving whole populations from the Stone Age into the 20th century with great rapidity.

Modern African leaders are themselves awake to the meaning of national and human equality and modern progress. Their own enlightenment, however, can have lasting significance only if it is shared with their own peoples. They will need great compassion and patience for that. They will also need wisdom if they are to choose with discrimination from among the welter of ideas and ideologies which bear down on Africa from all sides, those which will benefit their peoples. As the Soviet drive into the continent gains momentum, the pressures on these leaders will increase and the confusion of alternatives will be further compounded.

I believe it will be well to recognize that while the ideological choices which are made will be those of the African leaders and their peoples, the policies of the free nations will profoundly influence them. To the extent that these policies reflect a firm devotion to the concepts of freemen—to the concepts of national and human equality, to the extent that they reflect a willingness to assist in the progress of the African people—they can make a great contribution to the growth of human freedom. By the same token, irreparable harm can be done if these policies are short-sighted, fearful, and repressive.

It seems to me that a foreign policy which serves the total interests of this country, must welcome the present transition in Africa and the inevitability of change which it brings. We have already had an expression of congressional sentiment to that effect with regard to all dependent people throughout the world. In the 84th Congress, a resolution was adopted unanimously by both Houses calling for the administering of foreign policies and the exercising of our influence in support of other peoples "in their efforts to achieve self-government or independence." House Concurrent Resolution 149, 84th Congress, 1st session.

I can conceive of no long-range interest worthy of this country which would be at variance with this fundamental expression. How could it be otherwise? Can we reject the desire for national equality on the part of any people? Similarly, can we frown upon their desire for human equality? Or can we deprecate their efforts to improve their social and economic existence? To those who can answer these questions in the affirmative, I respectfully suggest a rereading of the Declaration of Independence and the Constitution of the United States.

*   *   *

At the same time, we ought to have clearly in mind our limitations in this connection. The achievement of rights is primarily the responsibility of peoples directly involved, both African and European. We can assist but we cannot impose.

I fully realize the difficulties of interpreting the principles of the charter, as they apply to Africa, in the countless decisions which must be made by the executive branch of the Government. It seems to me, however, that we have compounded these difficulties by our own neglect, by clinging to what seems to me to be an outmoded approach to that continent.

I would suggest, therefore, that the first step toward a more effective policy on Africa involves an increase in the flow of direct information on that continent into the formulation of policy. Would such a flow not be facilitated if the African Branch of the Department of State were separated from Near Eastern and south Asian affairs and consittuted as a bureau under an Assistant Secretary of State for African Affairs? And would the Senate not be better equipped to advise with the President on African matters if more Members found occasion to include Africa in their travels abroad?

Even with the limited and inadequate knowledge we now possess, it is possible to see the beginnings of a sound policy for Africa.

As I have already noted, the growing aspirations of the African people for national and human equality must have the consistent sympathy of this country. This sympathy must be reflected more clearly than is presently the case in the general course which we pursue in the United Nations and elsewhere. I hope that few occasions will arise in which we will be at variance with the western Europeans on this matter. When they do, however, our position ought to be forthright. If we disagree with them, let us disagree honestly. And if overriding circumstances compel us to accept temporary compromises, let us be equally prepared to acknowledge them frankly. Accommodation has a place in the foreign policy of this Nation, no less than in that of others, but hypocrisy does not.

I believe this country should also be prepared to enlarge the technical assistance program in Africa if it is clear that such assistance can be effective and that it is sought by the indigenous peoples. If other practicable ways can be developed which will hasten the economic and social progress of the African peoples, we should be prepared to give them sympathetic consideration. Again, the test of any such measures must be their contribution to the development of national and human equality in Africa and to the well-being of the African people.

I noted earlier in these remarks that we were at the beginnings of policy on Africa. Because we are, we have an unusual opportunity to set a firm foundation for our future relations with that continent. If we do so, we shall serve the interests of this country far beyond the present generation.

The key to an effective policy on Africa, I believe, will be found in the perception with which we treat the developing transition on that continent. If we understand and appreciate its vast implications and assist in the adjustments it requires, we will facilitate the emergence of a new Africa. It will be an Africa which will do willingly what it cannot be coerced into doing. It will be an Africa which will pour its original and as yet incalculable contributions into the general progress of freemen and into the maintenance of world peace.

*   *   *

Remarks by Representative Powell on the First Anniversary
of the African-Asian Conference*

April 18, 1956

*   *   *

Bandung has placed a time limit on indecision. It is absolutely impossible for the United States to continue to hope for any more support from the people of Asia and Africa if we continue to abstain on the question of colonialism before the United Nations. Congress on June 6, 1955, by record vote in the House of Representatives and Senate, established the following as a part of our foreign policy:

[84th Cong., 1st sess. H. Con. Res. 153]
Whereas Communist imperialism and other forms of colonialism constitute a denial of the inalienable rights of man; and
Whereas the people of the United States have traditionally supported other peoples in their aspirations to achieve self-government or independence and in their struggle against tyranny or domination: Now, therefore, be it
Resolved by the House of Representatives (the Senate concurring), That it is the sense of the Congress that the United States should administer its foreign policies and programs and

exercise its influence through its membership in the United Nations and in other international organizations so as to support other peoples in their efforts to achieve self-government or independence under circumtances which will enable them to assume an equal station among the free nations of the world.

Despite the fact that the foregoing resolution on colonialism was passed by both Houses of the Congress and thus became the law of the land, our delegates to the United Nations completely ignored this. . . .

    *   *   *

I am, therefore, requesting the Foreign Affairs Committees of the House and Senate to sharply question the appropriate officials as to why.

I recognize that Britain and France and other Western powers have for centuries stood at our side and fought with us, even though the fighting has ofttimes been our men fighting with them to protect their national sovereignty and integrity. I do not believe that for 1 minute we should turn our back upon these ancient allies. We should very vigorously and emphatically state that in Europe they are our allies and we can always be counted upon to give them the fullest measure of every kind of support.

I do believe that a historic break must be made and that we must just emphatically tell them that we can no longer support either with aid or with arms any form of imperialism sponsored by these nations in Asia and Africa. The cold stark fact confronts us that whether we take this stand or not, imperialism is finished. The natives, country by country are going to drive out the colonial powers and if we continue to stand with these powers on the question of colonialism then we are going to suffer diplomatic defeats. The full force of freedom is now sweeping over the earth and there are no powers that can stop it—short of a complete war of annihilation. This I don't believe the most rabid isolationist or warmonger would dare to suggest. From here on in the Western powers can no longer decide the fate of Asians and Africans without their leaders being present.

    *   *   *

Africa is the No. 1 problem of our world. That dark, vast continent stretching for 5,000 miles is shaped like a question mark and it is. For there in Africa will be won or lost the world battle for freedom. This our Foreign Office is not aware of or, if so, is doing nothing about it. Communism in the West under the leadership of Soviet Russia and in the East under Red China is supposedly waving the flag of peace even if it is a little dirty and blood-stained. While they are doing this, north Africa and south Africa represent soft spots to establish new beachheads of subversion by Communist agents. We went to Africa centuries ago carrying a cross. It is time to go back to Africa again carrying an offer of full equality, dignity, mutual respect and direct and adequate assistance for social change. This is the only way to stop the wave of communism in Africa.

We need to channel as much of the aid that we give in Asia and Africa through international organizations. We know that the United Nations has a limited role but we should seek to build its strength through concrete demonstrations of our belief in its principles.

    *   *   *

*Address on United States Foreign Policy in Africa by George V. Allen,
Assistant Secretary for African Affairs**

April 21, 1956

*   *   *

A responsible foreign policy toward Africa requires of the United States a deep understanding of the aspirations and problems of the individual African countries both in their relationship with the European powers and in their urge toward self-determination so that we may lend our good offices and assistance in promoting an orderly progress toward independence and nationhood.

*   *   *

The United States attitude toward colonialism is known. In the light of our historical origins and our traditions this attitude could hardly be different. But the application of this principle to present-day foreign-policy problems all over the world requires patient understanding and a high sense of responsibility regarding the ultimate and basic security interests of the United States. All of the so-called colonial powers represented on the continent of Africa are our friends and allies in the worldwide contest between the free and Communist worlds. Relationships established by them with countries in Africa date from an era when the concepts of international relations were different. No one but a demagogue would deny that basic advantages were brought to the African territories by this process of opening wider horizons and that, in fact, the impetus toward modern nationhood grew out of these contacts with Western civilization.

Furthermore, in the course of this relationship between the metropolitan powers and the African territories, there grew up interlocking economic relations, the violent disruption of which would seriously weaken our European allies. Similarly, a sudden break of these lifelines would create conditions of political and economic instability most harmful to our African friends. It is more largely a question of transforming this relationship into a cooperative endeavor by which the newly emerging states in Africa achieve and maintain their national self-respect and apply in their own way the benefits of their national resources to improving the lot of their own people. A strong, free, and friendly Africa is extremely important to United States security. Our security interests and our moral interests are both effectively served by the same general line of action—we need friendly and cooperative relations with Europe and Africa, just as their own interests require the maintenance of intimate ties with each other.

In Africa our allies are aware of the basic attitude of the United States toward colonialism, but they are equally aware of our intention to work as friends of both sides toward an orderly solution of these problems. Great Britain has publicly announced its policy of helping the countries of Africa toward independence, and its record in Asia is an earnest of its sincerity. In line with its poilcy as a responsible power, however, it does not wish to create perhaps greater problems by precipitate

Department of State Bulletin, Apr. 30, 1956, pp. 716-18.

action which granting of immedaite independence might create. This is a time when political vacuums are a great danger to world peace.

In North Africa, France has recently recognized the independence of Morocco and Tunisia and is engaged in trying to find a liberal solution to the problem of Algeria. Spain has also recognized the independence of its zone of Morocco, and that country has now the opportunity to become unified. Both Spain and France are engaged in working out arrangements by which the mutual economic benefits derived from their past association with Morocco can be continued in the light of the new relationship. In other areas of Africa, France is also looking toward creating a new relationship with the groups which are gradually developing a higher degree of political consciousness. The Belgians have recently established two universities in the Belgian Congo to meet the educational needs of the Congolese.

The United States attitude toward nationalism is not so easily definable. After World War II, when the threat of international communism endangered our security, United States opinion was inclined toward promoting a greater faith in federations in Europe which cut across—and, we hoped, would eventually obliterate—nationalistic rivalries. But in other areas of the world we recognized the strength of nationalism in resisting the threat of international communism. Communism cynically exploits the passions of revolt for the sole purpose of creating unrest, chaos, and revolution so that the small organized minority may seize power and permanently bury the instincts of healthy nationalism under the requirements of blind and absolute obedience to Moscow. This issue assumes a special importance in Africa, where the varying degrees of political experience, the large amount of illiteracy, and the insecurity of the individual in the process of exchanging his old loyalties for new ones make the population particularly vulnerable to exploitation of this issue by unprincipled demagogues.

Again the principle of understanding and responsibility in the conduct of foreign relations should guide us and other nations in relations with the countries of Africa so that the elements of nationalism which contribute toward genuine independence and stability will be encouraged and those which tend to be purely negative, anarchic, and disruptive be curbed.

*   *   *

The United States, as a nation, has no selfish interests in Africa except the preservation of our own security, which we consider, in present world circumtances, inextricably bound up with the kind of future the African countries desire for themselves. We are dedicated to the preservation of world peace, which we consider an indispensable corollary to the kind of development Africa needs. Because of our origins and traditions we are basically in sympathy with the desire for independence and nationhood of the emerging states, but we are also friends and allies of the powers who must help to shape this new status. This places us in a position from which we hope and believe our influence can be exerted to make the transformation of Africa a process of orderly evolution and not one of violent revolution.

Statement by Assistant Secretary Allen on the Mutual Security Program for the Near East, South Asia and Africa*

May 8, 1956

*   *   *

The problem of developing policies which further our national intersts in Africa is complex indeed; for this is a continent of as great diversity in social, economic and political features as in climate and topography. Here we must deal with both independent countries and territories in varying stages of political evolution. All of them also are in varying stages of social and economic underdevelopment and are faced with all the usual impediments to progress. With those areas in a dependent status our relationships must fall into a triangular pattern with the colonial powers. This requires that our policies relating to the dependent territories must be reconciled to our national intersts in both the metropoles and the territories and to their respective interests, which are at times conflicting.

The United States desires that the peoples of Africa progress and share in the social, economic, and political freedoms and advantages of the West. Beyond this the continent's human and natural resources contribute very significantly to the strength of the Western World. Our interest includes continued access to Africa's important and, in some cases, vital supplies of a number of essential materials including uranium, industrial diamonds, copper, manganese, cobalt, beryl, asbestos, chrome, rubber, zinc, lead, corn, cocoa, and sisal. It includes also strategic air bases and communications facilities, particularly those spotted across the northern part of the continent.

Africa, probably more than anywhere in the world, is a crucial testing ground of the good judgment and leadership of the Western powers. It is essential that the United States, through the mutual security program, strengthen its ties with, and support, the development aspirations of the independent nations of Africa. It is equally important we work with our allies in recognizing the aspirations for independence and development of dependent peoples. We and our Western European allies are directly involved, and the eyes of the underdeveloped peoples everywhere are upon us. Here we must collaborate in demonstrating conclusively the superior values of free-world ideals.

The bilateral country aid which is proposed in the mutual security program is essential to assist in meeting the problems of the area. But the Soviet economic offensive, the emergence of major economic crises, and the growing awareness within the area of the multilateral nature of some economic problems dictate a new approach in achieving our objectives through the mutual security program. It is for this reason that we are requesting a new, flexible Middle East and Africa authorization of $100 million.

*   *   *

**Ibid.*, May 28, 1956, pp. 877-78.

Report by Vice President Richard M. Nixon to President Dwight D. Eisenhower on the Emergence of Africa*

April 7, 1957

On the basis of my visits to Morocco, Ghana, Liberia, Uganda, Ethiopia, Sudan, Libya, Italy, and Tunisia, from February 28 to March 21, I submit the following observations and recommendations:

No one can travel in Africa, even as briefly as I did, without realizing the tremendous potentialities of this great continent. Africa is the most rapidly changing area in the world today. The course of its development, as its people continue to emerge from a colonial status and assume the responsibilities of independence and self-government, could well prove to be the decisive factor in the conflict between the forces of freedom and international communism.

*   *   *

Africa is emerging as one of the great forces in the world today. In a world in which, because of advances in technology, the influence of ideas and principles is becoming increasingly important in the battle for men's minds, we in the United States must come to know, to understand and to find common ground with the peoples of this great continent. It is in this context that the recommendations in this report, together with others previously made to the appropriate government agencies, are presented.

Appraisal of African Leadership

Africa is producing great leaders, dedicated to the principles of independence, world responsibility and the welfare of their peoples. Such men as the Sultan of Morocco, Prime Minister Nkrumah of Ghana, President Tubman of Liberia, the Emperor of Ethiopia, and Prime Ministers Abdullah Khalil of the Sudan, Ben Halim of Libya and Habib Bourguiba of Tunisia, certainly compare most favorably with the great leaders of the world. Nor should one omit King Idris of Libya, whom I unfortunately missed seeing on this trip because of an engine failure, but whose wisdom and statesmanship I remember most vividly from my previous trip to that country in 1953. These are all men who command respect beyond the borders of their own country. They are backed up by other equally dedicated leaders who have much to contribute both to the problems of their own countries and to those which plague the world today.

Recommendation

The United States must come to know these leaders better, to understand their hopes and aspirations and to support them in their plans and programs for strengthening their own nations and contributing to world peace and stability. To this end, we must encourage the greatest possible interchange of persons and ideas with the leaders

**Ibid.*, Apr. 22, 1957, pp. 635-40.

and peoples of these countries. We must assure the strongest possible diplomatic and consular representation to those countries and stand ready to consult these countries on all matters affecting their interests and ours.

Attitudes Toward the United States

There is no area in the world today in which the prestige of the United States is more uniformly high than in the countries which I visited on this trip. The President is respected as the acknowledged leader of the Free World. There is a most encouraging understanding of our programs and policies. These countries know that we have no ambitions to dominate and that the cornerstone of our foreign policy is to assist countries in resisting domination by others. To understand that the United States stands on principle and that this was the motivating force example, which led us to act as we did in the recent Suez crisis. They approve the stand which we took at that time and look confidently to us to act consistently with that stand in the future. They understand that the American Doctrine of the Middle East is dedicated to the principle of assisting the states of the Middle East to maintain their independence. They know that the United States stands for the evolution of dependent peoples toward self-government and independence, as they become able to discahrge the responsibilities involved.

Recommendation
This understanding of the principles for which we stand as a nation is a tremendous asset to us in this area. The maintenance of the present high prestige we are fortunate to have in Africa will depend upon whether the people of the Continent continue to understand our dedication to the principles of independence, equality and economic progress to which they are so deeply devoted. We must staff our diplomatic and information establishments in these countries with men and women capable of interpreting and explaining our policies and actions in a way which will guarantee that they are so understood.

Effect of Discrimination in U.S. on African Attitudes

As a result of skillful propaganda primarily inspired by the enemies of freedom, a consistently distorted picture of the treatment of minority races in the United States is being effectively presented in the countries I visited. Every instance of prejudice in this country is blown up in such a manner as to create a completely false impression of the attitudes and practices of the great majority of the American people. The result is irreparable damage to the cause of freedom which is at stake.

Recommendation
We must continue to strike at the roots of the problem. We cannot talk equality to the people of Africa and Asia and practice inequality in the United States. In the national interest, as well as for the moral issues involved, we must supply necessary steps which will assure orderly progress toward the elimination of discrimination in the

United States. And we should do a far more active job than we are presently doing in telling the true story of the real progress that is being made toward realizing this objective so that the people of Africa will have a true picture of conditions as they really are in the United States.

Economic Assistance

All of the African states which I visited are underdeveloped. Most of them have great economic potential. Their leaders are anxious to strengthen the economies of their countries in order to assure for their peoples a larger share of the advantages of our modern civilization. They seek economic as well as political independence so far as this is possible in the world of today. Their needs are great in terms of education and public health. They require roads and other communications in order to open inaccessible parts of their territory to economic development. They need agricultural development to sustain their expanding populations. They want assistance in developing their great mineral and forest resources. They foresee great opportunities for developing small industrial enterprises. In most areas these developmental needs are beyond their capacity to finance.

All of the leaders with whom I talked expressed preference for developing their economies through encouraging the investment of private capital and through loans from international agencies such as the World Bank where feasible rather than through government-to-government grants. It can truly be said that the welcome sign is out for investment of foreign private capital in Africa. African leaders are aware of the great role that such private capital can play in the development of their countries and many of them have adopted, or are in the process of adopting, special legislation designed to create an atmosphere conducive to expanded foreign investment.

Recommendation

Consistent with the desires of African leaders, the United States Government through its agencies should, as appropriate, draw the attention of private American capital to opportunities for investment in those areas where the conditions for such investment are propitious. Strengthening the economic sections of American Embassies in this area is needed if this objective is to be carried out.

We should support applications before the appropriate international agencies for financing sound economic development projects in the area.

To the extent that our resources and the demands of other areas permit, we should extend economic and technical assistance to the countries of Africa in helping them to further their economic development.

In this connection, I think it is appropriate to place in proper context the United States economic assistance programs. These progams should be approved only when they are in the mutual interests of the United States and the recipient country. They should be administered as efficiently as possible.

But while these programs should be constantly re-examined and improved so that they can better serve the national interest, shotgun attacks on our foreign assistance programs as such cannot be justified.

Special Relations With Other Countries

Africa and Europe have much in common. To a large extent, their economies are complementary. Certain of the independent states on the African continent maintain close ties of an historical, cultural and economic nature with the states of Europe. The maintenance of these relationships, on a basis of equality, can greatly benefit both Africa and Europe.

Recommendation

We should encourage the continuance of these special ties where they are considered mutually advantageous by the states concerned. We should take them in account in formulating our own policies to the extent compatible with the fundamental requirement of conducting our own relations with those states on a fully equal and independent basis.

The task of providing the economic assistance which is needed by the newly independent countries of Africa cannot be done by the United States alone. We should make it clear that we desire no exclusive position in any country in that area and that we want to work with other Free World nations in providing the assistance which will build strong, free, and independent nations in this area of the world.

Communism

Africa is a priority target for the international communist movement. I gathered the distinct impression that the communist leaders consider Africa today to be as important to their designs for world conquest as they considered China to be twenty-five years ago. Consequently, they are mounting a diplomatic propaganda and economic offensive in all parts of the continent. They are trying desperately to convince the peoples of Africa that they support more strongly than we do their natural aspirations for independence, equality and economic progress.

Fortunately, their efforts thus far have not been generally successful and, for the present, communist domination in the states of the area is not a present danger. All of the African leaders to whom I talked are determined to maintain their independence against communism or any other form of foreign domination. They have taken steps to bring under control the problem of communist subversion of their political, economic and social life. It would be a great mistake, however, to be complacent about this situation because the Communists are without question putting their top men in the fields of diplomacy, intrigue, and subversion into the African area to probe for openings which they can exploit for their own selfish and disruptive ends.

Recommendation

The communist threat underlines the wisdom and necessity of our assisting the countries of Africa to maintain their independence and to alleviate the conditions of want and instability on which communism breeds. The importance of Africa to the strength and stability of the Free World is too great for us to underestimate or to become complacent about this danger without taking every step within our power to assist the countries of this area to maintain their effective independence in the face of this danger.

Trade Unionism

In every instance where my schedule permitted, I made it a point to talk to the leading labor leaders of the countries I visited. I was encouraged to find that the free trade union movement is making great advances in Africa, particularly in Ghana, Morocco, and Tunisia. The leaders of these countries have recognized the importance of providing an alternative to communist dominated unions and they, thereby, are keeping the Communists from getting a foothold in one of their favorite areas of exploitation. In this connection, I wish to pay tribute to the effective support that is being given by trade unions in the United States to the free trade union movement in the countries which I visited. These close and mutually advantageous relationships are in the national interest as well as in the interest of developing a strong labor movement.

Recommendation

It is vitally important that the United States Government follow closely trade union developments in the Continent of Africa and that our diplomatic and consular representatives should come to know on an intimate basis the trade union leaders in these countries. I believe, too, that American labor unions should continue to maintain close fraternal relationships with the American free trade union movement in order that each man has the greatest possible advantage of the wisdom and experience of the other.

*   *   *

For too many years, Africa in the minds of many Americans has been regarded as a remote and mysterious continent which was the special province of big-game hunters, explorers and motion picture makers. For such an attitude to exist among the public at large could greatly prejudice the maintenance of our own independence and freedom because the emergence of a free and independent Africa is as important to us in the long run as it is to the people of that continent.

It is for this reason that I strongly support the creation within the Department of State of a new Bureau of African Affairs which will place this continent on the same footing as the other great area groupings of the world. I recommend similar action by the ICA and USIA. These bureaus, properly staffed and with sufficient funds, will better equip us to handle our relationships with the countries of Africa. But this in itself will not be enough. There must be a corresponding realization throughout the executive branches of the Government, throughout the Congress and throughout the nation, of the growing importance of Africa to the future of the United States and the Free World and the necessity of assigning higher priority to our relations with that area.

*Speech by Senator John F. Kennedy (Massachusetts) in the Senate
on Algeria and Imperialism* *

July 2, 1957

Mr. President, the most powerful single force in the world today is neither communism nor capitalism, neither the H-bomb nor the guided missile. It is man's eternal desire to be free and independent. The great enemy of the tremendous force of freedom is called for want of a more precise term, imperialism—and today that means Soviet imperialism and, whether we like it or not, and though they are not to be equated, Western imperialism.

Thus the single most important test of American foreign policy today is how we meet the challenge of imperialism, what we do to further man's desire to be free. On this test more than any other, this Nation shall be critically judged by the uncommitted millions in Asia and Africa, and anxiously watched by the still hopeful lovers of freedom behind the Iron Curtain. If we fail to meet the challenge of either Soviet or Western imperialism, then no amount of foreign and, no aggrandizement of armaments, no new pacts or doctrines or high-level conferences can prevent further setbacks to our course and to our security.

*   *   *

The basic theme which I shall attempt to develop is that unless the French are willing to make some concessions and adjustments in their basic policy toward Algeria today—and I hope they will do so—any hope that the French will occupy in North Africa a position of any real constructive value to France will in my judgment, disappear.

So I believe that in the true sense of the word—at least, that is my intention—this is a speech from a friend of France, in what I consider to be the best interest of France as well as the best interest of the United States and Africa.

*   *   *

American and French diplomats, it must be noted at the outset, have joined in saying for several years that Algeria is not even a proper subject for American foreign policy debates or world consideration—that it is wholly a matter of internal French concern, a provincial uprising, a crisis which will respond satisfactorily to local anesthesia. But whatever the original truth of these cliches may have been, the blunt facts of the matter today are that the changing face of African nationalism, and the over-widening byproducts of the growing crisis, have made Algeria a matter of international, and consequently American, concern.

*   *   *

No, Algeria is no longer a problem for the French alone—nor will it ever be again. And though their sensitivity to its consideration by this Nation or the U.N. is

Congressional Record, July 2, 1957.

understandable, a full and frank discussion of an issue so critical to our interests as well as theirs ought to be valued on both sides of an Atlantic alliance that has any real meaning and solidarity.

This is not to say that there is any value in the kind of discussion which has characterized earlier United States consideration of this and similar problems—tepid encouragement and moralizations to both sides, cautious neutrality on all real issues, and a restatement of our obvious dependence upon our European friends, our obvious dedication nevertheless to the principles of self-determination, and our obvious desire not to become involved. We have deceived ourselves into believing that we have thus pleased both sides and displeased no one with this head-in-the-sands policy—when, in truth, we have earned the suspicion of all.

*   *   *

On the one hand, there is the French claim that its policies protect metropolitan France. On the other hand, the French in Algeria refuse to accept the responsibility which such a point of view entails.

It is for that reason I contend that France, as a practical matter, has, through these statements, recognized Algeria as an independent entity. In my opinion, the situation should be treated in that light and France should carry on negotiations with the Nationalists on that basis. Until that is done, obviously the situation will continue to deteriorate.

This dismal recital is of particular importance to us in the Senate, and to the Foreign Relations Subcommittee on U.N. Affairs which I have the honor to serve as chairman, because of the attitude toward the Algerian question which has been adopted throughout this period by our spokesmen in Washington, Paris, and U.N. headquarters. Instead of contributing our efforts to a cease-fire and settlement, American military equipment—particularly helicopters, purchased in this country, which the natives especially fear and hate—has been used against the rebels. Instead of recognizing that Algeria is the greatest unsolved problem of Western diplomacy in North Africa today, our special emissary to that area this year, the distinguished Vice President, failed even to mention this sensitive issue in his report.

*   *   *

No matter how complex the problems posed by the Algerian issue may be, the record of the United States in this case is, as elsewhere, a retreat from the principles of indepdnence and anticolonialism, regardless of what diplomatic niceties, legal techni-calities, or even strategic considerations are offered in its defense. The record is even more dismal when put in the perspective of our consistent refusal over a period of several years to support U.N. consideration of the Tunisian and Moroccan questions.

I realize that no magic touchstone of "anticolonialism" can overcome the tremen-dous obstacles which must confront any early settlement giving to the Algerians the right of self-determination, and which must distinguish them from the Tunisians or Moroccans. But let us consider the long-range significance of these objections and obstacles, to determine whether our State Department should remain bound by them.

*   *   *

Should we antagonize our French allies over Algeria? The most important reason we have sided with the French in Algeria and north Africa is our reluctance to antagonize a traditional friend and important ally in her hour of crisis. We have been understandingly troubled by France's alarmist responses to all prospects for negotiations, by her warning that the only possible consequences are political and economic ruin, "the suitcase or the coffin."

Yet, did we not learn in Indochina, where we delayed action as the result of similar warnings, that we might have served both the French and our own causes infinitely better, had we taken a more firm stand much earlier than we did? Did that tragic episode not teach us that, whether France likes it or not, admits it or not, or has our support or not, their overseas territories are sooner or later, one by one, inevitably going to break free and look with suspicion on the Western nations who impeded their steps to independence? In the words of Turgot:

Colonies are like fruit which cling to the tree only till they ripen.

I want to emphasize that I do not fail to appreciate the difficulties of our hard-pressed French allies. It staggers the imagination to realize that France is one nation that has been in a continuous state of war since 1939—against the Axis, then in Syria, in Indochina, in Morocco, in Tunisia, in Algeria. It has naturally not been easy for most Frenchmen to watch the successive withdrawals from Damascus, Hanoi, Saigon, Pondicherry, Tunis, and Rabat. With each departure a grand myth has been more and more deflated. But the problem is no longer to save a myth of French empire. The problem is to save the French nation, as well as free Algeria.

*   *   *

My criticism is not meant to be a partisan one, but is meant only to indicate that I believe our policy has failed.

*   *   *

The one ray of hope that emerges from this otherwise dark picture is the indication tha the French have acknowledged the bankruptcy in their Algerian policy, however they may resent our saying so, by legislating extremely far-reaching and generous measures for geater self-government in French West Africa. Here, under the guidance of M. Felix Houphouet-Boigny, the first Negro cabinet minister in French history, the French Government took significant action by establishing a single college electoral system, which Algeria has never had, and, by providing universal suffrage, a wide measure of decentralized government, and internal self-control. Here realistic forward steps are being taken to fuse nationalist aspirations into a gradual and measurable evolution of political freedom.

*   *   *

New York Times *Editorial on Senator Kennedy's Algeria Speech**

July 3, 1957

Senator Kennedy has probably added fuel to a raging fire with his speech and resolution yesterday suggesting that the United States use its good offices to solve the Algerian problem. It took courage—perhaps rashness—to present a case so critical of French policies. As a Democrat and a Senator he is certainly entitled to criticize our own Administration's policies on this issue, but considering the sensitivity, jealousy and distrust the French have shown of our motives, an intervention of this type is at the very least risky.

One can hope that the gamble comes off, but the chances are heavily against the Senator. After all, he has attacked the French on a problem they consider to be internal. Granting that he has said some harsh truths, there are also inaccuracies in his picture and a certain degree of superficiality. Neither from the French nor American point of view is the problem as clear or simple as Senator Kennedy tries to make it.

Perhaps the strongest criticism which can be made of the Senator's efforts is that he has run a strong risk of making the situation worse. Even Frenchmen who have been critical of their Government's policies will resent interference from a foreigner who, as they will undoubtedly see it, has no right to intervene.

Moreover, the impression that the United States may try to mediate on behalf of the Algerian nationalists, will surely stiffen their resistance against the French. A compromise solution is made more difficult by an intervention of this type.

So far as the United States is concerned, Secretary Dulles is on sensible ground when he says, as he did yesterday, that we should not in present circumstances become more deeply involved in Algerian affairs then we are today. Algeria is not a simple question of imperialism, as Senator Kennedy suggests. It is an extraordinary complex problem in the relationship of two peoples and two territories, with historic, racial, economic, political and military factors all intermingled. The comparisons Senator Kennedy makes with Indochina, Tunisia and Morocco are only partly valid.

Algeria is a unique and baffling problem which may prove insoluble in the long run but which should be left for the time being in French and Algerian hands. Senator Kennedy undoubtedly has a sincere desire to be helpful. However, to be of service in a situation like this requires the most delicate exercise of diplomacy and not a smashing public attack on the floor of the United States Senate.

Address on the Problems and Prospects of Subsaharan Africa, by Joseph Palmer 2d, Deputy Assistant Secretary for African Affairs†

December 9, 1957

*   *   *

To summarize on the question of colonialism and nationalism: The African people quite naturally look to the United States for support for their aspirations for political

---

*The New York Times, July 3, 1957, p. 22.
†Department of State Bulletin, Dec. 9, 1957, pp. 931-33.

progress. The European powers equally naturally look to us for support for their efforts to assure peace and stability. We in the United States have a very real interest in a politically stable Africa and believe that this stability is dependent upon steady and orderly political progress. We believe that only in this way will responsible, moderate, and positive elements emerge—in contrast to the extremist, disruptive, and negative nationalism which poses such dangers for us all.

In general I believe that we in this country are encouraged by the remarkable progress which is being made in effecting the transition from colonial to self-governing and independent regimes. This has been particularly true in those areas where the population tends to be homogeneous. The problem is, of course, vastly more complicated in those areas in which there are important plural communities. This whole problem of relations between peoples of different races living together in multiracial states involves deep-seated emotions and prejudices which can only be overcome gradually. There are, of course, a number of different approaches to race relationships in Africa today, the spectrum ranging from countries in which the intermingling of races on an equal basis has become an accepted and unquestioned fact to countries in which separation of the races is a legal requirement.

In the light of our own experience in developing harmonious race relations and balancing precept with practice, it behooves us to approach racial problems elsewhere in the world in all humility. Nevertheless, the principles for which we stand are clear. They are embodied in our Constitution and in our Bill of Rights. They have recently been dramatically reaffirmed by our Supreme Court and by our President. In accordance with our traditions we are attempting to solve these problems by the process of orderly law enforcement.

It would not be appropriate for us, even if we wished, to become identified with any conflicting faction in Africa. We can, however, and while preserving our adherence to our own basic principle of racial equality, attempt to exert a moderating influence upon extremists and to oppose those who seek to exploit racial tensions for ulterior purposes. We have, in this connection, the strongest hopes for the success of the administering powers in their search for a basis for racial cooperation. In addition to the vital moral considerations involved, it is not, we know, an easy matter to bring about a full understanding of the extent to which races in a particular community are interdependent.

This leads me to another of the great problems facing sub-Sahara Africa—that of economic development. The economic evolution of the area is moving rapidly from the barest subsistence to the point where the African is beginning to enjoy an increasing share of the world's great supply of consumer goods. This, in turn, is providing incentives to production and creating corresponding increased demands for capital. It is, perhaps, not too strong a statement to say that the success or failure of the moderate regimes in power today in the self-governing and independent areas of Africa may well ultimately depend on the extent to which they are able to bring about the economic and social development of their countries in a manner which will meet the aspirations of their people for a greater share of the world's bounty.

The Western World is generally agreed that Africa must have a faster and more balanced economic development. Articulate Africans will not be satisfied with a mere increase in productivity of raw-material exports. They clearly desire a more diversified use of their countries' overall productive capacities and to avoid the danger of excessive dependence on one or a limited number of crops which may fluctuate widely in price on the world market. Most of the European countries are undertaking extensive economic development programs which attempt to avoid concentration on raw-material production. Progress is limited by available capital funds—both public and private—and deficiencies in African physical and human resources.

It appears likely that the total capital requirements of sub-Sahara Africa will increase substantially in the critical years ahead. Certainly the demands will exceed the capabilities of any one Western nation to meet, and it therefore becomes a matter of the greatest importance and urgency that all of the Western nations should seek to assure that the necessary funds are available for a progressive and orderly development of the subcontinent. The United States has already demonstrated its willingness to assist in this task to the extent that it can, taking into account the heavy demands which are made upon it on a worldwide basis. We have been providing and intend to continue to provide, in accordance with administration policy and subject to congressional approval, assistance to countries in the sub-Sahara region. Moreover, through the instrument of the Export-Import Bank we have made important loans in various parts of the area.

The amount of public capital available will, of course, be able to accomplish only a small part of the enormous task of development which lies before Africa. The demands for private capital will continue to be immense, and perhaps one of the most crucial tests which lies ahead is the extent to which the African areas are able to create the conditions of stability and confidence conducive to the attraction of private capital and to make known in the proper quarters each and every opportunity for attracting investment capital. Some areas of the subcontinent have already shown considerable success in creating such an atmosphere and in attracting capital. It is, I believe a matter of the utmost importance that those of us who are in a position to do so seek to encourage the creation of such conditions everywhere.

Before concluding I wish to say a few words about the problem of communism in the area as we see it. Thus far the Communists appear to have made only limited gains in this part of Africa. Nowhere does a Communist Party openly exist. Trade with Communist countries is still at a comparatively low level. African trade union movements have affiliated with the ICFTU [International Confederation of Free Trade Unions] rather than with the Communist-dominated WFTU [World Federation of Trade Unions] . But there is no room for complacency.

The Communists are openly eager to exploit the soft spots wherever they find them. Thus they have already shown some progress in penetrating individual labor organizations, youth groups, and nationalist organizations. They have assiduously cultivated students, particularly those studying abroad, with some success.

The greatest dangers of Communist penetration arise from factors affecting the attitudes of the West. Should the West falter in its determination and its ability to show steady progress in the solution of the range of problems which we have been discussing here, the road for Communist exploitation will be clearly opened. I am confident, however, that there is too much wisdom in Africa and in the West to permit this to happen.

The political map of Africa has undergone tremendous changes in the 12 years of the post-war period. The number of independent states in the continent as a whole has more than doubled. The number of self-governing entities has shown an even greater increase. The dynamism of this situation becomes every day more apparent.

The response of the West to the challenge which Africa presents has, I believe, thus far been both rapid and effective. In all of the newly emerged independent and self-governing states we have moderate regimes which are friendly to the West and genuinely dedicated to the protection of their newly acquired status. This, I believe, is cause for great satisfaction, because this situation has not come about by accident. It has resulted from planning, cooperation, compromise, and mutual good will. It represents a recognition, by the administering powers involved, of the fact that the African peoples are capable with education and experience of conducting responsibly their own affairs.

The leaders of these new states have, for their part, recognized that in a sense their problems begin—not end—with independence and that their only real hope of building and maintaining the stable, peaceful, and prosperous regimes which their peoples demand is through continued cooperation with the West. They will, I am sure, be able to maintain these positions as long as the West continues to show itself sympathetic to their efforts at adjustment and responsive to their needs.

This is a situation, however, which will continue to require imagination and dedication. We must assure that the dynamism which is so apparent in Africa today is met by a corresponding dynamism in the West and that both forces are harnessed together to achieve the same objectives. In this way we can build a relationship based on equality, confidence, and mutual benefit which will provide an effective answer to the disruptive and self-seeking objectives which the Communists seek in this continent, as elsewhere.

*Speech by Deputy Secretary Palmer on Emerging Africa**

May 20, 1958

The march of events during the last few years and months has brought the erstwhile "dark" continent into the center of the world arena. I am sure that as a result of the lectures you have heard during participation in this pioneering course on "Africa South of the Sahara" you, too, will agree with Vice President Nixon's statement in his report to the President on his trip to the area last year that "the emergence of a free and independent Africa is as important to us in the long run as it is to the people of that continent."

I have been asked to outline United States policy toward Africa. I shall therefore attempt to speak in general terms but know that you will bear in mind that there are, in fact, many Africas, even south of the Sahara, and our policy has to be molded to fit the facts and circumstances of the different regions and the particular countries and territories there.

*   *   *

The interdependence of Africa and Western Europe is indisputable. The two continents are essentially complementary areas. The economies of the Western European powers would suffer greatly if they were denied access to African markets, raw materials, and investment opportunities. Africa, on the other hand, cannot expand its

Ibid., June 16, 1958, pp. 993-96; 998.

less highly developed economies without technical know-how, capital accumulations, export markets, and finished goods such as those which Western European and other free-world countries are in a position to provide.

Without exception the European metropolitan powers recognize the importance of a continued relationship between them and their African territories, however widely they may differ in the philosophies underlying their policies in their overseas territories and in the methodology employed to achieve this objective. Similarly, the moderate African regimes now in power recognize in most cases the mutual advantage of the continuance of close ties with the Western World. The evolution of mutually satisfactory arrangements, adjusted to changed conditions, may well be decisive in determining the future stability and prosperity of both continents.

The United States and the Western World have a basic interest in increased African economic development, which is clearly essential to its sound political evolution. The size, diversity, and needs of the continent are so great as to require the sympathetic attention of all the countries in the free world in a position to help, for the needs are beyond the capability of any one country to meet. Nor should one forget that, whereas private capital can make a tremendous contribution, it cannot always do this job alone.

*   *   *

It is evident that the dynamic trend in postwar Africa is the movement toward self-government and independence.

This great movement is both old and new. For example, Liberia this July celebrates its 111th independence day while Ethiopia's independence dates back to Biblical times. In their postwar manifestations the same forces which began in Asia and the Middle East and swept across North Africa have now spread to sub-Sahara Africa, where on March 6 last year we saw Ghana gain its independence and thereby join the new nations of Libya, the Sudan, Morocco, and Tunisia, all of which have acquired their independence since 1951.

It is obvious that the success which the free world demonstrates in accommodating itself to this dynamic African nationalism may well be decisive in determining the future orientation of the continent.

An important indication of the current rend of African nationalism is found in the resolutions adopted by the representatives of the eight independent African states attending the pan-African conference held at Accra from April 15 to 22 on the invitation of Prime Minister Nkrumah. These resolutions made clear that, generally speaking, independent Africa today is led by moderate men; is zealous to strengthen and safeguard its independence, sovereignty, and territorial integrity; is vitally interested in advancing itself economically, socially, and culturally; and is intent on playing an important and responsible role in world affairs. Although we are not in accord with all that was said or advocated at Accra, we happily find ourselves in broad agreement—or at least broad understanding—with much that emerged from the conference.

Despite the dynamic trend of African nationalism, however, there are still large areas of the continent where the impact of Western civilization has left less of an imprint and the African remains politically inarticulate. Consequently the current problem is how to create the most desirable conditions for orderly development by educating an informed, discriminating citizenry, building durable representative institutions, and creating a stable economic and social structure in the very limited time available before pressures become too great to control.

In general it would appear that the present tempo of African development—the transformation to self-government and to independence—is proceeding at a rate commensurate with the requirements of the situation in most areas.

The United Nations has been an immensely constructive force in this development. The trust territories, of course, have been most directly affected. Under terms of the United Nations Charter, each administering power is charged with promoting the advancement of its trust territories toward self-government or independence. As a result of progress in this respect, the former British Togoland voted to join Ghana in 1957, the Italian East African Trust Territory of Somalia is due to obtain its independence in 1960, and other African trust territories such as French Togo and Cameroun are evolving rapidly toward the ultimate objectives of the trusteeship system.

The United Nations has not only provided opportunities for African nationalism to appeal to international conscience; it has also induced a sense of responsibility in holding out the prospect of membership in the community of nations when statehood is realized. Once membership in the United Nations has been obtained, it provides a framework for continued responsibility, as well as security, by relieving leaders of new states from excessive preoccupation with the danger of external attack. Conversely, the obligations of United Nations membership also enable African leaders to demonstrate more easily to their citizens the danger of resorting to national adventure themselves.

*   *   *

Some conclusions are perhaps now in order:

First, a stable interdependent relationship between Africa and the West will emerge in the long run only to the extent that it is based on considerations of dignity, sovereignty, equality, and mutual advantage, both as among peoples and among states.

Second, we of the West must convince the Africans that we desire close, friendly, equal relationships for the value of those associations per se and not solely for any advantage which may accrue to us in the balance-of-power situation in the world today. The West must, at the same time, continue to recognize the force of nationalism and, as partners, to encourage its evolution into constructive, responsible channels.

Third, while avoiding identification with any faction in Africa and preserving our basic principle of racial equality, we should conitnue to exert a moderating influence as appropriate and oppose those who seek to exploit racial tensions in Africa for ulterior purposes. In our own experience in this country, we must continue to demonstrate by example our ability to make progress in developing beneficial and harmonious racial relationships.

Fourth, the Communists give evidence of girding themselves for a determined effort to deny Africa to the free world. The success of the West in preventing this may depend less on our ability to convince the Africans of the dangers of communism than on our demonstrating to them in positive terms the advantages of cooperation with the West.

Finally, the United States Government alone cannot achieve all the objectives in Africa of this nation and its free-world associates. It is essential that "peoples to peoples" diplomacy—the whole private-enterprise system—assist in doing the total job. This diplomacy truly represents the full strength, the unique versatility—in fact, the very soul—of America.

Speech by Representative Powell Before the House on a New Policy for Africa*

March 23, 1959

*   *   *

So intense has been our concentration upon the struggle of the Soviet-Western world that we failed to observe that a new world was being born. It is in this new world arena that the struggle for peace and freedom in our time is going to be waged and our very survival will depend on its outcome. Our survival, our freedom, our beliefs in the dignity of man are inextricably tied in with the ultimate outcome of the struggle against oppression in central Africa and the Union of South Africa. However much we of the West talk about the Union of South Africa's membership in the free world and the resonsibility of the free world to close ranks to maintain that freedom, the African is fighting mad today for he knows it is freedom for whites only. So all of us of the United States in a holy crusade against communism that threatens our way of life are banded as one under the banner of freedom together with the Union of South Africa and other powers are ourselves subverting the cause of freedom in the eyes of the African people. Moreover, the entire Afro-Asian bloc expresses itself from time to time against Western indifference to the suffering there.

Nor is the unrest limited to certain geographical areas and certain tribes against a particular European military and political force. If that were the case we might pass a resolution here and take some positive action there on Nyasaland, on the Cameroons, on Algeria, on Egypt, on the Union of South Africa and be done with it. But it is not that simple. All over the vast continent of Africa in addition to the determination to remove the European rider from his back there is a revolution against the continuance of colonial traditions of any kind.

*   *   *

I have attempted to spell out the most obvious dilemmas which await us around the corner as we move to another position in this new world. It would be ironic, indeed, if we deliberately choose the losing side. For it is written, Africans will play a large role in our country's future, in fact, in the future of all the nations of the West. Have we forgotten that ultimate security depends on decisions made beyond the borders of the United States as much as on those made within our country?

We are challenged today and have but little time left to decide whether or not to abandon our double-edged policy in Africa, to decide whether to permit our sympathies for our European heritage to take precedence over the welfare of mankind even when there is clear recognition that the period of European ascendancy in Africa is drawing to an end.

**Congressional Record*, March 23, 1959.

To the dilemmas imposed we inquire again how long can we operate under a policy, "To be or not to be, to do or not to do" as a program of action?

*   *   *

Remarks of Senator John F. Kennedy Before Second Annual Conference of American Society of African Culture*

June 28, 1959

*   *   *

As chairman of the new Subcommittee on African Affairs in the Senate Foreign Relations Committee, I have become increasingly aware in recent months of our interest in Africa south of the Sahara—of our concern for developments in that area—and of the changes needed in our current attitudes and policies. Some may look at it from the viewpoint of vital natural resources and strategic materials. Some may be interested in military bases or new allies against Communism. Some may feel a responsibility in Africa because the West thrust itself upon the area and cannot be indifferent to the consequences. Some may have a real concern for Africa and her people. But whatever one's point of view, one fact cannot be denied—the future of Africa will seriously affect, for better or worse, the future of the United States.

*   *   *

In the light of such fantastic variety and revolutionary progress, it is a mistake for the United States to fix its image of Africa in any single mold. We an no longer think of Africa in terms of Europe. We dare not think of Africa in terms of our own self interests or even our own ideologies. But neither should we shrink from the tremendous problems Africa presents, with an excess of caution, conservatism or pessimism. For they are the problems of the greatest triumph modern man might ever known. They are the problems attendant upon newly won, or nearly won, freedom. They are the problems of a continent with an unlimited future—not a poor continent, let me stress in that regard, not even a poor continent today—but a rich continent filled with millions of poor people.

For today, years after the white man supposedly took up Kipling's predestined burden, most of the exploited natives live a life that holds no greater meaning for them than the unending search for enough food for themselves and their children. While non-African nations fattened and prospered materially from African natural resources, the tribes remained destitute. Per capita income—amidst acres of diamonds, lush pastures and now uranium itself—is generally below $50 a year.

In tropical Africa seven out of ten babies born will not live until their first birthday. Average life expectancy in America today is seventy years—in some areas of Africa it is twenty-eight.

In spite of splendid missionary efforts—many of them American—the pathetic

*Summary Report, Second Annual Conference, American Society of African Culture, The Waldorf-Astoria, New York, June 26-29, 1959, pp. 8-10.

shortage of medical care accounts for the deaths of legions of natives–deaths that could be prevented–from malaria, trachoma, worm infections and leprosy. Because of the absence of the barest educational facilities, the prevalence of illiteray has denied to history the body of literature any culture needs to record and perpetuate itself.

But our purpose here tonight is not merely to criticize the past or deplore the present. We want to help the states of Negro Africa. We have already given some help. It was not enough. We are giving some help today. It is not enough.

Our goal, for the good of Africa, for the good of the West, is a strong Africa. A strong Africa can only result from a strong people. And no people can become strong in a climate of servitude and social indignity. What can the United States do?

Through our Mutual Security Program, economic aid to Africa has been increased from 10 million dollars in 1956 to 100 million dollars this year. But this is still less than 3 percent of our total foreign aid budget–less than three percent for the most under-developed continent of them all covering one-fifth of the earth's inhabited surface. Even this represents a substantial increase–between 1945 and 1955, Africa received less than one-sixth of one percent of American foreign aid[1] –and most of this went to South Africa and the Rhodesias.

It is in this area of economic development that a new American policy toward Africa must begin. Our leaders may talk of "winning the battle for men's minds," which the Vice President stressed upon his return from that continent. There may be importance attached to the prompt recognition of new states, improved diplomatic relations and membership in international organizations. But the people of Africa are more interested in development than they are in doctrine. They are more interested in achieving a decent standard of living than in following the standards of either East or West.

For the present, this cannot be the development of large industry. There are still, for the most part, primitive economies. There is an acute shortage of technical, managerial and skilled labor. Our aid now should be concentrated not on large scale monuments to American engineering but on the village and the farm–on increasing agricultural productivity and diversifying one-crop economies.

And that is why it is not enough to say that private capital should take the lead in Africa. Private overseas investment in Africa has been concentrated largely in the few metropolitan areas–in the cities and districts dominated by whites–on mining gold, diamonds, copper and uranium. It avoids the jungle village in need of light industry, the farm in need of modern equipment, the hungry and illiterate people in need of a better way of life. I do not overlook all that private capital from America and Europe has done for the African continent–but it cannot do the job alone. It will not be attracted to nonprofit schools, hospitals and social services, or even to the necessary network of communication and transportation.

To meet this shortage of development capital in the underdeveloped areas of the world, the Congress has in recent years established the Development Loan Fund. That fund is our best tool for African economic policy today. Unfortunately, only a negligible amount of an already inadequate appropriation has been used for Africa to date. It is essential that this Congress strengthen the Development Loan Fund this year–and thus strengthen Africa's participation in it.

At the same time, far more must be done by way of technical assistance, under the so-called Point Four program. With more than 80 per cent of the population struggling

[1] There was no "foreign aid" to Union or Rhodesia.

to get by on a meager subsistence, we have made available to the entire continent in the current budget only 14 million dollars for the promotion of education, technical training and public health. A 50 percent increase has been proposed for 1960—but a 500 percent increase would hardly begin to do the job.

Let me stress, however, that economic progress in Africa is not the responsibility of this nation alone. It is primarily the responsibility of the Africans. It is also the responsibility of those European nations who have for centuries extracted the wealth of that continent. Perhaps the most effective way to provide financial help for investment, development and personnel might be through multilateral cooperation with African, European, American and other countries in an African regional economic plan. Such a program should properly be initiated by the African independent states, and be sufficiently elastic to negotiate and coordinate bilateral and multilateral arrangements. The African states would participate on a basis of complete equality—as givers as well as receivers.

*   *   *

Tied in closely with Africa's problems of economic development are her problems of education. Illiteracy is prevalent—schools are inadequate—teachers are in short supply—and the problems of language, diversity and change all pose an unprecedented challenge to educators. It is not enough to tell them how we did it here. Their conditions, their needs, their circumstances are different—and they cannot wait for a century of educational evolution. An African educational development fund—with particular emphasis on the exchange of students, teachers and trained personnel—making available our technicians and specialists in a whole variety of fields, while at the same time opening our universities and college doors to several times as many African students as now come over—this would be an investment which would be repaid to this country many times over in increased goodwill, trade and national security.

But while the benefits to our national security from a new approach to Africa cannot be overlooked, I have not stressed this evening the economic and educational activities now being carried on in Africa by the Soviet Union. We know such activities exist. We know they are a threat. But let us never assist Africa merely because we are afraid of Russian assistance in Africa. Let us never convince the people of that continent that we are interested in them only as pawns in the cold war. Nor do we want them to regard us only as a military guardian, a giver of goods, or a lender of cash.

*   *   *

Study on Africa Prepared by Program of African Studies, Northwestern University *

October 23, 1959

*   *   *

THE UNITED STATES, THE UNITED NATIONS, AND AFRICA

The degree to which the position taken by the United States on questions having to do with Subsaharan Africa demonstrates an alinement with the colonial powers has

*Senate Committee on Foreign Relations, *Africa, A Study*, 86th Cong., 1st sess., (Washington, 1959), pp. 73-77; 13-17.

given rise to much discussion. Conclusions, in general, have followed the biases of those intent on proving American sympathy for the colonial or anticolonial point of view. As far as can be determined, no analysis of the facts is available; that is, no study has been made of the comparative voting record of the United States on questions affecting Africa, as these have come up in the General Assembly or the various organs of the United Nations. From United Nations published sources, it is not possible to ascertain more than the numbers of delegations voting for or against a given resolution, or abstaining.

The Historical Division of the Bureau of Public Affairs, Department of State, has furnished the voting records of member nations on some of the more important resolutions treating of Africa for use in preparing this report, plus the vote of the United States on other questions where rollcalls had not been taken. Of the 97 votes thus reported, 40 provided data for the analysis of rollcall responses. These run the gamut of the African questions that have been before the United Nations. The treatment of the Indians in the Union of South Africa and the status of South-West Africa figure most prominently on the list. Also included are the votes on the future of French and British Togoland and the Cameroons, on requiring the transmission of information on non-self-governing territories by metropolitan powers, on the Ethiopia-Somaliland frontier question, and on the disposal of the former Italian colonies.

We have analyzed these votes to clarify the position of the United States on African matters as this is reflected in its degree of consonance with other voting members. Specifically, we have inquired into the extent to which the votes of the United States have been in accord with those of the colonial powers, as represented by the United Kingdom and France, with such anticolonial powers as India and Liberia, with Latin American countries as represented by Chile and Brazil, with Canada, and with Russia. We have also asked how these results compare with the voting record on African questions of some of the countries that belong to caucus or regional groups.

To ascertain the answers, we computed the percentages of agreement in the 40 votes cast by those countries on African issues. Only exact coincidences were counted —"yea" for "yea," "nay" for "nay," and abstention for abstention. This understandably introduces a bias toward lowering the percentages, and thus accentuating disagreement, since the difference between "nay" and "abstain" need not represent a real divergence in point of view. Thus, if we take Brazil as an example, only in one instance did the United States vote "aye" and Brazil "nay"; the other seven disagreements were between abstention and a position vote. Such instances, however, indicate the presence of something less than solidarity, and in all cases express the absence of complete agreement.

Turning to the results, we may first of all consider how the votes of the United States agreed with those of the majority, and with those of each of the other countries whose votes were tabulated. In reading these figures, it must be remembered that the higher the percentage, the greater the agreement:

	Percentages of agreement
United States, with—	
Majority	.77.5
Brazil	.80.0
Canada	.72.5
Chile	.70.0

India *60.0*
Liberia *52.5*
United Kingdom *47.5*
France *42.5*
U.S.S.R. *27.5*

As far as our data are representative, they show that the United States was in greatest agreement with the countries of the Americas, and that we agreed substantially more with the anticolonial powers than with our NATO associates. The low figure of concordance with Russia reflects divergence on wider world issues.

Further analysis of the data throws light on our second question. The U.S.S.R. was in agreement with Liberia on 62.5 percent of the issues, as against our 52.5 percent; with India 65 percent as against our 60 percent. The U.S. figure of 27.5 percent agreement with the Soviet Union may also be compared with that of 17.5 percent between the U.S.S.R. and the United Kingdom, or of 30 percent between it and France. Turning to the anticolonial countries, we may compare our 60 percent of agreement with India with that of the United Kingdom, which was ranged at the side of her fellow member of the Commonwealth on only 27.5 percent of the votes. The index for Franco-Indian concordance in 47.5 percent. The United Kingdom agreed with the Liberian vote to the same extent she agreed with that of India, 27.5 percent; France was on the same side as Liberia in 40 percent of the voting. Both these contrast with the United States-Liberian index of concordance, which is 52.5 percent. As regards consistency between powers having similarity of interests, the solidarity of the United Kingdom and France on African issues is reflected in the percentage of agreement in their voting, the figure being 72.5 percent. Even greater agreement is to be seen in the record of our two anticolonial countries, India and Liberia, the figure here being 82.5 percent.

It is clear that, as far as these results permit generalization, the United States, belonging to no caucusing or geographical group, has nonetheless taken what may be called a New World position on African matters. To what extent the degree of agreement found between the votes of New World powers represents U.S. influence on Latin American countries where questions not to their immediate interest are involved cannot be said, and in any event is outside the terms of reference of this report. The fact that the coefficient of agreement between Canada and the United Kingdom, 72.5 percent, is identical to that between her and the United States would seem to indicate that in respect to African affairs, Commonwealth ties have not over balanced her role as a great New World power.

The cumulative devolution of power to African peoples will for the United States both simplify the problem of voting in the United Nations, and make it more complex. It will do this in much the same way as these changes affect our operations in Africa itself. Each new commitment by one of our NATO associates to the principle of self-government for an African territory renders less difficult our ambivalent position. Concomitantly, each time the principle of self-government is implemented, the number of African states in the United Nations increases, and the complexity of mediating specific issues increases as well.

The change in the position taken by the United States in the Trusteeship Council on the future of Tanganyika provides an illustration of the first of these points. In 1955 a statement of the American representative concerning a timetable for the attainment of self-government was withdrawn because U.S. policy at that time held that "as a general rule the setting of a timetable tends to be too rigid." In 1959, however, when the situation in Tanganyika was under review, two "basic requirements" were declared essential, in American opinion, "if effective and orderly progress toward independence is to be maintained." The first was "a clear understanding and acceptance by the Africans of the political goals which they are headed for." The second was that "Africans must have satisfactory evidence of the plans being made for their progress toward independence." This, it was felt, "can best be accomplished by expressing from time to time the period within which the Government hopes to accomplish the next step in its program heading toward self-government." The first of these suggested steps was to institute a "fully responsible ministerial government in the territory." The second, provision for universal suffrage, was justified by reference to the fact that this system had been instituted in various of their possessions by the British, the French, and in limited form by the Belgians.

The most difficult questions having to do with Africa that the United States faces in the United Nations are those of Algeria and of the Union of South Africa. In each, the tensions responsible for bringing it before the United Nations have arisen out of a conflict between a large European minority and an indigenous majority. In both, the minority holds political control, and uses it as an instrument to maintain and enhance its economic and social status.

The case of Algeria presents us with our classical dilemma in sharpest outlines. Pressure from France, and policy decisions based on a predominantly European orientation, pull us in one direction, while our traditional sympathy for independence movements and pressures from the Africa group constitute strong counterinfluences. The difficulty of decision has in this instance been compounded by three factors. The first is that France has made the continuation of Algeria as a part of the metropole a matter of principle, so that any challenge to this position arouses the emotional responses of affronted national pride. Not so immediately on the surface, but very influential, is the economic reason for the preservation of metropolitan control. This derives from the proved existence of vast oil and other mineral resources in the Sahara, that are just beginning to be tapped. They are so great that, if retained under French control, they will not only free France from dependence for oil on outside sources by 1963, but will make of her a substantial petroleum exporter. The third factor is the strength of the counterpressures of the Asia-African group, more especially those of the newly formed African Caucusing Group, which can be measured by the fact that for them the Algerian issue today has first priority, and has become the symbol of its continental solidarity.

The tale of this African Caucusing Group is told in the spread of self-government in Africa. It is a development out of the Asian-African group, which began on an ad hoc basis in 1950, and was formally organized 5 years later. The possibility of forming a separate African Caucusing Group was discussed at the Ghana independence celebration, and it took shape after the 1958 Conference of African States in Accra. The problems of primary concern to these states were declared to be "self-determination, racial equality, as well as economic development and matters regarding collective measures for the reduction and control of armaments." During the 2 years this group has been in existence, the overall voting record of its members shows that they cast identical ballots 46.7 percent of the time, and were divided in 20 percent of the votes. The group has consistently promoted its objectives, as is evident from its voting record in the General Assembly for the two sessions it has been in existence. An analysis of this record shows that its members, in voting with the Assembly majority 60 percent of the time, were in accord on questions of human rights, collective measures, peaceful settlement of disputes, and economic cooperation.

This group has a coordinating body, chaired by each African state in turn. It meets once a month, or at the request of any member. Ghana, Liberia, Tunisia, and the United Arab Republic are members of its secretariat, which is selected on a revolving basis. Ghana's representative is its executive secretary. In 1958, the group sent three ambassadorial delegations to South America, Central America, and northern Europe to solicit support for its stand favoring Algerian independence. The recognition by Ghana of the Provisional Algerian Government in July 1959, the position of this topic on the agenda of the Saniquelli meeting of the heads of state of Ghana, Guinea, and Liberia, and the fact that it was a principal question discussed at the Monrovia meeting of African foreign ministers indicates the importance assigned to it by this group. The African states have also urged the setting of specific dates for the independence of Trust Territories; they have pressed hard to require Portugal to submit reports on its African possessions. The group has presented its own candidates for United Nations committee posts; it has assumed the role of sponsor for newly independent African states seeking membership, and acted to help obtain this for Guinea.

The position of this group is to be seen as one of growing influence. As to its internal composition and its relations to other groups, many possibilities suggest themselves which must be anticipated where questions bearing on future United States-African relations are concerned. The fact that its members also belong to the Asian-African group cannot be overlooked. The problem will present itself regarding the future relations between the North African and Subsaharan members of the African group itself, as well as that of the future relations between the organizing countries of the group and new Subsaharan member states, such as Nigeria and the Congo, whose size and population will give them major standing among the countries of the world.

In U.S. relations with Africa, the United Nations is a world forum, from whose platform our actions are closely followed. Here we are called on to take a stand for all to see, on issues that arise principally out of colonialism or that are the legacy of colonial systems that are giving way to self-government. The declarations we make, no less than our voting record, can gain us added African good will or cause us to forfeit it. This is not intended to suggest that in all cases we follow the lead of the African countries. Africans are as capable as any other people of understanding, and respecting, honest disagreement. But if they are to agree in such cases to disagree with us, they must see that the position we take on a particular issue reflects a consistent point of view, and arises out of basic aims unambiguously stated.

*   *   *

CONCLUSIONS AND RECOMMENDATIONS

The following conclusions and recommendations, which derive from the findings in the preceding section, and the materials of the pages that follow, are presented in paired form to facilitate reference and analysis of the points made, and suggestions for U.S. action deriving from them.

Conclusions

Recommendations

1. The dynamic character of the drive of African peoples toward self-government makes it apparent that in the near future we will be dealing in Africa with many governments controlled by Africans.

2. U.S. policy during the past decade has been based on the assumption that Africa, as a continent under the control of our NATO associates, can be given minor consideration.

3. The broadest interests of the United States lie in furthering amicable relations with the peoples and governments of Africa and in promoting mutual understanding as an instrument of world peace.

4. It is important that communism and African nationalism not be confused. The choices that African States will make as regards the world struggle will be influenced by the use of perceptive insights into African needs cast in African terms, and by understanding African aspirations in the light of patterns based on pre-existing traditional values and modes of behavior.

5. Africans have shown concern about the problem of "balkanization" of the continent, and of strong states preying on weak ones. They are insistent that future

1. U.S. policy, in furthering its own best interests and in accord with the action of some of our NATO associates, should be guided by expectation of the primacy of Africans in all Subsaharan Africa.

2. The United States must treat Africa as a major policy area, to be approached on a level of equality with other policy areas, particularly Europe, where African-American interests are involved. U.S. policy in Africa must be flexible, in view of the variations in the African Continent and the rapidity of the changes occurring there; imaginative in view of our traditional sympathy with the aspirations of peoples to direct their own affairs; and positive in shaping aid programs with a view to African needs rather than cold war instrumentalities.

3. U.S. policy in Africa must facilitate the implementation of mutual interests with African countries. It should favor their development free from outside interference, with governments that will live at peace with their neighbors and serve the best interests of their peoples, as these are defined in terms of their own values, functioning so as to reduce racial tensions where these are a factor.

4. The United States should recognize that for African states a policy of non-alinement is in the best interests of the West and of Africa. On the assumption that most of Subsaharan Africa will soon be released from colonial controls, the United States must take the position that our strategic requirements there will be subsidiary to political considerations, and military aid secondary to technical assistance.

5. The United States should view with sympathy efforts to create wider associations of African States which will promote political and economic stability,

independent African States be free to assert their own personalities while benefiting from wider affiliations within the continent.

6. The experience of the United Kingdom in West Africa and of France in the French related territories, like that of the United States in the Philippines, has demonstrated that elimination of uncertainty as to the future of non-self-governing peoples by the establishment of specific timetables or specific measures for the legal attainment of independence is particularly effective in lessening tensions and assuring future good relations.

7. Examined in historical perspective, the present differences in opportunity and reward between African, Asian, and European groups in the multiracial societies of Africa are found to be the end result of the circumstances of early contact. Resistance to change in the existing system of stratification is based on long-established attitudes which are reinforced by tensions of the kind found wherever entrenched social, economic, and political positions are challenged.

8. The problems in international relations presented to the United States by the multiracial countries of eastern and southern Africa arise from the handicaps that racial inequalities in these countries and the tensions resulting from them impose in furthering the cause of the democracies in world opinion.

9. The fact that we have never had, and never have aspired to have African dependencies, plus the attitudes generated over the years by the work of missionaries, scientists, and others, have made

and facilitate the extension of aid in the economic and technical fields.

6. The United States should extend to all African dependent territories the policy applied to Tanganyika, favoring the issuance of specific statements by the responsible authorities about when and how self-government is to be attained, since the more peaceful the transition to self-rule, the greater the likelihood that present orientations toward the West will be maintained by newly independent states.

7. The United States should exert its influence to assure peaceful resolution of conflict in the multiracial states of Africa. It should urge recognition of the interests of all concerned and the implementation of their rights, without regard to ethnic affiliation.

8. The United States must demonstrate that in Africa it applies its domestic policies aimed at achieving interracial good will and equality. Examples of this would be the extension to all government operations there of existing legislation forbidding dealings by government agencies with firms that practice racial discrimination; having U.S. missions apply nondiscriminatory rules in personnel policies as regards local staff; and requiring U.S. firms operating in Africa to show that they have used all legal means to comply with this principle in order to receive tax concessions.

9. The United States should greatly increase appropriations for African exchanges and educational programs of all kinds. Support should be given to projects that link Amerian scholars and their

our contacts with Africa essentially of the person-to-person variety. Private organizations, however, can no longer provide the amounts needed to carry on the educational and research activities that are requested of us. Hence, substantial government contributions are essential if the historic continuity of our earlier contacts with Africa, and the resulting benefits from them, are to continue.

10. The rapid shift of power and responsibility to independent African States, with the resultant withdrawal of overseas administrators, has created a shortage of trained and experienced management and advisory manpower that is likely to persist for some time. Africans fully recognize the needs created by this situation, and look to the United States, the United Nations, the former metropoles, and other countries and agencies for aid in providing essential personnel.

11. The proportion of U.S. loans, grants, and technical assistance to African territories has in past years comprised but a minute part of its total world commitments. Metropolitan countries have provided important assistance to their overseas dependent territories, but new provisions must be worked out as these territories become independent.

12. As in most nonindustrialized areas, a basic problem of Subsaharan Africa is the low level of average income with resulting deficiencies in health, education, and standard of living. Though the countries of Africa have shown a determination to rectify these deficiencies, they are handicapped by the fact that their essen-

counterparts in Africa, thereby making available to African countries our best educational resources. The number of fellowships for Africans to study in American institutions of higher learning and technology should be materially increased. Existing programs to train specialists sent to Africa as technical experts or members of the Foreign Service, in the human aspects of their work, should be extended.

10. The United States, in order to play its role in providing technical aid for newly independent and emerging African countries, should facilitate steps to establish career services for technical assistance personnel on the international level in cooperation with other countries, through the United Nations and through its own governmental operations.

11. The United States should immediately reappraise its aid programs for Subsaharan Africa in order to determine their adequacy in the light of the needs of the area and of American interests. To compound the effectiveness of future contributions, efforts should be made to develop regional arrangements, roughly analogous to the Colombo plan, that will provide a framework for cooperation among the countries of Subsaharan Africa, the European Economic Community, the British Commonwealth, the United States, and other nations willing to participate in measures to promote economic growth in the area.

12. U.S. grants, loans, and technical assistance, whether given directly or through international agencies, should be channeled toward aiding countries of Subsaharan Africa in building up an infrastructure of facilities in such fields as transporation, communications, health, and education, where local resources of

tial capital resources, like those of trained personnel, are inadequate.

13. Despite its subsoil resources, and the industrialization that is possible in view of the hydroelectric potential in Subsaharan Africa, farming will continue to constitute a major sector of African economies. The needs of farmers, however, are not customarily taken into account when loans and grants are projected, because of the difficulties in organizing and administering programs of aid on this level.

14. There are still great gaps in American knowledge about the ways in which African economic problems can be overcome. In order that technical assistance and loans and grants may best be used to develop stable and prospering states in Africa, a great deal more needs to be learned about the character of these societies.

15. There is little evidence that moves looking toward expropriation or unduly heavy taxation of foreign holdings by newly independent African States are to be anticipated. Thus far, U.S. private investment has been relatively restricted in Africa, both as to number of firms involved, total amount invested, and geographical spread. Enough data are in hand, however, to indicate that greater opportunities for profitable operations exist than has been realized.

capital and personnel are inadequate to permit these countries to implement these basic aspects of their developmental plans.

13. U.S. fund-granting agencies and international bodies on which the United States is represented should extend the range of their operations to provide for research into problems of soil management and the development of effective methods for growing, processing, and marketing crops. These matters should be included in the agenda of discussions and negotiations for loans or grants to the governments of African countries.

14. U.S. Government agencies, including the International Cooperation Administration, should be authorized and encouraged to initiate studies of how technical assistance and loan or grant funds can best stimulate long-term economic growth and stability. In fulfillment of this objective, U.S. Government agencies should make maximum use of the growing body of knowledge about African societies gathered by nongovernmental institutions.

15. To encourage American capital investment in that continent, the Department of Commerce should extend the series of economic studies of African countries treating of their commercial and industrial potentials. The United States should also extend the use of methods developed for guaranteeing private investments in newly independent African States, such as the International Cooperation Administration's investment guarantee program, which at the same time will promote the interests of these countries.

Hearings Before the Committee on Foreign Relations on
United States Foreign Policy with Africa*

January 28, February 11, March 16, 1960

         *   *   *

Mr. Satterthwaite [Joseph C. Satterthwaite, Assistant Secretary for African Affairs] : I am talking informally this morning and will, therefore, not speak point by point to the 15 conclusions and recommendations of the report.

What I have to say indicates a number of differences but, as you will have noted, you have had before you this morning a real authority on Africa, and I myself very much enjoyed being here. I am sure all of us from the State Department will benefit from his testimony.

One of the criticisms of U.S. foreign policy which the report makes is that the United States is too considerate of its NATO allies with respect to their African dependencies.

Now, it is evident to this committee that the United States cannot carry out its foreign relations in a vacuum.

Furthermore, I feel that some of this criticism is not particularly pertinent any longer in view of the fact that three of the metropolitan powers with large African territories; namely, the French, the British, and the Belgians, have taken steps either to grant full independence to their territories or to grant them self-government or are in the course of studying future constitutional changes for their territories.

Now, in the case of Portugal, it is evident and well known that Portugal for many years now has maintained the position that its overseas territories are an integral part of Portugal, and it is also known that there is no evidence that they intend to change this policy.

I should also point out, however, that this is a country with which we maintain friendly relations, and with which we have important base agreements.

Spain has a certain amount of territory left in Africa, and we see no indication of change there.

Italy, of course, returned to Africa only for a period of 10 years in the role of administrator of a trust territory.

Is Africa Treated as a Major Policy Area?

Another criticism of the study is that we do not treat Africa as a major policy area.

Now, gentlemen, in my bureau sometimes I am inclined to share this opinion, but I do not believe that it is entirely valid.

Certainly, as the study points out, the Department of State has for the last year and a half had a regional bureau dealing exclusively with African affairs, and other departments and agencies of the Government are following suit, although not as rapidly as I might wish.

I would like to assure the committee, however, that the top command of the State

*Committee on Foreign Relations, U.S. Senate, *Hearings Before the Committee on Foreign Relations*, Part 1, 86th Cong., 2d sess., (Washington, 1960), pp. 134-45.

Department is readily accessible to the African Bureau, and is fully sensitive to the great importance of this area.

Problems Regarding Multiracial Areas

The Northwestern University study seems to give the impression that the United States is not forthright enough in its approach to the multiracial aspects of the problems of the area.

It seems to me that one answer to this point has already been pointed out this morning by Professor Herskovits which is; namely, the record of our voting at the United Nations; and I would like to say in this respect that our delegations to the General Assembly and the Trusteeship Council and other organs have always tried to develop moderate constructive solutions in order to bring the colonial and anticolonial extremists together.

Some of this has been done through speeches. We think that our General Assembly statements on the Apartheid in recent years are excellent examples. Even more has been done, however, in negotiations behind the scenes.

I would like to express a few thoughts further on this question of the multiracial areas.

The U.S. Government has consistently and repeatedly made known its oposition to racial discrimination in all its forms everywhere it may exist in the world. Our record on this is clear. The problem arises, however, as to what one government can do to counter racialism in another country with which it maintains diplomatic relations and whose foreign policies at least strongly support the United States in the overriding issues of our times. Private individuals and organizations can, of course, freely denounce such countries, can raise funds in an attempt to alleviate the situation and can focus the spotlight of public opinion on the racial practices in question. This freedom of action is not available to a government.

I should like to point out this remark is not specifically aimed at Dr. Herskovits' report.

There is an article in the New York Times this morning on the statement by Prime Minister Macmillan which leads me to point out also that he is able to speak in a Commonwealth context, a platform which is not available to the United States.

Position of the United States in the United Nations

In the United Nations the situation is somewhat different and it is here in the last few years that the United States has made crystal clear its views on discriminatory racial practices throughout the world in general and in the Union of South Africa in particular. There has been some feeling among some of our private organizations in this country interested in Africa that the position of the U.S. delegation to the United Nations on this issue is fine but that that of the State Department leaves much to be desired. I can assure you that we speak with one voice and that remarks made and positions taken by our representatives in New York have been carefully coordinated with the Department in advance and represent official U.S. policy.

The rather complicated situation in the Federation of Rhodesia and Nyasaland is currently sub judice with the Monckton Commission now taking testimony on the spot. It is manifestly impossible for the U.S. Government to take any public position on this question at this time.

There seems to have been considerable progress in British East Africa in recent months, particularly in Tanganyika and even in Kenya, and the racial problem in those areas may well resolve itself in the very near future.

Policy of Nonalignment

Another interesting point made by Dr. Herskovits is that the United States should recognize that for African states the policy of nonalinement is in the best interest of the West and of Africa. While we may have to accept a policy of nonalinement in most emerging African states, we doubt that it will be universally the case. The African desire expressed so forcefully by Mr. Nyerere of Tanganyika recently on television not to become involved in the cold war is very understandable and one we should regard sympathetically. The fact remains, however, that in this day and age there is little that happens in the world which does not have a cold war aspect. Merely being a member of the United Nations involves the Africans in the cold war and they cannot expect to operate as an isolated entity immune from the currents that are sweeping the rest of the world.

Importance of Labor Problems in Africa

It seems to me also that the study could have given greater emphasis to Communist efforts in the labor field. While we have little evidence of trade union affiliations of a Communist character, we are, of course, aware of Communist activities in labor groups which are potentially dangerous to say the least.

In this connection, I believe the study might have given greater emphasis to the importance of labor problems in Africa in general. For instance, no reference is to be found to the well-known role played by labor leaders and labor organizations in a number of the independence movements. Furthermore, there is no reference in the report to the important role played by the International Labor Organization in Africa.

Statements on Self-Government

Another recommendation made in the study, on which I should like to comment, is that favoring the issuance of specific statements by the responsible authorities about when and how self-government is to be obtained.

Our feeling on this is that the pace of recent events has shown that timetables are rather unrealistic and can seldom be adhered to except in the last stages of negotiation.

Moreover, there are some areas where we feel that a premature timetable might result in increased unrest and even in disturbances leading to bloodshed.

Tribute to Missionary and Other Groups

Dr. Herskovits has paid tribute to the contributions made by American missionaries to Africa, and also to those of American private foundations. I would like to associate myself with these tributes and to express the hope that these nongovernmental activities will continue in even larger measure.

Diplomatic Representation in Liberia

There is one statement in the report on page 48 which I think was just a mistake in language, but I would like to correct the record.

This indicates that we had no diplomatic representation in Liberia between 1930 and 1934. The fact is that at all times during this period we maintained diplomatic relations, and were represented by a chargé d'affaires when the minister was not present. As a matter of fact, the minister, Mr. Charles E. Mitchell, was promoted from Minister-Resident to Minister Plenipotentiary during that period.

Special Program for Tropical Africa

The Northwestern study also expresses concern that the United States may not be extending sufficient economic assistance to Africa or extending it in the most beneficial manner. The study was of course written before our special program for tropical Africa had been made public and I trust that Dr. Herskovits will agree that this is a start in the right direction. The committee will, I believe, be interested in hearing about the special program at this time, even though I will be discussing it later, perhaps next week, in my appearance before the committee on the Mutual Security Program.

The executive branch is proposing a special program for tropical Africa with an initial appropriation request of $20 million. In preparing this request, we have sought to find a way properly responsive to the African aspirations. We have a fresh situation; we are attempting to meet it in a fresh manner.

The purpose of this program would be to provide assistance in those areas which constitute the greatest impediments to sound, longrun social and economic developments in Africa.

There can be little argument that this development depends in the first instance on a major improvement in the education and training of Africa's human resources and their productive use.

Major Portion of Special Program Funds to be Used to Accelerate Education and Training

In my travels in Africa, I have found one of the principal concerns of the responsible leaders to be the lack of experienced African civil servants, entrepreneurs, technicians—in general, the need for skills and professional knowledge which are so vital to modern national economies.

In November of 1958 I had the privilege of traveling to Africa with a number of prominent scientists under the direction of Dr. Serge Harrar, who had been commissioned by the National Academy of Sciences, under a contract with ICA, to see if some way could not be found whereby perhaps by the use of science, we could make what was then called a dramatic breakthrough in our assistance to Africa.

It is interesting to note that the conclusions which this study reached were that, to quote:

Future development of Sub-Sahara Africa depends, in the first instance, upon the rate at which progress can be made in strengthening education. Every other consideration is subordinate to that of education.

A major portion of the funds in our special program will be applied in a manner which will help to accelerate the education and training of Africans for the numerous essential administrative and technical jobs their countries require.

The importance of upgrading African skills, in general, has convinced us that this program should be broad enough to provide special training to those who will not have the opportunity for formal education. We thus propose to support many activities in such areas as agricultural extension, community development and public health.

Question of Regionalism

It is also clear that longrun stability and the most effective framework for the improvement of human resources are to be found in closer association of the African nations, and the development of multicountry planning and cooperative effort in order to solve their common problems.

The whole question of regionalism in Africa is a complex and difficult subject. The variety of forces on the continent—the different status of political evolution, the intense nationalism, the competition among African leaders for preeminence—make it extremely difficult to find an approach which will reverse the trend toward further fragmentation of the African Continent. While I believe that closer associations of African countries will develop, it will be a long process.

Funds to be Used to Foster Cooperative Approaches to
Developmental Problems

Much can be done, now, however, to help encourage cooperative approaches to the many common developmental problems which confront all the African countries. We are thus proposing to use a portion of the funds requested to support and sponsor multicountry conferences, workshops, and seminars as training programs in themselves and as a means of developing cooperative approaches to special developmental problems such as, for example, the tsetse fly which closes large parts of the continent to livestock development. A training grant program which will permit Africans from several countries to attend the various African schools and colleges now operating is also being proposed. This interchange of students between African countries should serve to facilitate the efficient use of available African institutions as well as promote friendships and ties between Africans from several countries. Other activities in this category include a regional English language training program, educational research, and an educational materials and documentation center.

Program for Tropical Africa to Seek Assistance from Other Free World Sources

One of the important criteria we had established for this program is that it should not become a competitor to, or substitute for, assistance from other free world sources. It is our hope, rather, that it may serve to help encourage an increase in assistance from other free world countries and international and national organizations. This area of tropical Africa is now receiving over $500 million annually from European countries for major development projects. Increasing amounts of technical and other forms of assistance are coming from a number of private organizations.

A number of U.S. foundations are making important contributions in a number of fields. The United Nations, through its technical assistance program and its Special Fund, is stepping up its assistance to this continent. It is our intention to seek the participation of these various organizations and countries on specific projects where feasible. We also hope that out of the multicountry conferences will come proposals for joint efforts on important develoment problems.

Role of Special Program for Tropical Africa

All of Africa will be included under the program except for the northern tier of Morocco, Algeria, Tunisia, Libya and Egypt, and the Union of South Africa.

The United States and the European countries have a great reservoir of good will and common interest built up in tropical Africa. Most of the educated Africans have studied in Western schools and universities; many have grown up with Western political institutions and principles, and with the Western private and public enterprises. This reservoir provides the United States with a valuable relationship on which to build our new ties with the African people. The Africans are looking to the United States to see how it will respond to their needs and problems. The special program for tropical Africa, I believe, can have an important role in demonstrating that the United States is willing in word and deed to identify itself with the aspirations of the African people.

I will be talking about this program before your committee, as I said, later on.

Now that, in effect, concludes my informal testimony.

*   *   *

Defense Agreement with Liberia

The Chairman: What has been the reaction among neighboring countries to our defense agreement with Liberia?

Mr. Satterthwaite: We have had no expressions of concern that I can recall, except possibly on the part of one country, and I believe that country was no longer concerned when we pointed out that this was an agreement of cooperation, which does make it clear that we take a great interest in the defense of Liberia, but goes no further, of course, than an agreement to consult in case Liberia's integrity should be endangered.

The Chairman: We did not furnish arms to Liberia?

Mr. Satterthwaite: We have furnished some small arms for the Liberian frontier force. We furnished a small quantity just in December.

These were arms which were very badly needed, and in view of our relationship with Liberia we were very glad to do so. They were not, however, a grant, but a purchase.

The Chairman: Of small arms?

Mr. Satterthwaite: Yes, sir.

Situation in Somalia

The Chairman: We were discussing some time ago in the committee the situation in Somalia. If Somalia would request arms, what would our position be? What is the policy of the Department?

Mr. Satterthwaite: Somalia has at the present time only a small police force. Actually, a request has been made of us for some arms for this force, but we have taken the position that while we are sympathetic with the need and realized the need, we thought that it was the primary responsibility of the administrative power, Italy, to furnish these arms.

The Chairman: You did not furnish them?

Mr. Satterthwaite: No; except that we have provided some transportation and ICA equipment under the ICA program.

Policy in Regard to Appointment of Ambassadors to African Countries

The Chairman: What is the policy of the Department with regard to the appointment of ambassadors to African countries?

Mr. Satterthwaite: Our policy is, with possibly some exceptions, that we will recommend to the President the appointment of ambassadors to the new African countries.

It is possible, although this still has to be determined, that some ambasssadors can perhaps be moved to two or more countries because of not only the expense involved but the minimal number of problems that these countries will have with the United States.

One of our problems, however, which has been brought out indirectly here, is that each of these new countries fully intends, and is probably sure of membership in the United Nations. It is therefore highly important to us to have an ambassador, or certainly someone of sufficiently high rank at each capital who has the confidence of the leaders of that government and has access to them, if only in connection with the United Nations matters and our general interest in world affairs.

The Chairman: Do we appoint members of the Negro race to these ambassadorships?

Mr. Satterthwaite: We have at the moment two Negro ambassadors, although one actually is a minister—one in Africa and one in Europe.

The Chairman: Do you have any difficulty in finding qualified ambassadors to serve in these newly created countries?

Mr. Satterthwaite: The problems in some of these countries are so complicated that the President has appointed experienced professional Foreign Service officers.

*   *   *

U.S. Policy Regarding Independence for African States

Senator Lausche: On page 1 of the report Dr. Herskovits pointed out statements made by Mr. Acheson, Mr. McGhee, Mr. Dulles, and Mr. Satterthwaite. They are supposed to be declarations of our attitude with respect to the aspirations of African peoples for self-government. He asserts that these statements contain entirely too many conditions and qualifications.

I would first like to ask Dr. Herskovits to make a statement on what he feels our policy ought to be. I do not want you to point out what you call the conditions, but to declare what the policy should be.

Mr. Herskovits [Melville J. Herskovits, Director, Program of African Studies, Northwestern University]: I think, in a sense, Mr. Satterthwaite has answered your question by saying that the events of roughly the last 6 months have made much of the point here irrelevant, because we would not have to say today what was said about being in favor of independence provided the people are ready for it.

I object most, I think, to these qualifying statements.

Senator Lausche: Would you say that we favored independence for all people of a similar race living within a geographical boundary that provides resources and the ability to live?

Mr. Herskovits: I do not think I would bring race in it.

Senator Lausche: All right. How would you declare it? I would like to have you declare what you believe should be the policy. Forget Africa—take some other country.

Mr. Herskovits: I believe the policy of the United States, granting the present climate of world opinion, should not hedge on the matter of favoring independence for nonindependent people.

Seator Lausche: Then would you say that we favor independence regardless of the conditions which prevail and regardless of the ability of the people to govern themselves?

Mr. Herskovits: If we have to say something, I would prefer that to these heavily qualified statements. But I am not so sure we have to make pronouncements about this.

Senator Lausche: I notice that each one of these persons, Acheson, McGhee, Dulles, and Satterthwaite, generally declared that they favored the independence of the people, providing they are prepared, providing they are willing and able to assume their obligations among the nations of the world, and so forth.

Let me hear your view. Have you read your statement, Mr. Satterthwaite?

Mr. Satterthwaite: I have; yes, sir.

Senator Lausche: Do you depart from it now or do you stand by it?

Mr. Satterthwaite: I stand by it because I think that it is only realistic to think that a government which has responsibility for conducting relations with all parts of the world has to have qualifications in almost any statement it makes.

One could go, if one were an international lawyer, into a long analysis of our traditional policies on the question of recognition of states, of new states, and one of the essential qualifications has always been a willingness on the part of a new state to recognize its international obligations, for instance, and that involves the ability to take responsibility.

Basic Policy Favors Right of Self-Determination

I personally feel that our basic policy in favoring the right of self-determination is well known, and it is not unreasonable in our public statements to clarify these to the degree we have.

I do believe that the statement which is, perhaps, the most authentic statement of all, was made by the late Secretary Dulles in 1958 in which he said:

> The United States supports political independence for all peoples who desire it and are able to undertake its responsibilities. We have encouraged and we rejoice in the current evolution.

Senator Lausche: What are some of the dangers of unequivocally and unconditionally saying that our policy is that a people shall have independence and the right to establish their own governments regardless of conditions?

Mr. Satterthwaite: Well, the obvious dangers or problems, Senator Lausche, are how do we define a people. Are we going to say that we feel the people of northern Nigeria should be independent from the people of the western region and the eastern region, all three of which have been federated? Our feeling is that the more unity there can be among diverse people the better it is.

Senator Lausche: I repeatedly make an effort to decide in my own mind what our primary policy in this is, and my final judgment is that our policy is to encourage people to gain their independence without intervention of other governments.

But then I get stuck on the question of what people. Are they to be mixed? Are they to be divided geographically by mountains, and so on? But I would say that our policy is to establish throughout the world independent governments when ethnological and geographical conditions are of a nature that would indicate the ability of those people to survive as a government.

Mr. Satterthwaite: I think that is a very good statement with the qualification you have in it, Senator.

Senator Lausche: That is all.

Supplementary Report by Senator Wayne Morse (Oregon) to the Foreign Relations Committee on the United States in the United Nations*

February, 1961

I would have no complaint if United States deeds—that is, votes—matched our fine words on colonial questions involving non-Communist nations. The verbal stance of the United States is not bad.

For instance, in President Eisenhower's speech of September 22 to the General Assembly there appear the following worthy passages:

> The drive of self-determination and of rising human aspirations is creating a new world of independent nations in Africa, even as it is producing a new world both of ferment and of promise in all developing areas. An awakening humanity in these regions demands as never before that we make a renewed attack on poverty, illiteracy, and disease.

*   *   *

> It is imperative that the international community protect the newly emerging nations of Africa from outside pressures that threaten their independence and their sovereign rights.
> To this end, I propose a program which contains five major elements:
> First, a pledge by all countries represented at this Assembly to respect the African peoples' right to choose their own way of life and to determine for themselves the course they wish to follow. . . .
> We believe that the right of every man to participate, through his or her vote, in self-government is as precious as the right of each nation here represented to vote its own convictions in this Assembly. I should like to see a universal plebiscite in which every individual in the world would be given the opportunity freely and secretly to answer this question: "Do you want this right?" . . .

*   *   *

As succeeding paragraphs will try to show, official expression of sympathy for the principles of self-determination have too seldom been followed in practice by the necessary United States votes.

The first instance of an unfortunate United States position, concerns a resolution which has usually been offered in General Assembly sessions (but not yet at the 15th session) inviting states to work out target dates for independence or self-government of their non-self-governing territories. Such a resolution would seem to be an appropriate implementation of the obligation under article 73b of the charter; namely, for members having colonies:

> b. To develop self-government, to take due account of the political aspirations of the peoples, and to assist them in the progressive development of their free political institutions, according to the particular circumstances of each territory and its peoples and their varying stages of advancement;

The instructions of the Department of State to the United States delegation to the United Nations have been to vote "no" on a resolution inviting administering authorities to set up independence target dates. If we are to match our deeds with our words, the United States should cosponsor such a resolution or at least vote "yes."

A second instance was our vote on a resolution which expressed the opinion of the

*Committee on Foreign Relations, U.S. Senate, *The United States in the United Nations, 1960—A Turning Point,* 87th Cong., 1st sess. (Washington, 1961), pp. 8-10; 12-13; 16-24.

General Assembly that territories of Portugal, such as Angola and Mozambique in Africa, are not self-governing (as Portugal claims) but are non-self-governing territories concerning which Portugal has an obligation under article 73e of the charter to submit information to the United Nations. Such a resolution was adopted by a vote of 45-6-24 in the Fourth Committee of the General Assembly in 1960 but instead of voting "yes" on the question the United States delegation was instructed by the State Department to abstain.

On October 13, 1960, I had spoken on behalf of the United States in praise and support of the Committee's Report on Information from Non-Self-Governing Territories. My speech covered the report in general, and found its objectives praiseworthy.

When we got down to specific cases of noncompliance in submitting information, the United States' position began to shift away from our fine words.

United States Stand on Portuguese Colonialism Costly

The vote of abstention by the United States delegation on what became known as the Portugal colonial issue was very costly to United States prestige in both the Fourth Committee and the General Assembly. As the United States delegate on the Fourth Committee, I was confronted with many criticisms and protests of the United States vote by delegates from nations who have every desire to be friendly to us. Yet, our vote on this resolution was so irreconciliable with the clear meaning of articles 73 and 74 of the U.N. Charter and with our professed ideals about supporting indigenous people in their struggle for independence that many of our friends in the Fourth Committee were at a complete loss to understand our vote. They did not want to believe what they feared and suspected, but they didn't hesitate to tell me that they suspected that Pentagon influences, military bases, and the NATO alliance were the controlling factors that dictated the United States vote.

It is common knowledge in the United Nations that Portugal has threatened the United States with the loss of the use of the Azores as an airline landing base if the United States joined other nations in rejecting Portugal's absurd claim that she does not have foreign territories but only overseas metropolitan provinces.

During the course of the debate in the Fourth Committee on this resolution, the Portuguese delegate sought to rationalize Portugal's claim that articles 73 and 74 of the U.N. Charter do not apply to her, because she has exercised the prerogative under domestic Portugal law of defining and designating her oversea land holdings as Portuguese metropolitan provinces. Thus, by such a legal fiction, the Portuguese argue that Goa in India is not a Portuguese territory but a Portuguese metropolitan province. Angola and Mozambique in Africa, by such tortured Portuguese reasoning, are not Portuguese territories but are Portuguese metropolitan provinces, and therefore, by Portuguese definition are not covered by the word "territory" as used in articles 73 and 74 of the Charter.

When this issue first arose in the Fourth Committee during the 15th General Assembly, we were engaged in a procedural debate. As yet, we had not received insructions from the State Department as to what our Government's position was going to be on the substantive issue, once the resolution was submitted for a vote. However, the argument of the Portuguese delegate raised a procedural question as to the jurisdiction of the Fourth Committee over the subject matter of the resolution. Although I had not, as yet, received instructions from the State Department on my Government's position in respect to the substantive issue, I was free to speak out in the procedural debate in defense of the Fourth Committee's jurisdiction over the subject matter, and I did so.

My extemporaneous remarks took the form of sustaining the jurisdiction of the Fourth Committee by answering what I considered to be the unsound interpretation of articles 73 and 74 of the Charter presented by the delegate from Portugal. Many delegates told me later, after the United States delegation under instructions voted to abstain on the substantive aspects of the Portugal colonial resolution that my speech was a fortunate face saver for the United States.

Because this particular incident is such a good example of the frequent failure of the State Department to face up to the realities which confront the United States delegation at the United Nations, I shall quote rather extensively from the speech I made in the Fourth Committee in support of the Fourth Committee's asserting jurisdiction, under articles 73 and 74 of the Charter, over Portuguese territories.

If the State Department had allowed the United States delegation to cast its vote on the legal merits of the issue, our vote would not have been one of abstention but would have been with the overwhelming majority of nations who voted against Portugal on the issue.

*　　　　　　*　　　　　　*

Another sorry example of United States alignment on the wrong side of a colonial issue was the final United States vote of abstention on the South West Africa resolution. The United States delegation had no choice in the matter, because the vote was dictated by instructions from the State Department. Here again, if the United States delegation to the United Nations had been allowed to follow its own best judgment based upon the best interests of the United States, as they developed in the course of the debate at the United Nations, the delegation would have voted in favor of the resolution.

Again, too, the opening speech I made on behalf of the United States was full of sympathy for the general welfare of the inhabitants of South West Africa. But as we got down to specifics, the State Department edged away.

This issue was so grossly mishandled by the State Department that I propose to discuss it in some detail in this report. It illustrates the need for a much better coordination between the State Department and the United States delegation; whenever an issue so impregnated with questions involving the best interests and good standing of the United States at the United Nations produces such a serious conflict in judgment between the United States delegation and the State Department.

My experience with this issue convinces me that when such a serious conflict develops between the United States delegation and the State Department over an issue of vital importance to the prestige of the United States within the United Nations, the coordinating procedure should call for a full discussion of the issue by the head of the United States delegation and the Secretary of State, with the right of appeal to the President himself. Judicial notice should be taken that rarely, if ever, would such an appeal be made to the President. As a matter of course, the United States ambassador at the United Nations and the Secretary of State, after a discussion in almost every instance, would reach a common accord. However, it should be remembered that an ambassador is an ambassador of the President.

Furthermore, the responsibilities of the ambassador to the United Nations are worldwide, and a procedure which would entitle him to submit a United Nations issue to the President of the United States should be formalized and regularized so that no reflection that he had gone over the head of the Secretary of State could be cast against him.

What I am suggesting is that the President of the United States should make clear to the Secretary of State and to his ambassador at the United Nations that in case a difference of opinion arises between them on a major issue at the United Nations, it should be understood to be within the rules of proper protocol to have the matter presented to the President for his consideration. With such an understanding, a request for Presidential consideration will more likely be a joint appeal than a one-sided appeal.

I make this recommendation because I am convinced that during the 15th session of the General Assembly, several of the instructions to the United States delegation would have been modified if either the Secretary of State or the President of the United States had been fully aware of the harm that the United States was bound to suffer within the United Nations as a result of some of the votes the United States delegation was instructed to cast.

*   *   *

The final resolution on South West Africa passed the Fourth Committee by a vote of 65 to 0, with 15 nations abstaining, including the United States. The resolution was clearly within the jurisdiction of the U.N. Charter, and was salutary in its objectives. The United States delegation should have voted for it. The United States vote of abstention on this resolution was very harmful because once again, we appeared to be sustaining policies of a colonial power whose policy in South West Africa has aroused deep resentment among many African nations.

A series of long-distance telephone calls, by me and the head of the United States delegation, to the Assistant Secretary of State who had been given charge of the issue at the State Department level, succeeded only in changing the original State Department instructions from an instruction to vote "no," to an instruction to abstain. However, in the eyes of the delegates from the overwhelming majority of nations which supported the resolution, the United States vote of abstention was seen as a vote in support of the position and the policies of the government of the Union of South Africa. It was my view at the time that this issue was of such serious importance to the interests of the United States that it should have received the direct intervention and consideration of the Secretary of State, himself, and, if necessary, even the President.

Negotiations for Missile Tracking Station in South Africa

It is my opinion that the real reasons for the instructions which were given us were never made known to the United States delegation. This was not the first time that the position first taken by the United States delegation at the United Nations was in conflict with the wishes of the Government of the Union of South Africa. On another occasion, the Ambassador of the Union of South Africa in Washington had protested to the State Department the position which the delegate of the United States on the Fourth Committee had taken on an issue involving the Union of South Africa.

On that occasion, the Ambassador of the Government of the Union of South Africa in Washington used his diplomatic channels to indicate that if this course of action in respect to the Union of South Africa's affairs continued, there might have to be a suspension of further negotiations for the establishment of a United States missile tracking station in the Union of South Africa. Knowledge of this attitude on the part of the Ambassador of the Union of South Africa was reported to me by delegates from several other nations.

*   *   *

Although the Assistant Secretary of State denied it, I am of the opinion that a reason for the State Department instructions on the South West African resolution was the protest by the Government of the Union of South Africa, including the matter of negotiations over a missle tracking station.

I would not mention these negotiations if they were in fact a secret, but United States plans to establish a missile-tracking station in the Union of South Africa were told to me by African delegates before I even knew about them from my own Government. These African delegates were not only critical, but they were bitter in their criticism of such a United States policy. Their objections followed two main lines of reasoning:

First, they fear that the chances of a nuclear war will not be reduced by the building of United States missile-tracking stations in Africa or for that matter, elsewhere. They are equally critical of Russia's missile armament race.

Secondly, they take the position that if the United States is determined to build a missile-tracking station in Africa, it should not be built in the Union of South Africa. Our contention that such a location may be the best and most strategic military location for a tracking station fails completely to impress them.

To the contrary, they argue that there are plenty of places outside of the Union of South Africa to build such an installation if one is to be built. They look upon such an installation in the Union of South Africa as nothing more than a direct economic subsidy to the Union of South Africa. They point out that a tracking station will call for an original investment of a good many millions of dollars plus additional large expenditures each year for its maintenance and personnel.

The expenditure of such a sum of money in the Union of South Africa, as seen through their eyes, is a concealed form of economic aid to the Union of South Africa, and so it is. As long as the Union of South Africa continues its inhumane apartheid policy, the United States cannot justify any form of economic aid to the Union of South Africa, even though it is clothed in the rationalization of military defense.

It is my opinion that our policymakers in the Pentagon Building are not sufficiently sensitive about the policies and practices of some of the colonial powers in respect to human rights of the indigenous people whom they rule and dominate. In the name of military defense, the United States has spent huge sums of money for bases and military installations in dictator countries, resulting in great economic benefit to colonial powers and dictatorships. It is very doubtful that the overall effect of any of these military installations has been to strengthen the security of the United States.

*   *   *

If military considerations, plus the influence of the British and other colonial powers had not been so dominant in the consideration of the South West Africa issue in the last session on the United Nations General Assembly, I am satisfied that the United States delegation would have been placed in a position so that it could have voted for the very reasonable resolution on South West Africa. The time has come to make it very clear to the Government of the Union of South Africa that it can no longer count on such United States support as it received in the last session of the General Assembly.

The Declaration on the Granting of Independence to Colonial Countries and Peoples

Undoubtedly the most glaring instance of an unwise policy by the United States on the colonial question was our failure to support the resolution called the "Declaration on the granting of independence to colonial countries and peoples." This resolution was sponsored by 43 Asian and African states (Doc. A/L. 323 of Nov. 29, 1960). This question was not referred to the Fourth Committee but was put directly on the agenda of the full Assembly for debate and decision. The procedure in itself is indicative of how important the subject was considered to be in the minds of a great majority of the members of the United Nations delegations.

*   *   *

The operative portion of the resolution reads as follows:

The General Assembly . . . Declares that:

1. The subjection of peoples to alien subjugation, domination, and exploitation constitutes a denial of fundamental human rights, is contrary to the Charter of the United Nations and is an impediment to the promotion of world peace and cooperation.

2. All peoples have the right of self-determination; by virtue of that right they freely determine their political status and freely pursue their economic, social and cultural development.

3. Inadequacy of political, economic, social, or educational preparedness should never serve as a pretext for delaying independence.

4. All armed action or repressive measures of all kinds directed against dependent peoples shall cease in order to enable them to exercise peacefully and freely their right to complete independence, and the integrity of their national territory shall be respected.

5. Immediate steps shall be taken, in Trust and Non-self-governing Territories or all other territories which have not yet attained independence, to transfer all powers to the peoples of those Territories, without any conditions or reservations, in accordance with their freely expressed will and desire, without any distinction as to race, creed, or colour, in order to enable them to enjoy complete independence and freedom.

6. Any attempt aimed at the partial or total disruption of the national unity and the territorial integrity of a country is incompatible with the purposes and principles of the Charter of the United Nations.

7. All States shall observe faithfully and strictly the provisions of the Charter of the

United Nations, the Universal Declaration of Human Rights, and this Declaration on the basis of equality, noninterference in the internal affairs of all States, and respect for the sovereign rights of all peoples and their territorial integrity.

This resolution was adopted by the General Assembly by a vote of 89 to 0, with 9 abstentions. The United States abstained along with Australia, Belgium, the Dominican Republic, France, Portugal, Spain, South Africa, and the United Kingdom.

*   *   *

Great astonishment over the United States vote was expressed by many friendly countries, followed in the next few days by open criticism of our position on the colonial resolution. Many of our friends in the United Nations felt that the United States had let them down. They expressed concern about the public reaction in their own countries. Many of them stated quite frankly that our vote was grist for the Communist propaganda mills in their countries. Because this vote undoubtedly did serious damage to United States prestige in the United Nations, the subject matter is deserving of some discussion in this report.

Let me turn now to the explanations given by the delegation of the United States under State Department instructions for abstaining in the vote. As pointed out earlier in this report, Ambassador Wadsworth always did an able job in presenting the best possible case in explanation of the United States vote even when the State Department instructions placed the United States delegation on the wrong side of an issue. Our delegation was placed in just such a position on this major colonial item. In explaining our vote, the United States representative stated full agreement with the purposes of the resolution. He went on, however, to say that—

> . . . there are difficulties in the language and thought of this resolution, which I shall comment on more specifically in a moment, which made it impossible for us to support it, because they seem to negate certain provisions of the Charter.

The United States representative mentioned four specific criticisms of the resolution:

1. He said:

> . . . it is hard to understand why a resolution on this broad subject should be completely silent on the important contributions which the administering powers, including my own Government, have made in the advancement of dependent peoples toward self-government or independence.

Yet the resolution was not silent on the contributions of the administering powers. A paragraph in the preamble to the resolution welcomes the emergence of a large number of dependent territories into freedom and independence in recent years. Aside from this consideration, however, the declaration as a whole did not purport to deal with anything except unfinished business; namely, with the need to move toward independence for those peoples who have not yet attained it.

2. He said:

> Although we are sure that this was not the intent of the sponsors of the resolution, paragraph 3 permits the interpretation that the question of preparation for independence is wholly irrelevant.

This criticism was unwarranted and the interpretation a tortured one. If operative paragraph 3 is read properly the word "pretext" should be mentally underlined. If that is done the obvious meaning of paragraph 3 is that if adequate preparation for independence is really lacking—as distinguished from a fraudulent claim by an administering authority that such preparation is lacking—then the attainment of political, economic, social, or educational preparedness is an appropriate reason for delaying independence.

3. He said:

> Paragraph 4, written in unqualified language, seems to preclude even legitimate measures for the maintenance of law and order. . . .

This criticism goes out of the way to find fault. The paragraph makes it rather clear that what is forbidden is the use of oppressive measures in cases where people are attempting "peacefully and freely" to exercise their right to independence.

4. He said:

> As for paragraph 5, here again is a very strong statement that only complete independence and freedom is the acceptable political goal for dependent peoples.

Again, I believe the United States State Department bent over backward to read the paragraph incorrectly. The paragraph does not seem to me to exclude political goals other than complete independence. If people become indpeendent, they can then, if they choose, unite with other people in some form of association as, for example, Egypt and Syria united to form the United Arab Republic. Moreover, operative paragraph 5 of the resolution speaks of steps which would "enable" peoples to "enjoy complete independence." The ability to enjoy complete independence would include the ability to enjoy a status of self-government within a federation with other peoples.

In short, the objections voiced by the United States State Department in explanation of abstaining in the vote on A/L. 323 were very unsubstantial.

Statement by Joseph C. Satterthwaite, Assistant Secretary for African Affairs, on the Mutual Security Program in Africa*

March 9, 1960

*   *   *

Of no less importance than the swift pace of political developments on the Africa scene is the pressing need for accelerating the sluggish rate of economic growth and improving living standards. Africa's economic and social structures are not developing at a pace comparable to its political evolution. It is fairly easy to recognize that the political revolution is at hand, and by and large its pressures are irresistible. It is essential that the pace of economic development match or at least not fall further behind the rate of political change now sweeping the African Continent. Very few of the emerging countries are economically viable, and their leaders very quickly recog-

*Department of State Bulletin, Apr. 18, 1960, pp. 603-609.

nize the importance of economic development and a higher living standard as necessities to sustain and fortify their political independence.

Countries are becoming politically independent without adequately trained leadership and technical skills and without the basic economic and social institutions and systems which provide the foundations for secure, confident, African-led nations. Present U.S. foreign assistance programs are not adequate in scope or size to be responsive to the dramatic changes taking place. The facts of this situation, and U.S. sympathy for the newly independent or about-to-be independent countries, and compelling recommendations for a new and creative U.S. approach.

The executive branch is, therefore, proposing to the Congress a special program for tropical Africa with an initial appropriation of $20 million within the special assistance category. In preparing this request we have sought to find a way properly responsive to the African aspirations. We have a fresh situation; we are attempting to meet it in a fresh manner. There are a number of general criteria which guided us. First, we wanted something which would provide a close identification of the United States with the African people. Second, we wanted to find some way of encouraging closer cooperation and interchange between the many African countries. Third, knowing that Africa's need for economic help is almost unlimited, we wanted to concentrate on a key problem area, one which stands as a major block to development. Fourth, we wanted to avoid competition with large-scale assistance from Europe but serve rather as a catalyst for stimulating an even higher level of this assistance. Fifth, we wanted as much as possible to avoid getting into a position of annual aid-level negotiations with many new countries pressing for external assistance. Finally, we wanted a program which would provide sufficient flexibility to permit effective adaptation to a very fluid situation.

The purpose of this program would be to provide assistance in those areas which constitute the greatest impediments to sound, long-run social and economic development in Africa. There can be little argument that this development depends in the first instance on a major improvement in the education and training of Africa's human resources and their productive use.

*   *   *

One of the important criteria we had established for this program is that it should not become a competitor to or substitute for assistance from other free-world sources. It is our hope, rather, that it may serve to help encourage an increase in assistance from other free-world countries and international and national organizations. This area of tropical Africa is now receiving over $500 million annually from European countries for major development projects. Increasing amounts of technical and other forms of assistance are coming from a number of private organizations. A number of U.S. foundations are making important contributions in a number of fields. The U.N., through its technical assistance program and its Special Fund, is stepping up its assistance to this continent. It is our intention to seek the participation of these various organizations and countries on specific projects where feasible. We also anticipate that out of the multicountry conferences will come proposals for joint efforts on important development problems.

We are proposing that assistance under this program be on a grant basis. Because of the nature of the activities to be undertaken and the limited resources of many of the African countries, grant assistance appears to be the most effective means for accomplishing our objectives. It is important to note, however, that we intend to operate this program on a project-by-project basis to avoid the difficult problems which often stem from situations where countries come to expect certain levels of assistance tied to what has been provided in previous years or related to levels received by neighboring countries.

All of Africa will be included under the program except for the northern tier of Morocco, Algeria, Tunisia, Libya, and Egypt, and the Union of South Africa.

The special program would not replace bilateral technical cooperation, although it is anticipated that it would be closely related to technical cooperation programs. The essential character of the special program for tropical Africa which differentiates it from the technical cooperation program lies in its intensive concentration on key education and training problems and on regional activities.

*   *   *

The question might well be asked whether the magnitude of this request is sufficient to meet the problems of Africa. It is the view of the executive branch that this is sufficient for the first year of a new program in education and training. I am convinced, however, that an expanded program will be necessary in subsequent years. As the President has stated in his mutual security message to Congress:

> It is my belief that this initial effort must grow significantly in the immediate years ahead and complement similar efforts on the part of other free world nations so that the capacity of the new and other developing nations in Africa to manage and direct their development can be strengthened and increased rapidly and effectively.

There are, of course, other major African needs, especially for capital development. It is expected that the Development Loan Fund will increase its activities in tropical Africa. The rate at which this can be accomplished, however, will depend in large measure on the volume and quality of proposals presented. As the preparation of development projects advances and the supply of technical skill grows, we expect that the flow of proposals will expand and that, increasingly, more external investment funds from all sources will be available. The Export-Import Bank has already made substantial loans to Africa and has indicated it expects to increase its activity. The International Bank for Reconstruction and Development now has in process a number of country and project economic surveys which should lead to more loans for Africa in addition to those already made.

As this committee is well aware, the pace of events in Africa has been so rapid it has been difficult to plan with any degree of precision. It is for this reason that I consider the availability of the contingency fund, in the amount requested, of particular importance in order to provide the administration with the flexibility we will need as new countries emerge and we are required to respond to new situations.

In certain countries we have been able to identify the problems we face in fiscal year 1961 which cannot be met through the special program for tropical Africa or through other economic instruments of U.S. foreign policy, and therefore are programing bilateral grant special assistance, The countries for which this bilateral special assistance is programed are Somalia, Ethiopia, and the Sudan. These three countries in the eastern part of the continent, bordering on the Red Sea and its approaches, are important and of immediate concern to the United States. During the past year we have observed major changes in their political and economic situation.

Full independence will be granted to Somalia on July 1st. Somalia suffers from a chronic and serious deficit in its operating budget and has no capital resources available for economic development. It is almost complete dependent upon external assistance to maintain and possibly increase its level of economic activity. This is particularly important in bolstering its political stability during the early period of independence. We are now discussing with the Italian Government possible arrangements by which they could continue their major role in support of the Somali economy. Just how these discussions will end up it is too early to predict, but I believe our approach in this situation is indicative of our general effort to encourage the continuance of assistance from our European friends to African countries. Our proposal for bilateral special assistance is designed to supplement the Italian effort.

Ethiopia has hitherto been a firm supporter of free-world interests and has made important contributions as a moderating influence in African and Afro-Asian conferences. It has been a particularly strong supporter of the principle of collective security. Ethiopia's recent acceptance of the $100 million credit from the Soviet Union may temper this position somewhat; however, U.S. relations with Ethiopia continue to be close, in part a result of the effective work carried out under our economic programs. The special assistance for Ethiopia will help to meet requirements for important development projects in agriculture, health, and education and strengthen our activities during this period when the Government is facing serious budgetary and foreign-exchange problems.

The political and economic situation in the Sudan has improved markedly. The balance-of-payments crisis has now passed. The present regime has provided an effective government, friendly to the United States. We are gratified over the prompt improvement in the Sudan's economic condition. We recognize, however, that progressive economic betterment will be required after the long run if the Sudan is to evolve a healthy and Western-oriented political life. Soviet-bloc activity in Egypt and Ethiopia should forewarn us of the greater vulnerability of this area which also serves as a bridge to other parts of Africa. The bilateral special assistance we are proposing for fiscal year 1961 will provide an important means for strengthening key areas of the Sudan's economy.

Our proposals for the continuation of technical cooperation programs in Africa are an essential element of the U.S. response to Africa's problems. We are requesting $24.3 million for this program, which is an increase of about 20 percent over the level for fiscal year 1960. The major portion of the increase is for programs in the area south of the Sahara. There are now technical cooperation programs in 13 African countries and territories, and we expect to initiate programs in 3 or 4 others within the year.

*   *   *

Turning briefly to military assistance programs on Africa, I must emphasize that our approach there is different from that in other areas. The African states, especially those that are just entering into independence, have only small military forces. None of these states is linked to the United States by collective security arrangements, and we would not expect any of them to play a major role in a global war. Our small military assistance programs in Africa are designed for different and essentially political purposes.

It is essential that the continent of Africa remain free from domination by the Sino-Soviet bloc. It is essential that the African states remain free to develop their own political, economic, and social institutions in cooperation with the rest of the free world. It is also essential for the United States to retain its rights to operate certain key bases in Africa and that the United States and its allies have continued access to a wide range of important materials in Africa, principally minerals.

To achieve these strategic and political objectives, the United States has undertaken to assist a few of the African states in providing equipment and training for the maintenance of their internal security. The small, lightly armed forces of the African nations which are receiving military assistance will not be expected to make a substantial contribution of forces in support of our worldwide strategy in the event of a global war. However, the support of these forces is essential to the degree of security and political stability required to maintain a pro-Western orientation.

The military assistance program for Africa is the smallest of all the regional programs. Cumulative programs through fiscal year 1960 have amounted to $57.8 million, whereas actual deliveries under these programs through June 30, 1959, have totaled $44.8 million.

For fiscal year 1960 we requested funds totaling $7.4 million. The fiscal year 1960 presentation of the Mutual Security Program to the Congress contemplated only one country program in the African region. In addition to a program for Ethiopia in fiscal year 1960, other programs were developed during the fiscal year for Liberia, Libya, Morocco, and Tunisia. After making the necessary adjustments to take into consideration these four additional country programs our area figure for fiscal year 1960 is $13.1 million instead of the $7.4 million which the executive branch proposed last year. For fiscal year 1961 we are requesting funds totaling $18.2 million. The difference between the adjusted fiscal year 1960 program and the proposed fiscal year 1961 program is accounted for by a slight increase in the proposed fiscal year 1961 programs for Ethiopia, Liberia, and Morocco. This request will enable us to meet new requirements in Africa and to strengthen the internal security of five countries— Ethiopia, Libya, Liberia, Morocco, and Tunisia—whose independence, political stability, internal security, and continuing friendship are important to us.

*Address by Assistant Secretary Satterthwaite on the United States
Role in African Independence**

April 8, 1960

*   *   *

I would like to turn to our proper contemporary role in Africa. I shall confine my remarks largely to the role of government. I use the word "proper" advisedly because, as this audience well knows, we are admonished by some to "keep hands off" and

Ibid., May 2, 1960, pp. 687-88.

urged by others to champion the growing nationalist movements in Africa. We are charged on the one hand with interference, on the other with irresponsible indifference.

*   *   *

I say "proper" also because we did not play a major role in Africa during the last century, whereas our European allies have major interests of long standing on that continent.

*   *   *

In tropical Africa the evolution toward independence has been and continues to be remarkable for the speed and nonviolence of the transition. This has required statesmanship, tolerance, and good will of a high order on all sides—by the Africans who are imbued with ardent nationalism and are impatient of delay, and by the European powers who are faced with major political, economic, and psychological decisions and adjustments. Our proper role as a government is to play the role of a friend contributing to orderly transition while hoping that new, strong, and voluntary ties will be established between the new countries and the former administering states. Certainly both stand to gain from such a relationship.

I do not mean to indicate from the foregoing that the United States has no official presence in African countries while these changes are going on or until they become independent. On the contrary we have one or more Foreign Service establishments in most of the political subdivisions of the continent, 29 United States Information Service establishments, as well as International Cooperation Administration representatives and programs in overseas territories. We have embassies in 11 independent countries. Significant, if modest, educational exchanges are taking place, and the President's cultural presentations program is bringing American artists, musicians, and athletes before African audiences. In 1958 and 1959 Prime Minister Nkrumah and President Touré of Ghana and Guinea, respectively, paid visits to the United States at the invitation of President Eisenhower. Such visits express the profound interest and respect of the American people and Government for these new nations and their leaders as they embark on the difficult course of liberty.

I should like to comment here on the frequently expressed doubts or fears as to whether the people of Africa are yet ready to run their own affairs, whether they have sufficient experience with self-government to assume its responsibilities, whether they will not fall victims of governments of the extreme right or left. As to their "readiness," I believe history has shown that this is almost an academic question. Peoples tend to acquire independence, ready or not, according to a timetable more or less of their own making. As to the degree of experience with self-government, this varies with the type of tutelage received from the mother country. In tropical Africa, for example, we are witnessing the imaginative evolution of the French Community. Its members have moved in a short period of time from typically colonial status toward self-government or independence. Nigeria, a British colony, has benefited in an exemplary manner from education and civic training and guidance provided by Great Britain in preparation for independence in October 1960. We have the dramatic instance of the Belgian Congo, where 6 months ago neither the people of that area nor the Belgian Government would have predicted the independence which will come on June 30 of this year. Yet the colonial government with outstanding statesmanship has negotiated with Congolese leaders for the transfer of power under the optimum conditions time will allow.

*　　　　　*　　　　　*

Speech by Senator Mansfield Before the Senate on the Congo and New African Policy*

August 29, 1960

*　　　　　*　　　　　*

Let me say at the outset that the conduct of African policy for the past few years by the President, the Secretary of State, and Mr. Lodge at the United Nations, in my opinion, deserves the support of the Senate. They have acted with insight and dispatch in dealing with a most uncertain situation.

It is no criticism of them to note that, of late, the waters of African affairs and particularly those in the Congo have become more turbulent.

What is taking place in the Congo may spread to other parts of the African Continent. Indeed, in the last few days the short-lived unity of Senegal and the Soudan Republic in the Mali Federation has threatened to come apart in factional dispute.

In short, we are likely to be in for a protracted period of difficulties in Africa. It is not easy to define the sources of these difficulties even though it is essential for the Senate to make the effort. Africa, from the point of view of our comprehension, is a new continent. It has burst upon our awareness suddenly, after having been shut off almost entirely by barriers of nature and the closed doors of colonial enclaves. What we need to know now for effective policies is not to be derived from the old travel books on Africa and the attitudes which they induced. It is the emergent Africa, the Africa of today and, even more important, the Africa of tomorrow which we must seek to fathom. For it is to this new Africa that we must address our policies.

*　　　　　*　　　　　*

I would suggest that our policies must now from the following principles:

First. This Nation should give its support, diplomatically and otherwise, to the end that independence and human equality will eventually be achieved throughout Africa. Our support must go, as it has begun to go under this administration, to those who work soberly in Africa for these ends. May I say, in all candor, that this principle grows easier to maintain with consistency and dynamism as the nations of Europe with whom we are associated in other matters increasingly espouse it in their own African policies. The difficulties, however, are great and will remain great in those areas in Africa of heavy European settlement, and I do not wish to make light of the task of those who must conduct our policies affecting those areas.

**Congressional Record*, Aug. 29, 1960, pp. 18122; 18124.

It seems to me particularly important that this principle find expression in the character and conduct of our expanding network of embassies in the new African Republics. I hope that these establishments will be kept modest in size and character. I hope, further, that our official representatives will seek a fresh and full understanding of the situations which they encounter, based upon direct and broad contact with the peoples of these new nations. I hope, finally, that these embassies will be conducted in a manner which reflects the simple good will of this Nation toward the new Republics of Africa and our sympathetic appreciation of their struggles. In sum, it seems to me of the utmost importance that now, at the beginnings of contact with the new Africa, our official representation be kept free of those characteristics which would invite a deflection of the political propellant of colonialism to this Nation.

Second. In the absence of overriding considerations to the contrary, this Nation should use whatever influence it can against a centrifugal fragmentation of existing political units in Africa. However powerful the divisive forces of an ancient tribalism may still be, they are the forces of the dying Africa; they are not the strengths of the Africa that is struggling to come into being. May I say that to hold to this principle is not to stand against adjustments in present political boundaries. Such adjustments are to be anticipated and are to be encouraged if they lead to more practical political and economic units. We should resist these tendencies, however if they derive either from a narrow tribalism or a sweeping racist pan-Africanism.

I realize that these particular problems must be dealt with primarily by the African peoples themselves. There is every indication, however, that the United Nations may be drawn increasingly into them. Since that is the probability, we must be prepared to exert our influence affirmatively in that organization and, in other ways, on the side of modern political progress in Africa.

Third. We should recognize that the hopes for freedom and progress in Africa during this period of transition depend, perhaps, more on the caliber of men than on the forms of governments and we should lend a most understanding ear to those African leaders who, with sincerity, personal dedication and realism seek to move their nations forward.

We must learn, quickly, as much as we can about the emergent African leadership and, if we are to learn accurately, we will eschew such inapplicable frames of reference as pro-Communist or pro-Western. The leadership that matters for the future of Africa will be neither one nor the other. It will be pro-African in the finest sense of the term in that it will be dedicated to the welfare of its own peoples and will drive soberly but relentlessly to increase their capacity for survival and expression in the modern world.

Fourth. We should join with all nations so inclined in an effort to lend a genuinely helpful hand to the vast needs of Africa for training in modern skills and for prompt economic and social development.

If Africa is to make the most of this help, and if the rest of the world is to gain from it in terms of peace, then it seems to me that this help must go to Africa free of any extension—expressed or implied—of the power conflicts and rivalries which divide the world. The challenge of Africa is not a call to greater propaganda battles between us and the Soviet Union. The challenge of Africa is to the world. It is a challenge to help open in peace the doors of modern life for the peoples of Africa, for their benefit and for the still unfathomed benefits which may flow to mankind from that opening.

If we accept this as the deeper challenge of Africa then it seems to me that we must begin to seek arrangement through our policies, in the U.N. and elsewhere, on the following points:

First. That all requests for military training missions and military aid from the African nations henceforth be referred to the United Nations and that such missions, as approved by the Security Council, be supplied solely under the aegis of the U.N.; further, that existing military aid missions in Africa be converted into U.N. missions at the request of any independent African nation and, as rapidly as possible.

Second. That the United States seek agreement with the Soviet Union to the end that both nations shall refrain from seeking military bases in Africa and from sending military forces to any part of Africa except as the Security Council may direct; further, that existing bases of either nation in Africa be closed out in due course and any military forces of either nation on the African Continent be withdrawn as the Security Council may direct.

Third. That the United Nations effort in the Congo, and similar efforts which may be required and sought elsewhere in Africa, henceforth be financed by a four-quarter fund: One-quarter supplied by the United States; one-quarter by the Soviet Union and Eastern Europe acting, as willing, in concert; one-quarter by Western Europe acting, as willing, in concert; and one-quarter by the other members of the United Nations.

Fourth. That the four-quarter fund be used, further, as the principal instrument for financing a substantial program of technical aid to Africa, to be pursued predominantly through an expansion of educational and training facilities in that continent, with technicians and teachers supplied on a similar four-quarter division, under the general direction of the U.N. Secretary General; and further, as this effort comes into operation, that bilateral assistance by all nations in Africa be progressively curtailed.

*   *   *

Address by President Dwight D. Eisenhower to the U.N. General Assembly on Africa*

September 22, 1960

Mr. President, Mr. Secretary-General, members of the General Assembly, and guests:

The people of the United States join me in saluting those countries which, at this session of the General Assembly, are represented here for the first time. With the admission of new members, mainly from the giant continent of Africa, almost 100 nations will be joined in a common effort to construct permanent peace, with justice, in a sorely troubled world.

The drive of self-determination and of rising human aspirations is creating a new world of independent nations in Africa, even as it is producing a new world of both ferment and of promise in all developing areas. An awakening humanity in these regions demands as never before that we make a renewed attack on poverty, illiteracy, and disease.

Side by side with these startling changes, technology is also in revolution. It has brought forth terrifying weapons of destruction which, for the future of civilization, must be brought under control through a workable system of disarmament. And it has

*Department of State Bulletin, Oct. 10, 1960, pp. 551-53.

also opened up a new world of outer space—a celestial world filled with both bewildering problems and dazzling promise.

This is, indeed, a moment for honest appraisal and historic decision.

We can strive to master these problems for narrow national advantage, or we can begin at once to undertake a period of constructive action which will subordinate selfish interest to the general well-being of the international community. The choice is truly a momentous one.

Today I come before you because our human commonwealth is once again in a state of anxiety and turmoil. Urgent issues confront us.

A Program for Africa

The first proposition I place before you is that only through the United Nations Organization and its truly democratic processes can humanity make real and universal progress toward the goal of peace with justice. Therefore I believe that to support the United Nations Organization and its properly constituted mechanisms and its selected officers is the road of greatest promise in peaceful progress. To attempt to hinder or stultify the United Nations or to deprecate its importance is to contribute to world unrest and, indeed, to incite the crises that from time to time so disturb all men. The United States stands squarely and unequivocally in support of the United Nations and those acting under its mandate in the interest of peace.

Nowhere is the the challenge to the international community and to peace and orderly progress more evident than in Africa, rich in human and natural resources and bright with promise. Recent events there have brought into being what is, in effect, a vast continent of newly independent nations.

Outside interference with these newly emerging nations, all eager to undertake the tasks of modernization, has created a serious challenge to the authority of the United Nations.

That authority has grown steadily during the 15 years since the United Nations pledged, in the words of its own charter, "to bring about by peaceful means, and in conformity with the principles of justice and international law, adjustment or settlement of international disputes or situations which might lead to a breach of the peace." And during those years the United Nations successfully supported Iran's efforts to obtain the withdrawal of foreign military forces; played a significant role in preserving the independence of Greece; rallied world resistance to aggression against the Republic of Korea; helped to settle the Suez crisis; countered the threat to Lebanon's integrity; and, most recently, has taken on an even more important task.

In response to the call of the Republic of the Congo, the United Nations under its outstanding Secretary-General, has recently mounted a large-scale effort to provide that new republic with help. That effort has been flagrantly attacked by a few nations which wish to prolong strife in the Congo for their own purposes. The criticism directed by these nations against the Secretary-General, who has honorably and effectively fulfilled the mandate which he received from the United Nations, is nothing less than a direct attack upon the United Nations itself. In my opinion, he, the Secretary-General, has earned the support and gratitude of every peace-loving nation.

The people of the Congo are entitled to build up their country in peace and freedom. Intervention by other nations in their internal affairs would deny them that right and create a focus of conflict in the heart of Africa.

The issue thus posed in the Congo could well arise elsewhere in Africa. The resolution of this issue will determine whether the United Nations is able to protect not only the new nations of Africa but also other countries against outside pressures.

It is the smaller nations that have the greatest stake in the effective functioning of the United Nations. If the United Nations system is successfully subverted in Africa, the world will be on its way back to the traditional exercise of power politics, in which small countries will be used as pawns by aggressive major powers. Any nation, seduced by glittering promises into becoming a cat's-paw for an imperialistic power, thereby undermines the United Nations and places in jeopardy the independence of itself and all others. It is imperative that the international community protect the newly emerging nations of Africa from outside pressures that threaten their independence and their sovereign rights.

To this end I propose a program which contains five major elements:

First: A pledge by all countries represented at this Assembly to respect the African peoples right to choose their own way of life and to determine for themselves the course they choose to follow. And this pledge would involve three specific commitments:

> To refrain from intervening in these new nations' internal affairs—by subversion, force, propaganda, or any other means;
> To refrain from generating disputes between the states of this area or from encouraging them to wasteful and dangerous competition in armaments;
> And to refrain from any action to intensify or exploit present unsettled conditions in the Congo by sending arms or forces into that troubled area or by inciting its leaders and peoples to violence against each other.

These actions my country—and many others—are now avoiding. I hope this Assembly will call upon all its members to do likewise and that each speaker who follows me to this platform will solemnly pledge his country to honor this call.

Second: The United Nations should be prepared to help the African countries maintain their security without wasteful and dangerous competition in armaments.

United Nations experts are being asked to train the Congo's security forces. If the Secretary-General should find it useful to undertake increased activity in order to meet requests of this nature elsewhere, my country would be glad to join other member states in making essential contributions to such United Nations activity.

More importantly, I hope that the African states will use existing or establish new regional machinery in order to avert an arms race in this area. In so doing they would help to spare their continent the ravages which the excesses of chauvinism have elsewhere inflicted in the past. If, through concerted effort, these nations can choke off competition in armaments, they can give the whole world a welcome lesson in international relations.

The speed and success of the United Nations in dispatching substantial forces to the Congo should give these states assurance that they can rely on the United Nations to organize an effective response if their security is threatened. This should reduce any pressures on them to raise larger forces than are required to maintain internal security. Thus they would help to free their resources for more constructive purposes.

Third: We should all support the United Nations response to emergency needs in the Republic of the Congo which the Secretary-General has shown such skill in organizing. I hope that states represented here will pledge substantial resources to this international program and agree that it should be the preferred means of meeting the Congo's emergency needs. The United States supports the establishment of a United Nations fund for the Congo. We are prepared to join other countries by contributing substantially for immediate emergency needs to the $100-million program that the Secretary-General is proposing.

Fourth: The United Nations should help newly developing African countries shape their long-term modernization programs. To this end:

The United Nations Special Fund and Expanded Technical Assistance Program should be increased so that in combination they can reach their annual $100-million goal in 1961. The Special Fund's functions should be expanded so that it can assist countries in planning economic development.

The United Nations operational and executive personnel program for making available trained administrators to newly developing countries should be expanded and placed on a permanent basis. The United States is prepared to join other countries in contributing increased funds for this program, and for the Special Fund, and for the United Nations Technical Assistance Program.

The World Bank and International Monetary Fund should be encouraged increasingly to provide counsel to the developing countries of Africa through missions and resident advisers. We should also look forward to appropriate and timely financial assistance from these two multilateral financial sources as the emerging countries qualify for their aid.

Of course, many forms of aid will be needed: both public and private, and on a bilateral and multilateral basis. For this assistance to be most effective it must be related to the basic problems and changing needs of the African countries themselves.

Fifth: As the final element of this program I propose an all-out United Nations effort to help African countries launch such educational activities as they may wish to undertake.

It is not enough that loudspeakers in the public square exhort people to freedom. It is also essential that the people should be furnished with the mental tools to preserve and develop their freedom.

The United States is ready to contribute to an expanded program of educational assistance to Africa by the family of United Nations organizations, carried out as the Secretary-General may deem appropriate and according to the ideas of the African nations themselves.

One of the first purposes of this assistance, after consultation and approval by the governments involved, might be to establish, staff, and maintain—until these governments or private agencies could take over—institutes for health education, for vocational training, for public administration and statistics, and perhaps other purposes. Each institute could be appropriately located and specifically dedicated to training the young men and women of that vast region, who are now called upon to assume the incredibly complex and important responsibilities inherent in an explosive emergence into nationhood.

If the African states should wish to send large numbers of their citizens for training abroad under this program, my country would be glad to set up a special commission to cooperate with the United Nations in arranging to accommodate many more of these students in our institutions of learning.

These then are the five ingredients of the program I propose for Africa:

Noninterference in the African countries internal affairs;
Help in assuring their security without wasteful and dangerous competition in arma-
ments
Emergency aid to the Congo;
International assistance in shaping long term African development programs;
United Nations aid for education.

*United States Note to Ambassador of Nigeria in Washington Concerning Refusal of
Service in Virginia to C. C. Uchuno, Second Secretary of the Nigerian Embassy**

January 12, 1961

I have the honor to refer to reports appearing in the local press since January 6
indicating that Mr. C. C. Uchuno, Second Secretary of the Nigerian Embassy, was
refused service at a restaurant located in the railway station in the city of Charlottes-
ville, Virginia, on January 5, 1961.

I am requesting the Chairman of the Interstate Commerce Commission, which has
jurisdiction in the matter, to make a full investigation and the Department of State
will communicate further with you once his report is received. In the meantime, I wish
to express my profound regret for any discriminatory treatment shown to Mr.
Uchuno, with the hope that you will understand that this discourteous act is in no way
indicative of the feeling of the Government or the people of the United States toward
the Government and people of the Federation of Nigeria.

Accept, Excellency, the renewed assurances of my highest consideration.

Christian A. Herter

*Remarks by G. Mennen Williams, Assistant Secretary-Designate for
African Affairs, on the Challenge of Africa to the American Citizen†*

January 30, 1961

*   *   *

First of all let me say that I sincerely believe that the African challenge to the world
is, as President Kennedy said in appointing me, "second to none." The kind of world
you and I know and believe in may well prosper or decline according to whether the
people of Africa have the opportunity to enjoy the blessings of freedom and the more
abundant life now so fervently sought by them.

The challenge of Africa to our sense of brotherly love and human dignity is likewise
a challenge to our perception of our own self-interest and sense of survival. Africa
today, at what for us is a late hour in history, is consumed by a hunger for freedom,
for human dignity, and for the good things of this world. Everything takes color from
this. America has stature with these peoples because of our own great Revolution and

*Ibid., Jan. 30, 1961, pp. 156-57.
†*Ibid.*, Feb. 20, 1961, pp. 259-61.

for our espousal of human dignity and self-determination. But America suffers when there is any appearance that we are somehow supporting colonialism and when we fail at home to support our philosophy of human dignity.

What can we do for our country with respect to the great revolution that is sweeping over the continent of Africa as it seeks to bridge several centuries in the march of human freedom and in some instances a millenium or more in the economic life of its peoples?

Tonight I would like to suggest that there are four things that each of us can do for our country to help Africa establish itself in freedom:

1. Know Africa and the Africans so that we may better support our Government in effective policies and programs for Africa.

2. Make the United States a hospitable host for our African visitors.

3. Accelerate our progress in seeing that we have no second-class citizens in America.

4. Encourage every American city to adopt an African city.

If America is to be the friend to Africa that most of us want it to be, we must understand the nations and peoples of that vast continent and help them to know us better. For too long most of Africa has truly been a Dark Continent to most Americans.

Yet Africa by its very geographic mass commands attention. It is the second largest continent, one-fifth of the land surface of the earth. It is as large as the United States, Western Europe, India, and China put together. In Africa there live about 220 million people, speaking somewhere between 600 to 800 languages. In the northeast, in Egypt, its cultural heritage can be traced back to the very cradle of human civilization. In the lofty mountains of Ethiopia lives a people independent since ancient times. Elsewhere in the continent there is a rediscovery of old kingdoms and cultures whose influences still enrich the lives of the African peoples.

Africa's resources have exceptional promise. The continent produces about 98 percent of all diamonds, 55 percent of gold, 22 percent of copper, and has rich stores of industrially useful minerals such as bauxite, uranium, and oil. Yet with these riches, great areas of the land are not arable and the continent as a whole is not self-sustaining in foodstuffs.

But although these are important indices of Africa, our attention is drawn above all to the life and movement of the African peoples, and here the theme is freedom. Until recent years only Liberia and Ethiopia were independent, and Ethiopia lost her freedom for a time. Today, hoever, there are 27 independent countries in Africa (including the Malagasy Republic), and 17 of these achieved their independence last year. These 27 nations make up better than one-fourth of the U.N. General Assembly. I need hardly observe that this emergence of new African nations has literally changed the shape of the political world in which we live.

Like our own Revolutionary America, these new nations want most of all to be free to develop their own institutions. We welcomed the loans and help we got from Europe, but the last thing we wanted was to be brought again under alien rule. So, too, with Africa, where there is a compelling desire to develop a distinctly African personality." From this it follows that few Africans are interested in the cold war, least of all being forced to choose sides. The peoples of Africa prize independence as the doorway into the larger world in which they can find their own self-expression and national development.

It was to this central truth that President Kennedy, during the election campaign, addressed himself. He said:

> We want an Africa which is made up of a community of stable and independent governments . . . where men are given the opportunity to choose their own national course, free from the dictates or coercion of any other country.

It is along this line of sight that we must look at what is happening in Africa if we would understand its peoples and develop friendly and constructive relationships with them.

People from these new African countries come to America in two generaly capacities—as traveling dignitaries or as students. In either case we can offer them our best help and in so doing perform a true service to our country. It is up to us to extend to them the welcome we would wish to receive were we visiting their countries. I have experienced African hospitality, and I can assure you that we shall be hard pressed to match it.

Occasionally a visiting African dignitary is not received here as he should be. While I am sure this audience here tonight possesses the understanding and sensitivity to know whereof I speak I just want to emphasize that one untoward incident can undo a world of good.

So I suggest that each one of us make a special effort whenever we can assist in the entertainment of our African visitors. We have much to offer to the world, but we must begin at home.

The African students who come to study in our schools are, in truth, the future leaders of the countries. They have come here to learn, to equal themselves for service to their governments, their industries, their farms, their schools, and to their families they will guide. Let us be sure they know America as it really is, not without blemishes but yet a source of strength to free minds and dedicated spirits.

I can testify that our efforts to realize these aims are not lost on other peoples. I am thinking of the time when I was sitting in a restaurant in Beirut, in Lebanon, when a Ghana delegation walked up and asked to be introduced. These were people who wished to assure me of their appreciation of the international student days we had sponsored at the capital in Michigan. They had not forgotten.

American policy is hampered in Africa, as it is in almost every part of the world, by our failure to life up to giving first-class citizenship to every American. I'm not going to elaborate on this because it is too obvious to everyone.

All I am going to say is that every American can help see that a better job is done in this regard wherever he lives—and you can help right here in Philadelphia, as I know I can in Michigan and now in Washington.

In the final analysis dignity is a personal thing, and so is friendship.

I suppose we could pour billions of dollars of aid into Africa or anywhere else and still fail in our desire to elevate human dignity and promote brotherhood. There is no point in expecting our African friends to jump through so many hoops to get aid that they will exhaust the good will which we presently can claim. I strongly believe that real personal respect and the implementation of that feeling can go a long way toward communicating a sense of personal dignity.

All of which causes one to wonder whether it would not be a service to our country and Africa of a number of our American cities were to choose a sister city in Africa and exchange expressions of interest by visits back and forth, by cultural exchanges, and the like.

Just think what the impact would be if a group of Philadelphia high school youngsters visited some African city on a good-will trip—perhaps a glee club, perhaps a marching band, or an athletic group. Of course there would be more formal events, such as an exchange of visits by mayors and city officials.

This would be a person-to-person recognition of human values and importance that would make national and international values and policies more meaningful. I do honestly think we could promote understanding and friendship in this among other ways.

I commend to you, then, these four points and ask of you that you consider them in the spirit of the President's inaugural. Our standing in Africa is in your hands, the hands of an enlightened American citizenry.

*   *   *

*Speech by Representative Barrett O'Hara (Illinois), Before the House, on Africa**

February 28, 1961

*   *   *

One reason we missed the boat in Africa was because of our alliances with the colonial powers. As the spirit of independence engulfed Africa it was increasingly difficult to maintain in African minds the old image of the Uncle Sam who had been the first to break away from the bonds of colonialism.

It was increasingly difficult because the European powers that were our loyal allies in NATO were sensitive as a reflection upon them to what we said and did in assistance to new emerging nations. I think it might have been better for them, and certainly better for us, if we had taken a more positive position. After all, colonialism in Africa had gone, and for the future there was the job of aiding the peoples of Africa in the establishment of sound, stable, and free governments and in the change to do no violence to the legitimate rights of those who under colonialism had made their contribution to the African economy.

Had the old image of Uncle Sam remained fixed in the African mind as the sturdy old pioneer who had shown the way from colonialism to independence, the United States would have been in a much stronger position of influence, beneficial to everyone with legitimate interest in the African Continent.

As it was, when the colonial possessions were becoming one by one independent and sovereign nations, we were put in the position, and under the false accusation, of being the heir and the benefactor of colonialism. I wish to make it very clear that this accusation, assiduously promoted by the Communist world, was entirely without any foundation in the facts. Nevertheless, when in respect to the feeling of our NATO allies we refrained from taking a positive position on a moral question seeking by avoidance of the subject or a softness in diction to avoid the rubbing of sensitive nerves, the net result was that the old image of Uncle Sam in the African mind gradually retreated.

Congressional Record, Feb. 28, 1961, pp. 2902-03.

Governor Williams has been given by President Kennedy the mission of restoring that image. Upon his accomplishment of that mission hangs the place of our Nation in world influence and leadership in the struggle for government of, for, and by the people, in the awakening continent of Africa and of all the world. It is just that important.

When I visited Africa in December I found everywhere a tremendous lift in spirit, unmistakable signs that the old image of Uncle Sam was being restored to the African mind, because President Kennedy had given priority to Africa by making the second appointment of his administration that of the Under Secretary of State for Africa. The news that the President had selected for this post a man of the stature of Governor Williams, many times Governor of a great American State and himself one of the Democratic presidential possibilities in 1960, this was a shot in the arm to the African leaders in all of the countries that I visited. I cannot overstate the importance of this.

If Governor Williams on his first visit to Africa had tailored his words to the sensitivities of the colonial powers, his mission would have been foredoomed. If that mission were to succeed it was necessary that the new Under Secretary of State for Africa should catch the spirit of the new nations of Africa and should express it in the language of the present. He has done exactly that.

He has found, as the members of our study mission found last December, that with most of the leaders in Africa, including Nyerere of Tanganyika, is a determination to avoid in the new countries of Africa the dangers of racial and class ruptures by applying the test of the American melting pot.

Let me illustrate. Tanganyika has been for centuries an occupied country, first by the Phoenicians, then by the Chinese, later by European powers, and now after all these centuries at long last Julius Nyerere, an African of the Negro race, is the head of the government of his country.

In Tanganyika Africans of Negro blood outnumber the other people of Tanganyika on the ratio of 125 to 1. Beginning about a century ago settlers came from India and Pakistan, and they prospered and by their efforts made a substantial contribution to the upbuilding of their adopted land.

The present speaker of the elected legislative council of Tanganyika is of Indian descent. He and his children all were born in Tanganyika, and there is his heart and his sole interest. A lady member of the 80-seat legislative council is American born, the widow of an English nobleman, and she is working for her adopted country of Tanganyika, just as many persons who came from many lands into our own American melting pot.

All call themselves and are accepted as Africans. Just as in our own United States, the sole test is their loyalty to Tanganyika over and above that of any interest in any other land. If one meets that test in our United States, he has the proud right of calling himself an American, and no one can dispute his right. So it is in Tanganyika, good people of many races and of many sorts, working together in the glorious adventure of launching a new free nation. So it is in the other countries in Africa. He who gives his heart and his sole interest to the African country of his home is an African and is so accepted.

Governor Williams was in Tanganyika, I believe, when he made some reference to Africa for Africans, and, being thrilled as I had been by the spirit of tolerance in all the leaders in Tanganyika, explained, as I have sought in my humble way here to explain it, that Africans did not mean just those of one race, but of all persons whose heart and interest first were in Africa.

Would anyone in our country seriously have taken issue with Governor Williams if he had said that America is for the Americans? That is the very spirit of the hemispheric solidarity for which President Monroe stood, which President Franklin Roosevelt so effectively promoted, and which President Kennedy, in one of the strongest passages in an inaugural address that will live forever, reaffirmed. If we believe that hemispheric solidarity means much to our own well-being in our pursuit of security and happiness then should we not accept the truth that what is good for us in our part of this great big world is good for all other peoples in our continents, including that of Africa.

Under Secretary of State Williams, recently Governor of a great American State, talked as forthrightly to the people of Africa and in the same American way as he has talked to American audiences. He has earned the gratitude of the American people by the first test of his ability and his dedication to perform the mission given him by President Kennedy, that of restoring in Africa the old image of Uncle Sam.

*   *   *

Remarks of Representative Member George Meader (Michigan) Before the House on Assistant Secretary Williams' Trip to Africa*

February 28, 1961

Mr. Speaker, Michigan's former Governor, currently Assistant Secretary of State for African Affairs, Soapy Williams, is on a tour of Africa which has not gone unnoticed in the world press. This, of course, is not surprising. It is difficult not to notice Soapy Williams.

*   *   *

I believe some who are not as well acquainted with Mr. Williams as we in Michigan might misconstrue his speeches in Africa, and might also be inclined to ascribe his attitude and conduct to the Kennedy administration, assuming Mr. Williams to be a bright and shining apostle of the New Frontier.

For this reason, I feel that I, as one who has been a constant, if somewhat unwilling, witness of Mr. Williams' performances over the last decade, should undertake his defense and that of the administration in which he was given, in the words of President Kennedy, a position of responsibility "second to none" in what is probably the most sensitive, delicate, and potentially explosive area of international affairs.

I do not believe, for example, that Mr. Williams intended any slight to our friends, who may be attempting to deal skillfully with a very sticky situation. I do not believe he intended to intervene and dictate to Africans, black or white, how their destiny should be worked out. He just had an unfortunate lapse—he thought he was still campaigning in Michigan. For 12 years he wore the mantle of the champion of the downtrodden and shook his fists at the evil businessmen and vested interests.

*Ibid., Feb. 28, 1961, p. 2889.

I think Mr. Williams' intentions were the best in the world—he simply and sincerely wished to assure the underprivileged and underdeveloped areas of Africa of the deep and abiding concern of the new administration in their welfare.

That Mr. Williams' choice of words may have been unfortunate may possibly be ascribed to the absence of his former incomparable press agent, Paul Weber, who, for a decade, successfully portrayed "Soapy" as the knight in shining armor tilting unceasingly, even though unproductively, with the Republican Michigan Legislature, in behalf of the welfare of the common man.

But I assure my colleagues, and also our friends abroad, that Mr. Williams meant no harm. His ideals and his objectives are laudatory. Nor should the New Frontier be blackened by one unfortunate lapse of Michigan's irrepressible former Governor.

Mr. Speaker, Mr. Williams has made great progress. It took him 12 years to wreck Michigan. It only took him 1 month to wreck our African relations. Has he not made his contribution to public service and earned retirement?

Remarks by Secretary of State Dean Rusk on Relationships with New African Nations*

March 25, 1961

               *   *   *

Q. On the subject of colonialism which you mentioned just now, perhaps we could turn to Africa. President Kennedy has come out very strongly supporting Mr. Mennen Williams' [Assistant Secretary for African Affairs] statement about Africa being for the Africans. Now, do you think the previous administration was perhaps a little insufficiently categorical in backing such a view?

A. Well, if I could go back to the remarks that I have just made, I think that one of the fresh approaches which the new administration can make is to take a look at some of these revolutionary changes and try to decide what our relation to these changes ought to be.

Now, to a considerable extent you and we in the West should be thinking about how we can regain the leadership of our own revolutions—independence. I mean, if you walk into the General Assembly of the United Nations, you will see sitting there more than 20 independent members who used to be a part of the British Empire. You people—beginning with the United States, of course—you people carried notions of freedom with you wherever you went. You couldn't help it.

Well, now, we in the West have tended to lose the leadership of our own revolutions for economic and social progress, for national independence, for freedom itself, for constitutional government. And you have the curious phenomenon that Mr. Khrushchev stands up in the General Assembly proposing that he is the leader of the nationalist revolution, that he is the champion of national independence—Mr. Khrushchev, who never gave away anything. And he makes some headway with this notion at the expense of you and us, who invented this idea.

Q. Do you therefore think that governments such as, for instance, the South

*Department of State Bulletin, Mar. 27, 1961, pp. 441-42.

*African Government and even the Portuguese Government in Africa are prejudicing
the cause of the West?*

A. Well, I believe that it is important for us in the West to come to a right and
reliable relationship with people in the non-West and that the whites come to a right
and permanent relationship with people of other colors. I think that everyone has a
great admiration for the way that you people have been able to work out national
independence on the one side followed by close, friendly relationships with those same
peoples after the divorce has occurred. This is a remarkable performance.

*Q. What would you say is the most important lesson we must learn from the
Congo?*

A. That the road to independence must be planned with care, that leadership
should be trained along the way, that a cadre of responsibility must be in place in
order to take responsibility effectively, and that, when areas of this sort go through
this painful sometimes traumatic experience, the rest of us should be careful not to
embroil these areas in the great, tumultuous rivalries that are going on in other parts of
the world if we can avoid it.

*   *   *

*Address by Assistant Secretary Williams on Africa's Challenge
to America's Position of Free-World Leadership**

May 19, 1961

*   *   *

The leaders I met define Africa's new freedom in three principal ways. It means for
them and for their peoples the right, first of all, to shape their own political destinies,
their future as independent nations. Secondly, it means the right to full racial equality.
And, finally, it means freedom from debilitating and degrading poverty—it means the
prospect of a better standard of living.

For Americans, also, freedom has always meant these things. And it is in these
common meanings that we see Africa's challenge to America's position of free-world
leadership.

In simplest terms the challenge is whether we will live up to our own ideals—the
ideals of freedom and human dignity which inspired our Founding Fathers and which
now inspire the revolutionary founders of the new nations of Africa. These leaders say
to us in effect, "If you would have us choose and uphold freedom, show us you know
its meaning. Stand up and be counted when the United Nations votes on self-determination for Algeria and Angola. Stand up and be counted when apartheid is condemned, and lend us a helping hand that we too may have a full belly and hold our
heads up knowing that our children, with work, can have a better life."

This challenge is put to us urgently, and we must respond. No other course is right;
no other course is human. And any other course is dangerous.

Our response was clearly pledged by President Kennedy in these words from his
inaugural address:

Ibid., June 12, 1961, pp. 912; 914.

To those peoples in the huts and villages of half the globe struggling to break the bonds of mass misery we pledge our best efforts to help them help themselves. for whatever period is required--not because the Communists may be doing it not because we seek their votes but because it is right.

In fulfillment of this pledge we intend, first of all, to stand up and be counted when issues of political self-determination and racial equality are debated at the United Nations. Already, in the General Assembly session this spring we have made this intention clear in our votes on Angola, on South-West Africa, and on apartheid in the Union of South Africa.

President Kennedy proposes also to use the full powers of the Federal Government to expand the area of respect for human rights here at home. To the colored two-thirds of the world's peoples our unresolved racial problem is an emotion-charged issue. We must accept it as a disgrace to the United States when diplomats and other visitors from Africa—among them students and leaders here at our invitation—suffer from incidents of racial discrimination. We can hope these visitors will understand that the prejudices of a few are not the true measure of the spiritual fiber of America; we can hope they will recognize that the problem is deep-rooted in some areas, that our national policy is dead-set against these injustices, and that we have made considerable progress. But we cannot really expect such understanding unless it is clear that we mean to press forward to rid our house of this blight, entirely apart from considerations of receiving visitors.

Beyond these vital issues of anticolonialism and racial equality, there is the challenge presented by African hopes for a rising standard of living. And here we confront a series of complex problems deserving the very careful attention of all who would see American leadership gain in strength in a perilous world.

*   *   *

. . . what policies should govern American help to Africa? Let me state a few key points.

We must seek the support of other developed nations of the free world who are able to take part in the great effort that is called for.

We must encourage by practical measures, including political guarantees, the fullest response of private investors to the opportunities to be found in opening up the African potential—being sure they understand that African benefit is a necessary condition and goal, apart from return on investment.

We must encourage regional economic and development planning. Indeed, this was one of my first missions after taking office. I made it a point to attend the meeting at Addis Ababa last February of the United Nations Economic Commission for Africa, where such regional problems were dealt with.

Finally, we must suit our government aid programs to this framework of planned development which we find in Africa—as elsewhere in the less developed world.

It is to fit that framework that President Kennedy has shaped his new economic aid proposals to Congress. The heart of the proposed procedure is to be able to make forward-looking commitments to developing countries. Instead of an annual scramble to fill only the needs of the moment—and the wastefulness and errors of that process--we want to be in a position to encourage rational medium-range and long-range planning. We want to make sure our dollars serve coherent and positive goals, and we can do so better in a number of cases with 2-year, 3-year, even 5-year commitments.

$$* \qquad\qquad * \qquad\qquad *$$

Speech by Senator Frank Church (Idaho) Before the Senate on New African Policy *

June 29, 1961

$$* \qquad\qquad * \qquad\qquad *$$

Today I wish to discuss one facet of these relations, the political aspect of U.S. policy. . . .

By "political aspect of American policy" I have in mind the response of the United States to African nationalism and to African neutralism. Without question, these are two of the mos potent forces in African politics today, and the future of American interests in Africa may depend in no small degree upon the policies we develop in respect to them.

How should the United States treat Africa's twin ambitions of national and international independence? I returned convinced that American interests can be best served in only one way. The European orientation of our past relations with Africa must be abandoned in favor of an independent approach of our own.

What would such an approach require? In regard to African nationalism, it calls for policy rooted in our historic role as a country which believes in the right of national self-determination. In regard to African neutralism, it calls for a recognition that it is a Communist-dominated, rather than an independent, though uncommitted, Africa, that constitutes the threat to our national interest.

In recent months, I have been pleased to see developments in American policy that seem to be founded upon these two principles. It would appear that the Kennedy administration is fashioning a positive new policy toward Africa that identifies the United States with both of these dominant African aspirations. If this is so, it represents a hopeful change of policy for which the President and his State Department deserve strong commendation.

The task we face in Africa is not easy. The overall impression that I brought home was that the United States will have difficulty persuading Africans that this country actively sympathizes with their aspirations for independence, and that we do not seek ti involve them in the cold war. Past American policies, particularly as manifested in the United Nations, have tended to draw down our reservoir of good will in Africa. This is especially true with respect to our past positions on the colonial issue.

Although the colonial issue is of central importance to the Africans, our past attitude has been highly equivocal. We sought to find a compromise between what we apparently believed to be the requisites of western unity and what we know to be the legitimate aspirations of the African peoples. Caught in dilemma, we looked for a middle ground between the extremes of open opposition and active support of African nationalism. Our policy thus tended to consist of lofty tributes to the principle of

Congressional Record, June 29, 1961, pp. 11759-62.

self-determination, combined with the avoidance of actual support of African causes which we feared might antagonize certain of our NATO allies.

This balancing act between Europe and Africa was particularly evident in the votes we cast in the United Nations. It is hard to avoid the conclusion, for example, that the abstention of the United States on the anticolonialism resolutin of last December intensified African suspicions that this country could not be counted upon to back up its declarations of belief, and served to confirm the impression that we put smooth relations with our European allies above our interest in Africa.

I appreciate the great distinction to be made between the colonialism practiced, say, by the British, and that practiced by the Portuguese. But these considerations were not really relevant to our decision, taken in the U.N. last December 14. We were there given the opportunity to vote in favor of the general beliefs we had so often enunciated, and we chose to abstain. African leaders were left to conclude that the United States was unwilling to risk the possible disruptive effects of a favorable vote upon the NATO alliance.

Further evidence was given last year to support this conclusion, in the votes we cast on Angola and southwest Africa. In each instance we abstained, and thus gave no support to the efforts of the anticolonial members of the U.N. organization to extend its activities in Africa. And in each case the apparent reason for the American abstention was the fear that an affirmative vote would adversely affect our relations with certain colonial powers within the Western alliance.

In regard to African neutralism, our past record has been little better. We know that the African States are absorbed in their own internal problems. Newly born, they tend to regard neutralism as proof of their independence, and they are as zealous to avoid entangling alliances as we were during the years of our national infancy. Yet we have only recently abandoned our strictures against their neturalism, and have shown little appreciation for the motives which give rise to it, or to the fact that it is not, in itself, inimical to American interests.

There are, of course, other factors which contribute to the skepticism in Africa concerning the United States. Africans look about them and see that the bulk of American private investment is located in the Union of South Africa and other territories with substantial white populations. They are also well aware that an average of roughly two-thirds of our mutual security program expenditures in Africa over the past few years have gone to north African countries where U.S. military bases are situated.

Finally, it must be said that, despite continuing efforts to point out that our official national policy is totally opposed to segregation, even those Africans who understand our problems and respect our efforts to solve them, find it hard not to be resentful over the widely advertised instances of racial intolerance or violence in this country. This reaction is especially intense when an African diplomat or visiting dignitary is affronted.

All of these factors, whether they be natural obstacles to better understanding or the fruits of past policy, when taken together now create a difficult situation for the United States. Despite this, the administration is forging a new approach to Africa that holds much promise for the future.

The appointments of Rusk, Bowles, Stevenson, and Williams laid the foundations for the new policy. All are widely identified with a sympathetic point of view toward the emerging countries in the old colonial areas, and with an appreciation for their strategic importance in world affairs.

The appointment of Governor Williams, in particular, asserted from the very start the responsiveness of the new administration to the special problems of Africa, and signaled that African issues are now to be dealt with on their own merits. These facts were emphatically communicated to the African people and their leaders by Governor Williams' trip to 16 African countries, made at the earliest possible moment after he assumed office as Assistant Secretary of State for African Affairs.

The administration has subsequently built on this foundation through a series of efforts both within and without the United Nations.

In the United Nations, a major step forward was taken by reversing the position of the United States on the colonial issue. In contrast to our record of abstentions of a few weeks earlier, Mr. Stevenson's affirmative votes on the Angola, southwest Africa, and apartheid resolutions, at last placed the United States in a pro-African posture.

In Africa itself, these votes were widely acclaimed as a new departure in American policy. But in a more fundamental sense, these actions were not new at all. Rather, they represented, as Tunisia's President Bourguiba remarked in his recent address to the Congress, a return to our traditional anticolonial policy and support of national self-determination.

Mr. Stevenson, himself, made this clear in presenting the American position on the resolution, when he said:

> Angola is but a part of the overall picture of evolution on the African Continent The views of the United States have not changed since Jefferson wrote, "We hold these truths to be self-evident, that all men are created equal, that they are endowed by their Creator with certain unalienable Rights."

Consistent with this principle, the United States then voted with the African delegates calling upon Portugal to plan, step by step, for Angola's full self-determination.

On the following day, the United States joined with a majority of the General Assembly to censure the Union of South Africa for its occupation of southwest Africa. Again, this was in contrast to our abstention on a comparable measure a few weeks earlier.

Only a few days ago, our new policy was reaffirmed by the support we gave to the resolution in the Security Council deploring the large-scale killings in Angola and admonishing Portugal to cease repressive measures.

Mr. Stevenson has also worked in the U.N. to cultivate a friendship with the African delegates themselves in ways that go beyond either his votes or statements. He has made his interest in them a personal hallmark. He has sought them out socially and has frequently consulted them on matters of policy. All of these efforts, while less evident than our recent U.N. votes, have been extremely important, for they have added the element of personal commitment to the objective evidence, showing the depth and degree in which our policy toward Africa has changed.

Outside the United Nations, our efforts to build a stronger United States-African relationship have paralleled our labors within the organization.

Secretary Rusk's reception for African Ambassadors on African Freedom Day last April, and President Kennedy's appearance and speech there, were further indication of our interest and support in the emerging community of independent African States. In his speech, the President summarized the spirit of the administration's policy in noting that we are a revolutionary country, and thus close in spirit to the people and problems of Africa. The President said:

> I think all of us who believe in freedom feel a sense of community with all those who are free.

He then added very significantly:

> but I think we also feel an even stronger sense of community with those who are not free but who someday will be free.

In many ways, the President has sought to extend and strengthen this sense of community. He invited President Kwame Nkrumah of Ghana to a meeting at the White House during the latter's visit to the United Nations. His initiative was well received by Nkrumah, and widely noted in Africa. It did much to restore some normalcy to United States-Ghana relations, despite the continued presence of serious problems.

The President's reception of courtesy calls by the African nationalist leaders, Mboya, Kaunda, and Banda, who were in the United States in April, is also to be noted in this regard, as was Vice President Johnson's representation of the United States at the independence celebration in Senegal, which was so favorably received in west Africa.

The fact that Tunisia's President Bourguiba was the first chief of state to be welcomed to Washington by President Kennedy on an official state visit is also indicative of the new significance being given our relations with Africa.

I believe these labors to build stronger bonds with Africa, through policies and actions identifying the United States more closely with the aspirations of Africa's people and leaders, to be steps in the right direction.

But some disagree. Indeed, the emergence of an American policy toward Africa, premised on the development of a community of independent African states, which are free, to the greatest possible degree, from the tensions of the cold war, has been subject to heavy assault.

African neutralism, it is argued, can only serve to undermine essential American interests. I believe the argument to be wrong. African neutralism, if it is genuine, is not adverse to the interests of the United States. The West has no need for military alliances spanning the African Continent. In fact, to pursue policies, the success of which depends upon the maintenance of strongly pro-Western regimes in Africa, would be as self-defeating there as it has been in certain parts of Asia. Moreover, genuine neutrals can be a useful balance wheel in a world that has become precariously polarized between two gigantic powers.

No, it is not neutralism that threatens the interests of the United States in Africa. What we need to fear is that these newly independent African countries might be drawn behind the Iron Curtain, and thus lose their capacity to be neutral. If we can help the Africans avoid this, then I am confident that, on most cold war issues, we can anticipate their support. Certainly the Africans' response to the abortive Russian effort to scuttle the U.N., through bitter attacks on the Secretary General, demonstrated their capacity and willingness to support the West, once the merits of the issue became clear.

What, then, of our developing African policy based on a firm affirmation of our historic opposition to colonialism?

Such a policy has been labeled sentimental. It has been suggested that our emotional attachment for the anticolonial character of our own national birth has led us to adopt a foreign policy which ignores the hard realities of international politics.

Some have even called the new policy foolhardy, asserting that an independent approach to Africa will loosen our ties with the strength of highly developed Western Europe, and wed us, instead, to the weakness of underdeveloped Africa.

In both these criticisms, the burden is the same. The new African policy, so the argument goes, is a luxury we cannot afford. Each time we part company with a NATO ally, on a matter relating to Africa, the alliance is weakened. To persist in such a policy will diminish the alliance, at the very least; at the very worst, it might even divide and destroy it. So rabid have some of these critics become, that any pro-African statement is at once construed as anti-NATO.

When these critics objected to our vote in support of the U.N. resolution to investigate Portuguese colonial policies in Angola, or the more recent Security Council vote condemning these policies, I am sure it was not because they, themselves, uphold the policies; it was not, in other words, because they feel we were mistaken on the merits. No one of them has yet spoken in defense of Portuguese colonial policies in either Angola or Mozambique. What they are saying, really, is that we should have voted wrong on the merits, for the sake of maintaining solidarity with a NATO ally.

How would these critics have us vote on the general issue of colonialism? I am certain they would concede that, on the merits, we should oppose it, the right of self-determination having been the basis of our own war for independence, and a venerable principle of our political code. Yet, when the issue was put squarely before us in the United Nations, last December, these critics upheld our abstention. They contended we were obliged to join company with such bitter-end colonial powers as Portugal and the Union of South Africa, engaged in a futile rearguard action on the tail of the 20th century, because to vote for the resolution generally condemning colonialism would have obliged us to differ with some of our NATO allies. Again, the critics reasoned, it was right for us to vote wrong, for the sake of NATO unity. Just imagine: In the name of NATO unity, we abstained, while the majority of our own NATO partners deserted us, to vote for the resolution.

Let me make clear that it is the doctrinaire quality of such a foreign policy to which I object. I do not argue that, for the sake of improving our relations with Africa, we should uphold the African side of every controversy involving a European ally. I ask only that, as each new question arises, we reach our judgment on its merits, and that we take our stand or cast our vote accordingly.

Let us remember that while an imprudent policy toward Africa cannot strengthen NATO, a prudent policy there can do much to further the long-term interests of the alliance. After all, the prosperous, industrial countries of Western Europe are in little danger of Communist uprising. Their governments are stable; their peoples are less interested in, or attracted to, the Communist ideology, than at any time since the end of the Second World War. It is, rather, in volatile Africa, now in its formative period, where multitudes are destitute and demoralized, that the danger of Communist subversion is real. If these African countries are drawn into the Communist orbit, then the NATO alliance is outflanked, and a Red hammerlock will tighten upon the free economies of Western Europe, which depend, in no small degree, on African raw materials to feed their industrial plants.

So our present effort to establish a better bond between the United States and the new African nations also serves the ultimate interests of our NATO allies. The era of Western colonialism is over. Should we, Mr. President, having avoided all connection with it while it was still robust in Africa, now permit ourselves to be linked with it in its death agonies? It would be better that we applaud the British and the French for the statesmanlike manner in which they are peacefully relinquishing their African possessions, and urge some of our other NATO allies to follow their example. Italy and Germany, deprived of their African possessions by the two World Wars, are clearly better off without them. Belgium will never return to the Congo, and the days of Portuguese dominion over Angola and Mozambique are fast running out. Within a little while, none of our NATO partners will have any territory left in Africa. Then their interests in that continent will be identical with our own; and we, in the meantime, by pursuing an independent course in regard to Africa, shall have helped secure a bridge of friendship between the new African countries and the Western World.

If, to do this, means that we must, from time to time, anger a NATO ally, such is the price we have to pay. But let us be clear about one thing: Nothing we are apt to do in regard to Africa will weaken or destroy the NATO alliance. This alliance is the shield that protects Western Europe from Russian invasion. It stands on its own base; no part of it is anchored in Africa. If the day ever comes when NATO means less to Germany, Belgium, France, Italy, or Great Britain than it means to the United States, it will no longer be a shield, but will be a sieve.

Mr. President, I say this as one who believes that NATO is the cornerstone upon which we most depend in our power struggle with the Communist world. I was a sponsor of the resolution establishing a citizens committee on NATO, and I think we mus do all within our power to strengthen the alliance. As with every alliance since the days of the Delos League, NATO will either grow or it will wither; it cannot remain static. But we do not serve the alliance by trying to placate one or another of our NATO partners on matters relating to Africa. We serve it only by common agreement on wise policies relating to Europe, where the alliance functions and has its being.

For these reasons, Mr. President, I submit that, contrary to the fears of its critics, our emerging policy of active support for the cause of African freedom will not only help to better our position in Africa, but will serve the long-term interests of the NATO alliance itself.

*   *   *

Statement by Pedro Sanjuan, Assistant Chief of Protocol,
Urging Maryland to Pass Public Accommodations Bill*

September 13, 1961

I have had the honor to be asked to come before you as a representative of the Department of State to acquaint you with a most serious situation affecting the lives of all Americans.

*Department of State Bulletin, Oct. 2, 1961, pp. 551-52.

The key to the solution of this problem is largely in the hands of the Legislature of the State of Maryland. Before some of you start wondering why the Department of State is interested in what may appear to some to be an internal matter within the State of Maryland, let me beg you to consider this rather as a request by the Department of State for the assistance of the State of Maryland in insuring the success of the foreign policy of the United States.

I have come to inform you that the Department of State strongly supports the public accommodations bill which is up for your consideration and to explain to you why the Department of State supports such legislation.

*   *   *

How can we persuade these Africans and these Asians, whose skins range from dark to black, that we believe in human dignity when we deny our own citizens the right to this basic dignity on the basis of skin color? How can we expect the respect and friendship of new nonwhite nations when we humiliate the representatives of these nations by denying them the right to be served in a highway restaurant or in a city cafe? How can we expect these diplomats, on whom their governments have placed the full responsibility to make decisions in the name of their country and whose duty it is to see that their national prestige is not tarnished during their tour of duty here—how can we expect these diplomats not to notice when the proprietor of a roadside cafe on Route 40 or a waitress in a Howard Johnson's restaurant informs them that they cannot be served because they are automatically presumed to be inferior to the average white American citizen?

*   *   *

Recently during a period of 2 weeks four African ambassadors were humiliated by private restaurant owners on Route 40 in Maryland. One of them was refused a cup of coffee while he was en route to present his credentials to the President of the United States. I would like to put this in the clearest terms possible—that when an American citizen humiliates a foreign representative or another American citizen for racial reasons, the results can be just as damaging to his country as the passing of secret information to the enemy.

Why does the Federal Government at this time seek the assistance of every loyal American in the State of Maryland? The State of Maryland has come a long way in recognizing civil rights and in insuring equal opportunities to all its citizens regardless of color. But the much-traveled route between the United Nations in New York and the White House in Washington is through the State of Maryland, and it is here, as statistics prove, that the majority of these incidents are likely to take place in spite of your desegregated schools or the Governor's Mansion, where visitors are welcome regardless of their color.

*   *   *

Address by Assistant Secretary Williams on Algeria, Angola, and Apartheid*

October 31, 1961

*   *   *

My travels in Africa have taken me among peoples who want this kind of world—a world of free choice, built on the foundations of self-determination and independence. I found this to be true in my first trip, to central Africa; on my second trip, to southern Africa; and most recently in visiting nine countries which lie beside or reach into the great desert of the Sahara. Six of these latter nations border on Algeria, where the issues of self-determination and independence have been bitterly fought over for 7 years.

*   *   *

... in my talks with African leaders I have sought a sympathetic understanding, a sense of common cause with our point of view, on this question. Frankly, I have had only partial success.

We can and do share important convictions with the Africans. The germinal ideas of freedom and self-determination, planted from the Western tradition which America has done so much to nurture, have burst into vigorous life in Africa. But the difference comes, usually, in what is in the forefront of the mind when these great principles are evoked. To us it may be Berlin; to them Algeria, or Angola, or apartheid.

*   *   *

... we must open our minds fully to consideration of those issues which have most immediate force for Africans. We are committed to freedom and self-determination. We must expect to be held to it. We must reckon with its dynamic force not only in areas we have known as battlegrounds but in the lives of peoples and nations we are just beginning to know.

In several issues our position is not an easy one. The interests of countries beside whom we have fought and bled are sometimes seemingly at odds with the interests of other countries or of peoples under their administration. These issues, forcing them-selves on the world's attention, we must inevitably face. Where they occur in the context of Africa's changing order—of Africa's future—we must consider them on their merits according to our traditional beliefs and within that basic framework of political and social order, the U.N. Charter.

*   *   *

In every country on my latest trip, and especially in the Arab nations flanking Algeria, the final issue of the Algerian struggle is awaited with—at one and the same time—sympathy and apprehension. The citizens of these neighboring nations, remem-bering their own recent emergence to independence, feel a deep, sympathetic identity

*Ibid., Nov. 27, 1961, pp. 885-88.

with the Algerian people's aspirations for self-government. And they are apprehensive over the uncertainties of how Algerian self-determination is to be realized.

*   *   *

Our policy reflects President Kennedy's long and well-known interest in the Algerian question. It comes down to this: We feel that the key to a solution lies in negotiations between France and the FLN [National Liberation Front]. We hope these negotiations can soon be resumed and that a settlement based on the principle of Algerian self-determination will be achieved.

The United States has always believed that a settlement, to endure, must be democratic and fast—that is, it must fulfill the aspirations of the Algerian people, and it must respect minority as well as majority interests. The goal of a sovereign, independent, peaceful, and prosperous Algeria is commonly accepted by Algerian nationalists and the French policy as publicly stated by President de Gaulle. We, too, support this goal.

The final test, however, lies ahead, and it calls for the highest order of statesmanship. Negotiations are the key to a settlement, and their success in turn depends on the elaboration of assurances sufficient to inspire confidence in the future on the part of all who have legitimate interests at stake. It is my own hope that wisdom and magnanimity will now prevail in the final negotiations between the French and Algerian representatives.

*   *   *

A second important question is Angola. This Portuguese overseas territory has become the focus of important international discussion. It is a key African issue and one that faces the United Nations General Assembly in the days immediately ahead.

A resolution adopted by the General Assembly last April, which the United States supported, took the view that Portugal had not accorded the inhabitants of Angola adequate opportunities for social, economic, and political advancement. The resolution in question called for appropriate reforms, for the establishment of a U.N. committee of inquiry, and, perhaps most importantly, for acknowledgment of the principle of self-determination for Angola. The note of urgency in this question was heightened by disturbances in Angola itself, involving considerable loss of life and property on both sides. The presence in the Congo of some tens of thousands of refugees from Angola contributes further to the concern of the world community.

The history of relations between the United States and Portugal is long and amicable, and it has been a source of regret to us that past votes at the U.N. on Angola have been construed by the Portuguese as hostile to their interests. That we have not agreed with Portugal does not mean that our purposes run contrary to the spirit of constructive friendship, and we have sought to clarify to the Portuguese Government the necessities which we believe are bound up in this question.

We believe that Africa is experiencing a revolution of expectations based upon the profound human desire for greater political and social self-expression and that the Portuguese territories are not immune to its influence. Portugal, in our view, has the power to make a positive contribution, as other metropolitan powers have done, by giving direction to these forces in her African territories.

Portuguese racial philosophy has a constructive aspect which can be usefully built upon. Moreover, continuing economic development in Angola cannot afford to lose the services of Portuguese technicians and their skills. We believe that these benefits could ultimately be lost if there does not occur a significant and timely accommodation to the legitimate aspirations of all inhabitants of these territories.

As the delegates of the United Nations again take up the Angolan question, I believe they will find a measure of encouragement that is quite new. At the end of August the Portuguese Government announced a series of reforms affecting its African territories. Not the least of these reforms are ones providing for a system of local self-government and the elimination of a separate status for "unassimilated" natives. There are clear indications that additional reforms will be announced, particularly in the important field of education in the African territories.

It is, of course, too early to judge the effectiveness of these reform measures. But they are positive steps, and we trust they will be implemented in a prompt and comprehensive fashion. They should, we feel, be accorded due weight in the minds of all who have in mind the well-being of the people of Angola.

It is out of basic obligations to the world community, rooted in the U.N. Charter, and to the goal of a just and peaceful settlement of differences that we have upheld the desirability of a progressive evolution for Angola. So, too, we support the need for cooperation with the United Nations, which we see as one avenue for resolving this problem. These have been and are today our purposes in the Angola question.

The question of apartheid in the Republic of South Africa presents itself with increased force each year at the U.N. General Assembly. We think apartheid is a wrongheaded policy fraught with dangers not alone to the peoples of South Africa but to international peace and security. We oppose it out of our convictions, out of our own experience with questions of racial discrimination, and in recognition of the clear injunctions of the U.N. Charter.

We do not suppose that racial accommodation can be achieved overnight and without the strain of a major social adjustment. We have our own shortcomings to answer for in this matter in parts of the United States, and it behooves us to press on and make good on the national policy of bringing discrimination rapidly to an end. But we cannot hold any sympathy for the policy of South Africa, which, in the words of a U.N. commission, is "contrary to the dignity and worth of the human person."

That is why, not only at the U.N. but in direct, official representations, we have felt obliged to bring our views strongly to the attention of the South African Government. We are mindful of valuable South African contributions to the victory over Hitlerite Germany and to turning back Communist aggression in Korea. But we cannot expediently note only what the right hand of South Africa does, if at home the left is raised to turn aside the wind of change or fend off the U.N. Charter's insistence on fundamental human rights for all peoples.

*Report by Senators Albert Gore (Tennessee), Philip A. Hart (Michigan)
and Maurine B. Neuberger (Oregon) on Aid and Politics in Africa**

September-October, 1961

*　　　　　　*　　　　　　*

We concluded as a result of our observations that the United States must continue to provide substantial amounts of grant aid to newly independent African countries. We concluded that such aid should be provided not simply to counteract Soviet bloc aid, but for the positive reason that, properly administered, free world aid will assist these new nations to develop in a pattern conducive to the maintenance of their independence, to their economic growth, and to the expansion of individual freedom. We believe that the existence of strong, free African states will help create the kind of world in which the values of a free society such as ours will be maintained.

The problem for the United States in assisting in the economic development of African nations is to make aid available in form and in amount to encourage economic and political independence. American foreign policy objectives will not be promoted if aid is viewed by Africans as a form of "neocolonialism" or if aid bolsters countries which deny basic rights of life and liberty and free expression to their peoples. United States aid must not become an instrument to bolster totalitarianism of either the right or the left. It must rather, be an instrument for the promotion of human rights and freedom.

This is not easy. The sensitivity of new nations is so near the surface that what seem to be safeguards to a donor country or to the private investor tend to become suspicious or onerous conditions to the receiver; what seem normal precautions for governmental grants or loans become "political strings" to recipients. The dilemma in administering aid programs in these circumstances is well illustrated by the large Volta River project in Ghana.

*　　　　　　*　　　　　　*

These figures show that the total cost of the Volta River project, including transmission lines and the aluminum smelter, is estimated, including overrun, to be $366 million, of which more than half—$201 million—will come from United States sources, of which up to $54 million (covered by a political risk guarantee) would be from private investors. The total planned United States resources to be devoted to the Volta River project during the next seven years, therefore, will be equivalent to almost one-half of the amount of aid that the United States is expected to provide to all Africa during the current fiscal year.

We do not here undertake to assess the economic feasibility of the Volta project, and for the sake of this report we assume it is economically feasible. Neither do we undertake to judge whether the past actions of this Government were such as to commit us morally or legally to providing assistance. . . .

We venture, however, to comment on the political considerations bearing upon the United States decision to proceed with assistance in the Volta project.

Committee on Foreign Relations, Study Mission to Africa, September-October, 1961 (Washington, 1962), pp. 11-14.

There should be no illusion but that the highest policy considerations were involved in this decision which, in the final analysis, had to be made by the President. A decision not to proceed with the United States portion of the project would have created vast bitterness in Ghana as well as in a few other African states. American private investments in Ghana might have been expropriated, and the Ghanain Government might have taken still another leap toward the left. It is doubtful if Ghana would have been as tempted to seek Soviet aid as Egypt was in the case of Aswan, because of the absence of any utility of the project unless an aluminum smelter, with free world markets, were constructed to utilize the electricity. In any event anti-American sentiment would have been fanned by our denial. The Soviet bloc would certainly have been invited in to fill part of the vacuum.

On the other hand, the undertaking to proceed with the project seems to many Americans and to many Africans as a reward granted to a state and government not truly neutral in conduct and committed in recent months to the suppression and oppression of the basic right of free expression and political disagreement.

We do not deny that the new states of Africa must be free to develop their own brands of political organization. But we do not believe American aid should be used to assist governments engaged in the systematic suppression of free expression.

There are many states in Africa badly in need of external assistance which adhere to the basic principles of the rule of law, which do not deny fundamental human rights to their opponents, which do not imprison their citizens without trial, which permit the existence of a free press, and which do not utilize their communications facilities and oversea missions for proselyting their neighbors. Is it proper for the United States in its aid policies to consider these things?

We must, of course, be careful in undertaking to apply the standard of what has been good for us to these new states. Their situations are different in many ways, in many degrees. We must be careful not to confuse nationalism with totalitarianism or communism. But with these cautions in mind, we do believe that United States aid must be related to the basic principles for which we stand. Only in this way can it commend the sustained support of our people.

Unfortunately, the domestic policies of Ghana in recent months, including the imprisonment of some 400 political opponents and the enactment of laws apparently designed to intimidate those who would express anti-Government views, have raised in our minds serious doubt as to whether United States aid for the Volta River project will in fact promote independence and individual freedom for the people of Ghana. We hope we are wrong!

We believe that if the long-range interests of the United States are to be served by the creation of free and independent states which respect the fundamental rights of the individual, American aid can in good conscience be provided only to governments which respect those basic rights and freedoms.

We hasten to add that the principle we have enunciated must be applied on a continent-wide basis. There are other states in Africa receiving United States assistance which do not, in our opinion, measure up to the minimum standards of free societies.

We found instances, for example, in which the United States has permitted strictly short-term national security considerations to affect adversely what seem to us are our longer term interests. In some countries we found that our officials took the position that the United States found it necessary to put up with a certain amount of blackmail simply because there were certain installations there that we wished to maintain. As one Ambassador remarked: "We tread a narrow line here, trying not to give in to blackmail requests for glamorous projects and providing aid in practical items under reasonable conditions."

Yet in these countries we found our policies tied to the demands of reactionary regimes, maintaining themselves in power by controlled press and radio, by limiting educational opportunities of promising critics, by skillfully playing off opponents against each other, and by stifling opposition.

Although African needs for education and development are virtually limitless, American resources which can justifiably be made available for assistance in Africa are not.

Year after year Members of Congress are subjected to increasing criticism for helping foreign nations solve power, water, and other development projects while postponing similar ventures in the United States. It is obvious that at some point the United States will reach a limit beyond which its aid cannot be increased. While that limit is related to our capacity to provide assistance, far more important is the relationship between what we provide and the results achieved. When the Congress, under its authority to appropriate funds "to pay the Debts and provide for the common Defense and general Welfare of the United States," decides to build a dam in Africa rather than in the United States, it does so because it believes that decision serves a national interest. In the words of the Act for International Development, Congress believes "survival of free institutions in the United States can best be assured in a worldwide atmosphere of freedom" and that it is "a primary necessity, opportunity, and responsibility of the United States" to demonstrate that "economic growth and political democracy can go hand in hand to the end that an enlarged community of free, stable, and self-reliant countries can reduce world tensions and insecurity."

Unless there is reason to believe that a particular expenditure promotes the "worldwide atmosphere of freedom" most likely to assure "survival of free institutions in the United States," the expenditure is not justified.

New York Times Editorial on Senators Gore, Hart and Neuberger and Aid to Ghana*

January 17, 1962

To aid or not to aid is one of the knotty questions United States Congressmen are facing. Senators Gore, Hart and Neuberger, all first-rank liberals fresh from a study mission to Africa, warn the Administration against extending aid to newly independent nations that do not respect "basic rights and freedoms."

Their hearts are in the right place but, in this case, not their judgment. Of course, the United States does not want to help regimes that commit themselves irrevocably to dictatorial policies of a totalitarian nature. We do want to give the fullest encouragement to governments that are trying to lay the foundations for real democracy.

But what about governments—in Africa, the Middle East, Asia and Latin America— that are not democracies today but that aspire to achieve democracy in the future? What about governments that might or might not end up as democracies if we and

The New York Times, Jan. 17, 1962.

other Western nations are patient and helpful? What about governments that we could feel fairly certain would commit themselves to the Communist bloc if we turn our backs on them?

We live in a dangerous, uncertain world nowadays. The newly independent nations of Africa are floundering. They do not have populations or politicians trained to Western styles of politics. They do not have adequate civil services, or administrators, or traditions that would help them make speedily and effectively the difficult transition from tribal life to modern independence.

The three Senators singled out Ghana, where the United States is committed to help build a hydroelectric project on the Volta River. As an article in Sunday's *New York Times Magazine* by our correspondent Henry Tanner pointed out, Ghana's President Kwame Nkrumah has developed dictatorial tendencies very quickly. He has cast sheep's eyes toward Moscow. This is too bad; but it is not very surprising nor is it a development that need forever condemn Ghana to an anti-democratic regime. At least, it need not do so if we display some patience and persuasion. But Ghana would probably be driven further into the Communist camp if the United States should back down on economic aid.

The basic purpose of our assistance is not to force the underdeveloped countries into our own image, but, as the President has repeatedly made clear, to help them maintain their own freedom and independence from foreign control. There will be an interim period in which these countries will have to find themselves as they establish their own governmental institutions; and if we can assist them to do so along democratic lines, so much the better. But while we certainly want to help embryonic democracies, this does not mean that we have to cut off all aid to non-democracies. That would be the surest way to block their progress toward freedom.

Address by Assistant Secretary Williams on Africa's Challenge to American Enterprise*

December 1, 1961

*   *   *

What is the role of American private enterprise in fostering the economic growth of Africa? Briefly, in the course of normal business activity it can assist by providing capital, by making available qualified technicians and business administrators, and by helping to improve the quality of African management.

Among the business areas in which African nations require immediate economic assistance are those of insurance, banking and loan associations, low-cost housing, and cold storage. There is room for commercial, financial, extractive, and industrial activities, exporting and importing businesses, large and small. As an example, I am intrigued by the number of African craft and folk art items I am beginning to see in American stores.

What is the climate for United States business in Africa? . . .

Admittedly these are turbulent times in Africa, when newly emerging nations are attempting to develop personalities and institutions of their own. The framework in which foreign private investment will operate in many of these nations is still unclear.

*Department of State Bulletin, Feb. 8, 1962, pp. 61-63.

At the same time the need for such investment is almost universally recognized, and we can be certain that, one way or another, it will play an important role.

There is no point in hiding the fact that risks for the private investor are high in some parts of Africa—because the place of foreign investment has not yet been determined, because adequate safeguards have not yet been devised, and in some areas simply because the possibility of political instability exists. But we should not let the headlines which dramatize the areas of unrest and governmental irresponsibility obscure the fact that in much of Africa conditions are peaceful and that, with the enthusiastic support of the mass of the people, energies are being devoted to the constructive tasks of economic development and the maintenance of political stability.

For those of us who have been close to the African scene, broad outlines of the future are becoming increasingly clear, even though the ferment of transition still obscures many of the details. Africa must be accepted on its own terms. We cannot expect, with rare exceptions, that the African nations will immediately develop all the institutions of democracy in our sense of the word.

African nations are now developing their own forms of government and their own institutions, based on cultural patterns that are familiar to them and that they can make work effectively. I am confident that they will move in the direction of free choice and self-expression.

At the risk of considerable oversimplification, we might say that many of the new states of Africa are atempting to substitute national loyalties for tribal loyalties and that, to obtain acceptance as a substitute for the tribe, the nation must take on certain characteristics familiar to the people. In practical terms, for the time being, this often means a strong leadership with paternal overtones and a rather different and more difficult role for political opposition. It often means a high degree of state responsibility for the well-being of the individual citizen, which derives less from modern welfare theory than from the traditional claims of a member of a family or a tribe on its chief. Government ownership tends to fit well into this kind of structure, and the lack of entrepreneurial skills and private capital in much of Africa accentuates the tendency. It is thus no accident that even some of the most pro-Western leaders of Africa in large measure think automatically in terms of state enterprise.

We must, of course, encourage the African nations to develop the plurality of institutions that we have found to be the greatest bulwark of freedom. In particular we must help them find a place for private enterprise. But we would be remiss if we did not say very candidly that private enterprise itself must be prepared to make major adjustments. It may well be that Africa will provide the proving ground for new forms of cooperation between private foreign investment and underdeveloped societies.

First of all, the new pattern of cooperation, to be effective, is likely to emphasize the management functions. If the major emphasis is placed on management rather than ownership, many new possibilities are opened which provide opportunities for us and which are fully acceptable to the Africans.

Second, the new pattern of cooperation is likely to show a somewhat different relationship between investment in capital and investment labor than we are accustomed to. Much of Africa has great labor resources, although woefully shy of capital. Even assuming a sharp increase in capital made available from outside, the net will far exceed the amount received if there is simply an attempt to reproduce the capital-insessive development of the industrialized West. If, with good planning and management, human resources can be used as a substitute for capital, not within the harsh framework of Communist exploitation but through humane and progressive enterprise. We in America may have a reputation abroad of efficiency and wealth through machines, but a far more accurate statement of America's contribution to the modern world has been its development of techniques through which large-scale production can be achieved in a genuinely free society. If we are to provide the managerial skills for labor-interests production as well as we have for production based on high capital investment, there is an assured place for us in Africa.

Stated another way, there are limitations in African development but there is also a tremendous potential. Political and social factors may be given very special recognition. American private enterprise can make a major contribution; it shows a flexibility in meeting African conditions that goes beyond anything we have experienced in the past.

Robert L. Garner, former President of the International Finance Corporation, has suggested certain particular aspects of responsibility to foreign businessmen operating in developed countries. They are worth noting. Foreign businessmen, he believes, "need to make special efforts to associate themselves with the local communities—first through maximum use of local sources and people, with positive efforts to provide training and opportunity for advancement to senior positions." Garner points out the mutual advantages in joint ventures with local enterprises, or in sharing ownership with local investors." He cites the role of business in setting the example and stimulating their local counterparts in supporting education, technical and business training, and other constructive community activities.

I hope that those of you who are already engaged in foreign business will keep those in mind, aware that the posture of American enterprise abroad greatly influences the attitudes of foreign peoples and governments toward the United States.

I am convinced that there are among you businessmen who can turn their capital, know-how, and experience to the promotion of the broad interests of our nation in aiding African development. Negro Americans are already among those of our citizens demonstrating the benefits which good private business can contribute to economic growth. Needless to say, stalwart sons of Michigan were among the pioneers. I speak of a Liberian-American timber firm run jointly by a group of young men from Detroit in collaboration with Liberian citizens. I understand also that Wilson Hines, a graduate of Howard and M.I.T., has established a liquid-air manufacturing company in Liberia. Another successful venture is the insurance company established in Ghana by a group of enterprising New Yorkers.

Some of the larger United States firms in Africa have hired Negro Americans in professional positions. These include a major aluminum company and leading soft-drink and cigarette manufacturers. This is a welcome sign of the extension of the American principle of fair employment practices that our Government is enforcing with increasing vigor. It is a development which I hope will spread throughout American business overseas.

I might say here parenthetically that our AID [Agency for International Development] missions in Sierra Leone and in Mali are directed by Negro Americans of high skills and competence.

The United States has great need for the participation and assistance of talented people in its activities to build security by increasing worldwide economic development, and larger participation of the Negro American in this task is no more and no less than an integral part of his full integration into American life.

To stimulate appropriate participation of private enterprise, the United States Government has worked out a program of providing insurances against various kinds of political risks and in some cases business risks as well. Certain loans are available to private enterprise on high-priority projects. Also the United States Government is in a position to provide financial help in surveys undertaken by potential investors to acquire the information essential to investment decisions.

As I have said, the magnitude of the task of African economic development is tremendous. Therefore it is reassuring to think that our Government can count upon the support of private enterprise in its efforts to meet the challenges of Africa and contribute toward the development of a stable and prosperous world.

Report by Senator Allen J. Ellener (Louisiana) on United States Foreign Operations in Africa*

December 4, 1962

*   *   *

I was met at the plane [at Dar-es-Salaam airport] by Ambassador William Leonhart and all the heads of our missions here. As I started to walk down the steps, the Ambassador suggested that I not go to the airport building, that he wanted to see me aboard the plane. I then walked back up the steps to talk with the Ambassador aboard the plane. All I could learn from him was that a statement attributed to me while at Salisbury, Southern Rhodesia was given as the reason why I could not visit Tanganyika. I asked what the statement was but no one seemed to know.

I was informed that the Prime Minister of Uganda had made a move to deny a visit by me to Uganda, and Tanganyika followed suit. In the meantime, a local immigration official came aboard the plane and handed me a document which read as follows:

Form 25–Tanganyika #886
The Immigration Regulations, 1957, Regulation 34 (1)
NOTICE TO PROHIBITED IMMIGRANT
To: Mr. Allan Ellender of Louisiana, U.S.
    Take notice that you are a prohibited immigrant on the ground that you have no Pass or Permit to enter Tanganyika. You are hereby ordered to leave the country immediately.
    Dated this 4th day of December, 1962.

[Could not read signature]
Principal Immigration Officer

I asked for what reason I was denied admission. The officer did not answer. I told him I had a visa, but he paid no attention and walked out.

*   *   *

May I say that I did not feel offended or even insulted by the treatment accorded me by the officials of Tanganyika. On the contrary, I felt sorry for them. Freedom of speech seems foreign to them, and they are evidently thin skinned politicians. I did not relish the idea of being denied admission because of newspaper reports taken out of

*U.S. Senate, *A Report on United States Foreign Operations in Africa*, 1962, 88th Cong., 1st sess., (Washington, 1963), pp. 146-49.

context and headlines, as was evident from a newspaper report handed to me before I left the airport. All my views should have been printed.

Excerpts from one of the large Rhodesian newspapers (the Sunday Mail) which reported on my interview read as follows:

> If you can get somebody to stay with you for 50 years, you might be able to take over. But believe me, you won't be able to do it overnight.

I was referring, of course, to the new countries that are still heavily dependent upon European civil servants and other forms of outside aid for the operation of their governments.

The second quote read:

> The African people in some countries like Nyasaland will not reach the goal their leaders aim for in 50 years.

Both of these statements, which I do not deny having made, appeared far down in the story which dealt with an interview that lasted more than an hour. Yet above the story, a banner headline read:

"YOU WILL NEED WHITE HELP FOR 50 YEARS"

I can understand how this might be considered antagonistic by some, but surely this was not a correct headline for a story which covered many, many other topics at much greater length. I did not use the word WHITE.

The report from Salisbury, or this particular part of the interview, was picked up by other African papers and greatly played up by the press. In my opinion, that one headline, which was not responsive to what I said, formed the basis for the subsequent action taken against me. If nothing else, it shows the negative power of the press.

The story that appeared in the papers of Tanganyika originated in Uganda. The Prime Minister of Uganda, as I previously stated, made the first move. I was not quoted in full in the local press, but I must confess that although I believe what I said to be the truth, perhaps Salisbury was not the best place to say it. There was quite a commotion going on at the time about dissolving the Federation of the Rhodesias and Nyasaland. My remarks as a whole were in reference to Nyasaland and the Federation. I was quoted:

> I have yet to see any part of Africa where Africans are ready for self-government.

I did say that. It is the truth.

I do not have any quarrel with full independence or self-government for any country, if that country has the capability to achieve and maintain that independence

I mean capability in resources, both human and economic. So far, I have not visited one newly formed government that did not need outside help on a grant basis and where technical assistance was not badly needed and provided by Western Europeans and Americans. The truth of the matter is that France is deeply involved in developing the economies of most of the countries formed out of French West and Equatorial Africa. We, too, have programs in all of them, including all former British colonies.

I also intended to say that most of the electorate in many countries was not fully qualified to vote. Of course, that is not peculiar to Africa, but to many other areas of the world; even in our own country some of the voters are not fully qualified.

I was further quoted as saying:

> . . . the average African is incapable of leadership without *white* assistance.

I did say that if there is any place in Africa where brick and mortar had been used by the natives to build a civilization through no assistance or without the assistance or guidance of Europeans, I would like to see it. I never used the word "white" as above quoted. It was taken from the headlines.

I further stated that the average new African country is incapable of progress except through the assistance of the Europeans; that it was through the assistance of the Europeans that schools have been established and some industries have been developed. Some Africans in some of the countries have since learned the techniques of progress.

I wish to say that I have never before been denied entrance to any country in the world, and I have visited all of them except Albania. I sincerely try to do an objective job on my inspection tours in the hope that I can bring back home the true picture of the countries that I visit. I admit I have been critical of what I have seen on some of my past visits, but I believe the criticism was in every instance well founded and given objectively.

State Department Statement on Senator Ellender's Remarks on African Self-Government*

December 4, 1962

The Department of State has received inquiries regarding remarks attributed to Senator [Allen J.] Ellender in Salisbury, Southern Rhodesia, on December 1.

Senator Ellender made clear in his remarks at a press conference that his comments on African governments were entirely personal and did not reflect the policy of the United States Government.

The United States has repeatedly demonstrated its support for the aspirations of the peoples and governments of Africa for the achievement and maintenance of freedom and independence, personal and national dignity and equality, and economic and social progress.

We have welcomed the independence of new African nations and support the application of the principles of self-determination for peoples in a dependent status. This Government opposes any abridgment of human rights and encourages the protection of the just rights of minorities in Africa.

*Department of State Bulletin, Dec. 24, 1962, p. 961.

*Address by Assistant Secretary Williams on Communism's Impact on
African Nationalism**

May 13, 1963

*   *   *

To date, Communist penetration of the southern regions of Africa has not been considerable, but the number of students from the area going to bloc schools is rising steadily. At present, estimates indicate that there are some 250-300 in the bloc from the Federation of Rhodesia and Nyasaland, South Africa, the Portuguese territories, and the High Commission territories. There also has been a sharp rise in the number of Africans from these areas going to the bloc for training in guerrilla warfare and sabotage. The number of hours of Portuguese-language broadcasting from the bloc has increased. In addition arms have been made available to various insurgent groups through independent African nations.

The Communists' principal aim in southern Africa appears to be to dominate all nonwhite opposition elements to the existing government in the Republic of South Africa. Although the South African Communist Party has been outlawed, it continues to exploit the tensions and frustrations generated by the Government's apartheid program. The party's membership is relatively small—only an estimated 800 hard-core members—but it has some 6,500 sympathizers. Its importance is not found in its size, however. Its importance lies in its long history of support for the African nationalist movement.

Since 1959, Communist efforts have met strong opposition from the Pan-Africanist Congress, which, partly because of its racial outlook, has opposed the white Communist leadership and is resentful of its efforts to direct protest movements toward strengthening the Communist apparatus rather than toward the organization of a nonwhite nationalist movement.

During recent months, the South African Government has moved to curb alleged Communists more severely and prevent further outbreaks of organized sabotage. In its zeal, however, it has failed to make a distinction between Communists and genuine liberals and nationalists and, as a result, has sharply restricted the freedoms of all South Africans.

The Government has placed some 30 persons under house arrest for violation of the harsh and extremely broad "Sabotage Act," and it has published a list of more than 400 "named Communists" who are banned from political activity under the new act. Statements made by any banned or restricted person may not be published anywhere in the country. This stricter Government surveillance has not materially diminished Communist activity in South Africa, which has operated clandestinely since 1950. In addition the Communists have moved part of their base of operations outside the country.

One of the more unfortunate aspects of South Africa's tighter control of Communist activities is its refusal to distinguish between Communist opposition and legitimate opposition to the South African Government. In their zeal to brand all opposition "Communist," they appear to be lending strength to the Communist cause. The editor of the *Rand Daily Mail*, a liberal, non-Communist newspaper, made this point very clear in a front-page editorial directed to the Minister of Justice. He wrote:

**Ibid.*, June 3, 1963, pp. 880-81.

Communism has never had wide support among non-Whites in South Africa. You are giving it the stature of a mass movement. . . . Do not hand to the Communists a monopoly of fighting for the rights of non-Whites. For if you do these things . . . you will have sealed South Africa's fate . . . having delivered a great country into the hands of the Communists.

The attitude that opposition to the governments in power in southern Africa automatically is Communist-inspired could lead to the very type of penetration that we seek to prevent in Africa.

This brings me to one of the paradoxes the West faces today. Throughout the southern part of Africa there are a number of movements directed toward racial accommodation and self-government. These movements seek Western assistance and do not desire a commitment from the Communist world. The response of the West traditionally is to call for peaceful transition by both the disenfranchised majorities and the ruling minorities. However, if hopes for achieving legitimate demands for racial and political equality through such peaceful methods are disappointed and the question becomes one of survival for these political movements, any compunctions they might have about accepting the Communist aid could be expected to disappear.

Such an eruption of African frustrations in the southern part of the continent is what the Communists are counting on in the long run. They believe that this could so maneuver the Western nations that the West's influence and political credit among Africans will rapidly diminish.

Unless there is a discernible movement toward more progressive policies in those parts of southern Africa not enjoying majority rule, and unless there appears to be vigorous leadership from the West to accomplish such progress, there is a good possibility that Western influence could be replaced by that of the Communists. Aided by a deterioration of the Western position, the Sino-Soviet bloc could become the leading outside influence in the painful transition in southern Africa and in the minds of Africans everywhere.

*   *   *

The basic answer the West must give to the Communist challenge in Africa is a program of action which responds to the pressing political, economic, and social needs of the peoples of Africa rather than simply an attack on communism. The best way to stop communism is to eliminate the conditions in which it flourishes—conditions not only of poverty, illness, illiteracy, and malnutrition but also of lack of self-expression and self-government.

*Address by J. Wayne Fredericks, Deputy Assistant Secretary
for African Affairs, on African Policy**

July 18, 1963

*   *   *

African influence in the United Nations and its specialized agencies in the past year has grown startlingly. We have the best examples of this influence today in their actions in the International Labor Organization, in the United Nations Economic and

*Ibid., Aug. 19, 1963, pp. 285-87.

Social Council, and in the UNESCO [United Nations Educational, Scientific and Cultural Organization] education meeting in Geneva in the past month as the African nations have sought to expel Portugal and South Africa from these organizations because of their inflexible positions.

A new degree of effectiveness of African organization is traceable to the meeting of African chiefs of state in Addis Ababa in May, where they, among other things, established an African Liberation Committee. The committee is already functioning in Dar-es-Salaam in support of African nationalist movements in the still dependent areas of the continent.

At Addis Ababa also the cause of African unity was advanced with the signing by 30 heads of state of a charter establishing an Organization of African Unity. The charter has already been ratified by more than two-thirds of the signatory states and will, therefore, formally enter into force in the near future.

In my opinion the establishment of the OAU is indeed a significant and historic event. It indicates that Africa is on the treshold of an exciting new chapter in the advance toward unity, a unity which was denied to them because of long years of colonial domination.

The United States, as in Europe and Latin America, heartily supports the stablishment of institutions which will promote political, economic, and cultural cooperation in Africa. Among the institutions called for in the OAU is the establishment of a Commission of Mediation, Conciliation and Arbitration to settle all disputes among themselves by peaceful means. Other important commissions to be established by the OAU are for economic and social affairs, education and culture, defense, and health, sanitation, and nutrition.

The establishment of a workable OAU could give further impetus to the activities of important regional organizations already functioning, such as the African and Malagasy Union, comprising 13 French-speaking states, the United Nations Economic Commission for Africa, and the East African Common Services Organization, which provides a considerable degree of economic integration in that area of Africa.

Kenya, Tanganyika, and Uganda are reported to be negotiating for the establishment soon of an East African federation with strong central powers to more effectively pool their national resources for the common good. Zanzibar, a self-governing British territory, is also considering joining this East African federation. Tanganyika and Uganda are independent, while Kenya, which only recently elected an African government, is expected to obtain her independence soon. Such a federation, if successful, could also have a powerful influence upon neighboring African areas where the African people have not yet obtained self-determination and self-government.

Nothing in the past year has altered my conviction that one-party government in Africa does not exclude the practice of democratic principles like free discussion and universal adult suffrage, although in some places freedoms we cherish are restricted. Independence-minded Africa remains determined to be free of both Soviet bloc controls and undue Western influence. In the past year the Communists have initiated a review of their African policies because of the clear rebuffs administered by the Republic of Guinea and newly independent Algeria. Communism, which demands uniformity, has made no enduring friends in Africa; the Western World of free choice tolerates, indeed welcomes and thrives on, African national individuality.

The United States must remain a progressive, dynamic, democratic nation, and it must avoid identification with reaction if it is to maintain its leadership and win the cooperation of Africa. In recent weeks the United States has faced a special test, not in the foreign field but in its domestic racial crisis. President Kennedy's honest recognition of our racial injustice and his expression of determination to see this wrong righted have, initially at least, maintained Africa's respect.

*   *   *

As the African people are busily engaged in building up their new states and properly utilizing their hard-won independence, they at the same time are not unmindful that American Negroes are seeking to gain equality of citizenship in our own country. Examples of racial discrimination and acts of violence in the United States have been widely reported abroad. Soviet propaganda organs have been inundating the world with pictures and lurid stories about hostile acts committed against Negro demonstrators in Birmingham and elsewhere.

Secretary Rusk, commenting upon this situation, said that we ought all to recognize that "this nation is now confronted with one of the gravest issues that we have had since 1865 and that this issue deeply affects the conduct of our foreign relations." In our effort to support the great causes of freedom in the world, Mr. Rusk noted, we in this country "are running this race with one of our legs in a cast."

Until the present, the internal question of civil rights—with all it involves for the American Negro—and the international question of United States and Africa have only occasionally been directly related. For example, the 1954 Supreme Court decision with respect to segregation helped improve our image in Africa, just as Little Rock made our position more difficult. At the same time, American Negro interest in Africa has been sporadically increasing, with ensuing implications for American policy. But because avowed Federal Government policy has been on the side of integration and equality of treatment the pressures on governmental leaders were neither intense nor prolonged as far as African policy was concerned, and the foreign reaction to events in this country was blunted.

In my opinion the situation is rapidly changing. The consequences of this change for United States policy toward Africa need searching examination. The principal reason for this change lies in the fact tha our racial crisis coincides with the new confrontation of forces in Africa over colonialism and apartheid.

At home Negroes are clearly not going to put up with further delay on the civil rights issue. This means there may be more incidents, with pictures such as that of the Birmingham policeman with a dog leaping at a Negro. Our strife will remind people of strife in South Africa.

As tension mounts the Negro elements of the population become a more articulate force in the public life of this country. As a matter of practical politics, they may be expected to exercise this force in other fields than domestic civil rights. This trend is both an opportunity and a problem in the conduct of policy toward Africa, for if Negro opinion is well informed it will be helpful but if it is merely a reflection of its frustration at home it could easily be harmful to our long-term interests in Africa.

The significant developments in Africa which may bring about a dangerous situation are these:

We have increasingly endorsed self-determination in Africa and have welcomed the emergence of the independent African nations. With one exception this transformation has been amazingly peaceful. However, we are down to the hard core of dependent Africa. We have been hopeful that Portugal and South Africa will find it in their interest to cooperate in peaceful political change. There has been little evidence that this is their intention, and African nations demand that the world choose now to support more positive actions.

In our relations with the rest of Africa we may find ourselves having to acquiesce in more extreme action or face sharply reduced influence, to the detriment of other important objectives. At the U.N. we shall more and more be branded as hypocrites by the Afro-Asians and branded as traitors to the West by their opponents.

Speech by Senator Ellender Before the Senate on the Foreign Assistance Act of 1913*

December 13, 1963

*   *   *

I must iterate that I deeply regret that the Senate conferees were unable to retain more of the Senate amendments when the Foreign Aid Authorization Act, as approved and passed by the Senate, was taken to conference with Members of the House. I am sure that each of those amendments, if they had prevailed, would have done a great deal to strengthen our foreign aid program. Certainly their adoption indicated that the aid administrators had better look to their laurels and begin a businesslike review of the program for the coming fiscal year.

I was particularly disappointed to note the changes which occurred in the amendment, sponsored by me, designed to limit military aid to African countries to not more than $25 million in any fiscal year.

*   *   *

Now the foreign aid authorization bill, as it came to the Senate from the House, also included a section dealing with aid to African countries. It provided that military aid could be given only for internal security requirements, and for public works, or civic action programs authorized by section 505(b) of the act. I have some arguments with the latter section, but I am completely opposed to allowing "internal security requirements" be the basis for the granting of military aid. This is exactly what I was striving to avoid. These three words "internal security requirements" are to blame for a large part of the current situation in Latin America. Once we get a military aid program off the ground in Africa, it will not be long before our friends to the south of us appear to be living in the utmost peace and prosperity by comparison.

*   *   *

The compromise language states that grant programs of defense articles for African countries for fiscal year 1964 shall not exceed $25 million. Notice that the limiting figure applies only to fiscal year 1964. Nothing is said of future fiscal years, and it is

Congressional Record, Dec. 13, 1963, pp. 24458-59.

the future that we mus look to in the present. Action should be taken now to make as sure as possible that a tight lid is clamped, and kept closed, on the military aid program as it applies to Africa. Bear in mind that Africa is a new continent, so far as our military aid programs are concerned. I am certain that our military missions, if not kept reined in, will make sure that it grows up very rapidly until it becomes like so many other areas which are struggling under the armies built up and maintained by the American taxpayer.

The language adopted by the conference committee provides that grant military assistance may be furnished to African countries only for internal security unless the President determines otherwise. That is a far cry from my original language, adopted by the Senate, which stated very plainly that:

> Internal security requirements shall not, unless the President determines otherwise . . . be the basis for military assistance programs for African countries.

The committee of conference reversed that language; its intent is negated completely.

The danger in this matter lies in the definition of "internal security." When do armaments provided for "internal security" become the agents for external aggression? As I pointed out in my African report, I discovered our country had spent over $600,000 to train paratroopers for the newly emerging and desperately poor country of Mali. By what definition I asked, and I again ask, by what definition can the training of paratroops be justified as internal security? There cannot, of course, be any valid answer.

But beyond this, consider the injustice we are doing these newly independent nations, and their people, by encouraging their governments to build up large military forces which must be maintained, at least someday, by taxes on the native population. We are doing them a grave wrong, and apparently are doing it, with our eyes wide open and of our own free will.

*   *   *

The conference committee action would require no positive action by the President, and that is where the trouble is.

The conference committee has allowed the military authorities to do as they please. They may alone determine the requirements. Military missions exist in many countries of the world. If my memory serves me correctly, there are only six or seven military missions in Africa, although I do not remember the exact number. Those missions abroad continually send recommendations to the Department of Defense, in Washington. I have even known of places—such as Pakistan, Afghanistan, or India—where the military missions have said that a certain amount of money was needed to supply the needs of a certain number of soldiers.

Then the host country will say, "That may be true, but we cannot afford that much."

The reply is, "Do what you can, and we will do the rest."

Let us consider the case of Mali, which I have already presented. We spent $600,000 in Mali, to train paratroopers. But anyone with commonsense knows that paratroopers are not necessary in order to protect the citizens of Mali. That training was requested in order to make possible some action against the neighbors of Mali.

There is also the case of Somali, to which we have furnished much aid. When that country asked us for weapons, we said, after conferring with the British and the Italians, "We think we can furnish you with about $17 million in hardware."

They replied, "Oh, no; that is not enough. Russia will give us $26 or $30 million. So we do not want yours." Now they will be getting that equipment from Russia while continuing to receive economic aid from us. Is that for internal security purposes? No; it is to enable Somali to take over part of Kenya. Somali is getting ready to annex a considerable part of Kenya, because Somali says that in that area there are more Somalis than Kenyans.

Such situations will continue; and if we let these countries have more military equipment than is necessary for their own police forces, we can expect trouble in the future.

*   *   *

*Speech by Senator Church Before the Senate on "Our Overinvolvement in Africa"**

February 17, 1965

*   *   *

If the inhabitants of Western Europe tend to see the world as we do, as a global arena in which "free" people are arrayed against Communists, it does not follow that Africans and Asians share this view. They have been participants in a different revolution, more potent and widespread than the Communist brand—a revolution foreshadowed two centuries ago, by the American War for Independence, and whipped into flame by Woodrow Wilson's ringing reaffirmation of the right of self-determination. Neither Marx nor Lenin fathered the revolt against colonialism, and we need not permit their successors, in Moscow or Peiping, to exploit the colonial issue to Communist advantage.

To avoid this, we must understand that, for most Africans and Asians, our concept of self-government and individual freedom is totally unreal, having never been experienced. In many, if not most, of these emergent lands, it is capitalism, not communism, which is the ugly word. The very term evokes images of the old colonial plantation and white man supremacy. Furthermore, any attempt to acquaint Africa and Asia with the miracles of modern capitalism, as witnessed in such places as the United States, Western Europe, and Japan, is relatively meaningless. The underdeveloped world lacks the private capital with which to industrialize. Government is often the only source available to underwrite development programs. Thus, popular repugnance to capitalism combines with economic necessity to cause most of the new governments in Africa and Asia to proclaim themselves Socialist states.

Because these facts are so well known, it puzzles me that American foreign policy in Africa and Asia has not been tied to them. We have plunged into these former colonial regions as though we had been designated on high to act as trustee in bankruptcy for the broken empires.

Ibid., Feb. 17, 1965, pp. 2869-71.

First of all, we strained relations by trying to induce governments to line up with us in the cold war, a struggle in which few felt any real interest. Forgetting that we ourselves had insisted upon our right to stay neutral for most of our history, we assailed "neutralism" as a kind of Communist trick. Later, having painfully learned that cold war neutrality always served as a badge of, and sometimes even as an umbrella for, independence, we changed tune, but, even then, we kept on administering our aid programs in ways designed to freeze out the Russians and Chinese.

In regions craving aid from any source, our freeze-out policy was bound to give rise to cries of undue interference. Soon, African and Asian governments were demanding aid "without strings attached," while accusing the United States of practicing "neo-colonialism." Worse still, sensing that we feared competition from Communist sources, many a government craftily raised the "ante" on us, threatening to go to the Reds for help if we failed to meet some new demand.

Neither AID nor the State Department will acknowledge submitting to this sort of diplomatic blackmail in the handling of our foreign aid program. But I have no doubt about it. Too often I have questioned an American Ambassador about a misfit project in some forlorn little country, only to be told: "If we hadn't done it, the Russians would have been asked." Knuckling under to such crude pressures has caused our prestige to go down, even as our costs have gone up.

Worst of all, we have permitted ourselves to be drawn into the internal political affairs of so many African and Asian countries that anti-American feeling is rising at an alarming rate. Our embassies are being subjected to increasingly frequent attacks, our information libraries are being sacked, and demagogs from Cairo to Djakarta court popular favor by rebuking us. Afro-Asian delegates at the U.N. castigate us with words of extraordinary violence. Clearly, the policy of intervening too much in the volatile ex-colonial regions of Africa and Asia, is backfiring on the United States.

Much of this could have been avoided. I visited Africa in 1960, immediately after John F. Kennedy's election, in company with two of my colleagues and the President's youngest brother, Ted. Wherever our presence became known, eager crowds would gather to shout, "Kennedy, Kennedy." The word had spread through Africa that the newly elected President of the United States had, as a Senator in 1957, spoken up for Algeria in her war for independence against France. For the first time, our country was being identified, by Arab and Black alike, with legitimate African aspirations. Opportunity was beckoning our way.

If we had continued to champion African nationalism, the cause that counts with the people; if we had declared ourselves strongly in favor of rightful independence for the Portuguese Territories, the flaming issue in Africa today; if we had held ourselves at arms length from the shifting factional fights for power within the seething young African countries, regardless of the labels chosen to solicit outside support, I have no doubt that our influence in Africa would have kept on growing.

But we have not yet managed to harness our zeal. Rational restraints give way to emtional involvement which, in turn, leads to more intervention. Fortunately, the Russians have made the same mistake in Africa, and now the Chinese seem eager to repeat it. Here are two examples, one Russian, one American, which constitute, in my judgment, showcase illustrations of how not to conduct a winning foreign policy in Africa:

Six years ago, Nikita Khrushchev scurried to the rescue of Sekou Touré, strong man of Guinea, after this little west African country had been stripped bare by the departing French. It seemed a perfect marriage, since the Guinean leaders, raised in the radical tradition of the French labor movement, were Marxists anyway, and anxious to establish a model Marxist state.

When I arrived in Conakry, the country's capital, in December of 1960, Guinea had taken on all the appearances of a satellite. The government had been persuaded to abandon the franc in order to impede further trade with the West, and the entire economy seemed welded into the Red bloc. Communist advisers sat beside every Governmenr minister. Numerous Red-donated projects were under construction, including a big printing plant, and the place swarmed with Communist technicians, transplanted from countries behind the Iron Curtain. Guinea had plainly been taken over.

Into this captured country, President Kennedy sent a young Ambassador, Bill Atwood. His instructions were to play it cool. He was not to lecture the Guinean dictator on the virtues of democracy, or belabor his commissars with the glories of free enterprise. He was to say it was their business, not ours, to choose the system they preferred; that we were interested only in helping them, in a modest way, with some of their problems of human suffering. Kennedy felt, if we did not press too hard, that Guinea would soon discover the Russians were not 9 feet tall.

And so it happened. It was not long before Guinea began to resent the heavy-handed interference of the Russians. Relations became so strained that the Soviet Ambassador was declared persona non grata, and ordered to leave the country. Meanwhile, Guinea began to reassume control over her own course. Today, her attitude toward the United States is much improved, and her ties with the West are growing again.

The mistake of too much intervention, which the Russians made in Guinea, we seem determined to duplicate in the Congo. Africans wonder why the United States, having no historic, economic, or security interests in the Congo, should so involve itself in that country's civil war. I also wonder why.

I know, of course, that the State Department regards the Congo rebels as a Communist front, though their source of supply—Algerian and Egyptian—would seem African enough. Our own envoy in Stanleyville, whose long agony with the rebels was climaxed when they forced him to eat an American flag, declared, after his rescue, that he believed the rebellion to be purely African, not Communist, in character. His statement met a response of stony silence from the American press.

For the fact is that our embrace with Moise Tshombe is popular in the United States. We see him as a vociferous anti-Communist. What matters, however, is how the Africans see him. And African animosity toward Tshombe is so intense that he is even barred from associating with other African leaders, having been physically excluded from their meetings. To them, he is the African equivalent of an "Uncle Tom," a puppet of the imperialists who uses white mercenaries to subdue his own countrymen. I doubt that Tshombe will ever win African acceptance. Our involvement with him serves only to turn the tide of African opinion increasingly against us.

*   *   *

Speech by Senator Church Before the Senate on the Military Assistance and Saks Act of 1966*

July 27, 1966

*   *   *

The harmful effects of military assistance are even greater in Africa. Here, Communist penetration has met with stubborn nationalist resistance. Such threat as may exist is political in character and, so far as the record indicates, Africans have shown an admirable capacity to handle the problem if left to themselves. That, at least, is what has happened in Ghana and Algeria.

*   *   *

No continent has less need for an incipient arms race than Africa. To nourish it along by the gift of arms is wrongful. And justification cannot be found in the excuse that we do it to prevent the Russians from doing it in our place. The notion that Russian interests would somehow be advanced thereby is simply not supported by recent history. The evidence, in fact, is preponderantly to the contrary. In hearings on the bill before the committee, no one made the point better than former Ambassador Galbraith, who testified:

Let me take note in passing of the recurring argument that if we do not provide arms to a country it will get them from the Soviets or possibly China. This is another example of that curious obtuseness which excessive preoccupation with cold war strategy produces in otherwise excellent minds. It was Soviet tanks that surrounded Ben Bella's palace in Algeria when that Soviet-supported leader was thrown out. It was a Soviet and Chinese equipped army which deposed the Indonesian Communists, destroyed the Communist Party in that ruthlessness on which one hesitates to dwell and which left Sukarno's vision of an Asian socialism in shambles. It was a Soviet-trained praetorian guard which was expected to supply the ultimate protection to the government of President Nkrumah and which did not. One can only conclude that those who worry about Soviet arms wish to keep the Russians out of trouble. This could be carrying friendship too far.

If the adoption of this amendment were to have no other effect than to put the damper on the spread of American arms in Africa, it would serve to benefit donor and donees alike.

*   *   *

Address by Under Secretary of State Nicolas Katzenbach on America and Africa†

June 5, 1967

*   *   *

America was able to devise answers to development alone and at its own pace for two reasons—reasons which make it possible for Americans to be thankful that our thirteen colonies won their independence in a simpler day.

*Ibid., July 27, 1966, pp. 17340-41.
†Ibid., June 5, 1967, pp. 14604-06.

One of these reasons is that we came to independence at a time when it was possible for us to be truly independent—to hold ourselves aloof from the rest of the world.

Though we were impoverished, we were left alone to build a nation and find our destiny. For decades, we found a watchword in Washington's farewell address: "It is our true policy to steer clear of permanent alliances, with any portion of the foreign world."

For us, non-alignment was an easy task.

The second reason is that, unlike some thirty new African nations, we became independent in a time when technological change was slow and slight.

Our arms were rudimentary, but they fired as well—sometimes better—than the Naval cannon and muskets of imperial Britain.

Our economy was simple, but then so was that of every country, in a time when concepts like gross national product were a century away from definition.

And our industry was primitive—for there was no other sort of industry. It was conducted on spinning wheels and blacksmiths' anvils. The world had not yet even dreamed of megatons or megawatts, aluminum smelters of titanium airplanes.

In short, newly independent America had time—time to explore itself, time to educate itself, time to learn new vocabularies and new technologies as they were devised.

By contrast, the new nations of Africa have been called to the main stage immediately—to go from the spear to the slide rule, from disunited tribes to the United Nations virtually in months.

Can this transition be made with the speed which the influential young men and women of Africa believe necessary?

That is not a question for an outsider to answer. It is a central question in virtually every new African nation. Their answers undoubtedly will vary. I would suggest, however, that there are two irreducible factors to which we must reconcile ourselves, factors which must limit the telescoping of time on this continent.

The first of these factors is human capabilities. The education of intelligent men and women in complex skills can be improved in quality. It can be enlarged in quantity. But no amount of good motives, nor wealth, nor wisdom can, without the passage of time, produce the pool of skilled and educated African men and women who are required to manage the affairs and fuel the spirit of a modern nation.

You here in this eminent institution will be frontiersmen in that effort. But not until your numbers swell—as surely they will—can this country and your sister countries on this continent find the manpower with which to generate widespread growth.

The second factor to which I believe we must reconcile ourselves follows the first. It is suggested occasionally that the development time gap could be overcome if only developed nations like the United States would more fully meet responsibilities of assistance to the underdeveloped world.

As a son of a free country and as a friend of Africa, I am unable to accept this case. It is theoretically possible for major industrial powers to send huge sums and corps of technicians to build and operate factories, or transportation systems, or railroads. And by doing so, they would help build nations in Africa. But they would not be African nations in Africa. As we oppose neo-colonialism, so should be oppose such a false solution.

President Johnson has observed accurately that development cannot be exported. And President Nyerere has said of his people, they "recognize that the task of economic development is a long and heavy one . . . our people do not believe that it is better to be a wealthy slave than a poor free man."

By no means do I wish to suggest that African nations can avoid losing their independence only by refusing outside assistance. Nor do I wish to suggest that already-developed nations should not assist those parts of humanity who are coming late to political manhood. What I do believe is that, in the interests both of developed and developing nations, developmental assistance must be carefully offered—and it must be carefully received.

In his speech on Africa a year ago, President Johnson outlined a policy for such assistance, noting that "The world has now reached a stage where some of the most effective means of economic growth can best be achieved in large units commanding large resources and large markets. Most nation-states are too small, when acting alone, to assure the welfare of all of their people."

This is the principle which underlies our present policy of aid for Africa—cooperation among donors and cooperation among recipients.

This is not a new philosophy for us. Nearly a third of the aid we have provided in the past has been for projects benefitting not merely one country but several.

*   *   *

New York Times *Editorial on Vice President Hubert H. Humphrey's Visit to Africa**

January 16, 1968

Vice President Humphrey seems to have accomplished admirably the twin purposes of his brief visit to nine African countries; he saw their problems at first hand and he was able to reassure his hosts of an enduring American interest in them.

There was some risk that as this energetic and sensitive observer became caught up in African problems his natural exuberance might arouse expectations of American assistance not likely to be fulfilled in the near future. The White House must have been interested in reports from Ghana quoting Mr. Humphrey as saying that he and President Johnson would take the fight for more foreign aid directly to the American people and that the aid program "should be doubled or tripled."

The only aid programs Mr. Humphrey announced en route, however, were modest ones long in preparation. His hosts, well aware that Africa's share of the smallest aid appropriation in twenty years is unlikely to exceed $160 million, made no specific requests. They were more interested in acquainting him with their long-range development plans.

We are glad to note that the Vice President stopped off in Zambia, not on his original itinerary. It would have been regrettable and misunderstood had he passed up this opportunity to demonstrate solidarity with President Kaunda and reiterate American opposition to the rebel regime in Rhodesia.

His trip obviously restoked a long-standing interest of Mr. Humphrey in Africa. He must now persuade an Administration with many higher priorities that a more constant and more consistent American effort in Africa is necessary and possible.

The New York Times, Jan. 16, 1968.

*Speech by Senator Edward Brooke (Massachusetts) Before
the Senate on African Objectives and American Policy**

April 20, 1968

    *   *   *

Let me make clear at the outset my conviction that our preoccupation with Southeast Asia is leading us to neglect other areas of growing significance in the developing world. My attempt to assess the current status of Africa's economy and politics from this standpoint is an individual effort to insure that, in the midst of the Asian conflict, the major issues in Africa receive attention in the American Government. In my opinion, one of the most important roles which Members of the Senate can play is to see that the intense focus of our Government on today's urgent business does not cause us to lose sight of other questions we must be prepared to meet if tomorrow's affairs are not to be even more troubled.

The crisis in Asia, in which we are so embroiled today, was brewing at a time when our attention was focused on other matters: on Europe, on the international monetary sysstem, on winning the Second World War. For many years Asia was regarded as the domain of our allies in Europe, of American missionaries and businessmen, and of a few "Asian experts" in the State Department.

Today, the situation has changed. We are deeply involved in Asia, in a contest that has many fronts and many ramifications. Now it is Africa that is regarded as the domain of our allies in Europe, of American missionaries and businessmen, and of a few experts in the State Department. We tend to think of Africa as a maze of tiny independent states—41, in fact—which are economically nonviable, politically tumultuous, and relatively outside the range of our immediate national interest.

This is not so. Botswana, one of the countries which I visited, is larger than the State of Texas: Yet it had never, in almost 2 years of independence, received an official American visitor. Another state, with one-quarter the territory and population of the United States itself, has been engaged in a bloody civil war for many months, using sophisticated weapons, tanks, and jet aircraft. Yet until recently its plight had received relatively little attention in the American press, despite the massacre of untold thousands of men, women, and children on both sides of the conflict.

In the five states of Southern Africa, over 23 million people are denied the right to participate in making the laws by which they are governed, and are segregated and classified on a purely racial basis. Trouble is brewing in this area, for as the white minority governments have become more repressive, numerous well-organized liberation groups have turned to violence to secure the rights of the majority. It behooves us to acquaint ourselves with trends and conditions in this vital region.

Africa is already an important force in world affairs, and this importance will inevitably increase as the Africa nations come into their own. The continent is three times the size of the United States; it accounts for 20 percent of the land mass of the world. It has a population of over 250 million, which is larger than that of the United States. It has 40 percent of the world's potential hydroelectric power; 65 percent of the world's gold supply; 96 percent of the world's diamonds; and at least 25 percent of

**Congressional Record*, April 20, 1968, pp. 4558-60; 4566-67.

its known copper reserves. In addition, large deposits of offshore oil have been discovered along the western coast of Africa. The bulge of West Africa, notably Guinea and Ghana, possesses some of the world's richest sources of bauxite, from which aluminum is made. Africa has twice the uncut forest area of the United States, more arable land and grazing land than the entire Soviet Union. Africa, in short, is a wealth of untapped resources. Its present level of crop production can be multiplied many times over by the use of mechanical implements, by improved methods of water control, by using fertilizers and insecticides, and by bringing more acres under cultivation.

In terms of conventional warfare, Africa occupies a strategic position in the world as well. During World War II, it was from North Africa that the great battles were fought to determine who would control the vital supply route of Suez, the Mediterranean and Gibraltar. It was from the French-speaking states to the south that a large portion of the supplies and reinforcements were derived. Naval bases in southern Africa kept open the alternate supply route around the Cape of Good Hope.

Even today, Europe depends heavily on access to the Suez Canal and the Mediterranean supply route for its oil supplies. This water route is still the most effective means of exchanging goods with the nations to the east—including such important trading partners of Western Europe as Australia, India, and New Zealand. At times when the Suez Canal is closed, as it has been since last year's Middle East war, the alternate route around the cape of Africa assumes a new and greater importance. South Africa has the only harbor south of the Sahara where major naval and commercial vessels can dock, refuel, and undergo repairs, though several of the countries of West Africa, such as Senegal, Guinea, Nigeria, and the Ivory Coast, are deepening their shipping channels and may assume a larger role in the years to come.

Ethiopia, South Africa, and the Malagasy Republic have cooperated in the American space program, providing valuable sites for radar and tracking installations. Other African states have played helpful roles in a variety of joint scientific technical, and commercial ventures with the United States.

African nations have also attracted a growing share of U.S. trade and investment. American private investment in Africa now totals more than $2 billion, while the volume of trade with all the African states has more than doubled in the last decade. Our annual exports to Africa increased from $623 million in 1955 to $1.2 billion in 1964. At the same time our imports from Africa rose from $534 million in 1955 to nearly $1 billion in 1964.

All of these statistics are important. By any yardstick—economic, political, geographical—Africa's role in the world is large and expanding.

*   *   *

The United States has enjoyed three political assets in its relations with Africa: It is not and never has been a colonial power, it has a large population of African descent, and it is a nation whose own democratic revolution gave it a certain kinship with the new nations. From the standpoint of the new African states and of this country, these factors argued for warm and cordial relations.

But those relations have not developed as rapidly or as richly as might have been expected. There are many reasons for this, but the dominant one has probably been the problem of scale. So many African states have become independent so quickly that the United States has not been able to cope with them as effectively as we might desire.

*   *   *

There were two primary factors involved in the revisions of U.S. aid to Africa, which were decided on in 1968 and put into effect this year. One was the report of the former American Ambassador to Ethiopia, the Honorable Edward M. Korry, on "U.S. Policies and Programs" in Africa. The other was a congressional limitation on the total number of developing countries which could receive U.S. assistance.

The main thrust of the Korry report was that because African development will be a long and difficult process, American assistance should concentrate as much as possible on regional and multinational programs which will have a long-term impact. The report argued that bilateral aid should be given only to those few countries whose size, population resources, and performance afford the best opportunity for significant progress.

*   *   *

There is, of course, merit to the approach advocated by the Korry report, and there were defensible justifications for a congressional limit to the number of nations eligible to receive direct U.S. assistance.

For many nations, regional cooperation may be the best solution to a number of their development problems. The regional approach to assistance received the endorsement of two Vice Presidents of the African Development Bank with whom I spoke; they pointed out that the Bank itself is emphasizing regional programs, and hopes to receive some capitalization from the United States.

But while regional assistance is important, African countries still need considerable bilateral assistance as well. The two forms of assistance can and ought to be complementary, not mutually exclusive.

*   *   *

I believe that American assistance should retain more of its original, bilateral character and should be geared to the development of human resources. Bilateral programs may be hard to administer effectively, but they are certainly worth the additional effort. We should grant longer term loans at less interest; schools, health centers, and even small businesses will not liquidate their initial costs in short periods. Such programs, designed to supplement the assistance of international bodies and former colonial powers, would be of greater value to the African states than an exaggerated emphasis upon regional planning. In recommending such an approach, I am also taking into consideration the benefits which such a program would have to the United States.

*   *   *

First. While there are good reasons for the United States to support various regional efforts, there are also good reasons for this country to maintain ample bilateral relations, both economic and political, with many African states. Trade, as well as aid, ought to be expanded.

Second. We should avoid any obsessive concern with the risks of the cold war in Africa. To be sure, the struggle for influence still exists. But it is contained both by the growing maturity of the great powers and their increased desire to limit the hazards of direct confrontation, and by the strongly independent spirit of the Africans themselves. We should respect this independence, and the policy of nonalinement which is has engendered. The African nations are friendly to the United States, but as Uganda's President Obote observed to me, "One cannot say that because someone is your friend, that friend's enemy is your enemy."

Third. We should make certain that our relations with the majority of African states are not clouded by the slightest suspicion of special interest in or sympathy for the minority regimes in southern Africa. If we are to enjoy beneficial relations with Africa as a whole, it is imperative that we be willing to sacrifice the ephemeral advantages of good relations with South Africa, Rhodesia, and Portugal, so long as they persist in oppressing millions of Africans. Only by standing with the just demands of the African majority, only by fidelity to our own principles, will we be able to lay a sturdy foundation for our future relations with the continent at large.

Fourth. We should judge African political development according to the distinctive situation of the Africans themselves, not by our standards. A country which is 90-percent illiterate cannot be expected to operate an elaborate two-party system with the range of choices available to a more advanced nation. In some cases, one-party government may be the lesser evil in the initial stages of national evolution. We should neither condone nor condemn such regimes in general, but should measure them individually by their responsiveness to the perceived needs of their people and by the efficacy of their attempts to build a more democratic system in the shortest possible time. Where the alternatives are chaotic tribalism or fierce dictatorship, a humane central government based on a single party with wide popular participation is hardly to be despised.

Fifth. We must put issues ahead of personalities in our relations with African countries. We should gear our own decisions to our mutual needs and interests, not to the individual characteristics of particular leaders.

In building a sound basis for future relations, it is especially important that Africans and Americans come to know each other better. In particular, I hope that other Members of Congress will have occasion to visit Africa, to become acquainted personally with the peoples and governments of that continent, and to assess for themselves the vital business now under way there. It is of particular concern to me that in recent years, of all the funds spent on congressional travel, less than 2 percent was expended on travel to Africa. Similarly, I hope that increasing numbers of African students, officials, businessmen, and others will have the opportunity to spend time in the United States. A closer association of this character can be mutually rewarding, both in terms of human understanding and in terms of joint accomplishment.

Nothing the United States does will be sufficient to assure the success of African development; as always, the outcome hinges primarily on the efforts of Africans themselves. But it is no small accomplishment to be an ally in the struggle for the freedom and welfare of over 250 million people. That role America can play in Africa, together with other developed nations. That role America should play, to the limit of its capacity.

*   *   *

Speech by Senator George McGovern (South Dakota) Before the Senate on Revenues and Expenditure Control Act of 1968, Opposing Military Aid to African Countries*

June 21, 1968

*   *   *

Here is a chance to save hundreds and hundreds of millions of dollars. That is where some of this $6 billion should be saved. Tell me why I should vote for hundreds of millions of dollars of American taxpayers' money for American military aid in Africa, where the per capita income of most of the people is less than $100 a year. We are sending them bullets when we should be sending them bread and literacy. Bread and literacy will not only make them free in a course of time but also will get us out of supporting dictatorships, military juntas, and tyrants, for which our money is being used around the world in the form of military aid. And we call ourselves a democracy. What hypocrisy. So much of our action in foreign policy is anything but supporting freedom. We support tyranny when we support the group in South Vietnam that we are maintaining and for whom we are sacrificing the lives of American boys. Most of them are former officers in the French military establishment. We can make some savings there. Also, we could save hundreds of millions of dollars in Africa.

*   *   *

Speech by Secretary of State William P. Rogers on
"U.S. Foreign Policy: Some Major Issues"†

April 6, 1969

*   *   *

Our relations with that other great continent—Africa—are as new as our relations with Latin America are old and established. In the space of two decades, Africa has been transformed from an externally dominated continent to one of over 40 free and independent states—states now playing an important role in the councils of nations.

Yesterday the United States, in conformity with our belief in the self-determination of people, welcomed the emergence of Africa to independence. Today Africa is engaged in consolidating its nationhood and in struggling with the problems of economic development. The former administering authorities in Africa are currently making the largest external contributions to help strengthen and develop the young institutions of these new nations. We have contributed as well, both in economic and social terms. Over 50,000 African students have studied in the United States in the postwar period; in a continent seriously deficient in highly trained professions, training here has made a major contribution to the building of their nations.

We hope to continue to contribute toward that economic and social development. And in particular we wish to encourage the increased regional political and economic cooperation which African leaders have seen as necessary for their growth and stability.

*Ibid., June 21, 1968, p. 7488.
†*Department of State Bulletin*, Apr. 14, 1969, pp. 310-11.

Progress in the southern part of Africa also remains a vital goal of the new African states and one with which we basically sympathize. Self-determination, majority rule with minority rights, and human equality are the product of our own practical experience and our practical idealism; it will be our policy to support them in Africa as well. Our dedication to these goals is the result of our history, a product of our search for basic answers to human aspirations. By the same token, Africa's effort to realize these goals throughout the continent is a product of its history and its aspirations. In this situation, there exists a broad community of understanding between Africa and the United States, dramatized by the fact that some 22 million Americans trace their origin to Africa. There will no doubt be differences between us and some of our African colleagues on methods and timing, but to the extent that they are committed to the above goals there will be none on objective.

Because of our interest in the peaceful development of the independent African nations, our concern is also deep when it is disrupted. It is now manifest over the crisis in Nigeria.

The situation in that bitterly divided land is as complicated as it is tragic and—so far—as elusive of solution. Moderation and reason are having difficulty in overcoming the legacies of ancient tribal feuds and hatreds.

The suspicions each side feels toward the other and their respective doubts about each other's objectives continue to block a negotiated settlement.

The United States has honored the wishes of the African nations to settle the conflict under their own auspices and we intend to resist any temptation for United States political intervention. We are refusing to permit the sale of United States arms to either side. We continue to support the efforts of the Organization of African Unity and the Commonwealth Secretariat to bring the fighting to an end and would support a United Nations role should it become feasible.

At the same time, the United States Government, reflecting the deep humanitarian concern of the American people, has made massive contributions to the relief effort and has exerted strenuous efforts to break the impasse hampering deliveries of desperately needed food and medicine. More than $31 million has already been contributed for the relief of persons on both sides of the battleline.

To improve our contribution in this regard I recently appointed Mr. Clyde Ferguson as Special Coordinator for relief in the Nigerian conflict. He is now exploring means of expanding the flow of supplies to both sides. He has consulted with international relief officials, with governments contributing to the relief effort, with the OAU, and with authorities in both Nigeria and the Biafran area. We hope that the international relief effort can be substantially increased as a result of his labors.

*Report to the Congress by President Richard M. Nixon on a New Strategy for Peace**

February 18, 1970

We know you have no easy task in seeking to assure a fair share of Africa's wealth to all her peoples. We know that the realization of equality and human dignity throughout the continent will be long and arduous in coming. But you can be sure as you pursue these difficult goals that the United States shares your hopes and your confidence in the future.
President's Message to the Sixth Annual Assembly of the Organization of African Unity, September 6, 1969.

Ibid., Mar. 9, 1970, pp. 305-8.

In this greeting last September to the summit meeting of the Organization of African Unity, I expressed America's determination to support our African friends as they work to fulfill their continent's high promise. The unprecedented visit of the Secretary of State to Africa this month is a confirmation of this support.

One of the most dramatic and far-reaching changes of the last decade was the emergence of an independent Africa.

Only ten years ago, 32 countries covering nearly five-sixths of the Continent were still colonies, their voices silent in world affairs. Today, these are all sovereign nations, proudly determined to shape their own future. And contrary to fears so often voiced at their birth, these nations did not succumb to Communist subversion. Africa is one of the world's most striking examples, in fact, of the failure of the appeal of Communism in the new nations. African states now comprise one-third of the membership of the United Nations. African issues have become important moral and political questions. African views justly merit and receive the attention of the world.

But this rebirth of a continent has been hazardous as well as hopeful. Africa was the scene of many of the recurrent crises of the 1960's. There was the factional strife and international rivalry in the Congo, an arms race between Ethiopia and Somalia, the establishment of white minority rule in Southern Rhodesia, and the agonizing human loss in the Nigerian civil war.

The Continent still faces grave problems. The imbalances of economies and institutions once under full external control are only too evident today. Arbitrary boundaries drawn in European chancelleries left many African countries vulnerable to tribal strife; and nowhere is the task of nation-building more taxing. Not least, Africans face the formidable task of strengthening their sense of identity and preserving traditional culture as their societies make the transition to modernity.

Over the last decade, America has not had a clear conception of its relationship with post-colonial Africa and its particular problems. Because of our traditional support of self-determination, and Africa's historic ties with so many of our own citizens, our sympathy and friendship for the new Africa were spontaneous. But without a coherent concept to structure our policies, we allowed ourselves to concentrate more on temporary crises than on their underlying causes. We expressed our support for Africa more by lofty phrases than by candid and constructive dialogue.

Just as we focus our policies elsewhere to meet a new era, we will be clear with ourselves and with our African friends on America's interests and role in the Continent. We have two major concerns regarding the future of Africa:

—That the Continent be free of great power rivalry or conflict in any form. This is even more in Africa's interest than in ours.

—That Africa realize its potential to become a healthy and prosperous region in the international community. Such an Africa would not only be a valuable economic partner for all regions, but would also have a greater stake in the maintenance of a durable world peace.

These interests will guide our policies toward the most demanding challenges facing Africa in the 1970's.

The primary challenge facing the African Continent is economic development.

If the 1960's were years of high hopes and high rhetoric, the 1970's will have to be years of hard work and hard choices. The African nations and those who assist them must decide together on strict priorities in employing the relatively limited development capital available to the Continent. In doing this, Africa and its friends can benefit from several lessons of the past decade.

Certainly development will not always proceed as rapidly as the Africans and their friends hope. In many countries, needs will outrun local and international resources for some time. But solid and steady progress will be made if our common development investment concentrates on those basic if undramatic building blocks of economic growth—health, education, agriculture, transportation and local development. In particular, Africa will realize the full advantage of its own rich material resources only as it nurtures the wealth of its human resources. In close coordination with the Africans' own efforts, the United States will direct our aid at these fundamental building blocks.

Another lesson we have learned from the 1960's is the need for close regional cooperation, in order for Africa to get the most from development resources. The United States will work with other donors and the Africans to help realize the potential for cooperative efforts—by the support which we are giving, for example, to the East African Economic Community and the promising regional groupings in West Africa. We will recognize, however, that regional action is not the only road for African development. In some cases, for geographic or political reasons, it will not work.

Our assistance throughout the Continent will be flexible and imaginative. We will make a particular effort—including programs of technical assistance and new encouragement of private investment—to help those countires not in a position to participate in regional projects.

We have learned that there are no panaceas for African development. Each country faces its own problems, and the solutions to them must spring from the national experience of each country. Foreign ideologies have often proven notoriously irrelevant, and even tragically wasteful, as designs for African progress. The most creative conceptual approaches to African development should come, of course, from the Africans themselves. Outsiders cannot prescribe the political framework most conducive to Africa's economic growth. In some countries, progress has depended upon stability. Yet elsewhere, solutions to local problems have been found amid periods of uncertainty or even turmoil.

The United States will measure African progress in terms of long-run social and economic accomplishment, and not in the political flux which is likely to accompany growth.

In Africa, as throughout the developing world, our goal in providing development aid is clear. We want the Africans to build a better life for themselves and their children. We want to see an Africa free of poverty and disease, and free too of economic or political dependence on any outside power. And we want Africans to build this future as they think best, because in that way both our help and their efforts will be most relevant to their needs.

As Secretary Rogers said in Ethiopia on February 12:

> As a developed nation, we recognize a special obligation to assist in the economic development of Africa. Our resources and our capacity are not unlimited. We have many demands at home. We will, however, continue to seek the means, both directly and in cooperation with others, to contribute more effectively to economic development in Africa.

Africa's second challenge in the 1970's will be to weather the inevitable strains which will come with the further development of nations which house a great diversity of peoples and cultures.

We have witnessed tragic manifestations of this problem in the civil strife in the Congo and Nigeria. The process of national integration may be stormy elsewhere.

Such turmoil presents a tempting target to forces outside Africa ready to exploit the problems of change to their own advantage. But foreign intervention, whatever its form or source, will not serve the long-run interests of the Africans themselves.

The United States approaches these problems of national integration with a policy which clearly recognizes the limits as well as the obligations of our partnership with Africa:

—We will not intervene in the internal affairs of African nations. We strongly support their right to be independent, and we will observe their right to deal with their own problems independently. We believe that the national integrity of African states must be respected.

—However, we will distinguish between noninterference politically and the humanitarian obligation to help lessen human suffering.

Finally, consulting our own interests, we will help our friends in Africa to help themselves when they are threatened by outside forces attempting to subvert their independent development. It is another lesson of the 1960's, however, that African defense against subversion, like African development, must be borne most directly by Africans rather than by outsiders.

The third challenge facing Africa is the deep-seated tension in the southern sixth of the Continent.

Clearly there is no question of the United States condoning, or acquiescing in, the racial policies of the white-ruled regimes. For moral as well as historical reasons, the United States stands firmly for the principles of racial equality and self-determination.

At the same time, the 1960's have shown all of us—Africa and her friends alike—that the racial problems in the southern region of the Continent will not be solved quickly. These tensions are deeply rooted in the history of the region, and thus in the psychology of both black and white.

These problems must be solved. But there remains a real issue in how best to achieve their resolution. Though we abhor the racial policies of the white regimes, we cannot agree that progressive change in Southern Africa is furthered by force. The history of the area shows all too starkly that violence and the counter-violence it inevitably provokes will only make more difficult the task of those on both sides working for progress on the racial question.

The United States warmly welcomes, therefore, the recent Lusaka Manifesto, a declaration by African leaders calling for a peaceful settlement of the tensions in Southern Africa. That statesmanlike document combines a commitment to human dignity with a perceptive understanding of the depth and complexity of the racial problem in the area—a combination which we hope will guide the policies of Africa and her friends as they seek practical policies to deal with this anguishing question.

American policy toward Africa, then, will illustrate our general approach to building an enduring peace. Our stake in the Continent will not rest on today's crisis, on political maneuvering for passing advantage, or on the strategic priority we assign it. Our goal is to help sustain the process by which Africa will gradually realize economic progress to match its aspirations.

We must understand, however, that this process is only beginning. Its specific course is unclear. Its success depends in part on how we and the Africans move now in the climate as well as the substance of our relations.

—Africa's friends must find a new tone of candor in their essential dialogue with the Continent. All too often over the past decade the United States and others have been guilty of telling proud young nations, in misguided condescension, only what we thought they wanted to hear. But I know from many talks with Africans, including two trips to the Continent in 1957 and 1967, that Africa's new leaders are pragmatic and practical as well as proud, realistic as well as idealistic. It will be a test of diplomacy for all concerned to face squarely common problems and differences of view. The United States will do all it can to establish this new dialogue.

—Most important, there must be new and broader forms of mobilizing the external resources for African development. The pattern of the multilateral consortium which in the past few years has aided Ghana should be employed more widely elsewhere. This will require the closest cooperation between the Africans and those who assist them. There is much to be gained also if we and others can help devise ways in which the more developed African states can share their resources with their African neighbors.

—The United States is firmly committed to noninterference in the Continent, but Africa's future depends also on the restraint of other great powers. No one should seek advantage from Africa's need for assistance, or from future instability. In his speech on February 12, Secretary Rogers affirmed that:

> We have deep respect for the independence of the African nations. We are not involved in their internal affairs. We want our relations with them to be on a basis of mutual respect, mutual trust and equality. We have no desire for any domination of any country or any area and have no desire for any special influence in Africa, except the influences that naturally and mutually develop among friends.

The Africa of the 1970's will need schools rather than sympathy, roads rather than rhetoric, farms rather than formulas, local development rather than lengthy sermons. We will do what we can in a spirit of constructive cooperation rather than by vague declarations of good will. The hard facts must be faced by Africans and their friends; and the hard work in every corner of the Continent must be done. A durable peace cannot be built if the nations of Africa are not true partners in the gathering prosperity and security which fortify that peace.

State Department Statement on the United States and Africa in the Seventies Submitted by Secretary Rogers to President Nixon*

March 26, 1970

Africa, for many reasons, deserves the active attention and support of the United States. It is in our national interest to cooperate with African countries in their endeavors to improve conditions of life and to help in their efforts to build an equitable political and economic order in which all can effectively share.

*Ibid., Apr. 20, 1970, pp. 513-21.

The energy and talent of the peoples of Africa represent a significant force in world development and world trade. It is a continent of impressive opportunities for future growth and development—one destined to play an increasingly important role in the world. Africans have taken much of their political inspiration from the United States. Their thousands of students in the United States today—and the many Americans studying and teaching in Africa—continue the tradition of this exchange. More than a few Africans who studied in America became leaders of independence of their countries.

Many of our ties to Africa have been long-standing. The Sultan of Morocco recognized our own independence at an early date and exchanged diplomatic correspondence with George Washington. The oldest American treaty which has been continuously in force was signed with Morocco in 1787. We signed a similar treaty with Tunisia in 1797. Close U.S. ties to Liberia date from 1816 and with Ethiopia from 1903. And Americans have long identified themselves with the pursuit of independence and freedom in Africa, as elsewhere.

Africa is growing closer to the United States. Communications with Africa are rapidly developing, and communication links with other continents through Intelstat are now in operation and more African earth stations are being constructed. Two major American airlines serve the continent. Overflight rights are important to our commerce and to our scientific efforts. We have important communications facilities in both West and East Africa. Our space and scientific programs rely on the cooperation of the peoples and governments of Africa.

The resources of Africa are products which we purchase substantially in international trade: rubber, petroleum, bauxite, timber, coffee, cocoa, minerals and precious stones, to name a few. They are important to the Africans as a primary source of their wealth.

America's links with the peoples of Africa have been extensive. Missionaries have established schools and hospitals throughout the continent and have lived and worked in Africa many years before official relations were established. We have demonstrated humanitarian concern for the people of the continent in our provision of help and relief in countless ways.

And, finally, we are linked by the cultural fact that one out of every ten Americans has his origins in Africa.

We seek a relationship of constructive cooperation with the nations of Africa—a cooperative and equal relationship with all who wish it. We are prepared to have diplomatic relations under conditions of mutual respect with all the nations of the continent. We want no military allies, no spheres of influence, no big power competition in Africa. Our policy is a policy related to African countries and not a policy based upon our relations with non-African countries.

As early as 1957, when he returned from a mission to Africa on behalf of President Eisenhower, the then Vice President Nixon recommended that the U.S. assign a higher priority to our relations with an Africa, which he recognized to be of growing importance to the United States. Specifically he said:

> The United States must come to know these leaders better, to understand their hopes and aspirations, and to support them in their plans and programs for strengthening their own nations and contributing to world peace and stability. To this end, we must encourage the greatest possible interchange of persons and ideas with the leaders and peoples of these countries. We must assure the strongest possible diplomatic and consular representation to

those countries and stand ready to consult these countries on all matters affecting their interests and ours.

Personal relationships between members of the Administration and African leaders have been widely expanded. President Nixon met leaders from 10 African countries during the past year. I met a number of African leaders during 1969 and in the fall met and discussed common issues with 26 African Foreign Ministers at the United Nations General Assembly. The meetings included and contributed to closer understanding even with states with which we have no current diplomatic relations; in the case of Mauritania the discussion with the Foreign Minister in New York was the first step toward a resumption of relations which has now taken place. In February I became the first Secretary of State to tour Africa. I visited 10 African countries. I also spoke with leaders of the Organization of African Unity, the UN Economic Commission for Africa and other regional bodies. I met in Kinshasa with the American chiefs of mission and principal officers from the African countries in which we are represented.

It is through open and honest exchanges such as these that we can better understand the needs and aspirations of the peoples and governments of Africa and they can learn of the objectives and problems we Americans face at this time and place in history.

Some of my countrymen used to long for the luxury of isolation behind the protection of two great oceans. But the time for that has passed. The continental size of the United States, its vast productive power, its technological capabilities, its interdependence with other parts of this planet impel us into active participation in world affairs.

But in this participation we do not seek any kind of domination. We seek with all nations the closest relationship which is mutually acceptable and beneficial, but seek it with full respect for diversity among nations.

An effective relationship with Africa depends on an understanding of Africa and its needs. We have sought in our discussions and visits with African leaders and African peoples to determine how they define these needs.

They have spoken to us first of their strong desire to satisfy the aspirations of their people for a better life. They want to do this through economic cooperation. They want economic assistance now to make themselves less dependent later on foreign resources. They look to trade as a more equitable relationship than aid. They want investment in which they are partners.

After decades of being governed from afar, they want respect for human dignity. They want to abolish discrimination. They want equality throughout the continent.

They want self-determination throughout the continent. They want respect for the independence of the new nations and for their sovereignty. They welcome cooperation with other nations but they do not want intervention.

They want to build political and social institutions based on their own cultural patterns. They want to adapt ideas from abroad to their own psychology and spirit.

They want respect for the boundaries of Africa and security for each nation within these boundaries. They want recognition that, within its infinite diversity, Africa has a cohesion and a unity of its own, such as represented by the Organization of African Unity.

The United States desires to be responsive to Africa, even though there are limitations on our capacities and our resources.

We desire economic relations on a basis of mutual benefit and respect. Recognizing the need for capital and technical assistance, the United States directly and in cooperation with others will continue to help. The U.S. will pursue more active programs of trade and private investment, with full recognition of African sovereignty.

We will continue to support wider cooperation on a regional and continental basis among African countries.

The United States will continue to stand for racial equality and self-determination looking for peaceful and evolutionary solutions to advance these goals. We will help to provide economic alternatives for the small independent states in southern Africa.

We will avoid supplying arms in southern Africa, and we will persist in our support for self-determination.

We will respect the institutions which the Africans themselves create. While we in this country have a preference for democratic procedures, we recognize that the forces for change and nation-building which operate in Africa may create governmental patterns not necessarily consistent with such procedures.

*   *   *

An American economic assistance program in Africa is in United States national interests. We wish to see African countries develop and take their rightful place in cooperative international efforts to resolve worldwide problems. The drive and determination to develop must come from the African countries themselves. But at this point in their development, when per capita annual incomes average about $135, most of these countries need substantial external assistance to achieve rates of progress responsive to the minimum aspirations of their more than 300 million people for a better life. Our principal concern, therefore, is how most effectively to make capital assistance and technical knowledge from the developed nations available to these developing nations.

Ever since the wave of independence swept through Africa in the late '50's and early '60's, Western European nations and multidonor organizations have provided 60 to 70 percent of economic assistance to Africa. Because of their strong traditional and historic links to Africa, we hope the European nations will continue to provide the bulk of foreign assistance to Africa. But the United States also has deep and special ties to Africa. We should do our fair share in support of the independence and growth of Africa nations.

The total U.S. share has, in fact, averaged about $350 million a year for the past several years. This is about 20 percent of all external assistance to Africa. We intend to maintain a substantial contribution, hopefully with a larger share in economic development programs.

Our bilateral assistance program has included resources from A.I.D., PL-480, the Export-Import Bank and the Peace Corps. In the form of loans, grants and personnel, it has reached some thirty-five African countries. It has assisted national development programs, as well as regional projects. We have worked through regional organizations, and jointly with other donors. The United States will continue to provide assistance to those nations which have been given emphasis in the past. At the same time, mindful of the needs throughout the continent, we have decided to make our approach to African assistance more flexible than it has recently been:

—We will to the extent permitted by legislation also provide limited assistance in other African countries to projects which contribute significantly to increased production and revenues.

—We will continue to emphasize aid to regional programs and projects, giving special attention to innovative ways to make our efforts effective.

—We wish to do more to strengthen African economic institutions including the UN Economic Commission for Africa, the African Development Bank, the OAU's Scientific, Technical, and Research Commission and subregional organizations.

—We will utilize food aid to advance economic development objectives and to help tide nations over emergency food shortages.

—We will more and more orient the program of the Peace Corps to meet the technical, educational and social development needs of African nations.

—We will concentrate our economic assistance in the coming years in the fields of agriculture, education, health including demographic and family planning, transportation and communications.

—We are actively studying the requirement that U.S. loans to Africa be used almost exclusively for the purchase of American goods and services.

We intend to provide more assistance to Africa through international institutions and multidonor arrangements. We contribute 40 percent of the budget of the UN Development Program; 40 percent of its program is now being directed to Africa. We also contribute 40 percent of the budget of the International Development Association; in the past year its loans to Africa have risen substantially to 20 percent of all its loans, and the prospect is that this proportion will continue to rise.

We are seeking a substantial increase in the absolute amount of United States contributions to these institutions. The United States is now engaged in discussions with other members of IDA, under the leadership of the World Bank, which we hope will lead to larger contributions by all donor members of IDA. We have proposed to Congress an increased contribution to UNDP.

In addition to our participation in international organizations, we are working more closely with other donors in World Bank and IMF [International Monetary Fund] sponsored consultative groups for several African countries, and in projects involving several donors. With limited total aid resources, we believe these mechanisms greatly increase the effectiveness of foreign aid.

We also look forward to joining with other non-African donors in support of the African Development Bank. This young institution, which has the financial backing of thirty-one African governments, has prospects for promoting significant pan-African cooperation in economic progress. It has already raised $67 million from its members in fully convertible currencies. It needs, however, a source of funds that could be loaned to its members on concessional terms. We are participating in discussions with other non-African donors which we hope will lead to the creation of special funds for this purpose. In the meantime, we are assisting the Bank directly in its efforts to develop and carry out urgently needed projects in its member countries.

An important portion of our assistance to Africa supports regional projects and regional institutions. In Addis Ababa, in the United Nations Economic Commission for Africa, one sees one of the most successful forms of international economic cooperation. Any serious appraisal of the development prospects in Africa makes clear the need for much greater regional cooperation. Many African nations are small; their national boundaries frequently split natural economic regions. Most national markets are too small to support industry using modern technology. Africans have already demonstrated their recognition of the need for regional cooperation by establishing regional educational, technical and research institutes, economic communities, common markets, common financial arrangements and even common currencies. We hope to remain in the forefront of cooperative efforts to foster regional cooperation in Africa.

Our Food for Peace programs have been a major means of economic assistance in many African countries, through credit sales, food-for-work, donations and emergency relief efforts. In the past few years, 40 percent of our aid to Africa has taken these forms. We will maintain this assistance wherever food aid can make an important contribution to economic development or help meet serious emergencies.

The Peace Corps conducts programs in twenty-three African countries. This, too, will be continued as long as African governments find the Peace Corps' efforts useful to them. The Peace Corps is seeking to intensify its recruitment of experienced and highly qualified personnel in order to emphasize technically oriented positions needed in development efforts. The Peace Corps is also moving ahead to make qualified volunteers available to international organizations working in the development field.

In our programs for youth, we shall intensify our efforts to establish personal relationships between African and American young political leaders, technicians, students and businessmen.

We shall expand inter-African scholarships and third-country training programs for youth within Africa, while maintaining traditional exchanges with the United States.

We shall encourage more of our own country's diverse public and private groups to learn about and from Africans.

We shall encourage the greater utilization of American citizens from the private sector to meet development needs in Africa. The International Executive Service Corps, an American private organization which recruits American businessmen for short-term service in developing nations has pointed the way.

*   *   *

The U.S. Government recognizes the great potential of African labor to play a constructive role in the sound economic development of free and independent African nations. We have, therefore, consistently sought friendly understanding of the labor movements of African countries. We hope we can continue to make some significant contributions.

It is our policy to continue to support and encourage African governments in the development and execution of comprehensive labor manpower programs. And while recognizing African preferences for a distinctive African approach to trade union matters, we encourage close fraternal relations between the leaders and members of the African trade unions.and Western national and international labor organizations.

There has been a steady growth in U.S. private investment in Africa since most of the African nations achieved their independence. By the end of 1968 the value of U.S. private investment in OAU member states was almost $2 billion. Between 1963 and 1968, U.S. private investment in Africa grew at an average annual rate of about fourteen percent.

We believe that private investment can and should play a growing role, above and beyond public assistance, in African development. Africans themselves desire to participate in such investment. In many countries, in the face of limited capital resources, it is the government rather than the private sector which has the financial wherewithal to join with foreign private investors. Thus, "joint ventures" frequently involve a combination of foreign private and African governmental capital. We are prepared to encourage American investors to cooperate in such endeavors under adequate investment protection.

Our investment policy should be creative and flexible. It should be deeply concerned with the social environment in which it operates. When investing abroad, modern American businessmen offer training, profit-sharing and other opportunities. At the same time, as businessmen, they expect stability for the enterprises in which they join and a reasonable return on their investments. While the United States Government has guaranty programs available to many American investors, these are insurance and not the basis on which businessmen make investment. Thus, they pay great heed to African government programs to foster a favorable investment climate. Therefore, an investment code, assurances from the African government and reasonable entry, work and tax arrangements, can make the difference between an American's willingness or unwillingness to work out an investment.

Mineral and petroleum development account for nearly three-fourths of current U.S. private investment in Africa. The industry is exceptionally able to seek out new sources and new opportunities to meet growing demands.

The same is not the case, however, for investments in manufacturing, agro-business and commerce. Thus, we are already conducting certain programs to stimulate American private efforts in these fields.

—We have an increasingly successful, albeit modest, effort at getting American investors to look at integrated, large-unit agricultural schemes in Africa. In the past three years, American companies have made 27 preliminary studies, leading to ten in-depth studies and four investment commitments. Several more and currently being negotiated.

—We are also seeking to interest medium size American investors to look at opportunities to help contribute to African markets, i.e., flour milling, bus transportation; and for meeting specialized markets which Africa could fill, such as plywood, shrimp fishing and food processing.

Success in these and other programs depends on the already-mentioned favorable investment climate, on enterprises tailored to realistic market size, and ultimately on getting the prospective American investor to go to Africa to see for himself what the conditions are and what his opportunity costs are.

The new Overseas Private Investment Corporation is authorized to provide guaranties, some equity, local currency loans and sound investment project advice to form the basis for a more efficient, flexible and aggressive approach to the promotion of U.S. investment in developing nations. It will be an important element in stimulating further American private investment in Africa.

I was deeply impressed on my recent trip by the great dependence of so many African countries on exports of one or two agricultural or mineral commodities. Sudden changes in world market prices for these commodities can cause violent fluctuations in export earnings and can disrupt development programs. In recognition of this instability the United States over the years has participated in international efforts to stabilize prices and incomes of primary products.

*   *   *

Several months ago the President set forth proposals for generalized tariff preferences for all developing nations, so that they could more readily find markets for their manufactured and semi-manufactured products in the developed nations, including the United States. To this end, we are actively seeking agreement with other developed nations on some generalized preference scheme.

We are mindful of the special relationship which exists between some African and some European countries. Our purpose, however, is to give all developing nations much improved access for exports of their manufactures to the markets of all developed nations on an equal basis. We are also urging the elimination of discriminatory tariffs—sometimes called "reverse preferences"—which put our goods at a competitive disadvantage in many African markets. We hope that European nations see no linkage between eliminating the preferences they currently receive in some twenty African nations and their levels of aid to those countries.

In the meantime, we have been most encouraged to learn of the important first step taken by the member nations of the Central African Customs and Economic Union (UDEAC), to reduce their general tariffs on most imported goods by fifty percent. They thus move closer to a nondiscriminatory tariff position.

This measure offers the prospect of greater American trade with these countries.

One of the most critical political problems of continental concern relates to southern Africa. The problems of southern Africa are extremely stubborn. Passions are strong on both sides. We see no easy solutions.

Yet the modern world demands a community of nations based on respect for fundamental human rights. These are not only moral and legal principles; they are poweful and ultimately irresistible political and historical forces. We take our stand on the side of those forces of fundamental human rights in southern Africa as we do at home and elsewhere.

In Southern Rhodesia, we have closed our consulate. Our representatives in Salisbury were accredited to the Queen of England. When the Queen's authority was no longer recognized by the regime we withdrew our consulate. We have also determined not to recognize the white-minority regime in Salisbury and will continue to support UN economic sanctions.

To alleviate the difficulties of certain refugees in the United States, particularly of those from southern Africa, with respect to travel abroad, the United States expects in the near future to issue travel documentation as provided under the Protocol to the 1951 Geneva Convention on the Status of Refugees.

In the matter of Namibia (South West Africa), the United States has respected the international status of that territory since 1920. It has sought in the United Nations, before the International Court of Justice and in direct exchanges with South Africa, to defend that status. We have sought equally to defend the rights of the inhabitants, which that status was established to protect. We are now participating in UN deliberations on this matter. Any further actions which the U.S. may take, in the UN or elsewhere, will continue to be consistent with our historic support of the law.

Our relations with the Republic of South Africa have been a matter of particular attention. We do not believe cutting our ties with this rich, troubled land would advance the cause we pursue or help the majority of the people of that country. We continue to make known to them and the world our strong views on apartheid. We are maintaining our arms embargo. We oppose their continued administration of Namibia (South West Africa) and their implementation of apartheid and other repressive legislation there. We will continue to make clear that our limited governmental activities in South Africa do not represent any acceptance or condoning of its discriminatory system.

As for the Portuguese Territories, we shall continue to believe that their peoples should have the right of self-determination. We will encourage peaceful progress toward that goal. The declared Portuguese policy of racial toleration is an important factor in this equation. We think this holds genuine hope for the future. Believing that resort to force and violence is in no one's interest, we imposed an embargo in 1961 against the shipment of arms for use in the Portuguese territories. We have maintained this embargo and will continue to do so.

The smaller independent states south of the Zambesi also deserve attention. They are seeking to create multiracial societies free of the predominant influence of the minority-dominated states adjoining and surrounding them. They cannot exist without a realistic relationship with their neighbors. At the same time it is in the interest of all those who wish to see these states develop and prosper to provide alternative sources of assistance and means of access to these states. This the United States, in cooperation with other donors, will seek to do. At the same time, the United States will seek to be responsive to requests from these states for a higher level of U.S. diplomatic representation.

In all these ways, as well as in positions taken in the United Nations and through diplomatic channels, we shall work to bring about a change of direction in parts of Africa where racial oppression and residual colonialism still prevail.

At the same time, we cannot accept the fatalistic view that only violence can ultimately resolve these issues. Rather we believe that solution lies in the constructive interplay of political, economic and social forces which will inevitably lead to changes.

*   *   *

Statement by Ambassador Seymour M. Finger, U.S. Alternate Representative to the U.N. General Assembly, and Text of Resolution on Implementation of Declaration on Decolonization*

October 12, 1970

Statement by Ambassador Finger

It is with deep regret that the delegation of the United States will be obliged to cast a negative vote on this resolution. Decolonization is a process which we strongly endorse, and we should most sincerely have desired to support this Program of Action.

*Ibid., Nov. 16, 1970, pp. 635-37.

To this end, while expressing its reservations in detail in the Committee of 24, my delegation offered specific amendments which, in our view, would have made the document not only acceptable but practical.

It is therefore a matter of regret and concern that despite the long association of the United States as a member of the Committee of 24, not a single amendment suggested by my delegation on this highly important resolution was adopted.

I do not propose to detail again our specific objections. However, the Program of Action—while laudable in objective—does not represent a useful or constructive approach to a problem of deep concern. In particular, it proposes courses of action in the Security Council which experience has shown cannot obtain the measure of support necessary to make them practicable.

It is not an easy matter for my delegation to be forced to cast a negative vote. In the area of southern Africa, which has so preoccupied the Committee of 24, our support for the principle of self-determination is clear. We have been as conscientious as any nation in support for the arms embargo against South Africa. We have conscientiously embargoed arms for use in the Portuguese territories. We have supported the United Nations position on Namibia, and we have unilaterally taken steps to demonstrate that support. We have firmly implemented the sanctions against Rhodesia. We justifiably feel that we stand with those seeking self-determination and human dignity in southern Africa. We shall continue to do so.

Text of Resolution

The General Assembly,

Having decided to hold a special commemorative session on the occasion of the tenth anniversary of the Declaration on the Granting of Independence to Colonial Countries and Peoples,

Considering that, by arousing world public opinion and promoting practical action for the speedy liquidation of colonialism in all its forms and manifestations, the Declaration has played and will continue to play an important role in assisting the peoples under colonial domination in their struggle for freedom and independence,

Conscious of the fact that, although many colonial countries and peoples have achieved freedom and independence in the last ten years, the system of colonialism continues to exist in many areas of the world,

Reaffirming that all peoples have the right to self-determination and independence and that the subjection of the peoples to alien domination constitutes a serious impediment to the maintenance of international peace and security and the development of peaceful relations among nations,

1. Declares the further continuation of colonialism in all its forms and manifestations a crime which constitutes a violation of the Charter of the United Nations, the Declaration on the Granting of Independence to Colonial Countries and Peoples and the principles of international law;

2. Reaffirms the inherent right of colonial peoples to struggle by all necessary means at their disposal against colonial Powers which suppress their aspiration for freedom and independence;

3. Adopts the following programme of action to assist in the full implementation

of the Declaration on the Granting of Independence to Colonial Countries and Peoples:

(1) Member States shall do their utmost to promote, in the United Nations and the international institutions and organizations within the United Nations system, effective measures for the full implementation of the Declaration on the Granting of Independence to Colonial Countries and Peoples in all Trust Territories, Non-Self-Governing Territories and other colonial Territories, large and small, including the adoption by the Security Council of effective measures against Governments and regimes which engage in any form of repression of colonial peoples, which would seriously impede the maintenance of international peace and security.

(2) Member States shall render all necessary moral and material assistance to the peoples of colonial Territories in their struggle to attain freedom and independence.

(3) (a) Member States shall intensify their efforts to promote the implementation of the resolutions of the General Assembly and the Security Council relating to Territories under colonial domination.

(b) In this connexion, the General Assembly draws the attention of the Security Council to the need to continue to give special attention to the problems of southern Africa by adopting measures to ensure the full implementation of General Assembly resolution 1514 (XV) of 14 December 1960 and its own resolutions, and in particular:

(i) To widen the scope of the sanctions against the illegal regime of Southern Rhodesia by declaring mandatory all the measures laid down in Article 41 of the Charter of the United Nations;

(ii) To give careful consideration to the question of imposing sanctions upon South Africa and Portugal, in view of their refusal to carry out the relevant decisions of the Security Council;

(iii) To give urgent consideration, with a view to promoting the speedy elimination of colonialism, to the question of imposing fully and unconditionally, under international supervision, an embargo on arms of all kinds to the Government of South Africa and the illegal regime of Southern Rhodesia;

(iv) To consider urgently the adoption of measures to prevent the supply of arms of all kinds to Portugal, as such arms enable that country to deny the right of self-determination and independence to the peoples of the Territories under its domination.

(c) Member States shall also intensify their efforts to oppose collaboration between the regimes of South Africa and Portugal and the illegal racist regime of Southern Rhodesia for the preservation of colonialism in southern Africa and to end the political, military, economic and other forms of aid received by the above-mentioned regimes, which enables them to persist in their policy of colonial domination.

(4) Member States shall wage a vigorous and sustained campaign against activities and practices of foreign economic, financial and other interests operating in colonial Territories for the benefit and on behalf of colonial Powers and their allies, as these constitute a major obstacle to the achievement of the goals embodied in resolution 1514 (XV). Member States shall consider the adoption of necessary steps to have their nationals and companies under their jurisdiction discontinue such activities and practices; these steps should also aim at preventing the systematic influx of foreign immigrants into colonial Territories, which disrupts the integrity and social, political and cultural unity of the peoples under colonial domination.

(5) Member States shall carry out a sustained and vigorous campaign against all military activities and arrangements by colonial Powers in Territories under their administration, as such activities and arrangements constitute an obstacle to the full implementation of resolution 1514 (XV).

(6) (a) All freedom fighters under detention shall be treated in accordance with the relevant provisions of the Geneva Convention relative to the Treatment of Prisoners of War of 12 August 1949.

(b) The specialized agencies and international institutions associated with the United Nations shall intensify their activities related to the implementation of resolution 1514 (XV).

(c) Representatives of liberation movements shall be invited, whenever necessary, by the United Nations and other international organizations within the United Nations system to participate in an appropriate capacity in the proceedings of those organs relating to their countries.

(d) Efforts shall be intensified to provide increased educational opportunities for the inhabitants of Non-Self-Governing Territories. All States shall render greater assistance in this field, both individually through programmes in the countries concerned and collectively by contributions through the United Nations.

(7) All States shall undertake measures aimed at enhancing public awareness of the need for active assistance in the achievement of complete decolonization and, in particular, creating satisfactory conditions for activities by national and international non-governmental organizations in support of the peoples under colonial domination.

(8) The United Nations as well as all States shall intensify their efforts in the field of public information in the area of decolonization through all media, including publiations, radio and television. Of special importance will be programmes relating to United Nations activities on decolonization, the situation in colonial Territories and the struggle being waged by colonial peoples and the national liberation movements.

(9) The Special Committee on the Situation with regard to the Implementation of the Declaration on the Granting of Independence to Colonial Countries and Peoples shall continue to examine the full compliance of all States with the Declaration and with other relevant resolutions on the question of decolonization. The question of territorial size, geographical isolation and limited resources should in no way delay the implementation of the Declaration. Where resolution 1514 (XV) has not been fully implemented with regard to a given Territory, the General Assembly shall continue to bear responsibility for that Territory until such time as the people concerned has had an opportunity to exercise freely its right to self-determination and independence in accordance with the Declaration. The Special Committee is hereby directed:

(a) To continue to assist the General Assembly in finding the best ways and means for the final liquidation of colonialism;

(b) To continue to give special consideration to the views expressed orally or in written communications by representatives of the peoples in the colonial Territories;

(c) To continue to send visiting missions to the colonial Territories and to hold meetings at places where it can best obtain first-hand information on the situation in colonial Territories, as well as to continue to hold meetings away from Headquarters as appropriate;

(d) To assist the General Assembly in making arrangements, in co-operation with the administering Powers, for securing a United Nations presence in the colonial

Territories to participate in the elaboration of the procedural measures for the implementation of the Declaration and to observe the final stages of the process of decolonization in the Territories;

(e) To prepare draft rules and regulations for visiting missions for approval by the General Assembly.

Letter from Charles W. Yost, U.S. Representative to the U.N., to Secretary General U Thant on the United States Withdrawal from the U.N. Committee on Colonialism*

January 11, 1971

Upon instructions from my Government, I have the honour to inform you that the United States has decided to withdraw from membership of the General Assembly's Special Committee on the Situation with regard to the Implementation of the Declaration on the Granting of Indepenedence to Colonial Countries and Peoples [Committee of 24].

As you know the United States has been a member of the Special Committee since it was first constituted in January 1962, since which time there have been a number of changes in the membership of the Committee.

The United States will, of course, continue to submit information on Territories under its administration in accordance with its obligations under the Charter and will be prepared to attend meetings of the Special Committee, at the Committee's invitation, when such information on United States Territories is being discussed.

I should be grateful if you would bring the text of this letter to the attention of the President of the General Assembly.

New York Times *Editorial on United States Withdrawal from U.N. Committee on Colonialism*†

January 16, 1971

The United Nations Colonialism Committee has long been run in high-handed fashion by its African and Asian members with loud verbal backing from the Soviet bloc. Totally ineffective in hastening the end of white minority rule in southern Africa, the stridency of its resolutions and the unreality of its demands have but increased in proportion to its frustrations.

It has squandered scarce U.N. resources in extravagant junketing to interview leaders of southern African liberation movements who could be consulted far less expensively at Turtle Bay, and to mount propaganda campaigns often designed to put Britain and the United States (but somehow France only rarely) in the dock with the white rulers of Rhodesia, South Africa and the Portuguese territories.

By supporting all this activity and the endless resolutions, the Soviet Union—almost the only authentic colonial power left on earth but immune from this committee's

Ibid., Jan. 23, 1971, p. 186.
†*The New York Times*, Jan. 16, 1971.

attacks—manages inexpensively to discredit the United States and Britain while expanding its own possibilities for penetrating black Africa.

Consequently, it is not surprising that the United States and Britain have notified Secretary General Thant of their withdrawal from the committee, the first time the United States has ever walked out of any U.N. body. But for Washington, at least, this is the wrong decision.

The African and Asian members are far from being as united on strategy and tactics as their committee behavior suggests. Some are keenly aware of the hypocrisy of the Soviet position and uneasy about the castigating of the United States and Berlin even if they are unwilling at present to say so publicly.

It would have been wiser for the United States to persevere despite frustrations in the long-run task of persuading the Africans that this country will support realistic measures to advance the goal of black majority rule in southern Africa. To walk out of the committee will only deepen African suspicions that the United States pays lip service to self-determination while steadily diluting its opposition to white minority rule and the monstrous doctrine of apartheid.

*Speech by Representative Charles C. Diggs, Jr. (Michigan) Before the House on the Black Caucus' Recommendations to President Nixon**

March 30, 1971

Mr. Speaker, on March 25, 1971, the 13-member congressional black caucus submitted to the President its recommendations for action in the areas of economic security and development, community and urban development, justice and civil rights, and foreign policy.

The issues and concerns of this caucus are not partisan ones. We are including these recommendations in the Record to bring them to the attention of the leadership of both parties in the Congress and the public at large.

The Members of the congressional black caucus are: Charles C. Diggs, Jr., of Michigan, chairman; Augustus F. Hawkins of California, vice chairman; Charles B. Rangel of New York, secretary; Shirley Chisholm of New York; William L. Clay of Missouri; Louis Stokes of Ohio; George W. Collins of Illinois; John Conyers, Jr., of Michigan; Ronald V. Dellums of California; Ralph H. Metcalfe of Illinois; Parren Mitchell of Maryland; Robert N. C. Nix of Pennsylvania; and the Reverend Walter Fauntroy, Delegate-Elect of Washington, D.C.

STATEMENT TO THE PRESIDENT OF THE UNITED STATES
BY THE CONGRESSIONAL BLACK CAUCUS, U.S. HOUSE OF REPRESENTATIVES,
MARCH 25, 1971

Part I. Opening Statement

We sought this meeting, Mr. President, out of a deep conviction that large numbers of citizens are being subjected to intense hardship, are denied their basic rights, and are suffering irreparable harm as a result of current policies.

Congressional Record, Mar. 30, 1971, pp. 3-4.

As you may know, all of us were elected by substantial majorities. We were given clear and unmistakable mandates to articulate the problems of our constituents and to work for prompt and effective solutions to them. Most of the districts that we represent are predominantly black, though our constituencies also include whites, Spanish-speaking, Indians, Japanese-Americans. and Chinese-Americans, some suburbanites as well as residents of the central cities, poor, middle income, and even some well-to-do Americans.

But our concerns and obligations as Members of Congress do not stop at the boundaries of our districts; our concerns are national and international in scope. We are petitioned daily by citizens living hundreds of miles from our districts who look on us as Congressmen-at-large for black people and poor people in the United States. Even though we think first of those we were directly elected to serve, we cannot, in good conscience, think only of them—for what affects one black community, one poor community, one urban community, affects all.

* * *

D. Foreign Policy

Recommendation 1: We call upon you to effect disengagement from Southeast Asia as soon as possible, preferably by the end of 1971, and definitely within the life of the 92nd Congress.

Recommendation 2: We call for drastic reduction in our military expenditures, and the redirection of these funds to finance much needed domestic programs—such as economic security and economic development, community and urban development, justice and civil rights, and many other unfulfilled interests of the black community.

Recommendation 3: Mr. President, following World War II Europe was the recipient of massive aid through the Marshall Plan and Japan was rebuilt essentially through American assistance. In the sixties the Alliance for Progress was conceived and funded for the benefit of Latin America, and the Middle East continues to receive a significant input of our resources. We feel strongly that Africa's turn is overdue. Africa must be given priority and attention on an equal basis with other parts of the world. Over the past few years, Africa has received only 8.5% of American aid; we believe this percentage should be increased significantly—to at least 15%.

We recommend that a special Task Force be created in the Executive Branch, composed of ranking members of the Departments of State, Commerce, Defense, and other pertinent agencies, where the variety of American policies dealing with Africa can be reviewed in a comprehensive manner and whose recommendations would be effectively implemented. In addition, several recognized experts of long time interest in this continent should be included (e.g., Members of Congress, academicians, journalists, and businessmen.)

U.S. representatives to the World Bank, the International Monetary Fund and the International Development Association should request those organizations to allocate increasing shares of multi-lateral resources for Africa.

We support broader U.S. participation in the African Development Bank and we urge that our government provide soft funds with other donors for the Bank.

Recommendation 4: United States relations with Southern Africa are in need of a major overhaul. This country should take the lead in isolating the Republic of South Africa, the world's most racist nation. Disincentives should be developed to discourage the expansion of further private American investment there. On the other hand, private American enterprise should be encouraged to seriously examine the potential for profitable investment in other parts of Africa.

We urge the Administration to actively support legislation proposing the withdrawal of the United States sugar quota for the Republic of South Africa, and its reallocation to other African countries. We further urge the Administration to implement the United States pronouncements in the United Nations to help liberate the remaining areas under colonial rule in Africa.

The House Subcommittee on Africa submitted a comprehensive report on Southern Africa to the Administration as a result of its extensive travels and hearings. The recommendations of this report and others it has rendered should be seriously considered.

Recommendation 5: Of all major industrial nations, the United States has for years allocated less proportionately for international development efforts. We propose that the United States direct at least 1% of its annual gross national product for international aid, with priority attention to Africa. (It must be noted that about 75% of all United States foreign aid funds have been spent for U.S. goods and services.)

Recommendation 6: We urge that blacks and other minorities be given a greater role in the making of foreign policy. We also ask the Administration to increase its recruitment of minority Americans for foreign policy positions, as well as to improve the upgrading procedures regarding minorities within the State Department and related agencies.

*Speech by Representative Diggs Before the House on a Report to the Nation**

June 3, 1971

Mr. Speaker, on May 24, 1971, the 13-member congressional black caucus responded to the President's report of May 18, 1971, in which he addressed himself to 60 recommendations for governmental action on major issues of today which said group previously submitted to him on March 25, 1971.

In their response, a "Report to the Nation," the caucus expressed disappointment in the 115-page report which failed to introduce new policy in the way of economic security and development; community and urban development; justice and civil rights, and foreign policy. The President's report merely reiterated policy already familiar to the caucus which we feel is totally inadequate in addressing itself to the areas so stated. We are including statements drawn up by the caucus expressing our reaction to the President's report.

     *   *   *

Ibid., June 3, 1971, pp. 4638; 4646.

D. Foreign Policy

Recommendations 1 and 2: It is clear that the positions of the President and the Congressional Black Caucus on Vietnam and budgetary priorities for domestic spending are irreconcilable.

Recommendation 3: The Congressional Black Caucus had recommended that Africa be given priority and attention on an equal basis with the rest of the world. Africa now receives approximately 8.4 percent of the total U.S. AID assistance. Our request that this amount be significantly increased was not even addressed.

b. The Administration rejected the Caucus' request for a special Task Force composed of a broadly representative policy group to provide a comprehensive review of the variety of U.S. policies affecting Africa. But, there is no better evidence of the need for such input than the few visible results of the review of "key African issues" by the National Security Council, such as the relaxation of our arms embargo policy against South Africa and the relaxation of our adherence to UN sanctions against Rhodesia.

Recommendation 4: a. The Caucus does not find the Administration's advocacy of the use of communication to support peaceful change in South Africa persuasive since the reply lacks any evidence that the policy is being pursued to establish communication links with the majority Black South Africans or among those liberal elements working for peaceful change in South Africa.

b. The Caucus finds it impossible to reconcile either our denunciation of the use of violence by the liberation movements or the President's statement ("The United States will not condone the violence to human dignity implicit in apartheid") with the nation's continuing moral, economic, and military support of South Africa, which subjugates the people of South Africa and of Namibia (South West Africa) by force and violence.

c. We welcome the Administration's advocacy of the goal of attracting private business interests to Black Africa. We would have also welcomed a more concrete explanation of its specific efforts to implement that commitment and accomplishments to date.

d. The Administration rejected our recommendation that the annual outright subsidy to South Africa of $20 million under sugar quota laws be ended. This is a clear reflection of this Administration's policy towards South Africa. Four developing countries of Black Africa each will now have approximately one-fourth of the sugar quota of South Africa, a developed country. There is absolutely no economic or political justification for continuing this support of South Africa for a two or three year period.

e. The Caucus endorses the Administration's interest in increased support for the majority-ruled states of Southern Africa, Botswana, Lesotho and Swaziland. The U.S. should further implement this interest by facilitating and actively supporting feasibility studies into the mineral resources of these nations to lessen their dependence on South Africa.

f. The citation of a limited scholarship program, which is currently being substantially reduced, cannot be considered a serious answer to the recommendation that the U.S. implement its UN obligations and pronouncements, to support self-determination for minority-ruled Africa. The Caucus believes that a decision not to support a violent solution cannot excuse the failure to provide other types of significant assistance (e.g., health and educational) directly to liberation movements to persons within the liberated areas.

g. In view of U.S. recognition, in the present case before the International Court of Justice of Namibia (South West Africa), of our obligation to respect and assist the UN's responsibility for the international territory, the Caucus can only characterize as frivolous the Administration's reply, which ignored our recognized obligations and equated the Ad Hoc Subcommittee with the Council for Namibia. The Caucus called upon the United States to join the Council and to cooperate fully with the UN.

Recommendation 5: The Administration's treatment of the recommendation for allocation of one percent of the gross national product to international development assistance was specious and failed entirely to address the point that priority attention be directed to Africa.

Recommendation 6: Statistics, as given by the Administration on improved hiring policies for black foreign service officers, however commendable, do not correct the overall picture. Instead of a numbers game, the Caucus called for an all-out effort to secure black representation in the foreign service, worldwide, at all levels and in all career specialties.

UNITED STATES ECONOMIC POLICY
TOWARD SUBSAHARAN AFRICA

*Report by Senator Theodore F. Green (Rhode Island) on
Economic Aid and Technical Assistance in Africa**

February 21, 1957

SCOPE OF UNITED STATES ECONOMIC AID PROGRAMS IN AFRICA

In comparison with our Government's overall program of foreign economic aid, the amount budgeted for Africa has been very small, both in proportion to the funds allocated, as well as in relation to the size and accelerating importance of that continent. Of a total sum of approximately $1,546.7 million appropriated for fiscal year 1957, it is estimated that somewhat less than $25 million will be allocated to Africa, or 1.6 percent of the total. Here, as elsewhere throughout this report, all program sums referred to are given in United States dollars, unless otherwise indicated.

The following table shows the distribution of sums provided under the current program:

[In dollars]

	Fiscal year 1956[1]	*Fiscal year 1957 to Mar. 31*
Belgian	18,892	5,000
British territories	920,180	50,000
Egypt	6,962,369	400,000
Ethiopia	2,923,156	287,000
French territories	19,003	5,000
Liberia	1,781,695	300,000
Libya	7,641,269	670,000
Portugese territories	70,033	15,000
Somalia	60,240	15,000
Regional	16,940	12,000
Total	20,413,777	1,759,000

[1]Includes reallotments in fiscal year 1956 of prior year's funds deobligated in fiscal year 1956.

As of March 31, 1956, Africa had received since 1948 a total of approximately 738 millions of dollars in United States assistance, including loans in the amount of $191 million from the Export-Import Bank. The cumulative totals, by countries are as follows:

*Committee on Foreign Relations, Economic Aid and Technical Assistance in Africa, Report of Senator Theodore Francis Green on a Study Mission Pursuant to S. Res. 162, 84th Cong. (Washington, 1957), pp. 4-7; 14-23.

CUMULATIVE SUMMARY OF UNITED STATES ASSISTANCE TO AFRICA

[Through Mar. 31, 1956, unless otherwise noted]

[In thousands]

	Strategic and basic materials[1]	Overseas development fund (special reserve fund)[2]	European fund	Technical coopera- tion	Develop- ment assist- ance	Export- Import Bank	Total United States
Belgian Congo	$1,550.0	$17,073.0		$133.9			$18,756.9
British Africa	51,602.0	8,637.0		1,638.0	[2]$4,964.0		66,841.0
French Africa	32,347.0	29,472.0	$297,670.6	1,210.2	[2]4,933.3		·365,633.1
Somalia (Ex-Italian Somaliland)				736.2	[2]300.0		1,036.2
Portugese Africa	4,630.0			161.0		$17,000.0	21,791.0
Ethiopia and Eritrea				12,351.0		3,000.0	15,351.0
Liberia				7,647.0		21,350.0	28,997.0
Libya				8,075.0	5,000.0		8,075.0
Egypt[3]				21,667.0	40,000.0		61,667.0
Sudan							
Union of South Africa						149,685.0	149,825.0
Total	90,269.0	55,182.0	297,670.6	53,619.3	55,197.3	191,035.0	737,973.2

[1] April 1968 to Dec. 31, 1955, from report to Senate Subcommittee on Minerals and Materials, May 1, 1956.
[2] Local currencies made available through sec. 550 surplus agricultural commodity sales.
[3] Figures as of June 30, 1956.

In addition to Egypt (which was not visited on this study mission) the only African country to receive straight economic aid or "development assistance" is Libya. The Libyan Government received from the International Cooperation Administration and its predecessor agencies $3 million in fiscal year 1955 and $5 million in fiscal year 1956. Seven million dollars has been programed for fiscal year 1957. All of this aid has been on a grant basis, supplementing special funds made available by the United States Government. Currently, the remaining programs in Africa are primarily concerned with technical cooperation. The only independent countries of Africa which are receiving neither development funds nor technical assistance under our aid program are the Sudan and the Union of South Africa. The latter, however, has had a loan from the Export-Import Bank.

*   *   *

Until 1954, apart from limited amounts of technical assistance, most of the aid from the United States went to finance development projects in such fields as transportation and power and was in the form of loans or grants. Today the emphasis in the dependent territories has shifted over to technical cooperation with varying degrees of support from the home countries. In the fiscal year 1956, technical assistance was furnished in the following amounts: $1.8 million for Liberia; $3 million for Ethiopia; $2 million for Libya (in addition to $5 million for development assistance), and $1.2 million for the dependent overseas territories of the Gold Coast, Nigeria, Uganda, Somalia, and the Central African Federation.

The character of the United States program in the dependent areas necessarily differs from that in the independent territories, in view of the substantial assistance furnished by the metropolitan countries. Primarily, our aid is designed to supplement that assistance in fields where we have shown we possess unique qualifications and experience. Its principal contribution is in agricultural extension education, technical and vocational training and transportation, for which the need is widespread through-out most of Africa.

*   *   *

It is to the solution of these problems that the United States effort, which is limited solely to technical assistance, has been directed. The program got underway in 1952 under an agreement signed the preceding year. In the early years major emphasis was placed upon education, first agricultural education, then general and industrial trades education. Now the emphasis is being gradually shifted to those projects which will have a direct effect on economic productivity, particularly, agriculture. Starting with $800,000 in 1952, United States technical assistance for the fiscal year 1956 amount-ed to $3 million, in addition to administration costs of $185,000. In the 4 years that the program has been operating, the total cash contribution of the United States into a joint fund for cooperating services has amounted to approximately $5 million, which has been more than matched by a contribution of over $5 million on the part of the Ethiopian Government. In addition to their joint cash contribution, the Ethiopians furnish land, buildings, and local personnel.

*   *   *

The relations between our operations mission and the Ethiopian Government are on an excellent basis, despite the open dissatisfaction expressed by the Emperor with respect to matters of military assistance. Yet this could well be the touchstone upon which continued harmonious relations with the Ethiopian Government depends.

The United States has important military bases in other countries which promise to be somewhat hazardous, if not unreliable, in the kind of crisis now facing the West. I fail to see the advantage in continuing our dependency upon areas where our potential enemies may outnumber our friends, especially when there are countries in the world which would warmly welcome our presence, and which could furnish terrain satisfac-tory for base purposes. I believe, therefore, that consideration should be given to ascertaining the feasibility of establishing such a base in Ethiopia, as an alternative to some one or more of our existing sites elsewhere.

E. SOUTH AFRICA

The great national wealth of South Africa is so generally familiar as to require no comment in this report. It is one of the most advanced countries of the world, in which modern technology is used extensively in manufacturing, in mining gold, diamonds, uranium, manganese and iron, and in agriculture. There is, therefore, no United States aid program here either on a grant or on a technical cooperation basis. Apart from some limited military assistance involving the use of a team of Air Force radar experts the only transactions which might be regarded as official United States aid consist of a few self-liquidating loans by the Export-Import Bank to private companies for the development of uranium extraction. These loans have amounted to about $44.5 million since 1953.

On the other hand, a number of American institutions are engaged in privately financed assistance programs. The Carnegie Corporation of New York provided funds during 1956 to send 5 South Africans to the United States and 2 Americans to South Africa. It has also sent selected United States sociologists to teach at the University of Natal's Institute for Social Research. The Rockefeller Foundation in 1951 provided the Durban Medical School at Natal with $127,000 for a 5-year program to train nonwhite doctors. $150,000 was granted by the Ford Foundation to the South African Institute of Race Relations to further its work. To the extent that the private foundations assume this function, just to that degree will United States Government action become less needed.

Valuable technical assistance is likewise furnished to South African enterprises in connection with normal business operations. For example, Westinghouse Electric, instead of entering the manufacturing field through a subsidiary company in South Africa, has undertaken research projects and planning for local capital, to assist in setting up manufacturing plants, with licensing and royalty arrangements between the American and South African companies.

Nevertheless, despite the advanced economy of the country, the future is not free from anxiety. If racial tensions were to exceed the breaking point, serious economic disruption would take place, because native labor has been heavily integrated in South Africa's major industries. At the same time, unless more native workers are brought into the country, its rate of expansion will inevitably be retarded. Continuation of present Government policies seems to be risking this eventuality with disturbing overtones.

Against the inexorable tide of nationalism and the gathering desire for improved social and political status elsewhere on the continent, the Union of South Africa has been pursuing a reverse course called "apartheid." The avowed objective of this policy is to maintain a supremacy of the European white races over the native population.

We in America may not fully realize that this is not merely a program of racial segregation. It is a program calculated to suppress those rights of professional, economic, and social liberty without which an entire class must remain in an inferior position.

        *   *   *

I cannot believe that this policy will succeed. Nor do I believe that such injustices as enforced abandonment of homes long owned, the prohibition against acquisition of title to real property, and the creation of a lower class professional and economic group can fail to fan into flame the smoldering embers of resentment. Such efforts to turn the clock back are bound, I believe, ultimately to create conditions favorable to a tragic explosion. Faced with this unhappy dilemma, America in setting the course of its policy toward South Africa must balance, on the one hand, its desire for friendship with the Union Government and its policy of noninterference in the domestic affairs of another nation with, on the other hand, its traditional interest in the preservation of human rights and freedoms everywhere.

E. LIBERIA

Liberia's is primarily a rubber economy, which, like the Gold Coast's cocoa crop agriculture, is highly vulnerable to world price fluctuations. It is an underdeveloped country, which is not self-sufficient in food, with inadequate roads, a high incidence of malaria, yaws, and other debilitating diseases, and vast areas of unutilized natural resources. Its people are 90 percent illiterate and there is an almost paralyzing lack of professional and scientific personnel, skilled and unskilled workers, and managerial personnel generally. Yet the future of the country holds much promise. Iron mining, with ore assayed at 60 percent or better, has become a major industry. Great timber reserves await transportation facilities.

Such, in a nutshell, is the problem of Liberia's needs, a country for which the United States has felt special responsibilities ever since emancipated slaves from America settled the western coast of Africa.

United States aid to Liberia has sought to meet these needs by projects in agriculture, health, transportation, cooperative education, and public housing. These projects are designed primarily to train Liberians in skills needed to raise their standard of living. The program is exclusively one of technical assistance, and its accomplishments, while limited by the funds made available, are, on the whole, very gratifying.

Since 1944, when an American economic mission was established in Monrovia, a total of $12.6 million in aid has been furnished, most of this ($10 million) being provided in the past 8 years. A breakdown of program costs during the period 1952-56 is contained in the following table:

TOTAL COST, UNITED STATES AID PROGRAMS, 1952-56

[Thousands of dollars]

Fields of activity	Fiscal year				
	1952	1953	1954	1955	1956
Agriculture and natural resources	215	273	431	315	317
Industry and mining	116	372	19	106	112
Transportation	86	106	114	244	256
Health and sanitation	217	316	231	390	327
Education	94	145	212	498	559
Public administration	7	43	31	13	46
Community development and housing	10	30	101	36	33
Miscellaneous and technical support	339	396	25	269	163
Total	1,084	1,681	1,164	1,871	1,813

During the same period, the extent of the Liberian Government's contribution was as follows:

LIBERIAN GOVERNMENT'S CONTRIBUTION TO AID PROGRAM, 1952-56

[In thousands of dollars]

Fields of activity	Calendar years				
	1952	1953	1954	1955	1956
Agriculture and natural resources	288	261	462	237	410
Industry and mining	343	368		80	79
Transportation	212	449		480	652
Health and sanitation	311	291	205	180	216
Education	189	194		334	411
Public administration	91	21		13	50
Community development and housing	42	166		50	36
Miscellaneous and technical support	169	92		38	10
Total	1,645	1,862	667	1,522	1,864

There were no counterpart contributions inasmuch as Liberia uses only United States currency.

United States loans to Liberia since 1948 have totaled $14.8 million (including $19.5 million provided under lend-lease for construction of the free port of Monrovia). Of this amount, loans extended by the Export-Import Bank have amounted to $21.35 million during 1951-55, of which $1.35 million was for a water and sewage system, and $20 million for a road construction program which is not yet completed.

The Government of Liberia sets aside 20 percent of its annual revenues for development purposes. A Joint Liberian-United States Commission for Economic· Development plans, supervises, and evaluates all development work. It has been an effective programing device.

*   *   *

No comment on Liberia would be complete without referring to the tremendous contribution of the Firestone Rubber Co. to the life and development of the country. Firestone has been a principal catalyst in the evolution of Liberia from a primitive, tribal society, toward a modern economy with the help of private capital. Almost 40 percent of the Republic's tax revenues are derived from Firestone's operations, along with more than 70 percent of its exports. Its impact has permeated almost every phase of the people's life. It is a heartening example of the mutually profitable and beneficial relationship which can be achieved by good will and enlightened restraint on the part of both business and government.

To conclude: the American aid program in Liberia, on the whole, has been successful. Its accomplishments are not only statistical, but visible. To cite a few examples: the country has increased its rice self-sufficiency from 90 to 95 percent in 2 years. Substantial increases have been realized in other agricultural products including cash export crops of coffee, cocoa, rubber, and palm produce. More dramatically, an entire marine fishing industry has been brought into existence as a result of United States assistance in fish refrigeration processing.

The scope of the program has been fairly well adapted to the country's capacity. But the pace of development has begun to quicken, and the point has now been reached where Liberia is not only ready for more technical assistance, but will need development funds to accompany progress in mining and other industries.

In a very real sense much of Africa is watching closely the results achieved in Liberia and the degree to which American assistance is enabling the Liberian people to attain a viable economy. As a kind of American fosterchild, Liberia is more than another candidate for economic aid, no matter how worthy. It is also a symbol of our country's willingness to support an underprivileged African people in their efforts to vindicate the democratic way of life.

AID PROGRAM IN THE DEPENDENT OVERSEAS TERRITORIES (DOT)

A. In General

Prior to 1954 aid to the African dependent overseas territories was tied closely to the European reconstruction program. As a consequence, its purpose was to improve the economic position of Europe through development projects which would also increase exports. Little attention was given to the fundamental problems characteristic of underdeveloped colonial areas, such as inadequate food production, lack of a trained labor supply, and the absence of facilities for training native personnel.

During the past few years metropolitan countries generally have come to recognize the need for facing up to these problems. In 1954 the United States policy toward the dependent areas shifted away from development financing to the more limited objective of technical cooperation. In this new policy we have had excellent cooperation from the United Kingdom in developing programs for British East and West Africa. There we have drawn on funds which included $5 million in sterling acquired as the result of the sale of surplus agricultural commodities to the British in 1954 and 1955. Among other things, the United Kingdom program has included assistance for a western Nigerian agriculture project and training of African medical assistants in Kenya. France alone has failed to show interest in pursuing a technical cooperation program, divorced from a large development program financed by the United States. As of 1956, the French effort had shrunk to less than $20,000 per year.

Throughout most of the United Kingdom's dependent overseas territories, United States aid has been characterized by delays and inadequate action. This is partly attributable to the fact that program arrangements must be processed through the Colonial Office. Further disadvantages result from the fact that all preliminary negotiations and the decision on agreed projects are not handled between our consular officials and the local authorities of a dependent territory, but between the central International Cooperation Administration mission and the metropolitan government. As a consequence, detailed information of the projects is often not available either in the files of our consulates, or in the archives of the local government itself. The Gold Coast program has suffered from the same cumbersome procedure, although this factor will no longer be operative after independence is acquired next March.

If there is to be a continuation of aid activities in such countries as Nigeria, for example, during the period prior to its acquisition of independence, it would seem advisable for our field representatives to have more direct liaison with Washington, rather than compelling them to operate indirectly through a European office. Project selection would then benefit by the active collaboration of those most familiar with local problems. It would have the further advantage of enabling our representatives to speak to the local officials with greater authority.

Report of Senator Hugh Scott (Pennsylvania) on a Trade Study Mission to Asia and Africa*

February 26, 1960

*   *   *

The trade mission discussed the U.S. relations with east Africa as a whole. The economic aspects of our relations comprise trade, private investment, technical and economic assistance under ICA. Insofar as trade is concerned, we were told that our exports to east Africa until very recently had been severely limited by the existence of dollar import controls. Essential goods not obtainable in the sterling area and the OEEC countries could be obtained from the dollar areas and consisted mainly of agricultural and industrial machinery and equipment, lubricating oils, motor vehicles, and unmanufactured tobacco.

Our investments in east Africa have been rather small except in some branches of oil companies, agricultural machine companies, and some insurance companies. It was noted also that several American shipping companies have connections with the main importers and the local agencies of American companies which sell their products throughout east Africa. Significant was the fact that many American companies located in the sterling area are actually supplying these British areas with products and brand names well known in the dollar area. In this connection goods from America will no doubt be sold in larger quantities as a result of the recent liberalization of dollar controls.

Our consular officials and private businessmen told us that, in the absence of exploitable deposits of minerals, there were rather few investment opportunities of real interest to American businessmen unless they were interested primarily in opening trade channels or producing for the local market.

*   *   *

Recommendations

1. The status of the ICA administrator should be clarified as soon as possible; either by being recognized on his own or being made part of the American consulate general, with the rank of consul, so as to obviate the anomalous position he occupies

---

*Committee on Interstate and Foreign Commerce, *Foreign Commerce Study, Asia and Africa: Japan, Taiwan, Hong Kong, Vietnam, Cambodia, India, Israel, Kenya, Federation of Rhodesia and Nyasaland, the Union of South Africa, (Washington, 1960), pp. 16-26.

at present. This clarification of status seems to be most important before profitable results can be expected.

2. Note should be taken of the need for commercial personnel in our representation to take care of the commercial and investment leads which seem to be available.

3. Note should be taken of the lack of response by American businessmen to trade inquiries from the general area. Has there been a decline in the American nose for business, or is the American businessman doing so well at home as to be disinterested in foreign markets?

4. A wide dissemination of the investment and trading possibilities of east Africa should be made available by the Commerce Department in Washington, D.C., because of the expectation for increased trade with the dollar area following the sterling-liberalization program.

5. As a result of a visit with Mr. Gikonyo Kiano, of Kenya, one of the noted African leaders, it seems advisable that greater cognizance should be taken of the aspirations of African leadership for increased scholarship grants for their peoples in the United States and increased assistance to the technical institutions in the area.

6. A compilation of local laws dealing with foreign firms, taxes, labor rates and laws, investment taxes, and other pertinent financial and commercial data not readily available from the U.S. Department of Commerce might be welcomed by our American businessmen.

*   *   *

The Federation depends heavily on foreign capital and assistance to finance its economic development. During the past few years the United Kingdom has furnished the bulk of the development funds but the United States is beginning to contribute heavily to the area's economic advancement through both public and private channels. Since World War II the U.S. Government has loaned this area almost $63 million, and the International Bank for Reconstruction and Development has loaned the Federation and Territorial Governments a total of $122 million. These loans were primarily for the expansion of electrical production by the building of the famous Kariba Dam. American businessmen have also found the Federation to be a profitable source for mining investments and have expended around $200 million for such purposes.

In addition to the great problem of race relations, which is common to all the "settler" countries of Africa, the main problem deals with economic development. The Government is following a program of so-called partnership by assisting the Africans in their economic development by allowing them certain additional lands and assisting them in the production of profitable crops, such as tobacco and tea.

The United States is the Federation's third most important trading partner, being preceded by the United Kingdom and the Union of South Africa. Our imports approximate 10 percent of their total exports which are averaging around $450 million per year, and we are supplying approximately 4 percent of their total imports of around $500 million per year.

The principal U.S. exports to the Federation comprise tractors, agricultural, industrial and mining machinery, motor vehicles, lubricating oils, fertilizers, and wrapping paper. The U.S. imports from the Federation are copper ores and concentrates, chrome, beryl, manganese, tantalum, lithium, ferrochrome, cobalt, and crude asbestos.

At the moment the Federation has a four-column tariff under which preferential rates are granted to the British Dominions and other British areas. As a member of the sterling area, it has also restricted its expenditures of hard currencies for nonessential dollar imports by placing such imports on a restricted list. However, this list has been progressively reduced and may eventually be eliminated.

Insofar as investments are concerned, the Federation is most anxious to obtain additional investments so as to continue its rapid rate of industrial growth. Lately the United States concluded a double taxation agreement with the Federation and eliminated the last remaining restrictions on repatriation of dollar investment capital.

The South African and Federation Governments are in process of negotiating a new trade agreement and the United States is vitally interested in this agreement insofar as it concerns new opportunities for expanded U.S. commercial relations with both countries.

*   *   *

Recommendations

1. A complete story of the Rhodesia tobacco industry, production and markets, and sales agreements, from the agricultural officer in Salisbury, might clarify the situation for the Department of Agriculture in Washington, D.C.

2. An expansion of our commercial representation, so as to take note of all possible leads in commercial and investment opportunities, might be useful.

3. Greater propaganda concerning the U.S. assistance, especially technical assistance in all spheres, might prove to be useful.

4. U.S. assistance to the multiracial university at Salisbury, or, at least an exchange program, might prove most beneficial.

5. Greater dissemination of data concerning the future possibilities of the Federation by the U.S. Department of Commerce might prove useful to U.S. manufacturers and businessmen in their planning for future operations.

6. It might prove beneficial for American consular officials on the spot to make a comprehensive statement on business taxes, employment regulations, labor rates, land taxes, tariff rates, railway-transportation charges, franchise laws, and other important facts for U.S. businessmen. The availability of such data in compact form in addition to the commercial facts readily obtainable from the U.S. Department of Commerce might result in large-scale increases of our trade with the Federation.

Union of South Africa

The trade mission spent the period from December 13 through 22 in the Union of South Africa. In appointments with Government officials and businessmen in Johannesburg, Pretoria, and Capetown, many inquiries were directed to the trade mission concerning U.S. objectives regarding South Africa. On the sensitive question of race relations, the Indian question and the general "apartheid" policies of the South African Government, no opinion was expressed. Time and again the trade mission asserted that its primary function was merely to check on United States-South African trade relations and the possible expansion in the future. However, in discussions with businessmen and during interviews with the English and Afrikaans' press a clarified statement was made as regards U.S. objectives.

It was stated categorically that South Africa and the United States have traditionally maintained friendly relations and it was hoped that South Africa would continue to look to the United States for leadership in free world affairs. U.S. basic objectives were stated as assisting in the maintenance of economic stability and progress in the Union. In order to emphasize the desirability of continuing friendly relations with South AFrica, attention was drawn repeatedly to the strategic importance of its geographical location and its position as a producer of raw materials—uranium, chrome, manganese, gold, wool, and fruit. Insofar as trade was concerned, the consensus was that American-South African trade relations had been profitable in the pas and hope was expressed that the same conditions would obtain in the future. As it was, South Africa was offering U.S. businessmen a most favorable investment climate and this situation augured well for future investment of American risk capital.

The South Africans noted with pride the absence of any American grant aid to the Union. Such assistance as was accepted came in the form of loans through the Export-Import Bank to various gold-mining companies for the extraction of uranium and also the Electrical Supply Commission fo;the expansion of electricity for use in uranium plants. South Africa also has a mutual defense assistance agreement with the United States but does not get any war materiel except on a cash basis. Another agreement of cooperation concerned the use of atomic energy, but here it was noted that a grant for $750,000 for research in "atoms for peace" was refused on the grounds that there were "strings" attached to this money—namely, that the reactor had to be bought in the United States. As part also of this agreement the United States has undertaken to purchase uranium oxide in the Union and has an agreement for the buying of this commodity until 1962. A question asked repeatedly was whether the United States would continue to buy uranium oxide in the Union or whether this contract would be reduced in quantity, but no definitive answer could be given.

In general, the feeling as regards trade relations was that U.S. trade performance in South Africa has been somewhat of a disappointment. The to al level of imports into South Africa was controlled by licensing agreements under which exchange allotments are given to registered importers in Africa for certain categories of goods. This import-control system has been progressively relaxed, so as to permit of a larger increase in total world imports.

The Union of South Africa represents the largest market in Africa for America which is currently supplying approximately 45 percent of all South African imports. U.S. exports have averaged around $275 million per year, whereas imports from South Africa have averaged $100 million per year. The United States is second only to the United Kingdom as a supplier of imports, but lately West Germany and France have increased their totals and U.S. trade has suffered from competition in various fields. U.S. goods have made an enviable reputation for quality and serviceability in the South African market, but time and again the trade mission was told that price factors have become an important element in South African demands for overseas goods. It seems that much closer attention to local market requirements and a greater care in the selection of trading agents should be exercised; also that price quotations to meet competitive import duties as well as competitive credit terms should be determined in advance. U.S. exports have diminished also because large-scale local production is increasingly sheltered by protective tariffs.

Traditionally, the South African Government has always maintained a favorable climate for private foreign investment in the country's economic development. Taxation on foreign firms has been moderate and no differentiation is made between local and foreign capital. The Government has also followed a policy of unrestricted remittance of profits and dividends. The U.S. total investment in all of Africa is around $700 million, of which total the South African investment ranges around $380 million. Approximately 160 American firms have subsidiaries or interests in the Union, ranging in activity from processing and distribution to manufacturing and mining.

*   *

Recommendations

1. The U.S. Department of Commerce trade mission of 1957 had initiated literally hundreds of trade leads for American businessmen, but it seems that few had been followed up to the extent necessary to bring such leads to fruition. The U.S. official commercial representation had to deal not only with trade, but also with investments and seemed to be understaffed to do both jobs adequately. Additional personnel might be needed to take advantage of the favorable climate for trade and investment to bring to the attention of South African businessmen the exact type of merchandise and machinery produced by the United States. On the other hand, reciprocal trade channels might be publicized for South African exporters.

2. Since South Africa is on the verge of another round of industrial expansion, U.S. businessmen might find it profitable to keep in close touch with our official representatives in South Africa insofar as new opportunities for investment are concerned.

3. A specific attempt should be made to initiate an expanded credit program for commercial goods since under such a program a large-scale expansion of U.S. exports might result.

4. Although the trend of tourism from the United States has shown a favorable increase in the receipts of South Africa of such tourist dollars, an intensive program should be developed whereby South African businessmen could be invited to the United States by publicizing our travel facilities and commercial opportunities.

5. A much greater representation allowance for our various consular and other officers in South Africa might bring much more favorable results because of increased contacts between our official family and South African business interests.

6. A much more intensive effort should be made to get men for representative positions in South Africa who speak the language of the country because of the marked schism between the English and Afrikaans-speaking people. Any foreigner who takes the trouble to learn the language of the greater percentage of the people is welcomed with open arms because of his greater identification with their interests and means of communications.

*   *   *

Address by W. Michael Blumenthal, Deputy Assistant Secretary for Economic Affairs, on Commodity Stabilization and Economic Development in Africa*

September 26, 1962

*   *   *

The problems of the new and old nations of tropical Africa are manifold. You have no doubt been hearing much these days about the rapidity of political evolution, the pressures of social change, and the imperatives of economic development.

*   *   *

Large parts of tropical Africa are poor, extremely poor. Per capita national incomes are under $100 per year in a majority of countries and even in the relatively richer countries, such as Ghana and Nyasaland, do not exceed $200. While little can be done about underlying climate, soil, and resource deficiencies, much can and is being done to raise educational and health standards, to import technical and managerial skills, to build ports, roads, railways, and airports essential to tie formerly subsistence economies into an African and world trade network and to develop indigenous power resources to support industrialization.

Clearly areas such as the Congo, which are rich in mineral wealth and in untapped hydro resources, have a great potential for economic development once unity and stability are restored. Elsewhere the future is also bright if capital, skills, and resources can be effectively combined. The mushrooming of new enterprises and the growth, for example, of a Nigerian entrepreneurial class give promise that this will be done in much of Africa.

But the process of modernization requires resources: human, material, and financial. Let it be clearly understood that most of these resources must, of necessity, be local in origin for private foreign investment, economic assistance, and other unilateral transfers of resources into the African area can form only a small though valuable part of the total required. Moreover, the resources coming in from the outside must first and foremost be directed toward speeding up the process of generating indigenous assets. They must also be employed to broaden the economic base and to help move resources out of commodities in overproduction into new lines of endeavor.

But there can be no question that, since the possibilities for local savings are limited, the need for private investment and economic assistance from the rest of the world is great. In particular, foreign exchange resources to finance essential imports of consumer and investment goods alike are often inadequate to foster rapid economic growth.

To help meet capital and foreign exchange requirements, our European allies will this year provide aid to countries in tropical Africa to the tune of over $600 million. Our aid effort, while comparatively modest—roughly $175 million in grants and loans for tropical Africa during fiscal year 1962—will usefully supplement aid from France, the United Kingdom, the European Economic Community, and elsewhere. So too will the flow of private American risk capital into tropical Africa, which may have added net new resources of about $60 million in 1961.

**Department of State Bulletin*, Oct. 22, 1962, pp. 616-19; 620.

Yet the fact remains that the export earnings of these countries are roughly four times as important a source of foreign exchange for them as aid and private investment.

Moreover, aid is temporary, but the development of a sound and growing volume of trade lays a more permanent and lasting foundation. The need to stimulate stable and growing income from export earnings is, therefore, of overriding importance.

Thus the African stake in trade is crucial. Yet these countries face serious trading problems. Let me mention five:

First: There is the fact that one or two primary commodities often account for between 60 percent and 90 percent of a nation's total export earnings. For example: Nigeria earns two-thirds of its export proceeds from cocoa and oilseeds; the Ivory Coast earns about 90 percent from coffee, cocoa, and timber; Senegal 85 percent from peanuts; Ghana 75 percent from cocoa and timber; and Uganda 75 percent from coffee and cotton.

Second: The commodities on which African countries are highly dependent are subject to wide short-term price fluctuations. For example, in recent years declines in coffee and cocoa prices have been dramatic. Spot cocoa is today quoted in New York at under 20 cents a pound whereas in 1958 high was over 50 cents. Even though Ghanaian production and exports have increased markedly in the past 2 years, cocoa earnings have merely held steady. For Nigeria, where production has grown more slowly, earnings from cocoa have declined, as they have for peanuts, where world prices are also soft. Although African coffee producers have fared relatively better than most Latin American producers in the last few years, the sharp fall in coffee prices has hurt them also. Nigeria did benefit from a 25 percent increase in tin prices from the first to the third quarter of 1961, although the price has subsequently declined again.

For agricultural commodities the major source of instability is found on the supply side. Yields fluctuate markedly as a result particularly of weather variations and crop diseases. Also, production of tree crops adjusts to changes in market conditions only with significant time lags. This fact appears frequently to work to increase price instabilities.

For the minerals the major source of short-term instability is found on the demand side, the level of economic activity in the developed countries being the leading influence on price.

Third: Not only do the prices of most primary commodities fluctuate widely, but also the long-term composite trend has been down for the past 10 years. The U.N. price index for primary products in international trade is down over 10 percent since 1953. During the same period the index for manufactured goods has risen by about 10 percent, with the consequence that African countries as well as the other predominantly primary producing areas are greatly concerned with what they refer to as the deterioration in their "terms of trade."

It is a fact that demand for primary commodities has grown less rapidly than demand for manufactured items and services. Technological change has led to economy of use of raw materials and the development of substitutes. And, even at higher incomes and lower prices, there is a limit to how much coffee Americans will drink; in technical language the elasticities of demand for primary commodities are often low.

These facts doubtless make the process of development slower and more difficult than it would be if demand for African products were growing more rapidly and if long-term price trends were not adverse.

Fourth: The pattern of trade for many African countries is directed predominantly toward the former metropoles. This is particularly true of franc area countries. For example, over 60 percent of Ivory Coast exports go to franc area countries, and over 75 percent of Ivory Coast imports in 1960 came from France. Moreover, the Ivory Coast is far from an extreme case of trade dependence.

Fifth: The efforts of African producers to industrialize are hampered by protectionalism in much of the rest of the world. The pattern is all too often that they labor under artificial handicaps even in processing their own products. For example, cocoa butter is often subject to higher duties than cocoa beans, and freight rates on processed items may be disproportionately high. Unfortunately, production of light manufactured goods faces still more difficulties.

As the leading world power, dedicated to expanding peacefully the area of freedom, the United States is necessarily concerned with the trade and commodity problems of African states, committed as they are to economic progress by one means or another. Peace and prosperity are in fact indivisible, . . .

What then would we like to do about commodity stabilization? What are the objectives of U.S. policy?

Our overriding objective is to keep commodity price fluctuations or declines from jeopardizing the development effort of producing nations—and, hopefully, to stimulate commodity trade so that it can increase its contribution to development.

We want to find solutions compatible with a growth of the freedom in the world and to minimize the temptation for the nonindustrial nations to seek the illusion of an allegedly easy Communist road to rapid economic development.

More specifically our objectives are, insofar as feasible (and this is an important caveat):

1. To dampen disruptive cyclical price fluctuations.

2. To arrest the secular decline in commodity prices. This is probably the most difficult objective of all to attain, because the downward secular price trend appears in good measure to be implicit in rapid technological progress and more efficient use of materials and primary products.

3. To mitigate problems of acute supply-demand imbalance which have arisen, for example, with respect to coffee.

4. To solve commodity problems in ways which promote the industrialization and diversification of the producing country. Indeed, industrialization and the development of trade within and among developing nations will be an important part of a solution of many of the trade problems of these nations.

5. To develop global, not regional, solutions to commodity problems or at least to find national and regional measures not incompatible with a global, multilateral, nondiscriminatory approach.

6. To avoid excessive or unworkable controls which might jeopardize the growth of free economic and political institutions. We would like to make maximum use of market forces supplemented, where necessary, by financial mechanisms and to place minimum reliance on such devices as quotas and the more direct types of price support.

7. To assure that any commodity stabilization arrangements, which necessarily will

vary from commodity to commodity, operate in ways which benefit both producers and consumers.

We are under no illusions that commodity stabilization will be easy within the framework which I have outlined. But we are making a concerted effort involving both study and action. I would like to describe the major components of the strategy we are following in our commodity stabilization efforts.

To deal with the purely short-term price instabilities, we are studying a global compensatory financing scheme which might partially offset cyclical fluctuations in export earnings of producing countries by providing short-term finance to permit imports to remain fairly stable and thereby to avoid sharp stops and starts in carrying out development plans.

Our efforts to work out compensatory financing mechanisms to offset cyclical fluctuations in export earnings are focused, primarily, in the U.N. Commission on International Commodity Trade (the CICT), although the Organization of American States had made major contributions to the study of possibilities in this field, developing a specific proposal which is under consideration. In addition the International Monetary Fund, which already provides a form of compensatory financing through its balance-of-payments assistance, is also considering the problem.

Final consideration of what type of compensatory financing system, if any, appears best suited for the long-term development needs of all developing nations depends on many factors both of a policy and of a technical nature. The United States is prepared to consider any approach, or combination of devices, which promises to stimulate long-term economic growth. We do, however, have doubts as to the desirability of using compensatory financing as an aid mechanism rather than as a short-term credit mechanism. Aid transferred in such a manner might too often go to nations whose aid needs were relatively less than other developing nations, and there appear to be difficult technical problems of assuring that aid in this form would be used as effectively as other forms of capital inflows.

National and regional marketing boards also can be fairly effective in smoothing out seasonal price fluctuations. These bodies also have a useful role to play in improving earnings through quality controls and distribution of better seeds, fertilizers, and technical information.

To deal with the longrun secular price declines and with problems of supply-demand imbalance, commodity agreements may provide a partial and interim answer. Thus for a few commodities with particularly serious structural problems—such as coffee and possibly cocoa—we have developed or are developing international commodity agreements with worldwide participation of producing and consuming nations. In such cases, for the agreements to be effective, producing nations must curb overproduction and shift excess resources out of primary commodities in oversupply into other areas. We believe all of the industrial nations should coordinate their aid programs to facilitate such a resource shift.

*   *   *

We are not "taking sides" between developing nations; we are not interested in the development of one nation or region at the expense of another nation or region. We are equally concerned with the development of the Ivory Coast, Nigeria, and Brazil—and of Senegal, Tanganyika, Indonesia, and Colombia. The United States is aware that the gradual phasing out of duties and other preferential arrangements must generally be cushioned by adjustment measures to provide at least equivalent benefits to Africans, including acceptable safeguards. The development prospects of nations now inside preferential systems must not be jeopardized in the course of abolishing preferential arrangements. Our task is to find arrangements alternative to preferences which will help to assure all developing nations equivalent export opportunities and which will provide the maximum resources and incentives to speed the creation of diversified and industrialized economies. These alternative devices must necessarily link the flow of economic assistance from industrialized to developing countries with our efforts to stabilize commodity prices and to improve commodity trade arrangements.

There is one final point which, although it is sometimes embarrassing to industrialized nations, including the United States, cannot be ignored in an analysis of commodity problems. This is the question of import restrictions and other devices such as internal taxes which curtail export markets for primary commodities. The United States imposes import quotas on petroleum, lead, zinc, and peanuts—to mention a few key commodities. It is difficult for us to ask other nations to take the often painful steps involved in, for example, curtailing coffee production or dismantling preferential devices when we ourselves retreat, on occasion, behind import quotas. We in the United States, too, must face our worldwide responsibilities of working out the most effective global arrangements for commodity trade.

*   *   *

Address to the International Executive Convention by
Assistant Secretary Williams on New Patterns of African Trade*

April 1, 1964

It gives me great pleasure to meet today with a group of businessmen interested in expanding American economic relations with Africa. We are in a period when new patterns of trade are beginning to reshape the African market of the future. It is an especially good timyto embark upon new business ventures on that continent.

Frankly, I am optimistic about Africa's future. My optimism is based on the years of intimate contact I have had with the African peoples and their leaders, for whom I have great respect. Africa's nations—both old and new—are seeking to develop themselves as rapidly as possible, and they are working arduously to build modern economies. In these efforts they are encouraging foreign investors to help them create modern, independent societies, and they are anxious to increase their import and export trade with the United States. To these goals we can only give our hearty concurrence and encouragement.

There are many reasons why we can be optimistic about the economic future of Africa, and there are many reasons why American business should take a closer look at the opportunities offered by Africa's developing nations.

*Ibid., Apr. 27, 1964, pp. 664-70.

The richness of Africa's mineral resources is well known, and the importance of these resources to the United States is substantial. Africa is a major world supplier of gold and diamonds, of cobalt and chrome, of copper, of manganese, of antimony. Recently, large deposits of petroleum, iron ore, and bauxite have begun to be developed, in many cases with substantial U.S. investment. Yet much of the continent has not been fully explored by U.S. businessmen. Undoubtedly many new opportunities await the more enterprising firms.

Prospects also are favorable in other resources. There is generally little, if any, population pressure in Africa, and in some areas there is even unused agricultural land to be made fruitful. Electric energy potential abounds in many areas—among them, the Congo River basin alone is estimated to have one-third of the total world hydroelectric generating capacity.

Then there are social factors favorable to economic growth. There is no highly rigid caste or class structure, as in other areas of the world, and there are few land tenure patterns which restrict mobility. The more enterprising African is able to move to the city and rise quickly in business or the professions when he has the necessary skills and capital.

At the same time there are drawbacks and hazards in expanded American business relationships with Africa, and I think we must recognize such risks frankly.

There are a number of factors which seriously limit progress in Africa; a low level of education; the lack of a substantial number of upper- and middle-level administrators, technicians, and professional people; low productivity rates; a shortage of entrepreneurs and indigenous capital; and an inadequate network of transportation, communications, and other services. It would be difficult for Africa to overcome those conditions with its own resources, and it is in those areas that foreign trade, aid, and investment can make important contributions to African progress.

On another plane, there have been severe political disturbances in many parts of the continent in recent months, and it is likely that there will be more unrest as long as aspirations remain unfulfilled. There is no need for me to catalog recent troubles; they have been widely reported in the American press. Those serious matters cannot be dismissed lightly, but we should, nevertheless, view such disturbances in perspective. Most of the current conflicts and crises are typical of the trouble newly independent countries encounter on the road to nationhood. The problems spring from the frustrations crated by poverty and the lack of swift progress, from the inevitable struggles between the old and the new, from the problems of societies moving from rural to urban life.

Our concern with those troubles, however, should not lead us to lose sight of the quiet, steady progress being made throughout the African Continent. Increases in gross national product, rising electric power production, or improved secondary schools cannot compete in the headlines with news about an army mutiny. Yet in terms of human involvement, the quiet progress is really the big news in Africa, and it is far more widespread and lasting than Africa's troubles.

A third problem that American businessmen should be awrae of is found in the artificial barriers to trade and investment which arose during Africa's colonial era. This is a system which tended to bind, almost inextricably, the economy of a colony to that of a colonial power. Although much of Africa—and, indeed, the most populated part of the continent—is relatively open to American trade and investment, there are some areas, such as the Spanish and Portuguese territories and some former French territories in tropical Africa, in which it is difficult for American and other foreign business to trade. Through such devices as preferential tariffs, bilateral trading arrangements, licensing systems, and exchange controls, nationals of the present and former metropolitan powers protect a predominant influence in the economies of those areas by sharply limiting commodity exchanges with third countries. At the same time, however, the European powers are providing significant amounts of aid and related public funds to those areas, and maintenance of their commercial privileges there is often defended on that basis.

While the United States recognizes the desirability of encouraging the European nations to continue to provide a high level of aid to Africa, we do not feel we should be precluded from efforts to improve the U.S. business position. We feel that a broadening of our trading relations in these ars is not only in our own interest but in the interest of the African areas and of the European nations themselves. For that reason we have studied with interest the recent Jeanneney report, which recommended that France diversify its assistance programs to embrace areas of Southeast Asia and Latin America. And we have noted President de Gaulle's overture to Mexico only 2 weeks ago, when he encouraged Mexicans to rely on more than one source for their economic associations. We hope that such diversification of economic interests will also occur in those parts of Africa which now have trade relations with one predominant source.

Now let me hasten to assure you that, despite the hazards and problems I have mentioned, there is a great deal of progress being made in Africa. There is much going well on that continent, both politically and economically.

One instrumentality that is contributing much to Africa's progress is the Organization of African Unity, which came into being last May at the historic African heads-of-state conference at Addis Ababa. It is now a 34-member, Africa-wide organization, embracing all independent states except South Africa. The OAU already has begun to function as a vehicle of continental political, economic, social, and cultural cooperation. It has made an impressive record for itself in the 10 months of its existence—notably in encouraging a cease-fire and then a settlement of the Moroccan-Algerian border dispute. Last week it played a similar role in bringing Ethiopia and Somalia together for talks aimed at arranging a cease-fire and at ending the sporadic border clashes between those two nations.

Another Africa-wide body making an important contribution to Africa's growth is the Economic Commission for Africa, a U.N. body operating under able African leadership. The ECA has begun to play a vital role in Africa's economic planning. In particular, it is building a philosophy of regional economic integration and a program of regional projects to realize economies from large-scale enterprises and to avoid the duplication and competition inherent in basing development on a large number of small economic units in Africa.

At its most recent meeting at Addis Ababa last month, the Economic Commission for Africa marked an important milestone in the efforts of the African states to achieve economic integration. That conference reflected a greater determination among African nations to find a common approach to the wide range of problems impeding Africa's economic development.

In addition there was a growing awareness that the existing fragmented markets of the continent restrict Africa's efforts to develop. Prevailing economic units, it was argued, are too small to permit the use of the most up-to-date technology and mass market techniques. For these and related reasons, Africans showed an increasing desire to enlarge the size of their markets to enable them to realize the benefits that can be derived from large-scale operations. In this respect, ECA missions have been working in East, North, and West Africa to explore the possibilities of setting up such industries as iron and steel complexes and chemical operations, to be located at sites considered optimum for natural resources and markets.

One important result of all of these efforts by the Economic Commission for Africa will be the expansion of opportunities for foreign trade and investment in many parts of the continent.

For its own part the United States Government is encouraging the growth of a climate in Africa which will be conducive to an expansion of U.S. trade and investment. This is a coordinated effort in which the principal instruments are the Department of Commerce, the Department of State and its African posts, the Agency for International Development, the Department of Agriculture, and the Export-Import Bank.

At this time of year I am particularly concerned with the United States AID program. In a few days I will appear before Congress to explain why I think AID is an essential element of our African foreign policy. I am well aware that our AID program has critics—and I concede that constructive criticism is needed to keep the program healthy. However, I do believe that some of the dissatisfaction with AID is due to misconceptions about its nature and its goals.

The true purpose of AID is to encourage and enable countries to develop and preserve their independence and stability. We believe that economic and social well-being and progress are integral parts of true independence and stability. While we recognize the importance of efforts undertaken by Africans themselves—and our AID program is geared to encourage Africans to help themselves—it is in the best American tradition to assist where we are able and where our aid is desired.

All Americans have an important interest in the economic growth and betterment of life in Africa because of the long-range bearing these factors have on world peace and order. You as businessmen, however, have an even more direct stake in foreign aid. United States economic aid programs in Africa provide many opportunities for U.S. exporters and investors. These opportunities stem from the present requirement that aid dollars be spent for U.S. goods and services and from the inducements offered by AID to encourage United States investment abroad. Combined with the growth of Africa markets resulting from an accelerating pace of economic development, our AID efforts provide a wide variety of business oportunities.

So successful have these efforts been that Farrell Lines *African News Digest* has written:

> Because of A.I.D., the entrepreneur of today, if his ideas are truly worthwhile, stands less risk than at any other time in our commercial history. The potential of American investment and interest in Africa is therefore dependent upon the creativity and imagination of American businessmen.

Although not the largest single donor in Africa, the U.S. Government in fiscal year 1962 and again in fiscal year 1963 provided about $500 million in economic assistance to 34 African countries. Surplus food and fiber, under the Food for Peace program, accounted for nearly half of this amount. In contrast, other free-world governments provided $1,200 million, and the Sino-Soviet bloc extended $200-250 million in credits. Thus the United States contributed roughly one-fourth of Africa's $2 billion in external economic assistance from government sources. In addition, important contributions are made by U.S. private foundations, religious organizations, and other nongovernment groups.

In carrying out our AID program, we strive in various ways to encourage the fullest participation of U.S. private concerns in African operations. While we are naturally interested in having American business take advantage of all opportunities for profitable new business ventures, we also are interested in the participation of United States concerns because of the entrepreneurial skills which American business can help transfer to Africa. A good example of such participation is the new Education Center at the University of Ibadan in Niberia, which was opened only 2 weeks ago by IBM World Trade Corporation to help English-speaking Africans acquire basic and technical education in such fields as data processing, accounting, government, economics, and mathematics. Next year, in Dakar, Senegal, IBM will open a second such center for French-speaking Africans.

One part of our program that stands in direct support of American business is a series of investment guaranties which have been arranged between the United States and 20 African countries. Through these agreements, U.S. investors in Africa are protected against the risks of inconvertibility of currency and expropriation. In addition, 17 of these agreements cover war risk and 14 of them cover extended-risk guaranties and guaranties against loss caused by revolution and insurrection.

Even before deciding to invest in Africa, however, an American firm may be able to obtain financial assistance from AID to make a feasibility study to determine whether a proposed African business venture is sound. Three such investment survey grants have been made in Africa, and five applications for grants are being processed.

There are also the so-called Cooley loans available in Guinea, Morocco, Sudan, and Tunisia. These loans are made from local currency accounts that have been built up by the AID program and are available to United States firms getting established in those countries—particularly to businesses which will increase sales of U.S. farm products.

Even if you are not immediately interested in establishing plant or sales operation in Africa, you should be aware of the stake of American business in our AID program. Between 80 and 90 percent of our economic aid expenditures, for example, are for U.S. goods and services. The approximately $500 million spent last year on African aid provided jobs, income, profits, and service contracts for tens of thousands of workers and farmers, and hundreds of U.S. factories, universities, engineers, building contractors, and many others.

AID estimates that 550,000 nongovernment jobs in the United States were provided by our worldwide aid expenditures in 1962. In New York State alone, major AID contracts amounted to more than $30 million in 1962 and some $45 million in 1963. And between 1960 and 1963 AID-administered cargoes on American-flag cargo liners rose from just over $40 million to approximately $108 million.

When our AID program provides a bulldozer, telecommunication equipment, or a shipload of wheat from our farm surplus, the story does not end at that point. The first shipment may be paid for by a grant or loan provided by the U.S. taxpayer. But bulldozers need spare parts and must be replaced one day, and telecommunication networks are often extended. Even dietary habits may change through increased use of American food products. New tastes and needs for American products can lead to new commercial sales, and this development can be an important end result of our AID program around the world. But unless the countries of Africa are helped to grow out of their low-level economies at an early date, they may not become important markets for our products.

In addition to United States aid, both trade and investment with Africa have been of rapidly growing importance to America in recent years. Total direct investment by United States firms grew fourfold in Africa from 1950 to 1962, far more than our rate of increase of foreign investment in any other continent. In 1962 United States investments in Africa totaled nearly $1.25 billion, an increase of $200 million over 1961. This increase was spread throughout Africa. In a similar manner, our total exports to Africa have more than doubled in value since 1950. In 1962 these exports amounted to almost $1 billion. Our imports from Africa came to $750 million in 1962 and were about 50 percent above the 1950 level.

Thus it is clear to me that many American businessmen are betting on Africa as a good place to do business, to invest, and to make a profit.

The largest African markets for U.S. products are the United Arab Republic, South Africa, Congo (Leopoldville), Liberia, Morocco, and Nigeria. Nigeria, with a growing economy, the largest population in Africa, and a central location, bears careful consideration as a place for exports, a place to set up a regional sales office, or a place to build a branch plant. The Arthur D. Little Company of Boston, on a contract with the Nigerian Government, has been seeking out investment opportunities for foreign firms in Nigeria for several years. There has been a remarkable increase in U.S. business activity in that country since it became independent in 1960. In these 4 years U.S. firms in Nigeria have increased from 9 to 72, including 3 banks, 6 petroleum companies, 13 manufacturing and assembly plants, and 20 service companies.

Regional, rather than national, markets also bear watching, as closer relations develop among African nations. In terms of regional cooperation, the East African nations of Kenya, Tanganyika, and Uganda provide a well-developed example of how sovereign nations can work together in harmony. Through the East African Common Services Organization—a multinational body—the area's 25 million people share a common currency, common communications and transportation facilities, common tax administration, common research facilities, and common customs and tariffs. And outside of the framework of the EACSO, they have pooled their intellectual resources in the University of East Africa.

All of these joint efforts make those three countries one of the world's advanced areas in cooperation and provide the area's people with services of a quality that would be difficult for individual nations to match. In addition, the effectiveness of such international cooperation makes a significant contribution to the area's overall stability. A further factor is that this cooperation has helped to make foreign assistance more effective in the area. Although U.S. efforts are primarily directed to individual countries, there are some programs we conduct on an East African regional basis.

Throughout the continent there is a whole range of immediate opportunities open to American private business. There is room for export and import businesses, large and small. Transportation and communication facilities are also among the very highest priorities of African leaders. In addition, opportunities include such areas as insurance, banking and loan associations, hotels and low-cost housing.

There will be many sales opportunities in Africa as that continent's purchasing power rises and its population grows. Africa already is a significant market for a variety of U.S. products. In 1962 the most important of these products were foodstuffs, which accounted for $178 million. Other products and their value were textile fibers and manufactures, $72 million; industrial machinery, $140 million; tractors, $53 million; and chemicals, $46 million.

There also are opportunities for purchasing in Africa that I want to touch upon. Admittedly, the range of goods available for such purchases is not as great as the range of opportunities for investment and sales, but some do exist and others can be sought and found.

Most of our principal imports from Africa—minerals, cocoa, coffee, and precious stones—are accounted for by American firms that have invested in extractive and production facilities in Africa. But there are some purchasing opportunities and markets for such products as African handicrafts and art objects, which are exotic and profitable items in this country. There are also various raw materials of a specialized nature that are available to American purchasers, such as spices, sisal, and scarce minerals needed for technological research and development.

A relatively unexplored and growing field for purchasers is that of processed and semiprocessed goods. As Africa's economic development progresses, there is increasing interest among the nations of Africa to process their raw materials domestically for export to foreign markets. Thus, sisal is being exported as twine, as well as a raw material. Another example is iron, which is being sold not only as ore but as ferromanganese or ferrochrome. This is a trend which will accelerate in the future, and it opens up many possibilities for American buyers.

In conclusion, there are five steps I would suggest to businessmen interested in looking into the African market:

1. Make a serious survey of the African market. Talks with banks and with other American firms experienced in African business would enable you to get a view of what the continent has to offer and what are some of the special problems of operations there. You should become acquainted with the Agency for International Development and with the Department of Commerce Field Office in New York, or wherever you operate, to be fully aware of the services the U.S. Government offers to the foreign trader and investor. The foreign trade publications of the Commerce Department can be especially helpful to you. In the last 13 months alone, the Commerce Department in Washington had 2,174 conferences with businessmen and processed 2,671 written inquiries on trade or investment in Africa.

2. Make a survey trip to Africa to look over opportunities on the spot. Here again you can enlist the services of the Department of Commerce, and the Department of State can advise its embassies in Africa and their staffs, particularly the commercial officers, of your visit. Thus, when you arrive in, say, Lagos, Dar-es-Salaam, or Tunis, the U.S. Embassy will be prepared to assist you in understanding the area and making important contacts there. The number of our commercial officers in Africa has risen from 4 in 1959 to 13 in 1964, to give you an idea of our increasing desire to provide services in Africa to American businessmen. In addition to these special commercial officers, there are economic officers at every post who are ready to help you.

3. To give the African market a fair chance, I would recommend the following procedure. Allow enough time in visiting a country to learn about it; no one can adequately survey a market in a day or two. Sales representatives and sales literature should use the commercial language of the country, and prices should be quoted in local currency. Businessmen have often had difficulties in French-speaking Africa in particular because they were unable to use that language.

4. Most important in any business operation in Africa, in my view, is the need to make a business venture a cooperative venture involving Africans in all phases. This is not only good politics but good business as well, because it means sharing American business know-how and developing Africans for more sophisticated work. Much attention should be given to the training and upgrading of Africans into increasingly responsible positions. It should be readily apparent that costs will be much lower if you employ Africans instead of sending Americans and their families abroad.

5. Finally, gear your products and sales to the needs of the market. Some businessmen rather quickly decide that the African capacity to buy expensive or sophisticated products is too limited to be worth the trouble. If you should so decide, perhaps you should consider African or U.S. manufacture of special products more suited to the current stage of development in Africa and gradually develop a market for more complex or more costly items.

The principal fact to remember is that you are dealing with a changing market. Past patterns of production and trade are being radically altered in Africa. New urban communities are coming into being. Large-scale mining, industrial, and agricultural projects are under way in many parts of the continent. Purchasing power is rising.

In some instances there are promising prospects for immediate opportunities for marketing and investment. In other cases the prospects are for the long term.

In any event, the future of Africa is in African hands, and American business can assist those hands as they approach their tasks of nation building. From such joint efforts, Africans and Americans alike have much to gain.

*Hearings Before the Subcommittee on Africa and the Challenge of Development**

July 25, 1967, April 24, May 8
and 14, 1968

*   *   *

Mr. O'Hara: What would you say is the investment climate in most of the countries of Africa? Is it good, or bad?

Mr. Rivkin: The investment climate varies considerably in Africa. I don't know of any African country which closes its doors entirely to private foreign investment. I think one has to look at Africa almost on a country-by-country basis.

You have all degrees of enthusiasm for external private investment. There are countries which are open-door countries, if you like, which welcome foreign private investment and make very substantial concessions to attract it.

---

*Committee on Foreign Affairs, *Africa and the Challenge of Development*, Hearings Before the Subcommittee on Africa of the Committee of Foreign Affairs, 90th Cong. 2d Sess., (Washington, 1968) pp. 82-87.

There are other countries that would like to exercise more selectivity, and welcome foreign private investment only in particular sectors or particular types of investment.

Then there are others that are really quite suspicious and uneasy about private investment from abroad, and although they may nominally welcome it, they make it somewhat difficult. And there are areas that are mildly hostile to external investment, but not entirely closed.

*   *   *

Mr. O'Hara: On the whole, would you say that the investments are secure?

Mr. Rivkin: I think this, too, varies considerably in Africa. There has been in a variety of countries, as you know, a fair amount of expropriation. The problem has been whether there would be reasonable compensation. Most African countries that have gone in for expropriation have made a serious effort to provide compensation.

There are countries where there has been no expropriation, and these generally are countries that welcome foreign investment warmly.

But I think you have the whole gamut, but there has been an increasing tendency for the state to take over particular types of industry, or particular types of external investment, generally with compensation.

*   *   *

Mr. O'Hara: The fear of the property being taken away is not a factor that deters the World Bank from its investments in Africa?

Mr. Rivkin: As part of its lending operation, the Bank is concerned with the total economic performance of a country. Hence, if the credit position of a country is impaired by the existence of a dispute over the default on its foreign debt or over compensation for property expropriated from a former foreign owner, the Bank must take account of such a situation before deciding on a loan to the country in question. The Bank is charged, under its articles of agreement, to encourage international investment. It has, therefore, a direct interest in the creation and maintenance of satisfactory relations between member countries and their creditors. Accordingly, the normal practice is to advise countries involved in expropriation compensation disputes that the Bank and its associate institution, the International Development Association, will not assist them with loans or credits unless or until they make appropriate efforts to reach a fair and equitable settlement of existing disputes.

Mr. O'Hara: What is the total of the investments of the World Bank in Africa?

Mr. Rivkin: I would have to get the precise number for you, Congressman O'Hara. The order of magnitude is $1.5 billion. In addition, IDA has invested about $275 million.

I could say that it has increased dramatically from a very low level, as you might have anticipated, say, 7 or 8 years ago, when there were a few independent countries, and where the World Bank operations were limited essentially to loans basically to metrpolitan countries for use in Africa.

(The requested information is provided in the following tables:)

TABLE A

Statement of World Bank and International Development Association Loans and
Credits to Africa—1946/47 to 1967/68 (as of April 30, 1958)

		Bank loans		*IDA credits*	
	Number	*Net amount*	*Net amount less sales and repayments*	*Number*	*Net amount*
AFRICA					
Algeria	3	$80,500,000	$27,803,000		
Botswana				1	$3,600,000
Burundi	1	4,800,000	1,820,000	1	1,100,000
Cameroon	1	7,000,000	7,000,000	2	11,550,000
Congo (Brazzaville)	1	30,000,000	30,000,000		
Congo (Democratic Republic)	5	91,582,854	32,587,346		
Ethiopia	9	70,200,000	55,110,340	3	28,400,000
Gabon	2	47,000,000	16,116,200		
Ghana	1	47,000,000	46,331,000		
Guinea	1	1,700,000	1,700,000		
Ivory Coast	1	7,091,567			
Kenya	5	85,200,000	55,938,974	6	26,200,000
Lesotho				1	4,100,000
Liberia	2	4,250,000	3,950,000		
Malagasy Republic	1	4,800,000	4,800,000	1	10,000,000
Malawi				5	27,500,000
Mali				1	9,100,000
Mauritania	1	66,000,000	2,645,100	1	6,700,000
Mauritius	1	6,973,119	2,022,520		
Morocco	4	59,749,041	55,803,620	1	11,000,000
Niger				1	1,500,000
Nigeria	6	185,500,000	170,443,094	2	35,500,000
Rhodesia	3	86,950,000	34,174,486		
Senegal	1	4,000,000	3,755,339	1	9,000,000
Sierra Leone	1	3,800,000	3,460,000		
Somalia				1	6,200,000
South Africa	11	241,800,000	26,767,294		
Sudan	5	129,000,000	113,781,000	1	13,000,000
Swaziland	2	6,950,000	4,790,000	1	2,800,000
Tanzania	1	5,200,000	5,110,000	4	26,600,000
Tunisia	4	33,985,481	33,024,373	3	23,062,598
Uganda	1	8,400,000	84,464	3	18,400,000
United Arab Republic	1	55,500,000	33,500,000		
Upper Volta					
Zambia	4	84,850,000	44,741,478		
Total	79	1,460,782,062	818,259,628	40	276,112,598

TABLE 8

Summary of International Finance Corporation Investments and Standby and
Underwriting Commitments in Africa—1956/57 to 1967/68 (as of Mar. 31, 1968)

	Number of investments and standby and underwriting commitments	Operational investments	Standby and underwriting commitments	Total commitments
AFRICA				
Ethiopia	3	$9,743,582	$3,708,501	$13,452,083
Ivory Coast	1	204,081		204,081
Kenya	1	2,794,179		2,794,179
Liberia	1		250,000	250,000
Morocco	2	2,884,260		2,884,260
Nigeria	3	1,571,031	1,400,000	2,971,031
Senegal	1	3,459,766		3,459,766
Sudan	1	688,893		688,893
Tanzania	2	4,657,485		4,657,485
Tunisia	2	4,075,926		4,075,926
Uganda	1	3,508,436		3,508,436
Total	18	33,587,639	5,358,501	38,946,140

Mr. O'Hara: What has been the percentage of losses in Africa?

Mr. Rivkin: Of the World Bank?

Mr. O'Hara: Yes.

Mr. Rivkin: None. The World Bank has never had a loss on a loan anywhere in the world, including Africa.

*   *   *

*Statement by Abba P. Schwartz, Administrator of the Bureau of
Security and Consular Affairs, on a Refugee Relief Program in Africa**

January 21, 1965

*   *   *

There are over 490,000 refugees in Africa today who have left their homelands because of changing conditions in Africa and have crossed international frontiers into other African countries offering asylum. These refugees, comprising six separate and conspicuous refugee problems, are grouped according to the following countries from which they have fled: Angola, Rwanda, the southern Sudan, South Africa, Portuguese Guinea, and Mozambique.

*Department of State Bulletin, Feb. 15, 1965, p. 224.

*   *   *

Apart from our educational program in behalf of refugee students, which Governor Williams has already discussed, United States assistance to the African countries which have granted asylum to these groups of refugees has been given in two principal ways: through our contribution to the program of the United Nations High Commissioner for Refugees (UNHCR) and our strong support in this connection of projects for African refugees, and through the provision of P.L. 480 food commodities. This food is provided on a government-to-government basis, through American and international voluntary agencies or through United Nations channels.

*   *   *

Speech by Senator Eugene McCarthy (Minnesota) Before the Senate on the Problems and Challenge of Emerging African Nations*

August 22, 1967

*   *   *

About the only time Africa engages the attention of the Senate, or the attention of our Government, is during a crisis. We must respond not only to crises. The question of priorities has no relevance here. We must give continuous attention to Africa.

The Subcommittee on African Affairs of the Foreign Relations Committee will hold educational hearings about Africa and U.S. relations with Africa. With this background, the Senate will, I hope, be able to make more informed judgments about the crises that will occur and also about how our Government reacts to them, and may influence policy so as to prevent crises from developing.

Compared with the historical commitments of the United States in other parts of the world, our commitment to Africa is a tabula rasa. At the end of World War II, there were only four sovereign nations on that continent: Egypt, Ethiopia, Liberia, and the Union of South Africa. Today there are 39, and over 29 of these nations have achieved independence since 1960.

It is a continent where societies are attempting fundamental social change and the development of new economic systems—not Western or Communist—but African systems that will enable them to convert traditional, subsistence agricultural systems into modernized, industrial, market-oriented economies. The very old and the very new will be side by side there for many years before these nations fully realize their potential at home and in the world.

In its "Summary Presentation to the Congress" for fiscal year 1968, the Agency for International Development announced a new policy for Africa. Based initially on Ambassador Edward M. Korry's 1966 report, this overhaul envisions four major changes:

First. The reduction of regular bilateral programs from 30 to 10 by phasing out existing programs and not undertaking new ones. The 10 countries to retain bilateral

*Congressional Record, Aug. 22, 1967, pp. 23458-60.

programs are those "where development prospects are best or where there is a special United States interest or relationship."

Second. "As soon as possible AID projects in other African countries will be limited to support for regional institutions, regional projects, and multidonor projects."

Third. "As soon as possible the possible transfer of funds to multilateral institutions for their use in providing capital and technical assistance."

Fourth. A renewed and expanded emphasis on self-help by African governments.

It is encouraging that the Agency for International Development is experimenting with its policy to Africa. Because of our limited involvement there, our policy can be more flexible than in any other area of the world.

I am encouraged to see a concentration of our aid to 10 so-called development-emphasis countries. The present practical possibilities of our aid program indicate that 10 is a sensible number of countries for concentration. It is unfortunate, however, that AID named the 10 countries implying that our special "interests or relationships" are fixed.

Although we have been assured that we can change our concentration, this flexibility should be emphasized. For instance, AID listed Sudan as one of our development-emphasis countries. At present we do not have diplomatic relations with Sudan, and while we continue to have concern about the Sudanese people and their problems, we cannot offer major assistance at this time.

Further, while discounting bilateral aid in the remaining African aid recipient countries, we must recognize that we still have interests throughout all of Africa which are political in the broadest sense. A new policy must not suggest disengagement from the continent, for that is not our intention.

I am wary of fashionable "isms" such as "regionalism" or "multilateralism" when used to describe a new policy. Initially, each sounds like the cure-all we have been awaiting. On closer examination, although they may represent improvements over our present policy in certain areas, neither "regionalism" nor any other single aid policy will bring the millenium for Africa during the next few decades, and it should not be presented as such.

My intention is not to debunk regionalism, but rather to raise questions concerning its limitations and realistically to outline its possibilities.

*   *   *

We should now ask for a series of comprehensive research studies on the effects of our aid both abroad and at home. The Agency should assemble a more detailed study of the economic effects of our foreign aid program in the United States.

A more realistic and a more objective approach by both the Congress and the administration is called for in our response to the problems of the underdeveloped countries, particularly those in Africa.

Let us relate our policies to those of many African leaders. For example, Tom Mboya of Kenya, Chairman of the Economic Commission for Africa, said in February:

> Development needs in Africa differ in so many ways from requirements in other developing parts of the world. These differences mean that a development program in Africa must be especially designed to solve our problems. Indeed, many of the global policies and institutional arrangements that now govern thydistribution of development capital were

created before Africa threw off the yoke of colonialism and in many ways are better fitted to the needs of the older developing nations. New policies and institutions may be needed to achieve more rapid development in Africa.

Similarly, Julius Nyerere, President of Tanzania and traditionally one of the foremost advocates of African unity, offered a policy of self-reliance in his Arusha Declaration on February 5, 1967. Many other African leaders—whether radical or conservative, English speaking or French—are facing up to their economic problems.

The complete development process—political, social, and economic—is a slow, often fearsome but also an irresistible and stirring process which will take many decades to complete. We are challenged by the emergence of these nations to demonstrate that we still stand by those men who pledged "our lives, our fortunes, and our sacred honor" to establish the ideal of freedom.

The problems of Africa are too serious to be left entirely to the State Department. I hope that Congress will lend its attention to these problems in the hope that through our judgment and the best kind of understanding as to what the Africans want and need, we may be able to make a most constructive contribution to the developing nations in Africa.

*   *   *

Table on United States Foreign Aid for the Fiscal Year Beginning July 1, 1971*

July 10, 1971

FOLLOWING IS THE TABLE RELEASED TODAY BY SENATOR WILLIAM PROXMIRE LISTING (IN THOUSANDS OF DOLLARS) UNITED STATES MILITARY AND ECONOMIC ASSISTANCE TO 43 COUNTRIES:

Country	Military assistance program	Foreign credit sales[1]	Economic supporting assistance[2]	Subtotal
Cambodia	200,000		110,000	310,000
Nationalist China	19,500	45,000		64,500
Indonesia	24,990			24,990
Korea	239,400	15,000		254,400
Laos			50,550	50,550
Malaysia	134	7,500		7,634
Singapore		7,500		7,500
Thailand			40,000	40,000
South Vietnam			565,000	565,000
Greece	19,875	60,000		79,875
India		5,000		5,000
Iran	942			942
Pakistan		5,000	250	5,230
Turkey	99,770			99,770
Portugal	1,000			1,000
Spain	13,000			13,000

The New York Times, July 10, 1971, p. 6.

Country				
Congo	477	2,000	1,016	3,493
Ethiopia	12,790			12,790
Ghana			106	106
Liberia	500		203	703
Nigeria			4,400	4,400
Argentina	897	15,000		15,897
Bolivia	666		115	781
Brazil	892	20,000	174	21,066
Chile	856	5,000		5,856
Colombia	844		340	1,184
Costa Rica			198	198
Dominican Rep.	539		370	909
Ecuador	645		135	780
El Salvador	374		56	430
Guatemala	336	5,000	377	5,713
Guyana			99	99
Haiti			3,000	3,000
Honduras	467		171	638
Mexico	107			107
Jamaica			96	96
Nicaragua	568		91	659
Panama	173		203	376
Paraguay	387			387
Peru	792			792
Uruguay	400	2,000	225	2,625
Venezuela	734	15,000	200	15,934
Philippines	17,000		800	17,800
Worldwide	$731,500	$582,000	$825,000	$2,138,500

Source: U.S. State Department.
[1]Estimates.
[2]Previously unclassified.

BLACK AFRICA:
FROM THE SAHARA TO THE ZAMBEZI

BLACK AFRICA:
FROM THE SAHARA TO THE ZAMBEZI

WEST AFRICA

Commentary

Had other things been equal, an observer might have expected the new states of West Africa to draw the special attention of American policy makers as the pace of African political changes picked up tempo in the late 1950's and early 1960's. West Africa was the part of Africa with closest historical ties across the Atlantic, the region from which Americans of African descent came through the slave trade to the New World. The earliest official American contacts in Africa were with oft-mentioned Liberia.

Moreover West Africa was in the political lead with Gahna's independence in 1957, and its Prime Minister, Kwame Nkrumah, was an energetic spokesman for African self-determination. Guinea's *"non"* to De Gaulle's 1958 referendum offering semi-autonomous states within a French community had made Sékou Touré the first leader of an independent French-speaking African country. Plans were well under way towards Nigeria's independence in 1960, and Togo and Cameroun had similar prospects with U.N. blessing.

Although 1960 was called "The Year of Africa," it might more accurately have been dubbed "West Africa's Year." The Congo, of course, claimed much attention that year too, but for much of the world the Congo was a United Nations problem more than an African one. Indeed, the diplomatic and military role played at the U.N. by the new West African states only served to highlight their new importance.

Independence and influence came first to West Africa for one key reason: West Africa had virtually no white settlers. Indeed, only tact and aesthetics prevented one African country from taking up the suggestion that the mosquito be placed on the new national flag in gratitude for preventing permanent European settlement.

African pressures combined with those elsewhere to force Britain and France to move quickly to end formal colonial rule. Clearly those steps came more easily in the absence of the entrenched land-holding interests of influential white populations in the Rhodesias or Kenya and, for France, Algeria. A few French-speaking West Africans had sat in the French National Assembly in Paris since the end of World War II; Ghana (or, more accurately, the Gold Coast) and Nigeria became internally self governing with government in African hands in the early 1950's. It was the white settlers who had jealously guarded devolving political power; in politics as elsewhere, there were different entrances and different facilities. The Africans and the British government in response had only begun to reverse that trend by 1960.

Yes, an observer might well have thought that West Africa was the place for imaginative, energetic American initiatives, given a new American awareness of Africa, and at least the language of its importance. He would have been wrong. Although official congratulations and thanks were exchanged, consulates raised to embassies, staffs increased both in the African Bureau of the State Department and at the African posts themselves; although the second major thrust of the Peace Corps was West Africa (the first was the Philippines); although G. Mennen Williams with known sympathy for African aspirations was President-elect Kennedy's first appointment—despite all those gestures the new West African countries rarely drew significant American attention. The gestures were scarcely more than gestures.

The reasons were two. The first was that the Congo, whether read by the United States for its African meaning or not, was thought to be consuming what energy America had for African matters. The second and more basic one was that policy towards Africa had not changed in fundamental ways. That is, in the absence of a crisis Africa was still the lowest priority. Pressure from the European desks at State often meant that America continued to defer to the NATO allies' views; after all, even if they no longer governed in Africa, they had had years of experience behind them that such deference might shield a calculated strategy of preventing any American "encroachment" on European "spheres of influence" was believed a small price to pay for friendship and knowledge.

This second determinant of policy was especially striking in the case of France. It was also a particularly easy course to follow; or, more accurately, in most of French-speaking Africa, it would actually have been made difficult to follow a different one. For except in Guinea, and possibly Mali, the French role and presence in the former colonies was imposing and crucial.

Furthermore, the exigencies of French African policy combined with growing stresses in Franco-American relations to make French officials in African countries often actively discourage what they saw as American cultural or economic encroachment. Because most Francophone African leaders had chosen not to follow the path of Sékou Touré who had cut all ties with France, and because the French permitted little middle ground between that stand and full cooperation, the United States would have been forced to make a major policy decision in order to have the range of international options with those countries.

Such a decision held far reaching implications: to strain further already tense relations with an historically important ally, a NATO ally already balking at NATO commitments. More, it would have meant a genuine commitment in Africa, for the French played a larger economic role, in aid, trade, investment and other financial support than did any other European country in former colonies. For the poorer, land-locked new states of West and Equatorial Africa, such help was desperately needed. The United States was quite unprepared to take on that burden. Why, indeed, should American policy makers take on any of these tensions and responsibilities and expenditures for the lowest of priorities? And so, almost by default, the United States "wrote off" Francophone Africa.

The Cold War thinking of the late 1950's and early 1960's had two effects on American relations with the new African states. One, already pointed out as a theme of policy seen globally, was to slow what might have been a quickening interest towards Africa, in deeds as well as words. The other seems in partial contradiction to relegating African matters to the position of low priority: outside the Africa bureau, policy makers were prone to see Africa as a potential or actual Cold War battleground.

In the late 1950's runs a refrain of official statements fitting Africa into a Cold War context—would the Communists "win" there? Would the Free World "win" there? Would America and its ideals triumph? Would the Soviet system exploit the issue of colonialism and emerge victorious? Always the motif was military, even if the policy proposed was not. And against these assumptions came the challenge from those whose perspective was African and from African spokesmen themselves: Africa did not need, did not want, would not allow itself to be thrust into (and the vehemence mounted) the Great Powers' great power game. They would not be trapped in the formulas of others; they would not exchange one outside domination for another, any other direct or indirect. That the challengers to interpreting Africa's problems through Cold-War-colored glasses did eventually carry the day was a victory for an Afro-centered view of African events; that it would have the ironic consequence of downgrading Africa's claims on America's economic commitment was not yet clear.

Most vocal in their insistence on Africa's right to a neutral *African* stance on world issues were West African leaders. There was, of course, to be no single stance; Africa, even just West Africa, was too vast and too diverse in history, culture and experience for unanimity to be more than a rallying cry at best, or a dream. Despite the fact that events in the former Belgian Congo reinforced both American and Soviet inclinations to view Africa in Cold War terms, such leaders as Kwame Nkrumah and Sékou Touré, William Tubman of Liberia and later Abubakar Tafawa Balewa of Nigeria insisted that Africa must have ideological independence and would not be fitted into anyone else's mold.

Much of official America, still refusing to abandon a Cold War mentality, saw countries like Liberia and Nigeria as "safe" in the early 1960's. Liberia, of course, had decades of ties with the United States; American investment in rubber and iron ore strengthened them, as did a 1959 open treaty unique in United States relations with Subsaharan Africa, of "Cooperation" between the two governments. The treaty provided that "in the event of aggression or threat of aggression against Liberia, the Government of the United States of America and the Government of Liberia will immediately determine what action may be appropriate for the defense of Liberia," followed by the continuing American pledge to assist Liberia in "the effective promotion of its economic development and in the preservation of its national independence and integrity."

Nigeria was a different case, but from the American Cold-War perspective, also promising. An extraordinarily complex country, it was widely advertised outside (and even inside) its borders as Africa's "model of democracy," a description not totally false but simplistic. Still, it was one agreeable to Americans burdened with ideological conflict and instability elsewhere. Also, so their thinking went, such a Nigeria was a monument to Britain's efforts, and British influence would help "reason" prevail.

Ghana and Guinea were different: the two countries in West Africa provided the rhetorical forum if one wanted to argue about leftist-Communist ideological penetration and commitment in Africa. They seemed to be in the vanguard of Africa's leadership. It was, of course, true that African leaders perceived a usefulness to their own national interests in dangling before any Cold War antagonist the threat of cooperation with his opponent. This could provide needed development projects, or lead to other ventures being funded, all in the interest of ideological courtship.

Divisions of African states into camps—Casablanca group, Monrovia group, Brazzaville (Francophone) group—those divisions belied the ideological unity propounded in 1958. They suggested that beneath non-alignment might be Cold War leanings, or at least old colonial influences. They reinforced American reluctance to see Africa as quite outside the United States-Soviet struggle.

Those Americans who had asserted Africa's genuine determination not to fall into Cold War power blocs were correct. This became clear, however, to the United States the Soviet Union and mainland China through their West African experiences. But in the early 1960's the battle, carried on through economic aid, loans, grants, technical assistance and all the paraphernalia of development, was joined.

Opposition came in the early 1960's to American contributions to building Ghana's Volta River dam and hydroelectric project. Those contributions were both government backed and private, for the Kaiser Corporation was keenly interested in Ghanaian bauxite. Political questions were raised, especially in Congress and not just by staunchly anti-Communist cold warriors frightened by the leftist sound and look of Nkrumah's Pan-Africanist words and internal deeds. Senators Gore, Hart, and Neuberger had learned subtlety in interpreting African pronouncements and actions during their tenure on the Foreign Relations Subcommittee on Africa. But they protested a continuing American role in the Volta development because they deplored the measures, starting with a preventive detention act, by which President Nkrumah was limiting expression of political opposition to his policies. That their protests brought no change was testimony to widened State Department thinking about African internal affairs, and the role of self interest in such decisions. Ghana was neither the first nor last country whose internal affairs would not, from a pristine American point of view, be in perfect order but with whom America would treat cordially nonetheless. Nor was the United States the first or last country to incorporate such contradictions in diplomacy. It was simply the standard operating procedure of diplomacy.

When Kwame Nkrumah was overthrown by a military coup d'etat in February 1966, some Americans with little chance of obtaining corroborating evidence, insisted that the Central Intelligence Agency had brought his downfall. A frequent African reaction from inside and outside Ghana was an interesting contrast. It asserted two points: such a view assumed C.I.A. omnipotence, a quality disputed in light of ventures exposed elsewhere and, to so read the situation was to misjudge Ghanaian politics and the capabilities of Ghanaians, in recognizing and dealing with their own problems. It surprised no one, however, that the United States was cordial to the military government that succeeded Nkrumah and to the civilian one, headed by Nkrumah's long-time political opponent, Kofi Busia. The bauxite was still there, and the language was more congenial.

In Guinea the situation had been different at almost every point, and it continued to be so. The United States, vacillating after the abrupt French pullout, had let a key psychological moment slip by in 1958. Sékou Touré, truly bitter that he had needed to beg even for American recognition, had turned towards the only help he could get—distinctly not of the Western bloc. Thus the United States entered the 1960's expecting only antagonism from Guinea. Officials watched in wonder and delight as Russian nations and Chinese technicians and government representatives were invited to leave, usually hurriedly, for "interfering in Guinea's internal affairs." Guinea's earlier quiet overtures to American aid and even capital became more energetic. She later invited France to join in. The policy of avoiding ideological hysteria had paid off; Guinea too has bauxite, more accessible than Ghana's, and iron as well.

Guinea's most troublesome international problem comes from her sharing a border with Guiné-Bissau, still a Portuguese colony despite Portuguese insistence that it, like Angola and Moçambique, is an "overseas province." As in the Portuguese-dominated countries in Southern Africa, Guiné-Bissau has a liberation movement, a guerrilla army that is challenging Portuguese denial of self-determination. The independent states of Africa are committed to self-determination for all Africa, and though they have clearly stated a preference for peaceful solutions, they refused to rule out any necessary measures or to deny whatever assistance they can give. As with other such movements, the one seeking to free Guiné-Bissau from the Portuguese needs a base of relative safety in territory it controls or, especially at first, in friendly countries across borders.

The Portuguese-designed invasion of Guinea (Conakry) in the Fall, 1970 showed Portugal's fury at the sanctuary Guinea supplied to the African "rebels." Though a U.N. investigation bore out the accuracy of Sékou Touré's contention that the invasion was fundamentally a Portuguese attack, the United Nations' inability to meet his pleas for assistance lessened already-waning African faith in the international organization's utility in times of genuine crisis. The fact that Guinea was able to quell the invasion spared both African and non-African countries from facing the crucial issues that might necessitate action.

A broader question does arise, however. Was the invasion, disguised as simply an attempt by Guineans to overthrow their own government, a trial run of a new Portuguese offensive strategy for the far more important setting of Southern Africa? Is it a matter of their training, supplying, and paying African guerrillas to counterattack inside African states bordering Guiné. In Angola and Moçambique, were they thinking of aiding rival factions in order to disrupt and even bring down unfriendly African governments, or at the least keep Subsaharan Africa in continual instability? Such a possible strategy calls minimally for a serious American reexamination of her position in relation to a favored NATO ally, Portugal.

But the greatest challenge that faced American policy makers in West Africa of the 1960's was Nigeria. Quickly perceived by other Africans as well as Americans, Britons, French, and Soviets as possibly the most important country in Black Africa, Nigeria is a land of monumental complexity. Large, populous, in African terms rich in natural resources, especially since the discovery of substantial oil reserves and deposits of high quality, Nigeria had to be central to anyone's thinking about Subsaharan Africa.

The trouble was that so much of the thinking was ill-informed. True, Nigeria was in some respects a model of democracy, for there were elections and multiple parties and freedom for most people—at least in the south. But Nigeria's politics worked within a constitutional framework that was only partly suited to its historical and cultural diversity. Nigeria's constitutions of the 1950's over which her political leaders hammered out differences among themselves and between themselves and the British, were nonetheless conceived in London and Oxford. They followed a score composed elsewhere, on assumptions that were not derived from Nigerian experience, and that did not necessarily serve the best interests of Nigeria's long-range stability and full political and economic opportunities for all her peoples.

Nigeria, as was the view of many, is not a land divided into three groups—Yoruba and Ibo in the south, Hausa-Fulani in the north. True, these groups existed, numbering in the millions each; true, under the constitutional arrangements at independence, each one was dominant, indeed a "majority," in one of the three regions the country comprised. But through literally thousands of years of historic movements of peoples and state-building and break-ups and rebuilding, the land Britain christened Nigeria came to contain peoples speaking some 250 mutually unintelligible languages, of a variety of political organizations and cultural orientations, all seeing themselves as distinct from one another, each with a vital sense of identity. Nigeria's greatest challenge was to make all these peoples feel themselves truly Nigerians, while at the same time not being denied opportunities because of local identities with deep historical roots. It was on that question that stability, prosperity, and influence in Africa and the world depended.

Nor was Nigeria a country troubled by violent religious strife. True, much of the population of the North was Muslim, and much of the population of the South was Christian. What most outsiders did not understand, however, was that all of Nigeria's population was African. That fact affected more than the details of religious belief and practice. It also should have forced second thoughts on those who would fit Nigeria into patterns of Muslim-Christian conflict elsewhere in the world.

The coup d'etat that in January, 1966 felled Nigeria's civilian government after months of apprehensive unrest drew world attention. A second military coup the following July increased it. Mobs rampaging and killing made headlines. Governments at least should have been prepared for the outbreak of civil war following the May, 1967 declaration of secession of a new state, "Biafra," drawn from Nigeria's southeast. Compounding it all were the vast oil resources—in that same southeast.

The details of that conflict—in human, and political, and economic terms as fraught with pain and complexity as in any war, are of concern here only as they were perceived from the outside, not as they were seen by the opposing sides, or "as they were" in as honest a reality as any human observer can recreate.

For the independent African states, initially the issue was clear: would the breakup of an African nation, for any reason whatever, be an eventuality, or an immediate reality, they would support? The answer at first was equally clear: no! Because almost none of the new nations was without internal tensions, only a minority of African states wavered from that position; of those only four recognized an "independent Biafra" during the course of the war. The Organization of African Unity sought to mediate, but it never shifted its stance from commitment to "One Nigeria."

The United States took its lead, as the official statements said, from the Africans, that is, the OAU. More, the American government insisted on neutrality, to the point that, although they continued full diplomatic relations with Nigeria, they never expressed the slightest official support for the "secessionists," and they would not sell arms to the Nigerian government.

Britain, after some hesitation and inaction shared by most outsiders in the early confusing months of the conflict, not only supported Nigeria verbally, but did sell arms. That position was never really in doubt: Britain was not in favor of the splintering of Nigeria; her historical partiality to the Hausa-Fulani of the north was only one factor among many. Undoubtedly important in the calculations of Britain, as of everyone else, was oil. And yet the dictates of oil were not perfectly clear. British (and Dutch and some American and Italian) oil companies had been prospecting offshore and in the Niger Delta for over a decade; the richness and the importance of their finds had only become clear since independence, and drilling and extracting were proceeding apace with production soaring. What was important to those with heavy investments and lucrative prospects was not to lose out; what mattered most was that the fighting, if it had to take place at all, be brief, and that one back the winner. After some early wavering, the established oil interests, and the countries of which they were part, bet on Nigeria. Britain and, some argued, the United States were among them. They argued, too, that Britain was again calling the tune to which American policy danced in Africa; for despite public outcry about starvation of war victims, especially children, the United States did not take the Biafran side. Here, however, as in some other cases, it seems that the European ally and former colonial power might set the direction of policy but not its precise terms.

Indeed, the standard interpretations of alignments on African issues did not work in other respects. What had happened to Cold War reckoning when England and the Soviet Union supported the same side? For, blocked from buying arms from the United States, Nigeria had turned to the U.S.S.R., herself extraordinarily eager—not for massive African involvement any more than were other outside nations—but for a foothold, a success of some sort, after disasters of diplomacy elsewhere in Africa. And Nigeria's importance was recognized as keenly in Eastern Europe as in Western. So was her oil.

On the other side came other anomalies: a "Biafra," created and led by people in no way historically or ideologically congenial with some of the allies; circumstances forced upon them direct and open assistance from Portugal, for instance and clandestine military gestures from South Africa. Even France, whose considerable support was never fully official or announced, was not, with her policy of a continuing presence in Africa, part of the kind of African independence the Ibo had long worked for. But the exigencies of war have often brought paradoxical alliances. And the aims of Biafra's "allies" seem discernible.

French policy in Africa since 1960 had a strong geopolitical orientation. There is some evidence that the Gaullist displeasure with matters "Anglo-Saxon" extended to what might be called "Anglo-Saxon Africa," or more accurately, Anglophone West Africa. That Nigeria was not only a former English colony, but that it was proving, as some predicted, a magnet for the whole of African development, was not part of a French design. Further, French oil companies did not have sizeable options in a Nigerian-controlled Niger Delta. Might French interests do better under another regime?

Thus whatever the internal considerations, a successful Biafran secession from Nigeria would accomplish for France several ends: it would displace Nigeria from its compelling African place; and, a Francophone (and at least French-influenced) country might emerge or a French-influenced "Biafra." But either of those alternatives, should they have arisen, would have fitted long range plans. The oil, of course, was in itself of as much interest as to others. Further, that oil, if combined with the resources of Francophone countries, could present all sorts of possibilities based on economic strength as well as the political force it would mean. Finally, Portugal, and even South Africa, had their particular interests—interests that, given France's continuing arms sale to South Africa despite the U.N. embargo and her growing investments in Moçambique, may not have been totally out of phase with those of France.

Portugal's and South Africa's aims seemed clear. Given their ever increasing entrenchment against the African drive for self-determination south of the Zambezi, and given an OAU commitment to oppose their ends in whatever ways possible and necessary, disarray in Black Africa could only work to their advantage. A war involving Nigeria, further, had special benefits for them: 1) Nigeria, among the strongest and wealthiest of African states, had supported materially as well as in words the southern African liberation movements sanctioned by the OAU. To end that support was obviously desirable. 2) Further, to splinter such a country could remove it from such far-flung enterprises for some time. 3) Any division among the states of Black Africa (as came when the Ivory Coast, Gabon, Zambia, and Tanzania recognized Biafra) was of benefit; the more dissension the better. 4) Any issue that diverted world, and of course African, attention from Southern Africa was to be encouraged. If world opinion could be prompted to draw conclusions about African inability to achieve political stability, that was a large, if fringe, benefit.

With the end of that war in January, 1970 and reconstruction in Nigeria under way, that policy brought only short-run success to its planners. The South African government's "dialogue" proposals may well be a new approach to the same strategy: one designed to encourage the all-important division among Black African states that would aid long-term white rule in Southern Africa.

With the fighting over, American policy toward the states of West Africa relaxed into decreasing concern—not the choice of a relatively neutral stance in a difficult situation, as during the Nigerian war, but the relegation of those states to the lower-keyed attention that lack of crisis in an area of low priority produces. In general a lessening political interest and a steady decline in economic aid have set the tone of the 1970's. Investment may increase somewhat, though capital seems more drawn south of the Zambezi. But foreseeably, both investment and declining aid will continue selective, as they have been all along, and, in the larger scheme of things, minimal.

WEST AFRICA

GOLD COAST (GHANA) AND NIGERIA

Senate Joint Resolution 183 on Self-Government in the Gold Coast and Nigeria*

August 27, 1954

Whereas it is the policy of the United States to encourage efforts toward independence and self-government truly expressive of the desires of the peoples and as they show their capability to establish and protect free institutions; and

Whereas the continent of Africa is a vital part of the free world area; and

Whereas a revised constitution of the Gold Coast was approved on April 29, 1954, and the first formal meeting of the legislature of that territory under this constitution will take place on July 29, 1954, and

Whereas a revised constitution of Nigeria is expected to be approved during August 1954, and the first meeting of the federal legislature of that territory under this constitution is expected to take place shortly thereafter; and

Whereas these occasions mark important milestones in their progress toward self-government and independence: Now, therefore, be it

Resolved by the Senate and House of Representatives of the United States of America in Congress assembled, That the Congress of the United States extend its most cordial greetings to the representative bodies of the Gold Coast and Nigeria on the occasion of the first meeting of their legislatures under the revised constitutions, in recognition of the democratic ideals shared by the United States and those territories, and in reaffirmation of the friendship of the United States for the peoples of Africa; and be it further

Resolved, That the Secretary of State is hereby requested to appoint a United States delegation at the appropriate time to represent the United States at ceremonies marking the achievement of complete self-government for these territories.

Address by Assistant Secretary Satterthwaite on a Survey of Relations Between the United States and West Africa†

May 1, 1959

* * *

American policy toward West Africa is based on a desire for mutual understanding and friendly cooperation.

On the question of federation the United States clearly views with favor political associations of African states. We feel, of course, that such associations should contribute to political stability and economic viability and should be formulated in

---

**Department of State Bulletin*, Jan. 10, 1955, pp. 67-68.
†*Ibid.*, May 25, 1959, p. 749.

accordance with the democratically expressed desires of the populations concerned. In the final analysis, however, West African federation is a West African problem and will be solved by the people of this area.

On other basic issues United States policy is equally clear and unequivocal. We believe in the right of self-determination for all peoples. We agree with Vice President Nixon that "the emergence of a free and independent Africa is as important to us in the long run as it is to the people of that continent."

We favor an orderly, steady development of African countries to the point where they may join the community of free nations as equal members, able to stand on their own feet. We also maintain that there is a community of interest between Western Europe and African that should be maintained, regardless of the nature of political ties. The economies of Western Europe and Africa are complementary, and it would be difficult for one to exist without the other.

The United States is accused by some of its friends in Africa of being anticolonialist and working against the Europeans in Africa. We have also been accused by the Africans of working hand in hand with our NATO allies to repress African freedom. I think, however, that our record is clear and that there is no inconsistency in our policy. We support African political aspirations where they are moderate, nonviolent, and constructive and take into account their obligations to and interdependence with the world community. We also support the principle of continued African ties with Western Europe. We see no reason why there should be a conflict between these two concepts.

As I told members of the House Foreign Affairs Committee a few weeks ago:

> I am convinced that the yearning of the peoples of Africa for a better way of life presents us with one of the great challenges of our time. If we fail to respond adequately, we may stand accused as a people who proclaim our own satisfaction with the benefits of freedom and well being but who are insensitive to the yearnings and needs of others.

The United States has always risen to the occasion when the issues and course of action were clear. A responsible West Africa is emerging. We must stand prepared to give it our sympathy and our understanding support in order to assist it to achieve its great potential in a manner which will benefit all concerned and bring us the friendly cooperation we seek.

Report by Representative Diggs on a Special Study Mission to West and Central Africa*

March 29-April 27, 1970

FINDINGS AND RECOMMENDATIONS

It became quite obvious from the questions asked of the study mission at press conferences, and by Government leaders, as well as the rank and file that there is a great lack of real information concerning the United States. There were numerous

---

**Committee on Foreign Affairs, *Report of Special Study Mission to West and Central Africa,* March 29 to April 27, 1970, by Hon. Charles C. Diggs, Jr., Michigan, Chairman, Subcommittee on Africa (Washington, 1970), pp. 3-6; 9-10.

questions regarding foreign aid—why is the United States reducing aid to underdeveloped countries in Africa—why does Africa have lowest priority in American foreign aid? There were always questions concerning U.S. relations with South Africa, Rhodesia, and the Portuguese Territories. Great interest was shown in the status of race relations in the United States. In this connection the study mission was asked to differentiate between race policies of South Africa and the United States. Other typical questions asked were—why are there not more black Americans in Africa, either with the U.S. Government or in private capacities? Why is there not more American private capital invested outside of South Africa? Also, why doesn't the United States exert more pressure and influence on Portugal to make her liberate her African colonies?

It was evident that Secretary of State Rogers recent visit to 10 African countries was appreciated as a sign of American interest in Africa and the contents of his report to President Nioxn was appreciated as the first definitive pronouncement from this administration. The Africans are beyond the point of being satisfied with pronouncements and are "watching for the performance rather than words." It is difficult for them to understand why the richest and most resourceful nation in the world cannot share more of its assets with the developing nations.

The intense feeling of independence and national identity amongst Africans is a shield against Communist penetration. Although they are searching for new political and economic institutions to reflect their own traditions and the realities of the modern world, the people of Africa instinctively resist external domination, whether it be Communist or colonial. But they understand and welcome genuine gestures of assistance to institutions which they devise and will control. For this reason the efforts of the Peace Corps have been generally more successful and more appreciated in Africa than in any other continent.

Peace Corps Technicians

Men with technical skills are urgently needed in all of Africa and any help the United States can give to train Africans in this field will not only be beneficial, but will also be greatly appreciated. Consequently, the mission highly commends the "New Directions" announced by Peace Corps Director Joseph Blatchford, under which Peace Corps volunteers would be engaged in various kinds of technical projects in the different countries they are sent to.

Indeed, in Conakry, Guinea, there are 25 Peace Corps volunteers—mechanics, electricians, and machinists engaged in such activities as the repair and maintenance of buses and trucks. This constitutes the first technical program of the Peace Corps and it might be hoped that the new venture will be successful.

African Development Bank

In Abidjan, Ivory Coast, the study mission met with the Acting President of the African Development Bank, Mr. Abdilwahab Labidi, and Vice President, Mr. Ola Vincent. The African Development Bank was inaugurated in November 1964, and now has 31 independent African countries as its members. In order to supplement its resources the Bank formulated a proposal for the establishment of an African Development Fund which would be a multilateral Fund and would receive contributions in grants. There are some 27 donor countries including the United States listed in the special section of this report concerning the Bank. There has been a detailed exchange of views between the U.S. authorities and the Bank on several occasions. It is hoped that the United States and the other potential donors for participation in the Fund will take positive action to provide financial support for the Bank; especially, with regard to such projects involving substantial capital which is more than what the Bank can provide from the contributions of its African member countries.

Special Self-Help Fund

Of the 12 countries visited only two, namely, Congo (K) and Uganda, are among the 10 development emphasis countries that receive about two-thirds of AID assistance to Africa. Among the other 25 aid recipient African countries, it was decided over 2 years ago to phase out bilateral programs and concentrate on strengthening their regional and subregional economic links. Some African countries are not in a position to cooperate easily with their neighbors for geographic and political reasons springing largely from the great disparities in the levels of development within those countries. Consequently, it would not be realistic nor politically desirable for the United States to insist upon the multinational concept in our AID policy. Meanwhile, the Special Self-Help Fund which presently ranges from $50,000 to $100,000 per country, should be increased to help those countries falling outside the group of development emphasis countries.

In fact, all the American Ambassadors in these self-help countries did state that the funds have proved to be highly rewarding by providing much needed assistance to low-cost, but high-impact projects supplementing village and community development efforts. Many of our Ambassadors have therefore proposed that those funds be increased to $200,000. The study mission wholly agrees with such a proposal.

There are some restrictions applied to these self-help activities that prevent maximum effective use of the funds. Among these restrictions is a general limitation of $10,000 for any one project. Two other restrictions, however, are binding: the prohibitions against contributing more than one time to any single project and against funding of former bilateral AID projects. Congress has placed a limitation on the total number of countries to which regular continuing bilateral assistance can be given; thus many of Africa's countries must remain ineligible for assistance other than under the Special Self-Help Fund and regional programs. There is a basic difference between the regular bilateral projects, which are undertaken by agreement between two governments, and self-help projects, which frequently involve grants to community or other smaller organizations. There is need for maximum flexibility not only in administering of Self-Help Funds, but also in the granting of regional and bilateral aid.

Recognizing the need to evaluate the above-mentioned points of the Special Self-Help Fund, AID has fielded a joint AID-State Department team to study the problem and to make recommendations as necessary.

1971 Kinshasa Trade Fair

The study mission recommends that the United States should participate in a larger way in trade fairs in Africa and more trade missions should be sent to explore in some detail, what market possibilities are in the continent. At the moment, there is very little interest among American businesses and potential investors in Africa. But this unsatisfactory condition is likely to persist if no efforts were made to increase our knowledge of the African market. Consequently, it would be worthwhile for the United States to participate substantially in the forthcoming Kinshasa Fair. The fair director, Mr. Thomas Tumba, has expressed the belief that U.S. business firms could expect sales up to the order of some $3 to $4 million to result directly from their participation in the fair.

It is anticipated that U.S. investment and private sector activity can make a contribution in developing natural and human resources in more African countries. As an example the Pan American World Airways is negotiating a major technical assistance contract with the Congolese national airline, Air Congo. This would be the largest technical assistance program in Pan Am's experience, encompassing a maximum of 47 Pan Am technicians and advisors to streamline and modernize every facet of Air Congo's operations and conduct a major training program. While this does not qualify as private investment, the program nevertheless has considerable developmental value since a more efficient Congolese airline can be expected to play a vital role in improving the Congo's domestic transport services and contribute to the development of tourism as a significant source of foreign exchange earnings.

Public Health Service's Smallpox Eradication and Measles Control Program

The Public Health Service's NCDC Smallpox Eradication and Measles Control program, an AID-financed, 5-year project in 20 West African countries, began field activities in January 1967. The program's 100 millionth smallpox vaccination ceremony, which took place in Niger in late 1969, coupled with the almost total eradication of smallpox cases and the decline in measles in West Africa demonstrate the overall success of the project. However, although Niger has experienced a very successful program in terms of a fall in the incidence of these diseases, there is still room for greater efforts and achievement. It may be emphasized that the success of these services depend a great deal on the provision of good transport facilities. The mission would express the hope that this aspect of our health programs in Africa should always be seriously considered.

U.S. Programs for African Students

The U.S. programs for African students from Francophone countries have not been very successful due to several reasons. There is the concern of some African students about our unpleasant race relations here in the United States. Understandably too, students trained in the French educational system prefer to continue their studies in French universities because of the language difficulty they might encounter studying in America. There are also some misgivings about the value of some American university degrees due to the fact that there are differences in educational standards among some of our universities. Such a situation is unfortunate; but not until a national standard is established, some doubts will continue to plague African students who might otherwise have liked to study here in the United States.

Another factor limiting the effectiveness of our scholarship programs is procedure for applications and the processing of these. The procedure is said to be complicated and full of delays between the time of filing applications and eventual placement in the university.

The mission strongly considers that the scholarship procedure be thoroughly reexamined by the appropriate authorities to see what changes can be made to facilitate the processing of these applications.

Redistribution of U.S. Sugar Quota for Africa

Production of sugar in developing countries of Africa is increasing rapidly. Uganda, for instance, has stepped up its sugar production from 128,000 tons in the first half of the 1960's to 163,000 tons in 1968-69. It seems ironic that countries like Uganda which need all the help we can afford to give in their economic development should be left almost uncatered for in an area most vulnerable to price fluctuations, while South Africa enjoys a protected position.

The study mission is of the opinion that as a further demonstration of our interest in the development of the countries of Africa, and our condemnation of the policy of apartheid, the sugar quota for South Africa be revoked and that economic privilege be extended to Uganda and any other countries more urgently in need of our assistance.

*   *   *

Specific Recommendations

The major weakness in U.S. foreign policy in Africa relates to the timetable–U.S. policymakers treat African affairs with a lack of a sense of urgency. The United States has a tendency to formulate policies based upon current controlling interests without the proper respect for the predictability and suddenness of change. Africa is still on the back burner because our policy makers think there is more time to consider the necessity for change than there really is. I submit that it is appropriate for our policy makers not only to consider the necessity for change but to positively work toward effecting this change by implementing the following recommendations:

1. We should establish a timetable indicating where we would like to be in Africa 5 years from now; 10 years from now, and develop policies designed to keep us on schedule and associated with certain developments that are obviously going to take place.

Our attention and support might be directed toward such projects as:

(a) the joining of the Niger and the Volta Rivers to promote progress in Upper Volta and its surrounding area.

(b) the construction of a network of trunk and feeder roads within regions to facilitate greater economic cooperation among African countries north and south of the Sahara.

(c) the mining of uranium and the exploration of oil and natural gas, etc., to improve the economy and aid in the process of modernization.

2. The phasing out of U.S. bilateral aid in these countries is undoubtedly one of their greatest concerns. This is particularly aggravated because the United States has thus far failed to implement the regional concept substitute in a meaningful way. Therefore, the American AID program must be reviewed to assure flexibility, despite the phasing out of bilateral aid so that those countries, development should not be halted.

3. The recommendation made by our Chiefs of Mission at the Kinshasa Conference with Secretary Rogers to increase the self-help fund to $200,000 per eligible country should be instituted.

4. Stronger efforts should be made to expose American business, big and medium size to the potentialities in black Africa.

5. Officials from all branches of the U.S. Government ought to be encouraged to get off the beaten path and make some visits to the smaller interior African countries. Likewise, the United States ought to encourage more francophone Africans to travel to the United States.

6. The United States should take the lead in supporting the African Development Bank and to encourage other non-African donors to do likewise.

7. The U.S. Government should devise ways to reach foreign correspondents and other members of the communication media in an effort to generate more constructive stories rather than the present crisis oriented image in our country about Africa.

GHANA

State Department Announcement on the American Recognition of Ghana*

March 5, 1957

The U.S. Government has officially recognized the new state of Ghana, which becomes independent and a member of the British Commonwealth on March 6.

With the permission of the Government of Ghana, the American consulate general at Accra will be raised to the status of an embassy at 1 minute past midnight on March 6. At that time, Donald W. Lamm, consul general, will be named chargé d'affaires pending the appointment of an ambassador to Ghana.

The U.S. Government has also informed the Government of Prime Minister Kwame Nkrumah that it would welcome the establishment of a Ghanaian embassy at Washington as soon as practicable.

American Foreign Policy, Current Documents. 1957, (Washington, 1962), pp. 1079-80.

*Report by Senators Gore, Hart and Neuberger on a Study Mission to Africa**

September-October, 1961

*　　　　　*　　　　　*

We concluded as a result of our observations that the United States must continue to provide substantial amounts of grant aid to newly independent African countries. We concluded that such aid should be provided not simply to counteract Soviet bloc aid, but for the positive reason that, properly administered, free world aid will assist these new nations to develop in a pattern conducive to the maintenance of their independence, to their economic growth, and to the expansion of individual freedom. We believe that the existence of strong, free African states will help create the kind of world in which the values of a free society such as ours will be maintained.

The problem for the United States in assisting in the economic development of African nations is to make aid available in form and in amount to encourage economic and political independence. American foreign policy objectives will not be promoted if aid is viewed by Africans as a form of "neocolonialism" or if aid bolsters countries which deny basic rights of life and liberty and free expression to their peoples. United States aid must not become an instrument to bolster totalitarianism of either the right or the left. It must, rather, be an instrument for the promotion of human rights and freedom.

This is not easy. The sensitivity of new nations is so near the surface that what seem to be safeguards to a donor country or to the private investor tend to become suspicious or onerous conditions to the receiver; what seem normal precautions for governmental grants or loans become "political strings" to recipients. The dilemma in administering aid programs in these circumstances is well illustrated by the large Volta River project in Ghana.

The Volta River Project

According to the Department of State—

The Volta River project consists of two major construction projects. The first is a dam to be built on the Volta River at Akosombo. This dam will provide a powerplant supplying electrical power for all of southern Ghana. a fisheries industry to be instituted on the reservoir made by the dam, flood control, irrigation, and health and sanitation measures through a fresh supply of drinking water and swamp drainage. The total cost of the dam and power station will be $168 million. This money will be supplied by—

[Dollars in millions]

	Amount	Percent	Number of years
Development Loan Fund	$20	3½	30
Eximbank	10	5¾	25
International Bank for Reconstruction and Development	40	5¾	25
United Kingdom	14	5¾	25
Ghana	[1] 84	--	--

[1] As equity.

*Committee on Foreign Relations, *Study Mission to Africa, September October 1961, Report of Senators Albert Gore, Philip A. Hart and Maurine B. Neuberger*, 87th Cong., 1st sess., (Washington, 1962), pp. 11 13.

In order to bring power to central Ghana, a transmission grid will also be constructed at a total cost of $28 million to be financed by

	Million
United States loan	$7
International Bank for Reconstruction and Development loan	7
Ghana	14

Loans for these projects have been agreed upon in their basic terms. Remaining negotiations concern details of reconciling various loan agreements.

The second major construction portion of the project is an aluminum smelter to be built at Toma on the coast of Ghana by Valco (Volta Aluminum Co., Ltd.), formed by the Kaiser Aluminum & Chemical Corp. and the Reynolds Metal Co. This smelter will serve as the prime customer of the powerplant and therefore will make the dam economically feasible. This project will cost $128 million. However, since substantial delays in the completion of the project resulting in increased costs could occur, financing also is assured for an overrun of $42 million should the cost increase. The smelter will be financed by an equity investment of $32 million made by the two corporate shareholders. Overrun may bring this portion of the cost to $54 million. The Export-Import Bank will provide a loan of $90 million for the remaining cost of construction. Overrun could bring this total to $110 million. Amortization of this loan and expenses of Valco will be paid through receipts of tolling contracts obligating the investors to buy the services of the Valco smelter.

These figures show that the total cost of the Volta River project, including transmission lines and the aluminum smelter, is estimated, including overrun, to be $366 million, of which more than half—$201 million—will come from United States sources, of which up to $54 million (covered by a political risk guarantee) would be from private investors. The total planned United States resources to be devoted to the Volta River project during the next seven years, therefore, will be equivalent to almost one-half of the amount of aid that the United States is expected to provide to all Africa during the current fiscal year.

We do not here undertake to assess the economic feasibility of the Volta project, and for the sake of this report we assume it is economically feasible. Neither do we undertake to judge whether the past actions of this Government were such as to commit us morally or legally to providing assistance. We note, however, on the basis of our visit to the damsite at Akosombo, that extensive work is already underway and that representatives of the Italian contractor and the Kaiser Corp. are already at work on the project.

We venture, however, to comment on the political considerations bearing upon the United States decision to proceed with assistance in the Volta project.

There should be no illusion but that the highest policy considerations were involved in this decision which, in the final analysis, had to be made by the President. A decision not to proceed with the United States portion of the project would have created vast bitterness in Ghana as well as in a few other African states. American private investments in Ghana might have been expropriated, and the Ghanaian Government might have taken still another leap toward the left. It is doubtful if Ghana would have been as tempted to seek Soviet aid as Egypt was in the case of Aswan, because of the absence of any utility of the project unless an aluminum smelter, with free world markets, were constructed to utilize the electricity. In any event anti-American sentiment would have been fanned by our denial. The Sovie bloc would certainly have been invited in to fill part of the vacuum.

On the other hand, the undertaking to proceed with the project seems to many Americans and to many Africans as a reward granted to a state and government not truly neutral in conduct and committed in recent months to the suppression and oppression of the basic right of free expression and political disagreement.

We do not deny that the new states of Africa must be free to develop their own brands of political organization. But we do not believe American aid should be used to assist governments engaged in the systematic suppression of free expression.

There are many states in Africa badly in need of external assistance which adhere to the basic principles of the rule of law, which do not deny fundamental human rights to their opponents, which do not imprison their citizens without trial, which permit the existence of a free press, and which do not utilize their communications facilities and oversea missions for proselyting their neighbors. Is it proper for the United States in its aid policies to consider these things?

We must, of course, be careful in undertaking to apply the standard of what has been good for us to these new states. Their situations are different in many ways, in many degrees. We must be careful not to confuse nationalism with totalitarianism or communism. But with these cautions in mind, we do believe tha United States aid must be related to the basic principles for which we stand. Only in this way can it command the sustained support of our people.

*   *   *

Testimony by Senator Gore Before the Senate on the Volta River Project in Ghana*

February 7, 1962

Mr. President, on December 16, 1961, the President of the United States announced his decision to commit U.S. funds to assist in financing the construction of the Volta River project in Ghana. I have previously publicly expressed by view that this decision was unwise. Today I shall undertake to explain in some detail why I consider U.S. participation in this project to be contrary to our own best interests and, in the long run, contrary to the principles of freedom and perhaps not in the best interests of the Ghanaian people. I shall also indicate why I think the President would be well advised to reconsider the question.

Our overall national objective in our foreign aid programs to insure national security in a world at peace, a world in which human beings everywhere may enjoy individual freedom and an opportunity to participate in the increasing benefits of a free and productive society. We have long since recognized that we cannot expect to retain in perpetuity for ourselves alone the benefits of a free society. A go-it-alone policy simply will not work in today's world.

In our own self-interest, then, we aid those who are allied with us in the cold war struggle. We do this by providing direct military aid. Moreover, we provide economic aid to shore up the economies of some of our allies so as to enable them to support the military establishments which our military aid helps to build. In this way, we seek to maintain overall military superiority for the West vis-a-vis the Soviet bloc. Let me make it plain that I endorse these principles, that I have been a constant supporter of collective action by free nations and a consistent supporter of mutual security programs.

The second major aspect of our aid program involves the assistance we extend to

Congressional Record, Feb. 2, 1962, pp. 1979-82.

those nations which are not now, and cannot in the foreseeable future become, significant military powers. These are so-called underdeveloped nations. Here we are motivated in part by our basic humanitarian desire to assist others to achieve the things we now enjoy. But here, too, our own self-interest is heavily involved.

Simply stated, we desire freedom for others, both for their sake and to preserve freedom for ourselves. Political freedom cannot long exist without economic freedom.

Thus, the Mutual Security Act attempts "to strengthen friendly foreign countries and to assist, on a basis of self-help and mutual cooperation, the efforts of free peoples to develop their economic resources and free economic institutions." I support these objectives, let me repeat.

The Volta project fails the test set forth in the quoted policy declarations of the act. Moreover, it violates the principles that ought to guide our foreign aid program, particularly in Africa where the need for aid is so great. In the first place, the Volta project is the wrong kind of aid. In the second place, it is given under the wrong kind of conditions and is in the wrong place.

*   *   *

Mr. President, if our aid program in Africa and in other underdeveloped nations is to succeed, we must orient it so as to improve the lot of the people rather than merely to entrench the political regime which happens to be in power. The overwhelming needs of the people in Ghana, as elsewhere in the new nations of Africa, are elemental—education, health, food and water. The Volta Dam and its power will not supply these needs. It will create but few jobs for the Ghanaian people. It is not even planned, at least initially, to develop the low-grade bauxite deposits in Ghana. Under the agreement between the Kaiser consortium and Nkrumah, Kaiser will be the sole judge as to whether and to what extent Ghanaian labor will be employed in the smelter which is to be constructed.

Nowhere is it seriously suggested that there is any need in Ghana for any significant portion of the aluminum that will be smelted. It is contemplated that shipment of aluminum to Europe and the United States will generate foreign exchange for Ghana, but there is no indication as to for what or where this foreign exchange will be used.

On the basis of presently available evidence, I must conclude that the principal beneficiaries of this project will be the huge U.S. corporations which have sponsored it and Mr. Nkrumah and his political group.

It is argued that failure to proceed with the project might have created bitter anti-American feeling in Ghana where Nkrumah could be expected to have ignited violent anti-American propaganda through his controlled communications media. He has been doing so constantly and, therefore, could be expected to do so again.

In country after country, during the month I spent in Africa, I found anti-American and anti-Western propaganda that had emanated from Ghana. So we should not be surprised if it occurs again.

But there is another side to the coin. By proceeding with the project, we have, to say the least, discouraged and raised doubts about the future of those who are sincerely dedicated to the promotion of individual liberty and democratic self-government, not only in Ghana but elsewhere in Africa.

If Volta is to serve as a guideline, no longer will progress toward democracy and freedom be considered the pathway toward United States assistance. Indeed, some may justifiably regard Volta as demonstrating that dictatorial methods, with a strong leftist slant, pave the way to Fort Knox. It surely will not go unnoticed by other political leaders in Africa that the amount of aid from U.S. sources—$201 million as now specified—which has been earmarked for this one project, is approximately equivalent to one-half of the total amount of aid it is expected to provide to all of Africa during the current fiscal year.

Mr. President, we must remember that it is the taxpayers' money which will be committed tomorrow by final signature to the contract, if that signature is fixed. I realize that the stakes for which we play in this rapidly changing world, particularly in Africa, are high. I am prepared, and I believe most patriotic Americans are prepared, to make whatever sacrifices are necessary, provided the expenditure promotes achievement of our national objectives.

I do not believe the Volta project will promote those objectives. Indeed, it may well hinder the achievement of those objectives.

Moreover, this project will produce adverse economic tax and balance-of-payments results which give promise of being unusually serious. Under the contemplated plan of operation, the Kaiser consortium will ship bauxite from Jamaica to the United States, where it will be processed into alumina. The alumina will then be shipped to Ghana, where it will be smelted into aluminum. The aluminum will then be marketed either in Europe or in the United States. There is no demand in Ghana for aluminum to come from this size production facility.

*   *   *

I have no objection, Mr. President, to legitimate activities by American companies to develop proposals for economic development in other areas. I believe, however, that projects actively promoted by U.S. companies which have a financial interest in their construction should be considered solely on the merits of the project itself and with the understanding that it is just barely possible that the interests of the private U.S. company is not always identical with that of the United States.

If this project is constructed as planned and operated as planned, I can foresee complication rather than simplification of future United States-Ghana relations. Un doubtedly, the Ghanaian people will take great pride in this project, at least initially, but after passage of a few years it is possible, if not probable, that they will view the situation merely as an operation under which a U.S. corporation is the principal beneficiary of Volta power. We have heard cries of dollar imperialism before and we will likely hear them again. An example of this can be found today in Guinea.

Mr. President, I wish to acknowledge that our entire foreign aid program has an important bearing upon the serious problem of the balance of payments. I would not stop our foreign aid program because of the particular difficulties which it raises. I think, however, we must distinguish between foreign aid—both economic and military aid—directed to meet the needs of people of the recipient countries and a huge industrial project, of which the principal beneficiary is a subsidiary of a U.S. corporation, which will operate for at least 10 years in a complete tax haven and compete unfairly with respect to U.S. concerns.

New York Times *Editorial on Anti-Americanism in Ghana**

February 6, 1964

The United States Government had no choice but to recall Ambassador William P. Mahoney Jr. from Ghana in the wake of the recent outrageous anti-American demonstrations in Accra.

Along with anger, Americans feel deep perplexity about these developments since it is impossible to see any rational basis for such conduct. The United States Government has been seeking for years to help, not hurt, Ghana, and American aid has taken such tangible forms as massive assistance with the Volta River hydroelectric project. Peace Corps volunteers are in Ghana at the request of the Accra regime.

The temptation exists, of course, to take retaliatory measures such as reducing or eliminating American economic aid. It may be that the elements in Accra that instigated the outrage hoped precisely to provoke such retaliation, which could then be used to raise anti-American sentiment much higher.

A wiser course of action for this country would be to exhibit patience and to refuse to be provoked. The Volta project in particular is a long-term endeavor designed to improve Ghana's economy for many years to come. It would be a mistake to allow even so brutal a provocation as the present one to blind us to the mutual interest of Americans and Ghanaians in our policy of friendship toward and aid for Ghana.

TOGO: FROM TRUSTEESHIP TO INDEPENDENCE

United States Statement Made Before the U.N. General Assembly on the Future of Togoland Under British Administration†

December 13, 1956

The vote which we are about to take is unique in the annals of the United Nations. We are for the first time taking the final action by which a trust territory will achieve the status of independence—in this case by a freely chosen integration with a neighboring country which is about to achieve its own independence. Although this Assembly is directly concerned only with the trust territory of British Togoland, its indirect interest and concern with the new forthcoming State of Ghana is very great. Ghana, we hope, will be one of the new members of the United Nations in the near future.

This action, Mr. President, is significant in the view of my delegation because it marks the first termination of a trusteeship agreement, one which in one form or another has existed for nearly half a century. We are thus bringing to an end a trusteeship and replacing it by independence. The role of the United Nations in this development has, in our opinion, been most significant, and in particular we wish to pay tribute to the expert work and indefatigable energy of Señor Espinosa as the agent of this [sic] United Nations in supervising the plebiscite by which the people of British Togoland freely chose to join the new state of Ghana.

*The New York Times, Feb. 6, 1964.
†*Department of State Bulletin,* Jan. 21, 1957, pp. 108-09.

The United States, Mr. President, will vote in favor of terminating the trusteeship agreement and integrating British Togoland with the new state of Ghana because this is the free choice of the people of British Togoland. This body must, in our opinion, affirm and reaffirm the right of the people in any part of the world to make such a free choice.

Unfortunately, another type of imperialism has emerged in certain areas which has had the effect of suppressing former independent societies and peoples and subjugating them to a cruel and heartless form of alien rule. We have been struggling with such a situation in these Assembly halls during the past several weeks. It is one of the striking paradoxes of our time that just as the old colonialism is giving way, a new and worse form of imperialism is being imposed upon people who deserve a better way of life.

Mr. President, I cannot conclude these remarks without saying a word about the opinion of my delegation concerning the magnificent accomplishments of the Administering Authority, the United Kingdom, with the supervision of the trusteeship system. We have seen with our own eyes how the Administering Authority has brought a knowledge not only of modern medicine, education, and government administration, but has instilled in the people under its charge knowledge and experience in truly democratic government, honesty in administration, impartial judicial procedures, respect for minority rights, and many other principles and practices which form the basis for truly self-governing institutions. In fact, it is not too much to say that wherever the influence of the United Kingdom has extended, whether in my own country or those in Africa or elsewhere, they have through that influence reflected these principles which have become enshrined as the rule of law and practice in those countries.

And now in welcoming—as we hope the action being taken today by this General Assembly will welcome—Togoland and the new state of Ghana in a day not too distant in the future we hope, my delegation would like to pay tribute to Prime Minister Nkrumah and his colleagues for the way in which they have facilitated the good relations between the Togolese people and the present Gold Coast. We would, however, Mr. President, also like to utter one note of caution. It has been evident, from the words of certain of the oral petitioners from this area of Africa to which I have been listening during the past weeks in the Fourth Committee, that there are some West Africans who are somewhat dissatisfied with the decision of the General Assembly. One of these dissident groups seeks a federal form of government in Ghana; another seeks a form of independence for both British and French Togoland. We would strongly urge these groups to accept the principle that political maturity seeks to achieve political change by peaceful means and to operate on the democratic premise that minorities should yield to majorities as long as there is a complete freedom for the minorities to seek to become in the majority.

We are confident, Mr. President, as I conclude these remarks, that the soon to be independent people of the new state of Ghana, including the people of British Togoland, will prove themselves to be responsible, progressive, and politically mature—and thus play a major role as a strong, free, and democratic state which can be an example for the entire world.

United States Statement Made Before the U.N. General Assembly
on the Future of Togoland Under French Administration*

January 8, 1957

It is always a matter of great satisfaction to see the people of a trust territory assuming increasing responsibilities for their own government and thus realizing the objectives set out for them under the United Nations Charter. The people of Togoland under French administration are now being governed under a new statute which accords them a very large measure of self government.

The objectives of the trusteeship system, as we all know, are defined in article 76 (b): "to promote the ... progressive development [of the inhabitants of the trust territories] towards self-government or independence...." The essential question, therefore, which has been laid before this Committee is to ascertain the extent to which the objective of self-government has been realized in practice under the new statute, and how the governmental institutions established under it are operating in realizing the charter objectives.

The Administering Authority—the French Republic—has laid before us a large body of documentation and has fully answered our questions as to the meaning of the new statute and its possibilities for the future. The French Government is to be commended for the able manner in which it has discharged its responsibilities, both toward the people of French Togoland and toward the United Nations under the trusteeship agreement.

We have also had the great advantage of having seven petitioners who have, from several points of view, given us a frank and clear expression of their attitudes with respect to the new government and statute of Togoland.

With all this information, however, the General Assembly, mindful of its own serious responsibilities, would be wise in not coming to a definitive conclusion at this session. The problem is in many respects too complex and there are still too many unanswered questions to enable us to express our final views as to the future of French Togoland. The Administering Authority has expressed the view, both on its own behalf and that of the principal leaders of Togoland, that the self-government now enjoyed by the trust territory would justify the United Nations in agreeing to terminate the trusteeship agreement. Some of the petitioners supported this view, while several consider that it would be premature at this session to act on termination.

It is clear from the discussion, however, that no one wishes to prevent the people of Togoland from enjoying self-government in the largest degree. We can all appreciate that, like all other countries, they naturally desire to be allowed to govern themselves as fully as possible within their political and economic capacity. The United States delegation fully respects this natural desire and would be unwilling to see the Togolese people remain in a state of dependency longer than the people themselves, by free election and decision, feel necessary.

*Ibid., Feb. 18, 1957, pp. 282-84.

GUINEA

*Correspondence Between President Eisenhower and Guinea President
Sékou Touré on American Recognition of Guinea**

President Sékou Touré to President Eisenhower

October 2, 1958

I have the honor to inform you of the proclamation of the National Assembly of Guinea on October 2, 1958, establishing the Republic of Guinea. The Guinea Government was established on today's date. The sovereign and independent state of Guinea earnestly desires to establish diplomatic relations with the United States on an international cooperation basis.

October 13, 1958

Owing to the urgency of certain decisions of international significance, the establishment of embassies and of economic relations, the Government of the Republic of Guinea, earnestly desiring to protect American interests and hoping for the development of economic and cultural relations with the United States, has the honor to request your excellency to reply to our message of October 2. In the interest of the United States and the Republic of Guinea, please agree to cooperation between our two countries through international relations. High consideration.

President Eisenhower to President Sékou Touré

November 1, 1958

With reference to the messages which you kindly sent me on October second and October thirteenth, it gives me great pleasure to renew my sincere good wishes for the future of Guinea which were conveyed to you through our Consul General in Dakar and to extend to your Government the formal recognition of the Government of the United States.

New York Times Editorial on Dealing with President Sékou Touré of Guinea†

November 12, 1966

The United States hardly could have done less than to recall for consultations its Ambassador to Guinea after the utterly unjustified abuse heaped on this country by President Sekou Touré and the mobs he incited. There is a good case for doing more.

*Ibid., Dec. 15, 1958, p. 966.
†*The New York Times*, Nov. 12, 1966.

Mr. Touré admits that 62 Peace Corps volunteers have done good work, but he has ordered them out of Guinea within a week. He decreed the house arrest of Ambassador Robinson McIlvaine and aroused the demonstrators who smashed into the embassy residence and destroyed property.

Mr. Touré was understandably outraged at the detention in Ghana of his Foreign Minister and eighteen other Guineans. So was the United States—and said so. But to have held Washington "entirely responsible" for this incident because the Guineans were traveling on an American airline was ridiculous beyond reason.

In the stormy aftermath, even a cautious State Department must have been inclined to halt all aid—since 1962 Guinea has received $72-million worth from the United States—and consider a complete break with Guinea. But the matter was not so simple. Washington had to weigh possible debits against the satisfaction of showing Mr. Touré he could not flout decent diplomatic behavior and get away unscathed.

There are in Guinea many ill-wishers of the United States who would rejoice at a break and try to exploit it in many ways. These include Chinese Communists, Castro Cubans, former President Nkrumah of Ghana and even Gaullist Frenchmen.

At present, Washington seems disposed to try to persuade Mr. Touré of the folly of his behavior by means short of an outright break. We think this to be the wiser course.

New York Times *Editorial on the "Ebb of African Revolution"**

December 7, 1968

President Sekou Touré of Guinea must often ask himself whether survival is possible for an African leader bent on radical revolution. The army's ouster of Modibo Keita in nearby Mali leaves Mr. Touré the only remaining revolutionary head of state in West and Central Africa.

African radicals invariably blame "neo-colonialists" or "imperialists" for the downfall of a Keita, Nkrumah or Lumumba. What is true is that a host of factors—primarily economic and military—usually make it extremely difficult for a struggling young African government to sustain a course markedly independent of its former colonial ruler.

Mr. Keita was an intelligent politician who cut a large figure in the new Africa; yet he followed a familiar African path to his downfall. He had finally confronted economic reality last year, turning back to his French colonial tutors for help in launching an austerity program and an effort to restore a convertible Malian currency. However, he was unable to prevent sabotage of his plans by Cabinet extremists. Finally, he made the mistake that had helped bring down Ghana's Nkrumah and the Congo Republic's Massamba-Debat. He created a popular "militia" with enough arms and authority to provoke the regular army and precipitate West Africa's twelfth military coup in three years.

The young officers who overthrew Mr. Keita have wisely called in able, experienced civilians to help run the government, but they must confront familiar problems of a bankrupt "revolutionary" African state: clumsy economic machinery, including two dozen state enterprises, which braked Mali's economy and eroded even its traditional trade ties. And they must urgently seek foreign aid and capital.

**Ibid.*, Dec. 7, 1968.

Mr. Touré, meanwhile, still paying rhetorical service to revolution, is forging new economic links with the World Bank, the United States and the West. He may yet be able to avert the fate of his revolutionary neighbors.

Statement by Ambassador Yost, U.S. Representative to the
U.N. Security Council, on the Guinea Resolution and the U.S. Abstention*

December 8, 1970

The armed raid made on the Republic of Guinea which led to the creation of the special mission whose report is now before us is a matter of particular concern to the United States. I should like to emphasize at the outset that the Government of the United States deeply deplores the loss of life and injuries that resulted from the action, as well as the physical destruction that it caused. We view in the most serious way an attack of this nature, which appears to have been prepared and mounted outside the country. President Nixon made this clear in the message he sent to President Touré declaring:

> On behalf of my Government and the American people, I would like to express sympathy to you and to the Government and people of the Republic of Guinea in this difficult period. I would like to take this opportunity to renew to you my assurances that the United States opposes any infringement of Guinean national sovereignty or outside interference in the internal affairs of the Republic of Guinea.

Mr. President, I should like to join in the remarks that have been made commending the work of the special mission and to thank its members for a most useful report. The charges under consideration by the Council are extremely serious, and it is fitting and proper that the Council made an independent effort to determine the facts before considering what action it wished to take. Clearly, the special mission was not able to investigate all of the possible elements of this situation, but we congratulate it for its success in gathering a substantial body of data concerning the events of November 22-23.

It is evident that in drawing up its conclusions, the special mission considered all information made available to it with the care and considered judgment that a matter of this gravity deserves. Its conclusions were not arrived at lightly or in haste. My Government has no reason to question the mission's considered opinion and judgment concerning responsibility for the attack. The report concludes that elements of the Portuguese armed forces participated in the armed raid, an action which my Government must condemn as contrary to the charter's injunction that we refrain from the use or threat of force directed against the territorial integrity or political independence of any state or in any other manner inconsistent with the purposes of the United Nations.

An event of this nature leads us to ask why it occurred and what can be done to prevent its recurrence. In considering these questions, my Government can agree with those who believe we should view the particular events under discussion in a broader context. That context involves the unrest and violence to which differences over the question of the future of the Portuguese territories have given rise over almost a

*Department of State Bulletin, Jan. 18, 1971, pp. 98-100.

decade. My Government has repeatedly made clear, and it reaffirms now, its support for the exercise by the people of those territories of their legitimate right to self-determination. The United States continues to support this principle and will continue to work with those concerned to see it carried out.

In working toward this goal, however, my Government believes that we must avoid violence and seek peaceful solutions. Violence can only bring counterviolence with the attendant misery and suffering. No one involved in this situation, least of all the people of the territories whose interests we are trying to advance, can gain through resort to force. It is for this reason that the United States provides no arms to Portugal for use in Africa and is unwilling as well to provide them to those who would use them against the Portuguese territories in Africa.

Some of the speakers before this Council have objected that this Council did not on November 22 comply with the request of the Government of Guinea by sending at once a United Nations peacekeeping force instead of a fact-finding mission. Let me make two points in regard to this objection:

First, it is proper, indeed essential, that the Security Council, the principal organ for the maintenance of peace and security, do its best independently to ascertain the facts relative to any serious issue on which it is contemplating action. If it did not insist on doing, so, it would soon lose its credit and authority and would involve our organization in the gravest difficulties.

Second, members of this Council are well aware that the United Nations disposes of no forces which can be sent immediately to a troubled area. My Government has long worked without avail for improved procedures that would permit prompt dispatch of peacekeeping forces. I hope that those who have spoken out during this debate will in the future give firm support to efforts to strengthen peacekeeping procedures. Fortunately, in the present case the Guinea forces gained control of the situation successfully and rapidly without requiring the help of U.N. forces.

I would appeal once again to all concerned to examine their consciences and exert renewed efforts to develop fresh, imaginative approaches to the basic problem underlying so much of the violence that disturbs the normal lives of so many of the people of Africa today. The attack on Guinea must not be repeated. But beyond that, we must all redouble our efforts to resolve the more fundamental problem. The spirit and the letter of the Charter of the United Nations commits us—and the parties here concerned—to seek, first of all, a solution to disputes likely to endanger peace and security by discussion and by a common will to look for and find peaceful means of settlement.

In our view the resolution now before us would be more realistic and do more to promote a peaceful settlement if it also took this view into account.

Mr. President, I should like to pay tribute to the way in which the Afro-Asian members of the Council went about the development of the draft resolution which was tabled on their behalf by the Representative of Burundi yesterday. The authors of that resolution showed an awareness of some of the special problems associated with this particular complaint. They had the courtesy to seek the views of other members of this Council before deciding to introduce their draft, and we appreciate their consideration.

During the consultations which we have had with the cosponsors, we have made known our reservations about the Council acting under chapter VII in this instance.

We recognize that, in response to the concerns of my Government and certain other members of the Council, the cosponsors made substantial alterations in their original draft which was circulated informally.

Mr. President, I should like to comment briefly at this point on a few aspects of the draft resolution that has been submitted to the Council. I have already indicated the United States position concerning the action of Portuguese forces involved in the armed raid on the Republic of Guinea. There are a number of other provisions of the draft resolution before us, however, that my Government cannot support, and we will therefore abstain in the vote on the resolution.

In the view of the United States the draft resolution does not constitute a finding that a chapter VII situation now exists nor could it commit the Council to taking action under chapter VII in any future situation. Nevertheless, the draft resolution does seem to us to go much too far in this direction and to create presumptions about our future action, in a very broad range of situations, which are not warranted at this time. We view the events of November 22-23 as very serious, but we cannot support the very far-reaching conclusions that some of the provisions of the draft resolution seek to draw from them.

With regard to operative paragraph 6, I have already reiterated the well-known policy of the United States, in effect since 1961, of providing no arms to Portugal for use in Africa. In the view of my delegation, that policy fully meets the objectives of operative paragraph 6. An effort to broaden the scope of the Council's recommendations concerning assistance to Portugal would be unjustified, in our opinion, and not in the interests of the people of the African territories under Portuguese control.

New York Times *Editorial on the United States Position on the Invasion of Guinea**

December 10, 1970

The United States suffered a serious erosion of credibility with Africa and the Third World when it abstained as the United Nations Security Council condemned Portugal for the recent invasion of Guinea.

Ambassador Yost conceded that the United States has no reason to question a U.N. investigating team's report, fixing responsibility for the attack on Portugal's armed forces; that Washington condemns this action as contrary to the U.N. Charter, and that it reaffirms support for the "legitimate right to self-determination" by the people of Portugal's African territories.

Mr. Yost also noted that in an effort to gain the support of the United States and others, the five African and Asian sponsors had diluted the Security Council resolution, eliminating a reference to Chapter 7 of the Charter, providing for the use of force and sanctions.

But Mr. Yost abstained, along with Britain, France and Spain, because the resolution went "much too far" and created "presumptions" about future Council action. He viewed the attack on Guinea as "very serious," but could not support the resolution's "very far-reaching conclusions" about it.

The State Department's fears about the resolution are surely groundless and its analysis of the situation in Portuguese Africa is out-of-date and out-of-joint. Just prior

The New York Times, Dec. 10, 1970.

to the vote, Max Jakobson of Finland, a member of the U.N. investigating team in Guinea, emphasized that the resolution as revised did not bind the Council to any particular course of action.

What "far-reaching conclusions" does Washington regard as unwarranted? Does it doubt the resolution's assertion that Portuguese colonialism is "a serious threat to the peace and security of independent African states"? It cannot be unaware of the savage Portuguese bombings of Zambian border towns, supposedly in retaliation for guerrilla activities in Angola.

Lisbon's refusal even to discuss self-determination and independence with the black leaders of its African territories is the root cause of violence and guerrilla war in Portuguese Africa. So long as it persists in this refusal it will be futile for the United States to counsel those black leaders to "seek peaceful solutions."

Indeed, it will be worse than that. The United States cannot avoid taking sides in the great struggle now gradually escalating in southern Africa. It will not suffice to deliver occasional rebukes to our Portuguese ally while standing aloof from any meaningful action by the United Nations Security Council.

LIBERIA

Agreement of Cooperation Between the United States and Liberia*

July 8, 1959

The Government of the United States of American and the Government of Liberia,

Desiring to strengthen peace in accordance with the principles of the Charter of the United Nations;

Affirming their right to cooperate for their security and defense in accordance with Article 51 of the Charter of the United Nations;

Recalling the unique relationship which has obtained between the peoples of the United States of American and Liberia for more than one hundred years;

Considering that the Government of the United States of America and the Government of Liberia are founded upon similar constitutional principles;

Considering further that the peoples of the United States of America and Liberia share a common democratic heritage;

Recalling that the Government of the United States of America has traditionally regarded itself as the next friend of the Government of Liberia; and

Reaffirming the historic interest of the Government of the United States of America in the preservation of the independence and territorial integrity of Liberia;

Have agreed as follows:

Article I

In the event of aggression or threat of aggression against Liberia, the Government of the United States of America and the Government of Liberia will immediately determine what action may be appropriate for the defense of Liberia.

*Department of State, *United States Treaties and Other International Agreements*, Vol. 10, Pt. 2, 1959 (Washington, 1960), pp. 1598-99.

Article II

The Government of the United States of America, in accordance with applicable laws of the United States of America and with applicable agreements heretofore or hereafter entered into between the Government of the United States of America and the Government of Liberia, reaffirms that it will continue to furnish the Government of Liberia such assistance as may be mutually agreed upon between the Government of the United States of America and the Government of Liberia, in order to assist the Government of Liberia in the effective promotion of its economic development and in the preservation of its national independence and integrity.

Article III

This Agreement shall enter into force upon the date of its signature and shall continue in force until one year after the receipt by either Government of written notice of the intention of the other Government to terminate it.

For the Government of the United States of America:
Douglas Dillon
For the Government of Liberia:
Geo. Padmore

Statement by Byron H. Larabee, President of Firestone Plantations Company, Ohio, Before the Subcommittee on Africa Hearings on the Activities of Private United States Organizations in Africa*

May 8-June 1, 1961

Mr. Chairman, I have no written statement.

My name is Byron H. Larabee. I am president of the Firestone Plantations Co., which is a Liberian corporation, but a wholly owned subsidiary of the Firestone Tire & Rubber Co. I have been associated with the company for about 23 years, during all of which time I have been concerned with the operation of our plantations, principally in Liberia.

*   *   *

We began our operations in Liberia principally in 1926. However, we had present in the country, before that time, a staff of people engaged in exploration.

We operate under what is known as the planting agreement which is a combination lease and concession agreement inasmuch as, under the constitution of the Republic of Liberia, we cannot own real estate. We have a 99-year lease which has had great publicity because it entitles us to select up to a million acres for the planting of rubber.

---

*Committee on Foreign Affairs, *Activities of Private United States Organizations in Africa,* Hearings Before the Subcommittee on Africa, 87th Cong., 1st sess. (Washington, 1961), pp. 21-26.

Under the process of the planting agreement we were simply permitted to select areas which the Government theoretically guarantees the title to but which we found was not possible. We then acquired title to any areas that were occupied, placed them in the name of the Government, and leased them back.

Under that arrangement we have under lease from the Government approximately 200,000 acres of land on which we have planted somewhat over 90,000 acres of rubber. I think it should be noted, however, that we occupy larger areas than that because all of the areas within those boundaries are not susceptible to planting and also we occupy large areas for villages, factories, roads, houses, hospitals, et cetera.

                    *   *   *

Now, on this area of land, we have housing provided by the company and we provide all the facilities you might imagine necessary for some 50,000 people. We employ, depending on our planting program and the time of the year, from 22,000 to 27,000 people. Currently our employment runs about 23,000.

We are engaged in tapping today only 68,000 acres because of the replanting program underway under which we are replacing our old rubber trees with higher yielding material.

We operate on the plantation all of the facilities which ordinarily are found in the city. We do that because when we went into Liberia such facilities did not exist and in the main do not exist today. For instance, we have a medical department in which we have 12 physicians and surgeons who we bring in as foreign staff members. We have a total of 24 foreign medical staff and some 300 Liberian technicians.

We operate a research program which has nine foreign technicians. We operate a supply department which started out and grew like Topsy and today the two facets of it have sales in the neighborhood of $12 million and require hundreds of people to staff.

We represent many American companies there, as distributors and agents for American products.

In the beginning we were also engaged in the banking business because the British bank, which was there when we came in, gave up and went home and left the country without a bank so we operated a bank up until 1955 at which time we sold it to the First National City Bank of New York who now operate it quite successfully.

I am trying to cover in a broad stroke here what our general operations are. Of course, we are in Liberia to grow rubber and to make money, and let me say we have been successful in both.

By nature of the area in which we operate and the time at which we began, we are required to perform many services and carry on many programs which would be strange to corporations operating in this country.

For instance, in the beginning we had a finance corporation which loaned money to the Republic of Liberia and which was paid off—the loan was paid off well in advance in 1956, for which we were very thankful and the government also because it was a source, as you might guess, of annoyance.

We have supported and do support research of varoius kinds. Medical research, and research in the botanical sciences particularly.

We have introduced practically all of the economical cash crops that are known in the tropics; they have been introduced primarily through our research organization and we have developed high-producing rubber trees which are indigenous—these particular ones only—to Liberia.

We have a program for fostering development of rubber by the local farmers and today there are some 2,000 Liberian farmers who have their own plantations and from that has been crated a middle class which did not exist before in Liberia.

Some of these people have rather large, relatively stable incomes from this source. Many others have something above a subsistence level.

Our relations with the government have on the whole been somewhat better than good. We have had our disagreements from time to time but for many years these have been minor.

We carry on, on the plantation, educational programs. At the present time there are about 2,200 Liberian children in school. Under this program the government sets the curriculum and provides the teachers. We pay the teachers, house them, provide the school, the books, et cetera.

We also have a human relations program which carries on the fostering and assistance for such organizations as the YMCA, YWCA, Red Cross, Boy Scouts, Girl Scouts, et cetera. We also provide clubs and recreational facilities for the entire plantation. We have organized teams and coaching in the various sports.

In the course of the years we have been under criticism from time to time, as I am sure everyone operating in an underdeveloped country has, for not having more of the indigenous population in our high staff positions. I might say in passing that while we have a labor force approximating 25,000 people, we are now at our highest number of employees from foreign countries, which is 202.

Of those less than 150 are actually engaged in the productive side of the plantation and the rest of them in service facilities, the medical, research and other services.

Of that number, we have seven Liberian staff members who are full staff members, having all the responsibilities for staff.

We have others here in training in the United States. However, it isn't always possible to obtain the people that you want because the Government itself is in need of their services and other private industry competes. Also, the supply line has not always been full.

I think that generally covers our operation.

*   *   *

Mr. O'Hara: Do you think the United States has done enough for Liberia?
Mr. Larabee: Sir, I don't think we have even scratched the surface.

*   *   *

Now, the Secretary, I am sure, will correct me on this if I am wrong, but until perhaps very recently—and I say it because there is one effort we have made upon which I am not clear—Liberia has had not one grant from the United States.

She has had loans made under regular terms with the Export-Import Bank and the Development Loan Fund, and she has had assistance through ICA and its predecessors for which she has paid in roughly 20 percent of her own National Government income each year, by the way—and this wasn't a one-sided thing.

The assistance, if I may say so, many times was not worth what it cost. It has been difficult, as everyone recognizes, to always secure people of the right training and disposition and temperament and willingness to work together on ICA and predecessor projects. I agree very much with Mr. Osborne; it has been very difficult to recruit good people, capable personnel to serve abroad these days and particularly in Africa.

So it hasn't always been the best of assistance. Many times these people have gone out there and had to be trained there. They have had some background but as to the problems that exist in an underdeveloped country in Africa, the climatic conditions and the extent of education of the laborer, it is difficult.

So, outside of that, unless there is something else I don't know of, they have had no grants and they have had no grants because they have never asked for grants.

They are paying back their loans on time and without asking—I think there was one period recently in which there was some adjustment made on a payment date but if there has been anything other than that, I don't know, and I try to keep close tab.

So to answer you directly, sir, we haven't scratched the surface as to what we should have done. Presupposing that we are going to have an aid and development program, then I believe that we should look after our friends as much at least as we do our enemies.

*   *   *

NIGERIA

*Statement by Secretary of State Christian A. Herter on the Admission of Nigeria to the U.N.**

October 7, 1960

*   *   *

We are being asked to recommend to the General Assembly that the Federation of Nigeria be admitted to United Nations membership. The United States endorses this recommendation with great pleasure.

This is perhaps a good time to look briefly at the remarkable renaissance which is going on in Africa. I feel certain that historians when they examine the events of this year will single out as the outstanding political fact of the year, if not, indeed, of the decade, the remarkable advancement of political freedom in Africa. Other events may cause more passing furor, but the achievement of independence by 16 new African states during the first 10 months of 1960 is one of the stirring phenomena of our days. Today virtually all of west Africa is either independent or soon to achieve independence.

The people of Nigeria have won their independence, but they have won our warmest admiration by the way they have gone about the winning of it. They have done it by demonstrating, time and again and in many fields, that Nigerians are anxious to enjoy the satisfactions of independence and fully capable of assuming its responsibilities. They have done it also by reaching agreement among themselves on the form and structure of their federation in one of the most constructive acts of statesmanship of the past decade.

Department of State Bulletin, Oct. 24, 1960, pp. 659-60.

When the green and white Nigerian flag was raised at one minute past midnight on October 1, it marked the culmination of a process which began nearly a century ago. During a recent visit to New York a distinguished Nigerian said:

> Our country presents a picture of political stability. There is no absence of politics, and at times controversy runs high, as it does in any free country, but the basic factor in our political life is stability. We have not rushed unprepared into independence, but we have advanced step by step over the years. . . .

Through the enlightened policies of Great Britain, Nigerians have been trained in ever larger numbers for the responsibilities of leadership. This policy has been carried out right here at the United Nations, where Nigerian officials have for a number of years followed United Nations activities closely as members of United Kingdom delegations. Today they are thoroughly familiar with the practices and procedures of the United Nations and will be able to make an important contribution to our work without delay. Already Nigeria has agreed to send a battalion to the Congo to join the United Nations Force there, which is a signal service which we all applaud warmly.

It is no exaggeration to say that the world has watched Nigeria's progress toward independence with unparalleled attention. Certainly few recent events have so captured the imagination of the American people. This, I believe, is due to a number of related reasons.

First, Nigeria is the most populous country on the African Continent, containing about 15 percent of Africa's total population.

Secondly, Nigeria, with its great size and diversity, has become a functioning federation. To operate a federal structure effectively, as our 170 years of experience with this system of government shows, requires a willingness to accept diversity and to cultivate a spirit of accommodation and conciliation. Nigerians have already abundantly demonstrated these qualities. They have adopted a course of freedom and equality for all ethnic groups. This, we believe, is the real road to lasting national unity.

Thirdly, Nigeria has all the muscle and sinew required for great economic expansion. Not only does it possess great natural resources, but its people are hard working. Moreover, its Government, with its kind of experience and dedicated officers, can be expected to follow wise economic policies. With these essential ingredients for economic development, and with the assistance of the United Nations and of its friends—among whom the United States is proud to count itself—economic advancement can be confidently expected.

Nigeria will face serious challenges in the development of its new state. We believe, however, that Nigeria has the men, the resources, and the will to succeed.

*   *   *

New York Times *Editorial on the Nigerian Coup d'Etat Revolt**

January 17, 1966

The attempted revolution in Nigeria is a result of tribal, social, political and religious tensions breaking through a veneer of stability. This most populous nation of

*The New York Times, Jan. 17, 1966.

Africa has often been held up as a rare example of African democracy. It has, however, been in a state of thinly disguised ferment for years.

Great efforts have been needed to hold this diverse federation together since independence in 1960. Of the unusually strong and able leaders who accomplished this, two have now been killed and one—Prime Minister Balewa—kidnapped. The forces of disunity were spurred by fraudulent elections in the Western Region last October.

While awaiting a clarification of the still confused events, some understanding of the situation can be gained by contemplating the extraordinary complications of Nigeria's federal structure. As the latest census showed, the Northern Region, which takes up about three-quarters of the country territorially, still had a big population edge of 29,000,000 against 22,000,000 for the Western, Midwest and Eastern regions. Thus the Northerners—most of them Moslems—have been able to hold a majority in the federal legislature since independence. However, the real political control was at the regional level. Much of the nation's wealth and talent has been in the South.

The Northern Region, inhabited mainly by the Hausa and Fulani tribes, could only keep its domination by alliances with minority opposition parties in the southern regions. The North is conservative—the opposition says feudal—and there has been bad blood ever since the Fulani carried out a jihad, or religious war, in the South early in the nineteenth century.

Arrayed against the Moslems of the North have been many of the political activists of the Yorubas in Western Nigeria and of the Ibos in the East. The most far-sighted Nigerian leaders have sought to unify these different peoples and to make national rather than tribal loyalties hold sway.

The hope for the future, once peace is restored, is a true confederation in which the Southerners will get a fair chance at political power and office through proportional representation.

New York Times *Editorial on Nigeria in Political Crisis**

August 3, 1966

The skeptics who argued long ago that Nigeria was a geographic expression, not a nation, must feel themselves vindicated by the current upheavals there. These have brought that country to the brink of dissolution. On the evidence to date, tribal and regional loyalties are far more potent than any sense of common Nigerian nationality. It will require a political miracle for even a tenuously joined federal Nigeria to survive, let alone the unitary state General Ironsi was trying to create before last weekend's revolt.

In retrospect, the real surprise is that it took so long for the present Nigerian crisis to appear full blown. The groundwork for it was bloodily laid last January by the coup that overthrew Prime Minister Balewa's Government. The young Ibo officers who struck then slaughtered the flower of the elite among the northern Hausa people, including the Prime Minister and the Sardauna of Sokota. General Ironsi realized the tragic potentialities of a Hausa effort to gain revenge, and it was a major achievement for him to maintain relative peace for more than a half year. Last weekend the Northerners finally struck back and took blood revenge.

*Ibid., Aug. 3, 1966.

The key issue now was well stated by Colonel Ojukwu, the Ibo military governor of Eastern Nigeria, in a broadcast challenging the attempt of the Northernor, Lieut. Col. Gowon, to take power. He declared that the annihilation of Ibo officers had "cast doubts as to whether the people of Nigeria, after these cruel and bloody atrocities, can ever sincerely live together as members of the same nation." A Northern leader could have used identical language last January. And if Nigeria should now disintegrate, this background of reciprocal political murders raises the question of whether the successor states can soon learn to live together as peaceful neighbors. The outlook is tragic for Africa's most populous country, a land whose initial development after independence made it seem for a time an oasis of stability and orderly development in a disorderly continent.

New York Times *Editorial on the United States and the Nigerian Civil War* *

August 24, 1967

It is ridiculous for Nigeria's Federal Government to accuse the United States of seeking to "balkanize" that country to gain control of its oil. What is true is that unusually clumsy State Department tactics have spotlighted the schizophrenia in Washington's behavior toward a civil war that is wracking the biggest and most important country of black Africa.

In that conflict, the United States recognizes only the Federal Government in Lagos and hopes a way may be found to keep Nigeria intact as a country. That means Washington hopes the attempt of Ibo leaders of the East to set up a separate state of "Biafra" will not succeed. Yet Washington goes out of its way to publicize its refusal to "provide arms and ammunition to either side." And when the Soviet Union moves into the vacuum to supply arms to the Federal Government to help it put down the secession, the State Department promptly calls this "a matter of regret."

There are times when schizophrenia cannot be avoided in the conduct of foreign policy, but greater American foresight might have prevented this situation from arising. In any case, it might be possible even at this late hour to tidy it up.

Suppose the United States and Britain together had warned the Ibo leaders flatly in May that they would never support any attempt to break up Nigeria. Then suppose Washington and London had pressured the Federal Government quietly but relentlessly to hold up military action while accepting mediation and conciliation offered by Presidents Kaunda, Kenyatta, Obote and Nyerere or by the Organization of African Unity, with the goal of preserving a viable, peaceful Nigeria.

To suggest what might have been useful three months ago is to suggest what might conceivably still work. Once the shooting started it was obvious that both Lagos and "Biafra" would take arms from any available source. Once Washington had turned down Lagos it was inevitable that General Gowon would turn to Russia. If Washington really wants to persuade Moscow not to fish in Nigeria's troubled waters, the proper course is quiet diplomacy, not petulant press handouts.

Other African nations are worried about Nigeria's civil strife and as concerned as Washington that it be kept free of great power competition and ideological exploitation. The United States and Britain should try again to promote mediation by the O.A.U. or any combination of its members. Then they should try to persuade the Soviet Union and France to join them in a declaration of support for these African efforts.

With the Nigerian military situation in evident stalemate, this could be the best possible time for such an African attempt. It may, in fact, be the last opportunity.

State Department Statement on the Soviet Decision to Supply Arms to Nigeria*

August 21, 1967

Neither the United States nor the Soviet Union has in the past been an important supplier of arms to Nigeria. Consistent with that fact, the United States decided for its part on the outbreak of the current hostilities in Nigeria that it would not sell or otherwise supply arms and ammunition to either side. To have done so would have risked deepening the conflict and introducing an element of great-power competition in the internal affairs of a friendly state.

The United States has adhered fully to that policy. Its refusal to supply arms has been stated publicly and is well known to the Soviet Union. In these circumstances, it is a matter of regret to the United States that the Soviet Union has not shown the same forbearance but, on the contrary, has decided to engage in the supply of arms in this internal conflict.

While we do not know the reasons that prompted the Soviet Union to take this decision or the functions of Soviet personnel reported to have arrived in Nigeria, we believe all nations have a responsibility to avoid any exploitation of this situation for ideological or other political purposes.

It remains the hope of the United States Government that the present destructive internal conflict in Nigeria will yield to a peaceful settlement and that all who wish that country well will devote their energies to that end.

State Department Statement Reaffirming United States
Support of the Nigerian Government†

February 5, 1968

          *   *   *

We've been concerned with a number of insinuations recently alleging United States support of the "Biafra" regime. I wish to make very clear that the United States continues to recognize the Federal Military Government as the only legal government in Nigeria. We do not recognize "Biafra" nor, so far as we know, does any other government in the world. We have, from the outset of the Nigerian crisis, regarded it as an internal conflict which, in the last analysis, only the Nigerians themselves can resolve. At the same time, we had hoped that the conflict would yield a peaceful

*Department of State Bulletin, Sept. 11, 1967, p. 320.
†Ibid., Feb. 5, 1968, p. 278.

solution which would spare all Nigerians from further tragic loss of life. The private actions of a few American citizens over which we have no control should in no way be construed as an indication of United States Government support for an unrecognized regime.

The United States Government has in no way encouraged, supported, or otherwise been involved in this rebellion.

Statement by President Lyndon B. Johnson on Relief Efforts for Nigeria*

July 11, 1968

                 *   *   *

The American people have watched with growing grief and horror the terrible loss of life and suffering in Nigeria.

The war in that bitterly divided nation is daily becoming more costly. Civilian inhabitants are threatened not just by violance but by starvation.

Normal supplies of food have been cut off by the fighting. With foods containing protein increasingly unavailable, the lives of children are particularly endangered.

The United States has cooperated with other governments and private organizations in efforts to provide needed food and medicine. We stand ready to support the International Committee of the Red Cross with additional funds, supplies, and equipment.

Relief efforts thus far have been frustrated by disputes on how to get supplies through the lines of fighting.

While we have no intention of interfering in Nigerian affairs, we do not believe innocent persons should be made the victims of political maneuvering.

Deaths caused by warfare are tragic enough. But mass starvation that can be prevented must be prevented.

I urgently appeal to all those bearing responsibility to allow supplies to get to the people who so desperately need them.

Speech by Senator Brooke Before the Senate on the Civil War in Nigeria†

July 11, 1968

Mr. President, the civil war in Nigeria has been in progress for well over a year. During that time—and before—thousands of people have lost their lives, either in direct combat, through accident, or through other effects of war. The death of the innocent is always deplorable, but a situation is developing in eastern Nigeria where the suffering exceeds all tolerable bounds or expectations. The Federal Military Government and the government of Biafra are locked in a deadly impasse, which is resulting in the loss of hundreds of lives each day.

We must all be deeply concerned that mutual apprehension and distrust have

---

*Ibid., July 29, 1968, p. 124.

†*Congressional Record*, July 11, 1968, p. S.8121.

combined with diplomatic and military considerations to block the provision of desperately needed food and medical assistance to those who are starving. Their welfare is the principal concern of the peoples of the world; it must be the foremost consideration of the contending governments as well.

It is true that the Federal Military Government of Nigeria has made numerous efforts to permit relief supplies to enter the territory still in rebel hands. They have suggested a ceasefire along certain overland routes to permit goods to be brought in from Federal areas. Colonel Ojukwu and his government in the former Eastern Region have rejected this source of supply. The FMG has offered to permit some supplies to be flown in by the International Red Cross, with the sole reservation that Federal forces be allowed to approve the flight and the cargo to prevent the simultaneous transport of additional weapons. The Biafran regime insists on unrestricted air transit. The Nigerian government fears that this would make it possible for the Biafrans to fly in weapons as well as relief articles. Biafra has refused to accept supplies brought overland because of its firm opposition to any indication of reliance upon the Federal government.

The political considerations involved are certainly understandable. The leaders on both sides, and a large portion of the people, have pledged what the founders of the United States declared to be "their lives, their fortunes, and their sacred honor" in the cause of seemingly irreconcilable goals. The principles involved cannot be ignored. But neither can the suffering, the loss of life, and the bitterness which will remain for years to come if this situation is allowed to continue.

Underlying all the differences, the leaders of Nigeria and of Biafra share some common goals; they all want a better life for their people; they all want peace; they all want personal security and political freedom. Surely, there is a point at which all these goals can be accommodated with a political settlement.

But negotiations, as Americans know from hard experience, are time consuming. Thousands of people in imminent danger of death by starvation cannot be allowed to wait until all political differences have been resolved.

It is my urgent and sincere hope that the leaders of both sides will quickly accept, in the name of humanity, an arrangement whereby food and medical supplies can be brought into the region on a continuing basis under mutually acceptable international auspices. A recommended route for continuing provision remains the land route. The best organization to perform this function is, in my opinion, the International Red Cross. The Red Cross, presently, has the confidence of both sides in the conflict. It could bring in limited emergency supplies by air, and at the same time develop substantial overland transport facilities which could accommodate the immediate political sensibilities of both sides, while meeting the needs of the suffering people as well.

Presently, facilities in Biafra are inadequate to support an airlift large enough to meet the population's needs. As another alternative to the road route, international agencies should cooperate in an emergency construction program to improve runways and other facilities int he area in order to provide the necessary airlift capability.

Mr. President, a clear distinction must be made between humanitarian necessities and political considerations, and both sides should be willing to separate these issues. No leader, in Nigeria, Biafra, or anywhere else, has the right to sacrifice innocent men, women, and children on the brutal altar of political controversy.

State Department Statement on Nigerian Relief*

July 18, 1968

You will recall earlier statements expressing our deep concern over the problem of relief to the peoples of Nigeria, peoples affected by the civil war.

We are gratified at the action being taken by the International Committee of the Red Cross, with whom foreign governments and private organizations are cooperating, in bringing relief to the victims on both sides of that civil war.

In order further to assist in the planning and execution of that humanitarian mission, the Secretary of State, on behalf of the U.S. Government, has made avilable to the ICRC a guaranteed reserve fund of $1 million derived from AID funds. The reserve account may be drawn upon for immediate requirements to accompany anticipated pledges of assistance from other nations and private organizations. It will also be employed to expedite current programs that may be delayed because of limitations on money.

Statement by Secretary of State Dean Rusk During a News Conference
on Civilian Victims of Civil War in Nigeria†

July 30, 1968

I have a short statement on the situation in "Biafra."

We continue to be deeply concerned over the suffering of the civilian victims on both sides of the civil war in Nigeria. A major relief effort has been mounted by the International Committee of the Red Cross. We are cooperating fully in that effort, along with many other governments and a large number of voluntary agencies.

The United States contribution to this relief effort has now reached some $7.3 million, including estimated donations of some $2 million from private American sources.

The dispute over how to get supplies through the lines of fighting has thus far permitted only small amounts of assistance to reach the areas of actual suffering. The Red Cross has been working urgently with both sides and with the Organization of African Unity to find a means of breaking that bottleneck.

As President Johnson stated on July 11, we do not believe innocent persons should be made the victims of political maneuvering.

The spirit of humanity in every part of the world has been deeply moved by the suffering in Nigeria.

We therefore urge all those in positions of responsibility to allow this international effort to move forward.

We have noted with satisfaction that agreement has been reached on an agenda for peace negotiations beginning no later than August 5 in Addis Ababa. These talks are sponsored by the Nigerian Consultative Committee of the OAU, under the chairman-ship of His Imperial Majesty Haile Selassie, Emperor of Ethiopia.

---

*Department of State Bulletin, Aug. 5, 1968, p. 142.
†Ibid., Aug. 5, 1968, p. 186.

We join with all friends of the people of Nigeria in expressing the hope for the success of these talks under this wise and distinguished leadership and for the earliest possible negotiated settlement of the civil war.

We hope that both sides will show the utmost restraint in their military operations so that the peacemakers will have a full opportunity to find a basis for agreement in this tragic fratricidal strife.

Statement by Senator McGovern Before the Senate on Biafra*

August 2, 1968

Mr. President, I know that for a number of weeks Senators have been concerned about news stories with respect to the mounting hunger and starvation in the area of Biafra, a part of the State of Nigeria, which has been gripped in a serious military and political conflict for a number of months.

Reports have come to me, which I believe to be well grounded, which indicate if the blockade that is now isolating 7 to 10 million people in Biafra is not penetrated in some fashion with food relief, as many as 2 to 3 million people may starve to death in the next few months. Already thousands of people have fallen victim to starvation in the situation that developed there this spring and summer.

To try to arouse some positive action on the part of our Government and other countries which must be watching the situation, I have this afternoon drafted a letter to the President which I am now circulating among Senators. It has been signed by the Senator from Idaho [Mr. Church], the Senator from Minnesota [Mr. Mondale], the Senator from Pennsylvania [Mr. Clark], the Senator from Oregon [Mr. Morse], the Senator from New Jersey [Mr. Williams] and the Senator from Rhode Island [Mr. Pell]. I hope we will have a number of other signers before the end of the day. I shall read the letter into the Record:

U.S. Senate Committee on Agriculture and Forestry,
Washington, D.C., August 2, 1968.

Dear Mr. President: We are deeply concerned about the mass starvation that now threatens Biafra.

As you know, this area, which has attempted to secede from Nigeria, is now completely surrounded by Nigerian Federal Troops, and is under a blockade that can only be penetrated by aircraft. It contains seven to ten million people who are traditionally dependent on food imports. The present blockade and the exhaustion of their reserves has forced them into a state of acute hunger and starvation.

The complex political issues responsible for the blockade are currently being discussed by the parties involved, but it may be several months before these negotiations can resolve the issues and lift the blockade. Medical authorities estimate that by that time several million people will have starved to death. A large majority of these will be children, since children are far more sensitive to dietary deficiencies than are adults. Thousands have already died, and the starvation rate is increasing rapidly.

We wholeheartedly support our government's present policy of strict political neutrality in this civil war. At the same time, we believe firmly that the resulting starvation should not occur if it is within our power to prevent it.

Therefore, we urge you to offer assistance through the United Nations or voluntary religious and humanitarian organizations to enable them to deal with the food shortage that has resulted from this conflict.

*Congressional Record, Aug. 2, 1968, pp. S10133-34.

We suggest that the relief operation be conducted according to the following general principles:

(1) Food should be brought into the impacted areas of Nigeria in sufficient quantity to sustain the population until normal food acquisition can be resumed.

(2) While it is probable that most of the assistance will be supplied by the United States, other advanced countries should be urged to contribute.

(3) Since the political situation may require that the relief operation initially be conducted by air, our Government and others should make appropriate arrangements to provide the distributing agencies with aircraft, pilots and supporting equipment.

We feel it is of paramount importance that America avoid partisan involvement in armed conflicts that do not significantly affect our national interests. Therefore, we urge that U.S. assistance be channelled entirely through international or private voluntary organizations.

All individuals participating in the relief operation shall do so at their own risk, and they and their sponsoring agency shall bear the entire responsibility for their safety.

The children and adults of eastern Nigeria must receive swift attention and assistance, or millions of them will die while many of the remainder suffer permanent mental or physical damage.

We urge that action be taken with all possible speed.

                    *   *   *

*Message from President Johnson to Ethiopian Emperor Haile Selassie on an Arrangement for Relief of Nigerian Victims**

August 5, 1968

The starvation and suffering in Nigeria have aroused the conscience of men everywhere. Friends of Africa around the world share the profound hope that the negotiations you and your distinguished colleagues begin today will bring an end to this tragic conflict.

I know the task is complex and the bitterness deep. But I know all Americans join me in urging that means be quickly found to ensure that innocent civilians are no longer made the victims of war.

Relief supplies are already nearby. The International Committee of the Red Cross, supported by many voluntary agencies and governments, including our own, stands ready to mount a major relief effort in the affected areas. That effort has already been frustrated too long.

Your Majesty, we in the United States remain ready to continue in every possible way to help in the humanitarian task of providing and moving supplies to the people who need them so desperately. The political aspects of the problem obviously must be settled by the parties concerned, with the help of their African neighbors. But feeding the starving and easing the suffering of civilian populations are the most basic obligations of common humanity. I know that you and your fellow Statesmen will extend every effort to allow these obligations to be met.

Our thoughts and prayers are with you.

State Department Statement on a United States Mission to Confer on Nigerian Relief†

August 10, 1968

Secretary Rusk has asked Ambassador C. Robert Moore, our former Ambassador to the Republic of Mali and now Deputy Assistant Secretary for African Affairs, to fly to

*Department of State Bulletin, Sept. 2, 1968, p. 243.
†Ibid.

Geneva this evening for urgent consultations on the relief of victims of the Nigerian civil war.

Ambassador Moore will meet with officials of the International Committee of the Red Cross and with representatives of other governments and organizations who share our concern over the starving in Nigeria.

You will recall that the United States has on several occasions voiced its deep concern about the tragic situation in Nigeria.

On July 11, President Johnson said: "I urgently appeal to all those bearing responsibility to allow supplies to get to the people who so desperately need them."

And just a week ago, the President said: "We in the United States remain ready to continue in every possible way to help in the humanitarian task of providing and moving supplies to the people who need them so desperately."

The United States Government has already contributed a total of $6.3 million to the relief effort. Private American voluntary organizations have also contributed about $2.5 million in food and other supplies.

Although some of this food is reaching the suffering, ICRC attempts to move adequate amounts of food to the starving on both sides of the conflict are still frustrated by the political impasse.

Ramone Eaton, Vice President for International Relations of the American Red Cross, will accompany Ambassador Moore. Also accompanying the Ambassador will be Frank Sieverts, Special Assistant to Ambassador Harriman, and Stephen R. Tripp, the Disaster Relief Coordinator in the Agency for International Development.

Needless to say, we hope for the success of this vital humanitarian mission and once again urge the cooperation of both sides in the effort to allow food to get to starving civilians.

*Statement by Presidential Candiate Richard M. Nixon on Biafra**

September 9, 1968

The terrible tragedy of the people of Biafra has now assumed catastrophic dimensions. Starvation is daily claiming the lives of an estimated 6,000 Ibo tribesmen, most of them children. If adequate food is not delivered to the people in the immediate future hundreds of thousands of human beings will die of hunger.

Until now efforts to relieve the Biafran people have been thwarted by the desire of the central government of Nigeria to pursue total and unconditional victory and by the fear of the Ibo people that surrender means wholesale atrocities and genocide.

But genocide is what is taking place right now—and starvation is the grim reaper.

This is not the time to stand on ceremony or to "go through channels" or to absorb the Diplomatic niceties. The destruction of an entire people is an immoral objective, even in the most moral of wars. It can never be justified; it can never be condoned.

Voluntary organisations such as the Red Cross, the church world service and Caritas have rushed thousands of tons of protein high rich nourishments and baby foods to the vicinity of the stricken region. Much of the food remains nearby while these children starve to death.

*Markpress News Feature Service, Biafran Overseas Press Div., Press Release, Gen.—300.

The time has long passed for the wringing of hands about what is going on. While America is not the world's policeman, let us at least act as the world's conscience in this matter of life and death for millions.

The President of the United States is a man charged with responsibilities and concern all over the world, but I urge President Johnson to give to this crisis all the time and attention and imagination and energy he can muster. Every friend of humanity should be asked to step forward to call an end to this slaughter of innocents in West Africa.

America is not without enormous material wealth and power and ability. There is no better cause in which we might invest that power than in staying alive the lives of innocent men and women and children who otherwise are doomed.

Message by President Johnson Calling on OAU to Break Deadlock on Relief for Nigeria*

September 13, 1968

         *   *   *

America's thoughts and good wishes are very much with you in this most important meeting of the Organization of African Unity. In the five years since its birth the OAU has made major contributions to the solution of African problems. Your historic work for peace and cooperation is needed more than ever in this time of testing.

We in America share your dream of the African future—of a peaceful, prosperous continent where all peoples may live in freedom and dignity and enjoy the fruits of their labor. That dream can be won only by perseverance and steadfast cooperation. And we share your proud confidence that it will come true.

We also know the importance you attach—and rightfully so—to the solution of Africa's problems by Africans. In Lagos, Kampala, Naimey and Addis Ababa, you have carried the hopes of the world in your tireless efforts to end the tragic fighting in Nigeria. For we all know that the helpless victims of the Nigerian civil war have been denied succor too long and their anguish should not be allowed to continue. As you gather today, women and children far from the sound of battle are dying of starvation in that stricken land.

The Government and the people of the United States and many other countries outside Africa have already contributed food and medical supplies to help relieve the suffering. We stand ready to give further help.

Yet a terrible and paralyzing deadlock still prevents life-saving relief supplies from reaching those who so desperately need them. And it is to you—the Assembly of the OAU as the highest voice and conscience of Africa—that the world now looks to break that deadlock. I pray that your great influence and wisdom will lead both parties in the conflict to set aside partisan considerations and allow a prompt, effective solution to this agonizing problem.

I do not underestimate the difficulties of your task. But I have every hope that your common dedication in the spirit of African unity will meet the challenge.

*Department of State Bulletin, Oct. 7, 1968, p. 356.

Speech by Senator Edward Kennedy (Massachusetts) Before the Senate
on the Need to Meet Humanitarian Needs in the Nigeria Civil War*

September 23, 1968

*   *   *

Mr. President, the humanitarian problems of Nigeria have been of deep concern to me for nearly a year. Last fall, following conversations with officials in the Department of State and during a visit to Geneva in my capacity as Chairman of the Judiciary Subcommittee on Refugees, I discussed the beginnings of the tragedy and the early appeals for international assistance with the International Committee of the Red Cross. In the months that followed, I and members of my staff watched developments closely, consulted with the Department of State and voluntary agencies working in the field and strongly supported initiatives, in both the public and private sectors, to mobilize an international relief operation under Red Cross auspices.

These early initiatives were fruitless, and last May, through a member of my staff on official business in Geneva, I again urged action—and new initiatives—to head off what was clearly evolving from a ragged but forgotten war into one of the greatest nightmares of modern times.

The world has lived with this nightmare for more than 3 months. But there has been great public indignation in this country and abroad over the inability of governments and statesmen to devise a workable formula to effect a relief operation for adequate provisions of food and medicine. This is not to say that few efforts have been made to accomplish this objective. We are aware of what has been done—especially the highly publicized meetings and negotiations at Kampala, Naimey, Addis Abbaba, Geneva, and Algiers, involving several governments, the warring parties in Nigeria, the Red Cross, and the Organization for African Unity.

And we are aware of what our own Government has done to facilitate these efforts—although I strongly believe our own actions were belated and, like so much of our moral and humanitarian leadership in recent years, without a sense of urgency, creativity and deep compassion for those in dire need.

Mr. President, we are conditioned in the world we have created to accept suffering and injustice—especially in our time when violent conflict and oppression are active in so many areas.

But the newer world we seek will not evolve if we ignore these challenges to leadership and take comfortable refuge in the mundane patterns and attitudes of the past.

In the case of Nigeria—in the effort to help her people caught in the passion of fraticidal war—I cannot believe that our own Government and the international community stands paralyzed in the fact of recrimination and stalemate, as though the parties to the conflict were debating a centuries old political argument. No one can ignore the situation in Nigeria—least of all the combatant leaders, no matter how sophisticated their didactics, or how convincing their propaganda, at stake are human lives—innocent lives—African lives—thousands even millions of lives—whose destruction will burden the conscience of Nigeria and all mankind for generations to come, unless something more is done to save them.

*Congressional Record, Sept. 23, 1968, pp. S.1227-28.

And so today, as an individual American hopeful for the future of Nigeria—as an individual American concerned about the dignity and preservation of the ultimate resource on our planet, I appeal for immediate action through the United Nations. I appeal to the warring leaders of Nigeria, to the leaders of all nations, and to the President of the United States to take action in support of of initiatives I know are being made, to have the humanitarian problem of Nigeria placed on the agenda of the General Assembly which opens tomorrow in New York. I believe the extraordinary nature of this problem demands that it be considered by the General Assembly at the earliest possible time—hopefully before this week is out.

Specifically, I recommend:

First, that the General Assembly consider and pass a resolution recognizing the international humanitarian obligations in the present situation of Nigeria;

Second, that the resolution, employing the mandatory power of United Nations charter, direct the Secretary General to use his good office and all the resources available to him, to expedite the conclusion of a "mercy agreement" with the parties to the Nigerian conflict;

Third, that the mercy agreement be carried out under the auspices of the United Nations, in cooperation with the Red Cross and private voluntary agencies, whose dedicated personnel, often with great personal risk, are doing what they can with the meager support currently available to them—and I pay high tribute to their efforts;

And, fourth, that governments actively support this effort of the United Nations and prepare to make voluntary contributions of funds, commodities, personnel, and equipment to effect the mercy agreement, including the logistical support to mount an airlift into areas of needs.

Mr. President, I do not underestimate the political and logistic difficulties involved in taking or carrying out the initiatives I have outlined. But I believe the world will respond—for in resolving the difficulties, and in meeting the needs of the Nigerian people, the path to understanding among all can only be broadened.

And let the Government of the United States heed the historic role of this Nation and pursue initiatives through the United Nations with determination and compassion. Let us act because it is right to do so—because it is unconscionable to remain silent—and because the hope of all mankind for a better world will be strengthened.

*Statement by Assistant Secretary Palmer on the Magnitude and Complexity of the Nigerian Problems**

September 11, 1968

*   *   *

Where has the United States stood with respect to these events and what is being done about them? For the reasons outlined at the beginning of this statement, we have continued our recognition of the Federal Government and the unity of Nigeria. At the same time we have also sought to use our influence to encourage a peaceful resolution of the problems which have divided the parties. Thus, in the period before secession, we urged both sides to negotiate their differences When negotiations broke down, we

*Department of State Bulletin, Oct. 7, 1968, p. 360.

counseled against secession through our consul in Enugu and Ambassador [Elbert G.] Mathews flew to that city to try to dissuade Colonel Ojukwu [Lt. Col. C.O. Ojukwu of Biafra] from this course. We also used our influence in both Lagos and Enugu to try to forestall a resort to force of arms. We tried to keep our lines of communications open to both sides and, in fact kept open our consulate in Enugu for approximately 5 months after secession, until security conditions necessitated our closing it after the evacuation of the great bulk of American citizens in the region. Although our advice to negotiate was not taken, we persisted in our efforts and following the outbreak of hostilities on July 6, 1967, we continued to urge both sides to return to the negotiating table.

Four days after the outbreak of hostilities, we announced our decision that the United States would not sell or otherwise supply arms and ammunition to either side. We did so out of a desire to avoid any risk of deepening the conflict. Moreover, we hoped that by taking such a self-restraining position, the Soviets would be encouraged to do likewise. Unfortunately these hopes were not realized, and in August the Soviet Union agreed to sell the Nigerian Government military equipment including advanced-type aircraft. On August 21 the United States issued a strongly worded statement deploring this Soviet decision.

Neither the United States nor the Soviet Union had been traditional suppliers of arms to the Nigerian armed forces. The British Government, on the other hand, is the former metropole and has historically trained and equipped the Nigerian forces. This included the sale of arms and ammunition. Many of Nigeria's officers have been trained at Sandhurst. The United Kingdom took the position that to refuse to continue its sale of arms to a Commonwealth member facing armed rebellion would have amounted in fact to a prorebel action. It also felt strongly that such action would have reduced Western influence with the Nigerians and resulted in an increase in that of the Soviets. The British Government has, therefore, continued to supply essentially the same kind of equipment it had traditionally supplied.

From the beginning of the crisis, we have also been in close and frequent touch with African and other nations to try to find ways and means of bringing the hostilities to an end and to promote a negotiated settlement These efforts were not facilitated by the initial strong position of the Federal Government that this was an internal Nigerian conflict which Nigerians themselves must resolve and that discouraged all outside efforts—African and other—to intervene. Nor were our efforts facilitated by the similarly strong position of the Biafran government that its sovereignty was not negotiable and the fact that it spoke at that time from a position of relative military strength.

Nevertheless, we and others persisted, and we were encouraged when in September 1967 the heads of state of the OAU set up a Consultative Committee composed of Ethiopia, Ghana, Congo (K), Niger, the Cameroon, and Liberia with a mandate to try to resolve the conflict within the framework of one Nigeria. This decision by the OAU was accepted by the Federal Government, and the Committee finally met in Lagos in November. At that time, General Ankrah of Ghana was given a mandate to try to bring the two sides together. Unfortunately, he was not successful, and for some time the OAU Committee was inactive, despite a number of efforts to stimulate it to new initiatives.

*   *   *

Statement by President Johnson on Additional Funds for Nigerian Relief*

November 8, 1968

I have today [November 8] authorized a $2.5 million contribution to the International Committee of the Red Cross to aid the victims of the Nigerian civil war. This contribution is in addition to the $10 million in money, food, and equipment we have already given, and the more than $4.3 million given by American voluntary agencies. We hope other governments will also respond generously. Nigeria's need is great and urgent.

The United States Government is doing, and will continue to do, all within its power working with others to help the thousands now starving on both sides of the battlelines. The international relief effort is already reaching over 2 million people on both sides. We will do all we can, in cooperation with the International Committee of the Red Cross and other humanitarian agencies, to maintain and augment the flow of relief supplies.

But so long as this war continues, men, women, and children will continue to starve. So long as the fighting goes on, no relief effort—however bold, however efficient—can meet the great need. The political dispute underlying this war is a Nigerian and an African problem—not an American one. But conscience and humanity impel all nations to call again on both parties to bring this tragic struggle to an end.

Speech by Under Secretary Katzenbach on the Civil War in Nigeria†

December 3, 1968

*   *   *

The tragedy of Nigeria, like so many other human tragedies, is that what seems clearly moral and clearly imperative to most of us is not what seems either clear, moral, or imperative to the people who have it in their power to end the conflict. To us the morality of the Nigerian predicament seems easy enough to define. End the bloodshed, allow food to get through to the starving, let medicine be delivered to the sick and wounded.

Many Americans ask us: "Why can't something be done?" "Why don't we help stop the war?" "Why can't we deliver food to those who need it?" The answers lie not in a lack of willingness not in a lack of food or boats or trucks that we can make available. The answers lie in other people—in how they feel and what they are prepared to do or not do—with whom our influence is most distinctly finite.

The American interest in the Nigerian civil war is primarily and fundamentally humanitarian: We want to relieve suffering and end the killing. We have already taken a number of steps to seek to do this and are prepared to do more.

The real difficulty, of course, is that the humanitarian aspects of the problem are hopelessly tied to its political aspects. We would like to separate them; we would like to convince those responsible that innocent persons should not be made victim to

Ibid., Nov. 25, 1968, pp. 543-44.
†*Ibid.*, Dec. 23, 1968, pp. 653-58.

power plays and political maneuvering, that the lives of women and children should not be sacrificed for the sake of narrow parochial advantage.

But the conflict is too deeply rooted in ancient rivalries and suspicions, too compounded by past mistakes and misunderstandings, too engulfed in mistrust and bitterness, for it now to be so easily divided. Human pride and political maneuvering have so far prevented the concessions necessary for humanitarian aid to get through in a manner and at a rate that would be truly effective.

Some persons, faced with this heartbreaking panorama of slaughter and starvation, would have us take direct action. They would have us slice through the Gordian knot which twists together a thousand political and humanitarian strands in an attempt to separate them. To end our frustration in providing humanitarian relief, they would have us force a political settlement upon the warring parts of the torn Nigerian nation.

I wish that a solution were so simple. The hard fact of the matter is that it is extremely doubtful, at very best, that we could unilaterally impose a solution that would end the bloodshed. And secondly, it would be a most questionable proposition that we should do this. even were it within our power.

Many other nations are far more intimately connected by geography and by historical and cultural ties with Nigeria than we are. Regional organizations, like the OAU [Organization of African Unity], and international organizations, like the United Nations. with far more direct responsibilities are in existence. I have no doubt that this audience is familiar, perhaps too familiar. with the intense debate of the last few years on the size and nature of world commitments undertaken by the United States. You have heard it said that we should not be the world's policeman; and, of course, we are not and have never tried to be.

As the world's strongest and richest power, we have certain international obligations stemming out of treaties and commitments. But no one has appointed us, nor have we sought, nor have we the capacity, to intervene in every world dispute, no matter how grim or tragic it may be.

Certainly in the case of Nigeria it would be self-delusory in the extreme to see ourselves as a kind of *deus ex machina*, a Daddy Warbucks invited in by providence to magically decompose a situation as tenacious as it is appalling and as grim as it is vexatious.

I think it might be best at this point to back up a little and sketch in a bit of history and background so as to put the current crisis in better perspective.

You will recall that the process of decolonization in Africa, much of it having taken place over the last decade, has already brought into existence no less than 41 independent states. The important thing to remember about the new African countries is that their boundaries were drawn by European colonial powers. sometimes arbitrarily, sometimes to reflect the exigencies of a strategy or perhaps a trade route long since forgotten, but in any case more often than not ignoring the requirements and the ethnic and religious composition of the indigenous population.

The colonial legacy left a residue of other problems: Lateral communications among Africans remained undeveloped; institutional mechanisms which would bring diverse groups together remained unformed.

The colonial political structures that had been erected were largely nonparticipatory and authoritarian. The prevailing philosophy was to keep the natives quiet and when necessary to divide and rule. Such democratic institutions as were constructed came very late in the game and were fragile and limited.

The new nations emerged out of this gray and melancholy past with a deep fear of further balkanization and dissolution. With some 2,000 ethnic groups existing on the continent, it was apparent that the concept of self-determination would be quickly reduced to the absurd if units too small to be politically or economically viable were to seek to splinter off. Acutely aware of this danger from the very beginning the Africans themselves have taken very strong positions against territorial changes imposed by force and against secessionary and splinter movements.

That is why so few African nations—only four of the 40 members of the Organization of African Unity—have recognized Biafra or given it any support. When the heads of state of the OAU met in Algiers in September they passed a resolution, by a vote of 33 to 4, appealing for an end to hostilities and for the secessionist state to cooperate with the Federal authorities in restoring peace and unity. The resolution also called on all U.N. members to refrain from taking any action detrimental to the peace, unity, and territorial integrity of Nigeria.

The United States has supported the resolution and avoided any action contravening its objectives. For we believe that the work of the OAU is expressive of the strong African desire, stemming out of some of the same reasons I have already indicated, to solve African problems within African institutions and organizations.

*   *   *

From the moment the crisis began, the United States has been active in trying to help the two sides reach a settlement. But for reasons I have already suggested, our influence in the situation is quite definitely limited. So if a solution is to be found, it is of necessity going to have to be one that is preeminently Nigerian and African.

This, however, does not mean we have been idle or indifferent to the folly and the bloodshed. A few days following the outbreak of the fighting we announced that we would not sell or in any other way provide arms or ammunition to either side. We hoped that others, particularly the Soviet Union, would follow this example.

The Soviets, though they were not previously a military supplier to Nigeria, have, however, chosen to capitalize on this bitter conflict and have sold military equipment, including modern aircraft to the Federal Military Government. The latter, in its hard-pressed situation, has understandably not been especially choosy about where it procured its supplies.

The British, who have traditionally trained and supplied Nigeria, have continued to do so. I do not really see how they could have made any other choice. Their position is clearly different from others who have been interlopers or Johnnies-come-lately in the Nigerian arms picture. If they had stopped their sales they would, in fact, be helping to support the dismemberment of a fellow Commonwealth country with which they have had a special relationship since its independence.

Unfortunately, however, other nations have covertly provided arms to Biafra, a fact which, perhaps more than any other, has prolonged the fighting.

The United States has also been in close touch with concerned African nations. President Johnson has communicated with the Emperor of Ethiopia and other African leaders who have been active in this matter. We have also been in close contact with the OAU, with the Commonwealth Secretariat in London, and with U.N. officials.

We have also pondered the wisdom of bringing the matter before the United

Nations. Although we have thoroughly explored this course in many diplomatic channels it has until now proved unfeasible. The African countries themselves oppose taking the matter before the U.N., and without their backing it would be impossible to muster sufficient support. For the United Nations to take up an issue of this gravity and then fail would, aside from leading to a loss of prestige for the organization, only aggravate the situation in Africa itself.

As for humanitarian aid, the United States Government has already contributed over $17 million in money, food, and equipment to aid the starving. American private voluntary agencies have provided over $4 million more. Two-thirds of the world total of relief funds has come from the United States a proportion which, while demonstrating our concern, certainly ought to give other affluent nations pause.

The International Committee of the Red Cross, UNICEF [United Nations Children's Fund], and other private agencies have worked very hard under the most difficult circumstances in trying to get food through. The main impediments to relief efforts, however, have not been the lack of money, resources, or equipment. The main impediments have been political hurdles erected by both sides.

The position taken by the Federal Government that the war was one for national preservation and accordingly an internal matter of no concern to outsiders did not make the task of international agencies any easier. Moreover, the Federal Government initially feared that relief efforts would interfere with military operations.

Subsequently, as the suffering grew and international concern mounted, the Federal Government modified its position and authorized relief flights. It has shown itself willing to make certain political concessions that would protect Ibo rights within the framework of a reunited Nigeria. Biafra, on the other hand, has shown no interest in any peace which does not recognize its sovereignty. The latter, it says, is not negotiable.

The Biafrans fear another massacre, one on an even bigger scale. Their fear, while understandable in view of recent history, is, we believe, unfounded in the present context. Outside observers, including representatives of the U.N. and the OAU, were invited by the Federal Government to look into the conduct of the war, including the treatment of civilians. They found no evidence to support the charge of genocide.

There are some who believe that the Biafrans' objective is to continue the struggle long enough to hang this frightful charge around the neck of their enemy in world councils. Under this strategy (composed, perhaps, in equal parts of calculation and desperation) the imminence of death, starvation, and atrocity would generate sufficient sympathy and support about the world to ultimately bear salvation and sovereignty as its fruit.

As is so often the case in civil wars where passions run strong and deep, neither side can be said to have a monopoly on cynicism or stubbornness, however. Both, it has seemed at times, have been willing to subordinate the lives of innocents to the political struggle. Both, it has seemed, have been willing to frustrate relief efforts to make a political point or gain a tactical advantage. Each side has resisted the relief corridors proposed by the other, despite the safeguards offered by the ICRC and the OAU. The Biafrans, for example, have opposed the land corridors favored by the Federal Government, despite the generally held belief that adequate quantities of relief can only get through on land. The Biafrans, however, claim that such corridors favor their enemy or that the food destined to travel down them would be poisoned.

The Federal Government, for its part. long opposed the air corridors demanded by the Biafrans, although acquiescing in night relief flights. It argued that air corridors could be infiltrated by day, as they already are by night, by clandestine arms shipments. More recently, however, the Federal Government has announced its willingness to permit daytime relief flights into Uli, the remaining major airfield in Biafra, on the condition that the field be used for no other flights during those hours. Although this offer would make possible a significant increase in the flow of relief supplies into Biafra, the Biafrans apparently have not accepted it so far.

Thus, the suspicions and intransigence of both sides have brought us to the present situation, one that is more wretched and desperate than ever. Even in normal times the Eastern Region of Nigeria has had to import food during the winter and spring months. Because of the war, a severe shortage of protein-rich foods necessary to sustain life continues. A shortage of carbohydrate foods, now developing, may well reach massive proportions after the end of the year.

In these grim and violently abnormal times our best information indicates that millions of people on both sides of the fighting will require much or even all of their food from outside sources if they are to survive. This means that several thousand tons of food will have to be delivered each week in Biafra. Presently, only about five or six hundred tons are getting through.

The calculations that follow, then, are bare, stark, and uncomplicated. They add up to this: Millions, literally millions, of people face starvation in the next several months unless the war is ended very quickly.

We shall help to intensify in every way feasible the existing relief flights, but even this will not suffice to reach all those in need so long as the fighting continues.

The grisly equation served up to us brings me back to my original message: The political and humanitarian aspects of the situation are interlocked and inseparable. The ultimate decision of what will happen—the decision of life or death for millions—rests with the leaders on both sides. Without their cooperation or consent, outside aid cannot be effective. But one thing is clear: If both parties remain recalcitrant, if both parties continue to put political advantage ahead of people's lives, then one of the most terrible famines in modern times is certain and inevitable.

And so there you have it: a situation that is grisly, a situation where all our better instincts compel us to react and to react quickly, but a situation, also, in which the courses of action open to us are sharply delimited. They are delimited by other peoples whose passions and priorities are much different than ours.

You have here a tragedy which looms. a tragedy which you would think would concern everyone, a tragedy potentially so grave that half the world should clamor to bring relief.

But we are far too lonely in our belief that no political consideration imaginable can be of greater importance than the avoidance of so great and horrible a tragedy. If we are right in our view, then somehow we must bring others to the same realization.

We are not, by ourselves, able to impose a solution, but a solution must be found. And like most foreign policy problems, the solution will come, I expect, not out of grand gestures but out of the quiet, unglamorous, and, I think, often underappreciated work of diplomacy.

I believe that any solution must come within a framework that both preserves Nigerian sovereignty and unity and guarantees the future safety and development of the Ibo people.

In previous negotiations, the Federal Government has offered specific proposals to meet Ibo fears. They were designed to guarantee both their protection and their full participation in the life of the nation. But the Biafrans' fears are genuine and deep seated, and the proposals have not yet proved acceptable to them. The effort to overcome those fears must continue, and the guarantees made by the Federal Government must not only be manifestly just but credible and workable.

No one pretends that such agreements will be easy to produce. But they must come, and they must come quickly. Too much time has already been lost in bickering. Too many lives are being lost. Too many other lives are at stake. No one wins by obstinacy when millions die in the process.

It is about just such arid feuding and stubborn folly that the Prince of Verona spoke when he rendered his bitter judgment on the death of Romeo and Juliet: "All are punish'd."

"All are punish'd," but the most badly punished of all are those innocent persons with the least to say about their punishment.

State Department Announcement on the Availability of United States Planes in Nigerian Relief Efforts*

December 27, 1968

Despite a steady increase in international relief shipments to both sides of the battlelines in Nigeria, the prospects are for deepening tragedy as a shortage of carbohydrates develops in the Biafran-held area. As we have emphasized on past occasions, the situation requires the utilization of every possible channel of relief, including most importantly a surface corridor, which we continue to hope can be arranged.

In the meantime, we continue to seek means of strengthening the airlift of relief supplies. We are therefore making available for the international relief airlift eight C-97G "stratofreighter" cargo aircraft which are no longer required by the U.S. Air Force. Four will be provided to the American voluntary agencies and four have been offered to the International Committee of the Red Cross. We are discussing with the officials of these organizations the details of transferring ownership of these aircraft as soon as possible.

No U.S. military personnel will be involved in the operation of these aircraft. The planes are provided with the clear understanding that they are to be used solely for humanitarian purposes in transporting urgently needed food and medical supplies for noncombatants. We are prepared, therefore, to cooperate in establishing inspection procedures toward this end.

These aircraft can substantially increase the tonnage delivered. It remains true, however, that the aircraft now operating in the relief effort, not to mention this additional capacity, cannot be fully utilized into the present airstrip in Biafra unless daylight flights are permitted. The Federal Military Government has approved such flights on humanitarian grounds. We continue to regret the failure of the Biafran authorities to sanction daylight flights into the existing airstrip.

*Ibid., Jan. 13, 1969, pp. 30-31.

*Statement by the American Embassy in Lagos**

December 31, 1968

The December 27 decision by the United States Government to make available C-97G "stratofreighter" cargo aircraft to the international relief airlift to assist victims of the Nigerian civil war was motivated solely by pressing humanitarian concern. Furnishing these transport planes is simply an extension of the continuing American effort to help relieve suffering.

In no way does this relief action reflect, either directly or indirectly, U.S. Government political support of the rebellion. Nor does it portend such support. The United States continues to recognize only the Federal Military Government. It continues to believe that only a negotiated settlement, in the context of a single Nigeria, with realistic guarantees for the safety and protection of all Nigerians, will bring an end to the tragedy which has befallen Nigeria.

The aircraft are cargo carriers of a type which have been used widely by commercial airlines and have become available to relief agencies because they are no longer required by the U.S. Government. They will be sold, not loaned. No U.S. military personnel will be involved in their operation.

The United States Government informed the American voluntary agencies and has stated publicly that the aircraft are made available with the clear understanding that.

a. Their use will be in accord with the strictly humanitarian purposes and operations of the total ICRC relief effort;

b. They are to be used solely for the relief of noncombatants in transporting urgently needed food and other nonmilitary supplies;

c. Workable procedures will be instituted for inspection of cargoes.

Representatives of Joint Church Aid, USA, comprised of Catholic Relief Services, Church World Service, and the American Jewish Committee, have assured the United States Government that they agree with these points and that they will cooperate in their implementation.

The United States Government wishes particularly to emphasize that its humanitarian concern applies equally to both sides of the battlelines. It has, in fact, been assisting massively on the Federal side through the ICRC with large quantities of relief supplies to needy civilians in Mid-Western, South-Eastern, and Rivers States, as well as Federally controlled areas of East-Central State. The U.S. Government has agreed to provide financial support to the relief and rehabilitation programs of the Nigerian Red Cross and the Federal Rehabilitation Commission.

Speech by Representative Donald Fraser (Minnesota) Before the House on Nigerian-Biafran Relief†

January 23, 1969

Mr. Speaker, today I have joined with 103 other Members in introducing House Concurrent Resolution 97, a bill aimed at helping to alleviate the starvation and suffering brought about by the Nigerian-Biafran war.

*Ibid.
†*Congressional Record*, Jan. 23, 1969, pp. H424-25.

The large number of cosponsors is a clear indication, I think, that there is strong support in Congress for expanding American relief efforts to this beleaguered area of Africa. The support is bipartisan; joining me in obtaining cosponsors has been the distinguished gentleman from Massachusetts (Mr. Morse). Similar bipartisan sponsorship is being obtained for a Senate resolution.

In brief the resolution makes two proposals: First, for the administration to increase significantly the amount of food, money, and nonmilitary transportation vehicles needed for relief; and second, to seek international cooperation in the humanitarian effort.

The words "humanitarian effort" are especially significant, Mr. Speaker, because this resolution has been drafted only for the purpose of fulfilling our humanitarian obligations while avoiding military and political involvement. The conflict is complex and dangerous. Several other major powers already are supporting one side or the other militarily. The United States has, wisely in my opinion, avoided military assistance to either side, and should continue to follow this policy.

However a clear distinction must be made between the political and military aspects of the situation, on one hand, and the humanitarian aspects, on the other. As the gentleman from Massachusetts (Mr. Morse) and I pointed out in our letter to Members of the House, the United States has provided more than $22 million and eight aircraft to the relief agencies so far. With only 200 tons a day reaching a people whose minimum relief needs are estimated at 2,000 tons a day, it is obvious that much more must be done. The relief we are proposing would be furnished to the relief agencies operating in the area with the consent of Nigerian and Biafran authorities.

Apart from the rightness or wrongness of either side in the conflict, Mr. Speaker, our Nation should be doing all that it can to prevent the already appalling starvation in Nigeria-Biafra from becoming one of the major disasters of our time. Millions of lives are at stake.

The text of Concurrent Resolution 97 follows:

Whereas reliable reports indicate that there is a tragic loss of life in the Nigerian Civil War caused by starvation and disease in areas controlled by the Federal Government and under the control of the "Biafran" authorities

Whereas present relief operations are inhibited by poor roads. bad weather. inadequate transport, and the inaccessibility of certain areas to overland supplies; and

Whereas increased shipments of food and medical supplies are needed to reduce the tragic rate of starvation; Now, therefore. be it

Resolved by the House of Representatives (the Senate concurring). That it is the sense of the Congress (1) that the President should act to increase significantly the amount of surplus food stocks relief monies, noncombat aircraft, and such other vehicles of transportation as may be necessary for relief purposes; and this relief assistance should be made avilable to and at the request of the Organization of African Unity, UNICEF, the International Committee of the Red Cross. and such other suitable religious and charitable relief agencies now or hereafter operating in the area with the consent of the responsible authorities; and (2) the Government of the United States should solicit the cooperation of other nations in this humanitarian effort.

Following are the cosponsors:

Brock Adams, of Washington.
Joseph P. Addabbo, of New York.
John B. Anderson, of Illinois.
Leslie C. Arends, of Illinois.

Thomas L. Ashley, of Ohio.
Edward G. Biester, Jr., of Pennsylvania.
Jonathan M. Bingham, of New York.
John A. Blatnik, of Minnesota.

Edward P. Boland, of Massachusetts.
Richard Bolling, of Missouri.
John Brademas, of Indiana.
William S. Broomfield, of Michigan.
George E. Brown, Jr., of California.
John Buchanan, of Alabama.
Phillip Burton, of California.
Daniel E. Button, of New York.
Shirley Chisholm, of New York.
Barber B. Conable, Jr., of New York.
Silvio O. Conte, of Massachusetts.
John Conyers, Jr., of Michigan.
James C. Corman, of California.
John C. Culver, of Iowa.
Dominick V. Daniels, of New Jersey.
Harold D. Donohue, of Massachusetts.
John J. Duncan, of Tennessee.
Don Edwards, of California.
Marvin L. Esch, of Michigan.
Dante B. Fascell, of Florida.
Hamilton Fish, Jr., of New York.
Thomas S. Foley, of Washington.
Donald M. Fraser, of Minnesota.
Peter Frelinghuysen, Jr., of New Jersey.
Richard Fulton, of Tennessee.
Robert N. Giaimo, of Connecticut.
Jacob H. Gilbert, of New York.
William J. Green, of Pennsylvania.
Gilbert Gude, of Maryland.
Seymour Halpern, of New York.
Lee H. Hamilton, of Indiana.
James M. Hanley, of New York.
Julia Butler Hansen, of Washington.
William D. Hathaway, of Maine.
Ken Hechler, of West Virginia.
Margaret M. Heckler, of Massachusetts.
Floyd V. Hicks, of Washington.
Lawrence J. Hogan, of Maryland.
Frank J. Horton, of New York.
Andrew Jacobs, Jr., of Indiana.
Harold T. Johnson, of California.
Joseph E. Karth, of Minnesota.
Robert W. Kastenmeier, of Wisconsin.
Hastings Keith, of Massachusetts.
Edward I. Koch, of New York.
Donald E. Lukens, of Ohio.
Paul N. McCloskey, Jr., of California.

Joseph M. McDade, of Pennsylvania.
Martin B. McKneally, of New York.
Catherine May, of Washington.
Thomas J. Meskill, of Connecticut.
Abner J. Mikva, of Illinois.
Joseph G. Minish, of New Jersey.
Patsy T. Mink, of Hawaii.
Chester L. Mize, of Kansas.
William S. Moorhead, of Pennsylvania.
Bradford Morse, of Massachusetts.
Charles A. Mosher, of Ohio.
William T. Murphy, of Illinois.
Lucien N. Nedzi, of Michigan.
James G. O'Hara, of Michigan.
Thomas P. O'Neill, Jr., of Massachusetts.
Richard L. Ottinger, of New York.
Claude Pepper, of Florida.
Bertram L. Podell, of New York.
Tom Railsback, of Illinois.
Thomas M. Rees, of California.
Ogden R. Reid, of New York.
Henry S. Reuss, of Wisconsin.
Howard W. Robison, of New York.
Peter W. Rodino, Jr., of New Jersey.
Fred B. Rooney, of Pennsylvania.
Benjamin S. Rosenthal, of New York.
Philip E. Ruppe, of Michigan.
William F. Ryan, of New York.
Fernand St Germain, of Rhode Island.
Herman T. Schneebeli, of Pennsylvania.
Fred Schwengel, of Iowa.
Robert T. Stafford, of Vermont.
William J. Stanton, of Ohio.
Louis Stokes, of Ohio.
Robert Taft, Jr., of Ohio.
Charles M. Teague, of California.
Frank Thompson, Jr., of New Jersey.
Robert O. Tiernan, of Rhode Island.
John V. Tunney, of California.
Morris K. Udall, of Arizona.
Charles A. Vanik, of Ohio.
Jerome R. Waldie, of California.
Morris K. Udall, of Arizona.
Charles A. Vanik, of Ohio.
Jerome R. Waldie, of California.
Lowell P. Weicker, Jr., of Connecticut.
G. William Whitehurst, Jr., of Virginia.

Lawrence G. Williams, of Pennsylvania.   John W. Wydler, of New York.
Charles H. Wilson, of California.   Sidney R. Yates, of Illinois.
Lester L. Wolff, of New York.

Speech by Representative Lee H. Hamilton (Indiana) on the Concurrent
Resolution on Nigerian-Biafra Relief*

January 29, 1969

Mr. Speaker, as one of 87 cosponsors of the concurrent resolution expressing the sense of the Congress that the President should act to increase significantly the amount of surplus food stocks and relief moneys for the assistance of civilians affected by the Nigerian-Biafran conflict, I wish to support passage of the proposed resolution through the following remarks.

*   *   *

Because humanitarian, political, and military factors are interwoven, it has been the policy of the U.S. Government to avoid political-military involvement by channeling support for the international relief effort through the nonpolitical ICRC and those agencies, including UNICEF, operating under its aegis. Both the Federal Government of Nigeria and the Organization for African Unity—OAU—have taken the position that all international relief efforts should be coordinated through the ICRC.

The feasibility and probable effectiveness of a possible referral of the problem to the U.N. General Assembly has been strongly influenced by the views of the Secretary General and the African states that the matter should continue to be dealt with by the OAU under chapter VIII of the U.N. Charter. If the Assembly were prepared to take up the matter, it has been U.S. policy that the United States would cooperate fully in seeking U.N. action.

No political consideration is of greater importance than the prevention of wholesale famine in Nigeria. Former President Johnson consistently backed efforts by the OAU and the ICRC to bring about agreement on the opening of land and air relief corridors to the needy in Biafra. He has appealed to the needy in Biafra. He has appealed to the parties to set aside the political issues of the war in the interest of reaching agreement on relief. The former President publicly backed the December 21 appeal to both sides by the Emperor of Ethiopia for a 7-day truce.

On September 10, 1968, President Nixon stated:

> Until now efforts to relieve the Biafran people have been thwarted by the desire of the Central Government of Nigeria to pursue total and unconditional victory and by the fear of the Ibo people that surrender means wholesale atrocities and genocide. But genocide is what is taking place right now—And starvation is the grim reaper. This is not the time to stand on ceremony and to go through channels or to observe the diplomatic niceties. . . . The destruction of an entire people is an immoral objective, even in the most moral of wars. It can never be justified. It can never be condoned. . . . The time is long past for the wringing of hands about what is going on. While America is not the world's policeman, let us at least act as the world's conscience in this matter of life and death for millions.

Ibid., Jan. 29, 1969, pp. E596-97.

With only 200 tons of food a day reaching a people whose minimum relief needs are estimated at 2,000 tons a day, it is obvious that much needs to be done. I believe that the United States must find a way to bring relief to those in need without directly involving our country in the war itself.

Thus, as a cosponsor of this concurrent resolution, I call upon the President to significantly increase U.S. relief assistance to Nigeria-Biafra.

By passing the proposed concurrent resolution, the Congress will give public support to increased Presidential efforts to meet the human needs of those caught in the Nigeria-Biafra conflict.

*Speech by Senator Thomas Dodd (Connecticut) Before the Senate on the Need for an Immediate Ceasefire in Biafra**

January 31, 1969

Mr. President, I submit, for appropriate reference, a concurrent resolution which states that it is the sense of the Congress of the United States that our Government should do everything in its power for the purpose of bringing about an immediate cease-fire between the Nigerian and Biafran forces; and that it should thereafter lend its good offices and use its diplomatic resources on the African continent to promote the conclusion of a just and durable settlement of the Biafran conflict.

In submitting this resolution, I am honored to be joined as cosponsors by Senators Bennett, Byrd of West Virginia, Fong, Gravel, Hart, Hartke, Inouye, Magnuson, Miller, Moss, Murphy, Nelson, Pastore, Ribicoff, Stevens, and Williams of New Jersey.

Mr. President, the deep concern which Congress feels over the appalling loss of life in the Nigerian-Biafran conflict is evident from the many statements that have been made on the floor of the House and on the floor of the Senate. It is also evident from the fact that some 60 Members of the Senate have cosponsored a resolution calling upon the U.S. Government to take the lead in stepping up the scale of relief operations in Nigeria-Biafra.

This resolution represents a first step. But in my opinion, in order to give this resolution meaning and plausibility, a second resolution is necessary calling upon the Government of the United States to use its good offices and diplomatic resources in the interests of an immediate cease-fire.

*   *   *

The settlement of the Biafran conflict will have to be an African settlement, and the prime initiative will have to come from the African states themselves.

Our own diplomacy will have to be used with restraint and delicacy.

But I am certain that it can be used, and that an increasing number of African countries would welcome an American commitment to a cease-fire because events have compelled them to recognize the validity of the statement made almost a year ago by Felix Houphouet-Boigny, the esteemed president of the Ivory Coast. This is what he said:

Ibid., Jan. 31, 1969, pp. S1120-21.

I want . . to cry out my indignation in the face of the inexplicable indifference – culpable indifference – of the whole world with respect to the massacres of which Biafra has been the theatre for more than ten months. I rejoin my country, pained, indignant deeply upset and revolted by the prolongation of this atrocious war which rages in Biafra and which has already cost more than 200,000 human lives, not to count the immeasurable cost in destruction of all kinds, in a country definitely rich but still underdeveloped.

Unity will be the fruit of the common will to live together It should not be imposed by force by one group upon another.

Insofar as we Africans form a part of the world, we could not but be astonished at how little we are valued; at the indifference with which people treat everything that concerns us.

We must realize this ineluctable fact: even if as a result of this military superiority in men and materials, Nigeria succeeds in occupying the whole of Biafra, the problem of the secession will not be involved. There will, therefore, be no real peace in Nigeria as long as Biafra fights for its independence.

Mr. President, I ask unanimous consent that the full text of my concurrent resolution be printed in the Record at this point.

The Vice President: The concurrent resolution will be received and appropriately referred; and, without objection, the resolution will be printed in the Record.

The concurrent resolution (S. Con. Res. 8) was referred to the Committee on Foreign Relations as follows:

S. Con. Res. 8

Whereas the war that has been going on for 18 months now between the government of Nigeria and the breakaway state of Biafra has resulted in a tragic loss of life, including the death by starvation of many hundreds of thousands of women and children; and

Whereas the American people have been deeply moved by this tragedy, in a manner that cuts across all political, racial and religious lines, while Congress has manifested its concern through numerous individual statements in the House and Senate, and most recently through a Senate resolution calling for a greatly enhanced international relief operation to cope with the famine conditions now prevailing in Biafra and certain parts of Nigeria; and

Whereas, despite emergency relief shipments, more than 10,000 people are still dying every day from the mass famine which afflicts Biafra; and

Whereas, according to relief experts working in the area, the coming months are bound to witness a grave intensification of the famine because most of the seed for next year's crop has already been eaten, so that the protein starvation from which the Biafrans are now suffering will soon be compounded by carbohydrate starvation; and

Whereas the famine in Biafra has now grown to such dimensions that without a cease-fire it will be impossible to mount an adequate relief operation; and

Whereas, in addition to resulting in the mass starvation of the civilian population of Biafra, the war is impoverishing and exhausting Nigeria and imperiling its future security because of the machinations of the growing corps of Soviet technicians and advisors; and

Whereas the continuation of this tragic conflict does not serve the interests of the people of Nigeria or the people of Biafra or the peoples of Africa; and

Whereas it is clear from all that has happened that the Biafran people are prepared to fight to the last man rather than submit, and that there can therefore be no military solution to the Nigerian-Biafran conflict: Now, therefore, be it

Resolved by the Senate (the House of Representatives concurring), That it is the sense of the Congress that the United States Government, in the interest of putting an end to the killing and starvation, should lend its good offices and utilize all of its diplomatic resources for the purpose of bringing about an immediate cease-fire between the Nigerian and Biafran forces and to thereafter promote the conclusion of a just and durable settlement of the Biafran conflict; and

Be it further resolved, That it is the hope of the Congress that, whatever the political terms of such a settlement, the settlement will at least provide for some form of continuing economic integration because of the manifest advantages of the economic unity to the peoples on both sides of this conflict.

Remarks by Representative Allard K. Lowenstein (New York)
Before the House on Nigeria and Biafra*

February 19, 1969

Mr. Speaker, I have just concluded my second journey within 6 weeks to Nigeria and Biafra.

Until now, I have refrained from public discussions of these trips and of my impressions of the situation there, in the hope that I might thus be able to be more helpful in the effort to increase the flow of food and drugs into the afflicted areas. The effort to increase the flow of relief must remain a primary concern of men of good will, and since that problem—the problem of finding new ways of getting relief in—is still at a critical point, I will limit comments today to these general observations:

First. The charge that the Federal Military Government of Nigeria is engaged in a campaign of willful genocide cannot be sustained. The fear of genocide among many Biafrans, however, is very deep, and is reinforced by continued bombings which inflict heavy civilians casualties on what can only be described as a random basis not visibly connected to military considerations. The effect of these bombings, in addition to feeding fears of genocide in Biafra, has been to stiffen the general will to resist. This is not, perhaps, a suprising reaction in view of similar experiences elsewhere.

Second. Suffering in Biafra and in the war-torn areas of Nigeria is acute. On the Nigerian side of the front lines, relief operations have been relatively effective in easing the problem of starvation. The authorities in Lagos have generously cooperated with relief workers who have sought to make food and medical supplies available to those in need regardless of tribal origin or political viewpoint. On the Biafran side, the acute protein famine of last summer, which caused somewhat more than a half million deaths, has been eased, but the overall food situation continues to deteriorate. Carbohydrate deficiencies will reach catastrophic proportions in the near future as the last of the seed yams and casavas are consumed, and there is in fact no prospect that internal food production in Biafra will be able to meet more than a third of the need of the population now residing in Biafra. That population can reasonably be estimated at over 7 million people.

Third. Whatever the ultimate political or military resolution of the conflict, to await such a resolution as the best way to cope with the relief problem is to invite into

*Ibid., Feb. 19, 1969, pp. 1202-04.

existence an enormous graveyard which must haunt the conscience of the world and dominate the future of the area.

The battle lines have in fact, been largely stabilized for several months, and there is now no prospect of a military decision without great new military exertions. The outcome of these exertions, should they now be forthcoming, will clearly be a major determinant of how the differences between Nigeria and Biafra are ultimately resolved, but unless massive quantities of relief get into the afflicted area in the meantime, this ultimate solution may well be the final one for a great many people, who may by then be dead from starvation. So I think it would be most irresponsible to suggest that there is no need to press for emergency relief efforts pending military developments.

Fourth. On the other hand, the unhappy legacies and memories of colonialism make interventions by Western or white governments or groups, however nobly intentioned, precarious, at best, and potentially quite harmful if these interventions should appear to be in pursuit of particular political or military results.

Ultimately, the matters at issue will have to be worked out by the people of the area involved.

Fifth. Nigeria and Biafra are now much too far apart to hope that acceptable conditions can be found for an early truce or cease-fire, let alone for negotiations that might avert further efforts to achieve a military resolution to the conflict.

We may all continue to hope for developments that will make steps toward peace possible at the earliest possible date. But the fact is that the best hope at this time for decreasing suffering and avoiding greater tragedies lies in the effort to find ways to bring in relief which are not dependent on truce, cease-fire, or successful negotiations for an end to the conflict.

Sixth. In this connection, the outpouring of compassion and concern among people around the world is gratifying and helpful. It would be an appalling indictment of the human race were there not such concern. The great response of children and students to the suffering of faraway contemporaries is especially heartwarming.

In fact, this outpouring of compassion and concern can provide the most hopeful antidote to expanding tragedy, if it leads to intelligent, informed, concerted action by men of good will here and elsewhere. But this action should now be concentrated on the proper—and urgent—effort to implement programs that will ease the suffering of the civilian victims of the war, not futile efforts to impose political solutions on Nigerians or Biafrans.

The notion that it is somehow racist for white people to be concerned about starvation in Biafra puts the situation precisely backward; it would be the absence of such concern that in fact would be racist. To say that because the people starving are black it is no one's business except other people who are black, would be a most pernicious kind of racism.

Seventh. From their public statements—and private assurances—the Governments of Nigeria and Biafra must be assumed to be dedicated to finding ways to permit and expedite massive infusions of relief in the immediate future. I can see no value in doubting the good faith of either side on this critical question at this critical moment.

The world will be waiting to see which side, if either fails, by delay, pretext, or evasion to live up to these assurances. We can meanwhile express our gratitude to the Government of the Republic of Dahomey for allowing relief flights to operate from its territory. If the Dahomey Government had not responded with such compassion and wisdom, the slack caused by the sad decision of the Government of Equatorial Guinea to cancel rather precipitately such flights from its territory would have had tragic consequences for countless additional people.

Eighth. The attitude of the new administration on these questions has been most encouraging. The Government of the United States can do much to ease suffering. Our resources and skills should be more deeply committed. Our good offices should be available.

The magnificent efforts of Caritas, Nordchurch Aid, and the International Committee of the Red Cross have shown that private citizens and voluntary organizations are capable of heroic efforts to meet great needs.

But the need is clearly too great to be met by private citizens and voluntary organizations alone. The policies and energies of the great international organizations—the U.N., the Commonwealth, the OAU, OCAM—as well as those of the Governments of the United States, the United Kingdom, and other concerned countries, should now be coordinated to bring about the immediate acceptance and implementation of a massive emergency relief program.

We are at the point where the next fortnight will tell whether the appalling specter of enormous additional numbers of people needlessly dead from and crippled by hunger and disease is to hang over the rest of this century.

The intricacies of finding a way to get food in to the afflicted areas can be resolved if the forces of good will in and out of Nigeria and Biafra join in the determination to resolve them. I cannot believe that this will not be done in view of what is at stake.

*Speech by Senator James B. Pearson (Kansas) Before the Senate on a Nigeria-Biafra Relief Coordinator**

February 25, 1969

Mr. President, on January 22, I introduced a resolution (S. Con. Res. 3) calling upon President Nixon to de more to help the starvation victims of the Nigeria-Biafra civil war. In this effort I was joined by the able junior Senator from Massachusetts (Mr. Brooke) and 59 of our colleagues. In the other body, approximately 106 Members have added their endorsement. Such a degree of support for expanded relief efforts is encouraging, but as yet it has not been translated into meaningful action on the scale required.

One positive first step toward the implementation of this program has been taken, however, and deserves our support. I refer, of course, to the action of President Nixon this past weekend in appointing a special coordinator for relief to Nigeria-Biafra. Such an office could be quite useful if the level of our support for the international relief agencies is indeed to be expanded. And I hope, as I am sure do the other sponsors of the relief resolution, that such an expansion is in the offing.

The role will be an exceedingly delicate one, however, for the risks of incautious action are great. If Prof. Clarence Clyde Ferguson, Jr., the new aid coordinator, becomes enmeshed in political conversations, as a representative of the President, he cannot help but involve our Government as well. I have no objection to the United States offering its good offices to mediate differences. But I would object to linking

*Ibid., Feb. 25, 1969, pp. S1946-47.

our relief program to any such political initiatives. For should they fail, our relief efforts would probably fail also and with them the hopes of thousands of starvation victims would be dashed. And let us never forget that it is the saving of these lives that is our sole object of concern. The political issues at stake in the conflict are for the parties themselves to resolve. We must do more, of course, but we must be careful to do it in such a way as to maximize the effectiveness of the international relief programs already underway. To do otherwise, regardless of the motive, is to risk losing everything we are trying so hard to save.

In this regard, let me say that I fully realize the need for accurate, timely information about the character of the relief programs now being mounted by the voluntary agencies. Without such data, it is extremely difficult to determine the scope and method of any projected expansion of U.S. humanitarian aid. I also realize the close relationship between the problems of organizing a massive relief operation and the beneficient effect a cease-fire or any other halt to hostilities could have on such problems. These and other considerations make it extremely attractive to contemplate sending Dr. Ferguson into the war zone as soon as possible. This inclination is also no doubt reinforced by his reputation as a competent administrator and negotiator.

But to thrust Dr. Ferguson into the considerable physical and diplomatic hazards of operations in the war zone, particularly in the Biafran-held territory, is a step which must be carefully evaluated before it is taken. I do not suggest that this move is in preparation by the administration, but it is a logical one to consider and I only hope every effort is made to insure the acceptance of any such maneuver by both disputants before it is undertaken. For after all, under the current policy, we recognize only Nigeria, and given the history of friendly relations which we have had with that Government, an official U.S. presence in secessionist territory is a matter of great delicacy, to say the least.

Thus, while Dr. Ferguson's appointment is extremely encouraging to all of us who have been urging more U.S. support for relief programs, a cautionary note is indeed in order lest we find ourselves enmeshed in the political questions of this unfortunate conflict, and lest we assume direction of relief efforts which I for one wish to see remain international in scope and operation.

I commend the President for this first step and take encouragement from his statement that—

> U.S. policy will draw a sharp distinction between carrying out our moral obligation to respond effectively to humanitarian needs and involving ourselves in the political affairs of others.

*Speech by Senator Charles Goodell (New York) Before the Senate on the Biafra Study Mission**

February 25, 1969

*   *   *

Unless something dramatic is changed almost immediately, a minimum of 1 million and probably 2 to 2.5 million Biafrans will die in the next 12 months. The study

*Ibid., Feb. 25, 1969, p. S1976.

mission which I took to Biafra has made specific and technical recommendations in their fields of professional expertise. I make further recommendations in the political arena. There can be no acceptable solution to this massive human tragedy without a political solution.

First, there must be an immediate cease-fire, or if a cease-fire is impossible, a temporary truce for a limited period.

Second, there must be an immediate end to all arms shipments into Nigeria and Biafra. This means, among others, that the British and Russians must stop shipping arms to Nigeria and the French must stop shipping arms to Biafra. In the absence of such action, there is grave danger that Nigeria and Biafra will become suffering pawns in a calamitous great power confrontation.

Third, the United Nations should face its urgent responsibilities in this humanitarian crisis. If the United Nations cannot meet this kind of humanitarian crisis with effective compassion, it is even more debilitated than its worst critics contend.

Fourth, I am assured that the U.S. Government will make available to relief agencies on a feasible and emergency basis such cargo planes, ships, maintenance personnel, and parts as are found to be necessary to perform the humanitarian mission of getting food and medical supplies to the starving people in Biafra and in Nigeria.

Fifth, in any event, the United States unilaterally should make available more than obsolete C-97 cargo planes that are plagued with shortages of replacement parts and with numerous maintenance problems.

Sixth, the United States, the United Nations. the Organization of African Unity and all great powers should offer their good offices to bring about direct negotiations between the leadership of Nigeria and the leadership of Biafra.

*   *

*Statement by President Richard M. Nixon on the Nigerian-Biafran Relief Coordinator**

February 2, 1969

I know that I speak for all Americans in expressing this nation's deep anguish for the terrible human suffering in the Nigerian civil war. It is tragic enough to watch a military conflict between peoples who once lived together in peace and developing prosperity. But that tragedy has been compounded, and the conscience of the world engaged, by the starvation threatening millions of innocent civilians on both sides of the battle.

Immediately after taking office, I directed an urgent and comprehensive review of the relief situation. The purpose was to examine every possibility to enlarge and expedite the flow of relief. This very complex problem will require continuing study. I am announcing, however, the following initial conclusions of the review:

1. The Red Cross and the voluntary agencies are now feeding nearly 1 million people in areas of the war zone controlled by the Federal Military Government of Nigeria. They fully expect the numbers will grow in magnitude over the coming months. This, therefore, will require additional support for the international relief effort from donor countries and, of course, the continued cooperation of Federal authorities.

Department of State Bulletin, Mar. 17, 1969, pp. 222-23.

2. There is widely conflicting information on future food requirements within the Biafran-controlled area, where the relief operation is feeding an estimated 2 million persons. The United States Government therefore is urgently seeking a comprehensive internationally conducted survey of food needs in that area.

3. Whatever the results of such a survey, it is already clear that the present relief effort is inadequate to the need in the Biafran-controlled area. The major obstacle to expanded relief is neither money, food, nor means of transport. The main problem is the absence of relief arrangements acceptable to the two sides which would overcome the limitations posed by the present hazardous and inadequate nighttime airlift.

4. The efforts of outside governments to expand relief are greatly complicated by the political and military issues that divide the contestants. Unfortunately, the humanitarian urge to feed the starving has become enmeshed in those issues and stands in danger of interpretation by the parties as a form of intervention. But surely it is within the conscience and ability of man to give effect to his humanitarianism without involving himself in the politics of the dispute.

5. It is in this spirit that U.S. policy will draw a sharp distinction between carrying out our moral obligations to respond effectively to humanitarian needs and involving ourselves in the political affairs of others. The United States will not shrink from this humanitarian challenge but, in cooperation with those of like mind, will seek to meet it.

With the above conclusions in view, I am pleased to announce that Secretary of State Rogers has today [February 22] appointed Mr. Clarence Clyde Ferguson, Jr., a distinguished American civic leader and professor of law at Rutgers University, as Special Coordinator on relief to civilian victims of the Nigerian civil war. He will be charged with assuring that the U.S. contributions to the international relief effort are responsive to increased needs to the maximum extent possible and that they are effectively utilized. In so doing, he will give particular attention to ways and means by which the flow of relief can be increased to the suffering on both sides of the battleline. He will, of course, work closely with the ICRC [International Committee of the Red Cross] and other international relief agencies, the Organization of African Unity, donor governments, and with the parties to the conflict.

The Special Coordinator will not seek and will not accept a charge to negotiate issues other than those directly relevant to relief. Nevertheless, the United States earnestly hopes for an early negotiated end to the conflict and a settlement that will assure the protection and peaceful development of all the people involved.

*Report by Representatives Diggs and J. Herbert Burke on a Special Factfinding Mission to Nigeria**

March 12, 1969

INTRODUCTION

The factfinding mission left Washington on February 7, 1969, having already been extensively briefed on the Nigeria/Biafra situation by C. Robert Moore, Deputy

*Committee on Foreign Affairs, *Report of Special Factfinding Mission to Nigeria, February 7-20, 1969, by Hon. Charles C. Diggs, Jr., Michigan, Chairman, Hon. J. Herbert Burke, Florida* (Washington, 1969), pp. 1-2; 17-18.

Assistant Secretary, Bureau of African Affairs, and other officials from the Department of State.

In London, aside from the American officials, we met and exchanged views with British Foreign Office personnel, the Nigerian High Commissioner, a Biafran representative, and the Ivory Coast Ambassador to the United Kingdom.

In Lagos, Nigeria, the study mission received excellent cooperation from Ambassador Elbert G. Mathews and the country team. We were afforded the opportunity of meeting Red Cross personnel, priests, U.N. officials, and many of the principal Federal Military Government officials, including Maj. Gen. Yakubu Gowon, both before proceeding into Biafra and after our return. Our stay was not confined to Lagos; we were flown around the country in General Gowon's personal jet to inspect Enugu and refugee camps, as well as Red Cross centers in that area, where relief supplies were being distributed. At Calabar we met with the Military Governor and his executive council. While there the study mission viewed bombed out sections of the city and visited more refugee installations. We touched down at Port Harcourt long enough to exchange views with the commanding officer of the 3d Marine Division, Col. Benjamin Adekunle.

For the study mission to visit Biafra it was necessary first to drive for 4 hours to Cotonou, Dahomey, where we conferred with Ambassador Knox and met President Zinsou. From there we accompanied an ICRC (International Committee of the Red Cross) cargo plane loaded with 10 tons of dried stockfish to land at night at the Uli airstrip. The study mission spent 2 days in Biafra in and around Umuahia where Col. Odumegu Ojukwu welcomed the members, and the various commissioners cooperated in every way in giving information and answering questions. We had time to tour the countryside with Father Doheny and inspected refugee camps and the Mbaise Joint Hospital. We also inspected the bombed marketplace where only about a week earlier 200 persons had reportedly been killed and there had been some 300 casualties. We saw several of the victims in the hospital and talked to Sister Luke who admitted them.

The study mission also visited Kaduna and Kano in the northern area where meetings were held with the State officials, and an audience was granted with Alhaji Ado Bayoro, Emir of Kano. The study mission returned to Washington, February 20, 1969.

I. Summary of Findings

1. The study mission believes that the posture of the United States concerning the Federal Military Government of Nigeria is correct in recognizing it as the only legal government of that country.

2. However, we believe that if there is to be any negotiated settlement of the war short of complete subjugation of one side militarily, there must be concessions and guarantees of security to the Ibos and other tribes by way of some form of federalism. The future is questionable, economic or otherwise, for a completely independent Biafra as it is presently constituted.

3. The Nigerian conflict is uniquely an African problem. The Organization of African Unity is attempting to mediate the problem. Under the chairmanship of the

Emperor of Ethiopia, and others, efforts have been made to bring the two competing sides together at the conference table. We believe that any ceasefire arrangement which might be worked out should be under African auspices. Furthermore, the OAU has indicated that it would be opposed to the United Nations taking jurisdiction of the dispute.

4. Since the inception of the fighting in Nigeria, the United States has refused to supply armaments to either side. We commend this action. However, arms have been supplied by the United Kingdom, the Soviet Union, France, and others. It is our hope that the U.S. Government might conduct informal conversations with these powers looking toward a possible agreement for all countries to suspend arms shipments to the warring factions.

5. The study mission strongly believes that our policy in operating through established international organizations such as the International Committee of the Red Cross and the Joint Church Aid (JCA), is justified and should be continued. We would not want to see the U.S. Government become directly involved either through operating an airlift or having the U.S. Government personnel coordinate the local distribution of food. Our humanitarian concern applies equally to both sides of the battle lines. Channeling aid through ad hoc committees should not be undertaken.

6. We are convinced as a result of our study that it is possible through greatly increased delivery of food supplies to prevent mass starvation in both areas of Nigeria. The food is in the area or available. The problem is to provide the means of delivery and distribution to those in direct need. Not enough information has reached the outside world concerning the relief to civil conflict victims in Nigerian federally controlled territory where literally thousands of people are being competently cared for, rehabilitated, and returned to their homes. The Biafran refusal to permit daylight flights and land corridors is the primary reason that relief and rehabilitation procedures are not today as well developed in the east as they are elsewhere in the country.

7. We see no justification for Biafra's continued refusal to permit daylight operations by the ICRC and JCA mercy missions. We have heard all the arguments and justifications for this posture, but we believe that in the light of the grave necessity such rationalizations are unconvincing. If Biafra does wish to save the lives of those verging on starvation in the area which it controls, then it must recognize the necessity of increased airlifts and the advisability of land corridors. The fear of poisoned food has to be shown as unfounded. If military and political considerations are the basis for the rejection of daylight flights and land corridors then the Biafrans must take responsibility for the consequences.

8. While our immediate objective should be to relieve the suffering, the study mission believes that if the two factions can be brought into agreement for increased food delivery there is a good possibility that these discussions might be a bridge leading toward agreement on a cease-fire followed by negotiations.

9. We can only deplore in the strongest terms the willful bombing of innocent civilian populations by the Federal Military Government forces. As we were witnesses to the tragic results of these bombings, we know that no military objective is achieved. Therefore, if these bombings of civilian centers continue, we must conclude that the motivation is malicious.

10. The study mission saw no intent by the Federal troops to follow a policy of genocide toward the Ibo people, although the Biafrans gave the impression of being

genuinely fearful of such a development. The International Observer Team to Nigeria, which is made up of officers from Canada, Poland, Sweden, the United Kingdom, the OAU, and a U.N. representative, without exception have made the point that no evidence of genocide, based on detailed investigation, was found. We are not so naive as to believe, however, that the bitterness generated by the war has not resulted in some incidents of retribution nor that it will not be in further evidence during the postwar period.

11. The study mission is pleased to note the appointment of Professor Clarence Ferguson, Jr., former dean of Howard University School of Law and presently a distinguished professor of law at Rutgers University, as the special coordinator on relief to the civilian victims of the Nigerian Civil War as we believe that pursuing the various initiatives to find agreement will require full time attention, patience, tact, and perseverance in order to reach agreement on certain humanitarian steps which will allow vastly increased delivery of food to the starving populations on both sides.

*   *   *

U.S. Policy

U.S. concern for this human tragedy is deep. Humanitarian, political, and military factors are interwoven in this situation, and it has been the policy of the U.S. Government to avoid politico-military involvement by channeling our support for the international relief effort through the nonpolitical International Committee of the Red Cross and through UNICEF and the American relief agencies, which have cooperated with it. The Federal Government of Nigeria has taken the position that all international relief efforts should be coordinated through the ICRC.

In consultation with other governments and with the Secretary General of the United Nations, the United States has explored the possibility of U.N. consideration of the Nigerian crisis. The great majority of member states, including almost all of the African states as noted above, have viewed the crisis as an internal political problem of civil war and secession and have been opposed to formal United Nations consideration. In our search for practical measures to alleviate the suffering and to help bring about a satisfactory resolution of this tragic situation, we are, however, keeping the possibility of United Nations action under continuing review.

The U.S. Government has the deepest sympathy for the suffering victims of the war. We believe that the prevention of wholesale famine is of crucial importance. We continue to back efforts by the OAU and the ICRC to bring about agreement on daytime relief flights and on the opening of land corridors to the needy in Biafra. We have appealed to the parties to subordinate the political issues of the war in the interest of reaching agreement on relief. We have fully supported the Commonwealth Secretariat and the OAU efforts to bring about a negotiated settlement and both publicly and privately backed the December 21 appeal to both sides by the Emperor of Ethiopia for a 7-day truce. We are, of course, not able to impose a solution, but we continue to press for an early negotiated settlement to the conflict.

The Relief Effort

In the areas under the control of the Federal Government, thousands of tons of food, medicine, and other relief supplies are stockpiled. Supplies are distributed from Lagos. Enugu, Calabar, Agbor, and Port Harcourt by trucks and Land Rovers, cargo aircraft, helicopters, barges. and coastal ships. Most of the relief supplies for Biafra have been stockpiled on the offshore islands of Fernando Po and Sao Tome for delivery by airlift. Here thousands of tons have been accumulated, and large cargo aircraft have been used for transport. The amounts of relief supplies reaching Biafra have recently averaged 3,000 to 4,000 tons per month. The ICRC estimates that it has been feeding 850,000 in Biafra and 850,000 to 1 million in areas under Federal Government control. Additionally, Joint Church Aid, a group of religious organizations including Caritas and Church World Service, has delivered large quantities of food into Biafra from Sao Tome and estimates that it is distributing food to almost a million persons.

A problem which recently developed for the airlift was the banning on January 6 of ICRC night flights from Fernando Po by the Government of Equatorial Guinea (GEG). We and other governments actively assisted in efforts to iron out this problem. While the matter was under active discussion between the ICRC and the GEG, the Government of Dahomey concluded an agreement with the ICRC initiating relief flights to Biafra from Cotonou. On February 12 the GEG agreed to a renewal of night flights from Fernando Po for 30 days. We hope this agreement may be extended.

The United States has thus far made about 60 percent of the global contribution for relief in Nigeria/Biafra. The U.S. Government has donated a total of $25 million in cash and surplus food commodities. Of this total $6.2 million in cash has been provided to the International Red Cross which has used a major part for the chartering of aircraft for the airlift to Biafra. On December 27 the U.S. Government announced that it was making available for the airlift at nominal cost eight C-97G cargo aircraft no longer needed by the U.S. Air Force—four to the ICRC and an additional four to the American voluntary agencies participating in Joint Church Aid. Four aircraft have been delivered to the American agencies. The transfer of the remaining four aircraft to the ICRC is underway. These aircraft are to be used solely for transporting relief supplies

Surplus food commodities (dried milk, bulgar wheat, and high protein blended food products totaling over 23,000 tons) provided to Catholic Relief Services, UNICEF, Church World Service, and the World Food Program are valued at $17.3 million, including freight costs. The U.S. Government also pays overseas transport costs of the relief supplies donated by accredited American voluntary agencies.

The private voluntary organizations of the United States have made substantial donations of food and other supplies totaling more than $7.3 million on behalf of the relief effort.

Relief Summary

U.S. Government $24,991,700

Public Law 480 food and transport costs	17,291,700
ICRC	6,200,000
General relief items	285,000
Voluntary agency transport costs	1,215,000
Total	24,991,700
U.S. voluntary agencies (for which figures are available)	7,268,062
Grand total	32,259,762

Excerpt on United States Aid from the Report of the Special Coordinator
for Nigerian Relief, C. Clyde Ferguson, Jr. *

April 24, 1969

Total Contributions from U.S. Sources to the Relief Effort in Nigeria

U.S. Government $46,426,500

    ICRC contributions 12,520,000
    UNICEF-Ocean transport costs 555,600
    Voluntary agency transport costs 1,215,000
    Voluntary agency transport costs-Public Law 480 2,000,000
    General relief items 329,600

Public Law 480 food donations 29,806,300

    Catholic Relief Services 9,709,400
    Church World Service 5,450,300
    UNICEF 14,485,600
    World Food Program 161,000

U.S. private organizations (approximate) 10,000,000

    Total 56,426,500

Speech by Senator McCarthy Before the Senate on Biafra†

May 16, 1969

Mr. President, during the past year, the horrors of the Nigerian-Biafran war have become clearer. Widespread starvation has resulted from the compression of millions of refugees into an area one-quarter of the original homeland, from disrupted planting, and from the cutting off of trade routes by the Nigerian forces. It is reported that over a million Biafran civilians have perished from starvation and a million more deaths may occur within the next few months. Not since World War II has a civilian population been so affected by war.

The American people have responded compassionately by contributing to relief efforts, which operate under the most difficult conditions, to airlift food and medicine to Biafra. The U.S. Government also has donated food and equipment to relief organizations on both sides of the fighting line.

*Committee on Foreign Affairs, *Report of the Special Coordinator for Nigerian Relief*, Hearing before the Subcommittee on Africa, 91st Cong., 1st sess., Thursday, April 24, 1969, (Washington, 1969), p. 18.
†*Congressional Record*, May 16, 1969, p. S.5250-52.

Unfortunately, this relief effort can alleviate only a fraction of the suffering, for as long as the fighting continues only a small part of the desperately needed supplies can be brought in. As long as official U.S. policy awaits a "military solution," present relief efforts will remain superficial and inadequate, if not contradictory to official policy.

It is time to reexamine our policy of "one Nigeria," which has resulted in our accepting the deaths of a million people as the price for preserving a nation that never existed.

The pattern of American diplomacy in this area is a familiar one, not very different from that in Vietnam. It began with misconception, was followed by self-justification, and is ending in tragedy. Political preconceptions have kept us from recognizing that the boundaries of Nigeria imposed artificially by a colonial power are not so scared as to justify the deaths of several million people. The price of unity is too high.

*   *   *

From the beginning of the civil war, the British have supported the federal military government of Nigeria, partly for economic reasons and partly because of an emotional or intellectual stake in a unified Nigeria, which is represented as a triumph of the British colonial technique of indirect rule and of the successful transition from colonial rule to independence. The U.S. Assistant Secretary of State for African Affairs, Joseph Palmer, who was our first Ambassador to Nigeria, personally shared this commitment to "one Nigeria." He accepted the analogy of the secession of Biafra to the secession of the American Confederacy, entirely overlooking the fact that Nigeria, unlike the United States, was not unified by a common language, culture, and historical tradition, and had no background of stable, capable government.

Furthermore, 30,000 South Carolinians had not been massacred in 1861, and the inhabitants of the Southern States were neither pushed out of the Union nor were they living in fear for their physical security as is the case with the Biafrans in Nigeria. The U.S. State Department accepted a historical analogy without taking into account the complicated background to the secession. By putting its diplomatic and political weight behind the Nigerian position, the United States has committed itself to a purely military solution. In the summer of 1967, the Economis pointed out that the time for mediation was before war and destruction rigidified the positions of Nigeria and Biafra. Had the United States recognized this, perhaps we could have persuaded our British ally to put pressure on both sides for renegotiation of an Aburi-type agreement. However, we concurred in the hard line of Lagos, which inevitably resulted in complete rigidity and hostility.

We were and are, in fact, not neutral. The United States has been neutral only in refraining from shipping arms. Whereas Great Britain and the U.S.S.R. continue to send in arms, we have officially accepted the Nigerian explanation of the situation and have used our influence to gain acceptance for this viewpoint among other African nations.

Any review of past events clearly demonstrates the bankruptcy of American policy of "one Nigeria—at any cost." The "one Nigeria," which upon the most optimistic projections might survive from the war would have little resemblance to the carefully balanced federation of regions which many people had envisaged as essential to independence. The "one Nigeria" of the future would have to be postulated upon the inequality of different tribes. The Ibos and other eastern tribes who cooperated in forming Biafra would be stigmatized and penalized in many ways. The Ibos would—according to the new proposed division of the country into states—be confined to a crowded, infertile region smaller than their ancestral homeland, with no access to the sea. They would be deprived of all but token participation in the reconstituted unitary state.

*   *   *

The United States should immediately call for an arms embargo. We should actively seek a truce. We should use our good offices to promote negotiations for resolving the differences. We should press for a deescalation of great power involvement. We should seek to form a multinational effort to provide the logistic support required for an adequate relief effort. We should accept Biafra's right to a separate national existence and look to possibly early recognition of Biafra by the United States and other nations.

The reaction to these proposals by those who have shaped American policy in West Africa heretofore can be anticipated.

They will say that Biafran independence will be a first step toward the Balkanization of Africa.

They will say that the Rivers tribes and other minority tribes of the east will suffer if Biafra gains its independence.

They will say that these proposals will undermine the position of our British ally in Africa.

They will claim that U.S. diplomatic recognition of Biafra will constitute intervention into a purely African problem.

Let us look at each of these objections.

The prediction that Biafran independence would lead to the Balkanization of Africa is obviously the discredited domino theory transferred to a new locale. There is no more reason to think that it is correct or that it is an adequate basis for present policy in West Africa any more than it is in Asia. Local grievances, local animosities, and local injustices are more important than outside influences in accounting for revolutionary developments within a country. It is significant that four African countries—Tanzania, Zambia, Ivory Coast, and Gabon—have recognized Biafra. Each of them has large minority groups, but none of them seemed to fear that its recognition of a secessionist regime elsewhere would encourage secession within its own boundaries.

As regards the question of economic stagnation and retrogression, it should be recognized that eliminating the hostility generated by an artificial political union could release energy for economic development. Certainly the technical ingenuity of the Easterners will be stimulated by the independence of Biafra. Furthermore, independence does not preclude economic association. The Biafrans have already indicated their willingness to cooperate with Nigeria on vital problems of transportation and communication, particularly the use of the Niger River. Almost any advantage that can accrue from "one Nigeria" can also be achieved by regional economic arrangements such as a common market and a regional development board for redistributing revenues. Even without such arrangements it is clear that Nigeria is viable without the eastern region, since it has great resources, including vast amounts of oil in the midwestern region; it has been able to forego the eastern oil revenues for 2 years while fighting a costly war, and it would evidently be in far better economic condition without the expense of the war.

It is hard to credit the claims of the Federal Government of Nigeria that Biafra is governed solely by and for Ibos, who subjugate the minority tribes. In any case, the national preference of the minority tribes is a question which can be settled through plebiscites supervised by the United Nations or the Organization of African Unity. Even without some minority tribes, Biafra would be a populous country by African standards, larger than three-fourths of the African countries. Only 10 of some 40 African countries would be larger.

The argument that American recognition of Biafra would undermine the position of our British ally depends upon two premises, both doubtful. The first is that essential British oil interests would be threatened by Biafran independence. However, as pointed out before, much of the oil is in the Midwest, nor have the Biafrans expressed any intention of expropriating British oil. In any case, this should hardly be a major consideration of American foreign policy in this case.

The second premise is that the British support the Federal Government of Nigeria has diminished Soviet influence upon that government. However, all that can be said with assurance is that the Federal Government of Nigeria has shrewdly played off the Soviet Union against Great Britain in order to receive as many arms as possible from both. Who will come out ahead in this game of influence is uncertain.

In my opinion, the interests of the United States and of Great Britain may best be served by disentangling the Nigerian-Biafran war from the cold war and by reducing great power intervention in the area. It would be better to use this area as a testing ground for reducing tensions among the great powers—since their interests are less serious here than elsewhere—than to perpetuate cold war maneuvers out of habit. In addition, many African countries are already resentful of the involvements of the great powers in their lands and might welcome a reduction of great power competition in the Nigerian conflict.

To argue that diplomatic recognition of Biafra would constitute intervention into purely African affairs is irrelevant; nonrecognition is also intervention. There are faults of omission as well as of commission. The United States has already intervened repeatedly in the area; first by propping up General Gowan when he assumed power; later by backing him when Nigeria abrogated the Aburi agreements; and also by exerting pressure on a number of African nations not to recognize Biafra.

The steps I propose are diplomatic, not military. Our goal should be the recognition of Biafra which has demonstrated that it represents the interest of its people. We should begin by seeking an arms embargo. Our goal should be a truce with a view to reasonable negotiation. We should seek to deescalate great power involvement. We should provide massive relief. The alternative—to continue to give passive military support and active diplomatic support in the name of unity—is no longer defensible.

*Statement by Secretary Rogers on United States Efforts to Help
Nigerian Civil War Victims**

November 12, 1969

Over the past 9 months this administration has made a major effort to help relieve
the anguish and suffering of civilian victims of the Nigerian civil war. A further report
on our efforts is in order.

From the beginning of this tragic event the United States has sought to support and
ensure an effective means of delivering relief to the sufferers on both sides.

Some of the steps this Government has taken include the appointment of a
high-level coordinator of all United States activities relating to Nigerian/Biafran relief,
Ambassador C. Clyde Ferguson; the donation of over $65 million to the international
relief effort; and sustained diplomatic efforts, both bilaterally and in concert with
other concerned Governments, to obtain agreement on expanded international relief
arrangements.

Nevertheless, relief into Biafran-held territory remains tragically inadequate.

Relief supplies now reach the Biafran enclave only at night, in insufficient amounts,
by aircraft across Federally controlled territory lacking the approval of the Federal
Government and originating outside Federal jurisdiction. Furthermore, following the
shooting down of one of its aircraft on June 5, the International Committee of the
Red Cross suspended its night flight operations, which had provided roughly one-half
of relief supplies. ICRC flights have remained suspended since that time in view of the
Federal Government's reiteration on June 30 that it could no longer permit such night
flights across its territory. One major consideration cited by the Federal authorities
was the intermingling at night of arms flights and relief flights into the enclave. The
present arrangements for getting relief into the enclave are considered by the agencies
involved to be both dangerous and inefficient.

In recent weeks, the United States has vigorously supported efforts of the ICRC to
obtain agreement by both sides on a program of daylight relief flights.

On September 13 the ICRC, after extensive diplomatic efforts, concluded an
agreement with the Government of Nigeria allowing an internationally inspected and
militarily inviolable relief airlift during daylight hours for an experimental period, with
good prospects for renewal. The Biafran authorities, however, have refused to accept
such flights—principally on the grounds that they believed they could not rely on
either the Red Cross or the Federal Government to assure that the daylight airlift
would not be violated by a surprise attack on the Biafran airfield, the vital terminus
for their arms supply. They asked instead that they be given third-party assurances as
to the good faith of the Federal Government of Nigeria.

To meet this concern, at President Nixon's direction we took the following
initiatives designed to facilitate agreement on a safe and effective method of getting
relief into the enclave:

1. We sought and received the solemn assurance of the Federal Government of
Nigeria that it would ensure that no hostile military action would be taken against the
ICRC relief aircraft.

**Department of State Bulletin*, Dec. 1, 1969, pp. 469-70.

2. After consultations with us, other governments agreed to offer impartial observers to accompany ICRC aircraft on their relief flights.

3. Ambassador Ferguson went to West Africa to give the Biafrans the specific pledge of the Federal Government of Nigeria as to the inviolability of the ICRC daylight relief flights. On October 24, 1969, the Biafran authorities formally rejected this assurance.

On October 31 the Biafrans publicly announced their acceptance of an earlier U.S. plan for a surface route utilizing the Cross River in Eastern Nigeria. Under this proposal, relief supplies would be delivered by ship to a mutually agreed neutralized distribution point. We have stated our willingness to resume discussions on this.

In our view, however, this Cross River route cannot substitute for the immediate resumption of ICRC daylight flights. Even if the plan could be promptly implemented, the capacity of the river route will be greatly reduced by a low water level for several more months. The agreement of the two sides to this plan is so far in principle only, and there has been no meeting of minds on the specifics of inspection and guarantees. Nevertheless, our relief coordinator is continuing his efforts to bring about agreement on the Cross River proposal.

Daylight flights under agreed procedures therefore remain the only practicable scheme for an immediate and substantial expansion of relief operations.

We believe that the ICRC proposal is such a realistic and reasonable scheme. We consider that the Federal Government, in agreeing to the ICRC proposal, has acted constructively and in accordance with its humanitarian responsibilities. We also believe that the proposed arrangements for daylight flights meet in a reasonable manner the legitimate security concerns of the Biafran authorities.

Innocent civilians are in desperate need of food and medical supplies. The United States stands ready to continue its aid to these helpless victims of the Nigerian war. We earnestly hope that the Biafran leadership will reconsider its position regarding daylight flights.

Beyond these immediate measures, however, we clearly recognize that the ultimate solution to the problem of relief is an end to the war. The suffering and the fighting have gone on too long. As President Nixon has said, the United States earnestly hopes for the earliest negotiated end to the conflict and a settlement that will assure the security and peaceful development of all the people involved.

News Briefing by Under Secretary Elliot J. Richardson on Nigeria *

January 13, 1970

I want to take this opportunity just to say a few words to you about the situation in Nigeria and the Biafran enclave and the measures that are being taken to cope with the humanitarian aspect of the situation and also to try to assure that those individuals who had been engaged in hostilities against the Federal Military Government are themselves treated with clemency and magnanimity.

First, though, I think it is important to emphasize the feeling that we in the Department of State who have been working on various aspects of this problem for

Ibid., Feb. 2, 1970, pp. 120-21.

these many months must have, as well as I am sure other Americans do, about the fact that at long last—whatever may have been our sympathies toward the participants in this tragic struggle—at least now there is the opportunity to bring relief to all the victims in this situation.

The frustrating aspect of it, while the fighting was on, was that we knew there were people in need and yet the avenues of relief were many times blocked by one obstacle or another. Fortunately, through the efforts and energy of many people—including most particularly for the United States our Special Relief Coordinator, Ambassador Clyde Ferguson—a great deal was done. But we knew that it was never really enough; and so, in addition, through the efforts of many people, coordinated in this Department by Mr. William Brubeck, who headed a special task force in the Bureau of African Affairs, we have also tried to make the resources and assisance and support of the United States available to support efforts to bring about an end to the fighting.

We have had to recognize that too conspicuous an initiative by the United States in this respect might be counterproductive, and so we have generally followed a course of encouraging the initiatives of others and making available our help to them, making it known to them that we stood ready to assist in whatever way we could.

And so, on the relief side, Ambassador Ferguson and, on the side of seeking to bring about an end to the fighting, Mr. Brubeck have been our own frontline representatives.

We feel that from the standpoint of a constructive role for the United States, this has been on the whole a successful course. In the end, obviously, our role was not instrumental in bringing about an end to the fighting. And yet, now that it has come about, much of the work and planning that has been done on the relief and humanitarian side can be brought to bear.

Our contingency studies, preparing for the possibility of military victory, go back to early December. During that period, Ambassador Ferguson worked on the revival of the possibility of utilizing the Cross River route and daylight airlift. He went to Nigeria to conduct a detailed firsthand study of the situation. Various plans were made, including the plans that are now being brought to bear to provide expedited and expanded transportation facilities. We can go further into this if there are any questions on the subject.

Before, however, turning to questions, I do have several points to mention that bring you up to date on things that we are doing as of today.

As I think you know, Assistant Secretary [for African Affairs David D.] Newsom saw General Gowon [Maj. Gen. Yakubu Gowon, head of the Federal Military Government] today. We have not yet had a report of this. When we do, we will have a better idea of what we can usefully do to help the Nigerian Government in meeting its current problems, such as the C-130 aircraft and helicopters which the President has offered and assistance in expanding the international observer force.

Ambassador Ferguson is consulting with the Prime Minister in London on coordination of all relief efforts, following several days of similar consultation with the relief agencies in Geneva.

In response to the request of UNICEF [United Nations Children's Fund] , we have asked AID to consult with them urgently to provide any necessary assistance in moving 48 trucks for them from the United States to Nigeria by airlift, if required. In addition, we have located four prepackaged hospital units which we are prepared to move to Nigeria as rapidly as possible if the Nigerians can use them.

Ambassador Ferguson has already allocated to the Red Cross $2 million for direct support to the Nigerian Red Cross of the $10 million committed by the President for relief on Monday. Those funds will be immediately available.

        *   *   *

Statement by David D. Newsom, Assistant Secretary of State for African Affairs, on Relief Problems in Nigeria-Biafra*

January 21-22, 1970

        *   *   *

The Nigerians face the challenges of relief reconciliation, and reconstruction.

As you know, Mr. Chairman, we have for a long time been very deeply concerned. Now today when peace comes the world naturally expects that some of the obstacles that had been in the way of relief in the past can be removed so solution to the total problem will not be either quick nor simple. The Nigerians want the help of many outside nations and are seeking such help. We have pledged our fullest support.

The reports which are just now being received from the world press, which the Nigerians permitted into the former area just a few days ago reveal the full extent of the challenge. What were in the words of preliminary reports that we received from observers called merely pockets of need now in the press reports become stark pictures of human tragedy.

We are urging our people in Nigeria to follow up as quickly and as closely as possible to insure that all that can be done is done.

In our handling of this tragic problem, Mr. Chairman, we have the immediate concern of being fully prepared to assist in meeting the needs for relief and rehabilitation, and I might add in making sure that we share fully with the Government of Nigeria all such assessments as we have had from the communicable disease center and others of what the magnitude of the tragedy may be.

We wish at the same time to keep in mind our longer term relations with Africa's most populous country and to put them on a positive basis.

I have just returned from Nigeria where I met with General Gowon on January 13. I conveyed to him the interest and concern of President Nixon in assisting the Nigerian Government to the fullest extent in the arrangements of relief and rehabilitation. This expression of interest has continued the pattern of humanitarian concern which has characterized our policy throughout this tragic episode.

General Gowon expressed appreciation for the President's offer. He stressed that he wished to be certain that requests for relief which Nigeria made were based on genuine

*Committee on the Judiciary, *Relief Problems in Nigeria-Biafra*, Hearings Before the Subcommittee to Investigate Problems Connected with Refugees and Escapees, 91st. Cong., 2d sess., part 2, January 21, 22, 1970, (Washington, 1970), pp. 170-72.

need and were coordinated. As a preliminary result of coordination and study which the Nigerians have been undertaking we have been asked to supply 50 jeeps, 50 trucks, and three packaged disaster hospitals. The jeeps and hospitals will be on an aircraft bound for Nigeria on Friday. We anticipate further requests as needs—as the situation develops. I returned from Nigeria with a strong impression of the desire of the Nigerian leaders to demonstrate their ability to heal the wounds of the civil war. I might insert here, Mr. Chairman, and Senator Goodell, that I think the world has had two primary concerns, one has been a concern of calculated genocide. The other has been a concern of the magnitude of the starvation and medical problem. On the question of genocide, it is my impression that the Nigerian Government has moved in its assurances to the population and in its treatment of the Ibo people, in its reappointment of many of the officials of what was formerl Biafra into the Nigerian service, to demonstrate that their intentions are honorable and humane. It is the area of the food deficit, the medical problem, the movement of people, where the great tragedy today exists.

Now, several Nigerians stressed to me the importance which Nigeria attaches to being directly associated with the relief efforts in the former Biafran enclave in order to insure more rapidly and more completely the reconciliation of these people. There is both pride of person involved and pride of race and General Gowon speaks of this.

The war that left a mark of resentment against some agencies which helped provide relief to Biafra. But despite this, it is our impression that the Nigerians are utilizing relief workers of many different agencies and nationalities who were in the enclave at the end of the war. The former head of the Biafran Red Cross has been appointed as a deputy to the head of the Nigerian Red Cross and has already gone to work at Enuga.

Now, until the reports just coming in, which I mentioned, have been received, our information on current conditions was fragmentary and based largely on outside observers who entered the area in the first few days after the end of the war.

These included Hendrick Beer, the Secretary General of the League of Red Cross Societies, Lord Hunt, Prime Minister Wilson's relief coordinator, and the military observers who were there through arrangement with the United Nations.

They noted in their reports pockets of severe need, both of food and medical care, hospitals which had been abandoned by the doctors and nurses which were in immediate need of staff and supplies. Pockets of serious malnutrition, all of these were noted and they are now being amplified.

Observers have reported favorably, however, on the present relief operation under the general direction of the Nigerian Red Cross, and have found that the reports that large numbers of refugees having taken to the bush and still not found seem so far to have been exaggerated.

Refugees ae reported moving back to their villages in great numbers. They appear to be in fair condition. The elderly and the wounded are in the greatest need of care.

Federal troops in general have been reported to have been assisting the Nigerian Red Cross in relief work with no observed excesses on the part of the troops. Now, that some of the starker pictures of the war are coming in from the observers who most recently have been there, there are perhaps the inevitable incidents of such a conflict.

Nevertheless, neither we nor—we feel—the Nigerians are complacent about the situation even though conditions in some ways may be better than had been predicted.

*   *   *

Finally, one comes back from Lagos today with a feeling that the relationships of the United States and other governments with Nigeria during this period will have a broader significance. The Nigerians stressed to me their feeling that the ability of an important black African nation to manage its affairs is at stake. There is an acute sensitivity about advice and actions which do not acknowledge Nigeria's sovereignty. In consideration of the importance that we attach to our relations with Nigeria and to other nations of the organization of African unity we are maintaining the closest of consultations on these matters of concern. Through this policy we feel we will have the best chance to render the assistance that is needed and to place our relations with this significant nation on a sound footing.

EAST AFRICA

Commentary

East Africa's arbitrary boundaries accord least with geographical and cultural realities. There is no Sahara in the north; there is no physical marker in the south. The geographical openness has encouraged movement of peoples and ideas north and south through the centuries and into recent times.

That fluidity has created some of East Africa's problems and challenges. The eastern part of "Black Africa" usually includes the Sudan as well as Ethiopia. Yet among the Sudan's internal problems of longest standing has been conflict ranging from political tension to violence between groups seeing themselves as culturally and racially distinct from one another.

Similarly in the south, the cut-off between Tanzania and Zambia is quite arbitrary. Neither in terms of population movements in pre-European days, nor in terms of post-colonial contacts and influences (as for instance the important ties between Tanzania and Zambia) does it make sense.

Even in the colonial context it did not make sense, for after the First World War, Britain was administrator on both sides of the artificial line. But for a bit of historic time, the decade (1953-1963) in which the short-lived Central African Federation incorporating Northern Rhodesia/Zambia, Nyasaland/Malawi, Southern Rhodesia/ Zimbabwe existed, the two regions pointed in different economic directions. And because the different orientations brought crucial and divergent political and economic repercussions, the distinction continues useful for analytic purposes, despite the Tan-Zam Railroad, whose completion may literally move Zambia into East Africa.

The East African region may be seen to include Tanzania (Tanganyika and Zanzibar), Uganda, Kenya, Somalia, the Sudan, and—for the United States distinctively and most importantly—Ethiopia. Except for the Sudan, which became self-governing in 1956, terminating an Anglo-Egyptian condominium dating from the late 19th century, and of course Ethiopia, never dependent though occasionally invaded and once occupied by Italian forces—except for these two nations, independence of East African states followed the procession of 1960 elsewhere on the continent. (It seemed less an inevitability after 1965 and concerted white resistance to African self-determination in Southern Rhodesia.)

That East Africa had not set the pace was not surprising. There as to the south, but contrasting with the west, were the problems of the multi-racial state. There and especially in Kenya, were the European settlers with their yearnings for continued political control. There were the Asians, who had taken a middle ground. More privileged politically than the Africans, though not the equals of the whites, they kept a separate political identity. Economically, too, they played the middle, entrepreneurial role, complementary with white ownership and African labor.

Tanganyika, which shared some of Kenya's problems, faced a situation different because of trusteeship status: ultimately the U.N. would decide, and it could only grant the one-man/one-vote arrangements to which its diverse membership was committed. Tanganyika's leader, Julius Nyerere, was to greatly influence independence there and in neighboring countries, starting from his repeated appearances to testify before the Trusteeship Council of the U.N. Zanzibar, with its Arab population that had for over a century dominated the island's Africans politically and economically, was a political footnote for almost everyone.

Uganda's situation was different, too. Of all Britain's colonies in East and Southern Africa, the British had protected Uganda's African rights and political and economic opportunities most fully. The country's African past produced kingdoms, especially that of the Baganda, that so dealt with and impressed early British intruders that they preserved these rights. Most important was the refusal to alienate land to Europeans, which meant that Uganda did not need West Africa's mosquito to keep out settlers and their vested interests.

But Uganda's situation was nevertheless not a simple one. In common with many African states, she inherited diverse peoples from her complex past, with separate identities as strong as separate nationalities. Moreover, some of those peoples had been split between European-defined countries; this, too was a common legacy of Europe's 19th century map-making across the continent. But problems of irredentism were particularly severe across East African borders. Uganda and Sudan found themselves facing that issue as did Kenya and Somalia (after the departure of the English and Italians created Somalia in 1960), and as did Ethiopia with Somalia and Kenya.

Kenya, Uganda, Tanganyika, and Zanzibar had a special opportunity in the early 1960's. Many aspects of their economies, and many of their services—post and telegraph as one example, East African Airways as another—were jointly organized and run. There, some thought, the unrealized if oft-repeated ideals of Pan-Africanism might possibly find a beginning. Julius Nyerere, with independence scheduled for 1961, offered a delay so that the territories might become self-governing together. For many reasons, the plans did not work, though in 1967 new efforts did produce an East African Community. Tanganyika became self-governing in 1961, Uganda in 1962, Kenya in 1963, Zanzibar in 1963. All, of course, had non-racial—and universal—electoral franchise in their constitutional arrangements.

In 1964 military coups d'etat that would later spread like an epidemic through Subsaharan Africa, touched East Africa. (The Sudan had been through its first military coup in the 1950's.) Army mutinies brought a plea for aid from Tanganyika and Kenya, not to the U.N., but to Britain, whose paratroopers responded, and restored the status quo. Another appeal, this one to an African state, brought Tanganyika the help of the Nigerian batallion as well. A subsequent uprising in Zanzibar led to the ousting, amid considerable bloodshed, of the Arab-dominated government and its replacement by an African one. Eventually a merger that was more in name than in actuality between Tanganyika and Zanzibar produced Tanzania. Through it all, the major American concern was with a space-tracking station on Zanzibar, which was soon shifted to Madagascar when it was shown to be clearly unwelcome on Zanzibar.

Except for involvement in Ethiopia this concern over the Zanzibar installations was as great an issue as the United States chose to see in East Africa. Otherwise, as the spareness of documentation may well reflect, that region claimed least attention from American governments whose concern with Africa was slight enough. Investment was least there, aid was least; the inclination prevailed to let Britain prescribe and have an unchallenged free hand, even though Britain's commitment there was not her greatest.

Britain had taken care of the one East African episode that even grazed American consciousness—the Kikuyu "or Mau Mau" nationalist movement of the early 1950's connected with Jomo Kenyatta. But in the 1960's, Kenyatta was the Grand Old Man of African politics, President of Kenya, clearly with British sanction. All was stable; America did not need to add East Africa to more pressing concerns. The countries of East Africa scarcely drew even the brief flurry of American popular interest that the early 1960's had brought. This was partly for logical historical reasons: 1) the ties of Americans of African descent were to West Africa, not East; 2) other African states were independent, but as yet East African ones were not. When their independence came, only a few years later, the novelty for much of the world, not just the United States, had worn off.

Only the energetic efforts of Kenya's Tom Mboya, who had attracted some American attention because he was a trade unionist as well as a political figure, and Senator John F. Kennedy and his staff, focused some American attention briefly on bringing Kenya students to the United States in 1960.

By the late 1960's not even mainland Chinese participation in building the Tan-Zam railroad, with the foothold that effort and their cordial relations with Zanzibar would give them, could arouse more than passing open official comment. Concern for the increased activities of the Soviet fleet in the Indian Ocean was apparently left to Britain, despite her cutbacks east of Suez, and despite the United States Navy's efforts, in 1970, to lobby for an Indian Ocean force.

Ethiopia, however, was an entirely different matter. Characteristically, statements on United States policy there begin by proclaiming long historic ties. The date that comes to the fore is 1903, marking diplomatic relations between the two countries. But the far more important historic tie is also more personal. For since 1936, Ethiopia's Emperor Haile Selassie has been in touch at one time or another with every American president. If this continuity, combined with the Emperor's influence gained through time and stature as an international figure, is one key to American policy, Ethiopia's important geographical position is the other.

In June, 1970, during hearings held before the Senate Foreign Relations Committee's Subcommittee on United States Security Agreements and Commitments Abroad under Senator Stuart Symington's chairmanship, the depth of American involvement in Ethiopia began to emerge. With the heavy Defense and State Department censorship of testimony before publication, it could not appear in perfect clarity.

What America had with Ethiopia was not a warm, historically, friendly relationship; nor was it a relationship of simple military aid, supplied under a Mutual Defense Assistance agreement signed in 1953. The strategic needs of the United States had combined with the policies of the Emperor to produce commitments with far-reaching implications—very far-reaching, as the Senators saw them in the context of Southeast Asian Experience.

In 1960, the United States gave written and oral guarantees to support a 40,000 man Ethiopian army, while reaffirming "its continuing interest in the security of Ethiopia and *its opposition to any activities threatening the territorial integrity of Ethiopia*." [italics mine] From the time of that agreement to 1970, the United States gave more than $147,000,000 in military aid to Ethiopia, including supersonic jet fighters. The United States has supplied the ammunition and bombs used by Ethiopian forces against guerrillas in Eritrea, the recently-incorporated province of ambiguous status that provides Ethiopia's only access to the Red Sea, and in the Ogaden region, bordering in the south on Somalia. The United States has stationed about 3,200 American military personnel and their dependents in Ethiopia, mainly to run a large and important communications station at Kagnew, a station engaging in secret electronic intelligence. The United States has also supplied American military personnel to train Ethiopians in techniques of counter-insurgency.

Those are the main points. The explanations for so large an American commitment (that it was military might well have remained officially concealed without the Senate hearings) have been offered in the following terms: Haile Selassie is a very important man, a much-respected international and African figure, who has, since 1936, advocated the collective security American leaders also favored. Thus it is eminently suitable for the U.S. to maintain close relations and cooperate with him.

In addition, Ethiopia (like Liberia) had a greater claim on American aid of whatever kind, since she did not receive the attention of any European country committed by ties of one-time colonial rule and continuing influence. Further, partly through the Emperor's influence, Addis Ababa has become the key center for international activity in Africa. It is the headquarters of the Organization of African Unity, and of the U.N. Economic Commission for Africa. It is, therefore, a logical place for American interest, a place providing access to African opinion from all over the Continent on many subjects. The communications base at Kagnew, whose existence was known, was part of America's global communications system (incidentally run by the Defense Department). State Department testimony pointed out its usefulness in transmitting diplomatic messages to American representatives in East Africa.

A study of United States relations with Africa is not the place for details of the ties of this commitment in relation to global communication or Middle Eastern problems or Soviet-American relations. But East Africa does seem to be the part of the continent which has drawn attention least often for reasons of its own making.

SUDAN

*Statement by Secretary of State Dean Acheson on
the Egyptian Abrogation of Condominium in the Sudan**

October 10, 1951

The American Embassy in Cairo has confirmed that the Egyptian Prime Minister on October 8 introduced in the Egyptian Chamber of Deputies draft legislation which would abrogate the Anglo-Egyptian treaty of 1936 and the Anglo-Egyptian condominium agreements of 1899, which provide for joint Anglo-Egyptian administration of the Sudan.

The parties directly involved are the United Kingdom and Egypt and, in the case of the 1899 agreements, the Sudanese people as well. However, these matters are also of general concern to the free world for they affect the security and defense of the important Middle East area.

None of the agreements in question provides for abrogation. The U.S. Government believes that proper respect for international obligations requires that they be altered by mutual agreement rather than by unilateral action of one of the parties. Furthermore, it should be noted that procedures wholly in accord with such respect for international commitments have already been set in motion.

During past months, new proposals to be offered to Egypt have been under consideration and the Egyptian Government had been informed that proposals were to be presented to it within the next few days. It is the belief of the United States that a solution to the Anglo-Egyptian question can be found through these proposals. The United States considers that the new proposals shortly to be presented to the Egyptian Government should serve as a sound basis for an agreement which will not only satisfy the interests of all parties concerned but also contribute to the defense of the free world in which the Middle East plays such an important role.

*Note from Secretary Acheson to the Foreign Minister of Egypt
on the Anglo-Egyptian Agreement on the Sudan†*

February 14, 1953

The United States is gratified that an agreement on the Sudan has been arrived at by Egypt and the United Kingdom. This is a truly important occasion. It affords an opportunity for me to express my Government's pleasure at the spirit in which these difficult negotiations were carried out.

My Government trusts that the same spirit of good will and cooperation will characterize the transitional period preceding the decision by the Sudanese people of

*Department of State Bulletin, Oct. 22, 1951, p. 647.
†Ibid., Feb. 23, 1953, p. 306.

their future status. The amicable resolution of this long outstanding question goes far toward creating an atmosphere of mutual understanding and trust in the Near East which can only result in great benefits for all the nations of the free world.

My Government continues to follow with interest and sympathy the progressive attitude and energetic efforts of the Government of General Naguib to meet and overcome the international problems which face the Egyptian people. The United States wishes the Egyptian Government every success in its efforts.

State Department Statement on the United States Participation in the Mixed Electoral Commission for the Sudan*

March 23, 1953

In reply to requests received from the Governments of Egypt and the United Kingdom, the Government of the United States has agreed to participate on the Mixed Electoral Commission for the Anglo-Egyptian Sudan. Mr. Warwick Perkins, a Foreign Service Career Officer of Class One, has been nominated as United States representative on the Commission. Mr. Perkins departed for Khartoum on March 19, 1953, and has been accorded by the President the personal rank of Minister for the duration of his service on this Commission.

The Anglo-Egyptian Agreement of February 12, 1953 on the Sudan provided for the election of a Sudanese Parliament as a step towards self-government and self-determination in that country. The election is to be supervised by a Mixed Electoral Commission consisting of representatives of the Sudan, Egypt, India, the United Kingdom and the United States.

State Department Statement on Recognition of the Republic of the Sudan by the United States†

January 2, 1956

The United States has extended recognition to the Sudan as an independent sovereign state. This action followed termination of the Anglo-Egyptian condominium in the Sudan and recognition of the Sudan's independence by Egypt and the United Kingdom. The U.S. Liaison Officer in Khartoum, Mr. Arthur E. Beach, presented the letter of recognition quoted below to the President of the Supreme Commission, which will exercise the powers of the Head of State:

> "I have been requested by my Government to inform you that it has noted the declaration on December 19, 1955 by the Parliament of the Sudan proclaiming the Sudan as an independent sovereign state and is pleased to extend its official recognition. The Government of the United States contemplates the establishment of appropriate means for the conduct of formal diplomatic relations at an early date. The United States of America congratulates the people of the Sudan on their assumption of the powers, duties and responsibilities of independence and expresses the hope that in the adoption and maintenance of an independent form of government the rights liberties and happiness of the Sudanese people will be secure and the progress of the country insured."

*Department of State Press Release 154, Mar. 23, 1953.
†Ibid., 2, Jan. 2, 1956.

Mutual Defense Assistance Agreement Between the United States and Ethiopia *

May 22, 1953

The Government of the United States of America and the Imperial Ethiopian Government,

Desiring to foster international peace and security within the framework of the Charter of the United Nations through measures which will further the ability of nations dedicated to the purposes and principles of the Charter to participate effectively in arrangements for individual and collective self-defense in support of those purposes and principles;

Reaffirming their determination to give their full cooperation to the efforts to provide the United Nations with armed forces as contemplated by the Charter and to participate in United Nations collective defense arrangements and measures, and to obtain agreement on universal regulation and reduction of armements under adequate guarantee against violation or evasion;

Taking into consideration the support which the Government of the United States has brought to these principles by enacting the Mutual Defense Assistance Act of 1949, as amended, and the Mutual Security Act of 1951, as amended;

Desiring to set forth the conditions which will govern the furnishing of such assistance;

Have agreed:

Article I

1. The Government of the United States, pursuant to Section 202 of the Mutual Security Act of 1951, as amended, will make available to the Imperial Ethiopian Government arms and other equipment, materials services or other assistance in such quantities and in accordance with such terms and conditions as may be agreed. The furnishing and use of such assistance shall be consistent with the Charter of the United Nations. Such assistance as may be made available by the Government of the United States pursuant to this Agreement will be furnished under the provisions and subject to all the terms, conditions and termination provisions of the Mutual Defense Assistance Act of 1949 and the Mutual Security Act of 1951, acts amendatory or supplementary thereto and appropriation acts thereunder. The two Governments will, from time to time, negotiate detailed arrangements necessary to carry out the provisions of this paragraph.

2. The Imperial Ethiopian Government will use this assistance exclusively to maintain its internal security, its legitimate self-defense, or to permit it to participate in the defense of the area, or in United Nations collective security arrangements and measures, and Ethiopia will not undertake any act of aggression against any other nation; and Ethiopia will not, without the prior agreement of the Government of the United States, devote such assistance to purposes other than those for which it was furnished.

*United States Treaties and Other International Agreements, Vol. 4, pt. 1, 1953, pp. 422-26.

3. Arrangements will be entered into under wich equipment and materials furnished pursuant to this Agreement and no longer required or used exclusively for the purposes for which originally made available will be offered for return to the Government of the United States.

4. The Imperial Ethiopian Government will not transfer to any person not an officer or agent of that Government, or to any other nation, title to or possession of any equipment, materials, property, information, or services received under this Agreement, without the prior consent of the Government of the United States.

5. The Imperial Ethiopian Government will take such security measures as may be agreed in each case between the two Governments in order to prevent the disclosure or compromise of classified military articles, services or information furnished pursuant to this Agreement.

6. Each Government will take appropriate measures consistent with security to keep the public informed of operations under this Agreement.

7. The two Governments will establish procedures whereby the Imperial Ethiopian Government will so deposit, segregate or assure title to all funds allocated to or derived from any program of assistance undertaken by the Government of the United States so that such funds shall not, except as may otherwise be mutually agreed, be subject to garnishment, attachment, seizure or other legal process by any person, firm, agency, corporation, organization or government.

Article II

The two Governments will, upon request of either of them, negotiate appropriate arrangements between them providing for the methods and terms of the exchange of patent rights and technical information for defense which will expedite such exchanges and at the same time protect private interests and maintain necessary security safeguards.

Article III

1. The Imperial Ethiopian Government will make available to the Government of the United States Ethiopian dollars for the use of the latter Government for its administrative and operating expenditures in connection with carrying out the purposes of this Agreement. The two Governments will forthwith initiate discussions with a view to determining the amount of such Ethiopian dollars and to agreeing upon arrangements for the furnishing of such Ethiopian dollars.

2. The Imperial Ethiopian Government will, except as may otherwise be mutually agreed, grant duty-free treatment on importation or exportation and exemption from internal taxation upon products, property, materials or equipment imported into its territory in connection with this Agreement or any similar Agreement between the Government of the United States and the Government of any other country receiving military assistance.

3. Tax relief will be accorded to all expenditures in Ethiopia by, or on behalf of, the Government of the United States for the common defense effort, including

expenditures for any foreign aid program of the United States. The Imperial Ethiopian Government will establish procedures satisfactory to both Governments so that such expenditures will be net of taxes.

Article IV

1. The Imperial Ethiopian Government will receive personnel of the Government of the United States who will discharge in its territory the responsibilities of the Government of the United States under this Agreement and who will be accorded facilities and authority to observe the progress of the assistance furnished pursuant to this Agreement. Such personnel who are United States nationals, including personnel temporarily assigned, will, in their relations with the Imperial Ethipian Government, operate as a part of the Embassy of the United States of America under the direction and control of the Chief of the Diplomatic Mission, and will have the same status as that of other personnel with corresponding rank of the Embassy of the United States who are United States nationals. Upon appropriate notification by the Government of the United States the Imperial Ethiopian Government will grant full diplomatic status to an agreed number of personnel assigned under this Article.

2. The Imperial Ethiopian Government will grant exemption from import and export duties on personal property imported for the personal use of such personnel or of their families and will take reasonable administrative measures to facilitate and expedite the importation and exportation of the personal property of such personnel and their families.

3. The military assistance advisory group to be provided by the Government of the United States will include an appropriate number of military personnel designated for the training of the Ethiopian Armed Forces and advising in their organization in accordance with such terms and conditions as may be agreed.

Article V

1. The Imperial Ethiopian Government will:

   (a) join in promoting international understanding and good will, and maintaining world peace;
   (b) take such action as may be mutually agreed upon to eliminate causes of international tension;
   (c) fulfill the military obligations which it has assumed in multilateral or bilateral agreements or treaties to which the United States is a party;
   (d) make, consistent with its political and economic stability, the full contribution permitted by its manpower, resources, facilities and general economic condition to the development and maintenance of its own defensive strength and the defensive strength of the free world;
   (e) take all reasonable measures which may be needed to develop its defense capacities; and
   (f) take appropriate steps to insure the effective utilization of the economic and military assistance provided by the United States.

2. (a) Subject to mutual agreement hereafter, the Imperial Ethiopian Government will, consistent with the Charter of the United Nations, furnish to the Government of

the United States, or to such other governments as the Parties hereto may in each case agree upon, equipment, materials, services or other assistance in order to increase their capacity for individual and collective self-defense and to facilitate their effective participation in the United Nations system for collective security.

(b) In conformity with the principle of mutual aid, the Imperial Ethiopian Government will facilitate the production and transfer to the Government of the United States, for such period of time, in such quantities and upon such terms and conditions as may be agreed upon, of raw and semiprocessed materials required by the United States as a result of deficiencies or potential deficiencies in its own resources, and which may be available in Ethiopia. Arrangements for such transfers shall give due regard to reasonable requirements of Ethiopia for domestic use and commercial export.

Article VI

In the interest of their mutual security the Imperial Ethiopian Government will cooperate with the Government of the United States in taking measures designed to control trade with nations which threaten the maintenance of world peace.

Article VII

1. This Agreement shall enter into force on the date of signature and will continue in force until one year after the receipt by either party of written notice of the intention of the other party to terminate it, provided that the provisions of Article I, paragraphs 2 and 4, and arrangements entered into under Article I, paragraphs 3, 5 and 7, and under Article II, shall remain in force unless otherwise agreed by the two Governments.

2. The two Governments will, upon the request of either of them consult regarding any matter relating to the application or amendment of this Agreement.

3. This Agreement shall be registered with the Secretariat of the United Nations.

In witness whereof, the undersigned duly authorized representatives of the Government of the United States and the Imperial Ethiopian Government have signed this Agreement.

Done in duplicate at Washington this twenty-second day of May, 1953.

For the Government of the United States of America:
Walter Bedell Smith
For the Imperial Ethiopian Government:
Aklilou

Report of Senators Church, Gale W. McGee (Wyoming) and Frank E. Moss (Utah) on a Study Mission to Africa*

November-December, 1960

*   *   *

Emperor Haile Selassi I, in an effort to bring his country into the modern world, has given particular attention to the need for education, and has retained the post of Minister of Education in his own hands. He has welcomed efforts, not only by the United States but by a number of other countries, to assist in the economic development of his nation and in the training of its military forces. Behind this policy of dispersion is both the desire to avoid undue influence by a single foreign power and a reflection of the mild suspicion of outsiders which persists in a land isolated for so many years. He has led his country into the ranks of numerous international organizations, firmly supported the principle of collective security action through the United Nations, and welcomed the establishment of the United Nations Economic Commission for Africa in his capital.

However, what the Emperor has not been able to do, or has felt it dangerous to do, is perhaps of even greater significance. Because his claim to the throne was originally little better than that of certain of his relatives—a situation dealt with in the revised constitution of 1955 through establishment of primogeniture—he was forced to commend himself to existing sources of power in the land. This cautious approach was solidified during the Italian invasion when certain of the great nobles stood by him throughout. He is intensely loyal to these men and gives weight to their counsel. Feelings of insecurity may also account for his lack of action to reduce the power of the church, to embark on a significant countrywide land reform program, or to relinquish any of his virtually sole powers of decision. Perhaps most important, he has failed to meet the demands for change and posts of importance from those modernists—in the army as well as civilian life—whose education he personally promoted.

The revolution of December 14 has not as yet been fully explained. But it appears that it was less the work of "Young Turks" than of officials trusted by the Emperor, preeminently the commander of the imperial bodyguard and his brother a provincial governor. What is obvious is that the poorly organized rebels killed a number of high-level civil servants, thereby increasing the difficulty of administering the country. Whatever the circumstances, if the Emperor chooses to retrench his powers, the result is likely to be intesified discontent among the "intelligentsia." Now that the military has become involved in revolutionary action, even in a small way, new importance will be attached to the officer corps as a basic force in Ethiopian politics.

Since the Ethiopian Army is largely American trained, the question immediately arises as to the results of that training. In one particular there is cause for alarm: many Ethiopian officers apparently have suffered from racial discrimination in the United States and have returned deeply embittered. If this problem cannot be resolved because of the location of American service schools, then it would be better to eliminate such training.

The United States has been giving grant military assistance to Ethiopia at an average

*Committees on Foreign Relations, Appropriations, and Interior and Insular Affairs, *Study Mission to Africa, November-December 1960,* 87th Cong., 1st sess., (Washington, 1961), pp. 15-16.

annual rate of several million dollars since 1953. Most of the equipment, training, and technical help has gone to the Army (including the bodyguard) of over 30,000 men, but in recent years the Ethiopian Air Force and incipient Navy have also been assisted, to a much lesser degree. Apparently because the Emperor feels hemmed in by Moslem countries which might stimulate trouble among Ethiopia's large Moslem population, he is greatly interested in creating a competent defense and internal security establishment. The United States is equally interested in maintaining one of the world's biggest communications centers near Asmara.

Over the period from fiscal years 1952 to 1960 the United States has extended economic and technical assistance to Ethiopia in the total amount of roughly $38 million, of which about $27 million has represented technical cooperation funds. Approximately one-third of the total has been devoted to the field of agriculture, while education and public health have accounted for the next largest amounts. The projects undertaken to date aim at helping with a multitude of Ethiopia's long-term needs, such as livestock breeding, coffee exports, indigenous cotton development, and a list far too long to reproduce here. They are well planned and executed, but they are of a modest character. Moreover, most schooling and technical centers are distant from the capital and make little impact on the populace at large. It is plain that there is not much recognition of the scope of our assistance in Ethiopia. Since the Emperor is so vitally interested in education, it might be thought that our agreement to contribute an initial $100,000 to the projected Haile Selassie I University would have a very favorable effect. However, this is a prime example of the loss of good will incurred by our inability to move quickly in the foreign aid field; the Emperor requested such help several years ago and obtained no answer after a protracted wait.

In our view, there appears almost no chance for any but the slowest and most long-range successes in the basic fields of economic development in Ethiopia. In the likely continued absence of a substantial land reform program, there is little popular incentive for changes which are necessary before the country can absorb large increases in development loans. In this connection, only about $2 million have been drawn by Ethiopia from the heralded Soviet credit of $100 million equivalent. This sum, ironically enough, has been converted into dollar holdings in New York, which obtain over 3 percent interest, while only 2½ percent interest has to be paid on the original withdrawal. Under the circumstances, the United States would do well to concentrate a little more on those fields of assistance closest to the Emperor's heart and most popular among the Ethiopian people.

*   *   *

Speech by Assistant Secretary Williams on the Communist Bloc Interest in Africa*

November 18, 1963

The Somali Republic, located on the bulge of the east coast of Africa, recently agreed to accept arms from the Soviet Union. In doing so the Somalis rejected a Western proposal of military assistance.

*Department of State Bulletin, Dec. 16, 1963, pp. 929-32.

*   *   *

In offering to assist Somalia militarily the Western countries had several objectives: to provide enough assistance for an adequate defense establishment, to avoid an effort which would sorely tax Somalia's resources in money and manpower, and to assist in such a way that our goals of continued peace and stability in that area of Africa would be served.

Discussions between Western and Somali officials in the spring and summer of 1963 revealed a significant gap between what the Somalis wanted in the way of equipment and what the Western countries felt able to provide. Two other developments complicated the situation: the outbreak in the summer of 1963 of incidents involving the Somali tribesmen who inhabit Ethiopia which had repercussions in Somalia itself, and the breakdown of Somali-British talks over the future of the Somali-inhabited portion of neighboring Kenya.

Because of these developments, and mindful of the coming Somali elections, the Somali Government decided to strengthen its forces substantially and urgently. Thus it turned to the Soviet Union.

The Soviets made a much greater offer and immediately sent aircraft to take Somalis to the Soviet Union for training. At the same time the Somali Government turned down the Western offer. The Western countries—conscious of their common desire to avoid participating in an arms race in Africa, their wish to avoid unduly burdening African economies with military equipment, and their interests in neighboring countries—did not feel they could or should compete with this offer.

The acceptance of Soviet arms assistance does not mean that Somalia is a Communist country, however. The receipt of such military assistance will undoubtedly increase Soviet influence in the country. Yet there are strong ties between the Somali Republic and the West, and Western countries plan to continue to assist Somalia economically.

*   *   *

Yet, in spite of—or perhaps in part because of—international communism's major efforts in Africa, the Communists have to date failed to subvert or capture any African country as a satellite. The very aggressiveness and overtness of the Communist power thrust has made many Africans keenly aware of Communist tactics. Open Communist interference in African domestic affairs and overt attempts to sway African nations to support Communist cold-war aims have helped to arouse African suspicions of Communist goals.

The most important factor in precluding Communist successes to this point, however, has been Africa's increasing awareness of the divergence between the aspirations of international communism and the aspirations of the African nations. The emerging nations of Africa are determined to remain free and independent at home and nonalined in international affairs. More and more frequently, troubled African leaders are asking themselves if Communist assistance is worth the headaches it entails—and more and more frequently the answer is no.

Nevertheless we cannot be—and we are not—complacent about the Communist threat to Africa. It is there, it is real, it is dangerous. We must meet it within a framework of policy and financial limitations that does not bind the Communists. But we believe our methods are best for the long-term future, both for the United States and for Africa.

*   *   *

Hearings Before the Senate Subcommittee on United States Security Agreements and Commitments Abroad on Ethiopia*

June 1, 1970

The subcommittee met, pursuant to recess, at 10:05 a.m. in room S-116, the Capitol Building, Senator Stuart Symington (chairman of the subcommittee) presiding.

Present: Senators Symington and Fulbright.

Also present: Mr. Holt, Mr. Paul, and Mr. Pincus of the committee staff.

David Newsom, Assistant Secretary for African Affairs, Department of State; George Bader, office of the Assistant Secretary for International Security Affairs, Department of Defense: Sophocles H. Hero, Office of the General Counsel, Department of Defense; Lt. Col. Melvin G. Goodweather, OSAF; Elizabeth G. Verville, attorney, Department of State, Office of Legal Adviser; Charles N. Brower, Assistant Legal Adviser for European Affairs, Department of State; John G. Kormann, Regional Politico-Military Adviser for Africa, Department of State, Gordon R. Beyer, Country Officer for Ethiopia, Department of State: Capt. Carl C. Hilscher, staff assistant, Africa region, Department of Defense; Peter Knaur, Office of the Assistant Secretary of Defense, International Security Affairs; Joseph J. Wolf, Bureau of Politico-Military Affairs, Department of State; and H. G. Torbert, Deputy Assistant Secretary for Congressional Relations, Department of State.

Senator Symington. The committee will come to order.

Today we will take up the matter of U.S. commitments in Ethiopia. The principal witness is Mr. David Newsom, Assistant Secretary of State for African Affairs. He is accompanied by Mr. George Bader from the Office of the Assistant Secretary of Defense for International Security Affairs.

Will everybody rise, as it is the custom, and take the oath. Please raise your right hand.

Do you swear the testimony you give the subcommittee will be the truth, the whole truth and nothing but the truth, so help you God?

Mr. Newsom: I do.

Mr. Bader: I do.

Senator Symington: Please be seated. Will you identify yourself reading from left to right as to who you are and who you represent.

Mr. Hero. Sophocles Hero, Office of the Secretary of Defense.

Colonel Goodweather: Lieutenant Colonel Goodweather.

Mrs. Verville: Elizabeth Verville, Office of the Legal Adviser, Department of State.

Mr. Brower: Charles Brower, Assistant Legal Adviser for European Affairs, Department of State.

*Committee on Foreign Relations, *United States Security Agreements and Commitments Abroad, Ethiopia,* 91st Cong. 2d sess., part 8, (Washington, 1970), pp. 1881-93; 1897-1909; 1910-24; 1953-55.

Mr. Kormann: John Kormann, Regional Politico-Military Adviser for Africa, Department of State.

Mr. Beyer: Gordon Beyer, Country Officer for Ethiopia, Department of State.

Captain Hilscher: Capt. Carl Hilscher, staff assistant, Africa region, Department of Defense.

Mr. Wolf: Joseph Wolf, Bureau of Politico-Military Affairs, State Department.

Mr. Knaur: Peter Knaur, Office of the Assistant Secretary of Defense for International Security Affairs.

Senator Symington: Thank you.

I understand you have a statement, Mr. Newsom.

Mr. Newsom: I do, Mr. Chairman.

Senator Symington: Mr. Secretary, will you read it?

TESTIMONY OF HON. DAVID D. NEWSOM, ASSISTANT SECRETARY
OF STATE FOR AFRICAN AFFAIRS; ACCOMPANIED BY GEORGE W.
BADER, DIRECTOR, AFRICA REGION, OFFICE OF THE ASSISTANT
SECRETARY OF DEFENSE, INTERNATIONAL SECURITY AFFAIRS

Mr. Newsom: Right.

Mr. Chairman, at the suggestion of the committee, I am pleased to appear today to review our relations with Ethiopia.

Historical Relationship Between United States and Ethiopia

Ethiopia has occupied a special place in U.S. relations with Africa for many years. As an historic land and as one of two independent black African nations prior to World War II, this land was of particular interest to our country and to our Negro citizens. We established diplomatic relations in 1903. The interest widened when the Emperor appeared dramatically before the League of Nations in 1936, to protest the invasion of his country. He was one of the first apostles of collective security.

Our role in the liberation of Ethiopia by the Allied forces in 1941 was minor. Nevertheless, in gratitude for the support which the United States and President Roosevelt had given to Ethiopia's struggle for freedom, the Emperor provided a plot of land adjacent to a royal palace for our Embassy.

Official relations became somewhat closer in 1942 when Averell Harriman visited Eritrea, a liberated Italian colony, and made contact with Ethiopian officials. The possibility of the United States use of a communications center site at Asmara in Eritrea was raised shortly thereafter. The site was technically a particularly desirable one.

When North Korea invaded South Korea on June 25, 1950, the United Nations shortly thereafter authorized the United States to lead a U.N. force in defense of the South. Ethiopia, backed by the Emperor's consciousness of collective security responsibilities, responded with troops. Ethiopian units fought beside ours in one of the most significant contributions from any Afro-Asian country.

The close cooperation was further signaled on May 22, 1953, when two agreements were signed between the United States and Ethiopia. One permitted the use by the United States until 1978 of communications facilities at Kagnew Station in Asmara.

The second governed the provision of grant military assistance and training to the Ethiopian forces.

These agreements are a matter of public record.

In the 1950's, also, the march of African countries toward independence began. In the view of many, Africa hung in the balance during those years. European nations, no longer content to bear the burden of colonial rule, and under increasing world pressure to relinquish control, accelerated the pace of independence. The Soviets watched from the sidelines, expecting to have a place of particular influence in the post-independence world. Skeptics in Europe doubted Africans could manage their affairs. Extremists in Africa projected plans and issued slogans beyond reality.

Ethiopia's Contribution to a Unified Africa

During this critical period, the prestige and the voice of the Emperor was of critical value in guiding the new nations into responsible nationhood and into communication with one another. All nations, including our own, who sought stability and cohesion in the nations of Africa and who sought to insulate Africa from the wider world struggle, owe him a debt.

Quick to perceive the great desire of the Africans for a symbol of their unity, yet conscious of the unreality of many proposals, he worked with great skill and diligence to bring into being the Organization of African Unity. Addis Ababa became its headquarters.

We may not be in full agreement at all times with the actions and policies of the Organization of African Unity. We have on numerous occasions, however, expressed our support for the generally stabilizing and constructive influence it has exerted on African events. Once more it is the Emperor who shares a large measure of the credit for the results.

Both as a leader in the OAU and as an individual with prestige unsurpassed in Africa, the Emperor has personally used his influence to assist the solution of critical African problems. His efforts at mediation in the border dispute between Algeria and Morocco in 1963 averted a crisis which could have had significant consequences for all states interested in the Mediterranean area. In the several years of crisis in the Congo, Ethiopia and the Emperor supported the United Nations efforts and worked directly to bring about stability in that country. Today the recovery of the Congo shows the wisdom of the Emperor's approach and the benefits of Ethiopia's contribution.

In the Nigerian civil war, the Emperor worked quietly to avert a graver crisis among African nations and to bring about peace within Nigeria, itself. His willingness to share his thoughts and counsel with us during this critical period was of great value in our own assessments of African opinion and the course of events.

To recount these various ways in which Ethiopia and the Emperor have contributed to the stability of Africa and to our own interests in Africa, is not intended to eulogize, but to place in perspective the emphasis we have put on Ethiopia in the allocation of our official resources in Africa.

Events and a commonness of interest brought us into close cooperation with Ethiopia. These factors, also, inevitably brought us into direct contact with some of Ethiopia's own problems.

Ethiopia's Own Problems

Ethiopia is a country of more than 40 different ethnic groups. Two of the groups, the Amharas and the Tigres, have dominated in the governing of Ethiopia. The Emperor's rule is highly personal, but from its first days he has recognized the need to develop more modern institutions of government. Recently his efforts have begun to bear fruit. In such a land, it is not surprising that there are pressures from within for greater autonomy for the ethnic groups and for modernization of society and government.

Ethiopia is a poor land. Illiteracy is widespread (95 percent); the general health of the people is poor (malaria alone reduces the effectiveness of the labor force by 25 percent); the standard of living is low (gross national product is $64 per year per person); the impact of scientific and modern ways is a disrupting element in a traditional society; there is a paucity of reliable information concerning the country's true resources.

Two adjacent former Italian colonies present special problems.

U.S. Military Assistance to Ethiopia

Between 1953 and 1960 we began the provision of grant military assistance under the agreement previously mentioned. A military assistance advisory group was established in 1953. During these years we assumed the responsibility for equipping three Ethiopian divisions of 6,000 men each.

In 1960, the Somali Republic was formed out of the former British and Italian Somalilands. There were determined voices calling for the unity of all Somalis, including the large number who graze in Ethiopia's Ogaden.

[Deleted.] The government turned to us for further help. [Deleted.] They requested an increase in equipment for each division to support 8,000 men and equipment for a fourth division. After extensive discussions, we agreed to provide the equipment [deleted] for a fourth Ethiopian Army division.

[Deleted.]

Through the years, since——

Threat to Ethiopia

Senator Symington: What was the danger involved there?

Mr. Newsom: The Somali Republic, Mr. Chairman, came into independence claiming or calling for the reunion of what it considered all Somali territory, part of which was in the Ogaden Province of Ethiopia, [deleted].

Senator Symington: This was former British and Italian land.

Mr. Newsom: That is right. The southern half was an Italian colony, the northern half a British colony.

Senator Symington: How many people live there, roughly.

Mr. Newsom: Approximately two and a half million people in the Somali Republic.

Senator Symington: How many live in Ethiopia?

Mr. Newsom: Approximately 24 million.

Senator Symington: What was the size of the army of the Somali Republic, roughly?

Mr. Newsom: At the time of independence, it was quite small, but I believe, and I will check this figure, Mr. Chairman, but I believe it was around 2,000. [Deleted.] The activities of Somali nomadic tribesmen ranged far and wide within the Ogaden Province of Ethiopia.

Senator Symington: The reason for my question is, I am sure, clear to you. You give them an army of 18,000, and then we add 6,000 more, and then, apparently, add a new division that would be 14,000 more, that would be 32,000. Then, as a result of the 1960 commitment, we go up to 40,000, equip a country with 40,000 military to defend itself against a country that has 10 percent—less than 10 percent—of the same number of people.

Mr. Newsom: Since then, Mr. Chairman, the Somalis have received Soviet military equipment. Their army has been increased to about 12,000.

Senator Symington: Did this have anything to do with the differences between Eritrea and Ethiopia?

Mr. Newsom: No; that is a separate problem, Mr. Chairman.

Senator Symington: Does it have anything to do with pressures from Yemen?

Mr. Newsom: The Yemen comes into this whole question as—and I should distinguish, Mr. Chairman, between South Yemen and the regular former kingdom of Yemen, South Yemen, Aden, has been and is becoming a base for the Eritrean Liberation Movement which is supporting small bands of insurgents within the province of Eritrea. It has not become involved, so far as we know in Somalia.

Senator Symington: Did we raise the size of the army just because of Somalia, or because of additional dangers pressing on Ethiopia?

Mr. Newsom: We raised the size of the army because of the Government's concern for what they considered to be the Somali threat and also their constant concern with the security of all parts of the kingdom, including Eritrea and including also the western frontier where, however, there has been in our view less of a threat.

Senator Symington: You mean Sudan?

Mr. Newsom: Sudan; yes.

U.S. Economic Assistance to Ethiopia

Senator Symington: Ethiopia's average annual income you say is a very low figure, $64, that is a very low per capita annual income, right?

Mr. Newsom: That is; it is one of the lowest in Africa; yes.

Senator Symington: What did the Emperor do with the near quarter of a billion dollars in economic assistance we gave him?

Mr. Newsom: Well, Ethiopia has had an accelerated growth rate, and just in the last few years, the rate itself has increased to just under 5 percent per annum. We have been one of the principal suppliers of economic assistance to Ethiopia, and I think it should be added, Mr. Chairman, that Ethiopia is a country which did not have any colonial relationship other than a brief period when Italy was there, so it started with an extremely low base when it came into the modern world.

Cost of Military Assistance

Senator Symington: How much money do we give them to equip 40,000 men?

Mr. Newsom: Well, over the entire period of our military assistance to Ethiopia the figure has been about——

Mr. Bader: If you mean just to equip——

Senator Symington: No; the whole figure, counting airplanes and everything.

Mr. Bader: It is $142 million since 1953.

Mr. Newsom: Since 1955 it is $142 million.

Senator Symington: I think you will find it is $147 million, and that is only through 1969. That does not embrace what has been given in 1970. Do you know how much we have given in 1970.

Mr. Bader: $12 million.

Senator Symington: If I am right, the total is $159 million. And what does the $12 million consist of?

Mr. Bader: $12 million consist of?

I can break it down for you, Senator.

Senator Symington: Just give me a couple of the major items.

Mr. Bader: Major items, most of it goes for attrition items, vehicles, communications equipment, follow-on spare parts, and training, which is a large segment of it.

Types of Aircraft United States Has Given Ethiopia

Senator Symington: That is enough. What kind of airplanes, if any, have you given them.

Mr. Bader: We have given them [deleted] F-5's, [deleted] F-86F's, [deleted] C-52's, [deleted] C-47's, [deleted] utility aircraft, and [deleted] T-28's.

Senator Symington: What is a utility aircraft.

Mr. Bader: Such as L-19's.

Senator Symington: Have we given them any helicopters?

Mr. Bader: Yes; we have given them [deleted] helicopters.

Senator Symington: What kind?

Mr. Bader: UH-1H's.

Senator Symington: I see. Thank you, will you proceed.

Mr. Newsom: Yes, sir.

Somali Threat to Ethiopia

Through the years, since, the Government has remained concerned about the Somali threat. This concern was further aggravated by a Soviet decision to provide arms to Somalia in 1963. [Deleted.]

In 1967, the Somali Government moved toward a detente with Ethiopia. Despite the coup d'etat in Somalia in 1969, that detente has held. The Government remains concerned, however. [Deleted.]

Eritrea

Eritrea, half-Muslim, half-Christian, was placed by the United Nations in the custody of Ethiopia for 10 years, its fate to be decided after that time. In 1962 the Eritrean Parliament voted to become a Province of Ethiopia. Since that time, there has been incipient insurgency, fomented by the largely Moslem Eritrean Liberation Front. Recently the front has gained support from extremist Arab nations, and its activities have apparently increased somewhat.

[Deleted.] Ethiopian police and army units have been active in defense against the ELF or Eritrean Liberation Front. Israel provides equipment and advisors to the police. Though we have provided equipment to the army, our own MAAG group has not been involved.

Antoher area of concern is the French territory of Afars and Issas, Djibouti.

Role of Maag in Eritrea

Senator Symington: You say our own MAAG group has not been involved? Exactly what do you mean by that?

Mr. Newsom: I mean by that, Mr. Chairman, that we have not had MAAG personnel with army units operating in Eritrea. We have had, I think, four–three, MAAG people at Asmara who have been solely concerned with the normal MAAG function of the delivery of equipment and checking on its——

Senator Symington: The MAAG doesn't do any fighting itself, just military assistance, correct?

Mr. Newsom: That is right.

Senator Symington: Thus, if you are giving them military assistance and you have MAAG people there, how can you say they have not been involved?

Mr. Newsom: They have not been involved directly in the Ethiopian activities against the ELF, Mr. Chairman.

Senator Symington: Is it standard for MAAG to be involved directly?

Mr. Newsom: No, Mr. Chairman; but this is a point we thought we might reinforce in this particular case.

Senator Symington: Then, what you are saying is that, even though MAAG is operating normally in Ethiopia by giving them assistance and helping them get the equipment and know-how to handle it, they haven't been operating abnormally because they haven't been doing any fighting, is that right?

Mr. Newsom: That is correct, Mr. Chairman.

Senator Symington: Thank you. Will you proceed?

Mr. Newsom: Another area of concern is the French territory of Afars and Issas, Djibouti. Djibouti is one of the principal ports of entry for goods to Ethiopia, being the terminal of the railroad to Addis Ababa. Its population is partly Somali, and the Somalis lay claim to it. [Deleted.]

U.S. Assurances Given to Ethiopia

Given the problems of his many peoples and the threat he sees and the insurgency in Eritrea, the Emperor has been primarily concerned with the security of his state. He has looked to us to help provide him with the tools to preserve that security.

We have no security commitment to Ethiopia. We have, at various times, given assurances of our continued interest in the security and integrity of his country and our opposition to any activities threatening the territorial integrity of Ethiopia. [Deleted.]

Senator Symington: [Deleted.] If you say you are interested in the security of Ethiopia, and its opposition to any activities threatening its integrity, don't you think the people have a right to know about these assurances? It is a commitment, isn't it?

Mr. Newsom: Well, as I was——

Senator Symington: Go ahead.

Mr. Newsom: I will seek to elaborate on that, Mr. Chairman, in the next paragraph.

Senator Symington: OK.

Mr. Newsom: In stating this we had in mind our continuing grant military assistance and the clear intention, in the event of any attack against Ethiopia, to use all our good offices in the United Nations and elsewhere to insure the maintenance of Ethiopia's integrity. In so doing, we would act to recognize not only our own direct interests in the country, but the significance to us and to all of Africa of the continued integrity of this historic land. [Deleted.]

Since 1953, the United States has provided Ethiopia about $147 million in military assistance which, from fiscal year 1953 to fiscal year 1970, has amounted to nearly half the total U.S. military assistance to all African countries, $305 million. For fiscal year 1970, military assistance for Ethiopia was $12 million and equalled almost 2/3 of the total planned for all Africa–$20.5 million. Of the 6,733 African students trained under the military assistance program between fiscal year 1963 and fiscal year 1970, 2,813 have been Ethiopians.

Military Training Program

Senator Symington: Where were they trained?

Mr. Bader: They are trained throughout the United States.

Senator Symington: How were they trained?

Mr. Bader: They are trained in various career courses, various technical courses.

Senator Symington: In the military?

Mr. Bader: In the military.

Senator Symington: Then they go back to Ethiopia after being trained here?

Mr. Bader: Yes, sir.

Senator Symington: Does that include pilots?

Mr. Bader: That includes pilots.

Senator Symington: Do you know how many were pilots?

Mr. Bader: No; I don't, Senator. The Ethiopians now have a capability of training their own pilots and are developing a source——

Senator Symington: Are we training any here at all?

Mr. Bader: At the moment, I think we probably do but I don't know how many off hand.

Senator Symington: If they can train their own pilots, they can certainly train their own ground troops, can't they?

Mr. Bader: Well, it depends, Senator, some of the specialties in the context of our service training are much better than anything they can duplicate.

Senator Symington: Wouldn't the pilot training at Maxwell Air Force Base at Montgomery, Ala., be better than training in Ethiopia?

Mr. Bader: Yes, sir.

Senator Symington: Why do we keep training them in the lesser arts and—we are not training them in nuclear warfare, are we, anything like that?

Mr. Bader: No, sir, we are not.

Senator Symington: I should think the one thing they would want would be the training of pilots if they get the planes and techniques.

Mr. Bader: One of our objectives wherever possible and as the host country capability is developed sufficiently is to start incountry training programs.

Senator Symington: Okay. Thank you.

Mr. Newsom: All right, Mr. Chairman.

U.S. Agreements with Ethiopia

A U.S. military assistance group was sent to Ethiopia in 1953. I have already referred to the 1960 commitment.

In November 1962, we agreed to supply various items of equipment for the Army, Air Force, and the Navy. [Deleted.] In September 1963, the United States agreed to provide various items of civic action equipment for the Army, two transport aircraft for the Air Force, and several vessels for the Navy. [Deleted.] Following the Soviet-Somali military aid agreement of 1963, the United States agreed in December 1964, to provide a squadron of 12 F-5 aircraft—[deleted].

These four commitments were all subject to congressional appropriation and authorization; they were specific augmentations to our ongoing military assistance program. We have delivered all the equipment identified in the latter three discussions and virtually all the basic items identified in the 1960 discussions.

Senator Symington: How much have we agreed to give them that they have not yet received?

Mr. Bader: [Deleted.]

Senator Symington: How about others?

Mr. Bader: The only other offer of equipment, specific offer, we have made is for [deleted] C-119K's [deleted] of which are already programed.

Senator Symington: When did we make that offer?

Mr. Bader: That was last summer, last July.

Senator Symington: [Deleted.] What agreement was that?

Mr. Bader: Some of the agreements, Senator, don't have specific identifications. As they are developed, guidance is sent out to the Ambassador.

Senator Symington: Who developed this guidance?

Mr. Bader: These were all interagency decisions.

Senator Symington: By State or Defense.

Mr. Bader: A combination of the two.

Senator Symington: At what level was it decided?

Mr. Bader: In the Department of Defense at the Secretary of Defense level.

Senator Symington: And in the Department of State, the Secretary of State's level?

Mr. Bader: I believe at the Secretary of State level.

Senator Symington: To the best of your knowledge, the [deleted] are all that are left that we planned or agreed to give them?

Mr. Bader: Yes, sir.

Senator Symington: Thank you.

Mr. Newsom: The last agreement came out of discussions, Mr. Chairman, which took place during the Emperor's visit here.

Senator Symington: They always do.

Mr. Newsom: Last summer.

Emperor Seeks More U.S. Assistance

Senator Symington: This is the place to come when you want to get assistance. What did he get on this trip that he just made to Moscow?

Mr. Newsom: We don't know, Mr. Chairman. [Deleted.]

Senator Symington: The custom all over the world, and I say this in complete seriousness, has been to milk us as much as you can and then when we can't be milked any further to turn to the new cow.

Therefore, I was wondering if the Emperor was dissatisfied with what we had given Ethiopia and thus was trying to get additional materiel from the Soviet Union. Do you know about that?

Mr. Newsom: We have no indication, Mr. Chairman, that he is trying to get any additional equipment from the Soviet Union at this time.

Senator Symington: Mr. Holt points out for the fiscal year 1971 planned military assistance for Ethiopia, [deleted] million, would equal almost [deleted] of all Africa—$18.6 million. For [deleted] C-119's, and [deleted] dollars there must be something added to that, isn't there.

Mr. Bader: My reference was to the C-119, Senator, you asked was there anything else we had promised.

Senator Symington: Here is a figure of $[deleted] million planned for fiscal 1971.

Mr. Bader: That is right.

C-119 Aircraft

Senator Symington: What does that consist of?

Mr. Bader: I will give you the details of that. We have, you are familiar with the generic breakdown, we normally give, proposed fiscal year 1971 for aircraft including spares is $[deleted] million. Ships including spares, and entirely spares, in this case——

Senator Symington: I can promise you one thing [deleted] C-119's are not worth $[deleted] million today.

Mr. Bader: [Deleted] C-119's [deleted] are worth $[deleted] million to MAP.

Senator Symington: That has to do with their original cost, doesn't it.

Mr. Bader: That is what it costs us to rehab them. These are the [deleted] version and what the military assistance program has to pay for a C-119 [deleted] delivered in Ethiopia.

Senator Symington: [Deleted.] If you move them the Defense Department ought to take the writeoff. [Deleted.]

Mr. Bader: [Deleted.] It has to be rehabbed, it has to be put into like new condition and the Defense Department must do that.

Senator Symington: Who does the work?

Mr. Bader: Well, the Defense Department does it or we farm it out but through our auspices.

Senator Symington: Who decides how much it is going to cost?

Mr. Bader: If it is a private commercial manufacturer that is doing it, it is negotiated.

Senator Symington: What was the original price of the C-119, do you know?

Mr. Bader: No, sir, I don't know.

Senator Symington: One of the first jobs I had was to sell those C-54's you talked about back to private enterprise and I still shudder at the price from the standpoint of the taxpayer. But this is a pretty simple matter inasmuch as they don't put up any money for these C-119's—it is just an interoffice operation, is it not?

Mr. Bader: Inter-DOD operation, yes sir, but there are normally charges for rehabilitation of the equipment.

Senator Symington: Yes.

Thank you.

Items Included in Map Program

I am still not sure what the $[deleted] million consists of.

Mr. Bader: I will continue if you would like.

Senator Symington: Yes. You mentioned the planes at $[deleted] million and that is all that you told us in addition to the $[deleted].

Mr. Bader: $[deleted] for ship spares. $[deleted] million of vehicles and weapons including spares and those mostly attrition vehicles and follow-on spares, [deleted] million dollars in ammunition. No missiles.

Senator Symington: No missiles.

Mr. Bader: No, sir. No missiles. $[Deleted] in communications equipment and including spares, $[deleted] in other equipment and supplies. $[Deleted] in repair and rehab of equipment. $[deleted] in supply operations, that is the cost to transport the equipment. $[Deleted] in technical assistance, [deleted] in training support and [deleted] million in training.

Senator Symington: That is a good summary. I would respectfully present to you that is more than $[deleted] plus [deleted] C-119's. My question was what do you do beyond 1970?

Mr. Bader: I am sorry, I misunderstood your question, Senator. This continues to be an on-going program.

Senator Symington: That is all right.

Mr. Secretary: would you say that this is, in effect, payment of rent in order to keep this unit going [deleted.]

Mr. Newsom: [Deleted.] We have always considered, [deleted,] that the general importance to us of the Emperor, of the key position of Ethiopia, the need to keep it friendly in the total African context were justification for our programs in Ethiopia.

Soviet Aid to Somalia and Ethiopia

Senator Symington: I heard the Emperor was pretty critical of the Cambodian venture. This is your part of the world. Why was that—if we are doing so much for him?

Mr. Newsom: Well, Mr. Chairman, until we have fuller information on the Emperor's talks with the Soviets, I really am not sure I can say what may have motivated him to participate in this communique. He has always sought to maintain a nonalined posture in world affairs.

Senator Symington: You know you always get into this chicken or egg business when it comes to military aid. Do you think that maybe one of the reasons that the Soviets began giving aid to Somalia was in response to our increase of aid to Ethiopia.

Mr. Newsom: No, Mr. Chairman. The Somalis were casting about for military assistance from the day that they became independent. [Deleted.]

Senator Symington: Why didn't we give aid to Somalia, too, we give it to everybody else when they ask for it.

Mr. Newsom: [Deleted.]

Senator Symington: Was that not done at the advice of the Emperor——

Mr. Newsom: We were certainly aware of his views in reaching this decision.

Senator Symington: (continuing), when it came to Eritrea becoming consolidated into Ethiopia? Didn't you gloss over that a bit in your statement?

Mr. Newsom: [Deleted.]

Senator Symington: Reading your statement it sounded a little like the Eritreans were pleading with King Halie Selassi to take them over. That is not the way I understand the story.

Mr. Newsom: I anticipated, Mr. Chairman, that I would have an opportunity to elaborate on some aspects of my statement.

Senator Symington: Incidentally, have you a declassified statement, too?

Mr. Newsom: I understand that will be worked out.

Senator Symington: Generally when we have witnesses who come up in other committees I am on, they have a classified and declassified statement. Would you see that we get a declassified statement as soon as possible?

Mr. Newsom: Yes, Mr. Chairman.

Eritrean Liberation Movement

Senator Symington: I heard in the Middle East that this Eritrean Government in absentia in Syria was a pretty effective working group. Would you care to comment on that?

Mr. Newsom: Yes.

Mr. Chairman, the Eritrean Liberation Movement, which began with the amalgamation of two political organizations which were active during the British military occupation of Eritrea, has been an incipient insurgency force in Eritrea for a number of years.

It has become more active in the last few years and it has gained some support, both in terms of supplies and equipment and in terms of propaganda—I was describing the background and support for the Eritrean Liberation Movement, Senator.

The more extremist Arab States, Syria and Iraq particularly, working through the Republic of South Yemen, have provided support to the Eritrean Liberation Movement.

[Deleted.]

In addition, there has been on the ground in Eritrea an increase in activities largely by small bands, or bands of somewhere between 50 and 100 men, that has been operating largely in the northern part of the province.

Senator Symington: Do they operate under the direction of the people in Syria?

Mr. Newsom: The headquarters of this movement are actually in [deleted] different places, and I am not sure that we know precisely where the main direction is from. [Deleted.]

Plans for Future Military Assistance

Senator Symington: Now, summing up, as I understand it, you had the 1960, 1962, 1963, and 1964 agreements, each of which has resulted in more militlary aid of some sort to the Emperor. Also last summer there was an agreement [deleted].

Mr. Newsom: [Deleted.]

Senator Symington: The total is $375 million that we have given—all except $40 million has been given since 1961.

Mr. Bader: Were you referring to military assistance, Senator?

Senator Symington: Military and economic. The military is $147 million plus the [deleted] you say that is now planned, that is [deleted].

Mr. Bader: Yes, sir.

Senator Symington: Do you plan to give more military aid to Ethiopia?

Mr. Bader: Expecting to?

Senator Symington: Yes.

Mr. Bader: We are expecting to.

Senator Symington: Of what type and character?

Mr. Bader: Essentially the same as the last.

Senator Symington: Planes, ammunition.

Mr. Bader: No, sir: essentially a force maintenance program, excepting the C-119s. By that I mean cost to support the attrition replacements and spare parts of weapons and vehicles already provided.

*   *   *

U.S. Treaties with Ethiopia

Senator Fulbright: What treaties do we have, these agreements that we are talking about, are they just informal executive agreements?

Mr. Newsom: They are executive agreements.

Senator Fulbright: Do we have any treaties with Ethiopia?

Mr. Newsom: They are not treaties.

Mr. Bader: Do you have any treaties with Ethiopia?

Mr. Newsom: We have three treaties. We have a Treaty of Arbitration (entered into force August 5, 1929), a Treaty of Conciliation (entered into force August 5, 1929), and a Treaty of Amity and Economic Relations (entered into force October 8, 1953).

Senator Fulbright: Are any of them used as a justification for any of these expenditures?

Mr. Newsom: They are not, Mr. Chairman.

Senator Fulbright: None of these agreements have been submitted to the Senate for even its information, have they, at the time they were made?

Mr. Newsom: The agreements have been mentioned each year in the presentation of the military assistance.

Senator Fulbright: Appropriations.

Mr. Newsom: Appropriations and authorizations.

Senator Fulbright: To the Appropriations Committee. They are not specifically authorized in the authorization for this purpose but you tell the Appropriations Committee what it is for.

Mr. Newsom: I believe we also make the same presentation to the Foreign Relations Committee.

Agreement Was Not Submitted to Congress in 1960

Senator Fulbright: I don't want to delay it. Does the record show the nature of these agreements? Were they written; how were they effected, by a conversation or an exchange of notes?

Senator Symington: Will you detail that now?

Mr. Newsom: Yes; all right. We have provided the most significant agreement on a piece of paper, Mr. Chairman, to the subcommittee. [Deleted.]

Senator Symington: Did you give it to the committee in 1960?

Mr. Newsom: I don't believe so, Mr. Chairman.

Senator Symington: Do we have a copy of it this morning?

Mr. Paul: I saw it on May 18, and it was left with me on Saturday.

Senator Fulbright: What I am getting at is the procedure, not the substance.

Mr. Newsom: It made note in the paper that any equipment furnished under this would be subject to congressional authorization.

Senator Fulbright: All you mean there is that in a general appropriation of money, it doesn't specify it was for this purpose, just if money is made available out of which you make take it; is that the correct procedure?

Mr. Newsom: That is correct, Mr. Chairman.

Senator Fulbright: [Deleted] was that made available to this committee in 1960?

Mr. Newsom: Not so far as I know.

Senator Fulbright: Why is it classified?

Mr. Newsom: [Deleted.]

Senator Fulbright: So classified that the Congress should not be informed about it.

Mr. Newsom: The Congress was informed——

Senator Fulbright. How?

Mr. Newsom (continuing): of the various agreements to supply which were mentioned in this communication.

Senator Fulbright: But the communication was not conveyed to this committee or to the Congress.

Mr. Newsom: So far as I know.

Senator Fulbright: It was not.

Mr. Newsom: It was not.

Senator Fulbright: And this is true of all of them that you have mentioned.

Extent of Congress' Knowledge of Other Agreements

Mr. Newsom: The others are letters from officials of the Defense Department to the officials of the Ministry of Defense in Ethiopia, is that not correct?

Mr. Bader: That is correct.

Senator Fulbright: Have all of these letters not been made available to the committee?

Mr. Bader: No, sir, I don't believe they have.

Senator Fulbright: Shouldn't they be made available?

Mr. Bader: I would have to discuss it with my superiors.

Senator Fulbright: With whom?

Mr. Bader: And with our legal people. I think that there was no multiyear funding involved.

Senator Fulbright: What I would like to get on the record as clearly as we can is what the attitude of the Department is with regard to the Congress' role in this matter. I mean is it your attitude that these agreements are such that we are not entitled to know them.

Mr. Bader: No, sir, it certainly isn't. I think the record will show that during the appropriation hearings the 1960 commitment, for example, has been discussed periodically, I think every year, with the committees.

Senator Fulbright: Well, now, be specific, you mean with just the Appropriation Committee.

Mr. Knauer: No, also this committee.

Mr. Bader: No, also the authorization.

Senator Fulbright: Do they really know what was involved here?

Mr. Bader: Well, I think——

Senator Fulbright: Are you sure?

Mr. Bader: On several of the testimonies, the interrogations that I have gone through in the hearings, certain questions have been asked in the give-and-take on that.

Senator Fulbright: Before this committee?

Mr. Knaur: Excuse me, may I interpose something, that it has always, in our formal presentation statement before this committee where the Secretary of Defense testifies, as long as I have been involved with the military assistance and the Congress, the 1960 agreement has been mentioned in the Secretary of Defense's presentation.

Senator Fulbright: It has been mentioned. The exact detail of it has not been presented to this committee.

Mr. Knaur: It has not been presented.

Senator Fulbright: It has never been presented or completely identified in any of the hearings.

Mr. Knaur: Not during the MAP hearings; no, sir.

Senator Fulbright: Well, that is all you can testify to. The truth of the matter is you concealed the detail of these agreements throughout the years, and you have never allowed this committee to know what they are; is that not true?

Mr. Bader: No, sir; that certainly is not true.

Senator Fulbright: I think it is true.

Mr. Bader: I can refer to the congressional presentation document that we give the Congress each year.

Senator Fulbright: What?

Mr. Bader: I refer to the congressional presentation document that we give to the Congress each year where year after year we refer to the 1960 commitment.

Senator Fulbright: But without telling them what the 1960 commitment was, or as the [deleted] agreement as it has come to our attention. You refer to it, but do not give any details of it.

Mr. Bader: No, sir; that is not correct. For example, looking at the 1969 presentation, the program is explained by saying what we intended to do toward completing the 1960 commitment toward equipping a 40,000-man army, and I think, historically, this runs through these presentations.

Senator Fulbright: I don't think I have ever seen in the record the 1960 agreement itself, [deleted]. What I have here, I am told, is just a summary of a memorandum left with the Emperor.

Mr. Newsom: You have the text of the memorandum left with the Emperor. It represents——

Senator Fulbright: It is not a summary.

Mr. Newsom. No, not a summary. [Deleted.]

Senator Fulbright: Maybe I am not making it clear. Is there any reason why all of these agreements and the extent of them should not be made a part of this record and be made public.

Mr. Newsom: [Deleted.]

Public Knowledge of Commitments

Senator Fulbright: This whole series of hearings are for the purpose of trying to inform not only the Senate but the public about the extent of our involvement in these innumerable countries abroad. We can tell nobody, and I don't think you have any long-range justification for doing this especially in view of our economic situation. How can you justify the public not knowing how their money is being spent?

Mr. Newsom: The public is aware——

Senator Fulbright: No, they are not.

Mr. Newsom: Of the key points of this agreement.

Senator Fulbright: I don't think the public has the slightest idea how our money is being dissipated all around the world. They would have revolted long ago, as this committee would have. Senator Symington's inquiry—and this is the first time we have had one—not just about Ethiopia but in many places—has indicated that there has been a very artful, in-depth concealment of what we are doing.

You go to the Appropriations Committee, and in order to get the money, you tell them about these commitments, but the commitments themselves were never made public. In the Appropriations Committee all you have to do is convince a few people that this is necessary for the military, isn't that true?

Mr. Newsom: Well, Mr. Chairman, I would draw a distinction between making public precise documents which we exchange in confidence with foreign heads of state and through diplomatic channels. We feel there is certainly a great sensitivity among heads of state about our releasing private communications we give to them or that they give to us.

Senator Fulbright: But I am speaking here from the point of view of the American public. Whatever a foreign government thinks about these, that is determinative and whether we should know about it is up to the foreign government not the Congress or our own Government, that is your attitude, isn't it?

Mr. Newsom: Well, what I was suggesting, Mr. Chairman, is that you were asking about a precise document [deleted].

Senator Fulbright: Why not?

Mr. Newsom: We have made public the fact that we have committed ourselves to support and supply equipment for the 40,000 man Ethiopian army subject to the availability of funds through congressional action; that we were going to lend them a naval vessel, that we were going to help them with their university, that we were going to initiate a police program, all of these things which are the key points of this document.

Senator Fulbright: You told to the Appropriations Committee.

Mr. Newsom: We told to the Appropriations Committee and the Senate Foreign Relations Committee.

Senator Fulbright: I don't believe the latter part of that.

Mr. Newsom: In the context of authorization.

Senator Fulbright: Would you mind looking up just where and what you told this committee on the details of these agreements?

Mr. Newsom: It is in the presentation document.

Senator Fulbright: I don't think the presentation documents are complete on this point.

Mr. Bader: As far back as fiscal year 1962, which you happen to have in front of you, the statement was made in that document as well.

Senator Fulbright: And you have always said that this is highly secret and it couldn't be published. You determined whether it should be published or not, haven't you?

Mr. Newsom: I have——

Senator Fulbright: You still do; that is your attitude that this should not be known. The public shouldn't know; we can't be trusted, [deleted].

Mr. Newsom: Are we talking, Senator, about the document or the elements?

Senator Fulbright: The document, the essence of the agreement is what I mean.

Mr. Newsom: Well, I think that, am I not correct that the size of the——

Mr. Bader: The size of the force is probably public but what we are doing regarding the details of this 40,000-man commitment, no, that is not public.

Mr. Newsom: It has also been our policy to respect the desire of foreign states to whom we are supplying military equipment not to give out publicly the details of what we are supplying to their military forces. Broad commitments we have made public but the details we have not.

Senator Fulbright: Because the Ethiopian Government doesn't want it made public.

Mr. Newsom: Yes.

Reconditioned Yacht Given to Ethiopia

Senator Fulbright: I understand that. So it is a very broad general statement.

The only thing I have been aware of really of any significance was that we had this communication facility that our government said was necessary for our world-wide communications from Ethiopia [deleted] the main justification for putting the money into it. There was considerable objection on that ground. Also when you gave him a reconditioned Navy ship as a yacht, I think it was $3 or $4 million, which was for his private use primarily; wasn't it?

Mr. Bader: No, sir; it was not and is not.

Senator Fulbright: What is it for?

Mr. Bader: It is a training ship, it is a former U.S. Navy ship.

Senator Fulbright: That is right. I remember that.

Mr. Newsom: The gold wallpaper, Mr. Chairman, was at a cost of $120.

Mr. Bader: $120, commercial wallpaper.

Senator Fulbright: What did the yacht cost?

Mr. Bader: To really have it reconditioned was about $3½ million.

Senator Fulbright: That is what I remember, about $3 million. They have a very poor navy.

Mr. Bader: They have 95 footers and 40 footers and have the coastal patrol vessels.

Procedure for Reviewing Commitments

Senator Fulbright: Obviously aside from the waste of money, it is the procedure I object to. I don't support the idea that these are all secret agreements and we can dissipate our money around the world without the public knowing it. If we as a government are entitled to do it, I believe the American people are entitled to know it even if the Emperor doesn't like it.

Mr. Newsom: It has always been my understanding, Mr. Chairman, that the full details of our military assistance to Ethiopia and other countries is reviewed in the authorizations and appropriation process.

Senator Fulbright: Your understanding is incorrect. But because our circumstances today are so serious, I don't think we can, as far as I am concerned, tolerate keeping it secret any longer. What happens is we are unable to get the votes on these matters because we are not at liberty to explain what the programs are about. We have gone along, I think mistakenly, accepting your pleas about keeping it secret, and now we find ourselves in a very serious situation.

Mr. Bader: Senator, the entire program isn't secret. Certainly after the budget year has gone by the total value is declassified and so the public knows the amount of money that the U.S. Government is putting in military assistance each year to Ethiopia.

Senator Fulbright: The basis for what we put in there has not been clear at all, I don't think.

Mr. Bader: I thought that had been clear.

U.S. Economic Condition Related to International Policies

Senator Fulbright: I don't understand really why you think it ought to continue in view of our circumstances here at home. Doesn't the way our economy is doing and the internal turmoil impress you? Hasn't this caused you any questions about the wisdom of our former policies. Doesn't the State Department feel any responsibility for our domestic affairs or the economic situation in the country. I understand they are coming up asking for an $18 billion increase in the national debt. Doesn't this shake you a bit?

Mr. Newsom: We are all taxpayers, Mr. Chairman, and we are all similarly concerned. We also in that context are trying to present what we consider to be the national interest involved in another part of the world, and to put before this committee the bases on which we have over the years taken action with respect to Ethiopia, and it may well be in retrospect differences of views on how this may have been done, and the wisdom of doing it. But we feel, as I have tried to point out in my statement, that we have gained an important point of view in Africa, we have gained the use of a facility.

Admittedly any such relationship is a continuing negotiation between our limitations and our requirements and the particular outlook of the foreign state, and we have tried to keep it within the bounds to the extent possible.

Strategic Significance of Wheelus

Senator Fulbright: With the giving up of Wheelus and so on, isn't the importance of this communications center greatly lessened?

Mr. Newsom: There is really no relationship, Mr. Chairman, between Wheelus and Kagnew. Wheelus was a training base for the U.S. Air Force in Europe. It had no strategic value. It was primarily for squadrons to come down from Europe for gunnery, bombing practice on a range south of Wheelus. With the loss of Wheelus this training must still continue. It has been distributed to various other bases in Europe. [Deleted.]

Senator Fulbright: It is the first time I have heard Wheelus had no strategic significance. However, I was under the impression that it used to be a strategic base versus Russia. It never was?

Mr. Newsom: In the early years, I think it had a SAC function, but I have been dealing with Wheelus for the last several years, Mr. Chairman, in one capacity or another, and it had no strategic importance.

Ethiopian Forces in Korea and the Congo

Senator Fulbright: Did you say you considered Ethiopia an ally of this country?

Mr. Newsom: It has on two occasions sent its forces to participate in actions which were parallel with our own objectives at the time, once in Korea and once in the United Nations efforts in the Congo. It is not an ally in the sense that it is involved in any treaty arrangement or collective security organization.

Senator Fulbright: You used the word "ally" very loosely there. It is not an ally, as you say under any treaty obligation.

Mr. Newsom: That is right.

Senator Fulbright: Just that they are friends. How many did they send to Korea?

Mr. Newsom: 3,200, I believe.

Mr. Bader: 3,000.

Senator Fulbright: Combat troops?

Mr. Newsom: Combat troops. It is my understanding from American officers who served with them that they were very effective combat units.

Senator Fulbright: Were they? Did we pay all their allowances when they went there?

Mr. Bader: No, sir, we didn't.

Senator Fulbright: We equipped them and transported them.

Mr. Bader: I would assume so, but I don't know.

Senator Fulbright: We didn't pay, directly, their pay?

Mr. Bader: Not to my knowledge.

Senator Fulbright: But we were giving economic aid to the government at the same time.

Mr. Bader: Not in 1950.

Senator Fulbright: We weren't giving them aid?

Mr. Bader: We certainly weren't giving military assistance other than what they received in Korea.

Senator Fulbright: Were we giving any economic aid?

Mr. Newsom: We didn't have authorization for economic assistance until, I believe, 1954.

Commitments Call for Influence in the U.N., not U.S. Forces

Senator Fulbright: [Deleted.] You said in 1960 and thereafter we had affirmed the continuing interest of the U.S. Government in the security of the Ethiopian Government and its opposition to any activities threatening the territorial integrity of Ethiopia. Is that the [deleted] language of the agreement?

Mr. Newsom: That is an oral statement which was made by the Ambassador [deleted].

Senator Fulbright: What was his authority to make that kind of a statement? What do you base it on?

Mr. Newsom: [Deleted.]

He made this under instructions from the Secretary of State at the time, and as I point out in my statement, Mr. Chairman, the implication of this we have always understood to mean a readiness to use our good offices in the United Nations, in the event of an attack on Ethiopia. Because of the clear limitations on this constitutionally there was no implication in here of any commitment to defend Ethiopia with American forces.

Senator Fulbright: It could be read that way, if you could call them an ally. It doesn't say just use our good influence, or good will in the United Nations; "the security of Ethiopia and its opposition to any activities threatening the territorial integrity of Ethiopia" it seems to me goes much farther than saying a good word in the United Nations. Wouldn't you agree?

Mr. Newsom: To the extent we have ever been asked for clarification this is what we would have replied.

Release of Documents to the Committee

Senator Fulbright: Let me come back; I don't want to leave the record, although it is difficult to make it too precise. If you have not done so, will you supply to this committee exact copies of all these agreements, whether you call them aide memoires, memorandums or agreements with any nation, can you do that or not.

Mr. Newsom: We have supplied this one.

Senator Fulbright: All of them.

Mr. Newsom: Some are Defense Department documents.

Senator Fulbright: All that the State Department is responsible for.

Mr. Newsom: This key document that has been referred to over the years as the 1960 or [deleted] commitment we have supplied.

(The information referred to follows:)

1960 U.S. Commitment to Ethiopia

The precise substance of the 1960 commitment is as follows

Indicative of the deep and continuing interest of the United States in the welfare and progress of Ethiopia, the following are the responses of the United States Government to certain requests previously made by the Ethiopian Government, subject of course in each case to the action of the United States Congress in making available to the Executive Department the funds involved, and upon the mutual development of the usual detailed arrangements for implementation of the proposed projects:

1. The United States agrees to provide, in the current fiscal year, certain training, equipment and support for a fourth division of the Imperial Ethiopian Army.

2. The United States agrees to commence discussions with a view to reaching mutual agreement regarding modification of the existing Military Assistance Program to take into account the training and equipment of the fourth division and of such support units as may be mutually agreed upon.

3. The United States will provide to the Imperial Ethiopian Navy, on a loan basis, a seaplane tender (AVP) for use as a training ship and will provide training in the United States for the necessary officers and crew.

4. The United States agrees to study the needs of the Imperial Ethiopian Police with a view to seeing whether the United States is in a position to meet a part of them.

5. The United States is prepared to implement immediately the first stage in the establishment of the Haile Selassie I University, in general accordance with the recommendations of the University of Utah team headed by Dr. Bentley.

6. The United States is prepared to provide, through the Development Loan Fund acting in cooperation with the International Bank for Reconstruction and Development and subject to agreement on loan terms financing for two road sectors of the Third Highway Program plus additional highway equipment.

7. The United States is prepared to provide up to US $1.5 million in special assistance and to continue technical assistance in the current US fiscal year at approximately the present level for agreed projects and programs.

The United States Government also reaffirmed its continuing interest in the security of Ethiopia and its opposition to any activities threatening the territorial integrity of Ethiopia.

The United States Government announced its great interest in obtaining agreement to the extension of the facilities presently operated by the United States Government at Kagnew Station in Asmara.

Senator Fulbright: And all subsequent exchanges referring to it. I want a record, if I can get it, of what the State Department has said, whether it is done informally or in the nature of memorandums. I don't want to overlook it by leaving the record vague. I want to know whether you will or won't and then if you won't, I want to take it up with the Secretary. That is what I want.

Mr. Newsom: Yes, Mr. Chairman, I am just asking one question for clarification.

[Deleted.]

The other documents referred to are all letters specifying ongoing programed agreements, what we will supply——

Senator Fulbright: Letters from whom?

Mr. Newsom: From the Secretary of Defense in most cases, or the Assistant.

Mr. Bader: Assistant Secretary, Deputy Secretary.

Mr. Newsom: And we agreed, before you came in, Mr. Bader would take up with the Defense Department the release of these documents.

Senator Fulbright: All of them?

Mr. Newsom: All of those that are referred to here.

Senator Fulbright: Well, I would like all of them that aren't referred to. Have you got any that we don't know anything about?

Mr. Bader: I don't think we have anything that you don't know about, Senator.

Senator Fulbright: I believe you do. Do you have any agreements with regard to supplying Ethiopia money or arms or so on that we don't know about? I am just trying to make these inquiries as all inclusive as I can so that you can't say I didn't ask you about them. We have had some experiences lately in which we overlooked asking whether we were going into Cambodia or not and then we were later told: "Well, you didn't ask us that question." I am trying to ask about all of them.

Mr. Bader: I think our two departments will have to consult on what we do.

Mr. Newsom: I would like to say, Mr. Chairman, what we tried to do in preparing for this session today is to pinpoint those agreements which have represented significant and substantial augmentations of our ongoing program. There are in a program of this size—there are a very large volume of communications between the two governments over the implementation of the program and the discussions of whether there will be 10 trucks or 20 trucks or this sort of thing. These which we have pinpointed represent the major augmentations to an ongoing program. As I said, we will seek to get authority for its release of these to the committee.

Senator Fulbright: Well, of course, I hope you will release them. If you don't release them I would like a memorandum saying why you don't release them. I am trying to establish what is the policy and attitude of the department toward this commitment and the role of the Senate in this matter; whether you believe that these are not proper for our surveillance, that you think we are not entitled to them. This is what I am trying to get at.

Mr. Newsom: I fully understand the purpose of the committee.

Senator Fulbright: And if you make them available to me, fine. If you do not, I would like a very clear memorandum as to why you are not, and you will be governed by it in the future.

Mr. Newsom: That is understood, Mr. Chairman.

Senator Fulbright: About the Defense Department's attitude, will you do the same with the Defense Department?

Mr. Bader: Yes.

Senator Fulbright: Is the 1964 commitment a military commitment part of the State Department?

Mr. Bader: You are correct; it is part of the State Department.

Senator Fulbright: Then isn't it available from the State Department? They ought to be more responsive than the Defense Department.

Mr. Bader: No, sir; that is why I said we would consult the two agencies when we get back and make a review of all the documentation and subject to appropriation-authorization we will make available what we can to the committee.

Senator Fulbright: Can you do it fairly soon? This has become a rather critical matter when for the first time in the 27 years I have been in the Congress, the State Department says, "We are instructed not to answer your questions even in executive session." Are you familiar with that policy?

Mr. Newsom: I am familiar with that.

Senator Fulbright: Isn't this a new policy?

Mr. Newsom: I don't know, Mr. Chairman. This is the first time I have been involved in this particular——

Senator Fulbright: It is the first time I have too, and this is what I am trying to——

Mr. Newsom: We share this together.

Senator Fulbright: We are trying to establish our relations on an understandable basis.

Then you will also give us an answer about the other agreement.

Mr. Newsom: Right.

(The information referred to follows:)

United States-Ethiopian Agreements of 1962, 1963, and 1964

The 1962, 1963 and 1964 agreements between the U.S. and Ethiopia concerned deliveries of equipment to the extent funds would be available under the on-going U.S. military assistance program to Ethiopia. Deliveries to Ethiopia of equipment identified under these three agreements have all been completed. The substance of these agreements is as follows:

1962 Agreement–In a memorandum signed in 1962, the U.S. Government agreed to provide certain items of equipment for the Ethiopian Army, Air Force, and Navy. The Army items generally were contained in the 1960 commitment and hence this agreement was simply to speed up delivery of these items. The Army items provided were ammunition, armored personnel carriers, and corrugated roofing material. The Air Force portion of the agreement was to provide T-28D, F-86, and T-33 aircraft and to continue support of the T-28A and F-86 squadrons. The Navy portion of the commitment was to provide one LCM.

1963 Agreement–In a memorandum signed in 1963, the U.S. Government agreed to provide various items of civic action equipment e.g. woodworking shop equipment, road graders, D-7 bulldozers, road scrapers. scoop loaders, and well-drilling equipment. For the Navy, armed 40-foot Coast Guard utility boats (Sewart Cruisers) were provided. It was also agreed to discuss the organization of the Ethiopian Air Force and Navy.

1964 Agreement–In a message dated 18 June 1964, the U.S. Government authorized the Ambassador to inform the Emperor of Ethiopia that we would provide a squadron of 12 F-5 aircraft to the Ethiopian Air Force. Deliveries of the aircraft were conditioned upon the preparedness of the Ethiopian Air Force to receive them.

Policy with Regard to Internal Insurrection

Senator Fulbright: Wasn't there a threat of an internal insurgency against the Emperor not too long ago?

Mr. Newsom: In 1960 and then there were rumors of one——

Senator Fulbright: What is your policy about a threatened internal insurrection of any kind?

Mr. Newsom: Well, we have established it as a policy, and it is a policy, that I think we would try to do our very best to maintain, to not interfere in the internal affairs of Ethiopia. We recognize the Emperor as the legitimate government of Ethiopia [deleted].

Senator Fulbright: This question arose, you know, in the case of Spain. We had joint exercises with the Spanish Armed Forces on a scenario based upon an insurrection. Are you familiar with it?

Mr. Newsom: I am familiar with it. We have had none in Ethiopia.

Senator Fulbright: Are there any contingency plans that you know of to deal with insurgency in Ethiopia?

Mr. Bader: There are always contingency plans, Senator, especially with a country with as many American citizens. I can't add anything further than that.

Senator Fulbright: How many American citizens do we have in Ethiopia.

Mr. Bader: We have about 6,000.

Senator Fulbright: That is including those at Kagnew?

Mr. Bader: That is including those at Kagnew. We have about 3,200 in the Kagnew family and about 2,800 others.

Senator Fulbright: So we would feel free to intervene to protect the lives of our——

Mr. Bader: No, sir; I didn't say that.

Senator Fulbright: I thought that was the implication of what you said. What did you mean? We would not?

Mr. Bader: What I said is that in any country of that size with that many American people there are always contingency evacuation plans, but this does not imply we would intervene militarily.

Senator Fulbright: Is that the Emperor's understanding so far as you know that we would not come to his rescue if there was an international insurgency?

Mr. Bader: He has never had any reason to assume otherwise, but I know of no discussion about it.

Senator Fulbright: There has been no discussion with the Emperor about it?

Mr. Bader: I know of none.

Senator Fulbright: Do you know of any?

Mr. Newsom: I know of none.

Senator Fulbright: I think our policy in Ethiopia is no different from our policy in Spain as to what our commitments are. Since the executive branch is taking this informal role, it is hard for us to participate. There was no treaty with Spain, but they proceeded to execute, under Secretary Rusk's direction, an agreement which results in American troops being in Spain. Then our Chief of Staff tells the Spanish military leaders our military presence can be characterized as being more binding and more reassuring than a treaty. Is that not correct?

Mr. Newsom: Not in the case of Ethiopia.

Senator Fulbright: No, Spain.

Mr. Newsom: Well, I am not qualified.

Senator Fulbright: I was wondering if you had a similar thing in Ethiopia.

Mr. Newsom: We have done no joint contingency planning with Ethiopians or anything of that kind.

Senator Fulbright: You have no plans to support the Emperor in case of an insurrection?

Mr. Newsom: As I said, this has not been discussed with him, and what we would do in the case of an insurrection would depend on a number of circumstances hard to predict in advance.

Senator Fulbright: Well, this language in the assurances of continual interest seems to me to be subject to the interpretation that we will come to the aid of the Emperor. And I would ask you again to consider making this text part of the public record so that we can give due consideration to it.

Mr. Newsom: [Deleted.]

Periodic Cincstrike Meetings with the Emperor

Senator Fulbright: I am told that the commanding general of CINCSTRIKE meets annually with the Emperor. Do you know about that?

Mr. Newsom: Yes; he has the responsibility for the supervision of the military assistance program in Ethiopia.

Senator Fulbright: Does he confer with the Emperor annually?

Mr. Bader: Not necessarily on an annual basis. He has met and discussed.

Senator Fulbright: More frequently perhaps, at least on an annual basis?

Mr. Bader: It is periodic.

Senator Fulbright: And do you get reports in the State Department about the arrangements that the commanding general of CINCSTRIKE makes?

Mr. Newsom: Yes; our Ambassador always sits in on any such meetings and reports, but the commanding general's discussions are always on the operation of the program and in many cases have been helpful [deleted.]

Senator Fulbright: If there were any agreements or understandings you would know about it in the State Department.

Mr. Newsom: We would, I am sure.

Senator Fulbright: Well, proceed, Mr. Chairman.

Economic Assistance to Ethiopia

Senator Symington: Please go ahead with your statement.

Mr. Newsom: Thank you, Mr. Chairman.

Given our close relations with the Emperor, Ethiopian participation in Korea, and the significant role the Emperor plays in Africa, there is every possibility that we would provide grant assistance [deleted] .

Ethiopia's development emphasis has not been entirely military. Particularly in recent years, the Emperor has turned more and more to the problems of social development and economic improvement. We, together with other foreign donors, have played a role in encouraging this direction and supplying resources for it.

The original economic assistance agreement between the United States and Ethiopia was signed in 1951. In the initial years our efforts were directed primarily to the three fields of education, health, and transportation. We also made important contributions as well to projects in agriculture, communications, and mapping. Our program was characterized by a multiproject approach and concentrated on institution building and infrastructure. More recently we have moved in the direction of channeling our aid to the revenue producing sections of the economy. We are supporting programs which aim to assist Ethiopia to mobilizle its own resources and to expand the monetary economy. We have given Ethiopia as of the end of fiscal year 1969, $97.2 million in loans and $131.5 million in grants for these projects.

U.S. Relations after Death of Haile Selassie

Inevitably, the question arises in a country such as Ethiopia: What happens after the ruler passes from the scene?

Haile Selassie has been ruler of Ethiopia for 54 years. He is currently 78 years of age and continues to be in good health. [Deleted.]

Our presence in Ethiopia, both officially through the Government and by the presence of numerous American citizens on aid and educational projects, has put us in touch with a wide section of the Ethiopian population. While there are those who would identify our position solely with that of the Emperor, we feel this is a narrow evaluation. Our close ties with Ethiopia have every chance of surviving an orderly succession.

[Deleted.]

Of the many lands in Africa, our relations with Ethiopia have been among the closest. History, respect, and a commonness of interest have formed them that way. These relations have inevitably involved us in the affairs of a distant and complicated corner of the world. However, by emphasizing the building of Ethiopia's strength to deal with its security and economic problems, there has been no question of military involvement in the troubles of the area. We have gained important facilities and the cooperation of a significant political figure in Africa. Ethiopia has gained resources for its security and development. This is the pattern that we and the Ethiopians have sought and one which has been of benefit to both our Nations.

Thank you.

Need for a Communications Facility in this Tense Area

Senator Symington: [Deleted.]

Now, it worries me a great deal that we are sitting in the middle of a mess—you brought up Somaliland and Djibouti, and I brought up Yemen, South Yemen, and the Sudan. And then, of course, we have the absentee government of Eritrea in Syria, which brings up another problem that we have, namely, the problem today of the Middle East.

[Deleted.]

Mr. Newsom: I can understand your concern, Mr. Chairman, over the position of an American installation in the center of this area [deleted].

Senator Symington: In an interview Mr. Walter Lippmann had on his 80th birthday after he, in effect, had retired, he used the words "blue water" a good many times. It seems to me that is a very important aspect of our future. If we can get off the land masses where we run into so much nationalism, and get on the water, which is essentially an international situation, we would be in a better position.

What would your position be on that?

Mr. Newsom: [Deleted.]

Senator Symington: I am not talking about relations as much as I am about the presence of American military personnel in another country in the midst of a cauldron.

Mr. Newsom: That I can understand.

[Deleted.]

Mr. Bader: I believe I can add something about the communications function. [Deleted.]

Mr. Newsom: Mr. Bader is competent to talk about the worldwide military communications [deleted].

Senator Symington: [Deleted.]

Let us take them in order with you, sir. You start out. You represent the Defense Department, correct?

Mr. Bader: That is correct.

Senator Symington: Who do you report to in the Department of Defense?

Mr. Bader: Mr. G. Warren Nutter.

Senator Symington: For the record, what is his title?

Mr. Bader: He is the Assistant Secretary of Defense for International Security Affairs.

Senator Symington: All right.

Number of U.S. Personnel at Kagnew

Let us talk about communications. Why is it necessary for us to have 6,000 people in Ethiopia from the standpoint of communications?

Mr. Bader: Senator, they are not all related to communications at Kagnew.

Senator Symington: How many are?

Mr. Bader: We have about 3,200 people, including military, civilians and dependents at Kagnew.

Senator Symington: 3,200. Why is that essential?

Mr. Bader: Well, so far as those functions that Mr. Newsom mentioned, Department of Defense has the U.S. Army Strategic Communications Station at Kagnew. That is a primary installation of our worldwide defense communications system. Also there is an earth terminal for the Defense Satellite Communications System. It also provides a high frequency transmitter for the diplomatic telecommunication system.

Senator Symington: Couldn't you do all that from an island or from a ship?

Mr. Bader: There are other ways it could be done, if that is your question.

Senator Symington: Yes, that is my question.

I just do not like to see another Vietnam come up overnight or another Cambodia or another Laos or another Korea.

Couldn't we put those 3,200 people on communications somewhere else?

Mr. Bader: [Deleted.]

Senator Symington: I thought you said out of the 6,000, 3,200 were on communications.

Mr. Bader: No, sir. I said of the 6,000, 3,200 are at Kagnew.

Senator Symington: What do the others do there?

Mr. Newsom: May I clarify this? The 6,000 figure is the total number of American citizens in all capacities in Ethiopia; 3,200 is the total number at Kagnew.

Senator Symington: Yes. What are the other 2,800 doing?

Mr. Newsom: There are AID personnel, business people, educators.

Senator Symington: Nongovernmental people?

Mr. Newsom: Nongovernmental.

Senator Symington: Plus AID personnel. How many of the 6,000 are nongovernmental?

Mr. Newsom: Probably about 1,500.

Senator Symington: So then we cut the figure to 4,500.

Mr. Newsom: That is right.

Senator Symington: Of which 3,200 are at Kagnew?

Mr. Newsom: Yes, sir.

Senator Symington: Which is in Eritrea, right?

Mr. Newsom: Right.

Mr. Bader: Right.

Senator Symington: Near Asmara, right?

Mr. Bader: Right.

Senator Symington: How many of those people are involved in communications?

Mr. Bader: STRATCOM, which is the Strategic Communications Station, has approximately [deleted]. The next one which I have not yet mentioned is the NAVCOMSTA, Navy Communications Station, and they have about [deleted].

Senator Symington: These are all military?

Mr. Bader: These are DOD personnel.

Senator Symington: Yes.

Mr. Bader: Primarily military, but there are some civilians; yes, sir.

Senator Symington: [Deleted.]

What is 87, at the hospital?

Mr. Bader: At the hospital.

Personnel at Kagnew are Predominantly Young

Senator Symington: That is around 1800. Where are the other 900?

Mr. Bader: They are their dependents.

Senator Symington: Dependents. Generally it is 50-50 between the military and the dependents. Here it is about three-quarters military, right?

Mr. Bader: Yes. There are more unaccompanied people.

Senator Symington: Why?

Mr. Bader: I do not know any particular reason for it.

Senator Symington: There must be some reason.

Mr. Bader: They have not had children. They have not married.

Senator Symington: Do they allow noncommissioned officers to bring their families?

Mr. Bader: Yes, they do.

Senator Symington: So it is a question of money then, they could not afford it.

Mr. Bader: Not necessarily.

Senator Symington: Are they too young?

Mr. Bader: They just may not be married.

Senator Symington: Would they be draftees in the main or young volunteers?

Mr. Bader: Probably, or young volunteers, yes, technically.

Senator Symington: How many of this group are noncommissioned or in the private——

Mr. Bader: The overwhelming majority.

Senator Symington: Then it does not require great skills, that is what I was getting at, to do this.

Mr. Bader: On the contrary, it does require many great skills in some of the more technical areas, but if we are talking about the military housekeeping function by definition, not all of those jobs require great skills.

Senator Symington: How many civilians have you there that are in government but not military—I would say around 1,500, perhaps, the way you gave your figures. What do they do?

Mr. Bader: No. I said there was a total of about 1,800 DOD personnel, and of that about 100 are civilians.

Senator Symington. 100. The figures you have presented are not much over 3,000. What do the other people do there that are——

Mr. Bader: You are talking about all of Ethiopia.

Senator Symington: Right.

Mr. Bader: I was just talking about Kagnew.

Personnel in Military Advisory Group in Addis Ababa

Senator Symington: I understand, but I was talking about greater Ethiopia. In other words, have we military stations in other parts besides Eritrea?

Mr. Bader: Yes, sir. We have a military advisory group stationed in Addis.

Senator Symington: How many involved?

Mr. Bader: 101 military authorized and three civilians.

Senator Symington: How many officers are in that 101?

Mr. Bader: They are predominantly MAAG officers. I will give you a breakdown of it. We have just about half and half.

Senator Symington: What is the highest ranked officer there?

Mr. Bader: Brigadier General George McCaffrey.

Senator Symington: Has he any other generals there?

Mr. Bader: No, sir; he has not. He has colonels.

Senator Symington: How many colonels?

Mr. Bader: Offhand I could not give you that.

Senator Symington: Would you supply that for the record, how many colonels, how many majors, and how many captains.

Mr. Bader: Yes, sir.

(The information referred to follows:)

U.S. Military Assistance Group Ethiopia Officer Complement

The U.S. Military Assistance Group in Ethiopia is authorized (as of 1 July 1970) 48 officers divided by rank as follows:

Brigadier general 1
Colonel 5
Lieutenant colonel 17
Majors 21
Captains 3
Warrant officer 1

Total officers 48
Enlisted men authorized (E-5 through E-9) 53
Civilian authorized 6

Total (as of July 1, 1970) 107

Senator Symington: Do you get extra pay for serving in Ethiopia?

Mr. Bader: As Ethiopia per se, no. There are overseas allowances, and so forth, yes.

Mr. Paul: What did you say was the total number of American military personnel and DOD civilians at Kagnew?

Mr. Bader: 3,200.

Mr. Paul: Not including dependents?

Senator Symington: He said including dependents.

Mr. Bader: About 1,800 without dependents.

Senator Symington: About 1,800.

Mr. Bader: DOD personnel, of whom about 100 are civilians.

Senator Symington: Will you supply the various figures for the record, Mr. Bader, that we have been asking these questions against.

(The information referred to follows:)

U.S. Personnel At Kagnew Station (On Board) Asmara, Ethiopia (June 1, 1970)

Total DOD personnel 1,805
Dependents of DOD personnel 1,363

Total 3,168

Function of Military Advisory Group

Senator Symington: Why do we have to have 101 people as military advisors in Addis Ababa, especially as just up the road a bit we have several hundred military.

Mr. Bader: The military at Kagnew do not perform in an advisory or administrative function in the military assistance program. Their function is completely different.

Senator Symington: What do the ones in Addis Ababa do?

Mr. Bader: Well, they carry out the normal missions of the MAAG, which includes the administrative function of receipting the equipment, periodically checking into it, assisting the host country in the operations of the equipment.

Senator Symington: Do they go out as advisors with the Ethiopian Army?

Mr. Bader: Not in operational missions.

Senator Symington: They do training presumably?

Mr. Bader: They assist in training, yes. Normally, Senator, they would be training a trainer.

Location of Maag's in Ethiopia

Senator Symington: You said you have some in Addis Ababa and others around Asmara. Are there any other places where Americans are located in the country?

Mr. Bader: I said the headquarters of MAAG was in Addis. In Asmara, for example, we have three people who are associated with the military assistance program. One is with the division headquarters. The other two are with the Air Force.

Senator Symington: We have covered those two places. Are there any other places?

Mr. Bader: Yes, sir; Massawa.

Senator Symington: What do they do there?

Mr. Bader: One officer and two enlisted men. The same type of general MAAG function, periodically inspecting the equipment, making sure the Ethiopians are properly trained to operate the equipment.

Senator Symington: Is that all?

Mr. Bader: No.

Senator Symington: Where are the others?

Mr. Bader: The fourth place is Harar. Again we have two officers and one enlisted man.

Senator Symington: What do they do there?

Mr. Bader: The same as I said before.

Senator Symington: That is four places.

Mr. Bader: Yes, sir.

Senator Symington: That is all.

Military Training Program

Senator Fulbright: How many do we train?

Mr. Bader: Yes; we have——

Senator Symington: Have we brought any over?

Mr. Bader: About 3,000.

Senator Fulbright: What were they, army?

Mr. Bader: They would be from all services, but primarily army.

Senator Fulbright: Over what period?

Mr. Bader: The program dates from 1953.

Senator Fulbright: And 3,000 all together?

Mr. Bader: The exact figure, I think, is 2,813.

Senator Fulbright: What does it cost on the average to train them?

Mr. Bader: Senator, there is no average that would give a meaningful figure.

Senator Fulbright: What is the total cost of that program up to now?

Mr. Bader: Senator Symington and I had a dispute about the cost of the program, but the total cost of the training program——

Senator Symington: Excuse me, my figure was the figure used by Mr. Newsom of $147 million for military. Your figure was $142 million, so you want to get straightened out on that.

Mr. Bader: Mr. Newsom and I have a dispute on that. I will have to submit for the record the answer to your question, Senator Fulbright.

(The information referred to follows:)

Military Assistance to Ethiopia (Fiscal Years 1953-69)

The total grant military assistance provided to Ethiopia (FY 1953-69) is $141.2 million. The figure of $147.1 million shown in the *Special Report Prepared For the House Foreign Affairs Committee* statistical data presentation represents the total grant military assistance program amount $141.2 million) plus $5.9 million, the value of the USS ORCA (now HMS ETHIOPIA), which is on loan to the Ethiopians.

Senator Fulbright: I just wanted to know what the training cost was.

Mr. Bader: Total training costs?

Senator Fulbright: Yes. It is a substantial sum, is it not?

Mr. Bader: Yes, it is. If you are talking about fiscal year 1970 or 1971——

Senator Fulbright: No. You said first about 3,000 and then 2,813. What has that cost us?

Mr. Bader: I would like to submit that for the record.

Senator Fulbright: You could not estimate it now? Isn't it in the neighborhood of $10 million, $20 million, $50 million?

Mr. Bader: Unfortunately, I do not have an accumulated total, but I will supply that figure for the record.

(The information referred to follows:)

Cost of Training Ethiopian Students (Fiscal Years 1953-70)

A total of 2,813 Ethiopian military will have been trained in the United States and overseas (fiscal years 1953-70) at a total cost of approximately $6.8 million.

Senator Fulbright: You do have an estimate of what it cost to train one. There is no way we can presently estimate what that cost was?

Mr. Bader: I can give you an example of what we propose for fiscal year 1971.

Senator Fulbright: What was it?

Mr. Bader: $1.5 million.

Senator Fulbright: That would be for how many people?

Mr. Bader: That would be 141 people for fiscal year 1970.

Senator Fulbright: That is what, $10,000 each, if it is 141?

Mr. Bader: Not really, the total amount also includes costs for mobile training teams, MAAG, and command training support.

Number of People Trained Under Worldwide Program

Senator Fulbright: Do you bring them here and train them at Leavenworth?

Mr. Bader: Leavenworth is one of the facilities.

Senator Fulbright: How many will you bring over in 1971 from all sources; can you have that figure available?

Mr. Bader: Worldwide?

Senator Fulbright: Yes. I just wondered if it is 141 from Ethiopia, what is it from all countries. Is it 5,000? Do you know?

Mr. Bader: Well, it won't exceed the number of people that we bring over under civilian auspices, Senator.

Senator Fulbright: What is that figure?

Mr. Bader: In fiscal year 1971, prior to section 510 it would have been 5,778. After section 510 about 4,000.

Senator Fulbright: Is the Defense Department requesting a change in that limitation?

Mr. Bader: Not to my knowledge, Senator.

Senator Fulbright: I just wondered whether you were content with it or you planned to change it.

Somali Request for U.S. Assistance

I wonder if I could ask you a little history out of your statement about Somalia.

As I understand it, Somalia became independent about when?

Mr. Newsom: 1960.

Senator Fulbright: Did the Somalis ask the United States for military aid?

Mr. Newsom: Yes. The Somalis asked us for military aid very shortly after they became independent. They had the remnants of the Italian and the British police forces, part of which were made into the nucleus of the Somali Army.

Senator Fulbright: Did we give them aid?

Mr. Newsom: The only military assistance, I believe, that we provided was a civic action——

Mr. Bader: That is what we were contemplating.

Mr. Newsom: Yes. [Deleted.]

Senator Fulbright: We rejected their request for military aid [deleted] did we not?

Mr. Newsom: We were trying to put together a package in which we would provide a small civic action component; is that right?

Mr. Bader: That is right.

Mr. Newsom: But the bulk would be from other countries.

Senator Fulbright: But is it true to say when the Somalis became independent they did request military assistance from us, but we rejected it because of our relations with Ethiopia?

Mr. Newsom: [Deleted.]

Senator Fulbright: After that we tried to get other free world countries to give them military aid?

Mr. Newsom: That is right.

Senator Fulbright: And failed in that?

Mr. Newsom: That is right.

Senator Fulbright: Then is when the Russians came in.

Mr. Newsom: As a matter of fact, the Somalis accepted a Russian offer while we were in the process of putting together the package.

Senator Fulbright: The Russians were really the only ones who offered them this aid; weren't they?

Mr. Newsom: We were——

Senator Fulbright: Actually offered them.

Mr. Newsom: That is right.

Senator Fulbright: I just want to get the record clear.

Mr. Newsom: I am trying to recall because I was involved in that, but we never actually were able to get a proposal to them.

Senator Fulbright: So in order to understand the situation, if I do understand it, the Russians came in only after we or other non-Communist people failed to respond to their request. This has some bearing, I think, upon the way you judge their entry exactly.

Mr. Newsom: That is right.

Senator Fulbright: It is not generally presented that way in public discussions; is it?

Mr. Bader: May I add, Mr. Newsom that we had not said no in 1963 to Somali overtures. They went to the Soviet Union and came back with a $35 million arms deal.

Senator Fulbright: We had not said "Aye" either. That is all the point I am making, Mr. Newsom. After 4 years we had not said yes.

Mr. Bader: Well, the drift was definitely toward yes.

Senator Fulbright: A very slow drift, over 4 years.

Mr. Bader: We had discussions.

Mr. Newsom: Actually, the request was made in 1962 when their Prime Minister visited the United States and made the request of the President.

U.S. Supplies Weapons for Ethiopian Army

Senator Fulbright: We were giving aid to Ethiopia?

Mr. Newsom: We were giving it to Ethiopia.

Senator Fulbright: I would ask you, and you can correct me, but one of the reasons we were reluctant to give military aid to the Somalis was because, I understand, the Ethiopians, the Emperor, did not want it.

Mr. Newsom: [Deleted.]

Senator Fulbright: That is all I wanted to say.

Mr. Newsom: It should be pointed out the Soviets had made an aid offer to Ethiopia.

Senator Fulbright: Which we requested them to reject.

Mr. Newsom: Which they did reject when they agreed to the 1960 commitment.

Senator Fulbright: Is it true to say then at that time we outbid the Soviets?

Mr. Newsom: In effect, yes.

Senator Fulbright: That is what I mean.

Mr. Newsom: Yes.

Senator Fulbright. I am just trying to get a feel of the situation.

Mr. Newsom: Right.

Senator Fulbright: So we gave them a better offer.

Do we supply all the ammunition used by the Ethiopian Army, Mr. Bader?

Mr. Bader: Yes. To my knowledge, for those weapons that we have provided. They do have some other arms outside of the Army, the police forces.

Senator Fulbright: But the army we supply all weapons?

Mr. Bader: Yes, sir.

Senator Fulbright: Have they used that against their neighbors, the Somalis, or other places?

Mr. Bader: Against their neighbors? Not to my knowledge.

Senator Fulbright: How do the Ethiopians justify the need for the ammunition?

Mr. Bader: The ammunition that we provide, for example, in the fiscal year 1971 program, is that ammunition which we judged would be required to support their training.

Senator Fulbright: Training?

Mr. Bader: Yes.

Senator Fulbright: Do the Ethiopians justify the need on the ground that they have had trouble with some neighbor?

Mr. Bader: Yes.

Senator Fulbright: Haven't they had trouble in the Ogaden?

Mr. Bader: Yes; but the Ogaden belongs to Ethiopia.

Senator Fulbright: It is an internal insurgency; this is what they need it for?

Mr. Bader: There are some Somali tribesmen that inhabit it.

Senator Fulbright: Is this the justification for our supplying them ammunition?

Mr. Bader: No, sir; it is not.

U.S. Supplies Bombs to Ethiopian Air Force

Senator Fulbright: Have we supplied them with bombs for their air force?

Mr. Bader: We have supplied them with bombs for their air force; yes.

Senator Fulbright: Have we given them napalm?

Mr. Bader: We have never given them napalm.

Senator Fulbright: Have they requested it?

Mr. Bader: To my knowledge, they have never requested napalm.

Senator Fulbright: They have not.

Would we give it to them if they requested it?

Mr. Bader: No, Senator. We have a policy against providing napalm to African countries.

Use of American Weapons Against Insurgents

Senator Fulbright: [Deleted.] You said that we supplied the bombs, and they are using their aircraft against the insurgents, aren't they?

Mr. Bader: They used their aircraft in Asmara and, as you say, against insurgents. I am not entirely sure how I would define "against the insurgents." If you mean that they are shooting at the insurgents from the aircraft——

Senator Fulbright: I assume they dropped a bomb; isn't that the way they use a bomb?

Mr. Bader: They very well may, Senator. We do not keep track——

Senator Fulbright: How does this correspond with your former statements that we would not be interested in supporting the Government against an insurgency?

Mr. Bader: I did not say that.

Senator Fulbright: I thought that you had no plans to do this, or no obligation to do it.

Mr. Newsom: The question came up, Senator, in context, as I had understood it, of an insurgency against the Emperor of a major kind which resulted in a threat to the Emperor's position.

Senator Fulbright: What is this insurgency?

Mr. Newsom: This is a minor insurgency in Eritrea which is a threat to the internal security of that particular area, but which certainly does not, at this time, pose any major threat to the regime itself.

Senator Fulbright: Then would I be correct to say the policy is to supply bombs and ammunition against a minor threat to the Emperor but not against a major threat?

Mr. Newsom: The latter question has not arisen.

Senator Fulbright: Well, you make a distinction between a minor and a major one. I thought it might have had some significance. Would that be a conclusion to draw from your testimony?

Mr. Newsom: The conclusion we would draw about any involvement of our military assistance program in the major upheaval in Ethiopia would really depend upon a number of circumstances, the Emperor's position, what the request would be he might make of us, our own decision back here after appropriate consultations, the general nature of the situation within Ethiopia.

What we are talking here are exactly the kinds of incipient internal security problems which have been part of the Ethiopian scene for many years, Eritrea, and Ogaden in which the army has been used in action.

Senator Fulbright: So it is clear and fair to say that presently we are supplying bombs and ammunition which are being used by the military forces of Ethiopia against an internal insurgency; is that correct?

Mr. Bader: That is correct, that is true.

Mr. Newsom: That is correct.

*   *   *

Senator Fulbright: Who would know it?

Mr. Bader: He is not there to involve himself in the tactics or conduct of the operations of their counterinsurgency operations in Eritrea.

Senator Fulbright: We train them and advise them there as well as here; don't we?

Mr. Bader: We advise them there, and them; not necessarily at Asmara, but periodically it could be.

Senator Fulbright: Isn't, under the law, the MAAG mission, which supplies the material, required to know what the material is used for?

Mr. Bader: He is required to know that the material is used for purposes authorized by the Foreign Assistance Act.

Senator Fulbright: Then if it is used for bombing the insurgents, he is required to know it, is he not, if he does his duty?

Mr. Bader: But it is all for internal security and is undifferentiated, Senator, between training and operations. He will have no way of knowing it.

Senator Fulbright: You stretch my credibility. You mean these are small operations relative to Vietnam. When is it that big things can go unnoticed? But do you think really it would go unnoticed? They would not know they were bombing the insurgents in Ogaden, do you think it is reasonable?

Mr. Bader: Well, I think it is entirely reasonable, Senator.

Senator Fulbright: If the Ethiopians are using MAP supplied bombs and ammunition, the MAAG Mission is required to know what it is, isn't it?

Mr. Bader: How many rounds would be expended in an operational mission?

Senator Fulbright: If they are bombing an insurgency, MAAG officers are required to know that the bombs are being used for that purpose, are they not? What if they were bombing some other country; are they not supposed to know that? Can a U.S. adviser say, "Well, I didn't know; I thought they were training."

Mr. Bader: That is not what it has been authorized for.

Senator Fulbright: I was not asking you about authorization; I am asking about use.

Mr. Bader: We can ask but I do not believe the MAAG can differentiate in terms of specific quantities.

Senator Fulbright: The law requires him to know what the ammunition is used for.

Military Assistance is Authorized for Internal Security

Mr. Bader: But there is nothing wrong, Senator, with their using that ammunition for that purpose. After all, our program is authorized for and keyed to their internal security problems.

Senator Fulbright: Well, this was not clear a moment ago. I thought your testimony, the testimony of both of you, was that we are not there just to maintain this regime in power and against insurgency. I thought you said the policy has not been developed, but here we actually are——

Mr. Bader: Wasn't Mr. Newsom talking about a contingency? I thought the question was military intervention.

Senator Fulbright: Of course, this has really happened. It is going on now, and you are now supporting the Emperor against an insurgency.

Mr. Bader: And we so justified before Congress every year, and this has been stated.

Senator Fulbright: You do?

Mr. Bader: Yes, sir.

Senator Fulbright: You say this is for putting down an insurgency that is going on within a country.

Mr. Bader: Yes.

Senator Fulbright: Is this again the Appropriations Committee or this committee?

Mr. Bader: This goes to the Appropriations and Authorization Committee.

Senator Fulbright: What does it say, does it say that this may be used for training and also against insurgency?

Mr. Bader: Well, yes, and assist in the development of the Ethiopian military forces which, can maintain internal security, and our program is to maintain internal security.

U.S. Advisers Not Directly Involved in Insurgency

Senator Symington: Will you yield for just one observation? I do not think that you should think this is not pertinent to our problem. At one time, as a member of the Armed Services Committee, we were defending putting our people in South Vietnamese planes on the grounds that they were giving advice, that they were not actually participating in the fighting.

We then found out that the Vietnamese could not speak English, and the Americans could not speak Vietnamese, so the whole thing was a fraud, and unquestionably was but another step leading us into the quagmire we are in today in Indochina.

So these questions, in my opinion, are very pertinent to just what is our role. [Deleted.]

Mr. Newsom: Well, could I say something on this, Mr. Chairman? We have admittedly a very difficult question here. We have committed ourselves to equip and train the Ethiopians for forces to be used for internal security. At the same time, it has been our policy for many years to seek to avoid involvement in the internal security problems of Ethiopia. We have never put advisers down at lower units to advise them on tactics against insurgency. We have provided them with the equipment, we have taught them how to use the equipment, we have supplied them with what we thought was a reasonable amount of ammunition for the purposes of training.

The next step to move to monitor their activities against insurgents would put us into a position of involvement in their internal security affairs, which we have always sought to avoid.

There are, as a matter of fact, instructions in being to all MAAG personnel to avoid involvement in any type of Ethiopian activities against elements within the country.

Therefore, we have chosen to draw back from any adviser involvement in the kind of activities that have just been discussed.

Senator Fulbright: If you are actually supplying them with the weapons, the bombs, used against the insurgency, how do you reconcile that with the statement of policy you have just given?

Mr. Newsom: What they do with the bombs within their own country is a matter for their decision and their policy.

Senator Fulbright: As a practical, commonsense matter if we do actually do it we are identified with supporting the Government against any change.

Eritrean Problem

Let me review a minute. Wasn't Eritrea given Ethiopia only as a 10-year leasehold, so to speak?

Mr. Newsom: After 10 years there was to be a determination of its future course, and there was an action by the Eritrean Parliament calling for union with Ethiopia which [deleted].

Senator Fulbright: Is this related to the insurgency at all. Do the Eritreans think they ought to be independent of Ethiopia, at least some of them?

Mr. Newsom: There are three elements. There are those who favor union with Ethiopia, there are those who wish for more autonomy but within an Ethiopian union, and then there are the insurgents which, perhaps, number 1,500 or so, who want an independent Arab-oriented Eritrea.

Senator Fulbright: It has an Italian background, has it not?

Mr. Newsom: Yes, it has an Italian—it was an Italian colony for 80 years.

Senator Fulbright: Just like Vietnam. Don't you remember when France took Vietnam about 1865?

Mr. Newsom: It was all part of a worldwide colonial expansion.

Senator Fulbright: That is right. This was part of it. So we are now supporting with our arms and ammunition the Ethiopians to make Eritrea remain a part of their empire; that is about the effect of it.

Mr. Newsom: We are supporting them against armed insurgency about what all observers feel is a minority element within Eritrea.

Senator Fulbright: Nearly all insurgencies are minorities, are they not? They begin as minorities, do they not?

Mr. Newsom: I suppose one could argue that, I guess.

Senator Fulbright: Well, do you think if it were a majority——

Mr. Newsom: There wouldn't be need for insurgency.

Arms Are Used to Influence Internal Insurgencies

Senator Fulbright: There would not be need for insurgency. But this is a difficult point, it seems to me, and this lends credence to the allegation that we everywhere are supporting the status quo; we are using our arms and influence against change; is that right?

Mr. Newsom: Well, it presents us with a very difficult problem because if we assist a country which is sovereign within its territory, how far can we go or should we go in determining the exact policies in a country.

Senator Fulbright: This is one of the principal arguments very hard to answer, of why we should not pursue a bilateral program; and if we do have a program, it should be multilateral, so we should not become involved in it; isn't that correct?

Mr. Newsom: There are others more closely involved with the pursuit of the insurgency than we are, and that is the Israelis.

The Israelis have equipped and framed the police force in Eritrea, and our only involvement is with the if one can call it an involvement——

Senator Fulbright: Where do the Israelis get most of their funds to pursue those policies, from the United States?

Mr. Newsom: Well, I would carry it back only to the primary, to the first, source, Israel itself.

Senator Fulbright: Do the insurgents know that we are giving bombs to the Ethiopians to be used against them?

Mr. Newsom: I am sure they are aware of our military assistance to Ethiopia.

Senator Fulbright: Do you know whether the Syrians are giving aid to the insurgents?

Mr. Newsom: Arms are coming to the insurgents through channels which come from [deleted].

* * *

Mr. Paul: Since there were relatively few countries in Africa to which we give assistance, would you put in the record at this time the level of military assistance to Ethiopia and the other countries for the last unclassified year.

Mr. Bader: I can do it one way or the other. I can give you cumulative totals?

Mr. Paul: No; the annual amount.

Mr. Bader: In fiscal year 1970 we have $1.8 for the Congo, $12 million for Ethiopia, $100,000 for Ghana, $500,000 for Liberia, $200,000 for Libya, that was for support of MAAG, it is not assistance per se; $800,000 for Morocco, $100,000 that had been planned for Nigeria, $3 million for Tunisia, that was a total of $18.5 in 1970, and in 1971 the planned figure is [deleted].

Value of Kagnew

Mr. Paul: Now, in light of your comment earlier, Ambassador Newsom, that our military assistance to some extent is [deleted] and in light of these other figures for Africa, which are way below Ethiopia, would you have some concept of what the figure would be without Kagnew? Obviously it would not be precise.

Mr. Newsom: No; that would be speculative.

Mr. Paul: Let me ask this question: Twelve million dollars for Ethiopia in FY-1970, way and above other countries in Africa. Do you think Kagnew is worth this exceptionally high amount of military assistance?

Mr. Newsom: I think the value of Kagnew is something that has to be assessed in the total range of all of its activities, the possibility of replacing it in other places, together with the general importance of Ethiopia and its stability in that area of the world. [Deleted.]

So I think it is very difficult to say it is worth it or it is not worth it. [Deleted.]

Mr. Paul: Let me ask this question, which you frankly have addressed yourself to to some extent, but perhaps not in this context. Is it possible that Kagnew is a pretense for this large military assistance that is given to Ethiopia and that it is really an amount given to induce a favorable presence there, but that only as payment for base rights could it be justified to the Congress?

Mr. Newsom: No.

Mr. Bader: No.

Mr. Paul: Would you say that the Ethiopians need the military assistance which we provide them as much as we need that which we get for the military assistance?

Mr. Bader: [Deleted.]

Mr. Paul: We have a facility that is similar in some respects to Kagnew in [deleted] and we only provide the [deleted] with less than a million of military assistance.

I know no situation is exactly comparable to the other, but this striking disparity would suggest that assistance to Ethiopia is disproportionate to what we are getting.

Would you say that our assistance to Ethiopia is disproportionate to what we are getting?

Mr. Bader: No; I would not.

Mr. Paul: [Deleted.]

Gao Report

Mr. Paul: With respect to the relative needs of ours and the Ethiopians to us, I would appreciate the Ambassador's comment on this quote from the General Accounting Office report of December 19, 1969, which says:

[Deleted.]

It was not increased, though, was it, at that point?

Mr. Newsom: No; as I said the figure we ultimately reach each year is a matter of adjustment between a number of different perspectives and different interests.

The country team being on the spot is likely to perceive of greater requirements perhaps than in our judgment we can provide, and we have tried to come out at the lowest acceptable figure and it has sometimes been lower than what the country team felt right.

Mr. Paul: Would not our experience in a year and a half since then suggest that they were unduly concerned, too pessimistic, as to the American [deleted] position in this situation?

Mr. Newsom: They are out there.

We have to make allowances for that.

Economic vs. Military Assistance to Ethiopia

Mr. Paul: We provide, did your statement say, about $20 million of economic assistance to Ethiopia?

Mr. Newsom: That is the figure—16 for this year, fiscal 1970.

Mr. Paul: Even if we continue to give the Ethiopians a total package of $28 million of assistance, in light of their economic difficulties would it not be more appropriate to be giving more of it in economic assistance than in nonremunerative military assistance?

Mr. Newsom: I think we would probably agree [deleted].

Mr. Bader: Also could I just add it would not address the real security problem.

They do have security problems, and the end items that go into a country including training are very badly needed.

Mr. Paul: But wouldn't this be a much smaller figure than the $12 million for fiscal year 1970. Dollar for dollar, shouldn't the equation be less military assistance and more economic assistance?

Mr. Bader: What would be the end result? Would the end result mean more diversion from economic development funds from their own budget to pick this up?

I quote from a renowned study back in 1968, the Symington Amendment Study. One of its findings was that the IEG is not converting U.S. economic assistance nor its own resources to unnecessary military expenditures. If you give that, take that as given then that is about what we are doing, and about what they are doing, is about the right mix in order to maintain that level of effort. If you were to reduce the grant military assistance program the vacuum would have to be filled from some other source.

Mr. Paul: It is good you called my attention to that, but it seems from what we discussed already they are devoting too much to military expenditures, and we are devoting too much by comparison with the rest of Africa to military assistance.

Mr. Newsom: I would not say we would agree with the conclusion stated that way. We might feel and wish that there was greater emphasis on economic development, but given the situation in which the Emperor and his government feel themselves, the priorities that they have placed upon it to achieve the objectives we have, the present mix seems required.

*   *   *

New York Times *Editorial on the Commitment to Ethiopia* *

October 26, 1970

Many Americans, in and out of Congress, will be shocked to learn that the United States for the last ten years has been committed to oppose any direct threat to the territorial integrity of Ethiopia. This 1960 pledge by the Eisenhower Administration has been brought to light by a Senate Foreign Relations subcommittee investigating American overseas commitments.

The United States has long maintained several thousand service men in Ethiopia to operate the Kagnew communications station. Some members of Congress were also aware that this country had provided nearly $150 million in military aid to Ethiopia. What even Foreign Relations committee members evidently did not know was that the United States, as part of the agreement, had formally "reaffirmed" its interest in Ethiopia's security and "opposition to any activities threatening" its territorial integrity.

Senator Fulbright charges that the references to the Ethiopian involvement in the Administration's annual presentations to Congress on the military aid program constituted "very artful, in-depth concealment of what we are doing." It is impossible to disagree. Here again is the kind of vague commitment that could lead this country into trouble. It is precisely the kind of surreptitious commitment, made without Congressional advice or consent, that has opened a dangerous gap of confidence between the executive and legislative branches over a wide range of foreign policy matters. Whatever the arguments for or against an underwriting of Ethiopian security they should have been set forth frankly to Congress.

The Nixon Administration is not responsible for the deal with Ethiopia, but it showed comparable disregard for the role of Congress in foreign policy two months

The New York Times, Oct. 26, 1970.

ago when it concluded a new agreement with Spain, pledging this country to "support the defense system" of the Franco regime.

Commitments that could lead at some future date to the involvement of American forces abroad should be spelled out clearly in treaty form and submitted to the Senate for approval. An Administration that ignores the legitimate role of Congress must expect heavy-handed interference from an aroused Senate and House.

KENYA, TANZANIA AND UGANDA

*Report of Senators Church, Moss and McGee on a Study Mission to Africa**

November-December, 1960

The Crown Colony and Protectorate of Kenya has been preparing for late February elections which are likely to result in increases in the degree of African self-government, approaching the status already achieved in more politically advanced but less developed Tanganyika. Under the terms of the "Lancaster House Constitution" an expanded franchise will permit well over 1 million persons—in a population of about 6.3 million—to vote for an African majority in the legislative council. There will also be an African majority among the "unofficial," as distinct from the appointed "official," members of the Council of Ministers. Finally, and most important, the door may be opened for eventual appointment of an African Chief Minister following the election.

*   *   *

Whatever the outcome, the political die has been cast and Kenya is on a fairly direct road toward independence. Some violence may well accompany further moves, including possible pressures for Kenyatta's release. Over the longer term, however, sustained violence is more likely to derive from tribal and political feuds and reprisals among the Africans themselves than from British reluctance to turn over government controls. One can comprehend why African leaders feel unable publicly to give property and other guarantees to the European and Asian minorities in the preindependence period. But it is greatly to be hoped that the latter's future will not be made so bleak as to induce the worst reactions on all sides.

There has been one fortunate aftermath of the Mau Mau rebellion. The detention of many of the most conservative tribal elements among the Kikuyu removed the main barrier to the success of the government land consolidation program in Central Province. Kenya government officials, with infinite patience, have persuaded African farmers to make their holdings contiguous and to have them surveyed so that land titles may be registered and used as collateral for commercial bank and government loans to improve productivity. Some relatively small amounts of ICA money will be devoted to this latter purpose; a few agricultural technicians have been provided in the past. The work in Central Province, now about finished, will affect well over a million

Study Mission to Africa, November-December 1960, pp. 16-19.

Africans. On some holdings which have been developed under the program there has been a startling rise in individual income from roughly $35 to $700 a year.

This scheme has broad implications for Kenya's future in terms of raising agricultural production and reducing unemployment. When, or if, the program is extended throughout the provinces it should provide new employment to 400,000 Africans. Kenya is one of the poorer territories in Africa in resources and usable land. It has virtually no known minerals of commercial quantity and will have to concentrate upon promoting agricultural exports and the creation of light manufacturing industries. Much has been done in regard to both requirements, especially in native production of high grade coffee and good blends of tea, and programs to improve land use will accelerate this development. Some slow progress is also being made toward government purchase and redistribution of European settler estates in the so-called White Highlands, which represent much of the best and most productive land in the territory, as well as some which has not yet been cultivated but is barred to the Africans.

Because of Kenya's great need for education and educational facilities, we were very interested in the status of the "African Airlift" which in 2 years has sent over 300 students to the United States from Kenya, and a smaller number from neighboring Uganda and Tanganyika. While the original selection process certainly left much to be desired, a high proportion of these students have compiled good records. One very urgent problem has arisen: the great majority of the 470 Kenyan students in the United States will soon be without any subsistence funds. The U.S. Government should be doing more to encourage a larger, better-coordinated approach by American private agencies, and to support local programs in education which would preclude the need for hasty, ad hoc measures of this kind.

Tanganyika

The United Nations Trust Territory of Tanganyika, administered by Great Britain, over the past year has moved quietly to the verge of independence. An absence of headlined disorders does not mean that Tanganyika is out of the main current of African nationalism. On the contrary, nationalism has won its immediate goals as rapidly as anywhere in Africa, owing largely to the organizational talents which created a single powerful party, the Tanganyika African National Union (TANU), and to the generally cooperative attitude of the governing power. Nationalist pressure was exercised, but it stopped short of violence. Full self-government is in the process of being achieved under the leadership of a large majority of Africans in the legislative council and Chief Minister Julius Nyerere.

There are even more basic reasons for this advance. Unlike Kenya, the territory has not had a white settler problem or a related land shortage; few of the 25,000 Europeans (a little more than a third of the number in Kenya) have even settled on the land, of which all but a tiny fraction is held by the government and communally by tribes. There is also an absence of the tribal conflict which has retarded nationalist consolidation in Kenya.

Tanganyika apparently can have independence in the near future almost for the asking. The Chief Minister, however, has held back in order to propose a federation with Kenya, Uganda, and Zanzibar. He believes that such a project must be undertaken before independence, or else national zeal will prevent any real devolution of power to a larger entity. The jealously guarded sovereignty of the newly independent countries in West Africa indicates the validity of the thesis. A federation formed by the Africans themselves would probably bring great benefits to their complementary economies and transportation systems, as well as consolidate other common services now supervised by the East African High Commission. It would also preclude the division of certain tribes by national boundaries, and provide a means of avoiding conflict over such problems as the coastal strip in Kenya leased from the Sultan of Zanzibar.

The chances for the success of this idea depend mainly upon the early appearance in each of the other territories of a single nationalist leader able to speak for the great majority of his people. In the case of Kenya, there are almost too many possible candidates and no one agreed leader, unless Kenyatta could be considered as such. In Uganda, no prominent nationalist figure has been able to emerge and draw away misplaced African sentiment favoring the Kabaka of Buganda, who in fact represents tribal separatism and traditional rule. Zanzibar confronts different problems. Both major political parties on the islands support federation in principle, but it is not clear whether or not they seek independence first. They have just fought a close election to a disputed result. If the Zanzibar Nationalist (mainly Arab) Party is disappointed in its hopes for power, it may follow increasingly extreme policies which could inflame racial sentiment; it already has been subject to some Communist infiltration. More-over, the Chinese Communists and the Soviets have been concentrating great attention on educational and other exchanges with Zanzibar and seem intent on introducing external ideological conflicts into East Africa. They have fostered much of the antagonism to a U.S. Project Mercury satellite tracking station being constructed on the main island by misrepresenting it as a missile base.

Under the circumstances, the Nyerere proposal seems to face rather long odds. Much could depend upon the depth of the favorable British attitude and, if an incipient federation makes an appearance, upon the willingness of the United States to offer help speedily in the form of encouraging, easily visible economic benefits.

*　　　　　*　　　　　*

Final Report of the Committee on Commerce on Freedom of Communications on the Airlift of Students from Kenya*

August 1-November 7, 1960

SPEECHES REMARKS, PRESS CONFERENCES AND
STATEMENTS OF SENATOR JOHN F. KENNEDY

BACKGROUND MEMORANDUM PREPARED BY SENATOR KENNEDY'S OFFICE,
AUGUST 1960

---

*U.S. Senate, Subcommittee of the Subcommittee on Communications, *Freedom of Communications.* Final Report of the Committee on Commerce, part I, (Washington, 1961), pp. 1275-84; 1088-91.

The Facts on Grant to African Students Airlift
Summary

On July 26 when Tom Mboya of Kenya visited Senator Kennedy at Hyannis Port, the State Department, despite intervention by Mr. Nixon, had with finality turned down a request to provide an airlift for over 200 African students who had received U.S. scholarships.

Senator Kennedy arranged for the Joseph P. Kennedy, Jr., Foundation, established in the memory of his brother who was killed in World War II, to finance the airlift when other foundations were not prepared to do so. In order to keep this project out of politics, it was provided that no public announcement be made of the grant.

After the Kennedy Foundation had decided to provide the money and just before the meeting was held to make final plans, Mr. James Shepley of Mr. Nixon's office, learning of the Kennedy Foundation action and intervening with the State Department on behalf of Mr. Nixon, achieved—in a matter of hours over one weekend and one Monday morning—a reversal of the State Department's long-established negative position. Mr. Shepley's role in this has now been confirmed by the State Department's answer to Senator Fulbright.

The African-American Students Foundation, weighing the Kennedy Foundation's interest in the whole project, the value of non-governmental financing, and the Government's general hostility to the project but for Mr. Shepley's last-minute efforts, decided not to reject the private foundation grant which had already been made. It urged the State Department to use the newly allotted funds to expand its own African scholarship program.

The next day, after Mr. Shepley and the State Department had been infromed of the decision to go ahead with the Kennedy Foundation grant, Senator Scott, a member of Mr. Nixon's campaign board of strategy and of the Republican "truth squad," announced and hailed the State Department grant, making no mention of the prior Kennedy Foundation action. Then the following day Senator Scott alleged that since his announcement the Kennedy Foundation had "outbid" the U.S. Government and "attempted to pluck this project away from the U.S. Government" for "blatant political purposes."

Even after the facts had been disclosed by Senator Kennedy and the African-American Students Foundation, and were acknowledged by Mr. Nixon's office and by the State Department, Senator Scott went on nationwide TV to repeat and compound his wholly false charges.

The following memorandum gives a chronological account of the facts in detail. The key facts are supported by the accompanying documents.

I. 1959 Airlift Africa

Through the efforts of Tom Mboya of Kenya and the African-American Students Foundation, 81 students from Kenya were granted scholarships in the United States and a plane was chartered to bring them here.

Repeatedly the State Department was asked to help finance this project and repeatedly it turned the project down. Copies of the correspondence on this are available from this files of Congressman Diggs. The money was raised by a direct appeal to the public.

II. 1960 Airlift Africa

In response to letters from Mrs. Ralph Bunche, a director of the African-American Students Foundation (AASF), some 230 scholarships valued at over $1 million were offered for African students by Class I accredited colleges in the United States.

This 1960 program included not only Kenya as in 1959, but also Uganda, Tanganyika, Zanzibar, Northern Rhodesia, Southern Rhodesia, and Nyasaland. About 230 students were selected, and money was raised in Africa from Africans to provide about $1,000 per student for living expenses in the United States.

A. State Department's Decision Not to Finance Project

Repeatedly, beginning in November 1959, the State Department was asked to finance the air transportation of this, the largest student travel scholarship program ever to be undertaken in Africa. The chronology of these requests and the State Department's negative responses follows, with full documentation available:

(1) On November 18, 1959, Mr. Scheinman, the vice president of the African-American Students Foundation (AASF), wrote to the Assistant Secretary of State for African Affairs, Mr. J. C. Satterthwaite, outlining the program for the 1960 airlift of some 250 students from central and east Africa, and asking for transportation assistance.

(2) On December 10, Assistant Secretary of State Satterthwaite replied saying that he regretted "to have to respond * * * in the negative," and adding that "Perhaps you will wish to send a copy of this letter to Mr. Mboya so that he will not have any unfounded expectations regarding this matter."

(3) On January 15, 1960, Mr. Scheinman wrote to Mr. Satterthwaite asking for reconsideration. No reply was received by AASF.

(4) On June 9, 1960, Mr. Jackie Robinson, on AASF letterhead, wrote to Vice President Nixon asking for his assistance in the matter.

(5) On June 23, Mr. Nixon replied that he was urging the State Department to give the project serious consideration.

(6) On July 7, Assistant Secretary of State Satterthwaite, wrote AASF taking note of Mr. Nixon's interest but advising that it would not be possible for the U.S. Government to finance the air transportation.

(7) On July 13, in an effort to persuade the Department to change its negative decision, Mr. Frank Montero, the president of AASF and Mr. Scheinman, met in Washington with several State Department officials, including Mr. C. Kennety Snyder, Program Officer for Africa, Policy and Plans Staff, Bureau of Education and Cultural Affairs. After about a 3-hour conference, the Department officers had not changed their position and in fact had given addition reasons why the Department could not be involved in the project. They said the project had gone up to the "top" and been finally rejected.

(8) On July 21, Mr. Mboya telephoned from Africa to express his alarm about the

failures to secure transportation for the students. It was decided he would fly to the United States to make a direct appeal.

(9) On July 23, telegrams were sent to all members of the Senate Foreign Relations Committee by AASF telling of Mr. Mboya's trip and asking for appointments for him.

(10) On July 25, Mr. Mboya attended a conference called by the Phelps-Stokes Fund in New York of some 50 representatives of organizations concerned with higher education in east and central Africa. The African airlift program was discussed. Mr. Snyder represented the State Department. Also present were representatives of the Institute of International Education, the Carnegie Foundation, the Foreign Policy Association, the African-American Institute, the American Society of African Culture, the American Council on Education, and the Rockefeller Foundation. Mr. Snyder explained why the State Department was not in a position to support the project: It could not operate on a "crash" basis, and was limited in its work in colonial territories such as east Africa.

(11) On July 27, Senator Wiley, in response to the telegram requesting an appointment for Mr. Mboya, wrote to Mr. Montero as follows:

> I have your telegram requesting an appointment for the purpose of discussing the airlift of 250 African students to the United States this coming September.
>
> After consulting with our State Department, which is not unaware of your problem, I have been advised it does not look with favor on an airlift of foreign students at Government expense. You can readily understand that if an exception were made in one instance, a precedent would be established which would not only be difficult of control but would subject the United States to criticism at home, and abroad by those not so favored. Therefore, much as I approve of encouraging exchange of foreign students, I cannot be of assistance to the Foundation in this instance.

B. *The Kennedy Foundation's Support of the Project*

(1) In response to the telegram about Mr. Mboya's visit, Senator Kennedy invited him to come to Hyannis Port. They met on July 26 for a long discussion of the African situation. Mr. Mboya described the great opportunity of filling over 200 scholarships for Africans which was about to be lost because of lack of transportation. He asked Senator Kennedy, as chairman of the Senate Foreign Relations Subcommittee on African Affairs, to intercede with the State Department. Senator Kennedy said that if Mr. Nixon had already tried and failed, he could do little there. He suggested, however, that the Joseph P. Kennedy, Jr., Foundation might be able to help.

After consulting with the executive director of the Kennedy Foundation, Sargent Shriver, Jr., on the telephone, Senator Kennedy informed Mr. Mboya that the Kennedy Foundation would contribute at least $5,000 and would take the initiative in securing the rest of the funds needed from other foundations, perhaps on a matching basis with the Kennedy Foundation.

(2) On July 27 and 28, and later, Mr. Shriver called a number of other private foundations, including Carnegie, Ford, Phelps-Stokes, Rockefeller, the Institute of International Education, and the Foundation for All-Africa (of which Mr. Robert Kennedy is president). While some of the foundations were interested, none was prepared to move immediately.

(3) On July 29, upon learning that no progress had been made in securing other financing, Senator Kennedy asked that Mr. Shriver be advised that in his opinion, as a trustee of the Kennedy Foundation, the whole project should be financed by the

Kennedy Foundation, so that the planes could be chartered and the students could arrive here in time to take up their scholarships in September. Senator Kennedy said that a condition of the grant should be that there be no announcement of it, in order to keep the project out of politics.

(4) On August 5, 1960, Mr. Shriver wrote to Mr. Joseph P. Kennedy as follows:

> Last week, Jack met with Tom Mboya . . . up at the cape. Mboya told Jack that there was a million dollars worth of scholarships awaiting students of Kenya in the United States, but that Mboya did not have the money to transport these students to the United States. Jack offered to help in a modest way and asked me to find out if other foundations would be willing to join our foundation in providing money for the transportation of these Kenya students to this country.
>
> While I was in the process of contacting the foundations (none of which were flexible enough to move quickly on this urgent matter), Jack decided he would like us to go ahead with the project on our own.
>
> Approximately $90,000 is required for the transportation since 250 to 350 students are involved, and I am recommending to Jack that another $10,000 be appropriated so that we may have the expert services of the Institute for International Education or the Phelps-Stokes Fund to select the students and make sure they are assigned to institutions in the United States where they are capable of doing a good job.
>
> Over this weekend I will be talking to Jack and presumably getting his final OK. Jack's theory is that we would have no publicity about this matter.

(5) On August 10, in Washington, D.C., the AASF officers, Montero and Scheinman, were informed that the Kennedy Foundation would assure the transportation costs of the student airlift. They were also informed that a condition of the grant was that there be no public announcement about it. They agreed to this. While details remained to be worked out, Messrs. Montero and Scheinman left with the assurance that the commitment was made.

(6) On the same day, August 10, Mr. Shriver invited Congressman Diggs to serve on an advisory committee, which the Kennedy Foundation intended to establish to see that the best possible arrangements were made for the students both in their travel and in their studies here.

(7) On August 12, Mr. Shriver called a meeting for Monday, August 15, at 2:30 p.m. at which final details would be worked out and the advisory committee established, and to which the AASF president, Mr. Montero, would be invited, along with representatives of the Institute of International Education, the African-American Institute, the Phelps-Stokes Fund, the Foundation for All-Africa, and the Ford Foundation. At the time Mr. Montero received this invitation on Saturday morning, and agreed to be in Washington Monday to complete the plans, he says that he had received no indication that the State Department was considering reversing itself.

C. Mr. Shepley's Role

(1) On Saturday, August 13, after the Monday plans had been agreed upon, Mr. Jackie Robinson called Montero to say that Mr. James Shepley of Mr. Nixon's office wanted to talk to him. When Montero then called Shepley, Shepley expressed his interest in getting the State Department to support the project. Either in this call or in a call the following day, or in both calls, and Montero believes it was in both, Shepley stated that he knew that the Kennedy Foundation had offered up to $100,000 to finance the airlift. Montero says he neither confirmed nor denied this because of his agreement that there be no publicity, but he did tell Shepley that a private foundation

was prepared to finance the airlift. Shepley urged him to let him try to get an offer from the Government and said he would call back the next day. According to Montero, Jackie Robinson, as a member of the board of the AASF, was informed of the Kennedy Foundation decision; Robinson denies he knew any more than that the Kennedy Foundation would give $5,000 and seek to raise the rest from other foundations. Senator Scott's account is that in this Saturday telephone talk Montero related to Shepley "that during the period immediately after the Democratic National Convention the Kennedy people had offered to make $100,000 available for Airlift African, 1960." (Cong. Rec. Aug. 17, p. 15442.) This is in accord with the Washington Star's article (Aug. 14) in which Mr. Nixon's press secretary, Herbert Klein, is quoted as saying that Shepley found out that the Kennedy Foundation was involved on Sunday "when Mr. Montero called him to say the financing had been guaranteed." However he found out, it appears evident that at least by Saturday Mr. Shepley knew of the Kennedy Foundation grant.

(2) On Saturday, August 14, despite his knowledge that the airlift financing had already been arranged privately, Shepley called Montero to say that although he still had nothing firm to offer he hoped the Department would reverse itself before Montero's meeting with the Kennedy Foundation representative on Monday. He said he was taking the issue up with Undersecretary of State Dillon. He made arrangements to reach Montero on Monday before the meeting. Later the same day, Montero and Jackie Robinson talked about the situation and, according to Montero, agreed that it didn't matter who financed the airlift if the students got here in time for school.

(3) On Monday, August 15, Montero and Shepley talked on the phone several times, with Shepley each time saying that he hoped within a matter of minutes to get an affirmative answer from the State Department. During the noon period Shepley called to say that he would speak with Dillon as soon as Dillon finished testifying before the Senate Foreign Relations Committee. A few minutes later, Shepley called to say that he had been authorized to make a definite offer that the Government would provide transportation costs up to $100,000 for the airlift. He asked that Montero contact Mr. Robert Thayer, Special Assistant to the Secretary of State for Cultural Affairs, for further details. Montero said he would talk with Thayer but that there was already, as Shepley knew, a prior commitment agreed upon with the Kennedy Foundation.

Mr. Shriver, as executive director of the Kennedy Foundation, told Montero and Scheinman that they were entirely free to accept the Government's offer. The latter decided that in view of the Government's reluctance about the whole project, the preference of many Africans for nongovernmental support, and the Kennedy Foundation's concern for the interest of the students while in this country, the AASF should not reject the Kennedy Foundation grant. Rather, it should urge the Government to apply the proffered $100,000 to an expansion of its own scholarship program for east and central Africa. (Last year the Government's academic scholarship programs for all Africa amounted to 142 students.)

At the 2:30 p.m. meeting the following persons were present in addition to Shriver, Montero, and Scheinman: Dr. Fred Patterson, of the Phelps-Stokes Fund; Mr. Gordon Hagberg of the African-American Institute; the Reverend Gordon H. Fournier, executive vice president of the Foundation for All-Africa; and Mr. Albert Sims of the Institute of International Education. Mr. Shriver explained that the Kennedy Foundation had decided to finance the airlift and hoped they and Congressman Diggs would serve as an advisory committee to the project. It was agreed that several members of the advisory committee would shortly go to Africa to study the procedures used in selecting students and to accompany the students to this country in early September.

Later Montero called Shepley and Thayer to inform them of the decision. Montero says that Shepley protested their action in "turning down the U.S. Government" and that he implied that efforts might be made by his side to suggest in the press that this was a politically motivated act by Senator Kennedy.

D. Senator Scott's Role

(1) The next day, Tuesday, August 16, Senator Scott announced that the State Department had granted $100,000 to finance the African student's airlift. Senator Scott is a member of Mr. Nixon's campaign board of strategy. He has stated that although Mr. Shepley knew of the Kennedy Foundation grant on Saturday, the 13th, and the Department of State knew at least by Monday, the 15th, he (Senator Scott) did not know of it when he made this announcement on Tuesday. Who gave him the information about the State Department's offer or authorized him to announce it, or why such person did not tell him of the Kennedy Foundation's prior grant, is not known. One possible source is suggested by the Senator's references in the text of his release to Jackie Robinson, a strong supporter of Mr. Nixon.

(2) Early on the same day, August 16, Montero informed Jackie Robinson of what had happened Monday and of the decision to go ahead with the Kennedy grant. Robinson read Montero the draft of a column he had written for publication in the New York Post on Wednesday, August 17. The column essentially followed the line of Senator Scott's announcement, mentioning only the State Department's offer and not the Kennedy Foundation grant. It read in part:

> Good news is all too rare these days, but on Monday I received a call from Washington which added up to just that. Jim Shepley, an aid to Vice President Nixon, called to tell me the State Department has decided to pick up the tab for the three planeloads of African students which the African-American Students Foundation is bringing over this year to study at American universities.
>
> *   *   *
>
> Incidentally, it is no accident that an aid of the Vice President was the one to call me about this. When I conferred with Mr. Nixon in Washington several weeks ago, one of the points we discussed was this project. . . . Shepley was assigned to follow up on the matter, and Monday's phone call was the happy result.
> . . . And I congratulate Vice President Nixon, Under Secretary Dillon and Jim Shepley for the vital roles they played in bringing it about.

After hearing this read, Montero told Robinson that this was unfair and inaccurate reporting. He says Robinson told him he was going to print it anyway.

(3) After Senator Scott's announcement that Montero and Scheinman sent a telegram to Congressman Diggs stating that the State Department's "belated offer" was "only made after the foundation, which had repeatedly requested help during the past 12 months and was finally turned down late last month, was successful in obtaining a grant of $100,000 from a private foundation. . . . The fact is the State Department has repeatedly turned a cold shoulder to the airlift-Africa program." They suggested that the funds allocated by the Government should "be made immediately

available to other African students on a continuing basis." As agreed upon with Senator Kennedy and Mr. Shriver, they did not identify the Kennedy Foundation.

Congressman Diggs released this telegram to the press with an accusation that the State Department was playing politics by announcing a grant which it knew had been made too late. The Department "showed interest in the matter," said Congressman Diggs, who had tried diligently since 1959 to persuade the State Department to act, "only when their inaction was about to prove embarrassing to the Republican Party."

(4) On Wednesday, August 17, Senator Scott on the Senate floor stated that "since" the time (the previous day) when he had been "privileged" to announce the State Department grant (the day after it had already been turned down), he had "been informed that the long arm of the family of the junior Senator from Massachusetts has reached out and attempted to pluck this project away from the U.S. Government." He said he was "surprised" at the decision of the African-American Students Foundation but he could "understand the pressures brought by the Kennedy people and their anxiety to take over the functions of the Government in advance of an election." He said he was concerned "at the apparent misuse of tax-exempt foundation money for blatant political purposes." He asked why "the Kennedy people" were so anxious to commit themselves to this expenditure "just 1 day after learning of the action of the Department of State."

(5) In reply to Senator Scott on the Senate floor, August 17, Senator Kennedy outlined the facts in this memorandum, calling Senator Scott's statement "the most unfair, distorted, and malignant attack I have heard in 14 years of politics." He said in conclusion:

> . . . the Kennedy Foundation went into this quite reluctantly. I am chairman of the Subcommittee on Africa. I think this is a most important program. . . . Mr. Mboya came to see us and asked for help, when none of the other foundations could give it. when the Federal Government had turned it down quite precisely. We felt something ought to be done. To waste 250 scholarships in this country, to waste $200,000 these people had raised, to disappoint 250 students who hoped to come to this country, it certainly seemed to me, would be most unfortunate and so we went ahead.

He urged the State Department at this late date to use the funds "to bring other students to the United States."

(6) On August 18, Senator Fulbright addressed 13 questions to Secretary of State Herter on the role of Mr. Shepley and the Department in this whole matter, asking for answers by Monday, August 22. To the press Senator Fulbright stated that:

> If the facts are like they appear to be, I think it is an outrageous distortion of the facts on the part of Senator Scott. If it is true that the State Department was pressured into allocating funds, it was an unacceptable interference with the orderly conduct of our foreign policy by the State Department for partisan, political purposes.

(7) Later on August 18, Lincoln White, Director of the State Department's Office of News, stated that the Department had turned down the African airlift when it was originally proposed early in July because it was confined only to Kenya, because the specific request was for free transportation through MATS, because it felt the project should be conducted through the Institute of International Education, and because there was inadequate provision for the students' expenses in the United States. Mr. White stated that the project had been finally approved after assurances were given

meeting all these Department objections. He stated that the Department was informed on Monday that its offer was not accepted, because the airlift had already received private financing.

(8) On August 19, Vice President Scheinman of AASF wired Senator Fulbright that the Department's explanation that the decision was reversed "because we finally met requirements laid down by the Department is patently incorrect because the Department never laid downn any requirements at all." Specifically, Scheinman said that the 1960 airlift was never designed just for Kenya alone and that the other countries involved were listed in his letter to Assistant Secretary Satterthwaite on January 15, 1960. Nor was the request ever confined to Air Force transport. Nor had the other alleged objections been met, he said, unless the Department was counting on the support of the Kennedy Foundation for expenses of the students in the United States. Mr. Lincoln White conceded that he had been in error as to the original proposal for 1960 being limited to Kenya. But he insisted that the other conditions had been met, although he would not disclose the source of any such assurances.

(9) On August 19, Jackie Robinson published a second column on the matter, stating: "I don't mind admitting it: I was wrong." He said he would not dispute the account by the African-American Students Foundation that the Kennedy Foundation had already committed itself to support of the full project by the time the State Department offer was made. He stated that "as late as the time my column was written on Tuesday I was not told the State Department offer had been rejected." He did not add that after writing the column but before it went to press Montero had told him this and the other relevant facts refuting the main theme of that column.

(10) On Sunday, August 21, on ABC's television "College News Conference," Senator Scott was asked whether in view of the fact that the Kennedy Foundation had kept its grant quiet until he brought it to the forefront, wasn't he the one who was making it a political issue? Despite all of the above facts and the State Department's acknowledgment of them, Senator Scott replied:

> Well, I wouldn't think so, since the foundation did not move in this matter until after they had learned of the decision of the State Department last Saturday to make these funds available. . . . so the truth is that the Kennedy Foundation offered nothing until they had heard of the State Department offer.

Instead of conceding his error, as Jackie Robinson finally did, Senator Scott repeated as a fact that "the Kennedy people had no interest in this whatever until Monday of this week."

Saying "we are going to have an awful lot of questions of abuse of money in this campaign, and this is one of them. . . ." Senator Scott went on to make further charges such as "millions more" of Kennedy money "will be used if means can be found to evade the election laws."

SPEECH BY SENATOR JOHN F. KENNEDY, CITY HALL SQUARE,
BOWLING GREEN, KY., ON OCTOBER 8, 1960

*   *   *

When the crisis in the Congo recently erupted across the front pages of our newspapers it dramatized not only the dangers we face in Africa—but it also dramatized the failures of American policy which created those dangers.

It was only the intervention of the United States which prevented the immediate establishment of a Soviet satellite in the heart of Africa. Yet assembled here on this lawn is enough talent and skill, knowledge and education to have saved the Congo from chaos and confusion—permitting an orderly transition to independence—and halting the threat of Communist subversion without intervention.

But the Congo did not have the skills of the people assembled here. Instead the Belgians left behind them a country of 8 million people with less than a dozen college graduates—a country with only a single 21-year-old Government officer with a degree from a European university—a country which had never been given the education needed to run a nation. The result was inevitable—and it happened—we are still paying the high price on our failure to educate the people of the Congo.

To understand these failures—we must understand modern Africa.

In 1776, the year of the first successful revolt against colonial rule, Tom Paine wrote that "A flame has arisen not to be extinguished." Today that same flame of freedom burns brightly across the once "Dark Continent," creating new nations and driving old powers from the scene—kindling in men the desire to shape their own destinies as freemen.

Each of these newly emerging nations has, in varying degrees, the same problems, the same needs, and the same dangers as now beset the Congo. And in each of them wait the same tireless and implacable agents of communism watching for the opportunity to transform poverty or hunger or ignorance into revolt and Communist rule.

The new African nations are determined to emerge from their poverty and hunger. They are determined to build a modern and growing economy with a constantly rising standard of living. They are determined to educate their people—maintain their independence—and receive the respect of all the world.

The only real question is whether Africa will look West or East—to Moscow or Washington—for help and guidance in this effort.

This choice may well determine the course of the cold war—whether the world shifts toward communism or toward democracy—toward freedom or toward slavery in the years to come.

I believe that Africa will look to the West—that it will choose freedom.

For it was the American Revolution—not the Russian—which began man's struggle for national independence, individual liberty and freedom from colonial rule. When the African National Congress in Northern Rhodesia called for reform and justice—it threatened a "Boston Tea Party"—not a Bolshevik bomb plot. African leader Tom Mboya invokes the "American dream"—not the Communist manifesto.

And in the most remote bushlands of central Africa there are children named Thomas Jefferson and George Washington—but there are none named Lenin or Stalin or Trotsky. And those ties of history and spirit are strengthened by our common goals. What we wnat in Africa is what the nations of Africa want for themselves. We want an Africa where the standard of living is constantly increasing—where the economy is moving forward—where malnutrition and ignorance are disappearing.

And this is what Africa wants.

We want an Africa where there is a community of stable and independent and protected countries and where men are given the opportunity to choose their own national course, free from the dictates or coercion of any other country.

And this is what Africa wants.

We want an Africa which is not a pawn in the cold war or a battleground between East and West.

And this, too, is what the people of Africa want.

Yet—despite these powerful bonds—America is losing ground in Africa: The newly independent country of Guinea has moved steadily toward the Communist bloc—importing Soviet technicians, borrowing Soviet money, and signing trade agreements with Eastern Europe.

The newly independent country of Ghana has moved away from the West—and recently the President of the nation sent troops to the Congo by Soviet jet. In the strife-torn, newly independent country of the Congo one of the most powerful factions—that of Premier Lumumba—is pro-Russian and anti-American. And throughout Africa there is growing uneasiness about America's role and American motives.

We have lost ground in Africa because—in the past 8 years—we have neglected and ignored the needs and aspirations of the African people. We failed to foresee the growing importance of Africa. We failed to ally ourselves with the cause of independence and freedom. We failed to help the Africans develop the stable economy and the educated population on which their growth, stability and freedom depend. These were failures of vision, of leadership and of will.

Although by 1952 it was obvious that new African nations would soon be a growing force on the world scene—our State Department did not establish a Bureau of African Affairs until 1957—and, that same year, we sent more Foreign Service officers to Western Germany than to all of Africa. Even today less than 5 percent of all our Foreign Service officers are in Africa—and there are five newly independent nations that have no State Department representation at all. One reason that communism succeeded in Guinea is that we didn't bother to send an Ambassador there until 8 months after independence. However, the Soviet representative arrived on Independence Day.

Although the emerging nations of Africa desperately need the development capital which is essential to the creation of a growing economy—through the end of 1957 we had granted Africa less than two-tenths of 1 percent of our total foreign assistance. And as late as 1959, Africa was receiving only 5 percent of all our foreign aid—and only 2 percent of all the money spent by the Development Loan Fund—a fund which was specifically created to help the underdeveloped countries.

Although there are only a handful of college graduates in many African countries—and less than 1 percent of all Africans entering the primary grades ever finish high school—we are doing almost nothing to help educate the African people. Today our Government is aiding less than 200 African students in this country—and yet this is the largest number we have ever helped. Nor are we supplying the books and the technicians which could help the Africans train themselves—less than 5 percent of our technical help is allotted to Africa south of the Sahara.

This Republican record of neglect and indifference—of drift and failure and retreat—has resulted in a steady decline in American prestige in Africa—and a steady growth of Soviet influence.

If we are to create an atmosphere in Africa in which freedom can flourish—where long-enduring people can hope for a better life for themselves and their children—where men are winning the fight against ignorance and hunger and disease—then we must embark on a bold and imaginative new program for the development of Africa.

First, we must ally ourselves with the rising tide of nationalism in Africa. The desire to be independent of foreign rule—the desire for self-determination—is the most powerful force of the modern world. It has destroyed old empires—created scores of new nations—and redrawn the maps of Asia, the Middle East, and Africa. It is vital that we unequivocally place ourselves on the side of man's right to govern himself, because those are our historic principles—because the ultimate triumph of nationalism is inevitable—and also because nationalism is the one force with the strength and endurance to threaten the integrity of the Communist empire itself.

Second, we must make the United Nations the central instrument of our energies and policies in Africa. With limited resources and personnel, the United Nations has accomplished wonders in Africa—not only in the Congo, but in Togoland, and the Cmaeroons and Ruanda-Urundi and Tanganyika. The U.N. has eased the transition to independence for many African nations—and has won the support and confidence of most of the African people. By centering many of our activities in the U.N. we demonstrate that our principal desire is to build a strong and free Africa—rather than to use the African nations as pawns in the cold war.

We will cooperate fully in U.N. economic aid and technical assistance programs. We will send first-rate men to staff our own U.N. mission—and encourage talented Americans to work for the Secretariat.

But it will take time to establish effective United Nations programs over the delays, harassment, and opposition of the Soviet Union. And Africa's needs will not wait.

Third, to meet the need for education, we must greatly increase the number of African students—future African leaders—brought to this country for university training. And we must establish a multination African educational development fund. This fund—in which the African states would be full partners—will map the long-range educational needs of Africa, helping to build the school systems and universities which will ultimately permit Africans to educate their own people.

And while Africa builds its own educational system we will send a stream of experts and educators—engineers and technicians—to train Africa in the tools of modern production and modern agriculture—and in the skills and knowledge essential to the conduct of government.

Fourth, we must help provide the development capital which can transform the resources of Africa—the least productive area of the world—into a higher standard of living for the African people. We should establish a multlateral development loan fund—a fund directed by Western and African nations—a fund whose expense would be borne by all the Western allies—a fund which would make the long-term capital loans necessary to develop the roads, the power, the water, the hospitals, and all the other public needs which are vital to an industrial economy.

Fifth, we must stimulate private investment in Africa. For the capital needs of Africa are far too great ever to be met by government alone. Therefore we must expand our consular services—and use the resources of the Development Loan Fund to educate private industry to Africa's enormous economic potential.

With this program we can begin to reverse the disastrous errors and neglect of the past 8 years—we can begin to rebuild the strength of the cause of freedom in Africa—and we can begin to restore our historic ties with the people in Africa.

In a recent American film, "The Defiant Ones," two men, a white man and a Negro chained together, fall into a deep pit. The only way out is for one to stand on the shoulders of the other. But since they were chained—after the first had climbed over the top of the pit, he had to pull the other out after him—if either one was to be free.

Today, Africa and America, black men and white men, new nations and old, are bound together. Our challenges rush to meet us. If we are to achieve our goals—if we are to fulfill man's eternal quest for peace and freedom—we must do it together—and together we can and will succeed.

New York Times *Editorial on Zanzibar: "A Cuba Off Africa?"**

January 14, 1964

There are dangers for East Africa and the free world in the communal conflict in Zanzibar that now has led to an African revolt against the Arab elite.

Internal strife, a small population of 340,000, isolation from the mainland and the approach of independence have made the tiny island a tempting Communist target for several years. Many meddlers have stirred the pot—Chinese, Russian, Cuban, Egyptian and the East Africans of neighboring Tanganyika and Kenya. Britain's inevitable departure Dec. 10 has left a vacuum that others would like to fill.

Peking, Moscow and Havana all have been training and financing adherents within most of the island's factions. One Cuban-trained group, which calls itself "Fidelistas," has recently returned home. Communist activity has been increased by competition for influence between pro-Moscow and pro-Peking factions. The danger in the current disorder is that some of these elements may capture control. The attraction of little Zanzibar for the Communists is that it would make a manageable base for subversion in all East Africa.

The interest of the free world lies less in which political party rules the island than in keeping Zanzibar's independence in the hands of responsible national elements. There are such elements in most factions, including the Afro-Shirazi party, which is one of the two groups that have seized power.

There is little the United States can do directly. American intervention would be unwise, and the American space-tracking station there is already a target for Communist propaganda. Britain has little desire to reverse its colonial disengagement in that part of the world.

One heritage of British rule, however, is the existence of aviation, communications and other links among Zanzibar, Tanganyika, Kenya and Uganda. There long has been talk of forming a federation of these countries.

The best safeguard for Zanzibar's independence would be common action by its East African neighbors—the countries most directly endangered—to shore up responsible elements against the external threat.

New York Times *Editorial on China and the Tanzania-Zambia ("Tan-Zam") Railroad*†

August 29, 1965

There is concern in Africa and elsewhere over the arrival of a team from Communist China to study the projected railroad from Zambia's copper belt to the port of Dar es

---

**The New York Times*, Jan. 14, 1964.
†*Ibid.*, Aug. 29, 1965.

Salaam in Tanzania. Fear of a new foothold for Peking persuaded some American officials to urge that the United States plunge in with an offer to help build this Tan-Zam railroad. But Washington has wisely resisted pressure to act on a project that is questionable as well as costly.

The railroad would give Zambia an alternative to shipping out its copper through Rhodesia and Portuguese Mozambique, both under potentially hostile white minority governments. But it would not make Zambia economically independent of Rhodesia nor could it be decisive in persuading the two white regimes to modify their racial policies.

World Bank and United Nations teams both recommended against the railroad. The U.N. group said that Rhodesia Railways, of which Zambia is part owner, could meet "any foreseeable normal increase in copper export traffic." It said the Tan-Zam railroad might prove "an expensive mistake," setting back Zambia's economic development. Both teams urged consideration of all-weather roads for the opening up of northeastern Zambia and southwestern Tanzania.

The United States has not ruled out consideration of the railroad for all time but has urged delay pending a broader survey of over-all transportation needs in the area. Washington in fact has offered to finance a survey of the need for roads to parallel any new studies of the advisability of the rail project.

Belief is widespread that reports of a Chinese offer to build the road amount to a bluff—an attempt to force a positive decision by the United States and the West. Peking's highly advertised aid program for Tanzania to date has been short on performance. Economists are skeptical that China will now take on a project likely to cost upwards of $200 million.

So long as the United States keeps open its offer to help Zambia and Tanzania in other development projects for which the need is clearer, it is well advised to await proof that the railroad is something more than an expensive prestige symbol in an area that might be better served by highways.

CENTRAL AFRICA

Commentary

The Central African region, a purely geographic designation, comprises the former Belgian Congo (Congo-Kinshasa, now Zaïre) and the countries that succeeded the French-imposed and ended Equatorial African Federation—Congo-Brazzaville, Gabon, the Central African Republic, and Chad. The once Spanish enclave of Rio Muni is part of this regional grouping, and the Cameroun, whose independence brought the trust territories of (British) Cameroons and (French) Cameroun together by plebiscite, may also be included.

For a world attuned to crisis, the Congo was the country that drew attention when the events of 1960 broke. Few people even knew there was another Congo whose capital was across the river and named for the French explorer, de Brazza.

Indeed, in 1960 the Congo was all Africa for much of the world. The events were dramatic, the area vast—one-third the size of the United States—and it was truly central and rich. So central that a Cold War confrontation in the face of a vacuum there would have to damage all Africa and reach far beyond, and so rich—all that copper and the other minerals in the province called Katanga, whose separation from the Northern Rhodesian/Zambian copper belt made no historical or cultural or geographical sense. But it had made political and economic sense to Leopold II of Belgium and to the European powers from the late nineteenth century on.

King Leopold's personal administration of his personal colony, whose profits he had shared with European concessionaires with frank fixation on maximum profit, had raised a popular outcry especially in England and America at the turn of the twentieth century. Revulsion against forced labor (practiced more quietly by the Portuguese to the south) and the severity of corporal punishment forced a reluctant Belgian parliament to take over responsibility for the Congo. From 1908 on, the Belgians ruled the Congo with their special brand of profitable paternalism. They retained the centralization of King Leopold's days, but otherwise their intention was to right the earlier human wrongs, to atone for earlier excesses.

It was a policy unlike that of the other colonial powers in Africa. Though neither Britain nor France expected African self-determination in any foreseeable future (an attitude held to firmly until at least the mid-1950's and even beyond), they did intend it in the fullness of theoretical time. The Belgians did not particularly intend it. It was not that they actively opposed self-determination as the Portuguese or the whites in Southern Africa did. It was just that they did not much think about it; they certainly

883

did not plan for it, even in theory. A partial explanation may come from the fact that the British, French, and Portuguese were true imperial powers, they had far-flung empires, centuries of varied experience which combined with their own historic currents to give them theories of colonial rule and its eventualities. The Belgians had only the Congo, which in a sense had been thrust upon them by accident in the twentieth century.

Belgian rule in the Congo was three-pronged: a centralized administration controlled from Brussels; an educational system controlled by the Church and ultimately from Belgium; an economy planned and controlled through Belgium's Société Générale, an almost all encompassing operation that controlled much of her economy and of which the mining interests in the Congo (Union Minière) were a part.

The paternalism towards the Congolese was the theme running through all aspects of policy. The mid-1950's, when colonial rulers elsewhere were forced to confront political decisions, brought no such internal problems for the Belgian administration. In 1955, political participation by Africans had not even been suggested, let alone begun. The Belgians pointed out that Europeans living in the Congo did not have voting rights either, and that made it all equal. Why did the Africans need politics? Did not the Congolese enjoy the broadest-based system of primary education in Black Africa? (So it was claimed with near justice.) There was technical training, with no restrictions on African employment in skilled jobs as elsewhere (how often Belgian administrators pointed out that trains plying the copper belt had to stop for crew changes at the Northern Rhodesian border; in the Congo Africans were able to drive engines, but white Rhodesians asserted that Africans were unable to handle these skills).

Medical posts were being built every fifty kilometers throughout the Congo, to be manned throughout the territory by Belgian doctors and Congolese assistants. With all these oportunities, social services, roads and other critical contributions to economic growth, what else could the Africans want? What the Africans did want was quite another matter, but a question seldom posed.

Belgian policy seemed to rest on a commitment to insulation. If the Congolese had education, up to a point; if they had economic opportunities, up to a point; if they could hold administrative jobs up to a point—if indeed all non-political activity were open to them up to a point, and if that point were high relative to neighboring territories, then everything should be fine? Shouldn't the Congolese be content? Why would such a system fail to work far into the future without disruption?

In 1956 when a Belgian professor proposed that it might be sensible to consider possible independence for the Congo in thirty years' time, he was roundly attacked for unnecessarily stirring up needless and unrealistic desires. But on June 30, 1960, the Congo celebrated its independence with its first university graduates and its political leadership with but a few months experience in government. However, it soon plunged into chaos with the mutiny of African troops of a *force publique* still under Belgian officers.

Was it that Africa's winds of change had simply blown down the Belgians? Or was it that something else, a feeling some observers had that perhaps certain Belgians believed that independence would be a change of status in name only and that necessity would soon bring a return to the status quo, or something like it? Insulation had worked both ways, on the governing and the governed.

Politics, when it came to the Congo, had the metaphorical reality of a first draft. Time and circumstance had not yet edited for simplicity or coherence. The Congo was not only a large country in area, but also one of great ethnic diversity. Its complex past had produced traditional attitudes of cooperation among some of the peoples whose last political experience was pre-Belgian; among others there had been rivalry and hostility. The lack of opportunities for higher western-style education, either in the Congo or in Belgium, had not only kept the Congolese away from certain ideas and knowledge; it had also kept them away from each other.

For largely that reason, then, the Congo lacked a political leadership made up of men who, however they might compete for power, might know each other, might share certain assumptions and certain experiences and common goals. In other parts of Africa the possibility of such communication and the common experience of political leaders would contribute to a certain stability in the years just after independence. In later years, under military rule, the cohesiveness of the ruling group might in theory be greater; in fact it depended on the length and type of training army officers had shared.

In the Summer, 1960, little of this was understood in other parts of Africa, in Europe in the United States, the Soviet Union, and the United Nations. From everywhere came all sorts of explanations for the Congo's problems, but most were based on abysmal lack of knowledge, and the most pressing concerns, at least of non-Africans, had little to do with the people of the Congo.

For the independent African states what seemed to matter was the true political independence of the Congo and the preservation of its integrity and unity. For the European countries, feelings were more ambivalent. Belgium's policy and pace might not have met with complete approval from Britain and France, but as fellow colonial powers who had themselves shared certain pressures, a community of sympathy developed. There was shared resentment at "interference" of various kinds—certainly from the Afro-Asian states, the United States, the Soviet Union, the United Nations (acting for shifting combinations of outside interests, as the Europeans might have seen it). There was also a sharing of long-range economic interests in the Congo, but more diverse ones that might be threatened if a continuing, less formal European presence were denounced and ousted. Some Americans shared this particular aspect of their concern, shifting to irritation and resentment as the months passed.

For the leaders of the United States and the Soviet Union, however, the Congo was a Cold War problem. Both feared a vacuum in the very center of Africa that might draw them into a confrontation that neither wanted. If the primary motive on both sides was not pure altruism—to be of assistance to the peoples of Africa generally and the Congo in particular in troubled times—they also did not want to alienate African opinion at so crucial a moment. President Eisenhower, at the end of his last term, resisting pressures to involve the United States in land war in Asia, was unlikely to welcome a land war in Africa either. The first Congo government's requests for aid, dispatched jointly and somewhat ironically by President Kasavubu and Prime Minister Lumumba, were refused amind a clamor from the independent African states against "Great Power" or "Cold War" involvement in an Africa determined to insist on non-alignment. More important for American action, the United States did not want bilateral involvement and deepening commitment.

Nor apparently did the Soviets want bilateral involvement, although a second call for aid did not go immediately to them. When the whole Congo question moved into the U.N. arena, they initially supported that move. The Soviets seemed to have thought their aims could reach fruition through the U.N., that view combined with the wish to avoid confrontation at that time and place. Premier Khrushchev was also launching a bid for popularity among the world's newest nations and it was clear to all that whatever else, no one would be popular in Africa who precipitated a super-power competition on a Congolese battleground.

By the time of John F. Kennedy's election, the U.N. operation in the Congo was under way, and the daily intricacies of the problem were surfacing. The commitment to the U.N. action—and only U.N. action—had been made, and it was congenial to the new administration whose support for the U.N. was strong. It was an administration more inclined than some Americans and certainly than many Europeans to help newly-independent African countries fulfill *their own* goals. It was less automatically determined to follow uncritically the lead of European allies. It was not even thrown into hysteria at the mention of a changing status quo. But all that was secondary. Thinking about the Congo in a Cold War context predominated and brought decisions which were made always with one end in view: stability without Great Power confrontation. No other consideration, Congolese or other, really mattered, as the memoirs written about the time so vividly show. After all, with open crises over steel at home and Cuba off-shore, the new administration was decreasingly inlined towards a direct African crisis (and that inclination started from a zero point).

Further, if both the United States and the Soviet Union had hoped that the U.N. presence in the Congo might work to their own advantage, again seen in Cold War terms, it did look as though the Americans were "winning." The terms of reference of the U.N. Peacekeeping force were to keep the two sides apart and thus preserve the status quo. Not, of course, that such impeccably unpolitical action was humanly possible. But when Kasavubu toppled Lumumba, it did seem, if seen quite out of Congolese context, to produce a pro-Western status quo, and therefore that event encouraged continuing massive American financial support of the U.N. and solidified Soviet determination to withhold its levied contributions completely. Countries do not pay for undermining their own self interest.

Still in concert with the U.N., and therefore the Afro-Asian nations, the United States opposed the most severe threat to Congolese territorial integrity, the secession of Katanga. That such a secession, especially under so avowedly pro-Western a leader as Tshombe, would work to the advantage of European and American economic interests was clear; by itself Katanga would be stable, far easier to influence if not control than the unruly Congo, and its wealth could be concentrated without having to contribute to the budget of a huge country, many parts of which were far less well-endowed. But Katanga's economic resources and Belgian settler presence made it resemble its white-dominated southern neighbors more closely than its sister provinces within the Congo. Though Moise Tshombe surely believed that he could ride the settler tiger, men in the State Department's Africa bureau feared he could not. For them—as documentation will eventually show—policy had to prevent the line of white minority control from encircling Katanga. For in addition to the consequences there, to extend that line was to threaten already precarious prospects for Northern Rhodesia, still in the grip of the Central African Federation and its white-controlled government. An independent Zambia was by no means inevitable in 1961.

United States policy opposing secession angered some Americans who saw only through Katanga-colored glasses. But apart from other considerations, the American government feared that one secession might easily set the precedent for another. What was to prevent a further break-away, this time of Orientale province, with its capital, Stanleyville, already credited by the world press as the "left-leaning" headquarters of Lumumba and later Gizenga and others sympathetic, in Cold War terms, to Soviet aims and ambitions?

Finally but importantly, this American stance against secession dove-tailed with passionately-held African views. African states vehemently opposed Tshombe's actions in Katanga for two related reasons: first, they saw the threat of unmasked Belgian neo-colonialism that had to be stopped or all African independence would mean nothing. Second and ultimately of the utmost importance, Africa could not stand the precedent of splintering. Not only did the ideological soundings of the day all read bigness and consolidation of some kind—but more realistically, if the shattering began, where would it end—given Africa's overwhelming historical and linguistic diversity?

Thus the United States and nations of the "Third World" worked together for their own reasons through the U.N. to achieve some form of African stability in the Congo. A few years of continuing crisis followed—political coups and killings, mutinies and mercenaries inside and outside, accusations and counter-accusations, denunciations of action and inaction. But governments and publics grow accustomed to continuing crisis; only the participation of American helicopters and troops in 1964 in rescuing mainly Belgian and American civilians from Stanleyville, then in the throes of a kind of civil war, briefly brought the passions on all sides to their earlier pitch.

A military coup in 1965 brought Joseph Mobutu to power. With him a kind of stability and, no doubt, a sigh of relief came among United States policy makers. Senatorial reaction against Asian or African commitments was beginning to mobilize; the single overt attempt by the Johnson Administration to prop up the Mobutu government with three transport planes against a military threat (even an external threat, a Portuguese-financed attack across the Congo-Angola border) drew such furor in the Senate and in the Press that the planes flew home quickly. The reaction to involving cargo planes and crews and the merest suggestion of advisers was becoming Pavlovian: it scarcely mattered *what* the executive branch of the government said was at stake. But then what may really have been at issue inside the Congo never entered into the calculations.

The rest of the Central African region, American policy makers may have thought, was blessedly the concern of France. Virtually all of it had been part of the now-extinct Federation of French Equatorial Africa, split into separate states by France in 1956. In the climate of ever decreasing concern with Africa in the mid-1960's, Americans were more inclined than ever to leave it all to French policy and activity.

If there were a threatened coup d'etat in friendly Gabon, let the French paratroopers bolster President Mba (they did). If the government of Congo (Brazzaville) started sounding pro-Chinese, let the French worry about it (they did). If civil war in Chad, huge and landlocked (sandlocked might be more accurate), had implications for neighboring Niger's uranium and Libya's oil, let the French deal with it. (They did: under a 1958 mutual defense treaty they sent their first paratroopers in the Spring of 1969.) Critics in France call Chad "France's little Vietnam," and some Americans worried that United States weapons might in some way enter the picture. But few worried because in America's world as the 1970's began, those who had even heard about Chad tended to feel only relief that it was someone else's problem.

CENTRAL AFRICA

ZAIRE (THE CONGO-KINSHASA)

Message from President Joseph Kasavubu and Prime Minister Patrice Lumumba of the Congo to Secretary General Dag Hammarskjold Requesting Urgent Military Assistance*

July 12, 1960

The Government of the Republic of the Congo requests urgent dispatch to the United Nations of military assistance. This request is justified by the dispatch to the Congo of metropolitan Belgian troops in violation of the treaty of friendship signed between Belgium and the Republic of the Congo in 1960. Under the terms of that treaty, Belgian troops may only intervene on the express request of the Congolese Government. No such request was ever made by the Government of the Republic of the Congo and we therefore regret the unsolicited action of Belgium as an act of aggression against our country.

The real cause of most of the disturbances can be found in colonial mass actions. We accuse the Belgium Government of having carefully prepared the secession of Katanga with a view to maintaining a hold on our country. The government, supported by the Congolese people, refuses to accept a *fait accompli* resulting from a conspiracy between Belgian imperialists and a small gang of Katanga leaders. The overwhelming majority of the Katanga population is opposed to secession which means the disguised perpetuation of the Katangaist regime. The essential purpose of the requested military aid is to protect its national territory of the Congo against the present external aggression which is a threat to international peace. We strongly stress the extremely urgent need for the dispatch of United Nations troops to the Congo.

Message from President Kasavubu and Prime Minister Lumumba to Secretary General Hammarskjold Clarifying the Nature of Assistance Requested†

July 13, 1960

In connexion with military assistance requested of United Nations by the Republic of the Congo the Chief of State and the Prime Minister of the Congo make the following clarification: (1) the purpose of the aid requested is not to restore internal situation in Congo but rather to prorect the national sigtory against act of aggression posed by Belgian metropolitan troops. Our request for assistance relates only to a United Nations force consisting of military personnel of neutral countries and not of United States as reported to certain radio stations. (3) If requested assistance is not received without delay the Republic of the Congo will be obliged to appeal to the Bandung Treaty Powers. (4) The aid has been requested by the Republic of the Congo as an exercise of its sovereign rights and not in agreement with Belgium as reported.

**American Foreign Policy, Current Documents, 1960,* (Washington, 1964), p. 524.
†*Ibid.,* p. 524.

*Statement by Henry Cabot Lodge, U.S. Representative to
the Security Council, on U.N. Assistance to the Congo**

July 13, 1960

On July 7 the Security Council met to extend the hand of friendship to the people and Government of the Republic of the Congo for endorsing its application for United Nations membership. On this occasion the United States called attention to the pressing problems inherited by this great new central African nation and its request for sympathy, encouragement, and concrete aid from the United Nations.

No one could foresee at that time the rapidity with which general statements of support here in the Council would need to be translated into concrete action. This need tonight is self-evident and urgent.

The unfortunate sequence of events in the Congo which makes the speediest possible United Nations assistance imperative is well known to us all. In general we understand that certain elements of those responsible for the maintenance of public order are turning against a democratically elected and legally constituted government. While we have been concerned primarily with the loss of life and destruction of valuable national assets, the departure of many of the foreign technicians whose assistance to the new state was considered crucial by the Government must also be noted. The specter of famine and disease implicit in the breakdown of security and communications is appalling. While no aggression has been committed, certain aspects emerge from the confusion which do justify urgent United Nations action and which, we think, can be stated as follows:

First, there is a popularly elected, duly constituted Government of the Republic of the Congo. That Government has asked for a United Nations force on an urgent basis.

Second, speed is essential. The longer the present state of near anarchy continues, the heavier the toll of lives, the greater the prospect of hunger and epidemic, and the greater the difficulties in future economic development. We confront a situation which is developing hourly—not daily, or weekly, but hourly.

Third, it is not only futile but positively harmful to seek to apportion blame at this time for what has happened. What is required is an instantaneous response to the urgent request of the Congo Government rather than ill-advised or malicious attempts to make political capital of the serious difficulties of the Congolese people.

The United States, therefore, welcomes the initiative of the Secretary-General in requesting this meeting of the Security Council. We believe that the recommendation which he has made for a United Nations force is reasonable and proper. For its part the United States is prepared to respond to the call before us. Indeed, we will respond to any reasonable United Nations request in the fields of transport and communications. We have also taken measures to insure that food supplies adequate to the needs of the capital, where we understand a food shortage is threatening, will be forthcoming. These food supplies will be of assistance to the United Nations in Léopoldville. Surely the beleaguered Government and unhappy people of the Congo have the right to such assistance, and we will not fail them.

*Ibid., p. 526.

In the course of this statement, Mr. President, I have used the words "urgent" and "speed" several times. I mean them literally and precisely. United Nations assistance would be most useful this very evening. It will still be of great service if it arrives in the Congo before the weekend.

Finally, Mr. President, let me pay tribute here to the efforts of the Government of the Congo to restore peace, security, and tranquility in the country. It has our full moral support in this effort. Let us hope that it receives material assistance very soon. Then the people and Government of the Congo can get on with the all-important task of building a great, new, modern state in the very heart of Africa.

The Secretary-General has outlined a reasonable and effective plan of action. The United States believes this Council should move ahead speedily to approve a resolution giving effect to the proposal of the Secretary-General.

Statement by Ambassador Lodge in the Security Council on the U.S. Interpretation of the U.N. Authorization of Military and Technical Assistance to the Congo*

July 14, 1960

The United States voted for the Tunisian resolution in spite of its doubts about the wisdom of the first operative paragraph, and we did so because of the vital urgency which we attach to prompt United Nations action to meet the tragic and highly dangerous situation in the Congo.

In voting for this resolution the United States expressly interprets the first paragraph calling upon the Government of Belgium to withdraw its troops as being contingent upon the successful carrying out by the United Nations of the second paragraph, that is, in providing the Government of te Republic of the Congo with the military assistance necessary until national security forces are able to fulfill their task.

The situation we face in the Congo is unique. At the outset of its independence, as power was being passed from the Government of Belgium to the Government of the Republic of the Congo, public law and order collapsed. In these circumstances the United Nations must not contribute to the perpetuation of public disorder by insisting upon the withdrawal of military units capable of assisting in the protection of life and property without establishment of alternate methods to accomplish the task.

The resolution can only be read as a whole in this sense, and it is with this understanding that the United States has supported it.

The United States has confidence that the Government of Belgium will cooperate wholeheartedly with the United Nations along these lines, in accordance with the long tradition which it has of loyal membership in support of the Organization. May I say to the representative of Belgium [Walter Loridan] that he has in fact just this evening made a statement expressing his Government's willingness to withdraw its troops upon introduction of United Nations forces, a statement of Belgium's full cooperation with the United Nations for which the Belgian Government should be congratulated and which reflects credit on the Belgian representative here.

*Ibid., pp. 529.

Statement by Secretary Herter on United States Moral and Material Backing of the U.N. to Restore Peace in the Congo*

July 21, 1960

I want to report briefly on the situation in the Congo as it affects our interests.

Our first concern was for the welfare and safety of the some 2,000 Americans living in this widespread area. A number of them are members of our official family connected with the Embassy at Léopoldville and the consulate at Elisabethville. The vast majority, however, were missionaries of many denominations who have been carrying on their work for many years in remote areas. I am glad to say that our records indicate that over 1,500 American citizens have now been safely evacuated. Almost all of those who remain are doing so on their own decision.

The breakdown of public order in the Congo shortly after independence and the appeal of that young country to the United Nations for help drew immediate response from that body. On July 13 the Security Council adopted a resolution authorizing the Secretary-General "to take the necessary steps . . . to provide . . . military assistance" in the Congo, until the Congolese Government can maintain order.

The United States not only voted in support of this resolution but put its logistic and communications resources at the disposal of the United Nations. At the request of the Secretary-General we have, I think, set a remarkable record in bringing aid and assistance to the Congo. Starting from scratch on July 14, the United States had as of today transported approximately 3,500 troops with 300 tons of equipment from three African countries and one European country. We have flown in 400 tons of desperately needed flour and airlifted equipment essential to the proper functioning of the U.N. Command in the Congo. In this brief time a total of over 125 flights of transport planes provided by the United States have been made to the Congo. This support operation is continuing day and night. By the end of this week we shall have transported an additional 2,000 troops and approximately 100 tons of equipment to the U.N. Command in Léopoldville.

The United States effort, of course, is conducted entirely in response to a request of the United Nations. Our own troops are not involved in the United Nations action. You will recall that it was mutually understood that the major powers should not supply troops. The United States has abided by the letter and spirit of this understanding. However, we have been shocked by the attitude and statements of the Soviet Union regarding this matter. The representative of the U.S.S.R. voted in the United Nations Security Council for the same resolution as the United States which I quoted above. This action had hardly been completed, however, when Mr. Khrushchev was publicly assuring the leaders of the Congo that he was prepared to intervene militarily in the Congo if the United Nations did not proceed to his satisfaction. I submit that such statements and threats, whether intended to be carried out or not, are recklessly irresponsible. The resolution for which the Soviet delegate voted was designed to restore peace and order to the Congo. The threat to take unilateral action in the Congo, repeated again by the Soviet delegate at the Security Council last night, can only be designed to increase tensions in the area and make more likely the continuation of hostilities and disorder. We must ask ourselves which policy the Soviet Union

*Department of State Bulletin, Aug. 8, 1960, pp. 205-06.

really intends to pursue. I find it hard to believe that the Soviet Union is prepared to set itself against the United Nations in the effort to restore order to the Congo which is progressing so rapidly and well. Ambassador Lodge at the Security Council last night made clear United States policy in such event.

In the situation in the Congo the United States will continue to back with all its moral force and material resources the action of the United Nations to restore peace and order.

Statement by Deputy Assistant Secretary of State Davis on the Role of the American Military in the Congo *

July 21, 1960

With regard to the Soviet Government's statement of July 19 concerning the presence of American troops in the Congo, the United States Government wishes to inform the Soviet Government that it has no combat troops in the Congo. As the Soviet Union is aware, the United Nations requested the United States to provide airlift facilities in support of the resolution adopted by the Security Council on July 14. The small group of United States service personnel in Léopoldville are engaged with the approval of the United Nations, but not as part of the U.N. Force, in air traffic control, aircraft maintenance and communications work essential to the operation of the airlift of U.N. supplies, food, troops, and equipment. They will remain in Léopoldville only as long as the United Nations requires assistance from the United States for this airlift from abroad to Léopoldville.

The United States Government regards the Soviet Government's demand as a deliberate, unilateral attempt to obstruct the United Nations efforts in the Congo. The United States will continue to make its fullest contribution to this important U.N. effort and will not be deterred by Soviet attempts to misrepresent its actions.

Statement by Ambassador Lodge on New Difficulties in the Congo†

August 8, 1960

The decisions which we must take today follow from those which we took on two previous occasions. At that time the United Nations decided to assist in the establishment of order in the Congo, on the one hand, and, on the other, to achieve the withdrawal of Belgian troops from the whole country. The United Nations was on the right track then; it is on the right track now.

Since our fateful decisions of July 14 and July 22, what has happened?

First, the United Nations, with the Secretary-General leading the way, has so far transported 11,500 troops to the Congo and has deployed them to points in five of the six provinces. We commend the Secretary-General for his efficiency, his drive, and his courage.

Ibid, Aug. 8, 1960, pp. 206.
†*Ibid.*, Sept. 5, 1960, pp. 384-85.

Second, all Belgian troops from five of the six provinces have now been moved to their home base of Kitona on the western edge of the Congo. Fifteen hundred have actually left for Belgium, and we have Belgian assurances that this number is steadily growing.

Third, the gratifying speed and effectiveness of the United Nations action has come up against a thorny but, we believe, temporary obstacle in Katanga. The Secretary-General has now quite properly come back to the Security Council for support and instructions in completing his task.

This brings us squarely to the problem of Katanga. The Secretary-General in his latest report to the Council has wisely separated the internal political aspect of this problem, which lies outside the concern of the United Nations, from the task of the United Nations, which is to insure peace and security and thereby the withdrawal of Belgian troops.

The task of the Council today is to help the Secretary-General get on with his job in Katanga. To do this we must reinforce the Secretary-General's view that the United Nations cannot be drawn into the political struggle between Prime Minister [Patrice] Lumumba and Provincial President [Moise] Tshombe.

The United Nations Charter and United Nations practice for 15 years emphasize that the United Nations cannot be involved in internal political disputes.

Let me now speak of the presence of Belgian troops in Katanga. We understand the motives which led Belgium some time ago to reinforce her troops in the Congo, which includes Katanga. But the presence of those troops became a source of friction between Belgium and the Congo. The Belgian Government, therefore, pulled back its troops as United Nations forces came into position.

This process should now be extended to Katanga. United Nations forces are now in a position to move into Katanga. The time has come for Belgian withdrawal at the earliest moment under arrangements to be worked out by the Secretary-General for the preservation of law and order.

The United States considers that local authorities in Katanga will have no grounds to object to United Nations forces once the Council has assured them that the only task of the United Nations is to insure law and order and thereby Belgian withdrawal. Nor can Belgium have any reason any longer to postone speedy withdrawal from Katanga.

*   *   *

*Summary of United States Support for Airlift of U.N. Troops and
Equipment into the Congo* *

August 9, 1960

The airlift of United Nations troops and equipment into the Congo is now about completed. The following summarizes the part that the United States played in this phase of the operation.

As of August 7, U.S. Air Force planes had lifted to the Congo 9,190 troops from eight countries and 1,134.6 tons of equipment. These were:

Ibid., Sept. 5, 1960, p. 385.

2,400 Moroccan troops and 277 tons of equipment;
2,259 Tunisian troops and 232.8 tons of equipment;
637 Ghanaian troops and 55 tons of equipment;
625 Guinea troops and 57 tons of equipment and rations;
612 Swedish troops and 182.5 tons of equipment;
250 Liberian troops and 10 tons of equipment;
1,168 Ethiopian troops and 125.5 tons of equipment;
566 Mali troops and 93.5 tons of equipment.

In addition, the following items were furnished and transported by the United States: 400 tons of flour; 6 H-13 and 2 H-19 U.S. helicopters; 6 light U.S. reconnaissance aircraft; 10 C-47 and 5 C-119 U.S. transport aircraft; 20 U.S. jeeps; and 11,000 helmet liners. Additionally transportation was provided for 6 Swedish light aircraft and 2 Norwegian light aircraft.

All of this was done within a period of 16 days.

This is not only an impressive demonstration of the capability and effectiveness of our Defense Establishment but also a demonstration of this Government's firm commitment to the principles of the United Nations and its willingness and ability to implement that commitment in support of peace and security.

Statement by President Eisenhower on the Security Council Resolution on the Congo *

August 10, 1960

I believe that the Security Council resolution adopted early yesterday represents another step forward in the United Nations determination, under the Secretary-General's tireless efforts, to find a peaceful solution to the difficult situation in the Congo.

The United States welcomes the steps Belgium has already taken and has said it will take in conformity with the Security Council resolutions. Belgium has contributed much in past years to the development of the Congo. The United States hopes that loyal cooperation with the United Nations on the part of all concerned will restore confidence between the Belgian and Congolese peoples and enable Belgian civilians to continue their contributions in the development of the new Congolese state.

Message from President Eisenhower to President Touré of the Republic of Guinea on Recognition of M. Kasavabu as Chief of State†

November 25, 1960

Your cable of November 20, 1960, I regret to say, reflects a serious misunderstanding of the policy of the United States Government in support of African freedom. I am prompted, therefore, to recall to you that the United States has been in the forefront of those nations who have favored emancipation of all peoples, including Africans, in accordance with the purposes and principles of the Charter of the United Nations. The

*Ibid., Sept. 5, 1960, p. 385.
†Ibid., Dec. 19, 1960, p. 922.

record of our actions over many years in support of African emancipation is open for all to see.

With specific reference to the Republic of the Congo, the United States warmly welcomed its independence. We have recognized and upheld its unity and territorial integrity through United Nations actions. We have refrained from unilateral intervention in its internal affairs. Although considerable partisanship has been demonstrated by some states, our support for the recognition by the United Nations of M. Kasavubu as Chief of State, a constitutional position which is universally accepted and recognized in the recent report of the U.N., is not a question of partisanship but an attempt to strengthen one of the essential foundations of stable and effective government in that unhappy country. This, I believe, is in strict conformity with the interests of the Congolese Government and people. As you are aware, a large number of African states have taken a similar stand. In view of the support by most countries for the United Nations role in the Congo and the fact that United Nations success is vital for the welfare of the Congolese, I sincerely hope that you will give full support to the United Nations effort there.

[Note: President Toure's cable read as follows—

November 20, 1960

[I have the honor to inform you of our concern at the development of a partisan position by the United States in the situation in the Congo. We earnestly request that you cease supporting the position of the enemies of African emancipation, who are employing every possible means against the legitimate government of the Congo to attack the unity and territorial integrity of the Congolese Nation. If the United States maintains its present position the Government of Guinea will refuse to take any part in the Conciliation Commission and will take any position in African affairs consistent with Congolese interests. High consideration.

Sekou Toure]

Correspondence Between President Eisenhower and President Touré of Guinea on African Freedom and the Congo *

President Touré to President Eisenhower

November 20, 1960

I have the honor to inform you of our concern at the development of a partisan position by the United States in the situation in the Congo. We earnestly request that you cease supporting the position of the enemies of African emancipation, who are employing every possible means against the legitimate government of the Congo to attack the unity and territorial integrity of the Congolese Nation. If the United States maintains its present position the Government of Guinea will refuse to take any part in the Conciliation Commission and will take any position in African affairs consistent with Congolese interests. High consideration.

Ibid., Dec. 24, 1960, p. 922.

President Eisenhower to President Touré

November 25, 1960

Your cable of November 20, 1960, I regret to say, reflects a serious misunderstanding of the policy of the United States Government in support of African freedom. I am prompted, therefore, to recall to you that the United States has been in the forefront of those nations who have favored emancipation of all peoples, including Africans, in accordance with the purposes and principles of the Charter of the United Nations. The record of our actions over many years in support of African emancipation is open for all to see.

With specific reference to the Republic of the Congo, the United States warmly welcomed its independence. We have recognized and upheld its unity and territorial integrity through United Nations actions. We have refrained from unilateral intervention in its internal affairs. Although considerable partisanship has been demonstrated by some states, our support for the recognition by the United Nations of M. Kasavubu as Chief of State, a constitutional position which is universally accepted and recognized in the recent report of the U.N., is not a question of partisanship but an attempt to strengthen one of the essential foundations of stable and effective government in that unhappy country. This, I believe, is in strict conformity with the interests of the Congolese Government and people. As you are aware, a large number of African states have taken a similar stand. In view of the support by most countries for the United Nations role in the Congo and the fact that United Nations success is vital for the welfare of the Congolese, I sincerely hope that you will give full support to the United Nations effort there.

Statement by Senator George Aiken (Vermont), U.S. Representative in Committee of the U.N. General Assembly, on the United States Voluntary Contribution to the Costs of the United Nations Operations in the Congo*

November 29, 1960

The item before us is clearly the most important one that this committee has yet discussed. Its importance stems from a number of facts. Perhaps the most important of these is the fact that the United Nations is now, for the first time, really facing up to its responsibilities toward the newly independent countries of Africa.

The decision of the Security Council on July 14, 1960, was historic. It was a recognition of the fact that the welfare, the security, and the independence of the African peoples is a major responsibility of this Organization. It was a recognition of the fact that a threat to the peace in Africa is a threat to the peace everywhere.

The decision of the Security Council on July 14, 1960, was a dedication by this Organization of the resources of the entire membership to the task of restoring to the Congo the peace, law, and order which would enable the people of the Congo to govern themselves.

*Ibid., Dec. 26, 1960, pp. 975-76.

The United Nations Force in the Congo is the result of that decision. Many governments responded magnificently to the call for troops to man the force. Foremost among these were the countries of Africa. Other countries, far from Africa, also sent their young men to assist the people of the Congo. Some of the men of the force have already given their lives to assure the success of this historic effort. We pay tribute—the highest tribute—to them today. We trust that their example will guide and inspire us here.

     *   *   *

The United States is aware that the costs of this operation have been high and will be a burden to many countries. In order to ease this burden the United States is prepared to make a substantial voluntary contribution toward the expenses for 1960 over and above its normal assessed share of the expenses.

We offer this voluntary contribution on the assumption that these expenses for 1960 are incorporated in the regular budget of the United Nations for 1960. There must be assurance that no one will be tempted to argue in the future—as some have argued without foundation in the past—that there is no legal obligation to pay assessments for expenses which are not incorporated in a section of the regular budget.

The United States voluntary contribution is in two parts. First, the United States waives its costs for the initial airlift to the Congo of contingents of the United Nations Force. The amount waived is $10,317,621.52. This will reduce the budget estimates recommended by the Advisory Committee on Administrative and Budgetary Questions to a figure under $50,000,000 and will benefit all members. The second part of the United States voluntary contribution is a pledge of a cash contribution of the order of $3,500,000 to $4,000,000. The exact amount will depend upon the final assessment level. This will be determined in part by whether other governments are prepared to announce the waiver of claims against the United Nations which are included in the budget estimates. This cash contribution will be made on the understanding that it will be used to provide a 50 percent reduction in the contributions of those governments having a limited capacity to pay. We trust that a satisfactory formula can be devised to carry out this purpose.

Mr. Chairman, the United States is offering these voluntary contributions for several reasons. First, we believe that the United Nations operation in the Congo is the collective responsibility of all members of this Organization and that we must all contribute—and make our contributions commensurate with our ability to pay. Second, we offer this contribution as a tribute to the governments which have given troops to the United Nations Force and to the troops themselves who represent the United Nations—and all of us—in the Congo today. And, finally, we offer it as a tribute to those men who have given—again in the words of Abraham Lincoln—"the last full measure of devotion" in the service of the United Nations.

President John F. Kennedy's News Conference on the Congo *

February 15, 1961

Ambassador Stevenson in the Security Council today has expressed fully and clearly the attitude of the United States Government towards the attempts to under-

*Public Papers of the Presidents, John F. Kennedy, 1961, pp. 91-92.

mine the effectiveness of the United Nations organization. The United States can take care of itself, but the United Nations system exists so that every nation can have the assurance of security. Any attempt to destroy this system is a blow aimed directly at the independence and security of every nation, large and small.

I am also, however, seriously concerned at what appears to be a threat of unilateral intervention in the internal affairs of the Republic of the Congo. I find it difficult to believe that any government is really planning to take so dangerous and irresponsible a step. Nevertheless, I feel it important that there should be no misunderstanding of the position of the United States in such an eventuality.

The United States has supported and will continue to support the United Nations presence in the Congo. The United States considers that the only legal authority entitled to speak for the Congo as a whole is a government established under the Chief of State, President Kasavubu, who has been seated in the General Assembly of the United Nations by a majority vote of its members. The broadening of the government under President Kasavubu is a quite legitimate subject of discussion, and such discussions have been going on in Leopoldville and in New York. But the purported recognition of Congolese factions as so-called governments in other parts of that divided country can only confuse and make more difficult the task of securing Congolese independence and unity.

The United Nations offers the best, if not the only possibility for the resoration of conditions of stability and order in the Congo.

The press reports this afternoon that Prime Minister Nehru has stated, and I quote, "If the United Nations goes out of the Congo, it will be a disaster." I strongly agree with this view. Only by the presence of the United Nations in the Congo can peace be kept in Africa.

I would conceive it to be the duty of the United States and, indeed, all members of the United Nations to defend the Charter of the United Nations by opposing any attempt by any government to intervene unilaterally in the Congo.

*   *   *

*Statement by Adlai E. Stevenson, U.S. Representative to the U.N.,
on the Congo Situation**

February 15, 1961

A few days ago a new administration took office in the United States. This is the first occasion for the United States, under the leadership of President Kennedy, to speak formally in the Security Council on a question of substance.

*   *   *

It seems to be my lot, Mr. President, to address you and my colleagues for the first time in a moment of grave crisis in the brief and tragic history of the Congo and in a moment of equally grave crisis for the United Nations itself. I had hoped it would be otherwise.

*Department of State Bulletin, Mar. 13, 1961, pp. 359-63.

Within recent days we have seen successively the withdrawal of two national units of the United Nations forces, the violent death of former Prime Minister Patrice Lumumba, the reported recognition of the [Antoine] Gizenga regime in Stanleyville by the United Arab Republic, and a threat by the U.S.S.R. to provide unilateral assistance outside the United Nations. What we decide here in the next few days may, we believe, determine whether the United Nations will be able in the future to carry on its essential task of preserving the peace and protecting small nations.

This is a time for urgent and constructive action. In the midst of passions it is a time when the Security Council must be calm. In the midst of efforts to destroy the United Nations action in the Congo it is a time when we must persevere in the interests not only of the Congo but of all of us, large and small. The choice, as always, is a choice of us, the members of the United Nations. Either we will follow a path toward a constructive and workable solution or we will follow a path of negative recrimination and self-interest.

As a new arrival listening and talking to delegates, I have wondered sometimes in the past 10 days if everyone is actually thinking about the Congo—a new republic struggling to be born—or if the Congo has been obscured by passions and prejudices about the doctors—Kasavubu, Lumumba, Gizenga, Tshombe, and so forth.

Opinion seems to be polarizing about them, not about the patient. So it is more important than ever to rally support to the United Nations in order to save the patient.

*   *   *

As I said, Mr. President, I had hoped that my first formal remarks to the Security Council on the vexed problems of the Congo could be directed solely to constructive suggestions which would be helpful to the Congolese people in working out their own independence, free of outside interference.

Instead, I find myself compelled to comment on constructive suggestions but on a statement and a proposed resolution by the Soviet Union published in this morning's newspapers, which is virtually a declaration of war on the United Nations and on the principle of international action on behalf of peace.

Permit me to analyze what, stripped of intemperate rhetoric, this statement and this resolution propose. They propose the abandonment of the United Nations effort for peace in the Congo and a surrender of the United Nations to chaos and to civil war.

*   *   *

And now the cold war. Does the Soviet Government really want to chill what should be warm and temperate in Africa with the icy blasts of power politics? The United States does not. Its only interest in the Congo is to support the Congolese people in their struggle for real independence, free from any foreign domination from any source.

The United States deplores any war, cold or otherwise. Its only desire is to live in peace and freedom and to let all other peoples live in peace and freedom. It will resist with all of its power all assaults on its own peace and freedom, and it proposes to join with all other peace-loving peoples in resisting, in the cooperative framework of the United Nations, all assaults on the peace and freedom of other peoples.

In that spirit we declare that, so far as we are concerned, Africa shall never be the scene of any war, cold or hot. But we also declare that Africa for the Africans means Africa for the Africans and not Africa as a hunting ground for alien ambitions. And we pledge our full and unstinted support against any attempt by anyone to interfere with the full and free development by Africans of their own independent African future.

We believe that the only way to keep the cold war out of the Congo is to keep the United Nations in the Congo, and we call on the Soviet Union to join us in thus insuring the free and untrammeled exercise by the Congolese people of their right to independence and to democracy.

But, Mr. President, the position apparently taken by the Soviet Government involves more than the unhappy and despicable fate of three Congolese politicians. It involves the future of the 14 million Congolese people. They are the ones with whom we are concerned. We deplore the past, and we condemn those responsible for it, no matter who they may be. But we submit that it is the future that is all-important now and that the best efforts of this Council should be concentrated on the future security of the Congo and, indeed, on the future security of all peoples.

For, Mr. President, it is the security of all peoples which is threatened by the statement and by the proposals of the Soviet Government. Let me make my meaning abundantly and completely clear, if I can. The United States Government believes, and profoundly believes, that the single best and only hope of the peoples of the world for peace and security lies in the United Nations. It lies in international cooperation, in the integrity of an international body rising above international rivalries into the clearer air of international morality and international justice.

The United Nations has not achieved perfection nor has the United States, and they probably never will. The United States, like the United Nations, is composed of humans; it has made mistakes, it probably always will make mistakes; it has never pleased all people, it cannot please all people; in its desire and wholehearted determination to do justice it may offend one group of states in 1952, another in 1956, and perhaps still another in 1961. But always the United States has tried, and we believe it will always try, to apply evenhandedly the rules of justice and equity that should govern us all.

Are we callously to cast aside the one and only instrument that men have developed to safeguard their peace and security? Are we to abandon the jungles of the Congo to the jungles of internecine warfare and internal rivalry?

This issue, Mr. President, even transcends the fate of the suffering 14 million Congolese people. It involves the fate of all of us, of all mankind.

The issue, then, is simply this: Shall the United Nations survive? Shall the attempt to bring about peace by the concerted power of international understanding be discarded?

[At this point Ambassador Stevenson was interrupted by a disturbance in the public gallery. The gallery was cleared, and the meeting continued.]

Mr. President, may I say that I deeply deplore this outrageous and obviously organized demonstration. To the extent that Americans may have been involved, I apologize on behalf of my Government to the members of the Security Council.

To continue, shall any pretense of an international order, of international law, be swept aside? Shall conflicts of naked power, awful in their potential, be permitted to rage in Africa or elsewhere, unchecked by international cooperation or authority?

These are questions, Mr. President and my colleagues, which call for an answer, not so much by the great powers as by the smaller ones and the newer ones. My own country, as it happens is in the fortunate position of being able to look out for itself and for its interests, and look out it will. But it is for the vast majority of states that the United Nations has vital meaning and is of vital necessity. I call on those states to rise in defense of the integrity of the institution which is for them the only assurance of their freedom and their liberty and the only assurance for all of us of peace in the years to come.

      *   *   *

Now let me turn to the Congo and to what can be done to arrest the sad deterioration in that divided country. There are certain fundamental principles concerning the Congo which have had and will continue to have the full support of the American people and of the United States Government. It is on the basis of these principles that we have undertaken consultations this past fortnight. We believe that they are shared by others, and we are willing to work with any and all who show a willingness to find a solution. The essential principles of such a solution are, we believe, apparent to all.

In the first place, that the unity, the territorial integrity, the political independence of the Congo must be preserved. I am sure Sir Patrick will not object if I repeat that the United States was one of the first anticolonialists and that, during the 186 years since, we have stood steadfastly for the right of peoples to determine their own destiny. The United States desires nothing for the Congo but its complete freedom from outside domination and nothing for its people but the same independent freedom which we wanted for ourselves so long ago and have resolutely defended ever since.

Much as the United States was once beset by internal dissensions, so the Congo since its independence has been beset by secessionist movements—previously in the Katanga and now in Orientale Province too. The United States supports the continued territorial integrity of the Congo. So far as we are concerned, its borders are identical with its borders on July 1, 1960. The United States is ready to join with other states which support its independence and integrity to maintain this principle within the framework of the United Nations.

Secondly, the Congo must not become a battleground, as I have said, either for a cold or a hot war among the big powers. When the United States was first requested to provide troops for the Congo, we told the Congolese Government to appeal to the United Nations. We then supported the United Nations military assistance to the Congo. In contrast to others, the United States has never at any time provided a single tank, a single gun, a single soldier, a single piece of equipment that could be used for military purposes to anyone in the Congo.

We have, on the other hand, responded to every request made to us by the United Nations promptly and vigorously so that the entire control over our assistance passed from our hands to those of the United Nations. We remain firmly determined, as I have said, to do everything in our power to keep the cold war out of Africa.

Third, we support the United Nations action in the Congo to the fullest measure of our power. The best way to keep the cold war and the hot war out of the Congo, as I have said, is to keep the United Nations in. To those members who are still contemplating withdrawal, I suggest a long, hard, careful look at what might happen in the Congo if the United Nations Force collapses or if the United Nations mission fails because of lack of support from its members.

Finally, we believe that the Congolese people must be allowed to develop their own political settlement by peaceful means free from violence and external interference. The Congo's political problems must in the last analysis be worked out by the Congolese themselves. The United Nations can assist in this effort—by helping create peace and stability and through extending its good offices as it has done in the Conciliation Commission. But only a settlement demanding the support of the Congolese people will long endure.

*   *   *

*Statement by Secretary Rusk on United States Policy in the Congo**

January 18, 1962

*   *   *

United States policy with regard to the Congo is consistent with our general foreign policy and our attitude toward Africa as a whole. Briefly stated, that attitude is (a) to help the African peoples form societies and governments that will be truly independent and consonant with their own consciences and cultures; (b) to maintain and promote the strong ties of culture, friendship, and economic life that already exist between the new nations of Africa and the nations of Europe and America; and (c) to cooperate in every way acceptable to both the Africans and ourselves as these new countries strive to produce the political stability, economic progress, and level of education that are essential to a free society.

In pursuit of these broad objectives, the United States has strongly supported efforts to preserve the territorial integrity of the Congo. Like almost every country in the world, the United States has firmly opposed efforts by Kasai, Katanga, Orientale, or any other province to secede. This is our policy because there is no legal, moral, or practical basis for the secession of any of these provinces; nor is there reasonable evidence that secession is the will of the majority of the population of any province involved.

*   *   *

New York Times *Editorial on U.S. Civilians' Role in the Congo†*

June 18, 1964

The State Department has been showing a salutary sense of shock over the news—which curiously it was among the last to know—that American civilians were

*Ibid., Feb. 5, 1962, p. 216.
†The New York Times, June 18, 1964.

flying combat missions for the Congolese Government against rebels in Kivu Province. It looks like one of those cases where the left hand did not know what the right was doing.

The situation is that some United States civilian pilots have a contractual agreement with the Congolese Government to train pilots to fly T-28 planes the United States gave to Léopoldville. The technicians were not ever supposed to take part in combat themselves, but when the capital of Kivu Province, Bukavu, was threatened last week they did so. The understanding now is that they will not be called upon to carry out any more operational missions for the Adoula Government.

If there is any lingering suspicion it is because the pilots who are being trained to fly the T-28's are Cuban exiles, and the Congolese rebels are in part armed and financed by Chinese Communists. The connection between Cuban exiles and the Central Intelligence Agency has been uninterrupted since long before the Bay of Pigs invasion.

However, it does seem to have been made clear now that it is not United States policy to use Americans in the Congo for purposes that will involve us in operations parallel to those in Cuba, Vietnam or Laos. There are Belgian, Israeli and Italian as well as American technicians training Congolese troops in the use of military materiel. The purpose is supposed to be merely to maintain order in a large country with a desperate lack of trained men and transport.

The Congo is still a United Nations responsibility, although the U.N. troops are leaving on June 27. What happens afterward is something to worry about, but the cause for worry will be greater still if the United States should find itself blundering into an unsought role as policeman to fill still another vacuum, this time in Africa. The speed with which a brushfire can escalate into a crisis—our crisis—is disturbing enough, even when we know what we are getting into.

New York Times *Editorial on United States Military Assistance to the Congo* *

August 13, 1964

While President Johnson was telling the American Bar Association how troubled and turbulent the world is and how the United States lives with crisis and danger, American planes and soldiers were on their way to the Congo. There they will find as much trouble, turbulence and danger as exists at any spot on the globe. Thus the United States is getting itself militarily involved in still another conflict—and it is doing so unilaterally. This time the United Nations is not taking part. A vacuum has to be filled and, as is becoming the custom, the United States is to fill it.

Presumably, the calculation is that Premier Tshombe's Government would succumb to the rebels, or that the vast country would fall into anarchy, unless help were sent quickly. The fact that the Chinese Communists are supporting the rebels is certainly another reason for the American move. So now our troops and transport planes are being sent to prop up the man we helped drive into exile just a short time ago.

The United States is starting with only enough arms, men and materiel to put out a little bonfire. This may be sufficient, but as Southeast Asia showed, bonfires can grow

Ibid., Aug. 13, 1964.

into great conflagrations. Premier Tshombe will surely want the American transport planes for use against the rebels. United States soldiers are likely to get shot at. Are they going to shoot back? The Congolese rebels are surprisingly well organized and armed. Does Washington believe they can be defeated without a major effort?

These and many other questions need to be answered. The Johnson Administration may be justified in involving the United States in still another crisis in another faraway country, but the American people should be told, frankly and honestly, what the Government has in mind and how far it is prepared to go. Events are moving so oquickly that President Johnson did not include even a reference to the Congo in his speech yesterday about the sweep of our involvements as world policeman. A better explanation than the Pentagon and State Department have given is in order, while there is still time to assess the wisdom of our commitment.

New York Times *Editorial on "The Disintegrating Congo"**

August 21, 1964

When Moise Tshombe went back to Leopoldville at the end of June he proclaimed to his people and the world that he was going to give them "a new Congo" in three months. Nearly two of those months have gone and there seems a serious possibility that Premier Tshombe is not even going to be able to hang on to the old Congo.

The United States must either keep clear of this crumbling edifice or face serious damage if—or, more likely, when—the walls cave in. Even to have supplied transport aircraft with paratroopers, as President Johnson did last week, was risky because it could only be a beginning. Next, came a request for bombers—which are being supplied. More demands are sure to come, because this is a situation that will require massive military and economic aid simply to prevent a collapse.

The American position, for the moment, is unilateral. If Mr. Tshombe's African neighbors respond favorably to his appeal for aid, the situation would change. But his unpopularity among them makes the chances slim, and in any event help would be delayed. Meanwhile, the more help Mr. Tshombe gets from the United States the more he is branded with the old stigma of being a tool of the Western imperialists.

The Chinese Communists are providing advice, monyy and perhaps some arms to the Congolese rebels, but this does not make the Congo—so huge, backward and torn by tribal strife—a major testing ground in the cold war. It will only become so if the United States gets deeply involved.

Leopoldville has now lost the whole eastern portion of the country to the rebels. Kwilu Province in the southwest is also in rebel hands, Kasai Province in the south has been weakened by rebellions. A struggle for power is taking place all over the country. No one can predict who is going to come out on top. The United States must not be put in the position of seeming to impose a leader, especially when he is one we so recently were helping to depose.

The United States does not need to fill every vacuum, everywhere. The Congolese should have a chance to settle their own quarrels. The solution, whatever it is and whenever it comes, must be an African one, a Congolese solution.

Ibid., Aug. 21, 1964.

In the meantime, the American people have a right to know far more precisely than they know now what the Johnson Administration has in mind. The way events are developing, the United States could be drawn ever deeper into the Congolese jungle.

New York Times *Editorial on Mercenaries' Effect on the Congo**

August 26, 1964

Premier Moise Tshombe's decision to defend his Government with white mercenaries puts an ugly new aspect on the Congolese situation. It will, almost certainly, close the door to any help from his African neighbors, since these hired soldiers will be mainly South Africans, Southern Rhodesians and Europeans who fought for Mr. Tshombe when he was the secessionist President of Katanga Province. South Africa and Southern Rhodesia, with their white supremacist policies, are anathema to the other independent African nations.

Mr. Tshombe's decision makes the United States position in the Congo even more uncomfortable than it has been. Washington has been hoping that the Congolese conflict, being African, would be solved by Africans. Now this country is placed in the unhappy position of helping a government which is feverishly recruiting foreign white mercenaries from countries its neighbors loathe. The American position vis-a-vis the other African nations is bound to be adversely affected. Naturally Premier Khrushchev is making the most of this propagandistic opportunity.

The main question to be answered now is: What is the reasoning behind Premier Tshombe's policy? He must know that in recruiting the mercenaries and at the same time asking five African nations to help him he is contradicting himself. It is plausible that he figured in advance he would get no help from the Organization of African Unity and that his only hope is to defend himself by any means.

The mercenaries are obviously an act of desperation. They might win some skirmishes against the rebels and even some battles. But it seems hardly possible that they can crush the rebellion, or that Moise Tshombe can erect a strong and safe regime on a Praetorian Guard of white adventurers who fight for pay. The danger is that the United States, already involved in the Congo with transport planes and paratroopers, will keep expanding its commitment—without any real explanation of why we are there at all.

New York Times *Editorial on "The Disintegrating Congo"†*

September 9, 1964

When the Belgians left on July 1, 1960, the Congo, like Humpty Dumpty, fell off the wall and all the U.N.'s forces and all the U.N.'s men could not put it together again. The U.N. made a valiant effort, which for a while seemed to be succeeding. The then President Tshombe was forced out of Katanga Province and Leopoldville nominally became the core of a centralized government. Yet the forces of disintegration

---

Ibid., Aug. 26, 1964.
†*Ibid.,* Sept. 9, 1964.

continued to work, and by the time the U.N. forces had to quit just four years after they had begun, the Congo was falling apart again.

Moise Tshombe, returning as Premier, is now in his turn facing a secessionist move. Rebels in Stanleyville under Cristophe Gbenye have proclaimed a "Congolese People's Republic." This is more of a struggle for power than for ideology. It is gross oversimplification merely to identify the Tshombe Government with the West and the rebels with the Communist Chinese, though both the West and the Communists are involved.

When Moise Tshombe first came back at the end of June he thought his problem was political. Soon he decided that it was military and that the Congo could only be held together by force. His own Congolese troops, although better armed and no more inexperienced than the rebels, would not fight. So he needed help. He turned first to the United States, which is in no position to commit the troops and materiel to make another Vietnam of the Congo. He turned next to the recruitment of white merce-naries, who alienated the only people who could really help him—his fellow-Africans of the Organization of African Unity. Mr. Tshombe has finally turned to them. He was few friends in the organization, but if they want to see him give up his mercenaries, they must offer him African troops on terms that he can reasonably accept.

This is not a situation in which the United States can play a decisive role. However, Washington is certainly not going to recognize any "People's Republic" in the Congo. Perhaps the Communists would like to balkanize the country, but not the West, and least of all the African nations whose own stability will be threatened if the Congo cannot settle down.

*President Lyndon B. Johnson's News Conference on the Congo**

November 28, 1964

*   *   *

What has happened in Stanleyville has happened far too often to Congolese and foreigners alike on both sides in various conflicts in the Congo in recent years. The Congo has suffered through more than 4 years of violence and bloodshed and disunity. It has been an arena of power struggles and ideological wars. I hope now that it can have at last a chance for peace and order, and economic recovery, so that the ordinary people of the Congo can hope for improvement in their lot and for protection against the daily threat of violent death.

I have wired the relatives of our citizens who lost their lives there my feelings and expressed my great sympathy for them in this hour. We lost three Americans.[1] Undoubtedly we would have lost dozens more had we not acted promptly and decisively in cooperation with the Belgian paratroopers. As you know, more than 4,000 Congolese themselves, most of whom were people with education, more than 4,000 Congolese in recent months have lost their lives because of these disorders.

I would like to stress to those of you here at the ranch this morning that the United

Public Papers of the Presidents, Lyndon B. Johnson, 1963-1964, pp. 1611-12.
[1] Dr. Paul Carlson of California, Phyllis Rine of Mount Vernon, Ohio, and Joseph Tucker of Lamar, Ark., all missionaries.

States has no political goals to impose upon the Congo. We have no narrow interest. We have no economic gain to be served in the Congo. We seek to impose no political solution, neither our own nor that of some other outsider.

We have tried only to meet our obligations to the legitimate government, and to its efforts to achieve unity and stability and reconciliation in the Congo.

So we hope now that everyone who has had a part in this 4-year agony of the Congo will bury past differences and try to work together in a spirit of compassion, to help reach these goals of unity and stability and reconciliation. If this could happen, perhaps the hundreds of innocent lives, Congolese and foreign, that have been sacrificed will not have been sacrificed in vain.

We were necessarily a party to the decisions, and I assume full responsibility for those made for our planes to carry the paratroopers in there, in this humanitarian venture. We had to act and act promptly in order to keep hundreds and even thousands of people from being massacred. And we did act in time.

The paratroop force that we moved in there will be moved out tonight, and it will be moved out of the Congo to Ascension Island in the South Atlantic Ocean.

*   *   *

New York Times *Editorial on The Airdrop at Stanleyville**

November 26, 1964

The dramatic U.S.-Belgian airborne operation in the Congo was fully justified and effectively carried out but—in retrospect—it should have been done sooner, and it should have been kept secret until after the event.

The political and psychological disadvantages of the operation, illustrated by the expected automatic Soviet and African protests, were an inherent part of it no matter when it was done; the objective—the saving of lives—far outweighed these disadvantages. Prior permission of the Tshombe Government was of course necessary; but the last-minute nature of the airdrop and the publicity concerning it probably helped to cause loss of life.

If the airdrop had been undertaken sooner it might well have been even more effective. Certainly if press secrecy could have been maintained, the element of surprise would have tremendously aided the paratroopers in accomplishing their objective—the freeing of the hostages without loss of life. More resolution on the part of Government and more restraint on the part of press were called for under the circumstances.

New York Times *Editorial on "After the Congo Rescues"†*

November 29, 1964

Their mercy mission at an end—though not in time to save nearly 100 of the white prisoners held as hostages by the Congo rebels—Belgian paratroopers have begun their

---

The New York Times, Nov. 26, 1964.
†*Ibid.,* Nov. 29, 1964.

promised withdrawal from the Congo. They go even though the fate of hundreds of additional whites in rebelw-held territory remains unclear. All the circumstances of their arrival and departure testify to the humanitarian nature of their mission and to the total lack of justification for the protest demonstrations the paratroop drop has provoked in Communist and African countries.

As President Johnson made plain in his news conference yesterday, the real target for indignation should be those responsible for the savage massacre of the hostages, not those who came to save them. Many more Congolese than whites were murdered, a fact the demonstrators choose to ignore in the eagerness to fabricate a new excuse for excoriating "white colonialism."

The violent denunciations of the rescue operation voiced at the emergency conference of seven African states in Nairobi amounted almost to a call for overthrow of the Tshombe Government in the Congo. The attack on the United States and other embassies in Moscow, though nominally the work of African and Asian students, could scarcely have been carried out without the approval of the Soviet Government. The hypocrisy of the Russian and Chinese attitude in the entire affair is evident when one recalls how angrily both countries have reacted whenever their own citizens' safety or freedom of action has been threatened in a foreign land, under conditions far less outrageous than those that caused the present mercy move—a move carried out with the full endorsement of the established Congolese Government.

The emotional character of the African protests should bring a considerable easing of tension now that the paratroopers have begun evacuating. But it would be delusive not to recognize that the possibilities of fruitful cooperation between Western nations and the new African states have been set back. By the same token, the opportunity for increased Soviet and Chinese influence—and exploitation—in these states has increased. The outlook in the Congo remains a tortured and unhappy one—for it and the world.

Statement by Ambassador Stevenson at the U.N. Answering Charges of United States Interference in the Congo *

December 14, 1964

*　　　　　　*　　　　　　*

In the last few days the United States has been variously accused, and I quote, of "wanton aggression"; of "premeditated aggression"; of plotting a humanitarian mission as a "pretext" for military intervention; of a "nefarious action" designed "to exterminate the black inhabitants"; of "inhumanitarianism"; of a "wanton and deliberate massacre of Congolese people"; of a "murderous operation", of a "premeditated and coldblooded act"; of "not being truly concerned with the lives of the hostages"; of a "crude subterfuge"; of "massive cannibalism"; of having killed Lumumba "with cynicism and premeditation"; of genocide against an entire people; of being caught "redhanded"; of using the United Nations as a "Trojan horse"; of a racist attack to kill thousands of "blacks," an operation which, in the words of one of the speakers, proved to him that a "white, if his name is Carlson, or if he is an American, a Belgian, or an Englishman, is worth thousands upon thousands of blacks."

*Department of State Bulletin, Jan. 4, 1965, pp. 15-21.

And that's not all! We have heard words in this chamber either charging or implying that the United States Government was an accomplice to the death of Dag Hammarskjold—and even the assassination of President Kennedy!

I have served in the United Nations from its inception off and on for 7 years. But never before have I heard such irrational, irresponsible, insulting, and repugnant language in these chambers—and used to contemptuously impugn and slander a gallant and successful effort to save human lives of many nationalities and colors.

But even such a torrent of abuse of my country is of no consequence compared to the specter of racial antagonism and conflict raised in this chamber. I need no credentials as a spokesman for racial equality and social justice in this country, and the Government of this country needs none in the world. Yet at a time when all responsible men and governments are trying to erase every vestige of racial antagonism, when racism has become an ugly word in all nations, we hear its ominous undertones—in the United Nations.

Racial hatred, racial strife, has cursed the world for too long. I make no defense of the sins of the white race in this respect. But the antidote for white racism is not black racism. Racism in any form by anybody is an offense to the conscience of mankind and to the Charter of the United Nations, which enjoins us to promote and encourage "respect for human rights and for fundamental freedoms for all without distinction as to race, sex, language, or religion."

Mr. President, the verbal violence, the mistrust, the hatred, the malign accusations we have heard from a few representatives of African nations is not, I fear, just an echo of the language and tactics of the cold war, which for so long corrupted international discourse. And I heard with relief the statements last Friday by the distinguished representatives of the Ivory Coast and Morocco deploring the introduction into our debates of racial strife and hatred.

We share profoundly their concern. We had hoped that the era of racial discrimination which has poisoned the atmosphere of Africa was coming to an end. It is precisely because the policy of apartheid in South Africa is inconsistent with the concept of racial equality and harmony that it has been condemned by all of us.

Yet the Foreign Minister of Congo (Brazzaville) seems to attribute the difficulties that have so long beset his country's neighbor, the Congo, to a mythical struggle between blacks and whites.

The Government of Congo (Brazzaville) has for well over a year encouraged and supported rebellion against the legitimate government of Congo (Leopoldville) under President Kasavubu, Prime Minister Adoula, and Prime Minister Tshombe. It is precisely the rebellion, the civil war, supported by Congo (Brazzaville) and other states which has been responsible for the massacre, often in atrocious circumstances, of thousands of Congolese civilans, for the most part loca leaders and intellectuals formerly associated with the Adoula government. And yet the Foreign Minister of Brazzaville has without foundation accused the United States and Belgium of killing "thousands and thousands of Congolese" in the recent rescue operation.

The Council has heard the sober, factual account of that operation by the Foreign Minister of Belgium. In fact, only a very small number of rebels were killed as a consequence of that operation and these only in self-defense or because they were at the moment resisting the attempts to rescue the hostages.

The grim story of thousands of innocent civilians—many of them foreign—illegally seized, brutalized, and threatened, and many murdered by rebels against the Congo

Government, has already been related to this Council. Every means—legal, moral, and humane, including the United Nations—was exhausted to protect their lives and secure their release, all without avail. When it became apparent that there was no hope, the Belgian and American Governments, with the cooperation of the Government of the United Kingdom and with the express authorization of the sovereign Government of the Democratic Republic of the Congo, undertook an emergency rescue mission to save the lives of those innocent people.

The operation was carried out with restraint, courage, discipline, and dispatch. In 4 days 2,000 people—Europeans, Americans, Africans, and Asians—were rescued and evacuated to safe territory. These included Americans, Britons, and Belgians; Pakistanis, Indians, Congolese, Greeks, French, Dutch, Germans, Canadians, Spaniards, Portuguese, Swiss, and Italians; as well as citizens of Ghana, Uganda, Ethiopia, and the United Arab Republic.

The mission lasted 4 days from first to last and left the Stanleyville area the day its task ended; it returned immediately to Belgium; the episode is finished.

Yet the memorandum from certain African states supporting the request for this meeting charges that the United States and Belgium, in defiance of article 52 of the charter and as a deliberate affront to the Organization of African Unity, launched military operations in Stanleyville and other parts of the Congo with the concurrence of the United Kingdom and that these actions constituted intervention in African affairs, a flagrant violation of the charter, and a threat to the peace and security of the African Continent.

It makes no mention whatever of the repeated and repulsive threats made by those controlling Stanleyville, of the solely merciful objectives of the rescue mission, of its authorization by the Government of the Congo, of the fact that the mission withdrew as soon as it had evacuated the foreign hostages and other civilians who wished to escape, nor of the fact that some of the signatories of the letter are themselves intervening in the Congo against its Government, or of other relevant facts known to the members of this Council—and to the world at large.

The United States emphatically denies the charges made in this memorandum and in the debate. We have no apologies to make to any state appearing before this Council. We are proud of our part in saving human lives imperiled by the civil war in the Congo.

The United States took part in no operation with military purposes in the Congo. We violated no provision of the United Nations Charter.

Our action was no threat to peace and security; it was not an affront—deliberate or otherwise—to the OAU; and it constituted no intervention in Congolese or African affairs.

This mission was exactly what we said it was when we notified this Council at the beginning—nothing more an;nothing less than a mission to save the lives of innocent people of diverse nationalities, many of whom were teachers, doctors, and missionaries who have devoted their careers to selfless service to the Congolese people. To anyone willing to consider the facts—in good faith—that must be clear. To anyone who will face the facts, unobstructed by hatred for Tshombe or the Congo or Beligum or the United States and Great Britain, that must be clear.

While our primary obligation was to protect the lives of American citizens, we are proud that the mission rescued so many innocent people of 18 other nationalities from their dreadful predicament. We mourn the thousands of others—Congolese and foreign

—already sacrificed in the preceding months of their horrible civil strife in this tortured country. And we urge all nations to appeal for the safety of those who remain in danger.

No amount of detail—and certainly no extraneous issues—can obscure the stark outlines of that story. Yet questions have been raised—harsh statements have been made—about the motivations involved in launching the rescue mission. Let me therefore speak to that point.

For months before the rescue mission was undertaken, diplomatic efforts had been pursued through every conceivable channel to persuade the rebels to release the hostages.

Conscious of the legal and humanitarian issues at stake, the Secretary-General of the United Nations, the International Committee of the Red Cross, the Ad Hoc Commission of the Organization of African Unity, the Government of the Congo, and various other governments, including African governments, made repeated efforts to secure the rights and release of the hostages for three long, anxious, and frustrating months.

Every available avenue was tried; every approach was ignored or in effect rejected by the rebels; and in the process the Red Cross, the World Health Organization, and the United Nations were vilified by the military leaders of the rebels " as espionage organizations in the service of the neo-colonialists." These are the exact words used by the so-called General Olenga in a mesage on September 3, 1964. This accusation was also repeatedly broadcast by Stanleyville.

For some days before November 23 it was difficult to be sure who was in charge in Stanleyville—or indeed whether anyone was in control. It was impossible to know whether any agreement that might be made with any alleged representative of the rebels could in fact be carried out.

Nonetheless, when the possibility arose, through the good offices of the chairman of the Ad Hoc Commission of the Organization of African Unity, of a meeting with a representative of the rebels in Nairobi on November 21, my Government immediately named its Ambassador to Kenya, Mr. William Attwood, to represent it for the purpose of discussing the safety of the hostages.

Mr. Thomas Kanza, who was said to represent the rebels, did not appear. Instead, on that day, November 21, the Stanleyville Radio, mouthpiece of the rebel forces, suggested that the hostages be burned alive or massacred with machetes and "devoured."

On the following day, November 22, the rebel representative belatedly did appear in Nairobi, and a meeting was subsequently held with Ambassador Attwood on November 23. The rebel spokesman, however, refused to address the problem of the release of the hostages on its humanitarian merits; he persisted in callous efforts to barter their lives for political and military concessions from the Government of the Congo.

It must be obvious that my Government could neither legally or morally accept this as a satisfactory basis for discussion. Legally, we could not concede what lies within the competence of another sovereign government. Morally, we could not agree that our citizens could be illegally held for ransom.

Mr. Kanza categorically refused the request of Ambassador Attwood to make a public commitment with respect to the safety of the hostages. When Ambassador

Attwood reported this refusal and we continued to receive threats of imminent execution of the hostages, it was clear to my Government that all hope had run out and the time was short.

At that very moment, five members of the American consular staff in Stanleyville, who had been held in illegal captivity for 3 months, during which time they were repeatedly beaten, were under threat of public execution. Similarly held was Dr. Paul Carlson, charged with being a spy in spite of all the evidence that he was a dedicated medical missionary working solely to relieve human suffering among the Congolese, including the rebels. Day by day his imminent execution was announced to the world.

The fate that awaited these men and the hundreds of other hostages—men, women, and children—was clearly foreshadowed by the atrocious execution of Congolese officials, described to us by the representative of the Democratic Republic of the Congo, and by the public statement of the rebel leader, Christophe Gbenye, read to us by the Foreign Minister of Belgium, that "we will make our fetishes with the hearts of the Americans and Belgians, and we will dress ourselves with the skins of the Americans and Belgians."

I have heard in this Council, nevertheless, the astonishing thesis that nothing needed to be done, that the threats were not real. I heard it asked whether it was "not a sad fact that the hostages were killed only after the paratroopers landed" and then heard it asserted that it was "well known that no Europeans had been executed."

Mr. President, the threats were very real indeed; they had been carried out in the past, and we had every reason to expect that they would continue to be carried out in the future. From mid-August onward, after the rebel forces had taken Stanleyville, seizing and holding foreigners as hostages became a deliberate act of rebel policy. In the following months this medieval practice was widely applied. Many of these hostages were deliberately killed.

By the time the Belgian paratroopers arrived in Stanleyville, and before the outlaws even knew of their impending arrival, the total of those thus already cruelly tortured and slaughtered amounted to 35 foreigners, including 19 Belgians, 2 Americans, 2 Indians, 2 Greeks, 1 Italian, 2 Portuguese, 2 Togolese, and 4 Dutch, and 1 English, many of them missionaries who had spent their lives to help the Congolese people. That, at least, is the verified number. God alone knows how many others, long missing and out of touch with the outside world, had met a similar fate.

During this period of many months before the rescue mission arrived in Stanleyville, the rebels not only murdered these foreigners but systematically slaughtered local Congolese officials, police, teachers, intellectuals, members of opposing political groups, labor leaders, and rank-and-file members of labor unions who were considered unreliable or even undesirable by their captors. The exact number of Congolese so liquidated may never be known, but it had reached thousands long before November 24.

In case there is still any doubt in your minds that the rescue of the hostages was a matter of life and death, members of the Council might find of interest this photostat of a telegram from General Olenga to Major Tshenda in Kindu, dated September 30, 1964. It says: "Major Tshenda Oscar, Kindu: Reference your unnumbered telegram, Americans Belgians must be held in a secure place stop In case of bombing region, exterminate all without requesting further orders. signed General Olenga."

Again, if there is any doubt about what was happening before the rescue mission arrived, I call your attention—and I do so with reluctance—to what happened at Isangi, not far from Stanleyville, on November 19, 5 days before the paradrop. The entire Isangi religious community of 17 priests and 13 nuns were stripped of their clothes, beaten, and the nuns raped. Of these, an American nun, Sister Marie Antoinette, and a Dutch priest were murdered and thrown in the river. A Belgian Sister, Ann Francois, was beaten to death.

Mr. President, throughout this debate I have waited in vain to hear one word, spoken by those who have brought this complaint, in condemnation of the taking of hostages and the deliberate liquidiation of an intelligentsia. Whatever their fancied complaints about the Belgian and American rescue mission, I would have thought that the complainants would at least have shown an awareness of and a respect for accepted standards of humanitarian conduct, particularly as they are expressed in article 3 of the Geneva convention for the protection of war victims of 1949, which prohibits the taking of hostages in time of internal conflict and guarantees humane treatment to noncombatants located in areas of civil strife.

I find this absence of condemnation of such inhuman practices all the more surprising, not only because they are illegal but because they are at such fundamental variance with the ancient and proud traditions of the peoples of Africa themselves. Anyone who has visited and traveled in Africa, as I have, knows the kindness, consideration, and protection which the African tradition of hospitality and tolerance extends to strangers. We will do nothing here to strain that tradition; for it is clear to us that the barbarism of the rebels in the Congo cannot be considered as that of African nationalists and liberators.

*   *   *

It has been charged in this Council that, quite apart from the rescue mission, the United States has intervened militarily in the Congo.

I reject this charge. These are the facts:

As I have stated, Prime Minister Adoula earlier this year requested—and the United States provided—some military materiel and training assistance to the Congo. This is exactly what all other African states have done or are doing. There is not one of them that does not obtain military equipment or training or both from outside Africa in the exercise of its own sovereign right.

When, in accordance with the constitution of the Congo, President Kasavubu selected Prime Minister Tshombe to succeed Prime Minister Adoula, who had resigned, the United States continued this program. It did so upon specific affirmation by Prime Minister Tshombe that the Government of the Congo desired that the program be continued, As the need arose, the United States, at the request of the Government of the Congo, provided additional equipment and transport. It was not requested to, and did not undertake, military operations in the Congo.

Mr. President, statements have been made here which seem to add up to the astounding proposition that the United States has no right to provide assistance to the Congolese Government and that that Government has no right to accept it because the aid comes from outside Africa. I repeat that there is hardly an African state which has not requested and received military aid, in thyform of arms or training or both, from outside Africa. Certainly Algeria, for example, has received and is receiving massive foreign military aid in both these categories.

Is this sovereign right to be exercised by some and denied to others? Would other states in Africa who receive arms and military assistance from outside the continent relinquish this equipment or assistance, or ask its withdrawal, in the unhappy event that rebellion broke out within their boundaries? I very much doubt that they would or that anyone here really believes they should.

It is perhaps necessary to repeat that the United States furnished military assistance to the Congo in the form of transport and communications equipment, in the first instance to the government of Mr. Adoula, when it became quite apparent that the United Nations would be unable to undertake the necessary reorganization of the Congolese army. Our assistance was continued when it became clear that the U.N. operation was about to be terminated for lack of funds, after a rebellion fomented from abroad had broken out in the Congo and after Mr. Adoula had appealed to other African states for aid to maintain peace and security in his country.

Would any African country which has spoken at this table deny that, under similar circumstances, it would have urgently appealed for and gratefully accepted military aid from outside Africa? And, I must add, if these countries sincerely wish the Government of the Congo not to seek such aid, let them scrupulously refrain from stirring up rebellion and aiding the insurgents. If they demand that the Government cease to defend itself with the only means at its disposal, while at the same time themselves refusing aid to the Government and granting it to the rebels, what confidence in their good faith can anyone have? On what grounds and for what purpose do they appeal to a Council the duty of which is to maintain international peace and security? If the practice of supporting rebellion against a government which is disliked by other governments becomes prevalent in Africa, what security will any African government have?

Let us not be hypocritical. Either each government recognizes the right of other governments to exist and refrains from attempting to overthrow them, or we revert to a primitive state of anarchy in which each conspires against its neighbor. The golden rule is do unto others as you would have them do unto you.

The world has made some progress, and military invasions of one another's territory are diminishing, thanks in large measure to the United Nations. But a new practice has developed, or rather an old practice has developed new momentum—the more or less hidden intervention by nations in the internal affairs of their neighbors. Most of the fighting and killing that still goes on can be traced to outside interventions designed to undermine or overthrow governments.

In Africa nearly every country wants and needs the help of outsiders in achieving those "better standards of life in larger freedom" which are the goal of their rising expectations and the promise of their political independence. So outsiders are bound to be involved to some extent in their internal affairs. The question therefore is: Under what rules will the outsiders operate on the inside? Over the years, more through the practice of nations than the teachings of scholars, have we not developed some general principles to guide this widespread practice of mutual involvement? Where the government, recognized diplomatically by other states as the responsible government, exercises its sovereign right to ask for outside help, then it would seem that the response and the involvement of outsiders is all right.

But I concede that it is not an easy line to draw. The principle that outsiders should be invited and not crash the party is far from an infallible guide to good conduct. But still, the principle of permission is certainly the best one yet developed to prevent a reversion to imperialism and foreign domination. For if the outsiders, not the insiders, decide when intervention is right, the fragile fabric of nationhood will come apart at the seams in a score of new African nations.

Every nation has its dissidents, its internal struggle for power, its internal arguments about who should be in charge and how the country should be run. But if every internal rivalry is to become a Spanish Civil War, with each faction drawing in other Africans and great powers from other continents, the history of an independent Africa in this century will be bloody and shameful and the aspirations of Africa's wonderful peoples will be cruelly postponed.

That is why we supported the United Nations Operation in the Congo and were sorry that it had to be withdrawn, its mission incomplete, because of the United Nations' financial difficulties. And that is why we oppose unsolicited foreign intervention in the Congo.

*   *

U.N. Security Council Condemns Recruitment of Mercenaries*

Statement by Deputy Ambassador William B. Buffum

July 6, 1967

We readily agreed this afternoon to an urgent meeting of the Security Council to consider the complaint from the Government of the Democratic Republic of the Congo charging that forces from outside its own country have fomented disturbances in the eastern portion of the Congo and, with the cooperation of dissident local military elements, apparently gained control of several important cities. The charges are indeed serious ones, and they deserve our most careful consideration. Certainly the type of action that has been alleged would contravene not only the spirit but also the letter of the United Nations Charter.

The strong opposition of the United States Government to intervention by one state in the internal affairs of another has been demonstrated repeatedly. Such interference, whether it be with armed forces or through subversion or other less obvious means, cannot be countenanced. If any foreign government is in fact aiding and abetting those in the Congo who are seeking by force to wrest control of certain areas from the legitimate authorities, such action would violate the charter and accepted principles of international law. All U.N. member states, in our judgment, should refrain from any such activities and should take appropriate measures to discourage their nationals from participation in them.

Inasmuch as these charges are serious ones, the Council will naturally wish to be fully informed of the facts of the situation. We trust that the Government of the Congo will make every effort to ascertain the full facts and keep us informed of developments as they occur. In the meantime the United States believes it is incumbent on all of us to do nothing that will further exacerbate the situation there.

Since the day when the Congo became independent the United States has been

*Ibid., July 31, 1967, pp. 151-53.

prominent among those that have supported and assisted the government of that nation to develop strength and stability in order to insure the security and well-being of the Congolese people. We have made these efforts both through the United Nations and through mutually agreed bilateral arrangements. This record, if I may say in all humility, Mr. President, is one of which my Government is proud.

And it is for this reason, as well, that we are deeply disturbed over any threats to the steady progress which has been made in the Congo and we firmly support the efforts of the Central Government in the Congo to restore order and to exercise its legitimate authority throughout the country. We deplore any attempts by outside forces to interfere with those efforts. I am sure that this will also prove to be the attitude of other members of this Council and feel confident that within a short time it will again be possible for all of the people in the Congo to live in peace and free from fear, as they so richly deserve.

Ambassador Buffum's Statement

July 10, 1967

Mr. President, although the draft resolution which has just been introduced by the distinguished representative of Nigeria does not coincide with our preferences in every respect, the United States will vote affirmatively. We will do so because we fully support the efforts of the Democratic Republic of the Congo to exercise its legitimate authority throughout the country and to restore order wherever order is disrupted.

Mr. President, in our view, if any foreign government aids or abets any elements in the Congo, whether these be mercenaries or irregular forces seeking to overthrow the Government or to gain control of any part of the country, such action would be in clear violation of the United Nations Charter and deserving of our condemnation. This was our policy, sir, 3 years ago when secessionist elements in the eastern Congo were engaged in large-scale conflict, with substantial support from the Chinese Communists, to wrest control from the Central Government; and this remains our policy today.

We will vote for the resolution this evening because we support the principle of noninterference in the internal affairs of the Congo. In doing so, we do not consider that by this resolution the Council is making any specific finding with regard to any specific government.

Mr. President, the United States has not been content to give merely moral support to the principles endorsed in this resolution this evening. On the contrary, we have sought to provide the Government of the Congo with some of the tools which it needs to do the job in protecting its integrity and its political independence.

It was in this connection that over the past weekend the United States, in response to a request from President Mobutu and consistent with previous United Nations resolutions dealing with the Congo problem and calling for assistance in helping that government to maintain its independence and territorial integrity, dispatched three C-130 transport aircraft and crews to Kinshasa. These are aircraft, I should like to make clear to the Council, which are designed to provide long-range logistic support for the Congolese Government in meeting the mercenary-led rebellion. They will be there in a noncombatant status.

This action reflects our longstanding policy of supporting the Central Government and the unity of the Congo, and it is in this spirit that we will support the resolution sponsored by Ethiopia, Nigeria, Mali, and India.

Text of Resolution

The Security Council,

Having taken cognizance of the message of the Congolese Government contained in document S/8031,

Having discussed the serious developments in the Democratic Republic of the Congo,

Concerned by the threat posed by foreign interference to the independence and territorial integrity of the Democratic Republic of the Congo,

1. Reaffirms in particular paragraph 2 of Security Council resolution 226 (1966) of 14 October 1966;

2. Condemns any State which persists in permitting or tolerating the recruitment of mercenaries, and the provision of facilities to them, with the objective of overthrowing the Governments of States Members of the United Nations;

3. Calls upon Governments to ensure that their territory and other territories under their control, as well as their nationals, are not used for the planning of subversion, and the recruitment, training and transit of mercenaries designed to overthrow the Government of the Democratic Republic of the Congo;

4. Decides that the Security Council shall remain seized of the question;

5. Requests the Secretary-General to follow closely the implementation of the present resolution.

Speech by Representative Robert F. Sikes (Florida) Before the House on United States Military Forces in the Congo*

July 10, 1967

Mr. Speaker, I am shocked to note that the United States has sent military forces to the Congo, ostensibly as a show of support for the Congolese Government. We have no treaty obligations there. Congress has not been asked to authorize or to appropriate funds for such a venture. Nor would we.

May I sadly remind those in power that we already have a war. It is halfway around the world in Asia, and the progress we are making there is painfully slow. It is now costing the lives of nearly 1,000 Americans a month. We do not want another war in Africa. It was a token intervention, much like the one in the Congo, which led to full-scale involvement in Vietnam.

It is inconceivable to me that we would attempt to settle civil disorders for other nations throughout the world. We have not even shown that we can solve our own. Through token intervention, we can invite similar involvement by the forces of other nations and find ourselves in a contest to get there first in every danger spot. It is

*The Congressional Record, July 10, 1967, p. 18196.

altogether too obvious that this can lead to world conflict. There should be immediate withdrawal of American forces from the Congo.

Speech by Representative H. R. Gross (Iowa) Before the House
on United States Intervention in the Congo*

July 10, 1967

Mr. Speaker, the action by President Johnson in sending three C-130 transport planes to participate in the rebellion in the Congo ought to be condemned by every thinking American.

These military aircraft, manned by U.S. Air Force crews and paratroopers from the 82d Airborne Division, have been dispatched without the slightest approval of Congress. These planes, crews, and combat troops have not been sent to the Congo to evacuate American nationals. According to the State Department, they have been dispatched primarily to airlift Congolese troops and military equipment.

In other words, President Johnson has injected the United States into still another rebellion around the world, this time in support of the so-called President of the Congo, Lt. Gen. Joseph Mobutu, who clearly demonstrated a year ago that he is, in fact, one of the world's most brutal military dictators.

Mr. Speaker, what will happen if the Communists also decide to intervene in the Congo rebellion by sending Mig jet fighters to stop the use of U.S. transports?

Mr. Speaker, the United States cannot longer attempt to police and finance the rest of the world. Are we also scheduled to intervene in the rebellion in Nigeria and every other fracas in Africa?

Congress ought to take action immediately by telling Lyndon Johnson to get those planes, crews, and paratroopers out of the Congo and back to the United States as fast as it is possible to do so.

Speech by Representative Louis C. Wyman (New Hampshire) Before
the House on Disapproval of United States Involvement in the Congo†

July 11, 1967

Mr. Speaker, while not a member of the Foreign Affairs Committee, I want to associate myself with those who are critical of President Johnson's sending of military planes and personnel to the Congo these last 2 days. I believe it is unwise to directly intervene in the tempestuous, unstable, boiling pot of unsettled, restless, darkest Africa. The United States is already overextended. We ought not to invite further foreign involvements in this way at this time.

More particularly, this ought not to be done without the prior approval and authorization of the Congress of the United States. Telephone consultation with a few Senators is not enough. Congress is not a rubberstamp for any President, whatever his political party.

*Ibid., July 10, 1967, p. 18199.
†Ibid., July 11, 1967, p. 18266.

Although the conduct of foreign affairs is undeniably entrusted by the Constitution to the executive branch, when such conduct can lead to war by extensive predictable involvement of men and equipment it ought not to be undertaken without advance deliberation and approval of the Congress. Accordingly, I have today introduced a resolution of disapproval of this latest foreign involvement in the Congo. I would offer such a resolution whether the administration were Republican or Democrat. The United States can no longer afford the risk of one-man involvement in war of this entire Nation.

Speech by Representative George A. Goodling (Pennsylvania) Before the House on Involvement in the Congo*

July 11, 1967

Mr. Speaker, the distressing news comes to us that three U.S. Air Force planes and accompanying paratrooper guards have been sent to the Congo to shore up the forces of President Joseph D. Mobutu.

This is a dangerous situation, and we might be asking for real trouble, because the commitment of even a token force of Americans could well be an invitation to full-scale involvement. We need but think back on how our involvement mushroomed in Vietnam, starting with the assignment of a few mechanics in 1954 and escalating to an assignment of some 450,000 troops today. And even now there is a call for another 100,000 or more American troops in this area.

A wholesale involvement in the Congo—on top of our already heavy commitment in Vietnam—would place a terrible burden on our American manpower and resources. All of this raises the question of just how long America can play the role of "policeman of the world."

*   *   *

Mr. Speaker, the world is too big and has too many trouble spots for America to act as a world policeman.

The Congo is a point in order. What obligation do we have there? Why should we be committed with our men and materials in that area? Is there any good reason why we should invite the sacrifice of American lives on this continent?

Is it not about time we put a stop to trying to act as a lone policeman on a vast world beat and, instead, confine our police activities to what we can afford in men and materials—and what, in our national interest, are bona fide obligations?

New York Times *Editorial on the Sending of United States Planes to the Congo†*

July 12, 1967

Senatorial criticism of the Administration's dispatch of three military transport planes to the Congo is exaggerated.

*Ibid., July 11, 1967, p. 18296-97.
†The New York Times, July 12, 1967.

This is not a case of "unjustified" and "immoral" intervention in the internal affairs of the African nation, as Senator Russell of Georgia put it. Nor is there sufficient reason to be "shocked, surprised and dismayed," to use Senator Mansfield's words.

President Mobutu, beneficiary of the move, heads a sovereign state recognized by the United States. The American planes are to engage only in noncombatant operations. While the loan of the planes is obviously to advertise the fact tha the United States is not supporting the quasi-rebellion in the Eastern Congo, the American position would be stronger if at the same time there were official condemnation of the hijacking and capture of Moise Tshombe, now a prisoner in Algeria.

In lending thycargo planes to President Mobutu the United States has merely proved that it is not encouraging Mr. Tshombe or foreign business interests in the Congo that may be sympathetic to him. But the dispatch of the planes, intended to win the favor of most African governments, is not entirely without risks, because the Congo is still unstable and potentially inflammable. This was demonstrated when Congolese Government troops retook the town of Bukava from the rebels and went berserk, beating and killing Europeans and natives, looting and raping.

It was a savage explosion which contained the warning that the United States must take care not to get too deeply involved in Congolese affairs. Senatorial critics would be right to keep a close watch on what the United States does in the Congo; but as yet there is no real cause for complaint.

Speech by Representative Donald Fraser (Minnesota) Before the House on Support for President's Action in Sending Cargo Transport Aircraft to the Congo*

July 12, 1967

Mr. Speaker, I strongly support the action of President Johnson in sending the three cargo transport airplanes to the Congo.

What apparently happened in the Congo was that white mercenary members of the Congolese Army mutinied, resulting in racial tensions which threatened not only to jeopardize the security and safety of the people in the Congo but also threatened to exacerbate race relations in that part of Africa.

By responding to the request of the Central Government of the Congo in a very limited way, I believe the President has helped to moderate and to calm the situation, has maintained the excellent relationship which we have with the Central Congolese Government and has helped to maintain a strong and durable relationship with the rest of Africa.

I know some Members fear this limited assistance to the Central Congolese Government may possibly be the beginning of another major involvement of the United States in a war similar to Vietnam. I believe a close examination of the realities of that situation would suggest that there is no such risk.

*The Congressional Record, July 12, 1967, p. 18553.

The U.N. Condemns Use of Angola as Base for Congo Mercenaries *

Statement by Ambassador Buffum

November 8, 1967

Mr. President, it is a matter of some regret to my delegation that the Security Council once again finds it necessary to convene on a serious charge relating to the activities of armed mercenaries in the Democratic Republic of the Congo.

We we were reminded by the Deputy Foreign Minister of the Democratic Republic of the Congo, it has been less than 4 months since we were called upon to consider the potential threat to the independence and territorial integrity of the Congo posed by mercenaries then reported to be assembling in neighboring territory.

On July 10, in Resolution 239, the Security Council expressed its concern over this circumstance and condemned "any State which persists in permitting or tolerating the recruitment of mercenaries, and the provision of facilities to them, with the objective of overthrowing the Governments of States Members of the United Nations." This resolution also called upon "Governments to ensure that their territory and other territories under their control, as well as their nationals, are not used for the planning of subversion, and the recruitment, training and transit of mercenaries designed to overthrow the Government of the Democratic Republic of the Congo."

I have listened very carefully, Mr. President, to the statement made to us today by the distinguished Deputy Foreign Minister of the Congo. His account of these recent incursions into his country is a cause of deep concern. Now, it is admittedly very difficult under prevailing circumstances for any government in a short time to marshal and to present those concrete kinds of evidence which one would like to have before making a formal judgment on the merits of a complaint. However, his report on the current situation and our own knowledge of the history of the mercenary problem in the Congo create a strong presumption that the resolutions of this Council have been violated. Confirmation of his report would mean, notwithstanding the denials made by the Government of Portugal and which were repeated to us today, that Angola had indeed been used by mercenaries to prepare an armed incursion into the Congo.

It is very difficult for my delegation to understand how foreign mercenaries could be present in Angola, make preparation for such a misadventure, and then leave Angola for the Congo without the acquiescence or at least the knowledge of the Portuguese authorities. The implications of Portuguese responsibility, even if only tacit, would therefore appear to be serious. It was for this reason, sir, that my Government has made known to the Government of Portugal its concern about this matter.

It is the hope of the United States that the Government of the Democratic Republic of the Congo will be able to deal effectively with this latest mercenary threat so that it can continue the development of national unity and economic progress in a framework of peace and security.

It is the proper concern of this Security Council that the mercenary danger which

**Department of State Bulletin*, Dec. 11, 1967, pp. 807-8.

has threatened the Congo for so long be eliminated and not be permitted to recur. All countries, particularly those bordering on the Congo, have a very grave responsibility to insure compliance with the resolutions of this Council on the mercenary problem. My delegation, consequently, calls upon all countries to comply scrupulously with both the letter and the spirit of Council Resolution 239.

Text of Resolution

November 15, 1967

The Security Council,

Concerned by the serious situation created in the Democratic Republic of the Congo following the armed attacks committed against that country by foreign forces of mercenaries,

Concerned that Portugal allowed those mercenaries to use the territory of Angola under its administration as a base for their armed attacks against the Democratic Republic of the Congo,

Taking into consideration the support and assistance that those mercenaries have continued to receive from some foreign sources with regard to recruitment and training, as well as transport and supply of arms,

Concerned at the threat which the organization of such forces poses to the territorial integrity and independence of States,

Reaffirming resolutions 226 of 14 October 1966 and 239 of 11 [10] July 1967,

1. Condemns any act of interference in the internal affairs of the Democratic Republic of the Congo;

2. Condemns, in particular, the failure of Portugal, in violation of the above-mentioned Security Council resolutions, to prevent the mercenaries from using the territory of Angola under its administration as a base of operations for armed attacks against the Democratic Republic of the Congo;

3. Calls upon Portugal to put an end immediately, in conformity with the above-mentioned resolutions of the Security Council, to the provision to the mercenaries of any assistance whatsoever;

4. Calls upon all countries receiving mercenaries who have participated in the armed attacks against the Democratic Republic of the Congo to take appropriate measures to prevent them from renewing their activities against any State;

5. Calls upon all Member States to co-operate with the Security Council in the implementation of this resolution;

6. Decides that the Security Council should remain seized of the question and requests the Secretary-General to follow the implementation of the present resolution.

Report by Representative Diggs on a Special Study Mission to the Congo*

March 29-April 27, 1970

U.S. Military Mission to the Congo (Comish)

Background

In June 1962, a special DOD advisory team made a study to determine the basic essentials for the creation of an effective Congolese Armed Force. One of the main conclusions of this study (the Green report) was that foreign military materiel, training, and advisory assistance were needed. The first shipment of 20 jeeps and spare parts arrived in the Congo in October 1962. A U.S. military aid mission was activated in Kinshasa in August 1963 (known as COMISH, Congo Mission Headquarters). Today, COMISH is authorized a strength of 42 personnel. Included in this force is a USAF crew for the C-123 aircraft assigned for support of COMISH.

Mission

The mission assigned COMISH is: Prepare and implement, in coordination with the ANC and Western nations committed to helping the Congo, realistic programs which provide on an austere basis, the minimum logistic support and associated technical training required to assist the ANC to reach an acceptable degree of professional military competence to provide for its own internal security.

Activities

Since its inception in August 1963, COMISH has planned materiel and training programs through fiscal year 1976 The Field Advisory Teams assist the Congolese in the maintenance of MAP provided materiel, as well as providing advice, in conjunction with the Belgians, on all aspects of logistics and maintenance management. Constant upgrading and shifting of ANC personnel have made this task very difficult and seemingly endless.

Program

COMISH has two programs in existence. The materiel program is the major portion of the effort. The bulk of the materiel being supplied by the United States is transport and communication equipment. To date, we have delivered 2,589 trucks of various types, 1,154 radios, 46 aircraft together with assorted tools and support equipment. The training program also consists of two parts. Part one: Field teams working CJT shoulder-to-shoulder with the ANC in signal and automotive fields. Part two: In-country English language training and subsequent CONUS courses at U.S. Army schools. The U.S. service school programs have been modest because systems and procedures taught in the United States are rather sophisticated for the average ANC student in view of his educational level, and are often not directly compatible with the systems and procedures in use by the ANC; i.e., Belgian system.

---

*Committee on Foreign Affairs, *Report of Special Study Mission to West and Central Africa, March 29 to April 27, 1970* by Hon. Charles C. Diggs, Jr. Michigan, Chairman Subcommittee on Africa, (Washington, 1970), pp. 37-42.

U.S. Assistance Program (AID)

The basic interest of the United States in the Congo is to see a unified, viable, independent state capable of maintaining internal security and a reasonable rate of economic and social development adequate to meet the political and social aspirations of its peoples.

In support of these objectives the United States provides the following types of economic assistance to the Congo:

Import Support

This program has provided $190 million over the years in supporting assistance grant and loan funds to import industrial supplies and machinery as well as trucks and related transport equipment to keep the industrial sector of the economy operating during periods of foreign exchange shortage. The last $10 million of this amount is now being disbursed, after which no more funds of this type will be committed because a development program is replacing the supporting assistance program. The Congolese zaires generated by the sale of these imports are used for economic development projects. (See section on counterpart funds below.)

Public Law 480 Food Programs

Flour and tobacco are imported from the United States by agreement between the two governments to meet critical shortages. This program, which is now financed on a loan basis repayable in dollars over 20 years at 3 percent interest, is running at an annual rate of about $4 million. It is expected that the program will gradually decrease and phase out over the next year due to reduced requirements and greater availability of foreign exchange. As in the case of the import support program, the consumer pays for the commodities in Congolese zaires. (See section on counterpart funds below.)

A second part of the food-for-peace program is the distribution of food provided as a grant by the United States and made available through American voluntary agencies. Distribution is made to hospitals, refugees, school feeding programs and to individuals participating in food-for-work programs. Two voluntary agencies are working in the Congo—the Catholic Relief Services and the Church World Service. The program reaches over 300,000 persons. In fiscal year 1969, $2.2 million was obligated to the program. However, the program has been suspended since March 1969 because of Congolese Government difficulties in allotting sufficient funds to cover port charges and inland freight costs. It is expected to resume shortly.

Contribution to the United Nations

The United States makes a direct contribution to the United Nations program in the Congo, completely apart from its contributions to worldwide U.N. programs. This support is in the form of a contribution to a special U.N. funds-in-trust program which the U.N. operates in the Congo from contributions made by several nations. About 80 technicians of the U.N. will be provided this year by the funds-in-trust program, in addition to the more than 200 U.N. technicians working on regular U.N. projects. The United States contributed $970,000 in 1969 for this program which was also supported by Canada and Belgium. The program is now concentrated in the transport sector where experts and technicians are provided for the Public Works Department, the

Navigable Waterways Service, and the Civil Aviation Division. Other experts provide services in the field of public health and in the administration of counterpart funds.

Development Grants

Under this program, experts and material are supplied to the Congolese Government for certain projects. The United States advises and helps train and organize the Congo's National Police, supplies transportation and communications equipment, uniforms, and other items. Over the past several years, assistance has been given to the National Pedagogical Institute and the National School of Administration, among others. A labor education project is also supported by these grants. Scholarships and training grants for study in the United States have been provided to more than 600 Congolese. An important agricultural credit pilot scheme is just getting underway. The current fiscal year program will provide about $1 million for the continuation of technical assistance activities.

Development Loan Assistance

In 1967, a $2.5 million loan was authorized to assist in the financing of a 250-room hotel in Kinshasa. Additional financing has been provided by the Intercontinental Hotels Corp., a subsidiary of Pan American Airways, the Congolese Government, and from local currencies generated from the U.S. import support program. Construction began early in 1969.

Studies are now underway to determine the economic and technical feasibility of upgrading National Route 1 between Kikwit and Luluabourg and between Luluabourg and Mbuji-Mayi. It is expected that these studies will lead to further development loan assistance. Similarly a reconnaisance of the transport requirements of the northeastern Congo now being completed is expected to identify a considerable number of high-priority roads requiring rehabilitation and improvement. At least some of these projects may well qualify for development loan assistance. Final recommendations are now being prepared for the financing of a floating drydock at Boma to replace the antiquated and dilapidated facility now existing there. Final planning is well advanced for a loan to finance imports in support of the transport sector.

Counterpart Funds

The zaires generated under the import support and food-for-peace programs are made available for Congolese economic development projects through a joint consultation and programing effort of the USAID and the GDRC. Highest priority in these projects has been granted to the transport sector, where considerable sums have been invested in the maintenance and rehabilitation of roads, bridges, ferries, and the service fleet of the Navigable Waterways Service. In addition, new road, bridge, and airport facilities have been constructed. The agriculture sector has also benefited significantly from these funds through the support of agricultural production efforts, in addition to agriculturally important transport links and the construction of agricultural training facilities at the vocational and university levels. The third area of special concentration is that of education, where important facilities have been constructed at the four university level institutions, at a number of the postsecondary specialized schools, and most recently at teacher-training colleges. A major contribution will be made during fiscal year 1970 to the funding of the Congolese Development Bank, a project sponsored by the World Bank.

Summary of U.S. Economic Assistance to the Congo
[in millions of dollars]

	Fiscal years 1960-69	Fiscal year 1970 (estimated)
Import support program	190.0	---
Public Law 480 food programs	156.0	1.2
Assistance through the United Nations	30.0	---
Technical assistance TC/DG	16.0	1.5
Capital assistance loans	2.5	9.0
Counterpart fund activities	14.0[1]	15.0

[1] Fiscal year 1969 only

U.S. Investment and Private Sector Activity

In extractive industry, two American oil companies were recently granted exploration concessions. Mobil Exploration Congo is Mobil's Congolese company, formed to assume Mobil's share of "Socorep," a consortium composed of Mobil, Shell, and Petrocongo. Socorep is currently prospecting for oil onshore in the Bas-Congo.

Gulf Oil Congo has been granted an offshore concession and is now conducting seismic and geologic studies. The company plans to begin drilling in the near future and expects to invest perhaps $1.5 million over the next 3 years.

Union Carbide is associated with a Belgian mining company and the Congolese Government in a joint venture. The local company, called Somucar, has been granted exploitation and processing rights for colombium, tantalum, thorium, phosphorus, and associated minerals in Kivu Province. The company's authorized capital was increased recently to $2 million.

Anticipated U.S. investment in the Congolese mining industry includes an important consortium seeking prospection rights mostly for copper and tin in northern Katanga. This international group is composed of Standard Oil Co. of Indiana, Anglo-America, Mitsui, a French mineralogical research firm, and Leon Templesman & Son of New York, a company which took the initiative in forming the consortium and which is already engaged in purchasing Congolese diamond production on behalf of British Diamond. Englehard-Philipp Bros. Minerals & Chemicals is associated with a Belgian firm in an enterprise extracting cassiterite and columbo-tantalite and has also applied for a concession to extract monazite in northern Kivu.

In agriculture, there is as yet no American investment. However, both Goodyear and Firestone have expressed interest in developing rubber plantations in the Congo, and their plans have considerable developmental interest, not only in terms of increasing the Congo's production and export earnings but especially in terms of providing training, income, and permanent assets for sizable numbers of Congolese small planters. Both companies have also expressed interest in investing in a tire factory in the Congo, provided market studies show that with adequate protection from import competition, such a plant could be commercially viable.

In the field of manufacture, processing, and construction, the Continental Grain Co. has formed a joint enterprise (Minaco) to develop a 100,000-ton capacity flour mill at the Congolese seaport of Matadi. Construction is scheduled to begin this year. Total investment should reach $4.5 million by 1971. Ford-Europe and several European and Japanese automakers have expressed interest in full-scale assembly plants in the Congo, again contingent on the results of detailed economic and market studies. Four American construction companies are, or about to become active in the Congo. Bechtel is now building a $6 million, 26-room Intercontinental Hotel in Kinshasa, scheduled for completion in 1971. This is a 50/50 joint venture by Pan Am's Intercontinental Hotel Corp. and the Congolese Government. This and other hotel projects in Kinshasa and elsewhere can be expected to help develop a Congolese tourism industry and also to encourage more businessmen and potential investors to visit the Congo. In addition to Bechtel, the Kalicak Construction Co. of St. Louis is now entering the Congolese housing market, with planned construction of approximately 300 homes in Kinshasa.

There is a great shortage of housing at all income levels as well as need for additional office space and industrial plants. International Engineering Co., a branch of Morrison-Knudsen, is opening an office in Kinshasa with the intention of competing for design, engineering, and construction bids in all fields—buildings as well as civil engineering and heavy construction. Lyon Associates, a Baltimore firm, has already opened an office with the same intentions.

Pan American World Airways is now negotiating a major technical assistance contract with the Congolese national airline, Air Congo. This would be the largest technical assistance program in Pan Am's experience, encompassing a maximum of 47 Pan Am technicians and advisers to streamline and modernize every facet of Air Congo's operations and conduct a major training program. While this does not qualify as private investment, the program nevertheless has considerable developmental value since a more efficient Congolese airline can be expected to play a vital role in improving the Congo's domestic transport services and contribute to the development of tourism as a significant source of foreign exchange earnings.

GABON

New York Times *Editorial on the United States, France and Gabon*[*]

March 12, 1964

Some Frenchmen in the West African republic of Gabon are angry with the United States and are taking it out on the few American diplomats and businessmen there. The United States is blamed for the coup that momentarily overthrew President Léon Mba three weeks ago. It is sad to see Frenchmen descending to such tactics.

As the Swiss journalist and historian Herbert Luethy wrote: "France unquestion-

[*]*The New York Times*, Mar. 12, 1964.

ably possesses the oldest and greatest colonial tradition of all the European nations." It dates back to the Norman expeditions nearly a thousand years ago and to the early crusades. The French colonized North America, India and Africa before the English. As with the British, there was an enormous sense of self-confidence behind their drive; but where the British still have this serene sense of power, the French are profoundly frustrated. The loss of Indochina and all of North Africa brought on shattering crises in France.

It is surely not far-fetched to see in President de Gaulle's new reaching out to all parts of the globe a more or less conscious effort to recapture an empire that France had lost twice before. This time it is not a case of physical conquest or colonization, but of political influence, trade and cultural impact.

But in this postwar era, the French are no longer self-confident. From the arrogance of a de Gaulle down to the petulant gangsterism of the French terrorists in Gabon, one finds a note that approaches hysteria. Out of this come the suspicion, distrust and antagonism toward the United States which could lead Frenchmen to believe immediately after the Second World War that Americans wanted to take North Africa away from them, or that we are trying now to subvert a government like President Mba's in Gabon for economic or imperialistic purposes.

So far as Libreville is concerned, the Gabonese authorities could surely to more to protect American property and persons. President Mba has a strongly centralized government and, unless the recent coup weakened his position, he ought to be able to control the hoodlums. Gabon's motto is "Union, Work, Justice." Justice does not mean mob rule.

SOUTHERN AFRICA: THE WHITE REDOUBT

THE WHITE REDOUBT
SOUTHERN AFRICA

Commentary

The development of a separate policy towards Southern Africa is an outgrowth of events of the late 1960's. The importance of the Zambezi, marking a line between the nations moving towards self-determination and the entrenched white minority states had been recognized some years earlier; it appears in the report on African policy made to the Senate Committee on Foreign Relations in 1959 and in writings by observers of the African scene thereafter. Indeed, in the early 1960's–during the threat of Katanga's secession and before Zambia's independence in 1964–some African experts in the State Department feared the demarcation would move farther north still.

In late 1965, however, with Southern Rhodesia's Unilateral Declaration of Independence following the breakup of the Central African Federation and the independence of Malawi and Zambia, the Zambezi had to be recognized as more than a geographical marker with metaphorical possibilities. Inaction by a confounded Labor Party Government in Britain, followed by action by the U.N., forced rethinking outside and realignment inside the "White Redoubt."

The U.N. embargo on arms and oil in December, 1965 was followed by selective mandatory sanctions against key Rhodesian exports and a ban on sales of military equipment in December, 1966, and expanded mandatory sanctions encompassing all trade in May, 1968. At each stage the white governments of Southern Rhodesia, South Africa, and Portugal moved in more concerted reaction; geo-politics makes strange bedfellows.

The strangeness might not have been apparent at first glance, but coordination among these governments, if perhaps inevitable in the context of all of Africa, had not been building historically. Economic ties certainly existed, if mostly in the form of South African exports through Moçambique's ports, African labor finding work in the South African mines, and white South African tourists sunning themselves at resort-hotels in Lourenço Marques. Some labor had made its way across the Limpopo from Southern Rhodesia too, but both Portuguese territories and South Africa were important to Southern Rhodesia for communications: the roads and railroads by which goods came into and went out of that land-locked country.

But there had not been political identity. The differences between the Portuguese territories and the other two were multitudinous; one can encompass them here in the all-important mythology that they were part of metropolitan Portugal. There was no political or cultural place for either South Africa or Southern Rhodesia in Portuguese thinking.

Less obvious were the tensions between Southern Rhodesia and South Africa. They have deep historical roots, dating to the turn of the century and Cecil Rhodes' chartered company which "founded" and ruled the Rhodesias. Affected by the Anglo-Boer war, the whites who settled in the territories were committed to the English side of the "racial struggle," as the terminology of the day myopically called the tension between Britons and Boers. In later years the direct tie to the British crown reinforced differences. Though the whites of Southern Rhodesia hoped to travel South Africa's path to full independence within the British Commonwealth (and started with internal self-government in 1923) they did not want the growing Afrikaner political role to threaten their predominance. Although some Afrikaners did move north of the Limpopo, English-speaking control, with its linguistic and cultural certainties, was not threatened. The whites of the Rhodesias preferred to keep it that way, despite a growing inclination to favor aspects of South Africa's racial policies.

Nor was South Africa in the years after World War II eager to link up with Southern Rhodesia. The Nationalist (Afrikaner) government, in power after 1948, was not keen to acquire the problems more English-speaking whites might bring and the even greater burdens of additional millions of Africans. Further, the idea of buffer states between themselves and the rest of Africa—that is, Black Africa—appealed to them. Never unaware of their ultimately beleaguered position, they could conceive the usefulness of such buffers—the Federation as it then was, the Portuguese territories too—even before the days of African liberation movements. To be tied to the other white-dominated states was to be on the front lines, and South African leadership preferred the alternative.

But the events after 1965 changed that, as one suspects any serious challenge to one or another of the four territories would have done. With Southern Rhodesia virtually under siege, Portugal and South Africa rallied to their neighbor's aid, ignoring all the U.N. dictates and greatly decreasing the effectiveness of the U.N. measures thereby.

In turn, the outside world—African countries and non-African—were forced to think in Southern African terms. For nuances of policy towards one of these countries would have ramifications for the others and for entrenched white power south of the Zambezi. Relatively slight shifts in American policy would be instantly detected as indications of United States attitudes towards white domination in Southern Africa: for example, whether or not to change a vote (let alone cast a first and lonely veto) on a U.N. resolution to protest denial of a visa to a black American athlete, to have a United States naval vessel call at a port or not call there, or to expand commercial flights. Such actions and the more central policy to encourage (or not to discourage) American private investments, are closely watched by the states of Southern Africa, and at least as important, by those of Black Africa, who are constantly testing the American rhetoric of commitment to human dignity and freedom for all.

So seemingly small a step as a U.S.-A.I.D. grant of $850,000, given in November, 1970 to "assist the governments of Botswana and Zambia in improving facilities for commercial traffic between the two countries, and especially by improving the road in Botswana used by this traffic," was viewed out of all proportion to its size. Behind the dry official State Department language is an American life-line thrown to Botswana. One of the truly beleaguered states, with Lesotho and Swaziland in the economic and geographical clutches of white Southern Africa, Botswana has by a fluke of the drawing board a 500-yard access to the outside. It is that tiny border with Zambia which the road will cross, and its ramifications for "Fortress Southern Africa," however minute at present, are clear.

The United States has stressed one overriding theme in its official dealings and attitudes towards Southern Africa and its separate components: that change should come, but by *peaceful* means. The leaders of independent states of East and Central Africa who signed the Lusaka Manifesto in April, 1969 expressed their strong preference also for peaceful self-determination. But they tempered that wish with a realism they know first-hand: ". . . while peaceful progress is blocked by actions of those at present in power in the States of Southern Africa, we have no choice but to give to the peoples of those territories all the support of which we are capable in their struggle against their oppressors."

The broad feelings of black Africans are clear. But the leaders at Lusaka also saw that, whatever the arbitrary unity south of the Zambezi, ". . . the obstacle to change is not the same in all the countries of Southern Africa, and it follows therefore, that the possibility of peaceful means varies from one country to another." Two and a half years later, however, at their October, 1971 meeting, these leaders were less sanguine about achieving effective change by peaceful means.

Shortly after that meeting, the White House and Congress decreased African willingness to believe that the United States would genuinely work for such ends. Africans and other observers watched the lobbying, the Congressional voting, and the Presidential signing produce a military procurement act, amended to permit American violation of U.N. economic sanctions against Southern Rhodesia. That it was, as so often, an action taken more for non-African than African reasons, has not mitigated the reaction in Africa.

American intentions in Southern Africa seemed, indeed, to shift to open support of white domination with the signing of new agreements with Portugal in December, 1971 (see below, p. 958). So, at least, argued Congressman Charles C. Diggs, Jr., in explaining his unprecedented resignation from the United States delegation to the United Nations. For Africans, 1971 marked a change as important as that signaled by the United States arms embargo of 1963. But this change was in the opposite direction, undermining the prospects for African self-determination south of the Zambezi.

STATEMENTS OF GENERAL POLICY
TOWARD AFRICA SOUTH OF THE ZAMBEZI

New York Times *Editorial "The U.S. on Southern Africa"**

September 25, 1966

Ambassador Goldberg's Assembly address hardened appreciably the American position against white minority rule and racial discrimination in southern Africa.

It was the latest in a series of initiatives aimed at removing any doubts in the minds of Rhodesia's white rebels and South Africa's Nationalists about where the United States will stand in any showdown.

Mr. Goldberg moved closer than the British have to the African demand that Rhodesia be granted independence only on the basis of majority rule when he said: "We are not, and never will be, content with a minority government .in Southern Rhodesia."

His language on South-West Africa was perhaps the most severe ever spoken in public on that subject by an American official of Cabinet rank. He referred to that mandated territory as a place "where one race holds another in intolerable subjection under the false name of apartheid." He warned that all U.N. members would re-examine their relationships with South Africa if it continued to violate its mandate obligations.

Mr. Goldberg's remarks fleshed out President Johnson's more general pledge to African ambassadors last May that "We will not support policies abroad which are based on the rule of minorities or the discredited notion that men are unequal before the law," and it follows three other official American statements of the last few weeks citing South Africa's obligations under the mandate and Washington's expectation of their fulfillment.

This series of initiatives does not suggest any dramatic early move against South Africa. For the present, Washington is certain to resist any African demands for sanctions or force against Pretoria. The United States is trying, rather, to persuade South Africa that it is on a long-run collision course with most of the rest of the world, and that only a change in its racial policies—first of all in South-West Africa— can avert that clash. Ambassador Goldberg's warning before the General Assembly should help drive the point home.

The "Lusaka Manifesto" on Southern Africa, Issued by the
Leaders of Fourteen Independent African States†

Lusaka, Zambia, April 16, 1969

1. When the purpose and the basis of States' International policies are misunderstood, there is introduced into the world a new and unnecessary disharmony, disagreements, conflicts of interest, or different assessments of human priorities, which provoke an excess of tension in the world, and disastrously divide mankind, at a time

**The New York Times*, Sept. 25, 1966.
†*Congressional Record*, June 4, 1969, pp. E4601-03.

when united action is necessary to control modern technology and put it to the service of man. It is for this reason that, discovering widespread misapprehension of our attitudes and purposes in relation to Southern Africa, we the leaders of East and Central African States meeting at Lusaka, 16th April, 1969, have agreed to issue this Manifesto.

2. By this Manifesto we wish to make clear, beyond all shadow of doubt, our acceptance of the belief that all men are equal, and have equal rights to human dignity and respect, regardless of color, race, religion, or sex. We believe that all men have the right and the duty to participate as equal members of the society, in their own government. We do not accept that any individual or group has any right to govern any other group of sane adults, without their consent, and we affirm that only the people of a society, acting together as equals, can determine what is, for them, a good society and a good social, economic, or political organization.

3. On the basis of these beliefs we do not accept that any one group within a society has the right to rule any society without the continuing consent of all the citizens. We recognize that at any one time there will be, within every society, failures in the implementation of these ideals. We recognize that for the sake of order in human affairs, there may be transitional arrangements while a transformation from group inequalities to individual equality is being effected. But we affirm that without an acceptance of these ideals—without a commitment to these principles of human equality and self-determination—there can be no basis for peace and justice in the world.

4. None of us would claim that within our own States we have achieved that perfect social, economic and political organisation which would ensure a reasonable standard of living for all our people and establish individual security against avoidable hardship or miscarriage of justice. On the contrary, we acknowledge that within our own States the struggle towards human brotherhood and unchallenged human dignity is only beginning. It is on the basis of our commitment to human equality and human dignity, not on the basis of achieved perfection, that we take our stand of hostility towards the colonialism and racial discrimination which is being practiced in Southern Africa. It is on the basis of their commitment ot these universal principles that we appeal to other members of the human race for support.

5. If the commitment to these principles existed among the States holding power in Southern Africa, any disagreements we might have about the rate of implementation, or about isolated acts of policy, would be matters affecting only our individual relationships with the States concerned. If these commitments existed, our States would not be justified in the expressed and active hostility towards the regimes of Southern Africa such as we have proclaimed and continue to propagate.

6. The truth is, however, that in Mozambique, Angola, Rhodesia, South-West Africa, and the Union of South Africa, there is an open and continued denial of the principles of human equality and national self-determination. This is not a matter of failure in the implementation of accepted human principles. The effective Administration in all these territories are not struggling towards these difficult goals. They are fighting the principles; they are deliberately organising their societies so as to try to destroy the hold of these principles in the minds of men. It is for this reason that we believe the rest of the world must be interested. For the principle of human equality, and all that flows from it, is either universal or it does not exist. The dignity of all men is destroyed when the manhood of any human being is denied.

7. Our objectives in Southern Africa stem from our commitment to this principle of human equality. We are not hostile to the Administration of these States because they are manned and controlled by white people. We are hostile to them because they are systems of minority control which exist as a result of, and in the pursuance of doctrines of human inequality. What we are working for is the right of self-determination for the people of those territories. We are working for a rule in those countries which is based on the will of all the people, and an acceptance of the equality of every citizen.

8. Our stand towards Southern Africa thus involves a rejection of racialism, not a reversal of the existing racial domination. We believe that all the peoples who have made their homes in the countries of Southern Africa are Africans, regardless of the colour of their skins; and we would oppose a racialist majority government which adopted a philosophy of deliberate and permanent discrimination between its citizens on grounds of racial origin. We are not talking racialism when we reject the colonialism and apartheid policies now operating in those areas; we are demanding an opportunity for all the people of these States, working together as equal individual citizens, to work out for themselves the institutions and the system of government under which they will, by general consent, live together and work together to build a harmonious society.

9. As an aftermath of the present policies it is likely that different groups within these societies will be self-conscious and fearful. The initial political and economic organizations may well take account of these fears, and this group self-consciousness. But how this is to be done must be a matter exclusively for the peoples of the country concerned, working together. No other nation will have a right to interfere in such affairs. All that the rest of the world has a right to demand is just what we are now asserting—that the arrangements within any State which wishes to be accepted into the community of nations must be based on an acceptance of the principles of human dignity and equality.

10. To talk of the liberation of Africa is thus to say two things. First, that the peoples in the territories still under colonial rule shall be free to determine for themselves their own institutions of self-government. Secondly, that the individuals in Southern Africa shall be freed from an environment poisonsed by the propaganda of racialism, and given an opportunity to be men—not white men, brown men, yellow men, or black men.

11. Thus the liberation of Africa for which we are struggling does not mean a reverse racialism. Nor is it an aspect of African Imperialism. As far as we are concerned the present boundaries of the States of Southern Africa are the boundaries of what will be free and independent African States. There is no question of our seeking or accepting any alterations to our own boundaries at the expense of these future free African nations.

12. On the objective of liberation as thus defined, we can neither surrender nor compromise. We have always preferred, and we still prefer, to achieve it without physical violence. We would prefer to negotiate rather than destroy, to talk rather than kill. We do not advocate violence; we advocate an end to the violence against human dignity which is now being perpetrated by the oppressors of Africa. If peaceful progress to emancipation were possible, or if changed circumstances were to make it possible in the future, we would urge our brothers in the resistance movements to use peaceful methods of struggle even at the cost of some compromise on the tiring of

change. But while peaceful progress is blocked by actions of those at present in power in the States of Southern Africa, we have no choice but to give to the peoples of those territories all the support of which we are capable in their struggle against their oppressors. This is why the signatory states participate in the movement for the liberation of Africa under the aegis of the Organisation of African Unity. However, the obstacle to change is not the same in all the countries of Southern Africa, and it follows therefore, that the possibility of continuing the struggle through peaceful means varies from one country to another.

13. In Mozambique and Angola, and in so-called Portuguese Guinea, the basic problem is not racialism but a pretence that Portugal exists in Africa. Portugal is situated in Europe; the fact that it is a dictatorship is a matter for the Portuguese to settle. But no decree of the Portuguese dictator, nor legislation passed by any Parliament in Portugal, can make Africa part of Europe. The only thing which could convert a part of Africa into a constitutent unit in a union which also includes a European State would be the freely expressed will of the people of that part of Africa. There is no such popular will in the Portuguese colonies. On the contrary, in the absence of any opportunity to negotiate a road to freedom, the peoples of all three territories have taken up arms against the colonial power. They have done this despite the heavy odds against them, and despite the great suffering they know to be involved.

14. Portugal, as a European State, has naturally its own allies in the context of the ideological conflict between West and East. However, in our context, the effect of this is that Portugal is enabled to use her resources to pursue the most heinous war and degradation of man in Africa. The present Manifesto must, therefore, lay bare the fact that the inhuman commitment of Portugal in Africa and her ruthless subjugation of the people of Mozambique, Angola and the so-called Portuguese Guinea, is not only irrelevant to the ideological conflict of power-politics, but it is also diametrically opposed to the politics, the philosophies and the doctrines practised by her Allies in the conduct of their own affairs at home. The peoples of Mozambique, Angola and Portuguese Guinea are not interested in Communism or Capitalism; they are interested in their freedom. They are demanding an acceptance of the principles of independence on the basis of majority rule, and for many years they called for discussions on this issue. Only when their demand for talks was continually ignored did they begin to fight. Even now, if Portugal should change her policy and accept the principle of self-determination, we would urge the Liberation Movements to desist from their armed struggle and to co-operate in the mechanics of a peaceful transfer of power from Portugal to the peoples of the African territories.

15. The fact that many Portuguese citizens have immigrated to these African countries does not affect this issue. Future immigration policy will be a matter for the independent Governments when these are established. In the meantime, we would urge the Liberation Movements to reiterate their statements that all those Portuguese people who have made their homes in Mozambique, Angola or Portuguese Guinea, and who are willing to give their future loyalty to those states, will be accepted as citizens. And an independent Mozambique, Angola, or Portuguese Guinea may choose to be as friendly with Portugal as Brazil is. That would be the free choice of a free people.

16. In Rhodesia the situation is different insofar as the metropolitan power has acknowledged the colonial status of the territory. Unfortunately, however, it has failed to take adequate measures to re-assert its authority against the minority which has seized power with the declared intention of maintaining white domination. The matter

cannot rest there. Rhodesia, like the rest of Africa, must be free, and its independence must be on the basis of majority rule. If the colonial power is unwilling or unable to effect such a transfer of power to the people, then the people themselves will have no alternative but to capture it as and when they can. And Africa has no alternative but to support them. The question which remains in Rhodesia is therefore whether Britain will reassert her authority in Rhodesia and then negotiate the peaceful progress to majority rule before independence. Insofar as Britain is willing to make this second commitment, Africa will cooperate in her attempts to reassert her authority. This is the method of progress which we would prefer; it could involve less suffering for all the people of Rhodesia, both black and white. But until there is some firm evidence that Britain accepts the principles of independence on the basis of majority rule, and is prepared to take whatever steps are necessary to make it a reality, then Africa has no choice but to support the struggle for the people's freedom by whatever means are open.

17. Just as a settlement of the Rhodesian problem with a minimum of violence is a British responsibility, so a settlement in South West Africa with a minimum of violence is a United Nations responsibility. By every canon of international law, and by every precedent, South West Africa should by now have been a sovereign, independent State with a Government based on majority rule. South West Africa was a German colony until 1919, just as Tanganyika, Rwanda and Burundi, Togoland, and Cameroon were German colonies. It was a matter of European politics that when the Mandatory System was established after Germany had been defeated, the administration of South West Africa was given to the white minority Government of South Africa, while the other ex-German colonies in Africa were put into the hands of the British, Belgian, or French Governments. After the Second World War every mandated territory except South West Africa was converted into a Trusteeship Territory and has subsequently gained independence. South Africa, on the other hand, has persistently refused to honour even the international obligation it accepted in 1919, and has increasingly applied to South West Africa the inhuman doctrine and organisation of apartheid.

18. The United Nations General Assembly has ruled against this action and in 1966 terminated the Mandate under which South Africa had a legal basis for its occupation and domination of South West Africa. The General Assembly declared that the territory is now the direct responsibility of the United Nations and set up an ad hoc Committee to recommend practical means by which South West Africa would be administered, and the people enabled to exercise self-determination and to achieve independence.

19. Nothing could be clearer than this decision—which no permanent member of the Security Council voted against. Yet, since that time no effective measures have been taken to enforce it. South West Africa remains in the clutches of the most ruthless minority Government in Africa. Its people continue to be oppressed and those who advocate even peaceful progress to independence continue to be persecuted. The world has an obligation to use its strength to enforce the decision which all the countries cooperated in making. If they do this there is hope that the change can be effected without great violence. If they fail, then sooner or later the people of South West Africa will take the law into their own hands. The people have been patient beyond belief, but one day their patience will be exhausted. Africa, at least, will then be unable to deny their call for help.

20. The Union of South Africa is itself an independent sovereign State and a Member of the United Nations. It is more highly developed and richer than any other nation in Africa. On every legal basis its internal affairs are a matter exclusively for the people of South Africa. Yet the purpose of law is people and we assert that the actions of the South African Government are such that the rest of the world has a responsibility to take some action in defense of humanity.

21. There is one thing about South African oppression which distinguishes it from other oppressive regimes. The apartheid policy adopted by its Government, and supported to a greater or lesser extent by almost all its white citizens, is based on a rejection of man's humanity. A position of privilege or the experience of oppression in the South African society depends on the one thing which it is beyond the power of any man to change. It depends upon a man's colour, his parentage, and his ancestors. If you are black you cannot escape this categorisation; nor can you escape it if you are white. If you are a black millionaire and a brilliant political scientist, you are still subject to the pass laws and still excluded from political activity. If you are white, even protests against the system and an attempt to reject segregation, will lead you only to the segregation, and the comparative comfort of a white jail. Beliefs abilities, and behavior are all irrelevant to a man's status, everything depends upon race. Manhood is irrelevant. The whole system of government and society in South Africa is based on the denial of human equality. And the system is maintained by a ruthless denial of the human rights of the majority of the population—and thus, inevitably of all.

22. These things are known and are regularly condemned in the Councils of the United Nations and elsewhere. But it appears that to many countries international law takes precedence over humanity; therefore no action follows the words. Yet even if international law is held to exclude active assistance to the South African opponents of apartheid, it does not demand that the comfort and support of human and commercial intercourse should be given to a government which rejects the manhood of most humanity. South Africa should be excluded from the United Nations Agencies, and even from the United Nations itself. It should be ostracised by the world community. It should be isolated from world trade patterns and left to be self-sufficient if it can. The South African Government cannot be allowed both to reject the very concept of mankind's unity, and to benefit by the strength given through friendly international relations. And certainly Africa cannot acquiese in the maintenance of the present policies against people of African descent.

23. The signatories of this Manifesto assert that the validity of the principles of human equality and dignity extend to the Union of South Africa just as they extend to the colonial territories of Southern Africa. Before a basis for peaceful development can be established in this continent, these principles must be acknowledged by every nation, and in every State there must be a deliberate attempt to implement them.

24. We reaffirm our commitment to these principles of human equality and human dignity, and to the doctrines of self-determination and non-determination and non-racialism. We shall work for their extension within our own nations and throughout the continent of Africa.

Speech by Senator Edward M. Kennedy (Massachusetts) Before the Senate on the Lusaka Manifesto and the Proposed New Constitution of Rhodesia*

June 9, 1969

Mr. President, by a curious coincidence of history, within the brief period of a few weeks in April and May of this year, two events of major significance occurred that are likely to have a strong influence on the future course of the racial crisis in southern Africa. One of these events looks toward a new day of peace and racial harmony on the continent, in which the majority and minority races in all African nations will be able to live in concord, equality, and dignity with one another. The other event looks backward to a cruel era of slavery and oppression, and carries one of Africa's most highly developed nations further into the night of racial strife that threatens to engulf it.

The event that is bright with hope occurred in April in Lusaka, Zambia, where representatives of a number of forward-looking nations met in conference. The product of that conference is a remarkable document entitled "Manifesto on Southern Africa," signed by 13 nations of East and Central Africa—Burundi, the Central African Republic, Chad, the Republic of the Congo, the Democratic Republic of the Congo, Ethiopia, Kenya, Rwanda, Somalia, Sudan, Tanzania, Uganda, and the host nation Zambia.

In their manifesto, the 13 nations have joined together in a passionately reasoned condemnation of all aspects of racism and racial segregation. They call on all African nations to govern themselves in accord with the basic principles of human dignity, equality, and national self-determination, regardless of race or other discriminatory classifications.

In clear terms, the manifesto denounces the colonialist and racist doctrines now being promulgated by governments in six separate territories of southern Africa— Mozambique, Angola, Portuguese Guinea, Rhodesia, Southwest Africa, and the Republic of South Africa. The policies of segregation and apartheid, relentlessly applied in these territories, are the antithesis of the fundamental principles of humanity. The stand universally condemned not only by the African nations who signed the manifesto, but by the United Nations and the overwhelming majority of all free nations throughout the world.

Perhaps the greatest importance of the Lusaka document is its tone as a manifesto for peaceful revolution, not violent revolution in southern Africa. Today in Africa, the ancient repressions and denials of majority rule have begun to spawn increased levels of terrorism and guerrilla violence, not only in the Portuguese colonies but in Rhodesia as well. Not even the fortress which is South Africa feels secure, and wise men fear a spark that may ignite the continent. At times such as these, a document like the Lusaka manifesto is especially significant because its emphasis throughout is on peaceful and nonviolent change as the method to improve the plight of the oppressed black majorities. It gives us hope that reason and compassion may yet prevail over the violence that now sweeps so much of the world.

In contrast to the eloquent Lusaka manifesto, there stands the new Constitution proposed in May by the Government of Rhodesia. As published, the new constitution

*Ibid., June 9, 1969, pp. 6083-84.

is designed to entrench the doctrine of apartheid in Rhodesia and thereby to guarantee white domination of the country for all time. Later this month, the new Constitution will be submitted to a national referendum, in which the electorate will be overwhelmingly white. Most experts agree that the constitution is almost certain to be approved.

                *   *   *

If the new Rhodesian Constitution is approved in the coming referendum, there will be little possibility of a negotiated settlement between Rhodesia and Great Britain with respect to the basic issues raised by Rhodesia's unilateral declaration of independence in November 1965. The ruling regime in Rhodesia will no longer have any pretense whatever for the claim that it intends to move toward eventual majority rule, which is the fundamental condition laid down by Britain for settlement. Instead, under its new Constitution, Rhodesia will have moved inexorably into the South Africa mold of an apartheid republic, a nation bitterly divided between whites and blacks, controlled by a dominant white minority, and ruled by the racist principles of apartheid.

The striking juxtaposition between the proposed constitution of Rhodesia and the Lusaka Manifesto on Southern Africa raises a profound question as to who speaks for Western man in Africa today. The Lusaka Manifesto, issued by African nations governed by African majorities, is a convincing plea for the basic principles of human dignity and equality, principles long associated with the liberal tradition of the West and the noblest aspirations of man. By some cruel irony, it is South Africa and Rhodesia who today reject these honored principles of humanity, even though these two white-dominated nations are far and away the most advanced states of modern Africa, and consider themselves as the only truly civilized nations of Africa, the outposts of Western civilization on an alien continent.

Mr. President, for too long we as Americans have failed to recognize the crucial issues at stake in African development. It is entirely appropriate that we should state our position and demonstrate our sympathies on these basic issues of freedom and human dignity. The universal principles enunciated in the Lusaka Manifesto are precisely those that Americans have long accepted as the guiding principles for the evolution of our own society. However imperfect our application of these principles in practice, we remain committed to them as the fixed star of our constitutional development.

I believe, therefore, that the United States should make clear to the nations that signed the Lusaka Manifesto that we support their position and that we oppose racial discrimination in South Africa and Rhodesia and the rest of Southern Africa, just as we oppose it in the United States and wherever else it is found. We must stand firmly behind these principles and take positive action wherever it is appropriate.

Although our power may be limited, it is not negligible. To mention but two examples of immediate relevance to the recent developments I have discussed:

We should urge Great Britain, as the authority still legally responsible for the affairs of Rhodesia, to do whatever lies within its power to assure the well-being of all the people of that land.

We should renew our pledge of wholehearted support to the United Nations sanction program against Rhodesia, thereby halting the pressures now building up on the United States to agree to loopholes in the sanctions for the benefit of particular interest groups.

*   *   *

Nevertheless, through modest steps such as those I have suggested, the United States can help to fill the existing vacuum by providing strong moral leadership for other nations, and can begin to bring significant economic pressure to bear on this repressive regime. At the very least, we can offer fresh encouragement for the aspirations of the oppressed majorities of Southern African and other parts of the world.

*   *   *

*Speech by Assistant Secretary Newsom on the U.N., the United States and Africa**

September 17, 1970

No African problem has demanded and received greater attention from this administration than the problem of southern Africa.

Fundamental to our thinking about this area is our sympathy with aspirations for equality and dignity; we can readily understand how the policies of apartheid and colonialism generate demands for redress and change.

How that change is to be effected, however, raises important questions, including our posture toward force and violence.

Many Africans, faced with the continuation of systems which disregard the principle of human equality, see no alternative but violence. In the absence of change for the better in southern Africa, this feeling is likely to grow, despite the fact that most African leaders today earnestly hope for a more moderate solution.

We do not believe the use of force is the answer. We do not believe it is a feasible answer, given the strength of the white regimes in the area. We do not believe it is a just answer, because violence rarely brings justice to all. We do not believe it is a humane answer.

In our deliberations on these issues, therefore, we seek constantly to find ways and to encourage trends which will lead to peaceful change.

At the last General Assembly, we welcomed much of what was contained in the Lusaka Manifesto, which reflected the concern of African leaders over the human costs entailed in the use of force and expressed a preference for peaceful dialogue as a means to effect constructive change in southern Africa.

Where violence has broken out, we opt for those resolutions which will bring the parties together to sort out and resolve differences.

We seek to turn the white minority governments away from imposition of their policies by force—in the direction of the rule of law and respect for human rights.

We are giving support to the nonracial states of southern Africa—Botswana, Lesotho, and Swaziland—to help them develop increased economic and political independence and stability. We believe they can serve as examples of the constructive possibilities of peaceful change.

Department of State Bulletin, Oct. 12, 1970, pp. 420-23.

Another issue we face, and one which is closely related to the problem of violence, is that of the provision of arms to the white-ruled territories of southern Africa. This issue will dominate much of the debate on African and colonial questions at this year's session of the United Nations.

In 1963, the United Nations Security Council established an embargo on the sale of arms to South Africa. We voted for the resolutions calling for that embargo, and we have observed it faithfully since that time.

Recently, when the new government in Britain announced that it was considering the sale of arms to South Africa for maritime defense of the Capte Route, the Organization of African Unity protested vigorously—as did the Commonwealth countries, with which further consultations are being undertaken by the British.

While fully understanding the importance to Britain of the route around the cape, we have not associated ourselves with their proposed decision. We continue to give our full support to the 1963 arms embargo resolutions.

There is, however, a problem that inevitably arises in the implementation of an embargo. That is, simply, that the embargo is interpreted and implemented in very different ways by the major trading nations.

Some countries are much more permissive than we in deciding what can be sold under the embargo. Most countries take a very liberal attitude toward permitting the sale to the South African military of nonlethal items. This uneven implementation of the embargo creates great problems for a government earnestly attempting to hold to a rigorous definition of what goods are prohibited.

Our own adherence to the embargo is based on our respect for the United Nations Charter, our preference for peaceful over violent means, and our desire to avoid any action which would condone or strengthen the current racial policies of South Africa.

We, therefore, will continue to refuse to sell or license arms to South Africa. We do not intend to strengthen either its military capacity or its capacity to enforce its own racial policies internally.

There are inevitably borderline cases such as civilian-type items. Since the embargo went into effect, we have reviewed such items on a case-by-case basis, taking account of all the facts and of the 1963 U.N. resolutions and United States announcements. We have been urged in many cases to make decisions on the basis that other large industrial nations sell this or that type of equipment to South Africa. We have decided in these cases what to do and what not to do. In accordance with the principles of the embargo we do not, for example, license military aircraft or large transport aircraft for military use but would consider licenses for limited numbers of small unarmed executive civilian-type aircraft. These planes are freely sold by other nations and will not strengthen South Africa's military or internal security capacity. We intend to continue to treat civilian-type items in this way. Thus we will continue to give strong support to the arms embargo.

A separate problem concerns Portugal's African territories. The charge is still made in the United Nations and elsewhere that the United States supplies arms for Portuguese use in Africa.

The fact is, however, that consistent with our opposition to the use of violence, we have since 1961 maintained an embargo on all arms for use in Africa by any of the parties involved in the disputes over the Portuguese territories.

Our military assistance program to Portugal, a NATO ally, has in recent years averaged only $1 million a year. This assistance is used to enhance Portugal's capabilities in antisubmarine warfare and air and sea defense.

Charges that Portugal is diverting U.S. arms to Africa are untrue. Charges that our military assistance frees substantial stocks or resources for use in Africa are unfounded. Reports of U.S. arms in the Portuguese territories, when investigated, invariably prove to be World War II or Korean war vintage articles long since passed out of U.S. control. We do not, of course, place restrictions on sales of purely civilian items to civilian agencies of the Portuguese Government.

Despite our disagreements over Africa, we have sought nonetheless to maintain a relationship with Portugal which will, it is hoped, be useful in encouraging ultimate movement toward self-determination for the population of the Portuguese African territories. Portugal's espousal of racial equality provides some basis for hope that a peaceful and equitable settlement of this problem may be possible.

With regard to South Africa, the policies of apartheid and internal repression by the Government of Pretoria have been unequivocally condemned by the United Nations. Most of the nations of the world have manifested a lack of sympathy for a system which continues to confine rights and privileges to those of a single race.

Despite South Africa's emphasis on the concept of "separate development," there is considerable doubt in the minds of many that South Africa would be prepared to make the concessions necessary to create truly independent and viable black nations within the present area of South Africa.

South Africa argues that implementation of its apartheid policies is a matter of domestic jurisdiction in which the United Nations should not intervene. Such an assertion ignores South Africa's pledge under articles 55 and 56 of the United Nations Charter to promote human rights and fundamental freedoms without regard to race, as well as the U.N.'s own responsibility under these articles.

The United States will continue to emphasize in United Nations deliberations its fundamental abhorrence of the apartheid system and to press for practical measures in protection of the legal and human rights of all South Africans. We are aware, however, that rhetoric is not always an effective instrument in international affairs.

South Africa's administration of South-West Africa (also called Namibia) is another problem the U.N. faces. South Africa occupies this former German colony and League of Nations mandate in defiance of the direct authority of the United Nations. South Africa extends apartheid and repressive legislation to South-West Africa in violation of the rights of the inhabitants of that international territory.

We believe that South Africa should respect the legal rights of the inhabitants and we support the authority of the U.N. in Namibia. We do not recognize the South African right to administer this territory. We also support the Security Council's request to the International Court of Justice for an advisory opinion on the legal consequences for states of South Africa's occupation of the territory. The Court has set November 17 for filing statements in this matter.

In the meantime the U.S. Government officially discourages any new U.S. investment in South-West Africa. U.S. nationals who nevertheless invest there on the basis of rights acquired from South Africa since 1966 will not receive U.S. Government assistance in protecting these investments against claims of a future lawful government in the territory.

Rhodesia presents a very special problem. Events in that territory since 1965 have made it the focus of international and U.N. attention. Our actions and policies toward Rhodesia receive wide publicity and are looked upon as a concrete measure of America's commitment to self-determination, majority rule, and human rights.

As you may recall, in 1965 a white minority regime in Rhodesia proclaimed itself to be the lawful government and unilaterally declared Rhodesia's independence from the United Kingdom. The U.K. undertook lengthy but fruitless negotiations with the regime. Finally, the U.N. Security Council, on the initiative of the United Kingdom, undertook a series of actions designed to bring pressure on the Smith regime to reverse its course. The most important Security Council action was its resolution of December 16, 1966, imposing mandatory economic sanctions against Rhodesia.

In March 1970 we closed our consulate in Salisbury when the Smith regime unilaterally declared a republic and severed the last formal ties with the recognized sovereign power and instituted a new constitution which specifically denied the African majority from ever gaining a predominant voice in the government of their country.

The present situation is not accepted as wholly satisfactory by anyone—this includes many Rhodesians as well as Rhodesia's immediate neighbors.

We will continue to support fully the U.N. economic sanctions against Rhodesia and will seek ways to insure more uniform compliance with the sanctions.

In our enforcement of Rhodesian sanctions during the last 3 years, we have become aware of other special difficulties encountered by American firms.

We believe some relief can be given by permitting U.S. firms to sell their assets in Rhodesia. This is consistent with our commitments and with the U.N. sanctions. Each case, of course, has to be considered individually.

Because of controls imposed by the Smith regime, most American firms no longer have effective control over their Rhodesian assets. The sale of such assets, therefore, does not materially aid the Smith regime. The total book value of U.S. investments was estimated to be about $56 million shortly after sanctions were imposed. Of this total some $50 million is invested in chrome mining enterprises.

A special difficulty concerns firms which legally paid for goods in Rhodesia before the U.S. Government prohibited such imports. At the time our implementing regulations were published, the Treasury Department announced that such transactions would be licensed under a "hardship" provision. If any American firm can demonstrate that it did legally pay for the goods prior to the Executive order—and only one has to date—we consider that it may complete the transaction, thus denying to Rhodesia the benefit of keeping both the foreign exchange and the goods. The U.N. sanctions committee will, of course, be formally advised of any such transactions.

The real solution to the Rhodesian problem lies in an agreement which will gain for Rhodesia international acceptance through a formula reopening the door to eventual majority rule in that territory. The United States sincerely hopes that further exploration of this problem by the Government of the United Kingdom, and perhaps a recognition of common interest in such an exploration by Rhodesia's neighbors, will lead in this direction.

In the consideration of these matters at the United Nations, many Africans seek measures which call either for the complete isolation, economically and politically, of the states and territories of southern Africa or for other measures which we consider unworkable, either from the standpoint of international practice or our own laws and opinion.

We do not favor the isolation of South Africa or the cessation of contacts with the Portuguese territories. We believe that appropriate channels of communication and dialogue must be kept open. We believe contact with the outside world will help the nonwhite majorities and will help bring the white rulers to an understanding of the need for a change in their policies.

Beyond the question of communication lies that of economic sanctions. We voted for them in Southern Rhodesia because of the special legal situation and because of a reasonable hope that they might lead the Rhodesians to work out an acceptable agreement with the United Kingdom.

But the situation in South Africa is different. Mandatory economic sanctions are neither practicable nor likely to advance our goals. We continue to feel that the alternative to violent change in this land is internal change aided by the pressures of its own economy and those from the outside world. We favor contact by the outside world with all segments of the South African population.

It is our earnest hope that, given our firm endorsement of the peaceful principles which the African nations espouse toward southern Africa, especially as stated in the Lusaka Manifesto, we will be able on all matters to maintain an effective exchange with them.

*   *   *

*Address by Assistant Secretary Newsom on United States Options in Southern Africa**

December 8, 1970

Our own perspective, as many in this audience know, is mixed. Many of our citizens feel that South Africa's problems are its own; we should leave them to work them out. They are conscious that we have our own problems and are perhaps not in the best position to talk to others. There are a few of our citizens who view the white domination in southern Africa with a certain nostalgia.

Yet, whether we like it or not, we are involved in the problem of southern Africa because it has become a world problem. The southern African problem in its many forms preoccupies the United Nations. More and more of our own citizens, both black and white, share the feelings of those in the third world against the continuation of practices and policies based solely on the color of a man's skin. While there is debate on either the possibility or the imminence of violence in southern Africa, we cannot rule this out. And a violent confrontation between white and black in southern Africa would have an impact on our own society.

For those in our society concerned with our position in the world, the opportunity afforded the Soviets and Chinese by continued stalemate in southern Africa cannot beignored. Their inroads in central Africa are perhaps not solely related to African frustrations over southern Africa, but these frustrations are a major element.

There is a tendency on the part of many in South Africa and in our own and other countries to discuss this area by analogy. Why should we pressure the South Africans to change when there is racial discrimination in other parts of Africa? Why should we pressure Rhodesia and ignore Czechoslovakia? It is hard to see the relevance of such argumentation. The fact is that a situation of legal discrimination on the basis of race exists in southern Africa. This discrimination is an affront to the newly independent

Ibid., Jan. 18, 1971, pp. 82-84.

African as well as the Asian. It is an affront to the black citizens, as well as to many whites, in our own country. It is a problem constantly before the world and the United Nations. It has within it the seeds of violent explosion which could make it an even graver dilemma for us and the world.

Against this background, let us examine the various approaches suggested to us and other concerned nations.

The first we might call acceptance. South Africa's problem is its own. We have our own; we should not meddle in others. Let us accept it as it is, have normal relations with it, benefit from its economic possibilities. It is, moreover, anti-Communist; we should put our chips on it in the global struggle.

No American government has accepted this approach. We cannot do so and be consistent with our own efforts to solve the dilemma of prejudice. We cannot do so and maintain our bona fides with even the moderate African governments. We cannot effectively provide alternatives to Communist efforts in black Africa if we isolate ourselves with the white-dominated enclaves of southern Africa.

The second option might be called liberation. This calls for support for the liberation movements directed against the present regimes in white-dominated southern Africa. It has been manifested in the recent controversial decision of the World Council of Churches. It has been an issue in the recent meeting of the African Studies Association. It appeals to many who see no other alternative and who are concerned that, in the absence of Western support, the liberation movements will find help only from the Communist countries.

This is the road to violence. Many of those who are in the liberation movements are undoubtedly conscientious, capable men, frustrated by the lack of progress at home. Undoubtedly there are others who find in the movements more of a political than a military base. But even a sympathetic observer finds it difficult to see this path as being either right or effective.

More than any other acts of pressure against South Africa, those directly related to support for the liberation movements have the effect of increasing the fear and determination which lie at the base of the resistance of the white community to change. Given the formidable security and military power of South Africa and Rhodesia, it is difficult to see success for these groups within the foreseeable future. Armed intervention could well set back rather than advance progress toward change. As a Government, however much we might understand the frustrations leading to the espousal of the liberation approach, we cannot find in it a realistic or supportable solution.

A third approach is isolation. This approach suggests the breaking of diplomatic relations, the withdrawal of investment, the further isolation of South Africa in sports, communication, trade, and finance.

This is questionable, even if workable. United States investment in South Africa represents only 16 percent of their foreign investment. Even if it were possible to obtain congressional authority to force its withdrawal, an unlikely prospect, there is no assurance that its place would not be taken by other investors. Neither is it a foregone conclusion that U.S. investment in South Africa necessarily helps apartheid; it is also a factor in the economic pressure on apartheid which I mentioned earlier. The South African, particularly the Afrikaaner, is a determined, resolute man. There is no assurance that he would respond constructively to the pressure of total isolation. Further, such isolation would isolate also the African; not many of them want this.

There is a fourth option: communication.

The visiter to South Africa is impressed by the grave lack of communication among the principal elements of the scene in that area. White does not talk to urban black in any meaningful way. South Africa does not talk to black Africa, except in a limited way. Similarly, in black Africa there is an imprecise knowledge of current South Africa and the attitudes and circumstances of both black and white.

*   *   *

Communication can bring people to ask themselves questions. A Cape Argus editorial before Mr. Carter and I left South Africa mentioned that we had obviously not been persuaded that the separate development approach was correct. It asked whether they, the South Africans, should not take another look.

Communication does not mean acceptance. It means, in a sense, a greater challenge than isolation. It does not mean departing from the arms embargo, from the refusal to submit to apartheid in any of its forms, from our continued expression of abhorrence for the system. It could mean that each side knows better what the other is talking about. It could mean that greater hope could be given to both whites and blacks in South Africa who seek another way.

Address by H. E. Sir Seretse Khama, President of the Republic of Botswana on an African View of African-American Relations in the Seventies*

March 8, 1971

*   *   *

I should be very surprised if our American friends spoke with one voice. There are few constraints on them to do so. Africa is far from being the most pressing problem facing the United States today. The United States is engaged in a major internal debate on the extent to which it should involve itself in areas which in the last quarter of a century have been of immediate concern to it. The great power confrontations which are currently pre-occupying the world are in South East Asia and the Middle East. In addition the United States is today facing in acute form what many of us fear will face other developed industrial, urbanized societies—an internal problem of considerable dimensions which, in the U.S. case, is complicated by the issue of race. Indeed there are cynics who say that it is only the racial factor which makes it necessary for America, in its present mood of introspection, to have an African policy at all—rather than a set of bilateral relationships with individual African states. Certainly the enthusiasm for African independence which was a hallmark of the "new frontier" has been replaced by a mood which some might call disillusion but which might more neutrally and accurately be described as an absence of illusion. As President Nixon put it in his Foreign Policy Statement: "the excitement and enthusiasm of national birth have phased into the more sober period of growth." Perhaps this transition has not been without its moments of postnatal depression. I suspect much the same mood guides African attitudes to the United States and to other Great Powers. This is far from being a bad thing. Relations between states, like relations between people,

*Address before opening session of the "African-American Dialogue," held in Lagos, Nigeria.

prosper best when there is an absence of illusion. But an absence of illusion should not be allowed to degenerate into an atmosphere of indifference or mistrust.

*   *   *

I hope I shall be forgiven if for the remainder of my address I concentrate on the areas of our continent and those aspects of U.S. policy with which I am most familiar. I mean, of course, Southern Africa. I do not think my concern will be regarded as parochial, since the problems of my area take up a large part, some would say a disproportionate part, of the deliberations of international bodies.

We have reached the stage where we must question the effectiveness of the great expenditure of words devoted in the United Nations and elsewhere to the problems of Southern Africa. This is not, I want to make clear, because I do not share the objectives of those who draft, sponsor and speak to the manifold resolutions on Southern Africa which are endlessly debated at so many international gatherings. I recognize only too clearly that my country's prospects of fully independent development are inextricably bound up with the emancipation of all the minority-ruled populations of Southern Africa. Because of this I regret the situation in which we find ourselves. I see few signs that the peoples and governments of Asia and Latin America, much less the Great Powers and their allies, even though more is now known about conditions in Southern Africa. Indeed it may be the case that greater knowledge has led to pessimism about the prospects of change. Behind the screen of words, international activity has been directed towards areas where the dangers of great power confrontation and the risks of starting a Third World War are much more immediate. I find this understandable. Although I and my countrymen have first-hand experience of the inhumanities and indignities of apartheid and white supremacy, I cannot regard Africa, as some of my colleagues do, as the world's unhappiest continent.

*   *   *

Yet when we are drawing up the long and dready catalogue of man's inhumanity to man, the situation in Southern Africa does warrant a special entry. I should like to underline the unique character of the moral issue with which Southern Africa confronts the world. Its problems remain a matter for international concern because of the peculiar nature of the oppression and injustice involved which is, to a greater or lesser extent, based on race. Above all, South Africa is unique among sovereign states in its nation-wide institutionalization of racial injustice. It is precisely these elements of racial oppression and racial confrontation in the Southern African situation which make it a matter for world concern. In an increasingly interdependent world the problem of race is not only affecting situations within states but relations between them. Neither the U.S.A. nor the U.S.S.R. is racially homogeneous, though it is the problems of the former that have attracted more international attention. Britain, since the War has become a multi-racial and is striving to become a non-racial country. Everywhere in the world the destinies of different racial groups are too inter-linked to enable any single ethnic unit, however clearly it sees its own identity, to stand aloof. Even China, which at times in its history has opted for autarky and isolation is looking outward, and may involve itself, with as yet incalculable effect, in problems far from its borders.

*   *   *

We in Africa are watching with interest the growing influence of Black Americans in U.S. politics and I am happy that some of them are with us here in Lagos. Our interest in this, and not least in the developing black representation in Congress is not motivated by the hope that this as yet small group will press the United States to solve our problems for us. We recognize that the first duty of Charles Diggs, John Conyers, Louis Stokes and their colleagues is first to their constituents of all colors and to the Black American community. But we are not unaware of the past and present influence of ethnic pressure groups in U.S. policy-making. And the presence and increasing power of this group of legislators underlines what I was saying earlier about the essential indivisibility of the racial situation throughout the world.

It is this indivisibility which means that the problem of Southern Africa is at the core of U.S.-Africa relations. Questions of aid and investment are important, as they are in U.S. relations with other parts of the developing world. And they are not separate from the issue of freedom and human dignity in the South. But the guts of the relationship between Africa and America is race, and hence Southern Africa.

And just as the problem of violence has always been part of the problem of race within the United States from slavery to the ghetto, it is impossible to discuss the problem of Southern Africa without discussing the issue of violence. Botswana's policy is to work for peaceful solutions to the problems of our area and to minimize violence, but we cannot ignore its existence or bury its origins in a conspiracy of silence. I believe it is possible still to work for peaceful change, but there are no easy and wholly painless solutions to the dilemmas of Southern Africa—and violence already exists. Violence exists in the Portuguese territories where the African nationalists have resorted to armed struggle because peaceful means of achieving self-determination were denied them. Violence exists, albeit sporadically and on a smaller scale, in Rhodesia where the Republican constitution, which specifically excludes the possibility of majority rule presents an obstacle to peaceful progress quite as unyielding as Portugal's insistence that its boundaries extend to Africa. Violence of a kind, exists in South Africa. In that country, as we have been forcibly reminded in recent weeks, the machinery of oppression is all pervasive, and resistance, whether violent or non-violent, from whatever quarter, receives short shrift.

Western leaders in tones of varying severity have deplored the resort to violence by the oppressed throughout Southern Africa, and not all have been as forthcoming as President Nixon in recognizing the violence of apartheid. We can no more condemn those who resort to violence to gain freedom in such situations than we could condemn the violence of European resistance movements against German occupation or the violence of the Hungarians against the Russians in 1956. The United States of America was born in an act of violence against a colonial power, which would not respond to pleas for representative government. It is possible, of course, to be more or less skeptical about the success of violent tactics in different situations, but that is essentially a matter of political and military judgment, and not of morals.

And this is one reason why we should not overlook the need to examine separately the component parts of the Southern African situation. I am opposed to a general escalation and extension of violence in Southern Africa because, in President Nixon's phrase, it would "hurt the very people it would purport to serve." I base my view on an assessment of the balance of forces in Southern Africa. Wholesale violence, particularly if accompanied by greater external involvement, would assist not the independence movements nor the African governments who share their aspirations, but the minority regimes. I want to make it quite clear that this viewpoint is not based on special pleading, influenced by the peculiar vulnerability of my own country. Nor are my statements on the use of force in Southern Africa designed to please any particular audience. My concern is for the future of Africa. We should not overlook the essentially defensive position of independent Africa in the face of Southern African economic, political and military power.

But if we turn from the general situation to the particular, and look at Portugal's colonies, it becomes immediately clear that violence is not a negative element in the special circumstances of Angola, Guinea (Bissau) and Mozambique. Even such a subtle American apologist for the status quo in Southern Africa as George Kennan observed of Portugal, "Members of the Portuguese administration in these territories make no bones of the fact that the armed challenge with which they have been confronted in recent years has stirred them, and, more importantly has stirred the Lisbon authorities, to reforms and improvements that might otherwise have taken decades to complete." Violence has therefore achieved change in the Portuguese territories. One is bound to question whether the change would continue of the stimulus of violence was removed. As the Prime Minister of Ghana, Dr. Busia, has said in a different context, "Dialogue and armed pressures are not necessarily incompatible".

The offer of dialogue on the basis of a commitment to human dignity and self-determination has been made in the Lusaka Manifesto. Implicit also in the manifesto is a set of practical priorities which we must not lose sight of. We must not let our sense of outrage and moral concern about apartheid blind us to those points at which pressure can be most effectively applied. One of those points is Portugal. Nowhere is the West offered greater opportunity for promoting change by communication and pressure. But the West has not taken advantage of their defense and economic links with Portugal to press its rulers to take up the offer contained in the Manifesto. Instead, having been singled out for approval because it does not share South Africa's form of institutionalized racialism, Portugal has been encouraged in its present course. This may turn out to have been an opportunity tragically lost. To be sure Dr. Caetano has instituted new reforms which grant greater autonomy to the overseas provinces, but I fear that the effect of these reforms may be to push Angola and Mozambique closer to Rhodesia and South Africa. Their European minorities, if they feel threatened by African advancement within the official framework of *assimilado* multiracialism, may opt for the overtly racist pattern of their Southern African allies.

Again, concerned as we were with the arms sales issue at the recent Commonwealth Conference, Rhodesia was given only a perfunctory mention. I am glad that the option of communication which the American administration has chosen specifically excludes Rhodesia. I hope that United States influence will be exerted at the United Nations and elsewhere to ensure that sanctions are maintained until a settlement can be achieved which guarantees unimpeded progress to majority rule.

There is, of course, widespread skepticism about sanctions, and, because they are flouted by South Africa and Portugal, their effects are often lightly dismissed. But these are far from negligible, and are weakening the regime in a number of ways, which we can discuss in more detail later in our meeting. These weaknesses give rise from time to time to doubts about the long-term viability of Rhodesia as a white-ruled country. Some South Africans, including the *verligte* elements in the ruling Nationalist party are irritated by what they regard as an obstacle in the way of the outward-looking policy and in addition fear an open-ended financial and security commitment. A settlement between Britain and Rhodesia on any terms acceptable to the men who enunciated the five principles is far from sight. Sanctions are having a distinct economic, social and political effect. There are continuing indications of South African ambivalence to a white-ruled Rhodesia (an ambivalence, which, incidentally, I suspect extends to Angola and Mozambique). This is therefore not the moment for any relaxation of sanctions.

But an important part of establishing our priorities for Southern Africa is the analysis of South Africa itself, its internal situation and its external ambitions. I have already stressed the reality of South African power, which affects the situations I have just mentioned. South Africa has attracted world attention, by its outward-looking policy, especially its overtures to African states and the sharp focus into which this outward movement has placed its domestic anomalies and injustices. South Africa has left the *laager* and is pursuing its interests in a continental, indeed an international arena. It has the power, the resources and the will to do so. At times it has come close to proclaiming a Monroe Doctrine for Southern Africa. Its ambitions may grow with increasing confidence. Both the U.S. and Britain have tacitly welcomed the outward-looking policy, primarily because they have sought to work for accommodation between majority-ruled and minority-ruled Africa in order to relieve the pressure on themselves. If Africa can live with apartheid, no one can expect Western countries to do otherwise. Western observers and some Africans have also claimed that the outward-looking policy will, by ending South Africa's isolation, bring change within its borders. But we must be clear about the motives behind South Africa's strategies. The outward-looking policy is for export only—it has nothing to do with internal liberalization. The condition for dialogue with South Africa is acceptance of the status quo. Its rulers have made it quite clear that the dialogue with black Africa can be about many things, but it cannot at this stage be about political change or self-determination.

And yet white politics in South Africa are in an interesting condition. It remains to be seen whether any new policies will be born of the present unncertainty and confusion among white South Africa's leaders. But any significant change which does take place will not result from contacts with African states, though South Africa does mind desperately about western attitudes. The decisive forces for change, however, are internal. The nature of Afrikanerdom is changing following the new trek from the platteland to the cities. White opinion is becoming increasingly aware of the contradictions within South African society—the most notable of which is the contradiction between economic growth and straightforward white supremacy.

Black politics are changing too, although the limitations on self-expression make these changes hard to interpret. There are leaders emerging, some of whom are genuine and who, while working for their people within the framework of separate development, have lost no opportunity of pointing out the vast credibility gap between theory and practice. I reject sovereign political units based on ethnic criteria, but the potential significance of the Bantustan experiment should not be overlooked. Its consequences are feared by the white public, but increasingly politicians from the largely English-speaking United Party and the more liberal "Progressives" are accepting that the consolidation of the Bantustans and the development of quasi-democratic institutions in them is a policy which would be difficult to reverse completely. Much remains to be done, however, before these fragmented and over-populated areas could begin to look like even remotely credible mini-states. Botswana, Lesotho and Swaziland are a constant challenge to their credibility. Bantustan development cannot be condoned, but its implications deserve careful analysis.

It is developments such as these which I imagine prompted David Newsom's statement in his interesting address at Northwestern University, "Communication does not mean acceptance. It means, in a sense, a great challenge than isolation". The United States and Britain have expressed their abhorrence of apartheid. They seek to change the system in America's case by communication and moral pressure and in Britain's by contact and trade. Initial results of these new policies have not been encouraging. President Nixon's statement was greeted in South African Government circles as "realistic" and a visa was promptly refused to Arthur Ashe. Britain's announcement on Wasp helicopters came in the midst of an unprecedented campaign against the churches, which has involved the harassment and expulsion of both British and American clergy. The question is, given this unpromising beginning, how is the West going to pursue Mr. Newsom's challenge. If communication does not mean acceptance, where do we go from here?

These developments in US and UN policy have been interpreted as a triumph for South Africa's outward diplomacy. The contact has been accepted, the pressure for change brushed aside as rhetoric. But Botswana is the last country to call for the total isolation of South Africa. Can anything be achieved by a policy of communication on the part of Western countries whose friendship South Africa clearly values? Only, I suggest, if the West does not behave as if it needs South Africa more than South Africa needs the West, when, in fact, the reverse is the case. The advocates of contact and communication must spell out what they hope to achieve by these means. Perhaps this meeting can consider some possibilities. The case of the Polaroid Corporation and some of Carl Rowan's statements before the Diggs Committee might make a starting point.

Moreover, if South Africa is to be pressed to make concessions in return for a measure of respectability, which is the only way communication could differ significantly from acceptance, then concessions abroad might come more easily than concessions at home. The attitude of South Africa is clearly critical in determining the future of Rhodesia and the Portuguese territories.

Progress could be made towards common objectives if we were to recognize a mutual interest in limiting violence and working for peaceful change. Peaceful change will not be secured if existing minority-ruled situations are allowed to harden and South Africa's outward-movement encouraged. Separate solutions must be sought for the problems of Portugal, Rhodesia, South-West Africa and eventually South Africa itself. This involves restraining South Africa's outward expansion, eroding the outer edges of the white bastion developing in Southern Africa, driving wedges between its constituent parts, preventing its further consolidation, and maintaining contact and communication with all the forces for change throughout the region. Unless a positive overall strategy is developed along these lines, then communication will slip into acceptance and moral pressure will be reduced to mere rhetoric.

*Address by Assistant Secretary Newsom on African Issues at the U.N.**

September 21, 1971

*   *   *

The stand we have taken on the African issues is clear. We have demonstrated, as unequivocally as any major nation, our support for the principles involved.

President Nixon said last year in his address to the 25th anniversary session of the General Assembly:

> We do hold certain principles to be universal:
> —That each nation has a sovereign right to its own independence and to recognition of its own dignity.
> —That each individual has a human right to that same recognition of his dignity.
> —That we all share a common obligation to demonstrate the mutual respect for the rights and feelings of one another that is the mark of a civil society and also of a true community of nations.

We have maintained conscientiously the arms embargo against South Africa recommended by the United Nations Security Council in 1963, although under the terms of the resolution it is not mandatory.

We have supported fully the U.N.'s determination that continued South African occupation of South West Africa is illegal. We supported the referral of the Namibia case to the International Court of Justice. We discourage U.S. business from going into that territory.

We have been at the forefront in enforcing sanctions against Rhodesia, the only mandatory sanctions ever voted by the United Nations.

We have scrupulously maintained a voluntary arms embargo policy with respect to the Portuguese territories in Africa.

Most African leaders with whom I have spoken recognize and give us credit for what we have done and are doing. They wish only that we would do more.

They recognize, too, that actions in the United Nations are but one part of our total relationship. They know that our manifestation of interest in the causes and concerns of independent Africa occurs in other ways of importance to them. Not the least of these is our contribution to the economic and social development of their countries. Further, the varied currents of opinion in modern independent Africa are not fully manifested in the caucus approach taken by the Africans in the United Nations. The U.N. actions are therefore only a part of the picture. This does not diminish, however, the importance of United Nations action on both the world and the African scene.

It is not pessimism, but honesty, to say that we shall undoubtedly fail to achieve full agreements with the African nations on African issues in this General Assembly, just as we have during previous sessions. We hope our African friends and those deeply

Department of State Bulletin, Oct. 11, 1971, pp. 375-78.

concerned in this country will recognize that in these issues we are not challenging the principle.

*   *   *

... our differences with the African nations are essentially over how change in southern Africa will be achieved—not wheter. It is over how the United Nations can be most effectively used—not whether. In general, the Africans seek support for three broad approaches: isolation of the offenders, economic measures against them, and the use of military force. We have problems with each approach.

We believe change will come in southern Africa. Economic and demographic pressures make this inevitable. In South Africa itself there is a lessening of rigidity. Change is a central theme of discussion; there is psychological and intellectual ferment within the Afrikaner community; there have been isolated instances of acceptance of multiracial activities; there is a growing realism among businessmen that Africans are important to them as skilled workers and as a market. They are beginning to focus on the need for improvement of working conditions for non-whites. We cannot expect change to come quickly or easily. Our hope is that it will come peacefully.

Isolation can breed rigid resistance to change. Open doors can accelerate it. We believe the idea of expelling or suspending South Africa would represent a dangerous precedent, a move toward isolating South Africa's black population, and a move away from that universality of membership which the United Nations is gradually approaching.

Punitive economic measures are unpopular in this country. We have had experience in the problems of enforcement and control. These experiences do not encourage us to believe that such measusres are workable against countries which are important economic entities. By their wealth such entities are able to cushion themselves against economic pressures and encourage noncompliance by others to weaken and thwart these pressures.

We have supported the economic sanctions against Rhodesia, but this is a special case. We have supported them as a feasible, if difficult, short-term measure to create pressures for a settlement with the United Kingdom. Despite incomplete compliance by many nations, we feel this boycott is achieving its objective. We do not see it as a precedent for other, different situations.

We can understand the impatience which leads to demands for the use of force. Nevertheless, we see little prospect of its effective use in bringing change in southern Africa, and we cannot favor its use.

The United States is most unlikely to be involved in military intervention on any side in Africa. Moreover, actions of the U.N. itself to support force would not accord with the basic purposes of the organization.

This catalogue of potential differences is long. I have set it forth in order to put our response to the African issues in perspective. I have set it forth, also, as a means of frank communication with our African friends themselves. I have found they appreciate and respond to this type of diplomacy.

We do not expect the Africans to cease pressing their viewpoints on these issues. The United Nations represents one of the few means they have of continually mobilizing world opinion on their behalf. We, further, agree with them that the absence of substantial change in southern Africa will continue to create tensions and ultimately threaten the peace.

We do seek and hope for continuing discussions with the Africans on these issues and continuing cooperation in fidning acceptable and effective courses of action. We hope that in this way the substantial influence of the United Nations can be preserved and exercised so as to generate not the appearance of solutions, but fair and workable progress toward human rights and self-determination for all in southern Africa.

Press Conference Statement by Congressman Diggs on Resigning from the United States Delegation to the U.N.*

December 17, 1971

When I was informed of my assignment to the United Nations, I was fully aware, of course, that I would become a part of an instructed delegation. But I only undertook the assignment after being assured that there would be opportunity for input. Indeed, at the initial meeting of State Department officials with the delegation, we were assured that the Department would welcome our interest and that our concerns would be granted full consideration. On Monday, November 29, however, during a meeting of the General Assembly, I was informed that a vote was coming up within that hour on apartheid and that the United States was to vote against one part of that delegation and abstain on three parts relating to the Report of the Special Political Committee. Out of courtesy to the Government, I walked out of the Assembly and left a staff person to cast the votes. That afternoon, I dispatched a cable to the Secretary of State (copy of text is Attachment #1), emphasizing my position on consultation. Although, more than two weeks and several voting instructions later, I did receive a reply, my request for consultation was ignored insofar as decisions on voting were concerned. Admittedly, in the press of the work here at the Mission, there is not optimum time for discussion. Even so, time for consultation could have been found—is found—for matters of real interest on the part of the Administration in giving me opportunity for input into these vital questions on Africa.

I have been especially concerned with our position on many matters relating to the resolutions on the Arms Embargo; on the work of the Special Committee on Apartheid, and on the dissemination of information on apartheid. The reasons which have been furnished for these votes (Attachment #2: letter from Asst. Secy. De Palma of Dec. 14) appear tenuous and inadequate to me. Additionally, although I understand it is a long-standing position, I cannot accept the argument that apartheid is not a "crime against humanity" as anything except legal verbiage to support a policy position (see Attachment #3: cable to the Secretary on this. The Department classified its response).

In company with South Africa and Portugal, the United States voted against this year's resolution on the "Question of Territories under Portuguese Administration" (A/C.r/L.992). I believe that my problems with this position are evident from the following partial catalogue of the U.S. difficulties with this resolution:

*Press Release handed out at Press Conference.

—We objected to deploring Portugal's refusal to recognize the inalienable right of the people of those territories to self-determination and independence in accordance with GA Resolution 1514, the Declaration on the Granting of Independence to Colonial Counties and Peoples.

—We objected to the expression of deep concern over the "continued and intensified activities of those foreign economic, financial and other interests which contrary to the relevant resolutions of the General Assembly are directly and indirectly assisting the Government of Portugal in its colonial wars. . . ." To those who would argue that the Azores Agreement is a matter of bilateral concern, I would point to this and many other similar resolutions of the General Assembly.

—We objected to the statement that the colonial wars waged by Portugal in these territories seriously disturbed international peace and security. The United States continues to keep vigilance to avoid any steps which would indicate a frank acknowledgement that the situation in the Portuguese territories is a "threat to international peace and security," and therefore, constitutes a Chapter VII situation. Further, hiding behind an irrelevant "domestic jurisdiction" argument in relation to territories within Chapter XI of the Charter, we objected to interfering with Portugal and urgently calling upon it to end the wars and grant self-determination and independence to the peoples of these territories.

The United States abstained on the General Assembly resolution on Namibia. Inter alia:

—We had difficulty with a provision deploring support to South Africa, which enables South Africa to pursue its repressive policies in Namibia, and calling for the termination of such support.

—We found difficulty with a provision calling upon all States to refrain from economic relations concerning Namibia, although we acknowledge that the General Assembly is the legitimate administering authority for Namibia.

—We were concerned about the financial implications of a clause inviting the Specialized Agencies to give full publicity to Namibia and to the conditions prevailing there.

—Although we acknowledge that South Africa is illegally present in Namibia, we object to the clause calling upon States not to recognize rights or interests in property or resources in Namibia.

As in the case of the resolution on the Portuguese territories, the hypocrisy of our positions enumerated above is self-evident.

The United States has voted against the UN resolutions on the "Activities of Foreign Economic and Other Interests which are Impeding" the granting of independence to countries under colonial domination. This resolution (as contained in A/C.4/L 1005) affirms that the activities of foreign economic and financial interests constitutes a major obstacle to the political independence of these countries and deplores the support given by other States to such interests in exploiting the resources of these areas without regard to the welfare of the people. These positions are supported by much of the evidence resulting from the hearings and investigations of the House Subcommittee on Africa. Further, irrefuted testimony has shown that the condition of the majority in South Africa has actually worsened economically and financially since the development and industrialization of that country. For, regardless of the growth of an economy, unless all the people are given an opportunity to participate fully and freely, a full economy does not mean benefits to those segments whose free participation is excluded. In South Africa, economic growth has not meant greater spending power for the Africans. A study prepared by a UN agency for the Unit on Apartheid, "Poverty, Apartheid and Economic Growth," deals directly with this question. The position of the United States on "the need for trade to help Black Africans" is not based on fact. I am also concerned with an indication that the United States is allying itself with South Africa's so-called "outward policy."

We would have supported the resolution and effort to have more information on apartheid disseminated, but this would have been an addition to the UN budget, was the explanation, and we are opposed to anything that increases the UN budget. Therefore, we abstained. I find this explanation inadequate, because we do support changes in the structure in the UN that will call for more money.

As a firsthand witness, I have found stifling the hypocrisy of our Government which, while uttering its abhorrence of apartheid, unflaggingly votes in opposition to any attempt to act, rather than orate, with respect to apartheid and the minority regimes of southern Africa.

The deterioration in U.S. policy on Africa, reflected here at the UN in our votes on critical resolutions on Southern Africa was continued by the hypocrisy shown by the Administration during the hard fight we made in Congress against the Byrd Amendment to the Military Procurement Bill. This amendment would permit the importation of Rhodesian chrome. If enforced, it would make the U.S. an international law breaker and put us in violation of our UN obligation under Article 25 of the Charter to enforce the Security Council decisions to embargo all trade with the illegal Smith regime in Zimbabwe. The Administration, while emitting soft noises of adherence to sanctions, utterly failed to convey the cues to Congress which sophisticated people look for to determine the seriousness of the Administration's interest in defeating a particular measure. It was clear that the White House was not concerned in stopping the effort to undercut the sanctions. Consistent with that posture of this Administration is a suspicion that out of the Nixon-Heath meeting in Bermuda this coming Monday or Tuesday, there may come an understanding that the United States will support the British on the Rhodesian settlement proposals—settlement proposals which do not accord with the inalienable right of the people of Zimbabwe to self-determination. A position of supporting a unilateral British decision that the rebellion of the Smith regime was ended would be consistent with our opposition to a resolution (A/C.4/ L.998) providing that it is the UN which must find that "a non-self-governing territory" has attained a full measure of self-government in terms of Chapter XI of the Charter.

At this point, I wish to make it perfectly clear that the people here at the U.S. Mission to the UN have not been responsible for this situation. Many people at the Mission, including Ambassador Bush, have been frustrated in their desires for a more enlightened policy because of the instructions that have come down. They have fought for a more enlightened position and have lost to the European Bureau to the economic and to the military groups which have been dominating policy of the United States vis-a-vis African issues, as well as to those "watch dogs" of Southern African policy who have relegated unto themselves the decision-making authority so that positions on this area are the peculiar responsibility of the White House at the National Security Council level.

My concern about the drift in our decision-making was heightened last week when the State Department announced the conclusion of an agreement with Portugal continuing U.S. base rights in the Azores and providing a $436 million quid pro quo for Portugal. This enormous, unprecedented and anomalous commitment was made to a country which has not only refused to recognize its obligations, under the UN Charter, of self-determination for the people of Angola, Mozambique, Guinea-Bissau and Cape Verde, but is waging wars against the peoples of each of these African territories.

The Government of Portugal has been undergoing severe financial difficulties, because of its expenditure of approximately one-half of its budget to fight these wars against the legitimate aspirations of Black people in Africa for freedom and independence.

The Caetano Government has also been subject to much domestic criticism for this diversion of 50% of its annual resources away from the development of its own country, which is the least developed in Western Europe, to maintain a colonial empire.

Having visited two of the so-called Portuguese territories in Africa, Angola and Mozambique in 1969, I visited the other two—Guinea-Bissau and Cape Verde, last August. I have seen first-hand the exploitation by the Portuguese of their African colonies and their subjugation of the people, and the inordinately low state of the economy of these territories.

I have seen that whatever the Portuguese are doing for the people of these areas is attributable to the pressures of the Liberation movements. At the same time, it was clear that the Portugese do not admit their legal obligations to grant self-determination to the peoples of these areas. Entering into a pact to provide Portugal with vast amounts of economic assistance is, therefore, incredible.

What is the justification for the extraordinary economic assistance program for Portugal in this agreement, in which the aid proposed for Portugal through loans from the Export-Import Bank of the United States is more than four times the Exim assistance program to Portugal in the whole period from 1946 to 1970?

Does this agreement not add a new dimension to the already deeply perturbing indications of NATO interest in buttressing the white minority-ruled areas of Africa?

Does not our Azores agreement with Portugal appear to represeent a feeling that Portugal is threatened by the successes of the freedom fighters militarily and economically? Portugal is suffering a trade deficit of approximately $498.8 million dollars. The liberation forces hold substantial territory in Angola, Mozambique and Guinea-Bissau. Has there been a call to the NATO countries to come to Portugal's rescue to which the United States has responded?

I should stress that my quarrel is really much deeper than the injection of such huge sums into Portugal—although (when I consider our alleged inability to put money into crucial areas for the 23 million Blacks in the United States) I find the amount staggering. But, I object most strenuously to the U.S. commitment to bail Portugal out from the economic and political consequences of its nefarious policies in Africa without any commitment and definitive action by Portugal towards ending the wars and towards granting independence to the peoples of these areas.

This decision by our government dramatically climaxes a series of actions which this Administration has taken both against the true foreign policy interests of the United States vis-a-vis Africa, and against the interests of Africa itself.

The very character of this Administration's support to South Africa and Portugal has changed. Until now, there has been a sub rosa alliance with the forces of racism and repression in southern Africa, as indicated:

—by the relaxation of the arms embargo to permit the sale of light aircraft to the South African military and of troop transport planes to Portugal;
—by the sale of Bell helicopters to the Portuguese;
—by the quiet reversal of our former policy of limited Exim involvement in South Africa for a policy of substantial Exim exposure in South Africa;

–by the erosion of our policy here at the United Nations on African questions beginning in 1969, first to abstaining on important issues on African policy and, finally, to actually voting against such resolutions,.

In the Azores Agreement, this Administration has announced both an open alliance with Portugal and a decision which I can interpret only to mean "partnership" in the subjugation of the African people. The hard line on African issues with which I have been confronted here at the United Nations must have been a precursor of this decision to become directly involved with Portugal in a pact which is in flagrant violation of numerous General Assembly resolutions on Portugal and the territories under Portuguese Administration (For text of statement submitted to the President with request for point-by-point response, see Attachment #4.)

As a member of the United States delegation to the United Nations, I have tried in vain to get underway a real consultative process on U.S. positions here at the United Nations. However, the Azores Agreement is a watershed. After much thought I have decided that considerations of integrity and of the now depserate need to turn U.S. policy around from the perilous course on which it has embarked require that I completely disassociate myself from this Administration on African policy.

The conclusion of the Azores Agreement compels me to cut any ties tha might bind me to the foreign poliy of this Administration. Although it is nearly the final hour of this General Assembly, the new commitment of this government to actively assist Portugal in waging wars against Black people constrains me to act. I am therefore submitting my resignation to the President.

I have today submitted by resignation from this delegation to the President of the United States.

New York Times *Editorial on Congressman Diggs' Resignation from the United States Delegation to the U.N.* *

December 18, 1971

When Representative Charles C. Diggs Jr. of Detroit accepted an appointment as a United States delegate to the United Nations this year he knew he would have to follow instructions. Where he erred was in taking seriously the Administration's rhetoric against apartheid and white minority rule in southern Africa, as well as its promises to consult members of the delegation in advance about positions to be taken in the General Assembly.

The Michigan Democrat is a member of the House Foreign Affairs Committee and the active, widely-traveled chairman of its subcommittee on Africa. He is also head of the Black Caucus on Capitol Hill. He says he had supposed that the Administration might be interested in "giving me an opportunity for input into these vital questions on Africa." He now knows better.

Yesterday, Mr. Diggs quit the delegation in anger and frustration. It was the first time in U.N. history that an American delegate had resigned during the General Assembly. With Washington increasingly unwilling to back any U.N. actions aimed at

The New York Times, Dec. 18, 1971.

prodding the white rulers of South Africa, Rhodesia and the Portuguese colonies toward self-determination for black majorities, life had become a series of embarrassments for Mr. Diggs.

The "watershed" for Mr. Diggs was Washington's decision to revive an agreement with Portugal for the use of air and naval bases in the Azores and to prop up the Lisbon Government's floundering economy with up to $435 million in credits. Mr. Diggs interprets this as an American commitment to assist Portugal in carrying on its colonial wars in Africa and as suggestive of an increasing "NATO interest in buttressing the white minority ruled areas of Africa." It is, in any event, part of an emerging pattern of far greater Washington concern for the sensibilities of white rulers of southern Africa than for the struggle of the black majorities for justice and self-determination.

Congressman Diggs is not alone in finding this policy hypocritical and disastrous in the long run for the United States.

SOUTH AFRICA

Commentary

Just as geopolitically as South Africa looms in importance over the southern sixth of the continent, so it also commands greatest attention on the issues of self-determination and human dignity. The policies by which it lives are the most rigid; its ruling minority is the most determined; and most important, its wealth is the greatest on the continent. Wealth is the key not just because of strength, power and size, but because an African governed South Africa would long since have solved the problems of Southern Rhodesia, Angola and Mocambique. These countries are, in detached, objective terms, South Africa's buffers—and South Africa's continued existence guarantees a chance for their own. It is a special reciprocity.

American attitudes towards South Africa are based on partial knowledge of that country's past. The emotional reactions that grow on such a base are often contradictory; depending not only on a mix of idealism and self-interest, but on which ideals one espouses. It is no condemnation of turn-of-the-century American opinion to point to its emotional support for the Boers against British imperialism. But the sensibilities of the 1960's and 1970's are quite different from those of the earlier decades. It is important to notice that this support rested on a notion advanced ever since with enthusiasm by South Africa's rulers: that there is greatness and virtue in hardiness, individualism, triumph over the wilderness—in other words the pioneer spirit—and that white South Africans and Americans (they do not say white Americans) have built-in empathy with each other for sharing such traditions. For South Africa's rulers own sensibilities have changed little over the decades, even centuries, and they expect that the whole white world will be as unvarying in outlook as they.

There are those in the United States to whom these parallels appeal; they choose to dwell on the pioneer side of American tradition (ignoring the price exacted from the American Indians) and subordinate the Declaration of Independence and the Bill of Rights. Apart from those among them who are personally committed to a virulent brand of racism, those who advance admiring arguments about white South African achievements are also, perhaps coincidentally, figures committed to Cold War thinking.

For it is in such thinking that mid-twentieth century characterizations complement these of earlier eras: The Europeans of South Africa, especially the Afrikaners are valiant builders of an admirably developed country (never mind the labor, in which the whites scarcely shared, of Africans who outnumbered them in ratios from hundreds to one to the four to one of the present). More, they are a bastion against instability and Communism (the two are often assumed to be related in the non-western world) and they are stalwarts of the free enterprise system. And they therefore deserve support because they give support to the "Free World," despite their many and complicated problems, a caveat that always appears coupled with ritualistic, if genuine, deploring of South Africa's racial policies.

Statements growing from these assumptions appeared less frequently as official American policy towards South Africa reflected changes in attitude during the early sixties, both towards the Cold War and African problems. But when such established spokesmen of earlier administrations as Dean Acheson and George Kennan have come forth in apparent understanding of, if not sympathy for, South Africa's white rulers and their problems, it has not been without impact in South Africa and in Black Africa. To many Americans and outsiders such figures represent a deeply entrenched United States foreign policy making "Establishment." When their pronouncements appear in the pages of *Foreign Affairs*, and the *Washington Post* and *New York Times*, they seem to carry added authority, though their authors lack specific expert knowledge of South Africa itself. They contribute to making policy, as much as do countervailing official speeches and explanations of votes, and statements by others of equal stature but different views.

For there are quite different views within the United States, views resting on quite different premises: that the fundamental American—indeed, human—commitment must be to dignity and freedom for all men. That, whatever the history of South Africa (and these views deny the argument that the past supports white supremacy south of the Limpopo), now, in the present, the whites-only government and its *apartheid* policies make flagrant man's inhumanity to man, as bad or worse because it is white man's inhumanity to black.

This position has had spokesmen who also command a national and international audience, sometimes official, but more often ex-official or official-by-association; they, like their counterparts of the "pro-pioneer" school also carry an "Establishment" aura; they too contribute to making American policy.

Most notable of all in the 1960's was Robert F. Kennedy, who spoke out not only in the United States but, as no other American has done, or perhaps could do, in South Africa itself. And there were others, former Supreme Court Justice and U.N. Ambassador Arthur Goldberg, who, with credentials to equal Acheson's, locked horns in newsprint with the former Secretary of State over the legal intricacies of South Africa's claims to South West Africa.

Many start their thinking on South Africa from abhorrence of apartheid; they are also diverse; black and white, young and older, official and quite unofficial. There is no consensus among them on the hardest question: what to do about it? Solutions run a gamut, usually based on the degree of insistence on peaceful change. Solutions do not run the *whole* gamut, though, for they do not admit one position: cooperation, however indirect, however attenuated, with the white South African government, no matter what end it may be said to achieve. For those holding these views have a deep conviction that such cooperation can only entrench and further legitimize minority rule in South Africa. And that it will seriously damage America's relations with the countries of Black Africa. They base that conviction on South Africa's past and Africa's present.

The history of South Africa, as they examine it, reveals several telling points. The first is that the Afrikaner government now in power and its Afrkanns-speaking constituency have one of the world's longest traditions of purposeful isolation and determination not to yield to external influences. Their early treks in the 1830's and even before showed an unequalled determination to avoid outside pressure. From the "second trek" in the 1840's, through the "First War of Independence" to wrest the Transvaal from British rule in 1881, through the inflexible treatment of "Uitlanders" in the South African Republic, through the Anglo-Boer War with its "bittereinders" (those who would fight to the bitter end) outnumbering those who would give in, its "hensoppers"—through it all, the dominant theme was absolute refusal to yield to peaceful pressure, let alone simple entreaty. It was not just resistance to British authority, it was to a British authority that did regard the Africans as "hewers of wood and drawers of water" in the literal Biblical interpretation.

The guilt of the post-Anglo-Boer-War British Liberal Party, whose leaders were bent on atoning for what they saw as British imperialist sins against the Boers, removed whatever counterweight or influence that might have modified the direction of white-dominating policy. The Union of South Africa, independent after 1910, moved steadily (if not quite inexorably) towards ever-greater exclusion of Africans from even the chance of sharing, except as a labor force, in their country's destiny.

For those who asserted that the Africans (and other non-whites) would find room for maneuver in divisions between English-speaking and Afrikaans-speaking whites, history has had more disillusionment. Since 1948, when the Nationalist Government of the Afrikaners came to power, all but a few English-speaking whites have supported government policies on crucial issues, even over the symbolically important issue of becoming a republic and leaving the British Commonwealth. There as elsewhere, self-interest has taken precedence over other considerations. The economic, political—indeed, total—self-interest of the South African whites in preserving the status quo is obvious in a situation of unrivaled prosperity based on cheap labor without political rights, with the labor force outnumbering the privileged minority four to one.

Nor have countervailing pressures, some by the few whites who oppose the government in the face of vast personal risk, succeeded in affecting the direction of policy. A study of the varied African attempts to organize resistance, protonationalist, and nationalist movements along lines quite usual elsewhere in Africa (some, paradoxically drawing on early South African experience) shows this point clearly.

From the organization of the South African National Congress in 1912, through its first anti-pass campaign in 1919, the organization of Natal sugar growers in 1936, the Great Mine Strike of 1946, the A.N.C. Defiance Campaign of 1952, and the sad events of Sharpeville in 1960, the pattern of government response has been constant. It has been to close every loophole that each successive attempt to bring change has revealed. Even a few of the measures taken make the point: the 1913 Land Act, which first restricted Africans to a small proportion of the country; the retrogressive Native Land and Trust Act of the 1936 Herzog government, which cut to 12% the land that later came to be called "Native Reserves"—these measures were just a start.

The Nationalist government enacted voluminous legislation in the 1950's and 1960's, most notably the Suppression of Communism Act (where "Communism" is defined as any doctrine or scheme "which aims at bringing about any political, industrial, social or economic change within the Union by the promotion of disturbance or disorder, by unlawful acts or omissions or by the threat of such acts or omissions or by means which include the promotion of disturbance or disorder, or such acts or omissions or threats"); the Bantu Education Act, which destroyed African chances for equal education, separate or otherwise; the Group Areas Act that carved the country into a multitude of fragments, mainly to keep different peoples apart. Capping it all was a definition of treason of the greatest latitude, with most severe penalties for violators. The government has supposed that its "Bantustan" policy, setting up "homelands" for Africans on parts of that 12% of South Africa's least productive land, would somehow make all these measures more rather than less palatable, both inside the country and outside.

It is in this context that Black African states look at South Africa, and at expressions of what direction American policy towards it may take, and at the subtle shifts that give direct indication of what policy is. For there is a range of possibilities within the commitment to working for peaceful change which, along with abhorrence of *apartheid*, has been a theme of American policy. It is clear that even if open support of the South African status quo is not an option for the United States, there are many ways to give aid and comfort and indirect support to the status quo, or even to a further entrenched government with its ever more repressive measures.

Options arise over many issues: American trade, American investments, the activities and employment practices of American firms with branches in South Africa, an American space tracking station, South Africa's place in the American sugar quota, commercial flights between South Africa and American cities, American athletes—black and white or only white?—competing in South Africa. And all that is quite apart from formal U.N. votes as key, if general, indicators.

When an Assistant Secretary of Commerce says, "We neither encourage nor discourage investment in South Africa," what does that mean? It means at least that the Commerce Department makes known possibilities, and apparently the facts speak for themselves. For since American investors picked up the slack in South African investment in the crucial years when it was declining in the aftermath of Sharpeville, American capital has in ever increasing sums apparently found South Africa an attractive—and stable—prospect.

Some argue, of course, that it is on economic realities that the South African government's apartheid policies will run aground; that an increase in economic activity and prosperity will force the government to permit more highly skilled opportunities to Africans, and that such economic changes are bound to have political repercussions (a side point is that Africans also benefit from rising wages). It is difficult not to wonder, however, why the spectacular economic growth of the past decade has, if this reasoning is correct, produced more repressive measures rather than fewer.

Those who oppose America's private financial ventures in South Africa found heartening the November, 1969 announcement that a consortium of ten United States banks (the Bank of America, Chase Manhattan Bank, National City Bank, Manufacturers Hanover Trust Co., Morgan Guaranty Trust Co., Chemical Bank of New York Trust Co., Bankers Trust Co., Irving Trust Co., Continental Illinois Bank and Trust Co., First National Bank [Chicago]) had discontinued their $40 million revolving loan to the South African Government. Whether the decision came solely for reasons of international economics, or whether mounting pressures from churches, universities, and legislators contributed is not clear.

Shifting from purely economic to military-technological interest, what does it mean when NASA does not number black Americans among its personnel at the space tracking installations in South Africa to put the government to the test, and hires South African Africans only for menial jobs (and on South African wage scales)?

There can be little ambiguity in the inclusion of South Africa in the American sugar quota, in act whose wording specifically favors producing countries with a "need for economic development." Clearly South Africa has no such need and yet the Congress of the United States continues to include it. In the words of Representative Jonathan Bingham (New York), that inclusion grants ". . . a subsidy paid by unknowing American consumers to South African sugar plantation owners—a subsidy which strengthens the base of an apartheid policy which is totally repugnant to most of those who pay it."

But probably the most important immediate issue is the sale of arms or of equipment that could be used for military purposes. A corollary is investment in plant which could permit South Africa the even greater self-sufficiency of being able to produce her own military hardware (hence the debate over the South African activities of such American enterprises as General Motors, the Ford Motor Company, Union Carbide, and the Polaroid Corporation).

The reason the arms issue is central is that, however much the outside world including the African states may want a peaceful solution to South Africa's problems, the South African government has been engaged in a military build-up for over a decade. "Bittereinders," to use the Boer War phrase, the Afrikaner leadership is taking no chances with internal uprising; easily able to suppress even the smallest signs, they are nonetheless prepared for retaliation as massive as may be necessary; indeed, all indications are that they are more than massively equipped for all possible contingencies, at least in the geopolitical present. Some African states even fear that South Africa's outward political thrust of the 1970's may one day have its own aggressive military component, though the activities of liberation movements legitimize the government's language of defense.

The American declaration of its own arms embargo against South Africa, announced by Adlai Stevenson on August 2, 1963, had immediate impact, and it has continued in force. But in international relations as in constitutional law, there may be strict constructionists and those whose interpretations range more widely. The strict constructionism, in this sense, achieved through the efforts of the Africa Bureau of the State Department in the months after the embargo was taken up by other U.N. members, persisted relatively undamaged for some years. But watchers of United States policy towards South Africa noted a shift in a speech by Assistant Secretary of State for Africa, David Newsom, in September, 1970: "There are inevitably borderline cases such as civilian-type items. . . . In accordance with the principles of the embargo we do not, for example, license military aircraft or large transport aircraft for military use but *would consider licenses for limited numbers of small unarmed executive civilian-type aircraft*." (italics mine) Requests to license such planes had been turned down before and it was well-known that executive civilian-type aircraft can be used for military reconnaissance; they can even be armed.

In this connection, the continuing American tendency to follow Europe's lead in African policy raises questions of a shift in policy; certainly strict constructionism has been widened. But more, this change comes in the context not only of uninterrupted French arms sales to South Africa (for France never observed the U.N. embargo). The Conservative government in Britain has moved towards resuming such sales themselves. It was fortuitous for the South African government that the closing of the Suez Canal, which brought forth a torrent of nineteenth century thinking about protecting the sea-routes to the Far East, and the condition of Britain's economy, combined to give new leverage with England's rulers. A Soviet navy increasingly active in the Indian

Ocean had further raised the strategic value the American military place on the Cape.

What could become a reversion to following the dictates of Europe (and the needs of one's own balance of payments amid heightened concern, given world monetary problems, with the foremost producer of gold) has implications for Black African nation's views of the United States position, and what position it might take in future. Is there, indeed, to be a white solidarity? Will the United States side with her NATO allies on Southern African questions, and does that mean that in the (unlikely) event of imminent violence, it will be that much feared international confrontation of white and black?

These questions come to the fore in one other context: South Africa's "forward policy" towards Black Africa, initiated in the late 1960's and picking up momentum in 1971 over the issue of dialogue with the Black African states. For South Africa is combining her military defense with political offense. South Africa's leaders propose to enter into discussions with the leaders of Black African states, but on South African terms: no discussion of "internal affairs"—that is, apartheid policies—but only of such matters as trade and investment.

Some leaders in Black Africa are lured by a chance to try, through contact and communication, to affect the minds and hearts of South Africa's leaders; others are strongly opposed to pursuing such overtures. In the words of the Nigerian Head of State, General Gowon,

> I believe really the best thing they [the South African government] can do is first of all to enter into meaningful dialogue with the black people in South Africa, give them the human dignity they deserve and treat them as human beings. . . . I think anybody that speaks of talking and having dialogue before this is realised is betraying the black South Africans in South Africa.

Whether or not dialogues actually take place, South Africa can only profit. If they do, she will receive *de facto* legitimacy, despite disclaimers, from some Black African states; if they do not, she will have succeeded, even if only temporarily, in creating dissension within Black Africa on the one subject that had united them: refusal to countenance in any way apartheid-based authority in the "white redoubt."

Hope for "dialogue" has recurred in American policy statements, but before the South African initiative, it was phrased as dialogue *within* South Africa, among the Africans, Asians, Europeans there. Changes in wording with that initiative in 1969, and repeated in 1970 and 1971, suggest American willingness to approve any attempt at communication. However admirable the long-range goals, American policy makers run the same risks in their relations with Black African nations in this seemingly minor and well-intentioned shift as in dealing with other equally ambiguous problems—all difficult, all with intricate implications, all part of that central problem for Africa and the world that is South Africa.

SOUTH AFRICA

Statement by James J. Wadsworth, U.S. Representative to the
U. N. General Assembly, on the Problem of Apartheid in South Africa*

December 6-8, 1955

The question of race conflict in the Union of South Africa has been before the General Assembly for 2 years. It involves the subject of race relations within a member state and is a matter which my Government views with deep concern. Our primary desire is to promote, within the framework of the charter, the objectives of the United Nations in the field of human rights.

*   *   *

A key point which the United States has sought to stress during consideration of this item at previous sessions is the importance of determining how the United Nations can best play the part laid down for it in the charter with respect to the advancement of human rights. This brings us at once to the question of the competence of the organization in this field.

We have no doubt that the drafters of the charter believed that the United Nations had a positive role in the field of human rights. How otherwise can we explain the presence of those provisions of the charter such as articles 55 and 56? Article 55 specifies that the United Nations shall promote "universal respect for, and observance of, human rights and fundamental freedoms for all without distinction as to race, sex, language, or religion." Article 56 provides that all members "pledge themselves to take joint and separate action in cooperation with the Organization for the achievement of the purposes set forth in Article 55."

While the United States Government is not in accord with some of the extreme views regarding the application of article 2 (7) to this case, we believe it is essential that the Assembly should at all times bear in mind the domestic jurisdiction provisions of the charter. Ambassador Lodge reiterated this year in the General Committee our view that items of this character invite questions concerning the competence of the Assembly under article 2 (7) of the charter. He also emphasized our concern over a tendency in the Assembly to include in the agenda items whose international character is subject to question and which could affect the authority and sound development of the United Nations.

*   *   *

My delegation believes that the way the Assembly should deal with the present item is to reaffirm its belief in the basic wisdom and the universal validity of the human-rights provisions of the charter as a standard to which all members should aspire.

This is the basis for our view that the Assembly should not consider this problem in terms of conditions in the Union of South Africa alone but in relationship to

*Department of State Bulletin, Jan. 3, 1955, pp. 32-36.

developments throughout the world. This was why we did not support the establishment of the United Nations Commission on the Racial Situation in the Union of South Africa. We seriously doubted its usefulness. We were convinced that this was not the way to encourage and nurture a constructive solution to the problem before us.

*   *   *

In so doing, it [the Commission] has fallen into the regrettable error of seeking to judge one country by the situation in another. Unfortunately, its summaries of the situation elsewhere suggest in some instances perfection, where in fact the situation is far from satisfactory. For example, the Commission states flatly that—

> in the Union of Soviet Socialist Republics, racial problems have been resolved as a result of continuous and effective action by the government and authorities. Racial discrimination has been abolished and any attempt to practice it constitutes an offense.

The Commission then cited appropriate provisions of the Soviet Constitution to demonstrate that the principle of nondiscrimination was an important part of the Soviet system.

*   *   *

EXPLANATION OF VOTE

As I indicated in my speech in the general debate on this item, the United States does not regard the perpetuation of the United Nations Commission on the Racial Situation in the Union of South Africa as the proper means of dealing with the situation. We continue to believe that the most useful way in which to approach this problem of human rights is, first, to relate its consideration to developments and conditions throughout the world and, second, for the Assembly to state, and where appropriate to reaffirm, the objectives to which all members should aspire in the promotion and encouragement of human rights. In the long run, we think this course would be more effective in bringing about the result we all desire than any other action within the competence of this body.

*   *   *

To sum up, the United States is voting against three paragraphs of the 20-power resolution, operative paragraphs 4, 6, and 7, for the reasons I have already given. We will abstain on all other paragraphs of the resolution and on the vote on the resolution as a whole. We are abstaining because we do not believe that this resolution is the best way to achieve results. On the other hand, the United States Government, as every member of this organization knows, opposes every form of racial discrimination, and it is abstaining because it does not wish to cast a vote that could be regarded as in any way condoning the racial policies of the Union of South Africa.

*   *   *

Statement by Francis T.P. Plimpton, U.S. Representative to the U.N.
General Assembly, on Apartheid in South Africa*

April 5, 1961

I wanted to say once again that the United States is squarely, utterly, and irrevocably opposed to the policy of racial discrimination epitomized in the term apartheid. Let there be no mistake about our position. But our paramount consideration must be, and I repeat my words of the other day, "the welfare of apartheid's unfortunate victims themselves" and "not punitive action against a recalcitrant government."

Two resolutions are now before this committee. The first, set forth in SPC/L.59/Rev. 1, was submitted by Ceylon, the Federation of Malaya, and India. In firm and unequivocal terms it again calls upon the Government of the Union of South Africa to bring its policies and conduct into conformity with its obligations under the charter. The condemnation of apartheid in this resolution is clear and strong. The language of the operative paragraph is dignified, appropriate, and just.

The second resolution, set forth in SPC/L.60, was submitted by 24 African members of the United Nations. I can understand the justified indignation that prompted this draft. Some of the cosponsors have emphasized their desire to present in the strongest possible form their feelings about the policy of apartheid. Operative paragraph 5 of this resolution states, "Solemnly recommends to all States to consider taking"—and then it sets forth a series of sanctions. Let us be in no doubt about the language of this introductory sentence. We do not believe the word "consider" makes any significant change in the effect of this paragraph of the resolution. We believe that anyone who votes for this resolution as it is presently worded is in effect voting in favor of sanctions and should feel an obligation to put them into effect, otherwise there would be no need to go beyond the language of operative paragraph 3 of the previously introduced three-power draft. These sanctions range from the severance of diplomatic relations to a complete economic blockade.

Our primary objection to these harsh measures is that they simply will not accomplish what they are intended to do. If sanctions as extensive as these were to be approved and carried out, the effect could be an internal explosion in South Africa, the brunt of which could be borne by the very Africans we are striving to help. Beyond that, the peace of the whole continent of Africa could be in jeopardy.

Also, despite our total rejection of apartheid, we will vote against the proposal for sanctions because we do not believe its adoption will bring an end to apartheid or improve the lot of the victims of that abhorrent policy.

There are those who say that a vote in favor of a sanctions resolution is the way to express the maximum disapproval of apartheid. But the sanctions contained in the resolution go well beyond disapproval since specific measures are recommended whose effect could have the most serious consequences. We believe that this would not produce the end of apartheid but would result in embittered chaos threatening African and world peace and security. We will not vote in favor of sanctions which we believe would endanger the victims of apartheid and the peace of Africa.

*Ibid., Apr. 24, 1961, pp. 602-04.

Since the African resolution is a call to the members of the United Nations to take concrete action against the Union of South Africa, we wonder how many members of the United Nations stand ready to take such drastic action should the resolution be adopted. To vote for this resolution which we do not believe would ever be fully implemented if adopted would tend to weaken the United Nations without weakening apartheid. We must not let the United Nations become an instrument of empty threat.

There are many of us who believe that a change in the policies of the South African Government will come only as the proponents of apartheid feel their increasing and forlorn political isolation and realize the hopelessness of apartheid. Apartheid in the last analysis is a moral question. If the views of the United Nations are to have weight, this Assembly must state its opposition to apartheid in a single, unequivocal voice. The three-power text before us is one we believe all can support. Through it we can and will speak with a united voice. The 24-power text will divide us.

We are prepared to vote for the three-power resolution because it casts a judgment on apartheid which we believe is just. We are prepared to speak out against apartheid and consider practical and realistic measures to achieve this end. We believe the three-power resolution, representing as it does the maximum disapproval of apartheid, is such a measure. It expresses the unanimous judgment of thyworld that apartheid is an evil offense against the conscience of mankind.

Let us be realistic. A sanctions resolution if put into effect would endanger the welfare of the very people we are trying to aid. The racial conflict that it would bring about would leave a new scar on the African Continent increasing the very racial intolerance we are seeking to eliminate. I urge my colleagues to join in unanimous approval of the sound and statesmanlike resolution proposed by the Governments of Ceylon, the Federation of Malaya, and India, and to reject sanctions.

Statement by Ambassador Plimpton on the Problem of Apartheid in South Africa*

November 19, 1962

*   *   *

Today we are addressing ourselves to the problem of apartheid in the Republic of South Africa. The view of the United States on this matter is clear. We are unalterably and irrevocably opposed to apartheid in all its aspects. Our traditions and our values permit us no other position. We believe that the continuation of apartheid can only lead to profound human tragedy for all races in South Africa. We are firmly committed to use our best efforts to encourage South Africa to abandon these policies and to live up to its obligations under the charter.

Our concern—and that of the United Nations—with the question of apartheid derives not only from our dedication to the principle of human rights, not only from the clear violation by the South African Government of articles 55 and 56 of the charter, and not only from the repeated refusal of that Government to heed the recommendations of the General Assembly and the Security Council. It derives most of all from concern for the millions of men, women, and children whose lives this harsh and rigid policy thwarts and stunts. It derives from the conviction that persistence in this policy will only increase tensions among the races throughout southern Africa—a heightening of animosity which can well result in disaster for all its races.

The arguments used to justify apartheid ring in our ears with melancholy familiarity. These were the same arguments used a century ago in our own country to justify a system of human bondage by which one race claimed its right to own another. Such arguments are refuted equally by the advance of morality and the advance of knowledge.

*   *   *

We believe that this committee and the General Assembly should begin by reaffirming its condemnation of apartheid and by declaring again that it is South Africa's solemn duty to bring its racial policies into conformity with the charter.

We believe further that the Assembly must again urge the Government of South Africa to meet its obligations to the charter with respect to the treatment of peoples of Indian and Indo-Pakistan origin.

We believe that the nations represented here must take every opportunity to make known to the Government of South Africa the sentiments of the world community, and we believe that any resolution to be adopted must call on individual states to exert as much influence as they can on that Government.

I would propose that member states be instructed to report back to the 18th General Assembly the steps they actually have taken to influence South Africa to abandon these regressive policies. Such reports will enable the Assembly to determine more accurately the actual effect of various measures which might be used to hasten apartheid's inevitable end.

Finally, in recognition of the explosive character of affairs in South Africa, we suggest that the Security Council be requested to maintain a close and continuing watch on the situation as one which might precipitate a serious threat to world peace and security.

Some nations have raised the question of the application of sanctions to South Africa. But would the passage of a resolution recommending sanctions bring about the practical result we seek? We do not believe this would bring us closer to our objective—the abandonment of apartheid in South Africa. We see little value in a resolution which would be primarily a means for a discharge of our own emotions, which would be unlikely to be fully implemented, and which calls for measures which could be easily evaded by the country to which they are addressed—with the result of calling into question the whole efficacy of the sanction process.

The hard fact is that in answer to such a resolution sanctions would be applied only partially, feebly, and ineffectually. Supplies cut off from one source could be easily furnished from other sources. I could not sympathize more with the sense of frustration which lies behind the appeal for sanctions, but I submit that that frustration would be exacerbated by the adoption of a program inherently doomed to failure.

What would be the impact on the United Nations and its members of the adoption of such a resolution, unimplemented by many members?

For one thing, bitterness might arise between members as to who is and who is not fully complying with the resolution, with a resulting unfortunate disunion which would benefit only South African apartheid.

But, more important, the adoption of a sanctions resolution which would not be fully implemented and which would not achieve the desired result would seriously weaken the authority of the United Nations, debase the effectiveness of its resolutions, and generally impair its reputation. This is something which I am sure that all of us, particularly the smaller nations, would wish to avoid. We should all recall that the decline of the League of Nations was precipitated in large part by its inability to make good on a resolve to apply sanctions.

Members of this committee will recall that last year the General Assembly adopted, with near unanimity, a resolution which called on all members to take such individual or collective actions to end apartheid as were open to them in conformity with the charter. The United States has supported that resolution and has complied with it. We believe that each member state can and should take measures which, given its particular circumstances, will be most effective to bring about the result that we all desire. There is, however, a vital distinction, both practically and in terms of the charter, between such a resolution and a resolution recommending specific sanctions, such as the one which the General Assembly rejected last year. The latter type the United States will continue to oppose.

The call for sanctions is based on the natural but insubstantial hope that there is a shortcut to the solution of the terrible problem of apartheid. Similarly the expulsion of South Africa from the United Nations has been suggested as a way of dealing with apartheid; but the practical result of expelling South Africa would be to remove its Government from the one place where the full weight of world opinion can be brought to bear on it. We believe that apartheid can be ended, not by the contraction of relationships between South Africans—black, colored, or white—and the rest of the world but on the enlargement of those relationships and by the full and continued exposure of the South African Government to world opinion.

Ending apartheid will not, we believe, be achieved by any one or another dramatic action but only by the steady and repeated impact of the mobilized conscience of the world community, and we call on all nations to continue to mobilize the influence of world opinion on South Africa.

My own Government fully recognizes its duty to mankind, as well as to this organization, to try to bring the South African Government to change its disastrous policy.

To be concrete, the United States has already adopted and is enforcing the policy of forbidding the sale to the South African Government of any arms, whether from governmental or commercial sources, which could be used by that Government to enforce apartheid either in South Africa or in the administration of South-West Africa. Furthermore, my Government has made and will continue to make official representations to the South African Government on all aspects of apartheid. It has told and will continue to tell that Government that it owes it to the world, to its obligations under the charter, and to the welfare of its own people to abandon apartheid. We call on all nations to join with us in speaking in a single voice to express the world community's condemnation of apartheid and its concern lest the continuation of South African policies lead to bloodshed, war, and disaster for all races.

THE UNITED STATES BAN ON SALE OF ARMS TO SOUTH AFRICA *

Statement in Support of Security Council Ban by Ambassador Stevenson

August 2, 1963

All of us sitting here today know the melancholy truth about the racial policies of the Government of South Africa. Our task now is to consider what further steps we can take to induce that Government to remove the evil business of apartheid, not only from our agenda but from the continent of Africa.

The policy of apartheid denies the worth and the dignity of the human person. And for this very reason we must try to express our feelings, we believe, with as much restraint as we can muster. Self-righteousness is no substitute for practical results.

                *   *   *

We also believe that all members, in the words of the resolution passed almost unanimously by the 16th General Assembly should take such separate and collective action to bring about an abandonment of apartheid as is open to them in conformity with the charter. The United States supported that resolution and has complied with it.

I should like to take this occasion to bring up to date the record of the measures the United States has taken to carry out this purpose.

First, we have continued and, indeed, have accelerated our official representations to the Government of South Africa on all aspects of apartheid in that country. We have done this through public words and private diplomacy, expressing our earnest hope that the South African Government would take steps to reconsider and to revise its racial policies and to extend the full range of civic rights and opportunities to nonwhites in the life of their country. And we have observed to the South African Government that, in the absence of an indication of change, the United States would not cooperate in matters which would lend support to South Africa's present racial policies.

We have utilized our diplomatic and consular establishments in South Africa to demonstrate by words and by deeds our official disapproval of apartheid.

And as the United States representative informed the Special Political Committee of the General Assembly on October 19, 1962, the United States has adopted and is enforcing the policy of forbidding the sale to the South African Government of arms and military equipment, whether from Government or commercial sources, which could be used by that Government to enforce apartheid either in South Africa or in the administration of South-West Africa. We have carefully screened both Government and commercial shipments of military equipment to make sure that this policy is rigorously enforced.

But I am now authorized to inform the Security Council of still another important step which my Government is prepared to take.

*Ibid., Aug. 26, 1963, pp. 333-37.

We expect to bring to an end the sale of all military equipment to the Government of South Africa by the end of this calendar year in order further to contribute to a peaceful solution and to avoid any steps which might at this point directly contribute to international friction in the area. There are existing contracts which provide for limited quantities of strategic equipment for defense against external threats, such as air-to-air missiles and torpedoes for submarines. We must honor these contracts.

The Council should be aware that, in announcing this policy, the United States as a nation with many responsibilities in many parts of the world naturally reserves the right in the future to interpret this policy in the light of requirements for assuring the maintenance of international peace and security. If the interests of the world community require the provision of equipment for use in the common defense effort, we would naturally feel able to do so without violating the spirit and the intent of this resolve.

*   *   *

It is clear to my delegation that the application of sanctions under chapter VII in the situation now before us would be both bad law and bad policy.

It would be bad law because the extreme measures provided in chapter VII were never intended and cannot reasonably be interpreted to apply to situations of this kind. The founders of the United Nations were very careful to reserve the right of the organization to employ mandatory coercive measures to situations where there was an actuality of international violence—or such a clear and present threat to the peace as to leave no reasonable alternative but resort to coercion. We do not have that kind of a situation here. Fortunately for all of us, there is still time to work out a solution through measure of pacific settlement, and any solution adopted by this Council must be reasonably calculated to promote such settlement.

It is bad policy because the application of sanctions in this situation is not likely to bring about the practical result that we seek, that is, the abandonment of apartheid. Far from encouraging the beginning of a dialog between the Government of South Africa and its African population, punitive measures would only provoke intransigence and harden the existing situation.

Furthermore, the result of the adoption of such measures, particularly if compliance is not widespread and sincere, would create doubts about the validity of and diminish respect for the authority of the United Nations and the efficacy of the sanction process envisioned in the charter. Also on this matter, views differ so widely that we cannot hope to agree on the necessary consensus to make such action effective even if it were legitimate and appropriate.

And as for suggestions of diplomatic isolation, persuasion cannot be exercised in a vacuum; conflicting views cannot be reconciled in absentia.

Instead, we believe still further attempts should be made to build a bridge of communication, discussion, and persuasion. It the human race is going to survive on this earth, wisdom, reason, and right must prevail. And let us not forget that there are many wise and influential people in that great country who share our views.

It is regrettable accomplishments in so many fields of human endeavor in South Africa are being obscured by a racial policy repugnant to Africa and to the world. Certainly one ultimate goal for all of us is to assist South Africa to rejoin the African Continent and to assist in the development of all the peoples of Africa.

And this, Mr. President, is why my Government has looked with such favor on the idea of appointing special representatives of the Security Council who can work energetically and persistently and be free to exercise their own ingenuity and to pursue every prospect and every hint of a useful opening.

We cannot accept the proposition that the only alternative to apartheid is bloodshed.

Statement by Ambassador Charles W. Yost Explaining Security
Council Vote on Embargo on Arms to South Africa

August 7, 1963

My Government is able to support this resolution because it reflects the attitude of the United States toward the racial policies of the Republic of South Africa. We particularly appreciate the cooperation of the sponsors of the resolution which has facilitated our desire to vote in favor of it.

We have over a period of years expressed our strong disapproval of the policy of racial discrimination being pursued in South Africa contrary to the obligations of the Republic Government under articles 55 and 56 of the charter. Thus we wholeheartedly endorse the appeal to South Africa to abandon these policies and to liberate those persons who have been imprisoned, interned, or subjected to other restrictions merely because they are opposed to thypolicy of apartheid.

My delegation also supports the request that all member states cease forthwith the sale and shipment of arms and military vehicles. As you will recall, Ambassador Stevenson announced in this chamber on August 2 that the United States Government had taken another important step demonstrating its concern at the continued lack of progress in ending racial discrimination in South Africa by voluntarily deciding to end the sale of all military equipment to the Government of South Africa by the end of this year.

Mr. President, the Council will also recall that at the time the United States representative announced this new policy he explained that our decision not to sell armaments after the end of this year to South Africa was without prejudice to the completion of delivery of certain strategic equipment, such as air-to-air missiles and torpedoes on which contracts had already been signed. In addition, it will be recalled that we naturally reserved the right to interpret this policy in light of any future requirements for the common defense effort in assuring the maintenance of international peace and security.

Security Council Resolution 181 (1963) Banning Sales of Arms to South Africa*

August 7, 1963

The Security Council,
Having considered the question of race conflict in South Africa resulting from the

*U.N. Security Council, *Official Records*, 18th Year Supplement for July, August. September 1963, 1964, pp. 73-74.

policies of apartheid of the Government of the Republic of South Africa, as submitted by the thirty-two African Member States,

Recalling its resolution 134(1960) of 1 April 1960,

Taking into account that world public opinion has been reflected in General Assembly resolution 1761 (XVII) of 6 November 1962, and particularly in its paragraphs 4 and 8,

Noting with appreciation the interim reports adopted on 6 May and 16 July 1963 by the Special Committee on the Policies of apartheid of the Government of the Republic of South Africa,

Noting with concern the recent arms build-up by the Government of South Africa, some of which arms are being used in furtherance of that Government's racial policies,

Regretting that some States are indirectly providing encouragement in various ways to the Government of South Africa to perpetuate, by force, its policy of apartheid,

Regretting the failure of the Government of South Africa to accept the invitation of the Security Council to delegate a representative to appear before it,

Being convinced that the situation in South Africa is seriously disturbing international peace and security,

1. Strongly deprecates the policies of South Africa in its perpetuation of racial discrimination as being inconsistent with the principles contained in the Charter of the United Nations and contrary to its obligations as a Member of the United Nations;

2. Calls upon the Government of South Africa to abandon the policies of apartheid and discrimination, as called for in Security Council resolution 134 (1960), and to liberate all persons imprisoned, interned or subjected to other restrictions for having opposed the policy of apartheid;

3. Solemnly calls upon all States to cease forthwith the sale and shipment of arms, ammunition of all types and military vehicles to South Africa;

4. Requests the Secretary-General to keep the situation in South Africa under observation and to report to the Security Council by 30 October 1963.

Adopted at the 1056th meeting
by 9 votes to none, with
2 abstentions (France, United
Kingdom of Great Britain and
Northern Ireland).

Decision

At its 1073rd meeting, on 27 November 1963, the Council decided to invite the representatives of India, Liberia, Madagascar, Tunisia and Sierra Leone to participate, without vote, in the discussion of the report submitted by the Secretary-General in accordance with resolution 181 (1963) above.

*Security Council Resolution 182 (1963) Forbidding the Sale
and Shipment of Arms to South Africa* *

December 4, 1963

The Security Council,

Having considered the race conflict in South Africa resulting from the policies of apartheid of the Government of the Republic of South Africa,

Recalling previous resolutions of the Security Council and of the General Assembly which have dealt with the racial policies of the Government of the Republic of South Africa, and in particular Security Council resolution 181 (1963) of 7 August 1963,

Having considered the Secretary-General's report contained in document S/5438 and addenda,

Deploring the refusal of the Government of the Republic of South Africa, as confirmed in the reply of the Minister of Foreign Affairs of the Republic of South Africa to the Secretary-General received on 11 October 1963, to comply with Security Council resolution 181 (1963) and to accept the repeated recommendations of other United Nations organs;

Noting with appreciation the replies to the Secretary-General's communication to the Member States on the action taken and proposed to be taken by their Governments in the context of paragraph 3 of that resolution, and hoping that all the Member States as soon as possible will inform the Secretary-General about their willingness to carry out the provisions of that paragraph,

Taking note of the reports of the Special Committee on the Policies of apartheid of the Government of the Republic of South Africa,

Noting with deep satisfaction the overwhelming support for resolution 1881 (XVIII) adopted by the General Assembly on 11 October 1963,

Taking into account the serious concern of the Member States with regard to the policy of apartheid, as expressed in the general debate in the General Assembly as well as in the discussions in the Special Political Committee,

Being strengthened in its conviction that the situation in South Africa is seriously disturbing international peace and security, and strongly deprecating the policies of the Government of South Africa in its perpetuation of racial discrimination as being inconsistent with the principles contained in the Charter of the United Nations and with its obligations as a Member of the United Nations,

Recognizing the need to eliminate discrimination in regard to basic human rights and fundamental freedoms for all individuals within the territory of the Republic of South Africa without distinction as to race, sex, language or religion,

Expressing the firm conviction that the policies of apartheid and racial discrimination as practised by the Government of the Republic of South Africa are abhorrent to the conscience of mankind and that therefore a positive alternative to these polices must be found through peaceful means,

1. Appeals to all States to comply with the provisions of Security Council resolution 181 (1963) of 7 August 1963;

2. Urgently requests the Government of the Republic of South Africa to cease forthwith its continued imposition of discriminatory and repressive measures which

Ibid., pp. 8-10.

are contrary to the principles and purposes of the Charter and which are in violation of its obligations as a Member of the United Nations and of the provisions of the Universal Declaration of Human Rights;

3. Condemns the non-compliance by the Government of the Republic of South Africa with the appeals contained in the above-mentioned resolutions of the General Assembly and the Security Council;

4. Again calls upon the Government of the Republic of South Africa to liberate all persons imprisoned, interned or subjected to other restrictions for having opposed the policy of apartheid;

5. Solemnly calls upon all States to case forthwith the sale and shipment of equipment and materials for the manufacture and maintenance of arms and ammunition in South Africa;

6. Requests the Secretary-General to establish under his direction and reporting to him a small group of recognized experts to examine methods of resolving the present situation in South Africa through full, peaceful and orderly application of human rights and fundamental freedoms to all inhabitants of the territory as a whole, regardless of race, colour or creed, and to consider what part the United Nations might play in the achievement of that end;

7. Invites the Government of the Republic of South Africa to avail itself of the assistance of this group in order to bring about such peaceful and orderly transformation;

8. Requests the Secretary-General to continue to keep the situation under observation and to report to the Security Council such new developments as may occur and in any case, not later than 1 June 1964, on thyimplementation of the present resolution.

Adopted unanimously at the 1078th meeting.

Testimony by Assistant Secretary Williams Before the Subcommittee on Africa of the House Committee on Foreign Affairs on United States-African Relations*

March 1, 1966

We believe that the forces for change in southern Africa are increasing their tempo. While, on the one hand, this is encouraging, it also increases the threat of violence. As intensified pressures for change meet intensified resistance, as peaceful avenue to change are blocked off one by one, fewer and fewer alternatives to violence remain open.

I am not here as a prophet of doom. I do not mean that violence cannot be avoided. What I do mean is that the search for peaceful accommodation of the forces for change in southern Africa, both inside and outside the area, must be intensified before it is too late.

The U.S. Government has no prescription for South Africa. But if South Africa's peoples are to devise their own solution, it seems to us that a good way to begin would

---

*Committee on Foreign Affairs, *United States-South African Relations*, Hearings Before the Subcommittee on Foreign Affairs, 89th Cong., 2d sess., part I, (Washington, 1966), pp. 4-5; 7; 8-10.

be to start some form of dialog among the racial groups in South Africa. We are alarmed at the severance one by one of constructive contacts between the whites and nonwhites in South Africa.

If we and other like-minded nations could contribute to the creation in South Africa of an atmosphere of free discussion and mutual effort to understand and respect the other person's real interests and aspirations, a great stride would have been made toward stable human relations in the subcontinent. It is clear that a lasting solution in South Africa can only be one devised by the South Africans themselves. But it must be the creation of all groups. Whether imposed paternalistically or by force, a formula imposed by one group upon the others will not endure.

It must be recognized that there are serious obstacles in South Africa to the free discussion and compromise we consider indispensable if the long-range trend toward large-scale violence is to be arrested and reversed. While accommodation of conflicting aspirations and interests is vital, the forces within South Africa making for such accommodation are being repressed.

* * *

The broad aims of U.S. policy toward South Africa are essentially political. We support freedom, equality, and justice for the people of South Africa for the same reasons we support them elsewhere, both at home and abroad. We support them because they are the keystones of our heritage. We support them because we believe that at home they safeguard and enhance our enjoyment of life, liberty, and the pursuit of happiness and that abroad in doing the same thing they strengthen the basis for a just and lasting peace.

These basic freedoms are, of course, fundamental to our role of leadership as a nonracialist nation in a multiracial world. We support renewed efforts to initiate in South Africa a peaceful, evolutionary process toward these goals.

Despite the frustrations we must persist in the search for a peaceful solution. A resort to violence would be enormously costly, not only to the peoples of South Africa, but also to the peoples of Africa generally. It would also be costly to us and to the free world and would undoubtedly be exploited by forces hostile to us.

These political aims are paramount. In scientific, economic and strategic respects our bilateral relationships with South Africa are useful to us—even in some fields important—but they are not essential to our national security.

* * *

The U.S. Government over the years has sought to dissuade South African officials at all levels from discriminatory and repressive laws and from employing various oppressive measures. We have, through diplomatic channels, warned against the extension of apartheid practices to the international territory of South West Africa. The U.S. Government has expressed its critical views to South Africans on the basis of a large accumulation of first-hand evidence.

American officials have devoted much time and effort to the study of apartheid in its many aspects. Despite the many frustrations we have encountered in our efforts to persuade South African leaders to change their policies, the increasingly manifest contradictions and unrealities of apartheid give at least some grounds for hope that the situation in South Africa has not rigidified irreparably.

Along with our policy of persuasion, we have followed a policy of continuing certain forms of cooperation with South Africa and keeping open the lines of communication. Pursuing these policies simultaneously has faced us with some difficult dilemmas. Our representatives in South Africa are exposed to strong pressures from the South African Government and its supporters to conform with apartheid practices.

Wherever it is legally possible to do so, our representatives resist these pressures. Our Embassy and consulates hold nonracial receptions and individual officers entertain nonracially. Our diplomatic and consular posts hirylocal employees on a nondiscriminatory basis. The U.S. Government makes clear that it disapproves of the appearance of Americans, whether as amateurs or professionals, before segregated audiences in South Africa. It will not sponsor visits to South Africa of perofrmers who would appear before such audiences.

As a result this aspect of our exchange program is virtually suspended. More importantly, we have canceled operational port calls in South Africa of U.S. naval vessels and aircraft rather than accept the application of racial conditions to our personnel.

*   *   *

As concrete evidence of our abhorrence of apartheid and our determination not to contribute to its enforcement, we do not sell to South Africa any arms, ammunition, military equipment or materials for their manufacture and maintenance. Our first step in this direction was when we placed a ban on arms that could be used in enforcing apartheid within South Africa. As international opposition to apartheid increased in tempo, along with repression in South Africa, the growth of violence, and the flight of refugees, we took a further step in August 1963.

We extended our arms ban against South Africa to all arms, ammunition, and military equipment, except those under existing contracts and those which might be required in the interests of world peace.

*   *   *

We adopted this comprehensive ban prior to the adoption of a U.N. Security Council resolution calling on all U.N. members to apply such a ban. We supported the resolution and have strictly observed the ban. In the Security Council the late Ambassador Stevenson explained this policy as intended to contribute to a peaceful solution and to avoid actions adding directly to international friction in the area. In December 1963, in support of another resolution of the Security Council, our ban was extended to equipment and materials for the manufacture and maintenance of arms and ammunition in South Africa.

Aside from the arms embargo, the U.S. Government does not interfere with trade and investment in South Africa. This is in keeping with our traditional policy of keeping world trade and other economic relations as free as possible from Government interference. An exception is where the national security is directly affected, as in the cases of Communist China and Cuba.

The U.S. Government neither encourages nor discourages investment in South Africa. Potential investors who seek our advice are briefed on the political and racial situation, the outlook, and American policy and interests. The decision about whether to invest remains with the individual or company.

The U.S. Government of course encourages both new and old companies to maintain high standards in the treatment of personnel employed in South Africa. We believe American companies abroad should lead in such respects as fair wages, nondiscrimination, pension systems, and the like. While American companies operating in South Africa are, of course, obliged to abide by South African laws, we are encouraged by their generally progressive record.

Despite strong pressures in the U.N. and from various American organizations concerned about civil and human rights in South Africa, we have not been prepared to support U.N. economic sanctions against South Africa. Several problems are involved. These are:

(1) The problem of a legal basis for such actions;

(2) The problem of economic effectiveness; and

(3) The problem of psychological effectiveness.

With regard to the legal problem, the U.S. Government believes that the conditions envisaged in chapter VII of the U.N. Charter for the imposition of compulsory sanctions; that is, the existence of a threat to international peace or an act of aggression, do not apply to South Africa at this time.

Much thought has been given in this Government and in the U.N. to the problem of the economic effectiveness of sanctions. In the summer of 1964 the U.N. Security Council established a committee of experts to study the feasibility, effectiveness, and implications of sanctions, or as it described them, "measures which might be taken against South Africa within the framework of the U.N. Charter." The Committee was requested to make a technical and practical study of sanctions without reference to the circumstances in which their application might be considered. The United States participated actively in the work of the Committee. Its report was submitted to the Security Council in February 1965. It emphasized the view that, although South Africa would not be readily susceptible to economic measures, South Africa is not immune to impact from such measures. It concluded that the degree of effectiveness of economic measures would directly depend on the universality of their application and on the manner and the duration of their enforcement. Should a situation arise in which the U.N. appropriately might consider resort to sanctions, the United States believes the availability of this detailed, practical study will be helpful.

Cessation of investment is most often urged as a first step in applying graduated economic pressures. Could the United States exert effective pressure on South Africa by withholding investment? A generation ago the South African economy depended to a very large extent on foreign investment. Now foreign investment plays a much smaller role in the economy. The United States provides only a small proportion either of total investment in South Africa or of foreign investment there. Our investment in South Africa is only 14 percent of all foreign investment there.

From 1950 to 1963 U.S. direct investment in South Africa by companies amounted to only 2.3 percent of the total net domestic capital formation there. If one includes portfolio investment the percentage is still only 3.5.

South Africa is one of the countries which is subject to all aspects of the U.S. program to improve its balance of payments. This means that all types of U.S. private capital flows to South Africa are subject either to the interest equalization tax or to the President's program of voluntary restraints on private corporate investment and bank lending abroad. It is probable that new U.S. investment in South Africa will be reduced as a result. Even before this program was begun American companies had been financing their investments largely by profits made in South Africa, advances from South African banks, and the issuance of stock both in South Africa and Europe. From 1955 to 1963 the net outflow to South Africa of new American capital amounted to only $9 million.

American investment in South Africa is minor compared with that of the United Kingdom, about one-fourth. The United States alone would have little leverage. Since U.S. investment is not essential to South Africa, the argument for such action is largely psychological; that is, that it would jar South African whites into a better appreciation of the worldwide opposition to their policies.

Discouraging or prohibiting U.S. investment in South Africa would, of course, improve our relations with much of the world. It is also undoubtedly true that the stopping of American investment would have a considerable impact on South Africans. Even though the economy were not shaken, the confidence of those relying on apartheid as a permanent pattern for South Africa's economy and society would be undermined. The cessation of investment would be seen as one of a long series of developments tending to isolate South Africa. Many who profit from apartheid would be induced to reflect on its long-term disadvantages more seriously than they do now.

Whether increased doubt about the advantages of apartheid would affect South African policies beneficially is questionable. It might harden South African policies even further and undoubtedly would impel South Africa to turn to other sources of investment and to accelerate its already considerable efforts to achieve economic self-sufficiency.

While cessation of investment might increase our credibility and influence with African countries in our efforts to encourage a nonviolent solution, it would seriously handicap our ability to carry on a dialog with South Africa. It would cause some damage to our own economic, scientific, and strategic interests.

The United States, at both public and private levels, has a wide variety of cultural and scientific contacts with South Africa. Such contacts are intended to promote mutually beneficial relations in these fields. We hope they may also have the effect of combating the tendency of South Africa to drift off into sterile isolation.

Both public and private U.S. educational and exchange programs, though small, include all cultural groups as well as supporters of the Government and opposition. A special effort is made, particularly in Government programs, to reach nonwhites, in view of their greater need and the many obstacles encountered. The South African Government's reluctance to give travel documents to nonwhites is one such obstacle, but we do not believe the effort should be abandoned.

*   *   *

Mr. O'Hara: Ambassador Goldberg made certain statements to the United Nations and I made some. I said, and the Ambassador said it in a different way, that the United States had sold no arms to South Africa and also we had turned down orders for I think $60 million worth of goods, commercial goods that might have been used for military purposes.

Recently I have been told there had been some thought of our Government, the United States, consenting to the sale of airships to the Government of South Africa.

Have you heard anything about that?

Mr. Williams: Yes, sir. We have refused to sell. There was a question about airships recently. They have not been sold, sir.

Mr. O'Hara: I do appreciate, of course, because such a sale with the approval of our Government would make a liar out of Ambassador Goldberg and a liar out of me. I can think of nothing that would do our country greater harm in playing into the hands of the Soviet Union which has been questioning our activity in South Africa than the sale to South Africa of those airplanes.

Mr. Secretary, we have almost an hour before noon and I would like to allow time for questioning by all the members of the subcommittee and other members of the full committee who are here.

*   *   *

Mr. Adair: Mr. Chairman, Governor, what kind of aircraft were those? I was not aware of this matter abou which the chairman was speaking. Were those commercial craft or military craft?

Mr. Williams: Mr. Congressman, this matter has come up not once but a number of times. It has come up with respect to aircraft of different qualities, but they all have had a potential of military use.

I think in most cases they actually were intended to be used by the military.

Mr. Adair: They were then fighter aircraft as opposed to passenger aircraft?

Mr. Williams: Not necessarily, sir. They may have been transport aircraft.

Mr. Adair: It is your opinion they were not designed for civilian use?

Mr. Williams: It would be my judgment, if I may put it the other way, these were craft susceptible to military use.

Mr. Adair: And were purchased on that basis—were sought to be purchased on that basis?

Mr. Williams: Yes, sir.

*   *   *

Mr. Diggs: Thank you, Mr. Chairman.

Mr. Secretary, I would like to concur in the statement made by the chairman of our committee when he stated that the policy of our government toward South Africa appears to be lip service. I am unable to see in our policy, in the net effect of our policy, any support for all of the principal theories that have been enunciated. I am particularly concerned about it because as you have so eloquently pointed out, the situation in South Africa appears to be worsening and yet I am not aware that our policy is changing.

Is that a fair assessment, that there has not been any change in our policy despite the worsening situation in South Africa?

Mr. Williams: I think that is a little strong, sir. I think your original statement also that there had been no effective—I shouldn't use "effective"—concrete measures taken is a little strong because I think we immediately can refer to the arms embargo that we have discussed.

I think this is one immediate example. I think our efforts diplomatically have been continuous. I think the question really goes to whether some of the other methods of persuasion or pressures should be used.

Mr. Diggs: With respect to the arms ban and our support of that, what is to keep American banking interests in South Africa, which represent, I believe, a considerable amount of our private investment in that country, from loaning money to the South African Government so that they can purchase arms?

Mr. Williams: You mean loaning American funds——

Mr. Diggs: To the South African Government, the American banks, the Bank of America, I believe, and other banks that are there, from loaning money to the Government so they can purchase arms wherever they want to purchase it, thus getting around, negating our support of a so-called arms ban?

Mr. Williams: I couldn't answer directly that question, except that I don't think that there is any real problem on the part of South Africa of having the funds with which to purchase the arms that they use. I don't know that we would have any specific control over a U.S. bank lending money for an object that we wouldn't know.

Certainly as to the export of arms from the United States, that is prohibited.

*   *   *

Mr. Rosenthal: That leads me to a point I don't understand. In November 1963 the U.N. voted on an oil embargo to force South Africa to abandon the very policies which are in the statement which you now yourself condemn and the only countries which voted against the resolution besides South Africa were Great Britain, the largest investor in South Africa, the United States, the second largest investor in South Africa, France, the third largest investor in South Africa, and Spain and Portugal, who still have colonies in Africa.

Could you draw any inferences from these facts as I have stated them if they are true?

Mr. Williams: I think, sir, what is involved here is what the chairman opened his remarks with, and that is the question of whether it is a chapter 6 or a chapter 7 situation. The United States has voted in many votes in the United Nations to condemn the system of apartheid, but it does not feel that the use of the embargo is warranted because it is a chapter 6 situation rather than a chapter 7.

Mr. Rosenthal: If you were a representative of an independent African nation and you were referred to these facts and you saw that the only countries that voted against that resolution were the first, second, and third largest investors in South Africa, and Spain and Portugal, would you draw any inferences from that?

Mr. Williams: I think the fact is that many of the countries of Africa feel that the investors, the countries with investments have been voting for that reason. But I pointed out in my main statement that this is a consideration, but it is not a dominant or a determining part of the decision of American policy.

Mr. Rosenthal: In your opinion, Governor, are we losing good will among the other African nations because of American investment policy in South Africa?

Mr. Williams: I think that this is an element which causes Africans to regard less highly Americans, yes, indeed.

Mr. Rosenthal: How many, if you know, Governor, resolutions have there been where we have voted concerning censure or an embargo on South Africa where the United States has voted with the minority?

*   *   *

Mrs. Bolton: . . . I wonder what our policy aims at in the world. I was deeply interested in Mr. Adair's question. If we take this aspect of it in South Africa, what about Lithuania and what about Poland and the central European states which are constantly begging us for help and wanting us to take some stand, some action that will help them to be liberated from this slavery?

Mr. Williams: Mrs. Bolton, on this I must testify as an individual, because in the Department I have no jurisdiction. My personal feelings in this are that we must pursue the matter of liberty, of course in appropriate ways, and I personally have a great concern in all of these areas. I think that South Africa presents a case really of our own political interest because what South Africa is doing, as I tried to point out in my statement, is jeopardizing our relations with the rest of Africa, and with a great deal of the rest of the world. Obviously two-thirds——

Mrs. Bolton: That is her business if she wants to do that.

Mr. Williams: By the same reason I would say it is our business to try and protect our relations with the rest of the world and with this particular matter which causes us this difficulty we ought to use all legal means within our power to eliminate this difficulty.

The question then comes down to what are the appropriate means that we can use.

This is very difficult situation. This raises the question that the chairman and Mr. Diggs raised, that we don't seem to be using those instruments that might be open to us to compel the changes, and from the other side it is argued that this really isn't something about which we should have concern. I think we do have a concern. I think we must strive to find legal ways in which to exercise that concern.

Mrs. Bolton: Of course, everything is in timing, isn't it? Isn't South Africa about the only stable country at the moment? Do we trust any of the others? Do we count on any of the others? South Africa is comfortably off. Seventy percent of the gold we get from her. They must do well financially from us. Therefore she would hold together longer perhaps than some other countries.

Mr. Williams: I think, Mrs. Bolton, there is no question that there are growing pains in the rest of Africa. If South Africa didn't have within it the elements of instability——

Mrs. Bolton: I didn't say that. I said it is the most stable country today.

Mr. Williams: If I may put it the other way, I think that this is only momentary. I am delighted when any country has the ability to have stability. I think in the long run it has either to accommodate itself to this force wtihin it or it may have the kind of explosion which would be worse than in some of the areas we have already seen.

Mrs. Bolton: It has interested me very much when I have talked to Afrikaners that so many of them are very earnest people, who believe apparently quite as deeply as we do that we are on the wrong track and they are on the right track, to make it possible for the nonwhite to develop himself, and that if he is forced by too much contact with the white he will go beyond himself. He won't know what to do. But if he goes at his own speed, it is the way of evolution. We don't think so.

Mr. Williams: We had that same argument in our own country, Mrs. Bolton. And I don't think you accepted that completely any more than I did.

Mrs. Bolton: For myself I am against apartheid. I don't believe in it, any phase of it. But I do think it has gone on so long there that to do away with it without a blood bath is going to be a difficult thing.

I think it is up to the South Africans to work out methods of doing it. I don't see how we can do much. Sanctions, what do they mean? We can't even get our best allies to help us in other parts of the world by not shipping and so on. They can't trust sanctions very much can they? Of what value are they?

Mr. Williams: Mrs. Bolton, there is no question this is an extremely difficult problem. I think that we can't leave it completely defeated because I think the repercussions of apartheid in the long run can be so serious as to affect a great part of the world.

Mr. Rosenthal: You are not serious when you say that you hope they will enter into a dialog to work this out? Their past actions don't lead you to that conclusion, do they?

Mr. Williams: Well, may I answer your first question directly. I do hope this. Without such a dialog I see no possibility of a solution. On the second part of your question, there has been nothing in recent history in South Africa to indicate that they were moving toward that dialog.

Mr. Rosenthal: If anything it was indicated to the contrary?

Mr. Williams: That is true, that they seem to become more intractable, but I think that this is part of our diplomacy and human relations to keep working at this and not accept defeat.

Mr. Rosenthal: Diplomacy means that you should never give up, but it also means you have to be realistic about what the prospects are.

Mr. Williams: I agree. I think it is indicative that we may have to, or that we must reexamine the situation from time to time. As I related, the U.N. resolutions originally, they never mentioned South Africa when they condemned discrimination. But after a time, particularly after Sharpeville, they discovered they had to, in order to be realistic, include South Africa. So that certainly our search for methods of bringing about a dialog have to be dynamic.

Mr. Rosenthal: It seems to me, Mr. Secretary, if I may, Mr. Chairman and Mrs. Bolton, that the most that has been said for South Africa today is that she is stable and prosperous. There were other countries that people said similar things about in the 1930's that were following physical and political discrimination. I don't see the difference.

Mr. Williams: I am not present to defend the situation in South Africa. I find it most obnoxious. The thing that I am trying to address myself to as I am sure you are, is what methods can we find that are lawful and effective to bring abou a change, and we certainly prefer to see this change evolutionary and peaceful.

The thing that worries me so much about the South African situation is that by their methods they may be buying time for stability and enjoyment of the status quo, but that these seeds of change are going to keep sprouting, so that they may come to the time when the only possibility of change is through violence.

That is why I am hopeful that we may be able to find ways of persuasion and pressure which may be more compelling to South Africans to reassess their situation and to begin a dialog in order to achieve accommodation.

Mr. Rosenthal: In other words, what you are suggesting it seems to me, and I thoroughly agree with you, and I am hopeful—a little less so than you are—that what you want to do is a good deal better than have a violent racial confrontation which seems inevitable unless there is a change in South African policy.

Some people suggest it is not to our moral interest to intervene, but it seems to me it is in our national interest to prevent that conflagration taking place when we will become involved on a much larger scale than we might be by economic sanctions.

Mr. O'Hara: Mr. Secretary, I wish to make clear at this time the reason for these hearings. As chairman of the subcommittee, I do not think that we have the right to go into a foreign country and to examine its political institutions and to make political recommendations for that foreign country.

We have an interest here. It is the American interest we are serving. It is the matter of the United Nations. During the last General Assembly we were losing very rapidly our African friends.

Mr. Secretary, you are acquainted with that fact. In the 21st General Assembly if this continues we will be in the position of having very few friends left in Africa, Africa having an increasingly large number of membershhip in the United Nations. So we have a legitimate American interest.

Not going into South Africa, passing judgment upon its political institutions, but we must make clear in the United Nations not just by words but by actions, and I would say, as I see it, in my humble way, that the chief objective of these hearings is to bring out whether the United States in the 21st General Assembly should vote for sanctions against South Africa.

That would be one of the reasons that I would say for these hearings. Our position vocally is well known. But words are not sufficient. There must be action.

One matter that I think should be inquired into, and properly so, is the effect of American investments. I don't think any of us would wish to put restrictions on American business, undue restrictions, but certainly I can remember the time when we had a bad situation in Latin America. Our banana companies had bad labor conditions. They paid bad wages.

Our American nationals in business in Latin America were requested—and I think many of them voluntarily did—to reform their ways so that American employers were the best employers in those areas. Certainly what the conditions are, labor conditions and investments are, I do not know at this time.

When this subcommittee has concluded its hearings, I think we will know pretty definitely what those conditions are. But they do affect us.

*United States Subsidiaries, Affiliates and Branch Offices in South Africa**

March 1, 1966

JOHANNESBURG CONSULAR DISTRICT (TRANSVAAL AND ORANGE FREE STATE)[1]

South African Subsidiary, Affiliate, or Branch	U.S. Firm
(S) Abbott Laboratories S.A. (Pty), Ltd.	Abbott Laboratories, North Chicago, Ill.
(S) Adams Brands (Pty), Ltd	Warner-Lambert International, division of Warner-Lambert Pharmaceutical Co., 201 Tabor Rd., Morris Plains, N.J.
(B) Aetna Insurance Co.	Aetna Insurance Co., Hartford, Conn.
(S) Afamal Advertising (Pty), Ltd	The Interpublic Group of Companies, Inc., 1271 Avenue of the Americas, Rockefeller Center, New York, N.Y. 10020.
(B) Allis-Chalmers International	Allis-Chalmers International, Milwaukee, Wis.
(S) American Abrasives Co. S.A. (Pty), Ltd.	American Abrasives, Inc., Westfield, Mass.
(S) American Ethicals (Pty), Ltd.	Ayerst Laboratories International, 685 3d Ave., New York, N.Y. 10017.
(B) The American Express Co., Inc.	The American Express Co., 65 Broadway, New York, N.Y. 10006.
(B) American Foreign Insurance Association	American Foreign Insurance Association. New York, N.Y.
(B) American Insurance Co.	American Insurance Co., Newark, N.J.
(S) American International Under-writers (S.A.), Ltd. (an indirect subsidiary through Bermuda).	(various individual U.S. stockholders).
(S) American Motors S.A. (Pty), Ltd.	American Motors Corp., 14250 Plymouth Rd., Detroit, Mich.
(C) Amrho International (service office)	
(S) Armco (Pty), Ltd.	Armco Steel Corp., Middletown, Ohio
(S) Armstrong Cork (Pty), Ltd. (an indirect subsidiary through Switzerland).	Armstrong Cork Co., Lancaster, Pa.
(C) Balkind's Agencies (Pty), Ltd.	
(S) Baltimore Investments (Pty), Ltd.	Eastern Stainless Steel Corp., Baltimore, Md.

Ibid., pp. 15-26.
[1] See footnotes at end of Table.

South African Subsidiary, Affiliate, or Branch	U.S. Firm
(S) Bechtel International, Ltd. (an indirect subsidiary through Panama).	Bechtel Corp., 220 Bush St., San Francisco, Calif.
(S) Black, Clawson (S.A.) (Pty), Ltd. (an indirect subsidiary through Trinidad).	The Black Clawson Co., 200 Park Ave., N.Y.
(S) B.L. Pharmaceuticals (Pty), Ltd.	Bristol Laboratories, division of Bristol Myers Co., Syracuse, N.Y.
(S) The Borden Co. (S.A.), (Pty), Ltd.	The Borden Co., 350 Madison Ave., New York, N.Y. 10017.
(S) Bristol-Myers (Pty), Ltd.	Bristol-Myers International, 630 5th Ave., New York, N.Y. 10020.
(S) Burroughs Machines, Ltd.	Burroughs Corp., Post Office Box 200, Detroit, Mich.
(S) The Butterick Publishing Co. (S.A.) (Pty), Ltd.	The Butterick Co., Inc., 161 6th Ave., New York, N.Y.
(B) The Calabrian Co., Inc., of New York	The Calabrian Co., Inc., of New York, 26 Broadway, New York, N.Y. 10004.
(S) J. I. Case (S.A.) (Pty), Ltd.	J. I. Case Co., Racine, Wis.
(S) Caterpillar (Africa) (Pty), Ltd.	Caterpillar Tractor Co., Peoria, Ill. (Caterpillar Overseas S.A., Geneva, Switzerland).
(S) Champion Spark Plug Co., of South Africa (Pty), Ltd.	Champion Spark Plug Co., Post Office Box 910, Toledo, Ohio.
(S) Chesebrough-Pond's International, Ltd.	Chesebrough-Pond's, Inc., 485 Lexington Ave., New York, N.Y., 10017.
(S) Chrome Corp. (South Africa) (Pty), Ltd.	Union Carbide Corp., 270 Park Ave., New York, N.Y.
(B) The Coca-Cola Export Corp.	The Coca-Cola Export Corp., 515 Madison Ave., New York, N.Y., 10022.
Do	Do.
(S) Colgate-Palmolive, Ltd.	Colgate-Palmolive International, 300 Park Ave., Box 2250, Grand Central Station, New York.
(B) P. F. Collier, Inc.	P. F. Collier, Inc., 640 5th Ave., New York, N.Y.
(B) Collins Radio Co. International CA	Collins Radio Co., Cedar Rapids, Iowa.
(S) Control Data (Pty), Ltd.	Control Data Corp., 8100 34th Ave., Minneapolis, Minn.
(S) Crown Carlton Paper Mills (Pty), Ltd.	Crown Zellerbach Corp., 1 Bush St., San Francisco, Calif.
(S) Crown Cork Co. S.A. (Pty), Ltd.	Crown Cork & Seal Co., Inc., Philadelphia, Pa.

	South African Subsidiary, Affiliate, or Branch	U.S. Firm
(B)	Cyanamid International Corp.	Cyanamid International Corp., Wayne, N.J.
(S)	De Leuw Cather Rosen & Partners	De Leuw, Cather & Co., 165 West Wacker Dr., Chicago, Ill.
(S)	Denver Equipment Co. S.A. (Pty), Ltd.	Denver Equipment Co., 1400 17th St., Denver, Colo.
(S)	Derby & Co. (South Africa) (Pty), Ltd. (an indirect subsidiary through the United Kingdom.	Minerals & Chemicals Philipp Corp., Menlo Park, N.J.
(S)	Dodge & Seymour (Pty), Ltd.	Dodge & Seymour, Ltd., 53 Park Pl., New York, N.Y. 10007.
(S)	Dow Chemical Africa (Pty), Ltd.	Dow Chemical International, Abbot Road Bldg., Main St., Midland, Mich.
(S)	Dun & Bradstreet (Pty), Ltd.	R. G. Dun & Bradstreet Co., 99 Church St., New York City, N.Y.
(A)	Eimco (South Africa) (Pty), Ltd.	The Eimco Corp., 537 West 6th South St., Box 300, Salt Lake City, Utah.
(S)	Emery Air Freight Corp.	Emery Air Freight Corp., Piersall Bldg., Wilton, Conn.
(S)	Encyclopaedia Britannica (S.A.) (Pty), Ltd., (an indirect subsidiary through the United Kingdom).	Encyclopaedia Britannica, Inc., 425 North Michigan Ave., Chicago, Ill.
(S)	Engelhard Hanovia of Southern Africa (Pty), Ltd.	Engelhard Hanovia, Inc., 100 Chestnut St., Newark, N.J.
(S)	Esso Standard South Africa (Pty), Ltd.	Esso Standard Eastern, 15 West 51st St., New York, N. Y. 10019.
(S)	Eutectic Welding Alloys Corp. of S.A. (Pty), Ltd.	Eutectic Welding Alloys Corp., 40-40 172d St., Flushing, N.Y.
(B)	Farrell Lines International Corp.	Farrell Lines, Inc., 1 Whitehall St., New York, N.Y. 10004.
(S)	Ferro Enamels (Pty), Ltd.	Ferro Corp., 4150 East 56th St., Cleveland, Ohio.
(A)	Fiberglass South Africa (Proprietary), Ltd.	Owens-Corning Fiberglass Corp., Toledo, Ohio.
(A)	First Consolidated Leasing Corp. (Pty), Ltd.	First National City Overseas Investment Corp., 399 Park Ave., New York, N.Y. 10022.
(S)	First National City Bank of New York (South Africa), Ltd.	First National City Bank, 399 Park Ave., New York, N.Y. 10022.
(C)	Forsyth Udwin (Pty), Ltd.	
(S)	Fox Theatres South Africa (Pty), Ltd.	20th Century-Fox Film Corp., Delaware.
(S)	Frib Africa Trading (Pty), Ltd.	Continental Grain Co., 2 Broadway, New York, N.Y.

South African Subsidiary, Affiliate, or Branch	U.S. Firm
(S) Friden (South Africa) (Pty), Ltd.	Friden Inc., 2275 Washington Ave., San Leandro, Calif.
(S) Galion (Pty), Ltd.	The Jeffrey Co., Columbus, Ohio
(S) Gardner-Denver Co. Africa (Pty), Ltd.	Gardner-Denver Co., Quincy, Ill.
(S) Gates South Africa (Pty), Ltd.	The Gates Rubber Co., 909 South Broadway, Denver, Colo.
(A) The General Tire & Rubber Co. (South Africa), Ltd.	General Tire & Rubber Co., Akron, Ohio.
(A) A. J. Gerrard Steel Strapping Co., (S.A.) (Pty), Ltd.	A. J. Gerrard & Co., 426 East Tuohy Ave., Des Plaines, Ill.
(S) Gillette South Africa (Pty), Ltd. (an indirect subsidiary through the United Kingdom).	The Gillette Co., Gillette Park, Box 2131, Boston, Mass.
(S) Grant Advertising, Ltd.	Grant Advertising, Inc., 919 North Michigan Avenue, Chicago, Ill.
(B) Grolier International, Inc.	Groller, Inc., 575 Lexington Avenue, New York, N.Y. 10022.
(S) Heinemann Electric (South Africa), Ltd.	Heinemann Electric Co., Trenton, N.J.
(S) Helena Rubinstein S.A. (Pty), Ltd. (an indirect subsidary through the United Kingdom).	Helena Rubinstein, Inc., 655 5th Ave., New York, N.Y.
(S) Hochmetals (Africa) (Pty), Ltd.	South American Minerals & Merchandise Corp., 425 Park Avenue, New York, N.Y., 10022.
(S) Hoover (S.A.) (Pty), Ltd. (an indirect subsidiary through United Kingdom).	The Hoover Co., North Canton, Ohio.
(S) Ingersoll-Rand Co., South Africa (Pty), Ltd.	Ingersoll-Rand Co., 11 Broadway, New York, N.Y. 10004.
(B) Insurance Co. of North America	Insurance Co. of North America, 1600 Arch St., Philadelphia.
(S) International Business Machines South Africa (Pty), Ltd.	IBM World Trade Corp., 821 United Nations Plaza, New York, N.Y. 10017.
(S) International Flavors & Fragrances I.F.F. (S.A.) (Pty), Ltd.	International Flavors & Fragrances, Inc., 521 West 57th St., New York, N.Y. 10001.
(S) International Harvester Co. (S.A.) (Pty), Ltd.	International Harvester Co., 180 North Michigan Ave., Chicago, Ill.
(B) International Johns-Manville Corp.	Johns-Manville International Corp., 22 East 40th St., New York, N.Y. 10016.
(S) Jeffrey-Gallon (Pty), Ltd.	The Jeffrey Co., Columbus, Ohio.

South African Subsidiary, Affiliate, or Branch	U.S. Firm
(S) Jeffrey Manufacturing Co. (Pty), Ltd.	Do.
(S) John Deere-Bobans (Pty), Ltd.	Deere & Company, John Deere Rd., Moline, Ill.
(S) Joy Manufacturing (Africa) (Pty), Ltd.	Joy Manufacturing Co., Henry Oilver Building, Pittsburgh, Pa.
(S) Kellogg Co. of South Africa (Pty), Ltd.	Kellogg Co., Battle Creek, Mich.
(S) Kelly-Springfield Tyre Co. S.A. (Pty), Ltd.	Kelly-Springfield Tire Co., Cumberland, Md.
Kendall Co. of South Africa (Pty), Ltd.	The Kendall Co., International Div., 140 Federal St., Boston, Mass.
(S) Kimberly-Clark of South Africa (Pty), Ltd.	Kimberly-Clark Corp., Neenah, Wis.
(S) Lakeside Laboratories (S.A.) (Pty), Ltd.	Affiliated with Lakeside Laboratories Inc., Milwaukee, Wis., 53201, *but* a subsidiary of Colgate-Palmolive International.
(S) Lavino South Africa (Pty), Ltd.	E. J. Lavino & Co., 3 Penn Center Plaza, Philadelphia, Pa.
(S) L. W. Manufacturing Co. (Pty), Ltd.	Le Tourneau Westinghouse Co., 2301 W. Adams St., Peoria, Ill.
(A) Lease Plan International Corp. of South Africa, Ltd.	Lease Plan International Corp., Great Neck, N.Y.
Le Carbone (South Africa) (Pty), Ltd. (an indirect subsidary through Paris).	The Carbone Corp., Boonton, N.J.
(S) Ledlab Proprietary, Ltd. (an indirect subsidary through Cyanamid International Corp., Panama).	Cyanamid International, Berdan Avenue, Wayne, N.J.
(C) A. R. Lilly & Son (Pty), Ltd.	
(S) Lilly Laboratories (S.A.) (Pty), Ltd.	Eli Lilly & Co., Indianapolis, Ind.
(S) Link-Belt Africa, Ltd.	Link-Belt Co., Prudential Plaza, Chicago, Ill.
(B) Mack Trucks Worldwide, Ltd.	Mack Trucks Worldwide, Hamilton, Bermuda.
(S) Masonite (Africa), Ltd.	Masonite Corp. 29 North Wacker Dr., Chicago, Ill.
(B) Max Factor & Co.	Max Factor & Co., Inc., Hollywood, Calif.
(B) McGraw Hill, Inc.	McGraw Hill, Inc., 330 West 42d St., New York, N.Y.

South African Subsidiary, Affiliate, or Branch	U.S. Firm
(S) McKinnon Chain (South Africa) (Pty), Ltd.	Columbus McKinnon Corp., Post Office Box 72, Tonawanda, N.Y.
(S) Mer-National Laboratories (Pty), Ltd.	Merrell National (Overseas) Laboratories, Division of Richardson-Merrell, Inc., 122 East 42d St., New York, N.Y.
(S) Metro-Goldwyn-Mayer Films (S.A.) (Pty), Ltd.	Metro-Goldwyn-Mayer International, Inc., 1540 Broadway, New York, N.Y. 10036.
(S) Geo. J. Meyer (South Africa) (Pty), Ltd.	Geo. J. Meyer Manufacturing Co., Post Office Box 452, Milwaukee 1, Wis.
(S) Mine Safety Appliances Co. (Africa) (Pty), Ltd.	Mine Safety Appliances Co., Pittsburgh, Pa.
(S) Pfizer Laboratories (South Africa), Ltd.	Pfizer International, Pfizer Bldg., 235 East 42d St., New York, N.Y. 10017.
(S) Pipe Line Technologists (Netherlands), N.V.	Pipe Line Technologist, Inc., Houston, Tex.
(S) Playtex Africa (Pty), Ltd.	International Latex Corp., Empire State Bldg., New York, N.Y.
(S) Preload Africa (Pty), Ltd.	Preload International Corp., Box 804, Springdale, Conn. 06879.
(S) Procter & Gamble Co. of South Africa (Pty), Ltd. (an indirect subsidiary through Switzerland).	Proctor & Gamble Co., Cincinnati, Ohio.
(S) Remington Rand S.A. (Pty), Ltd.	Sperry Rand International Corp., 1290 Avenue of the Americas, New York, N.Y.
(S) Republic Aluminium Co. (Pty), Ltd.	Kaiser Aluminum & Chemical Corp., Kaiser Center, 300 Lakeside Dr., Oakland, Calif.
(S) Revlon S.A. (Pty), Ltd. (an indirect subsidiary through Venezuela).	Revlon, Inc., 666 5th Ave., New York, N.Y.
(A) Richelieu Pearls S.A. (Pty), Ltd.	Richelieu Corp., Inc., Holbrook, Long Island, N.Y.
(S) Robertson Thain (Africa) (Pty), Ltd.	H. H. Robertson Co., Farmers Bank Bldg., corner 5th and Wood Sts., Pittsburgh, Pa.
(S) Robins Conveyors (S.A.) (Pty), Ltd.	Hewitt-Robins, Inc., 666 Glenbrook Rd., Stamford, Conn.
(S) A. S. Ruffel (Pty), Ltd.	Smith Kline & French Laboratories, 1500 Spring Garden St., Philadelphia, Pa.
(A) Saphar Laboratories, Ltd.	Baxter Laboratories, Morton Grove, Chicago, Ill.
(S) Scherag (Pty), Ltd.	Schering Corp., U.S.A., Bloomfield, N.J.

South African Subsidiary, Affiliate, or Branch   U.S. Firm

(S) G. D. Searle (Africa) (Pty), Ltd.	G. D. Searle & Co. Post Office Box 5110, Chicago, Ill.
(S) Seaway International (Pty), Ltd.	Seaway Associates, Inc., 808 Oakland St., Ann Arbor, Mich. 48107.
(S) Simplicity Patterns (S.A.) (Pty), Ltd.	Simplicity Pattern Co., Inc., 200 Madison Ave., New York, N.Y.
(S) Singer South Africa (Pty), Ltd.	The Singer Co., 30 Rockefeller Plaza, New York, N.Y.
(S) SKF Laboratories (Pty), Ltd. (Smith Kline & French).	Smith Kline & French Laboratories, 1500 Spring Garden St., Philadelphia, Pa.
(B) A. O. Smith International (S.A.)	A. O. Smith, Milwaukee, Wis.
(S) Socony Southern Africa (Pty), Ltd.	Mobil International, Inc., 150 East 42d St., New York, N.Y., 10017.
(S) South African Cyanamid (Pty), Ltd. (an indirect subsidiary through Canada).	American Cyanamid Co., Wayne, N.J.
(S) South African General Electric Co. (Pty), Ltd.	I.G.E. Export Division (Division of General Electric Co.), 159 Madison Ave., New York.
(A) Southern Cross Steel (Pty), Ltd.	Eastern Stainless Steel Corp., Baltimore, Md.
(S) Squibb Laboratories (Pty), Ltd.	Olin Mathieson Chemical Corp., 460 Park Lane, New York, N.Y., 10022.
(S) Standard Telephones & Cables (S.A.) (Pty), Ltd.	International Telephone & Telegraph Corp., New York, N.Y.
(S) Minnesota Mining & Manufacturing Co. (South Africa) (Pty), Ltd.	Minnesota Mining & Manufacturing Co., St. Paul, Minn.
(C) Monarch Cinnabar (Pty), Ltd.	
(S) The Montrose Exploration Co., Ltd.	Allied Chemical Corp., 61 Broadway, New York City, N.Y.
(S) Moore-McCormack Lines (S.A.) (Pty), Ltd.	Moore-McCormack Lines, Inc., New York.
(B) Moore-McCormack Lines, Inc.	Do.
(S) MSD (Pty), Ltd.	Merck, Sharp & Dohme International, Division of Merck & Co., Inc., New York.
(S) Muller & Phipps Africa (Pty), Ltd.	Muller & Phipps (Asia), Ltd., 1 Park Ave., New York, N. Y.
(S) National Cash Register Co. (S.A.) (Pty), Ltd.	The National Cash Register Co., Dayton, Ohio.
(A) National Packaging Co., Ltd.	St. Regis Paper Co., 150 East 42nd St., New York, N.Y.
(S) Nordberg Manufacturing Co. (South Africa) (Pty), Ltd.	Nordberg Manufacturing Co., Post Office Box 383, Milwaukee, Wis.

South African Subsidiary, Affiliate, or Branch   U.S. Firm

(S) Nordberg Ramsey Africa (Pty), Ltd.   Nordberg Manufacturing Co., Post Office
                                               Box 383, Milwaukee, Wis., and Ramsey
                                               Engineering Co., 185, West Country
                                               Rd. C., St. Paul, Minn. 55113.
(S) Norton Abrasives S.A. (Pty), Ltd.   Norton Co., Worcester, Mass.
(S) Otis Elevator Co., Ltd.   Otis Elevator Co., 260 11th Ave., New
                                               York, N.Y.
(A) Palabora Mining Co., Ltd.   Newmont Mining Corp., 300 Park Ave.,
                                               New York, and American Metal
                                               Climax, Inc., 61 Broadway, New
                                               York, N.Y.
(B) Pan American World Airways   Pan American World Airways, Inc.,
                                               Panam Bldg., New York, N.Y., 10017.
(A) Parachute Industries of Southern   Irving Air Chute Co., Inc., 1315 Versailles
     Africa (Pty), Ltd.   Rd., Lexington, Ky., and Pioneer
                                               Parachute Co., Inc., Manchester, Conn.
(S) Parke, Davis Laboratories (Pty),   Parke, Davis & Co., Detroit, Mich.
     Ltd.
(S) Parker Pen (Pty), Ltd.   The Parker Pen Co., Janesville, Wis.
(S) Pepsi-Cola Africa (Pty), Ltd.   Pepsi-Cola Co., 500 Park Ave., New York,
                                               N.Y.
(S) C. J. Petrow & Co. (Pty), Ltd.   Keystone Asbestos Corp., 1005
                                               Investment Bldg., Washington, D.C.
(S) Stein, Hall South Africa (Pty), Ltd.   Stein, Hall & Co., Inc., 605 3d Ave., New
                                               York, N.Y., 10016.
(S) Tampax (S.A.) (Pty) Ltd.   Tampax, Inc., 161 East 42d St., New
                                               York, N.Y.
(S) Timken South Africa (Pty), Ltd.   Timken Roller Bearing Co., Canton, Ohio.
(S) Tokhelm South Africa (Pty), Ltd.   Tokheim Corp., Fort Wayne, Ind.
     Trans-World Airlines, Inc. (Service   Trans-World Airlines, Inc., 605 3d Ave.,
     Office)   New York City, N.Y.
(S) Tuco (Pty), Ltd.   The Upjohn Co., Kalamazoo, Mich.
(A) Underwood Africa (Pty), Ltd.   Olivetti-Underwood Corp., 1 Park Ave.,
                                               New York, N.Y., 10016.
(S) Union Carbide South Africa   Union Carbide International Co., Division
     (Pty), Ltd.   of Union Carbide Corp., 270 Park
                                               Ave., New York, N.Y.
(S) United Artists Corp. (S.A.)   United Artists Corp., 729 7th Ave., New
     (Pty), Ltd.   York, N.Y., 10019.
(B) United Cargo Corp.   United Cargo Corp., 563 West 35th St.,
                                               New York, N.Y.
(S) United States Rubber Co. (S.A.)   United States Rubber Co., 1230 Avenue
     (Pty), Ltd.   of the Americas, New York, N.Y.,
                                               10020.

South African Subsidiary, Affiliate, or Branch	U.S. Firm
(S) Valvoline Oil Co. S.A. (Pty), Ltd.	Ashland Oil & Refining Co., Ashland, Ky.
(S) Vendo (South Africa) (Pty), Ltd.	The Vendo Co., 7400 East 12th St., Kansas City, Mo., 64126.
(S) Vick International (Pty), Ltd.	Vick International, Division of Richardson-Merrell, Inc., 122 East 42d St., New York, N.Y.
(S) Warner Bros. 1st National Pictures (S.A.) (Pty), Ltd.	Warner Bros. Pictures International Corp., 666 5th Ave., New York, N.Y.
(S) J. R. Watkins Co. (Africa) (Pty), Ltd.	Watkins Products, Inc., Liberty St., Winona, Minn.
(S) Western Knapp Engineering Co. (division of McKee of Panama, S.A).	Arthur G. McKee, Cleveland, Ohio.
(S) Westinghouse Electric International S.A. (an indirect subsidiary through Geneva, Switzerland).	Westinghouse Electric International, 200 Park Ave., New York, N.Y.
(S) Whitehall Products S.A. (Pty), Ltd.	American Home Products Corp., 685 3d Ave., New York, N.Y.
(S) Willys Afrika (Pty), Ltd.	Kaiser Jeep Overseas S.A., Toledo, Ohio.
(S) Wyeth Laboratories (Pty), Ltd.	Wyeth International, Ltd., division of American Home Products Corp., 685 3d Ave., New York, N.Y., 10017.

CAPETOWN CONSULAR DISTRICT (WESTERN CAPE PROVINCE AND SOUTH-WEST AFRICA)

(S) Addressograph-Multility (Pty), Ltd.	Addressograph-Multigraph Corp., 1200 Babbitt Rd, Cleveland, Ohio.
(C) Argus Africa (Pty), Ltd.	
(S) Armour-Africa (Pty), Ltd.	International Packers Ltd., 135 South La Salle St., Chicago, Ill.
(S) Artnell Exploration Co.	Artnell Co., 101 South Wacker Dr., Chicago, Ill.
(S) Ault & Wilborg Co. of South Africa (Pty), Ltd.	Interchemical Corp., 67 West 44th St., New York, N.Y., 10036.
(S) Beckman Instruments (Pty), Ltd.	Beckman Instruments, Inc., 2500 Harbor Blvd., Fullerton, Calif.
(S) Black & Decker South Africa (Pty), Ltd.	The Black & Decker Manufacturing Co., Towson, Md.
(S) Burlington Hosiery Mills (S.A.), Ltd.	Burlington Industries, Inc., Greensboro, N.C.
(S) Caltex Oil (S.A.), Ltd.	California Texas Oil Corp., 380 Madison Ave., New York, N.Y., 10017.
(S) Chamberlains (Pty), Ltd.	Warner-Lambert Pharmaceutical Co., Morris Plains, N.J.

South African Subsidiary, Affiliate, or Branch	U.S. Firm
(S) Chrysler South Africa (Pty), Ltd.	Chrysler Int. S. A. Geneva, Switzerland (wholly owned by Chrysler Corp., U.S.A.)
(S) Chrysler South Africa (Pty), Ltd., Parts and Accessories Division.	Do.
(S) Connell Bros. Co., Ltd.	Connell Bros Co., Ltd., San Francisco, Calif.
(S) Etosha Petroleum Co., (Pty), Ltd.	Kewanee Overseas Oil Co., Post Office Box 591, Bryn Mawr, Pa. (B)
(B) Fairbanks, Morse & Co., Ltd.	Fairbanks, Morse & Co., Inc., International Division, Fair Lawn, N.J.
(S) FMC South Africa, Ltd.	FMC Corp., Post Office Box 760, San Jose, Calif.
(S) Gabriel S. A. (Proprietary), Ltd.	Gabriel International, Inc., Apariado 4504, Panama, Republic of Panama.
(A) J. Gerber (Factors) (Pty), Ltd.	J. Gerber & Co., Inc., 855 6th Ave., New York, N.Y., 10001.
(S) Gilbarco (S.A.) (Pty), Ltd.	Gilbert & Barker Manufacturing Co., West Springfield, Mass.
(S) Grace, W. R. Africa (Pty), Ltd.	W. R. Grace & Co., 7 Hanover Sq., New York, N.Y., 10005.
(S) Richard Rudnut (Pty), Ltd.	Warner-Lambert Pharmaceutical Co., Morris Plains, N.J.
(S) Kodak (South Africa) (Pty), Ltd.	Eastman Kodak Co., 343 State St., Rochester, N.Y., 14650.
(S) Koret of California SA (Pty), Ltd.	Koret of California, Inc., San Francisco, Calif.
(S) Mobil Oil Southern Africa (Pty), Ltd.	Mobil Petroleum Co., Inc., 150 East 42d St., New York, N.Y., 10017.
(S) Ocean Science & Engineering (South Africa) (Pty), Ltd.	Ocean Science & Engineering Inc., Ocean Science Bldg., 4905 Delray Ave., Washington, D.C., 20014.
(S) O'OKlep Cooper Co., Ltd.	Newmont Mining Corp., 300 Park Ave., New York City, N.Y.
(S) Pepsi-Cola Bottling Co. (Pty), Ltd.	Pepsi-Cola Co., 500 Park Ave., New York, N.Y., 10022.
(A) Phoenix Assurance Co., Ltd.	Continental Insurance Co., 80 Maiden Lane, New York City, N.Y.
(C) Premix Asphalt Co.	
(C) Robert Page & Associates	
(S) Royal Baking Powder (Pty), Ltd.	Standard Brands, Inc., International Division, 625 Madison Ave., New York, N.Y.
(S) Scholl Manufacturing Co., S.A. (Pty), Ltd.	The School Manufacturing Co., Inc., West Schiller St., Chicago, Ill.

South African Subsidiary, Affiliate, or Branch	U.S. Firm
(S) South African Preserving Co. (Pty), Ltd.	Del Monte International, Inc., 804 Ponce de Leon, Santurce, PR.
(C) Tedd-Hill Products (Pty), Ltd.	
(C) Tedd McKune Investment Co. (Pty), Ltd.	
(A) Tidal Diamonds S.W.A. (Pty), Ltd.	Tidewater Oil Co., 4201 Wilshire Blvd., Los Angeles, Calif., 90005.
(S) Tidewater Minerals S.W.A. (Pty), Ltd.	Do.
(S) Tsumeb Corp., Ltd.	American Metal Climax Inc., 1270 Avenue of the Americas, New York, N.Y., and Newmont Mining Corp., 300 Park Ave., New York.
(S) Tupperware Co.	Tupperware Home Parties, Orlando, Fla.
(C) Universal Mineral Discoveries (Pty), Ltd.	
(S) Vitreous Enamelling Corp. (Pty), Ltd.	Symington Wayne Corp., Salisbury, Md.
(S) Warner Pharmaceuticals (Pty), Ltd.	Warner-Lambert Pharmaceutical Co., Morris Plains, N.J.,
(S) Wayne Pump Co. (S.A.) (Pty), Ltd.	Symington Wayne Corp., Salisbury, Md.
(S) Wilbur Ellis Co. (Pty), Ltd.	Wilbur-Ellis Co., 320 California St., San Francisco, Calif.

DURBAN CONSULAR DISTRICT (NATAL PROVINCE)

(A) Airco Engineering, Ltd.	Carrier Corp. (International., division), 385 Madison Ave., New York, N.Y., 10017.
(S) Amalgamated Packaging Industries, Ltd.	St. Regis Paper Co., 150 East 42d St., New York, N.Y., 10017.
(S) Bayer-Pharma (S.A.) (Pty), Ltd.	Sterling Products International, Inc., 90 Park Ave., New York, N.Y., 10016.
(S) Beech-Nut Life Savers, Ltd.	Beech-Nut Life Savers, Inc., Canajoharie, N.Y.
(S) Carnation Co. (Pty), Ltd.	Carnation Co., 5045 Wilshire Blvd., Los Angeles, Calif.
(B) Coca-Cola Bottling Co. of Durban	Coca-Cola Export Corp., 515 Madison Ave., New York, N.Y. 10022.
(S) Corn Products Refining Co. (S.A.) (Pty), Ltd.	Corn Products Co., 717 Fifth Ave., New York, N.Y.
(S) Diamond H Switches (S.A.) (Pty), Ltd.	Oak Manufacturing Co., Crystal Lake, Ill.
(B) Lykes Lines Agency, Inc.	Lykes Bros. Steamship Co., 821 Gravier St., New Orleans, La.
(C) Millburg Industrial Painters (Pty), Ltd.	

South African Subsidiary, Affiliate, or Branch	U.S. Firm

PORT ELIZABETH CONSULAR DISTRICT (EASTERN CAPE PROVINCE)

South African Subsidiary, Affiliate, or Branch	U.S. Firm
(S) Berkshire International (S.A.), Ltd.	Berkshire Knitting Mills, Wyomissing, Pa.
(S) Carborundum-Universal S.A., Ltd.	Carborundum Co., Niagra Falls (Carborundum Ltd, Manchester, England).
(S) Firestone South Africa (Pty), Ltd.	Firestone Tire & Rubber Co., Akron, Ohio.
(S) Ford Motor Co. of S.A. (Pty), Ltd.	Ford Motor Co., Dearborn, Mich.
(S) General Motors S.A. (Pty), Ltd.	GM Overseas Operations, 1775 Broadway, New York.
(S) General Motors Acceptance Corp., Ltd.	Do.
(S) Goodyear Tyre & Rubber Co. (S.A.) (Pty), Ltd.	Goodyear International Corp., 1144 East Market St., Akron, Ohio, 44316.
(S) Johnson & Johnson (Pty), Ltd.	Johnson & Johnson, 1940 George St., New Brunswick, N.J.
(S) Phillips Carbon Black Co. (Pty), Ltd.	Phillips Petroleum Co., Bartlesville, Okla.
(S) Rexall Drug Co. S.A. (Pty), Ltd.	Rexall Drug & Chemical Co., 8480 Beverly Blvd., Los Angeles, Calif.
(S) Mobile Refining Co. Southern Africa (Pty), Ltd.	Mobil Petroleum Co., Inc., 150 East 42d St., New York, N.Y., 10017.
(C) Perth Products (Pty), Ltd.	
(C) P.M. Products (Pty), Ltd.	
(S) Quix-River Brand Rice Mills (Africa) (Pty), Ltd.	River Brand Rice Mills, Inc., 350 West 4th St., New York, N.Y.
(S) Robertson's (Pty), Ltd.	Corn Products Co., 717 5th Ave., New York, N.Y.
(S) Sterling Drug (S.A.) (Pty), Ltd.	Sterling Products International, Inc., 90 Park Ave., New York, N.Y., 10016.
(S) Triton Chemicals (Pty), Ltd.	Rohm & Haas Co., Washington Sq., Philadelphia, Pa.
(A) Weyerhauser South Africa (Pty), Ltd.	Weyerhauser Co., Tacona, Wash.
(S) Winthrop Laboratories (S.A.) (Pty), Ltd.	Sterling Products International, Inc., 90 Park Ave., New York N.Y., 10016.
(S) Rockwell South Africa (Pty), Ltd. (an indirect subsidiary through Switzerland).	Rockwell International S.A., 81 rue de la Servette, Geneva, Switzerland.
(S) Thompson Ramco (S.A.) (Pty), Ltd.	Thompson Ramco Woolridge, Inc., 23555 Euclid Ave., Cleveland, Ohio.

Note.—Total number of U.S. firms represented in South Africa, 243. Key: (S) American firm controls 50 percent or more of capital. (A) American firm controls less than 50 percent of capital. (B) Branch (primary service organization). (C) Company owned by resident American.

Votes on Resolutions Adopted by the U.N. General Assembly and Security Council on Racial Policies in South Africa*

March 1, 1966

A. GENERAL ASSEMBLY

Shown below are all resolutions concerning the racial policies of the Government of South Africa adopted by the General Assembly from its 1st through its 20th session. The total vote is shown beside the resolution number in this order: Yes-No, Abstain. The titles of the resolutions are identified as follows: 1—Treatment of People of Indian Origin; 2—Policies of Apartheid; 3—Treatment of People of Indian and Indo-Pakistan Origin. The votes of five selected countries are shown (where rollcall votes were taken) under appropriate columns using the following key: Y—Yes; N—No; A—Abstain; AB—Absent; NP—Not Participating.

Resolution No.	Total vote	Title	United States	South Africa	United King-dom	France	USSR	Date adopted
44 (I)	32-15, 7	1	N	N	N	Y	Y	Dec. 8, 1946
264 (III)	47-1, 10	1	Y	N	A	Y	A	May 14, 1949
395 (V)	33-6, 21	1	Y	N	A	A	A	Dec. 2, 1950
511 (VI)	44-0, 14	1	Y	AB	A	A	Y	Jan. 12, 1952
615 (VII)	41-1, 15	1	Y	N	A	A	Y	Dec. 5, 1952
616 A (VII)	35-1, 23	2	A	N	A	A	Y	Do.
616 B (VII)	24-1, 34	2	Y	N	A	A	A	Do.
719 (VIII)	42-1, 17	1	Y	N	A	A	Y	Nov. 11, 1953
721 (VIII)	38-11, 11	2	A	N	N	N	Y	Dec. 8, 1953
816 (IX)	45-1, 11	1	(^{1})	(^{1})	(^{1})	(^{1})	(^{1})	Nov. 4, 1954
820 (IX)	40-10, 10	2	A	N	N	N	Y	Dec. 14, 1954
917 (X)	41-6,8	2	(^{1})	(^{1})	(^{1})	(^{1})	(^{1})	Dec. 6, 1955
919 (X)	46-0,8	1	(^{1})	(^{1})	(^{1})	(^{1})	(^{1})	Dec. 14, 1955
1015 (XI)	42-0, 12	1	(^{1})	(^{1})	(^{1})	(^{1})	(^{1})	Jan. 30, 1957
1016 (XI)	56-5, 12	2	(^{1})	(^{1})	(^{1})	(^{1})	(^{1})	Do.
1178 (XII)	59-6, 14	2	A	NP	N	N	Y	Nov. 26, 1957
1179 (XII)	64-0, 15	1	Y	NP	A	A	Y	Do.
1248 (XIII)	70-5, 4	s	Y	NP	N	N	Y	Oct. 30, 1958
1302 (XIII)	69-0, 10	1	Y	NP	A	A	Y	Dec. 10, 1958
1375 (XIV)	62-3, 7	2	Y	NP	N	N	Y	Nov. 17, 1959
1400 (XIV)	66-0, 10	1	Y	NP	A	A	Y	Dec. 10, 1959
1597 (XV)	78-0, 2	3	(^{1})	(^{2})	(^{1})	(^{1})	(^{1})	Apr. 13, 1961
1598 (XV)	95-1, 0	2	Y	NP	Y	Y	Y	Do.
1662 (XVI)		3	(^{3})	(^{3})	(^{3})	(^{3})	(^{3})	Nov. 28, 1961
1663 (XVI)	97-2, 1	2	Y	N	Y	Y	Y	Do.
1761 (XVII)	67-16, 23	2	N	N	N	N	Y	Nov. 6, 1962

*Ibid., pp. 32-41.

^{1} No rollcall.

^{2} South Africa did not participate.

^{3} No rollcall: adopted unanimously.

^{4} The 19th General Assembly agreed without vote to note receipt of reports on this subject, but took no other action.

Source: Prepared by IO Reference and Documents Section, Mar. 3, 1966.

Resolution No.	Total vote	Title	United States	South Africa	United King- dom	France	U.S.S.R.	Date adopted
1881 (XVIII)	106-1, 0	2	Y	N	Y	Y	Y	Oct. 11, 1963
1978 A (XVIII)	100-2, 1	2	(^{1})	(^{1})	(^{1})	(^{1})	(^{1})	Dec. 16, 1963
1978 B (XVIII)	99-2, 0	2	Y	N	Y	Y	Y	Do.
2054 A (XX) Rev. 1[4]	80-2, 16	2	A	N	A	A	Y	Dec. 15, 1965
2054 B (XX) Rev. 1[4]	95-1, 1	2	(^{1})	(^{1})	(^{1})	(^{1})	(^{1})	Do.

B. SECURITY COUNCIL

Shown below are all five resolutions adopted as of March 3, 1966, by the Security Council with regard to the racial policies of the Government of South Africa. Shown are the resolution number, the total vote arranged in the order of Yes-No, Abstain, with the vote of the four selected countries indicated in parentheses. The Government of South Africa has never been a member of the Security Council and hence did not participate in any of these votes.

Resolution No.	Total vote	Date adopted
S/4300	9 (United States, U.S.S.R.)–0, 2 (France, United Kingdom)	Apr. 1, 1960
S/5386	9 (United States, U.S.S.R.)–0, 2 (France, United Kingdom)	Aug. 7, 1963
S/5471	(^{1})	Dec. 4, 1963
S5761	7 (U.S.S.R.)–o, 4 (United States, France, United Kingdom)	June 9, 1964
S/5773	8 (United States, United Kingdom)–0, 3 (France, U.S.S.R.)	June 18, 1964

Resolutions Adopted by the General Assembly With Regard to South-West Africa

Shown below are all resolutions concerning South-West Africa which have been adopted by the General Assembly from its 1st through its 20th session. The total vote is shown beside the resolution number in this order: Yes-No, Abstain. The votes of five selected countries are shown (where rollcall votes were taken) under appropriate headings using the following key: Y—Yes; N—No; A—Abstain; AB—Absent; NP—Not Participating.

Resolution No.	Total vote	United States	South Africa	United King-dom	France	U.S.S.R.	Date adopted
64 (I)	37-0, 9	Y	A	A	A	Y	Dec. 14, 1946
141 (II)	41-10, 4	Y	N	N	Y	Y	Nov. 1, 1947
227 (III)	43-1, 5	(¹)	(¹)	(¹)	(¹)	(¹)	Nov. 26, 1948
337 (IV)	33-9, 10	N	N	A	N	Y	Dec. 6, 1949
338 (IV)	40-7, 4	(¹)	(¹)	(¹)	(¹)	(¹)	Do.
449 A (V)	45-6, 5	Y	N	Y	Y	N	Dec. 13, 1950
449 B (V)	30-10, 16	Y	N	N	A	Y	Do.
570 A (VI)	45-5, 8	Y	AB	A	Y	N	Jan. 19, 1952
570 B (VI)	36-0, 26	A	AB	A	A	Y	Do.
651 (VII)	45-2, 8	(¹)	(¹)	(¹)	(¹)	(¹)	Dec. 20, 1952
749 A (VIII)	46-0, 12	Y	N	A	A	A	Nov. 28, 1953
749 B (VIII)	47-1, 11	Y	N	A	A	Y	Do.
844 (IX)	33-3, 15	Y	N	N	N	A	Oct. 11, 1954
851 (IX)	34-8, 0	(¹)	(¹)	(¹)	(¹)	(¹)	Nov. 23, 1954
852 (IX)	40-3, 11	(¹)	(¹)	(¹)	(¹)	(¹)	Do.
904 (IX)	25-11, 21	Y	N	A	A	N	Do.
934 (X)	54-0, 4	(¹)	(¹)	(¹)	(¹)	(¹)	Dec. 3, 1955
935 (X)	44-2, 11	(¹)	(¹)	(¹)	(¹)	(¹)	Do.
936 (X)	47-0, 8	(¹)	(¹)	(¹)	(¹)	(¹)	Do.
937 (X)	50-0, 9	(¹)	(¹)	(¹)	(¹)	(¹)	Do.
938 (X)	45-7, 4	(¹)	(¹)	(¹)	(¹)	(¹)	Do.
939 (X)	45-2, 9	(¹)	(¹)	(¹)	(¹)	(¹)	Do.
940 (X)	43-2, 9	(¹)	(¹)	(¹)	(¹)	(¹)	Do.
941 (X)	45-1, 10	(¹)	(¹)	(¹)	(¹)	(¹)	Do.
942 (X)	32-5, 19	(¹)	(¹)	(¹)	(¹)	(¹)	Do.
943 (X)	34-6, 14	(¹)	(¹)	(¹)	(¹)	(¹)	Eo.
1047 (XI)	60-0, 9	(¹)	(¹)	(¹)	(¹)	(¹)	Jan. 23, 1957
1054 (XI)	47-0, 16	(¹)	(¹)	(¹)	(¹)	(¹)	Feb. 26, 1957
1055 (XI)	52-0, 17	(¹)	(¹)	(¹)	(¹)	(¹)	Do.
1056 (XI)	55-4, 7	(¹)	(¹)	(¹)	(¹)	(¹)	Do.
1057 (XI)	57-2, 9	(¹)	(¹)	(¹)	(¹)	(¹)	Do.
1058 (XI)	55-0, 14	(¹)	(¹)	(¹)	(¹)	(¹)	Do.
1059 (XI)	40-11, 19	(¹)	(¹)	(¹)	(¹)	(¹)	Do.
1060 (XI)	40-3, 23	(¹)	(¹)	(¹)	(¹)	(¹)	Do.
1061 (XI)	58-0, 13	(¹)	(¹)	(¹)	(¹)	(¹)	Do.
1138 (XII)	62-0, 16	(¹)	(¹)	(¹)	(¹)	(¹)	Oct. 25, 1957
1139 (XII)	64-0, 15	(¹)	(¹)	(¹)	(¹)	(¹)	Do.
1140 (XII)	65-0, 15	(¹)	(¹)	(¹)	(¹)	(¹)	Do.
1141 (XII)	60-3, 17	(¹)	(¹)	(¹)	(¹)	(¹)	Do.
1142 (XII)	55-3, 17	(¹)	(¹)	(¹)	(¹)	(¹)	Do.
1143 (XII)	50-10, 20	Y	AB	Y	Y	N	Do.
1243 (XIII)	61-8, 7	(¹)	(¹)	(¹)	(¹)	(¹)	Oct. 30, 1958
1244 (XIII)	64-0, 13	(¹)	(¹)	(¹)	(¹)	(¹)	Do.
1245 (XIII)	64-1, 13	(¹)	(¹)	(¹)	(¹)	(¹)	Do.
1246 (XIII)	62-0, 14	(¹)	(¹)	(¹)	(¹)	(¹)	Do.
1247 (XIII)	68-0, 8	(¹)	(¹)	(¹)	(¹)	(¹)	Do.

¹ No rollcall.

² No rollcall; adopted unanimously.

³ This matter was not considered at the 19th session of the General Assembly.

Source: Prepared by IO Reference and Documents Section, Mar. 3, 1966.

Resolution No.	Total vote	United States	South Africa	United Kingdom	France	U.S.S.R.	Date adopted
1333 (XIII)	40-21, 11	(¹)	(¹)	(¹)	(¹)	(¹)	Dec. 13, 1958
1356 (XIV)	57-1, 10	(¹)	(¹)	(¹)	(¹)	(¹)	Nov. 17, 1959
1357 (XIV)	57-1, 12	(¹)	(¹)	(¹)	(¹)	(¹)	Do.
1358 (XIV)	62-1, 12	(¹)	(¹)	(¹)	(¹)	(¹)	Do.
1359 (XIV)	56-1, 13	(¹)	(¹)	(¹)	(¹)	(¹)	Do.
1360 (XIV)	55-5, 11	(¹)	(¹)	(¹)	(¹)	(¹)	Do.
1361 (XIV)	55-4, 16	(¹)	(¹)	(¹)	(¹)	(¹)	Do.
1362 (XIV)	65-9, 2	(¹)	(¹)	(⁷)	(¹)	(¹)	Do.
1563 (XV)	82-0, 5	(¹)	(¹)	(¹)	(¹)	(¹)	Dec. 18, 1960
1564 (XV)	84-0, 7	(¹)	(¹)	(¹)	(¹)	(¹)	Do.
1564 (XV)	86-0, 6	Y	NP	A	A	Y	Do.
1566 (XV)	86-0, 0	(¹)	(¹)	(¹)	(¹)	(¹)	Do.
1567 (XV)	83-0, 7	(¹)	(¹)	(¹)	(¹)	(¹)	Do.
1568 (XV)	78-0, 15	A	NP	A	A	Y	Do.
1593 (XV)	74-0, 9	Y	NP	A	A	Y	Mar. 16, 1961
1956 (XV)	83-0, 9	Y	NP	A	A	Y	Apr. 7, 1961
1702 (XVI)	90-1, 4	(¹)	(¹)	(¹)	(¹)	(¹)	Dec. 19, 1961
1703 (XVI)		(²)	(²)	(²)	(²)	(²)	Do.
1704 (XVI)	93-0, 0	(¹)	(¹)	(¹)	(¹)	(¹)	Do.
1705 (XVI)	94-0, 1	(¹)	(¹)	(¹)	(¹)	(¹)	Do.
1804 (XVII)		(²)	(²)	(²)	(²)	(²)	Dec. 14, 1962
1805 (XVII)	98-0, 1	(¹)	(¹)	(¹)	(¹)	(¹)	Do.
1806 (XVII)		(²)	(²)	(²)	(²)	(²)	Do.
1809 (XVIII)	84-6, 17	(¹)	(¹)	(¹)	(¹)	(¹)	Nov. 13, 1963
1900 (XVIII)		(²)	(²)	(²)	(²)	(²)	Do.
1902 (XVIII)		(²)	(²)	(²)	(²)	(²)	Do.
1979 (XVIII)	89-2, 3	Y	N	A	A	Y	Dec. 17, 1963
2074 (XX)³	85-2, 19	(¹)	(¹)	(¹)	(¹)	(¹)	Do.
2075 (XX)²		(²)	(²)	(²)	(²)	(²)	Do.
2076 (XX)³		(²)	(²)	(²)	(²)	(²)	Do.

*Statement by Alexander Trowbridge, Assistant Secretary of Commerce for Domestic and International Business on South Africa, Before the Senate Foreign Relations Committee**

March 2, 1966

*   *   *

South Africa has traditionally represented the most important trading area for the United States in Africa. During 1965, U.S. sales to South Africa amounted to $438 million, accounting for approximately 35 percent of all U.S. exports to Africa. At the

*Ibid., pp. 44-47; 53-55.

same time, U.S. imports from South Africa were $225 million, or about 26 percent of total purchases from Africa. Our trade with South Africa in 1965, therefore, provided the United States with a favorable bilateral trade balance of well in excess of $200 million.

$$*\qquad\qquad*\qquad\qquad*$$

The commodity composition of U.S.-South African trade has remained fairly constant in recent years. U.S. exports to South Africa have been largely in the capital and producer goods areas, with machinery and transport equipment constituting, by far the largest single category of exports.

Other important U.S. exports have been chemicals and related products, textile fibers and manufactures, and certain other manufactured goods. In turn, principal U.S. imports from South Africa have consisted of a wide variety of metals and metallic ores, uranium, diamonds, wool, asbestos, and various fish and fish products.

The book value of U.S. direct private investment in South Africa amounted to $467 million as of the end of 1964, according to the latest available official U.S. data. This represented about 28 percent of total U.S. direct private investment in Africa and about 1 percent of global U.S. direct investment abroad.

Total U.S. investment in South Africa—direct plus portfolio—has been estimated by South African sources at $600 million. This represents about 11 percent of total foreign investment in South Africa, which, as of the end of 1964, was estimated by the South African Reserve Bank to total over $4.3 billion. The largest foreign holdings, by far, in South Africa belong to the United Kingdom whose direct and portfolio investments at the end of 1964 were approximately $2.7 billion.

$$*\qquad\qquad*\qquad\qquad*$$

Areas where U.S. firms historically have been most strongly represented are automobile manufacture and assembly, drugs and cosmetics, industrial machinery and equipment, oil refining, mining, tire and rubber manufacture, and tractor and farm equipment manufacture and distribution. U.S. firms in South Africa include some of the largest and best known companies of American industry.

Since the mid-1950's the increase in the value of direct U.S. private holdings has resulted largely from the reinvestment of earnings by American companies in South Africa rather than from the inflow of new capital. Thus, between 1955 and 1963, the total net outflow of new U.S. capital to South Africa amounted to only $9 million; the remainder of the growth in the value of U.S. private investment came from reinvested earnings totaling $209 million.

It is noteworthy, however, that even including the amount of reinvested earnings, the contribution of U.S. private capital to the overall growth of the South African economy has been relatively marginal for many years. In this regard, U.S. investment for the past 15 years has accounted for only a relatively small portion of total capital formation in South Africa, the bulk of which is now derived from domestic savings in the country.

Thus, between 1950 and 1963, for example, U.S. direct investment provided only about 2.3 percent of total net domestic capital formation in South Africa. Even if U.S.

portfolio investment are included, the comparable percentage would be only 3½ percent.

*   *   *

At the same time, however, the presence of U.S. business in South Africa has, in certain limited areas, exerted a positive influence on some aspects of racial practices in South Africa, particularly in the industrial sphere. In many instances, U.S. firms have been in the forefront in introducing progressive labor-management practices, such as employing nonwhite labor at high job and skill classifications.

Similarly, certain U.S. firms have taken the lead in instituting multiracial pension and insurance plans, while other companies have been noted for setting up and operating fully integrated production facilities and assembly lines.

In terms of the pattern of U.S. overseas investment, it is noteworthy that South Africa ranks as the 17th largest area for U.S. private foreign investments.

South Africa's importance to the American business community is reflected in the substantial foreign earnings accruing to U.S. investments. On an annual basis, these earnings amounted to $87 million in 1964 and $82 million in 1963. Our business investments in South Africa also contribute directly to our export trade with that country. Many U.S. businesses in South Africa are engaged in manufacturing activities which traditionally utilize component parts for assembly and industrial raw materials from U.S. sources of supply.

*   *   *

In conclusion, it has been a characteristic of U.S. policy to permit the maintenance of normal commercial relations with all foreign countries except where national security considerations would dictate otherwise. In the absence of such considerations, in the case of South Africa, the United States continues to carry on normal commercial relationships with that country with the major exception of commerce in items covered by the arms embargo. . . .

The U.S. Government neither encourages nor discourages new investment in South Africa. However, the Department and other agencies of the executive branch insure that potential investors are given full information and briefing on all factors, both negative and positive, which may bear on the investment situation in South Africa.

With respect to American business already established in South Africa, the United States recognizes its traditional obligation to protect the interest of existing U.S. investment in that country. In this connection, the maintenance of a significant business community in South Africa may provide a useful channel of communication with influential South African private and official circles.

*   *   *

Mr. O'Hara: Mr. Secretary, do you know anything about a plan to sell some air equipment to South Africa?

Mr. Trowbridge: There have been a number of applications, Mr. Chairman, for permits to export aircraft to the Republic of South Africa. Licensing of military aircraft is under the jurisdiction of the Office of Munitions Control of the Department of State. Military aircraft are denied licenses in accordance with the U.N. Security Council resolutions which have dealt with the questions of arms, ammunition, and military equipment. Most civilian aircraft is licensed for export by the Department of Commerce. In implementing the U.N. arms embargo, the Department of Commerce has denied licenses for the sale of civilian aircraft to South Africa where it was determined that the aircraft would likely be used for military purposes. There have been other cases where the end use was of a purely commercial nature and the export has not been prevented.

Mr. O'Hara: At the time you had under consideration those proposals had you read the statement at the 20th General Assembly of the United Nations by Ambassador Goldberg and myself?

Mr. Trowbridge: There have been a number of different cases of aircraft. Could you pinpoint the particular one that you are thinking of?

Mr. O'Hara: These statements in substance were this: that we had not only refused to sell South Africa military equipment but we had turned down over $60 million in orders for civilian equipment that possibly might be converted to military use. Are you acquainted with those——

Mr. Trowbridge: Yes.

Mr. O'Hara: You know I made one of those statements?

Mr. Trowbridge: Yes, sir.

Mr. O'Hara: You know that if you were to sell, if our Government were to sell any airplanes that could be used for military purposes, you would be making a liar out of me and also a liar out of our permanent Ambassador to the United Nations, Arthur Goldberg, you appreciate that?

Mr. Trowbridge: Yes, sir.

Mr. O'Hara: Can the Ambassador and I feel our honor is safe in your hands?

Mr. Trowbridge: Yes, sir.

*   *   *

Mr. Secretary, what types of planes were these for which permits were refused?

Mr. Trowbridge: We have had several cases. One case I can recall very clearly was a so-called civilian version of a military cargo aircraft. The item was judged on its end use and we did not issue a permit.

Mr. Adair: Manufactured by what company? Do you recall?

Mr. Trowbridge: I am not sure whether under our regulations I am allowed to give you that information in open session, Mr. Adair.

Mr. Adair: I will withdraw that question. We can get it later.

Mr. Trowbridge: I would be happy to furnish the information to this committee on a confidential basis.

Mr. Adair: I understand. Were some of the planes for which licenses were refused Cessna-type planes?

Mr. Trowbridge: Once again, Mr. Adair, under the Export Control Act we do not divulge in public the companies who are affected by these particular policy decisions.

Mr. Adair: From your statement in general I take it that commercial and business relations between the United States and the Republic of South Africa, insofar as the Department of Commerce is concerned, have been quite satisfactory?

Mr. Trowbridge: I think they are going forward under what we would call normal commercial relations. As I pointed out, we do not get into some of our more widely used trade promotion activities such as trade missions and commercial exhibits which show substantial U.S. Government participation or sponsorship.

We neither encourage nor discourage investment. We feel that the trade which has been going on obviously has benefits for an export balance-of-payments situation. But in adopting a governmental policy toward South Africa, I think we have to fit this into the total context of the whole series of considerations.

The trade level is high in comparative terms with the rest of Africa. The trade level is much lower in comparative terms of our total trade pattern.

Mr. Adair: Is it the highest in Africa?

Mr. Trowbridge: It is the highest single country of all Africa as far as U.S. exports and imports go; yes, sir.

*   *   *

Mr. Diggs: . . . . Mr. Secretary, the general weight of your testimony in my opinion does encourage American business interests in South Africa. The various phrases that you use about it, being the most important trading area for the United States—

Mr. Trowbridge: In Africa.

Mr. Diggs: The favorable U.S. balance-of-trade position and all such expressions as that, if I were a business person looking for investments outside this country and read this testimony, I would be encouraged to make such an investment. Therefore I think that it is according to my interpretation erroneous to say that the Department takes a neutral position with respect to this matter.

*   *   *

United States Direct Investment in South Africa by Major Industrial Sector, 1964*

March 2, 1966

Table A: U.S. direct investment in South Africa by major industrial sector, 1964[1]

	Value (in millions of U.S. dollars)
Mining and smelting	68
Petroleum	([2])
Manufacturing	192
Public utilities	([3])
Trade	51
Other	157
Total	467

[1] "Survey of Current Business" September 1965 edition.
[2] Combined in "Other industries."
[3] Less than $500,000.

Source: "Survey of Current Business," Office of Business Economics, Department of Commerce.

Table B: Total (indirect plus portfolio) foreign investment in South Africa—
South Africa's total foreign liabilities[1] of the direct and nondirect investment sectors, Dec. 31, 1964

[Millions of South African rands]

	Total direct and indirect investments in South Africa[2]	*Country or area percentage of total figure*
1. United Kingdom	1,902	61
2. Continental Western Europe	468	15
3. United States	349	11
4. Other sterling area countries	194	6
Total	3,135	--

[1] Neither the United States nor the United Kingdom maintains official figures relating to foreign indirect or portfolio holdings. The only current figures relating to total direct and indirect foreign investment in South Africa are those compiled by the South African Reserve Bank.

[2] The Reserve bank itself regards these figures as only extremely rough approximations, which for several reasons, can be regarded as substantially understating the real values of foreign holdings, perhaps by as much as 20 percent. For example, shares held by foreigners in South African organizations which are controlled by local (South African) residents, are tallied at nominal values or, if quoted on the Johannesburg Stock Exchange, at prices of December 1956, the date of the initial foreign investment survey.

Source: South African Reserve Bank Quarterly Bulletin of Statistics, South African Reserve Bank, Pretoria, December 1965.

*Ibid., p. 48.

Statement by Bernard Blankenheimer, Director of African Division, Office of International Regional Economics, Department of Commerce, Before the Subcommittee on Africa of the House Committee on Foreign Affairs*

March 2, 1966

*   *   *

Mr. Diggs: Mr. Secretary, I was interested in getting further information about the machinery that you refer to here in your testimony and some assurance comparable to that you just gave our distinguished chairman that this machinery cannot be converted for use in connection with the manufacture of arms or anything pertaining thereto.

Mr. Trowbridge: Machinery is a rather large category of trade. In the listing in the table D, which is entitled "U.S. Exports to South Africa by Leading Commodity Groups in 1965," and is part of the annex to my statement, table D the major categories are manufactures of metal and machinery other than electric. This is all types of machinery. I can't honestly say to what end product all of these machines are being put.

Mr. Diggs: Why isn't the same criteria applied to machinery as is applied to aircraft, because obviously they could certainly circumvent our ban on the sale of munitions and arms by getting the machinery and doing it themselves.

Mr. Trowbridge: As you know, the end use of aircraft to the extent that it is identified as being of military end use I think is a bit different than the normal commercial exports of machinery to a commercial private customer in South Africa. To move into controls on machinery as a broad category would probably be under some rather broader policy of economic sanctions. I might say that machinery used primarily for the production of arms is expressly included under our policy of denial. This includes anything that would contribute to the actual production of rifles or other military weapons.

Mr. Diggs: Are you saying that you are satisfied that none of this other machinery might be converted to such use?

Mr. Trowbridge: When you are talking about such a broad category as machinery, there are always certain problems. For example, you could have a machine that makes electric light bulbs. These could be used in the barracks. Similarly, a piece of machinery that turns out textiles could be used to make uniforms. But the machinery directly used in the production of arms or military support weapons would not be exported.

Mr. Diggs: Under those circumstances it isn't actually fair to say that we are carrying out to the fullest extent the arms ban to which we have been a party and because obviously there are ways of circumventing that according to your response to that question?

Mr. Trowbridge: I believe that we have a very strict control in support of this arms embargo on not only the arms and munitions themselves but the machinery that can make them. I think we are implementing a very tight control in this area.

**Ibid.*, pp. 55-56.

There is no denying that there are types of machinery that could make products of use to not only the entire civilian market of a country, but also make certain products which, in some circumstances, could be used by the Government for military purposes as well. However, under present policy guidelines, any machinery or related equipment specially designed for the manufacture or maintenance of arms or other military equipment would be denied.

*   *   *

*Testimony of William E. Lang, Deputy Assistant Secretary of Defense for the African Region Before the Subcommittee on Africa of the House Committee on Foreign Affairs**

March 8, 1966

Summary Statement

Mr. William Lang testified in executive session about the strategic significance of South Africa's geographic position and the value to us of port and other facilities in South Africa.

He discussed the importance of its location athwart the approaches to the Atlantic and Indian Oceans and thus the convergence of the maritime routes at Africa's southern tip. Continuing, he described its potential value to an ASW effort during wartime. Further, he noted that it has the only harbors in Africa south of the Sahara where major naval vessels can fuel, dock, and undergo repair—which could be of particular usefulness at this point in time as a result of the need for some of our large aircraft carriers to proceed to the waters off Vietnam from the east coast of the United States via this route and that this line of communication would assume increased importance were the usage of the Suez Canal denied.

In conclusion, he emphasized that regardless of the requirement, the USG had never compromised basic national principles for the sake of these facilities.

Mr. O'Hara: Mr. Secretary, would you state that the Republic of South Africa under present conditions is essential to the strategic interests and military security of the United States?

Secretary Lang: If we use the word "essential," sir, in its literal sense, I would say no, that South Africa is not essential, that we could live without South Africa.

Mr. O'Hara: On pages 1 and 2 of your statement you discuss the usefulness of the facilities of South Africa from a military standpoint. In the event that the facilities were not made available to the United States, what are the alternatives?

Secretary Lang: The alternatives, sir, are such as that which we did in the case of

Ibid., pp. 105-10.

the *Independence*, when we sent a fleet tanker from the eastern shore of the United States off South Africa to refuel the carrier. If by some chance there were a breakdown which required some form of major repair, we would have to bring the vessel back to the United States, the Mediterranean, or to Argentina, perhaps, those are the closest areas where equivalent port repair facilities are available.

Mr. O'Hara: [Security deletion.]

You have noted that the South Africans have sought to impose restrictions and the United States has responded by not using their facilities. Now, to the best of your knowledge, have we ever faced up to this issue by having Negroes aboard ships stopping at South African ports? If so, are they required to stay on board?

Secretary Lang: The answer to your question, Mr. Chairman, is that ships calling at ports in South Africa have had Negro crews aboard, that these crews have been free to go ashore, and, in fact, do go ashore in mixed groups. A report from the commander of the last naval vessel to visit South Africa, which was in November, indicated that the Negro members of the crew enjoyed their stay in South Africa.

Mr. O'Hara: They went ashore?

Secretary Lang: They went ashore, sir.

Mr. O'Hara: And they met no discrimination that was uncomfortable to them?

Secretary Lang: From the reports we have from the Navy, sir, I would say that statement is accurate.

Mr. O'Hara: In this same connection, you note that the alternative to not docking the U.S.S. *Independence* was to have a tanker dispatched from the east coast for its refueling. You further note that this is expensive [security deletion]. Is it fair to say tha in each instance where one of the large ships is required to refuel in this manner because of this restriction it is costing the United States [security deletion].

Secretary Lang: The answer is "Yes," sir.

Mr. O'Hara: Mr. Adair.

Mr. Adair: Mr. Chairman, Mr. Lang, are these American technicians in South Africa military or nonmilitary or both? Do you know?

Secretary Lang: The technicians, sir, are employees of a contractor.

Mr. Adair: So they are civilian?

Secretary Lang: There are three military personnel [security deletion] but they are not technicians.

*   *   *

Mr. Diggs: Mr. Secretary, I was interested in your statement that South Africa has the only harbors in Africa south of the Sahara where major naval vessels can dock and undergo repair. That is a pretty revealing statement.

Secretary Lang: Yes, sir.

Mr. Diggs: Are there any other harbors in Africa that approach such usefulness for our purposes?

Secretary Lang: As I recall, sir, the harbor at Lagos has a depth of about 12 or 15 feet. The draft of a carrier is 35 feet.

Mr. Rosenthal: Mr. Diggs knows where that is, don't you?

Mr. Diggs: Yes. Thirty-five feet are necessary. And that is the only other harbor that even approaches the kind of facilities that would be required, is that correct?

Secretary Lang: That is correct, sir. Accra does not have really what might be considered as harbor facilities. It is more of a roadstead.

Mr. Diggs: You said Accra or Dakar?

Secretary Lang: Accra.

Mr. Diggs: Accra.

Secretary Lang: You will find that even the commercial vessels at Accra off-load use lighters. They do not have modern docking facilities there.

*　　　　　　*　　　　　　*

Mr. Diggs: Now you state on page 3 that you want to make it clear that we, quoting you "have never for these reasons compromised our basic national principles." Yet, of course, the whole weight of your testimony here emphasizes the strategic value of South African facilities for these purposes and would seem to question that kind of conclusion. To me it is analogous to the testimony made by the Department of Commerce, which said that they were not encouraging American business people to make investments here, yet the whole weight of the testimony would seem to encourage it.

Are not the national interests of the United States, with respect to this subject, the same as South Africa's? In other words, if South Africa has the same security interests that we have, presumably they would be just as much interested in our using those facilities because they derive a certain amount of mutual protection from it as we would, is that not true?

Secretary Lang: I believe that is correct, sir.

Mr. Diggs: So that any agitation with respect to their internal policies would not necessarily result in their depriving us, would you not say, of the use of these facilities?

Secretary Lang: I am not quite sure I understand your question, Mr. Congressman.

As I understand what you have said is that there is in a sense a mutuality of interest, that it is both in our interest and in the South African interest that these strategic facilities be available to the free world. And with that I would agree, yes, sir.

Mr. Diggs: Of course the followup question is whether or not any kind of agitation or what they consider to be interference with their internal policies would not necessarily be followed by their refusing us the use of these facilities, because their own interest is involved in this matter.

Secretary Lang: We do have the case of where, for whatever reasons the South Africans deemed best, they stopped the *Independence* from coming in by imposing what to us was an unacceptable condition. This illustrates what I meant when I said that we have not compromised our basic national principles, because of the importance of South African facilities. Another illustration would be the case where the South African Government sought to buy some Orion aircraft, these aircraft are specially configured with electronic equipment for antisubmarine warfare. From the defense viewpoint we considered it would be important for South Africa to have this capability, because of the sumbarine threat in the area. Yet we did not press this importance, when the State Department judged that it would be in our national interest not to sell the aircraft.

*   *   *

Mr. Rosenthal: How does this enter into your thinking in making use of South African facilities and committing money to the building of facilities, including the tracking stations?

Secretary Lang: Mr. Congressman, the facilities were built in 1960, basically for a phase of our space development program which was extremely important at that time.

That work has in large measure been completed. This does not mean to say that the usefulness of the tracking facilities is over. We will continue to need the tracking facilities. For example, they will continue to be useful in connection with the defense communications satellite proejct.

We can see a future need, a future usefulness of the facilities. These facilities are also being used to support NASA operations. But we have not in recent years, by that I mean the last year or two, expended great amounts of money in developing the facilities. Most of our equipment there is in what we call transportable vans.

Now of some of the equipment, the radar, for example, must be mounted in a concrete pad, but the other equipment is in transportable vans and could be removed.

Mr. Rosenthal: Now, have you taken into consideration as to whether or not the continued use of South African facilities, including ports and the tracking station affects our relationships with those countries north of the Zambezi River? What are their attitudes? Have their attitudes changed by the use of these facilities?

Secretary Lang: I personally have not seen any reaction on the part of the nations north of the Zambezi to our use of the ports, airfield facilities in South Africa.

Mr. Rosenthal: Do you have sort of high level discussions with your counterparts in the State Department on this matter?

Secretary Lang: Yes, indeed, sir.

Mr. Rosenthal: [Security deletion.]

Secretary Lang: [Security deletion.]

*   *   *

Statement by Earl D. Hilburn, Deputy Associate Administrator of National Aeronautics and Space Administration Before the Subcommittee on Africa of the House Committee on Foreign Affairs*

March 8, 1966

*   *   *

Summary Statement

Mr. Hilburn described NASA's operations in South Africa, which include an optical tracking station, an electronic satellite tracking and data acquisition facility, and a deep space instrumentation facility (DSIF). The latter, near Johannesburg, is part of a worldwide network of such facilities separated by 120° of longitude which provides the necessary 24-hour-per-day coverage of lunar and planetary missions. NASA's operations in South Africa support the U.S. program for the peaceful exploration of space, which consists of a broad spectrum of space activities, both manned and unmanned. Mr. Hilburn said that every space mission in order to be successful levies certain specialized demands for ground support, including (1) tracking, (2) data (telemetry) acquisition, and (3) command and control. All three functions are carried out by the South African stations, which are well positioned to support missions launched either from Florida or California. Mr. Hilburn described the history and current status of administrative arrangements covering the NASA installations in South Africa. All of these facilities are operated and managed by the Council of Scientific and Industrial Research of the Republic of South Africa. He pointed out that the Surveyor series of unmanned lunar soft-landing spacecraft was a necessary precursor to our manned lunar mission scheduled for the end of this decade. In conclusion, Mr. Hilburn stressed the importance of our meeting this target in moving toward our goal of preeminence in space.

Mr. Hilburn: That concludes my statement, Mr. Chairman.

We are ready now to try to answer any questions that you may have.

Mr. O'Hara: [Security deletion.]

Mr. Hilburn: [Security deletion.]

Mr. O'Hara: Has the space agency ever faced the issue of attempting to place Negroes or other nonwhite personnel in any of the facilities which operate on South Africa soil?

Mr. Hilburn: We have not had any occasion to, Mr. Chairman.

Mr. O'Hara: And all of the Africans employed, and from your statement, we spend about $1½ million a year, do we?

Mr. Hilburn: A little more than that.

*   *   *

Mr. Hilburn: (The information supplied is as follows:)

*Ibid., pp. 111-12; 115-18; 127-30.

The custodial and groundskeeping services required in support of station operation are performed by local unskilled nonwhite laborers. CSIR provides approximately 45 laborers to carry out these services; the number actually employed at any one time varies with the requirements of the station.

There are no white employees engaged in similar functions; conversely, there are no nonwhites among the professional engineers and technicians that comprise the technical complement of the station. Technical staff salaries range from approximately $2,000 to $7,000 per year, and are estimated to average $4,000 per year. No quarters are provided for this technical staff. Salaries for the nonwhite laborers are estimated to average approximately $1,000 per year, plus living accommodations provided in the vicinity of the station for these personnel.

* * *

Mr. Diggs: Did I understand you to admit that the facilities that are used by black Africans at the NASA stations are segregated?

Mr. Hilburn: I don't know whether the facilities are segregated. It is my understanding there is separation of the personnel there. I think this is typical of the South African——

Mr. Diggs: Do you know how they are segregated or what special conditions are imposed on them?

Mr. Hilburn: I don't personally know, sir.

Mr. Diggs: What reason do we have for permitting segregated patterns of that nature?

Mr. Hilburn: Well, this is a station operated by the South African Government and it is operated by them in accordance with their own procedures and regulations.

We don't attempt to impose our restrictions or regulations on them.

Mr. Diggs: Well, it is operated by them but it is our station, is that not true?

Mr. Hilburn: Well, I would say that it is a station in which there is a joint interest on the part of both Governments.

* * *

Mr. Diggs: If the United States insisted that the black Africans who work at these stations be treated the same as they would be if the station was, for example, located here in the United States, what do you think would happen?

Mr. Hilburn: I don't really believe I am in a position to make a judgment on that, Congressman.

Mr. Diggs: Do you think that they would——

Mr. Hilburn: I would guess, offhand, that the Government would object under the terms of the established agreement because we do not have that prerogative under the agreement as it was entered into by the two Governments.

Mr. Diggs: What is the date of the agreement?

Mr. Hilburn: September 1960.

Mr. Diggs: And for what period of time does it cover?

Mr. Hilburn: It runs for 15 years.

Mr. Diggs. Fifteen years. Well, does it say specifically in there that they have complete control over the employment policies or conditions of employment of the people that are working there?

Mr. Hilburn: I have here a copy of the agreement, Mr. Diggs.

UNION OF SOUTH AFRICA
TRACKING STATIONS

Agreement Effected by Exchange of Notes
Signed at Pretoria September 13, 1960;
Entered Into Force September 13, 1960

The American Ambassador to the South African Secretary for External Affairs

September 13, 1960

Sir: I have the honor to refer to the cooperative program initiated during the International Geophysical Year between our two countries under which certain facilities for space vehicles tracking and communications were jointly established and operated in the Union of South Africa for scientific purposes. In view of the resutling mutual benefits, the Government of the United States of America proposes that this cooperative program be continued and extended.

The object of such further and extended cooperation would be to facilititate space operations contributing to the advancement of our mutual scientific knowledge of man's spatial environment and its effects; the application of this knowledge to the direct benefit of man; and the development of space vehicles of advanced capabilities, including manned space vehicles.

It is proposed that the program be carried out in accordance with the following principles and procedures:

1. The program shall be conducted by Cooperating Agencies of each Government. On the part of the Government of the United States, the Cooperating Agency will be the National Aeronautics and Space Administration. On the part of the Government of the Union of South Africa, the Cooperating Agency will be the Council for Scientific and Industrial Research.

2. a. The nature and location of facilities required in the Union of South Africa for the program are as follows:

(1) Minitrack radio tracking station presently located at Esselen Park (originally established under an arrangement of October 11, 1957, between the United States Naval Research Laboratory and the Government of the Union of South Africa).

(2) Baker-Nunn camera optical tracking station presently located at Olifantsfontein (originally established in February 1958 under an arrangement between the United States National Committee for the International Geophysical Year and the South African National Committee).

(3) Deep space probe radio tracking station (85 foot diameter antenna) in the vicinity of Johannesburg.

The foregoing list of facilities and locations may be amended from time to time by agreement of our two Governments.

b. The Government of the Union of South Africa will provide sites for each facility at the agreed locations at no cost to the Government of the United States; these sites to remain the property of the Government of the Union of South Africa.

3. The Government of the Union of South Africa will, in so far as practicable, prohibit the operation of radio interference-producing devices (such as power lines, industrial facilities, electric trains, primary highways, etc.) within the vicinity of sensitive radio receiving equipment.

4. In connection with each facility to be operated under the program, the Cooperating Agencies will agree upon arrangements with respect to the duration of use of the facility, the responsibility for and financing of the construction, installation, and equipping of the facility, and other details relating to the establishment and operation of the facility.

5. Each facility established may, unless otherwise agreed, be used for independent scientific activities of the Government of the Unionof South Africa, it being understood that such activities would be conducted so as not to conflict with the agreed schedules of operations and that any additional operating costs resulting from such independent activities would be borne by the Government of the Union of South Africa.

6. The Government of the Union of South Africa will, upon request, take the necessary steps to facilitate the admission into the territory of the Union of South Africa of materials, equipment, supplies, goods or other items of property provided by the Government of the United States in connection with activities under this Agreement.

7. a. Title to all the aforementioned property provided by the Government of the United States for use in connection with each facility will remain in the Government of the United States.

b. If, upon terminating its use of a facility, the Government of the United States should desire to dispose of all or part of the property to which it holds title within the territory of the Union of South Africa, the two Governments will consult beforehand on arrangements therefor.

8. Such personal and household effects as shall have been brought into the Union of South Africa free of all taxes and duties by United States personnel, including contractor personnel, assigned to the Union of South Africa under the program, shall not be sold or otherwise disposed of within the territory of the Union of South Africa, except under conditions approved by the Government of the Union of South Africa.

With reference to paragraphs 6, 7, and 8, the matter of exemption from duties, taxes and other charges will be the subject of subsequent discussion and agreement between the two Governments as to the specific categories of personnel, goods, and materials to which such exemptions will apply, and the degree of exemption, if any, which will be applicable.

9. The Government of the Union of South Africa will, subject to its immigration laws and regulations, take the necessary steps to facilitate the admission into the territory of the Union of South Africa of such United States personnel, including contractor personnel, as may be assigned by the National Aeronautics and Space

Administration to visit or participate in the cooperative activities provided for under this Agreement.

10. The resident directors of the facilities will be officials of the Government of the United States, and they will relay the operational directions of NASA to the South African Station Managers who will be in control of the Stations.

11. This Agreement relates to cooperation between the signatories for the peaceful uses of outer space and the facilities established shall not be used for purposes of a military nature.

12. The program of cooperation set forth in this Agreement shall, subject to the availability of funds, remain in effect for a period of fifteen years, and may be extended as mutually agreed by the two Governments. This Agreement is subject to review and possible termination in the event of either party failing to comply with the provisions of the Agreement, or in the event that either party is involved in hostilities.

If the foregoing principles and procedures are acceptable to the Government of the Union of South Africa, I have the honor to propose that this note and your note in reply shall constitute an Agreement between our two Governments to enter into force on the date of your reply.

Accept, Sir, the renewed assurances of my highest consideration.

Philip K. Crowe

The South African Secretary for External Affairs to the American Ambassador

Unie Van Suid-Afrika
Union of South Africa
Department Van Buitelandse Sake,
Department of External Affairs,
Pretoria, 13th September, 1960

I have the honour to acknowledge receipt of your Note of today's date which reads as follows:

"I have the honor to refer to the cooperative program initiated during the International Geophysical Year between our two countries under which certain facilities for space vehicles tracking and communications were jointly established and operated in the Union of South Africa for scientific purposes. In view of the resulting mutual benefits, the Government of the United States of America proposes that this cooperative program be continued and extended.

The object of such further and extended cooperation would be to facilitate space operations contributing to the advancement of our mutual scientific knowledge of man's spatial environment and its effects; the application of this knowledge to the direct benefit of man; and the development of space vehicles of advanced capabilities, including manned space vehicles.

It is proposed that the program be carried out in accordance with the following principles and procedures:

1. The program shall be conducted by Cooperating Agencies of each Government. On the part of the Government of the United States, the Cooperating Agency will be the National Aeronautics and Space Administration. On the part of the Government of

the Union of South Africa, the Cooperating Agency will be the Council for Scientific and Industrial Research.

2. a. The nature and location of facilities required in the Union of South Africa for the program are as follows:

(1) Minitrack radio tracking station presently located at Esselen Park (originally established under an arrangement of October 11, 1957, between the United States Naval Research Laboratory and the Government of the Union of South Africa).

(2) Baker-Nunn camera optical tracking station presently located at Olifantsfontein (originally established in February 1958 under an arrangement between the United States National Committee for the International Geophysical Year and the South African National Committee).

(3) Deep space probe radio tracking station (85 foot diameter antenna) in the vicinity of Johannesburg.

The foregoing list of facilities and locations may be amended from time to time by agreement of our two Governments.

b. The Government of the Union of South Africa will provide sites for each facility at the agreed locations at no cost to the Government of the United States; these sites to remain the property of the Government of the Union of South Africa.

3. The Government of the Union of South Africa will, in so far as practicable, prohibit the operation of radio interference-producing devices (such as power lines, industrial facilities, electric trains, primary highways, etc.) within the vicinity of sensitive radio receiving equipment.

4. In connection with each facility to be operated under the program, the Cooperating Agencies will agree upon arrangements with respect to the duration of use of the facility, the responsibility for and financing of the construction, installation, and equipping of the facility, and other details relating to the establishment and operation of the facility.

5. Each facility established may, unless otherwise agreed, be used for independent scientific activities of the Government of the Union of South Africa, it being understood that such ctivities would be conducted so as not to conflict with the agreed schedules of operations and that any additional operating costs resulting from such independent activities would be borne by the Government of the Union of South Africa.

6. The Government of the Union of South Africa will, upon request, take the necessary steps to facilitate the admission into the territory of the Union of South Africa of materials, equipment, supplies, goods or other items of property provided by the Government of the United States in connection with activities under this Agreement.

7. a. Title to all the aforementioned property provided by the Government of the United States for use in connection with each facility will remain in the Government of the United States.

b. If, upon terminating its use of a facility, the Government of the United States should desire to dispose of all or part of the property to which it holds title within the territory of the Union of South Africa, the two Governments will consult beforehand on arrangements therefor.

8. Such personal and household effects as shall have been brought into the Union of South Africa free of all taxes and duties by United States personnel, including

contractor personnel, assigned to the Union of South Africa under the program, shall not be sold or otherwise disposed of within the territory of the Union of South Africa except under conditions approved by the Government of the Union of South Africa.

With reference to paragraphs 6, 7, and 8, the matter of exemption from duties, taxes and other charges will be the subject of subsequent discussion and agreement between the two Governments as to the specific categories of personnel, goods and materials to which such exemptions will apply, and the degree of exemption, if any, which will be applicable.

9. The Government of the Union of South Africa will, subject to its immigration laws and regulations, take the necessary steps to facilitate the admission into the territory of the Union of South Africa of such United States personnel, including contractor personnel, as may be assigned by the National Aeronautics and Space Administration to visit or participate in the cooperative activities provided for under this Agreement.

10. The resident directors of the facilities will be officials of the Government of the United States, and they will relay the operational directions of NASA to the South African Station Managers who will be in control of the Stations.

11. This Agreement relates to cooperation between the signatories for the peaceful uses of outer space and the facilities established shall not be used for purposes of a military nature.

12. The program of cooperation set forth in this Agreement shall, subject to the availability of funds, remain in effect for a period of fifteen years, and may be extended as mutually agreed by the two Governments. This Agreement is subject to review and possible termination in the even of either party failing to comply with the provisions of the Agreement, or in the event that either party is involved in hostilities.

If the foregoing principles and procedures are acceptable to the Government of the Union of South Africa, I have the honor to propose that this note and your note in reply shall constitute an Agreement between our two Governments to enter into force on the date of your reply.

Accept, Sir, the renewed assurances of my highest consideration."

In reply thereto, I have the honour to inform you that the Government of the Union of South Africa are in agreement with the foregoing and that your Note and the present reply shall be regarded as constituting an Agreement between our two Governments, such Agreement to enter into force and effect on today's date.

I have the honour to be,

Your Excellency's obedient Servant,

G. P. Jooste,
Secretary for External Affairs

    *   *   *

Mr. Adair: Now, other members have addressed questions to you concerning the relative efficiency of certain installations upon land and upon sea. Am I correct in understanding your answer to a question concerning certain radar facilities that it is less efficient, perhaps nonexistent upon ships, as compared to upon the land?

Mr. Hilburn: Yes.

* * *

So, in summary, I guess you could say that we think there would have to be a tremendously large investment in the additional research and development necessary to bring about the equipment, both in terms of the ship or the platform on which such an antenna would be mounted, as well as the stabilization equipment for it. We are studying this problem, however, and have transferred funds to the Navy Department as part of a long-range continuing study to look and see what can be done in these areas, but the initial reactions and the reports that we have had, and the studies that our own people have made in looking at this, make it a very pessimistic situation.

Mr. Adair: [Security deletion.]

Mr. Hilburn: [Security deletion.]

Mr. Rosenthal: In the last year or 6 months have you or your people detected any note of urgency on behalf of the State Department people with a warning to you that the situation was deteriorating and we ought to be alert to some potential changes?

Mr. Hilburn: I think certainly we have been aware of that, sir.

Mr. Rosenthal: [Security deletion.]

Mr. Hilburn: [Security deletion.]

Mr. Rosenthal: I think you have made an excellent presentation and you have convinced me of the essential character of those facilities and I don't expect you to make foreign policy judgments, but I do think that you are under obligation to be aware of what is going on and either the State Department isn't bringing you up to date as quickly as they should or maybe your folks have been somewhat sluggish in appropriately evaluating that information.

Mr. Hilburn: [Security deletion.]

Mr. Rosenthal: How much money does your argency spend each year in South Africa?

Mr. Hilburn: In terms of the annual operating costs it is just a little short of $2 million; $1,833,000 is the current figure.

Mr. Rosenthal: In terms of capital investment?

Mr. Hilburn: No, sir; that is annual operating costs. Our capital investment at the present time is $14½ million.

Mr. Rosenthal: Thank you, Mr. Chairman.

Mr. O'Hara: [Security deletion.]

Mr. O'Hara: Mr. Administrator, how much money did we have invested in Zanzibar? It was a large facility.

Mr. Hilburn: About $1½ million, Mr. Chairman.

Mr. O'Hara: A large facility, wasn't it?

Mr. Hilburn: Not compared to these, very much smaller. It is about $1½ million as compared to $14½ million. So it is just about an order of 10 times different in size.

Mr. O'Hara: I took them a long time to build it?

Mr. Hilburn: Yes, sir. [Security deletion.]

Mr. O'Hara: What happened at Zanzibar?

Mr. Hilburn: Well, I believe that Mr. Pozinsky might give you some information.

Mr. O'Hara: Briefly.

Mr. Pozinsky: The revolutionary element which took over the government did not welcome us there as a part of the space effort. We were obliged simply to move.

Mr. O'Hara: What did you do with the equipment?

Mr. Pozkinsky: We moved it to the island of Madagascar.

Mrs. Bolton: That is where it came from?

Mr. Pozinsky: They allowed us to establish it there.

Mr. O'Hara: I was in Zanzibar there when the unrest was starting. It largely started by the circulation of a report among the people that this was war material. They didn't understand the difference between a peaceful use and a warlike use.

Mr. Pozinsky: Yes.

Mr. O'Hara: But you salvaged most of the material, did you?

Mr. Pozinsky: Most of it, the vast majority of it.

Mr. O'Hara: Who took up the work formerly done by that tracking station?

Mr. Pozinsky: The station at Madagascar took up the functional workload of that station.

Mr. O'Hara: And did the personnel go with the equipment?

Mr. Pozkinsky: Yes, sir.

Mr. O'Hara: I might say one of the brightest young men of 21 or 22 that I ever met in my life was one of our personnel over there. He spent half a day explaining to us how every part of this equipment worked.

Thank you very much, Mr. Administrator, and thank you, Mr. Secretary. I would say it has been a very profitable afternoon.

Mr. Hilburn: Thank you.

Mr. O'Hara: [Security deletion.]

Mr. Hilburn: [Security deletion.]

Mr. O'Hara: I think it would be prudent if you should go over your testimony, and return to us with any security deletions you think proper.

Statement by Kenneth Robinson, Regional Director, United Automobile, Aerospace & Agricultural Implement Workers of America (UAW), Grand Rapids, Mich., Before the Subcommittee on Africa of the House Committee on Foreign Affairs*

March 10, 1966

*   *   *

Beyond these declarations, the UAW has, from its own resources supported by contributions and other actions the defense of men and women persecuted by the Government of South Africa, and we now in various ways give help to refugees from South Africa, to the families of imprisoned martyrs to the tyranny of South Africa,

Ibid., pp. 131-39; 154; 159-61.

and seek by all the means at our disposal to urge action that will bring an end to the crime of apartheid, which, we believe, is intolerable in a civilized world, an abrasion on the consciences of the international community, a threat to the world peace, and a monstrous economic growth which concerns every wage earner in that it has joined the most advanced technology and the resources of the richest and most powerful corporations in the world to a system of slavery and feudalism which produces and sells products on the world market in competition with articles that are made by free workers.

For all of these reasons, we believe that the U.S. Government, which has responded unhesitatingly and with overwhelming power to lesser threats to our national purpose and concern on other occasions should drastically amend its present policy toward South Africa so that it reflects the true interests and moral commitments of the American people.

At this moment, our Government and our economy, in violation of our central beliefs, are powerful allies of the Verwoerd government.

American corporations, like the German industrial combines under Hitler, are fattening and prospering on the evil profits of apartheid.

In this senseless and immoral venture, they contravene the declared policy of the Government to exercise restraint in overseas investments in consideration of our critical balance-of-payments crisis.

Moreover, as the result of the failure of the Government to act in accord with its own expressed principles, they have carried on this program with financial assistance from the Federal Government and with the encouragement of certain tax benefits.

Culpability is public as well as private, for the American Government, by granting a sugar quota to South Africa and by its own purchases in South Africa, sometimes at prices which are substantially above the economic price, reinforce and help finance the Verwoerd rule.

Business Week of June 19, 1965, describes the immoral and undignified rush of American corporations to cash in on apartheid:

> Despite its touchy racial and political problems, South Africa is caught in a business boom. U.S. companies. as well as giants from Western Europe, Britain, and Japan, are cashing in on it Some 230 U.S. companies have operations in South Africa. They range from small import and sales offices to factory complexes. Total U.S. investment there runs about $600 million, the bulk of which has been invested since World War II. . . . Says one U.S. businessman, "Profit margins there are the highest in Africa running an average of 14 to 15 percent " The list of U.S. companies operating in South Africa reads like a rollcall of the bluest of blue chips Detroit's Big Three–Ford Motor Co., General Motors Corp., and Chrysler Corp.–have large plants there.

End of quote from Business Week.

> General Electric Goodyear, Firestone, Link-Belt

the article continues—

> are also there. Moreover U.S. business investment in South Africa is still growing. Caltex has a $25 million refinery scheduled to come on scene next year. Chrysler is working on a $35 million expansion of its auto production facilities; GM recently opened a new engine-producing plant. Goodyear, Ford and others are also expanding there.

Reports in the business press almost daily describe the corporation lineup to collect on the apartheid jackpot:

Says the New York Times on January 31, 1966:

American capital up in South Africa. Despite President Johnson's appeal to American companies to cut back on capital outflow in 1965, investments from the United States continued to rise in South Africa. The major expansions were in the automotive industry.

The Wall Street Journal, March 5, 1965:

Scripto will open a new plant in South Africa, May 1.

International Commerce, January 31, 1965:

New subsidiary of Rheem International, Inc., New York, to be established here (South Africa) to manufacture market steel shipping containers.

Die Metallwerker of South Africa in September 1965 reported that Rockwell Standard is joining with other companies to manufacture commercial vehicle components.

The Journal of Commerce, September 10, 1965, reports that Templet Industries of Philadelphia is licensing a Japanese auto company to manufacture its products in South Africa.

The publication, "The Automobile in South Africa," in March 1965 announced in a banner headline that "Prestolite Introduces New 'Thundervolt' Spark Plug to South African Trade."

Automobile International in June 1965:

Thompson Rameo South Africa (Pty.) Ltd. has been formed by Thompson Ramo Woolridge, Inc., and the Anglo American Corp. of South Africa, Ltd. It will produce automotive parts for the original equipment and replacement market.

These business decisions are read as political commitments by South Africans. The distinguished Protestant theologian, Henry P. Van Dusen, president emeritus of Union Theological Seminary, reports that in a conversation with one of the foremost South African political spokesmen in Johannesburg, he was told, "We know the world despises us. But we can carry on as long as American banking and business support us."

It is not suggested that American businessmen and American bankers are ideological supporters of apartheid. Rather, they direct private corporations which are, as the board hairman of the largest industrial corporation in the world said, not American, or Dutch, or German, or French, but international, presumably owing allegiance to no government and under no compulsion except their own profit concern.

A top official in one of the Big Three, referring to the South African situation declared that it is the purpose of the company to go where it makes profits, and the 27 percent annual return on investment which prevails in South Africa is all the inducement and justification that are required. [Reading:]

"There are not many countries in the world," said Charles Engelhard, Jr., who is reported to be the most powerful individual American investor in South Africa, "where it is safe to invest, and South Africa is about the best of the lot."

South Africa is not the best of the lot because of the rule of justice that prevails there. In the mines controlled by Mr. Engelhard, Africans are forbidden to bargain collectively, a prohibition which also prevails in the Ford, General Motors, Chrysler, and other American manufacturing facilities there.

They may not vote, travel internally without special permission from the police.

They are most frequently forbidden to live with their families in the areas where they work. They are subject to arbitrary abuse and brutality day and night, and they may not own land in the 87 percent of South Africa which is set aside as "white areas."

The wage in the Engelhard mines averages 70 cents a day, while the lowest paid underground white miner receives a minimum of $7.82 a day.

Apartheid, which by every human criterion is evil, by the measurement of profit, makes South Africa among the "best" places to invest.

*   *   *

Yet, if an official publication of the U.S. Department of Commerce is to be taken seriously, the South African venture in apartheid is given approbation and encouragement as an attractive business opportunity. International commerce, according to the Journal of Commerce of January 12, 1966, glowingly reports on the "growth plans to boost U.S. exports to South Africa."

We in the UAW believe that the present commerce with South Africa is both immoral and unwise.

American companies in South Africa conduct themselves in ways that violate their statements of compliance with American civil rights laws.

The American Government itself is helping to finance a system of government which violates the basic laws and principles of our country. We believe this coexistence with evil, whether intended or inadvertent, should end.

At this time the UAW urges on this subcommittee that it give the most thoughtful consideration to the presentation of a joint resolution in the Congress which would call on the administration strongly to support and to vote for the application of sanctions by the United Nations for the purpose of isolating that country from the rest of the world until such a time as it is determined that the basic human and civil rights of all the people in that country are recognized in law and protected by the processes of government.

In the meantime we believe there are immediate measures that this subcommittee can recommend to the Government, until just government is established in South Africa:

(1) No government agency or any U.S.-supported financial agency underwrite, guarantee, or grant a loan for any purpose whatever in the Republic of South Africa;

(2) No purchases be made by the American Government of any product produced in South Africa;

(3) The licensing powers in connection with exports which are now available to the administration be applied to the Republic of South Africa and that no export licenses of any kind be granted;

(4) The authority possessed by the Secretary of the Treasury to forbid the

importation of any articles into the United States which are produced by forced labor be invoked against the appropriate products from South Africa;

(5) Legislation be enacted which denies tax benefits or credit of any kind to the profits earned by American corporations under the conditions of apartheid; and

(6) The provisions of the civil rights laws and of Executive orders which require companies doing business with the United States to maintain equal employment conditions be enforced against American corporations now applying the ugly apartheid rule in South Africa.

*   *   *

Mr. Diggs: Thank you, Mr. Chairman. . . . I would like to make an observation based on the statement which was contained in a release made today by our chairman, and that is that although a number of business firms having large investments in South Africa have been invited to appear and present testimony to this committee, to date not one single firm has accepted.

*   *   *

Mr. O'Hara: So it might be well for the Congress to have such a sense resolution.

Now, you have other recommendations that no Federal agency should give financial support in the way of guaranty, loans, and so forth, for any purposes in the Republic of South Africa. Now, that might be a good thing to include in a sense resolution. Then we come to—then also you have something with regard to purchases made by our Government.

Then we come to the matter of the undertakings and activities of an American firm or an American investor in a foreign land, should we give him instructions and prohibitions? I don't know. I would like your opinion on it.

*   *   *

Mr. Robinson: Yes. Well, we understand, Mr. Chairman, that the loans granted from the World Bank are not a U.S. decision. So that the thrust of our point, our recommendation No. 1, would be that we use our influence in the councils of the World Bank with respect to loans to South Africa as long as these conditions continue.

Now, the other point that you made as to whether we ought to regulate American industry in their operations overseas, I am not totally acquainted at this point in time with our tax structure as it relates to the operation of American companies overseas. But, again, I make the point that corporations are a creature of our laws, the laws of our society. I think they are subject to regulation in the public interest. And, to any extent, that American corporations operating in South Africa have tax advantages, I think these should be examined, and that we ought to use that as one of the means of helping to correct the situation that exists there.

Mr. O'Hara: That is, we have a moral obligation to see that the American does not have certain advantages in the way of tax and loans and all of that sort for doing business under this immoral form of government.

*   *   *

Mr. Robinson: Mr. Chairman, if I might add a specific objection on this question of loans. Something was handed to me here just a moment ago. This of course is looking back to 1961, but we had a situation in 1961, after the massacre in Sharpeville became a worldwide problem, the consciousness of the world to this event was sharpened by the events in Sharpsville in 1961, and there was a drying up immediately after that of foreign investment and the South African economy was in trouble. There was at that point in time $100 million raised by the World Bank, by the Export-Import Bank in Washington and by direct loans from U.S. banks, the three in combination created loans totaling $100 million to bail out the difficulties that the South African economy had gotten in as a result of this incident in Sharpsville that got worldwide attention. So that this, of course, is reaching back to an event of the past, but it is this type of assistance that the record makes clear we have been involved in, that we ought to avoid in the future.

Mr. O'Hara: Well, I would like to make it plain that this is a problem that the members of this subcommittee have recognized, and the purpose of these hearings is to get the judgment and the counsel of Americans in labor, in business, in every line, and I do hope and I expect that before these hearings are closed we will have representatives of American business and American finance doing business in South Africa appear before this subcommittee. I think they should come. I think they should present their case and their reasons and their thinking.

Now, I am not making any threats. I have quarreled with congressional committees who use threats and practice exposure in the name of legitimate legislative inquiry. But I do hope that before we are through with these hearings we will have the full cooperation of American business and American finance.

*   *   *

Statement by George M. Houser, Executive Director of American Committee on Africa Before the Subcommittee on Africa of the House Committee on Foreign Affairs*

March 10, 1966

*   *   *

Let me at the outset express my dismay about American policy toward South Africa. At best, one can characterize it as being a policy of reluctant concern. The

Ibid., pp. 190-91; 194-201.

United States has reluctantly been pushed by the African countries to state an increasing concern about the injustices in South Africa. But the United States has dragged its heels at almost every point.

The U.S. policy lags as far today behind the demand for action by the African people as it did a decade ago, although the whole debate is now on a higher scale. Whereas a decade ago the United States was abstaining on resolutions in the U.N. asking for South Africa to reconsider its apartheid policy and to observe the U.N. Charter, now the United States will condemn apartheid but will abstain or vote negatively on any form of economic sanctions.

I have read carefully the testimony of Gov. G. Mennen Williams and Mr. Alexander Trowbridge. They fall well within the policy of "reluctant concern." They point to some of the positive actions the United States has taken, such as the arms ban; disapproval of American performers appearing before segregated audiences—and here parenthetically I state that I hope someone from the Government expressed strong disapproval of Jack Nicklaus' recent golf exhibition matches with Gary Player before segregated galleries; if so, nothing was made public—canceling operational calls at South African ports by U.S. naval ships and aircraft. This is fine as far as it goes, but it doesn't begin to meet the crisis.

The United States has a divided mind in its policy toward South Africa. On the one hand, eloquent condemnatory statements are made about apartheid. In the last U.N. General Assembly debate, you, Mr. Chairman, very capably presented U.S. policy in one discussion when you said:

> The policy of apartheid, "racist in its origin and arrogant in its implementation," is a violation of the charter and the declaration of human rights, and contains all the elements of a racial conflict which could seriously trouble peaceful progress on the African Continent and throughout the world.

And Governor Williams, in his testimony before this subcommittee, said:

> Time and again, in recent years. attempts to shine the light of free discussion on at least the dark places of apartheid excesses and absurdities have been shut off by the police power or the behind-the-scenes pressure of Afrikaans organization.

Or again:

> While accommodation of conflicting aspirations and interests is vital, the forces within South Africa making for such accommodations are being repressed.

But on the other hand, it is pointed out that South African ports are "highly useful" to the U.S. Navy, that the tracking station facilities are "important," that American business provides a "useful channel of communication with influential South African private and official circles," that disinvestment "might harden South African policies," that in any event American disinvestment would have no effect on the South African economy.

Time and again our general policy statements are contradicted by our actions. This looks like hypocrisy to much of the world.

It is not true to maintain that the United States can't do anything about apartheid. Rather, the will to do something effective is absent. The United States is the most powerful country in the world economically and militarily. It sounds ridiculous to most of the world for the United States to say, "we can't do anything effective." This just isn't believed. Certainly it isn't believed by Africans who see such vigorous commitment in the Dominican Republic or in Vietnam.

*   *   *

My specific recommendations are based on the position that the United States should begin the process of disengagement with South Africa. Both morally and strategically, disengagement represents a sound policy for the United States. Dr. Henry Pitney Van Dusen, former president of Union Theological Seminary, put the issue well in its moral dimension in a letter to the New York Times, when he said:

> Every American who is a stockholder or depositor in commercial firms doing business in South Africa is indirectly a participant in the cruel repression of the majority of the South African populace, in the aggravation of violence, bloodshed, and brutality which daily increases, and it may well be, in the ultimate loss of American financial investment.

*   *   *

First, the United States should disengage itself from the South African economy.

Disengagement should begin where there is greatest involvement: in the economic sphere, which is significant, as Mr. Trowbridge pointed out in this testimony. U.S. investments, according to his figures, amount to at least $600 million. We think his estimate conservative—2 years ago South Africa claimed more than $800 million from the dollar zone. We shall nonetheless stick by the Department of Commerce figures for the sake of argument. Six-hundred million dollars is 11 percent of all foreign investment in South Africa. Some 240 American firms are represented by these holdings. The average rate of profit, according to 1963 Department of Commerce figures, was 17.1 percent, a sum exceeded only by gains from investment in West Germany. U.S. exports to South Africa last year approached half a billion ($438 million) and imports were $225 million. Thus there was a favorable balance amounting to more than $200 million.

This involvement indicates both that adopting a policy of discouraging trade and investment may find resistance, and that such a course would have significant effects.

Our reasons for recommending this policy of disengagement are as follows:

(a) Our present trade and investment helps the South African economy and encourages the architects of apartheid. As Dr. Van Dusen has pointed out in his letter quoted earlier, South African business says, "So long as U.S. banks and business back us, we can go ahead." Mr. Trowbridge, in his testimony, belittles the contribution of American trade and investment, and the effect it would have on the South African economy if it were ended. It should be noted that in 1964, South Africa exported 18 percent of her goods to the United States. Between 17 and 19 percent of South African imports in recent years were from the United States. This is second only to Britain in South Africa's total volume of trade. Furthermore, the South African imports from the United States were in economically strategic commodities. For example, one notes almost $12 million in petroleum and petroleum products in the first 11 months of 1965, over $15 million in chemical elements and compounds (one wonders if any of this can be used for explosives); almost $125 million in non-electric machinery and over $83 million in transport equipment—again, one can ask can any of this possibly be converted for military use?

Mr. Trowbridge points out quite rightly that the bulk of capital formation in South Africa is derived from domestic savings. Between 1955 and 1963 the net outflow of new capital that went to South Africa was only $9 million. The rest was from reinvestment. The $9 million outflow shows how profitable apartheid is—so profitable that little new outside capital apparently has to be found. But C. D. Richards, professor of economics at the University of Witwatersrand, stated at a 1961 Conference of the International Economic Association that—

> it has been on the basis of oversea risk capital investment that domestic investment has been induced and stimulated, and national income and standards of living greatly increased.

He made this statement while showing that domestic savings were, even at that time, "accounting for 90 percent of total requirements."

American companies are heavily involved in major industries in South Africa. The U.S. oil companies have almost 50 percent of South African refining capacity; U.S. motor companies produce about 60 percent of all vehicles; American rubber companies dominate rubber production, with Dunlop, a British company, being a major non-American firm. An American citizen controls 15 percent of South African gold and 20 percent of South African uranium production. As a prominent member of the Transvaal and Orange Free State Chamber of Mines, he is to some extent responsible for the recruiting system and wage structure for African mine labor.

We are not claiming that a withdrawal of American capital alone would destroy the South African economy. We are saying that American trade and investment are and have been of great value to South Africa's economic development.

(b) Our present trade and investment in South Africa discourages the opponents of apartheid. To the extent that American capital is of assistance to those who maintain the racist system, it is looked upon an inimical to the cause of those who struggle to bring the system down. Conversely, opponents of apartheid would be heartened by a policy of disengagement.

(c) Our present trade and investment in South Africa involves American business in basic compromises with democratic standards. The South African economy is based on cheap nonwhite labor. Unskilled workers (nonwhites) receive only 20 to 30 percent of skilled pay rate as compared to 60 to 80 percent in most industrial economies of the West. Nonwhite labor is kept both cheap and unskilled by a complex system of legislation including job reservation, limitation on apprenticeship training for nonwhites, the almost total lack of pension and unemployment plans for nonwhites, no collective bargaining for nonwhites. These are conditions business accepts.

In his statement, Mr. Trowbridge defended American business involvement in apartheid by saying that—

> the maintenance of a significant business community in South Africa may provide a useful channel of communication with influential South African private and official circles.

We ask for proof. When has such a significant dialog taken place? How did it affect nonwhites for the better? Year by year we see U.S. involvement becoming more obvious and year by year we see increases in political and social repressions. What a curious dialog must be taken place.

It is easy to find quotes from the lips of American businessmen on the confidence they have in South Africa. It is difficult to find critical statements. For example, Mr. Milton P. Higgins, chairman of the Norton Co. of Worchester, Mass., said on the occasion of opening a new abrasives factory near Johannesburg in January 1965:

> I think South Africa is going to remain a strong country, led by white people. I think foreign countries should leave South Africa alone. If they leave you alone you will get on and do a great job.

Mr. J. H. Fulford, president of the Jeffrey Co., of Ohio, said, when opening a new factory in Germiston in February 1965:

> We have complete faith in the soundness of the South African economy, full confidence in the stability of your country, and know that the substantial investment we have made in the past and the further investment we are presently making are all in good care.

Gen. Lauris Norstad, retired NATO supreme commander, now president of Owens-Corning Fiberglass Corp., recently in South Africa to negotiate new investments announced:

> We have full confidence in South Africa—not only we as individuals but the United States and the American people as well.

      *   *   *

Remarks such as these reinforce the basic convictions of opponents of apartheid that the United States is a willing partner in racism. All the USIS libraries in Africa will not blot out this shame.

      *   *   *

It seems a curious fact that businessmen have been so reluctant to appear before this subcommittee. Is it because they think they will be asked embarrassing questions about business under apartheid, or that by speaking critically of apartheid they will jeopardize their business opportunity in South Africa?

(d) Ending trade with and investment in South Africa would not essentially hurt the United States. Investments are only 1 percent of our total foreign investments. Our trade with South Africa amounts only to 2 percent of total foreign trade. Compared with the losses countries like India and Kenya suffered when they cut off trade with South Africa, the United States would hardly feel the change.

To implement a policy of disengagement we suggest the following:

First, as in the Rhodesian crisis, let the Government call leading businessmen involved in South African trade and investment together and ask compliance with a governmental policy of disengagement, emphasizing that continued trade with South Africa is contrary to the United States national interests. Some would comply, some would not; but at least a policy would be set.

Second, the bulk of United States exports to South Africa should be placed under the provisions of the Export Control Act. At the moment the principal control of trade with the Republic is the license system of the Munitions Board falling under the State Department. We recommend that trade with South Africa be placed, like that with Bulgaria for example, under a licensing system operated by the Department of Commerce in order to prevent the export of all goods and commodites which might be used in the defense of the regime.

Third, legislation should be passed making it illegal for U.S. firms abroad to practice racial discrimination.

Fourth, could a system be devised of taxing companies continuing to do business in South Africa, after these other efforts are made, perhaps by a special levy on dividends of the parent body in the United States, the proceeds to be used to aid victims of apartheid?

Fifth, financial disengagement with South Africa, to be successful, involves coordinating action with other countries. Therefore, we recommend that steps such as those above, be carried out with other countries, and that the U.N. be the forum for planning joint strategy.

Our whole first section then dealing with suggestions has to do with economic disengagement.

Our second proposal: The United States should eliminate altogether the quota for South African sugar.

It is shameful that this Congress and this administration could have, a few short months ago, agreed to increase subsidies to South African sugar producers. The annual quota was raised from 20,000 metric tons to 48,000 tons—and that was a compromise with the administration, which had recommended a quota of 96,000 tons.

No South African sugars were imported into the United States before 1962. But between 1966 and 1971. South Africa will be the 10th largest quota sugar exporter to America. I might note that a considerably larger movement of this commodity enters this country in the nonquota category.

Even more amazing is that, in order to meet our quotas, South Africa has occasionally imported sugar from the Dominican Republic and elsewhere.

Congress could not have been altogether unconscious of these startling developments. Senator Morse drew attention to them only last fall when he proposed lowering the South African quota to 10,000 tons. His amendment was defeated by a voice vote. The lobbyist to whom part of South Africa's success must be credited was John R. Mahoney from the law firm of Casey, Lane & Mittendorf in New York. In 1965, Mr. Mahoney received $19,320 from the South African Sugar Association. In 1964, the firm received a fee of $24,000.

May I remind this committee that one of the purposes of the Sugar Act was to—

permit nearbly friendly foreign countries to participate equitably in supplying the U.S. sugar market for the double purpose of expanding international trade and assuring a stable and adequate supply of sugar.

South Africa is not, by any stretch of the imagination, "nearby"; nor should it be considered "friendly," and we certainly hope that Congress will not be a party to "expanding international trade" with her.

We strongly feel that, to use the words of Public Law 89-331, 89th Congress, "... the continuation of a quota or a part thereof ... would be contrary to the national interest of the United States," and that the President consequently ought to withhold or suspend the South African sugar quota.

The third recommendation we have has to do with political asylum for South Africans against apartheid.

The United States is unique among Western nations in having provided no official legal status for those seeking political asylum.

* * *

Refugees from Eastern Europe and China, on the other hand, are favored, but only as immigrants—and not as a special category of refugees from political persecution. I note, however, that the Federal Government does make special funds available through the State Department, which then in turn contracts with agencies, to facilitate the smooth flow of such political refugees to these shores.

South Africans, however, do not benefit from such Federal generosity and concern. In the first place, they have no way of getting here, except perhaps as students or as temporary visitors. They must then play out a customary battle against immigration authorities involving: (1) an order for deportation; (2) an appeal to an immigration board or hearing officer based on the contention that, should the deportee be sent home, he will be subject to physical and mental persecution; and (3) a ruling by immigration authorities who follow the advice of the State Department. A person who goes through this procedure and is permitted to stay, then becomes subject to all sorts of discriminatory practices—he may not leave the country, he may not become a citizen, and so on. But the worst is that, no matter how often such cases are brought before immigration, no general policy is every established. Each deportee must prove anew he is in danger of life and limb if he were to return.

We have had experience in helping a number of political refugees already in this country from being deported. But we have never yet reached that final stage where the State Department admitted that apartheid is tyranny as far as black people go.

* * *

We would recommend that—

1. Basutoland and Swaziland, the United States should insist upon the freedom of access of nationals and visitors through or over South Africa and Mozambique to and from these countries.

2. For the three territories the U.S. Government should join with the United Kingdom in diplomatic initiatives to assure the sovereignty of the territories, and make it clear that any violation would be considered an unfriendly act.

3. Regarding Bechuanaland, the United States should cooperate with the United Kingdom in undertaking feasibility studies of the Okavango Swamp scheme and note the possibility of establishing communications between that high potential area and Zambia and South-West Africa.

Our fifth proposal, the United States should categorically demand the right to practice integration in its own South African facilities.

This means that on principle the United States cannot accept apartheid either in dealing with nonwhites in South Africa, or as regards American personnel serving in South Africa. In 1965 there was tension between the Governments of the United

States and South Africa on this point. Because of race restrictions, the aircraft carrier *Independence* did not stop at a South African port. The United States rejected the "whites only" demand of only white personnel manning the tracking stations in South Africa. The United States Ambassador was attacked for staging the annual July 4th interracial affair. But beyond verbal exchanges, nothing was essentially done.

We recommend that—

1. Every American-sponsored event be looked upon as integrated, in line with U.S. Government policy.

2. Qualified Negro personnel be assigned to some posts in South Africa.

3. American officials be directed to pay South African employees without discrimination. If nonwhites do not hold the same jobs as whites, they should be paid whatever a white man would earn for doing the same work.

Our sixth proposal, the United States should remove the tracking station from South Africa.

The tracking stations in South Africa are an embarrassment to the United States. Since they are strategically important to the United States, they certainly should be located in a country that is much less controversial than South Africa. Because of the strategic character of the tracking stations, information about them is not made public. Highly competent scientists from whom I have received information, say that they see no essential scientific reason that the tracking stations must be in South Africa. Therefore, disengagement through removal of the tracking stations should be undertaken without delay.

Our seventh point, the U.S. Atomic Energy Commission should cease cooperation with the South African Atomic Energy Board.

In mid-1965 South Africa inaugurated its first nuclear reactor of Pelindaba near Pretoria. At that time the following facts came out: (1) many South African staff members were trained at Oak Ridge; (2) Oak Ridge supplied a consultant for the Pelindaba reactor; (3) the director of Oak Ridge was an honored guest at the inaugural ceremonies; (4) the United States supplied the enriched uranium to start the reactor; and (5) nine American organizations were involved in the project, the major contractor being Allis-Chalmers.

Public announcements have assured all concerned that the South African reactor is not capable of producing fissionable material for use in nuclear weapons. But in such a highly secret field as this represents, suspicions are easily aroused. Why should the United States be so helpful to South Africa in such a sensitive project?

We recommend a congressional investigation about the extent of U.S. involvement in the Pelindaba project to gain assurances that fissionable material for weapons is indeed impossible.

Our eighth recommendation: The United States should lodge strong diplomatic protest each time South Africa refuses to grant visas to Americans on racial grounds or because of their views on integration.

Many Americans are refused visas to South Africa. It is most unusual for a Negro American to be permitted to enter South Africa. Any American who is a known participant in civil rights activities here, would probably be refused a visa to South Africa. Yet there seems to be no limitation on white South Africans with the most vicious racist views coming to the United States.

The South African Government even refuses transit visas to some Americans merely wishing to cross a section of South Africa to go to one of the former High Commission Territories such as Basutoland. This has even led to distinguished American scholars being prohibited from essential research, or from discharging responsibilities toward institutions in the territories.

Our ninth recommendation: The United States should contribute generously to the newly established United Nations Trust Fund for South Africa.

This fund was set up by action of the General Assembly in its 20th session. The purpose is to provide a channel through which governments can contribute for—

(a) Legal defense to prisoners charged under repressive legislation in South Africa;

(b) Relief of dependents of persons persecuted by the South African Government for opposition to apartheid;

(c) Education of prisoners and their children;

(d) Relief for South African refugees.

There are between 5,000 and 10,000 political prisoners in South Africa at present—the number fluctuates. It is estimated there are at least 2,000 dependents of prisoners. The need for legal defense and aid to dependents is estimated at between $600,000 and $700,000 in 1966. This is based on a food allowance of less than $9 a month per family, educational needs of children, and of prisoners, plus legal defense.

Last year, on the basis of a U.N. resolution asking for voluntary contributions to private funds, 12 countries gave about $300,000. This must be increased through the U.N. Trust Fund.

Our final and 10th recommendation: The United States should plan speedy implementation of the International Court decision on South-West Africa.

*   *   *

*Statement by Assistant Secretary Williams on the United States
Policy Toward South Africa**

March 1, 1966

*   *   *

The broad aims of U.S. policy toward South Africa are essentially political. We support freedom, equality, and justice for the people of South Africa for the same reasons we support them elsewhere, both at home and abroad. We support them because they are the keystones of our heritage. We support them because we believe that at home they safeguard and enhance our enjoyment of life, liberty, and the pursuit of happiness and that abroad in doing the same thing they strengthen the basis for a just and lasting peace.

These basic freedoms are of course fundamental to our role of leadership as a nonracialist nation in a multiracial world. We support renewed efforts to initiate in South Africa a peaceful, evolutionary process toward these goals. Despite the

*Department of State Bulletin, Mar. 21, 1966, pp. 433-38.

frustrations we must persist in the search for a peaceful solution. A resort to violence would be enormously costly, not only to the peoples of South Africa but also to the peoples of Africa generally. It would also be costly to us and to the free world and would undoubtedly be exploited by forces hostile to us.

These political aims are paramount. In scientific, economic, and strategic respects our bilateral relationships with South Africa are useful to us—even in some fields important—but they are not essential to our national security.

Before discussing the specific policies implementing our broad aims, a review of our specific interests may be helpful. Many of these interests, while not decisive in determining our policy, are important. They are and should be taken into account in formulating our policy, though they do not, as is sometimes alleged, dominate it. Our basic policies regarding South Africa stem from broad principles much more than from immediate specific interests largely because in southern Africa the clash of basic principles and values threatens our long-range interests in much of the world.

U.S. Facilities in South Africa

The position of southern Africa athwart the sea route around the Cape of Good Hope makes its ports highly useful logistically to the U.S. Navy, particularly in support of Atlantic Fleet ships en route to and from Viet-Nam waters. If the Mediterranean route were closed [as it was less than a year later] the importance of the Cape route would be enhanced.

Space-tracking facilities in South Africa have been, and continue to be, important, particularly for the lunar and other deep-space programs. Sudden removal of these facilities would adversely affect the progress of these programs. However, these considerations cannot override the greater imperatives of the larger principles to which we are committed.

Economic Interests

Other specific interests are economic.

Direct U.S. investment in South Africa was valued at $467 million at the end of 1964. We have no figures for portfolio investment, but according to our best estimates it would bring total U.S. investment in South Africa up to about $650 million. American direct investment in South Africa is about 28 percent of our total direct investment in Africa, and the 72 percent outside South Africa is growing more rapidly. Our investment in South Africa is only about 1 percent of our total foreign investment.

U.S. trade with South Africa has a favorable balance amounting in 1965 to about $213 million. Our exports, largely machinery, vehicles, and industrial goods, amounted to $392 million in 1964 and our imports, largely minerals, to $250 million. This was a considerable increase over previous years. In 1963 the trade balance was favorable by $19 million, in 1962 unfavorable by $34 million. Our trade with South Africa is about 1½ percent of our foreign trade.

Minerals

South Africa is an important source of strategic minerals, including industrial diamonds, chemical chrome, several types of asbestos, platinum, and gold. The U.S. has been buying uranium oxide under an agreement of 1950. The contract expires at the end of 1966 and is not expected to be renewed, as U.S. sources are adequate for our needs. South Africa's importance as a source of industrial diamonds has greatly diminished because of the availability of industrial diamonds elsewhere in Africa. Furthermore, the U.S. manufactures synthetic industrials. Other minerals, including chemical chrome, asbestos, and platinum, have been stockpiled or are available from other sources, including substitutes.

These specific interests must be viewed against the broad aims of U.S. policy. We have expressed our policy aims with respect to South Africa repeatedly both in the U.N. and bilaterally. Time and again we have pointed out the dangers we see in the policy of apartheid and have urged a change in approach more consistent with U.N. principles and present day realities.

U.S. Policy of Persuasion

The U.S. Government over the years has sought to dissuade South African officials at all levels from discriminatory and repressive laws and from employing various oppressive measures. We have, through diplomatic channels, warned against the extension of apartheid practices to the international territory of South-West Africa. The U.S. Government has expressed its critical views to South Africans on the basis of a large accumulation of firsthand evidence. American officials have devoted much time and effort to the study of apartheid in its many aspects. Despite the many frustrations we have encountered in our efforts to persuade South African leaders to change their policies, the increasingly manifest contradictions and unrealities of apartheid give at least some grounds for hope that the situation in South Africa has not rigidified irreparably.

U.S. Nonracial Policies in South Africa

Along with our policy of persuasion, we have followed a policy of continuing certain forms of cooperation with South Africa and keeping open the lines of communication. Pursuing these policies simultaneously has faced us with some difficult dilemmas. Our representatives in South Africa are exposed to strong pressures from the South African Government and its supporters to conform with apartheid practices. Wherever it is legally possible to do so, our representatives resist these pressures.

Our Embassy and consulates hold nonracial receptions and individual officers entertain nonracially. Our diplomatic and consular posts hire local employees on a nondiscriminatory basis. The U.S. Government makes clear that it disapproves of the appearance of Americans, whether as amateurs or professionals, before segregated audiences in South Africa. It will not sponsor visits to South Africa of performers who would appear before such audiences. As a result this aspect of our exchange program is virtually suspended. More importantly, we have canceled operational port calls in South Africa of U.S. naval vessels and aircraft rather than accept the application of racial conditions to our personnel.

U.S. Policy in the U.N.

In the U.N. the United States strongly supports the application to South Africa and to the mandated territory of South-West Africa of the basic principles of the U.N.

Charter's affirmation of respect for human rights, the dignity and worth of the individual, and the equal rights of men and women. We support the aim of promoting respect for international law. We have supported a number of resolutions against apartheid in the U.N. General Assembly.

The shooting of many unarmed men, women, and children at Sharpeville in March 1960 marked a watershed in U.N. treatment of apartheid. For the first time the Security Council considered a South African issue. The United States then supported a resolution deploring apartheid and the loss of life at Sharpeville and calling for abandonment of repressive policies. We have supported several similar Council resolutions since then condemning repression and injustice in South Africa.

Arms Ban

As concrete evidence of our abhorrence of apartheid and our determination not to contribute to its enforcement, we do not sell to South Africa any arms, ammunition, military equipment, or materials for their manufcture and maintenance. Our first step in this direction was when we placed a bad on arms that could be used in enforcing apartheid within South Africa. As international opposition to apartheid increased in tempo, along with repression in South Africa, the growth of violence, and the flight of refugees, we took a further step in August 1963. We extended our arms ban against South Africa to all arms, ammunition, and military equipment, except those under existing contracts and those which might be required in the interests of world peace.

Ambassador Stevenson, in announcing the arms ban, said that

> . . . the United States as a nation with many responsibilities in many parts of the world naturally reserves the right in the future to interpret this policy in the light of requirements for assuring the maintenance of international peace and security. If the interests of the world community require the provision of equipment for use in the common defense effort, we would naturally feel able to do so without violating the spirit and the intent of this resolve.

We adopted this comprehensive ban prior to the adoption of a U.N. Security Council resolution calling on all U.N. members to apply such a ban. We supported the resolution and have strictly observed the ban. In the Security Council the late Ambassador Stevenson explained this policy as intended to contribute to a peaceful solution and to avoid actions adding directly to international friction in the area. In December 1963, in support of another resolution of the Security Council, our ban was extended to equipment and materials for the manufacture and maintenance of arms and ammunition in South Africa.

Aside from the arms embargo, the U.S. Government does not interfere with trade and investment in South Africa. This is in keeping with our traditional policy of keeping world trade and other economic relations as free as possible from Government interference. An exception is where the national security is directly affected, as in the cases of Communist China and Cuba.

The U.S. Government neither encourages nor discourages investment in South Africa. Potential investors who seek our advice are briefed on the political and racial situation, the outlook, and American policy and interests. The decision about whether to invest remains with the individual or company.

The U.S. Government of course encourages both new and old companies to maintain high standards in the treatment of personnel employed in South Africa. We believe American companies abroad should lead in such respects as fair wages, nondiscrimination, pension systems, and the like. While American companies operating in South Africa are, of course, obligated to abide by South African laws, we are encouraged by their generally progressive record.

Opposition to Economic Sanctions

Despite strong pressures in the U.N. and from various American organizations concerned about civil and human rights in South Africa, we have not been prepared to support U.N. economic sanctions against South Africa. Several problems are involved. These are:
1. the problem of a legal basis for such actions;
2. the problem of economic effectiveness; and
3. the problem of psychological effectiveness.

With regard to the legal problem, the U.S. Government believes that the conditions envisaged in chapter VII of the U.N. Charter for the imposition of compulsory sanctions, i.e., the existence of a threat to international peace or an act of aggression, do not apply to South Africa at this time.

Much thought has been given in this Government and in the U.N. to the problem of the economic effectiveness of sanctions. In the summer of 1964 the U.N. Security Council established a committee of experts to study the feasibility, effectiveness, and implications of sanctions, or as it described them, measures which might be taken against South Africa within the framework of the U.N. Charter. The committee was requested to make a technical and practical study of sanctions without reference to the circumstances in which their application might be considered. The United States participated actively in the work of the committee. Its report was submitted to the Security Council in February 1965. It emphasized the view that, although South Africa would not be readily susceptible to economic measures, South Africa is not immune to impact from such measures. It concluded that the degree of effectiveness of economic measures would directly depend on the universality of their application and on the manner and the duration of their enforcement. Should a situation arise in which the U.N. appropriately might consider resort to sanctions, the United States believes the availability of this detailed, practical study will be helpful.

Cessation of investment is most often urged as a first step in applying graduated economic pressures. Could the United States exert effective pressure on South Africa by withholding investment? A generation ago the South African economy depended to a very large extent on foreign investment. Now foreign investment plays a much smaller role in the economy. The United States provides only a small proportion either of total investment in South Africa or of foreign investment there. Our investment in South Africa is only 14 percent of all foreign investment there. From 1950 to 1963 U.S. direct investment in South Africa by companies amounted to only 2.3 percent of the total net domestic capital formation there. If one includes portfolio investment, the percentage is still only 3.5.

South Africa is one of the countries which is subject to all aspects of the United States program to improve its balance of payments. This means that all types of U.S. private capital flows to South Africa are subject either to the interest equalization tax or to the President's program of voluntary restraints on private corporate investment and bank lending abroad. It is probable that new U.S. investment in South Africa will be reduced as a result. Even before this program was begun American companies had been financing their investments largely by profits made in South Africa, advances from South African banks, and the issuance of stock both in South Africa and Europe. From 1955 to 1963 the net outflow to South Africa of new American capital amounted to only $9 million. American investment in South Africa is minor—compared with that of the United Kingdom, about one-fourth. The United States, alone, would have little leverage. Since U.S. investment is not essential to South Africa, the argument for such action is largely psychological, i.e., that it would jar South African whites into a better appreciation of the worldwide opposition to their policies.

Discouraging or prohibiting U.S. investment in South Africa would, of course, improve our relations with much of the world. It is also undoubtedly true that the stopping of American investment would have a considerable impact on South Africans. Even though the economy were not shaken, the confidence of those relying on apartheid as a permanent pattern for South Africa's economy and society would be undermined. The cessation of investment would be seen as one of a long series of developments tending to isolate South Africa. Many who profit from apartheid would be induced to reflect on its long-term disadvantages more seriously than they do now.

Whether increased doubt about the advantages of apartheid would affect South African policies beneficially is questionable. It might harden South African policies even further and undoubtedly would impel South Africa to turn to other sources of investment and to accelerate its already considerable efforts to achieve economic self-sufficiency.

While cessation of investment might increase our credibility and influence with African countries in our efforts to encourage a nonviolent solution, it could seriously handicap our ability to carry on a dialog with South Africa. It could cause some damage to our own economic, scientific, and strategic interests.

The United States, at both public and private levels, has a wide variety of cultural and scientific contacts with South Africa. Such contacts are intended to promote mutually beneficial relations in these fields. We hope they may also have the effect of combating the tendency of South Africa to drift off into sterile isolation.

Both public and private U.S. educational and exchange programs, though small, include all cultural groups as well as supporters of the Government and Opposition. A special effort is made, particularly in Government programs, to reach nonwhites, in view of their greater need and the many obstacles encountered. The South African Government's reluctance to give travel documents to nonwhites is one such obstacle, but we do not believe the effort should be abandoned. Particular aims of these programs include familiarizing South Africans with how the United States is dealing with its own problems, including civil rights, and providing leaders and especially young potential leaders with opportunities for training and observation in the United States. Of the approximately 400 South (and South-West) African students in U.S. institutions of higher learning, 137 are supported by U.S. Government funds. Of this number 122 are nonwhite. The U.S. Government has specific programs in Africa and the United States to help refugees from South Africa and South-West Africa obtain training and education. We have also contributed to U.N. programs for the education of South-West Africans and South Africans.

*   *   *

Speech by Senator Robert. F. Kennedy (New York) at the
University of Capetown in South Africa*

June 6, 1966

We stand here in the name of freedom.

At the heart of that Western freedom and democracy is the belief that the individual man, the child of God, is the touchstone of value, and all society, groups, the state, exist for his benefit. Therefore the enlargement of liberty for individual human beings must be the supreme goal and the abiding practice of any Western society.

The first element of this individual liberty is the freedom of speech.

The right to express and communicate ideas, to set oneself apart from the dumb beasts of field and forest; to recall governments to their duties and obligations; above all, the right to affirm one's membership and allegiance to the body politics—to society—to the men with who we share our land, our heritage and our children's future.

Hand in hand with freedom of speech goes the power to be heard—to share in the decisions of government which shape men's lives. Everything that makes life worthwhile—family, work, education, a place to rear one's children and a place to rest one's head—all this rests on decisions of government; all can be swept away by a government which does not heed the demands of its people. Therefore, the essential humanity of men can be protected and preserved only where government must answer—not just to those of a particular religion, or a particular race; but to all its people.

And even Government by the consent of the governed, as in our own Constitution, must be limited in its power to act against its people; so that there may be no interference with the right to worship, or with the security of the home; no arbitrary imposition of pains or penalties by officials high or low; no restriction on the freedom of men to seek education or work or opportunity of any kind, so that each man may become all he is capable of becoming.

These are the sacred rights of Western society. These are the essential differences between us and Nazi Germany as they were between Athens and Persia.

They are the essence of our difference with Communist today. I am inalterably opposed to Communism because it exalts the state over the individual and the family, and because of the lack of freedom of speech, of protest, of religion and of the press, which is characteristic of totalitarian states.

The way of opposition to Communism is not to imitate its dictatorship, but to enlarge individual human freedom—in our own countries and all over the globe. There are those in every land who would label as "Communist" every threat to their privilege. But as I have seen on my travels in all sections of the world, reform is not Communism. And the denial of freedom, in whatever name, only strengthens the very Communism it claims to oppose.

For two centuries, my own country has struggled to overcome the self-imposed handicap of prejudice and discrimination based on nationality, social class or race—

*The New York Times, June 7, 1966.

discrimination profoundly repugnant to the theory and command of our Constitution. Even as my father grew up in Boston, signs told him that "No Irish need apply."

Two generations later President Kennedy became the first Catholic to head the nation; but how many men of ability had, before 1961, been denied the opportunity to contribute to the nation's progress, because they were Catholics, or of Irish extraction.

In the last five years, the winds of change have blown as fiercely in the United States as anywhere in the world. But they will not—they cannot—abate.

For there are millions of Negroes untrained for the simplest of jobs, and thousands every day denied their full equal rights under the law; and the violence of disinherited, insulted and injured, looms over the streets of Harlem and Watts and Southside Chicago.

But a Negro American trains as an astronaut, one of mankind's first explorers into outer space; another is the chief barrister of the United States Government, and dozens sit on the benches of court; and another, Dr. Martin Luther King, is the second man of African descent to win the Nobel Peace Prize for his nonviolent efforts for social justice between the races.

We must recognize the full human equality of all our people—before God, before the law, and in the councils of government. We must do this, not because it is economically advantageous—although it is; not because the laws of God and man command it—although they do command it; not because people in other lands wish it so. We must do it for the single and fundamental reason that it is the right thing to do.

And this must be our commitment outside our borders as it is within.

It is your job, the task of the young people of this world, to strip the last remnants of that ancient, cruel belief from the civilization of man.

Each nation has different obstacles and different goals, shaped by the vagaries of history and experience. Yet as I talk to young people around the world I am impressed not by diversity but by the closeness of their goals, their desires and concerns and hope for the future. There is discrimination in New York, apartheid in South Africa and serfdom in the mountains of Peru. People starve in the streets in India; intellectuals go to jail in Russia; thousands are slaughtered in Indonesia, wealth is lavished on armaments everywhere. These are differing evils; but they are the common works of man.

And therefore they call upon common qualities of conscience and of indignation, a shared determination to wipe away the unnecessary sufferings of our fellow human beings at home and particularly around the world.

It is these qualities which make of youth today the only true international community. More than this I think that we could agree on what kind of a world we want to build. It would be a world of independent nations, moving toward international community, each of which protected and respected basic human freedoms. It would be a world which demanded of each government that is accept its responsibility to insure social justice.

Just to the north here are lands of challenge and opportunity—rich in natural resources, land and minerals and people. Yet they are also lands confronted by the greatest odds—overwhelming ignorance, internal tensions and strife, and an often destructive and hostile nature. Many of these nations, as colonies, were oppressed and exploited. Yet they have not estranged themselves from the broad traditions of the

West; they are hoping and gambling their progress and stability on the chance that we will meet our responsibilities to help them overcome their poverty.

In another world, cleansed of hate and fear and artificial barriers, South Africa could play an outstanding role in that effort. This is without question a pre-eminent repository of the wealth and knowledge and skill of the continent. Here are the greater parts of Africa's research scientists and steel production, most of its reservoirs of coal and electric power. In your faculties and councils, here in this very aduience, are hundreds and thousands of men who could transform the lives of millions for all time to come.

But that help cannot be accepted if we—within our own countries or in our relations with others—deny individual integrity and the common humanity of man.

Our answer is the world's hope; it is to rely on youth. The cruelties and obstacles of this swiftly changing planet will not yield to obsolete dogmas and outworn slogans. It cannot be moved by those who cling to a present which is already dying, who prefer the illusion of security to the excitement of danger.

It demands the qualities of youth: not a time of life but a state of mind, a temper of the will, a quality of the imagination, a predominance of courage over timidity, of the appetite for adventure over the love of ease.

As I have seen, and as I have said—in Europe, in Asia, in Latin America, and now in South Africa—it is a revolutionary world we live in; and thus, I have said in Latin American, in Asia, in Europe and in the United States, it is young people who must take the lead.

"There is," said an Italian philosopher, "nothing more difficult to take in hand, more perilous to conduct, or more uncertain in its success than to take the lead in the introduction of a new order of things." Yet this is the measure of the task of your generation and the road is strewn with many dangers.

First, is the danger of futility: the belief there is nothing one man or one woman cna do against the enormous array of the world's ills—against misery and ignorance, injustice and violence. Yet many of the world's great movements of thought and action have flowed from the world of a single man. A young monk began the Protestant Reformation, a young general extended an empire from Macedonia to the borders of the earth, and a young woman reclaimed the territory of France.

Each time a man stands up for an ideal, or acts to improve the lot of others, or strikes out against injustice, he sends forth a tiny ripple of hope, and crossing each other from a million different centers of energy and daring, those ripples build a current that can sweep down the mightiest walls of oppression and resistance.

The second danger is that of practicality; of those who say that hopes and beliefs must bend before immediate necessities. Of course if we would act effectively we must deal with the world as it is. We must get things done.

But if there was one thing President Kennedy stood for that touched the most profound feeling of young people across the world, it was the belief that idealism, high aspirations and deep convictions are not incompatible with the most practical and efficient of programs—that there is no basic inconsistency between ideals and realistic possibilities—no separation between the deepest desires of heart and mind and the rational application of human effort to human problems.

A third danger is timidity. For every 10 men who are willing to face the guns of an enemy there is only one willing to brave the disapproval of his fellow, the censure of his colleagues, the wrath of his society. Moral courage is a rarer commodity than bravery in battle or greater intelligence. Yet it is the one essential, vital quality for those who seek to change a world which yields most painfully to change.

For the fortunate among us is comfort; the temptation to follow the easy and familiar paths of personal ambition and financial success so grandly spread before those who have the privilege of education. But that is not the road history has marked out for us. There is a Chinese curse which says, "May he live in interesting times." Like it or not, we live in interesting times. They are times of danger and uncertainty; but they are also more open to the creative energy of men than any other time in history. And everyone here will ultimately be judged—will ultimately judge himself—on the effort he has contributed to building a new world society and the extent to which his ideals and goals have shaped that effort.

So we part, I to my country and you to remain. We are—if a man of 40 can claim that privilege—fellow members of the world's largest younger generation. Each of us have our own work to do. I know at times you must feel very alone with your problems and difficulties. But I want to say how impressed I am with what you stand for and the effort you are making.

Like the young people of my own country and of every country I have visited, you are in many ways more closely united to these brothers of your time than to the older generations in your nation; determined to build a better future; that you know, as President Kennedy said to the youth of my country, that "the energy, the faith, the devotion which we bring to this endeavor will light our country and all who serve it—and the glow from that fire can truly light the world."

Statement by Ambassador Goldberg on United States Implementation of U.N. Embargo on Arms to South Africa*

December 16, 1967

*   *   *

Mr. Chairman, I would not wish to conclude my statement tonight without referring to the extreme and ridiculous allegations which we have heard in the past several days with regard to the implementation by the United States of the United Nations embargo of the supply of arms and military equipment to South Africa. My country has adhered scrupulously to the terms of this embargo. Despite this unequivocal position on the implementation of the Security Council's resolution on the shipment of arms and military materiel, the United States has been cited by two delegations during this debate for alleged violations in this field. I would like to cite these allegations and insinuations briefly and refute them categorically.

The distinguished delegate of the Soviet Union stated that the United States and certain other countries "continue to deliver bombers to the South African racists, as well as their missiles and various types of small arms." It is significant that the Soviet delegation did not provide any details on this sweeping allegation, either in the statement from which I have quoted or in its earlier statement on South West Africa.

*Department of State Bulletin, Jan. 15, 1968, p. 94.

On earlier occasions when similar statements have been made, we have directly challenged the Soviet delegate to furnish details, details which the Soviet delegation has been unable to provide. These charges were fabricated out of thin air. It is impossible to provide details because they do not exist.

Faced with this fact, other delegations have resorted to inference and insinuation rather than direct statements such as the one I have quoted. The distinguished delegate of Hungary, speaking at the 1624th meeting on December 11, 1967, said that "according to press reports in March 1967, the South African Army and Air Force were interested in an American executive aircraft." Mr. President, I cannot confirm or deny exactly what possible purchases interests South African military authorities, but I can deny categorically the suggestion, which the distinguished delegate of Hungary obviously sought to get across, that the United States is furnishing such aircraft.

*   *   *

Now, Mr. President, while the United States and other countries continue to strictly enforce an embargo on the sale of arms and military equipment to South Africa, that country does continue to receive large quantities of modern and sophisticated weapons. The real sources of these weapons are seldom mentioned. Those who criticize the United States, which scrupulously enforces the embargo, might better direct themselves to those countries which do not do so and to ways by which the embargo might be made more effective.

*   *   *

Speech by Senator James Eastland (Mississippi) before the Senate on Communist Boldness in the Far East*

February 28, 1968

*   *   *

There is one strong and stable pro-western nation which has been our ally in three wars and which occupies a very strategic position on the sea routes of the world.

The Republic of South Africa, commanding the cape route like a friendly lighthouse and representing a major influence throughout the Indian Ocean must not be forgotten.

*   *   *

In the light of these evaluations of the strategic value of South Africa to the free world it is somehow difficult tl understand why this country refuses to sell any military equipment to South Africa.

Some of the liberals in our country have decried the sale of arms to South Africa on the basis of South Africa's racial policies. These same poeple were all in favor of selling arms to Tito.

*The *Congressional Record*, Feb. 28, 1968, pp. 1811-13.

But, even giving the liberal do-gooders their say, I cannot see how submarines, destroyers, and long range antisubmarine aircraft could possibly be used in any way to enforce racial policies.

Mr. President, we are denying South Africa weapons with which she is willing to use to help support our struggle against Communist aggression.

The policy of the United States regarding the sale of military equipment to South Africa is made almost ridiculous by the fact that on November 16, 1967, it was announced that the U.S. Army had placed orders for $1,250,000 worth of special military equipment from South Africa.

The U.S. Army can purchase the South African tellurometer, a device which measures ranges by microwave, bu the South African Army cannot purchase nine Cessna aircraft for coastal patrol.

A year ago the U.S. aircraft carrier *Roosevelt* visited Capetown for refueling, at a saving to the American taxpayer of more than $250,000. We would not allow the crew to go ashore in Capetown because of our supposed concern over South African racial policies and since then we have prohibited our ships from refueling in South African ports.

This prohibition has already cost the taxpayers of our country more than $2.5 million. In addition, we must send tankers and sailors to the Far East to refuel our fighting ships and to make repairs at sea.

Recently one of our carriers visited Japan and strong demonstrations were held to protest her arrival. No such protests were encountered at Capetown.

Mr. President, The United States has for some years had satellite and missile tracking stations in South Africa in the operation of which the fullest support is obtained of the South African Government.

On renewing arrangements for tracking and telemetry installations on June 15, 1962, the U.S. Ambassador was authorized to state, inter alia, that—

> The United States Govermment can assure the South African Government that it will give prompt and sympathetic attention to reasonable requests for the purchase of military equipment required for defense against external aggression.

Four months later on October 19, 1962, the U.S. representative at the United Nations declared that the United States had adopted and was enforcing the policy of forbidding the sale to the South African Government of arms and military equipment which could be used to enforce apartheid.

In August, 1963, the question of arms for South Africa was raised in the Security Council. Mr. Adlai Stevenson declared:

> We expect to bring to an end the sale of all military equipment to the Government of South Africa by the end of this calendar year in order further to contribute to a peaceful solution and to avoid any friction which might at this point directly contribute to international friction in the area. . . .

He added:

> The Council may be aware that in announcing this policy, the United States as a nation with many responsibilities in many parts of the world, naturally reserves the right in the future to interpret this policy in the light of requirements for assuring the maintenance of

international peace and security. If the interests of the world community require the provision of equipment for use in the common defense efforts, we would naturally feel able to do so without violating the spirit and intent of this resolve.

Since then the United States has consistently refused to sell any military equipment to South Africa.

Mr. Barratt O'Hara declared at the United Nations on November 2, 1965:

> The United States had strictly observed the embargo on all arms and military equipment for the South African government. Indeed it had extended that embargo to cover items normally used for civilian purposes but easily convertible for military purposes; the loss of profits resulting from the embargo amounted to at least $115 million in less than two years.

He added:

> His government estimated that an additional $285 million of orders which normally would have been placed in the United States had been placed elsewhere during the same period.

Mr. President, at a time when our balance-of-trade deficit is so critical the President is calling for travel restrictions, it is hard to understand a policy which, in addition to being of questionable merit, is costing the United States millions of dollars in trade.

Trade with South Africa helps the United States counter its balance-of-payments difficulties. The United States is running an increasingly favorable balance of trade with the Republic.

Mr. President, in the first 11 months of 1967 the United States exported goods to the value of $397.5 million to South Africa and imported only $204.2 million. During the comparable period in 1966 exports totaled $366.2 million and imports $226.1 million. Only about 14 other countries in the whole world take more from the United States than South Africa does—foreign aid included. Over 30 percent of American exports to the African Continent are taken by South Africa.

The United States has passed one insulting and condemnatory remark after another about South Africa's racial policy while remaining silent on the bloodshed, turmoil, tribal warfare, collapsing economics and falling standards in many other parts of Africa.

Mr. President, South Africans are now understandably beginning to resent this attitude on the part of the United States. Four members of the South African Cabinet recently reflected this public feeling by asking whether South Africa has not made a mistake by alining itself on the side of the West and whether loyalty to the West is not more burdensome than advantageous.

Whatever one may think of South Africa's policy of apartheid or separate development, the Republic has the highest general standards of living, education, and health for all races on the continent. About 1 million foreign Africans work in South Africa. Thousands of others enter the Republic illegally in order to seek the benefits of life it has to offer.

Britain is reducing her commitments in the Far East and the Indian Ocean. Further burdens are now falling on American shoulders. Is this a time to be insulting to South Africa and alienate her still further?

Article by Ambassador Arthur J. Goldberg on the United States
Should Sever All Ties with South Africa*

October 9, 1698

In light of South Africa's unyielding and intensified policy of apartheid—so abhorrent to our commitment to equality for all races—the United States Government immediately should disentangle itself from remaining economic, military and scientific ties with that country.

We have long recognized that South African race policies offend human dignity today and might threaten peace tomorrow. We have long sought through diplomatic channels to induce changes in South Africa racial policies. Unfortunately, our efforts have had little impact of consequence.

The South African government has ignored United States representations while continuing to build its repugnant system of total racial segregation—apartheid. It has increased its suppression of democratic liberties for its people, blacks and whites alike.

Now, even at some cost to ourselves, our Government should take steps which would visibly disengage us from South Africa.

By so doing we will protect our moral and political position in the world. We will also lend practical support to those who are working toward the reconciliation and equality of the races in South Africa. And we will strengthen the defense of American interests in the rest of Africa and the non-white world—including the high level there of U.S. investments and trade.

Among these fast-growing, large-magnitude economic American interests, are oil in Libya and Nigeria, copper in Zambia, rubber and iron ore in Liberia, bauxite in Ghana.

We often overlook the fact that the value of these interests in Africa north of Rhodesia now substantially exceeds our economic interests in Southern Africa. And we tend also to overlook the political value of fostering the goodwill of more than 30 black African governments representing 150 million people. This should not be.

I propose the following major governmental steps:

Arms embargo. Stricter enforcement of the South Africa arms embargo, including a ban on sales of American "dual-purpose" items such as trucks and executive-type planes which can be used by their military.

We should close loopholes such as the recent authorization for sale of American components in some "nonweapons" military equipment sold to South Africa by other countries.

We should use our influence to halt such sales by Japan, France and other countries. In the United Nations Security Council, we should see that such violations are cited by name if they do not cease. By so doing, we could help assure that orders not filled by American suppliers are not thereby lost to foreign competitors.

Missile and Space Program. We should close our missile and space tracking stations in South Africa and shift to facilities elsewhere as soon as physically possible.

Nuclear Agreement. We should carefully examine whether continuance of the U.S.-South African nuclear cooperation agreement is in our over-all interest.

Fueling by Official Ships. No American official ships should use South African ports. Alternative fueling arrangements should be provided for research and

*Ibid., Oct. 9, 1968, p. 8849.

communications vessels as well as Navy ships such as the aircraft carrier Franklin D. Roosevelt. The additional expense is worth bearing.

(The carrier FDR stopped in segregated Capetown, South Africa, in February, 1967. After protests by U.S. Negro leaders and 40 members of Congress, shore leave for 3800 sailors was cancelled.)

Economic Ties. Government Export-Import Bank loans and investment guarantees for South Africa should be disallowed across the board. The present case-by-case consideration should be discontinued.

The United States Government should actively discourage private loans and investment by American businessmen and bankers in South Africa. Those who engage in such enterprises are profiting from and strengthening a system which (as our official speeches have made clear) is built on racism.

Commerce Department trade promotion publications for South Africa should be discontinued.

The United States sugar quota for South Africa should be abolished.

We also should support a realistic and peaceful United Nations program of bringing independence to the Territory of South-West Africa, now illegally held by South Africa.

As in the case of South Africa, I urge visible disengagement from Portugal in the Portuguese-ruled African territories of Angola, Mozambique and Portuguese Guinea.

We should make it an announced policy to reject AID investment guarantees for Portuguese African ventures.

We should reject Export-Import Bank participation in Portuguese Africa in the future. The reduction of Ex-Im participation in the recent large-scale American project for Angola did not go far enough.

As a result of UN Security Council action, we have embarked upon a similar policy of disengagement and disassociation with regard to Rhodesia. We should under no circumstances relax our support for this UN embargo.

All that I propose with respect to Southern Africa is peaceful action. I do not advocate the use of force; on the contrary, I oppose it.

But at the same time that we reject force, we must offer more than words to prove our moral abhorence of the racist cancer in Southern Africa.

We must take all peaceful and practical steps, within the capacity of our Government, to help stop the spread of that cancer and, with all reasonable speed, to eradicate it.

Note from Assistant Secretary for Economic Affairs, Anthony M. Solomon, to South African Ambassador H. L. T. Taswell on United States-South Africa Air Transport Agreement *

June 28, 1968

I have the honor to refer to the consultations which took place in Washington in December 1967 in accordance with the United States-South Africa Air Transport

*Department of State Bulletin, July 29, 1968, pp. 134-35.

Agreement signed on May 23, 1947, as amended, and to propose, on behalf of my Government, that this agreement be further amended as follows:

1. Substitute for the words "Union" and "Unie", wherever they appear in the English and Afrikaans texts of the agreement, the words "Republic" and "Republiek."

2. Delete Section VII of the Annex to the agreement.

3. Delete Schedule I and Schedule II of the Annex to the agreement and substitute therefor Schedule I and Schedule II as attached to this note, in both the English and Afrikaans languages.

If these proposals are acceptable to the Government of the Republic of South Africa, I have the honor to propose that this note and your reply thereto constitute an agreement between our two Governments, further amending the Air Transport Agreement, which will enter into force on the date of your reply.

I should also appreciate receiving confirmation, as agreed during the consultations, that the Government of the Republic of South Africa will consider at a later stage the grant to the Government of the United States of America of traffic rights at Capetown and traffic rights to points beyond South Africa.

Accept, Excellency, the renewed assurances of my highest consideration.

ATTACHMENT TO U.S. NOTE

Schedule I

Airlines of the Republic of South Africa authorized under the present Agreement are accorded rights of transit and non-traffic stop in the territory of the United States of America, as well as the right to pick up and discharge international traffic in passengers, cargo and mail at New York on the following routes in both directions. On each of the routes described below, the airline or airlines designated to operate such route may serve the points on such route n any order on any flight and may operate non-stop flights between any of the points on such route, omitting stops at one or more of the other points on such route.

1. South Africa via points in Africa south of the equator, the Cape Verde Islands, the Canary Islands, Spain, and Portugal to New York.

2. South Africa via points in Africa south of the equator and South America to New York.

Schedule II

Airlines of the United States of America authorized under the present Agreement are accorded rights to transit and non-traffic stop in the territory of the Republic of South Africa, as well as the right to pick up and discharge international traffic in passengers, cargo and mail at Johannesburg on the following routes in both directions. On each of the routes described below, the airline or airlines designated to operate such route may serve the points on such route in any order on any flight and may operate non-stop flights between any of the points on such route, omitting stops at one or more of the other points on such route.

1. United States via points in the Azores, the Canary Islands, the Cape Verde Islands, Portugal, Spain, Germany, Italy, Greece, and Africa to Johannesburg.

2. United States via points in the Caribbean, South America, and Africa to Johannesburg.

*TESTIMONY ON AIR TRANSPORT AGREEMENT
BETWEEN THE UNITED STATES AND SOUTH AFRICA
BEFORE THE SUBCOMMITTEE ON AFRICA OF THE
HOUSE COMMITTEE ON FOREIGN AFFAIRS**

April 2 and 15, 1969

Statement of Joseph B. Goldman, General Counsel, Civil Aeronautics Board

The origins of the route award are found in the Air Transport Services Agreement between the United States and South Africa, an executive agreement negotiated in 1947. The 1947 Agreement gave the United States two air routes to South Africa and granted South Africa rights to serve New York, with the actual routing to be determined at a later date. As a consequence of this Agreement, Pan American has been operating a service to South Africa since 1947. Last year, the Agreement was amended at the request of South Africa to specifically define South Africa's air routes to New York. The amendment was effectuated by an exchange of notes between the Department of State and the South African Ambassador on June 28, 1968.

Less than a month later, on July 25, 1968, South African Airways applied to the Board under Section 402 of the Federal Aviation Act for a permit to operate to New York via Rio de Janeiro, a route provided for in the amended Agreement.

On September 20, 1968, a hearing examiner of the Board issued his decision, in which he recommended that South African Airways' application for a foreign air carrier permit be granted. No objections to the examiner's recommended decision were filed. The Board adopted the examiner's recommendation by a decision of October 2, 1968, and President Johnson approved the Board's decision on November 7, 1968. The South African Airways permit became effective immediately, and the time for reconsideration expired on November 29, 1968.

Two months later, on January 28, 1969, the Board and President Nixon received letters from the American Committee on Africa, requesting that the South African Airways case be reopened. The letter to President Nixon was answered by Mr. Robert Ellsworth, Assistant to the President, who stated that "it does not appear within President Nixon's power to reopen the South African Airways case at this time." That conclusion was in keeping with the general rule that the grant of a foreign air carrier permit or certificate of public convenience and necessity cannot be recalled after the time for reconsideration of the action has expired and the authorization has become effective. In view of these facts, the Board replied to the American Committee on Africa, stating that the Board did not deem it appropriate to take any further action at this time with respect to the South African permit.

*Committee on Foreign Affairs, *South Africa and United States Foreign Policy*, Hearings before the Subcommittee on Africa, 91st Cong., 1st sess. (Washington, 1969), pp. 2-3; 17-21; 73; 81-82.

The complaint has been made that the Board gave no notice of the public hearing on the application of South African Airways. Our rules of procedure, which are applicable to all cases, contemplate that all persons who wish to become "parties" to a Board proceeding will file petitions for intervention prior to the prehearing conference, and that a notice of hearing shall be served upon all the "parties." Over the years, foreign air carrier permit cases have often been expedited through a practice whereby all persons at the prehearing conference agree to waive further notice and to proceed directly to the public hearing. This procedure has been followed routinely in numerous foreign air carrier permit proceedings without objection. In the South African Airways case, no persons opposed to the grant of a permit indicated any interest in the case by filing petitions for intervention or by appearing at the prehearing conference. Consequently, with the agreement of all those present at the prehearing conference, further notice of hearing was waived and the examiner followed the customary expedited procedure by hodling the hearing immediately following the conclusion of the prehearing conference. In sum, the South African Airways case was conducted under the same procedures applicable in all similar Board matters.

Even under the expedited procedures, persons interested in air transportation between South Africa and the United States had several opportunities to learn about the Board's proceedings. The 1968 amendment of the bilateral Air Transport Services Agreement with South Africa was the subject of a Department of State press release on June 28, 1968. The filing of the application was noted in the Board's weekly summary of filings which is freely available to the public. Public notice of the prehearing conference was published in the Federal Register on August 27, 1968; and the examiner's recommended decision was given wide public distribution. The Board's decision, approved by the President, was noted in a Board press release on November 8, 1968. It was not until January 28, 1969, two months after the time for reconsideration had passed, that the Board was first informed of the objections to the procedure employed.

As a matter of law, the only procedures now available for further Board review of the South African Airways permit are found in Section 402(f) of the Federal Aviation Act. Under Section 402(f) the Board is authorized, after notice and hearing, to modify, suspend, or revoke a foreign permit when that action is in the "public interest." Under present circumstances, however, starting a new proceeding under Section 402(f) would not be consistent with the basic statutory plan under which foreign air carrier permits are granted.

In processing the original application under Section 402, the Board found that the carrier was fit, willing, and able, and that granting the application was in the public interest from a transportation standpoint. Furthermore, under Section 1102 of the Act the Board was required to act consistently with any obligation assumed by the United States in any international treaty, convention, or agreement. Since we have an outstanding air transport agreement with the Republic of South Africa providing for the route, the grant of the permit also discharged the obligation under the air transport agreement. Since the permit is justified on economic grounds, the only basis for withdrawing it would be on diplomatic or foreign relations considerations. These considerations, however, are embodied in the air transport agreement and involve matters which are properly for the decision of the President and the State Department.

Unless and until the Agreement is terminated, the Board regards the Agreement as controlling on the diplomatic and foreign relations aspects of the public interest.

Essentially, those who object to the Board's grant of a permit are seeking to challenge the Department of State's recent decision to amend the 1947 Agreement. Though the objectors seek hearings before the Board, their aim is to gain a forum for stating their grievances against the Agreement on diplomatic and foreign relations policy grounds. Those are not proper subjects for Board proceedings.

Under the statutory plan for granting foreign air carrier permits, it is the President who grants the permits, and he must necessarily look to the Secretary of State for guidance on diplomatic and foreign relations matters. It is the Department of State, not the Board, which is the President's advisor on those matters. The Board's role is essentially economic. While it makes recommendations to the President that take into account the views of other Departments, the Board does not undertake to substitute its judgment on matters specially within the competence of those Departments.

Statement of Frank E. Loy, Deputy Assistant Secretary, for Transportation and Communications, Bureau of Economic Affairs, Department of State

Mr. Chairman and members of the committee, I welcome this opportunity to discuss with you the way the State Department approached the question of the recent implementation of the 1947 agreement granting South African Airways landing rights in New York. If I may, I would like to make a few general background remarks.

It is the normal and traditional practice of the United States to encourage peaceful trade with other countries, even those with which we have serious differences. Historically, the United States has considered trade in peaceful goods a normal and desirable part of its relations with other countries. We normally do not base our economic relations with other countries on whether we approve or disapprove of their forms of government or conduct. Exceptions have been rare and have generally been made where security interests were directly affected.

In addition to trade, we have fostered the free exchange of persons and ideas, and the expansion of cultural relations on a worldwide basis. Proud of our dynamic ideas, our convictions and our aspirations, we have furthered contacts of all kinds with peoples all over the globe, convinced that over time we can develop mutual understanding and promote our democratic values.

Turning from these general concepts to the case of South Africa, we find that our Government has taken every opportunity to express its abhorrence of the South African Government's efforts to give the force of law to repugnant discriminatory practices and to elevate racial discrimination to the dignity of an official ideology. Our own experience with racial discrimination, and our Government's efforts to eliminate it, have made us acutely aware of the tragic mistake being made by the South African Government and have made it impossible for us, as a Government, to refrain from taking a strong stand on apartheid in our bilateral relations with South Africa and at the United Nations. Considering the deprivation of human rights and fundamental freedoms to be matters of international concern, we have made repeated representations to South Africa and we have voted in the United Nations for resolutions condemning apartheid.

As concrete evidence of our determination not to contribute to the enforcement of apartheid or the further development of a white redoubt in southern Africa, we do not send to South Africa any arms, ammunition or military equipment, nor materials for their manufacture or maintenance.

Despite the depth of our differences with South Africa, and in harmony with our general policy, we permit normal and lawful trade with South Africa and neither encourage nor discourage investment there. We do this because we believe it is important to keep open the lines of communication, in order to continue to bring to bear a constructive influence, and to keep in touch with the many people in South Africa, both white and nonwhite, who question the direction of apartheid policy. Moreover, we do not believe that the system of racial repression in South Africa would be changed for the better, if we were to follow a policy of economic quarantine or isolation.

It was in this framework that the United States considered the South African request to have routes for its carrier defined under our Air Transport Agreement. Our decision to proceed with negotiations was made with full understanding that there were negative factors to be taken into account, but was in keeping with our general policy on peaceful economic exchanges and toward South Africa.

Another consideration we could not ignore concerned the terms of our existing agreement. In 1947 we granted South Africa landing rights in New York, with the exact routes to be determined later. When South Africa recently came forward to claim its side of the bargain, we were faced with a choice. We could either honor our commitment or we could put at risk continued air service between the two countries, with consequent damage to our economic interests as well as to our general trade policy. We concluded that we would gain nothing by reneging: in the absence of direct air service, the traffic between the two countries would be shifted to the many carriers of other countries that serve South Africa; and in any case our action was not likely to improve racial conditions in South Africa. On the other hand, by honoring our commitment we would also safeguard our economic interests. I should add that our carrier has benefitted from its rights for more than 20 years.

Regarding the United Nations General Assembly resolution that requested member states to deny landing and passage facilities to South African aircraft, I would like to point out that that resolution is not mandatory in character and did not receive United States support when it was passed.

*   *   *

In response to a message from the Apartheid Committee, forwarded to the U.S. Government by the U.N. Secretary General, the United States made clear its view that it was in no way acting contrary to its obligations under the United Nations Charter in fulfilling its longstanding contractual obligation to South Africa.

That statement is contained in the letter from Ambassador Yost dated March 5, 1969. It is quite recent.

I would like to submit that for inclusion in the record, if I may.

(The letter referred to follows:)

The Policies of Apartheid of the Government of South Africa—Letter
Dated 5 March 1969 From the Permanent Representative of the United
States of America to the United Nations Addressed to the Secretary-General

I have the honour to refer to your letter of 20 February 1969. conveying the views of the Special Committee on the Policies of Apartheid of the Government of the Republic of South Africa regarding the South African Airways link to New York.

The 1947 United States-South Africa Air Transport Agreement gave the United States two air routes to Johannesburg and granted South Africa rights to serve New York with actual routing to be defined at a later time. The South African Airways link to New York, therefore, represented the fulfillment by the United States of a contractual undertaking going back to 1947. South African Airways could have activated its rights under the agreement at any time since 1947 but only chose to do so recently. In this context, it is incorrect to state, as the Special Committee does, that the South African Airways link to New York represents the grant of a "new" facility or right by the United States to South Africa.

I would also point out that General Assembly resolution 1761 (XVII), which requested Members States to deny landing and passage facilities to South African aircraft, was non-mandatory in character and did not receive United States support. In fulfilling its long-standing contractual obligation to South Africa, the United States was in no way acting contrary to its obligations under the United Nations Charter.

The implementation of the agreement does not represent any change in the well-known United States policy with respect to apartheid.

I would be grateful to you if you would bring this letter to the attention of the Special Committee and circulate it as an official document of the General Assembly and the Security Council.

(Signed) Charles W. Yost

Mr. Diggs: Mr. Secretary, in 1966 when the subcommittee conducted some rather extensive hearings on the whole complex of our relations with South Africa, representatives of the Department of Commerce defined their policy as one which does not encourage or discourage economic relationships with the representatives of South Africa. Now, in your second paragraph you defined the policy through the eyes of the State Department as one which encourages peaceful trade with other countries, even those with which we have serious differences.

I would like to know just what does represent our policy, the Commerce Department which says we don't encourage or discourage or your policy which says we do encourage trade even with those countries with which we have serious differences.

Mr. Loy: Mr. Chairman, I don't believe those two are at war with each other. In describing our attitude toward South Africa, I did say in my statement that we neither encouraged nor discouraged trade or investment with it. The problem that you refer to is a quite fundamental one which the Department has considered rather frequently. But the basic proposition is that the trade in peaceful goods is a normal and desirable part of our relations with other countries and that does include countries with whom we have very deep differences. That policy may be right or wrong, but we have considered it for a long time and it is fairly deeply enshrined in our attitude. I don't think it differs from what you quote.

Mr. Diggs: On page 2 of your testimony, you cite as concrete evidence of our determination not to contribute to the enforcement of apartheid, or to the further development in South Africa, the fact that we do not send South Africa any arms, ammunition or military equipment and supplies, meaning hardware, for manufacturing or maintenance. You let it stand based on that fact alone, without any reference to our other involvement in South Africa's economic development, from the private sector, for example, and indirectly from the public sector. You don't really believe that this is concrete evidence of our determination not to involve ourselves in the economic development of South Africa, the fact that we don't send any military supplies over there?

Mr. Loy: Mr. Chairman, I had intended to limit really my testimony to matters dealing with the air service between our two countries, but it certainly is quite clear that we have very numerous economic ties with South Africa; and to that extent we are involved in their economy. But the point that I made in the paragraph to which you refer is that we have been quite careful to avoid becoming a partner of South Africa in any effort on their part to enforce by military or forceful means the apartheid policy.

*   *   *

Statement of Congressman Ogden R. Reid

Mr. Chairman, I very much appreciate your giving me this opportunity to submit a statement for the hearing record, as I am concerned by the foreign policy implications of the granting of a permit authorizing South African Airways to transport persons, property and mail between Johannesburg and Kennedy International Airport.

The route granted to South African Airways is the most direct route in operation between this country and Johannesburg, and I am deeply concerned that its authorization diminishes our dedication to justice in the eyes of black Africans and black Americans alike. The granting of the permit can easily be interpreted by sensitive observers in both Africa and America as official "sanction" of the system of apartheid which prevails in all institutions under the direct control of the Government of South Africa. South African Airways, which is administered by the Minister of Transport as a subdivision of the South African Government, is one of those institutions; one can reasonably expect that the airline will extend its discriminatory policies toward United States citizens.

In my judgment, the implied sanction of the policy of apartheid is unfortunate for two reasons. It comes at a time when we are trying to strengthen our relationships with the nations of black Africa, which recognize the inconsistency in our policies toward them and toward South Africa. In addition, the granting of a permit to South African Airways is in direct opposition to United Nations policy, as set forth in a resolution passed by the General Assembly in 1962. That resolution, which requested that member states act against apartheid, specifically supported action to refuse landing and passage facilities to all aircraft belonging to the Government of South Africa and companies registered under South African laws.

I would hope, Mr. Chairman, that the views expressed in these hearings will lead the Civil Aeronautics Board to reexamine its position in the granting of a permit to South African Airways. The reciprocity agreement under which the permit was granted was signed May 23, 1947—before apartheid became the national policy of the South African Government—and no route was defined. I see no justification for granting any route, but especially the most direct route between New York and Johannesburg, to an airline which is operated by a government intent on perpetuating injustice.

Appendix C, Group 1: List of Inaugural Guests to South Africa

Depart per SA.202 on April 7, 1969.
Return per SA.201 on ˙April 13, 1969 (except where indicated differently).

1 and 2: General and Mrs. S. L. A. Marshall.

3 and 4: General and Mrs. Mark W. Clark; the Citadel, the Military College of South Carolina, Charleston, S.C.

5 and 6: Dr. and Mrs. Chas Moore; executive vice president, International Copper Research Association, Inc., New York, N.Y.

7 and 8: Ambassador and Mrs. Joseph C. Satterthwaite.

9 and 10: Ambassador and Mrs. H. L. T. Taswell; South African Embassy.

11 and 12: Mr. and Mrs. J. Alexander Black; senior vice president (International Division), Otis Elevator Co., New York, N.Y.

13 and 14: Congressman and Mrs. Samuel N. Friedel; chairman of the Transportation and Aeronautics Subcommittee.

15 and 16: The Honorable and Mrs. A. Burks Summers, Rockville, Md.

17: Mr. Thomas L. Wrenn; chief examiner, Civil Aeronautics Board.

18: Mr. Allen Craig; deputy director, Bureau of Accounts and Statistics, Civil Aeronautics Board.

19: Mr. F. Lordan; staff director of the Senate Committee on Commerce.

20 and 21: Mr. and Mrs. Thomas B. Lovejoy; Dillon Read and Co., Inc., New York, N.Y.

22 and 23: Mr. and Mrs. Felix M. Mansager; president and chairman of the board, the Hoover Co., North Canton, Ohio.

24 and 25: Mr. and Mrs. Jerome B. Temple; senior vice president, Inns and Restaurants, Holiday Inns of America, Inc.

26: Mr. Leo Bernstein; president, District of Columbia National Bank.

27: Mrs. Rose Saul Zalles; Washington, D.C.

28: Mr. R. M. Lee; Hunting World Inc., New York, N.Y.

29: Seat Blanked-Off for Mrs. Kruger; wife of general manager, South African Railways, Johannesburg.

30 and 31: Mr. and Mrs. R. G. Brett; manager for North America, South African Airways.

32 and 33: Mr. and Mrs. L. F. Corea; senior vice president, Riggs National Bank.

Report of Representatives Diggs and Lester L. Wolff (New York) on a Special Study Mission to Southern Africa *

August 10-30, 1969

A. General Observations

Nowhere in the world is the black-white crisis more starkly unclothed than on the African Continent. The Republic of South Africa, the illegal regime of so-called Southern Rhodesia, and the Portuguese administrators of Mozambique and Angola have apparently turned their backs on the moral requisites of the 20th-century doctrine of uncompromising equality. In so doing, they have helped to lay the foundation for an eventual black-white collision of explosive proportions. Most of

*Committee on Foreign Affairs, *Report of Special Study Mission to Southern Africa*, August 10-30, 1969, by Hon. Charles C. Diggs, Jr., Michigan, Chairman, Hon. Lester L. Wolff, N.Y., Pursuant to H. Res. 143, 91st Cong., 1st sess., (Washington, 1969), pp. 2-6.

Africa's freedom movements are committed to change through constitutional reorganization based upon majority rule. But South Africa's and Southern Rhodesia's racist reluctance and Portugal's brooding hesitancy, while differing more in degree than in kind in their oppressive policies, are nonetheless equally responsible for the surging proliferation of Africa's freedom movements. As that dedicated and peace-loving freedom fighter, South African Chief A. J. Lutuli, declared in 1964 at the Rivonia trial:

> In the face of uncompromising white refusal to abandon a policy which denies the African and other oppressed South Africans their rightful heritage—freedom—no one can blame brave and just men for seeking justice by the use of violent methods; nor could they be blamed if they tried to create an organized force in order to ultimately establish peace and racial harmony.

The members of this study mission wish to make unerringly clear one conclusion as the result of their conversations with various African leaders: should an extremely unfortunate racial bloodbath engulf South Africa, Southern Rhodesia, or the Portuguese territories of Angola and Mozambique, such an eventuality would be the direct consequence of the economic exploitation, political dispossession, and other forms of degradation imposed by the white minority in those countries.

An even more ominous portent is the possibility of heavy Communist involvement in the African freedom struggle as it turns away in frustration from the western nations and seeks, and in turn receives, help from Communist states, anxious for a determinant role in African affairs.

In southern Africa, 4 million whites rule 28 million blacks (about 2½ million are mixed races or Asian). While most of the freedom movements seem to be multiracial in outlook, there also appears to be a danger of their efforts becoming a rigid black-white confrontation if their progress is frustrated by long, drawnout struggle. Some reports to the study mission indicate that the freedom movements are not all really multiracial in outlook—for example, it was stated that the South-West African Peoples Organization wants "whites" out of South-West Africa, and that the Zimbabwe African Peoples Union includes individuals who would drive out white "settlers," who outlawed the party in 1962.

It is too soon to predict with any certainty not just when, but even whether, the freedom movements will be successful in their efforts to end white minority rule in southern Africa. Yet, without a change in the present policies of the existing governments and in view of the continuing determination of the movements themselves and the international support which they receive, it appears that time and history are on the side of the revolutionary forces. Details on the major freedom fighters organizations of southern Africa are covered later in this report.

B. U.S. Policy Considerations

American foreign policy toward Africa can be summarized in one word: schizophrenic.

On the one hand, the United States, the most powerful symbol of democracy in the world, is committed to freedom and equality and opposed to tyranny and injustice.

And on the other hand, America has made an immoral entangling alliance with one of the most tyrannical governments in the world, the Republic of South Africa. Not only do we maintain intimate economic ties with South Africa, but we have also forged other links such as a NASA tracking station and landing rights for South African Airways that have endowed her with respectability and security. Nor have Africans been impressed with our bumbling policy of confusion toward Southern Rhodesia.

Understandably, a nation's foreign policy is governed primarily by its self-interest or what former State Department policy planner Charles B. Marshall defined as "enabling our constitutional values to survive."

U.S. self-interest is dramatized by the presence in our midst of over 25 million black citizens who are increasingly identifying with their cultural heritage and who are on the threshold of linking up with the goals of the African liberation movement. Once the struggle becomes internationalized in this fashion they may also expect support from their traditional allies in the labor movement, on the campuses, among the churches, and other liberal elements. This will also give impetus to Africanists, foreign policy organizations, and the thousands of returned Peace Corps volunteers with interest in Africa. The activation of this kind of constituency is much nearer than many of our policymakers realize. Those who think they can buy time with short-range concepts that cater to certain present controlling interests are courting disaster. Africa is "the continent of the future." The United States should ask itself, "What will be our posture in Africa 5, 10, 25 years from now?" If it is to be on the side of the vast majority of Africans, our present policies and plans should reflect an enlightened projection and drastic revisions are demanded.

The United States is indeed confronted with difficult policy decisions as it attempts to balance the advantage of political stability against the traditional American aim of supporting the development of broadly based and fully representative governments. The foundation of the American attitude toward Africa has been the principle of self-determination and its corollary of government by the consent of the governed. In Rhodesia, the Portuguese territories, and South Africa, nonwhites generally acquiesce in the authority of existing governments, but this is essentially because they have little alternative due to repression and police state methods. Tribal society is still strong in some areas and allowed to exist and even encouraged. At the same time, support for peaceful transition is also a cornerstone of United States-African policy.

The United States has attempted to isolate Africa from the arms race as much as possible and advocates refraining from active military intervention in African affairs. It has been the consensus of American leaders that Africa should be left free to seek African solutions to its problems and be encouraged to act through African institutions. Thus, while American sympathies may lie with the principle of African self-rule which the revolutionary movements represent, the United States has confined its activity in support of the principle only to United Nations action and bilateral discussions with established governments, which has been tragic for our reputation as a democratic leader.

The U.S. Government neither encourages nor discourages new investment in South Africa. However, the agencies of the executive branch insure that potential investors are given full information and briefing on all factors, both negative and positive, which may bear on the investment situation in South Africa. Total U.S. investment in South Africa has been estimated at $800 million. In comparison the United Kingdom has an estimated investment there of around $3 billion. See appendix E5 for further discussion of U.S. investment in South Africa.

As a NATO ally of Portugal, the United States has unilaterally attempted to encourage that country to take a more enlightened view of its role on the African continent. Moreover, the United States voted for the U.N. resolution (1742-XVI) which called for self-determination in Angola and for Resolution 1699 (XVI) which censured Portugal for noncompliance with U.N. regulations concerning reporting on non-self-governing overseas territories.

The Portuguese Foreign Minister in discussing his Government's policies in Africa with our study mission admitted that, on the surface, the policies of the U.N. might appear right. However, the Portuguese consider themselves experienced and in the long run they are not impressed by the U.N. resolutions. The Foreign Minister contended that not a single country has implemented any resolution of the U.N. contrary to their vital interest. He also maintained most U.N. resolutions are irresponsible and not realistic.

In spite of its record within the United Nations in support of self-determination for the Portuguese African territories, the United States has been condemned by freedom fighters for its cooperation with Portugal in the form of arms supplies, bases, and trade. The United States has received reassurances from its NATO ally that arms supplied under NATO agreements are not being diverted for use in Portugal's defense of her African territories, but leaders of the revolutionary movements insist that NATO weapons are being used against them and that provision thereof releases funds which the Portuguese use to finance the war against them. In answer, the United States has stated that the arms embargo is effective and pointed out that any American arms involved in the conflicts are usually of World War II origin, available commercially from markets outside the United States.

The U.S. Ambassador in Lisbon advised the study mission that materiel furnished to Portugal by the United States under the military assistance program is not being utilized by the Portuguese in her African Provinces. Since 1961 no materiel usable in Africa has been furnished the Army. Military aircraft furnished under the military assistance program is limited to that required for NATO training and for NATO committed units. The principal effort of the military assistance program for the Navy in recent years has centered around cost sharing construction of three destroyer escorts, modernizing electronic gear on NATO committed ships, furnishing necessary follow-on spare parts and training ammunition. Such assistance is not directly relevant to African wars of liberation.

U.S. policy toward Rhodesia has also centered around U.N. action by supporting the mandatory sanctions against the Ian Smith government. Neither the United States nor any other nation formally recognizes the illegal government of Prime Minister Ian Smith and the United States continues to recognize British sovereignty over the territory. The United States, under Executive Order 11322 of January 5, 1967, in support of U.N. Security Council sanctions, prohibited Americans from engaging in trade of selected goods with Rhodesia. The United States also joined in unanimous approval of the 1968 Security Council resolution which imposed even more stringent economic sanctions upon Rhodesia.

On November 11, 1965, the United States withdrew all but a token staff from its consulate in Salisbury. The acting U.S. Consul in Salisbury is accredited to the British

Government. Since the break between Britain and Rhodesia following the June 20, 1969, constitutional referendum, the United States has not indicated if it would withdraw the remaining members of its mission although this has been recommended by the State Department and the present Consul. It now awaits decision by the President.

The United States has long been on record in opposition to South Africa's policies of apartheid and rule over South-West Africa. The United States supported the Security Council's 1963 resolutions requesting member states to embargo the sale of arms to South Africa and scrupulously implements such an embargo. The United States also supported the landmark Generaly Assembly resolution (2145 (XXI), Oct. 27, 1966), which declared that South Africa's League of Nations Mandate for South-West Africa was terminated and that the territory came under the direct responsibility of the U.N. During the 1967 trial of South-West African nationalists, the United States joined other U.N. members in calling upon South Africa to cease the illegal application of the Terrorism Act in the territory of South-West Africa and for the release and repatriation of the defendants. To obtain South African compliance with U.N. resolutions, the United States pledged its support for such peaceful and practical measures as might be desired. Though the United States has continued to maintain its relations with the Republic of South Africa, it has made clear, as our Ambassador to the United Nations had stated, that:

> We will provide full and faithful support to the people of South-West Africa in the peaceful pursuit of their goals, in their efforts to assert and to exercise fully the rights to which all men everywhere aspire and are entitled.

It can be seen that the freedom movements in southern Africa present the United States with delicate policy considerations. In formulating our policy we must take into account the liabilities as well as the benefits from our relations. Perhaps the foremost issue for U.S. policy is what one American Senator has described as ". . . our moral and political credit with all of Africa." American leaders who share this outlook ask whether the United States can afford not to give substantial encouragement to the freedom movements which represent the aim of self-government for Africans within these territories; to fail to do so, they contend, would be to sacrifice Africa's faith in the genuineness of America's dedication to self-determination for all peoples.

In the interest of the free world and Africa itself, the manner in which the United States implements the basic principles of its African policy significantly affects the future political pattern of that continent. Specifically, does the situation in southern Africa demand a more forceful U.S. position against minority rule, or should the United States leave the intiative to the Afro-Asian bloc in the U.N. to formulate international action against the offending governments? Can the present forces supporting political stability be directed toward the development of representative government? Would a unilateral or international attempt to alter the status quo in southern Africa represent, as former Secretary of State Dean Acheson has suggested, "barefaced aggression . . . unjustified by a single legal or moral principle"? Are the freedom movements, in fact, operating in the interest of the native Africans, with the goal of establishing government by consent of the governed? Who determines what native people want, really? To indicate the complexity of this question, for instance, do the chiefs in Rhodesia—who are salaried employees of the government—speak for Africans or do ZANU and ZAPU exile leaders represent African sentiment? Several hundred Africans are imprisoned inside Rhodesia for antigovernment activities; do they speak for Africans?

African representatives in Rhodesia's Parliament have spoken out against recent political developments and racial policies espoused by the regime and some of these have opposed violence as a solution; do those who advocate peaceful change speak for the Africans; As a protest, followers of the banned ZANU and ZAPU parties have refused to register or otherwise participate in Rhodesian politics for several years; does this action provide us with an answer as to what the Africans really want? It is the answers to these and other complex questions which will determine the nature and future direction of U.S. policy toward freedom movements in southern Africa.

*   *   *

Statement by Christopher H. Phillips, U.S. Representative to U.N. General Assembly Urging Negotiation and Dialogue in Southern Africa*

October 16, 1969

The general debate on Namibia, Southern Rhodesia, and the territories under Portuguese administration has held the attention of this committee for the past week. My delegation has listened with interest to the views of the numerous delegations that have taken part. We have been struck by the virtually unanimous agreement in certain conclusions which ran like a thread throughout the discussion. If one were to summarize this agreement it was: (1) that there is a profound sense of disillusionment, nay of frustration, over the lack of progress in the achievement of self-determination for the people of southern Africa; (2) that there is widespread dissatisfaction with the adoption of increasingly shrill yet meaningless resolutions; (3) that there is growing concern with the hardening of positions between the mass of peoples striving for self-determination on the one hand and those in power on the other, which bodes ill for a peaceful settlement.

My delegation shares this frustration, this dissatisfaction, this concern. We, too, are disillusioned by the lack of progress in achieving self-determination. We are deeply concerned by the tendency to adopt resolutions which are more and more unrealistic, which even their authors do not expect to see implemented. This concern is not limited to the fact that no relief is being efforded to those concerned; we are seriously concerned by their effect on the credibility and prestige of the United Nations. Finally, we are deeply troubled by the increasing intractability of South Africa and the Ian Smith regime [in Southern Rhodesia]. Each passing day without progress, each unrealistic and unenforceable resolution from these halls, each act of defiance by these regimes constitutes a setback to the cause of peace and to a negotiated solution acceptable to the parties in dispute.

In his eloquent address to the General Assembly last week, His Excellency President Ahidjo of the Federal Republic of the Cameroon commended the Lusaka Manifesto to us. The fact that this distinguished African statesman spoke to us as President of the

*Department of State Bulletin, Nov. 24, 1969, pp. 458-59.

Assembly of Heads of State and Government of the Organization of African Unity, which had recently given its endorsement to this important document, gave added weight to President Ahidjo's recommendation. For this document, the Lusaka Manifesto, is undoubtedly one of the most important political and human documents to have emerged from modern Africa. Its adoption first by the 14 Central and East African states that participated at the Lusaka conference last April and its recent endorsement by the Organization of African Unity, representing 41 independent states, make it worthy of the attention and most careful study by the world community.

My Government finds itself in agreement with much that is contained in this moving document. The manifesto presents in memorable terms the aim of the authors: first, that the peoples of the area "shall be free to determine for themselves their own institutions of self-government" and, secondly, that they shall be "given an opportunity to be men—not white men, brown men, yellow men, or black men."

The categorical rejection of racialism embodied in the manifesto accords with our own views. Equally encouraging is its advocacy of dialogue as the first and perhaps the best way to achieve the manifesto's stated objective of freedom for all the people of southern Africa.

We wholeheartedly applaud the manifesto's declaration that the authors still prefer to achieve their goals without physical violence and that "We would prefer to negotiate rather than destroy, to talk rather than kill. We do not advocate violence; we advocate an end to the violence against human dignity which is now being perpetrated by the oppressors of Africa."

With the certain knowledge that his words were not spoken lightly but represented the most careful and considered thoughts of the leading statesmen of Africa, we are pleased to echo the words of President Ahidjo before the General Assembly of these United Nations, when he said:

> Our campaign, therefore, implies the condemnation of all racialism and not the establishment of a racialism in reverse. It is nourished by thyunshakable conviction that. in denying human value to a single man, the dignity of all men is under attack.
>
> By thus appealing to the universal conscience, we intend not only to demonstrate our attachment to peace and the ideal of human brotherhood, our desire to contribute through dialogue and negotiation to the world's great problems. but also to revive our faith in man and our attachment to his dignity, to foster aspirations, in these troubled times, to the highest values of mankind, and the orientation of history towards the recognition of man by man.

Mr. Chairman, we wish to suggest most earnestly that those now in power in southern Africa accept this offer to negotiate, accept this invitation to a dialogue. If they were to do so, we believe that their action would receive wide endorsement not only among their neighbors in Africa but in Europe, in the Americas, and elsewhere throughout the world. For herein lies the only true hope for a solution to a situation that anguishes the conscience of civilized men everywhere and does violence to the legitimate rights and aspirations of millions of men who are also our brothers.

*Hearings before the Subcommittee on Africa on Foreign Policy
Implications of Racial Exclusion in Granting Visas**

February 4, 1970

Hon. Charles C. Diggs, Jr.: There is no question that there are masses of facts, decisions, testimony from various sources proving that the South African Government practices overt and universal racialism in its sports field. Moreover, the South African Government is not very subtle about it, it is actually part of their national policy, and therefore, part of their political policy. One just cannot separate the question of the denial of a visa to an Arthur Ashe from the political questions that are generally involved and which have implications for the United States.

I might add that this policy not only covers sports participants but also spectators, because by law whites and blacks in South Africa cannot be spectators at a sports event except on a segregated basis. There have been some exceptions to that, the South Africans are very skilled at the technique of minor exceptions, and these exceptions notwithstanding, policy has continued to be maintained.

The announcement on January 28 of this year denying Mr. Arthur Ashe a visa confirms my conviction that they maintain this policy and, as has been previously stated, this policy is perverse and twisted. Mr. Ashe, the top ranking tennis player in the United States, had applied for a visa to participate in the 1970 South African National Tennis Championships and on applying for a visa stated that his principal desire in visiting South Africa was only to play tennis. It is quite obvious that he was denied entrance solely because he is black because there have been other athletes that have been critical of South African policy and still have been permitted to come into that country and therefore this arbitrary action reinforces our contention that something should be done. We are hopeful that our Government is going to develop some kind of policy to implement the pronouncements that they have made here in Washington and other international forums that this policy on the part of South Africa is a part.

*   *   *

STATEMENT OF OLIVER S. CROSBY, DIRECTOR FOR SOUTHERN AFRICA, DEPARTMENT OF STATE

*   *   *

The Department greatly regrets the refusal of the South African Government to allow Mr. Ashe to play in the national tennis championships. This is particularly regrettable because of the overtones of racial bias in the case that you have already mentioned. Over the years the U.S. Government has made clear its unalterable opposition to the policy of apartheid, or racial separation, in South Africa. It has done this in bilateral representations and in the U.N. and other multilateral organizations. As we have so often stated, it is our conviction that it is in South Africa's deepest

---

*Committee on Foreign Affairs *Foreign Policy Implications of Racial Exclusion in Granting Visas, Hearing before the Subcommittee on Africa,* 91st Cong., 2d sess., (Washington, 1970), pp. 1-4; 15-16.

interests to foster foreign contacts and exchanges–not to shut itself off in sterile isolation.

There is unfortunately a limit to our ability to bring the South African authorities to a reasonable stance in such matters, as one of the attributes of national sovereignty is thyright of a state to determine for itself who shall be allowed to enter its territory. However, this does not render any more tolerable the South African Government's decision in cases such as that of Mr. Arthur Ashe.

The story is not over as this kind of case will come up again and again as long as the South African Government persists in pursuing apparently discriminatory policies with respect to American citizens. And again and again we will do our utmost to defend the rights and interests of our citizens before the Government of South Africa.

*   *   *

Mr. Diggs: Mr. Crosby, you stated what the committee expected you to say about American policy on this whole question, that "unfortunately, there is a limit to our ability to bring South African authorities to a reasonable stance in such matters."

Are you saying that there was no way in which the United States can, for example, reciprocate in kind with respect to athletes who come from that country to this country and who have been coming to this country and enjoying all of the benefits pertinent thereto without any kind of restrictions at all? Are you saying that our hands are tied and we cannot do anything about this matter from the reciprocation standpoint?

Mr. Crosby: Mr. Chairman, from the standpoint of possible reciprocation; retaliatory visa refusal, there are two general categories of considerations that pertain to the U.S. position, one concerning visa regulations, on which I will ask Mr. Smith to speak to you, and one of general principle I would like to discuss very briefly for a moment.

It is our strong feeling and a source of pride to us that the United States is an open country. We cherish this fact and we are determined to keep it so. Part of this quality that we value so highly is the objective basis on which we admit foreigners to the country; we believe that an exchange of ideas and the exchange of people is a fruitful thing. We very strongly regret the restrictions that the South African Government places on this, but we don't think that it is in our interest to emulate them in such actions, and we believe that for policy reasons we should continue to handle these applications for South African athletes in the fashion that the regulations call for.

One particular consideration we have in mind when examining this type of problem is what the consequences would be. It is my belief that the consequences of rejection of a visa for Mr. Player would not cause the South African Government to change its policies, would not cause the South African Government to adopt a more lenient stance with regard to the issuance of visas to Mr. Ashe or other black Americans of any category.

And at the same time it would simply move us out of the part of the forest we find more comfortable and put us in the same category as the South African Government. This would not be to our advantage. At the same time, I think it would be to their advantage because it would remove, I would expect, much of the opprobrium that attaches to their arbitrary action in a case such as this one.

Mr. Diggs: Well, that is a very interesting comment because it is this kind of concept that I think that too often in our policy vis-a-vis South Africa and that is whether or not it is going to have an effect upon South African policy. Given the intransigence of that administration and the official policy of that Government on this subject, you may be correct; however, we have here in this sports subject something that has a little extra dimension to it because the South African people are great sports enthusiasts, and there is, from what I can gather, a developing resentment against this sort of situation.

There are some people who have spoken out, athletes and whatnot, who have spoken out against their governments in this instance because of the Ashe incident, so that it has had some effect inside. But in addition to that, what about the effect? We talk about the effect on South African policy. What about the effect on the degradation that this represents for the 30 million black Americans here in the United States. What about the effect of this kind of incident and the kind of implications of this matter with respect to the other African countries and their supporters. In each instance that the United States identifies itself either through some kind of policy pronouncement, that is not implemented or in some other fashion on the wrong side of this question, our rating in the rest of black Africa goes down another notch.

So you are confining the issue to the question of whether or not what we do is going to have some effect on South African policy, as a very disturbing statement if it reflects the opinions of our administration in that matter.

Mr. Crosby: Mr. Chairman, that was part of the comment I made, that it could not be expected necessarily to change their policy over the short run. There is another major reason why I believe our present policy is correct in relation to our own values, and this has to do with the view other countries take of the United States itself.

You mentioned the reaction of other African countries. I don't have a reading on how they have felt about this, but I expect they would respect the efforts in this particular case to get a visa for Mr. Ashe. At the same time, I think they would particularly respect our strength of character in maintaining the policy, in maintaining a position of openness. It is this contrast that sets us off so positively in comparison with the policies of the South Africans. I honestly believe it is not in our interest to take on the characteristics that we criticize in them. I believe this is the way a change of position would be regarded in Africa, because the African countries themselves so strongly dislike what is at the root of the problem in South Africa.

Mr. Diggs: Well, it has not been my experience, Mr. Crosby, that they do have this reaction. We are continually criticized in all parts of Africa despite the pronouncements that have been correct. We have made all kinds. We are the greatest country in the world for making pronouncements that are correct, not only as it relates to this matter but all aspects of Africa. Yet we know these people are not naive, they are much more sophisticated than they are given credit for. We make a correct statement that we are abhorring apartheid and we are against racism and yet on the other hand one of our leading citizens is denied entrance into a country like South Africa and yet one of their people can come over here. I am positive this lack of implementing these pronouncements is seen for what it is, and we are not fooling anybody because I have had this kind of criticism directed at our Government on missions that I have made to all parts of Africa, not only on the part of private individual citizens but on the part of leading members of the Government.

*   *   *

UNITED STATES ABSTAINS ON SECURITY COUNCIL RESOLUTION
ON SOUTH AFRICA*

Statement by Ambassador Buffum

July 23, 1970

* * *

We have strongly and repeatedly urged the Government of South Africa to change its racial policies, and we have warned that Government of the dangers inherent in the continued pursuit of its policies.

The United States does not believe it is in the interests of a long-term solution in this area to send arms and lethal equipment to South Africa. The United States has itself scrupulously avoided any contribution of lethal weapons to South Africa and continues to believe that it is in the interest of the total international community to do likewise. Mr. President, as early as 1962—before there was a Security Council embargo—the United States voluntarily prohibited the sale to South Africa of arms which could be used to enforce apartheid. In August 1963—again on our own and before there was a Security Council embargo—we informed the Council that, effective the end of that calendar year, we would not sell any military equipment to South Africa, subject only to our honoring existing contracts and our right to interpret our policy in the future in the light of requirements for assuring the maintenance of international peace and security. The United States solemnly and formally affirmed these obligations we had freely undertaken in voting in favor of the Security Council's resolutions of 1963 and 1964 which established an arms embargo against South Africa.

We have faithfully carried out these obligations. We intend to continue to carry them out. Our own embargo on the sale of arms to South Africa was reaffirmed as late as March of this year. Let me reaffirm once again before the Security Council that the United States supports the Council's resolutions on the sale of arms to South Africa and that our Government would not be able to associate itself with any measures which might result in an increase in the flow of arms to South Africa.

Mr. President, some of the preceding speakers have referred to arms supplied to South Africa by the United States over the last few years. I again affirm that deliveries currently being made consist entirely of some spare parts and stemmed from contracts entered into prior to the effective date of the United States embargo, specifically, December 31, 1963. I would also point out that deliveries of major items of military equipment under these contracts have long since been completed. It is a basic tenet of United States trade policy that valid contracts should be honored.

Mr. President, the United States is able to support the basic intent of the draft resolution before us and many of its specific provisions. In particular, we fully endorse the expression of total opposition to the policy of apartheid and the reaffirmation of Resolutions 181, 182, and 191. We supported them, we have fully and faithfully abided by them, and would wish that all states had done likewise.

However, while the present text is a welcome improvement over the draft origianlly circulated, we cannot support it in its entirety. It is clear that the more sweeping

*Department of State Bulletin, Aug. 17, 1970, pp. 204-05.

provisions contained in this draft resolution—provisions which go beyond the limits to which my Government can commit itself—cannot command the wide support in the Council that would make them effective. On the contrary, we would in all seriousness ask whether they may not carry with them the danger of weakening instead of strengthening the measure of compliance required to give practical effect to resolutions of this Council. We are concerned that their embodiment in this resolution may serve only to divide the Council, fail to fulfill their intended purpose, and thus operate to the detriment of both the people of South Africa and the United Nations.

We will therefore abstain when the Council votes on this text. We particularly regret the necessity for this decision in view of our long-standing record of support for and observance of earlier Council resolutions on this subject. We would have been happy to support a resolution which had unanimous support in the Council. We believe that such a conclusion to the recent debate would have contributed effectively to the achievement of our common objective. We have been and remain eager to assure that there is no misunderstanding, particularly in South Africa, that this Council remains unanimous in its condemnation of the policies of apartheid.

Text of Resolution

July 23, 1970

The Security Council,

Having considered the question of race conflict in South Africa resulting from the policies of apartheid of the Government of the Republic of South Africa as submitted by forty Member States,

Reiterating its condemnation of the evil and abhorrent policies of apartheid and the measures being taken by the Government of South Africa to enforce and extend those policies beyond its borders,

Recognizing the legitimacy of the struggle of the oppressed people of South Africa in pursuance of their human and political rights as set forth in the Charter of the United Nations and of the Universal Delcaration of Human Rights,

Gravely concerned by the persistent refusal of the Government of South Africa to abandon its racist policies and to abide by the resolutions of the Security Council and of the General Assembly on this question and others relating to southern Africa.

Gravely concerned with the situation arising from violations of the arms embargo called for in its resolutions 181 (1963) of 7 August 1963, 182 (1963) of 4 December 1963 and 191 (1964) of 18 June 1964,

Convinced of the need to strengthen the arms embargo called for in the above resolutions,

Convinced further that the situation resulting from the continued application of the policies of apartheid and the constant build-up of the South African military and police forces made possible by the continued acquisition of arms, military vehicles and other equipment and of spare parts for military equipment from a number of Member States and by local manufacture of arms and ammunition under licenses granted by some Member States constitutes a potential threat to international peace and security,

Recognizing that the extensive arms build-up of the military forces of South Africa poses a real threat to the security and sovereignty of independent African States opposed to the racial policies of the Government of South Africa, in particular the neighboring States,

1. Reiterates its total opposition to the policies of apartheid of the Government of the Republic of South Africa;

2. Reaffirms its resolutions 181 (1963), 182 (1963) and 191 (1964);

3. Condemns the violations of the arms embargo called for in resolutions 181 (1963), 182 (1963) and 191 (1964);

4. Calls upon all States to strengthen the arms embargo

(a) by implementing fully the arms embargo against South Africa unconditionally and without reservations whatsoever;

(b) by withholding supply of all vehicles and equipment for use of the armed forces and paramilitary organizations of South Africa;

(c) by ceasing supply of spare parts for all vehicles and military equipment used by the armed forces and paramilitary organizations of South Africa;

(d) by revoking all licenses and military patents granted to the South African Government or to South African companies for the manufacture of arms and ammunition, aircraft and naval craft or other military vehicles and by refraining from further granting such licences and patents;

(e) by prohibiting investment in or technical assistance for the manufacture of arms and ammunition, aircraft, naval craft, or other military vehicles;

(f) by ceasing provision of military training for members of the South African armed forces and all other forms of military co-operation with South Africa;

(g) by undertaking the appropriate action to give effect to the above measures;

5. Requests the Secretary-General to follow closely the implementation of the present resolution and report to the Security Council from time to time; and

6. Calls upon all States to observe strictly the arms embargo against South Africa and to assist effectively in the implementation of this resolution.

Commerce Department Views on South African Economic Trends and Their Implications for the United States*

December 22, 1969

South Africa is a growing and dynamic market. The trend is for continued expansion of total imports with special emphasis on machinery and electrical equipment, transport equipment, textiles and many types of consumer goods.

While local industry has continued to take over more and more of the finished product market with some expansion of raw material and semi-finished imports, high quality finished product imports have remained competitive. The pace of new investments or expansions of old operations continues. Since foreign investment and licensing in industry tend to orient materials supply to the investor's sources, these developments have a profound and enduring effect on the relative roles of various country suppliers in the import picture. Long established SA policy is to welcome foreign investment. Details are worked out on a case by case basis. The prospect,

---

*Department of Commerce, *Foreign Economic Trends and Their Implications for the United States,* Dec. 22, 1969, pp. 8-11.

however, is for more effort to channel investment in accordance with central government and local planning.

The US has been maintaining about a 17% share of SA's 3 billion plus dollar import market. US trade continues to benefit from big increments in the sale of civil aircraft and in major capital equipment as well as semi-finished goods, particularly for long-established US firms and licenses. The US continues to be only moderately active in the finished consumer goods market.

A good deal of South Africa's growth, especially in heavy industry, has a government role, manifested not only in tariff protection, but also in quasi-governmental agencies such as the IDC (Industrial Development Corporation), ISCOR (iron and steel), ESCOM (electric power supply) and SASOL (petroleum industry). The current budget also has provision for a continuing major infrastructure program.

Basic current government financial capital expansion programs include electricity generation and transmission (to extend the national grid), ports and harbors expansion, SASOL's refining and petro-chemical processing program and ISCOR's iron and steel expansion program. Major specific projects which offer important trade opportunities are:

1. ESCOM's 12 year expansion program involving outlays of nearly 3 billion dollars, with concomitant opportunities for US suppliers of power plant and equipment.

2. A 3000-megawatt, 33.6 million dollar thermal power station in the eastern Transvaal, to be commissioned in 1977, which could be one of the biggest of its kind.

3. South African engineering firms looking for trading connections to put them in front running for the construction of nuclear power stations, the first of which is projected for the Cape.

4. Harbor improvement programs in Cape Town and Durban involving outlays of 140 million and 56 million dollars, respectively. Cape Town's scheme embraces a ship repair quay, a new two-mile sea wall and a new deck shed, geared specifically to container handling. The SA Railways and Harbours Administration plans to extend Durban harbor and improve its facilities.

5. Expected long-term iron-ore contracts between South Africa and Japan, involving 60 million tons over the next decade, requiring the construction of ore handling and harbor facilities at a yet undetermined site.

6. Huge construction projects, such as the Orange River Project, already underway, providing continuing markets for heavy construction equipment.

7. Oil exploration and drilling as well as oil transportation and refining.

8. ISCOR's expansion of its present iron and steel facilities involving the expenditure of 1.2 billion dollars over the next ten years. 420 million dollars alone will be spent on its Vanderbylpark Steel works for such items as combination slabbing and plate mill, blast furnace, electric arc furnaces and a wide strip mill complex. A third ISCOR works is planned for Newcastle in Natal and a fourth and fifth steel mill will be eventually built.

These and other programs require industrial raw materials and finished goods such as construction equipment, including road building machinery and vehicles, materials handling machines, electrical measuring and control equipment and mining machinery (both open face—a new trend—and deep mining).

Ample spring rains filling reservoirs over much of the Republic should mean prosperity for the agricultural sector. Farm machinery and implement sales will almost certainly rise from last year's drought depressed levels. Moreover, sales of other items for the rural market will rise, bringing opportunities for exporters of such diverse items as irrigation equipment, light aircraft, house paints, air conditioning units and other household appliances, dairy equipment, generators and lighting plants.

Relaxation of import restrictions on many consumer goods and continuing strong consumer demand suggest a growing market for a greater variety of durable and non-durable consumer goods of the kind in which US industry excels. Specific products, noted in more detail in an April 7, 1969 International Commerce article on trade trends in South Africa which remains relevant, include air-conditioning, hi-fi equipment, sporting goods and other leisure equipment.

Tourism, already a 140 million dollar per year industry, can be expected to grow at or near world growth figures. Demand for hotel and catering equipment will rise proportionately.

Competition for the South African import market in all categories of capital and consumer goods continues to grow. The South African is constantly looking for better products and present US suppliers must be watchful of their place in the South African market. A large number of trade missions have visited South Africa in recent months. In 1970, foreign exhibitors in South Africa's many trade fairs and trade missions (15 are due from Britain alone) will provide the South African an opportunity to compare his present suppliers' products with the finest their competitors provide. Over the past few months, major suppliers such as Britain, West Germany, France and Switzerland have further increased their investment links which in turn help support exports to industry in the country. West Germany, Japan, France and Italy—among major trading partners—increased their share of the import market in 1968 over 1967. The UK share—the highest at about ¼ of the market—declined somewhat in 1968.

Price and delivery are, of course, competitive factors but quality is a major consideration. Supplier credit terms have a particular bearing in private sector trade, given the continuing restraints on credit locally.

Advertisement Placed by the Polaroid Corporation Entitled
*"An Experiment in South Africa"**

January 13, 1971

Polaroid sells its products in South Africa as do several hundred other American companies. Our sales there are small, less than one half of one percent of our worldwide business.

Recently a group has begun to demand that American business stop selling in South Africa. They say that by its presence it is supporting the government of the country and its policies of racial separation and subjugation of the Blacks. Polaroid, in spite of its small stake in the country, has received the first attention of this group.

We did not respond to their demands. But we did react to the question. We asked

The New York Times, Jan. 13, 1971, p. 23.

ourselves, "Is it right or wrong to do business in South Africa?" We have been studying the question for about ten weeks.

The committee of Polaroid employees who undertook this study included fourteen members—both black and white—from all over the company. The first conclusion was arrived at quickly and unanimously. We abhor apartheid, the national policy of South Africa.

The apartheid laws separate the races and restrict the rights, the opportunities and the movement of non-white Africans. This policy is contrary to the principles on which Polaroid was built and run. We believe in individuals. Not in "labor units" as Blacks are sometimes referred to in South Africa. We decided whatever our course should be it should oppose the course of apartheid.

The committee talked to more than fifty prominent South Africans both black and white, as well as many South African experts. They heard from officials in Washington. They read books, papers, testimony, documents, opinion, interpretation, statistics. They heard tapes and saw films.

They addressed themselves to a single question. What should Polaroid do in South Africa? Should we register our disapproval of apartheid by cutting off all contact with the country? Should we try to influence the system from within? We rejected the suggestion that we ignore the whole question and maintain the status quo.

Some of the black members of the study group expressed themselves strongly at the outset. They did not want to impose on the black people of another country a course of action merely because we might feel it was correct. They felt this paternalistic attitude had prevailed too often in America when things are done "for" black people without consulting black people.

It was decided to send four of the committee members to South Africa. Since this group was to include two black and two white members, it was widely assumed they would not be granted visas. They were.

It was assumed if they ever got to South Africa they would be given a government tour. They were not.

It was assumed they would not be allowed to see the actual conditions under which many Blacks live and would be prevented from talking to any of them in private. They did see those conditions in Soweto and elsewhere. And with or without permission they met and talked to and listened to more than a hundred black people of South Africa. Factory workers, office workers, domestic servants, teachers, political leaders, people in many walks of life. They also talked to a broad spectrum of whites including members of all the major parties.

Their prime purpose in going to South Africa was to ask Africans what they thought American business should do in their country. We decided the answer that is best for the black people of South Africa would be the best answer for us.

Can you learn about a country in ten days? No. Nor in ten weeks. But our group learned one thing. What we had read and heard about apartheid was not exaggerated. It is every bit as repugnant as we had been led to believe.

The group returned with a unanimous recommendation.

In response to this recommendation and to the reports of the larger study committee, Polaroid will undertake an experimental program in relation to its business activities in South Africa.

For the time being we will continue our business relationships there (except for sales to the South African government, which our distributor is discontinuing), but on a new basis which Blacks there with whom we talked see as supportive to their hopes and plans for the future. In a year we will look closely to see if our experiment has had any effects.

First, we will take a number of steps with our distributor, as well as his suppliers, to improve dramatically the salaries and other benefits of their non-white employees. We have had indications that these companies will be willing to cooperate in this plan.

Our business associates in South Africa will also be obliged (as a condition of maintaining their relationship with Polaroid) to initiate a well-defined program to train non-white employees for important jobs within their companies.

We believe education for the Blacks, in combination with the opportunities now being afforded by the expanding economy, is a key to change in South Africa. We will commit a portion of our profits earned there to encourage black education. One avenue will be to provide funds for the permanent staff and office of the black-run Association for Education and Cultural Advancement (ASECA). A second method will be to make a gift to a foundation to underwrite educational expenses for about 500 black students at various levels of study from elementary school through university. Grants to assist teachers will also be made from this gift. In addition we will support two exchange fellowships for Blacks under the U.S.-South African Leader Exchange Program.

Polaroid has no investments in South Africa and we do not intend to change this policy at present. We are, however, investigating the possibilities of creating a black-managed company in one or more of the free black African nations.

Why have we undertaken this program? To satisfy a revolutionary group? No. They will find it far from satisfactory. They feel we should close the door on South Africa, not try to push it further open.

What can we hope to accomplish there without a factory, without a company of our own, without the economic leverage of large sales? Aren't we wasting time and money trying to have an effect on a massive problem 10,000 miles from home? The answer, our answer, is that since we are doing business in South Africa and since we have looked closely at that troubled country, we feel we can continue only by opposing the apartheid system. Black people there have advised us to do this by providing an opportunity for increased use of black talent, increased recognition of black dignity. Polaroid is a small economic force in South Africa, but we are well known and, because of our committee's visit there, highly visible. We hope other American companies will join us in this program. Even a small beginning of co-operative effort among American businesses can have a large effect in South Africa.

How can we presume to concern ourselves with the problems of another country? Whatever the practices elsewhere, South Africa alone articulates a policy exactly contrary to everything we feel our company stands for. We cannot participate passively in such a political system. Nor can we ignore it. That is why we have undertaken this experimental program.

Polaroid Corporation

*Speech by Representative Ogden R. Reid (New York) Before
the House on Banking and "Non-Renewal of Credit" to South Africa**

November 26, 1969

Mr. Speaker, on the first of this month, my colleague from New York (Mr. Bingham) and I, along with Mr. Brademas, Mr. Conyers, Mr. Diggs, Mr. Fraser, Mr. Mosher, Mr. O'Neill of Massachusetts, and Mr. Whalen, wrote letters to the presidents of 10 banks which had formed a consortium extending a $40 million annual line of credit to the Republic of South Africa.

The credit agreement was up for renewal and our purpose in writing was to urge that the banks not continue this financial assistance to a country whose apartheid policies are repugnant to all who love freedom.

The banks involved are Bank of America, Bankers Trust Co. of New York, Chase Manhattan Bank, Chemical Bank, First National Bank of Chicago, Irving Trust Co. of New York, Manufacturers Hanover Trust Co., Morgan Guaranty, Continental Illinois Bank & Trust Co. of Chicago, and First National City Bank of New York.

We pointed out in our letter that "the moral question raised by such a revolving credit arrangement to the racist government of South Africa is quite clear" and that the banks have helped "to strengthen the regime in South Africa and have not served to affect that government in any positive way." The full text of the letter will be inserted in the Record following my remarks.

Just yesterday, it was announced that the Government of the Republic of South Africa had requested that the line of credit not be renewed. The Finance Minister in Pretoria stated that "The Republic's strong gold and foreign exchange position" made the credit unnecessary, and that it had not, in fact, been used for the last 3 years.

Frankly, I consider the decision more a victoy for civil rights and for the cause of justice and freedom everywhere. It is a clear indication that the continued and concerted efforts of private groups and committed public officials can make a difference in an action with enormous moral significance.

The American Committee on Africa and the executive council of the Episcopal Church are two of the groups which have applied pressure on the banks for at least 4 years to refrain from financial dealings which benefit the white-minority regime in the Republic of South Africa. In addition, Mr. Bingham's efforts at mobilizing congressional opinion have been most valuable.

I am hopeful that these developments will be studied seriously in the White House and the State Department where a review of our policy toward Africa is now taking place.

In addition, I would hope that other private investors in South Africa will consider carefully the implications of their financial involvement in that country. In my view, financial institutions cannot be indifferent to the serious erosion of the rule of law in South Africa, the increasing denial of human rights, and the evermore rigorous enforcement of apartheid. Banks and other private investors are not, in short, absolved of responsibility for the conditions around them in South Africa.

*Congressional Record, Nov. 26, 1969, pp. 10137-38.

*Hearings Before the Subcommittee on Africa of the House Foreign
Relations Committee on South Africa and the Sugar Quota**

April 2 and 15, 1969

STATEMENT OF TOM O. MURPHY, DIRECTOR, SUGAR POLICY STAFF,
AGRICULTURAL STABILIZATION AND CONSERVATION SERVICE,
U.S. DEPARTMENT OF AGRICULTURE

Mr. Chairman, members of the subcommittee: I appear here today to present economic information about the sugar program, and the quota of South Africa under the U.S. Sugar Act.

South Africa did not export sugar to the United States until 1962. Under the 1962 amendments to the Sugar Act, South Africa received a small quota equal to 0.71 percent of the quantity reserved for foreign countries other than the Republic of the Philippines, Canada, the United Kingdom, Belgium, and Hong Kong.

That amendment also provided that 55.77 percent of the same quantity would be reserved for Cuba, but in the absence of diplomatic relations with that country, the sugar would be supplied by any friendly foreign country subject to the payment of a fee representing the approximate premium of the domestic market price over the world market price.

The quotas assigned to South Africa amounted to 8,325 tons in 1962, 21,823 tons in 1963, and 20,326 tons in 1964. In those years, South Africa also exported sugar against the Cuban reserve (global quota). Total imports into the United States in these years amounted to 93,000 tons in 1962, 132,000 tons in 1963, and 120,000 tons in 1964.

The quota provisions of the act for countries other than the Republic of the Philippines expired at the end of 1964. The Secretary of Agriculture exercising his general powers under the act assigned quotas to foreign countries in 1965.

Since there was serious legal question as to his authority to collect a variable import fee in the absence of specific authorization, the global quota was discontinued, and total requirements for foreign countries other than the Republic of the Philippines were assigned individually to those countries on the basis of their performance in supplying sugar to the United States in 1963 and 1964 at a time when significantly larger returns could have been earned from sales in the world market. South Africa was assigned a quota of 103,862 tons in 1965.

Under the Sugar Act amendments of 1965, South Africa was granted a quota of 1.06 percent of the total quantity available for foreign countries other than the Republic of the Philippines, Ireland, and the Bahama Islands.

That amendment also assigned 50 percent of such requirements to Cuba and provided that in the absence of diplomatic relations with Cuba that quota, with certain minor modifications, would be prorated to other foreign countries with percentage quotas on the basis of the percentages assigned to each.

The quotas assigned to South Africa (including its share of the Cuban reserve) amounted to 55,292 tons in 1966, 56,103 in 1967, 59,854 in 1968 and 56,808 tons

*South African and United States Foreign Policy, pp. 46-47; 64-68; 70-71.

for the present year. The global quota provision of the act was discontinued under the amendments of 1965.

To provide a little perspective for those quotas, let me say that during the 3 years, 1963 through 1965, shipments to the United States accounted for about 19.5 percent of South Africa's sugar exports. Since then, such shipments have accounted for about 6.5 percent.

The change was brought about because shipments to the United States were halved while total exports increased substantially in response to sharply expanded production.

On terms of our own sugar needs, sugar from South Africa accounted for about 3 percent of total importants of quota sugar by the United States during the 3-year period 1963 through 1965. Since then, about 1¼ percent of such imports has come from South Africa and the quantity which has come from South Africa is of the order of one-half of 1 percent of all the sugar consumed in this country, from both domestic and foreign sources.

Sugar accounted for about from 5 to 7 percent of the total value of all imports from South Africa during the period 1963 through 1965. Since then, sugar has accounted for about 3 percent of the value of total imports.

The United States had a favorable balance of trade with South Africa in the period 1963 through 1965, with exports exceeding imports by about 50 percent. Since then, the favorable balance has continued—imports have remained at about the same level while exports have expanded and have exceeded imports by about 75 percent.

Although a large exporter of sugar before the war, South Africa was thereafter relatively unimportant in the world sugar trade until the middle fifties. Since then, sugar production has doubled. Presently South Africa is one of the largest sugar exporting countries. In terms of net exports, it ranks after Cuba, Australia, the Republic of the Philippines, Brazil and China (Taiwan).

*   *   *

STATEMENT OF JULIUS L. KATZ, DEPUTY ASSISTANT SECRETARY OF STATE, BUREAU OF ECONOMIC AFFAIRS

Mr. Murphy, of the Department of Agriculture, has just explained the derivation of the South African sugar quota from the time it was first granted by the Congress in 1962.

I would, however, like to say a few words about the amendments made to the Sugar Act of 1965, the last time this legislation was reviewed by the Congress.

The 2 years preceding this review, Mr. Chairman, can only be described as the most hectic years the world's sugar economy has ever seen. Cuba, for many years the world's principal supplier of sugar, had 3 years of unprecedentedly low production under the Castro regime, sugarbeet harvests in Europe were poor.

As a result, consumer bid frantically for scarce supplies, and world sugar prices skyrocketed to alltime high levels, reaching 12.60 cents per pound in 1963 and 11.18 cents in 1964.

Our own sugar system was not immune to the pressure on world supplies, and prices in the United States for raw sugar, on a comparable basis, reached 12.29 cents in 1963 and 8.58 cents in 1964:

The United States managed to secure adequate supplies of sugar for its consumers during the difficult years of 1963 and 1964. This accomplishment was made possible through the cooperation of a number of the large foreign suppliers of our market who sold sugar to the United States although there were times during that 2-year period when they could have obtained substantially higher prices in the world market.

It was this fact that led the administration in 1965 to recommend to the Congress that the relative dependability of our suppliers in time of emergency should be recognized and rewarded. To accomplish this, the administration recommended that the Congress in enacting new legislation should assign import quotas among foreign countries on the basis of their performance in supplying this market during the critical 1963-64 period. The criteria recommended as a basis for assigning import quotas were thus objective and impartial.

The Congress gave substantial weight to this recommendation of the executive branch in assigning import quotas in 1965. There were some departures from the standard suggested, however, and the South African quota was a notable exception.

This, while its performance during 1963-64 would have entitled South Africa to a basic quota of about 97,000 tons, the Congress actually assigned a quota of 48,000 tons, or 50 percent less.

Imports of sugar into the United States have been regulated by a series of Sugar Acts over a long period of years, beginning in 1934. Traditionally, this legislation has been enacted for extended periods of time—4, 5, or 6 years. When the legislation was last reviewed by the Congress in 1965, it was amended and extended for 6 years, through 1971.

There is an important reason for enacting sugar legislation for an extended period of time. Five domestic sugar-producing areas and 31 foreign countries or areas are directly affected by the provisions of the Sugar Act. There are many conflicting interests affected by this legislation, both domestic and foreign.

When these problems are resolved by the Congress, it is essential that the role of each segment of our domestic industry and of each foreign country be clearly established for a period of years. This permits domestic and foreign-producing areas to make the necessary investments and commitments to enable them to comply with the provisions of the Sugar Act and thus assure U.S. customers of dependable supplies of sugar. For this reason, we believe that the present act should be allowed to run its course.

As you are aware, Mr. Chairman, a special provision of the Sugar Act, section 202(d)(1)(B), authorizes the President to suspend the quota for any country if this is deemed to be in the national interest. Such action was in fact taken against Southern Rhodesia on November 20, 1965, when President Johnson determined that the unilateral declaration of independence by the Smith regime and the tensions that arose therefrom made it contrary to our national interest to continue the sugar quota for Southern Rhodesia for 1965 or to establish one for 1966.

Cancellation of the sugar quota was one of a number of measures taken against Southern Rhodesia at that time, in concert with the United Kingdom. Among other things, we then imposed a total arms embargo, withdrew our consul general from

Salisbury, suspended action on all Rhodesian applications for U.S. Government loans and credit and investment guarantees, embargoed the shipment of petroleum products from the United States to Southern Rhodesia, and announced the decision to control all U.S. exports to Southern Rhodesia.

Since 1966, the sugar quota for Southern Rhodesia has been denied pursuant to Executive Order 11322 which prohibits imports of certain products including sugar from Southern Rhodesia.

The political and other tensions referred to in President Johnson's initial directive were subsequently determined by the United Nations Security Council to represent a threat to international peace and security and formed the basis for Security Council Resolution 232 of December 16, 1966, which called for the application of mandatory economic sanctions against Southern Rhodesia.

In the case of South Africa, however, despite our abhorrence of apartheid and its attendant repressive measures, we do not believe that the situation existing in that country is a threat to international peace and security. Nor has the United Nations Security Council made any such finding.

As I indicated earlier, the provision of the Sugar Act and the allotment of quotas to domestic- and foreign-producing areas was part of a complex and interrelated package. An attempt to alter one element of that package runs the risk of upsetting the delicate balance worked out in the Sugar Act of 1965. The Congress will during 1971 review this matter thoroughly and will have the opportunity to make such amendments as it believes desirable.

I am constantly amazed at statements from the Executive that absolve our Government from any kind of responsibility for its continued support of the economic development of a country which is unique in the world in its racial policies, which has been condemned, as you have already indicated, in certain forums, of which the United States has been a part, and then, after all of these high-flown statements and phrases, to turn right around and become involved in its economic development, by providing it with financial subsidies and all the rest.

It is difficult for me to understand the inconsistency of condemning this system of government, and then turning around and helping to finance its continuance. Would you care to comment on that?

Mr. Katz: Mr. Chairman, I can see your problem, but I don't think it is fair to say that we are financing the existence of this government, nor are we subsidizing it. We are carrying out a relatively normal economic relationship with this country, as we do with other countries whose governments and whose policies we disagree with, and those with whom we have very serious and basic disagreements.

Our relations with the Republic of South Africa are on a commercial basis. We don't provide loans; we don't provide aid to them.

Mr. Diggs: There are other countries in Africa who are in a position to provide whatever sugar we need to get from that area, and I am curious as to why these countries have not been accorded additional quotas, rather than to channel to South Africa.

I have specific reference to Mauritius, for example, which is about 98 percent dependent upon sugar crop. I have reference to Swaziland, Uganda, Malagasy Republic, even Congo (Brazzaville), which hasn't been too friendly to our Government, and to a lesser extent, Morocco, Tunisia. None of these countries practice this unique exploitation of labor and other resources based on race.

Why does South Africa have this preferred status over, say, Mauritius?

* * *

Mr. Katz: What the administration did, in 1965, when it made its proposals to the Congress, was to use the only equitable basis that it could find, and that is to take historical performance, and, particularly recently historical performance, which had an additional justification, because it took into account the relative dependability of foreign suppliers at a time when we were in some difficulty.

Now, the result of that, as I have explained in my statement would actually have given South Africa twice the amount of the quota that the Congress finally decided upon. But at the present time, under the present act, we do not have the authority to increase the quotas of other producers in Africa. We have been troubled by this ourselves, Mr. Chairman.

We have had representations from some of the producers in Africa, such as Mauritius, and our hands are really tied. Even if the quota were to be taken away from South Africa, through Presidential determination, it would not go to other African producers; it would be redistributed to producers in the Western Hemisphere.

* * *

Mr. Morse: . . . it certainly seems to me to follow that one of the purposes of the Sugar Act is to achieve U.S. foreign policy objectives. Is that correct, Mr. Katz?

Mr. Katz: Mr. Chairman, I think the purposes of the act are primarily related to defending the system of sugar production in the United States, and to provide dependable supplies of sugar to consumers at reasonable prices. I think those are the primary purposes of the act.

Mr. Morse: Well, you spoke earlier about the reallocation under the law, the reallocation of quotas to Western Hemisphere producers.

Why was that limitation imposed in the law, in your opinion?

Mr. Katz: I think obviously, to give special consideration to the Latin American economy.

Mr. Morse: Which is certainly a U.S. foreign policy objective, is it not?

Mr. Katz: Yes, sir.

Mr. Morse: Therefore, the Sugar Act certainly is an instrument for the achievement of the U.S. foreign policy objectives, is it not?

Mr. Katz: Well, I think it certainly has that effect, but I think the basic purposes are related to our domestic economy.

Mr. Morse: Well, I would agree with that, but there is certainly this ancillary purpose that you have just described.

Mr. Katz: Yes, sir.

Mr. Morse: Has there ever been a revocation, apart from the Rhodesian situation, of a quota under that section of the act which permits the suspension of a quota, section 292(d)(1)(B)?

Mr. Katz: No, no; Rhodesia is the only one.

Mr. Morse: Are there any guidelines in the law which indicate what standards should be considered in determining whether or not a suspension is in order?

Mr. Katz: Well, the language of the provision reads, "Whenever and to the extent the President finds that the establishment or continuation of a quota or any part thereof, for any foreign country, would be contrary to the national interest of the United States, such quota or part thereof shall be withheld or suspended and such importation shall not be permitted."

It doesn't go beyond the reference to the national interest.

Mr. Morse: Until Mr. Bingham's proposal to the President, has there been any proposal made to discontinue the South African quota, with which you are familiar?

Mr. Katz: Yes, sir. I could not identify any particular person with it, but we are getting a certain amount of correspondence.

Mr. Morse: Is this a fairly new phenomenon?

Mr. Katz: I don't believe so. It goes back a number of years.

Mr. Morse: Has your office ever considered any recommendations to the President with reference to suspension under section 202(d)(1)(B) of the South African quota?

Mr. Katz: This question was considered, at the time the administration recommendations were formulated, in 1965, for submission to the Congress, and the decision was made at that time to use straight historical basis for the recommendation.

*   *   *

*Speech by Representative Jonathan Bingham (New York) Before
the House on Legislation to Eliminate Sugar Quota for South Africa**

October 20, 1969

Mr. Speaker, last April, along with a number of colleagues, I introduced a bill—H.R. 10239—to end the current subsidy to South Africa's sugar producers by eliminating its sugar quota. That legislation stated clearly that—

It is not in the interest of the United States to provide official support in any form to a country whose racial policies are anathema to the conscience of the world.

An identical bill was introduced in the Senate by Senator Edward Kennedy.

Not only is our sugar quota a subsidy to South African apartheid—it is also a form of scarce foreign economic assistance. South Africa, however, is a highly developed nation which does not require the aid through trade offered by the sugar quota it currently enjoys. By contrast, the developing nations of Africa and the rest of the world do have great need for such assistance.

With these considerations in mind, I am today, with the support of 16 of my colleagues in the House, introducing legislation which amplifies my earlier bill to cut off the South African sugar quota. The legislation we are today introducing would redistribute the South African quota among the other four sugar exporting nations of Africa: Uganda, Mauritius, Malagasy, Swaziland.

*Congressional Record, Oct. 20, 1969, p. 9728.

Passage of this legislation would represent a concrete gesture of American support for and confidence in the developing nations of Africa. More specifically it would be an appropriate means of commemorating the seventh anniversary of the independence of Uganda, which was celebrated on October 9.

Uganda is a new nation richly deserving of our assistance. So far, despite a thriving sugar export capacity, Uganda has not been included in the group of nations permitted to export sugar to the United States under our sugar quota system. This legislation would permit such exports on a par with Mauritius, Malagasy, and Swaziland. The sugar quotas currently delegated to the latter three nations are well below their export capacity, and this legislation would provide significant increases in their quotas.

I hope this legislation will be given prompt consideration and approved.

*Speech by Representative John Dow (New York) Before the House on
Termination of Sugar Quota Allocated to Republic of South Africa**

April 1, 1971

Mr. Speaker, today I am introducing legislation to amend the Suga; Act of 1948 to terminate the sugar quota allocated to the Republic of South Africa.

The Sugar Act expires this year and is presently before the Congress for review. Now is the most appropriate time to discuss the policy of continuing support by economic means a government which practices an apartheid policy repugnant to the principles and ideals of all Americans.

My bill simply eliminates the quota presently given to South Africa and redistributes it to the other countries who receive a quota under the act. This approach emphasizes the issue before this country and the Congress: Should we in any way lend economic support to this regime unless it changes its racial policies?

We must also remember that it was U.S. support which absorbed the sugar market previously imported by Great Britain before it stopped trading with South Africa in 1962. The economic benefits to South Africa are substantial, they are worth more than $5 million above the market price.

For many years it has been the policy of the U.S. Government to preserve within the United States the ability to produce a substantial portion of our sugar requirements. In earlier years protection of our domestic producers was provided by a tariff policy, then, in 1934 a quota system which protected the domestic market by quotas for both domestic producers and foreign suppliers was enacted. This quota system was revised in 1937 and further revised in 1948 under the present act. The House Agriculture Committee report on the sugar program of December 31, 1920, states on page 29 that—

> It is unlikely any significant quantity of sugar would be grown in the United States if American producers had to compete on the open world market with sugar produced with cheap tropical labor or under subsidy in other countries.

The committee report highlights the economic fact that the U.S. price is above the world price and, therefore, under the quota, any country trading with us does

Congressional Record, Apr. 1, 1971, pp. 2414-15.

therefore receive a form of economic aid. A recognition of this view was made by our Government on November 20, 1965, when the quota of Southern Rhodesia was suspended pursuant to the terms of the Sugar Act after a Presidential finding that it would be contrary to the national interest of the United States to continue the sugar quota for Southern Rhodesia.

The other precedent of suspension was the withdrawal of the entire quota for Cuba by President Eisenhower in 1960 in response to the expropriation of American property by the Castro regime.

I believe that the continuation of a quota for South Africa is very much against our national interest. The racial policies of the South African Government have been deplored by our own officials but no governmental act has followed these pronouncements. The treatment by the South African Government of our own citizens is the ground on which to base the withdrawal of the quota. Two of our colleagues, Congressman Charles Diggs and Congressman Ogden Reid, were refused visas to that country as was an American well known to the world of sports, Mr. Arthur Ashe. I have asked the Congressional Research to provide me with a complete list of other U.S. citizens who were denied visas or expelled by the South African Government.

Mr. Speaker, one of the factors considered by the Congress in the apportionment to individual countries of the portion of the market reserved for imports is, according to the House Agriculture Committee print of December 31, 1970, page 48:

> Friendly government to government relations. *including non-discrimination against U.S. citizens in the quota country* and indemnification for property owned by U.S. citizens in cases of expropriation. (Emphasis added.)

I strongly believe that the Government which clearly stands for a policy abhorrent to our own citizens and which has practiced discrimination against our citizens and our Congressmen should not continue to be rewarded with a quota when the Sugar Act is reviewed by the Congress. My amendment would simply extinguish this benefit and redistribute it to other importers.

*   *   *

Address by Robert S. Smith, Deputy Assistant Secretary for African Affairs, on Foreign Investment in South Africa*

April 30, 1971

I wish to begin by stating that I am second to no one in my contempt for a legal system which so blatantly discriminates against so many people, purely on the grounds of skin color and racial origin, as does the Republic of South Africa's system of apartheid. I share with most of you the profound hope for change in this system— change to equal rights and equal opportunities for all.

Nevertheless, I am equally convinced that the ability of the Government and people of this country, or of any other country outside of the Republic, to bring about a change in this system is limited. Further, I do not believe that violence or boycott would be desirable or even potentially successful ways to do so.

*Department of State Bulletin, June 28, 1971, pp. 825-27.

It is the view of the Government of the United States that the best policy we can adopt at this time toward the Republic of South Africa, while making our stand against apartheid absolutely clear, is to maintain and increase communication with all of the people of South Africa: communication intended to maintain human contact with nonwhite South Africans and to persuade and ultimately convince white South Africans that change, which can best come from within, is both necessary and inevitable.

The object of a policy of communication is not retaliation, punishment, or clearing our own consciences, but peaceful change.

We continue to make clear our abhorrence of apartheid.

We continue to ban the shipment of any military equipment to South Africa. . . .

     *   *   *

Thirdly, it encourages—even obliges—white South Africans to ask themselves about their policies.

And fourthly, a policy of communication seizes upon the possibility of peaceful change, rather than rejecting it through violence or enforced isolation.

How does a policy of "communication for change" relate to U.S. private investment in South Africa?

There is no doubt that foreign investment strengthens the regime and, to some extent, supports its racial policies:

—It provides revenues.

—It increases productive capacity.

—It stimulates the economy.

—It constitutes foreign involvement in and cooperation with the system.

—It is a psychologically significant symbol of outside acceptance.

At the same time foreign investment can be a force for change in that:

—It adds to the economic pressures to bring more nonwhites into the labor force and at increasingly higher levels.

—It increases communication with the outside world, through foreign businessmen and technicians.

—It provides an opportunity to inject enlightened employment policies to improve the well-being of and opportunities for nonwhites.

—It is a channel through which outside influences can be felt, as we have recently seen in the case of Polaroid.

What about purely business considerations involved?

Business in and with South Africa is certainly profitable Much American investment there goes back many years. In 1969 there was a return of about 14 percent on U.S. manufacturing investment in South Africa. U.S. exports to South Africa in 1970 were worth $563 million. Together, these represented one-fourth of our investments and one-third of our exports to the whole of Africa. Our imports from South Africa include major sources of important minerals, such as gold, platinum, industrial diamonds, antimony, chromite, and uranium.

At the same time, Americans doing business in South Africa are beginning to come under serious criticism from diverse groups in this country, in Africa, and in major international bodies. Church, labor, university, and racial minority groups have been challenging American investors. Polaroid, General Motors, and Gulf are particular targets. In the past few months about 20 major American companies have sent their representatives to talk to us in the State Department about the future of their investments in South Africa.

What is U.S. Government policy toward investment in South Africa?

We neither encourage nor discourage American investment in the Republic itself. Direct Export-Import Bank loans are not available for this purpose. Restrictions on U.S. investment in developed countries apply to South Africa. The U.S. Government does not participate in trade fairs and exhibits in the Republic. The Department of Commerce makes the facts of investment available upon request, including facts about the racially discriminatory labor laws and associated deterrents to investment. Where investment occurs, we seek to encourage enlightened employment practices by American firms.

Our policy toward South West Africa, the League of Nations mandate territory that the Republic continues illegally to maintain, is a different matter. It is as a result of this illegality that President Nixon decided last May that we would actively discourage investment in the territory, that we would deny all Export-Import Bank facilities for trade and investment in the territory, and that we would deny U.S. Government assistance for the production from claims of a future lawful government against investments made on the basis of rights acquired since the U.N. General Assembly revoked South Africa's mandate in 1966.

What are the choices available to American investors?

A. Withdrawal. We understand the point of view of those investors who would withdraw, and recognize that the South Africans would be distressed if a firm should take that step. However, we do not believe a general American policy of withdrawal would be an effective blow to apartheid. To implement such a policy would probably require legislation, and we have little reason to believe that other industrialized nations would follow suit. In fact, they would be much more likely to fill the gap—an investment which only represents 15 percent of direct foreign investment in South Africa. General withdrawal would have moral value, but it would probably harden the resolve of the South African Government to maintain its present system, reduce opportunities for the communication for change of which I have been speaking, and probably not upset the economy of South Africa.

b. No New Investment. Similar considerations apply to this choice.

C. Increased Investment. We do not discourage U.S. firms from investing, because we believe U.S. firms can exercise an influence for good, even within the system.

D. Enlightened Employment Practices by American Firms. We believe that much can be done, within the laws of South Africa, to improve salaries, increase worker education and training, provide health and welfare benefits, including educational assistance to children of workers, and generally improve working and living conditions and opportunities for non-white labor. Such practices are already carried out by a number of South African firms, as well as by certain American firms. An extension of enlightened employment practices is consistent with communication for change and may significantly ameliorate labor conditions and thus provide some of the ingredients for more fundamental changes in the apartheid system.

I am well aware that such a gradualist approach will not satisfy many outspoken critics of apartheid. But I believe that many critics would be willing to reconsider their positions if there were evidence that American business was having a favorable impact on the South African situation.

E. Investment in Black Africa. An additional opportunity is the expansion of American investment in the majority-ruled states of Africa. Already half of American private investment on the continent of Africa is in black Africa, and it is growing at a higher rate than U.S. investment in South Africa. We definitely encourage this development. It demonstrates our support for the economic development of one of the least developed continents in the world, a continent which offers rich mineral resources, and growing agro-business, industrial, and tourist possibilities. It also reflects our preference for countries which do not have a legally imposed system of racial discrimination.

The successful development of black Africa cannot but have influence on the racial attitudes and theories of South Africans. Particularly significant is investment in the nonracial states of Botswana, Lesotho, and Swaziland, land islands in the South African sea. Investment in these three very poor nations has the benefits of investment in the other black African states, as well as the commercial advantage of participation in the Southern African customs union and rand currency zone, and are directly visible in South Africa itself.

To conclude: While foreign investment, including American investment, has helped South Africa's economy to grow, we are not persuaded that general withdrawal of this investment or stopping all new investment would cause South Africa to abandon its policy of apartheid.

We neither encourage nor discourage new investment in South Africa. Such investment as there is can, if properly managed, contribute to peaceful and constructive change in South Africa. At a minimum, this requires enlightened employment practices within the limits of South African law. And American commercial interests located in South Africa can provide channels of contact needed to bring home to the South Africans the realities of the world around them.

New York Times *Editorial on the Sugar Quota and South Africa* *

June 8, 1971

The United States officially condemns apartheid and enforces a United Nations arms embargo against South Africa—and then hands South Africa an annual present of $4.8 million in the form of a sugar subsidy. This "foreign aid"—the General Accounting Office called it that in 1969—to a highly advanced country with a booming economy, a country that practices a virulent brand of racial discrimination, is only one of many disgraceful effects of the Sugar Act.

If the House Agriculture Committee has its way, the United States will continue for at least three more years this bonanza to a South African industry based on what can only be called indentured labor. The committee has approved a bill that would let South Africa sell 60,000 tons annually—about 6.5 per cent of its sugar crop—in a protected United States market at double the world price. The whole arrangement flouts one of the committee's own criteria, namely that in allocating sugar quotas Congress will take into account the "need for economic development" in the producing countries.

It also violates the spirit of a provision in the Foreign Assistance Act aimed at

The New York Times, June 8, 1971.

denying aid to governments that violate basic freedoms and practice racial or religious discrimination. But the Agriculture Committee's arbitrary behavior does not stop there. Its chairman, W. R. Poage of Texas, will try to persuade the House Rules Committee to bring the Sugar Act to the floor under a rule barring amendments.

Such a rule would foreclose any opportunity for a direct House vote on the South African subsidy—in effect a vote on apartheid—which a group of Congressmen, including New York Representatives Dow, Reid and Bingham, are seeking. The House would have to accept or reject the entire act, and in that case its heavy subsidies for domestic as well as foreign producers probably would insure passage.

At best, little can be said in defense of the Sugar Act, founded as it is on protectionism and forged in a murky climate dominated by lobbyists, special interests and sordid logrolling. One of the few compensating factors in the current bill is that it does assign modest quotas to some of the poorer African countries.

But nothing at all can be said for an annual gift by the American taxpayers of nearly $5 million to the practitioners of apartheid in South Africa; Congressmen ought to have to stand up and be counted for or against this monstrosity.

New York Times *Editorial "Vote on Sugar—And Racism"**

June 9, 1971

The House of Representatives has an unusual opportunity today to accomplish three useful goals in one series of votes. It can break out of an outrageous legislative straitjacket fashioned by Agriculture and Rules Committee majorities, expose the corruption written into the Sugar Act, and remove an appearance of hypocrisy in United States policy toward South African racism.

On the Agriculture Committee's recommendation, the Rules Committee yesterday voted to bring the Sugar Act to the House floor under a rule that would bar any amendments. This would mean, among other things, that the House as a whole could not vote directly on a provision of the act that would give South Africa an annual gift of nearly $5 million in sugar subsidies.

Congressmen of both parties have fought hard to eliminate this largesse for a country that enforces racial apartheid and uses indentured labor to harvest sugar. Their effort with the Rules Committee fell short only by the margin of eight to six. There is a chance that they can persuade the whole House today to reject the rule or open it for amendment so that Representatives in effect would have to vote yes or no on apartheid.

It is a fight that involves the nation's good faith and common decency, as well as the use of taxpayers' money. It is a fight worth making.

**Ibid.*, June 9, 1971.

NAMIBIA (SOUTH WEST AFRICA)

Commentary

The case of Namibia (South West Africa as it was known until the U.N. formalized its African name, offers a specific test of policies towards South Africa. It is a special case, for by historical circumstance international authority has a claim to special concern for its fate.

Except for its single port, Windhoek, seized as an enclave by Britain in the nineteenth century "Scramble for Africa," the territory known as South West Africa came under German control at the end of that European competition. After World War I, South Africa, which had inherited the coastal enclave from Britain, assumed a mandate over all of South West Africa under provisions of the League of Nations. Following the Second World War the mandated territories—in Africa, the others were Cameroons, Togo, Tanganyika—became U.N. Trust Territories; the shift was, so most nations agreed, automatic. Only South Africa refused the conversion, and the ensuing controversy in international law has continued through the decades. Indeed, most arguments about the territory turn on precisely that point; is Namibia a separate territory, and is South Africa imposing her own apartheid and other policies in violation of her mandatory (or trusteeship) obligations? Or is Namibia an "integral part" of South Africa, and therefore no one else's legitimate business? That is South Africa's position; the international community has refused to accept it.

Rising interest in the fate of South-West Africa[1] coincided with the aftermath of "Africa's Year," 1960; that year had also seen the South African governments' actions at Sharpeville—brutalities from which the world generally recoiled.

Because of the international status of the territory and because the early 1960's were a time of willingness to hope for United Nations effectiveness, South West Africa's problems were placed before the highest of international legal tribunals, the International Court of Justice. It was fitting that litigation should have been started by the two African states longest self-governing, Liberia and Ethiopia (though they saw themselves as representatives of all Africans). It is important that Americans participated with Liberians in preparing and arguing these cases and that in both judgments of the 1960's, opinions opposing South Africa's position were filed by America's judge on the World Court, Philip Jessup, himself highly praised for his role by African heads of state.

---

[1] I shall use the historically appropriate terminology, referring to the country as South West Africa until the 1966 action by the General Assembly, and as Namibia thereafter.

Both cases, culminating in decisions in 1962 and 1966, turned on the most technical of legal technicalities: whether or not the Court could (or would) rule on substantive issues at a later date. Whether South Africa would abide by World Court decisions if they went against her, was a matter of important speculation. In view of her refusal to heed or even notice scores of U.N. directives, her compliance seemed unlikely. What the world's nations would do then was the ultimate question, but in the early 1960's it was premature.

The Court's ruling in 1962, "that it has jurisdiction to adjudicate upon the merits of the dispute," led African nations and the United States to think that the issue might be joined in a matter of years. It also led to confidence in the Court on the part of those seeking self-determination for the peoples of South West Africa.

In the years between the 1962 decision and the judgment of 1966, American policy on the South West African issue was keyed to the role of the Court. Such policy made broader American sense: it meant support for the U.N. when the United States was strongly backing the U.N.; it meant supporting the position of most African states when such support seemed important, and when the stand on principle conflicted little with other pressures. It meant opting for peaceful change and legality, stances very congenial to United States policy makers.

For the Americans, whose support for the Court's role was quite genuine, and for the African states, whose representatives shared that approach, the Court's second decision was awaited with eager anticipation in 1965 and early 1966. No statements on the subject, inside the U.N. or out of it, failed to reflect the conviction that the Court's ruling would be all important, that entirely new plans, policies, actions would follow. The less explicit assumption was that the Court would rule again, as it had in 1962, that South West Africa's problems as presented to it by Liberia and Ethiopia were within its jurisdiction.

The decision of 1966, then, sent the South African government into jubilant, if irrelevant, statements that apartheid was vindicated, and placed the African nations and their supporters into a state of shock. For the decision, handed down on July 18, 1966, found that the "Applicants" (Ethiopia and Liberia) lacked a "legal right or interest regarding the Subject-matter of their claim" and thereby dismissed it. What with the 1962 ruling as precedent and the world climate of the mid-1960's, literally no one had expected this abdication, this refusal to move on the merits of the case. South Africa did not expect it, nor did the United States Government, nor African governments, nor any other governments. Nor did the world of international law.

The only consolation for the "self-determinists" was that the decision had turned on niceties of interpretation of high legal principles, not on substance. They firmly denied that South Africa could legitimately draw vindication, support, or even comfort from the ruling. It was, in the words of Ernest A. Gross of the New York Bar, agent and leading counsel for Ethiopia and Liberia at the Hague, a debate between "the respective principles of contemporaneity and effectiveness;" on the side of the slim court majority ". . . the philosophically operative phrases [were] 'the situation as it was at that time' (viz. 1920), and 'the setting of their period.' "[2] On the dissenting side Justice Jessup gave his view: "The law can never be oblivious to the changes in

_____

[2] E. A. Gross, et al., *Ethiopia and Liberia Vs. South Africa: The South West Africa Cases.* Occasional Papers No. 5, African Studies Center, UCLA (1968), p. 6.

life, circumstances and community standards in which it functions. Treaties—especially multi-partite treaties of a constitutional or legislative character—cannot have an absolutely immutable character." He stressed that moral commitment as well as legal formality had underlain the mandate system created by the League of Nations (in the contemporaneous words, indeed, a "sacred trust of civilization"). Further, the U.N.'s Trusteeship system continued that moral commitment and it must be recognized and honored.

The U.N. General Assembly did not fail to react; if the Court would refuse to confront the issue, it would not. Almost unanimously, the Assembly adopted in October a resolution declaring, as the then U.S. Ambassador, Arthur Goldberg, put it: "By virtue of the breach of its obligations and its disavowal of the Mandate, South Africa forfeits all right to continue to administer the Territory of South West Africa. Indeed, it is because of South Africa's own action that it can no longer assert its rights under the Mandate, and apart from the Mandate South Africa has no right to administer the Territory."

Not only did the General Assembly resolution terminate South Africa's mandate, it asserted the international status and territorial integrity of South West Africa, and declared that thenceforth that territory came under the General Assembly's *direct* responsibility, a responsibility it would discharge after study and by means worked out, in and through the vehicle of an ad hoc committee.

The South African government, delighted by the Court's refusal to rule, and undaunted by the volume of words delivered at the U.N., continued to treat Namibia (as 1966's events rechristened South West Africa) in her own way. That way is to insist that Namibia does not exist, that South West Africa is, as "always" a part of South Africa, and accordingly to implement their own policies there. The 1967 arrest and trial for "terrorism" of thirty-seven South West Africans was one proclamation of their defiance. (A fifty-nine nation sponsored condemnation of this action made no difference; nor did Ambassador Goldberg's description—he said that application of the Terrorism Act "constitutes a repudiation of South Africa's claim to a tradition of respect for the rule of law".) Their 1967 declaration that Ovomboland in the north of Namibia would become a "native homeland" à la Transkei or Zululand, thus entrenching South Africa's formalized geographical apartheid in the territory, was even more flagrant.

In this setting stands taken by the United States are carefully watched. Precisely because the issues are so clear—except to those of a certain turn of legal mind, such as Dean Acheson—American policy is particularly vulnerable to African criticism if there is the slightest retreat from the General Assembly's general determination to wrest Namibia from South Africa's *de facto* control.

Thus the United States decision to block American investment in Namibia, a decision announced by Ambassador Yost in May, 1970, mattered as much for the stand it was seen to express as for what effects it might genuinely have. There are those in Africa and the United States who hope that such a step to new American policies might point the way in South Africa. But the two situations are very different—strategically, economically, legally. Only morally are the issues much the same, and policy is not always dictated by moral congruences.

Meanwhile, since international law and organization do hold a key in Namibia, the early months of 1971 found the world community again waiting for the International

Court of Justice ruling. But they waited with less assurance, and because of 1966, with less willingness to let it make definitive differences in their policies and actions. When that decision came, in June, 1971, declaring the South African Mandate to have ended, it may have restored some African confidence in the Court. What it did or could not do was to alter the realities of South Africa's control. The next step would have to come from the United Nations, and on its collective wish and ability to enforce compliance would rest issues most immediate in Southern Africa but reaching far beyond, not least to the U.N. itself.

NAMIBIA (SOUTH WEST AFRICA)

Statement by John F. Dulles, U.S. Representative to the U.N.,
Relative to United Nations Resolution II (1) on Non-Self-Governing People *

February 9, 1946

It gives me great pleasure to move the adoption of the resolutions which have been read to you. The matters which have come before this first Assembly of the United Nations have, in large part, as has been said, been organization matters. Our first job has been to get organized, and we have done that, and done it well. But the doing of it could not arouse great enthusiasm. It could not answer the question which the world puts: Will the United Nations draw the peoples together in tasks of human welfare? Only if this Organization becomes a positive and unifying force will it survive.

There was one matter which the Preparatory Commission proposed which could significantly test the spirit of the United Nations. That was a suggested resolution which touched the fringes of the problem of dependent peoples. Your Fourth Committee took hold of that resolution and transformed it into a bold and significant advance. By the resolution now before you, the United Nations speaks out in relation to the whole colonial problem, involving hundreds of millions of dependent peoples, and not merely the fifteen millions who might come under trusteeship.

We make it clear once and for all that the declaration regarding Non-Self-Governing Territories contained in Chapter XI of the Charter is not merely the concern of the colonial Powers, but also the concern of the United Nations.

By the resolution, the United Nations, while recognizing the importance of promoting the economic, social and educational aspirations of democratic peoples, is not afraid to single out for special mention thyobligations of Chapter XI to develop self-government, and free political institutions as well as the goals of self-government and independence to be sought under Chapter XII. By this resolution, the United Nations will implement the provisions of Chapter XI requiring reports from all colonial Powers.

The Secretary-General is to make those reports available as progress reports in relation to the economic, social and educational state of dependent peoples. By the resolution, the United Nations records with satisfaction that the Members holding mandates from the League of Nations, responsive to and sharing the conscience of this Assembly, have all made declarations of intention. These declarations in most cases indicated an intention promptly to negotiate trusteeship agreements, and in one case, an intention to establish independence.

By this resolution, the United Nations calls upon the mandatory States, in concert with the other States directly concerned, to conclude trusteeship agreements for subsequent submission to this Assembly, preferably not later than our next meeting. Thus, progress in this matter need not await a prior legalistic definition of that elusive phrase, "States directly concerned." Such a definition could have been found only after great delay, and, moreover, any abstract definition might have given States not

*U.N. General Assembly, *Official Records*, 1st sess., 1st part, 1946, pp. 367-68.

genuinely concerned in establishing the trusteeship system a legal position which might in practice have impeded the full and prompt establishment of that system.

*   *   *

*Statement by Ambassador Dulles Relative to U.N. Resolution 65 (1) on the Future Status of South West Africa**

December 14, 1946

This joint resolution is a good illustration of how the processes of this Assembly can bring about harmony. We started out with a statement by the delegation of the Union of South Africa, which reported to this Assembly that on the basis of its information, the peoples of the mandated territory of South West Africa desired to be incorporated into the Union of South Africa. It suggested that this Assembly should approve that step. That South African proposal at once gave rise to sharp and strongly expressed differences of opinion. Most of the Member States here came quickly to feel that this Assembly ought not to accede to that suggestion of the Union of South Africa, but there was much difference of opinion among us as to thylegal and practical reasons for that conclusion and as to the terms in which it should be couched. Several proposals were strongly debated. Gradually, as views were exchanged, the differences came to seem less momentous, until now it is possible to put forward a resolution sponsored jointly by States which initially were in disagreement.

This joint resolution does not give satisfaction to the suggestion of the Union of South Africa. But that denial is couched in terms which, while firm, are courteous and avoid offence and which make a constructive suggestion as to the future.

We believe that this joint resolution constitutes a solution which we can all welcome as a good product of our fellowship here.

Statement by Francis B. Sayre, U.S. Representative to the U.N., Relative to Resolution 141(II) on the Trusteeship of South Africa†

November 1, 1947

The question of South Africa is one of great delicacy and difficulty. Debates in the Committee revealed an honest difference of opinion as to whether the Union of South Africa is under a legal or moral obligation to submit a trusteeship agreement for the mandated Territory of South West Africa. As a consequence, there has been a similar difference of opinion as to the terms and tone of the proposed resolution.

With respect to the question of obligation, the United States believes . . . that Article 77 of the Charter does not legally require a mandatory Power against its will to place a mandated territory under Trusteeship. The language of this Article is very clear:

Ibid., 1st sess., 2d part, 1946, pp. 1325-26.
†*Ibid.*, 2d sess., 1947, pp. 577-78.

"The Trusteeship System shall apply to such territories in the following categories as may be placed thereunder by means of trusteeship agreements."

Article 77, paragraph 2 states:

"It will be a matter for subsequent agreement as to which territories in the foregoing categories will be brought under the Trusteeship System and upon what terms."

These are not the words of a binding legal obligation. The United States Government played an active role, both at the Crimean Conference and at the San Francisco Conference, in the formulation of the basic principles of the Trusteeship System. It was always of the view that nothing in the Charter could or should compel the placing of any territory under the Trusteeship System.

The present text of the resolution involves, in its ninth paragraph, a specific and rigid time-limit. It is proposed in that paragraph that the General Assembly should urge the Union of South Africa to submit a trusteeship agreement for consideration by the Assembly at its third session. But is it wise to include a provision which could be misinterpreted as an ultimatum? Moreover, long diplomatic experience reveals that it is usually rash to set a fixed time-limit in a matter of such delicacy, since all the parties concerned may be embarrassed if, for some reason, the objective is not attained by the exact date prescribed. The United States delegation therefore welcomes and supports the amendment . . . which sets forth the time-limit in a less arbitrary and rigid manner.

* * *

Statement by Ambassador Sprague on Apartheid*

November 15, 1962

Mr. Sprague (United States of America) after referring to the statements of the sponsors of the item under consideration in support of their views and of other delegations who stressed the limitations imposed by Article 2, paragraph 7, of the Charter, said that his delegation wished to avoid both excess of zeal and timid legalism in dealing with the South African racial problem and, above all, to promote the objectives of the United Nations within the framework of the Charter. It endorsed a national policy of attempting steady progress toward removal of discriminations which the Charter condemned and considered that no lasting solution of racial problems could be attained short of full participation of all races in the life of a nation. The belief in the equality and freedom of all men, consecrated in the Declaration of Independence, was the foundation of American democracy.

With regard to the legal issue of competence, the United States delegation felt that the South African motion was too broad in that it would preclude discussion of the agenda item under consideration. The exercise of the right of discussion did not contravene Article 2, paragraph 7, of the Charter; the legal restriction contained in that Article should not prevent adequate consideration of the vital question of human rights in a dynamic world. On the other hand, it would be unwise to leave the door

*Ibid., 7th sess., 1952-53, Ad Hoc Political Committee, pp. 90-91.

open to every kind of proposal. In the light of its own experience with a written Constitution, the United States felt that the General Assembly should steer a middle course and continue, as it had done in the past, to feel its way in dealing with the legal aspects of such difficult problems as the racial situation in South Africa.

The United States Government fully respected the sovereignty of South Africa and paid tribute to the fine contribution of its armed forces both in the Second World War and in the current struggle against aggression in Korea. It had no intention of making any accusation against the South African Government. However, interest in the present and future well-being of the peoples of the Union of South Africa led to serious concern over the matter at issue. It recognized the complexity of the racial situation and the conflicts within as well as among various groups. Without presuming to sit in judgment on South Africa's internal affairs, it questioned the practical wisdom of that policy at a time when the trend in other societies was towards progressively wider and more equal participation of all groups in the political and economic life of the community. Not only was a policy of increased restriction incompatible with the generally accepted interpretation of the obligations of the Charter, but its long-term repercussions might be adverse to the South African Government itself and harmful to thydevelopment of racial harmony elsewhere in the world.

The role of the United Nations was considerably limited. It was not a super-government and could not intervene in matters essentially within domestic jurisdiction of States. It had no power to impose standards, but only to proclaim them. It could reaffirm the principles of respect of human rights and call upon all Member States to orient national policy towards embodying those principles in law and custom as rapidly as local conditions permitted. Such an appeal, in general terms, would avoid the vexing issue of competence and obviate the danger to the stability of the Organization inherent in singling out for direct action special legislation of a Member State. Moreover, it might be more effective than any recommendation which might injure national pride.

The United States delegation doubted the desirability of joint draft resolution in its present form. The proposed commission, another in the large number of subsidiary groups set up by the United Nations, could add little to the already well-known facts of the situation. The General Assembly provided the best forum for discussion of their international implications. It could not enforce change; it could only seek to influence and persuade. The appointment of a fact-finding commission was not a practical means of exerting influence on the South African Government to moderate its policy and might serve only to stiffen its resistance to persuasion.

On the other hand, the Scandinavian amendment offered a broad basis for agreement in the Committee and the best method of persuasion. It expressed in more specific terms the obligation of all Member States under the Charter and called on all States—not merely one single State—to conform to their pledges. The representative of Ecuador, who had found it too theoretical and philosophic, should bear in mind that the United Nations was founded on the principle of the triumph of appeals to the mind and heart and not on resort to compulsion. The Scandinavian amendment was the most likely to rally overwhelming support. It would not satisfy those eager to crack down on a Member State regarded as delinquent, nor those who, not recognizing the limitations of the United Nations, wanted it to do something about distressing situations. In the long run, the course proposed in the Scandinavian amendment, however, might prove more effective and more constructive than direct action. Enforcement of the principles it set forth should be left to the conscience of the citizens of each country and to the power of world public opinion.

Statements by Jonathan Bingham, U.S. Representative to the
General Assembly, on U.N. Resolution 1596(XV) on Apartheid*

March 13 and 21, 1961

Mr. Bingham (United States of America) observed that the question of South West Africa was one of the most distressing and intractable problems that had confronted the Fourth Committee and that any such change as had occurred in the situation during that period had been for the worse. In spite of the repeated urging of the Fourth Committee and the General Assembly, the Union Government had refused to recognize any of its international obligations with regard to the Territory and had rejected or ignored the resolutions of the General Assembly and the decisions of the International Court of Justice. At the same time its administration of the Territory had grown increasingly harsh and repressive. The policy of apartheid which had been introduced there was repugnant to all the people of the United States, as it was to all the Governments represented on the Committee, save one. The picture presented by the petitioners of repression and persecution was truly appalling and had not been contradicted by any evidence that the Union of South Africa might have seen fit to introduce by way of reply or mitigation. In accordance with its policy of rejecting any competence of the United Nations with respect to the Territory, the Union had chosen to take no active part in the Committee's proceedings. It could not, therefore, complain if the members concluded that the statements of the petitioners had presented an accurate view of conditions in the Territory.

The Union Government's attempted justification of its refusal to permit the Committee on South West Africa to visit the Territory on the grounds that the matter was *sub judice* was especially unconvincing coming from a Government which had ignored or rejected the prior decisions of the International Court of Justice and had given no assurance that it would accept the Court's decisions in the contentious proceedings brought by the Governments of Ethiopia and Liberia. He would like to ask the South African delegation the same question which had been addressed to it by the representative of Mexico during the earlier part of the session: namely, whether the Union, to establish its sincerity in advancing the *sub judice* argument, would assure the Members of the United Nations that it would abide by the decisions of the International Court of Justice.

His delegation regretted that the Union Government had not permitted the Committee on South West Africa to visit the Territory; it could only conclude that the Union Government did not want the Fourth Committee or the General Assembly to have the information which the Committee on South West Africa would have laid before them.

He had no draft resolution to submit, at least for the time being, nor was he prepared to comment on any of the suggestions that had been made. He would merely

*Ibid., 15th sess., 1960-61, Committee 4, Trusteeship, pp. 19-20.

express the hope that the members of the Committee would keep constantly in mind that the primary objective was to achieve some tangible improvement in the situation of the people of South West Africa and that an important secondary objective was to preserve the prestige and the authority of the United Nations. Care should be taken, therefore, to avoid making recommendations which could not conceivably be carried out or which, if carried out, would not contribute to an improvement of the situation and might even be harmful to the basic objectives. It would be most unfortunate, for example, if the Committee were to take any action endangering the existence of the Mandate, upon which the United Nations position in the matter so largely depended. Likewise, nothing should be done to jeopardize the success of the contentious action brought in the International Court of Justice by Ethiopia and Liberia. His delegation considered those proceedings to be of great importance and felt that in instituting them the Governments of Ethiopia and Liberia had performed a signal service on behalf of all peoples who believed in the essential dignity of man, regardless of race, colour or creed.

By urging that the Committee should approach its task realistically he did not mean to suggest that it should become discouraged and give up any attempt to solve the problem. To do that would be to betray the interests and aspirations of great numbers of human beings within the Territory and the ideals of the United Nations itself. On the contrary, every effort must be made to find a solution, or at least a beginning of way to a solution. It was inconceivable that the Union Government should be able indefinitely to resist the moral pressure of world opinion as brought to bear through the medium of the United Nations.

*   *   *

Mr. Bingham thanked the Venezuelan representative for the kind words he had addressed to the United States delegation and congratulated the sponsors of the draft resolution on their proposal and the great care they had taken in drafting it. The text was well expressed and served a legitimate purpose, especially in regard to the instructions given to the Committee on South West Africa.

The core of the draft resolution was in operative paragraphs 5 and 6, and it was to be hoped that the measures proposed there would bring about a distinct improvement in the situation in South West Africa. His delegation was willing to support the main thrust of the draft resolution, on the understanding, however, that operative paragraphs 5 and 6 could not be construed as implying the use of force or deception to achieve the purposes mentioned. He would welcome some clarification of that very important point from the sponsors.

His delegation wished, however, to draw the attention of the twenty-three sponsors to certain questions of wording which, in his opinion, warranted reconsideration. In particular, the wording of the various paragraphs of the draft should be made consistent. The final preambular paragraph and operative paragraph 7 referred to a "threat to international peace and security", which was the wording used in Chapter VII of the Charter, while in operative paragraph 4, just as in the draft resolution on the situation in Angola which had recently been considered by the Security Council, it was recognized that the present situation might "endanger international peace and security," the words used in Chapter VI of the Charter. Since Chapters VI and VII of the

Charter dealt with different situations, and since part of draft resolution A/C.4/L.675 was addressed to the Security Council, it would seem to be highly important to use the appropriate wording, preferably that of Chapter VI. He therefore proposed that the final preambular paragraph should read:: "Reiterating that this situation, if allowed to continue, is likely to endanger international peace and security," and that operative paragraph 7 should read "Decides to call the attention of the Security Council to the situation in South West Africa which, if allowed to continue, is likely to endanger international peace and security."

With regard to operative paragraph 1, it would probably be better, considering the inadequacy of the information available to the Committee on South West Africa, to recognize the yearning of the people of South West Africa for self-determination rather than to presume that they would choose independence. The paragraph might therefore be redrafted to read "Recognizes and supports the passionate yearning of the people of South West Africa for freedom and the exercise of their right to self-determination."

Operative paragraph 3 was somewhat unclear. If there was any need to repeat the idea embodied in that paragraph, it would be better to use the wording of the sixth preambular paragraph of resolution 1593 (XV) adopted by the Assembly, namely: "Considering that attempts at the assimilation of the Mandated Territory of South West Africa, culminating in the so-called referendum held on 5 October 1960, are totally unacceptable." The present version of the paragraph was inaccurate because it was wholly based on the reference to the referendum. The question which had actually been put in the referendum was: "Do you wish the Union to become a republic?" While the fact of voting "yes" might be construed by some as signifying approval of the assimilation of the Mandated Territory, there was equal justification for the claim that the referendum in no way affected the status of South West Africa. The Committee and the General Assembly would certainly not wish to do anything that might be interpreted by the Union Government as recognizing a termination of the Mandate. His delegation approved of the decision taken by the Ethiopian and Liberian Governments to bring the dispute before the International Court of Justice, and nothing should be done which might jeopardize the success of that endeavour.

A similar question arose in regard to the phrase "and to their immediate accession to national independence" in operative paragraph 4. It might be asked whether that phrase was not contrary to the letter and spirit of the Mandate and, consequently, whether it might not jeopardize the success of the proceedings before the International Court. In no other part of the draft resolution was it said that the Committee or the General Assembly favoured the immediate accession of South West Africa to independence. The problem thus raised was one of capital importance and should, if it were to be included at all, be dealt with separately, rather than as part of paragraph. If that were what the sponsors of the draft really intended, the validity of the Mandate would be seriously challenged. If the Committee was to take a decision on the accession of a Territory to independence, it should do so only when it had all the relevant information before it and only in the light of that information. The paragraph went further than the declaration on the granting of independence to the colonial countries and peoples, which dealt only with immediate steps to be taken for that purpose. It would seem that a policy statement was being made in the present case, that the General Assembly had already decided in favour of immediate independence. He accordingly proposed that the phrase should be deleted. If it was deleted, the paragraph would end, at least in the English text, on a very firm and solemn note.

With regard to operative paragraphs 5 and 6, his delegation, like the sponsors of the draft, could not accept the arguments of the Government of the Union of South Africa, first, that the present recommendation would run counter to the *sub judice* rule and, secondly, that the mission of the Committee on South West Africa would be contrary to the Mandate. It also regretted that the representative of the Union Government had not replied to the question whether his country would be willing to accept the Court's decision. In that connexion, he pointed out that his own delegation's position had changed since the time of the vote on resolution 1568 (XV), when it had abstained.

As the Liberian representative had said, parts of the draft resolution might entail certain consequences which would have to be considered by the Assembly's Steering Committee for the contentious proceeding.

It might be more appropriate to defer the proposed appeal in paragraph 8 until the Committee on South West Africa was in possession of fuller information.

He hoped that the sponsors of the draft resolution would take his observations into consideration and find it possible to accept them.

*Statement by Ambassador Bingham
on the Question of South West Africa* *

March 13, 1961

*   *   *

In spite of the repeated urgings of this committee and of successive sessions of the General Assembly, the Union of South Africa has been adamant in its refusal to recognize any international obligations whatsoever with regard to the Territory of South-West Africa. Year after year it has rejected or ignored General Assembly resolutions urging that it enter into a trusteeship agreement with respect to the Territory. It has ignored or rejected—sometimes in the rudest of language—the decisions of the International Court of Justice defining the nature of its continued obligation with respect to the Territory under the mandate granted to it following the First World War.

Over these same years, while the Union of South Africa has continuously refused to recognize any international obligation with respect to the Territory, its policies for the administration of the Territory have grown increasingly harsh and repressive. The policy of apartheid has been introduced and more and more rigorously imposed.

Mr. Chairman, we in the United States share with the rest of the world in our Declaration of Independence a magnificent statement of the faith of free men everywhere. The words of Thomas Jefferson and his associates reflected the inspiration of a revolution on these shores and have expressed the aspirations of human beings struggling, through all the decades since, for equality of opportunity, for human dignity, and for freedom. Permit me to recall these deathless words:

Department of State Bulletin, Apr. 17, 1961, pp. 569-71.

> We hold these truths to be self-evident, that all men are created equal, that they are endowed by their Creator with certain unalienable Rights, that among these are Life, Liberty and the pursuit of Happiness. That to secure these rights, Governments are instituted among Men, deriving their just powers from the consent of the governed. . . .

Now, Mr. Chairman, I will not pretend for a moment that we in the United States have been wholly successful in our efforts to live up to the ideals represented by those words, but, along with most of the nations of the world, we recognize the validity of those ideals and we have striven with considerable success, and will ever continue to strive, to achieve them. The appalling thing about the policy of apartheid is that it rejects those ideals in principle, as well as in practice. The policy of apartheid is founded on a hateful concept that human beings of different races are not entitled to equality of opportunity. Moreover, it rejects the principle that governments derive their just powers from the consent of the governed. I feel confident, Mr. Chairman, that all members of this committee, without exception, would agree that in the case of South-West Africa the government exercised by the mandatory power is not derived from, and does not have, the consent of the vast majority of the governed. I say without exception, because the Union of South Africa itself apparently does not believe that the governed, when their skins are of a darker hue, have any right to expect that they should have any choice whatsoever with regard to the government imposed upon them.

Thus the policy of apartheid is repugnant to us in the United States of America, as it is to all the governments represented here, save one. It is particularly deplorable that such a policy should be exercised in an area such as the Territory of South-West Africa, where the administering authority has international obligations, even though it refuses to recognize those obligations.

*   *   *

Mr. Chairman, my delegation regrets that the Union of South Africa did not see fit to permit the Committee on South-West Africa to visit the territory. This would have been an excellent opportunity for the Union Government to demonstrate its willingness to cooperate with the sincere and protracted efforts of the United Nations to find a solution consistent with the terms of the charter and of the mandate. We can only conclude from its noncooperation that the Union did not want this committee or the General Assembly to have before it the information which the Committee on South-West Africa would have obtained and would have brought back to lay before us.

Mr. Chairman, I do not have at this time any draft resolution to submit, nor am I prepared to comment on any of the suggestions which have been offered for possible approval by this committee. As I began by saying, the rocklike refusal of the Union of South Africa to accept in any slightest degree the repeated expressions of opinion by the world community, as represented by the United Nations, has made this problem an extraordinarily difficult and intractable one. I would merely like to express the hope that the members of this committee, in considering the various kinds of action which the committee might recommend to the General Assembly, would keep constantly in mind that our primary objective is to achieve some tangible improvement in the situation of the people of South-West Africa and that an important secondary objective is to preserve the prestige and authority of the United Nations. Let us be careful, therefore, to avoid the temptation of making recommendations which are impractical and cannot conceivably be carried out, or which, even if carried out, will not contribute to an improvement of the situation or may even be harmful to our basic objectives. It would be extremely unfortunate, for example, if this committee were to take any action endangering the existence of the mandate, upon which the United Nations position in this matter so largely depends. Likewise we must be careful not to do anything to jeopardize the success of the contentious action brought in the International Court of Justice by Ethiopia and Liberia. As indicated by my Government's support of General Assembly Resolution 1565 last fall, we believe that this proceeding is of great importance and that, in instituting it, the Governments of Ethiopia and Liberia have performed a signal service on behalf of all peoples who believe in the essential dignity of man, regardless of race, color, or creed.

*   *   *

New York Times *Editorial on the United States and International Court of Justice Decision on South West Africa**

July 18, 1966

Today's decision of the International Court of Justice in the South-West African case will—whichever way it goes—add a new dimension to the fight of the African nations against perpetuation of white minority rule in southern Africa. It will be deeply significant not only for the Africans but for the United States and Britain, for the Court itself and for the United Nations, with which it is linked.

The Court must decide two things: Is the League of Nations mandate for South-West Africa, assigned to the South African Government in 1920, still valid, with the United Nations inheriting the League's supervisory powers? Does South Africa's extension of racial apartheid into the territory violate its obligation under the mandate to "promote to the utmost the material and moral well-being and the social progress of the inhabitants"?

In an advisory opinion in 1950 the Court held that South Africa was still bound by the mandate and that the U.N. had inherited the League's authority. But in 1962 the Court accepted jurisdiction in the South-West African case by only an 8-to-7 margin, so the outcome is uncertain.

Today's decision will be legally binding on the parties, though the Court has no obligation to specify how it should be carried out. In bringing the case in behalf of the other African nations, Ethiopia and Liberia asked the Court for a "cease and desist" order with regard to the apartheid issue. Article 94 of the U.N. Charter authorizes the Security Council to act to enforce compliance with the World Court decisions.

The black African states are aiming both to settle the status of South-West Africa—a territory bigger than Texas, with a population of 526,000, of which only 75,000 are whites—and to build pressures on South Africa itself to change its system of apartheid, under which 3.4 million whites rule a country of eighteen million.

The United States has condemned-apartheid in U.N. debates for years and has

The New York Times, July 18, 1966.

encouraged recourse to the World Court and compliance with its decisions. Up to now, however, Washington has said no legal basis exists for U.N. action against South Africa itself. With its other world burdens the Administration would be reluctant to join now in collective action against South Africa. Britain, with its vastly greater economic stake in South Africa, and the question of Rhodesia's white rebellion still far from resolved, would be even more reluctant.

But if the decision should go against South Africa and if the Pretoria Government then should flout the Court, it is difficult to see how the United States and Britain could argue against some Security Council action aimed at forcing compliance.

The winds of change seem about to blow fiercely once again on southern Africa, and not even the United States can escape the consequences.

New York Times *Editorial on the International Court of Justice Decision on South West Africa* *

July 20, 1966

The decision of the International Court of Justice to throw out the South-West Africa case will baffle laymen and arouse fierce debate among international lawyers.

It is bound to affect the stature and usefulness of the World Court. It will necessarily alter the means employed by African governments, in the U.N. and elsewhere, to press the fight against white domination and racial segregation in southern Africa.

One reason why the decision will provoke enduring argument among lawyers is the remarkable seven-to-seven deadlock of the justices on so important a case. This required the vote of the Court's President, Sir Percy Spender of Australia, to produce a verdict, which in effect reversed a previous verdict of the same Court on the same case.

Another reason is the devastating nature of some of the dissents, particularly that of the American justice, Philip C. Jessup, who said the judgment was "completely unfounded in law."

The question about the ruling that both lawyers and laymen find most puzzling is this: Why did the Court take jurisdiction in the case if Ethiopia and Liberia could not establish "any legal right or interest in the subject matter of their claims" against South Africa? As Justice Jessup posed it in his dissent:

"Why would the Court tolerate a situation in which the parties would be put to great trouble and expense to explore all the details of the merits, and only thereafter be told that the Court would pay no heed to all their arguments and evidence because the case was dismissed on a preliminary ground which precluded any investigation of the merits?"

The answers can only be: Because the Court line-up had changed—due to death, illness and disqualification—between the acceptance of jurisdiction in 1962 and the verdict of 1966. And because this Court majority (given the President's vote) drew a fine, legalistic line between the right to jurisdiction and the right to a decision on the merits of the complaints of the two plaintiffs.

Prior to deciding not to rule on the merits, Sir Spender and his colleagues probed deeply into the claims of the plaintiffs. In the most protracted case it has ever heard, the Court studied sixteen printed volumes of written pleadings and listened to nearly 6,000 pages of oral argument in 112 sessions.

After all this, the majority declined to rule even on whether the League of Nations mandate for South-West Africa, conferred on South Africa in 1920, is still in force. And it evaded the question of whether extension of racial segregation (apartheid) into South-West Africa violates South Africa's mandate obligation to "promote to the utmost the material and moral well-being and the social progress" of the 526,000 inhabitants, all but 75,000 of them nonwhite.

This verdict will disappoint all who had hoped for a valuable addition to the body of international law. On the South-West Africa question it represents retrogression of a sort, for in an advisory opinion in 1950 the Court had held that South Africa was still bound by the mandate and that the U.N. has inherited the League's supervisory functions.

For South Africa, the decision is a victory beyond the fondest hopes of Prime Minister Verwoerd. The verdict means that for the foreseeable future South Africa can continue to administer South-West Africa, including the extension of apartheid, unhindered by international supervision or interference.

With the legal route to change in South-West Africa and an international legal judgment on apartheid barred indefinitely, the new African nations will now turn to other channels. Moderate African voices will have vastly greater difficulty gaining a hearing; the language of the African majority in the U.N. or the Organization of African Unity will become more strident and its actions more violent.

It will be a long time before the United States or anyone else will be able to persuade any African government that it can obtain justice from the International Court of Justice.

Statement by Seven Republican Congressman (Morse, Maillard of California, Frelinghusen of New Jersey, Conte of Massachusetts, Horton, Reid, Kupferman of New York) on South West Africa*

August 5, 1966

It has traditionally been the faith of the United States that disputes between nations can and should be resolved through the rule of law. But broad acceptance of the rule of law requires that it afford justice to those appealing to it. Perhaps the most significant result of the decision by the International Court of Justice on July 18, 1966 in the South West Africa case is that it may make the concept of peaceful settlement of disputes more difficult to accept by nations anxious for change.

The decision was an unfortunate setback for those who have counseled restraint and moderation in dealing with apartheid in South West Africa. Strong United States leadership is needed now to encourage African leaders to continue the search for a peaceful settlement of the controversy. Overwrought aggressiveness would result in needless human suffering and loss of life—and would diminish the chances for constructive change.

*Congressional Record, Aug. 5, 1966, p. 18430.

In dismissing the suit of Ethiopia and Liberia, the International Court of Justice made what Judge Mbanefo of Nigeria, in his dissenting opinion, termed two "impermissible" distinctions; first, between the right to bring a case and the right to have that case decided, and secondly, between the "conduct provisions" and the "special interests provisions" of the Mandate agreement. These distinctions are legally dubious and historically myopic. But they form the basis of the decision, and that decision will stand, despite American Judge Phillip C. Jessup's brilliant dissenting opinion that it is "completely unfounded in law." The Africans will not let the matter rest there—nor should the United States.

The Court stated that it had to "apply the law as it finds it, not to make it." In fact, the Court majority appears to have ignored the law as it found it in the 1962 Judgement, by which the Court accepted jurisdiction, which was then considered to be final and without appeal. Instead the Court made law by giving the sanction of silence to de facto annexation and racial discrimination. Thus, the decision seems to be an unfortunate example of legal politics and judicial avoidance. Because it appears to be a political determination, the decision could cast doubt in the minds of many Africans about the efficacy of the rule of law.

In addition, the decision of the all-white members of the Court majority could severely curtail the influence of their countries in Black Africa. If the United States fails to take the initiative in seeking an end to racial discrimination in South West Africa, the western countries may be increasingly precluded from any effective influence in this issue. Thanks to the learned dissent of Judge Jessup, the United States is in a unique position to take such an initiative.

The painful silence of the Administration since the decision has been punctured only by the belated and limp State Department release of July 27th. The release contents itself with a recounting of past Court opinions while failing to acknowledge the serious political implications of this Court decision, the wisdom of the Jessup dissent, or the need for United States leadership. Only U.S. leadership now will convince the African States of the sincerity of U.S. concern for the future of non-discriminatory development and non-violent transition in Africa. Only U.S. leadership now can assure that we will be welcome in Africa when prudent leadership is most critical.

Therefore, we strongly recommend that the President:

1. Initiate a resolution at the forthcoming Session of the United Nations General Assembly, convening in September, to call an immediate Charter Amendment Convention to review Chapters XI and XII of the Charter, relating to Non-Self-Governing Territories and the International Trusteeship System, respectively. In such a Convention, the United States should support Charter amendments providing for:

(a) the automatic inclusion of former mandated territories under the League of Nations (such as South West Africa) as United Nations Trust Territories;

(b) the explicit prohibition of racial discrimination in any Trust Territory;

(c) the establishment of the right of the Secretary-General to bring action in the International Court of Justice upon a finding that racial discrimination is practiced by the administering power in the Trust Territory.

The Convention should be required to recommend any Charter amendments to the 21st Session of the General Assembly by January 1, 1967.

2. Appoint a high-level official delegation, headed by the Secretary of State, to visit African states and the Organization of African Unity in Addis Ababa, and to

confer with African Foreign Ministers. This would demonstrate American concern and facilitate the development of a responsible United States policy for the resolution of the South West African crisis.

3. Call a White House Conference of American businessmen and bankers with economic interests in South Africa to examine in detail all proposals for a unified private and public economic policy of the United States to encourage the Government of South Africa to abandon its abhorrent policy of apartheid.

Statement by Ambassador Goldberg Before the General Assembly on the International Court of Justice Ruling on South West Africa*

September 22, 1966

＊   ＊   ＊

My Government holds strong views on these problems. We are not, and never will be, content with a minority government in Southern Rhodesia. The objective we support for that country remains as it was stated last May: "to open the full power and responsibility of nationhood to all the people of Rhodesia—not just 6 percent of them."

Nor can we ever be content with such a situation as that in South West Africa, where one race holds another in intolerable subjection under the false name of apartheid.

The decision of the International Court, in refusing to touch the merits of the question of South West Africa, was most disappointing. But the application of law to the question does not hang on that decision alone. South Africa's conduct remains subject to obligations reaffirmed by earlier advisory opinions of the Court, whose authority is undiminished. Under these opinions, South Africa cannot alter the international status of the territory without the consent of the United Nations and South Africa remains bound to accept United Nations supervision, submit annual reports to the General Assembly, and "promote to the utmost the material and moral well-being and the social progress of the inhabitants."

This is no time for South Africa to take refuge in a technical finding of the International Court—which did not deal with the substantive merits of the case. The time is overdue—the time is long overdue—for South Africa to accept its obligations to the international community in regard to South West Africa. Continued violation by South Africa of its plain obligations to the international community would necessarily require all nations, including my own, to take such an attitude into account in their relationships with South Africa.

＊   ＊   ＊

Department of State Bulletin, Oct. 10, 1966, p. 523.

New York Times *Editorial on South Africa's Control Over South West Africa**

September 23, 1966

As its first item of political business, the General Assembly in extraordinary debate will try to decide what the United Nations should try to do about South Africa's League of Nations mandate over South-West Africa.

Without even waiting for the start of that specific debate today, United States Ambassador Goldberg has called on South Africa to accept U.N. supervision of the mandate and warned that continued violation of its "plain obligations" would bring serious consequences.

The World Court barred the shortest route to international collective action in July when it threw out the case brought by Ethiopia and Liberia without ruling on its merits.

Now African governments have prepared an Assembly resolution that would declare South Africa's mandate revoked or terminated. The sponsors are confident they can muster a two-thirds majority for such a resolution, which might call for establishment of a U.N. supervisory commission for South-West Africa and for Security Council action to effect the transfer of responsibility.

This resolution would be based on advisory opinions of the World Court in 1950, 1955 and 1956. These held that the mandate was still valid, that the United Nations was the legal heir of the League, and that South Africa had to accept U.N. supervision.

The Assembly in overwhelming majority will doubtless agree that South Africa has violated its obligations and deserves to be stripped of its mandate to "promote to the utmost the material and moral well-being and social progress" of South-West Africa's inhabitants. The nagging question is: Could such an Assembly resolution have any practical effect on the South-West African situation?

South Africa has flouted more than seventy Assembly resolutions and ignored those earlier Court decisions. It knows, as the other African states know, that in present circumstances the United States and Britain—the only two powers that could act effectively—will not go to war to "liberate" South-West Africa.

The most the Africans can realistically expect is that the Assembly will express itself forcefully on the mandate and that the Council will use every practical means to persuade South Africa to comply while keeping open all its options for enforcement action. This also seems to be the least unpalatable among the policy positions open to the United States.

Statement by Ambassador Goldberg Before the General Assembly Urging Concrete U.N. Action in South West Africa†

October 12, 1966

We of the United States delegation have listened with close attention to this debate on the future of South West Africa. The extraordinary importance attached to this issue was dramatically demonstrated by the General Assembly when it decided to

---

*The New York Times, Sept. 23, 1966.
†*Department of State Bulletin, Oct. 31, 1966, pp. 690-91.*

begin the debate without delay and to hold it in plenary session. We share the general view of the importance of the issue, and we believe this may prove to have been one of the truly decisive debates of the United Nations if, as we earnestly hope, it results in effective action.

I should like to pay tribute to you, Mr. President, and to the participants in this debate, for the seriousness with which this very difficult question has been treated. My delegation has great respect for the views expressed, both in the statements made and in the 54-power draft resolution.

We are encouraged to find that, as regards the status of South West Africa, virtually all of the membership, with very few exceptions, is in agreement. This near-unanimity finds strong support in the legal framework clearly defined by the three advisory opinions of the International Court of Justice, which remain an authoritative statement of the law on this matter.

It may be useful at this stage of our debate to sum up at this point the essential elements of this broad agreement, which we believe exists in this Assembly.

First, the people of South West Africa, like all peoples, have the right to determine their own future.

Second, South West Africa is a territory having an international status and will remain so until its people exercise this right of self-determination.

Third, South Africa's right to administer the territory arose solely from the mandate.

Fourth, as the mandatory power, South Africa incurred certain obligations toward the people of the territory—including the promotion of their material and moral well-being and their social progress. It has not fulfilled these obligations. Indeed, it has even gone so far as to impose on the territory the abhorrent system of racial segregation known as apartheid.

Fifth, as the mandatory power, South Africa incurred certain obligations to the international community, for which the General Assembly has supervisory responsibilities. Among these are obligations to report annually on its administration of the territory and to transmit petitions from the inhabitants. South Africa has repeatedly refused to carry out these obligations. We are thus confronted with a continuing material breach of obligations incumbent upon the mandatory power.

Sixth, South Africa itself has disavowed the mandate, asserting that it ceased to exist upon the dissolution of the League of Nations.

Seventh, by virtue of the breach of its obligations and its disavowal of the mandate, South Africa forfeits all right to continue to administer the Territory of South West Africa. Indeed, it is because of South Africa's own actions that it can no longer assert its right under the mandate; and apart from the mandate, South Africa has no right to administer the territory.

Eighth, in these circumstances the United Nations must be prepared to discharge its responsibilities with respect to South West Africa.

On these eight points, Mr. President, we believe all but a very few members are in essential agreement. We agree on the nature of the problem. We agree on the objective. It is highly important that our near-unanimity on these fundamentals should be made manifest.

This is all the more true when we come to decide on the best means of implementing our common aim. To be effective in this most important issue, we need more than world opinion voiced by words in a resolution. We need world cooperation manifested by concrete action.

And with this in mind, the United States is prepared to work with all delegations committed to our common goal.

In our view, the General Assembly should begin by expressing explicitly the decision with respect to the status of South West Africa in a form acceptable to virtually all the membership. Having done this, it should create a practical instrumentality to give effect to its decision.

In considering what form this instrumentality should take, we are very much helped by the eminently sensible suggestion made by a number of representatives during this debate; namely, the establishment of a United Nations commission for South West Africa. The United States would be glad to serve on an appropriately representative body if that is the desire of the General Assembly.

This commission, it seems to us, should have very explicit and strong terms of reference. It should be asked to recommend means by which, in accordance with a prescribed timetable, an administration for South West Africa can be set up which will enable the people of the territory to exercise their right of self-determination. The commission should report as soon as practicable and in any event not later than a specific and early date to be agreed upon, a date consistent both with the urgency of the matter and with the need for effective discharge of its important responsibility. All principal organs of the United Nations should be asked to take appropriate action with respect to the commission's report, and the cooperation of all members in its work should be requested.

This, let me emphasize, Mr. President, is an action proposal. It contemplates steps which can be immediately and practically implemented and which lie within the capacity of this organization. It is designed to provide the community of nations promptly with a considered blueprint for united and peaceful action for the benefit of the people of South West Africa.

It is extremely important, Mr. President, that the action which the General Assembly takes on this transcendantly important issue should be both intrinsically sound and widely supported. This is necessary in the first place for the sake of the people of South West Africa, who have a right to expect from us not only words but also concrete, helpful, and meaningful actions. And it is equally necessary for the sake of the United Nations itself—for the authority and prestige of this world body.

These are the views of the United States on this important subject. We do not suggest that we have spoken the last word on this matter. We are flexible in our approach. But we are also firm in our determination that the United Nations, with all the unanimity and effectiveness we can muster, shall proceed to bring practical relief to the people of South West Africa in their time of need.

New York Times *Editorial on the U.N., the United States and South West Africa**

October 13, 1966

The United States has finally thrown its weight behind a United Nations effort to divest South Africa of its control over the mandated territory of South-West Africa.

**The New York Times*, Oct. 13, 1966.

That is the meaning of Ambassador Goldberg's declaration in the General Assembly that South Africa "has lost and forfeits all right to continue to administer" the mandate. He set forth American willingness to participate in a United Nations Commission, not simply to restudy conditions in South-West Africa but to recommend means for establishing a U.N. administration that would enable its inhabitants "to exercise their right of self-determination."

The United Nations has set up four previous missions or committees to deal with South-West Africa. None produced meaningful results, but none was armed with the "very explicit and strong terms of reference" advocated by Mr. Goldberg.

In previous U.N. efforts the United States opposed coercion and the imposition of a deadline for South African compliance. Now it recommends "a prescribed timetable" for setting up a U.N. administration in South-West Africa and urges that all principal organs of the U.N. be asked to take "appropriate action" on the Commission's report. This clearly includes action by the Security Council if necessary, a step the United States has opposed in the past.

Mr. Goldberg's statement does not imply that the United States is ready or eager to impose sanctions on South Africa or mount an invasion of the mandated territory. Obviously, the best outcome would be South Africa's voluntary surrender of the mandate. But the American recommendation is "an action proposal" that envisions neither indefinite delay nor steps that could not be implemented.

So the African delegates have a choice. They may have the votes to push their own extreme resolution through the General Assembly, but the practical among them know they cannot implement it without American support.

The other course is to engage the United States and like-minded governments— almost the entire U.N. membership—in a more careful approach to an extremely complicated problem that could open the way to meaningful action. No one can yet spell out that action, but this is obvious: The United States is committed as never before and could not reverse its direction.

New York Times *Editorial on the U.N. and South West Africa**

October 30, 1966

The United Nations has broken new political and legal ground with the Assembly's declaration that South Africa's mandate over South-West Africa is "terminated" and that the territory now comes under "the direct responsibility" of the U.N.

How much this bold language will mean depends first on whether a fourteen-member U.N. Committee will be able by next April "to recommend practical means" for administering South-West Africa and giving self-determination and independence to its 526,000 inhabitants. Ultimately, it depends on the willingness of the Security Council to agree on action to enforce the Assembly declaration and throw the South Africans out of the territory they have administered since 1920.

But there is no reason to doubt that South Africa will resist by all possible means any U.N. encroachment on South-West Africa and it is difficult at present to envision effective U.N. action.

It was with these problems in mind that Latin-American nations moved successfully

**Ibid.*, Oct. 30, 1966.

to substitute an ad hoc U.N. Committee to recommend measures by next April for the African bid to establish immediately a U.N. Administering Authority for South-West Africa. Some of the same considerations plus the desire to get Britain's support prompted the last-minute attempt by Arthur J. Goldberg to diffuse immediate U.N. responsibility—an attempt that ended in a humiliating American defeat.

In light of Mr. Goldberg's earlier commitment on this issue, however, he had no alternative but to vote for the resolution in its final form, and the United States will serve on the U.N. Committee if asked.

The abstentions of Britain and France plus the Soviet Union's well-known distaste for any U.N. enforcement machinery seem likely to circumscribe Security Council action. To cite these evident limitations on early enforcement is not to disparage the Assembly resolution. The dramatic fact is that 114 nations joined in this attempt to vacate South Africa's mandate.

In a sense, then, the "legislation" to deal with this crucial matter is now on the record books. The fact that it may not be promptly enforced discredits it no more than the failure of universal enforcement discredits civil rights laws in the United States.

Statement by Ambassador Goldberg on the United States Decision to Serve on the U.N. Ad Hoc *Committee on South West Africa**

November 21, 1966

As the President of the General Assembly has announced, the United States is among the countries which will be serving on the United Nations *Ad Hoc* Committee on South West Africa.

We have accepted his invitation to serve, despite our great regret that France and the United Kingdom have not found it possible to take part. We would have welcomed their participation in the resolution of this grave and important problem.

Our acceptance is based on our understanding that, as indicated in the General Assembly's resolution on South West Africa, the Committee will proceed to its highly responsible task with all deliberate speed and concern, in full recognition of the many complex and difficult problems involved. I have already expressed my country's view that we must seek a peaceful solution consistent with the United Nations Charter and with the principle of self-determination, a principle to which the United States has been committed from the earliest days of its history.

In short, United States participation is based on the expectation that the Committee will explore all avenues to a peaceful solution to this problem and on our conviction that its recommendations, if they are to be acceptable and effective, must be realistic and practicable and within the capacity of the U.N. to achieve.

New York Times *Editorial on the U.N.* Ad Hoc *Committee on South West Africa†*

November 23, 1966

It is unfortunate, but not unexpected, that Britain and France should decline to serve on the fourteen-member United Nations *ad hoc* Committee on South-West

Department of State Bulletin, Dec. 19, 1966, p. 937.
†*The New York Times, Nov. 23, 1966.*

Africa. Apart from this setback, Abdul Rahman Pazhwak of Afghanistan, President of the General Assembly, has named a committee that reflects fairly well the geographic and power distribution among U.N. members.

The refusals of Britain and France were foreshadowed last month by their abstentions on the Assembly's declaration that South Africa's mandate over South-West Africa was "terminated." Given President de Gaulle's distaste for the General Assembly and for U.N. interventions, France probably would not have participated under any circumstances. Britain might have been willing to do so if an American attempt to broaden the committee terms of reference and blunt any immediate U.N. responsibility for South-West Africa had been accepted. But the British decided against joining a committee whose majority might demand an embargo on trade with South Africa that could magnify Britain's trade and payments crisis.

So the U.N. committee must determine how to implement the Assembly resolution and bring self-determination to South-West Africa without the advice of three permanent Security Council members (Nationalist China was not invited). These absences raise doubts as to whether the Council will order any action the committee recommends by its deadline next April.

Explaining American participation, Arthur J. Goldberg put such emphasis on the committee's responsibility to seek a "peaceful" solution in South-West Africa that Africans asked if Washington had retreated from its strong stand on the issue. There has been no retreat, but obviously it will be extremely difficult for the committee to fill Mr. Goldberg's prescription for recommendations that are "realistic and practicable and within the capacity of the U.N. to achieve."

New York Times *Editorial on "Futility on South West Africa"**

May 11, 1967

The United Nations General Assembly is grinding to the end of one more frustrating debate on South West Africa. It will have been mostly an exercise in futility, whether or not the Assembly adds yet another strongly worded resolution to the seventy-plus it has adopted during the past twenty years.

Black African governments might muster a substantial majority for a resolution calling for "mandatory sanctions" against South Africa, but many of them realize this would be meaningless. None of the great powers intends to take any significant action to deprive Pretoria of control over the territory it has ruled for half a century but never owned.

Britain and France have been consistent during recent U.N. deliberations. They abstained on a resolution supported by the United States and Russia last October that declared South Africa's League of Nations mandate over South-West Africa "terminated," and that added: "Henceforth, South-West Africa comes under the direct responsibility of the United Nations."

While accusing the United States of being the ally of South Africa's white minority Government, the Soviet Union has made it plain that it would not support any U.N. attempt to take over South-West Africa or to install a U.N. administration there.

*Ibid., May 11, 1967.

Ambassador Goldberg insists the United States has not retreated from his tough stand of last fall; but his emphasis has shifted and the proposals he now backs ignore most of the U.N. history on South-West Africa. In October, he asked that a special U.N. committee recommend "a prescribed timetable" for setting up a U.N. administration for South-West Africa to give its people the right of self-determination. He still endorses a proposal for a special U.N. representative and a U.N. Council for South-West Africa, but now urges caution and delay pending an attempt to open a "dialogue" with South Africa.

But what has the U.N. been trying to do about South-West Africa for twenty years? Its record is full of abortive attempts to open "dialogues" with Pretoria and includes the failure of four U.N. missions or committees for South-West Africa of the kind the United States now proposes.

Mr. Goldberg warns the U.N. against "confrontation" with South Africa, but he surely has matters reversed. It is Pretoria that repeatedly has chosen "confrontation" with the U.N. and with three World Court decisions holding that it had to accept U.N. supervision of its mandate. He warns against "coercion," but General Assembly attempts to "coerce" South Africa to accept U.N. supervision for the mandated territory began long ago and were brought to a dramatic climax by the 1966 resolution terminating the mandate.

Nobody in his right mind would wish anything but a peaceful solution of the South-West African question and Mr. Goldberg is welcome to try his hand at a "dialogue" with a Government that has heaped scorn on the 1966 resolution he supported.

The point, however, is that if the United States is unwilling to do anything to implement such a resolution it might have been wiser not to support it in the first place.

Letter from Ambassador Goldberg to the Editors of the New York Times
on Solving the South West African Question *

May 9, 1967

I read with great interest your May 8 editorial "Futility on South-West Africa," but I do not agree that the United States position in the current debate is ill-founded.

There are three new factors which have substantially altered the nature of the long-standing South-West Africa problem.

First, the 1966 U.N. resolution declared the mandate of the South African Government terminated by its own default. Second, the South African Government appears to be moving toward some flexibility in its diplomatic policies in Africa, although it continues to apply and in certain respects to extend its repressive and abhorrent apartheid laws. Third, and as corollary to the foregoing, the South African Government, according to an April 21 dispatch in The Times, has agreed in principle to enter into a "dialogue" on South-West Africa with the United States and other members of the United Nations.

None of these factors has existed heretofore.

Ibid., May 11, 1967.

In view of these changes in the situation, the United States believes, as you seem to agree in your editorial, that such a "dialogue" should be conducted. There can be no assurance that the dialogue will be fruitful; however, it would be unreasonable on our part to ignore this development and the possibility of peaceful progress on the issue.

Our support for such a dialogue should not be taken as a withdrawal from, or modification of, the United States position in favor of the 1966 U.N. resolution on South-West Africa, a position which The Times approved in its editorial columns of Oct. 30, 1966. Rather, we believe circumstances indicate that the next step should stress diplomacy and not force and coercion. Our stated goals of independence and freedom for South-West Africa are unchanged, and we remain consistent in our commitment to those fundamental principles.

There are many problems in world affairs which are not susceptible of a quick and easy solution. However, attempts must be made to find solutions; such attempts are not "an exercise in futility," even when they do not meet with immediate or complete success.

In voting for the 1966 resolution on South-West Africa last fall, the United States made clear its view that a difficult search for a peaceful and practical solution lay ahead. We are continuing and will continue to push forward in that search.

Statement by Ambassador Yost on the United States Stake in an Effective United Nations*

May 19, 1970

I should not wish to end without saying a few words about two other related subjects of major United Nations concern: decolonization and human rights. One of our greatest achievements in these 25 years has been to welcome into the U.N. family new members which have won self-determination and independence during that time. Progress has also been made—though far less than is needed—in the pursuit of that other great objective of the charter, the strengthening of fundamental human rights. Much of our concern and much of our debate at the United Nations centers, as you know, around that part of the world, southern Africa, where we are still farthest from these two goals, where human rights are still outrageously flouted and majority rule shamelessly denied. Before concluding, I should like to report specific action which the United States is taking about one part of this region—Namibia, or as it was formerly known, South-West Africa.

Namibia suffers not only from a denial of human rights; it also suffers a unique international wrong in the unlawful perpetuation of South African rule. It is 3½ years since the General Assembly, after other remedies had been exhausted, declared the South African mandate at an end and with it South Africa's right to govern the territory. Yet South Africa remains in possession in defiance of the United Nations and has compounded the offense by introducing into Namibia the apartheid system and the whole apparatus of arbitrary South African police laws and political trials.

In this situation there has been an unhappy division of counsel in the United Nations. Some members have urged the use of armed force. We oppose this course. As

*Department of State Bulletin, June 8, 1970, pp. 708-09.

my predecessor Justice Goldberg said, the world is already suffering from too many confrontations and we should not add one more to the list. Mandatory economic sanctions against South Africa would also heighten confrontation and would require the use of force to ensure their effectiveness and do not command our support as an appropriate step.

In these circumstances the United States, among others, pursues other courses. We have vigorously protested to South Africa over the application of laws violative of human rights and fundamental freedoms in an international territory where it has no right to be. We have joined with other members of the U.N. Security Council in a search for means better to discharge the U.N.'s direct responsibility for the territory. We have accepted over the years 39 Namibians as refugee students in the United States; and we are also taking steps, as Secretary Rogers announced in March, to issue travel documents, under the 1951 Geneva Convention on the Status of Refugees, to certain refugees in the United States, including Namibians as well as others from southern Africa. It is pertinent also to recall that since 1963 the United States has maintained its embargo on the shipment of all military equipment to South Africa.

We have given careful consideration in our Government to further peaceful and practical steps which the United States, and other powers, could take to demonstrate more concretely to South Africa the strength of our opposition to their policy in Namibia and our strong belief that they should reconsider. As a result of this review I can tell you that the President has decided on the following steps:

1. The United States will henceforth officially discourage investment by U.S. nationals in Namibia.

2. Export-Import Bank credit guarantees will not be made available for trade with Namibia.

3. U.S. nationals who invest in Namibia on the basis of rights acquired through the South African Government since adoption of General Assembly Resolution 2145 (October 27, 1966) will not receive U.S. Government assistance in protection of such investments against claims of a future lawful government of Namibia.

4. The United States will encourage other nations to take actions similar to these.

We are under no illusion that these steps, taken alone, will quickly induce South Africa to abandon its present policy in Namibia. They should, however, make clear to South Africa that its illegal occupation cannot be condoned. We hope that others may take similar steps, and we are consulting with other governments on possible further moves. We hope, moreover, that the accumulation of such steps may cause the South African Government to reflect whether in truth its interests are better served by the lonesome road it is traveling than they would be by a return to legality and peaceful resolution of the international issue of Namibia. Sooner or later, equality of political rights is bound to come to all of southern Africa. Better that it should come soon than late, and far better that it should come by peaceful and orderly stages than after explosions of violence.

*   *   *

UNITED STATES U.N. SECURITY COUNCIL'S NEW MEASURES CONCERNING NAMIBIA *

Statement by Ambassador Buffum

July 29, 1970

The United States is pleased to have been able to vote in favor of the resolutions just adopted by the Council. The substantial support accorded them is a fitting tribute to the ad hoc subcommittee whose work they endorse. We would like to make our congratulations to the subcommittee a matter of record.

Mr. President, on May 20 this year my Government announced new policy steps it intends to take to discourage investment by our citizens in Namibia and to deny credit guarantees and other assistance for trade with that territory. We are grateful to note that the economic measures which states are called upon to take in operative paragraphs 4 through 7 of draft resolution S/9891 are consistent with and in fact reflect the policy already enunciated by my Government. In our view, such steps constitute a meaningful contribution to the Council's efforts to deal effectively with the problems of Namibia.

In explaining our vote, Mr. President, I must recall that the United States did not vote in favor of Resolution 282 and therefore cannot join in its reaffirmation as provided in preambular paragraph 6.

With regard to operative paragraphs 2, 10, and 12, the positions taken previously by my Government on the matters of substance dealt with in those paragraphs remain unchanged.

As for operative paragraph 2, my Government continues to maintain that member governments must remain free to take appropriate action to protect their own citizens and the people of Namibia. On operative paragraph 10, my Government's position on General Assembly Resolution 2248 is well known. Finally, I would reiterate that our support for operative paragraph 12 constitutes no undertaking on our part to contribute to a special fund for Namibia in the event such a fund is established.

Mr. President, my Government particularly welcomed the draft resolution in S/9892, which requests an advisory opinion of the International Court of Justice. This is the first time the Security Council has availed itself of the procedures in article 96, paragraph 1, of the charter. We are pleased at this historic development—which is consistent with Secretary Rogers' statement of last April advocating greater use of this major organ of the United Nations.

We believe that the international community has a serious need for impartial and authoritative legal advice on the question of Namibia. The Court, in its advisory opinions of 1950, 1955, and 1956, has already provided some useful guidance to the General Assembly on legal issues concerning South-West Africa.

The question posed to the Court in the resolution just adopted is: What are the legal consequences for states of the continued presence of South Africa in Namibia notwithstanding Security Council Resolution 276? Operative paragraph 2 of that resolution states that "the continued presence of the South African authorities in

Ibid., Sept. 7, 1970, pp. 284-86.

Namibia is illegal and that consequently all acts taken by the Government of South Africa on behalf of or concerning Namibia after the termination of the mandate are illegal and invalid." The Court can and should give the Council the benefit of its impartial and authoritative views as to the duties of South Africa and the responsibilities of other members of the United Nations in the light of that resolution.

Mr. President, my delegation is under no illusions that the resolutions adopted today will solve the problem of Namibia. We believe, however, that both resolutions, embodying as they do peaceful and practical steps, make a useful contribution to furthering our efforts to find a solution. Again, we congratulate the ad hoc subcommittee for its effective work and look forward to further constructive suggestions from the subcommittee. For our part, the United States will continue its bilateral efforts to persuade South Africa to acknowledge United Nations responsibility for Namibia and would hope that other member states will do likewise.

Texts of Resolutions

July 29, 1970

FIRST RESOLUTION

The Security Council,

Reaffirming once more the inalienable right of the people of Namibia to freedom and independence recognized in General Assembly resolution 1514 (XV) of 14 December 1960,

Reaffirming its resolution 264 (1969) and 276 (1970) by which the Security Council recognized the decision of the General Assembly to terminate the mandate of South West Africa and assume direct responsibility for the territory until its independence and in which the continued presence of the South African authority in Namibia as well as all acts taken by that Government on behalf of or concerning Namibia after the termination of the mandate were declared illegal and invalid,

Recalling its resolution 269 (1969),

Noting with great concern the continued flagrant refusal of the Government of South Africa to comply with the decisions of the Security Council demanding the immediate withdrawal of South Africa from the territory,

Deeply concerned that the enforcement of South African laws and juridical procedures in the territory have continued in violation of the international status of the territory,

Reaffirming its resolution 282 (1970) on the arms embargo against the Government of South Africa and the significance of that resolution with regard to the territory and people of Namibia,

Recalling the decisions taken by the Security Council on 30 January 1970 to establish, in accordance with rule 28 of the provisional rules of procedure, an Ad Hoc Sub-Committee of the Security Council to study, in consultation with the Secretary-General, ways and means by which the relevant resolutions of the Council including resolution 276 (1970), could be effectively implemented in accordance with the appropriate provisions of the Charter in the light of the flagrant refusal of South Africa to withdraw from Namibia, and to submit its recommendations to the Council,

Having examined the report submitted by the Ad Hoc Sub-Committee (S/9863) and the recommendations contained in that report,

Bearing in mind the special responsibility of the United Nations with regard to the territory of Namibia and its people,

1. Requests all States to refrain from any relations—diplomatic, consular or otherwise—with South Africa implying recognition of the authority of the South African Government over the territory of Namibia;

2. Calls upon all States maintaining diplomatic or consular relations with South Africa to issue a formal declaration to the Government of South Africa to the effect that they do not recognize any authority of South Africa with regard to Namibia and that they consider South Africa's continued presence in Namibia illegal;

3. Calls upon all States maintaining such relations to terminate existing diplomatic and consular representation as far as they extend to Namibia and to withdraw any diplomatic or consular mission or representative residing in the territory;

4. Calls upon all States to ensure that companies and other commercial and industrial enterprises owned by, or under direct control of the State, cease all dealings with respect to commercial or industrial enterprises or concessions in Namibia;

5. Calls upon all States to withhold from their nationals or companies of their nationality not under direct government control, government loans, credit guarantees and other forms of financial support that would be used to facilitate trade or commerce with Namibia;

6. Calls upon all States to ensure that companies and other commercial enterprises owned by the State or under direct control of the State cease all further investment activities including concessions in Namibia;

7. Calls upon all States to discourage their nationals or companies of their nationality not under direct governmental control from investing or obtaining concessions in Namibia, and to this end withhold protection of such investment against claims of a future lawful government of Namibia;

8. Requests all States to undertake without delay a detailed study and review of all bilateral treaties between themselves and South Africa in so far as these treaties contain provisions by which they apply to the territory of Namibia;

9. Requests the Secretary-General of the United Nations to undertake without delay a detailed study and review of all multilateral treaties to which South Africa is a party, and which either by direct reference or on the basis of relevant provisions of international law might be considered to apply to the territory of Namibia;

10. Requests the United Nations Council for Namibia to make available to the Security Council the results of its study and proposals with regard to the issuance of passports and visas for Namibians and to undertake a study and make proposals with regard to special passport and visa regulations to be adopted by States concerning travel of their citizens to Namibia;

11. Calls upon all States to discourage the promotion of tourism and emigration to Namibia;

12. Requests the General Assembly at its twenty-fifth session to set up a United Nations Fund for Namibia to provide assistance to Namibians who have suffered from persecution and to finance a comprehensive education and training programme for Namibians with particular regard to their future administrative responsibilities of the territory;

13. Requests all States to report to the Secretary-General on measures they have taken in order to give effect to the provisions set forth in the present resolution;

14. Decides to re-establish, in accordance with rule 28 of the provisional rules of procedure, the Ad Hoc Subcommittee on Namibia and request the Ad Hoc Subcommittee to study further effective recommendations on ways and means by which the relevant resolutions of the Council can be effectively implemented in accordance with the appropriate provisions of the Charter, in the light of the flagrant refusal of South Africa to withdraw from Namibia;

15. Requests the Ad Hoc Sub-Committee to study the replies submitted by Governments to the Secretary-General in pursuance of operative paragraph 13 of the present resolution and to report to the Council as appropriate;

16. Requests the Secretary-General to give every assistance to the Ad Hoc Sub-Committee in the performance of its tasks;

17. Decides to remain actively seized of this matter.

SECOND RESOLUTION

The Security Council,

Reaffirming the special responsibility of the United Nations with regard to the territory and the people of Namibia,

Recalling Security Council resolution 276 (1970) on the question of Namibia,

Taking note of the report and recommendations submitted by the Ad Hoc Sub-Committee established in pursuance of Security Council resolution 276 (1970),

Taking further note of the recommendation of the Ad Hoc Sub-Committee on the possibility of requesting an advisory opinion from the International Court of Justice,

Considering that an advisory opinion from the International Court of Justice would be useful for the Security Council in its further consideration of the question of Namibia and in furtherance of the objectives the Council is seeking,

1. Decides to submit in accordance with Article 96 (1) of the Charter, the following question to the International Court of Justice with the request for an advisory opinion which shall be transmitted to the Security Council at an early date:

"What are the legal consequences for States of the continued presence of South Africa in Namibia, notwithstanding Security Council resolution 276 (1970)?"

2. Requests the Secretary-General to transmit the present resolution to the International Court of Justice, in accordance with article 65 of the Statute of the Court, accompanied by all documents likely to throw light upon the question.

UNITED STATES POLICY ON NAMIBIA *

Statement by Aloysius A. Mazewski, U.S. Alternate
Representative to the U.N. General Assembly

November 16, 1970

One of the main characteristics that has usually permeated our debates on Namibia has been the effort by all delegations to work together. Since the adoption of

*Ibid., Jan. 18, 1971, pp. 101-03.

Resolution 2145 of the General Assembly, efforts have been made to seek practical and peaceful means by which the responsibility of the U.N. would be exercised over the Territory of Namibia.

In addition, we are all aware that at the request of the General Assembly the Security Council has been seized with the question of Namibia and has examined at length various steps which would lead to a satisfactory conclusion of the problem. As a result, it has adopted constructive suggestions as recommendations for action with respect to the territory. Its two resolutions, 283 and 284, which were based on the report of the ad hoc subcommittee of the Security Council, represented, in our view, an effort to assist through practical means the people of the territory. The adoption of these resolutions marked a genuine attempt for the United Nations to act in concert in trying to achieve for the people of Namibia the right of self-determination and independence.

Since the adoption of Resolution 2145, my delegation has participated on a number of committees relating to the future of Namibia and more recently devoted considerable time in the ad hoc subcommittee of the Security Council which made recommendations on the kind of steps that member states could take vis-a-vis Namibia.

Our position on Namibia is clear. We support Resolution 2145 and regard South Africa's continued presence in Namibia as illegal, and we agree that the United Nations has a direct responsibility for that territory. The United States will continue to exert all efforts in seeking to assist the people of Namibia in their legitimate right of self-determination.

In conformity with this position the United States announced on May 20 and in the Security Council and the General Assembly a variety of steps which we were prepared to take vis-a-vis Namibia. Let me recall for the benefit of the members here these steps. We announced first that the United States would henceforth officially discourage investment by U.S. nationals in Namibia. Second, credit guarantees and other facilities of the U.S. Export-Import Bank would not be made available for trade with Namibia. Third, United States nationals who invest in Namibia on the basis of rights acquired through the South African Government since adoption of General Assembly Resolution 2145 will not receive United States Government assistance in protection of such investments against claims of the future lawful government of Namibia.

Prior to the steps that we announced in May, the United States had taken other steps both in the United Nations and in South Africa. In this connection let me recall that we have repeatedly brought to the attention of the Government of South Africa its duty to account for and release inhabitants of Namibia which it reportedly holds under section 6 of the Terrorism Act. We have admitted over the years Namibians as refugee students, and we are also taking steps to issue travel documents under the 1951 Geneva Convention on the Status of Refugees to certain refugees in the United States including Namibians as well as others from southern Africa. In addition we have taken steps to recognize travel documents issued by the Council for Namibia for Namibians. And finally, we have urged the Government of South Africa to be more responsive to the United Nations.

Mr. Chairman, these are steps which the United States has taken and which are included, to some degree, in the resolution adopted by the Security Council last July which we supported, Resolution 283.

It is regrettable in looking over the resolution tabled by the cosponsors contained in document A/C.4/L.964 to find that no mention was made of the activities of the Security Council. Indeed, in examining the resolution, one would suspect that the Security Council has not done anything on the question of Namibia. The calls on the Security Council to take chapter VII action seem unrealistic in light of the various resolutions of the Council. In addition my delegation need not remind the committee that the Security Council has not determined that a threat to international peace and security exists in Namibia. There are other specific provisions new to the resolution this year which my delegation cannot support—among others, operative paragraphs 5, 6, 8, and 9.

We regret the general tone of this particular resolution. It appears to be retrogressing from previous resolutions of the General Assembly. We note that no attempt has been made to reconcile varying views on this very important subject. Rather than seek a means by which it may be possible to resolve the problem through peaceful means, the resolution places its emphasis on drastic action. This, in the opinion of my delegation, is not the way to help the people of Namibia. There are many features in this resolution which we could have supported. Because of its extreme language and its absence of recognizing the realities of the situation as well as its apparent refusal to acknowledge and consider work of the Security Council in this matter, my delegation regretfully has no other alternative but to vote against the resolution. This is regrettable to us because we are in sympathy with the objective we all seek with regard to the future of the Territory of Namibia and we have done out utmost, particularly in the Security Council, which is now seized with the matter, to find ways and means by which the United Nations determination and responsibility over the territory could be fulfilled. The United States, despite this negative vote, will for its part continue in the Security Council and other appropriate bodies to seek all peaceful and practical means for helping the people of Namibia to achieve their just goals.

Text of Resolution

December 9, 1970

The General Assembly,

Recalling its resolutions 1514 (XV) of 14 December 1960, 2145 (XXI) of 27 October 1966 and subsequent resolutions on the question of Namibia, as well as Security Council resolutions 264 (1969) of 20 March 1969, 269 (1969) of 12 August 1969 and 283 (1970) of 29 July 1970,

Recalling further the relevant provisions of General Assembly resolution 2621 (XXV) of 12 October 1970 containing the programme of action for the full implementation of the Declaration on the Granting of Independence to Colonial Countries and Peoples,

Bearing in mind the special responsibility of the United Nations with regard to the Territory of Namibia and its people,

Deeply concerned at the deteriorating situation in Namibia due to the continued illegal presence of South Africa in the Territory in deliberate defiance of the United Nations, a situation which threatens international peace and security,

Gravely concerned that the continued refusal of South Africa to comply with the decisions of the Security Council and the General Assembly seriously undermines and encroaches on the authority of the United Nations,

Taking into consideration the fact that South Africa has persistently violated the principles of the Charter of the United Nations, and mindful of the obligations of Member States under Article 25 thereof,

Considering that the basic condition for the fulfillment of the responsibilities of the United Nations towards Namibia is the application of effective measures to ensure the removal of South Africa from the Territory,

Noting with appreciation the report of the United Nations Council for Namibia,

1. Reaffirms the inalienable right of the people of Namibia to self-determination and independence in conformity with General Assembly resolution 1514 (XV), and the legitimacy of their struggle against the foreign occupation of the Territory;

2. Recommends the report of the United Nations Council for Namibia to all States and to the subsidiary organs of the General Assembly and other competent organs of the General Assembly and other competent organs of the United Nations as well as to the specialized agencies and other international organizations concerned, for appropriate action, acting in conformity with the relevant resolutions of the General Assembly and the Security Council;

3. Condemns the Government of South Africa for its persistent refusal to comply with the decisions of the Security Council and the General Assembly and to withdraw from the Territory;

4. Further condemns the Government of South Africa for the extension of the internationally condemned policies of apartheid to the Territory, and for its policies aimed at destroying the unity of the people and the territorial integrity of Namibia through the creation of the so-called separate "homelands";

5. Condemns the support given to South Africa in the pursuit of its repressive policies in Namibia by the allies of South Africa and, in particular, by its major trading partners and financial, economic and other interests operating in the Territory;

6. Calls upon the Governments concerned to cease immediately any assistance to and co-operation with South Africa;

7. Invites the Security Council to consider taking effective measures, including those provided for under Chapter VII of the Charter of the United Nations, in view of the continued refusal by the Government of South Africa to comply with its resolutions 264 (1969) and 269 (1969);

8. Calls upon all States, particularly the permanent members of the Security Council, to lend their full support to the Security Council in the application and implementation of all measures which the Council has decided or may decide upon to obtain the withdrawal of South Africa from the Territory;

9. Appeals to all States to take appropriate steps, through action in the specialized agencies and other organizations within the United Nations system of which they are members, with a view to discontinuing any collaboration with the Government of South Africa;

10. Reaffirms its solidarity with the people of Namibia in their legitimate struggle against foreign occupation and calls upon all States, in consultation with the Organization of African Unity, to provide increased moral and material assistance to the Namibian people in their struggle;

11. Calls again upon the Government of South Africa to treat the Namibian people captured during their struggle for freedom as prisoners of war in accordance with the Geneva Convention relative to the Treatment of Prisoners of War of 12 August 1919 and to comply with the Convention relative to the Protection of Civilian Persons in Time of War of 12 August 1949;

12. Endorses the measures taken by the United Nations Council for Namibia with a view to the issuance of identity certificates and travel documents to Namibians, and appeals to all States which have not already done so to communicate to the Secretary-General their willingness to recognize and accept such documents for purposes of travel to their countries;

13. Requests the United Nations Council for Namibia to continue to perform the functions entrusted to it in the relevant resolutions of the General Assembly, including consultations with the representatives of the Namibian people and of the Organization of African Unity in Africa or at United Nations Headquarters;

14. Requests the Secretary-General to continue to provide the necessary assistance and facilities to the United Nations Council for Namibia to discharge its duties and functions;

15. Calls upon all States to co-operate fully with the United Nations Council for Namibia in its efforts to discharge its responsibilities.

SOUTHERN RHODESIA

Commentary

That the first show-down between the irreconcilable forces for African self-determination and white minority rule would come in Southern Rhodesia took much of the world by surprise. Everyone recognized that the country's position was pivotal and that conditions there did contain potential conflict. But not until Ian Smith's governments' Unilateral Declaration of Independence from Britain on November 11, 1965 did observers or even the principals (excepting, perhaps, the Smith government) expect the uncompromising confrontation that transpired.

Terminology provides a short-hand to the intricate historical issues: the British call the territory Southern Rhodesia; the Africans call it Zimbabwe; the white minority in power call it Rhodesia. Unravelling the reasons provides the background against which the United States and the rest of the world had to take a stand.

The land between the Limpopo and Zambezi Rivers had, like many other parts of Africa, known the existence of a powerful and prosperous state before pressures of internal African history and European intrusions combined to undermine it. That state, in later years referred to by its capital, Zimbabwe, gave its name to the new nation African peoples of the territory hoped (and expected, in light of continent-wide developments of the 1960's) would be theirs.

The European presence, dating to the 1890's and the activities of Cecil Rhodes' chartered company, had in the early years a characteristic dominance. The settlers' goal, there and to the north (in Northern Rhodesia/Zambia), was to follow what they saw as the standard path of British colonies. It was not exactly the South African model, more that of Canada, Australia, New Zealand, where by stages full representative government moved completely into the hands of settlers of British descent. But the independence of South Africa in 1910 encouraged the whites in Southern Rhodesia in their demands, and Britain yielded internal self-government to them in 1923.

In the decades that followed further steps were deferred, partly because of complex possibilities of association with the territories of Northern Rhodesia and Nyasaland, where Britain guaranteed "protected status" to the Africans. Plans for amalgamation, and for separation were discarded over the years; finally in 1953, for largely economic reasons, the Federation of Rhodesia and Nyasaland came into existence. The politics of the unhappy decade that followed were extraordinarily intricate. The two northern territories were Nyasaland/Malawi (densely populated and a supplier of labor) and Northern Rhodesia/Zimbabwe (the Federation's greatest economic prop, with rich copper mines that only Europe's politics had divided in two from the Congo (Katanga). These two territories contained far fewer whites than did Southern Rhodesia. Nationalist agitations within them, and the African "winds of change" combined to place severe pressure on Britain to grant them full self-determination. That meant breaking up the Federation, since an African-governed Federation was impossible; the Federal and Southern Rhodesian constitutions contained elaborate franchises severely restricting African participation in government.

Finally, in 1963 Britain gave her consent to the end of the Federation. That had been a crucial issue, a test for Africans of Britain's true beliefs and intentions toward them. Zambia's and Malawi's independence followed; Southern Rhodesia reverted to its 1923 status, internal self-government by a still-severely restrictive constitution. Its white government, which rapidly moved to the right on the key racial issue, limited both political and social opportunities for the Africans; the system seemed to many to resemble more and more that of Southern Africa, despite official disclaimers. In any event, the direction of change seemed clear.

It was Southern Rhodesia's refusal to make a commitment to eventual majority rule that led to confrontation with Britain. Increasing settler rancor at the British refusal to grant full independence on their terms emboldened Ian Smith; his Unilateral Declaration of Independence proclaimed his government's determination not to compromise its racial-political stand.

Much of the controversy over these events played itself out on the U.N. stage. Initiatives both from Britain and from the African states had brought measures ranging from an arms embargo and economic sanctions including the British-sponsored oil embargo (passed on the General Assembly on November 20, 1965, the United States voting in favor); British-introduced selective sanctions against twelve key Southern Rhodesian exports and banning sales of military equipment (passed in the Security Council December 16, 1966, the United States voting in favor); expansion of mandatory sanctions to include all trade (passed May 29, 1968, the United States voting in favor).

Without the cooperation of Portugal and South Africa, complete success of sanctions was impossible; from those countries (and some others) came the opposite of compliance. A Security Council resolution, introduced on Afro-Asian initiative, sought to extend mandatory sanctions to South Africa and Moçambique in reprisal (it was defeated, with the United States abstaining along with Britain and France). Later measures concerning the use of force were rejected (the United States abstaining).

And then the United States cast its first veto in the U.N. Security Council on a resolution condemning Britain for not using force to bring down the Smith regime. It was not likely that the American Government would support such condemnation, but abstention as an alternative to veto existed as it had so often before. The American veto, then, could only be seen as a decisive statement of a changing position, one that inevitably shifted American policy in the eyes of Africans, reinforcing an impression of wavering. Because the veto came in tandem with Britain, it further reinforced impressions of an American inability—or refusal—to declare its own independence of European allies' dictates. But American actions were even more suspect to Africans, for though Britain had broken completely with the Smith regime following Southern Rhodesia's constitutional referendum of June 20, 1969, the United States did not withdraw its consulate until March 1970, a belated step whose significance the Security Council veto seemed to some to negate.

Although American policy seemed clear from the start—rigorous enforcement of the military embargo and economic sanctions—there were continuing counter-pressures. Other American interests were brought into play, and protests came from several quarters, though the spokesmen were often the same. Many spokesmen were part of what may be termed loosely a "Rhodesian Lobby" in Congress. In the Senate the main voice was that of James Eastland of Mississippi, with additional major statements by Harry Byrd of Virginia and Strom Thurmond of South Carolina; in the House the contingent was larger; John R. Rarick of Louisiana, Albert W. Watson of South Carolina, William M. Colmer of Mississippi, Joel T. Broyhill of Virginia, John M. Ashbrook of Ohio, Jesse Younger of California, James G. Fulton of Pennsylvania, H. R. Gross of Iowa—these men, especially Rarick, were most vocal. Outside Congress Dean Acheson commanded greatest attention.

Loudest in support of State Department policy—majority rule in and sanctions against Southern Rhodesia—were Edward Brooke and Edward Kennedy of Massachusetts in the Senate and, in the House, Charles C. Diggs of Michigan, Donald M. Fraser of Minnesota, Jonathan B. Bingham of New York, and George E. Brown of California.

The forces in support of Rhodesian independence and against economic sanctions used several arguments. First came the spurious parallel between 1965 and 1776, a supposed appeal to principle. (An implicit corollary of this position was support for the racial policies of the white redoubt which was not openly expressed.) Then came an argument against American support for Britain in Rhodesia in the face of British refusal to support every aspect of American policy in Vietnam and Cuba.

But the argument most strongly advanced combined economic, military, and Cold War reasoning. It centered on chrome, for Southern Rhodesia is the world's largest producer of chromite, essential in the manufacture of steel, and therefore in defense industries. One factor was the impact on American extractive investment in Rhodesian chromium mines (Union Carbide and other smaller firms had substantial operations there), but the fact that the Soviet Union is the second-largest producer added a more important dimension. Rhodesia was staunchly anti-Communist, so the argument ran, and by implication, therefore, the United States was acting against an ally—and then came the rub—and adding to the economic strength of an enemy in the process. For with stockpiles of chromite decreasing, the United States was forced, through military and industrial necessity, to buy from the Soviet Union. It was even alleged that the Soviets were with impunity breaking the U.N. embargo, buying Rhodesian chromite which they then sold to the American market.

It was in the face of such pressures that American policy seemed to waver after 1968. Supporters of sanctions, both in the United States and in Africa, wondered at the configuration: military and industrial pressures seemed to combine with a "Southern Strategy" taking on Southern African overtones.

Precisely because there were such pressures, and because Southern Rhodesia forced clearly identifiable choices in policy, American actions in that developing situation were as closely watched as those anywhere in Africa. But they were watched closely by very few Americans. Thus, in October and November, 1971, the Senate and then the House of Representatives passed a military procurement bill, permitting—through an amendment introduced by Senator Harry F. Byrd, Jr. of Virginia—importation of chrome from Southern Rhodesia. The arguments were not new; the "Rhodesia Lobby," with its industrial backers and southern sympathies, had been advancing them ever since the U.N. Security Council had voted mandatory sanctions.

The success of these Senators and Congressmen came when it did for reasons having little to do with Africa. The military procurement bill raised other, more pressing issues (having mostly to do with Southeast Asia), both for the Administration and for Congressional supporters of sanctions. Further, feeling against the U.N. was running high; the issues were many, but foremost among them was the recent expulsion of Nationalist China from the world organization (perhaps some Congressmen had decided to share the President's pique that African delegates had too expressively shown their approval of replacing Taiwan with Peking).

In this climate neither the White House nor the State Department had acted energetically to prevent passage and inclusion of the amendment; protests by opponents in the House of Representatives especially and in the press had no effect. Almost by default, then, President Nixon and the Congress defied the United Nations, and—as important to African critics if not American ones—lessened substantially moral and economic pressure on the Smith regime, and had done so in contrast to British adherence to sanctions. Moreover, the reversal came just when sanctions seemed to be having an economic impact, serious if not crippling. And it came as Britain was reopening negotiations with the Smith regime, talks designed to gain concessions on African political rights. The American action only strengthened the hand of the white *de facto* rulers of Southern Rhodesia against the NATO ally who, from ex-colonial experience and knowledge, had so long been seen as the most suitable guide to United States policy. (It also undermined thereby the efforts inside the British Parliament to hold out for extensive concessions from Smith in a possible settlement).

An overwhelming General Assembly vote (106 to 2—Portugal and South Africa—with 13 abstentions and the United States not voting) "cautioned" the United States that to import chrome from Rhodesia would be deliberately to violate the U.N. Charter and the treaty obligations and commitments that bind those who signed it. Truly a massive censure, this vote had no effect. Perhaps it had come too late, as so many other measures by an otherwise preoccupied opposition. The whole episode showed fine tactical maneuvering of the Rhodesia-philes in the Senate especially. The White House would find it impossible to veto a military procurement bill.

Explaining this drastic change in policy would not be easy. Only weeks before the Congressional and Presidential action, Assistant Secretary of State for African Affairs, David Newsom, had said flatly that, "The stand we have taken on African issues [at the U.N.] is clear. . . . We have been at the forefront in enforcing sanctions against Rhodesia, the only mandatory sanctions ever voted by the United Nations."

However the American government might try to explain, the most charitable African reaction was that, once again, Africa was the lowest priority. The more prevalent one, however, was that the United States would not only tolerate but support white domination in Southern Africa.

SOUTHERN RHODESIA

*Speech by Representative Barrett O'Hara (Illinois) Before the House Incorporating G.
Mennen Williams Statement of U.S. Policy Made in Salisbury, Southern Rhodesia**

September 22, 1961

*   *   *

I have taken the time of the House today to call the attention of my colleagues to a truly remarkable speech of Assistant Secretary of State Williams before the Rhodesia National Affairs Association at Salisbury in Rhodesia and Nyasaland. That is a zone of tensions. Mr. Williams spoke on the "Basic U.S. Policy," and when I describe his address as truly remarkable that evaluation is substantiated by the fact that following its delivery both the Evening Standard, the white settler newspaper, and the Daily News, the black African newspaper, editorially commended it.

*   *   *

BASIC U.S. POLICY

(Address by the Honorable G. Mennen Williams, Assistant Secretary
of State for African Affairs, to the Rhodesia National Affairs Association,
Salisbury, Rhodesia and Nyasaland, August 25, 1961)

It is a great pleasure and honor to be invited to address the Rhodesia National Affairs Association. This is our third and final day in Salisbury before going on to Blantyre, the Copperbelt, and Lusaka. We also slipped into your country about 10 days ago for a first glimpse of your magnificent Victoria Falls.

My wife and I have been tremendously impressed by this vital city of Salisbury. We have met and talked with a great many of your citizens and have noted many evidences of the progress you have been making in housing, education, and welfare. This morning it was a special pleasure to attend the greatest tobacco auction in the world where we heard the familiar sounds of an American tobacco auctioneer. Later today we are looking forward to our visit to the University College of Rhodesia and Nyasaland.

This is my second visit to Africa since President Kennedy appointed me to the Department of State. My mission is, first of all, to become acquainted with the leaders and public of Africa and to convey to them renewed assurances of the keen interest and friendship of the United States. Second, and quite simply, I have come to learn of your aspirations and your problems so as to offer effective counsel of my Government in the formulation of its foreign policy.

The U.S. Government under the new administration of President Kennedy finds itself faced by a host of critical and fundamental problems of foreign affairs. Some of these are of grave and immediate urgency. Others have a long-range but equally profound significance.

**Congressional Record* Sept. 22, 1961, pp. 20824-26.

These problems manifest themselves in many ways and in many different parts of the world. Yet there seem to be ties that bind quite a number of them together. People the world over want governments of their own choosing. They want a better life for themselves and their children. And they want to enjoy the full recognition of their dignity as human beings. When the continued enjoyment of these conditions is threatened, or the prospect of achieving them is denied, the result is a restiveness which more often than not smolders or explodes into unpleasant problems.

The United States is concerned about these things because of our moral and political heritage but also because we believe that the denial of these values jeopardizes the world of peace and justice we want for ourselves and our children.

In these terms one of the most pressing challenges today is that of Berlin. Berlin is a vitally important symbol of freedom and self-determination to a large part of the world. It represents the desire and the determination of 2¼ million West Berliners to continue under a government of their own choosing, and it is a focus of the hopes of other millions now under the imperialist rule of the Kremlin. What West Berlin means has been demonstrated in recent weeks by the repressive measures taken by the Communists to stop the flow of refugees who streamed by the thousands and thousands into the West Berlin sanctuary of liberty and hope. I need only add that the Soviet Union maintains 22 divisions of occupation troops in the countries of middle and Eastern Europe to subjugate these aspirations for freedom.

President Kennedy has plainly told the American people that the Soviet threat to continued freedom and self-government in West Berlin has brought the unsought choice of war or peace dangerously close. You may be sure, and President Kennedy has stated it in so many words, that "the challenge is not to us alone" but "to all who want a world of free choice." Surely many of you here have known war. And all of you can read the omens of this shrinking planet in the trace of satellites whirling through the heavens overhead. My country, like yours, has known a time of isolation, but that time is gone with the wind.

We have made our pledges, with the support of the Atlantic Community, to meet the peril of Berlin. We hope, with God's help, to preserve the peace and defend the human rights of the people of that city. At the same time, we look out upon another and broader field in which the future of countless millions of human beings will be determined—a future equally bound up with peace and security for all of us. I am speaking here of the less developed areas inhabited by some two-thirds of the world's peoples.

Is the question of freedom any less vital here? Surely it is not, for we hold that freedom is indivisible. That is why President Kennedy has pledged the United States to assist the less developed countries to build up the strong and independent societies to which their peoples aspire. That is the underlying support for our policy toward Africa.

We recognize that the new nations of Africa do not wish to be involved in the cold war. And we believe that they need not be directly involved, provided they can work out solutions to the basic problems of misery and despair, of human rights and essential justice. The Communist aim of course is to aggravate the tensions and discontent that may be attendant on this process, but the problems themselves are inherent in the transitional process. Our purpose is to help these peoples and govern- ments to help themselves, because in this ever more interdependent world that concerns all of you here in Africa sooner or later will concern us, if it does not affect us already.

On my visits to the newly independent countries of tropical Africa, I have been impressed by the sincerity and convictions with which national leaders have told me of their aspirations.

First among these aspirations is the desire to be free from any form of outside domination, to be independent in the fullest sense. The United States recognizes the dynamics of nationalism in Africa today. Coupled with this is an awareness and assertion of what is often referred to as the African personality. Also related is a fierce desire for racial equality and sensitivity to problems of color wherever they trouble the world.

Then there is the compelling, burning aspiration for education. To provide educational opportunities to millions of young Africans is a tremendous challenge to responsible governments and to those from outside who would help. Yet I submit we cannot evade this challenge.

Another basic aspiration is for economic development to raise living standards and assure political stability. The prevailing pattern is one of economic planning for rapid development, in which there is a mixture of private and government-owned enterprise. Very little in this pattern is rigid or doctrinaire. And we must of course expect these new African States to develop governmental institutions which fit the values of their particular societies.

This may sometimes mean a greater reliance on some aspects of centralized authority than in the democracies of the Western World. The evidence suggests, however, that democratic forces will continue to make themselves felt. In the history of Europe and America, there is much evidence that the early processes of nation-building are formidable and often turbulent. Yet to date, the broad consensus of the peoples of the new African States has been responsive to their leadership.

The newly independent countries of Africa face a great many problems. They are short of capital, short of skills, short of broad experience in self-government. Their leaders seem to be in a great hurry, new and changing groupings among them appear to be developing, and there are a good many borders in dispute.

In our view, it is not reasonable to expect to find fully mature governments firmly in place in these new countries. What is striking, and reassuring, is that the great majority of the new leaders are conducting responsible independent governments, despite all their burdens. The Congo has been an important exception, but clearly it is an exception and not the rule. And let me add that the United States has steadfastly supported the United Nations in the Congo with one purpose; to allow the Congolese people to develop their own national destiny.

If all these leaders can keep abreast of the rising expectations of their peoples, responsible government will prosper and mature. That is why they deserve our help. For the alternatives are surely demagoguery, disorder and subversion.

There has been an unprecedented transfer of power in Africa and we must accept the plain facts that there are now 28 sovereign nations in Africa, of which 18 have attained their independence in the past 2 years. This represents an enormously significant transformation in our world community.

This new play of forces on the world stage may seem poorly rehearsed and we are not very well acquainted with many of the actors. But this drama of change is a text for our times. It cannot be buried by angry men or hidden in the midst of the sea by those who dislike or fear its unrolling. It is inexorably written in the lifestream of our times.

Around this central theme there is, in Africa, much diversity in political and social development, and I do not suppose that what is true of one area is necessarily true everywhere. On the other hand, no part of Africa is set apart from this great process of transition, which is so much in your thoughts today.

Whatever may be said of the tensions inherent in the colonial experience, it is striking that the great majority of the new African nations have emerged to freedom peacefully. A considerable degree of preparation, perhaps lacking in some respects but nevertheless vital, was extended to these dependent peoples in the field of economic development, education, political expression, and self-government. Confusion has resulted, and could result again on the continent, largely through failure to make this preparation or from undue delay in the political process which it is intended to facilitate.

Where preparations for inevitable change have not yet begun, the hour is dangerously late. But even in those areas determined reform coupled with genuine good will may in God's grace find success. Let us pray that this course will be chosen.

Your own Government institutions and your peoples are engaged in a vital process not only of constitutional transition but of accommodation between races. Certainly these problems of transition and accommodation must be resolved primarily by the peoples and governments concerned. It is our genuine hope that political, social and economic progress will occur without reference to the race of individual citizens, and certainly without the derogation of the full rights of any element of the population.

There are some who feel you are going too fast and there are some who feel you are going too slow. But the important thing is that you have not set your face against the course of history. You are working toward the commendable goals of self-government by all the people and an interracial society. It is the speed with which you approach these goals which is the substance of your political dialog. We take it that it is your intention to get on with the job.

We in the United States are humbly aware that we have yet to achieve the full promise of racial equality. But it is the declared law of the land, it is the vigorous policy of our new national administration, and we shall attain it.

American foreign policy is based on a set of principles to which we hold most seriously. Self-determination is one of these principles. In fact it is a universally recognized principle which asserts the right of people to determine the kind of government under which they want to live. This is the very basis of the world order which makes possible the area of freedom and which, I am sure, is the goal of your own evolution.

From this basis, the United States will seek to evaluate its policies toward Africa according to the merits of each individual case and problem. We do not propose to apply formulas nor have we any desire to export any particular concepts of our own. We shall instead, adhere to principle and try to use our influence judiciously and in concert with men of good will, of all races and creeds, in whose hands the future of Africa rests.

In conclusion, may I express again my appreciation for the opportunity to visit this part of Africa. I am gratified at the good will I find among so many, and at the dedicated efforts being made, by people of all races, to create a society in which all can fully enjoy a good life in peace and harmony.

I think I can understand the disappointment of those who find things moving too slowly and even the concern of those who find things moving too fast. Certainly, I would not minimize the tasks of transition which are yours to solve.

Speaking for the Government of the United States and on behalf of its people, I wish you Godspeed in bringing those tasks to a successful conclusion.

Reaction to the Williams Address

Here is the editorial from the Evening Standard, the white settlers newspaper:

The Truths Earnestly Spelled Out

The U.S. Assistant Secretary of State for African Affairs, Mr. Mennen Williams, was certainly "telling us" in his speech in Salisbury today.

For that reason, more than anything else, there are many who will criticize him, but nobody who is prepared to look at, and analyze, his speech dispassionately can deny the truth of what he says.

Nor can anybody who reads the speech carefully, and with perception, fail to appreciate the principle which is basic to American policy toward Africa—and the other countries of the world as well.

Whether it is Berlin or Africa, America believes that the people have the right to determine the kind of government under which they want to live. The United States is pledged to assist the less developed countries to build up the strong and independent societies to which their people aspire—and which it considers basic to peace and freedom.

*   *   *

Mr. Williams made his speech today with that earnestness which is characteristic of the Americans. In that spirit he had a special word for us in the Federation (though he seemed studiously to avoid use of the word; "Federation" does not appear once in the text of his speech): "The important thing is that you have not set your face against the course of history. You are working toward the commendable goals of self-government by all the people in an interracial society. It is the speed with which you approach these goals which is the substance of your political dialog. We take it that it is your intention to get on with the job."

As we have already commented, he was certainly "telling us." Equally certainly he told countries like Portugal and South Africa what America's attitude is, what it thinks they should do, and of the grave dangers it believes inevitable if they do not "get on with the job" of coming to terms with their peoples' aspirations.

America will not be loved any the more as a result, but it would be a tragedy (in the real sense of the word) if the truths he spelled out today were hidden and lost in the mists of anger.

The Black African Reaction

Here is the editorial from the Daily News, the black African newspaper:

Williams Speaks

The declaration of policy by Mr. Mennen Williams, the Assistant Secretary of State for Africa in the United States today, will be received with interest and widespread approval by those persons of all races and background genuinely interested in the development of self-governing African states, and dynamic nonracial new nations.

The subject of freedom for a people to choose governments under which they will live, is a vital one in Africa today—it is the cry on the lip of every articulate African from Cairo to

Cape Town, and from the Atlantic to the Indian Ocean. It is gratifying for people in Salisbury to hear, firsthand, that America tends to assist in this delicate but vital process.

Mr. Williams has not minced words. Some of his statements will be hard for local politicians to swallow and digest—even if they did they may suffer from indigestion. This is mainly because many of our people take too parochial a view of the current world problems and have attitudes of the past century. If they were to have their own way, the prospects of world peace would be endangered as Mr. Williams warned.

We are also heartened by Mr. Williams' acceptance of the fact that new African nations do not (and should not) wish to be involved in the cold war, where, of course, they would only be used as pawns. The acceptance of the neutral position of African states is one of the new, but encouraging lines of thought in the new Kennedy administration.

The pace of constitutional transition and accommodation of the races here, particularly the latter, is too slow for our liking. We hope there is the intention to get on with the job. If that intention were not there, or new men tried to slow it down, we expect Mr. Williams to put the full weight of his administration in the direction of greater speed, even if it means hurting old, or newly won friends.

Speech by Assistant Secretary Williams, On United States Policy Towards Southern Rhodesia*

June 15, 1965

*   *   *

Although we recognize the legal and constitutional limitations upon the British, we have stated publicly in the United Nations and told them privately that we believe they must be the catalyst in this situation. We believe that their undoubted influence— political, financial, psychological, and moral—is the most effective means to bring all the parties together to negotiate a settlement of the problem by peaceful means. We also have appealed to all parties concerned not to resort to force and violence in seeking a solution.

We have gone on record at the United Nations several times in favor of the application of the right of self-determination to Southern Rhodesia in a way that will (a) lead to timely universal adult suffrage and (b) preserve the rights of all the country's inhabitants, regardless of their color. Furthermore, and most importantly, we have supported Britain's determination not to relinquish sovereignty over Southern Rhodesia until the government of that country is representative of the majority of its population.

A unilateral declaration of independence could not alter the basic legal or policy views of the United States. Southern Rhodesia is a British colony accorded internal autonomy by the United Kingdom. The American consulate general in Salisbury deals with the Southern Rhodesian Government on this basis. Our relations may be charac- terized as "correct but cool." We continue to support all reasonable proposals for a peaceful solution of Southern Rhodesia's problems that will be satisfactory to all parties.

Neither a unilateral declaration of independence by the Southern Rhodesian Gov- ernment nor the establishment by African nationalists of a government-in-exile would warrant a different position regarding the legal status of Southern Rhodesia. Nor would they change the policy we follow of supporting peaceful and agreed achieve-

**Department of State Bulletin*, July 12, 1965, p. 75.

ment of independence under a government established by the consent of the governed and ready to honor its international obligations.

Let me make our position crystal clear, so there will be no misunderstanding. The United States will support the British Government to the fullest extent, if asked to do so, in its efforts to reach a solution of the Southern Rhodesian problem. We would also support the British Government to the fullest extent in case of a unilateral declaration of independence in Southern Rhodesia. A unilateral break in the constitutional relations of Southern Rhodesia with the United Kingdom by the Southern Rhodesian Government would cause inevitable political, economic, and social chaos in the country. I am firmly convinced that an illegal minority government in Southern Rhodesia would not find international support or recognition. I therefore urge in the most serious manner, and with the utmost of good will, that the Southern Rhodesian Government recognize the full consequences of an act of rebellion.

On another matter, the United States has been charged recently with supplying arms to the Southern Rhodesian Government. I would like to set the record straight on this point once and for all. The United States is not, I repeat not, supplying military arms or equipment to Southern Rhodesia. Nor have we supplied these items since the dissolution of the Federation in December 1963.

The operations of the Agency for International Development in Southern Rhodesia, which were never very large, were terminated completely on June 30, 1964.

We do, however, maintain an active and successful information program in Southern Rhodesia.

*   *   *

New York Times *Editorial on the United States and British Efforts in Southern Rhodesia**

November 8, 1965

Britain's Harold Wilson has come up with yet another "last ditch" effort to head off a unilateral declaration of independence (U.D.I.) by Rhodesia's white minority Government.

The question now will be: Does Prime Minister Ian Douglas Smith any longer have enough room for maneuver with his own Rhodesian Front to accept Mr. Wilson's suggestion that they meet on Malta for a fresh attempt to negotiate a peaceful settlement? Mr. Smith may not be able to turn away once again from the brink of U.D.I. without provoking a revolt by Front extremists.

Yet Rhodesia has been at the brink for so long, and the consequences of U.D.I. for Africa and the world could be so calamitous, that the universal disposition is to cling to hope that it will not happen. It would be more realistic to prepare for the worst.

In that connection, a major question will be whether Mr. Wilson's Conservative Opposition will back the Prime Minister if he tries to impose financial and economic sanctions against a rebel Rhodesian regime.

Another question will be what action the United States will take to demonstrate

*The New York Times, Nov. 8, 1965.

the strong support for Britain that President Johnson underscored in his reported letter to Mr. Smith. This country has negligible trade with Rhodesia and thus could provide only marginal practical support for a British embargo.

The United States might influence events most effectively through action directed at Rhodesia's neighbors. Washington could, for instance, warn South Africa and Portugal—which controls neighboring Mozambique—that it would take a grave view of any support given Rhodesia's white rebels.

Perhaps more important, the United States must demonstrate its determination to help keep afloat the economics of Zambia and Malawi if they are jeopardized by U.D.I. A suggestion under study is a huge British-American airlift of the copper on which Zambia's economy depends, should the rail line through Rhodesia to the port of Beira in Mozambique be cut.

Solid evidence that Washington means business along these lines might prevent disaster for Zambia and Malawi, so dependent on their economic ties with Rhodesia. The Johnson Administration's brave words may soon have to be backed' up with purposeful economic action.

New York Times *Editorial on the United States and Southern Rhodesia**

November 12, 1965

There are grave dangers for Africa and the world in the act of rebellion against the British Crown by a Government in Rhodesia that represents only 220,000 whites in a population of more than four million. It was just a situation that Britain's Ambassador to the United Nations had in mind last year when he warned his U.N. colleagues that the potential explosion could be "something far bigger than anything we have known before, such as the Congo or Cyprus or Suez."

If Britain means business, and gets the support promised by its Commonwealth partners and its allies, including the United States, Ian Douglas Smith and his colleagues will not get by with this attempt to seize independence and perpetuate white minority rule. The trouble is that Britain and everyone else involved must maneuver with great skill to prevent racial war from erupting and to minimize the damage to innocents, white as well as black, in Central Africa.

On the stark facts of trade and finance, Britain, with Commonwealth cooperation, can strangle Rhodesia's economy over a period of months. The United States has little trade with Rhodesia, but it can help to deny the Smith regime access to the world's money markets.

But such stiff action cannot be selective. If it ruins Smith and his backers it will also ruin those Rhodesian whites who oppose his policies and many among the country's four million Africans. Neighboring Zambia can join a trade embargo against Rhodesia only at great peril to its own delicate economy. Nearby Malawi is likely to be badly hurt. Britain itself will imperil investments in Rhodesia estimated at $560 million and will lose $100 million in exports.

The United States could easily replace the tobacco for which Britain has been paying Rhodesia £25 million a year—but Britain, still in balance of payments trouble, can hardly spare the dollar equivalent ($70 million).

There is no moral or political choice for the United States: We must give Britain full support. Washington must try to dissuade South Africa and Portugal, to which neighboring Mozambique belongs, from forming an alliance with the Smith regime. The United States certainly can help keep Zambia and Malawi afloat and ease Britain's economic burden.

Of all the ironies in this situation none is richer than the attempt of the Smith regime to equate its act with 1776, even to the extent of issuing a clumsy paraphrase of the American Declaration of Independence. Conspicuous by its absence, needless to say, was that truth, held by Jefferson to be self-evident, that "all men are created equal and are endowed by their Creator with certain unalienable rights. . . ."

If Ian Smith and his men had accepted that principle, Rhodesia would have had its independence long ago and there would be no crisis today in Central Africa.

THE UNITED NATIONS CONDEMNS UNILATERAL DECLARATION OF INDEPENDENCE BY SOUTHERN RHODESIA AND CALLS FOR ECONOMIC SANCTIONS *

Statement by Ambassador Goldberg

November 12, 1965

The event which has brought us into this Council this morning is one of the most shocking that has transpired since the dawn of the present era of decolonization and fraught with the gravest of consequences. A small, stubborn, and sadly mistaken minority has seized sole power in an effort to dominate the lives of the vast and unwilling majority of the population of Southern Rhodesia. Defying the stern warnings of the sovereign authority, the United Kingdom, this white minority regime, in a desperate and what will certainly prove to be a futile gesture, has unilaterally declared the independnece of Southern Rhodesia, not in the interests of a majority of the people upon which a genuine declaration of independence might depend but in the interests of a privileged minority, making this a spurious declaration of independence.

           *   *   *

My Government has repeatedly made clear its position on this issue, and today I wish to reaffirm it.

That position, briefly, is as follows: First, we are firmly and irrevocably dedicated to the principle of self-determination and independence for the people of Southern Rhodesia, self-determination by and for all the people, independence on a basis acceptable to the people of the country as a whole. Second, we hope and believe that the means of achieving this goal should be through peaceful negotiation to reestablish-

*Department of State Bulletin, Dec. 6, 1965, pp. 912-16.

ment of the broken lines of contact among the various factions in Southern Rhodesia. And, third, we have supported the United Kingdom as the sovereign authority in its monumental efforts to find a peaceful and responsible solution to meet Southern Rhodesia's aspirations in conformity with the United Nations Charter and the principle of paramountcy of the interests of the inhabitants.

*   *   *

It is now for all of us to stand behind the United Kingdom to lend it all necessary assistance and support in making effective the measures that it has taken. We must do this with a single purpose: to bring to an end the rebellion in Southern Rhodesia. We must close ranks, all of us, the members of the United Nations, to insure that the full effect of these stern measures shall be felt.

As a first step, the United States yesterday recalled its consul general from Salisbury. We have also informed the British Government that the Minister for Southern Rhodesian Affairs in the United Kingdom Embassy in Washington, and his four staff members, no longer have any diplomatic status in the United States.

We are immediately instituting a comprehensive embargo on the shipment of all arms and military equipment to Southern Rhodesia.

We will withhold the establishment of any quota for the importation of sugar from Southern Rhodesia in 1966.

The United States Government will suspend action on all applications for United States Government loans and credit guarantees to Southern Rhodesia and will make clear to any potential American investors in Southern Rhodesia the risks which we perceive in any further investment of American capital.

Finally, we will discourage all American private travel to Southern Rhodesia.

We are also considering what further steps might be taken.

*   *   *

Statement by Ambassador Goldberg

November 20, 1965

*   *   *

Permit me to say, Mr. President, that not only are we proceeding quickly to implement the steps which I outlined in my statement of November 12 but we are already going beyond them, where we find additional moves that can be made to reflect the seriousness with which we view the situation and to impress upon the illegal regime in Salisbury that their rebellion cannot be permitted to succeed.

For example, I announced on November 12 that the United States Government would suspend the sugar quota for Southern Rhodesia for 1966. In the meantime, after learning that the entire 1965 Southern Rhodesia quota amounting to approximately 9,500 tons is now on the high seas in transit to the United States, the President of the United States has suspended the sugar quota from Southern Rhodesia for 1965 and has directed that this shipment will not be accepted.

We will continue to consider urgently what other steps we can take to assure that no action is taken which would assist and encourage the illegal regime in Salisbury.

It is in that spirit, Mr. President, and in the spirit of the action which we have taken in connection with the 1965 quota, that my Government has voted for and interprets paragraph 8 of this resolution. That is to say, we understand the call upon states "to do their utmost in order to break all economic relations with Southern Rhodesia, including an embargo on oil and petroleum products" to require an immediate examination of the feasibility and effectiveness of additional trade sanctions against Southern Rhodesia. My Government will proceed urgently to this end.

*   *   *

New York Times *Editorial on the United States and Consequences for Zambia of Economic Sanctions Against Southern Rhodesia**

December 21, 1965

The difficulty about economic sanctions against Rhodesia has always been the certainty that they would first hurt neighboring Zambia. This grim fact may now sink in on African leaders impatient with Britain for not taking more drastic action to bring down the white rebel regime in Salisbury.

Once Britain attempted to embargo crude oil shipments to Rhodesia, it was inevitable that Prime Minister Ian D. Smith would react by cutting off Zambia's oil and gasoline supply—200,000 tons a year—from the Umtali refinery. The result has had to be the launching of a massive British-American oil airlift from Dar-es-Salaam to Lusaka, supplemented by dispatch of oil-carrying trucks over the primitive dirt road network that links Tanzania and Zambia.

It was certain that if Britain were to impose meaningful sanctions, the Smith regime would react sooner or later by boosting the price of the coal from Wankie—700,000 tons a year—that powers Zambia's copper-mining industry. Mr. Smith now has raised the royalty on Wankie coal to Zambia from 14 cents to more than $14 a short ton, and for good measure has slapped an export tax of $22.40 a ton on coke. With British and American assistance, Zambia is developing its own coal field at Kandabwe, but production is still some weeks away and at best this will be an inadequate substitute for the Wankie coal.

Zambia is going to have to pay a heavy price for its contribution to the effort to restore constitutional government in Rhodesia. In this emergency, the United States has the clear obligation to do everything it can to assist President Kenneth Kaunda, one of the most admirable and sensible leaders of the new Africa.

State Department Statement on the End of the United States Airlift to Zambia†

April 30, 1966

The emergency mission of the United States petroleum airlift to aid Zambia has been accomplished and therefore is being terminated, as is the Canadian airlift. The

*The New York Times, Dec. 21, 1965.
†Department of State Bulletin, May 16, 1966, p. 783.

other supply routes—through Tanzania, Kenya, Democratic Republic of the Congo, Malawi, Mozambique, and Angola—by road, rail, river, lake and sea, as well as continuing British air transport, are now regarded as sufficiently well developed to meet Zambia's current petroleum consumption levels and to continue to build up Zambia's petroleum reserves.

Farewell ceremonies to commemorate the American-Canadian contribution to this multinational effort were held by the Zambian Government April 30.

The Vice President of Zambia, Mr. Reuben Kamanga, expressed his country's appreciation of the United States and Canadian airlifts in a broadcast April 21 over Zambian radio and television. He said in part:

> We have now assured our supplies of petroleum products and have built up our stocks to the highest levels there have ever been in this country. The American and Canadian airlifts have made a great contribution to meeting our needs and to building up our stockpiles. I would like to bid them farewell and place on record our great appreciation of the work that they have done and of the vital contribution that they have made to the solution of our petroleum problems.

Both the Pan American and Trans World Airlines jets commenced service in the airlift in early January of this year, carrying petroleum products from Leopoldville to Elisabethville. The products were then transported from Elisabethville to Zambia by rail and road. The Congolese Government as well as many commercial enterprises in the Congo cooperated actively in carrying on the airlift. The two United States airlines have carried more than 3.6 million gallons of petroleum products in this airlift.

The United States Agency for International Development in late 1965 and early 1966 signed the airlift agreements with Pan American Airways and TWA. The multi-national transport effort to Zambia was initiated in order to minimize the impact upon Zambia of the cessation of petroleum supplies normally received from and through Southern Rhodesia.

New York Times *Editorial on the United States and U.N. Action Against Southern Rhodesia* *

December 17, 1966

With American backing, the United Nations Security Council has taken an unprecedented step. It has voted mandatory but selective economic sanctions against Rhodesia in an effort to bring down the white rebel regime. The most that can be said for this Council action is that it was the least damaging of the courses open to a hard-pressed Britain.

It satisfied no one, including Prime Minister Wilson, who reluctantly proposed it. African governments pressed Britain to use military force against Salisbury. At minimum they wanted sanctions covering South Africa and Portugal's territories of Mozambique and Angola as well as Rhodesia. Mr. Wilson's Conservative opponents urged him to keep trying to reach a settlement with the rebel Prime Minister, Ian Smith, despite his promise to the Commonwealth of a year-end deadline on such moves.

*The New York Times, Dec. 17, 1966.

Some Tory leaders and several distinguished American critics said flatly that Mr. Wilson should have scuttled—allowed the Smith regime to get away with its unilateral declaration of independence, whatever happened to Rhodesia's four million Africans. But a distinguished pro-Tory British journalist, Peregrine Worsthorne, gave the answer to these suggestions when he wrote:

"The truth is that Britain can no more boldly advance towards imposing a solution than she can supinely retreat from further responsibility."

The Security Council action is the result. If enforced, sanctions eventually could wreck Rhodesia's economy. It does not follow that this would promptly end white minority rule in Salisbury. South Africa and Portugal have said all along that they will not apply sanctions, whatever the Security Council orders. These outlets would make enforcement difficult. In particular, they probably would render totally ineffective the very limited oil embargo Britain finally accepted in the Council resolution.

Where sanctions could be effective is in preventing Rhodesia from selling its exports, particularly its tobacco crop. The voluntary sanctions in the last year are estimated to have cut Rhodesia's exports by about $115 million. In time, South Africa might tire of making up such a trade and payments deficit.

As we have said previously, the United States had no reasonable alternative to supporting the sanctions resolution. This country cannot take its stand in the world forum on the side of an illegal regime representing a white minority outnumbered eighteen to one by the African population.

Having taken its stand, the United States has the obligation to enforce the sanctions and to exert its influence to persuade other governments to comply with the Council order—but it should do so without illusions as to the probability of early success.

THE UNITED STATES SUPPORTS SANCTIONS AGAINST SOUTHERN RHODESIA *

State Department Statement

December 30, 1965

The Agency for International Development on December 29 concluded an agreement with Pan American World Airways to begin an airlift of gasoline and oil into Zambia as the U.S. contribution to the British efforts to minimize the impact upon Zambia of the cessation of petroleum supplies normally received from and through Southern Rhodesia.

Pan American is supplying a late-model jet cargo aircraft which is expected to leave New York for Léopoldville on January 1. At Léopoldville arrangements have been made for delivery of petroleum products to the airport (Ndjili Airport), from where the cargo will be flown to Elisabethville.

At Elisabethville, under arrangements made with the British and the Zambian Governments, the local oil companies will forward the cargoes by truck and railroad the short distance (60-100 miles) to major towns in the Zambian Copperbelt, where very strict gasoline and oil rationing has had to be imposed. The U.S. aircraft will

*Department of State Bulletin, Jan. 31, 1966, pp. 157-58.

operate between Léopoldville and Elisabethville, since airports in those cities are capable of handling large jet aircraft. The Zambian airports are not. The Congolese Government has promised complete cooperation in this airlift.

AID is currently engaged in arrangements to augment the U.S. airlift by procuring further aircraft sufficient to lift approximately 6,000 tons of gasoline, oil, and lubricants during the months of January and February. A further announcement will be made when these plans have been completed.

The U.S. airlift is a part of an overall effort to move 14,000 tons of petroleum products into Zambia during January and a higher amount during February. By March 1 it is expected that alternative overland supply routes through neighboring countries will have been sufficiently developed to terminate the airlift.

State Department Statement

January 10, 1966

The Department of State announced on January 10 two further measures designed to complement the British program of economic sanctions against Rhodesia.

The Agency for International Development has arranged to augment the American contribution to the airlift now supplying Zambia with petroleum products. Trans World Airlines will supply an additional jet cargo plane, a Boeing 707-321C, which will operate between Léopoldville and Elisabethville in conjunction with a similar Pan American Airways plane now in operation. It is expected that the TWA plane will be in operation on or about January 14. Together the two planes will be capable of delivering cargo to Elisabethville at the rate of about 3,000 tons a month. From Elisabethville, the lifted petroleum products are delivered by rail and road to Zambia's Copperbelt cities.

In further support of the United Kingdom and of the Security Council resolution of November 20, the Departments of State and Commerce have been holding talks with United States importers of various Southern Rhodesian commodities with a view to replacing such imports with goods from other sources. These talks are continuing, and U.S. consumers of Rhodesian asbestos and lithium have expressed their willingness to cooperate in finding alternative sources. Lithium and asbestos are two of the more significant U.S. imports from Southern Rhodesia.

New York Times *Editorial on United States Policy Towards Southern Rhodesia*†

January 19, 1967

Barry Goldwater's successor in the Senate calls President Johnson's order invoking sanctions against Rhodesia "dictatorial, deceitful and dangerous." In the House a California Republican introduces a resolution to end the sanctions.

Such efforts by conservative elements in behalf of the white rebel regime in Salisbury were inevitable in the new Congress. The danger is that moderate forces will

†*The New York Times*, Jan. 19, 1967.

be sufficiently persuaded by specious political and legal arguments to join in this attempt to embarrass the Administration in its support of mandatory sanctions voted by the United Nations.

First of all, there can be no doubt that Mr. Johnson acted legally and properly in issuing the Executive order barring trade with Rhodesia in the products listed in the United Nations resolution. The United Nations Participation Act of 1945 empowers the President to take action to enforce Security Council decisions made under Article 41 of the Charter, which deals with U.N. measures short of armed force.

But most critics argue that the Council action violates Paragraph 7, Article 2 of the Charter, which bars U.N. intervention "in matters which are essentially within the domestic jurisdiction jurisdiction of any state. . . ."

The short, pertinent answer is that Rhodesia is not a "state" and has not been recognized as one by any government. South Africa and Portugal have befriended the white minority regime; neither has acorded it diplomatic recognition nor given legal sanction to its "independence."

There is no U.N. "intervention" in the meaning of Paragraph 7 because the Council acted at the request of the legal authority, Britain. Moreover, that paragraph adds that the nonintervention principle "shall not prejudice the application of enforcement measures under Chapter VII" of the Charter, covering threats to the peace–a proviso the critics usually overlook.

Finally, critics say the white regime has only exercised the right of "self-determination," and in any event is not a "threat to the peace." But it is a bizarre act of self-determination when a regime representing 220,000 whites declares independence for a country of more than four million. And anyone who argues that this illegal act–aimed at perpetuating the rule of the 6 per cent white minority over the 94 per cent African majority–is not a long-run threat to peace simply ignores the realities in southeast Africa.

There can be legitimate doubts about the effectiveness of the sanctions, but no reasonable doubt that the United States acted honorably and legally in supporting them. Ambassador Goldberg has answered the critics effectively and it is high time that the Administration and informed members of Congress made use of his arguments on Capitol Hill.

Speech by Assistant Secretary Williams on the Crisis in Southern Rhodesia*

January 28, 1966

*   *   *

American reaction to the illegal seizure of power by the Smith regime was immediate and positive. In the weeks that have elapsed since November 11 we have given many concrete evidences of our support of the British program of economic, political, and psychological countermeasures. We are encouraged by and pleased to acknowledge the widespread support our actions have received in the U.S. press, in American business circles, and from the general public.

**Department of State Bulletin*, Feb. 21, 1966, pp. 266-67.

At the present time, the United States is enforcing an arms embargo, announced in the U.N. Security Council last November 12, against the Southern Rhodesian regime. Under the Mutual Security Act of 1954, as amended, we have put anything in the munitions line under Government license to prohibit the export of arms and ammunition to the rebel regime.

Under the Export Control Act of 1949, as amended, we have prohibited the export from the United States of all petroleum and petroleum products to aid the British oil embargo. As far as foreign oil operations of American companies are concerned, they are voluntarily respecting the British embargo, although export control regulations do not apply. Although we are not a major supplier of petroleum products to Southern Rhodesia, we did supply that country with about 15-20 percent of its heavy lubricants, and those can now be cut off. Under this act we also are in a position to stay in step with the British as their sanctions against exports to Southern Rhodesia become tighter and tighter.

Although controls over U.S. exports to Southern Rhodesia are provided for by existing legislation, there are no comparable controls over imports from Southern Rhodesia. The President has, however, employed powers given him under the Sugar Act Amendments of 1965 to suspend Southern Rhodesia's sugar quotas for 1965 and 1966. In fact, the entire Southern Rhodesian sugar quota for 1965 was turned back at sea in early December. But for the most part the United States has had to rely upon the voluntary cooperation of American industry and for their recognition of British Orders-in-Council that apply to their operations in Southern Rhodesia. Such cooperation has been forthcoming in commendable fashion from American importers of Southern Rhodesian commodities.

We have managed to cut our imports from Southern Rhodesia almost in half through the elimination of sugar imports and by obtaining the voluntary agreements of U.S. importers of lithium and asbestos to find other sources of these materials. Last week, the British Government issued an Order-in-Council banning exports of chrome from their Southern Rhodesian colony. If such exports are cut off, it would be another blow to the Smith regime's remaining foreign exchange earnings. This would go a long way in tightening the economic noose around the Southern Rhodesian regime.

Let me express here our regard for the oil companies who were partners in the consortium that operated the Southern Rhodesian oil refinery at Umtali. Those companies responded cooperatively to the British Order-in-Council banning the import of oil into Southern Rhodesia.

*   *   *

State Department Statement on Export of Rhodesian Chromite*

January 28, 1966

The Government of the United Kingdom has recently announced an Order-in-Council prohibiting the export and transactions intended to promote the export of

*Ibid., Feb. 21, 1966, p. 267.

chromite from Southern Rhodesia. The United States Government recognizes the legal authority of Her Majesty's Government to take this action and has requested all United States importers of Rhodesian chromite to comply with the Order.

*Statement by Ambassador Goldberg on the Security Council Authorization for Great Britain to Use Force to Divert Oil Shipments Bound for Rhodesia**

April 9, 1966

*   *   *

We are asked in the Security Council—and it should be a matter of deep consideration and concern for all of us—to put our sanction upon what will be a rule of international law when this Council acts: Vessels on the high seas can be arrested and detained in the interest of international law which we will be making here today if we adopt the resolution tendered by Great Britain, as I hope we will do.

It is not an easy decision for any government to put its support to a resolution of this character, both in light of our history and traditions and in light of all of the far-reaching implications that such a step as we are asked to take may envision. Indeed, for a major trading country such as the United States to put teeth into a program of denial such as the one called for by the Security Council last November involved an impressive array of steps on our part, which called into play very important decisions on our part. When I last spoke to the Council on this subject I mentioned some of the measures which we had taken and I said the United States would consider urgently what else remained to be done in order to apply an effective across-the-board program of trade sanctions against Southern Rhodesia. I am sure the members of the Council will be interested in hearing what this involved from the standpoint of the United States in terms of taking such action.

First, we refused recognition of the Smith regime.

Second, we immediately instituted a comprehensive embargo on the shipment of all arms and military equipment to Southern Rhodesia.

Third, we suspended action on applications for United States Government loans and credit guarantees and are issuing no further investment guarantees to Southern Rhodesia.

Fourth, we took action in support of the financial measures instituted by the British Government, including recognition of the authority of the newly appointed Board of Directors in London over the official deposits of the Reserve Bank of Rhodesia in the United States.

Fifth, we announced that at the request of our Government the United States importers of asbestos and lithium from Southern Rhodesia had agreed to find other sources.

Sixth, we informed United States companies that we recognized the legal authority of the British Government to take actions banning the trade in Southern Rhodesian chrome and tobacco, and we recommended in the strongest terms to the United States companies that they comply with the British Orders-in-Council passed for this purpose.

*Ibid., May 2, 1966, pp. 715-17.

Seventh, despite our great tradition and in part our constitutional commitment to freedom of private travel, we took measures to discourage private travel by Americans to Southern Rhodesia by announcing that the United States Government could no longer assure normal protective services to Americans planning to travel through or in Southern Rhodesia. And we also said that American travelers intending to go to Southern Rhodesia must have British visas, not Southern Rhodesian visas, for travel to that country.

Eighth, we instituted procedures which have cut off virtually all American exports of consequence. The exceptions are largely humanitarian items and not essential to the Southern Rhodesian economy.

Ninth, we suspended the United States sugar quota for Southern Rhodesia for the years 1965 and 1966. In fact, part of that quota was on the high seas for delivery to the United States when we took that action, and we have subjected ourselves, obviously, to legal action for the act we took with respect to a shipment on the high seas before the Security Council acted.

Tenth, we instituted a total embargo on shipments of all United States petroleum and petroleum products into Southern Rhodesia. And we also advised United States citizens and enterprises to comply in full with the British Government's Order-in-Council prohibiting import of such products into Southern Rhodesia.

In addition to these direct measures, we have joined the United Kingdom and other countries in establishing an airlift of petroleum products to Zambia in order to aid that landlocked nation in maintaining its economy, a consideration which must never escape the minds of this Council. United States aircraft are being used in this operation delivering vital cargo to Elisabethville at a total rate of 1 million gallons per month.

Mr. President, these measures cannot be taken overnight. We took them urgently and as quickly as we could. And the measures we have instituted against Southern Rhodesia will mean a trade loss to the United States of many millions of dollars. In addition, since the middle of January, the United States has allocated more than $4 million for the Zambian airlift and for planned emergency maintenance of the Great North Road from Tanzania to Zambia. It is interesting, Mr. President, to reflect that this figure represents more than the total United States contribution for the United Nations Force in Cyprus covering the same period of time and almost two-thirds of the United States contributions to the United Nations Emergency Force in the Middle East for the entire year 1966. In short, our support for Zambia in connection with the implementation of the Security Council's November resolution on Southern Rhodesia is comparable in cost to the support which we provide for the United Nations important peacekeeping operations.

I mention these costs not to use figures but to emphasize that these are costs which we accept gladly in support of the principles of legality, democracy, and self-determination in Africa. And we are glad that we were able to make this contribution because we deem the problem of Rhodesia to be a problem for all the world. We recognize, of course, the special concern of Africa in this problem, but we share that concern.

Mr. President, I think this is a proper occasion to strongly urge other countries which have not as yet moved to tighten this ring around the Smith regime to do so without delay. As for us, we continue to support the United Kingdom firmly as it discharges its responsibilities in this effort.

Now today we deal with a particular problem. The United Kingdom has brought to the attention of this Council the greatest current danger in our common effort: the risk of a serious breach in the program of oil sanctions as a result of the arrival and the potential arrival of tankers at Portuguese ports with cargoes apparently destined for Southern Rhodesia.

The United States fully concurs in the British proposal that the Council act vigorously and promptly to meet this danger. And this resolution is, indeed, destined to meet firmly and clearly the immediate danger before us by calling on the Portuguese Government, and on any government whose vessels may be involved, to prevent the movement of oil into Rhodesia through Beira and, in case this is not sufficient, it calls on the United Kingdom Government to prevent such movement, by force if necessary.

*   *   *

Speech by Ambassador Goldberg on the Crisis in Southern Rhodesia *

May 2, 1966

What is the United States stake in this Rhodesian crisis? Why do we feel it so important to take a strong stand on it?

First, the basic issue in Rhodesia is a moral one: to restore the constitutional authority in order that all of the people of Rhodesia may be enabled to join in determining their national future. Our country, founded on the proposition that all men are created equal and currently engaged in a vigorous nationwide program to make that equality real for our own Negro citizens, cannot honorably adopt a double standard on what is happening in Rhodesia.

Second, our history also gives us a strong anticolonial tradition. This is the teaching of our own Revolution. In recent times we have supported decolonization and self-determination in the Philippines, India, Pakistan, Indonesia, and indeed throughout the world; and it is this sime principle of self-determination which we are upholding in South Viet-Nam. We cannot stand aside and see these same principles turned into a mockery in Rhodesia.

Third, as a founder of the United Nations and a principal architect of the U.N. Charter, we have a special obligation to see that the charter's provisions concerning human rights and self-determination are upheld. These provisions are not merely exhortations; they are solemn treaty obligations.

Fourth, we have a practical interest in maintaining friendly relations with the newly independent countries of Africa, for whom this Rhodesian issue is of the highest importance.

Fifth and last, but not least, the success of a rebellion aimed at creating a new white minority state in southern Africa would inevitably harden the lines of political conflict and would tend to stir interracial violence on that continent.

A failure to resolve the Rhodesian crisis with justice to the African majority would inevitably strengthen the hand of extremism, violence, and racism in the heart of Africa. Moderate African leaders, who have recently gained ground in several coun-

Ibid., May 23, 1966, p. 801.

tries, might lose ground again. Such a prospect is not in the interest of African development and progress nor of world peace and security, nor is it in the interest of the United States.

For all these reasons the United States, in dealing with the Rhodesian question, intends to remain true to its best traditions—knowing that in so doing we also most effectively uphold our national interests. We shall continue to proceed step by step, weighing both the legality and the wisdom of each step as we go in the light of the situation and of the United Nations Charter.

White House Announcement on U.N. Sanctions Against Southern Rhodesia *

January 5, 1967

The President on January 5 signed Executive Order No. 11322 implementing the United Nations Security Council's Resolution No. 232 of December 16, 1966, which imposed selective mandatory economic sanctions against Southern Rhodesia.

The President acted under the United Nations Participation Act of 1945, as amended. Section 5 of the act empowers the President to implement Security Council decisions adopted pursuant to article 41 of the United Nations Charter. In its Resolution No. 232, the Council decided that all member states shall prohibit imports of Rhodesian asbestos, iron ore, chrome, pig iron, sugar, tobacco, copper, meat and meat products, and hides, skins, and leather, as well as dealing by their nationals or in their territories in such products originating in Southern Rhodesia. The resolution also obligates members to embargo shipments of arms, aircraft, motor vehicles, and petroleum and petroleum products to Southern Rhodesia.

This Executive order prohibits the activities proscribed by the resolution, including transactions involving commodities exported from Southern Rhodesia after December 16, the date of the resolution, and delegates to the Secretaries of State, Commerce, and the Treasury the authority to promulgate regulations necessary to carry out the order. These regulations will be issued by the Departments shortly and will be effective as of January 5.

A violation of the Executive order is a criminal offense. Provision will be made in the regulations to deal with cases of undue hardship arising from transactions commenced before the date of the order.

The selective mandatory sanctions imposed by the Security Council's resolution of December 16 supplement earlier voluntary measures taken by a large majority of U.N. members in response to the Council's appeal, contained in its resolution of November 20, 1965, that they break off economic relations with Southern Rhodesia. This resolution was adopted a few days after the Smith regime in Southern Rhodesia had unilaterally declared its independence on November 11, 1965. The United States joined with other states in implementing the voluntary measures called for by the Security Council by embargoing the shipment to Southern Rhodesia of all arms, military equipment, and related items and by suspending the 1965 and 1966 U.S. import quotas for Rhodesian sugar. Since early 1966, the United States has called upon U.S. firms to cooperate with the voluntary Security Council sanctions and has recommended that U.S. firms comply with British Orders-in-Council by avoiding trade

Ibid., Jan. 23, 1967, pp. 145-46.

in commodities of significant importance to the Southern Rhodesian economy, including petroleum, as well as Rhodesian exports of chrome, asbestos, and tobacco.

EXECUTIVE ORDERS RELATING TO TRADE AND OTHER TRANSACTIONS INVOLVING SOUTHERN RHODESIA *

Executive Order 11322

January 5, 1967

By virtue of the authority vested in me by the Constitution and laws of the United States, including section 5 of the United Nations Participation Act of 1945 (59 Stat. 620), as amended (22 U.S.C. 287c), and section 301 of Title 3 of the United States Code, and as President of the United States, and considering the measures which the Security Council of the United Nations, by Security Council Resolution No. 232 adopted December 16, 1966, has decided upon pursuant to article 41 of the Charter of the United Nations, including the United States, to apply, it is hereby ordered:

Section 1. The following are prohibited effective immediately, notwithstanding any contracts entered into or licenses granted before the date of this Order:

(a) The importation into the United States of asbestos, iron ore, chrome, pig-iron, sugar, tobacco, copper, meat and meat products, and hides, skins and leather originating in Southern Rhodesia and exported therefrom after December 16, 1966, or products made therefrom in Southern Rhodesia or elsewhere.

(b) Any activities by any person subject to the jurisdiction of the United States, which promote or are calculated to promote the export from Southern Rhodesia after December 16, 1966, of any of the commodities specified in subsection (a) of this section originating in Southern Rhodesia, and any dealings by any such person in any such commodities or in products made therefrom in Southern Rhodesia or elsewhere, including in particular any transfer of funds to Southern Rhodesia for the purposes of such activities or dealings: Provided, however, that the prohibition against the dealing in commodities exported from Southern Rhodesia or products made therefrom shall not apply to any such commodities or products which, prior to the date of this Order, had been imported into the United States.

(c) Shipment in vessels or aircraft of United States registration of any of the commodities specified in subsection (a) of this section originating in Southern Rhodesia and exported therefrom after December 16, 1966, or products made therefrom in Southern Rhodesia or elsewhere.

(d) Any activities by any person subject to the jurisdiction of the United States, which promote or are calculated to promote the sale or shipment to Southern Rhodesia of arms, ammunition of all types, military aircraft, military vehicles and equipment and materials for the manufacture and maintenance of arms and ammunition in Southern Rhodesia.

(e) Any activities by any person subject to the jurisdiction of the United States, which promote or are calculated to promote the supply to Southern Rhodesia of all other aircraft and motor vehicles, and of equipment and materials for the manufac-

*U.S. Treasury Department, *Rhodesian Sanctions: Regulations and Related Documents,* July 29, 1968, (containing all amendments through Sept. 29, 1968), pp. 1-9.

ture, assembly, or maintenance of aircraft or motor vehicles in Southern Rhodesia; the shipment in vessels or aircraft of United States registration of any such goods destined for Southern Rhodesia; and any activities by any persons subject to the jurisdiction of the United States, which promote or are calculated to promote the manufacture or assembly of aircraft or motor vehicles in Southern Rhodesia.

(f) Any participation in the supply of oil or oil products to Southern Rhodesia (i) by any person subject to the jurisdiction of the United States, or (ii) by vessels or aircraft of United States registration, or (iii) by the use of any land or air transport facility located in the United States.

Sec. 2. The functions and responsibilities for the enforcement of the foregoing prohibitions are delegated as follows:

(a) To the Secretary of State, the function and responsibility of enforcement relating to the importation into, or exportation from the United States of articles, including technical data, the control of the importation or exportation of which is provided for in section 414 of the Mutual Security Act of 1954 (68 Stat. 848), as amended (22 U.S.C. 1934), and has been delegated to the Secretary of State by section 101 of Executive Order No. 10973 of September 3, 1961.

(b) To the Secretary of Commerce, the function and responsibility of enforcement relating to—

(i) the exportation from the United States of articles other than the articles, including technical data, referred to in subsection (a) of this section; and

(ii) the transportation in vessels or aircraft of United States registration of any commodities the transportation of which is prohibited by section 1 of this Order.

(c) To the Secretary of the Treasury, the function and responsibility of enforcement to the extent not delegated under subsections (a) or (b) of this section.

Sec. 3. The Secretary of State, the Secretary of the Treasury, and the Secretary of Commerce shall exercise any authority which such officer may have apart from the United Nations Participation Act of 1945 or this Order so as to give full effect to this Order and Security Council Resolution No. 232.

Sec. 4. (a) In carrying out their respective functions and responsibilities under this Order, the Secretary of the Treasury and the Secretary of Commerce shall consult with the Secretary of State. Each such Secretary shall consult, as appropriate, with other government agencies and private persons.

(b) Each such Secretary shall issue such regulations, licenses, or other authorizations as he considers necessary to carry out the purposes of this Order and Security Council Resolution No. 232.

Sec. 5. (a) The term "United States," as used in this Order in a geographical sense, means all territory subject to the jurisdiction of the United States.

(b) The term "person" means an individual, partnership, association, or other unincorporated body of individuals, or corporation.

Lyndon B. Johnson

Executive Order 11419

July 29, 1968

By virtue of the authority vested in me by the Constitution and laws of the United States, including section 5 of the United Nations Participation Act of 1945 (59 Stat.

620), as amended (22 U.S.C. 287c), and section 301 of Title 3 of the United States Code, and as President of the United States, and considering the measures which the Security Council of the United Nations by Security Council Resolution No. 253 adopted May 29, 1968, has decided upon pursuant to article 41 of the Charter of the United Nations, and which it has called upon all members of the United Nations, including the United States, to apply, it is hereby ordered:

Section 1. In addition to the prohibitions of section 1 of Executive Order No. 11322 of January 5, 1967, the following are prohibited effective immediately, notwithstanding any contracts entered into or licenses granted before the date of this Order:

(a) Importation into the United States of any commodities or products originating in Southern Rhodesia and exported therefrom after May 29, 1968.

(b) Any activities by any person subject to the jurisdiction of the United States which promote or are calculated to promote the export from Southern Rhodesia after May 29, 1968, of any commodities or products originating in Southern Rhodesia, and any dealings by any such person in any such commodities or products, including in particular any transfer of funds to Southern Rhodesia for the purposes of such activities or dealings; Provided, however, that the prohibition against the dealing in commodities or products exported from Southern Rhodesia shall not apply to any such commodities or products which, prior to the date of this Order, had been lawfully imported into the United States.

(c) Carriage in vessels or aircraft of United States registration or under charter to any person subject to the jurisdiction of the United States of any commodities or products originating in Southern Rhodesia and exported therefrom after May 29, 1968.

(d) Sale or supply by any person subject to the jurisdiction of the United States, or any other activities by any such person which promote or are calculated to promote the sale or supply, to any person or body in Southern Rhodesia or to any person or body for the purposes of any business carried on in or operated from Southern Rhodesia of any commodities or products. Such activities, including carriage in vessels or aircraft, may be authorized with respect to supplies intended strictly for medical purposes, educational equipment and material for use in schools and other educational institutions, publications, news material, and foodstuffs required by special humanitarian circumstances.

(e) Carriage in vessels or aircraft of United States registration or under charter to any person subject to the jurisdiction of the United States of any commodities or products consigned to any person or body in Southern Rhodesia, or to any person or body for the purposes of any business carried on in or operated from Southern Rhodesia.

(f) Transfer by any person subject to the jurisdiction of the United States directly or indirectly to any person or body in Southern Rhodesia of any funds or other financial or economic resources. Payments exclusively for pensions, for strictly medical, humanitarian or educational purposes, for the provision of news material or for foodstuffs required by special humanitarian circumstances may be authorized.

(g) Operation of any United States air carrier or aircraft owned or chartered by any person subject to the jurisdiction of the United States or of United States registration (i) to or from Southern Rhodesia or (ii) in coordination with any airline company constituted or aircraft registered in Southern Rhodesia.

Sec. 2. The functions and responsibilities for the enforcement of the foregoing prohibitions, and of those prohibitions of Executive Order No. 11322 of January 5, 1967 specified below, are delegated as follows:

(a) To the Secretary of Commerce, the function and responsibility of enforcement relating to—

(i) the exportation from the United States of commodities and products other than those articles referred to in section 2(a) of Executive Order No. 11322 of January 5, 1967; and

(ii) the carriage in vessels of any commodities or products the carriage of which is prohibited by section 1 of this Order or by section 1 of Executive Order No. 11322 of January 5, 1967.

(b) To the Secretary of Transportation, the function and responsibility of enforcement relating to the operation of air carriers and aircraft and the carriage in aircraft of any commodities or products the carriage of which is prohibited by section 1 of this Order or by section 1 of Executive Order No. 11322 of January 5, 1967.

(c) To the Secretary of the Treasury, the function and responsibility of enforcement to the extent not previously delegated in section 2 of Executive Order No. 11322 of January 5, 1967, and not delegated under subsections (a) and (b) of this section.

Sec. 3. The Secretary of the Treasury, the Secretary of Commerce, and the Secretary of Transportation shall exercise any authority which such officer may have apart from the United Nations Participation Act of 1945 or this Order so as to give full effect to this Order and Security Council Resolution No. 253.

Sec. 4. (a) In carrying out their respective functions and responsibilities under this Order, the Secretary of the Treasury, the Secretary of Commerce, and the Secretary of Transportation shall consult with the Secretary of State. Each such Secretary shall consult, as appropriate, with other government agencies and private persons.

(b) Each such Secretary shall issue such regulations, licenses or other authorizations as he considers necessary to carry out the purposes of this Order and Security Council Resolution No. 253.

Sec. 5. (a) The term "United States," as used in this Order in a geographical sense, means all territory subject to the jurisdiction of the United States.

(b) The term "person" means an individual, partnership, association or other unincorporated body of individuals, or corporation.

Sec. 6. Executive Order No. 11322 of January 5, 1967, implementing United Nations Security Council Resolution No. 232 of December 16, 1966, shall continue in effect as modified by sections 2, 3, and 4 of this Order.

Lyndon B. Johnson

Rhodesian Sanctions Regulations

August 12, 1968

TITLE 31, CODE OF FEDERAL REGULATIONS,
CHAPTER V, PART 530

Subpart A—Relation of This Part to Other Laws and Regulations

530.101 Relation of This Part to Other Laws and Regulations.

(a) The Rhodesian Transaction Regulations (Part 525 of this title) issued as of January 5, 1967, as amended, are revoked and the regulations in this Part 530 are adopted in place thereof controlling certain financial and commercial transactions involving Southern Rhodesia or business nationals thereof: Provided, That the revocation of the Rhodesian Transaction Regulations shall not be deemed to authorize any unlicensed importation, transaction or transfer prohibited by the Rhodesian Transaction Regulations and all penalties, forfeitures, and liabilities under such regulations or any other applicable laws or regulations shall continue and may be enforced as if such revocation had not been made.

(b) A license or authorization contained in or issued pursuant to this part does not authorize any transaction that is prohibited by the provisions of any law, statute or regulation other than section 5 of the United Nations Participation Act of 1945, Executive Order 11322 issued January 5, 1967, thereunder, Executive Order 11419, issued July 29, 1968, thereunder, and the regulations contained in this part.

Subpart B—Prohibitions

530.201 Prohibitions   *530.201 Prohibitions.*

(a) All of the following direct or indirect transactions by any person subject to the jurisdiction of the United States are prohibited, except as authorized by the Secretary of the Treasury (or any person, agency, or instrumentality designated by him), by means of regulations, rulings, instructions, general or specific licenses or otherwise:

(1) The importation into the United States of merchandise of Southern Rhodesian origin;

(2) Transfers of property which involve merchandise outside the United States of Southern Rhodesian origin;

(3) Transfers of property which involve merchandise destined to Southern Rhodesia or to or for the account of business nationals thereof;

(4) Other transfers of property to or on behalf of or for the benefit of any person in Southern Rhodesia (including the authorities thereof); and

(5) The importation into the United States of ferrochrome produced in any country from chromium ore or concentrates of Southern Rhodesian origin.

(b) Any transaction for the purpose or which has the effect of evading or avoiding any of the prohibitions set forth in paragraph (a) of this section is prohibited.

(c) The effective date of this section is 11:59 p.m., e.s.t, July 29, 1968.

Subpart C—General Definitions

530.301 Persons.

The term "person" means an individual, partnership, association, corporation, or other organization.

530.302 Transfer.

The term "transfer" includes, but not by way of limitation, any actual or purported act or transaction, whether or not evidenced by writing, and whether or not done or performed within the United States, the purpose, intent, or effect of which is to create, surrender, release, transfer, or alter, directly or indirectly, any right, remedy, power, privilege, or interest, with respect to any property and without limitation upon the foregoing shall include the making, execution, or delivery of any assignment, power, conveyance, check, declaration, deed, deed of trust, power of attorney, power of appointment, bill of sale, mortgage, receipt, agreement, contract, certificate, gift, sale, affadavit, or statement; and the appointment of any agent, trustee, or other fiduciary.

530.303 License.

Except as otherwise specified, the term "license" shall mean any license or authorization contained in or issued pursuant to this part.

530.304 General License.

A general license is any license or authorization the terms of which are set forth in this part.

530.305 Specific License.

A specific license is any license or authorization issued pursuant to this part but not set forth in this part.

530.306 United States; Continental United States.

The term "United States" means the United States and all areas under the jurisdiction or authority thereof including the Panama Canal Zone and the Trust Territory of the Pacific Islands. The term "continental United States" means the States of the United States and the District of Columbia.

530.307 Person Subject to the Jurisdiction of the United States.

(a) The term "person subject to the jurisdiction of the United States" includes:

(1) Any person, wheresoever located, who is a citizen or resident of the United States;

(2) Any person actually within the United States;

(3) Any corporation organized under the laws of the United States or of any State, territory, possession, or district of the United States; and

(4) Any partnership, association, corporation, or other organization organized under the laws of, or having its principal place of business in, Southern Rhodesia which is owned or controlled by persons specified in subparagraph (1), (2), or (3) of this paragraph.

530.308 Property.

The term "property" includes, but not by way of limitation, money, checks, drafts, bullion, bank deposits, savings accounts, any debts, indebtedness obligations, notes, debentures, stocks, bonds, coupons, any other financial securities, bankers' acceptances, mortgages, pledges, liens or other rights in the nature of security, warehouse receipts, bills of lading, trust receipts, bills of sale, any other evidences of title, ownership or indebtedness, powers of attorney, goods, wares, merchandise, chattels, stocks on hand, ships, goods on ships, real estate mortgages, deeds of trust, vendors' sales agreements, land contracts, real estate and any interest therein, leaseholds, grounds rents, options, negotiable instruments, trade acceptances, royalties, book accounts, accounts payable, judgments, patents, trademarks, copyrights, contracts or licenses affecting or involving patents, trademarks, copyrights, contracts or licenses affecting or involving patents, trademarks or copyrights, insurance policies, safe deposit boxes and their contents, annuities, pooling agreements, contracts of any nature whatsoever, and any other property, real, personal, or mixed tangible or intangible, or interest or interests therein, present, future, or contingent.

530.309 Merchandise.

The term "merchandise" means all goods, wares, and chattels of every description without limitation of any kind.

530.310 Business National.

(a) The term "business national" of Southern Rhodesia means:

(1) Any business enterprise in Southern Rhodesia;

(2) Any person outside Southern Rhodesia to the extent such person is acting for or on behalf of or for the benefit of a business enterprise in Southern Rhodesia;

(3) Any person outside Southern Rhodesia owned or controlled by a business enterprise in Southern Rhodesia.

(b) The term "business enterprise" includes an individual to the extent he engages in business activities.

530.311 Free Account.

A free account is a licensed account held by a domestic bank for a person in Southern Rhodesia. Credits to free accounts may only be made in accordance with a general or specific license. Debits to free accounts may be made without further license, provided that the debit is not for a transfer prohibited under any other part of this chapter.

530.312 Suspense Account.

A suspense account is an account (other than a free account) held by a domestic bank for a person in Southern Rhodesia. Transfers to or from suspense accounts may only be made in accordance with a general or specific license.

Subpart D—Interpretations

530.401 Reference to Amended Sections.

Reference to any section of this part or to any regulation, ruling, order, instruction, direction, or license issued pursuant to this part shall be deemed to refer to the same as currently amended unless otherwise so specified.

530.402 Effect of Amendment of Sections of This Part or of Other Orders, Etc.

Any amendment, modification, or revocation of any section of this part of any order, regulation, ruling, instruction, or license issued by or under the direction of the Secretary of the Treasury pursuant to Executive Order 11322 or Executive Order 11419 shall not unless otherwise specifically provided be deemed to affect any act done or omitted to be done, or any suit or proceeding had or commenced in any civil or criminal case, prior to such amendment, modification, or revocation, and all penalties, forfeitures, and liabilities under any such section, order, regulation, ruling, instruction, or license shall continue and may be enforced as if such amendment, modification, or revocation had not been made.

530.403   Transactions Between Principal and Agent.

A transaction between any person within the United States and any principal, agent, home office, branch, or correspondent outside the United States of such person is a prohibited transaction to the same extent as if the parties to the transaction were in no way affiliated or associated with each other.

530.404   Officers and Directors of Foreign Firms.

Section 530.201 prohibits persons subject to the jurisdiction of the United States who are officers, directors, or principal managerial personnel of business enterprises in foreign countries from being involved in any transaction subject to Section 530.201. Such persons are involved in transactions when they authorize or permit the foreign business enterprise to engage in a transaction subject to Section 530.201, even if they do not themselves actively engage in the transaction.

530.405   Transactions by Persons in Southern Rhodesia.

Section 530.201 prohibits persons who directly or indirectly own or control any person in Southern Rhodesia from authorizing or permitting the latter to engage in any transfer of property prohibited by Section 530.201.

530.406   Alterations of Letters of Credit.

Section 530.201 prohibits the renewal, amendment, extension or other alteration of irrevocable letters of credit issued or confirmed by domestic banks prior to July 29, 1968 except in accordance with a specific license.

530.407   Proceeds of Insurance Policies Held by Persons in Southern Rhodesia.

Payments by domestic insurance companies to or on behalf of or for the benefit of persons in Southern Rhodesia are prohibited by Section 530.201. Section 530.512 authorizes such payments to be made into suspense accounts.

530.408   Insurance Operations in Southern Rhodesia.

(a) Section 530.201 prohibits domestic insurance companies from insuring or reinsuring:

(1) Merchandise in Southern Rhodesia produced there in whole or in part for export;

(2) Merchandise of any origin shipped to or from Southern Rhodesia unless the shipment has been generally or specifically licensed by the Office of Foreign Assets Control;

(3) Property in Southern Rhodesia which facilitates the export of merchandise from Southern Rhodesia, e.g., a factory or a mine whose output is chiefly for export purposes.

(b) Section 530.201 does not prohibit domestic insurance companies from insuring or reinsuring lives of persons in Southern Rhodesia, or property in Southern Rhodesia which is not related to import or export of or carriage of merchandise. Payments under such policies to persons in Southern Rhodesia may only be made by payment into a suspense account.

530.510   Publications and Films of Southern Rhodesian Origin.

All transactions incidental to the importation into the United States of publications and documentary or news films of Southern Rhodesian origin are hereby authorized.

530.511   Exportations to Southern Rhodesia.

All transactions ordinarily incident to the exportation of goods, wares and merchandise from the United States to any person within Southern Rhodesia are hereby authorized provided the exportation is licensed or otherwise authorized by the Department of Commerce under the provisions of the Export Control Act of 1949, as amended (50 U.S.C. App. Sec. 2023).

530.512   Payments to Suspense Accounts.

(a) Any payment or other transfer of property to a suspense account is hereby authorized provided such payment or transfer shall not be made from any other suspense account if such payment or transfer represents, directly or indirectly, a transfer of the interest of a person in Southern Rhodesia to any other person.

(b) This section does not authorize any payment or transfer from a suspense account in a domestic bank to a suspense account held under any name or designation which differs from the name or designation of the suspense account from which the payment or transfer is made.

530.513   Certain Transaction with Respect to Patents, Trademarks, and Copyrights.

(a) The following transactions are herewith authorized:

(1) The filing and prosecution of any application for a Southern Rhodesian patent, trademark or copyright, or for the renewal thereof;

(2) The receipt of any Southern Rhodesian patent, trademark or copyright;

(3) The filing and prosectuion of opposition of infringement proceedings with respect to any Southern Rhodesian patent, trademark, or copyright, and the prosecution of a defense to any such proceedings;

(4) The payment of fees currently due, either directly or through an attorney or representative, in connection with any of the transactions authorized by subparagraphs (1), (2), and (3) of this paragraph or for the maintenance of any Southern Rhodesian patent, trademark or copyright; and

(5) The payment of reasonable and customary fees currently due to attorneys or representatives in Southern Rhodesia incurred in connection with any of the transactions authorized by subparagraph (1), (2), (3) or (4) of this paragraph.

(b) Payments effected pursuant to the terms of paragraph (a) (4) and (5) of this section may not be made from any suspense account.

530.514   Checks, Etc., Dated Prior to July 29, 1968.

(a) Payment of any check, draft or acceptance issued by a person in Southern Rhodesia and drawn ona domestic bank is hereby authorized, provided that the individual item is in an amount of $500 or less and is dated prior to July 29, 1968.

(b) Payment of any such check, draft or acceptance dat4ed prior to July 29, 1968 which exceeds $500 is also authorized, provided the item was in the United States in the process of collection by a domestic bank prior to July 29, 1968.

530.515   Certain Remittances for Necessary Living Expenses.

(a) Remittances by any person through any domestic bank to any individual who is a citizen of the United States in Southern Rhodesia are hereby authorized on the following terms and conditions:

(1) Such remittances do not exceed $1,000 in any one calendar month to any payee and his household and are made only for the necessary living and traveling expenses of the payee and his household, except that an additional sum not exceeding $1,000 may be remitted once to such payee if such sum will be used for the purpose of enabling the payee or his household to return to the United States;

(2) Such remittances are not made from a suspense account other than from an account in a domestic bank in the name of, or in which the beneficial interest is held by, the payee or members of his household; and,

(3) Such remittances are not made directly or indirectly to any person if either the payee or a member of his household is engaged in business activities in Southern Rhodesia.

(b) As used in this section, the term "household" means:

(1) Those individuals sharing a common dwelling as a family; or

(2) Any individual not sharing a common dwelling with others as a family.

530.516 Letters of Credit.

Blanket licenses will in general be issued authorizing domestic banks to pay drafts drawn under irrevocable letters of credit issued or confirmed by domestic banks prior to July 29, 1968.

530.517 Remittances from Rhodesia to Persons in United States.

Specific licenses will in general be issued authorizing debits to suspense accounts for remittances from persons in Southern Rhodesia to persons in the United States when the remittance is for any of the following purposes:

(a) Payment of a legacy;

(b) Payment of principal or interest on a loan made prior to July 29, 1968, provided the loan was not renewed or extended thereafter;

(c) Educational and medical expenses of dependents in the United States of persons in Southern Rhodesia;

(d) Maintenance of relatives in the United States of persons in Southern Rhodesia;

(e) Pensions;

(f) Pension contributions in appropriate cases;

(g) Other personal remittances in appropriate cases;

(h) Travel and subsistence inthe United States of Rhodesian nationals;

(i) Personal insurance premiums;

(j) Taxes or fees payable to the United States or to any state or other political subdivision.

Subpart F—Reports

530.601 Records.

Every person engaging in any transaction subject to the provisions of this part shall keep a full and accurate record of each such transaction engaged in by him, regardless of whether such transaction is effected pursuant to license or otherwise, and such record shall be available for examination for at least 2 years after the date of such transaction.

530.602 Reports to be Furnished on Demand.

Every person is required to furnish under oath, in the form of reports or otherwise, from time to time and at any time as may be required by the Secretary of the Treasury or any person acting under his direction or authorization complete information relative to any transaction subject to the provisions of this part. The Secretary of the Treasury or any person acting under his direction may require that such reports include the production of any books of account, contracts, letters, or other papers, connected with any such transaction in the custody or control of the persons required to make such reports. Reports with respect to transactions may be required either before or after such transactions are completed. The Secretary of the Treasury may, through any person or agency, investigate any such transaction or any violation of the provisions of this part regardless of whether any report has been required or filed in connection therewith.

Subpart G—Penalties

530.701 Penalties.

(a) Attention is directed to section 5(b) of the United Nations Participation Act of 1945 (22 U.S.C. sec. 287(c)), which provides in part:

Any person who willfully violates or evades or attempts to violate or evade any order, rule, or regulation issued by the President pursuant to subsection (a) of this section shall, upon conviction be fined not more than $10,000, or, if a natural person, be imprisoned for not more than 10 years, or both; and the officer, director, or agent of any corporation who knowingly participates in such violation or evasion shall be punished by a like fine, imprisonment, or both, and any property, funds, securities, papers, or other articles or documents, or any vessel, together with her tackle, apparel, furniture, and equipment, or vehicle, or aircraft, concerned in such violation shall be forfeited to the United States. (Dec. 20, 1945, ch. 583, sec. 5, 59 Stat. 620; Oct. 10, 1949, ch. 660, sec. 3, 63 Stat. 735.)

This section of the United Nations Participation Act of 1945 is applicable to violations of any provisions of this part and to violations of the provisions of any license, ruling, regulation, order, direction or instruction issued pursuant to this part or otherwise under section 5 of the United Nations Participation Act, Executive Order 11322, and Executive Order 11419.

(b) Attention is also directed to 18 U.S.C. 1001 which provides:

Whoever, in any matter within the jurisdiction of any department or agency of the United States knowingly and willfully falsifies, conceals, or covers up by any trick, scheme, or device a material fact, or makes any false, fictitious or fraudulent statements or representations, or makes or uses any false writing or document knowing the same to contain any false, fictitious or fraudulent statement or entry, shall be fined not more than $10,000 or imprisoned not more than 5 years, or both.

Subpart H–Procedures

530.801 *Licenses.*

(a) General licenses. General licenses may be issued authorizing, under appropriate terms and conditions, types of transactions subject to the prohibitions contained in subpart B of this part. All such licenses are set forth in subpart E of this part. It is the policy of the Office of Foreign Assets Control not to grant applications for specific licenses authorizing transactions to which the provisions of an outstanding general license are applicable. Persons availing themselves of certain general licenses are required to file reports and statements in the form and in accordance with the instructions specified in the licenses.

(b) Specific licenses–(1) General course of procedure. Transactions subject to the prohibitions contained in subpart B of this part which are not authorized by general license may be effected only under specific license. Form TFAC-26, Revised, is the specific license form. The specific licensing activities of the Office of Foreign Assets Control are performed by the central organization and the Federal Reserve Bank of New York. When an unusual problem is presented, the proposed action is cleared with the Director of Foreign Assets Control or such person as the Director may designate. (2) Applications for specific licenses. Applications for specific licenses to engage in any transaction prohibited by or pursuant to this part are to be filed in duplicate on Form TFAC-25, revised, with the Federal Reserve Bank of New York. Any person having an interest in a transaction or proposed transaction may file an application for a license authorizing the effecting of such transaction, and there is no requirement that any other person having an interest in such transaction shall or should join in making or filing such application.

(3) Information to be supplied. Applicants must supply all information specified by the respective forms and instructions. Such documents as may be relevant shall be attached to each application as a part of such application except that documents previously filed with the Office of Foreign Assets Control may, where appropriate, be incorporated by reference. Applicants may be required to furnish such further information as is deemed necessary to a proper determination by the Control. If an applicant or other party in interest desires to present additional information or discuss or argue the application, he may do so at nay time before or after the decision. Arrangements for oral presentation should be made with the Control.

(4) Effect of denial. The denial of a license does not preclude the reopening of an application or the filing of a further application. The applicant or any other party in interest may at any time request explanation of the reasons for a denial by correspondence or personal interview.

(5) Reports under specific licenses. As a condition upon the issuance of any license, the licensee may be required to file reports with respect to the transaction covered by the license, in such form and at such times and places as may be prescribed in the license or otherwise.

(6) Issuance of license. Licenses will be issued by the Office of Foreign Assets Control acting on behalf of the Secretary of the Treasury or by the Federal Reserve Bank of New York, acting in accordance with such regulations, rulings, and instructions as the Secretary of the Treasury or the Office of Foreign Assets Control may from time to time prescribe, in such cases or classes of cases as the Secretary of the

Treasury or the Office of Foreign Assets Control may determine, or licenses may be issued by the Secretary of the Treasury acting directly or through any person, agency, or instrumentality designated by him.

530.802 *[Reserved]*
530.803 *Decision.*

The Office of Foreign Assets Control or the Federal Reserve Bank of New York will advise each applicant of the decision respecting applications filed by him. The decision of the Office of Foreign Assets Control acting on behalf of the Secretary of the Treasury with respect to an application shall constitute final agency action.

530.804 *Records and Reporting.*

(a) Records are required to be kept by every person engaging in any transaction subject to the provisions of this part, as provided in 530.601.

(b) Reports may be required from any person with respect to any transaction subject to the provisions of this part as provided in 530.602.

530.805 *Amendment, Modification, or Revocation.*

The provisions of this part and any rulings, licenses, authorizations, instructions, orders, or forms issued thereunder may be amended, modified, or revoked at any time. In general, the public interest requires that such amendments, modifications, or revocations be made without prior notice.

530.806 *Rule Making.*

(a) All rules and other public documents are issued by the Secretary of the Treasury upon recommendation of the Director of the Office of Foreign Assets Control or by the Director of the Office of Foreign Assets Control. Except to the extent that there is involved any military, naval, or foreign affairs function of the United States or any matter relating to agency management or personnel or to public property, loans, grants, benefits, or contracts, and except when interpretative rules, general statements of policy, or rules of agency organization, practice, or procedure are involved or when notice and public procedure are impracticable, unnecessary or contrary to the public interest, interested persons will be afforded an opportunity to participate in rule making through submission of written data, views, or argument, with oral presentation in the discretion of the Director. In general, rule making by the Office of Foreign Assets Control involves foreign affairs functions of the United States. Whenever possible, however, it is the practice to hold informal consultations with interested groups or persons before the issuance of any rule or other public document.

(b) Any interested person may petition the Director of Foreign Assets Control in writing for the issuance, amendment or repeal of any rule.

530.807 *Delegation by the Secretary of the Treasury.*

Any action which the Secretary of the Treasury is authorized to take pursuant to Executive Order 11322 and Executive Order 11419 may be taken by the Director of the Office of Foreign Assets Control, or by any other person to whom the Secretary of the Treasury has delegated authority so to act.

530.808   Customs Procedures: Merchandise Specified in 530.201.

(a) With respect to merchandise specified in 530.201, whether or not such merchandise has been imported into the United States, district directors of customs shall not accept or allow any:

(1) Entry for consumption (including any appraisement, entry, any entry of goods imported in the mails, regardless of value, and any other informal entries);

(2) Entry for immediate exportation;

(3) Entry for transportation and exportation;

(4) Withdrawal from warehouse;

(5) Transfer or withdrawal from a foreign-trade zone; or

(6) Manipulation or manufacture in a warehouse or in a foreign-trade zone, unless either:

(i) The merchandise was imported prior to July 29, 1968, and in the case of merchandise listed in 530.505(b) was imported prior to January 5, 1967.

(ii) An applicable general license appears in subpart E hereof,

(iii) A specific license issued pursuant to this part is presented, or

(iv) Instructions from the Office of Foreign Assets Control, either directly or through the Federal Reserve Bank of New York, authorizing the transaction are received.

(b) Wherever a specific license is presented to a district director of customs in accordance with this section, one additional legible copy of the entry, withdrawal or other appropriate document with respect to the merchandise involved shall be filed with the district director of customs at the port where the transaction is to take place. Each copy of any such entry, withdrawal, or other appropriate document, including the additional copy, shall bear plainly on its face the number of the license pursuant to which it is filed. The original copy of the specific license shall be presented to the district director in respect of each such transaction and shall bear a notation in ink by the licensee or person presenting the license showing the description, quantity, and value of the merchandise to be entered, withdrawn, or otherwise dealt with. This notation should be so placed and so written that there will exist no possibility of confusing it with anything placed on the license at the time of its issuance. If the license in fact authorizes the entry, withdrawal or other transactionwith regard to the merchandise the district director, or other authorized customs employee, shall verify the notation by signing or initialing it after first assuring himself that it accurately describes the merchandise it purports to represent. The license shall thereafter be returned to the person presenting it and the additional copy of the entry, withdrawal, or other appropriate document shall be forwarded by the district director to the Office of Foreign Assets Control.

(c) Whenever a person shall present an entry, withdrawal, or other appropriate document affected by this sectionand shall assert that no specific Foreign Asserts Control license is required in connection therewith, the district director of customs shall withhold action thereon and shall advise such person to communicate directly with the Federal Reserve Bank of New York to request that instructions be issued to the district director to authorize him to take action with regard thereto.

530.809   Rules Governing Availability of Information.

(a) The records of the Office of Foreign Assets Control required by 5 U.S.C. 552

to be made available to the public shall be made available in accordance with the definitions, procedures, payment of fees, and other provisions of the regulations on the Disclosure of Records of the Office of the Secretary and of other bureaus and offices of the Department issued under 5 U.S.C. 552 and published as Part 1 of this Title 31 of the Code of Federal Regulations, 32 F.R. 9562, July 1, 1967.

(b) Form TFAC-25, revised, and any other form used in connection with the Rhodesian Sanctions Regulations may be obtained in person from or by writing to the Office of Foreign Assets Control, Treasury Department, Washington, D.C. 20220, or the Foreign Assets Control Division, Federal Reserve Bank of New York, 33 Liberty Street, New York, N.Y. 10045.

Statement by Assistant Secretary Palmer on the Issue of Majority Rule in Southern Rhodesia*

February 28, 1967

*   *   *

The President of the United States, acting under the authority granted to him by the Congress in section 5 of the United Nations Participation Act of 1945, issued an Executive order on January 5 of this year to prohibit U.S. firms and individuals from engaging in the activities proscribed by the Security Council resolution, including transactions involving the commodities described therein.

It is primarily this action that has attracted the attention that we find in the United States today. This interest has been reflected in widespread comment, much of which is favorable. However, much is also critical. Doubts have been cast on the legality of the action as well as on its wisdom. The line between informed opinion and misinformation or misunderstanding has often become blurred. For example, we hear that U.S. support for the Security Council action derogates from our own sovereignty, that it constitutes misguided support of the British, and that its purpose is to curry favor with some members of the international community at the expense of others.

We are all aware of the fact that the United States as a permanent member of the Security Council has the power under article 27, paragraph 3, of the charter to prevent the Council from taking any action in any situation where we may deem it inappropriate. But in the case of Southern Rhodesia, we considered that the Council's finding of a threat to the peace and its decision to impose mandatory sanctions were appropriate and necessary. We voted for them only on the basis of a considered judgment that it was clearly in our national interest to do so.

This raises the question of the U.S. interest in the Rhodesian problem. As the leading free-world power and as a member of the United Nations, we have a direct interest in contributing responsibly to stability and progress in Africa, as in many other areas of the world.

The situation in Southern Rhodesia, where a racial minority has seized power illegally and attempts to continue its domination over the vast majority of Rhodesians, forms a basic threat to that stability. It has already served to heighten racial tensions in

*Department of State Bulletin, Mar. 20, 1967, p. 450.

and around Rhodesia itself. In time, there is a real danger that it could develop into a confrontation along racial lines between the African countries north of the Zambezi Rvier and the white-dominated nations of southern Africa. Black Africans, frustrated and embittered by vestiges of colonial or racial repression, are understandably concerned by the state of affairs in Rhodesia. At the same time, the continued defiance by the white minority regime of Ian Smith of legal authority and international opinion in Southern Rhodesia could serve to consolidate and extend the strength and attitudes of white supremacists in southern Africa. The result of such a continued polarization in Africa of extremist racial philosophies can only be instability, strife, and chaos.

To do nothing to avert such a confrontation would play into the hands of those forces seeking to undermine the stability and progress of Africa as a whole. Our national interest therefore dictates that we play our proper role in doing what we can to strengthen the forces of moderation among white and black alike, to try to minimize those conditions of instability that create the opportunity for Communist penetration and subversion, and above all to encourage peaceful and responsible change. Our policy on Southern Rhodesia supports these ends.

*   *   *

State Department Announcement on Banning Trade with Southern Rhodesia*

July 29, 1968

The President on July 29 signed an Executive order implementing United Nations Security Council Resolution No. 253 of May 29, 1968, which extends the program of mandatory economic sanctions against Southern Rhodesia.

The President acted under the United Nations Participation Act of 1945, as amended. Section 5 of the act empowers the President to implement Security Council decisions adopted pursuant to article 41 of the United Nations Charter.

In its Resolution No. 253, the Security Council unanimously decided that all member states shall extend the earlier prohibitions on imports from and exports to Southern Rhodesia to cover all commodities and products except exports to Southern Rhodesia of publications, news material, and articles needed for medical, educational, and humanitarian purposes. The resolution also obligates each member state to prohibit any activities promoting or calculated to promote such imports and exports, the carriage of such articles in ships and aircraft of its registry or under charter to its nationals, and transfers to Southern Rhodesia of funds and other financial or economic resources other than pensions, payments for news material, and transfers for medical, educational, and humanitarian purposes. Finally, the resolution decides that member states shall prevent their air carriers and aircraft of their registry or under charter to their nationals from operating to Southern Rhodesia or coordinating operations with airline companies constituted in or aircraft registered in Southern Rhodesia.

This Executive order prohibits these activities covered by the resolution, including

Ibid., Aug. 19, 1968, p. 199.

transactions involving commodities and products exported from Southern Rhodesia after May 29 (the date of the resolution). The order delegates to the Secretaries of Commerce, the Treasury, and Transportation authority to promulgate regulations necessary to carry out the prohibitions. The Secretary of Commerce on July 16 acted under authority of the Export Control Act to impose the further restrictions on exports to Southern Rhodesia called for by the resolution. The further regulations required under the Executive order will be issued shortly and will be effective July 29. The prohibitions of Executive Order No. 11322 of January 5, 1967, implementing Security Council Resolution No. 232 of December 16, 1966, continue in effect.

It is a criminal offense to engage in the prohibited activities. Provision will be made in the regulations to deal with cases of undue hardship from transactions commenced before the date of the order.

In Resolution No. 253 the Security Council also decided that member states shall prevent the entry into their territory of persons traveling on Southern Rhodesian passports and take all possible measures to prevent the entry of individuals ordinarily resident in Southern Rhodesia who are likely to further or encourage the illegal regime or evade the economic sanctions. The Departments of State and Justice are implementing these provisions under the Immigration and Nationality Act.

The mandatory sanctions imposed by the Security Council's resolution of May 29 supplement the selective mandatory sanctions imposed in December 1966 and the earlier voluntary measures taken by a large majority of the members of the United Nations in response to the Council's appeal of November 20, 1965, just after the Smith regime in Southern Rhodesia had unilaterally declared its independence, that economic relations with Southern Rhodesia be broken. The United States is fully supporting the Security Council resolutions.

New York Times *Editorial on "Wanted: A Rhodesian Policy"**

September 25, 1969

The United States claims that it adheres more strictly than any other country to the mandatory sanctions invoked against Rhodesia by the United Nations Security Council. At the same time, Washington continues to maintain a consulate general in Salisbury, seat of the white-minority regime it says is illegal and immoral.

For most black African governments the explanation for such schizophrenia is simple—and cynical: they do not believe the United States is really opposed to the regimes seeking to perpetuate white domination at any cost in southern Africa.

The valid explanation, however, is even simpler—and equally inexcusable: in Rhodesia, as in other critical areas, the Nixon Administration, after eight months in office, has no policy. In this as in other areas, the much-maligned State Department is not to blame. The responsibility for a policy of no-policy rests with the White House.

Mr. Nixon himself reportedly ordered the sanctions maintained despite some business and Congressional pressure for relaxation. But the White House to date has

*The New York Times, Sept. 25, 1969.

failed to act on the recommendation of Consul General Paul O'Neill and the State Department that the consulate general in Salisbury be closed.

It is not only the black Africans who are offended by this situation. Britain recalled its Governor General and ended diplomatic and consular ties with Salisbury in July, after Rhodesia's white electorate had approved a racist, despotic Constitution under which Prime Minister Ian Smith will soon proclaim a republic.

The British are astonished that the United States, while agreeing that the Smith regime is illegal, maintains its consulate in what seems to be a fundamental break with London. France, West Germany, Italy and the Netherlands have also kept their consulates open, reportedly awaiting the American decision.

If the Administration has any interest in retaining some influence in black Africa, as well as in upholding nonracialism, majority rule and the rule of law on that continent, there is only one decision it can make. It ought to be made without further delay.

New York Times *Editorial on "U.S. Presence in Rhodesia"**

March 5, 1970

Secretary of State Rogers made a point during his recent African visit of deploring the perpetuation by force of white minority governments. He placed the United States squarely on the side of the blacks aspiring to self-determination and majority rule in southern Africa.

Yet the United States continues to maintain a consulate general in Salisbury, even after the formal declaration this week of a white-ruled, racially segregated Republic of Rhodesia. Washington keeps this office open despite its claim to adhere strictly to the mandatory sanctions voted unanimously by the United Nations Security Council against a regime it regards as illegal, immoral and a threat to international peace and security.

The State Department insists the open consulate does not constitute recognizing Prime Minister Ian Smith's regime; but this is playing with words. Mr. Smith certainly regards it as a de facto recognition, and when Consul General Paul O'Neill returned to Salisbury after home leave in September a regime official told a reporter, "I can't think of anything that would have been a better morale booster for us at the moment."

For every black African government, the open consulate heightens the suspicion that the United States is really in league with all the remaining white minority regimes of southern Africa. The American presence in Salisbury also undercuts Britain, which severed its last ties with its former colony after the Smith regime rammed through a Constitution last July to permit the birth of the Republic and perpetuation of white rule.

Perhaps most serious of all is the effect this symbol of "business-as-usual" has on the standing of the United Nations. Here was an instance where the Security Council had unanimously invokved unprecedented mandatory sanctions, under Article 41 of the Charter. The question is not whether there may be more despotic governments on

*Ibid., Mar. 5, 1970.

earth than the one in Salisbury, where representatives of 225,000 whites rule a country of five million. The question is one of upholding the U.N. Charter and of sustaining a Security Council action to which the United States gave its backing.

Statement by Secretary Rogers on the Closing of the United States
Consulate General at Salisbury, Southern Rhodesia*

March 9, 1970

The United States has decided to close the American consulate general in Salisbury, Southern Rhodesia.

On March 2, 1970, the Rhodesian regime implemented a new constitution and a Rhodesian President is substituted for the British Crown as head of state. This constitutes the final and formal break with the United Kingdom. The United States has regarded and continues to regard the United Kingdom as the lawful sovereign.

In the above circumstances, we have instructed our consul in Salisbury to begin arrangements for closing as of March 17 and for the departure of the staff.

We have given particular attention to the ways in which the need of American citizens for consular and related services can be met in the future. We will attempt to have arrangements made for Americans to have available appropriate on-the-spot assistance, in addition to consular services which will be provided at American Foreign Service posts in neighboring countries.

Interview with Secretary Rogers on the NBC Television "Today" Show
on Closing the Salisbury, Southern Rhodesia Consulate†

March 17, 1970

*   *   *

Mr. Monroe: *Mr. Secretary, we're withdrawing our consulate in Rhodesia. Isn't that opposed to the idea that has been gaining currency that the matter of leaving a consulate or an embassy in a country, or recognizing a country, should not involve any moral judgments as to whether we approve or disapprove of that country or its policies?*

Secretary Rogers: Well, I think it could be considered in that light. But as you know, we have taken the position all along, as far as Southern Rhodesia is concerned, that it's an illegal regime; and we voted that way in the United Nations. And we have supported an embargo of goods to Southern Rhodesia.

In the light of that, it would be quite inconsistent for us to give legal recognition to the regime in Southern Rhodesia. And for that reason, we closed our consulate.

We will be able to take care of the American citizens who are there other ways.

**Department of State Bulletin*, Mar. 30, 1970, p. 412.
†*Ibid.*, Apr. 6, 1970, p. 443.

Mr. Monroe: *Was there considerable argument within the Government about closing that consulate?*

Secretary Rogers: No, I don't think so. There was a question about timing. Up until the time we closed it, we had credentials from the Queen of England, because it was a colony of Great Britain. And once the Rhodesians declared their independence, then we were faced with the proposition of whether we'd give legal recognition to the Southern Rhodesian regime.

Mr. Valeriani: *After your travels to that part of the world, Mr. Secretary, did you come away with any more concern about the possibilities of a black-white explosion in the southern part of Africa?*

Secretary Rogers: No, I wouldn't say that I had any more concern. I think that we're all concerned about that. I don't think it's likely in the immediate future, but I think sometime it's possible. And I think we have to do our part to avoid that. And I think that we have to have much closer and more effective relations with the African nations—black African nations—than we've had.

I was the first Secretary of State, as you know, who's ever visited black Africa. And I think that in itself speaks rather clearly about the fact that we have not had an active interest in African affairs, as we should have.

THE UNITED STATES VETO OF SECURITY COUNCIL RESOLUTION ON SOUTHERN RHODESIA AND SUPPORT OF COMPROMISE RESOLUTION*

Statement by Ambassador Yost

March 13, 1970

I have listened with great care and interest to the statements made before this Council and in particular to the statements made by the Minister of State for Foreign Affairs of Zambia and previous speakers. I also listened with great interest to the interventions made by my distinguished colleague Lord Caradon, who stressed the importance and need for urgency in acting in unison in not recognizing the so-called Republic of Rhodesia.

To say that we are meeting at a sad or shocking or deplorable time in the history of the Rhodesian question is but to state a truism. For indeed these adjectives apply to the entire period since the unilateral declaration of independence in November of 1965. And yet the situation with which we are confronted now does have a special significance, for we are told that a constitution which was approved by 1 percent of the Rhodesian population is now in effect and that a "republic" which was approved by a similarly small percentage of the electorate has been established.

I commented in some detail at our meeting last June on the specifics of that constitution—on the provisions which assure that political power will forever remain in white hands and on the ironically entitled Declaration of Rights. I would only like to remind the members of the Council of what I said at that time:

Ibid., Apr. 13, 1970, pp. 501-5; 506; 508-9.

Since these proposals—despite all the trappings of law in which they are dressed—are intrinsically unjust and since they emanate from an unlawful regime, they will be without legal effect regardless of the results of the voting on June 20.

My Government's view, Mr. President, has not changed since that time. Illegal acts perpetrated by an illegal regime can in no way be considered to lend any air of legitimacy to that regime. Attaching the word "republic" to the illegal minority regime in Salisbury will deceive no one.

My Government has assured the United Kingdom that we continue to regard it as the legal sovereign in Rhodesia. Consistent with this position and following the Smith regime's severance of the last formal ties with the United Kingdom, the Secretary of State on March 9 announced that the United States consulate general in Salisbury would be closed as of March 17 and that the staff would depart. We believe that this was an important step at a crucial time, a step which again made clear the posture of the United States toward the Smith regime's pretensions to legitimacy. This step may, we hope, help to discourage any prospect that the newly instituted republic might begin to gain acceptance by the nations of the world. We have not recognized, and we have no intention of recognizing, the illegal regime in Salisbury. I repeat these assurances to the members of this Council.

Mr. President, the United States has supported every resolution passed by the Security Council concerning Rhodesia since the unilateral declaration of independence by the Smith regime in 1965. We have implemented strictly the mandatory economic sanctions imposed by Resolutions 232 and 253. We believe that our implementation of the sanctions has been second to none.

We and six other members of the Council regretfully found ourselves unable to support the last resolution placed before the Council concerning Rhodesia last June. I pointed out at that time that the Council had "exerted an effective influence on the Rhodesian situation only when it worked on the basis of unanimity" and that the only ones who would find any solace in the division within the Council would be Mr. Smith and his friends.

Mr. President, I hope and trust that this will not be the situation we face during this Council session. The United States supports the view expressed by the distinguished delegate of the United Kingdom that we should urgently act in not recognizing the "Republic" of Rhodesia, and we support the draft resolution which was introduced by the United Kingdom at our meeting March 6. I hope that all other members of the Council will do so as well and that we will not become bogged down in attempts to call for measures which will divide the Council and will not assist the people of Rhodesia.

Let us, rather, pass this resolution speedily and unanimously so that Mr. Smith and his followers will be fully aware that the mind of the international community has not been changed by the "purported assumption of a republic status," that we still refuse to recognize his regime, and that we remain firm in our belief that majority rule will eventually come to Southern Rhodesia.

Mr. President, my Government shares the desire felt around this table for the need to achieve an equitable solution to the situation. This is indeed a most difficult and complex problem. We are convinced that all of us here in this Council must meet our responsibilities concerning Rhodesia with perseverance but also with prudence.

The Security Council has steadfastly condemned the actions of the present Salisbury regime and taken the unprecedented step of imposing mandatory economic
sanctions. These sanctions must be firmly maintained and strictly enforced. We must
persevere in our opposition to racism and repression. In charting our course for the
future, Mr. President, we will want to take particular care that we continue to act with
unanimity. My delegation is aware that the failure of South Africa and Portugal to
adhere to the sanctions program provided for in Resolution 253 is a major source of
concern. It is regrettable that these two countries continue to flout the sanctions.
Minister Nkama [Minister of State for Foreign Affairs Moto Nkama, of Zambia], when
speaking the other day, made a direct reference to this unfortunate situation, and I
note that this particular questionis included in the draft resolution tabled by the
Afro-Asian members of this Council. My delegation has had the occasion to state that
the application of sanctions to countries neighboring Southern Rhodesia would be
only following a dubious course which would introduce new and grave complications
in an already complicated situation.

There is no doubt that, in view of the continued refusal of the Smith regime to
heed the calls of the international community to alter its course, we all would prefer
to take more effective and decisive measures. The question, however, arises whether
these more extreme measures which have been suggested would be sufficiently supported by the international community, especially those most directly concerned, to
make them in fact effective or whether in seeking such action against economically
powerful states under existing circumstances they would merely demonstrate the
limitations of the U.N. and further entrench the Smith regime and its supporters in
southern Africa. We must therefore seek to avoid embarking on unrealistic courses of
action which, because they would overextend the capacity of the U.N. for effective
action, would reflect adversely on this body and give aid and comfort to Ian Smith and
his collaborators.

Mr. President, my delegation also doubts the wisdom and the effectiveness of
imposing a communications ban as envisaged in the draft resolution. We in the United
States have consistently attached the greatest importance to the maintenance of
communications with other states, even those with whom our relations were greatly
strained and in some cases even when hostilities were in progress between us. The
United States has a long history and tradition of freedom of movement and of speech
and would view most seriously the prospect of leaving United States citizens anywhere
in the world without the means to travel or communicate. Furthermore, we do not
believe that the cutting off of communications, the stemming of a free flow of
information, would contribute to a solution of the difficult problem with which we
are faced. Rather, it might tend to further harden the attitude of the white minority.

In our view, such measures tear the very fabric of international relations and would
tend to foreclose the free exchane of information and ideas upon which progress in
this unfortunate situation in part depends.

I should like to close my remarks, Mr. President, by quoting from President Nixon's
recent report to the Congress on U.S. foreign policy for the 1970's:

> Clearly there is no queston of the United States condoning, or acquiescing in, the racial
> policies of the white-ruled regimes. For moral as well as historical reasons, the United States
> stands firmly for the principles of racial equality and self-determination.

Statement by Ambassador Buffum

March 13, 1970

Mr. President, I shall be very brief indeed. Naturally we will wish to give very careful consideration to the remarks we have just heard from the distinguished Minister of State for Foreign Affairs of Zambia. I should like to say, however, by way of introducing this very brief comment, that the one thing that pleases me most about his intervention was that I think all of his remarks reflect—and, indeed, this is an accurate reflection that we do share, both of us—a very common objective in dealing with the problem of Southern Rhodesia. If I may say so, it emerges equally clearly that where we differ is with regard to the means of achieving that objective, and I think it is very frequently on such differences of tactics and methods that friends can honestly disagree. But I do appreciate the spirit in which he made his remarks, and we shall study them in exactly the same spirit.

There is only one specific that I should like to comment on at this point and would reserve a right, if I may, to intervene at a later stage with regard to the other questions which he has raised, some of which we will need to investigate. But he did, in his comment with regard to the purchase of chrome, imply that the United States is in fact still purchasing chrome in Southern Rhodesia. I can assure him and the members of the Council categorically that this is not the case; in fact, just the contrary is true. As a result of our prohibition on the importation of chrome from Southern Rhodesia, it has been necessary for us to secure alternative sources in other countries, often at considerable extra expense and difficulty and in many instances in a less satisfactory manner and quality, I think. But nevertheless we do abide scrupulously by the sanctions imposed by this Council. We do so willingly and wholeheartedly.

Just to make quite clear this is fully understood in all of its ramifications, I should like to add that chrome arriving in the United States from any source in southern Africa is carefully tested, and we have through a consistent and stringent checking system of this kind determined that there has been no disguised Rhodesian chrome entering this country. I would just like to submit that information as a partial reply to the remarks of the Minister this afternoon.

Statement by Ambassador Yost

March 17, 1970

Mr. President, under these rather extraordinary circumstances I should like to make another suggestion, and since I wish to be sure that we have time to consider it seriously, with all the seriousness that I think these circumstances warrant, I am going to ask for consecutive interpretation, and I announce that in advance.

I very deeply regret the decision of the Council. It is a procedural one, of course, but I must say I find it out of keeping with the normal spirit in which we conduct our operations.

I have had a great deal of experience on this Council, and I remember any number of occasions in which members, for reasons that seemed good to them because they were confronting difficult decisions on important matters, have requested postponements. The distinguished Representative of the Soviet Union, for example, has frequently done so, in my recollection. Almost invariably this request is granted in the spirit of courtesy and mutual accommodation which governs the business of this Council.

There are many differences of substance between us, and we try to resolve those as best we can over time. In order to help us do so, we try to conduct our procedures in such a way as to give rise to as little difference and as little dissatisfaction and resentment as possible.

Therefore, I must say that I do find this a legitimate request designed to give several members of the Council an opportunity to reflect on a new situation. This was not simply the text of a resolution with which, of course, as the distinguished Representative of Sierra Leone points out, we have been fully familiar for a long time. But a new situation was created by private consultations after the meeting had begun, I believe, as far as we are aware, in which we were not involved. This has presented a new set of circumstances of great gravity and moment on which we certainly would have wished to have further instructions from our Government.

Voting on a resolution of this magnitude, importance, and scope is not a matter to be undertaken lightly. We had previously considered, and I had explained in my comment on the resolution, some of the difficulties that confronted us.

As we are all quite aware, the exact composition and balance of the resolution makes a difference to some delegations; some can vote for one paragraph and not for others; and in other cases the situation is different. Therefore, a fundamental change may occur in the course of paragraph-by-paragraph voting.

Statement by Ambassador Yost

March 17, 1970

Mr. President, only the most serious of considerations would cause us to take the step of casting our negative vote on a resolution of such importance.

The United States has staunchly supported the economic sanctions which had been imposed on Rhodesia. We were prepared to look with favor on the suggestions put forward earlier in the debate by the distinguished Ambassador of Finland for taking further action in common. We shall still continue, of course, to explore all possibilities in this sense.

However, we are not able to support the resolution which, by implication, calls upon the United Kingdom to use force. We have repeatedly stated the view that force is not the answer to this problem. For this reason we oppose a resolution condemning the United Kingdom for failure to use it.

We closed our consulate in Southern Rhodesia, thus leaving our citizens in that country with no direct protection. We did so in the belief that it remained possible for our citizens at least to be in contact with their own country and with consulates elsewhere in Africa. We cannot now agree not only to cut off all their communications with the rest of the world but even to cut off all means by which they might leave Southern Rhodesia. Paragraph 6, in our view, would amount to barring American citizens in Rhodesia from contact with the outside world, and this we cannot support. Besides the grave effect this action would have on United States citizens, many of whom are there for the sole purpose of alleviating suffering among the black majority of the population, we do not think that such an action is in the interests of the oppressed majority in Rhodesia, nor indeed that it would have any decisive effect on the illegal minority regime.

It is with very great reluctance, therefore, that we take this step. We have felt, and continue to feel, that a little greater effort to find common ground might have obviated this necessity. Let us not now abandon the search for common ground but resolve to try all the harder to grapple together with the problem of Rhodesia, which so deeply concerns us all and which, sooner or later, must and will be resolved in the interest of the oppressed majority.

Five Power Draft Resolution[1]

March 17, 1970

The Security Council,

Recalling and reaffirming its resolutions 216 (1965) of 12 November 1965, 217 (1965) of 20 November 1965, 221 (1966) of 9 April 1966, 232 (1966) of 16 December 1966 and 253 (1968) of 29 May 1968,

Reaffirming in particular its resolution 232 (1966), in which it determined that the situation in Southern Rhodesia constitutes a threat to international peace and security,

Deeply concerned that the situation in Southern Rhodesia has deteriorated further as a result of the proclamation of a so-called republic and that the measures so far taken have proved inadequate to resolve the situation in Southern Rhodesia,

Gravely concerned further that the decisions taken by the Security Council have not been fully complied with by all States,

Noting that the Governments of the Republic of South Africa and Portugal, in particular, in contravention of their obligation under Article 25 of the Charter of the United Nations, have not only continued to trade with the illegal racist minority regime of Southern Rhodesia, contrary to the terms of Security Council resolutions 232 (1966) and 253 (1968), but have in fact given active assistance to that regime, enabling it to counter the effects of measures decided upon by the Security Council,

Noting in particular the continued presence of South African forces in the territory of Zimbabwe,

Affirming the primary responsibility of the Government of the United Kingdom to

---

[1] U.N. doc. S/9696/Corr. 1 and 2. On Mar. 17 the Security Council in two separate votes rejected operative paragraphs 8 and 9 by votes of 7 to 0, with 8 abstentions (U.S.). The vote on the five-power draft resolution, as modified, following the rejection of operative paragraps 8 and 9 was: 9 votes in favor, 2 against (U.S., U.K.), with 4 abstentions. The draft resolution was accordingly not adopted owing to the negative votes of two permanent members of the Council.

enable the people of Zimbabwe to exercise their right of self-determination and independence,

Reaffirming the inalienable right of the people of Zimbabwe to freedom and independence and the legitimacy of their struggle for the enjoyment of that right,

Acting under Chapter VII of the Charter of the United Nations,

1. Condemns the proclamation of a so-called republic in Zimbabwe by the racist minority regime in Salisbury and declares null and void any form of government which is not based on the principle of majority rule;

2. Decides that all States Members of the United Nations shall refrain from recognizing this illegal regime and urges States not Members of the Organization, having regard to the principles set out in Article 2 of the Charter of the United Nations, to act accordingly;

3. Calls upon all States to take measures as appropriate, at the national level, to ensure that any act performed by officials and institutions of the illegal regime in Southern Rhodesia or by persons and organizations purporting to act for it or in its behalf shall not be accorded any official recognition, including judicial notice, by the competent organs of their State;

4. Emphasizes the responsibility of the Government of the United Kingdom, as the administering Power, with regard to the situation prevailing in Southern Rhodesia;

5. Condemns the persistent refusal of the Government of the United Kingdom, as the administering Power, to use force to bring an end to the rebellion in Southern Rhodesia and enable the peole of Zimbabwe to exercise their right to self-determination and independence in accordance with General Assembly resolution 1514 (XV);

6. Decides that all States shall immediately sever all diplomatic, consular, economic, military and other relations with the lillegal racist minority regime in Southern Rhodesia, including railway, maritime, air transport, postal, telegraphic and wireless communications and other means of communication;

7. Requests the Government of the United Kingdom, as the administering Power, to rescind or withdraw any existing agreements on the basis of which foreign consular, trade and other representations may at present be maintained in or with Southern Rhodesia;

8. Condemns the assistance given by the Governments of Portugal and South Africa and by other imperialist Powers to the illegal racist minority regime in defiance of resolutions of the Security Council and demands the immediate withdrawal of the troops of the South African aggressors from the territory of Zimbabwe;

9. Decides that Member States and members of the specialized agencies shall apply against the Republic of South Africa and Portugal the measures set out in resolution 253 (1968) and in the present resolution;

10. Calls upon all Member States and members of the specialized agencies to carry out the decisions of the Security Council in accordance with their obligations under the Charter of the United Nations;

11. Calls upon all States Members of the United Nations, and, in particular, those with primary responsibility under the Charter for the maintenance of international peace and security, to assist effectively in the implementation of the measures called for by the present resolution;

12. Urges all States to render moral and material assistance to the national

liberation movements of Zimbabwe in order to enable them to regain their freedom and independence;

13. Requests all States to report to the Secretary-General on the measures taken to implement the present resolution;

14. Requests the Secretary-General to report to the Security Council on the progress made in implementing the present resolution.

Statement by Ambassador Yost

March 18, 1970

*   *   *

Mr. President, I have already expressed my regret over the unfortunate division of the Council yesterday. To a considerable extent this division no doubt arises from honest differences of perspective. It is natural and proper that the African members of our organization should feel deep frustration at the inability of our organization, thus far, to bring about the compliance of a regime, representing only 200,000 whites, and not even all of them, among 4½ million blacks, with the legitimate demands and decisions of this Council. It is equally natural that they should seek further means to make our decisions prevail.

However, as we are all aware, the United Nations does not have unlimited powers. The charter does not convey such powers upon it, nor have members been able to agree among themselves to give it in fact all the authority which the charter conveys in principle. As long as this situation obtains, we who believe in and cherish this organization, who place great hope in its future growth and reinforcement, must take great care not to place impossible burdens upon it, not to demand of it more than it can deliver. To do so will only emphasize its shortcomings, bring it into contempt, and lessen that public confidence and support on which its future growth and reinforcement depend.

In the present instance it seems to us both improper and futile to call upon the United Kingdom to overthrow the Smith regime by force—improper because starting a war anywhere is hardly what the United Nations should recommend and starting a war in southern Africa would be a particularly risky business; futile because we all know perfectly well that the United Kingdom is not going to engage in any such hazardous enterprise. As to cutting off communications, we have also expressed our view. Even if it were possible, we should not want to cut off all the inhabitants of Rhodesia, blacks as well as whites, foreigners as well as nationals, from the free flow of information from the outside. There might be nothing which would be more agreeable to the minority regime than to have our help in bringing down an iron curtain around its people. Certainly such an act would be totally ineffective in inducing the regime to change its oppressive policies.

Unpalatable as it may be to all of us, I think we have no alternative but to recognize the fact that the process of making the rule of law and the rights of the majority prevail in Rhodesia will not be a quick one. We must persist firmly and patiently in the course we are pursuing, in the strict and comprehensive application of the sanctions we have all agreed upon. In the long run, if they are persisted in, they are bound to have their effect.

My delegation has examined with great care the resolution tabled by the Representative of Finland. While we have reservations about some provisions, we support the resolution as a whole, believing it would make a substantial contribution to achieving the ends we all seek and would help to restore harmony and unanimity among us. Concerning operative paragraph 3, I should note that under our constitutional system our courts must be free to take judicial notice. We have serious doubts about the wisdom of seeking to impose a complete ban on all surface transportation, as envisaged in paragraph 9(b), having in mind the practical problems of implementation, the serious practical problems created for United States citizens in Rhodesia, and the economic consequences which would fall particularly on the neighboring state of Zambia, and would not very probably be without unforeseen consequences on others. We would have wished to have a separate vote on this paragraph and, if there had been such a separate vote, we would have abstained. However, as long as it is clear that the humanitarian and medical exceptions provided for in Resolution 253 are maintained, as the sponsor of the resolution has pointed out they would be, we will not oppose the resolution on account of this provision.

Having in mind the broader considerations I mentioned a moment ago, particularly the capital importance of harmony among us for the effect that harmony must have on the minority regime, my delegation is prepared to support the resolution tabled by Finland.

Resolution Tabled by Finland

March 18, 1970

The Security Council,

Reaffirming its resolutions 216 (1965) of 12 November 1965, 217 (1965) of 20 November 1965, 221 (1966) of 9 April 1966, 232 (1966) of 16 December 1966 and 253 (1968) of 29 May 1968,

Reaffirming that, to the extent not superseded in this resolution the measures provided for in resolutions 217 (1965) of 20 November 1965, 232 (1966) of 16 December 1966 and 253 (1968) of 29 May 1968, as well as those initiated by Member States in implementation of those resolutions, shall continue in effect,

Taking into account the reports of the Committee established in pursuance of Security Council resolution 253 (1968) (S/8954 and S/9252),

Noting with grave concern:

(a) That the measures so far taken have failed to bring the rebellion in Southern Rhodesia to an end,

(b) That some States, contrary to resolutions 232 (1966) and 253 (1968) of the Security Council and to their obligations under Article 25 of the Charter, have failed to prevent trade with the illegal regime of Southern Rhodesia,

(c) That the Governments of the Republic of South Africa and Portugal have continued to give assistance to the illegal regime of Southern Rhodesia, thus diminishing the effects of the measures decided upon by the Security Council,

(d) That the situation in Southern Rhodesia continues to deteriorate as a result of the introduction by the illegal regime of new measures, including the purported assumption of republican status, aimed at repressing the African people in violation of General Assembly resolution 1514 (XV),

Recognizing the legitimacy of the struggle of the people of Southern Rhodesia to secure the enjoyment of their rights as set forth in the Charter of the United Nations and in conformity with the objectives of General Assembly resolution 1514 (XV),

Reaffirming that the present situation in Southern Rhodesia constitutes a threat to international peace and security,

Acting under Chapter VII of the United Nations Charter,

1. Condemns the illegal proclamation of republican status of the Territory by the illegal regime in Southern Rhodesia;

2. Decides that Member States shall refrain from recognizing this illegal regime or from rendering any assistance to it;

3. Calls upon Member States to take appropriate measures, at the national level, to ensure that any act performed by officials and institutions of the illegal regime in Southern Rhodesia shall not be accorded any recognition, official or otherwise, including judicial notice, by the competent organs of their State;

4. Reaffirms the primary responsibility of the Government of the United Kingdom for enabling the people of Zimbabwe to exercise their right to self-determination and independence, in accordance with the Charter of the United Nations and in conformity with General Assembly resolution 1514 (XV), and urges that Government to discharge fully its responsibility;

5. Condemns all measures of political repression, including arrests, detentions, trials and executions, which violate fundamental freedoms and rights of the people of Southern Rhodesia;

6. Condemns the policies of the Governments of South Africa and Portugal, which continue to have political, economic, military, and other relations with the illegal regime in Southern Rhodesia in violation of the relevant United Nations resolutions;

7. Demands the immediate withdrawal of South African police and armed personnel from the Territory of Southern Rhodesia;

8. Calls upon Member States to take more stringent measures in order to prevent any circumvention by their nationals, organizations, companies and other institutions of their nationality, of the decisions taken by the Security Council in resolutions 232 (1966) and 253 (1968), all provisions of which shall fully remain in force;

9. Decides, in accordance with Article 41 of the Charter and in furthering the objective of ending the rebellion, that Member States shall:

(a) Immediately sever all diplomatic, consular, trade, military and other relations that they may have with the illegal regime in Southern Rhodesia, and terminate any representation that they may maintain in the Territory;

(b) Immediately interrupt any existing means of transportation to and from Southern Rhodesia;

10. Requests the Government of the United Kingdom as the administering Power, to rescind or withdraw any existing agreements on the basis of which foreign consular, trade and other representation may at present be maintained in or with Southern Rhodesia;

11. Requests Member States to take all possible further action under Article 41 of

the Charter to deal with the situation in Southern Rhodesia, not excluding any of the measures provided in that Article;

12. Calls upon Member States to take appropriate action to suspend any membership or associate membership that the illegal regime of Southern Rhodesia has in specialized agencies of the United Nations;

13. Urges Member States of any international or regional organizations to suspend the membership of the illegal regime of Southern Rhodesia from their respective organizations and to refuse any request for membership from that regime;

14. Urges Member States to increase moral and material assistance to the people of Southern Rhodesia in their legitimate struggle to achieve freedom and independence;

15. Requests specialized agencies and other international organizations concerned, in consultation with the Organization of African Unity, to give aid and assistance to refugees from Southern Rhodesia and those who are suffering from oppression by the illegal regime of Southern Rhodesia;

16. Requests Member States, the United Nations, the specialized agencies and other international organizations in the United Nations system to make an urgent effort to increase their assistance to Zambia as a matter of priority with a view to helping her solve such special economic problems as she may be confronted with arising from the carrying out of the decisions of the Security Council in this question;

17. Calls upon Member States, and in particular those with primary responsibility under the Charter for the maintenance of international peace and security, to assist effectively in the implementation of the measures called for by the present resolution;

18. Urges, having regard to the principle stated in Article 2 of the United Nations Charter, States not Members of the United Nations to act in accordance with the provisions of the present resolution;

19. Calls upon Member States to report to the Secretary-General by 1 June 1970 on the measures taken to implement the present resolution;

20. Requests the Secretary-General to report to the Security Council on the progress of the implementation of this resolution, the first report not to be made later than 1 July 1970;

21. Decides that the Committee of the Security Council established by resolution 253 (1968), in accordance with rule 28 of the provisional rules of procedure of the Security Council, shall be entrusted with the responsibility of:

(a) Examining such reports on the implementation of the present resolution as will be submitted by the Secretary-General;

(b) To seek from Member States such further information regarding the effective implementation of the provisions laid down in the present resolution as it may consider necessary for the proper discharge of its duty to report to the Security Council;

(c) To study ways and means by which Member States could carry out more effectively the decisions of the Security Council regarding sanctions against the illegal regime of Southern Rhodesia and to make recommendations to the Security Council;

22. Requests the United Kingdom, as the administering Power, to continue to give maximum assistance to the Committee and to provide the Committee with any information which it may receive in order that the measures envisaged in this resolution as well as resolutions 232 (1966), and 253 (1968) may be rendered fully effective;

23. Calls upon Member States as well as the specialized agencies to supply such information as may be sought by the Committee in pursuance of this resolution;

24. Decides to maintain this item on its agenda for further action as appropriate in the light of developments.

New York Times *Editorial on "The First American Veto"**

March 21, 1970

It probably was inevitable that the United States would be obliged one day to cast its first United Nations veto against an unrealistic resolution that commanded a Security Council majority. On two counts, however, it is unfortunate that the American no-veto record had to be sacrificed after a quarter-century on a Rhodesian resolution already doomed by the certainty of a British veto.

This action will appear to Africans as a pullback by the Nixon Administration after its decision to close the American consulate in Rhodesia and its strong recommitment by Secretary of State Rogers to the cause of black majority rule in southern Africa. The veto cast in tandem with Britain will also strengthen a widespread impression at the U.N. that the United States has no policy of its own for southern Africa but invariably follows London's lead in that part of the world.

Clearly, the United States could not support a resolution condemning Britain for refusing to use military force to bring down the white minority regime in Rhodesia. No British Government could survive that even contemplated such an expedition—even if it were militarily feasible, which it is not. The African leaders who incessantly demand such a British action understand this fully but still push their extreme U.N. resolutions with hypocritical support from the Asians, the Soviet bloc and Spain.

In the circumstances, Britain scarcely would have taken offense if the United States had abstained, along with four other council members. The end result—subsequent adoption of a milder council resolution asking members to sever relations with the Rhodesian regime and tightening U.N. sanctions against it—would have been the same; and the United States would have preserved the principle that a Security Council veto should be employed only in emergencies of the most extreme kind.

CONGRESSIONAL DEBATE ON RHODESIAN SANCTIONS

Remarks of Senator James Eastland (Mississippi) Before the Senate[†]

March 2, 1966

Mr. President, Vietnam and Rhodesia are half a world apart. But there is a reason why we should think of them together, in one particular connection.

This is what I want to discuss for a short time today.

---

*The New York Times, Mar. 21, 1970.
[†]Congressional Record, Mar. 2, 1966, pp. 4691-92.

In South Vietnam we are fighting a war to preserve the independence of that little country.

Britain is waging an economic war against Rhodesia to force that little country, which only recently declared its independence, to come back under British domination.

We are helping Britain in her Rhodesian struggle; but Britain is not helping us in South Vietnam. This epitomizes our relationships, today, with many of our allies.

*   *   *

We should be able to count upon substantial help from England, in our efforts to preserve the independence of South Vietnam, but we have not been getting it and there is no prospect that we will get it.

Yet Britain is getting our help in her efforts to destroy the independence of Rhodesia.

[Among other measures] The U.S. Government put pressure on American manufacturers who purchase raw materials from Rhodesia, and as a result various imports from Rhodesia have been discontinued. Imports of asbestos and lithium were discontinued on January 10. The State Department has been attempting to persuade American users of chrome to stop buying Rhodesian chrome or chrome ore, and it was recently reported that such purchases had been suspended. This seems a particularly shortsighted move, because in recent years nearly one-third of all chrome used in the United States has come from Rhodesia. Chromium is a material in short supply here, as well as being a strategic material; and the State Department's position in seeking a voluntary cutoff of Rhodesian chrome imports into this country seems hard to justify in the light of our own national interest.

The United States has not been a completely innocent bystander during the development, in recent years, of increased racial tensions in Rhodesia. Lest it be forgotten, let me recall an incident of about 4 years ago.

John K. Emmerson, U.S. consul general at Salisbury, Rhodesia, was recalled in March 1962, after 17 months in that post, as a result of charges by Roy Welensky, then Rhodesian Prime Minister, that after appointment of G. Mennen Williams as the U.S. State Department's African expert, U.S. representatives in Rhodesia had abandoned their "traditional line of noninvolvement in Rhodesian internal affairs" and had "pursued a line of not oversubtle alinement with African Nationalists."

Specific charges included these:

First. That the U.S. Information Agency had issued films and literature which "appeared to incite Africans to greater efforts to combat or boycott the federal and Southern Rhodesian systems of government."

Second. That certain films offered by USIA contained "scenes and episodes from past wars of liberation" coupled with "reminders that Africans, too, are struggling for their independence."

Third. That in Nyasaland, "American consular cars frequently have gotten mixed up in car processions of the Malawi Congress Party, making it appear as if U.S. officials and Malawi partisans are riding toward independence together."

Fourth. That in Southern Rhodesia, American consular men "have also been in close touch with Mr. Joshua Nkomo's Zambia movement." This liaison with Nkomo, it was charged, had been carried on "by both Americans and locally recruited African consular staff of U.S. diplomatic missions."

Sir Roy Welensky in June of 1962 ascribed what he called the present truculence of African leaders partly at least to American and United Nations encouragement.

Dissatisfaction was also expressed by the Rhodesians over the size of the U.S. diplomatic mission, which had a staff of nearly 200 persons, most of them locally employed Africans, and which was larger than any other diplomatic mission in the Federation, and even larger than the British High Commission in Rhodesia. These figures covered the two U.S. consulates in Lusaka and Zambia, as well as the Consulate General in Salisbury.

Throughout Africa, new countries have proliferated as the rising tide of black nationalism has spread across that continent. Every time a group of partially educated, half-savage tribes has constituted an alleged government and declared its country free and independent, we have been pressured by an unreasoning fear of world opinion into immediate recognition of that government. These new, instable, little so-called countries are immediately admitted to the United Nations where each is given a voting strength the same as our own in that international body. We are told that under no circumstances must force be used to retain or recapture any of these newly declared independencies as territories or dominions of one of the civilized nations of the world.

But when Rhodesia declared its independence, there was a vast cry that force must be used to restore British control; and representatives of the United Kingdom at the United Nations were snubbed and insulted because Britain had not used immediate force to destroy Rhodesian independence.

Does that sound like a double standard? In reality it is not. It is a single standard. The basic principle is increased power for the blacks; but no increased power for the whites.

The first white settlements in central Africa were made only 75 years ago. If we want to understand how the white Rhodesians feel, it may help to imagine how the early settlers in any State of our Union would have felt at being told, 75 years after settlement of the State began, that they should turn over their government to the Indian because they were the true majority.

Remarks of Senator Eastland Before the Senate on
United States Treatment of Rhodesia*

August 25, 1966

*   *   *

Of the 49 nations of Africa, the U.S. taxpayer contributes largely to the fiscal support of 38 of these countries.

No less than $2,936 billion has been pumped into the sagging economies of the fledgling nations by the United States. Of this amount nearly $2 billion is in the form of grants which, of course, means that there is no prospect of recovering these funds.

*Ibid., Aug. 25, 1966, pp. 20541-42.

We have been told that this foreign aid investment in the new nations of Africa has been required to keep these countries from falling prey to the Communists and to help them in the establishment of democracy.

With few exceptions Communist influence has not been lessened due to our foreign aid, the money has been squandered and pocketed by petty dictators and their henchmen and the economy of these countries has continued to decline. Fortunately, Mr. President, there are two bright spots on the Continent of Africa. One of these is the Republic of South Africa, a stable, prosperous pro-Western and anti-Communist government.

The other is Rhodesia, a country equally prosperous, anti-Communist and pro-Western.

The essential difference is that the United States does not recognize Rhodesia and her independence, while it does extend full diplomatic relations to the Republic of South Africa. Mr. President, as I have said in previous speeches, the legality of the Rhodesian independence is unquestioned and there is no doubt that our recognition would be in the best interest of the United States and Western civilization. I am offering a resolution which I hope will be acted upon promptly which will extend recognition to this gallant new nation.

Mr. President, opponents to recognition of Rhodesia appear to fall into two categories.

In the first category are those who believe we must support Great Britain as an ally in her dispute with Rhodesia. I do not agree with this philosophy. Britain and the United States has imposed economic sanctions on this peaceful country, yet, Britain has refused to recognize the same sanctions against North Vietnam, or to supply either naval or ground forces to fight communism in that country.

British trade with Cuba was further indication of how lightly Britain values cooperation with the United States on issues Britain chooses to ignore.

Mr. President, the second group of critics will claim that Rhodesia does not deserve recognition because its constitution and government are not fully democratic.

This is utterly untrue. The franchise in Rhodesia is extended to all men regardless of race, creed, or color, and the constitution of Rhodesia has been accepted by a vote of her population.

Let us look for a moment at some of the other countries of Africa to which we extend diplomatic relations and foreign aid.

*   *   *

Nor, does this list complete the expenditures of U.S. taxpayers' money in Africa to support corrupt and often unfriendly regimes.

By contrast Rhodesia and the Republic of South Africa have favorable balances of trade, as well as minerals and agricultural products needed and impoted by the United States.

To continue to deny legitimate recognition for Rhodesia is folly.

This is a time when we should treasure such allies and do our utmost to bring them closer to us.

I submit a resolution expressing the sense of the Congress about the treatment of Rhodesia by the U.S. Government, and ask that it be appropriately referred.

The Acting President pro tempore. The resolution will be received and appropriately referred; and, under the rule, the resolution will be printed in the Record.

The resolution (S. Res. 297) was referred to the Committee on Foreign Relations, as follows:

S. Res. 297

Resolved, Whereas Rhodesia has been a self-governing colony within the British Commonwealth since 1923;

Whereas the constitutionally elected Government of Rhodesia, with the full support of the Council of Chiefs, declared Rhodesia's independence on November 11, 1965;

Whereas the subsequent dispute concerning Rhodesia's declaration of independence is solely a matter for settlement between herself and Great Britain (just as our own independence was a matter between ourselves and Great Britain);

Whereas Rhodesia is not hostile to the United States nor an enemy of the United States either under international law or under the laws of the United States;

Whereas the Prime Minister of Rhodesia has offered Rhodesian troops and supplies to assist the United States in Vietnam;

Whereas United States citizens continue to be warmly welcomed in Rhodesia and our Government representatives there are still accorded full consular privileges;

Whereas Rhodesia is one of the very few countries in Africa which pays her own way and receives no U.S. aid and that trade between our two countries had been running two to one in our favor, all on a commercial basis with no subsidies, thereby assisting our balance of payments;

Whereas according to the Constitution (Article 1, Section 8, Paragraph 3) only the Congress has power to regulate commerce with foreign nations and the Executive has no legal authority to block trade except under laws which control trading with the enemy;

Whereas the United States Government, without any authority from the Congress or the American people, has adopted and encouraged a stringent policy of economic sanctions against Rhodesia;

Whereas as part of this policy, the United States Government is participating in a costly and totally unnecessary operation to transport oil and copper to and from Zambia by uneconomic and inadequate routes, the normal route being over Rhodesia railways which are still freely available to Zambia;

Whereas the integrity of United States banking institutions has been damaged by the action of the United States Government in ordering that assets of the Reserve Bank of Rhodesia held in the United States be frozen, this solely at the behest of the British Government whose authority over these assets has not been proved;

Whereas the United States Government turned back a cargo of Rhodesian sugar sold and shipped to United States citizens before Rhodesia's declaration of independence, thus causing forfeiture of a valid contract;

Whereas United States citizens have extensive commercial interests in Rhodesia which have been severely damaged by the arbitrary application of economic sanctions;

Whereas said United States citizens have even been prevented from performance of valid contracts and other legal and moral obligations, to their present and future great loss;

Whereas economic sanctions will deprive thousands of Africans from Rhodesia and from neighboring countries of their livelihoods in the virile Rhodesian economy, to force the closure of African schools and hospitals, to bring misery and starvation to many thousands of African families and to destroy one of the remaining stable governments on the African continent. Therefore, be it

Resolved by the Senate (the House of Representatives concurring), That it is the sense of the Congress of the United States that the United States Government immediately cease its inhumane, illegal, arbitrary, unfair, harmful, and costly policy of economic sanctions again Rhodesia; take necessary steps to compensate United States citizens for any financial losses incurred as a result of said policy; and resume this Nation's former policy of honorable self-interest toward this friendly country.

Report by Representative John R. Rarick (Louisiana) to the House on Rhodesia*

March 14, 1968

       *   *   *

We were tremendously impressed with Rhodesia and South Africa. Both are modern progressive nations with a high Western-type civilization second to none in the world. The backward, primitive image from movies and books is as out of date as cowboys fighting Indians in the United States.

Both nations are well governed. Employment is high and economies are expanding. Opportunity is unlimited. There is little evidence of poverty. The living standard for Europeans is as high as any place in our country, while that of the blacks is the highest—by far—of any nation on the African continent, including North Africa.

From my observations and interviews, I am convinced that the present governments of these two nations are the only hope for any stability on the African continent.

To any who might criticize the firmness in law and order in those countries—I remind them there is little or no crime, except that which is created or instigated from outside their borders.

In spite of sanctions, Rhodesia's economy shows every indication of expanding and continuing strong.

       *   *   *

While I was in Rhodesia, Vice President Hubert Humphrey arrived in neighboring Zambia and lashed out at the members of the Government of my host country, Rhodesia.

After referring to obstacles which left-leaning, black nationalist Zambia was supposed to face, Mr. Humphrey said:

> We all recognize that the problems you face have been made doubly difficult by the retrogressive policies of your neighbors to the South. They have turned their faces away from the inevitable triumph of self-determination.

He continued, saying:

> President Johnson has recognized the special burdens imposed on Zambia by the Rhodesian rebellion. He has pledged and provided American assistance to Zambia during the past two years.

He then announced that the United States would give Zambia the $200 million she desires for construction of a highway stretching from Dar-es-Salaam to Lusaka.

It is unfortunate Mr. Humphrey's speeches were based on political information rather than facts. For his facts were in reverse. It is Zambia that suffers from retrogressive policies. Rhodesia is threatened by terrorists, Communist trained in Moscow, Havana, and Peking, that strike at her from Zambia—with the full knowledge and approval of the Zambian Government—and now with the implied approval of our

*Ibid., Mar. 14, 1968, pp. E 1865-66.

U.S. foreign policy. It is the irresponsible Zambian Government which has destroyed the Central African Airways and Railroad System that our taxpayers are now being asked to rebuild. Conversely Rhodesia has threatened no attack on Zambia nor does she harbor terrorists intent on overthrowing the Zambian Government.

The intemperate remarks of the Vice President served only to undermine moderate stable African leaders seeking reconciliation with Southern Africa, while at the same time his demagoguery assisted such Communist nationalists as Simon Kawpepwe, Eduardo Mondiane, and Roberto Holden—who are set on overthrowing all responsible government in Africa.

Instead of helping Africa toward stability, the policies pronounced by Vice President Humphrey can but contribute to its turmoil and have thrown U.S. prestige behind the terrorists—terrorists of the same Communist school and operation as the Vietcong tearing out the hearts of American boys in South Vietnam. A strange double standard of foreign policy.

One wonders why our Vice President did not take the opportunity to visit Rhodesia, South Africa, the Portuguese provinces, or Malawi to see firsthand what he proclaims he wants destroyed. If he had, his unfortunate statements would never have been uttered like explosive charges to impassion the primitive minds of African peoples.

*   *   *

Report by Representative Albert Watson (South Carolina) to the House on Communist Activity in Southern Africa*

March 20, 1968

*   *   *

Mr. Speaker, news reports from Africa in the past few days indicate that stepped-up guerrilla action by Communist-trained forces from Zambia into Rhodesian territory is reaching mammoth proportions. In fact, the situation is so critical that South African police and Rhodesian military forces with air support are moving to Rhodesia's northern border with Zambia.

This is only the beginning of widespread Communist guerrilla activity designed to plunge the whole of southern Africa into war. The objective of this Communist-supported drive is simple: The Soviet Union and Red China desperately want to dominate the important shipping lanes around the tip of South Africa. Of course, the closing of the Suez Canal has demonstrated beyond contradiction that the sea route around the cape is of immense strategic importance both militarily and economically. It goes without question that, if a Communist power can overrun South Africa, the United States will lose a vital refueling port. As long as the Suez remains closed, the cape is the main link between India and America, and Western Europe. Lose control of the cape, and American influence in Africa and Asia will terminate. In my judgment, loss of the cape would contribute mightily to a U.S. defeat in Vietnam.

*Ibid., Mar. 20, 1968, pp. 1170-71.

Mr. Speaker, this Nation, if for no other reason than to protect its long-range self-interests in Africa, must move immediately to reexamine its official policy toward South Africa and especially Rhodesia. These two nations are firm allies. Where else on the African continent can we point to greater pro-Western governments?

Yet, our State Department continues on the futile and ridiculous course of supplying the supporting timbers for British foreign policy by taking part in the economic sanctions against Rhodesia. The ever-increasing abdication by Britain of her international responsibilities should make the U.S. Government all the more resolute not to sacrifice our major strategic interests simply because London is seeking the easy way out of her commitments by turning to the United Nations. The United States must now look for allies within the vacuum that British withdrawals have created. South Africa and Rhodesia are such allies, and we should invite their friendship. In the future the United States must look upon these nations as holding the true balance of power and as being the only pro-Western influence of any consequence in sub-Saharan Africa and on the western shores of the Indian Ocean.

This Nation has no quarrel with the Government of Rhodesia. Why should we pull British chestnuts out of the fire by taking part in these immoral and illegal sanctions? Without the support of Washington, the sanctions would collapse overnight. We destroy the credibility of our image as a champion of the smaller nations of the world by supporting the boycott. In the case of Rhodesia, we not only tarnish the image but we are running the risk of suffering a humiliating defeat by communism in Africa at a time when we are desperately trying to hold the line in Southeast Asia.

This Nation can prevent another Vietnam, at least in southern Africa. But, the administration must act now to withdraw its support of the British trade boycott against Rhodesia. Rhodesia has declared its independence, and it has no intention of knuckling under to the Wilson government. Rhodesians are fighting the same battle in Africa that we are fighting in Vietnam. The frontline is as clearly defined on the Zambezi as it is in Vietnam—the one arm of communism is being restrained in Vietnam while the other is being resisted in Africa.

Rhodesia at this moment is successfully resisting Communist aggression. But, its enemies are determined and ruthless in their design to destroy all remaining vestiges of Western influence in Africa. A military defeat would pave the way for Russian and Chinese domination of Africa.

*   *   *

*Speech by Representative Diggs Before the House on the Travesty in Rhodesia**

June 26, 1969

Mr. Speaker, it would be recalled that on Friday, June 20, 1969, the world witnessed yet another display of desperate courage by the Ian Smith regime in Rhodesia in the conduct of a referendum by which the people of that territory are said to have decisively voted to turn that colony into an independent Republic. By that

*Ibid., June 26, 1969, p. 1177.

act, the Smith government has severed all remaining links with Britain. And as we sit here today, it is very likely that a new constitutional bill is being placed before the Parliament of Rhodesia to give "legality" to the results of that referendum.

Our State Department has correctly labeled this referendum a "travesty." Commenting on the referendum, a State Department spokesman stated:

> The United States deplores the fact that constitutional proposals clearly designed to intensify and institutionalize political control by the small white minority are now about to be given effect as a result of the referendum.

He also indicated that the closing of the U.S. consulate in Salisbury accredited to the British Governor was under study.

    *   *   *

I would like to urge that the U.S. consulate be withdrawn immediately. It is clear that the prospect of a settlement between the illegal white regime in Rhodesia and the British Government is no longer possible. We should move decisively by withdrawing our representative.

Second, I would urge that our Government support action in the United Nations which would lead to the blockading of the sanction-breaking ports in the Portuguese-held territory of Mozambique and the minority-ruled country of South Africa. If a minority white regime is a travesty in Rhodesia, so are the same kind of regimes also a travesty in Mozambique and South Africa. We should support U.N. action against these countries which have aided and abetted the violation of the mandatory sanctions voted by the U.N.

Third, I would urge that our Government use all its diplomatic resources to protest the violation of sanctions by those states which are not upholding the sanctions on Rhodesia voted by the U.N. These states include not only South Africa and Portugal, but France, Switzerland, West Germany, and Japan.

These steps are the minimal measures which the United States can take to show its support for majority rule and nonracialism in southern Africa.

    *   *   *

*Speech by Representative James G. Fulton (Pennsylvania) on
Dean Acheson's Statement on Economic Sanctions**

November 19, 1969

Mr. Speaker, U.S. sanctions against Rhodesia were imposed by Executive order without action or approval by the Congress, with penalties of fines up to $10,000 and prison terms up to 10 years, blocking even U.S. importation of chrome mined and refined by U.S. citizens and U.S. corporations in Rhodesia.

Mr. Speaker, I read now into the Record the excellent statement of Dean Acheson against U.S. economic sanctions being imposed on free world countries, which was

*Ibid., Nov. 19, 1969, pp. 1067-69.

delivered before the Subcommittee on Africa, Committee on Foreign Affairs, House of Representatives, November 19, 1969:

Statement of Dean Acheson

The question whether Britain should, and on what terms might, grant independence to Rhodesia misses the essential operational reality. Britain had no power, and has no power, to grant or withhold Rhodesian independence. Rhodesia's independence of Britain is an established fact.

The dispute between Rhodesia and Britain focused on procedure for amending certain items in the Rhodesian constitution. The British official mind became befuddled by the concept of Parliament's supremacy. That idea has operational reality for the United Kingdom itself, where the instruments of administration are subject to Parliament's control. In view of Parliament's lack of leverage concerning the civil service, the courts, the police, the armed forces, the budget, revenue, commerce, or what not in Rhodesia, the idea of parliamentary supremacy projected to that land was an empty abstraction.

Rhodesia moved in 1965 to bring technicalities into line with operational realities by assuming full custody of its own constitution. It employed a power manifestly at its disposal, irrespective of the London government's acquiescence or objection. The action did not create the fact. It only registered the fact.

The British government invoked a parliamentary enactment which purportedly conveyed to it plenary powers to deal with the situation. It issued an Order-in-Council. That document purportedly abolished the governing structure in Rhodesia, assigned absolute control to the government in London, reduced Rhodesia to the status of a Crown Colony (which it has never been), and made the British-appointed figurehead governor in Salisbury a surrogate overlord of the land.

The provisions were fictitious. A more bizarre instance of fantasy decked out in trappings of law can scarcely be imagined.

To determine the pattern of rulership in another country requires conquering it. The British had neither appetite nor capabilities for doing anything of the sort. Nothing was farther from Prime Minister Harold Wilson's resourceful imagination than the intention to invade, to subjugate, to pacify, and to run Rhodesia.

International sanctions were what the British counted on to bail their policy out of bankruptcy. Wholesale commercial restrictions were to be a substitute for the war which the British lacked heart and means to fight.

We live in curious times. The British found the United Nations Security Council in a mood to be gulled. Chorusing anti-colonial cliches, assorted governments vowed to help Britain reduce a self-governing territory to Crown Colony status. British misrepresentations of the background and British misinformation about the prospects were accepted without question. When it came to a matter of declaring Rhodesia to constitute a threat to the peace, so as to rationalize application of mandatory sanctions under Article 41 of the Charter, the step was taken without the adducing of a scintilla of corroboratory evidence.

The actions which have been taken are, of course, in derogation of the Charter itself. The powers authorized by Chapter VII have been invoked not for the proper purpose of preserving peace but for doing something expressly forbidden by paragraph 7 of Article 2 of the Charter, which states that the United Nations is to keep hands off matters essentially within the domestic jurisdiction of states.

The idea of using commercial restrictions as a substitute for war in getting control over somebody else's country is a persistent and mischievious superstituion in the conduct of international affairs. As in other instances, it has proved delusory in the Rhodesian case.

The result, all contraproductive, have been to encourage the British in impeding a settlement with Rhodesia by insisting on untenable conditions, to solidify the Rhodesian electorate's support of the regime, to push Rhodesia sharply rightward in political outlook, to slow up economic progress for the Rhodesian blacks, and to make the United States improvidently dependent on the Soviet Union for chromite.

In view of the manifest failure of economic sanctions, the question for this government now concerns next steps.

One theoretic possibility is a resort to direct hostilities under Article 42 of the Charter, as urged by some black African governments.

That course seems to me to be absolutely out of the question. Britain has no will or means for such a venture. I cannot imagine this government's letting itself get involved in hostilities certain to encompass all of Southern Africa—a multifarious remote, difficult area equal to a dozen Californians in size. To blunder into war in Southern Africa would have a divisive effect on our society measurelessly greater than Viet Nam has had.

An alternate idea is to extend sanctions to all Southern Africa. That is a scheme for redeeming folly by compounding it. Even if our government were to take leave of its senses and go along in such an undertaking, the British, I am sure, could be counted on to veto it. They are not about to cut off their lucrative trade with South Africa. In this respect at least, they have not lost perspective about means and ends.

What else? A few souls, reflecting little familiarity and no competence regarding what they are talking about, have urged invocation of Section 5(b) of the Trading-with-the-Enemy Act, as amended, or some other and hypothetical Act of Congress, with undefined provisions, as a measure for what they paradoxically call disengagement from Southern Africa. The only sure calculable result would be to provide a golden opportunity for capital from other countries, including especially South Africa, to take over extensive Amiercan corporate properties, operations, and markets at distress prices.

I do not see any way, just as I do not see any reason, for pressing further into the bog to which British follow, abetter by our own improvidence, has brought us.

I have seen three sorts of arguments on behalf of continuing sanctions. None of them strikes me as having even a shadow of validity.

The first such argument rests on a concept germane to public relations rather than to foreign policy soundly considered. Its gist is that persistence will garner moral credits for us among black African governments.

I reject any argument for persisting in folly in hope of applause. In this instance I think the argument is downright patronizing. It rests on a premise that other governments can be fobbed off with tokenism. Some of the black African governments, have discerned the sterility of sanctions all along and insisted that war would be necessary if the purpose of redesigning the government in Rhodesia were to be realized. If we are not willing to go down that avenue—and I am devoutly hopeful and substantially sure that we are not—then the dignified course is to tell the black African governments concerned that they saw the matter correctly at the outset; that for manifest good reasons we are not of a will to take the steps necessary to the purpose; that the folly of economic hostilities under a guise of preserving peace has proved folly enough; that we are not in a mood to go as far as the ultimate foolishness of making war in the name of avoiding it; that, in reason, we must abandon a purpose that is beyond our jurisdiction anyway.

The second sort of argument for persisting in sanctions is a hope that somehow, in some unascertainable future through developments not now foreseeable, sanctions may produce deterioration of conditions to a point where Rhodesia's blacks will be incited to rise up against the regime and thus ignite war in Southern Africa. In hope of inducing the tragedy of war, this argument would have us cling to a policy originated ostensibly for the purpose of avoiding war. A more corrupted logic is hard to imagine.

The third argument for going on and on with sanctions is one uttered by a British government spokesman at a meeting of the United Nations Trusteeship Committee two weeks ago. While sanctions have proved inefficacious for the purpose of forcing the Rhodesian government to submit to being redesigned by others, they have had, according to his version, very important side effects in other directions in that they have denied Rhodesia the degree of economic development and outside capital investment necessary to the territory's economic if it is not to stagnate. So long as sanctions are maintained, Rhodesia's economy will never attain buoyancy. Thus he argued.

The prediction is at variance with observable trends. As its worst aspect, however, the argument is based not on principle but on malice. Sanctions, ostensibly designed for preserving peace, become a method of waging a mean war on prosperity. Impoverishment becomes a goal for international collaboration. The ethic of vengeance takes charge. One feels a touch of pity for the abjectness to which an old ally's policy has come. If we cannot dissuade the British from so shabby a goal, at least we should not feel impelled to accompany them further.

The question is how to get out of sanctions. We can and should do so by unilateral action if necessary, as well it may be.

One trouble is that the Charter does not take into account the eventuality of sanctions' coming a cropper. Neither does the United Nations Participation Act. Back at the time of their origin, almost a quarter century ago, it simply was not foreseen that Chapter VII would ever be invoked with such disregard for principles and practicality as we see in the Rhodesian instance.

It would be unwise and unnecessary to hold that the United States can extricate itself from sanctions only by the procedure by which it entered—to wit, by a vote of the Security Council susceptible of veto by any one of the Permanent Members. (I can scarcely imagine that the Soviet Union would fail to veto an action designed to free us from the predicament which we are in with respect to the availability and pricing of chromite ore.) My own belief is that the residual power remains with the United States, and rests specifically with the President, to determine whether and when an action under Chapter VII has failed and thereupon to declare an end to our obligation to continue the action.

I understand that the continued presence of the U.S. consular establishment in Salisbury is a matter of concern to the Subcommittee in view of the prospective proclamation of a Rhodesian republic. The allegation is that failure to close the consulate might be construed as a weakening of resolve to maintain sanctions and even as a prefiguration of eventual diplomatic recognition.

I do not see either of these results as a necessary corollary of keeping open the consulate. If the conclusion were otherwise, however, I would ask: So what?

It is high time to get the folly of sanctions over and done with.

As for the question of eventual recognition, I am content to leave the matter where the Constitution puts it—in the President's discretion, subject to coordination with the Senate serving as a sort of council of state.

On September 25, 1969, the Senate acted on Senate Resolution 205, introduced by Senators Cranston and Aiken. Its gist is: "That it is the sense of the Senate that when the United States recognizes a foreign government and exchanges diplomatic representatives with it, this does not imply that the United States necessarily approves of the form, idealogy, or policy of that government." The yeas were 77. The nays were 3. I call that an impressive majority.

At the Senate Foreign Relations Committee's hearing on June 17, 1969, on Senate Resolution 205, Mr. George H. Aldrich, Acting Legal Adviser of the Department of State, appearing in support of the resolution, said, "The proposed resolution reflects the established position of the United States that recognition of a foreign government does not imply approval of that government's domestic policies or the means by which it came to power."

Good! The Executive also goes along in what I regard as a sound approach.

The proper source of advice is the Senate, and it has spoken. The Executive branch appeas to concur. Without venturing a specific prediction, I think I see signs of the end of an error.

Speech by Representative Benjamin B. Blackburn (Georgia) Before the House on the Trade Embargo Against Rhodesia*

February 10, 1970

Mr. Speaker, many speeches have been made before this body concerning the trade embargo which has been placed against the Republic of Rhodesia. As you know, this embargo has forced the United States to purchase chromium ore which is vital to our defense effort from the Soviet Union instead of Rhodesia. Recently, Mr. L. G. Bliss, chairman of the board and president of the Foote Mineral Co., presented testimony before the Subcommittee on Africa of the House Foreign Affairs Committee regarding our need for chromium ore. For the information of my colleagues, I am hereby inserting Mr. Bliss' testimony into the Record:

Statement of L. G. Bliss

Mr. Chairman and Honorable Members: I am L. G. Bliss, Chairman of the Board, President and Chief Executive Officer of Foote Mineral Company, a Pennsylvania corporation. Since 1932 Foote Mineral Company has been the sole owner of Rhodesian Vanadium Corporation, a Delaware corporation, which owns and operates

Ibid., Feb. 10, 1970, pp. 1051-52.

chromium ore deposits and mines in the Great Dyke region near Salisbury, Rhodesia. Prior to the establishment of economic sanctions against the Rhodesian government, these deposits constituted one of Foote Mineral Company's principal sources of chromium ore for the production in the United States of ferro-chromium and other chromium-containing alloys. These alloys are essential to the production of stainless steel, tool steels, and other high performance metals and alloys.

The distribution of the mineral riches in the earth's crust having been decided many millenia before political boundaries were established, it has been customary through the ages to share the world's resources through trade between nations. This interchange of the materials vital to civilization is conducted between nations of widely divergent political and philosophic views, and is rarely interrupted except in the face of hostilities—in which case the supply of strategic materials becomes a matter of utmost importance to a nation's defense.

The principal sources of high grade metallurgical chrome ores carrying a ratio of chrome to iron of 3 to 1 or better are located in Rhodesia, the Soviet Union, Turkey, Iran, Yugoslavia, Albania and the Republic of South Africa. It is believed that the reserves in the Soviet Union are extensive, but reliable quantitative information is not available. Excluding Russia for the moment, it is significant that, of the chromium ore reserves of some 440 million tons estimated for the rest of the world, approximately 300 million tons are located in Rhodesia.

*   *   *

Clearly, Foote Mineral Company's economic muscle was inadequate to continue maintenance operations for an indefinite period of time. By the end of 1967, and prior to the imposition of so-called "hard" sanctions, we made it known to our Government as well as to Rhodesian officials that the one million dollars advanced for the protection of our assets and for the preventing of dispersal of our operating force was all we could afford. This sum covered the production of 57,000 tons of high grade metallurgical ore. The implications of this decision were quite clear. If the mines were abandoned at the end of the support period, 4,000 workers and their families would be dispersed with destinies unknown, and a valuable chromium source would be lost not only to the Company but to our nation.

This eventually was forestalled when, on January 2, 1968, Rhodesian Vanadium Corporation was mandated and the management of Rhodesian Vanadium Corporation was instructed by the Rhodesian government to continue the operations at the minimal level of 40,000 tons per year. This mandate continues in force, although there is no guarantee as to the future.

With regard to the economic impact on our Company, it must be appreciated that we had invested substantial sums of money prior to the imposition of sanctions for the purpose of exposing the ore to be mined in the future. This is a necessary requisite to the development of any mine.

*   *   *

Needless to say, the cost of the developed ore referred to above had been paid for well in advance of December 16, 1966. It equates to four to five years of total production at a minimal rate of 40,000 tons per year.

In the belief that the United States Government would not choose to discriminatorily penalize a U.S.-based company in the implementation of the Rhodesian sanctions, Foote Mineral Company submitted a special license request to the Foreign Assets Control Division of our Treasury Department on September 27, 1967 for permission to import 40,000 tons of metallurgical grade chrome ore, mined and paid for. Paradoxically, the Rhodesian regime did not then, nor do we believe it now would, prevent shipment of this parcel to the United States. The special license requested was denied. A second request for 57,000 tons mined and paid for was submitted on August 28, 1968. This request was also denied.

In the meantime, an offer was received to purchase our Rhodesian assets, including the ore above ground Obviously under existing circumstances, the price offered was well below what is considered to be a reasonable market value. We requested comments from various departments of our Government on the advisability and legalities of selling the properties. No formal response has been received albeit several unofficial observations were offered.

I believe some comments on the total chrome problem relating to sanctions are germane to your deliberations.

Based on an estimated consumption of 850,000 short tons of high grade chrome ore in 1969, there will be no shortfall. Of the amount required, the Soviet Union and Turkey will provide an estimated 629,000 tons; the contribution from Government stockpiles is expected to be 175,000 tons. Inventories and imports of South African ore will more than satisfy the modest deficit.

However, it is our understanding that all economically usable chrome ore in the excess stockpile has already been committed to the U.S. consuming industry. Beginning in 1971, a shortfall of available ore can be anticipated. Depending on the levels of producer stockpiles and specific purchasing arrangements, all producers of chromium alloys may not be equally affected by the shortfall, but the net effect to the steel industry will be a reduction in the availability of domestically produced ferrochrome products.

We have another concern in attempting to assess the magnitude of the shortfall. As the U.S. Government and the U.S.-based companies rigorously adhere to the intent of the United Nations sanctions and the resultant regulations, it is well known that many other countries party to the same agreements are not so disposed. The fact is that movements of Rhodesian ore to many of our competing friendly nations are increasing. How much and at what rate Rhodesian chrome ore will continue to find its way into world markets at substantially lower prices than those paid for by American industry for ore of a different origin, is difficult to predict. Whether the magnitude of these sales will be adequate to offset the anticipated shortfall by increasing the availability of Russian ore remains to be seen. Yet, regardless of the outcome it is clear that high priced ores will continue to be the only ones available to U.S.-based furnaces.

In our efforts to set an example in international morality we must be mindful of the practical considerations. It is well documented that countries such as Malawi, Botswana and Zambia, as well as others surrounding Southern Rhodesia, are quite realistic, as are those nations buying Rhodesian chrome ore. They point out the need to protect their own economies as justification for their trading behavior. Thus it is that, as we assess alternatives available to us, we must be mindful of the long range pragmatic aspect of any course we steer. To recount a few:

1. No amount of expenditure of U.S. dollars can cause redistribution of the world's high grade chromium deposits.

2. A shortfall of high grade chrome can only further contribute to the spiral of inflation.

3. A prolonged shortfall of chrome guarantees a major disturbance in the raw materials essential to our mobilization base. Above-ground stockpiles are exhaustible much sooner than known reserves of chrome ore in Rhodesia. Maintenance of our stockpiles, or replenishment of depleted stockpiles, through sources presently available to the United States, seems increasingly remote.

I cannot believe there was ever any intent in our support of the United Nations position on Rhodesia that we jeopardize our national security. Nor do I believe that inequitabilities were foreseen in the administration of that policy which would place upon any American company or segment of American industry a disproportionate share of the cost. In short, I believe we intended to treat ourselves as equitably as we intend to treat the rest of the world.

*   *   *

*Speech by Senator Harry F. Byrd (Virginia) Before the Senate on a Bill to Amend the U.N. Participation Act of 1945**

March 29, 1971

S. 1404. A bill to amend the United Nations Participation Act of 1945 to prevent the imposition thereunder of any prohibition on the importation into the United States of any strategic and critical material from any free world country for so long as the importation of like material from any Communist country is not prohibited by law. Referred to the Committee on Foreign Relations.

Mr. President, I am today introducing legislation aimed at ending the dependence of the United States upon the Soviet Union for its supply of chrome ore—a material vital to national defense.

The United States is now facing a critical shortage of chrome, which is essential to the manufacture of stainless steel. Jet aircraft and missiles are among the items vital to defense which make use of chrome.

Our current situation is the result of American participation in United Nations economic sanctions against Rhodesia, the small African country which is the world's richest source of chrome.

The U.N. sanctions were imposed after Rhodesia declared her independence from Great Britain. Rhodesia was labeled a "threat to international peace and security"—a ridiculous charge.

Unfortunately, the United States actively supported the embargo against Rhodesia. Since the first sanctions in 1966, the United Nations has twice tried to strangle Rhodesia with an ever-tighter boycott, each time actively supported by the United States.

These measures have not worked. The embargo policy is a failure. Rhodesian trade actually is increasing.

*Ibid., Mar. 29, 1971, pp. S3994-95.

Yet the United States persists in supporting the unethical U.N. sanctions, even though all Rhodesia has done is to declare her independence from Great Britain—a step the American colonies took in 1776.

It is today a criminal offense for any American to engage in trade with Rhodesia.

Now this situation would be bad enough if it were just a question of international law and relations between nations. Former Secretary of State Dean Acheson has called the U.N. action against Rhodesia "barefaced aggression, unprovoked and unjustified by a single legal or moral principle."

I concur.

But more than legal and moral principle is involved.

Before the U.N. sanctions were imposed, Rhodesia supplied the United States with most of its chrome ore.

With the embargo in effect, the United States has had to turn to the Soviet Union for chrome. Sixty percent of the chrome we are using comes from Russia.

The Russians have taken advantage of a monopoly situation and have more than doubled the price of the chrome ore they export to the United States.

But even more serious is the fact that we are dependent on the favor of the Russians for a strategic material.

The administration has requested that Congress pass a bill permitting withdrawal of 30 percent of thypresent supply of chrome in the Nation's reserve stockpile.

This would temporarily meet our needs, in combination with Russian chrome. But it is only a stopgap measure, for at this rate we would exhaust our stockpile in a little over 3 years.

To my mind, it is totally illogical for the United States to depend upon Russia for a strategically important commodity.

The legislation I am introducing today would enable us to end this dependency upon the Soviet Union.

Under my proposal, the President could not ban imports of a strategic material from a free world country if the importation of the same material is permitted from a Communist-dominated country. That seems logical to me.

Now technically, the administration could meet the requirements of this legislation by banning all chrome imports. But then of course there would be far too little ore for even the most elementary needs of the United States.

Therefore, the United States would have to end its participation in the U.N. sanctions against Rhodesia, insofar as chrome is concerned.

It would be my hope that the administration would drop all sanctions against Rhodesia. That would be the proper course to take.

But even if this course were not taken, at least the United States would end its reliance upon the Soviet Union for strategically vital chrome ore.

Legislation similar to mine has been introduced in the House of Representatives by Representative Collins of Texas. I hope that the Congress will take prompt action to change the absurd and dangerous position in which the United States now finds itself.

Mr. President, I send to the desk proposed legislation to accomplish this purpose, and I ask unanimous consent that the text of the bill be printed at this point in the Record.

There being no objection, the bill was ordered to be printed in the Record, as follows:

S.1404

A bill to amend the United Nations Participation Act of 1945 to prevent the imposition thereunder of any prohibition on the importation into the United States of any strategic and critical material from any free world country for so long as the importation of like material from any Communist country is not prohibited by law.

Be it enacted by the Senate and House of Representatives of the United States of America in Congress assembled, That section 5(a) of the United Nations Participation Act of 1945 (22 U.S.C. 287c(a) is amended by adding at the end thereof the following new sentence: "On or after the effective date of this sentence, the President may not prohibit or regulate the importation into the United States pursuant to this section of any material determined to be strategic and critical pursuant to section 2 of the Strategic and Critical Materials Stock Piling Act (50 U.S.C. 98a), which is the product of any foreign country or area not listed as a Communist-dominated country or area in general headnote 3(d) of the Tariff Schedules of the United States (19 U.S.C. 1202), for so long as the importation into the United States of material of that kind which is the product of such Communist-dominated countries or areas is not prohibited by any provision of law."

*House of Representatives Debate on the Military Procurement Authorization, 1972**

September 10, 1971

Mr. Bolling: Mr. Speaker, by direction of the Committee on Rules, I call up House Resolution 696 and ask for its immediate consideration.

The Clerk read the resolution as follows:

H. Res. 696

Resolved, That immediately upon the adoption of this resolution it shall be in order to consider the conference report on the bill (H.R. 8687) to authorize appropriations during the fiscal year 1972 for procurement of aircraft, missiles, naval vessels, tracked combat vehicles, torpedoes, and other weapons, and research, development, test, and evaluation for the Armed Forces, and to prescribe the authorized personnel strength of the Selected Reserve of each Reserve component of the Armed Forces, and for other purposes, and all points of order against said conference report for failure to comply with the provisions of clause 3 of rule XX and clause 3 of rule XXVIII are hereby waived. It shall also be in order, pursuant to clause 1 of rule xx, for a separate vote to be had upon demand on those individual parts of the Senate amendment now contained in the conference report and numbered as sections 503, 505, and 601.

The Speaker: The gentleman from Missouri (Mr. Bolling) is recognized for 1 hour.

Mr. Bolling: Mr. Speaker, I yield 30 minutes to the distinguished gentleman from California (Mr. Smith), pending which I yield myself such time as I may consume.

(Mr. Bolling asked and was given permission to revise and extend his remarks.)

Mr. Bolling: Mr. Speaker, I would like to explain this rule. It is a most unusual rule. I think the Members may be interested in what it contains. It was reported by the Rules Committee, I believe, unanimously.

It seeks to give all Members interested in this matter a fair opportunity under the rules of the House. The Reorganization Act which was passed by the House and become law last year provided for a new treatment of nongermane matter adopted in the other body which would not be germane when considered in the House when that matter is brought back in conference.

The other body originally had six such amendments in the bill that passed the other body on the military procurement matter. When the conferees returned to the House, three had been eliminated and three were left.

There was a provision dealing with chrome, a provision limiting the amount of assistance that could be given to Laos, and a modified version of the—whatever number it is—Mansfield amendment which the other body had adopted previously.

The Rules Committee provided a rule which would protect the conference report from any point of order which would have eliminated the consideration of the conference report.

As I said, I believe the Rules Committee acted on this rule unanimously.

The Rules Committee felt that it should protect the rights of all Members under the rules of the House which were adopted las year in effect in the reorganization plan as to the procedure on nongermane substance. The Rules Committee wrote the rule so as to accomplish that. So, there could be debate of 40 minutes—20 minutes on a side—on each of the matters that I have detailed.

*   *   *

Mr. Fraser: Mr. Speaker, I urge you to vote to strike this nongermane amendment known as section 503 in the conference report.

There are several reasons why I think the House should reject this section.

First, this matter originally came before the House Committee on Foreign Affairs, and came before the subcommittee of which I am the chairman. It came in the form of several bills offered by several Members of this House.

We held hearings on the question of whether we should amend our sanctions on Rhodesia with respect to the importing of chromium ore.

Here are the hearings. We had Members testify. We had representatives from the steel companies testify. We had the State Department testify. When we were through, at a meeting of the subcommittee, the conclusion was reached, among the Members present, that there was no justification for going forward with any of the bills which would amend sanctions on Rhodesia so far as importing chrome ore is concerned.

Mr. Speaker, let me dispose of certain issues which have been raised along the way. These sanctions are being undertaken by the U.S. Government by the President pursuant to international treaty obligations. There are only two countries in the world today who are openly defying their treaty obligations in this respect, and those are the countries of Portugal and South Africa. If we accept this nongermane amendment we will join South Africa and Portugal and be the third country to openly ignore their international treaty obligations.

It is abundantly clear that if we pass this provision and begin to import chrome ore from Rhodesia that we will be in violation of international law.

I do not believe that this is the time to argue whether there should have been sanctions against Rhodesia in the first place or not. The most important fact on this score is to know that the Conservative Party in Great Britain is trying to reach a conclusion with Rhodesia, and Lord Hume, the Foreign Minister of Great Britain, is headed for Salisbury, Rhodesia, within the week to try to conclude some kind of a settlement with Rhodesia that will lead, hopefully, to the end of international sanctions. But from the point of view of the U.S. Government there could not be a worse time to be saying that we are going to violate international law and turn our back on international treaty obligations because we want to import chrome ore.

There is no shortage of chrome ore. In fact, we have a stockpile that is in excess of our needs, and part of this stockpile is being released for domestic consumption. . . .

We are going to use this because we do not have the need for such a large stockpile.

Now the argument is made that we have become too dependent upon the Soviet Union for ore. But the fact is in 1963, 49 percent of high grade metallurgical chrome ore was coming in from the Soviet Union and today it is 58 percent, or 9 percent higher than it was in 1963, several years before the sanctions began.

So this is really a false issue. The fact is that the Soviet Union has only a limited supply of high grade ore and the fact that they are willing to ship it to us means that they are depleting their own resources.

If there should be an international emergency of some kind, of course, then we can change whatever restrictions we have on importations from Rhodesia. But there is no such emergency. We hae an excess in our stockpile so I believe that this House should support the President and the Secretary of State who have asked that we turn this amendment down and stay in compliance with our international obligations.

* * *

Mr. Dellums: Mr. Speaker, and Members of the House, shortly we will vote upon an amended version of the Byrd amendment that would end the embargo on Rhodesian chrome. I join with the gentleman from Minnesota and my colleagues of the Congressional Black Caucus in urging the House to defeat this amendment that would put us in violation of our international legal obligations and which can only be interpreted as a victory for the forces of racism and reaction. Can this country, committed as it states to racial equality and justice, feel comfortable in the company of South Africa and Portugal, the only other countries to defy openly the U.N. embargo? Why should the United States take the blame that propery belongs to other countries by breaking the Security Council sanctions against the Smith regime?

The Congressional Black Caucus has strongly opposed this nefarious amendment— nefarious because not only is it dealing with an illegal regime, not recognized by any state, not even South Africa, but it is in violation of U.N. sanctions which the United States voted for and supported.

If the attempt to lift the embargo is successful, it will confirm the pattern we have seen lately in domestic policy of indifference or even open hostility to the claims of the poor and underprivileged. It is obvious that the motivation for this action cannot be need for chrome, since the executive branch has introduced a bill to unload 1.3 million tons of excess chrome from our stockpile.

* * *

Mr. Speaker, the congressional black caucus urges its colleagues to reaffirm the historic and legal commitment of this country to law and self-determination, and I ask that all of you join in opposing the amended version of the Byrd amendment that would end the embargo on Rhodesian chrome.

*   *   *

Mr. Edwards of Alabama: Mr. Speaker, I rise in support of section 503, and urge that it be kept in the conference report.

Mr. Speaker, ever since President Lyndon Johnson issued an Executive order in 1966 pursuant to United Nations sanctions barring all trade with Rhodesia, the United States has been confronted with the gnawing problem of being able to obtain a very vital and necessary defense commodity—chromium.

Up until 1966, we were receiving nearly 40 percent of our total chromium imports from Rhodesia through the auspices of two American-owned chromium mines. At the same time, Communist Russia was supplying us with about 27 percent of our chromium at a healthy competitive price of about $30 to $33 a ton.

Since the advent of this embargo, we have been forced to channel more than twice that price to Russia which now is furnishing us with about 65 percent of our chromium needs. Compounding this dilemma is the suspected fact that the chrome ore we are purchasing from Russia is actually Rhodesian chrome which is being trans-shipped by an intermediary nation to Russia. I cannot say categorically that this is true, but I believe it is true. At any rate, the conference report refers to several U.N. nations who have purchased chrome ore from Rhodesia.

Mr. Speaker, I cannot think of a more absurd position for this Nation to be in. To have to rely on Communist Russia to furnish us with a vital defense commodity is beyond all sense of reason. To see other U.N. nations buying from Rhodesia while this great Nation doggedly abides by the U.N. sanctions is unbelievable.

Because of our need for chrome we find ourselves dipping into our chrome ore stockpile. If we continue to do this at the present rate our chrome stockpile could vanish within 3 years.

Nor does it help matters to learn that the Russians, fully aware of our predicament, have planned on raising their price on the chrome ore they supply us with from $72 to $82 per ton next year!

There is no secret about the fact that this Nation cannot easily function without chromium. Not only is it essential in the production of our military jet aircraft, missiles, and satellites, it is the all-important ingredient which makes stainless steel "stainless," and which is also vital in the production of everything from industrial tools, to automobiles, to home construction, to kitchen items.

By the same token, it is no secret that we are courting national disaster by continuing to depend on the Russians for our defense needs. This is an incredible situation. It runs afoul of what should be the first two words in all our foreign policy: "America First."

Mr. Speaker, the answer to solving this discouraging problem is as plain as the sun in the sky.

It can be accomplished simply by making certain that section 503 of the Conference Report is approved. If we are willing to buy chrome ore form from a Communist nation, then it certainly should be proper for this country to buy chrome ore from a friendly free nation such as Rhodesia.

As far as I can tell, the only thing wrong with Rhodesia is that England is not happy with it, and there are some in our own country who disagree with some of its internal policies.

Mr. Speaker, we have delayed too long. I urge full approval of this provision so that we may once again resume the importation of chrome ore from Rhodesia for the good of our own Nation.

*   *   *

Mr. Dent: Mr. Speaker, I hesitate to take the floor after the gracious treatment I had today on this floor, but I just cannot stand aside on this particular amendment.

I just talked today to the representatives of the steel companies of America. The difference in price for a ton of steel between American steel and foreign steel, on the basis of chrome coming from Rhodesia, is $35 to $40. That is $35 to $40 difference in price.

The entire American steel industry last year had an average profit on a ton of steel of $12. Believe me when I say to these Members, there was a difference of 115,555 steel workers between July and August of this year. That many steel workers were out of work between July and August.

I have the greatest respect for the man who preceded me. I have absolutely the greatest respect for him. His position is based on a social basis, but tonight I am talking to the Members on an economic basis. I say to the Members of this Congress, both the Senate and the House, this country must start to look inward, toward its own welfare, keeping in mind that only the inward welfare of this country can make us strong enough to help those countries who need help. If we go further down the drain in our economic standing we cannot do that.

Today the stock market industrial index of the United States lost 12 points. Maybe that does not mean anything to the Members, but it means this to me: We are in a very serious situation. Please do not vote for this.

Mr. Roush: Mr. Speaker, I rise in support of the Senate amendment, I appreciate the intent of the sanctions imposed by the United Nations against Rhodesia. I am in sympathy with the motives which prompted the imposition of those sanctions. But I am in sympathy with the minorities of those sanctions. But I am in sympathy with the minorities of this country as well as the plight of all those who work in the specialty steel plants of this country. They are being driven out of their jobs by reason of unfair competition.

I am informed that Japan buys chrome for $31.50 a ton and we pay Russia $72 a ton for a poor quality of chrome. Is it any wonder we cannot compete with Japan? The gentleman from Pennsylvania (Mr. Dent) has pointed this out very clearly. Is it any wonder that the tradition of free trade is under assault? If free trade is not accompanied by fair trade then it cannot survive.

Now concerning Russia's sale of chrome to this country: The argument has been made that the chrome we buy from Russia is not Rhodesian chrome. Russia imports steel from Rhodesia for $31.50 a ton. I would acknowledge that they are not selling us Rhodesian chrome. Is there any doubt as to what Russia is doing? I would surmise that they are using the high quality chrome of Rhodesia which can be purchased for $31.50 a ton for their own purposes and selling the inferior Russian produced chrome to us for $72 a ton. This increases the cost of our specialty steel and makes it impossible for us to compete with other nations—such as Japan.

The gentleman from Massachusetts tells us the administration is imploring us not to buy steel from Rhodesia and thus protest certain policies of that government. Within the past few days the administration has asked us, as a people, to approve the sale of 20 million bushels of grain to Russia for the going price. Well, I do not approve of the oppression that takes place in Russia, but I do approve of that proposed sale of grain, because it is in the best interest of this country. I do not approve all that goes on in Rhodesia, but I approve of the purchase of chrome from Rhodesia, because it is in our best interest.

Mr. Findley: Mr. Speaker, the Rhodesian sanctions I have always felt were unfortunate. They were ill considered. Yet they were invoked through the procedure to which our Government had committed itself under the United Nations Charter. I think it is unfortunate we are using this device to set aside an agreement to which our Government has bound itself.

Another unfortunate aspect of this is, it is my understanding that the State Department is opposed to this provision. I would be glad to yield to the chairman of the subcommittee for clarification on that point. I realize the parliamentary dilemma we face. I simply regret that we find ourselves in that fix. Can the gentleman clarify the attitude of the State Department on this point?

Mr. Fraser: Mr. Speaker, the State Department appeared before our subcommittee and opposed this, and we have a letter in the Congressional Record from David Abshire, liaison for the State Department. I understand the White House itself has made their view known as in opposition on this. It is clear the State Department and White House are opposed to its retention in the bill.

Mr. Findley: Is there any attitude on the part of the administration to this as far as other Members know? I have not heard anything contrary to what the gentleman from Minnesota has stated. If any others want to clarify that, I will yield.

We certainly pride ourselves as a nation that agrees on a rule of law. This situation is most unfortunate, and causes us to damage our posture as far as world opinion as a nation committed to the rule of law.

Mr. Dent: Mr. Speaker, will the gentleman yield?

Mr. Findley: I yield to the gentleman from Pennsylvania.

Mr. Dent: Mr. Speaker, evidently there was some misunderstanding as far as what some of us want. I am voting to sustain the chairman in the amendment.

Mr. Findley: Yes, I understand the gentleman's position.

Mr. Fraser: Mr. Speaker, I yield 4 minutes to the gentleman from New York (Mr. Bingham).

Mr. Bingham: Mr. Speaker, first I should like to point out that the issue here is not, as it was stated in the conference report, whether the United States needs the chrome ore, both from an economic and national security standpoint, or whether this should be subordinated to the policy position established by the United Nations in its sanctions against Rhodesia.

The issue is, very simply, whether we are going to live up to a treaty obligation entered into freely, and particularly the issue is whether there is any pressure on us to do so at this time.

The stockpile is adequate, and more than adequate. If some crisis arises in the future when we absolutely need Rhodesian ore we can reexamine the situation at that time. For us to move to do so now would be a violation of our treaty obligation with the United Nations.

On the question dealt with rather lightly here as to whether there has been some transshipment of ore from Rhodesia via the Soviet Union to us, there is a statement which has been in the Congressional Record from the U.S. Geological Survey stating on microscopic analysis that this is simply not the fact, that the ore we receive from the Soviet Union is not produced in Rhodesia.

It is interesting to note that the conference committee made no such claim.

Finally, with respect to the very persuasive appeal Members have heard from the gentleman from Pennsylvania about the position of the steel industry, I believe it should be noted that there is also in the Congressional Record, on page S15319, a letter from Mr. I. W. Abel, president of the United Steel Workers of America, in which he indicates his opposition to any change at this time in the sanction program unilaterally by the United States. He says, among other things:

> The United Steel Workers of America supports the intent of the embargo and its continuation. We feel that as a nation and in conjunction with other nations we must be concerned about basic human justice and if need be sustain an economic price for that conviction. Furthermore, this is one of the few occasions on which the United Nations acted as the moral conscience of the world.

That is the president of the United Steel Workers, Mr. Abel, speaking.

I would urge Members not to take this position at this particular time, when the British are in negotiation with the Rhodesian Government and when there is a very good chance that there may be a settlement of the problem. This would be the worst possible time for us to take this step, and there is no need for it at this time.

*   *   *

Mr. Dent: I happen to have been in contact with the steel workers today. The situation is one as to whether we decide whether the social aspect of legislation at this point in our economic situation shall take precedence over the serious economic problem we face.

I agree with the gentleman on the question of the treatment of the social aspects with respect to the Rhodesian Government, but there is also this fact: There are only two nations in the entire international agreement which are living up to the unanimous vote of the U.N., Great Britain, and the United States. West Germany is buying Rhodesian ore. Japan is buying Rhodesian ore. Every steel producing nation that signed and voted on the sanction against Rhodesia is buying Rhodesian ore.

*   *   *

Mr. Biaggi: Mr. Speaker, I rise in support of the conference report.

I can sympathize with many of the arguments put forth by the gentleman, particularly with regard to the denial of voting rights to the black majority in Rhodesia. However, I believe we can better bring about our goal of democratic practices in that country as a friend of Rhodesia rather than an enemy. Moreover, I cannot ignore the overriding national defense considerations involved here.

The United States has been dependent on the Soviet Union for more than 60 percent of its chrome ore since the embargo was placed against Rhodesia in 1967.

During this time the Soviet Union has raised the price 288 percent from the presanction level of $25 per ton to the present price of $72 per ton.

At the same time, the U.S.S.R., no friend of the United States, has been purchasing high grade Rhodesian chrome ore from other nations violating the embargo and selling the United States its poorer grade chromite at substantially higher prices. In the interests of national security, the United States cannot continue to be dependent upon the Soviet Union as a major source of a critical defense material. Moreover, it is highly hypocritical for the United States to get its chrome ore in this underhanded manner. The sanctions, frankly, are not working.

The arguments put forth that the stockpile of chrome is in surplus is not acceptable. The purpose of the stockpile is to have a reserve and this Nation should not be using its stockpile supplies as a regular source of chrome ore as some have advocated.

The high price of chromite has placed the U.S. steel industry in an unfavorable competitive position relative to other nations who are importing the Rhodesian ore.

As a result many Americans are unemployed, because of the increased importation of low-cost steel and steel products. While this problem could be alleviated through import controls, we have at hand today a ready means of accomplishing the same end.

To give you an example of the degree of penetration of the U.S. markets by foreign producers, I would like to quote a few figures from the conference committee report:

Imports of specialty steels are at an alltime high—20 percent of the total domestic market in the first quarter of 1971. For some individual speciality steels, the penetration is even greater; 35 percent of stainless cold rolled sheets, 68 percent of the market for stainless wire rods, and 54 percent for stainless wire.

This is a shocking set of figures and the cause can be directly traced to the embargo on Rhodesian chrome ore.

I can understand the desire of those who wish to maintain our strong support of the United Nations in this matter. However, the U.N.'s demonstrated lack of interest in fair play by rejecting Nationalist China makes one question whether the United States should continue to jeopardize its national defense interest to support the world body.

Mr. Speaker, I am pleased the House conferees have accepted the Senate amendment permitting the importation of Rhodesian chrome ore as I had urged last month. I believe this provision and the entire military procurement bill conference report deserves adoption by this body in the form finally agreed upon by the conferees.

Mr. Fraser: Mr. Speaker, I yield 3 minutes to the gentleman from Massachusetts (Mr. Morse).

Mr. Morse: Mr. Speaker, I rise in support of the effort of Mr. Fraser to delete section 503 from the military procurement bill. This is a nongermane amendment approved by the Senate providing for the importation of Rhodesian chrome. A resumption of chrome ore importation by the United States is clearly opposed by the Nixon administration. It has so advised many of the Members of this body on both sides of the aisle and, believe me, it would represent a clear violation of our international legal obligations as a signatory to the United Nations Charter.

Looking at the strategic considerations: Proponents of section 503 to resume importation of chrome ore from Rhodesia claim that the United States, as a result of the embargo, has become dependent on the Soviet Union for its supply of chrome ore.

Mr. Speaker, this is simply not valid. A significant U.S. trade with the Soviet Union in chrome ore existed long before the Rhodesian sanctions went into effect.

Additionally, large quantities of chrome ore are simply not necessary to maintain our defense requirements. This has been made unmistakably clear by the unqualified support of the administration—for S.773 which would authorize the release of 1.3 million tons of chrome ore over the next 3 years from the U.S. stockpiles, on the grounds that our current stockpiles of chrome ore do in fact exceed our national security requirements.

With regard to the current negotiations between Britain and Smith's government, it is clear that U.S. action to resume importation of chrome ore from the Smith regime at this time would undermine these ongoing efforts to reach a settlement by encouraging the Smith regime to hold out indefinitely, thus canceling whatever progress has been made in the talks.

Mr. Speaker, I urge Members on both sides of the aisle who are aware of some of the things that happened in the other body to recognize their responsibilities to respect the sanctions which are embodied in international law and which would be restored by the action of this House.

*   *   *

Mr. Fraser: Mr. Speaker, let me just straighten out a couple of facts.

The first is that the Soviet ore is a superior ore to that of Rhodesia and has always demanded a higher price.

Second, Mr. Speaker, the continent of Africa supported us on the China issue. The majority of the nations of Africa were with us as were a majority of the nations in Latin America. I say that where we lost on the China issue was in Europe. We lost the vote of every one of our NATO allies, and to penalize the area where the majority of them voted with us, I think is the height of irresponsibility.

I think what we have before us is a solemn treaty obligation. Many people do not take that treaty obligation lightly. But it seems to me that it is important for us to observe the rule of a treaty obligation in our country's conduct with other nations around the world. That is the fundamental issue. This is what the President has asked for, this is what the Secretary of State has asked for and this is what I asked the chairman of the subcommittee tha held the hearings on this issue.

Mr. Speaker, we have a letter from the head of the Steelworkers Union which says these import sanctions have nothing to do with the unemployment situation in the steel industry.

I think that we have to fully understand what our obligations are as a responsible people, leaders we like to think in the free world. I think we will make our true selves known in a way of which we can be proud in the Congress of the United States on this issue. . . .

Mr. Dent: I admire your position on treaty obligations, but I would like to say to all of you that we are in Vietnam because of a treaty obligation. Yet the gentleman for whom I have great admiration, as a person, is one of the greatest fighters on this floor against our participation in Vietnam, and that is a treaty obligation.

*   *   *

Mr. Dellenback: Mr. Speaker, I intend to be brief, but think this is a very troublesome time.

The issue that this Congress faces and that the United States faces tonight is in my opinion not an economic issue, important though that is. It is not a social issue, important though that is. The basic issue that the United States faces tonight is its own credibility in the world. I say this because we are here facing the question of whether or not we will live up to a solemn commitment made through a treaty.

Mr. Speaker, if there is to be a long-term peace in this world, it will not come through an escalation of arms. The long-term peace of this world depends upon our maintaining a military strength now which in the long run depends upon commitments between nations, which nations will believe the other nations intend to adhere to and which we in America will indeed adhere to.

If at this time for reasons that are not matters of law and order, not matters of national commitment, but matters of what we consider short-term self interest, we go back on this commitment, then what is to say to any other nation with which we may ever make a commitment that we will live up to it? What is to lead Germany to feel that we will obey our commitments to her? Or if we come out of the SALT talks with an agreement with Russia, how can she believe we will live up to those commitments? If we cannot live up to this commitment when, indeed, are our commitments to be trusted by any nation with which we may deal?

*   *   *

Mr. Edwards of Alabama: Mr. Speaker, as far as the committee report goes, Germany is buying chrome from Rhodesia. If we are supposed to be so concerned about our own commitments, I wonder what the gentleman from Oregon would say about Germany? There are many of us who believe, although it is hard to prove, that Russia is buying chrome from Rhodesia. I do not know why we should be so concerned about our commitments in view of Russian action. Or how about France or some of the other U.N. countries. Commitments?

I believe we have been Uncle Sap too long in this whole procedure.

The thing that has bothered me is this. It has been argued that we do not need to worry about this, if at some time in the future we get in trouble then we can go to Rhodesia for chrome. But I can tell you that if I were Rhodesia, and we got into that position, I would tell the United States to go jump in the lake—to go some place else to get its chrome. Mr. Speaker, we cannot have it both ways. It is time we cut out this foolishness and start dealing with our friends.

*   *   *

New York Times *Editorial on "More Than Chrome at Stake"**

October 10, 1971

Only President Nixon can now pull Congress back from an action that would damage the United Nations, tarnish the credibility of United States policy in Africa, jeopardize delicate negotiations between Britain and Rhodesia, and offend liberal opinion everywhere.

The Senate has inserted in the military procurement bill a provision for breaching sanctions twice invoked against the white racist regime in Rhodesia by the United Nations Security Council—with strong American backing. The provision would permit importation of Rhodesian chrome, supposedly to lessen American dependence on high-priced Russian chrome.

Senators Fulbright and McGee fought hard to leave the decision on chrome imports to the President. They failed at the showdown by six votes, partly because of absentees—including Democratic Presidential aspirants Harris, Jackson, McGovern and Muskie—and partly because the Administration kept silent.

This issue far transcends a narrow commercial interest. The Security Council voted sanctions for the first time in U.N. history because it regarded perpetuation of minority rule in Rhodesia—where blacks outnumber whites 20 to 1—as a formula for eventual racial war. For the U.S. Government unilaterally to violate that embargo would have grave consequences for the U.N. It would be serious business in any circumstance to amend the United Nations Participation Act of 1945, which empowers the President to enforce Security Council decisions. To do so in order to relieve chrome importers and to augment a chrome stockpile already adequate for the next two years would be extreme folly.

Such a move might encourage the white rulers in Salisbury to intransigence just when Britain sees a chance at last to negotiate an agreement for Rhodesian independence with a guarantee of unimpeded progress toward majority rule.

With the military procurement bill now in Senate-House conference, Mr. Nixon still has a chance to head off this mindless act—if he is interested enough to try.

Statement by the African Group of the U.N. on Southern Rhodesian Chrome[†]

November 8, 1971

The United States Congress took action on 4 November 1971 to allow chrome ore to be imported into the United States from Southern Rhodesia (Zimbabwe) in contravention of Security Council resolution 253 of 29 May 1968 which the Government of the United States has supported and until now executed.

By that resolution, the Security Council, with the support of the United States of America, imposed mandatory sanctions against the illegal regime of Southern Rhodesia, and, in the exercise of its authority, called upon all States, Members of the United Nations to observe the sanctions contained in its resolution 253 (1968), in

**The New York Times*, Oct. 10, 1971.
[†]U.N. Security Council, S/10385, Nov. 8, 1971.

particular and among other things, to "prevent the import into their territories of all commodities and products originating in Southern Rhodesia and exported therefrom after the date of this resolution (whether or not the commodities or products are for consumption or processing in their territories, whether or not they are imported in bond and whether or not any special legal status with respect to the import of goods is enjoyed by the port of other place where they are imported or stored). . . ." This was an important action taken by the Security Council in support of the legitimate rights of over 5 million Africans against the oppressive action of the white minority regime which continues to inflict indignities on the Africans.

If the amendment removing the United States President's authority to ban importation of Rhodesian chrome into the United States is implemented, it will undermine the basis for State responsibility for mandatory sanctions imposed by the Security Council, especially in the case of one of its permanent members.

The African Group at the United Nations deeply regrets this action taken by the United States Congress especially since such action would make the sanctions much more ineffective. The African Group nevertheless feels that there is still time for the United States Administration to recognize the importance of this matter and act in accordance with the degree of responsibility which such a matter demands.

The African Group views with grave concern any violation of the mandatory sanctions on Southern Rhodesian adopted by the Security Council. The African Group requests the Secretary-General to draw once again the attention of Member States to their responsibility under the Charter to adhere strictly to the decisions of the Council. In this connexion, the Group further requests the Secretary-General to use his good offices to draw the attention of the appropriate authorities of the United States on the effect of any violation of the mandatory sanctions against Southern Rhodesia.

Statement by William E. Schaufele, Jr., U.S. Representative, in Committee IV, on the Question of Southern Rhodesia*

November 11, 1971

I have listened to the statements before the committee yesterday and today. I appreciate the spirit in which most of them were given. Our aims remain the same, the achievement of majority rule in Southern Rhodesia. However, I categorically reject any idea that the U.S. has been violating the Sanctions Program.

The matter to which the draft resolution alludes is still under consideration in the U.S. Congress. It would be inappropriate therefore for my Delegation to take part in the vote.

We recognize the committee's concern in this matter, and the executive branch of the U.S. Government has made known to the Congress its own similar concern and position on this matter. Under these c-rcumstances we believe that the resolution would not serve any useful purpose.

With one exception which arose from the fulfillment of a contract entered into prior to the imposition of sanctions the United States has not imported any chrome from Southern Rhodesia since 1965. At the same time estimates in the latest Sanctions

*United States Mission to the U.N., Press Release USUN-183 (71), Nov. 11, 1971.

Committee report show that more Southern Rhodesian chrome is available and exported than was the case in 1965.

This can only have resulted from violations of the sanctions by other countries. It will not pass unnoticed in my country that no other nation is named in this resolution. Under these circumstances we can hardly consider this an even-handed resolution.

My Government will continue to adhere to the broad, overall sanctions program. Moreover we will be prepared, at the proper time, to make a report to the Sanctions Committee of the Security Council on this legislation and its possible effects on the sanctions program.

Recommendation of the U.N. Fourth Committee on the Question of Southern Rhodesia*

November 12, 1971

The General Assembly,

Having considered the question of Southern Rhodesia,

Recalling its resolution 1514 (XV) of 14 December 1960, containing the Declaration on the Granting of Independence to Colonial Countries and Peoples, and resolution 2621 (XXV) of 12 October 1970, containing the programme of action for the full implementation of the Declaration,

Recalling also the relevant resolutions of the Security Council, particularly its resolutions 232 (1966) of 16 December 1966, 253 (1968) of 29 May 1968, 277 (1970) of 18 March 1970 and 288 (1970) of 17 November 1970,

Recalling further all previous resolutions concerning the question of Southern Rhodesia adopted by the General Assembly and the Special Committee on the Situation with regard to the Implementation of the Declaration on the Granting of Independence to Colonial Countries and Peoples, and also the consensus adopted by the Special Committee at its 828th meeting, on 6 October 1971,

Expressing its grave concern at the recent legislative moves in the Congress of the United States of America which, if carried through and confirmed, would permit the importation of chrome into the United States from Southern Rhodesia and thus would constitute a serious violation of the above-mentioned Security Council resolutions imposing sanctions against the illegal regime in Southern Rhodesia,

1. Calls upon the Government of the United States of America to take the necessary measures, in compliance with the relevant provisions of Security Council resolutions 253 (1968) of 29 May 1968, 277 (1970) of 18 March 1970 and 288 (1970) of 17 November 1970, and bearing in mind its obligations under Article 25 of the Charter of the United Nations, to prevent the importation of chrome into the United States from Southern Rhodesia;

2. Requests the Government of the United States to inform the General Assembly at its present session of the action taken or envisaged in the implementation of the present resolution;

*U.N. General Assembly, A/C.4/L.989/, Nov. 12, 1971. Passed by General Assembly on Nov. 15, 1971 by vote of 93 to 2 (Portugal and S. Africa), with 12 abstentions, the U.S. not voting.

3. Requests the President of the General Assembly to draw the attention of the Government of the United States to the urgent need for the implementation of the present resolution;

4. Reminds all Member States of their obligations under the Charter to comply fully with the decisions of the Security Council on mandatory sanctions against the illegal regime in Southern Rhodesia;

5. Decides to keep this and other aspects of the question under continuous review.

New York Times *Editorial on "The Moral Cost of Chrome"**

January 26, 1972

The Nixon Administration has now taken an action that puts the United States in violation of the United Nations Charter and gives moral support, at a critical moment, to Rhodesia's white minority Government. Officials will doubtless say that the Treasury was bound by a provision in the Military Procurement Act of 1971 to lift restrictions on imports of Rhodesian chrome—in spite of the mandatory sanctions invoked against Rhodesia—with American backing—by the U.N. Security Council.

However, there was a thoroughly legal way out if Mr. Nixon had been interested in defending the United Nations as well as the integrity of this country's commitment to that organization. He could have removed chrome from the list of strategic materials on the sound ground that the United States now has a stockpile adequate to meet both military and civilian needs for the next two to three years.

It would be a grave matter at any time for the United States—which has given unlimited support to "the rule of law" and to adherence to international law—to breach unilaterally a Security Council decision, especially one for which it voted. Secretary General Kurt Waldheim must now have a clearer idea of what Mr. Nixon meant, in a White House talk Monday, when he promised "full support" for the United Nations.

Bad as is the undercutting of this newly given commitment to the U.N., it is doubly tragic to give a major boost to the white racists who rule Rhodesia at a time when that country's black majority is dramatizing daily its hostility to Prime Minister Ian Smith's regime. This action will further damage respect for United States integrity—and not just in black Africa.

The New York Times, Jan. 26, 1972.

PORTUGUESE AFRICA

Commentary

"As for the Portuguese Territories, we shall continue to believe that their peoples should have the right of self-determination. We will encourage peaceful progress toward that goal. The *declared Portuguese policy of racial toleration* is an important factor in this equation. We think this holds genuine hope for the future." (Italics mine)

So runs an American pronouncement at the highest level when the Secretary of State for Africa, William Rogers, and his President, Richard Nixon, turned their attention briefly as the decade began to the United States and Africa in the 1970's. The theme was not new; here as elsewhere there is continuity in the formulation of the American stance (although until 1961 the United States did not express views at all on the question).

Literal interpretation and acceptance of the Portuguese word underlie the American "genuine hope for the future," a hope, presumably, for the peaceful achievement of African self-determination. For the Portuguese have stressed, throughout their overseas history, the longest of any western country, their colorblindness, or at least as one might phrase it, their racial generosity. They deplore the racism explicit in "Anglo-Saxon attitudes," and declare that such discriminating thoughts have never crossed the collective Portuguese mind. They point with pride to Brazil; they try to point to the Portuguese experience in Africa. Their claims are repeated and accepted by outsiders almost by rote, the rote of good will and usually lack of knowledge. But no government can plead ignorance in formulating policy, and certain facts of Portuguese rule in Africa can be easily ascertained.

Portugal's rulers have asserted with unwavering consistency that she does not have, indeed has never had, colonies. Angola, Moçambique, Guiné-Bissau—all are "overseas provinces" of Portugal. This contrived legalism is central to all Portuguese arguments; it permits designating the affairs of those territories as "internal," say, as those of Czechoslovakia, the United States, Nigeria, or South Africa. They need not, then, report to the U.N. on what happens there, as other colonial rulers have had to do. Whether or not one accepts the legal fiction that the colonies do not exist—and few of the world's nations do—the claim that there is no differential treatment based on race does not stand up to scrutiny, even if the separation and discrimination are not proclaimed by South-African-like statutes. Sparse opportunities available to Africans for education and grossly differential economic conditions show flagrant violations.

The argument goes that for the Africans things are getting better all the time (thus the optimistic hope for peaceful change). But "better" from what base-line? And "better" *enough* to meet statements of high principle? Changes have certainly occurred in the last decade. Until then, (and still now) Portuguese colonial policy rested on a cultural justification: the possibility of "assimilation." There, as in French colonial policy, European ethnocentrism took the particular form of offering Africans entree into Portuguese (or western) culture; that such absorption was ideally desirable from an African perspective was never questioned.

But to become an *assimilado* was a process designed with such intricacy and difficulty that a miniscule number of Africans qualified. The almost total Portuguese denial of educational opportunities made control of social mobility easy; not least ingenious was the pre-elementary level of schooling called *rudimentar*, devised in 1941. According to an official statement this system aimed at "the perfect nationalization and moral uplift of the natives and the acquisition of habits and aptitudes for work." Stress was laid on "abandonment of indolence." The moral exhortation to hard, sustained, physical labor has been the refrain of all pronouncements, with the need to "fulfill ... social obligations" the rationale.

Without "assimilated" status, no African could, before 1961, be a Portuguese "citizen"; how then were these Africans like all metropolitan Portuguese, equal members of Portuguese society? Their status, called *indigena* and governed by a code called the *indigenato*, rested on a "social" distinction: By statute, "Individuals of the Negro race or their descendants who were born or habitually reside in the said Provinces (Angola, Moçambique, Guiné) and who do not yet possess the learning and the social and individual habits presupposed for the integral application of the public and private law of Portuguese citizens are considered to be *indigenas*." Such wording had to raise questions about the usual semantic escape from the charge of discrimination by race.

Certain realities followed from this status. Many decrees were phrased in the paternalistic language of "protection," but it was a protection whose end results were rooted in Portuguese economic interests. Registrations and permits, total administrative control of movement and law—all this combined into the skillful manipulation of an African population most important as a labor force. Indeed, apart from indirect means of forcing the *indigenas* into a wage labor pool (such means as taxation in money were used by all colonial powers in Africa at one time or another) the Portuguese actually maintained an explicit system of forced labor, legally ended only in 1960.

Politically all questions were—and are—moot within the Portuguese framework. Quite without discrimination, no one black or white in the "overseas provinces" has political self-determination, any more than do the Portuguese in metropolitan Portugal. Salazar's long-lived dictatorship, apparently unshaken substantively by his death and the succession of Marcello Caetano (interestingly a former minister in charge of thy "overseas provinces"), has combined with Portuguese poverty to keep minimal any attempts there to achieve political liberty. In the 1950's some thought that Portuguese settlers in Angola might try to break away from Lisbon's tight hold—a kind of Angolan unilateral Declaration of Independence, Rhodesian-style. But economic shifts, combined with fear in the face of guerrilla attacks in the early 1960's, brought that unity of self-defense that so characterizes southern African whites.

It is economics, however, that dominates Portugal's relations with her African colonies and her rigid refusal to adjust the relationship as England and France and even Belgium did elsewhere. In the standard rhetoric of economic interpretations of European imperialism, such factors are given not just priority but exclusive weight in controlling policy. Careful analysis of a century's global trade and investment have forced modification of that view for most industrialized countries of Western Europe. Perhaps the key is the word "industrialized"–for there is the difference even in the 1970's between Portugal and, in contrast, Britain, France, Germany, the United States, whose trade and movements of capital have been in overwhelmingly high proportion with other "developed" countries.

None of this is to say that economic self-interest has not mattered, and mattered importantly, in relations between the "West" and the "Third World." But for Portugal it mattered overwhelmingly. For Portugal is itself a poor, underdeveloped country with high illiteracy to this day. Portuguese economic dependence on the wealth of her "overseas provinces" was genuine. The potential wealth of Angola and Moçambique were long unsuspected; only in the 1960's has the off-shore oil and the subsoil mineral wealth been, literally, uncovered. But these territories provided hope, at least an outlet, for poor, crowded Portuguese of the metropole. In these "overseas provinces" cheap labor, in part altogether unpaid, made any economic enterprise profitable. It was not that Angola and Moçambique were the ideal places to raise the best cotton or coffee; but the plantations were highly profitable because labor, often obtained by force, cost little even for Africa. And the profit did not go, as in some places, just to the particular European planter or investor, taxed mildly then by the administration of the colony itself. It went massively to the government–and the government was ultimately Portugal's.

This system was worked out in perfect symbiosis with South Africa's economic needs. For, especially in the years from the gold rushes to the boom of massive economic diversification in the 1960's, South Africa was also built on the backs and lives of cheap labor.

As with Moçambique's cotton, more so with South African gold; its quality was not the best, but its quantities were vast. Only with low-paid labor would it be profitable to mine it in the quantities that would make South Africa the world's foremost producer, and escalate her importance to the world thereby.

But South Africa did not herself have enough cheap African labor, and the incentives of the "free market" might not, her leaders feared, produce enough. Asian labor, imported for the precise purpose of alleviating the problem, was seen as compounding other political difficulties. One solution was a mutually beneficial arrangement, reached with the Portuguese about Moçambique at the turn of the twentieth century and continually revised: permission to recruit thousands of Moçambiquans for short-term labor in the mines (the average annual figure is 100,000), in return for the guarantee that almost 50 percent of South Africa's exports be shipped from the port of Lorenço Marques.

Furthermore, Moçambiquan labor is paid only fractionally with South African money in South Africa; the remaining 80 percent South Africa by contractual agreement pays the Portuguese government *in gold*. The Moçambique workers receive their wages in local currency on their return, they lose two ways: by forced interest-less "savings" put to government uses, and in the conversion frogold to *escudos*.

Geo-political change in Africa in 1960 shook Portuguese complacency. The independence of the Congo from Belgium and the independence of Tanganyika and Zambia a few years later, gave both Angola and Moçambique common borders with free African states (the Portuguese faced a similar problem earlier in Guiné-Bissau). At least some Africans from Angola and Moçambique were convinced that the Portuguese would not peacefully allow African self-determination, or any steps towards it.

Geography then caused the white redoubt to face the threat of its first African "liberation movements" across Portuguese borders. Guerrilla warfare began in Angola in 1961, in Guiné in 1963, in Moçambique in 1964. Neither the Portuguese nor the South African and Southern Rhodesian whites underestimate the importance of these wars and their outcome. A coordinated policy to divert and splinter the energies of black African states is becoming clearer. Signs of selective guerrilla counter-offensives against such vulnerable bordering countries as Zambia are starting to surface. They fit into a continent-wide pattern whose first outlines emerged in 1967 with the attack launched from Angola into the Congo-Kinshasa. Later came bombing of Tanzanian villages from Moçambique, and, in West Africa, the 1970 invasion of Guinea from Guiné-Bissau. All thrusts aimed to keep key independent states of Black Africa in internal disarray, these steps may point to a white redoubt whose leaders deal increasingly with their northern neighbors through commitment to offense as, indeed, the best defense. Portuguese assistance to "Biafra" during the Nigerian Civil War fitted readily into this scheme, as does the continuing possibility of provocation launched from Sao Tomé, the Portuguese controlled island (another "overseas province") only miles off the Nigerian coast.

In this context the special relationship between the United States and Portugal seems to Africans especially ominous. That relationship grows from Portugal's membership in NATO. It is not that Portugal is the only NATO member with African interests—but she is the only one still holding African colonies, governed, furthermore, by policies of continuing white domination. Further, because Portugal is the one European country explicitly engaged in fighting Africans, and because NATO is a military alliance, the "NATO partners" inevitably play a role, direct or indirect, in determining the actions she can take in Africa. For despite massive economic growth in the "overseas provinces" in the last decade, Portugal is still a poor country, hardly a country able to afford military expenditures which have climbed to nearly 50 percent of total government spending.

It is at this point that military-industrial interests enter—especially military-industrial interests in the United States, working in concert and influencing policy in Washington and events in Africa. The pressures they exert and the results they attain are even more clear here then in American relations with South Africa.

For the military the argument is straightforward. To threaten cordial relations with Portugal is to place in jeopardy two items of supreme importance: the right of the United States to maintain a military base in the Azores (it was important once, it still must be, goes the argument), and even more crucial the fabric and morale of NATO, to which the American military (and some political leaders) are immovably committed. It follows from these premises that we must not offend Portugal, nor must we seem to treat her differentially within the alliance—whatever other NATO countries receive in military assistance (personnel, training, equipment) so must Portugal. In response to questions about the use of such personnel and equipment in Portugal's African wars,

American spokesmen insist that it has been made perfectly clear to Portugal that no NATO material is to be so used; Portugal is said to have agreed.

On the economic side—apart from the economic consequences of military aid, direct and indirect—come the complementary pressures of certain American businesses. For since 1965 when the Portuguese government lifted the restrictions on non-Portuguese capital in the "overseas provinces," a sizable influx of American capital especially in Angola (and Cabinda) and Moçambique has contributed to impressive economic expansion. In Angola the interest is in minerals, diamonds and sulphur especially; in Angola and Moçambique in construction and distribution; and everywhere in searching for oil. The greatest boon to the Portuguese has been the discovery of vast oil resources off-shore of that great colonial anomaly, Cabinda. A tiny enclave, bordering Congo-Brazzaville to the north, and separated from Angola by the tongue of Zaïre (Congo-Kinshasa) that reaches to the Atlantic Ocean, Cabinda is an historical fluke. But it was a very valuable one to Portugal in slaving days and today it is the headquarters of the enormous Gulf Oil Company's operation in off-shore oil. From prospecting beginnings in 1954 through its first strike in 1966, Gulf Oil has had a clear and present interest in stability in Portuguese West Africa. Only the worst fighting in 1961 stopped their activities momentarily; Gulf, like most investors in extractive industries, would go to some lengths to avoid repeating that stoppage.

Gulf's contributions to the Portuguese war effort are substantial, even when indirect. Through rents and royalties and taxes and other payments Gulf contributed about $20 million to the Portuguese government in 1969, almost half of that governments's estimated military expenditure in Angola. Further, Portugal's agreements with Gulf stipulate her right to a sizable percentage of the oil so produced; the connection between oil and the military needs no diagram.

As important for Portugal as the role of overseas oil companies, is a project at Cabora Bassa, on the Zambezi in Tete province, the part of Moçambique that juts into former British Central Africa and thus borders on Malawi, Zambia, and Southern Rhodesia. Tete province has seen some of the most intense fighting between FRELI-MO (the major Moçambique liberation movement) and Portuguese troops; it is crucial militarily as well as economically. What is planned at Cabora Bassa is an enormous hydro-electric project, resulting from a dam 70 percent larger than Aswan.

The power the project will produce will serve several economic ends with vast political implications. First, it will enable the Portuguese to develop the Tete region for a million white settlers, immigrating largely from Portugal—clearly a further bulwark against African self-determination, peacefully achieved or wrested by force. Second, plans for distribution of power fit into elaborate pan-white-Southern-African plans made in South Africa; cooperation with South Africa will further tie that country to Portugal's fortunes in Africa. Finally and similarly, all involvement of American and European finance and investment in the project will make more difficult the task of NATO allied governments' withdrawing their support for (let alone asserting their opposition to) Portugal's defiance of time and trend, all at the expense of the Africans. The plans testify to renewed faith in long-term white domination of Southern Africa.

Although some European countries, notably the Swedes and the Italians, have already pulled back from an initial involvement in the project, others, notably France and West Germany, are participating along with South Africa. From across the

Atlantic has come pressure from General Electric on the Export-Import Bank, an autonomous agency of the United States government, to finance for Portugal in export credits the $55 million contract for electrical systems that General Electric wishes to install for the project. The political message of such collaboration between United States business and government is there for Africa and the world to read.

It is partly because of the obvious implications as well as the concrete effects of such American business initiatives that efforts have been launched by some stockholders (relatively few, of course, who especially hope to influence Gulf, and also Polaroid for its South African activities) to force reconsideration of and, with sufficient pressure, withdrawal from such Southern African ventures.

Those who take the position that to discourage American investment in South Africa is, if not pointless, futile, since it constitutes only a small percentage of investment there generally, cannot so argue in the case of the Portuguese territories. Although the absolute sums are smaller, the proportion is far higher, and given the newness of that economic boom, a cut-back or elimination of American investment would be crippling. Africans argue that to continue according to the economic and military pattern of the 1960's is to give tacit comfort and active aid to the determined Portuguese effort to keep down the Africans under her control.

American policy, even as most generally expressed at the U.N., has been solicitous of Portuguese feelings. It is couched always in terms of the United States commitment to peaceful change, and encouragement for what measures of reform have been taken (formal abolition of forced labor, for example); the American representatives have consistently refused to support any proposals to aid actively in bringing self-determination to the Africans of Angola, Moçambique, and Guiné-Bissau (such resolutions are usually described as "unrealistic.")

The first American "no" vote was on a General Assembly resolution in December 1962. The shift from consistent votes of "yes" or abstentions on general condemnations of Portuguese colonial policy came over the call to member states to "refrain forthwith from offering the Portuguese government any assistance that would enable it to continue its repression . . . and for this purpose to *take all measures to prevent the sale and supply of arms and military equipment to the Portuguese government."* (italics mine)

A second "no" vote soon followed, over a proposal to impose sanctions against Portugal. Another "no" came in December, 1965 on a resolution condemning foreign economic interests that contribute indirectly to continuing the status quo oppressive to Africans, and calling on member states to "prevent such activities on the part of their nationals." Successive later resolutions along similar lines have met a consistent negative American response, with the explanations that the United States does not supply arms to Portugal for use in Africa; nor does it discourage or encourage private overseas American investment.

That these explanations do not convince African opinion is clear. Precisely because Portugal is a member of NATO, testing American priorities is especially easy where Portugese interests are vitally concerned. It is also clear that, for the same reason of Portugal's NATO participation, American ability to exert leverage on Portuguese policies, her sheer power to affect the course of events in Portuguese-dominated territories is great. Not only does the Portuguese case invite Africans to test American priorities, it permits them to confront American leaders, as almost nowhere else in

Africa, with a need to choose between self-interest and oft-spoken ideals, the two irreconcilable in the context of "Portuguese Africa."

Few observers, American or African, expected the Nixon Administration's renewal in December, 1971—after a lapse of nine years—of the World War II agreement permitting United States use of air and naval bases in the Azores. Still less did they expect the agreement to include some $435 million in credits to Portugal, which had not received economic aid before. Whatever the disclaimers from Washington, Africans were certain that the pact would help the Portuguese in their wars to assure white minority rule in Angola, Moçambique, and Guiné-Bissau. Suddenly, it seemed, the American administration had made its choice.

PORTUGUESE AFRICA

THE UNITED STATES SUPPORTS AFRO-ASIAN RESOLUTION ON ANGOLA*

Statement by Ambassador Stevenson

March 15, 1961

When he first raised the question of Angola in the Security Council, the distinguished representative of Liberia, Ambassador [George A.] Padmore, recognized that the recent disturbance in Angola was not of itself an immediate threat to the maintenance of international peace and security. At that time he said,

> I believe that there is still time for us to help build in Angola a future of which neither the Portuguese nor the Africans need be afraid. But we no longer have centuries or even decades in which to accomplish what should be a simple and humanitarian task.

He emphasized several problems with which the United Nations must concern itself: the urgency in this era of rapid communication of acting with dispatch, the recognition of Angola's problem being a part of the larger African scene, and the desirability of Portugal availing itself of United Nations cooperation and help in the development of its territories in Africa.

It was clear from his remarks that Ambassador Padmore was anticipating conditions which, if unchanged, might endanger the peace and security of Africa, if not of the world.

It is in a spirit of seeking a constructive elimination of not just the symptoms but the sources of friction that the United States approaches this problem. . . . We recognize full well that, while Angola and the conditions therein do not today endanger international peace and security, we believe they may, if not alleviated, lead to more disorders with many unfortunate and dangerous consequences.

We in the United States deplore the violence which occurred in Luanda and the tragic loss of life involving all elements of the community. Nothing we can do here will restore these people to life, but perhaps we can discourage further violence, which can only make constructive efforts toward the solution of basic problems more difficult.

It is only prudent to view the disorder in Luanda in the context of dramatic changes which have taken place in so much of Africa in the past few years. Angola is but a part of the overall picture of evolution on the African Continent.

The views of the United States have not changed since Jefferson wrote,

> We hold these truths to be self-evident, that all men are created equal, that they are endowed by their Creator with certain unalienable Rights, that among these are Life, Liberty, and the pursuit of Happiness. That to secure these rights, Governments are instituted among Men, deriving their just powers from the consent of the governed.

These words reflect, we believe, the basic principles which all governments would do well to observe and to implement with all of the energy at their command.

*Department of State Bulletin, Apr. 3, 1961, pp. 497-98.

It is no secret that the General Assembly has been interested for years in conditions within Portugal's African territories. There can be no doubt that the people of Angola are entitled to all of the rights guaranteed them by the charter, the right of unfettered opportunity to develop their full economic, political, and cultural potentialities. I am sure that Portugal recognizes that it has solemn obligation to undertake a systematic and rapid improvement of the conditions of the peoples of its territories, an evolution which is contemplated by the charter.

The United States would be remiss in its duties as a friend of Portugal if it failed to express honestly its conviction that step-by-step planning within Portuguese territories and its acceleration is now imperative for the successful political and ecnomic and social advancement of all inhabitants under Portuguese administration—advancement, in brief, toward full self-determination.

The practical difficulties facing Portugal in the immediate future are formidable. If the people of Angola are not given reason to believe that they too may hope to participate in determining their own future, the tension which exists today will grow and may well result in disorders which will indeed pose a threat to international peace and security.

On the other hand, we all know, and know all too well, the tragic events which have occurred in the Congo, that huge, unhappy state which lies just to the north of Angola. I do not think I would be straining the truth to conclude that much of the Congo's problems result from the fact that the pressure of nationalism rapidly overtook the preparation of the necessary foundation essential to the peaceful and effective exercise of sovereign self-government. The important thing for us, then, is to insure that similar conditions do not exist for the Angola of tomorrow. We believe that a beginning should be made promptly within that territory to foster that educational, social, and economic development of which political development is an integral part, and to insure the rapid attainment of political maturity within this area. As we know, political maturity is the crying need everywhere.

Last fall by Resolution 1542 the General Assembly considered that a number of Portuguese territories were non-self-governing within the meaning of Chapter XI of the charter. The Assembly spoke of an obligation which exists on the part of Portugal to transmit information under chapter XI of the charter concerning these territories. The Assembly further invited the Government of Portugal to participate in the work of the Committee on Information from Non-Self-Governing Territories.

I mention this because, in the view of my Government, the best course of action for Portugal is the best course of action to promote the interplay of the people of Portuguese territories seems to be through cooperation with the United Nations. In our view the resolution to which I have been referred was an invitation to Portugal to talk with members of this Organization to insure the more rapid progress of the peoples in Portuguese territories. I stress, gentlemen, the words talk with." The United States does not read any dark dangers into this resolution. This is a matter of concern, a gesture of good will, and, intend that, an effort toward genuine cooperation in achievement of goals which are shared by all of us and which are recognized in the charter of the Organization.

Statement by Francis W. Carpenter, U.S. Delegation Spokesman,
Concerning the United States Vote on the Angola Issue

March 17, 1961

The United States decision to vote for the resolution was made only after thorough consultation between Governor Stevenson and officers of the Department and after approval by the Secretary of State and the President. The policy decisions behind the vote, which were all reflected in Governor Stevenson's speech before the Security Council, had been carefully considered. Our allies were informed in advance. We have a deep and continuing common interest with them. The difficulty and complexity of African questions are, however, such that there are and may continue to be differences in approach on some of them.

Answer by Secretary Rusk to a Question Asked at a News Conference
*on the Angola Question**

March 20, 1961

Q. Mr. Secretary, do you think last week's vote in the United Nations on the Angola question marks a change in the United States' policy?

A. I think there has been some greater interest on the part of the new administration in the great forces which are producing changes in many parts of the world. I am commenting on that in my remarks later today.

We do believe that those who are responsible for the administration of overseas territories need to think hard about the development of those peoples and those territories. The great instinctive, traditional reaction of the American people on such questions has been well demonstrated over the years.

We hope very much these questions can be worked out in a peaceful way without the violence we have seen recently in Angola.

Statement by Ambassador Stevenson Explaining the U.S. Position
on Portuguese Territories †

July 26, 1963

*　　　　　　　　*　　　　　　　　*

The resolution also asks that member states refrain from the sale or the supply of arms and military equipment to Portugal for use in the Portuguese overseas territories in Africa. The United States has felt that arms supplied to Portugal for other purposes and used in its overseas territories might well contribute to an increase in friction and danger. With these considerations in mind, the United States has for a number of years followed a policy of providing no arms or military equipment to Portugal for use in

**Ibid.*, Apr. 10, 1961, p. 521.
†*Ibid.*, Aug. 19, 1963, p. 304.

these territories. And with these same objectives in mind, we have also prohibited direct export of arms and military equipment to the Portuguese territories. The United States will continue to adhere to this policy. We trust, Mr. President, that other states will exercise a similar restraint, avoiding actions of any kind which could further increase the tensions in the area and that they will cooperate fully to assure that the solution will be achieved through peaceful means.

*   *   *

Statement by Ambassador Goldberg Urging Portuguese-African Talks on Self-Determination*

November 11, 1965

*   *   *

Taking first the question of the supply of arms to Portugal, the United States has for some time, consonant with the recommendations of the Council, felt that arms supplied to Portugal for use in its overseas territories or arms supplied for other purposes and used in its overseas territories might well contribute to increased friction, tension, and danger. With these considerations in mind, the United States has for a number of years forbidden the provision of arms or military equipment from public or private sources without specific assurances that it will not be used in the territories. In line with the same objectives, the United States has also prohibited direct export of arms and military equipment to the Portuguese territories. This is a firm policy to which the United States will continue to adhere.

In this connection may I add, in response to the suggestion that NATO is making arms and armaments available to Portugal, that this is not the case. In the first place, NATO, as its name implies, is committed to the defense of the North Atlantic area and only to the defense of the North Atlantic area, and it is operative only within that area, an area which does not include the Portuguese African territories. In the second place, NATO does not supply arms. Individual nations supply arms to other nations in terms of common defense interests and commitments under the North Atlantic Treaty Organization. The Portuguese Government's attitude toward its territories is not to be attributed and is not attributable to Portugal's membership in NATO. In fact, the evidence is quite to the contrary since all those other members of NATO which have had colonies are following or have followed the process of decolonization based on self-determination principles voiced by the Assembly and the Security Council.

Yesterday our distinguished colleague, the representative of the Soviet Union, referred to a sizable loan by my Government to the Government of Portugal which he said had been made in January 1965. I would like to tell him and tell this Council that he has been misinformed. My Government has no programs of economic assistance either to Portugal or to its overseas territories.

Reference has also been made to the question of private foreign investment in the Portuguese territories. We cannot accept the contention that it is foreign private investments in these territories which are impeding the implementation of the declara-

*Ibid., Dec. 27, 1965, pp. 1034-35.

tion of the granting of independence in territories under Portuguese administration. Nor could we accept the proposal that the immediate withdrawal of foreign investments which relate to the welfare of the people of the territories would accrue to their advantage.

*   *   *

Statement by Ambassador Finger Concerning the United States Abstention on the U.N. Resolution on Portuguese Territories*

November 14, 1969

The United States believes very strongly that the Government of Portugal should in its own best interest grant self-determination to the peoples of Angola, Mozambique, and Guinea (Bissau). We also believe it is the proper business of this committee to debate the question of Portuguese administration of these non-self-governing territories and the duty of this committee to make constructive suggestions on the implementation of the goal of self-determination and majority government for the peoples of these territories.

The United States was encouraged by the statesmanlike emphasis in the Manifesto of the Organization of African Unity on the attainment of self-determination through peaceful means, and we are convinced that Portugal would serve its own best interests by accepting an offer to discuss and negotiate an equitable solution—equitable for people of all races in Angola, Mozambique, and Guinea (Bissau).

Mr. Chairman, in the view of my delegation the resolution now before us will not lead toward that goal. This resolution, while purporting to recall the Manifesto of the Organization of African Unity, negates the spirit of the manifesto; in fact, it tends to shut the door to a possible dialogue with Portugal. This resolution repeats prescriptions which have failed in the past and which obviously cannot help in achieving what we all desire: self-determination for the African peoples under Portuguese administration. By its uncompromising and condemnatory character, this resolution will only serve to discourage any tendency the Government of Portugal might have to reach toward conciliation.

My delegation believes that the sponsors of this resolution are also committing a serious error in tarring the Portuguese people with the same brush of racism which is so richly deserved by the illegal regime of Ian Smith and by the Government of South Africa. The tragedy of this error is that it tends to push the Government of Portugal toward the very racist regimes of southern Africa which it has been condemned for collaborating with.

Now, Mr. Chairman, it is not at all certain that a conciliatory approach toward Portugal would lead toward the goal of self-determination for the people of Angola, Mozambique, and Guinea (Bissau), but we are convinced it is worth trying. What is certain in the light of many years' experience is that the harsh approach which characterizes this resolution will fail.

Although we are compelled to express frankly our deep disappointment with the

*Ibid., Dec. 29, 1969, pp. 641-42.

draft before us, we would not want the sponsors of this resolution to think that we do not appreciate their attempt to engage in a constructive discussion with us. We regret, however, that that discussion had to be built on such an unsound foundation. The sponsor who talked with us had to base his consultations on a text which was very far indeed from what we would consider a useful approach. Though he showed great courtesy, patience, and understanding and tried to take our suggestions into account, the gap was much too wide and the time available for discussing changes was too short. How much better it would have been if consultations had taken place before a first draft had been written, rather than after several drafts and days of debate by the potential sponsors. Nevertheless, I want to reiterate our deep appreciation for the manner in which we were consulted.

In addition to our misgivings over the general thrust of this draft, which we consider misguided, certain provisions are particularly objectionable in our view. For example, paragraph 4 condemns Portugal's alleged policy of using the territories under its domination for violation of the territorial integrity and sovereignty of independent states. The United States, as a member of the Security Council, has carefully considered such evidence as has been presented to substantiate such charges and finds it far from conclusive. We find in paragraph 5 a new concept, not present in last year's resolution; i.e., a condemnation of the "colonial war" which is allegedly being waged by Portugal against people in its African territories. This type of blanket condemnation is hardly likely to achieve a constructive dialogue with the Government of Portugal. Paragraph 7 purports to condemn the alleged intervention of South African forces against the people in these territories. While there may be individual armed South Africans in these territories, we know of no evidence of "South African forces," as alleged in this paragraph.

Paragraph 12 recommends that the Security Council take effective steps "with a view to the immediate implementation of resolution 1514 (XV) in the Territories under Portuguese domination. . . ." This is in flagrant contrast with the Manifesto of the OAU, which envisages a more gradual movement toward self-determination. Paragraph 13 makes particular reference to the members of the North Atlantic Treaty Organization, with the implication that military assistance which some of its members give to Portugal enables that country to pursue the fighting in its African territories. In fact, the North Atlantic Treaty Organization is concerned exclusively with defense in the North Atlantic area, and there is no evidence whatsoever that any military equipment provided to Portugal is being used outside that area.

We recognize that many members of this committee have legitimate grounds for impatience when they see their hopes of bringing about an end to colonialism frustrated. We share that sense of frustration. Yet these delegations should, in our view, ask themselves whether it is by passing still more violent resolutions that they will achieve their objective. We would have thought it better to take a new approach along the lines suggested by the very manifesto which was endorsed by many of their governments.

Mr. Chairman, if my delegation abstains on this resolution when you bring it to a vote later this morning, it is for two reasons: first, because we desire thereby to signify our support for the concept of self-determination, even though we disagree with the route proposed in this draft; second, because we wish thereby to recognize the effort of certain of the sponsors to consult with us. We regretfully conclude that this is still a bad resolution, despite the last-minute efforts of the sponsors to correct some of its worst defects. It was for these reasons—and only for these reasons—that we could, after agonizing consideration, avoid voting against this draft. We are convinced that the main losers when this resolution is adopted and deposited in the archives of these United Nations will be the very people whom we would like to help in their search for self-determination and political dignity—the people of Angola, Mozambique, and Guinea (Bissau)—and along with them, this organization, whose credibility, relevance, and effectiveness will have been further undermined by the addition of this resolution to the long list of other misguided and ineffective resolutions already consigned to its voluminous records.

Statement Submitted by Congressman Diggs to President Nixon Requesting Point by Point Reply on the United States-Portuguese Agreement*

December 17, 1971

(a) That the United States Government must be required, and is herein called upon, to explain the enormous, unprecedented and anomalous commitments which the United States is making to Portugal in connection with the Agreement to extend U.S. base rights in the Azores—an Agreement under which Portugal is to receive in the next two years (the Agreement expires on February 3, 1974) the following quid pro quo:

$15 million in P.L. 480 agricultural commodities;
the loan of a hydrographic vessel at no cost;
$1 million for educational development programs;
$5 million in drawing rights for non-military excess equipment;
the waiver of MAAG support payments ($350,000) for the MAAG (Military Assistance Advisory Group) to Lisbon;
$400 million of Exim loans and guarantees for development projects.

(b) That specifically, the government is called upon to address each of the following points:

1. From the point of view of U.S. interests, the new Agreement with Portugal represents an unusual and anomalous commitment. There is no apparent justification for the quid pro quo in the new Agreement.

a. The general availability of funds for foreign economic assistance has been diminishing since 1967. In that year, funds for economic assistance totalled $5,120 million. In 1968, they were $4,634 million. In 1969, they were $4,067 million. Last year, they totalled $4,711 million. The Export-Import Bank is an exception to the rule; its funds have been increasing in the last few years. But the question must arise why loans and credit guarantees to Portugal are rising at a moment when federal funds are so scarce, and when total appropriations for economic assistance are falling.

b. The funds projected for commitment to Portugal are out of all proportion to previous development commitments through the Export-Import Bank to either Europe or Africa. The total of Export-Import Bank loans to Africa in the whole period

*Press release handed out at Press Conference, Dec. 17, 1971.

1946-1970 was less than $358 million. The total of long-term economic loans to Europe from the same source in that period was only $753.7 million.

c. The projected commitment is also out of proportion to any previous commitments to Portugal itself. That country received less than $50 million in the whole period from 1946-1970 through the Export-Import Bank. The present Administration is proposing to provide more than four times this amount in the next two years alone.

d. The projected new commitments would constitute a tremendous drain on the funds of the Export-Import Bank. They would represent about 10% of the average annual commitments to all countries from the Bank in the last few years; and this does not even take into consideration the $200 million in Exim credit guaranties.

e. The question which remains to be answered, therefore, and it is a most important question, is why a small nation of 8.6 million people should receive such extraordinary special treatment.

2. The United States, furthermore, is now going through the worst balance of payments crisis in its history. We now have the largest deficit on record. Unemployment has risen to high levels as a consequence of deflationary measures designed to remedy that situation. In this context the Administration has undertaken an Agreement with a small European country which will lead to a substantial increase in the foreign exchange costs of our economic assistance. Again, the question must arise why Portugal should qualify for such special treatment.

3. Total U.S. dollar flows to Portugal and its overseas territories now exceed $400 million. (See Table below). These flows are important to that country's balance of payments. The Administration is now proposing a substantial increase in these flows through the loans provided for in the new Agreement.

Portugal and Overseas Territories:
Gross Flows of Funds
from North America*
(1969, millions of $)

1. Imports from Portugal and Overseas Territories	$166 million
2. Freight and Insurance on Merchandise	3 million
3. Other Transportation	11 million
4. Travel	79 million
5. Investment Income	29 million
6. Other government	6 million
7. Other private	24 million
8. Unrequited transfers (pension remittances, etc.)	89 million
9. Non-monetary Sectors: Direct Investment	6 million
Total	$413 million

Source: IMF Balance of Payments Yearbook, August 1971, vol. 22
*These figures refer to flows from the U.S. and Canada. U.S. funds account for almost the whole of the total.

4. The Portuguese are now running a trade deficit of just under $500 million. This deficit is, to an important degree, the result of the drain on Portugal's economy created by the pursuit of three colonial wars in Africa. Additional, and substantial, assistance to Portugal in this context will have the effect of helping it to continue those wars at the very moment when it is being forced to consider seriously whether it ought to withdraw from its overseas territories.

5. It should be noted that parts of the new Agreement can easily become open-ended commitments. The expanded commitment under P.L. 480 may well be increased still further when the Agreement is reviewed two years from now. The

provision dealing with excess equipment is already open-ended. Secretary Rogers' letter clearly states that $5 million for this purpose is not to be considered a maximum ceiling.

6. Dollar flows to Portugal, from both the private and the public sector, are already on a scale amounting to "economic intervention that might just decide the outcome of the colonial war." The new Agreement increases that indirect assistance by a substantial amount and changes the character of our commitment to Portugal.

7. The political context cannot be ignored. Particularly:

—the liberation forces control large areas of Angola, east and south of the Central Plateau.

—in Mozambique the liberation forces control several provinces and operate freely south of the Zambesi River.

—in Guinea-Bissau, the PAIGC have forced the Portuguese to leave the countryside and to retreat to the urban areas and a few scattered military bases.

The obvious effect of the Azores Agreement is to enable Portugal to continue waging the three wars in Africa.

8. There is nothing to indicate that the military value of the Azores is of overriding importance to U.S. security so that it merits such an inordinate expenditure. Further, the fact that the base Agreement remained dormant for the past 10 years (since 1962) indicates this.

9. The injection of huge sums for economic and educational assistance, as well as aid in kind, into the Portuguese economy, in the existing internal situation of considerable domestic unhappiness with, and criticism of, wholly disproportionate budgetary expenditures on colonial wars, will greatly assist the Caetano Government in dampening the domestic antipathy to the wars and thus to continue their prosecution.

(c) That, if the Administration cannot provide a statement of compelling reasons for making this Agreement, it must be considered as admitting that it is the intention of the Administration to directly assist Portugal in waging these wars against the peoples of Guinea-Bissau, Angola and Mozambique.

(d) That the United States Government respond to the following questions:

1. What projects were reviewed, or are contemplated for Exim loans?
2. Are these projects in Portugal, that is in so-called "metropolitan Portugal" as distinguished from Guinea-Bissau, Angola and Mozambique?
3. Are similar increases in Exim loans being considered (i) for South Africa, (ii) for majority-ruled African countries?

(e) That, in view of the implications of this Agreement for the United States, the Administration explain why this Agreement was entered into by the executive agreement route rather than as a treaty and submitted to the Senate for its advice and consent to ratification.

(f) That the Administration explain the discrepancy between its claimed lack of funds to assist Black business in the United States, with its 23 million Blacks, on the one hand and, on the other, its expenditure of tremendous sums to assist the economy of Portugal, a country with only 8.6 million people, and thus to assist the waging of wars against Black people in Africa. According to its reports to the Congress, the Federal Government is now giving only $213.8 million in loans to minority businesses in this country (including Blacks and Spanish-speaking Americans), whereas the sums projected for Portugal in this Agreement are more than double that amount.

ACKNOWLEDGEMENTS

Roosevelt and the Russians by Edward Stettinius, Copyright © 1949 by The Stettinius Fund, Inc. Reprinted by permission of Doubleday & Company, Inc.

In The Cause of Peace by Trygve Lie, Copyright © 1954 by Trygve Lie. Reprinted with permission of The Macmillan Company.

Africa in World Politics by Vernon McKay, Copyright © 1963 by Vernon McKay. Reprinted by permission of Harper and Row Publishers, Inc.

New York Times Editorials, Copyright © 1957, 1960, 1962, 1964, 1965, 1966, 1967, 1968, 1969, 1970, 1971, 1972 by The New York Times Company. Reprinted by permission.

INDEX
The United Nations

INDEX
Subsaharan Africa